CW00959756

THE CAMBRIDGE HISTORY OF

ENGLISH POETRY

Poetry written in English is uniquely powerful and suggestive in its capacity to surprise, unsettle, shock, console and move. *The Cambridge History of English Poetry* offers sparklingly fresh and dynamic readings of an extraordinary range of poets and poems from *Beowulf* to Alice Oswald. An international team of experts explores how poets in England, Scotland, Wales and Ireland use language and to what effect, examining questions of form, tone and voice; they comment, too, on how formal choices are inflected by the poet's time and place. *The Cambridge History of English Poetry* is the most comprehensive and authoritative history of the field from Anglo-Saxon times to the present. It traces patterns of continuity, transformation, transition and development. Covering a remarkable array of poets and poems, and featuring an extensive bibliography, the scope and depth of this major work of reference make it required reading for anyone interested in poetry.

MICHAEL O'NEILL is Professor of English at Durham University. He has published widely on poetry and is a published poet himself. His recent publications include *The All-Sustaining Air: Romantic Legacies and Renewals in British, American and Irish Poetry* (2007) and *Wheel* (2008), a collection of poems.

THE CAMBRIDGE HISTORY OF ENGLISH POETRY

*

Edited by
MICHAEL O'NEILL

CAMBRIDGE
UNIVERSITY PRESS

CAMBRIDGE UNIVERSITY PRESS
Cambridge, New York, Melbourne, Madrid, Cape Town, Singapore,
São Paulo, Delhi, Dubai, Tokyo

Cambridge University Press
The Edinburgh Building, Cambridge CB2 8RU, UK

Published in the United States of America by Cambridge University Press, New York

www.cambridge.org
Information on this title: www.cambridge.org/9780521883061

First published 2010

Printed in the United Kingdom at the University Press, Cambridge

A catalogue record for this publication is available from the British Library

ISBN 978-0-521-88306-1 Hardback

Contents

Notes on contributors

PETER BARRY is Professor of English at Aberystwyth University. His most recent books are *Poetry Wars: British Poetry of the 1970s and the Battle of Earls Court* (2006) and *Literature in Contexts* (2007).

BERNARD BEATTY is Senior Fellow in the School of English at the University of Liverpool and Associate Fellow in the School of Divinity at the University of St Andrews. He is the author of *Byron's Don Juan* (1985) and *Byron's Don Juan and Other Poems* (1987), and edited *The Byron Journal* from 1988 to 2005.

JOHN BEER is Emeritus Professor of English Literature and Fellow of Peterhouse, Cambridge. His books include *Blake's Humanism* (1968), *Blake's Visionary Universe* (1969), *Romantic Consciousness: Blake to Mary Shelley* (2003), *Post-Romantic Consciousness: Dickens to Plath* (2003), *Romantic Influences* (1993) and *William Blake: A Literary Life* (2005).

MICHAEL BRADSHAW is the author of *Resurrection Songs: The Poetry of Thomas Lovell Beddoes* (2001), the co-editor with Ute Berns of *The Ashgate Research Companion to Thomas Lovell Beddoes* (2007) and has edited Beddoes's *Death's Jest-Book: the 1829 Text* (2003) and *Selected Poetry* (1999). He is currently Professor of English at Edge Hill University.

KATHARINE A. CRAIK is Senior Lecturer at Oxford Brookes University. She has published widely on Shakespeare and his contemporaries, and her book *Reading Sensations in Early Modern England* appeared in 2007.

RICHARD CRONIN is Professor of English Literature at the University of Glasgow. His most recent book is *Romantic Victorians: English Literature, 1824–1840* (2002).

ROBERT DOUGLAS-FAIRHURST is a Fellow of Magdalen College, Oxford. He is the author of *Victorian Afterlives: The Shaping of Influence in Nineteenth-Century Literature* (2002), and has edited Dickens's *'A Christmas Carol' and Other Christmas Books* (2006) and *Great Expectations* (2008), and co-edited, with Seamus Perry, *Tennyson among the Poets: Bicentenary Essays* (2009). He is currently writing a book about Dickens's early career.

PAUL EDMONDSON is Head of Learning and Research at The Shakespeare Birthplace Trust. His publications include *The Shakespeare Handbooks: 'Twelfth Night'* (2005). He has co-authored (with Stanley Wells) *Shakespeare's Sonnets* (2004) and *Coffee with Shakespeare* (2008). He is co-supervisory editor of The Penguin Shakespeare.

ALICE ENTWISTLE is Principal Lecturer at the University of Glamorgan. She co-authored *A History of Twentieth-Century British Women's Poetry* with Jane Dowson (2005), and is preparing a monograph on contemporary poetry written by women in Wales and co-editing with John Goodby an anthology of innovative Welsh poetries.

DAVID FAIRER is Professor of Eighteenth-Century English Literature at the University of Leeds. His books include *Pope's Imagination* (1984), *The Poetry of Alexander Pope* (1989), *English Poetry of the Eighteenth Century, 1700–1789* (2003) and *Organising Poetry: The Coleridge Circle 1790–1798* (2009).

CHRISTINE GERRARD is the Barbara Scott Fellow in English at Lady Margaret Hall, Oxford. She co-edited with David Fairer *Eighteenth-Century Poetry: An Annotated Anthology* (second edition, 2003) and edited *A Companion to Eighteenth-Century Poetry* (2006), as well as volumes I and II of *The Complete Correspondence of Samuel Richardson* (2010).

JOHN GOODBY lectures in English at the University of Swansea. He is the author of *Irish Poetry since 1950: from Stillness into History* (2000), editor of the *New Casebook on Dylan Thomas* (2001) and he has published widely on British and Irish poetry.

ANDREW HADFIELD is Professor of English at the University of Sussex. His books include *Shakespeare and Republicanism* (2005), *Literature, Travel and Colonialism in the English Renaissance,1540–1625* (1998), *Spenser's Irish Experience: Wilde Fruyt and Salvage Soyl* (1997) and *Literature, Politics and National Identity: Reformation to Renaissance* (1994). He is the editor of *Renaissance Studies*.

JASON HARDING is Reader in English Studies at the University of Durham and a Visiting Research Fellow at the Institute of English Studies, University of London. He is the author of a study of British interwar literary journalism, *The Criterion: Cultural Politics and Periodical Networks in Interwar Britain* (2002) and is co-editor of a collection of critical essays, *T. S. Eliot and the Concept of Tradition* (2007).

ELIZABETH HEALE taught in the Department of English at the University of Reading until 2008. She is now a Research Fellow in the department. Her publications include *Wyatt, Surrey and Early Tudor Poetry* (1998) and *Autobiography and Authorship in Renaissance Verse: Chronicles of the Self* (2003).

ALISON HICKEY is Associate Professor of English at Wellesley College, Massachusetts. She is the author of a book on Wordsworth (*Impure Conceits*, 1997).

HESTER JONES is Senior Lecturer in the Department of English at the University of Bristol, and was Lecturer in English at the University of Liverpool from 1994 to 2007. She has published a volume (2004) on the Rossettis in the Lives of Victorian Literary Figures series.

EDWARD LARRISSY is Professor of Poetry in the School of English at Queen's University, Belfast, and Research Director of the Seamus Heaney Centre for Poetry. He is the author, among other books, of *Reading Twentieth-Century Poetry: The Language of Gender and Objects* (1990), *Yeats the Poet: The Measures of Difference* (1994) and *Blake and Modern Literature* (2006).

BARBARA K. LEWALSKI is William R. Kenan Professor of History and Literature and of English at Harvard University. Her Milton books include *John Milton: A Critical Biography* (2000), *Paradise Lost and the Rhetoric of Literary Forms* (1985) and *Milton's Brief Epic: The Genre, Themes, and Art of Paradise Regained* (1966). She has edited *Paradise Lost* in an original spelling/punctuation edition (2007).

JAMIE MCKENDRICK has written five books of poetry, the most recent being *Crocodiles & Obelisks* (2007). A volume of his selected poems, *Sky Nails,* was published in 2000, and *The Embrace*, his translation of the Italian poet Valerio Magrelli, appeared in 2009.

BERNARD O'DONOGHUE was born in Co. Cork in 1945. He has lived in England since 1962, and he is currently a fellow in Medieval English at Wadham College, Oxford. His *Selected Poems* was published in 2008, and he is the editor of the *Cambridge Companion to Seamus Heaney* (2009).

FRANCIS O'GORMAN is Professor of Victorian Literature at the University of Leeds. Recent publications include essays on Wordsworth, Coleridge and Tennyson.

MICHAEL O'NEILL is Professor of English at Durham University. His recent books include *The All-Sustaining Air: Romantic Legacies and Renewals in British, American, and Irish Poetry since 1900* (2007) and *Wheel* (2008), a collection of poems.

SEAMUS PERRY is a Fellow of Balliol College, Oxford, where he is Tutor in English Literature. His publications include *Coleridge and the Uses of Division* (1999) and *Tennyson* (2005), and editions of *Coleridge's Notebooks* (2002) and *Coleridge on Writing and Writers* (2007). He co-edited, with Robert Douglas-Fairhurst, *Tennyson among the Poets: Bicentenary Essays* (2009).

CATHERINE PHILLIPS is a Fellow of Downing College, Cambridge. Her publications include an edition of Gerard Manley Hopkins's *Selected Poetry* (1996), *Robert Bridges: A Biography* (1992), an edition of Yeats's *The Hour-Glass: Manuscript Materials* (1994), a monograph on Hopkins and the Victorian visual world and articles on various aspects of nineteenth- and twentieth-century literature and its cultural context.

RALPH PITE has recently published *Thomas Hardy: The Guarded Life* (2006). He teaches at the University of Bristol.

JONATHAN POST is Professor of English at University of California, Los Angeles, where he has served as Department Chair. He is the author of three books of criticism: *Henry Vaughan: The Unfolding Vision* (1982), *Sir Thomas Browne* (1987) and *English Lyric Poetry: The Early Seventeenth-Century* (1999; reprinted 2002). He has also edited a number of collections of essays, including: *Green Thoughts, Green Shades: Contemporary Poets on the Early Modern Lyric* (2002).

MARK RAWLINSON teaches in the School of English, University of Leicester. He has written widely on the literatures of twentieth-century wars, including *British Writing of the Second World War* (2000).

CLAUDE RAWSON is the Maynard Mack Professor of English at Yale University, and General Editor of the Cambridge Edition of the Works of Jonathan Swift. His books include *Order from Confusion Sprung: Studies in Eighteenth-Century Literature from Swift to Cowper* (1985) and *God, Gulliver, and Genocide: Barbarism and the European Imagination, 1492–1945* (2001).

GARETH REEVES is Reader in English at Durham University. He is the author of two books on Eliot, *T. S. Eliot: A Virgilian Poet* (1989) and *T. S. Eliot's 'The Waste Land'* (1994), and of *The Thirties Poetry: Auden, MacNeice, Spender*, with Michael O'Neill (1992). He has also written two volumes of poetry, *Real Stories* (1984) and *Listening In* (1993).

STEPHEN REGAN is Professor of English at Durham University. He is the author of *Philip Larkin* (1992) and the editor of the volume on Larkin in the New Casebook series (1997). He has written essays on W. B. Yeats, Robert Frost, Louis MacNeice, Seamus Heaney and Paul Muldoon. He is also the editor of *Irish Writing: An Anthology of Irish Literature in English 1789–1939* (2004).

FELICITY RIDDY is Emeritus Professor of English at the University of York and a former Director of its Centre for Medieval Studies. A specialist in late medieval literature, she has published extensively on Scottish poetry, Arthurian romance and historiography, women's writing and gender issues and the culture of private life. She co-edited *Youth in the Middle Ages* (2004).

DAVID G. RIEDE, Professor of English at the Ohio State University, is the author of numerous articles and reviews on nineteenth-century British literature and of books on Romantic poetry and criticism, Swinburne, D. G. Rossetti and Matthew Arnold; and most recently *Allegories of One's Own Mind: Melancholy in Victorian Poetry* (2005).

ANDREW MICHAEL ROBERTS is Reader in English in the School of Humanities at the University of Dundee. His books include *Conrad and Masculinity* (2000), *Geoffrey Hill* (2004) and (with Jonathan Allison) *Poetry and Contemporary Culture: The Question of Value* (2002).

CORINNE SAUNDERS is Professor in the Department of English Studies at the University of Durham. She is the author of *The Forest of Medieval Romance* (1993), *Rape and Ravishment in the Literature of Medieval England* (2001) and *Magic and the Supernatural in Medieval English Romance* (2010). She has edited *Chaucer* (2001), *Writing War: Medieval Literary Responses* (2004), *Pearl* (2005) and *A Concise Companion to Chaucer* (2006). She is the English editor of the journal *Medium Ævum*.

WENDY SCASE is Geoffrey Shepherd Professor of Medieval English Literature at the University of Birmingham. She has published extensively on Middle English literature. She is founding co-editor of *New Medieval Literatures*, and chairs the editorial board of the book series Medieval Texts and Cultures of Northern Europe.

A. V. C. Schmidt is Andrew Bradley-James Maxwell Fellow and Senior English Tutor, Balliol College, Oxford. He is the author of numerous books and articles on Chaucer, the *Gawain*-poet and especially Langland, including a two-volume *Parallel-Text Edition* of *Piers Plowman*, a World's Classics translation of the B-text and a critical study, *The Clerkly Maker: Langland's Poetic Art*.

Alison Shell is Professor in the English Department at Durham University. She is the author of *Catholicism, Controversy and the English Literary Imagination, 1558–1660* (1999) and *Oral Culture and Catholicism in Early Modern England* (2007).

Vincent Sherry is Professor of English at Washington University, St Louis. His publications include *The Great War and the Language of Modernism* (2003), *Joyce: Ulysses* (1994), *Ezra Pound, Wyndham Lewis, and Radical Modernism* (1993) and *The Uncommon Tongue: The Poetry and Criticism of Geoffrey Hill* (1987). He has also edited the *Cambridge Companion to the Literature of the First World War* (2005).

Nicholas Shrimpton teaches English at Lady Margaret Hall, Oxford, where he is Thelma Herring Fellow and Vice-Principal. His recent publications include articles on pessimism in the late nineteenth century, money in Victorian literature and George Steiner.

Jane Stabler is Reader in Romantic Literature at the School of English, University of St Andrews. Her publications include *Burke to Byron, Barbauld to Baillie, 1790–1830* (2001) and *Byron, Poetics and History* (2002).

Richard Terry is Professor of Eighteenth-Century English Literature at Northumbria University. He is the author of *Poetry and the Making of the English Literary Past 1660–1781* (2001).

Heidi Thomson is Associate Professor in the School of English, Film, Theatre and Media Studies at Victoria University of Wellington, New Zealand. Her research focuses on the Age of Sensibility and British Romanticism.

Herbert F. Tucker holds the John C. Coleman Chair in English at the University of Virginia, where he is also associate editor of *New Literary History* and series co-editor in Victorian Literature and Culture for the University Press. His most recent book is *Epic: Britain's Heroic Muse 1790–1910* (2008).

Laura Varnam is Lecturer in Old and Middle English Literature at University College, Oxford. She is currently working on a monograph on sacred space in Middle English literature.

Peter Vassallo is Professor of English and Comparative Literature at the University of Malta, where he was Head of the Department of English from 1988 to 2006 and Chair of the

Institute of Anglo-Italian Studies. He has published widely on Anglo-Italian literary relations and is the editor of the *Journal of Anglo-Italian Studies*.

TIMOTHY WEBB is Senior Research Fellow and Professor Emeritus at the University of Bristol, where, for some years, he was Winterstoke Professor of English. His books include *The Violet in the Crucible: Shelley and Translation* (1976), *Shelley: A Voice Not Understood* (1977), *English Romantic Hellenism, 1700–1824* (1982), editions of Shelley and Yeats and an annotated edition of Leigh Hunt's *Autobiography* (just completed).

STEVEN N. ZWICKER is Stanley Elkin Professor of Humanities at Washington University, St Louis. He is author of *Dryden's Political Poetry* (1992), *Politics and Language in Dryden's Poetry: The Arts of Disguise* (1984) and *Lines of Authority: Political and English Literary Culture 1649–1689* (1993), and has written the essay on Dryden for the *Cambridge History of English Literature, 1660–1780*, and more recently on 'Dryden and Biography' in *Writing Lives in Early Modern England* (2008).

Acknowledgments

I would like to thank Ray Ryan at Cambridge University Press for inviting me to edit this volume, all the anonymous readers of my proposal for their helpful comments and the contributors for their patience and co-operativeness, as well as for their fine chapters. I am indebted to the Department of English Studies at Durham University for some financial support.

My chief obligation in preparing the initial typescript is to my research assistant, Ann-Marie Einhaus, who is writing a PhD on First World War short fiction at Durham University. Ann-Marie has taken responsibility for many tasks, including the formatting of chapters, and she has brought rare qualities of proactive intelligence and cheerful efficiency to the project. It is, in large part, due to her invaluable editorial assistance that the volume has taken material form. I am extremely grateful.

I am also indebted for helpful research assistance during the copy-editing process to Paige Tovey and Madeleine Collaghan. Audrey Cotterell has been a magnificent copy-editor: meticulously attentive to the detail in and through which poetry lives and has its being. I and the other contributors owe her a great deal. The index has been prepared by Peter Andrews.

Note

Line numbers for poetry are normally supplied when they are available. Occasionally page numbers are supplied instead. Where line numbers are not available, as is the case with much twentieth-century poetry, the reader is referred to the relevant edition or volume.

Introduction

MICHAEL O'NEILL

Scope and approach

'And Question five is, God help us, what is my definition of Poetry?' So Dylan Thomas wrote in 1951 in response to conundrums posed by a student. Among his answers is a reminder of 'the mystery of having been moved by words',[1] a 'mystery', not a mystification, to which subsequent pages in this volume bear witness, and which coexists with poetry's ability to provide greater clarification of the human condition. The poet, writes Yeats, 'is part of his own phantasmagoria and we adore him because nature has grown intelligible, and by so doing a part of our creative power'.[2] The phrasing here may be consciously on its stilts, its affirmations unashamedly ready to disconcert, even to embarrass, but Yeats comes close to smoking out the essence of the hold possessed by poets over their readers.

The poets discussed in this *Cambridge History of English Poetry* often exercise ways of making 'nature ... intelligible' that add to their readers' sense of 'creative power'. Milton using word-play, paradox and affecting rhythmic intensity to overcome mortality in *Lycidas* as he describes his drowned fellow poet as having 'sunk low, but mounted high, / Through the dear might of him that walked the waves' (lines 172–3); Coleridge making personification a means of mesmerically conveying tragic futility at the close of the reversed sonnet 'Work without Hope'; Ted Hughes inventively exploiting rhyme and line-endings to evoke how 'a black- / Back gull bent like an iron bar slowly' in 'Wind' (lines 15–16): the three examples give a taste of how English poetry embodies and irradiates 'creative power'.[3]

The present book is, in one of its central aspects, a robust if never simply uncritical celebration of that 'creative power'. It provides a literary-historical account of English poetry from Anglo-Saxon writings to the present. Principally the *History* deals with narrative and lyric poetry and does not include poetic drama written for the stage. Thus, Shakespeare's sonnets and narrative poems are included, but not his plays, except briefly. However, English poetry contains many fine poems which exploit possibilities associated with drama, even though they are not intended primarily for the stage: again, there are other dramatic works, which, though intended for the stage, have ended up mainly as texts experienced through private reading. Works such as Milton's *Samson Agonistes*, therefore, as well as Shelley's *Prometheus Unbound* and *The Cenci*, are discussed.

Some guiding principles are at work. First, contributors have been asked to highlight the formal and aesthetic features of poetry. 'Formal and aesthetic' is meant to draw attention to the fact that this is a history of poetry, and that 'poetry' involves artistic uses of language, as, indeed, many of the poets discussed in the volume insist. One subsidiary topic running through the volume is the discussion by poets in their poems of the nature of poetry. Contributors have been asked to explore ways in which poets use form, taking that term in its widest sense to include all aspects of poetry considered as an art: uses of genres; handling of metre, structure, image, metaphor, echo and allusion; deployment of diction, idiom, ambiguity; tone and mood. Multiple threads run through the volume as a consequence. If one stays solely with the question of echoes and allusions, one might note how subtle resonances link poets as various as Pope, Dante Gabriel Rossetti and Hill with Milton; how Yeats's *ottava rima* stanzas connect to and contrast with the same verse form's function in Byron; and how T. S. Eliot's *The Waste Land* is a mosaic of generic fragments and owes its power partly to the way in which it summons up, in however frustrated or ironic a manner, previous poetic styles.

Second, contributors have been asked to write in terms that are historical as well as literary, though it is *literary* history that is placed to the fore. There will be many occasions where literary history requires reference to the political and social history of the period in which poets are composing, and due attention is given to the intersection between these histories. That formal choices may reflect political, social, historical and gender preoccupations is clear.

The fifty-three chapters are centred on authors: sometimes on single authors, sometimes on authors considered as groups. The *History* departs from the practice of many literary histories[4] by singling out in a few chapters particular works at the heart of an understanding of English poetry. Sympathetic though the *History* is to the claims of the non-canonical, the purpose of the *History* is less to offer a critique of a supposedly inflexible canon than to give an overview of English poetry that is alert to continuity and change. Since the work is a 'history', it often considers works that many readers of poetry in their own and succeeding ages have regarded as particularly significant. But it is alive to the argument that what makes a text canonical is precisely its openness to various modes of reading, and it is aware of the fact that the notion of the 'canonical' is always shifting, always provisional. 'Literary history' is always a contentious and contested enterprise, raising questions about the validity of groupings and periodisation. The notion of 'transition', the passage from one era to another, is crucial for the *History* and is continually explored in its pages.

Above all, contributors have been asked to write with first-hand consideration and depth. The watchword for contributors and the volume has been 'attention': sustained, unremitting attention to the implications and meanings of verbal structures artistically shaped by poets. The poems themselves have been allowed to generate through their language appropriate frames of reference. So the *History* has much sympathy with Paul Muldoon's dual view that 'We know that no poem may be read as a completely discrete construct ... but we also know that part of the function of the poem is to present a construct that is *relatively* free-standing, to create a *relatively* squared-off stand of timber on the plain.'[5] Contributors have been invited to demonstrate, implicitly or explicitly, knowledge of relevant reception history, but never at the expense of independent response.

The *History* is a history of 'English' rather than 'British' or 'Irish' poetry: it focuses on poets writing in English in the political structure currently termed the United Kingdom, though there has been some fluidity here and a recognition of the shifting political definitions of 'English' and 'British' over the centuries. The *History* certainly makes no attempt to cover all poetry written in English. In practice, purity of principle has been hard to follow and may not, for good reasons, be wholly desirable. Thus, there is a chapter on Imagism in which the American poet Ezra Pound features, because of his centrality to English poetry in the twentieth and twenty-first centuries; a similar reason explains the inclusion of Sylvia Plath.

An evident principle of structure is chronological, tracking the time-line that runs from *Beowulf* through to, say, Alice Oswald. Closely linked with that principle is a geographical emphasis, stronger in some chapters than others, that attends to the importance of place and space in English poetry: the regionality of 'English' poetry features throughout the volume, including questions thrown up by what John Kerrigan calls 'the current devolutionary process'.[6]

Contents: brief description

Chapter 1 describes major trends and achievements in Anglo-Saxon poetry. The legacy of Anglo-Saxon poetry (in, for example, Pound's *Cantos*, the early work of Auden or Heaney's translation of *Beowulf*) indicates its continuing relevance, and anticipates the volume's emphasis on patterns of continuity and discontinuity. Chapter 2 discusses the productions of the *Gawain*-poet, especially *Sir Gawain and the Green Knight*, in relation to the Alliterative Revival of the late fourteenth century, the significance of courtly poetry and the awareness and use of French Arthurian romances. Chapter 3 maps and contextualises poetry written around and during the reign of Richard II (1377–99), an era which has been central to the development of subsequent English poetry. Chapter 4 is the first chapter to explore a single work, here *Piers Plowman*, a major poem of medieval English literature. Chapter 5 also explores in detail individual works, Chaucer's *Troilus and Criseyde* and *The Canterbury Tales*, two of the finest poems in the language. Chapter 6 discusses the literary phenomenon of medieval literature in Scotland, literature written in Scots English in the Lowlands of Scotland.

Chapter 7 considers major poets of the sixteenth century, writing during the reign of Henry VIII (1509–47), and studies, in particular, the work of three poets: Skelton, Wyatt and Surrey. Chapter 8 concentrates on the literary productions of Spenser, especially *The Faerie Queene*. Chapter 9 takes up the story of the sonnet begun in chapter 7, focusing principally on sonnet sequences by Sidney and Shakespeare, though it also consider other major Elizabethan sonnet-writers (especially Spenser and Drayton) and explores lyrics written by poets such as Campion. Chapter 10 examines the narrative verse of Marlowe and Shakespeare.

Chapter 11 considers the major poets writing in the first part of the seventeenth century, during the reign of James I (1603–25): John Donne and Ben Jonson. Discussion of the work of Wroth, Lanyer, Drummond, Herrick, Carew and King is also offered. The basis for the chapter division between this and the following chapter is essentially chronological (though Herbert is placed in the next chapter because of his influence on Vaughan). Chapter 12 examines the poetry of other major lyric poets of the seventeenth century, focusing, in particular, on religious poetry produced in the period. Figures considered include Herbert, Vaughan, Cowley, Marvell, Crashaw and Philips. Chapters 13 and 14 are devoted to the career of one of the greatest poets in the language, Milton. The first considers his shorter poems, the second *Paradise Lost*, *Paradise Regained* and *Samson Agonistes*.

Chapter 15 addresses the generation of poets associated with the period following the Restoration of Charles II, especially Dryden, Behn and others. Chapter 16 is given over to readings of three major poems by Dryden, *Absalom and Achitophel*, *Religio Laici* and *The Hind and the Panther*, to allow the contributor to dwell more fully than was possible in chapter 15 on Dryden's poetic achievement as exemplified by three of his major works. Chapter 17 focuses on Swift; chapter 18 on Pope and Samuel Johnson; chapter 19 on eighteenth-century women poets; chapter 20 on the longer eighteenth-century poem (by Akenside, Thomson, Young, Cowper and others); and chapter 21 on eighteenth-century lyric poetry (written by such authors as Gray, Collins, Smart, Joseph Warton, Thomas Warton, Macpherson, Chatterton and Burns).

Chapter 22 offers an overview of English Romantic poetry. Chapter 23 looks at Blake's major lyric poems, especially in *Songs of Innocence and of Experience*, and his prophetic poems. Chapter 24 studies shorter poems by Wordsworth and Coleridge, especially *Lyrical Ballads*. Chapter 25 focuses on Wordsworth's two major long poems, *The Prelude* and *The Excursion*. Chapter 26 examines the work of Hunt, Byron and Moore, and chapter 27 looks at Byron's *Don Juan*, one of the greatest (and funniest) long poems in the language. Chapter 28 analyses the work of Shelley and Keats. Chapter 29 looks at 'third-generation Romantic poetry', in particular the poetry of Beddoes, Clare, Darley, Hemans and Landon. Chapter 30 looks more specifically at poetry by Romantic-era women poets.

Chapter 31 provides an overview of Victorian poetry, before subsequent chapters address the work of individual poets (32 on Tennyson, 33 on Robert Browning and Elizabeth Barrett Browning, 34 on Emily Brontë, Arnold and Clough, 35 on Dante Gabriel Rossetti and Swinburne and 36 on Christina Rossetti and Hopkins). Chapter 37 looks at later Victorian poets (including James Thomson, Symons, Dowson, Lionel Johnson and Housman) and chapter 38 looks at a further grouping of such poets (including Davidson, Kipling, 'Michael Field' [Katherine Harris Bradley and Edith Cooper], Eugene Lee-Hamilton, Augusta Webster and May Kendall).

Chapter 39 supplies an overview of Modernist and Modern poetry; chapter 40 explores the work of Hardy and Mew. Chapter 41 is on Yeats, chapter 42 is on Imagism and chapter 43 is on T. S. Eliot. Chapter 44 looks at the achievement of First World War poets, including Owen, Rosenberg and Sassoon, while chapter 45 explores the thirties poetry produced by Auden, Day Lewis, MacNeice and Spender. Chapter 46 investigates the work of Dylan Thomas and other poets of the 1940s.

Consideration of poetry after 1945 begins with a chapter (47) on Larkin and the Movement, which is followed by a discussion of three twentieth-century women poets – Riding, Stevie Smith and Plath (chapter 48) – and by accounts of Ted Hughes and Seamus Heaney (49), Geoffrey Hill (50), poets from Northern Ireland (Mahon, Muldoon, McGuckian and Carson) and from the Republic of Ireland (Boland and others) (51), and by two chapters on poetry since 1980 (52 and 53).

Inevitably there will be lacunae, but the volume as a whole is intended to stimulate renewed interest in the history of English poetry, to narrate its developments and changes, to trace and explore its linguistic, generic and formal achievements and transformations and to offer illuminating accounts of a multitude of significant poems and poets.

Notes

1. Dylan Thomas, 'Notes on the Art of Poetry', in James Scully (ed.), *Modern Poets on Modern Poetry* (London: Fontana, 1966), pp. 201, 202.
2. 'A General Introduction for My Work', *The Oxford Authors: W. B. Yeats*, ed. Edward Larrissy (Oxford: Oxford University Press, 1997), p. 379.
3. These poems are quoted from *The Norton Anthology of English Literature*, seventh edition, general ed. M. H. Abrams, 2 vols. (New York: Norton, 2000).
4. Valuable predecessors of the present volume include George Saintsbury, *A History of English Prosody*, 3 vols. (London: Macmillan, 1923) and Herbert Grierson and J. C. Smith, *A Critical History of English Poetry* (Harmondsworth: Penguin, in association with Chatto and Windus, 1962). Many notable anthologies of English poetry have also undoubtedly shaped the editorial decisions informing this book.
5. Paul Muldoon, *The End of the Poem: Oxford Lectures in Poetry* (London: Faber, 2006), p. 171.
6. John Kerrigan, *Archipelagic English: Literature, History, and Politics 1603–1717* (Oxford: Oxford University Press, 2008), p. 2.

Chapter 1

Old English poetry

BERNARD O'DONOGHUE

Old English poetry is a somewhat improbable recent success story, in an era when formal study of classical literature and even the study of modern languages have been in decline in England. The most prominent success was Seamus Heaney's verse translation of *Beowulf* in 1999, a volume which won prizes in competition not only with other poetry books but with books in all literary categories. Important as the positive reception of Heaney's marvellous translation was, it was not a sole cause of the new popularity of Old English poetry. His book was also a confirmation of the popularity of this poetry with English poets dating back to the Victorian period and strengthening amongst Modernist poets in the earlier twentieth century.[1] Heaney's predecessors here include Longfellow, Hopkins, Auden, Pound and Edwin Morgan. Some Old English poems, such as *The Wanderer*,[2] *The Seafarer* and *Wulf and Eadwacer* are amongst the most widely translated items in the twentieth century. There have been a number of attempts to identify what quality it was that commended these poems so much to the modern taste, in particular to that of the Modernists; a recurrent phrase is 'the power of the half-stated'. Auden's enthusiasm is much quoted: 'I was spellbound. This poetry, I knew, was going to be my dish . . . Anglo-Saxon and Middle English poetry have been one of my strongest, most lasting influences.'[3] In the main part of this essay I want to concentrate on what Auden might mean by 'influences', trying to describe what qualities in Old English poetry were found useful and expressive for writers in English of later periods.

Hopkins had famously said in 1882 that the Anglo-Saxon language 'is a vastly superior thing to what we have now', and another crucial part of my intention here will be to suggest what it was in the poetry that Hopkins thought was superior.[4] The popularity of the poetry amongst modern writers is all the more notable when we recall how precarious its survival was. Chaucer could not read Old English; when the language and literature began to be studied again in the late sixteenth century, it all had to be done more or less from scratch.[5] The first attested reference to *Beowulf*, by George Hickes in 1700, is to tell his collaborator Humfrey Wanley that he can't find any trace of it.[6] It would be hard to exaggerate how precarious this survival was, and how spectacular its scholarly recuperation. One of the most effective introductions to the condition of that literature bears the ominous title 'The Lost Literature of Medieval England',[7] in which R. W. Chambers argued that the relative lack of overlap in the surviving texts (very little of the poetry is attested in more than one manuscript) suggests that what we have is the tip of a generic iceberg.

Yet, despite this paucity (there are only about 30,000 lines of Old English poetry altogether: some single Middle English poems have as many) and the precariousness of its survival, in one of the most authoritative accounts of the literature Stanley Greenfield says, 'Anglo-Saxon prose and poetry are the major literary achievement of the early Middle Ages. In no other medieval vernacular language does such a hoard of verbal treasures exist for such an extended period (*c.*700–1100) . . . If we had more of what must have been an even greater original creation, our wonder would grow in proportion.'[8] Naturally, in this chapter my attention will be on the principal surviving texts, but the fact that they occur in a major literary and cultural corpus must be emphasised first, if only because of the discredited but not quite forgotten notion of 'the Dark Ages'.[9] Greenfield's grand claim is even more remarkable in view of the late development of scholarly attention to the literature after its beginnings in the late sixteenth century. Tom Shippey's authoritative introduction to the Critical Heritage volume on *Beowulf* gives striking evidence of the late development of any kind of understanding of even this most canonical of Old English poetic works.[10]

The survival of Old English poetry, precarious as it was, is mostly owed to its preservation in four great manuscript collections (for which the neutral word 'codex' is usually used because at least some of them are gatherings of separate materials). When the general project of editing the poetry was undertaken for Columbia University Press by G. P. Krapp and E. V. Dobbie in the 1930s, these four codices were supplemented by two other volumes, *The Paris Psalter* and *The Meters of Boethius*, as *Anglo-Saxon Poetic Records* (hereafter *ASPR*) volume v, and a sixth volume of *The Anglo-Saxon Minor Poems*, containing items (including the historically based poems *The Battle of Brunanburh* and *The Battle of Maldon*) which did not occur in the four principal codices.[11] Outside of the four major volumes of the *Anglo-Saxon Poetic Records* then, there are some poems, including *Maldon*, whose survival was even more fortuitous. The major four codices are the Junius manuscript

(*ASPR* 1 – sometimes called 'the Caedmon manuscript'), the Vercelli Book (*ASPR* 2), the Exeter Book (*ASPR* 3) and *Beowulf* and *Judith* (*ASPR* 4 – sometimes called 'the *Beowulf* manuscript' or 'the *Judith* manuscript'). The six monumental editions of the *ASPR*, published between 1931 and 1953, are beyond the scholarly and economic compass of general poetry readers, but as a method of referencing the major manuscripts and their contents they remain definitive, so I will begin by describing their contents, as an introduction to the subjects and themes of the poetry, and as a way of embracing the principal texts. After using these major collections as an introduction to the poetry, I will end by summarising briefly the texts and techniques which led modern writers like Hopkins and Auden to make such high claims for this poetry and its language.

Considering the contents of the first four codices one by one is not an entirely satisfactory way of introducing their poetic materials; it will become obvious that there are more logical thematic and generic ways of looking at them. For example, Greenfield and Calder (*A New Critical History of Old English Literature*) have separate chapters devoted to poems dealing with Christ and to those dealing with Old Testament subjects, though this cuts across the four collections. Godden and Lapidge[12] assign chapters to their contributors along the same lines. Wrenn[13] gives prominence to the one named poet, Cynewulf, and thereafter organises the poems on thematic and generic grounds: lyric, heroic, elegiac. Alexander[14] does something similar, foregrounding what he sees (not unpersuasively) as the most attractive genres for the modern reader: riddle, elegy and heroic poetry – the last category in order to accommodate *Beowulf* and *Maldon*. Swanton,[15] in the rather quaint fashion of his era, uses impressionistic rather than descriptive chapter titles: 'Until the Dragon Comes', and 'The Ruin of Time', for example. O'Brien O'Keeffe[16] breaks away from both the codex-defined corpus and the attempts to define by subject or theme, by assigning to her contributors a series of critical approaches. Pulsiano and Treharne[17] and their team of contributors organise the material on grounds of theme and provenance. Shippey remains a good, critically alert introduction to the poetic corpus as a whole.

Before outlining the contents of the four codices, one wider general issue of categorisation should be raised. There has been some vigorous debate as to whether the corpus of Old English poetry is entirely religious. An important, and unusual, feature of the history of Old English poetry and its survival arises here. If any of the surviving poetry can be seen as secular and pre-Christian, its distant historical content is 'the fund of common narrative material associated with the Teutonic Migration Period (fourth to sixth centuries)'.[18] The complicating factor is that all the major surviving manuscript evidence dates from around the year 1000, long after the events (if we can call them anything so concrete) they deal with. It goes without saying that any poetry worthy of the name, religious or not, will draw on the natural world for its imagery, and Old English poetry often does so with unforgettable success. But was the objective of this poetry invariably to promote religious – and therefore, in its era, Christian – feeling and understanding? The question is pointedly raised by the different emphases in two major discussions: Greenfield's chapter 6 is called 'Secular Heroic Poetry', but in his important book *The Search for Anglo-Saxon Paganism* (1975), Eric Stanley argued that the corpus's only religious or ethical perspective is Christian. The poems which are solely heroic (*Deor* and*Widsith* for example) are not founded on some alternative 'pagan' morality. Stanley suggests that the old view that there was some pre-Christian secular heroic ethic in the literature was largely attributable to nineteenth-century German antiquaries, intent on constructing textual evidence for a distinctive Germanic-Teutonic past.

But to return to the corpus as included in the first four *ASPR* volumes: the first is an edition of Oxford Bodleian Library, Junius 11, assembled in the 1650s by the German-Dutch antiquary Franciscus Junius and given by him to the Bodleian Library in Oxford, where it still is. The principal poetic items in that manuscript are *Genesis A* and *B*, *Exodus*, *Daniel* and *Christ and Satan*. The Old Testament predominance is evident and earlier scholars thought – and hoped – that these poems might be the very poems written by the first attested English poet, the monk Caedmon, whose miraculous receiving of the poetic vocation was so spellbindingly described by Bede in his *History of the English Church and People*. After an angel had prompted this Whitby cowherd to sing, 'he sang of the creation of the world and of the origin of the human race and the whole narrative of Genesis, concerning the going out from Egypt of the Israelites and their entry into the land of promise'.[19] In fact the poems in the manuscript are very different both from each other and from the suggestion of Biblical paraphrase in this story. Although *Exodus* has attracted a good deal of modern scholarly attention, prompted by an impressive modern edition by Peter Lucas (1994), the subject of most critical discussion here has been *Genesis B*, lines 235–851 of the original poem traditionally called *Genesis*.[20] This section, dated to the mid ninth century rather than the (speculative) date of 700 for the rest of the poem (thereafter called *Genesis A*), is thought to be based on a Continental Saxon original. Most strikingly it features a vivid presentation of Satan which has provoked comparison with Book 1 of *Paradise Lost*, a comparison which was reinforced by the speculation that Milton might have been in contact with Junius, the owner of the codex, in London. The idea that the Bible-based poems of the Junius Manuscript are the work of Caedmon and that *Genesis B* might warrant the title 'Caedmonian Genesis' has long been abandoned; nowadays it is believed that the only thing that can be assigned to Caedmon is the nine-line 'Hymn' of creation, interpolated by Bede into his Latin *Historia*. Still, 'The Fall of the Angels' was one of the pieces of Old English found most exciting by Auden, and its figure of Satan, 'se ofermoda cyning, þe ær wæs engla scynost' ('the over-proud king who formerly was the brightest of angels') retains its compulsion for the modern reader.

ASPR 2, the Vercelli Book, has the most curious history of the great Old English codices. Discovered in Vercelli in North Italy in 1822 by a German lawyer, Friedrich Blume, criticism of it, as with the Junius Manuscript, has traditionally been dominated by attention to a single poem, *The Dream of the Rood*, a poem that has been greeted (by Helen Gardner, for example) as one of the greatest religious poems in the English language. The poem has a significant interest too in terms of its textual history. Though, as I have said, most of the surviving Old English poetry was written down around the year 1000, even when it is concerned with events several centuries earlier, a passage corresponding closely to a section of *The Dream of the Rood* is found in runes on the Ruthwell Cross in southern Scotland, a monument conjecturally dated to the period 670–750 (though to somewhat later dates too). The Vercelli Book as a whole is lacking in thematic coherence compared to the other codices. I will return later (in connection with the Exeter Book Riddles) to describe the imaginative brilliance of the verbal symbolism in *The Dream of the Rood*. For the poetry reader, the other significant contents in the book are *Andreas* and two poems by Cynewulf, the only known named poet in Old English, genuinely identified by his signature in runes at the end of four poems. The two poems by him here are *The Fates of the Apostles* and *Elene*. The latter, dealing with the finding of the Cross by St Helena, is related to *The Dream of the Rood* by the centrality of the Cross.[21]

The quality which made Hopkins think Old English poetry was a vastly superior thing to what we have now was its language: not surprising from a poet whose poetic language is seen as a crucial factor in his distinction. This linguistic excellence can be illustrated from many places in Old English poetry: from *Beowulf* or *The Dream of the Rood*, for example. But when we turn to the third of the four major volumes in the Anglo-Saxon Poetic Records, the Exeter Book, we encounter strikingly the quality that has principally appealed to the twentieth century from the Modernists onwards. This is a thematic rather than a linguistic feature: the wonderfully evoked elegiac note which has been so valued and practised in twentieth-century poetry.[22] This theme is most celebratedly prominent in the Exeter Book, the 'micela boc' already present in Exeter in the eleventh century in the time of Bishop Leofric, and dated on codicological and literary evidence to the decade 965–75.[23] And, although Auden famously responded too to the heroic-laconic spirit in Old English and Old Norse writings, it is also the elegiac note that made him confident that this poetry would be his 'dish'. The note is also prominent in *Beowulf*, of course: Tolkien memorably called the bulk of the great poem 'in a sense . . . the prelude to a dirge'.[24] In describing the great so-called 'elegies' of the Exeter Book – *The Wanderer*, *The Seafarer*, *The Wife's Lament* and *Wulf and Eadwacer*, all of which are among the texts most commonly translated into modern English poetry – some caution is called for. Since the early nineteenth century, when the poems were first named by their editors of the Romantic period, modern concerns and preferences were found mirror-imaged in the early poetry, and sometimes they sound like items in a Schubert song-cycle.[25] To take the most obvious example, *The Wanderer*, the title translates the word 'eardstapa' (line 6) aptly enough; but the first word used to refer to the poem's protagonist in the opening line is 'anhaga', the 'sole-thinker'. The poem therefore might have more naturally been called 'The Recluse', a title which would take the poem's subject nearer to the religious canon rather than to a secular one for which there is little evidence.

There has been a good deal of inconclusive debate about which poems precisely can be included in the category of elegy, or indeed whether it constitutes a category at all. However, this is no more true of this category than at the borders of any genre as discussed, say, by Todorov: the medieval romance is an obvious parallel. There are at least four poems in the Exeter Book which are universally agreed to have enough in common for them to be regarded as part of the genre of elegy: pre-eminent amongst them are *The Wanderer* and *The Seafarer*, the pairing that first came to major notice in the nineteenth century and which since then has been a standard presence in the canon of English poetry.[26] Increasingly, *The Ruin* and *The Wife's Lament* have been seen as central members of the elegiac group (nowadays *Wulf and Eadwacer* has been an equally common inclusion in the group, though perhaps with less justification, I will suggest). Other poems and parts of poems, both in the Exeter Book and outside it, are generically similar too, principally in their shared concern with transience. Two famous episodes from *Beowulf* fit here: the celebrated 'Lay of the Last Retainer' (again, also known by less lyrically romantic titles such as 'The Lament of the Last Survivor'), lines 2244–70 of the poem, and Beowulf's account of the misery of King Hrethel, one of whose sons killed another, an 'offence . . . beyond redress, a wrongfooting / of the heart's affections'.[27] The Hrethel passage is followed by one of the great set-piece elegies in the poem, the comparison with 'the misery felt by an old man / who has lived to see his son's body / swing on the gallows'.[28] Within the Exeter Book itself, the poems *Deor* and *The Husband's Message* are often added to the group of elegies, though there are other genres (heroic poem and riddle respectively) to which they might equally well be assigned.[29] Stanley Greenfield extended the group to 'nine (ten?)' by adding further items from The Exeter Book: *The Riming Poem* and the poem or poems – one or two, according to editorial division – which have been titled *Resignation (A and B)*[30] or *The Exile's Prayer*.[31] Muir, somewhat unhelpfully, calls the poem *Contrition (A and B)* without cross-reference in his contents, though his notes are the best succinct account of the poem's critical treatment in the modern era.[32]

The order in which Greenfield considers the poems is a useful guide both to their prominence in the modern era and to their degree of Christianisation. *The Ruin* is an eloquent reflection – the term for it since the early nineteenth century would be 'gothic' – on transience, prompted by the state of a decayed city, probably Bath. We might borrow the terminology once used for the chronological categorisation of epic (though of course we have no textual evidence for this periodisation): we could call *The Ruin* primary elegy, as an unadorned reflection on the tragedy of transience; *The Wanderer* would be secondary elegy, centring on the same tragedy but with book-ends of Christian consolation at the start and end of the poem; and *The Seafarer* would be tertiary, or applied elegy, where, despite the powerful evocativeness of the description of nature and of the desolation of life at sea, the argument is always under the control of a Christian allegorist from the moment that it is declared that everyone has to be concerned for his seafaring ('his saefore') as to 'what his lord will do to him' (lines 42–3).

But this is to push categorisation too far, failing to allow these great poems their independence or to acknowledge their difference from each other. As all commentators have noted, what the poems do have in common is a pattern well described by Shippey as 'Wisdom and Experience'. The poems' opening sections are typically powerful descriptions of worldly hardship:

Hægl scurum fleag –
þær ic ne hyrde butan hlimman sæ,
iscaldne wæg. Hwilum ylfete song
dyde ic me to gomene ganetes hleoþor
ond huilpan sweg fore hleahtor wera,
mæw singende fore medodrince.

(*The Seafarer*, lines 17–22)

(Hail flew in showers. There I heard nothing but the sea booming, the ice-cold wave. At times I took my pleasure in the swan's song, the gannet's scream and the curlew's music rather than the laughter of people, the gull's singing in place of mead-drinking.)[33]

I will return to the poetic felicities of this – the contrastive echo of 'hleoþor/ hleahtor' (scream/laughter), for example – at the end of the chapter, when I consider Old English poetics in general. What we might note for now is that this passage, which to us tends to read as a romantic or 'sublime' evocation of nature, in its era is an evocation of the misery of exclusion from the society of the hall-gathering: one of the most powerful recurrent themes of the culture. By the end of the poem, the wisdom of Christian consolation is totally vindicated, expressed through a paraphrase of the Beatitudes of the Sermon on the Mount (lines 106–7) and ending with the wording of the *Gloria Patri* ('thanks be to the holy one . . . the eternal lord, for ever and ever. Amen').

To the modern taste, the less reconciled consolatory conclusion of *The Wanderer* is more powerful. True, the poem also moves to its conclusion with the Beatitudes again ('it is well for him who seeks favour and comfort from the father in the heavens'), but what stays with the reader is the magnificent rhetoric of the *ubi sunt* passage, which equals Villon:

Hwær cwom mearg? Hwær cwom mago? Hwær cwom maþþumgyfa?
Hwær cwom symbla gesetu? Hwær sindon seledreamas?
Eala beorht bune! Eala byrnwiga!
Eala þeodnes þrym! Hu seo þrag gewat,
genap under nihthelm, swa heo no wære! (lines 92–6)

(Where has the steed gone? Where the rider? Where has the treasure-giver gone? Where the place of feasting? Where are the joys of hall? Alas the bright cup! Alas the armoured warrior! Alas the lord's power! How the time has passed, grown dark under the cover of night as if it had never been!)

It should be said that, even if it is this dark note that has been found so appealing in the era of the elegy of the past 200 years, part of the satisfaction of reading these poems lies in the elegant balance of story and moral.

I have mentioned already how the power of the half-stated in these poems was found so appealing to the early twentieth-century Modernists, with their mystique of doubt and fragmentation. Two poems manifest this particularly. The first is *The Wife's Lament*, a poem which is again founded on the experience–wisdom model, but in which the experience is so cryptically expressed and in such a compressed form that it is not clear exactly what the consolation is for. The poem begins almost identically to *The Seafarer* with the protagonist's claim that they (in this case she) are recounting their own experience and exploiting the common figure of journey ('siþ') as experience:

Ic þis giedd wrece bi me ful geomorre,
minre sylfre siþ.

(I compose this song about myself in my sorrow, of my own experience.)

This woman's lament – possibly a voice from the grave and thus a 'revenant' of the kind much favoured by the Modernists – also ends with a Sermon on the Mount motif, 'Woe is he who . . .' But here the separation from 'min freond' retains its unconsoled power to the end. This 'friend' or 'lord' seems somehow to be implicated in responsibility for the woman's isolation and his own, where he sits 'under stanhlifle storme behrimed' ('under a stone cliff, frosted by the storm', line 48; a location which we know from a famous passage in *Beowulf* has an infernal association).

Even more mysterious is the situation so memorably evoked in the poem traditionally named *Wulf and Eadwacer*. This also seems to be a woman's poem – the category of medieval poems referred to as *frauenlieder* in German, so not unparalleled – and a narrative can be speculatively constructed from its hauntingly baffling opening line:

Leodum is minum swylce him mon lac gife.

(It is as if someone should give a commemorative gift to my people),

to its equally evocative but uncertain moralising end:

Þæt mon eaþe tosliteð þætte næfre gesomnad wæs –
uncer giedd geador.

(That can easily be separated which was never joined together – the song of the two of us together.)

The romantic story that has been speculatively constructed is that the woman speaker is the wife of one Eadwacer, addressed in the lines before the concluding moral, and that her lover is Wulf, addressed in a remarkable apostrophe at the mid-point of the poem, 'Wulf, min Wulf!' Of the poems called elegy, this is the one that has least in common formally or thematically with the others, and indeed has the least claim to be termed an 'elegy' at all.[34] It has, like *Deor*, a refrain ('Ungelic is us ': 'it is not like that for us'), and no suggestion of a transience theme or any religious interpretation. Its closest connection is with *The Wife's Lament*, through the woman speaker and the suggestion of enforced separation and isolation.

Like another of the poems in the expanded elegy group, *The Husband's Message* (so called out of an excessive desire for balance on the part of the early editors, who wanted to link it with the very dissimilar *Wife's Lament*), the poems in the Exeter Book with which *Wulf and Eadwacer* has most in common are the groups of Riddles. The domination of the critical discussion of the 'micela boc' by the elegies has to some extent recently been modified by interest in these accomplished poems, with their significant classical parallels.[35] There is a significant overlap between the two categories, in fact; Greenfield and Calder's chapter before the one on elegy is entitled 'Lore and Wisdom', and, as Shippey's chapter title of his elegy discussion 'Wisdom and Experience' suggests, parts of the elegies might well be included under that heading. Greenfield and Calder deal with the Riddles in that chapter, as well as with several other varieties of 'wisdom literature': three series of *Maxims, Precepts*, a *Homiletic Fragment* and so on.

I am directing attention to the Riddles, though, not only because of their modern popularity. They are also one of the fundamental poetic genres in Old English, employing a kind of word-play that also underlies, as we will see, *The Dream of the Rood*. Furthermore, they represent an undeniable connection with classical literature and with the Latin writing of Aldhelm in the Anglo-Saxon period itself. Above all, they have a wit and verbal ingenuity which represent a major achievement in their own right. Their subjects cover a wide range of subjects, both religious and profane (to the point of indecency); often the wit consists precisely in the gap between the two. One of the most often-quoted of them, 'Moððe word fræt', is a good example of the operation of metaphorical style and resonance in these poems:

Moððe word fræt. Me þæt þuhte
wrætlicu wyrd, þa ic þæt wundor gefrægn,
þæt se wyrm forswealg wera gied sumes,
þeof in þystro, þrymfæstne cwide
ond þæs strangan staþol. Stælgiest ne wæs
wihte þy gleawra, þe he þam wordum swealg.

(Riddle 47, lines 1–6)

(A moth ate words. That seemed to me an amazing event when I heard of that marvel, that the worm – a thief in the darkness – swallowed the poem of one of mankind, his powerful saying and its strong subject. The thieving visitor was not the least the wiser for swallowing the words.)

First of all, this works excellently as a riddle; the curious story fills with meaning when the reader realises the solution: a bookworm. The way the poem moves from the literal operation of the noted event (a bookworm eating a manuscript: itself, of course, a minor crisis in the era when expensive vellum was the material of books) to the metaphorical reflection that this consuming of text does not lead to any increase in wisdom, sophisticated enough as that is, is only the beginning of the poem's meaning. It is also about reading: an inattentive reader, whether reading aloud or to themselves, may take the words on board without registering the meaning. This reader-theory interpretation reminds us to be cautious about patronising the works that develop from an oral tradition. It is not only the verbal form of the poem that is sophisticated; the understanding of literature here is also advanced.

Of the Old English poems that draw on the riddling tradition (I have already noted the links with it in the crypticism of *Wulf and Eadwacer* and possibly *The Husband's Message*), the most impressive is *The Dream of the Rood*, in the Vercelli Book. The poem begins with the report of a visionary dream, experienced in the middle of the night when 'reordberend' ('voice-bearers') are asleep and silent. The object seen is a wonderful tree, the 'brightest of beams'. We know from the Exeter Book that there was a tradition of Cross-riddles,[36] so the identity of this tree is not in doubt well before it is identified as the 'rood' (the specifically theological word for Christ's Cross) at line 44 ('Rod wæs ic aræred': 'as a cross I was raised up'). But the more important and poetically productive quality of the riddles that the poem draws on is the dazzling and profound use of imagery.

There is a striking use of this characteristic play of imagery early in the poem. The Cross of the vision is described as 'beama beorhtost' ('brightest of beams'): already in Old English the word 'beam' has a secondary sense of 'ray of light' as well as the primary 'plank of wood', so a constructive choice of interpretation is already offered.[37] The vision is then described in a strange conceit: 'Eall þæt beacen wæs / begoten mid golde' ('All that sign/beacon was suffused/soaked through with gold', lines 6–7). The word 'begoten' seems to belong particularly to contexts of suffusion by liquid (as in the later sense of begetting), so it seems mysterious to apply it to the appearance of the Cross. Can something look soaked *through* with gold: with a metal which can only be laid on its surface? But this metaphysical mystery is resolved forty lines later when the speaking Cross says that it was all soaked with blood, 'begoten of þæs guman sidan' ('shed from the man's side', line 49). This more idiomatic, liquid-related application of the participle 'shed/poured/suffused' is a retrospective identification and explanation of why the surface of the Cross was soaked with gold: the gold is a symbolic representation of the blood of Christ.

By an identical process of metaphorical substitution, in lines 13–14 of the poem the dreamer describes himself as 'synnum fah, / forwundod mid wommum' ('guilty / stained / adorned with sins, / wounded / pierced through with stains / blemishes'). How can a blemish – a word that means a superficial mark on the skin – wound or pierce *through*? Again, much later in the poem, the answer is provided by the repetition of the descriptive participle: the Cross describes itself as 'mid strælum forwundod' ('wounded or pierced through with shafts / arrows', line 62). The literal description again comes later to explain the puzzle of the earlier conceit, this time to make the symbolic identification of arrows and sins.

There is not room here to develop the extraordinary web of symbolism on which *The Dream of the Rood* is constructed, to show how the complex of meanings all serve the same dualist theological paradox. A non-speaking thing – the Cross – is endowed with the power of speech while 'reordberend' ('voice-bearers') are asleep and therefore speechless. The poem is a classic instance of the impossibility of translation (suggested by the need to give alternatives in the translations) because so much of its terminology is founded on contradictions and paradoxes, representing the triumph and tragedy of the crucifixion. The word 'fah' (quoted from line 14 above) recurs in the poem, to exploit its homonymic possibilities; helplessly but accurately, Mitchell and Robinson gloss the word as 'stained, guilty, outcast', but in brackets as 'decorated'. This is entirely in keeping with the paradoxical status of the event as tragic but also a cause for rejoicing; but what single modern English word can express that? At a famous point in the poem the Cross says that after the death of Christ the men began to make a tomb, 'beornas on banan gesyhðe' ('men in the sight of the slayer', line 66). When the Cross refers to itself as Christ's killer (the modern descendant of 'bana' is 'bane', and the Old English term seems no less pejorative), how can we represent the word?

If it is difficult to suggest in a brief essay how the dualist complexities of this poem operate, it is even more difficult to give a short account of *Beowulf*, incomparably the largest achievement in Old English poetry, in a satisfactory way.[38] It shares the fourth of the *ASPR* volumes with the poem *Judith* (itself perhaps the greatest of the Biblical-heroic poems in Old English)[39] and some lesser items. A consideration of *Beowulf* amongst the poems in Old English might start with thematic links to other texts: of things I have mentioned already, Tolkien's observation that it is 'a long prelude to a dirge' clearly links it with the elegiac, as do the passages on 'the last retainer' and the tragically bereaved father. The 'power of the half-stated' admired in the elegies is nowhere more impressive than in the mysterious and tragic opening of the poem's Finnsburh's episode (whose independence Heaney aptly acknowledges by using a different verse form for it in his translation). Without preamble King Hroþgar's 'scop', his court-poet, launches into the story of Hildeburh, the queen at the tragic centre of the war between her husband and brother:

> Nalles holinga Hoces dohtor
> meotodsceaft bemearn, syþþan morgen com,
> ða heo under swegle geseon meahte
> morþor-bealo maga, þær heo ær mæste heold
> worolde wynne.[40]

(By no means without cause did the daughter of Hoc lament her fate, when morning came and she could see under the sky the murder-feud of kinsmen, where before she had most enjoyed joy in the world.)

Although its manuscript dates, like the other major codices, from about the year 1000, *Beowulf* is the foundational case of Old English poetic style, for the same kinds of reason that Homer's work became the foundation-stone of Greek poetic rhetoric, which in turn became the model for Western poetics in general. Even in a short extract like the one I have just quoted, the principal poetic features are evident: the alliterative scheme on dominant word-roots with its ringing consonants ('meotod-', '-mearn', 'morgen' in line 1077), which was what Hopkins admired so much in his definition of 'sprung rhythm'; the noun–noun compounds which give such solidity to the word-formation ('meotodsceaft', 'morþor-bealo'); the figure of variation which has been seen as the essential device in the stately narrative pacing of Old English, by which – as most famously in the terms for God in Caedmon's Hymn – different terms are used to refer to the same subject (here 'Hildeburh' in the previous sentence, line 1071, 'Hoces dohtor', 'heo', in apposition to each other). One of the best books on the poetics of *Beowulf* sees apposition and duality as the founding principle of Old English poetic language: the morphological units build into compound words, the words into half-lines, the half-lines into full lines and the lines into units of sense.[41] This structuring principle has been taken a stage further, to demonstrate that the units of narrative – what might by analogy be called verse paragraphs – often start and end with the same details. For example, the Finnsburh episode just quoted begins by saying that there was a 'gid oft wrecen' ('a recitation often performed', line 1065) and ends 'Leoð wæs oft asungen / gleo-mannes gyd' ('A song was often sung, a gleeman's recitation', lines 1159–60). Similarly, the arming of Beowulf before his encounter with Grendel's mother begins 'Gyrede hine Beowulf / eorl-gewædum' ('Beowulf dressed himself in nobleman-arms', lines 1441–2), and ends 'syþþan he hine to guðe gegyred hæfde' ('when he had dressed himself for battle', line 1472).

This concentration on the poetics of the poem, brief as it is, is guilty of a further inadequacy in failing to deal both with the overall design of *Beowulf* and with the powerful set-pieces of epic-heroic literature throughout, from the opening description of Scyld Scefing's ship-burial[42] to the Wagnerian conclusion with Beowulf's own immolation. Neither is there room to describe in detail Hroþgar's account of the infernal landscape by Grendel's mere with its Tartarean iconography, reported by the locals, the 'londbuende':

Hie dygel lond
warigeað, wulf-hleoþu, windige næssas,
frecne fen-gelad, ðær fyrgen-stream
under næssa genipu niþer gewiteð,
flod under foldan. (lines 1357–61)

(They [the Grendel family] occupy a hidden land, wolf-slopes and windblown crags, a dangerous fen-path, where the mountain-stream travels downwards under the darkness of the cliffs, a river under the ground.)

Other great moments are the Song of Creation, the 'swutol song scopes' ('the clear song of the court-poet', lines 90ff.), translated separately by Heaney as 'The Fragment'.[43]

Beowulf of course also connects with the tradition of heroic poetry in Old English, mostly but not entirely Biblical. The most celebrated of the heroic poems (if it really is that) is *The Battle of Maldon*, edited in *ASPR* 6, whose preservation is even more precarious than the *Beowulf* manuscript's survival of the Cotton Fire at Ashburnham House in 1731. The manuscript containing *Maldon* was burned, so the poem's survival is owed to a transcript made by one David Casley a few years before the fire. The poem is famous for its ringing voicing of the spirit of heroic loyalty by Byrhtwold (not otherwise known), after the death of his leader Byrhtnoð in this tactically disastrous defeat of the English by the Vikings in 991:

Hige sceal þe heardra, heorte þe cenre,
mod sceal þe mare, þe ure mægen lytlað.[44]

(Spirit must be the harder, heart the braver, determination must be the more, as our number lessens.)

Maldon was probably written soon after the event, though of course we can't know, in the case of a poem surviving from an early eighteenth-century copy. In poetic terms, it is far from the finest example of Old English poetics, marked by a rather prosaic style, despite the interest of its subject which has caused it to be read as a – perhaps artificial – last rallying cry of the English in the generation before the Scandinavian domination of the country became complete.

With Old English poetry we are not just encountering a new poetic, founded on an unfamiliar version of the elegiac (*Beowulf* as Tolkien's 'prelude to a dirge'), or a set of formalities which are strikingly new to us: variation, alliterative patterns and the rest, forcefully effective as those are. Neither is it just a matter of Hopkins's 'vastly superior thing': the monosyllabic and consonantal force of the language, so brilliantly and unliterally captured in Pound's *Seafarer*: 'siþas secgan', 'speak of journeys', represented as 'journey's jargon'. Perhaps more important than any of these are the ways in which this poetry *is* familiar:[45] the Metaphysical figure for hailstones in *The Seafarer* as 'corna caldast', 'coldest of corn'; the Villonesque wistfulness in *The Wanderer*'s apostrophe to the 'bright cup': 'Eala beorht bune!'; above all the intricate dualist symbolism of *The Dream of the Rood*. Through these qualities Old English poetry has a place in a tradition of verbal wit and poetic imagination that is familiar to readers of poetry from the fourteenth century to the seventeenth and the twentieth, and for which no special pleading or allowances have to be made. It is probably futile to propose some enduring spirit in English poetry that survived the huge change in the language after the Conquest, as James Fenton says. But it is tempting to claim, after all, a continuity greater than that controversially proposed by Thomas Kinsella for Irish literature in the modern period: a continuity that witnesses 'a notable and venerable literary tradition . . . as it survives a change of vernacular'.[46]

Notes

1. See Chris Jones, *Strange Likeness: The Use of Old English in Twentieth-Century Poetry* (Oxford: Oxford University Press, 2006).
2. Throughout the chapter, I will italicise the titles of the individual poems for consistency. Many of them have been edited separately in the Methuen series of Old English texts, several later published by Exeter University Press.
3. W. H. Auden, *The Dyer's Hand and Other Essays* (London: Faber, 1963), pp. 41–2.
4. *The Letters of Gerard Manley Hopkins*, ed. C. C. Abbott (London: Oxford University Press, 1935), p. 163.
5. For a discussion of when Old English was intelligible or otherwise, see R. D. Fulk and Christopher Cain, *A History of Old English Literature* (Oxford: Blackwell, 2003), 'Conclusion', pp. 225ff.
6. Kenneth Sisam, 'Humfrey Wanley', in *Studies in the History of Old English Literature* (Oxford: Clarendon Press, 1953), p. 276.

7. R. W. Chambers, 'The Lost Literature of Medieval England', originally published in *The Library*, Fourth Series, 5:4 (March 1925). Reprinted in J. B. Bessinger and S. J. Kahrl (eds.), *Essential Articles for the Study of Old English Poetry* (Hamden, CT: Archon Books, 1968), pp. 3–26.
8. Stanley B. Greenfield and Daniel G. Calder, *A New Critical History of Old English Literature* (New York: New York University Press, 1986), p. 1. First edition by Greenfield alone, containing this passage, 1965.
9. 'The Dark Ages' received their literary death-blow from the great work of Ernst R. Curtius, *European Literature and the Latin Middle Ages*, trans. Willard R. Trask (New York: Pantheon Books; London: Routledge and Kegan Paul, 1953; originally published in German in 1948). Curtius established the unsurprising truth that medieval literature, far from being a new start *ex nihilo*, was firmly rooted in the late Latin classics. Peter Dronke has built powerfully in several books on Curtius's foundations. Also see Michael Lapidge, 'The Anglo-Latin Background', in Greenfield and Calder, *New Critical History*, pp. 5–37. It is worth remembering too, when stressing the paucity of Old English poetry, that it comprised less than 9 per cent of the surviving written corpus; there is a large volume of Old English prose which survived in the literary history more successfully than the poetry.
10. T. A. Shippey, *Old English Verse* (London: Hutchinson University Library, 1972). A useful brief outline of the history of the poetry in its own time is the Introduction to Fulk and Cain (eds.), *History of Old English Literature*.
11. G. P. Krapp and E. V. Dobbie (eds.), *The Anglo-Saxon Poetic Records*, 6 vols. (New York: Columbia University Press, 1931–53).
12. M. Godden and M. Lapidge (eds.), *The Cambridge Companion to Old English Literature* (Cambridge: Cambridge University Press, 1991).
13. C. L. Wrenn, *A Study of Old English Literature* (London: Harrap, 1967).
14. Michael Alexander, *The First Poems in English* (London: Penguin, 2008).
15. Michael Swanton, *English Literature before Chaucer* (London: Longman, 1987).
16. K. O'Brien O'Keeffe, *Reading Old English Texts* (Cambridge: Cambridge University Press, 1997).
17. Phillip Pulsiano and Elaine Treharne (eds.), *A Companion to Anglo-Saxon Literature* (Oxford: Blackwell, 2001).
18. Greenfield and Calder, *New Critical History*, p. 134.
19. Translation quoted from Wrenn, *Study of Old English Literature*, p. 94.
20. 'The Fall of the Angels' was the very successful title given by Henry Sweet to the extract he included in his *Anglo-Saxon Reader in Prose and Verse* (Oxford: Clarendon Press, 1876, much revised and reprinted). The often inspired titles given by Sweet are hardly less important than the names devised by the editors of the Romantic period. See, for example, Geoffrey Hill's adoption of one of Sweet's headings for his celebrated poetry collection *Mercian Hymns*.
21. The short discussion of the relations between the two versions in the 1934 Methuen edition of *The Dream of the Rood* by Dickins and Ross remains a good statement of the case (*The Dream of the Rood*, eds. Bruce Dickins and Alan S. C.

Ross, London: Methuen, 1963, pp. 1–19). The authoritative modern commentator is Éamon Ó Carragáin: see his *Ritual and the Rood: Liturgical Images and the Old English Poems of The 'Dream of the Rood' Tradition* (London: The British Library; Toronto: University of Toronto Press, 2005).

22. See for example Peter Sacks, *The English Elegy: Studies in the Genre from Spenser to Yeats* (Baltimore: Johns Hopkins University Press, 1985); Jahan Ramazani, *Poetry of Mourning: The Modern Elegy from Hardy to Heaney* (Chicago: University of Chicago Press, 1994).
23. Bernard J. Muir (ed.), *The Exeter Anthology of Old English Poetry: An Edition of Exeter Dean and Chapter MS 3501* (Exeter: University of Exeter Press, 1994), vol. I, p. 1.
24. J. R. R. Tolkien, '*Beowulf*: The Monsters and the Critics'. This was the Sir Israel Gollancz Memorial Lecture to the British Academy in 1936, but it remains much the most suggestive and thought-provoking short introduction to *Beowulf*. Quoted here from *The Monsters and the Critics, and Other Essays*, ed. Christopher Tolkien (London: George Allen and Unwin, 1983), p. 31.
25. This also applies to the familiar but, when we think about it, strange title, *The Dream of the Rood*, which might more neutrally but less evocatively be called – as it was for some time – 'The Vision of the Cross'.
26. It is a pity, and surprising, that James Fenton in his admirable *Introduction to English Poetry* (London: Penguin, 2002) excludes this poetry on the grounds that he finds no 'continuity between the traditions of Anglo-Saxon poetry and those established in English poetry by the time of, say, Shakespeare' (p. 1). This is regrettable both because it excludes from his consideration some unquestionably inspiring poems in English and because it blurs the connections between the poetics of Old English and some modern practitioners who drew directly on it, like Auden and Pound.
27. *Beowulf*, lines 2441–2, in Seamus Heaney's version (London: Faber and Faber, 1999). Like a few other passages from *Beowulf*, Heaney has also drawn on this for a section in a separate poem (*Electric Light*, London: Faber, 2001), pp. 62–3.
28. Heaney, *Beowulf*, lines 2444–6.
29. There are several excellent brief accounts of the elegies: for example Shippey, *Old English Verse*, ch. 3; Christine Fell's 'Perceptions of Transience' (ch. 10 in Godden and Lapidge, *Cambridge Companion to Old English Literature*); and ch. 12, 'Elegiac Poetry', in Greenfield and Calder, *New Critical History*.
30. Greenfield and Calder, *New Critical History*, p. 280.
31. Fell, 'Perceptions of Transience', p. 172.
32. Muir (ed.), *Exeter Anthology*, vol. I, pp. 339–43; vol. II, pp. 630–5.
33. The extracts from the Exeter Book here are mostly taken from Muir's edition, with occasional modified punctuation; the plain translations are mine. There are, however, excellent, readily available translations of Old English poetry, both into plain modern prose (R. K. Gordon, *Anglo Saxon Verse* (London: Everyman, 1926); S. A. J. Bradley, *Anglo-Saxon Poetry* (London: Everyman, 1982)), and into verse (Richard Hamer, *A Choice of Anglo Saxon Verse* (London: Faber and Faber,

1970), Kevin Crossley-Holland, *The Anglo-Saxon World: An Anthology* (Oxford: Oxford University Press, 1999) and Alexander, *The First Poems in English*). Gordon has particular significance for the subject of this chapter as the version of the poetry with which Auden seems to have been most familiar. See John Fuller, *A Reader's Guide to W. H. Auden* (London: Thames and Hudson, 1970).

34. The Exeter Book's first modern editor and translator B. L. Thorpe (London, 1842) called it Riddle 1, famously saying 'Of this I can make no sense, nor am I able to arrange the verses' (p. 527).
35. A convenient modern translation is Kevin Crossley-Holland, *The Exeter Book Riddles* (Harmondsworth: Penguin, revised edition 1993). A full edition is Craig Williamson, *The Old English Riddles of the Exeter Book* (Chapel Hill: University of North Carolina Press, 1977). It should be noted of course that as well as the various shorter poems, the Exeter Book also contains several significant longer religious works which bring its contents closer to the first two *ASPR* volumes: *The Passion of St Juliana*, the two lives of *St Guthlac* (*A* and *B*) and two major poems about Christ, *Christ in Judgement* and *The Ascension*.
36. See especially number 55 (Muir (ed.), *Exeter Anthology*, p. 327). For a translation, see Crossley-Holland, *Anglo-Saxon World*, p. 59. Alexander, who is the best translator of the Riddles, has not included this in *First Poems in English*, though it is in his full translation in *Old English Riddles: From the Exeter Book*, revised edition (London: Anvil Press Poetry, 2007).
37. I am quoting from the version of the poem in Bruce Mitchell and Fred C. Robinson, *A Guide to Old English*, seventh edition (Oxford: Blackwell, 2007), pp. 268–75, because some of their restoration of manuscript readings seem preferable to the emendations made in some earlier editions.
38. There are some good brief introductions: Tolkien, 'The Monsters and the Critics'; Shippey's *Old English Verse*; Heather O'Donoghue's introduction to Kevin Crossley-Holland's *Anglo-Saxon World*. Heaney's introduction to his translation is, amongst other things, a moving reading of the poem's tragic politics for the modern age. There are many crucial critical treatments of *Beowulf* since the late nineteenth century: Andy Orchard, *A Critical Companion to 'Beowulf'* (Cambridge: Brewer, 2003); T. A. Shippey and Andreas Haarder, *Beowulf: The Critical Heritage* (London: Routledge, 1998); R. E. Bjork and J. D. Niles (eds.), *A 'Beowulf' Handbook* (Lincoln: University of Nebraska Press, 1997). The time-honoured edition is by Fr. Klaeber (Lexington, MA: D. C. Heath, 1922); there is an excellent modern working edition by George Jack (Oxford: Oxford University Press, 1994) which glosses all the main words in the margin. The most attractive unannotated way of encountering the poem is the Norton 2000 text of Heaney's translation, set parallel to the Wrenn and Bolton original (Exeter: University of Exeter Press, 1988).
39. *Judith* also deserves far more extensive treatment than is possible here. Like *Maldon*, it is truncated at the start and there has been some inconclusive debate about how much is missing. It has a vivid and ironic style, and its treatment of Holofernes has been seen as part of a 'monsters' theme which was proposed

(not very persuasively) as a common element in the items in the manuscript. There is an excellent modern edition by Mark Griffiths (Exeter: University of Exeter Press, 1997).

40. *'Beowulf' and 'The Fight at Finnsburgh'*, ed. Fr. Klaeber, third edition (Lexington, MA: Heath, 1950), lines 1076–80.
41. F. C. Robinson, *'Beowulf' and the Appositive Style* (Knoxville: University of Tennessee Press, 1985). Other good accounts of the poetics of *Beowulf* and other Old English poetry are B. C. Raw, *The Art and Background of Old English Poetry* (London: Arnold, 1978); Bruce Mitchell, *An Invitation to Old English and Anglo-Saxon England* (Oxford: Blackwell, 1995); G. A. Lester, *The Language of Old and Middle English Poetry* (London: Macmillan, 1996), chs. 4 and 5. I have not discussed the ancient matter of the 'oral-formulaic' nature of the poetry, believing that in the restricted space available it was more constructive to deal with its distinction as major written material.
42. See Heaney, 'A Ship of Death', *The Haw Lantern* (London: Faber, 1987), p. 20.
43. Heaney, 'The Fragment', *Electric Light*, p. 57.
44. *The Battle of Maldon*, ed. E. V. Gordon (London: Methuen, 1949), lines 312–13.
45. For a model for the simultaneous appreciation of the familiar and 'alterity' in medieval literature, cf. H. R. Jauss, 'The Alterity and Modernity of Medieval Literature', *New Literary History*, 10:2 (Winter 1979), pp. 181–227. Though he is writing about the later medieval period, Jauss's essay is an immensely enlightening introduction to the reading process for earlier European literature.
46. *The New Oxford Book of Irish Verse*, ed. Thomas Kinsella (Oxford: Oxford University Press, 1986), p. xxvii.

Chapter 2

The *Gawain*-poet and medieval romance

CORINNE SAUNDERS

The romance genre

Romance, the most influential genre of imaginative writing in the Middle Ages, at once looks back to the tradition of epic poetry and forward to the genre of the novel. While prose romances developed in the thirteenth century, poetry was the traditional mode of romance, and there exists an immensely diverse collection of verse narratives. The earliest French romances retold classical epics while reflecting new cultural interest in chivalry, courtliness and the individual: thus the focus of the twelfth-century *Roman d'Eneas* was the love of Dido and Aeneas. Thebes, Troy and the exploits of Alexander offered popular story matter, and romance writers took up earlier twelfth-century *chansons de geste* to treat the heroes of French history. A more courtly type of romance also developed, which drew on the 'matter of Britain', Celtic folk material, and in particular, on legends of King Arthur and the Round Table. In the later twelfth century, the *lais* of Marie de France, written in sophisticated Anglo-Norman octosyllabic couplets for a highly refined audience and treating intense moments of rarefied emotion, were balanced by the extended and complex verse narratives of Chrétien de Troyes, which developed the pattern of quest and adventure in the context of the knight-hero's journey to self-realisation. These and the many French romances of the thirteenth century, along with a sophisticated tradition of lyric poetry, provided the substance of courtly entertainment in England, and in the fourteenth century French poets such as Froissart, Machaut and Deschamps shaped an international court culture in which poetry played a prominent role.

English romances, which began to be written in the late thirteenth century, occupied a rather different space. Not only were English romanciers using a highly developed mode and a storehouse of familiar conventions, applicable to a whole range of subject matters, but also they were writing for audiences who did not necessarily read French, and whose interest was in works that were more 'popular' than courtly: in particular, the country gentry and the new merchant class. The earliest English romances employ a four-stress couplet based on the French octosyllabic couplet. Tail-rhyme romances, with stanzas using the repetition of a shorter line rhyme after at least two longer rhyming lines, were swiftly developed, and may reflect the desire to create an English form amenable to memorisation and recitation. The flowering of alliterative poetry in the fourteenth century offered new possibilities for romance writers, and the various forms of romance were sustained through to the fifteenth century. Romances refer repeatedly to minstrels, audiences and music, and although it is unlikely that they were composed orally, they were certainly read aloud as well as privately, perhaps with musical accompaniment. This is a genre treating an archaic, stylised world, always already past, yet also a genre that can speak immediately and urgently to the present, engaging with contemporary themes and moral issues. English romance adds to classical, French and Celtic subject matters English history, as for instance the extended and long-lived dynastic romances of *Beves of Hampton* and *Guy of Warwick*, and romances of the greenwood such as *Gamelyn*, which underpin legends of Robin Hood. Classification by subject, however, may suggest too many similarities within a disparate group of texts while ignoring parallels between groups. Motifs, or, as Helen Cooper has recently termed them, 'memes', echo through the genre, forming the backbone of romance: exile and return, love, quest and adventure, family, name and identity, pagan and Christian.[1] Romances offer escapism and frequently open on to an exotic or in some way aggrandised world, whether of faery or Charlemagne's France, but they also allow for social comment, exploration of gender and relationships, and engagement with the deep structures of human existence, sometimes through a dream-like interweaving of fantasy and reality.

Two of the earliest known English works, *King Horn* (*c.*1225) and *Havelok the Dane* (*c.*1275), both translating Anglo-Norman romances, provide strikingly different versions of exile and return stories. *Horn* is set in a timeless romance world, in which the hero fights three symbolic battles against the pagans; his journeys across the sea are ritualised through the repetition of the lines, 'the see bigan to flowe / And Horn child to rowe'.[2] *Havelok*, by contrast, exploits material realism, for example, of the noble Havelok labouring as a porter carrying 'a carte-lode / Of sedges [cuttle-fish], laxes, of plaices brode, / Of grete laumprees, and of eles', or winning a shot-putting competition.[3] Both, however, treat the themes of love and arranged marriage with immediacy and empathy, and the princess Rymenhild's passion for Horn is described with notable frankness: 'heo luvede so Horn child / That negh heo gan wexe wild [she nearly went mad]' (lines 255–6). A third early romance, *Sir Orfeo*, is very different, reworking the legend of Orpheus and Eurydice as a Breton *lai* of faery. This work exploits a range of literary motifs in the sinister vision of the Queen, Heurodis, as she sleeps within her orchard; its enactment in her self-mutilation and then actual taking by the King of Faery; Orfeo's exile and life as a Wild Man; and his journey into the eerie world of the Un-dead, a 'fair cuntray' recalling 'the proude court of paradis', the inhabitants of which are frozen in various positions of violent death.[4] The happy ending of this version affirms the power of love, 'trouthe' and good government.

It is no surprise that this diverse, flexible mode, reliant on convention yet open to sophisticated and original individual treatment, also appealed to the imagination of the great English writers of the later fourteenth century. This period, marked by prolonged war with France, growth of the merchant class and a new sense of nationhood, saw the adoption of English in law, government and schools, and correspondingly, the development of sophisticated, courtly writing in English, including the original, self-conscious and learned works of Chaucer and Gower.

The *Gawain*-poet

Alongside these named poets stands the anonymous *Gawain*-poet, whose verse narratives, in particular *Sir Gawain and the Green Knight*, are now among the most renowned of the Middle Ages, although in their time they can have been very little known. Like Langland's *Piers Plowman*, they belong to the alliterative tradition of the second half of the fourteenth century, but by contrast to some fifty manuscripts of Langland's writings (and some forty each of Chaucer's and Gower's), there is only one manuscript of these poems. The loss of that in the Cotton Library fire would have changed as dramatically the canon of Middle English poetry as the loss of *Beowulf* would that of Anglo-Saxon poetry. The manuscript itself is far from *de luxe*, and its twelve illustrations are primitive. It seems most likely that the poet was a cleric, perhaps in minor orders, writing for a small aristocratic household in the north-west Midlands; his dialect is that of Staffordshire. The alliterative tradition was particularly strong in the north and west of England, and was used for both romance and religious writing, as is demonstrated by the roughly contemporaneous but very different alliterative poems, the *Morte Arthure* and *Wynner and Waster*, a dream vision in which Edward III intervenes to end the battle between the pope and friars, who win wealth, and the noble and warrior classes, who spend it. Poems within this mode hint tantalisingly at the continuation of the oral-formulaic, alliterative form of Anglo-Saxon poetry. *Sir Gawain* plays on this idea in its first stanza by identifying the story as an ancient tale that the narrator has heard 'in toun', which he will set down in alliterative verse, 'In stori stif and stronge, / With lel letteres loken, / In londe so has ben longe'. [5] Yet while the *Gawain*-poet engages consciously with English popular tradition, his work is also learned and literary, and is informed by a sophisticated knowledge of classical and Biblical writing, and Continental literature, including Dante's *Divine Comedy* as well as the great twelfth- and thirteenth-century French romances.

As might befit a clerical writer, three of the poems accompanying *Sir Gawain* are explicitly religious in subject: *Cleanness*, *Patience* and *Pearl*. An alliterative saint's life, *St Erkenwald*, composed in a very similar dialect, may also be this poet's work.[6] In its Arthurian and secular subject matter, *Sir Gawain* is puzzlingly different, although the similarities of poetic style and language are so notable that a single authorship for the four poems seems certain. All are structured in ways that reflect a heightened interest in formal and numerical patterns. *St Erkenwald*, for example, neatly divides into two parts of 176 long lines (each perhaps intended as 44 four-line stanzas). Both *Pearl* and *Sir Gawain* have 101 stanzas, and employ complicated verse forms; *Pearl* also uses a sophisticated scheme of rhyme and concatenation. The choice of the number 101 may be intended to gesture precisely through its slight imperfection towards the perfect number 100 (the number of cantos in Dante's *Divine Comedy*), and the line ratios of the sequence of the four poems may be analysed to produce the 'Divine Proportion', a continuous ratio leading to the infinite. The total number of lines of *Pearl*, 1212, is numerically significant: the product of its digits is reflected in the wall of the Heavenly Jerusalem, 144 cubits high, and in the 144,000 brides of Christ; the city has twelve foundations, gates and types of gem, and is 12,000 square furlongs. This poem, like *Sir Gawain* and like the endless circle of the pearl, is circular in form, the opening line echoed at the end. [7] Such features may be implied by the 'fayre formes' (line 3) of speech described by the poet at the start of *Cleanness*. The mathematical perfection of poetry seems for him to have presented a means of perfecting fallen language and approaching the subject of the divine. Yet this highly crafted and complex poetry is also immediately vibrant. The alliterative line provides the possibility of richly detailed and highly crafted description, dramatic narrative and dialogue, witty play and comedy, and moral and spiritual instruction. The poet was as ready to draw on dialect and colloquial terms as on the vocabulary of high-flown literary or archaic English, French and Norse: his poems include many unique words and usages, their vocabulary reminiscent of the poetic beauty of Old English, with its specialised treasure-chest of words and metaphors. Perhaps most striking is their ambiguity: they are experimental, edgy and questioning on all levels, moving in and out of convention, even while their formal and thematic aspects are tightly woven together.

All address the subjects of sin, virtue and heavenly reward: *St Erkenwald* treats justice; *Cleanness* offers three Biblical examples of the punishment of uncleanness: the stories of the Flood, Sodom and Gomorrah and Belshazzar's Feast; *Patience* probes that virtue through the story of Jonah. *Pearl* interweaves Biblical material and romance in a vision of the heavenly kingdom elaborated by the Dreamer's lost child. The pearl, image of spiritual perfection, also figures in *Cleanness* (lines 1113–32), and in *Sir Gawain* (lines 2364–5). *Sir Gawain* probes the virtues of chastity, loyalty and humility in the context of the chivalric ideal. The poems emphasise the difficulty of spiritual perfection and obedience, and the sometimes incomprehensible, apparently unfair ways of a God who may be fiercely punitive of the sinful. Yet this is also a courteous God whose qualities coincide with the chivalric ideal. The poet's interest in spiritual chivalry underpins his creative use of the romance form.

Cleanness and *Patience* take imaginative narrative in directions very different from romance, but they clearly demonstrate the poet's inventiveness. *Cleanness* commences with brief but vivid accounts of uncleanness and especially 'fylthe of the flesch' (line 202): the fall of the angels, 'hurled into helle-hole as the hyve swarmes' (line 223) within a 'styngande [stinging] storme' (line 225); the Fall of man 'thrugh the egging of Eve' (line 241); the angels' engendering of giants 'with her japes ille [evil tricks]' (line 272). They are complemented by a description of the 'mukel mangerye [great banquet]' (line 52) of the wedding feast at which the poor and weak replace the ungrateful rich (Matthew 2:1–14; Luke 14:16–24), here complete with bulls, boars, fatted fowls, pen-fed poultry, partridges, swans and cranes. Such delight in opulent detail is typical: the feast is rivalled later in the descriptions of Babylon and of Belshazzar's palace, musicians and ornately decorated, exotic dishes. Most extended is the description of the treasures fashioned by Solomon and stolen from the temple of Jerusalem, with their precious metals, gems and skilful shaping. Like the ornate craft of the poems themselves, their art reflects and venerates the Creator.

Divine power is vividly realised in *Cleanness*. The narrative of the Flood, which God wakens 'to wasch alle the worlde' (line 323), revels in the violence of the storm, evoked with sometimes onomatopoeic realism: 'Mony clustered clowde clef alle in clowtes [shreds], / Torent uch a rayn ryfte [each rain-rift tore open] and rusched to the urthe' (lines 367–8). The violence and absence of mercy in God's punishment of 'peple that he hated' (line 396) inspire fear, but there is humour too in the colloquial description of the animals on the ark, 'throly thrublande [impatiently jostling] in thronge' (line 504). Differently remarkable is the frank physical detail of the poet's discussion of sodomy, characterised as the worst of sins: 'Uch male mas [makes] his mach a man as hymselven, / And fylter folyly in fere [join together wantonly] on femmales wyse [in the manner of women]' (lines 695–6). The idea of the 'unkynde' (unnatural), which perverts God's creation, is a crucial aspect of the poet's understanding of sin. Sodomy is contrasted, again with striking explicitness, to natural, heterosexual love as God himself praises his creation of 'the play of paramores' (line 700), than which, when pursued privately and 'honestly' (line 705), 'Welnyghe pure Paradys moght preve no better' (line 704). The extremity of corruption is reflected in the violence of God's punishment: the destruction of Sodom and Gomorrah is imagined as a dreadful volcanic eruption of sulphuric smoke, fiery rain and earthquake. The poem also exploits the sinister, most strikingly in the eerie appearance of a wristless hand and pen at Belshazzar's Feast, 'That was grysly and gret, and grymly he wrytes' (line 1534). The horror of violence is not avoided: we are left with the stark image of Belshazzar in his bed 'beten to dethe, / That bothe his blod and his brayn blende on the clothes' (lines 1788–9).

The tone of *Patience* is similarly mixed: comedy is exploited in the image of the fearful Jonah slumbering ('sloberande he routes [snores]', line 186) through the storm, and the animated dialogue of the sailors who cast lots to discover the sinner. The use of vibrant, robust material description, which can readily shift from horror to humour, is most of all apparent in the description of the 'wylde walterande [wallowing] whal' (line 247), from his jaws so huge that they render Jonah a mere mote in a minster door (line 268), to his slimy gills and a hall-like 'stomak that stank as the devel' (line 274). Yet the angry deeps of the sea are also wonderfully opened out in Jonah's confession: 'I have greved my God and gulty am founden' (line 210), and his prayer, which draws directly on the words of the Biblical Jonah to characterise the plight of man: 'I am wrapped in water to my wo stoundes [pangs]; / The abyme byndes the body that I byde inne' (lines 317–18). The poetry looks forward to Cowper's some 500 years later in 'The Castaway', and perhaps also to Hopkins's use of sprung rhythm to characterise 'the dark night of the soul'. The difficulty of faith in an unjust world is most acutely rendered in the seemingly wanton destruction of the beautiful woodbine shaped by God to adorn Jonah's arbour, but as suddenly 'Al welwed [shrivelled] and wasted' (line 475) in the withering sunlight. The poet vividly realises both Jonah's innocent delight and bitter anger, but cunningly turns the meaning inside out, so that Jonah's distress at the destruction of an object he has not created functions to explain God's wish to preserve even the sinners of Nineveh, for all men are God's handiwork. Although all may seem dark to the sufferer, 'Lorde, colde was his cumfort, and God's care huge!' (line 264), yet there is a benign care in the workings of Providence that merits resistance to despair: 'pacience is a nobel poynt, thagh hit displese ofte' (line 531). The poem articulates compellingly the invisibility of that providential pattern to man and hence the difficulty of faith.

Sir Gawain and the questioning of romance

Although *Sir Gawain* is so different in its subject matter and tone, its stylistic and thematic qualities resonate with these poems: the emphasis on virtue, the interweaving of symbol and narrative, the vivid realism, dialogue and drama, and the emphasis on the incomprehensibility of the human predicament. The poet makes sophisticated use of and playfully undercuts the conventions and ideals of romance. His interest in structure is again clear: as well as following the demands of the alliterative form, each stanza (of variable length) ends with four rhymed lines of three beats, a 'bob and wheel', used to conclude paragraphs in something of the way that Shakespeare employs rhymed couplets at the end of scenes. The poem is divided into four 'fitts' and follows the cycle of the year, ending where it began. The number three recurs, including in the three strands of the story. The central strand, that of the beheading game, may be traced to the twelfth-century Irish tale of Cuchulainn; the poet is most likely to have known the version in the first continuation of Chrétien's *Perceval*, told in relation to the knight Carados. A temptation story not unlike that used in the poem also occurs in several forms with various protagonists, including French *Gauvain*-romances.[8] The tale of a contract and exchange of winnings is found in several Latin versions.

Gawain himself enjoys a long-standing and mixed literary history. His name occurs in the earliest Welsh Arthurian poems, among lists of heroes fighting alongside Arthur. As well as his prowess, however, Gawain's reputation for learning, elegant discourse and courtesy is repeatedly noted. In Chrétien's *Le Conte du Graal*, he is a foil to the naive hero, but whereas Perceval gains spiritual understanding, Gawain remains caught within secular knighthood, and in the thirteenth-century *Queste del Saint Graal*, he is unable to set aside his secular ideals to undertake penance and abstinence. A series of French romances builds on Gawain's secular reputation to depict him as womaniser. In a continuation of Chrétien's *Le Conte du Graal*, a beautiful maiden informs Gawain that she has long loved him, confirming his identity by comparing his face to an embroidered picture, and surrendering her body to him; in other versions Gawain must successfully pass a test such as escaping a magical sword to win the lady. Not all are positive: in one Gawain is abandoned by the lady; in another, when he discovers the lady intends to kill him, he takes her knife and rapes her. Gawain's name, then, is associated not simply with courtesy but also with a more active, potentially aggressive sexuality, an association recalled by the Lady in *Sir Gawain*, 'Ye ar stif innoghe to constrayne wyth strenkthe, yif yow lykes' (line 1496). The poem takes up and challenges the motifs of worldliness, courtesy, testing and seduction traditionally associated with its hero.

The poet also had English models, which until Malory's *Morte d'Arthur* tended to treat Gawain more positively. In the alliterative *Morte Arthure*, Gawain figures as the central warrior-hero, closer to Brutus, Roland or Beowulf than to his chivalric namesakes. This poem draws on English Arthurian chronicle, and is particularly striking for its realism: the rich depiction of Arthur's great feast, the geographically precise detail of his campaign on the Continent and most of all the descriptions of warfare. Gawain figures as the great epic hero, defying the Emperor Lucius, defeating the noble Priamus in single combat and overcoming the Saracen multitude with his few knights. As Arthur presses on in his imperialistic initiative, however, the poem raises questions concerning the limits of pride and ambition, and the destructiveness of war. The narrative is nowhere more masterful than in the account of the death of Gawain. He ventures in to the shore by galley while Arthur's ships wait offshore, and his few knights perform heroic feats against thousands, but he is eventually betrayed:

> His hand slipped and slode o-slant on the mailes
> And the tother [Mordred] slely slinges him under;
> With a trenchand knife the traitour him hittes
> Through the helm and the hed on high on the brain;
> And thus Sir Gawain is gone, the good man of armes.[9]

For a moment, even Mordred weeps. The passage captures the vivid, realistic mode of the poem, the violence of warfare and the fragility of human life, as one slip of the hand brings about the fall of the great knight. The tragic sense of loss recalls the *Battle of Maldon*: as in the case of Byrhtnoth, it is precisely Gawain's extreme heroism that is his downfall, yet that inspires the listener or reader and shapes the high drama and human impact of the poem.

Sir Gawain is much more obviously a romance, but it too insists on questioning ideals as the poet interweaves fantasy and reality, pagan and Christian, human and otherworld. The narrative is set at Christmas as the knights and ladies of the Arthurian court celebrate at Camelot, perhaps having forgotten the deeper significance of Christmas, although in this poem no didactic meaning is certain. The Green Knight's demand for a 'Crystemas gomen [game]' (line 283) is as ambiguous as his appearance, which evokes a range of natural and supernatural possibilities and is realised in strikingly material terms. His size, luxuriant hair and beard, violation of courtly behaviour by riding into the court, armed with an axe rather than a sword, and his rude challenge, 'What, is this Arthures hous?' (line 309), all place him as an outsider, a force of nature representative of the hostile world beyond the court. Yet his wild appearance is countered by his shapely limbs, ornate costume and fashionably ornamented horse. Most remarkable of all, both man and horse are 'overal enker [intense] grene' (line 150) – the detail dramatically concealed until the final line of the stanza. The poet revels in the strangeness of the colour, combining natural and artificial metaphors, 'such a hwe lach [take] / As growe grene as the gres and grener hit semed, / Then grene aumayl [enamel] on golde glowande bryghter' (lines 234–6), just as the Green Knight combines savagery and sophistication. The variety of terms used emphasises the difficulty of interpreting this supernatural phenomenon: he seems an 'aghlich mayster [awesome creature]' (line 136), 'half etayn [giant] in erde [earth]' (line 140), 'he ferde as freke were fade [he behaved like an elvish man]' (line 149), and the court is awestruck and silenced by this 'mervayle' (line 233), thinking it 'fantoum and fayryye' (line 240); later they characterise it as theatrical illusion. The poet exploits the horror and menace of the Green Knight's power over death itself in the account of the graphic beheading, the grotesque depiction of the court kicking around the head and finally the image of the torso holding up the 'lufly' (line 433), still-speaking head, to ride away 'runyschly [outlandishly]' (line 432) laughing. This triumph of life over death chillingly enacts the associations of Christmas, which not only celebrates the hope for salvation and resurrection made flesh in Christ, but also coincides with the pagan feast of the Midwinter Solstice marking the hope for regeneration of the seasons, symbolised by the burning of the Yule log.

The second fitt opens with a grand rhetorical pageant of the seasonal cycle, through 'crabbed Lentoun' (line 502) to 'the sesoun of somer wyth the soft wyndes, / Quen Zeferus syfles hymself on sedes and erbes' (lines 516–17), to the tempests of autumn, 'Wrothe [angry] wynde of the welkyn wrasteles [wrestles] with the sunne' (line 525), ending with Gawain's recollection of his 'anious [arduous] voyage' (line 535). This Gawain is anxious and reflective, and his resignation to fate, 'Of destinés derf and dere [harsh and gentle] / What may mon do bot fonde [try]' (lines 564–5), recalls the emphasis of Anglo-Saxon poetry. Gawain's shield, decorated with the Pentangle and with the image of Mary on the inside, symbolises the interwoven spiritual and secular virtues that must protect the knight against the unknown. The journey itself is especially remarkable in its precise, localised realism. Whereas conventional romance description tends to be limited to dark, deep or fair forests, Gawain's voyage takes him through the actual landscape of Britain: North Wales, Anglesey, Holyhead and the 'wyldrenesse of Wyrale' (line 701), towards the area from which the poem seems to originate, suggesting that the poet is playing a complex game of recognition with his audience. In a whirlwind parody of the romance hero's quest, Gawain fights with enemies at every ford, the traditional place of challenge, and with dragons, wolves, wild men, bulls, bears, boars and giants. Thus the normal subject matter of romance is turned inside out, relegated to less than a stanza. In a final twist, Gawain's worst enemy is none of these conventional opponents, but instead the English climate, evoked with a realism that recalls *The Wanderer* or *The Seafarer*:

> For werre wrathed [battle troubled] hym not so much, that wynter was wors,
> When the colde cler water fro the cloudes schadde,
> And fres er hit [froze before it] falle myght to the fale [pale] erthe.
> Ner slayn wyth the slete he sleped in his yrnes [irons]
> Mo nyghtes then innoghe in naked rokkes,
> Ther as claterande [clattering] fro the crest the colde borne rennes [runs],
> And henged heghe [hung high] over his hede in hard ysse-ikkles.
>
> (lines 726–32)

Like the later descriptions of the winter weather in which Gawain sets out to the Green Chapel, the poetry seems peculiarly, tangibly English.

The depiction of the castle at which Gawain finally arrives, Hautdesert, again merges romance and realism. It appears suddenly, in the manner of the Grail Castle that its name, 'High Wasteland', evokes, apparently in answer to Gawain's prayer on Christmas Eve, shimmering and seemingly 'pared out of papure' (line 802). Yet it is also a highly fashionable medieval barbican, complete with towers and turrets, ornamented and painted pinnacles, and chalk-white chimneys. Its rituals are Christian, but it is also a place of temptation and heightened material delight, focused in the surpassing beauty of Bertilak's lady. Here Gawain is cocooned in a feminised world, sleeping on in his luxurious bed while Bertilak rises early to hunt. The lady's advances are explicit,

'Ye ar welcum to my cors / Yowre awen won [pleasure] to wale [take]' (lines 1237–8), and the comedy of the bedroom scenes is situated partly in Gawain's desire elegantly to escape her wiles, rather than to enact the force she seems to suggest. At the same time, the poet emphasises Gawain's genuine sexual temptation, and his need for the protection of the Virgin: 'Gret perile bitwene hem stod' (line 1768). In balancing the demands of chastity, courtesy to his host's wife and loyalty to his host, Gawain's Christian virtue is set against his reputation as celebrated courtly lover, and the different facets of chivalry, spiritual and secular, are shown to coexist uncomfortably. Gawain survives the test of chastity but his integrity and faith are less sure: he accepts and conceals the lady's protective girdle, a secular symbol more resonant of pagan binding magic than of the Christian virtues of the Pentangle.

The peculiar menace of Gawain's test is heightened by the interwoven narrative of Bertilak's hunts of deer, boar and fox, which recall the violence of the beheading scene in their graphic images of chase, capture, death and dismemberment. But this is highly artistic violence: the poet draws on a medieval hunting treatise to offer elaborate instruction in the courtly art of venery. The repeated images of imprisonment used by the Lady parallel the vocabulary of the hunt, and the prey of the third day, the sly fox, may be seen as a counterpart for Gawain, who that day deceitfully keeps the Lady's gift, but this meaning is never made explicit. Rather, the narrator misleads his audience, claiming that Gawain is so 'clene' (line 1884) after making his confession that the morrow might be Judgment Day.

The final fitt returns ominously to the winter world outside: Gawain tosses and turns as 'The snawe snitered ful snart, that snayped the wylde; / The werbelande wynde wapped fro the hyghe [The snow showered very swiftly; it stung the wild animals; / The shrill wind struck from the high ground]' (lines 2003–4). His journey to the Green Chapel is evoked with equal realism: the bare boughs, raging streams, cliffs 'ther clenges [clings] the colde' (line 2078), and drizzling mist on moor and mountain that seems to give each hill 'a myst hakel [cape of mist] huge' (line 2081). The Green Chapel is in some ways anticlimactic, 'nobot an olde cave' (line 2182) by a boiling spring and waterfall, but also ominous, and with its 'balw berw [smooth barrow]' (line 2172) perhaps may be identified as a pagan burial site, associated with demonic magic. The poet's mastery of suspenseful, onomatopoeic realism is most evident in the sound of the Green Knight sharpening his axe, 'What! hit wharred [whirred] and whette [rasped], as water at a mulne [mill]. / What! hit rusched and ronge [rang], rawthe [horrid] to here' (lines 2203–4). Suspense is taken to new heights with the two feints, while Gawain's severed flesh and gushing blood at the third blow make real the threat to his life. The green girdle proves not to have been what it seemed: rather than offering magical protection, it is a mark of sin, the 'falssyng' (line 2378) that has taught Gawain cowardice and disloyalty. Yet although Gawain sees himself as having failed to live up to the perfection of the Pentangle, Bertilak commends his virtue and presents him with the girdle, which the court will wear as a badge of honour. Gawain has learned the one Christian virtue he lacked, humility; he has also acquired a new kind of knowledge, linked to experience, worldliness and imperfection, and symbolised by the non-Christian emblem of the girdle. We are left with questions concerning the possibility of reconciling secular and sacred, the value of chivalric ideals and most of all, the motivation of the Green Knight. Is he to be read as demonic tempter, divine arbiter and confessor, force of wild nature, faery knight or, as he states, the servant of Gawain's own aunt, Morgan le Fay, his shape shifted through her magical arts of illusion? The problem of interpretation opens on to the problem of individual perception and being in the world, and the poem ends in enigmas rather than answers.

Pearl and the sublimation of romance

Where *Sir Gawain* is witty and urbane in its ambiguity, *Pearl* is visionary and contemplative. The intricate and jewel-like effect created by its complex language and structure is fitting to a work that engages with some of the most enduringly difficult questions of human existence. Early readers were divided as to whether *Pearl* was a deeply personal elegy for a dead child or an allegory designed to teach the doctrine of salvation, but both elements are crucial: the poem moves between universal and personal; it is shifting, multifaceted and self-conscious. The structures of romance are again employed, but are merged with other conventions, in particular those of the dream vision and of mystical writing.

The courtly dream vision, with its setting of the springtime garden, use of allegorical figures and theme of secular love, finds its origins in the *Roman de la Rose*, begun by Guillaume de Lorris and completed by Jean de Meun, and was adapted by a long sequence of later poets, including Machaut, Froissart and Chaucer. *Pearl*'s opening depiction of an enclosed garden immediately suggests this genre, and fittingly, the narrator's reference to 'luf-daungere' [love-danger, love-sickness, line 11] establishes a context of *fin' amors* or 'courtly love'. The convention is elaborated as the narrator falls to the ground, the desolation of his heart enacted physically in his swoon-like sleep. Yet this is a garden with a difference, a garden not in springtime but in the ripeness of late summer, looking towards winter, and the images of decaying fruits and flowers and of the lost pearl evoke the ideas of death and the grave.

Correspondingly, the narrator's dream does not lead into a courtly love vision, but is directly associated with God's grace. The poem thus also situates itself within an ancient, more serious genre of dream-vision, employed in the Bible, Dante's *Divina Commedia* and Boethius's *Consolation of Philosophy*, as well as in the Old English *Dream of the Rood* and Langland's *Piers Plowman*. At the same time, the poet continues to exploit the motifs and language of romance as the spirit of the dreamer goes 'in aventure' (line 64), on a quest. The extraordinary, haunting evocation of a visionary world both depends on and transforms romance conventions, using the conventional motif of the earthly paradise, but making strange the beauty and riches of nature. The cliffs are of crystal; the trunks of the trees are 'blwe as ble [colour] of Ynde' (line 76), their leaves silver; the river bed is set with exotic gems; and precious pearls crunch beneath the Dreamer's feet. The Dreamer longs to cross the river to enter what seem to him to be the pleasure gardens of some great house, and when the Pearl Maiden appears she is a fitting inhabitant for such a place, her characteristics and costume those of the ideal romance lady. The narrator's dread and bliss at seeing her accord with the conventions of 'courtly love'. Yet, in one of the most striking oppositions of the poem, the joyless jeweller's lost pearl proves also to be a 'faunt' (line 161), a child, who is 'nerre then aunte or nece' (line 233); later we learn that she has lived less than two years. The confusion between child and lady is central to the poem, for the lesson of the Pearl Maiden's metamorphosis is the most difficult that the Dreamer must learn: she no longer belongs to him but to Christ.

The gradual process of the Dreamer's recognition, and the surreptitious hints at the Maiden's identity, are typical of the riddling quality of *Pearl*. The poem unfolds through a series of questions and answers concerning the enigmas of divine logic. The transient human world where roses flower and fade is countered by the brilliant, celestial sphere where no sun and moon are necessary and where the permanence of eternal life is expressed through the unchanging gems and metals of its landscape. Yet the very otherness of this world renders it difficult and often obscure, and the unsatisfying quality of some of the Pearl Maiden's explanations seems to gesture towards the ineffability of the divine. The Dreamer expresses comprehensible human feelings of confusion and doubt as he enters into a topsy-turvy dialogue where his child has become a divine instructress. Like *Patience*, the poem creates an uneasy sense that the bumbling efforts of men within this temporal world may be laughable to God. Again the questions central to the book of Job are asked, concerning the nature of a God who causes what seems needless suffering, and whose teachings are often paradoxical. Appropriately, the Pearl Maiden exploits the rhetorical modes of paradox and metaphor. Figurative, especially courtly, language plays a key role in explaining the inexplicable, but at the same time the use of highly sensual, sometimes secular images to elaborate sacred ideas and themes creates a strange tension.

The Dreamer faces one apparently illogical answer after another. He learns that, though young, his daughter is Christ's queen – but along with Mary there are 144,000 queens. The images of the bride and bridegroom, marital bliss, unity, love and possession are typical of the language of mystical literature, but do not normally describe young children, and the Dreamer's objection seems reasonable: it is 'to dere a date [too exalted a point]' (line 492). The parable of the workers who come late to the vineyard (Matthew 20:1–16) allows the Pearl Maiden to explain how those who die young may be saved without undergoing the process of Christian teaching: 'innoghe of grace has innocent' (line 625). The highly intricate, interwoven quality of her argument becomes apparent as one topic, usually represented by one symbolic and repeated word, leads directly on to the next. Thus the discussion of the spotless, sinless quality of children brings the Pearl Maiden to the heart of her theological narrative, the subject of the kingdom of heaven. The linking words of fitt XIII, 'mascelles' (spotless) and its near double 'makelles' (matchless), a word-play typical of the poem, become the two key qualities in the story of the perfect and peerless pearl for which the jeweller sells all his worldly goods (Matthew 13:45–6). The pearl is the kingdom of heaven: 'hit is wemles [spotless], clene, and clere, / And endeles rounde, and blythe of mode' (lines 737–8). The symbol resonates through the poem both figuratively and literally, written into landscape, costume and appearance.

The Pearl Maiden's description of her marriage to Christ, the Lamb, exploits the courtly language of love: he is her 'dere destyné' (line 757); she is his 'lemman [beloved] swete' (line 763); he calls her out of 'bonerté' (line 762), the courtly quality of generosity or bounty, and bestows on her the courtly virtue of 'bewté' (line 765). The use of French terms heightens the courtly ethos, and the images are strikingly, paradoxically sensual: the maiden leaves this 'wete' (line 761) world for the glittering heavenly one, and the Lamb's blood washes her clean, pure and white. In her depiction of the New Jerusalem (based on Revelation 14:1–5 and 21:1–22.5), the brides are dressed in their wedding garments, and Christ is depicted as the chivalric lover and ideal knight, 'In Jerusalem was my lemman slayn' (line 805), who sacrifices himself to the blows of 'boyes bolde' (line 806). Chivalry is invested with a new spirituality, manifested in Christ's loving sacrifice for mankind. The Dreamer responds comically by asking whether Jerusalem is not in the land of Judea, yet despite himself tumbles through the argument to attain the vision of the heavenly city. The poet links the stanzas describing the city with the name of St John, emphasising his Biblical authority, but considerably embellishes the details found in Revelation. The precious stones and metals of the walls and streets, and the gates of pearl, recall and fulfil the promise of the gems, gold, silver and crystal of the start.

The pearl takes on another level of meaning with the depiction of the Lamb himself, in clothing the semblance of 'praysed perles' (line 1112): the linking word 'delyt' (fitt XIX) points up the experience of heavenly bliss. The Dreamer's wonder and horror at the sight of the Lamb's wound, and of the blood spurting from his side, is replaced by more personal delight as he suddenly glimpses his 'lyttel quene' (line 1147) amongst the company of brides. As love-longing overcomes him, he leaps into the river, only to wake in the garden once more, alone and in sorrow. Yet if his dream vision has revivified and re-enacted his loss, it has also offered consolation in showing the happiness and transformation of his lost pearl. In the Dreamer's concluding prayer, the image of the pearl is extended to his own soul: 'He [Christ] gef uus to be his homly hyne [servants] / Ande precious perles unto his pay [pleasure]' (lines 1211–12). As with the other poems, however, there are no easy answers, but only the uneasy consolation of faith. The poem is deeply engaged with the difficulty of that faith, and with the gap between human and divine logic. Yet it also offers a visionary interlude that illuminates with its strange, otherworldly dream-light 'thys doel-doungoun [dungeon of sorrow]' (line 1187) of earthly life.

The enduring appeal of the *Gawain*-poet's works, and particularly of *Sir Gawain*, is affirmed by the remarkable number of writers who have tried their hands at modernisation of his work. Several acknowledge their debt to Ezra Pound, whose versions of Anglo-Saxon poems offer a kind of model, and whose treatise, *The Spirit of Romance*, engages with the intensity and influence of the genre. J. R. R. Tolkien not only produced the definitive edition of *Sir Gawain*, but also engaged over many years in translating the poem, its archaic, richly detailed style recalling that of *The Lord of the Rings*. Marie Borroff's remarkably fluent translations aimed to follow the verbal art of the originals in a more modern mode. Sustained interest is evident in the work of Ted Hughes, whose *Wodwo* (1967) plays on the Green Man legend, and who also translated sections of *Sir Gawain*. More recently, the extraordinary dramatic and visual potential of the poem led Harrison Birtwistle to create his opera *Gawain!*, using a verse libretto by David Harsent that places the enchantress

Morgan le Fay at the centre of the narrative, and employing ballet and mime.[10] Such works reflect a wider creative engagement with medieval poetry, particularly striking in Seamus Heaney's work, which includes translations of *Beowulf* and Henryson's *Testament of Cresseid*. In the last ten years, poets from Britain, America and Australia have translated *Sir Gawain*. Keith Harrison emulates the stress pattern of sections of *Four Quartets* in his attempt to convey in alliterative verse 'a rattling good story'.[11] Bernard O'Donoghue celebrates the English 'sprung rhythm' that appealed so strongly to Hopkins, Auden and Heaney. For W. S. Merwin, it is that 'spirit of romance', the Celtic mystery of *Sir Gawain*, that is crucial: his forceful, fluent translation attempts most of all to retain the movement and life of the poem. Simon Armitage writes persuasively of the need for 'a poetic response', both retaining the alliterative art of the original and translating its spirit. Armitage presents the translator as following the example of the *Gawain*-poet, who has 'set himself a series of rules, then consciously and conspicuously gone about bending them'.[12] Perhaps it is precisely that balance between artifice and adventure that has appealed so strongly to modern poets.

Notes

1. Helen Cooper, *The English Romance in Time: Transforming Motifs from Geoffrey of Monmouth to the Death of Shakespeare* (Oxford: Oxford University Press, 2004), p. 3.
2. *King Horn*, in *Middle English Verse Romances*, ed. Donald B. Sands, Exeter Medieval English Texts and Studies (1966; Exeter: Exeter University Press, 1986), pp. 15–54, lines 121–2.
3. *Havelok the Dane*, in Sands (ed.), *Middle English Verse Romances*, pp. 55–129, lines 895–97.
4. *Sir Orfeo*, in Sands (ed.), *Middle English Verse Romances*, pp. 185–200, lines 327, 352.
5. *Sir Gawain and the Green Knight*, in *Pearl, Cleanness, Patience, Sir Gawain and the Green Knight*, ed. A. C. Cawley and J. J. Anderson, Everyman Classics (London: Dent–Everyman's Library, 1976), pp. 159–254, lines 34–6. Subsequent references to the works of the *Gawain*-poet are from this edition, which modernises archaic letter-forms, and are cited by line number. For a full scholarly edition, see *The Poems of the Pearl Manuscript: 'Pearl', 'Cleanness', 'Patience', 'Sir Gawain and the Green Knight'*, ed. Malcolm Andrew and Ronald Waldron, fifth edition, Exeter Medieval Texts and Studies (Exeter: Exeter University Press, 2007). Includes prose translation on CD-ROM.
6. *Pearl*, *Cleanness*, *Patience* and *Sir Gawain and the Green Knight* are found in London, British Library, MS Cotton Nero A.x, dated to the last quarter of the fourteenth century (the twelve illustrations are contemporaneous or slightly later); *St Erkenwald* is preserved in London, British Library, MS Harley 2250, dated to 1477.

7. See Victor Watts's discussion in his *Pearl. A Modernised Version of the Middle English Poem*, ed. Corinne Saunders and David Fuller, intro. Kathleen Raine (London: Enitharmon, 2005), p. 8.
8. See further Elisabeth Brewer's anthology, *'Sir Gawain and the Green Knight': Sources and Analogues*, Arthurian Studies 27 (Woodbridge: D. S. Brewer, 1973, 1992) and Ad Putter, *'Sir Gawain and the Green Knight' and French Arthurian Romance* (Oxford: Clarendon Press, 1995).
9. *The Alliterative Morte Arthure*, in Larry D. Benson (ed.), *King Arthur's Death: The Middle English 'Stanzaic Morte Arthur' and Alliterative 'Morte Arthure'*, Exeter Medieval English Texts and Studies (1974; Exeter: Exeter University Press, 1986), pp. 115–238, lines 3854–8.
10. On Birtwhistle's opera (libretto by David Harsent, 1991) see further Barry Windeatt, 'Sir Gawain at the *fin de siècle*: Novel and Opera', in Derek Brewer and Jonathan Gibson (eds.), *A Companion to the 'Gawain'-Poet*, Arthurian Studies 38 (Cambridge: D. S. Brewer, 1997), pp. 373–83.
11. Keith Harrison (trans.), *Sir Gawain and the Green Knight*, intro. and annotated Helen Cooper, Oxford World's Classics (Oxford: Oxford University Press, 1998), p. xxxix.
12. Simon Armitage (trans.), *Sir Gawain and the Green Knight* (London: Faber, 2007), p. xii.

Chapter 3

Late fourteenth-century poetry (Chaucer, Gower, Langland and their legacy)

WENDY SCASE

Dryden's description of Chaucer as the 'Father of English Poetry' and Puttenham's demarcation of late fourteenth-century English poetry as a 'first age' have had varied fortunes in recent histories of poetry.[1] Although Chaucer's sobriquet was roundly defended on the occasion of his sexcentenary, the 'age of Chaucer' and 'Ricardian poetry', key terms for the New Critics, have yielded to more varied and nuanced periodisations.[2] However, there remain indisputable grounds for regarding the contribution of Chaucer and certain of his contemporaries as foundational in the history of English poetry, and for viewing the late fourteenth century as a distinctive and crucial literary period. Late fourteenth-century England produced the first English poetry that has continued to be read, and responded to, throughout all subsequent periods. We have incontrovertible evidence that the poetry of Geoffrey Chaucer, John Gower and the author of *Piers Plowman* (whom, following tradition, I shall call William Langland), all composed in the last three, perhaps four, decades of the fourteenth century, has never since fallen out of sight. This chapter outlines the opportunities and constraints that attended the making of poetry in English in the later fourteenth century, and explores the ways in which Chaucer, Gower and Langland responded to them. The final section of the chapter briefly turns to the legacy of these poets and the story of how they first became recognised as founders of a tradition of English poetry.

Several models of composition were available to and valued in late fourteenth-century England. None of these models was English. The metres and figures of the classical poets were transmitted as part of education in grammar and rhetoric. Schoolboys were required to compose Latin verse on set themes in prescribed metres. Valorised models of vernacular composition were available in French and Italian. The nobility and their servants moved in a multilingual environment where French was the language of polite intercourse, diplomacy and letters. War, diplomacy and marriage were among the circumstances that provided for the dissemination of French poetry in England. Richard II, born and brought up in Bordeaux until the age of four (1371), almost certainly spoke French as his first language, and he read French – 'very well' according to Jean Froissart, who presented him with a book of his verse in French in 1395.[3] Richard does not seem to have been an active patron of poets, but several English nobles and courtiers are known to have read French poetry or at least possessed books that included it.[4]

Dante, Petrarch and Boccaccio were internationally acclaimed as vernacular poets, being invested as laureates both in Italy and beyond. French provided access to these illustrious Italian writers, sometimes in turn through the medium of Latin.[5] *De obedientia ac fide uxoria mythologiae*, Petrarch's story of Griselda the patient wife that is the source of Chaucer's Clerk's Tale, was a translation from Boccaccio's version of the story in *The Decameron*. It is thought that Chaucer knew the Latin text, but that he also made use of a French translation of it.[6] Lydgate based his *Fall of Princes*, a translation of Boccaccio's *De casibus virorum illustrium*, on a French translation by Laurent de Premierfait.[7] But there were also means of direct contact between Italian poetry and English readers. Contact with Italian culture and society, and hence with the Tuscan poets, was facilitated by trade, pilgrimage, education and dealings at the papal court.[8] Knowledge of Latin and French must have permitted reasonably easy access to the Tuscan vernaculars.

An extensive corpus of verse composed in English before the later fourteenth century survives (much more must have been lost). But this poetry was not to be found in the schoolroom, nor in monastic libraries, nor in the university lecture halls, nor in the private libraries of the nobility. It offered no models for emulation, nor named poets for imitation. Much of it was explicitly targeted at audiences who could not understand Latin or French. A large amount of the surviving material answered to the needs of the Church for resources to teach congregations (and perhaps less educated priests) and to celebrate sacraments and feasts. Saints' lives, exemplary tales, homiletic and biblical material were translated or adapted from French (including Anglo-Norman) or Latin originals into rhyming syllabic metres and gathered into huge collections such as the *South English Legendary* (*c.*1270–85), the *Ormulum* (*c.*1200), the *Cursor Mundi* (*c.*1300) and the *Northern Homily Cycle* (before 1300).[9] Teaching associated with the sacrament of penance was transmitted in exempla collections such as *Handlyng Synne* by Robert Mannyng of Brunne (*c.*1300), while teaching on this world and the next was provided in texts such as the popular *Prick of Conscience* (before *c.*1350).[10] History, valuable for its edifying examples of good and bad governance and as a source of legal memory and precedent, was transmitted in verse translations such as Layamon's *Brut*, a rendering of Wace's *Roman de Brut* in informal alliterative long lines written in the Worcester diocese *c.*1200–25, and Robert Mannyng's *Chronicle* (before 1338), translated from the Anglo-Norman *Chronicle* of Pierre de Langtoft.[11] By translating into English, clerics provided edifying material to supplement (or supplant) popular English verse narratives and songs. Relative to the clerical translation, very little of the latter kind of material survives to this day, and it was apparently little recorded in manuscript even in its day. Short lyric poems, satires and romances in English were not, on the whole, regarded as useful resources that warranted systematic copying in manuscripts. Generally they survived in more haphazard ways. The famous lyric 'Sumer is icumen in', for example, survives with the music of the Latin hymn to whose tune it was to be sung.[12] Other lyrics survive because resourceful preachers saw them as memorable material that would catch their congregations' attention and give them a way of remembering religious teaching.[13]

While the vast majority of English verse dating before the later fourteenth century testifies to its status as material targeted at monolingual, and probably predominantly illiterate, audiences, some exceptions provide us with evidence of attempts to experiment with English as a medium for self-conscious poetic art. *The Owl and the Nightingale*, an anonymous 1,794-line poem in octosyllabic couplets (probably *c.*1272), explores poetics in a debate about the 'songs' of the two protagonists that alludes extensively to learned literary sources. Failing to resolve their debate, the two birds agree to put their quarrel to one Master Nicholas, an authority who 'diht [composes] & writ mani wisdom'.[14] The octosyllabics of this poem recall the metre of many French poems, though they are characteristically handled in a loose and lively way. Other poets set themselves demanding formal challenges of a different kind. 'Annot and John', for example, praises the lady Ann with tropes recommended by the rhetoricians. She is compared favourably with precious stones, flowers, birds, medicines and romance heroines in five ten-line stanzas, each of which rhymes aaaaaaaabb. In addition to needing eight rhymes on one sound in each stanza, the poet also alliterates each line, extending the alliteration over two lines in lines 8–9 of each stanza, bridging the a and b rhymes, as for example in a stanza in which the poet riddles on his lady's name:

> hire nome is in a note of þe nyhtegale;
> In an note is hire nome – nempneþ it non!
> Whose ryht redeþ roune to Iohon.[15]

Here the poet combines the disciplines of rhyme and alliteration with a riddle on the names of the lady and the poet himself.

A few exceptional manuscripts testify both to some frequency for verses that foreground poetic accomplishment in English and to a taste for and high valuation of such material among audiences. 'Annot and John' survives with many similarly ambitious love lyrics in London, British Library, Harley MS 2253, an anthology of French, Latin and English materials made in Shropshire around 1340.[16] The English poems are associated on dialect grounds with several different regions of England.[17] This suggests that poetic experiments of this kind may have been widespread, and that there were means by which they could be transmitted. Their copying in a single volume alongside French and Latin materials shows that they were accorded literary status and perhaps that they appealed to the tastes of cultivated readers.

Another important anthology of vernacular poetry dating from this period is Edinburgh, National Library of Scotland, Advocates' MS 19.2.1, the Auchinleck manuscript.[18] Narrative texts predominate, including saints' lives and religious legends (for example, stanzaic lives of Saints Margaret and Katherine, and the *Life of Adam and Eve* in octosyllabic couplets), and romances (for example, the stanzaic *Sir Beves of Hamtoun*, *Lay le Freine* in octosyllabic couplets and *Guy of Warwick* in couplets and in a stanzaic form). There are also examples of estates satire (*The Simonie)*, debates on secular and religious subjects (*The Thrush and the Nightingale*, *The Debate between the Body and the Soul*) and exemplary tales (*The Seven Sages of Rome*). The Auchinleck manuscript is thought to have been copied in London in the 1330s. It appears to be a 'commercial production', copied by several scribes under the supervision of an editor to fulfil the order of a purchaser.[19] Despite some uncertainty about the precise means of production, it is fairly safe to conclude that English poetry of the kinds in the manuscript was sought after and valued enough by readers and audiences to repay commercial production and even, perhaps, some financial speculation.

Many of the texts in MS Harley 2253 and in the Auchinleck manuscript do not occur anywhere else, and many occur in only one or two other witnesses. It must have been difficult to obtain exemplars for copying, and there was clearly no established means of written transmission of English poetry. The variety and discontinuities of production traditions must reflect patchy and discontinuous enthusiasm for this material among readers and patrons. Where relatively large numbers of manuscripts survive, they are usually of texts in whose dissemination the Church had an interest, such as the *South English Legendary* and the *Prick of Conscience*. Dissemination was inhibited too by the existence of regional varieties of English, and the lack of agreed standards of written representation of the language. Some texts were 'translated' from one regional dialect to another, for example, the Biblical history the *Cursor Mundi* is shown by rhyme and other linguistic evidence to have originally been composed in northern English, but manuscripts of the text in other dialects survive.[20] Those texts which did achieve some distribution, such as the lyrical meditation on the Passion 'Quanne hic se on rode', can evince enormous variety of spelling, vocabulary and morphology.[21] Such variations meant that written texts had limited comprehensibility beyond the region in which they were copied, even perhaps beyond the scribe and the circle around him familiar with the systems he used or developed, and dissemination would (and demonstrably did) involve much miscomprehension and error. There were sporadic attempts to standardise. One early, extreme example is the *Ormulum*, for which the poet-scribe developed a spelling system that indicated the lengths of vowels (perhaps to assist readers not familiar with the language).[22] That no accepted standard morphology or orthography was developed reflected, and in turn perpetuated, the low status of English as a medium for poetry.

We have seen that the models of excellence available to late fourteenth-century poets were written in Latin, French and Italian. The history of English poetry before the later fourteenth century includes experiments with self-conscious composition, attempts to create systems of spelling and morphology and some interest in collecting material into manuscripts that could serve as exemplars for copyists, models for poets and resources for readers. For a variety of reasons, however, these experiments remained just that. English poetry did not provide models for emulation or a sense of tradition in which an ambitious poet might work. The next section of this chapter examines the ways in which Chaucer, Gower and Langland responded to these circumstances.

One of Chaucer's most characteristic ways of tackling his relation with these models, negative and positive, is by indicating his own shortcomings in relation to the French and Latin examples and his links with 'lewed' ('unlettered/ignorant/lay') English composition. His invocation to the Muses at the beginning of Book 2 of *The House of Fame* to help him 'to endite [compose] and ryme' (*House of Fame*, line 520) is soon followed by the eagle's comically deflating explanation for why the dreaming poet has been snatched up into his claws: Jupiter has taken pity on him for serving Venus and Cupid without reward:

And never-the-lesse hast set thy wit –
Although that in thy hed ful lyte is –
To make bookys, songes, dytees,
In ryme or elles in cadence,

As thou best canst, in reverence
Of Love and of hys servantes eke,
That have hys servyse soght, and seke;
And peynest the to preyse hys art,
Although thou haddest never part.

(*House of Fame*, lines 620–8)

The poet has 'done his best' to compose love poetry, but, the eagle goes on to say, he has had no personal experience of the art of love, instead spending his time in his study reading and composing. The eagle views him as a 'lewed' (line 866) interlocutor who requires simple explanations in simple language (lines 853–64).

This inadequate Chaucer who fails to measure up as a poet is of course the product of a performance that is simultaneously comic and accomplished, and it is in his complex relation with the traditions of insular and continental poetry that he finds his subject. Chaucer's many well-known inflections of this poetic persona – the narrator of *Troilus*, the dreamers in the *Parliament of Fowls* and the Prologue to the *Legend of Good Women*, the dim-witted pilgrim-poet of *The Canterbury Tales* – provide many opportunities for him to ironise his relation with those whom his society considered poets. In every case Chaucer makes virtuoso poetry out of his affected distance from his society's literary models and standards.

Chaucer's metrical choices precisely reflect his uncomfortable positioning between the vernacular and his French, Latin and Italian models. Throughout his work he experiments ambitiously with a variety of demanding metres and verse forms. In the envoy to his 'Complaint of Venus', a short poem based on three French ballades by Oton de Grandson, he apologises for the shortcomings of his adaptation, blaming them on the difficulty of finding rhymes in English, as well as the intellectual infirmities of old age:

For elde, that in my spirit dulleth me,
Hath of endyting al the subtilte
Wel nygh bereft out of my remembraunce,
And eke to me it ys a gret penaunce,
Syth rym in Englissh hath such skarsete,
To folowe word by word the curiosite
Of Graunson, flour of hem that make in Fraunce.

('Complaint of Venus', lines 76–82)

He has, however, set himself a particularly exacting discipline here, in each three-stanza section restricting himself to two rhymes only. His apology draws attention to his achievement as measured against Grandson. That he aimed for a reputation for composing in the most challenging Continental forms is attested by his work (the roundel at the end of the *Parliament of Fowls*, and the many ballades). We may have lost some of his experiments in challenging verse-forms. In the Prologue to the *Legend of Good Women*, Alceste claims that the poet-figure's works include 'balades, roundels, virelayes' (F, line 423), though no virelays by Chaucer are now extant.

If Chaucer's translation of the *Roman de la Rose* is apprentice work aimed at experimenting with finding appropriate English verse-forms for celebrated models, as early as the *House of Fame* the poet was self-consciously measuring his verse against illustrious models. The invocation at the beginning of the third book of *The House of Fame* illustrates this well:

> O God of science and of lyght,
> Appollo, thurgh thy grete myght,
> This lytel laste bok thou gye!
> Nat that I wilne, for maistrye,
> Here art poetical be shewed,
> But for the rym ys lyght and lewed,
> Yit make hyt sumwhat agreable,
> Though som vers fayle in a sillable;
> And that I do no diligence
> To shewe craft, but o sentence.
>
> (*House of Fame*, lines 1091–100)

Here Chaucer is imitating Dante's invocation of Apollo in the *Paradiso* at the same time that he disclaims his own poetic ambitions, aiming only for his 'lewed' rhyme to be 'sumwhat agreable'. But the reference to 'lewed' properties and departures from strict syllable counting may also suggest that he is aiming to accommodate the French octosyllabic metre to the English language; he aspires not only to emulate, but to innovate. Perhaps he refers to his freedom with inflexional endings such as '-e' to create a fluid and responsive medium.[23] His most celebrated and historically significant innovation in versification, however, is his development of the iambic pentameter, the line later used in blank verse and Augustan heroic couplets, both in rhyme royal stanzas (for example, *Troilus and Criseyde* and the *Parliament of Fowls*) and in the rhyming couplets of many of *The Canterbury Tales*. The typical Chaucerian poetic voice, in which the disciplines of versification are enlivened with the illusion of colloquial, natural English speech, is most in evidence when he is using this metre.

Chaucer is aware of native verse-forms, but is uniformly disparaging of them.[24] In *The Canterbury Tales*, he allocates snatches of English love lyric to the disreputable Pardoner ('Com hider, love, to me'; General Prologue, line 672), and the absurd cockerel Chauntecleer and his hen ('My lief is faren in londe!'; Nun's Priest's Tale, line 2879). The six-line stanza of Sir Thopas hilariously parodies the jogging rhythms and banal rhymes of the stanzaic romances such as those found in the Auchinleck manuscript, prompting the Host to cry out for release from the torture with a rounding dismissal of the pilgrim Chaucer's 'lewednesse' and 'rym dogerel':

> 'By God,' quod he, 'for pleynly, at a word,
> Thy drasty rymyng is nat worth a toord!
> Thou doost noght elles but despendest tyme.
> Sire, at o word, thou shalt no lenger ryme.'
>
> (Sir Thopas, end link, lines 929–32)

Chaucer also distances himself from the alliterative long line, both by means of his own practice and more directly. After Sir Thopas, the Host proposes some alternative forms for Chaucer's tale:

> 'Lat se wher thou kanst tellen aught in geeste,
> Or telle in prose somwhat, at the leeste,
> In which ther be som murthe or som doctryne.'
>
> (Sir Thopas, end link, lines 933–5)

'In geeste' probably refers to the alliterative metre found in, for example, the late fourteenth-century *Morte Arthure*. Faced with these alternatives, Chaucer turns to prose. Later, the Parson makes the same choice, claiming that he 'kan nat geeste "rum, ram, ruf," by lettre', but that he also disapproves of 'rym' (Parson's Prologue, lines 43–4).

John Gower emulated French and Latin models by composing his own poems in those languages. In his Latin poem the *Vox Clamantis* (*c.*1385), he borrows freely from classical works, such as Ovid's *Heroides*, combining lines and fragments of lines and adapting them to fashion his attack on the estates of society.[25] He emulated French models in two Anglo-Norman ballade sequences, the *Cinkante Ballades* (*c.*1374), and a *Traitié* for married lovers (*c.*1398), and in the *Mirour de l'Omme* (1376–8), which is part estates satire, part manual of vices and virtues.[26] Like French poets such as Guillaume de Deguileville, who transformed the allegory of the *Roman de la Rose* into pious Christian teaching, Gower adapts the forms and genres of courtly poetry, replacing secular love with religious love. The metrical regularity of his French verse, especially the octosyllabic couplets of the *Mirour*, contrasts with the freedom (or technical shortcomings, as he may have thought) of Anglo-Norman and English octosyllabics. He seems to have aimed to outdo his models by maintaining a strict syllable count and rhyme scheme and combining them with the natural stresses of his vocabulary, as in these lines where he anticipates possible objections to his satire on the mendicant friars:

Mais s'aucun m'en soit au travers,
Et las sentence de mes vers
Voldra blamer de malvuillance,
Pour ce que je ne suy pas clers,
Vestu de sanguin ne de pers,
Ainz ai vestu la raye mance,
Poy sai latin, poy sai romance,
Mais la commune tesmoignance
Du poeple m'ad fait tout apers
A dire, que de fole errance
Les clercs dont vous ay fait parlance
Encore sont ils plus divers.

(*Mirour de l'Omme*, lines 21769–80)

Gower here invokes the authority of common talk against possible objections to his verses. The two instances of 'mais' here are rather difficult to construe, suggesting that he may have inserted them to maintain the syllable count and stress patterns of the lines, demonstrating his knowledge of 'romance' 'parlance'.[27]

Gower seems to have had similar ambitions for his English verse. He was one of the last poets to use octosyllabic couplets for a lengthy English work on a serious subject. His use of this metre in the *Confessio Amantis* (*c*.1386–93) was not simply traditional, however. In the prologue he announces that his work will be innovative in two ways:

Bot for men sein, and soth it is,
That who that al of wisdom writ,
It dulleth ofte a mannes wit
To him that schal it aldai rede,
For thilke cause, if that ye rede,
I wolde go the middel weie
And wryte a bok betwen the tweie,
Somwhat of lust, somewhat of lore

. . .

And for that fewe men endite
In oure englissh, I thenke make
A bok for Engelondes sake,
The yer sextenthe of kyng Richard.

('Prologue', lines 12–19, 22–5)[28]

Since books of unrelieved moral teaching are dull, he will attempt to write something that combines courtly desire ('lust') and moral teaching, and, because few have attempted serious composition in English, he will do so.

Like the works of Chaucer and Gower, *Piers Plowman* has a complex relation with Latin, French and English poetry. Structured as a series of visions in which the dreamer, Will, progresses uncertainly towards knowledge of how to save his soul, the poem is everywhere informed by the architecture and devices of the French allegorical love vision in its moralised iterations. Early in the poem the dreamer is 'ravysshed' by a vision of a lady:

> I loked on my left half as the Lady me taughte,
> And was war of a womman wonderliche yclothed–
> Purfiled with pelure, the pureste on erthe,
> Ycorouned with a coroune, the Kyng hath noon bettre.
> Fetisliche hire fyngres were fretted with gold wyr,
> And thereon rede rubies as rede as any gleede,
> And diamaundes of derrest pris and double manere saphires,
> Orientals and ewages envenymes to destroye.
> Hir robe was ful riche, of reed scarlet engreyned,
> With ribanes of reed gold and of riche stones. (II.7–16)[29]

Will's vision of the lady is informed by the tropes of love poetry – the superlatives and the medicinal stones recalling 'Annot and John' – but his enticement by this vision is immediately exposed as sinful by Holy Church. The vision of the lady is Holy Church's response to his request to be taught 'by som craft to knowe the false' (line 4) and the lovely lady is her example of 'mede', the bribery and corruption which lead men away from her.

Langland is also aware of Latin poetic models. Later in the poem Will's curmudgeonly guide Anima complains of a collapse of moral and intellectual standards in society, including education:

> Grammer, the ground of al, bigileth now children:
> For is noon of thise newe clerkes – whoso nymeth hede –
> That kan versifye faire ne formaliche enditen,
> Ne naught oon among an hundred that an auctour kan construwe,
> Ne rede a lettre in any langage but in Latyn or in Englissh. (XV.370–4)

Today's educated people ('newe clerkes') fail to teach children to read Latin, and themselves are unlearned in the crafts of versifying and formal composition, while (it is implied) fewer than one in a hundred can construe in French.

Although *Piers Plowman* is suffused with the vocabulary and tropes of French love vision poetry, the metre of the poem is not in the tradition of rhymed syllabic verse. Langland's choice is the alliterative long line, the metre described by Chaucer's Parson as 'rum, ram, ruf'. The basic unit is the line; it may comprise any number of syllables, and does not rhyme, but it must have two halves, each with at least one stressed syllable, divided by a caesura and linked by alliteration, with at least two alliterating syllables in the first half and one in the second.[30] Because Old English poetry was also written in alliterative lines, much critical energy has been expended on trying to trace lines of transmission from the Old English line to the long line of the later Middle English poets. The later fourteenth- and fifteenth-century corpus has often been seen as evidence of an 'alliterative revival' which is backward-looking, conservative, provincial and associated with some kind of English nationalism. However, the origins and development of the metrical models used by the poets remain unclear.[31] I would suggest that it may be more fruitful to regard the alliterative long-line corpus as an experiment in improving English poetry that precisely parallels those conducted by the poets who opted for syllabic metres. Whereas Chaucer and Gower experimented with reproducing the technical achievements of the French poets in English, Langland seeks to find an equivalent of the 'fair versifying' of the clerks with the alliterative long line.

The speech of Peace provides a good example of how Langland's verse relates to Latin models:

> Thanne pipede Pees of poesie a note:
> '*Clarior est solito post maxima nebula phebus;*
> *Post inimicicias clarior est et amor.*
> 'After sharpest shoures,' quod Pees, 'most shene is the sonne;
> Is no weder warmer than after watry cloudes;
> Ne no love levere, ne lever frendes
> Than after werre and wo, whan love and pees ben maistres . . .'
>
> (XVIII.410–14)

Peace quotes Latin verses ('poesie') from the *Liber Parabolorum* of Alanus de Insulis (a school text), then translates the chiastic construction of the two Latin lines ('clarior . . . post . . . post . . . clarior') into two pairs of four long lines: 'after sharpest shoures . . . after watry cloudes', amplifying and transforming the comparative into a superlative, 'clarior' becoming 'sharpest' and 'Clarior est . . . amor', being rendered 'no love levere, ne lever frendes'. So skilful is Langland's adaptation of Latin material in the alliterative metre that we are only now coming to recognise that many of his lines in fact have Latin sources.[32] Elsewhere, Langland brings Latin models in relation to English poetry by incorporating snippets of Latin into the metrical pattern and even the syntax of the English lines, as in this example from Peace's speech a little earlier in passus XVIII:

> 'Love, that is my lemman, swiche lettres me sente
> That Mercy, my suster, and I mankynde sholde save,
> And that God hath forgyve and graunted me, Pees, and Mercy
> To be mannes meynpernour for everemoore after.
> Lo, here the patente!' quod Pees, '*In pace in idipsum*,
> And that this dede shal dure, *dormiam et requiescam*.' (XVIII.181–6)

Here a line from a psalm (Psalms 4:9) serves as the second halves of two alliterative long lines, the words of the psalm becoming the title of the letters that authorise Peace and Mercy to save mankind.[33] Langland incorporates material from Latin texts and uses them as if they were English.

Langland's poetic art occupies an edgy, uneasy position between vernacular, secular models and discourses endorsed by the Church. The energetic disciplines of Langland's poetry are pointed up by the negative example of the figure of Sloth. Awakened from a sound sleep by Repentance, Sloth confesses that he is familiar with secular narratives ('rymes of Robyn Hood and Randolf Erl of Chestre', V.396) but not with religious poetry. He cannot read saints' lives, nor texts of canon law, nor construe the Psalms and teach them to his parishioners (V.416–22). Yet Langland does not align his poetry with the models of composition endorsed by the Church. In a famous passage, 'Imaginatyf' castigates the Dreamer for wasting time 'meddling' with 'makynges' when he could be saying prayers:

> 'And David in the Sauter seith, of swiche that loveth Jesus,
> "*Virga tua et baculus tuus, ipsa me consolata sunt*:
> Although thow strike me with thi staf, with stikke or with yerde,
> It is but murthe as for me to amende my soule."
> And thow medlest thee with makynges – and myghtest go seye thi Sauter,
> And bidde for hem that yyveth thee breed; for ther are bokes ynowe
> To telle men what Dowel is, Dobet and Dobest bothe,
> And prechours to preve what it is, of manye a peire freres.' (XII.13–19)

Will excuses his 'making' (a 'maker' being a much humbler figure than a 'poet') as a kind of solace (XII.22). Langland translates 'virga tua' with 'thi staf', and it is tempting to think that he cites this psalter verse because he is concerned about the part played by the 'staves' of the English alliterative line in the salvation of souls.[34]

The interest in metrical experiment that we have observed in all three poets is associated with a wider concern to 'improve' English as a vehicle for composition. Vocabulary was considered to be one area for improvement. Attempts to translate texts of learning into English were often made in the medium of prose. The great prose translation projects of the period include the Wycliffite Bible, the *Brut*, Nicholas Love's *Mirror of the Blessed Life of Jesus Christ* and John Trevisa's translation of Higden's *Polychronicon*. Poets contributed to this project, their metrical models and ambitions presenting them with particularly challenging problems to solve. Chaucer meets the challenges of 'scarcity of rhyme' in English by drawing on Latinate vocabulary that had come into English through French. For example, one of the rhymes in the first ballade of the 'Complaint of Venus' is on words with the suffix '-aunce': 'pleasaunce', 'remembraunce', 'governaunce', 'avaunce', 'suffisaunce', 'contenaunce'. The alliterative poet required a wide range of synonyms to alliterate on different sounds. For example, Langland deploys several synonyms for 'knight' in the passage where Christ is imagined as a knight jousting when he has his side pierced by Longeus. Christ is referred to as 'prikiere' (XVIII.25), 'knyght and kynges sone' (XVIII.76), and 'champion chivaler, chief knyght' (XVIII.99), and Longeus is referred to as 'knyght' (XVIII.78) and 'blynde bacheler' (XVIII.85).

Chaucer and Gower both distance themselves from the vocabulary associated with English syllabic verse. Chaucer registers disdain for vocabulary such as 'derne', 'gent', 'hende' and 'lemman' by allocating such terms to lower-class and morally repugnant characters.[35] For example, the pretentious and love-lorn parish clerk Absolon calls to Alison, 'Lemman, thy grace, and sweete bryd, thyn oore!' (Miller's Tale, line 3726), only to be rewarded with a kiss that is decidedly discourteous. In Sir Thopas, Chaucer parodies the formulas of stanzaic romance, the conventional 'Listen, lords!' opening line becoming increasingly absurd until it reaches its final iteration, 'Now holde youre mouth, *par charitee*' (Sir Thopas, line 891). John Burrow proposes that Gower similarly tries to exclude such vocabulary from his English verse, though not in as thorough a way as Chaucer.[36] Langland does not exclude such vocabulary from his lexis, though he does insist on adapting it to his moral and religious purposes. Holy Church accuses Lady Meed, for example, of having spoken ill of 'Leautee', her (Holy Church's) 'lemman' (II.21).

All three poets experiment with lexical sets associated with learned discourses. In the tale of Nactanabus, a story of a king who passes off sorcery as prophecy, Gower adds colour to his sources by describing how the king makes use of his 'Astellabre' (Book 6, line 1890, 'astrolabe'):

> He loketh his equacions
> And ek the constellacions,

He loketh the conjunccions,
He loketh the recepcions,
His signe, his houre, his ascendent,
And drawth fortune of his assent . . .
(Book 6, lines 1959–64)[37]

The specialised astrological terms used here are echoed by the description of the scientific paraphernalia to be found in the room of Chaucer's trickster Nicholas:

His Almageste, and bookes grete and smale,
His astrelabie, longynge for his art,
His augrym stones layen faire apart . . .
(Miller's Tale, lines 3208–10)

If Chaucer and Gower call such learned discourse under suspicion, even as they demonstrate that it can be used in English poetry, Langland's Dame Study leaves Will in no doubt about the deceiving properties of 'Astronomye', 'Geometry and Geomesie', 'sorcerie', and 'Alkenamye' (x.207–12):

'Alle thise sciences I myself sotilede and ordeynede,
Founded hem formest folk to deceyve.' (x.214–15)

Langland's diction positions his verse in relation both to Latin clerical discourses and to other late fourteenth-century alliterative poems. The poet of *Sir Gawain and the Green Knight*, for example, displays a dazzling command of the specialised vocabularies associated with polite living, deploying lexical sets associated with the arts of peace and war, such as hunting, armour, feasting and polite conversation. In many cases he draws on French-derived words, but he also uses other sources of vocabulary, such as Scandinavian topographical terms. As we have seen with the examples of the descriptions of Meed as a courtly lady and Christ as a knight, Langland redeploys 'courtly' vocabulary – whether fashionable or not – within an insistently moral and religious framework, and although he experiments with vernacularising clerical discourse, these specialised vocabularies remain problematic for him.

While ambitious poets might strive to improve the metres and vocabulary of English poetry, there was rather less that they could do about the problems of dialectal variety and scribal practice that threatened the comprehension, transmission and preservation of their works. *Troilus and Criseyde*, Chaucer's most sustained investigation of the enticing yet unstable properties of love, finishes with Chaucer's famous lament about those same properties in the English language:

And for ther is so gret diversite
In Englissh and in writyng of oure tonge,
So prey I God that non myswrite the,
Ne the mysmetre for defaute of tonge . . .
(*Troilus and Criseyde*, v.1793–6)

There is some evidence, however, that later fourteenth-century poetry was associated with the first attempts to remedy the situation. Chaucer's characteristic spellings seem to have been preserved by scribes, even when different and increasingly standardised usages were becoming the norm in official and legal documents. This suggests that Chaucer's characteristic spellings had developed some kind of authority, and that early scribes applied a notion of 'correctness' when copying his works.[38] Something similar is observable in the early manuscripts of Gower's *Confessio Amantis*. Gower's idiolect is distinctive, including some elements typical of Kent and some of Suffolk.[39] Manuscripts of the *Confessio* seem to have been produced to a standard format, and scribes respected Gower's characteristic spellings and morphology.[40] By contrast, the manuscripts of *Piers Plowman* are extremely diverse in format, readings and language. However, similar processes appear to have been at work. There are scribal corrections in the manuscripts, collation of various manuscripts to establish the text and scribal repair of faulty alliteration, while an 'editor' may have contributed to the production of the C-version of the poem.[41]

Even as new production processes and standards were being developed for the making of books of the new English poetry, great resource was being invested in the production of manuscripts of traditional verse. The example par excellence is the Vernon manuscript, Oxford, Bodleian Library, MS Eng. poet.a.1, a huge collection of edifying material, most of it Middle English verse, made for the benefit of pious lay readers in the final decade of the fourteenth century.[42] This manuscript includes saints' legends, homilies, exempla, prayers and devotional lyrics, biblical story, miracles and the A-version of *Piers Plowman* (the version that lacks the theologically troubling later sequences), but no Chaucer or Gower or other contemporary art poetry. Yet it was made no more than a decade, perhaps less, before the earliest surviving manuscripts of Chaucer and Gower were produced, and its physical magnificence and high standards of production testify to the investment of huge resources of time and funds in its making. Viewing this project, as its date requires us to do, alongside the poetic experiments of Chaucer, Gower and Langland, it appears as an alternative contribution to the improvement of English poetry. It brings together a vast quantity of material, comprising a huge resource of traditional Middle English poetry and translated material whose purposes were to transmit clerical instruction to the laity.

All of these projects are implicitly informed by awareness, not only of the vernacular's opportunities as a medium for serious poetry, but also of its dangers. With the calls of John Wyclif, convicted of heresy in 1382, and his followers the Lollards (or Wycliffites) for access to the Bible in English and their questioning of clerical textual practices, English lost its status as a medium that could communicate largely as the authorities chose, and became palpably a medium that could foment heresy and insurrection – perhaps, authorities feared, on the scale of the Peasants' Revolt of 1381.[43] Wycliffite literature and the approach to traditional English verse in the Vernon manuscript are two poles with which the experiments of Chaucer, Gower and Langland are in tension. The Wycliffites sought to improve English by developing a vernacular prose capable of giving unmediated access to scripture, rejecting what they saw as the misleading traditions of vernacular verse narrative. The Vernon manuscript offered a massive corpus of material in precisely that tradition of vernacular poetry as a resource for the transmission of clerical learning to the 'lewed'.[44] The edgy stylistic choices of Chaucer, Gower and Langland, are all, in their own ways, experiments in making a new future for English poetry.

All three poets immediately attracted imitators. *Piers Plowman* was imitated in a number of alliterative works on religious and political topics.[45] Chaucer was imitated by Thomas Hoccleve and John Lydgate, both of whom explicitly emulated their predecessor and lamented their shortcomings in comparison to their master. In the Prologue to his *Siege of Thebes* Lydgate imitates the opening of *The Canterbury Tales* and represents himself as another of the pilgrims called upon to tell a tale.[46] In his *Regiment of Princes*, Hoccleve pays tribute to Chaucer, praising him for embellishing the English language and claiming to have received guidance from him:

'But weleway, so ys myn hert wo,
That the honour of Englyssch tong is deed,
Of which I wont was han consail and reed.
'O mayster dere and fadir reuerent,
My mayster Chaucer, flour of eloquence . . .'

(lines 1958–62)[47]

Death may have slain Chaucer, but his books live on; Gower, likewise his 'master', is also dead ('Hastow nouȝt eeke my mayster Gower slayn, / Whos vertu I am insufficient / For to descryue?', lines 1970–7).

This is the beginning of a tradition of understanding of Chaucer's and Gower's importance that continued in the fifteenth century and over succeeding centuries.[48] Gower's reputation rested in part on Chaucer's dedication of *Troilus* to him, and in part on his own efforts to establish a reputation.[49] In the case of Langland, we cannot seek for tributes to a named poet, for it is not until the sixteenth century that we find John Bale referring to a William (or Robert) Langland, while Spenser still refers to the poet only as 'the Pilgrim that the Ploughman playde a whyle'.[50] The extent to which the numerous ploughman texts of the sixteenth century are tributes to the poem, and the meanings and circulation of the poem before its first printing by Robert Crowley in the mid sixteenth century, are matters of some debate.[51] The systematic study of the reception of the poem after Crowley is only just beginning.[52] The impact of *Piers Plowman* is one chapter in the history of English poetry which remains to be written.

Notes

1. See Dryden's 'Fables Ancient and Modern' (preface), in *The Poems and Fables of John Dryden*, ed. James Kinsley (London: Oxford University Press, 1958), p. 528; George Puttenham, *The Arte of English Poesy*, ed. Gladys Doidge Willcock and Alice Walker (Cambridge: Cambridge University Press, 1936), Book 1, chapter 31, p. 60.
2. Helen Cooper, '600 Years Dead: Chaucer's Deserved Reputation as "the Father of English Poetry"', *Times Literary Supplement*, 27 October 2000. Works in the tradition of New Criticism include J. A. Burrow, *Ricardian Poetry: Chaucer, Gower, Langland, and the 'Gawain' Poet* (London: Routledge and Kegan Paul, 1971) and Charles Muscatine, *Poetry and Crisis in the Age of Chaucer* (Notre Dame, IN: University of Notre Dame Press, 1972). Larry Scanlon and James Simpson (eds.), *John Lydgate: Poetry, Culture, and Lancastrian England* (Notre Dame, IN: University of Notre Dame Press, 2006) challenges the paradigm.
3. Nigel Saul, *Richard II* (New Haven: Yale University Press, 1997), pp. 12–13.
4. *Ibid.*, p. 360.
5. Michael Hanly, 'Courtiers and Poets: An International Network of Literary Exchange in Late Fourteenth-Century Italy, France, and England', *Viator*, 28 (1997), pp. 305–32.
6. *The Riverside Chaucer* ed. L. D. Benson (Oxford: Oxford University Press, 1988), p. 884 (note by Warren S. Ginsberg). All citations of Chaucer's works in this chapter refer to this edition.
7. Derek Pearsall, *John Lydgate (1371–1449): A Bio-bibliography* (Victoria, BC: University of Victoria, 1997), pp. 32–3.
8. Hanly, 'Courtiers and Poets', p. 332.
9. Manfred Görlach, *The Textual Tradition of the South English Legendary*, Leeds Texts and Monographs, n.s. 6 (Leeds: University of Leeds School of English, 1974), p. 38; R. Holt (ed.), *The Ormulum with the Notes and Glossary of R. M. White*, 2 vols.

(Oxford: Clarendon Press, 1878); Saara Nevanlinna (ed.), *The Northern Homily Cycle: The Expanded Version in MSS Harley 4196 and Cotton Tiberius E vii* (Helsinki: Société Néophilologique, 1972), Part 1, pp. 124–7; John J. Thompson, *The Cursor Mundi: Poem, Texts and Contexts*, Medium Ævum Monographs, n.s. 19 (Oxford: Society for the Study of Medieval Languages and Literature, 1998).

10. Robert Mannyng, *Handlyng Synne*, ed. Idelle Sullens, Medieval and Renaissance Texts and Studies (Binhampton, NY: Binhampton University Press, 1983); Robert E. Lewis and Angus McIntosh, *A Descriptive Guide to the Manuscripts of the Prick of Conscience*, Medium Ævum Monographs, n.s. 12 (Oxford: Society for the Study of Medieval Languages and Literature, 1982).
11. Judith Weiss and Rosamund Allen (eds.), *Wace and Lawman: The Life of King Arthur* (London: J. M. Dent, 1997), p. xxxiv; Robert Mannyng, *The Chronicle*, ed. Idelle Sullens, Medieval and Renaissance Texts and Studies (Binhampton, NY: Binhampton University Press, 1996).
12. London, British Library, Harley MS 978, fol. 11v.
13. Siegfried Wenzel, *Preachers, Poets, and the Early English Lyric* (Princeton: Princeton University Press, 1986).
14. *The Owl and the Nightingale*, ed. Eric Stanley, second edition (Manchester: Manchester University Press, 1972), line 1756. For the date see Neil Cartlidge, 'The Date of the *Owl and the Nightingale*', *Medium Ævum*, 63 (1996), pp. 230–47.
15. *The Harley Lyrics*, ed. G. L. Brook, fourth edition (Manchester: Manchester University Press, 1968), pp. 31–2, lines 28–30; my punctuation; I translate: 'Her name is in a note [song-sound] of the nightingale: in "a note" is her name – do not speak it! Whoever reads [the line] correctly, whisper [the answer] to John.'
16. Carter Revard, 'Scribe and Provenance', in Susanna Fein (ed.), *Studies in the Harley Manuscript: The Scribes, Contents, and Social Contexts of British Library MS Harley 2253* (Kalamazoo: Western Michigan University, 2000), pp. 21–109.
17. Frances McSparran, 'The Language of the English Poems: The Harley Scribe and his Exemplars', in Fein (ed.), *Studies in the Harley Manuscript*, pp. 391–426.
18. *The Auchinleck Manuscript*, ed. David Burnley and Alison Wiggins, National Library of Scotland, 2003, version 1.2. www.nls.uk/auchinleck/, accessed 26 March 2008.
19. *Ibid.* www.nls.uk/auchinleck/editorial/history.html.
20. Thompson, *The Cursor Mundi*, pp. 50–6.
21. For transcriptions see *Wessex Parallel WebTexts*, ed. Bella Millett, English, School of Humanities, University of Southampton www.soton.ac.uk/~wpwt/mouvance/melyric/MElyric.htm, accessed 26 March 2008.
22. R. W. Burchfield, 'The Language and Orthography of the *Ormulum* MS', *Transactions of the Philological Society*, 55 (1956), pp. 56–87 (p. 69).
23. Norman Davis, 'Versification', in Benson (ed.), *The Riverside Chaucer*, pp. xxxviii- xli.
24. Cf. Wendy Scase, 'The English Background', in Steve Ellis (ed.), *Chaucer: An Oxford Guide* (Oxford: Oxford University Press, 2005), pp. 275ff.
25. R. F. Yeager, *John Gower's Poetic: The Search for a New Arion* (Cambridge: D. S. Brewer, 1990), pp. 48–60.

26. *The Complete Works of John Gower: The French Works*, ed. G. C. Macaulay (Oxford: Clarendon Press, 1899).
27. 'If anyone is in dispute with me and would accuse my verse of malevolence, because I am not a cleric dressed in red or purple, but I am dressed in striped sleeves, and I know little Latin and little French, rather, the common testimony of the people has made me say everything openly which is that, concerning the foolish error of the clergy of which I have discoursed to you, they are more perverse than I have said.' Macaulay could find only about twenty lines in all of Gower's work which were not metrically correct (*ibid.*, p. xliv).
28. *The Complete Works of John Gower: The English Works*, ed. G. C. Macaulay, 2 vols. (Oxford: Clarendon Press, 1901). Some MSS have a dedication to Richard instead of 'A bok for Engelondes sake'.
29. All quotations from William Langland, *The Vision of Piers Plowman*, ed. A. V. C. Schmidt, new edition (London: J. M. Dent, 1987).
30. See the summary of types of line, *ibid.*, pp. 359–60.
31. See Thorlac Turville-Petre, *The Alliterative Revival* (Cambridge: D. S. Brewer, 1977), David Lawton (ed.), *Middle English Alliterative Poetry and its Literary Background* (Woodbridge: D. S. Brewer, 1982) and Thomas Cable, *The English Alliterative Tradition* (Philadelphia: University of Pennsylvania Press, 1991). Recent challenges to the revival narrative include Ralph Hanna, 'Alliterative Poetry', in David Wallace (ed.), *The Cambridge History of Medieval English Literature* (Cambridge: Cambridge University Press, 1999), pp. 488–512.
32. Traugott Lawlor, 'Langland Translating', paper presented at the Fourth International Conference for the Study of *Piers Plowman*, University of Pennsylvania, 17–19 May 2007.
33. For analysis of Langland's macaronic verse see A. V. C. Schmidt, *The Clerkly Maker: Langland's Poetic Art* (Cambridge: D. S. Brewer, 1987), pp. 93–102.
34. *Middle English Dictionary*, *staf* (n.) 2(b) 'a line of verse'. http://quod.lib.umich.edu/m/med/, accessed 10 April 2008.
35. E. T. Donaldson, *Speaking of Chaucer* (London: Athlone, 1970), pp. 13–29.
36. John Burrow, 'Gower's Poetic Styles', in Siân Echard (ed.), *A Companion to Gower* (Cambridge: D. S. Brewer, 2004), pp. 239–50 (pp. 243–5).
37. Macaulay (ed.), *The Complete Works of John Gower: The English Works* (p. 520) notes that 'the astrological terms in these lines are due to Gower'.
38. Simon Horobin, *The Language of the Chaucer Tradition* (Woodbridge: D. S. Brewer, 2003), pp. 16–35.
39. Jeremy J. Smith, 'John Gower and London English', in Echard (ed.), *A Companion to Gower*, pp. 61–72 (pp. 62–3).
40. Derek Pearsall, 'The Manuscripts and Illustrations of Gower's Work', in Echard (ed.), *A Companion to Gower*, pp. 73–97 (p. 80); J. J. Smith, 'Linguistic Features of Some Fifteenth-Century English Manuscripts', in Derek Pearsall (ed.), *Manuscripts and Readers in Fifteenth-Century England: The Literary Implications of Manuscript Study* (Woodbridge: Boydell and Brewer, 1983), pp. 104–12.

41. Wendy Scase, 'Two *Piers Plowman* C-Text Interpolations: Evidence for a Second Textual Tradition', *Notes and Queries*, n.s. 34 (1987), pp. 456–63; *Piers Plowman: The C Version*, ed. George Kane and George Russell (London: Athlone, 1997), p. 83.
42. *The Vernon Manuscript: A Digital Facsimile Edition*, ed. Wendy Scase (Oxford: Bodleian Library, forthcoming).
43. Margaret Aston, 'Lollardy and Sedition, 1381–1431' (1960), reprinted in *Lollards and Reformers: Images and Literacy in Late Medieval Religion* (London: Hambledon, 1984), pp. 1–48, and 'Wyclif and the Vernacular' (1987), reprinted in *Faith and Fire: Popular and Unpopular Religion, 1350–1600* (London: Hambledon, 1993), pp. 27–72; Anne Hudson, *The Premature Reformation* (Oxford: Clarendon Press, 1988), pp. 390–445.
44. Cf. N. F. Blake, 'The Vernon Manuscript: Its Contents and Organisation', in Derek Pearsall (ed.), *Studies in the Vernon Manuscript* (Cambridge: D. S. Brewer, 1990), pp. 45–59 (pp. 58–9).
45. Helen Barr (ed.), *The Piers Plowman Tradition* (London: J. M. Dent, 1993).
46. *Lydgate's Siege of Thebes*, ed. Axel Erdmann and Eilert Ekwall, 2 vols., Early English Text Society, extra series 108, 125 (London: Kegan Paul, Trench, Trübner, 1911, 1930).
47. M. C. Seymour (ed.), *Selections from Hoccleve* (Oxford: Clarendon Press, 1981).
48. Caroline Spurgeon, *Five Hundred Years of Chaucer Criticism and Allusion*, 3 vols. (Cambridge: Cambridge University Press, 1925).
49. Derek Pearsall, 'The Gower Tradition', in A. J. Minnis (ed.), *Gower's Confessio Amantis: Responses and Reassessments* (Cambridge: D. S. Brewer, 1983), pp. 179–97.
50. Anne Middleton, 'Introduction: The Critical Heritage', in J. A. Alford (ed.), *A Companion to Piers Plowman* (Berkeley: University of California Press, 1988), pp. 1–25 (p. 6).
51. Anne Hudson, 'Epilogue: The Legacy of *Piers Plowman*', in Alford (ed.), *A Companion to Piers Plowman* , pp. 251–66.
52. Sarah A. Kelen, *Langland's Early Modern Identities* (Basingstoke: Palgrave Macmillan, 2007) demonstrates the rich materials available for study of this area.

Chapter 4
Langland: *Piers Plowman*

A. V. C. SCHMIDT

In 1550 *The Vision of Piers Plowman* was published (without author's name) by the Protestant printer and controversialist Robert Crowley, and reprinted twice in the same year. Langland's great poem had previously been known only in manuscript copies, and as a product of a non-courtly tradition never interested William Caxton, who printed the works of Chaucer, Gower and Malory (1478; 1483; 1485). The first literary critics to notice it were William Webbe (1586), who thought the poet's 'dooinges . . . somewhat harshe and obscure' but judged him 'a very pithy writer' and George Puttenham (1589), who found his 'termes . . . hard and obscure', offering 'litle pleasure'.[1] Though read by Spenser, Marlowe and possibly Shakespeare, *Piers Plowman* sank from sight until Thomas Warton's *History of English Poetry* (1774–81). Warton found the poet's 'extremely perplexed' manner such as to 'disgust the reader with obscurities' but ascribed to the 'imposed constraint' of the alliterative metre his 'constant and necessary departure from the natural and obvious forms of expression'.[2] The poem's arresting first lines, which Warton quotes, hardly bear this out, however; and though Langland is not as linguistically accessible as Chaucer or Gower, his 'terms' will hardly seem 'hard' by comparison with the author of *Sir Gawain and the Green Knight*.

If Langland's poetry is 'difficult', this is due not to his language but his thought, his disconcertingly labile use of allegory and his unexpected and (at times) startling imagery, which contrasts strongly with the 'illustrative' mode typical of medieval writing. In his famous description of divine love (B-version, Passus I.148–58), heterogeneous conceits tumble forth, catching the light of semi-understanding before rolling into the shadow of semi-mystery. Love is a medicine, a spice, the plant of peace, the most precious virtue; heavy, it falls out of heaven, but after 'eating' earth grows light as a lime-tree leaf; it is easy to carry but sharp enough to penetrate chinks in armour or the walls of a fortified city. Langland's 'obscurity' here derives from the 'medling' or 'mingling' in his poetic figures of natural associations and learned tropes from patristic writings on the Incarnation:[3]

For hevene myghte nat holden it, so was it hevy of hymselve,
Til it hadde of the erthe eten his fille.
And whan it hadde of this fold [ground] flesh and blood taken,
Was nevere leef upon lynde lighter therafter,
And portatif [portable] and persaunt [piercing] as the point of a nedle,
That myghte non armure it lette ne none heighe walles (I.153–8)[4]

In some ways, this condensed and elliptical writing anticipates King Lear's tirade against corruption in law:

Through tatter'd clothes small vices do appear;
Robes and furr'd gowns hide all. Plate sin with gold,
And the strong lance of justice hurtless breaks;
Arm it in rags, a pigmy's straw does pierce it.
(*King Lear*, 4.6.164–7)[5]

But whether or not Shakespeare is directly echoing Langland,[6] what they share is an imaginative excitement generated from the rapid juxtaposition of contraries. Shakespeare sees the wealthy man in fine attire as impregnable to the force of Justice, while a poor man in coarse clothes is exposed to the smallest accusation; of two opponents armed for jousting, one is protected by gilt armour, the other vulnerable in rags. His bold opposition of poor and wealthy criminal (both personified by one word, 'sin') discloses to analysis that *gilt* armour connotes 'bribery', and 'plate' collocated with 'gold' suggests 'gold plate' as well as 'gilt plating', an object of monetary more than symbolic value. The metaphoric tension between justice's lance and the 'pigmy's straw' is higher than that between rags and furs, but recalls the tension between Langland's 'needle' (a little thing like the straw) and 'armour'/'high walls'. While both writers' images are electric with paradox, the medieval poet's figures have a further theological dimension; starting as literal, they pass into the wholly figurative, soliciting the reader's attentive interest. We are made to think how a material needle that could slip between the narrow openings in armour could never penetrate bonded masonry; yet the divine power of love can 'pierce' man's soul, however strongly defended. Despite evident differences, both poets offer not 'What oft was thought but ne'er so well expressed'[7] but 'What (if e'er thought) was ne'er at all expressed'.

One might reasonably wonder why the extraordinary qualities of Langland's poetry drew little comment from its early students. Thomas Whitaker, who edited the C-text of *Piers Plowman* in 1813, and Thomas Wright, whose edition of the B-text appeared in 1848, were antiquarian scholars interested in the poem especially as a document of medieval history and culture. Walter Skeat, who first edited the A, B and C versions, had the prime task of glossing and explaining rather than analysing its poetic qualities, which he profoundly admired (Skeat knew much of the poem by heart). In the nineteenth and early twentieth centuries, it was the poem's moral and religious 'message' that attracted most attention, and only as late as 1936 did C. S. Lewis recognise as 'truly exceptional about Langland . . . the kind, and the degree, of his poetic imagination', an 'intellectual imagination' that displayed (as in the 'Incarnation' passage) a 'power of rendering imaginable what before was only intelligible' unsurpassed even by Dante.[8] Less perceptive, however, is the same critic's assertion that Langland lacks Chaucer's variety and 'fine sense of language'.[9] Only Shakespeare among English poets does possess such variety; but properly to appreciate Langland's language we should relate him not to the lyric tradition that runs from Chaucer to Tennyson but to that of more dramatic poets like Wyatt, Donne, Browning and Hopkins. For, while not aiming at smoothness of versification and elegance of diction, Langland pursued his own kind of 'fineness'. This is evident in the way he controls the timbre of his lexis, varies the pace of his pausing alliterative line and exploits enjambment and deferred stress to create his distinctive union of metrical tension and speech-like immediacy.

What Langland's poetry does not display is Chaucer's 'divine fluidity of movement',[10] which appears to be what Lewis understood by 'fineness':

> And as the newe abaysed [suddenly frightened] nyghtyngale,
> That stynteth [ceases] first whan she bygynneth to synge,
> Whan that she hereth any herde tale [shepherd speak],
> Or in the hegges any wyght stirynge
> And after siker doth [makes] hire vois out rynge,
> Right so Criseyde, whan hire drede stente [ceased],
> Opned hire herte and tolde hym hire entente.[11]

Here, alliterating the iambically accented words enhances the pentameter line's fluid movement, while a similar melodic purpose motivates the assonantal -'yn'-patterning in lines 2 and 3, and the deferred full and 'rich' rhymes ('wyght' in line 4 with 'nyght' in line 1; 'herte' in line 7 with 'herde' in line 3), features that operate in concert with the three feminine end-rhymes. Chaucer's rhyme-royal stanza combines lexical amplitude with metrical ease to foster a leisurely expansiveness of syntax, enfolding sub-clause within clause ('That . . . Whan that . . . And after . . . whan'), while postponing the main verb so as not to lessen the conclusive force of the final assonating 'Opned . . . tolde'.

Whereas Chaucer's verse is 'fine' in the precise sense of 'possessing courtly refinement and elegance', Langland's staple manner exemplifies a proto-Shakespearean preference for 'working' the semantic force of non-lexical words, as in the passage describing Haukin the Waferer's lechery in Passus XIII (a powerful contrast with that on divine love discussed earlier):

> For ech a maide that he mette, he made hire a signe
> Semynge to synneward, and somtyme he gan taste
> Aboute the mouth or bynethe bigynneth to grope,
> Til eitheres wille wexeth kene [sharp], and to the werke yeden,
> As wel fasting dayes and Fridaies and forboden [prohibited] nyghtes,
> And as lef in Lente as out of Lente, alle tymes yliche –
> Swiche werkes with hem were nevere out of seson –
> Til thei myghte na moore . . . (B XIII.345–52)

Read slowly and with expression, this evidences a sense of language different from Chaucer's but equally fine, without which Langland could not count as the 'very great poet' Lewis calls him.[12] Unlike Chaucer's, Langland's melodic patterns, illustrated in his favourite device of pararhyme joining 'maide' to 'made', 'Semynge' to 'somtyme' and 'wille' to 'wel', are functionally secondary. For his verse (like Shakespeare's) is fundamentally dramatic, driving across the line-ends to a combined syntactico-semantic climax in 'myghte na moore'. Although only two verses run over, their impetus suggests an actor speaking to an audience; for Langlandian 'fineness' relates essentially to a movement of feeling that parallels the movement of thought. This is borne out by the need for complex editorial punctuation (as in the dash in the penultimate line) to bring out the colloquial naturalness of the writing.

Lewis is right about Langland's 'intellectual imagination' but mistaken that this is attained 'by thought rather than by sense' (here meaning 'sensuousness').[13] For in the variety of Langland's poetry illustrated here – and he has more 'variety' than Lewis allows – the most important aspect is not the visual but, as often in Donne, the 'kinetic'. The man and woman's sexual agitation is brilliantly evoked through a verse-mimesis of the stages by which 'eitheres wille wexeth kene': without specifying Haukin's 'signe', the poet implies its lascivious character by chiming the word with 'synne' in a glide of sibilants across the first and second lines. But Langland's melodic assonantal pattern, as deliberate as that formed by pararhyme, remains secondary to the alliteratively linked stress-pattern seen in -'tyme' and 'taste' (the latter verb run on with the assonating 'aboute' and 'mouth'). This last pattern repeats with mounting intensity in 'bigynneth to grope', a phrase marking the penultimate stage of the inevitable act of coition, with -'gynneth' now ironically rhyme-echoing 'synne'. At the end, the 'melodic' pattern of liquid consonants in 'And as *l*ef in *L*ente as out of *L*ente, alle tymes y*l*iche' is unexpectedly subordinated to the dramatic pattern (here coinciding with metrical accents) formed by the non-lexical vowel-staves 'in' and 'out' of the a-verse and the key-stave 'alle' in the b-verse. In the muscular deliberateness of such typical Langlandian lines, every word, whether lexical or grammatical, is made to pull its weight.

Three critics in 1962 turned from considering Langland's structure, themes and religious thought towards the details of his poetic achievement. Elizabeth Salter devoted a long chapter to his 'Art'; John Lawlor illuminated his imagery; and Nevill Coghill showed how Langland manipulated Latin and English lexical elements to generate the 'sublimity' Lewis had recognised but not analysed.[14] These studies began to answer the criticism that Langland 'hardly makes his poetry into a poem'. [15] That even specialists continued to suspect this might be true is clear from a revealing correlative admission nearly thirty years later (by a pupil of Lewis's sensitive to Langland's verbal and phrasal repetition) that he has 'long passages of sense – excellence of matter and meaning – which only rarely deviate into poetry'.[16] But as 'New Criticism' lit up the dusky vaults of medieval poetry, a bright beam directed by John Burrow upon the Second Vision in 1965 revealed Langland's capacity to achieve locally an 'Aristotelean' unity akin to Chaucer's or the *Gawain*-poet's.[17] In the same year P. M. Kean explored the allusive depths of the 'Incarnation' passage in her essay 'Langland on the Incarnation'; and the mode of analysis pioneered in R. E. Kaske's 1951 essay on the poet's figurative expressions[18] received fruitful development in Ben Smith's full-length study of his images of charity.[19]

Interest in Langland's poetry did not completely ebb as a new wave of interest in his content and context surged up.[20] Two decades after the last study mentioned, 'Langland's poetic art' found a champion[21]; and the thematic and structural significance of the poet's word-play received detailed scrutiny two years later from M. C. Davlin (1989).[22] But while growing scholarly enthusiasm was signalled by the publication of the *Yearbook of Langland Studies* (1989), that journal's twenty-two volumes to date contain only a handful of articles on metre or metaphor, and almost none on poetic language. The importance of all three aspects is certainly presupposed by the methods and aims of modern editors. But while the latter may be thought to have a vested interest in Langland's artistic excellence, other specialists have maintained that he suffered from a 'compulsion to tinker'[23] or 'felt uncompelled to ensure the accuracy of his text' but 'placed his credence in a copyist, whose work he shows no sign of having supervised and corrected'.[24] As Chaucer's 'Wordes' to his own scribe bear out, medieval poets were obliged to endure copyists' failure to reproduce their texts faithfully. But to go by Langland's tart comments on miscopied legal documents, he must have wanted *his* scribes to 'write trewe' after his 'makynge'[25] and protested if they 'parcelles overskipped' or 'ma[de] any defaute' (XI.305–8) in his meaning and metre 'witynge and wilfully' (XIX.374). This 'maker' took his art seriously enough to defend it (with subtle obliquity) against Imaginatif's attacks in Passus XII (lines 22, 27), where his dream-persona Will calls 'makynge' both his 'solace' and his 'work'.[26]

If *Piers Plowman* really contains 'a wider variety of fine poetry than any other work from the English Middle Ages',[27] its failure to occupy as central a place in our literature as *Troilus* or *Sir Gawain* may be due in part to its indeterminate genre. Religious poetry that is also satire is a potentially indigestible mix, since satire arises out of (and seeks to arouse) contempt, disgust and hatred of its object, while Christian writing leans towards love and forgiveness. But arguably the strong tension between these emotional poles may account for some of the poem's unique power. Modern readers also find difficult its troubled preoccupation with justice and mercy, knowledge and salvation, a preoccupation concentrated in the Third Vision (Passus VIII–XIV).[28] Earlier scholars from Skeat to Bennett accordingly limited their student editions to the first two visions, forming the so-called '*Visio*'. But while this opening section ends in a notoriously problematic scene, the Tearing of Truth's Pardon, it undoubtedly contains some of Langland's sharpest social satire and liveliest allegory. And here lies a third difficulty affecting the poem's appeal today. For despite the efforts of Elizabeth Salter, John Lawlor, John Burrow, David Aers and Priscilla Martin (who even formulates and answers 'Objections to Allegory'), the allegorical mode still seems to many (in Webbe's dismissive phrase) 'harshe and obscure'.[29] And since Langland displays less frequently than Chaucer or the *Gawain*-poet the realism or symbolism preferred today (though occasionally using both), the best way to defend his work might be to challenge directly Puttenham's assertion that in poetic allegory there is 'litle pleasure'. We may start with no less an authority than the 'symbolist-realist' author of *The Waste Land*, who confronted the *general* modern 'prejudice against allegory' in his 1929 essay on Dante, claiming for this method 'very great advantages' and judging it 'not a device to enable the uninspired to write verses, but really a mental habit, which when raised to the point of genius can make a great poet'.[30] Eliot stressed further that 'Dante's attempt is to make us see what he saw' (something that realist writers, in a different way, also do) and that 'he employs . . . very few metaphors, for allegory and metaphor do not get on well together'.[31] Eliot's last point has especial relevance for readers who see in Shakespeare and the Metaphysicals the quintessentially poetic; he argues that to appreciate Dante's greatness, we must not require great poetry to be exuberantly metaphorical.

However, compared with the *Commedia*, the supreme medieval allegory, *Piers Plowman* falls victim to a *particular* modern prejudice against which Eliot's defence of Dante cannot readily be adopted. For unlike Dante, making us 'see what he saw' is not his chief aim (notwithstanding such statements as 'Ac I shal seye as I saugh' at v 22); and this is because his method reflects a somewhat different 'mental habit'. Dante's Hell is an actual place, with a precisely realised topography, which also stands for the spiritual condition of the damned. Moreover, the occupants of the *Commedia*'s three regions are mainly human (or sometimes superhuman) beings, not personifications of abstract ideas. Dante writes mostly symbol allegory, in which his literal narratives have a symbolic meaning. But Langland, like the *Roman de la Rose* before him and Morality drama that followed him (and drew on his work), uses 'personification allegory'.[32] Meed, Hunger and Thought, though given words to speak or actions to perform, personify the abstract ideas their names denote. Their interaction with other personified figures, as R. W. Frank pointed out, is accordingly *literal* not symbolic. This is, admittedly, to simplify, for personification allegory is not Langland's exclusive mode. He produces memorable symbol allegory in his 'wilderness' with its tower on a hilltop, its second tower in a low valley and its field full of folk between them (Prologue 11–17), our interpretation of these images depending on their traditional use as symbols of Heaven, Hell and Middle-Earth. Langland also employs a 'figural allegory' related to the mode of Bible interpretation called typology, which discerned a reciprocal relationship of prefigurement and fulfilment between types and antitypes (whether events or persons or things) in the Old and New Testaments.[33] In this variety, the 'actants' or 'generators of action in any given narrative'[34] simultaneously exist on a historical level and personify concepts. Examples in Passus XVII–XVIII are Abraham/Faith, Moses/*Spes* and, in a more complex way, the Samaritan/Jesus; while at XVIII.10 and XIX.6 Piers himself, uniquely combining literal and symbolic significations, becomes a 'retro-type'[35] of Christ, the ideal of charity that he imitates and fulfils. Symbol and personification allegory are 'medled' in Passus XIII, where Haukin as a literal Wafer-Seller can interact with a Knight, Conscience and a Pilgrim-Hermit, Patience, but as a personification of 'Active Life', with the Knight and the Pilgrim-Hermit as personifications of respectively a mental faculty and a moral virtue. More broadly, Langland's poetry reflects a 'sacramental' attitude towards the whole creation, from the four elements that make up the material world to the living creatures that fill it and the 'earthly honest things' (XIX.94) made by men.[36] All of these are able to function as vessels of religious meaning, because for Langland nature brings news of God to eyes and ears that are ready to receive it. This attitude may affront another modern prejudice if it is taken (or mistaken) as an issue of belief. But the relevant question is not whether the poem's religious ideas are objectively true so much as whether the poet enables his reader to experience what it would feel like if they *were* true. For Langland, one suspects, 'realisation' of religious truth may have been inseparably bound up with the capacity of poetry to 'realise' experience.

To a large extent, it is not the diversity of Langland's figurative methods[37] so much as his bold 'medling' of them that (like his 'medling' of religious and satirical modes) can perplex even readers who 'buy into' the Modernist *mélange* of realism and symbolism in *The Waste Land* or *Ulysses*. Such readers' perplexity may stem from inappropriate expectations based on acquaintance with Spenser or Bunyan. For *Piers Plowman* not only has a complex structure of eight dream-visions (with two further embedded 'inner' dreams) and a wide thematic range (as indicated by the Prologue's panoramic opening vision), it is also more emotionally concentrated than *The Faerie Queene* (1589–96) and more intellectually daunting than *The Pilgrim's Progress* (1678), both of which may be enjoyed on the literal level as stories before being interpreted as allegories. Langland requires readiness to see the allegorical mode stretched to its limits, alertness to its narrative and 'generic' surprises, and imaginative resilience to engage sympathetically with the disclosures and enigmas thrown up in a series of frustratingly inconclusive dream encounters. These encounters sometimes seem less like those of Bunyan's Pilgrim than those of Carroll's Alice: the character 'Book' may remind us of Humpty Dumpty, or Conscience's Dinner of the Mad Hatter's Tea Party. Langlandian allegory is both less simply constituted and less clearly organised than that of an early Morality play like *The Castle of Perseverance* (*c*.1420–5), which derives from the Prudentian *Psychomachia* tradition.[38] *Piers Plowman* at times recalls the preaching tradition in the ways it develops its major theological themes;[39] but its one formal 'sermon' (at v.13–60) is delivered by a personified Reason to 'al the reaume' (v.11), while its wider audience (like that of Death in the Morality play *Everyman* (1520)) is 'all mankind'. Moreover, as a 'medling' of moral instruction and direct speech (v. 35–40, 42–7, 49, 52–9) halfway between homily and treatise, its primary purpose is dramatic – to arouse 'repentaunce' in the 'wille' of the folk (v.60–1). Again, Holy Church's long speech (I.12–209) is a rich medley of exposition and admonition, provoked by Will's initial request for clarification of the 'mountaigne', 'merke dale' and 'feld ful of folk' (I.11), and articulated in response to his six subsequent questions at I.45, 59–60, 73–4, 83–4, 138–9 and II.4. But while this crucial discourse offers a ground-plan for the entire poem,[40] setting the parameters for the cosmic battle between Truth and Wrong (God and the Devil) and emphasising the central importance of Christ's Incarnation, it does not presage a systematic development as does Canto I of the *Inferno* in relation to Dante's three successive *cantiche* of the world after death. For Holy Church's answer to Will's fourth question (lines 83–4), how he shall save his soul ('By pursuing Truth'), only begets a fifth question (about where Truth is to be found); and her reply to this prompts not the expected 'What *is* Truth?' but the (dramatically more promising) 'Teach me some means to recognise *the False*' (II.4).

If ever any work attempted 'by indirections' to 'find directions out', *Piers Plowman* is that work. Will's request to be *shown* 'the False' is adroitly used to effect a generic transition from religious poetry to social satire, via a thematic transition from transcendent Truth to this-worldly Reward. The connecting link between these two key ideas is that between the moral meanings of Truth and Meed. Next, since the answer Will receives comes not as words but as vision and action (Langland here aiming to make us 'see as he saw'), the poem is enabled to move back to the topical issue of political influence broached in the Prologue's Fable of the Rats and Mice. But possibly the real reason why Holy Church's answer is shown (ambiguously) and not stated (unequivocally) may be that spiritual education *has* to proceed in 'successive zig-zags' instead of following 'a straight, linear scheme'.[41] Moreover, the theological matters that now begin to be raised will sometimes be resolved not through the 'actants' reaching reasoned agreement but by one of them performing an unexpected action that propels both Dreamer and reader in another direction. When, towards the end of the Second Vision, a priest incredulously 'construes' the Pardon sent from Truth, Piers does not demand further explanation but tears the document 'atweyne' (VII.115), shunting Dreamer and reader off the direct path to Truth laid down in Piers's 'signpost-allegory' at V.560–629. The answer to Will's fourth question ('By pursuing Truth') has now become 'By doing well' because, according to Truth's Pardon, '*qui bona egerunt ibunt in vitam eternam* "Do wel" . . . and God shal haue thi soule' (VII. 110*a*, 112); but this answer only provokes him to ask 'What *is* Do-well?' (VIII.5, 13). Again, in the Fourth Vision, when the guests at Conscience's dinner become heated about this same question, Conscience's 'answer' takes the form of a curt farewell and sudden departure with Patience as his companion, 'pilgrymes as it were' (XIII.216). Finally, in the second inner dream, when Will, warned by Piers to question no more about the Trinity, asks instead to taste the fruits of the Tree of Charity, Piers 'answers' by shaking the tree vigorously, with dramatic results: 'For evere as thei dropped adoun, the devel was redy, / And gadrede hem alle togideres' (XVI.79–80). Whereupon the poem, with another abrupt zig-zag, embarks on its dazzlingly unconventional re-telling of Christ's Passion and death, a supremely dramatic answer to the overwhelming question of evil.

Even when a Langlandian *dialogus* (the name several manuscripts give the poem), does develop, it advances asymmetrically and is not unified by the unimpassioned reciprocity of the university *disputatio* but fissured by misunderstandings, warnings or threats. An apparently naive request for necessary information may receive only a mild rebuke, as when Will asks Conscience why Jesus is called 'Christ (XIX.25–6). But in the Dreamer's encounters with friars, the intellectual elite of the day, the tone quickly grows sharp. At the opening of the Third Vision, he is informed by two Franciscans that the 'Dowell' he is seeking lives with them (i.e. is found in the mendicant way of life). But when Will 'disputes' this, using the syllogistic form of which these '*maistres freres*' (Prologue 62) are master, their response (in the form of a simple parable) draws from him a provocative disavowal of the 'natural capacity' ('kynde knowing') to comprehend it (VIII.57). In another incident, the Dreamer's 'big issue' is, why do friars hear confessions and bury the dead rather than baptise infants, devoting themselves to two potentially lucrative sacramental rites rather than to one that offers no gain but is essential for salvation? Will accuses his confessor of wanting him to agree to be buried in the convent cemetery so that he can pick up the funeral dues, and perhaps a legacy (XI.63–83). But Langland allows the friar no chance to reply; instead, he brings on the forthright Lewtee (perhaps personifying his 'ideal' audience of truth-loving men), who laughingly encourages the scowling Dreamer 'To reden it in retorik to arate dedly synne' (XI.102). This kind of narrative 'abruption' could well qualify as one of those 'dooinges' that Webbe and Puttenham found 'harshe and obscure', but (like the one at XVI.79) it undeniably generates dramatic tension. Presumably, therefore, engaging his readers' interest and emotions was as important a motive for Langland as advancing a moral and religious lesson in sweetly lucid 'termes'. His *main* purpose may even have been to show what it is like to think about salvation, not to say what to think about salvation. Or the truth may be simply that Langland understood, like the fifteenth-century Morality playwrights later, how drama could help to make learning more effectual.

Whereas the confessor incident occurs in the first inner dream, Will's 'disputation' with the Friars Minor forms one of two longer 'waking episodes' (the other opens Passus xx). It ends with him wandering in a literal 'wildernesse' (VIII.63) that corresponds to the (not quite literal) 'wildernesse' of Prologue 12 which, unlike Spenser's Wood of Error (*Faerie Queene* I.i), resembles the real English terrain of uncultivated land bordered by forest, though without precise geographical location. Yet as the Vision Two wilderness imperceptibly grows out of the more 'Dantean' wilderness of the Prologue, it transpires that Will's emerging dream encounter (with 'Thought') is designed to precipitate a passionate struggle to escape from its 'maze' (I.6) of uncertainty. The struggle, that is, will be enacted in the Dreamer's mind, as he doggedly endeavours to reason with himself. Though as yet without the 'kynde knowynge' of Dowel that he desires (VIII.110), Will now declares not that he can't 'conceyve' (grasp) his interlocutor's words, but that he dislikes their 'savour' (line 109). In *this* pilgrim's progress the issue is to become less and less one of 'cognition' than of 'affect', and the learner's resistance to teaching will be seen as a product of temperament and personality even more than intellect and rational will. Will's painful struggle doesn't prove fruitless, however: it leads him to a wise instructor, 'Wit', who not only personifies the quest for moral understanding, but whose wife, Study, signifies the moral discipline of effortful desire.[42]

Will's succeeding encounters – with Fortune, Clergy, Scripture, Lewtee, Reason and Imaginatif – all occur in the poem's 'long middle', within an inner dream extending from XI.6 to XI.404. They are initiated and concluded by Latin rebukes ('harshe' but, to Will, *not* 'obscure') from Scripture and Reason respectively: '*Multi multa sciunt* . . .' ('Many know much but do not know themselves') and '*Nemo sine crimine vivit*' ('No one lives without blame'). The words '*Multi*' and '*Nemo*' 'bracket' 400 lines of deeply felt argument about whether right action is both necessary and sufficient for salvation, which (despite the case for the literary appeal of 'thinking in poetry' made by Burrow)[43] even educated medieval readers may have found hard going. However, as if anticipating the problem, Langland inserted between the two phases of this dense debate an idyllic vision of creation from the Mountain of Middle-Earth (XI.326–67). Through its intermedled 'Blisse and bale' (XI.332) gleam intimations of the Earthly Paradise, Will's report of how 'Kynde . . . nempned me by my name, and bad me nymen hede' (XI.321–2) audibly echoing God's invitation to Adam to summon the animals and name them (Genesis 2:19–20). Set almost at *Piers Plowman*'s 'sovereign mid-point',[44] it poignantly suggests 'the beginning / In Eden garden';[45] but Will's dramatic mood-change on witnessing the discrepancy between animal temperance and human excess immediately evokes 'the blight man was born for'[46] and inflames him to 'rebuke' Reason (XI. 372) for man's exile from the happy state (his very anger a symptom of his fallenness). The heat of their exchanges only dissipates after Will abruptly awakes from his inner dream and his consciousness ascends to the containing 'outer' dream, where an unnamed 'oon' asks *him* the original question 'What is Dowel?' to which (too late) he has realised the 'affective' answer: 'To se muche and suffre moore' (XI.410). Interestingly, it is this last interlocutor of Vision Three, Imaginatif, who implies the Middle-Earth/Paradise analogy, when he compares Will's lapse from reasonableness with Adam's original fall through 'pride and presumption' (XI.421) and urges him to think of the vexed problem of evil as something more in the nature of a mystery.

Such a proposal to 'feed his mind' with 'wise passiveness' looks forward, in certain respects, to Wordsworth's.[47] But while the unstated assumptions of the theological debate must be set in their medieval context, the real originality of Langland's vision of nature should not be overlooked. What he is inviting us to consider is how the 'unreasonable' acts of 'man and his make' (XI.370) might look from the point of view of God. For the poem's creator emphatically ascribes to the Creator of nature a positive desire to see as much as can be seen and endure/tolerate more than man ever can. Reason's pregnantly punning words 'Who suffreth moore than God?' (XI.387) express in effect what Peace, one of the Four Daughters of God, will claim later in Vision Five as the breathtaking reason for the Incarnation:

> Forthi God, of his goodnesse, the firste gome [man] Adam,
> Sette hym in solace and in sovereyn murthe [supreme joy];
> And siththe he *suffred* [allowed] hym synne, sorwe to feele –
> To wite what wele was, kyndeliche [directly] to knowe it.
> And after, God auntrede [ventured] himself and took Adames kynde
> To wite what he hath suffred in thre sundry places . . . (XVIII.217–22)

There is a profound lesson in this scene for the artist as well as for the receptive reader.

If the Middle-Earth passage (XI.326–67) attempts to 'make us see what he saw', it equally exemplifies his 'rendering imaginable what before was only intelligible'. But no less striking than these forty lines' ten variants of the word 'see' (such as 'beheld', 'toke kepe') are its terms describing the effect of visionary seeing, wonder ('merveille', 'selcouthe'). For just as Peace's account of the Incarnation highlights God's 'adventurous' desire to '*know* properly' (XVIII.208) what human suffering is (where Holy Church had emphasised *love* as its chief motive), so Will's vision of Middle-Earth focuses on the two ways in which (in Geoffrey Hill's phrase) 'landscape is like revelation'.[48] These too concern cognition and will, knowing and doing. For beholding attentively the variety and harmony that landscape 'reveals' may help man understand how to 'suffer' evil patiently; and reflecting on the behaviour of non-human creatures may assist him to work out the connection between right action and good art. Will is therefore shown to 'marvel' not only at how, after mating, the beasts 'Medled noght with hir makes' (XI.143) but also at how they 'made nestes' (line 343), displaying greater skill than 'wright' or 'mason' (lines 348–9). Langlandian nature does not foster man's moral life through beauty and fear (as in Wordsworth) but teaches him 'by ensaumples to knowe ... Kynde ... to lovye' (XI.324–5). Its specific lesson is that to follow reason rather than sensuality might empower Will both to overcome the *concupiscencia carnis* afflicting him at the start of his inner dream (XI.17–21) and to make (poetic composition) with a tempered mastery like that of the 'wonderful foweles' (line 328) who 'medle noght with hir makes' after mating. Such a reading of this important passage is not meant to privilege impulses from vernal woods over the moral teachings of the sages. For as Langland would have known, the Biblical sage Solomon had warned (as clearly as would Wordsworth) against the meddling intellect, and taught temperance and prudence from the ways of nature: 'Thou art ensnared with the words of thy mouth, and caught with thy own words ... Go to the ant ... and consider her ways, and learn wisdom ... Which, although she hath no guide ... provideth her meat ... in the summer, and gathereth her food in the harvest' (Proverbs 6:2, 6–8). The Middle-Earth scene's serene interval near the poem's centre holds but a moment; and ironically, it is meddling intellect that alters Will's mood to vexation at discovering 'That Reson rewarded [watched over] and ruled alle beestes / *Save* man and his make' (XI.368–9). Like his counterpart the Wafer-Seller in Vision Four, whose 'cote of cristendome' (XIII.274), a metonym for his soul, will be found soiled with every vice, Will learns the hard truth of how 'hard it is ... to lyve and to do synne'. Though seeing clearly how 'Synne seweth us evere' (XIV.322–3) he cannot yet see further, with Julian of Norwich, that though 'Synne is behovely ... alle maner of thynge shalle be wele'.[49] Will's pastoral vision of 'fleckede fetheres of fele colours' (XI.329) appears but a fugitive consolatory recollection of paradise lost when he looks on the unseemly 'moles and spottes' that have 'bidropped' the conscience of his alter ego Haukyn (XIII.315, 321). His bright memory of 'the sonne and the see and the sond' (XI.326) brings only anguish; for paradise cannot be regained. But it may be restored, if God 'aunters' himself by taking 'Adams kynde'.

Like the protagonist in the contemporary dream-vision poem *Pearl*, Will the believer aches for lost innocence: for baptismal purity, for the Church's pristine communal life. Will the maker, however, knows that he must rest content with 'perfection in imperfection', understanding his artistic vocation in accord with the teaching of St Gregory the Great that man grows perfect only through becoming 'spiritual in his flesh' (*carne spiritualis*).[50] If final perfection belongs to God, whose creative plan needs for its fulfilment the suffering of the individual and of mankind as a whole through the plotted course of 'Salvation History', poetry cannot (any more than history) remain unsullied by the 'foule plottes' (XIII.318) of political machination, greed, hypocrisy and lust. It must both embrace man's bodiliness and strive to liberate him from 'the body of this death' (Romans 7:24). Such a conviction produces in *Piers Plowman* at the level of both macrostructure (allegory) and microstructure (versification, word-play and metaphor), its distinctively 'medled' quality. Langland eschews an uninterruptedly high or low register, favouring a plain middle style like the Latin Bible's *sermo humilis*. But he is, above all, the great exponent of a mode that mixes tones and feelings usually kept apart by Chaucer, Gower and (if less often) the author of *Gawain* and *Pearl*. His coarsest episodes are 'flecked' with the sublime, his ostensibly heroic scenes 'moled' with racy humour.[51] This mode might be aptly called the 'medieval grotesque', if St Bernard's classic (but unfriendly) characterisation of the grotesque as *formosa deformitas* ('fair misfeature') can be thought of positively, as a kind of beauty rather than a kind of ugliness.[52]

To take an extreme example, the viscerally 'realistic' tavern scene in Passus V,[53] which seems to offer 'litle pleasure' in Puttenham's conventional sense:

> He pissed a potel in a *Paternoster*-while,
> And blew his rounde ruwet [trumpet] at his ruggebones [backbone's] ende,
> That al that herde that horne helde hir nose after
> And wished it hadde ben wexed [polished] with a wispe of firses [furze]
> (V.342–5)

Here Langland's yoking together of heterogeneous images (Glutton's pissing with the Lord's Prayer, his malodorous fart with doomsday's trumpet) by its grotesque 'medling' of discrepant experiences and ideas magnifies the drunkard's debauch to something bizarrely beautiful, rather as do the Elder Bruegel's paintings of Flemish peasant life. Another example is Will's complaint, towards the end of the poem, that old age has made him deaf, toothless and impotent:

> of the wo that I was inne my wif hadde ruthe,
> And wished wel witterly that I were in hevene.
> For the lyme [member] that she loved me fore . . .

. . .
I ne myghte in no manere maken it at hir wille.
So Elde and he[o] it hadden forbeten [enfeebled] (XX.193–8)

Satire could not get more mordant without becoming morbid; yet Langland's humour, though 'odd, grotesque and wild' is free of Swift's angry self-disgust.[54] Will may fear that his wife wishes him dead (so that she can marry someone more lusty?), yet she wants him 'in hevene', feels 'ruthe' for his 'wo'. And this collocation of high terms with harsh serves to moderate the speaker's animus, while hinting ruefully that if *he* is no longer 'hir wille', then *she* (as well as Elde) has made it so! Since for Langland, fallen 'man and his make' live necessarily against reason, man's endeavour of art can at best express yearning for what can never be regained, only recalled. So *Piers Plowman* offers neither the noble pity of Wordsworth's 'Ruined Cottage' nor the unalloyed loathing of Swift's 'Beautiful Young Nymph'; its pathos and irony, as in Hamlet's ideal of 'blood and judgement' (3.3.69), are always 'co-medled'.

Turning, finally, from the poem's grossest moments to its grandest, we find even a passage 'armed' in near-unbroken loftiness, Christ's great vindication speech at the Harrowing of Hell, admitting through a 'chink' a piercing needle-point of grotesque humour. In these soaring verses Langland's 'medled' macaronic high style generates deep theological resonances against which the high notes of the corporeal shrill out sharp.

For I that am lord of lif, love is my drynke,
And for that drynke today, I deide upon erthe.
I faught so, me thursteth yet, for mannes soule sake;
May no drynke me moiste, ne my thurst slake,
Til the vendage falle [grape-harvest take place] in the vale of Josaphat,
That I drynke right ripe must [wine from ripe grapes], *resureccio mortuorum*.
And thanne shal I come as a kyng, crouned, with aungeles,
And have out of helle alle menne soules.
Fendes and fendekynes [fiendlings] bifore me shul stande . . . (XVIII.366–74)

This is an inspired elaboration of the Biblical sublime of Genesis and St John – firm, clear and nobly simple. The ritualised repetitions of 'drynke' and 'mannes soule(s)' are heightened by cross-caesural assonance and pararhyme ('today / deide'; 'falle / vale'; 'lif / love'; 'helle / alle') and a surprising end-rhyme at lines 368 to 369; the potent extended metaphor culminates at line 371 in a sonorous credal Latin gloss ('the resurrection of the dead') on the 'harsh' but not 'obscure' vernacular 'must'. Here is religious poetry that need not fear comparison with Dante, possessing in full Arnold's 'two superiorities' of 'high poetic truth and seriousness' and 'a high poetic stamp of diction and movement'.[55] But Arnold – and it may be a measure of his limitation as a critic – would not have endured what only Langland could have done: introduce in so exalted a context the natural (but not obvious) coinage 'fendekyn'. For if 'ruthe' and 'hevene' in the passage on Will's impotence make one think of the *lacrimae rerum*, 'fendekyn' suggests a correlative *risus rerum*: a laughter on the far side of 'derknesse and drede' (XVI.85), 'deep down things',[56] assuring that all manner of things shall indeed be well.

Notes

1. It is not mentioned in Philip Sidney's *Apologie for Poetrie* (1583, printed 1595). The citations from Webbe, Puttenham and Sidney are all to be found in Gregory Smith (ed.), *Elizabethan Critical Essays*, 2 vols. (London: Oxford University Press, 1904), vol. I, p. 242 and vol. II, p. 65.
2. Thomas Warton, *History of English Poetry* (London, 1774–81), section VIII, p. 177.
3. P. M. Kean, 'Langland on the Incarnation', *Review of English Studies*, 15 (1964), pp. 241–61.
4. All Langland quotations are from my Everyman B-text, (*The Vision of Piers Plowman*, second edition (London: Dent, 1995)).
5. *Complete Works of Shakespeare*, ed. Peter Alexander (London: Collins, 1951).
6. See Haukin's words in XIII.28: 'And fewe *robes* I fonge or *furrede gownes*'.
7. Alexander Pope, *An Essay on Criticism*, line 298, in *Collected Poems*, ed. Bonamy Dobrée (London: Dent, 1969), p. 65.
8. C. S. Lewis, *The Allegory of Love* (London: Oxford University Press, 1936), p. 160.
9. *Ibid.*, p. 161.
10. Matthew Arnold, 'The Study of Poetry' (1880), in *Essays in Criticism: Second Series*, ed. S. R. Littlewood (1888; London: Macmillan, 1958), p. 17.
11. *Troilus and Criseyde* III.1233–9, in *The Riverside Chaucer*, ed. Larry D. Benson (Oxford: Oxford University Press, 1988).
12. Lewis, *Allegory of Love*, p. 161.
13. *Ibid.*, p. 160.
14. E. Salter, *Piers Plowman: An Introduction* (Oxford: Blackwell, 1962); J. Lawlor, *Piers Plowman: An Essay in Criticism* (London: Edward Arnold 1962); N. Coghill, 'God's Wenches and the Light that Spoke: Some Notes on Langland's Kind of Poetry,' *English and Medieval Studies Presented to J. R. R. Tolkien*, ed. N. Davis and C. L. Wrenn (London: Allen and Unwin, 1962), reprinted in *The Collected Papers of Nevill Coghill*, ed. D. Gray (Brighton: Harvester, 1988), pp. 199–217.
15. Lewis, *Allegory of Love*, p. 160.
16. A. C. Spearing, 'The Art of Preaching and *Piers Plowman*', in *Criticism and Medieval Poetry*, second edition (London: Arnold, 1972), pp. 107–34 (p. 127).

Spearing's allusion to Dryden's strictures on Shadwell (*Mac Flecknoe*, line 20) is not exactly complimentary to Langland.

17. See J. A. Burrow, 'The Action of Langland's Second Vision', *Essays in Criticism*, 15 (1965), pp. 247–68.
18. See P. M. Kean, 'Langland on the Incarnation', *Review of English Studies*, 15 (1964), pp. 241–61; R. E. Kaske, 'The Use of Simple Figures of Speech in *Piers Plowman* B', *Studies in Philology*, 48 (1951), pp. 571–600.
19. B. H. Smith, *Traditional Imagery of Charity* in *'Piers Plowman'* (The Hague: Mouton, 1966).
20. The thematic focus is prominent in James Simpson's widely used *Piers Plowman: An Introduction to the B-Text* (London: Longman, 1990), by contrast with Salter's thirty years previously.
21. A. V. C. Schmidt, *The Clerkly Maker: Langland's Poetic Art* (Cambridge: D. S. Brewer, 1987).
22. M. C. Davlin, *A Game of Heuene: Word Play and the Meaning of 'Piers Plowman'* (Cambridge: Brewer, 1989).
23. L. Warner, 'The Ur-B *Piers Plowman* and the Earliest Production of C and B', *Yearbook of Langland Studies*, 16 (2002), pp. 3–39, (p. 12).
24. R. W. Hanna, 'On the Versions of *Piers Plowman*,' in *Pursuing History: ME Manuscripts and their Texts* (Stanford, CA: Stanford University Press, 1996), pp. 203–43 (p. 226). This is incorrect. The unusually error-free state of the text of B XVI is probably due to the poet's having rubbed and scraped this portion of the (otherwise very corrupt) archetypal source of the extant B-text manuscripts. See further the discussion in my *Piers Plowman: A Parallel-Text Edition* (Kalamazoo, MI: Medieval Institute Publications, 2008), p. 125.
25. 'Chaucer's Wordes unto Adam, his Owne Scriveyn', *Riverside Chaucer*, p. 650, line 4.
26. See Schmidt, *The Clerkly Maker*, pp. 14–19.
27. E. Salter, *Piers Plowman: An Introduction* (Oxford: Blackwell, 1962), p. 1.
28. These passus are discussed in a major recent thematic study by N. Zeeman, *'Piers Plowman' and the Medieval Discourse of Desire* (Cambridge: Cambridge University Press, 2006).
29. See, as well as the article by Burrow cited in note 17, D. Aers, *Piers Plowman and Christian Allegory* (London: Edward Arnold, 1975) and P. Martin, *Piers Plowman: The Field and the Tower* (London: Macmillan, 1979).
30. T. S. Eliot, *Selected Essays*, third edition (London: Faber and Faber, 1961), p. 243.
31. *Ibid.* Eliot understands by 'metaphor' verbal tropes not large-scale structural figures.
32. It is the defence of works of this type, from the *Romance of the Rose* to *The Faerie Queene*, that C. S. Lewis undertook in *The Allegory of Love*. On the now standard distinction between the two types see R. W. Frank, 'The Art of Reading Medieval Personification-Allegory', *English Literary History*, 20 (1953), pp. 237–50.
33. *Piers Plowman*, ed. E. Salter and D. Pearsall (London: Arnold, 1967), pp. 20–8; Simpson, *Introduction*, pp. 191–200.

34. Simpson, *Introduction*, p. 14.
35. I owe this useful term to Professor Alan Deyermond.
36. A. V. C. Schmidt, *Piers Plowman: A New Translation of the B-Text* (Oxford: Oxford University Press, 1992), pp. xxxviii-xl, and 'Elementary Images in the Samaritan Episode of *Piers Plowman*', *Essays in Criticism*, 56 (2006), pp. 303–23 (pp. 307–12).
37. Salter, *Introduction*, pp. 65–81; Aers, *Piers Plowman and Christian Allegory*, pp. 71– 109.
38. Lewis, *Allegory of Love*, pp. 66–73.
39. See Spearing, 'The Art of Preaching and *Piers Plowman*'.
40. R. E. Kaske, 'Holy Church's Speech and the Structure of *Piers Plowman*', in B. Rowland (ed.), *Chaucer and Middle English: Studies in Honour of R. H. Robbins* (London: Allen and Unwin, 1974), pp. 320–7.
41. J. C. Chamberlin, *Medieval Arts Doctrines on Ambiguity and their Place in Langland's Poetics* (Montreal: McGill-Queen's University Press, 2000), p. 140.
42. Zeeman, *'Piers Plowman'*, pp. 119–31.
43. J. A. Burrow, *Thinking in Poetry: Three Medieval Examples* (London: Birkbeck College, 1993).
44. A. C. Spearing, *Medieval to Renaissance in English Poetry* (Cambridge: Cambridge University Press, 1985), p. 127.
45. Gerard Manley Hopkins, 'Spring', in *Poems*, ed. W. H. Gardner, third edition (London: Oxford University Press, 1956), p. 71.
46. Gerard Manley Hopkins, 'Spring and Fall', in *Poems*, p. 94.
47. 'Expostulation and Reply', lines 23–4, in *The Poetical Works of Wordsworth*, ed. T. Hutchinson (London: Oxford University Press, 1926), p. 481.
48. *The Mystery of the Charity of Charles Péguy*, section 5, in Geoffrey Hill, *Collected Poems* (Harmondsworth: Penguin, 1985), p. 188.
49. *A Book of Showings to the Anchoress Julian of Norwich*, ed. E. Colledge and J. Walsh, 2 vols. (Toronto: Pontifical Institute, 1978), vol. II, p. 405.
50. See C. Straw, *Gregory the Great: Perfection in Imperfection* (Berkeley: University of California Press, 1988), pp. 188–9.
51. Coghill, 'God's Wenches and the Light that Spoke' pp. 199–217.
52. St Bernard of Clairvaux, *Apologia*, XII.29, in *Opera Omnia* (Patrologia Latina 182: 916A).
53. An episode remembered by his most original Tudor admirer John Skelton in *The Tunnynge of Elynour Rummynge* (1517).
54. Jonathan Swift, 'To Mr Delany', line 25, in *The Complete Poems*, ed. Pat Rogers (New Haven: Yale University Press, 1983).
55. Arnold, 'The Study of Poetry', p. 13.
56. Gerard Manley Hopkins, 'God's Grandeur', in *Poems*, p. 70.

Chapter 5

Chaucer: *Troilus and Criseyde* and *The Canterbury Tales*

LAURA VARNAM

In Book II of Chaucer's *Troilus and Criseyde*, when Pandarus sets out for Criseyde's house to persuade her to reciprocate Troilus's love, the narrator declares: 'Now Janus, god of entree, thow hym gyde!'[1] Janus, the Roman god of entrances and exits, was commonly depicted with two faces, one looking forward and one looking back, an image which is suggestive of the poetic technique of Geoffrey Chaucer. He is a poet who hovers on the threshold, glancing back at the landscape of his literary forebears, but looking determinedly forward into his own poetic House of Fame. Centuries later, when William Blake painted the Canterbury Pilgrims, he placed Chaucer, 'the great poetical observer of men', at the far right of the picture enclosed in the gothic archway of the Tabard Inn, about to set forth on the road ahead of him.[2] Blake saw in *The Canterbury Tales* 'characters which compose all ages and nations'; they represented the 'physiognomies ... of universal human life'.[3] But in the fourteenth century Chaucer was venturing into new and potentially treacherous territory. He brought together characters and genres which had not shared the same poetic space before and he stretched the linguistic potential of the vernacular to its limits. Yet his apprenticeship for his role as 'Father of English Poetry', as Dryden was famously to dub him, began with dream visions in which he used contemporary dream theory such as Macrobius's *Commentary on the Dream of Scipio* to explore what it meant to be an English poet.[4]

In *The Book of the Duchess* and *The Parliament of Fowls* Chaucer's dreamers wander in the gardens and forests of medieval tradition. In *The Book of the Duchess* the bumbling dreamer interrogates the Man in Black's lament for his lady, raising questions about the efficacy of poetry and its role in memorialising the dead. In *The Parliament of Fowls*, the dreamer's vision of the courtly birds who do not choose a mate leaves him unsatisfied and reaching for his books in the hope that with further reading he will 'fare / The bet' (lines 698–9). But in *The House of Fame*, the aptly named 'Geoffrey' leaves the Temple of Venus through a wicket gate only to be confronted with an arid desert, an image of poetic sterility, rather than a garden of love in the manner of the *Roman de la Rose*. The dream-vision landscape is unpredictable and bewildering, but 'Geoffrey' is saved by an eagle who transports him to the House of Fame. The vision of classical *auctours* like caryatids bearing up the fame of the great story matters is no consolation to the dreamer poet, however. 'No wight', he declares, shall 'have my name in honde / I wot myself best how y stonde' (lines 1877–8), and he abandons the House of Fame with its arbitrary goddess and put-upon poets for the dynamism and energy of the House of Rumour. Never still, the House of Rumour spins 'as swyft as thought' (line 1924) and has 'of entrees as fele as of leves ben in trees' (lines 1945–6). The House of Rumour reflects Chaucer's mature poetics in its multiple entrances and exits. There is no single dominant perspective and when a 'tydyng' enters the House and passes amongst the crowd, each teller of the tale 'gan somewhat for to eche / To this tydynge', remaking it in their own image (line 2065–6). The stories which Chaucer takes as the basis for his greatest works, *Troilus and Criseyde* and *The Canterbury Tales*, fare similarly. He 'eches' them with his own style but he refuses to be the 'man of gret auctorite' (*The House of Fame*, line 2158) who determines their ultimate meaning.

Troilus and Criseyde

Chaucer's achievement in *Troilus and Criseyde* was to expand the significance of the narrative of Boccaccio's *Il Filostrato* by the introduction of more sophisticated characterisation and broader, more philosophical themes. Whereas Boccaccio used the story to fulfil personal ambitions in love by addressing it to his lady, for Chaucer it provided the raw material for an investigation of matters as diverse as literary authority, free will and predestination, love and war. In *Troilus*, Chaucer creates a narrator so uncomfortable with the implications of his material that he oscillates between comedy and tragedy, myth and history, romance and farce almost to the point of poetic breakdown. The narrator's conscious acknowledgment of Troilus's 'double sorwe' from the opening line of the poem and his attempts to stave off the inevitable recognition of Criseyde's guilt mean that the poem, like Troilus, is 'sterelees withinne a boot . . . bitwixen wyndes two' (I.416–17). Doubling is an important poetic technique in *Troilus* and Chaucer alerts us to the double nature of language when Diomede glosses the word 'ambages' (ambiguities):

And but if Calkas lede us with ambages –
That is to seyn, with double wordes slye,
Swiche as men clepen a word with two visages –
Ye shal wel knowen that I naught ne lie. (v.897–900)

Diomede's use of the word 'slye' here suggests that 'ambages' are intentionally ambiguous. Indeed, we might think of the entire poem as a text which intentionally presents 'two visages': the comedic visage of the love affair and the tragic visage of Criseyde's betrayal.

This poetics of dyads characterises the presentation of Criseyde. Chaucer frequently uses rhyme to reveal Criseyde's two visages, especially the pairing of 'entente' and 'mente'. Criseyde always means what she says but due to the reader's foreknowledge of the betrayal, her words are often read ironically. In Book IV, for example, the reader cannot help but see the ironic implications of her hyperbolic oaths to be true to Troilus ('Attropos my thred of lif tobreste / If I be fals!' IV.1546–7). When she shows the first signs of transferring her affections from Troilus to Diomede, she declares:

I say nat therfore that I wol yow love,
N'y say nat nay; but in conclusioun,
I mene wel, by God that sit above! (v.1002–4)

The complexity of the double negatives reveals Criseyde's subterfuge – she will indeed not say 'nay' to Diomede – and her attempted obfuscation collapses as she concludes feebly that she means well. Criseyde's meaning well is perhaps her tragedy. She truly means to 'mene wel' and if she were judged according to the economics of The Friar's Tale where intention is all, she would be saved. But Chaucer's Criseyde lives in the present moment as she herself, in Chaucer's insightful addition to the *Filostrato*, confesses:

Prudence, allas, oon of thyne eyen thre
Me lakked alwey, er that I come here!
On tyme ypassed wel remembred me,
And present tyme ek koud ich wel ise,
But future tyme, er I was in the snare,
Koude I nat sen; that causeth now my care. (v.744–9)

Criseyde, ensnared in her own narrative, is blind to future events, unlike the reader, whose foreknowledge pounces on every linguistic slip she makes. In Book III when she declares 'in thought ne dede untrewe / To Troilus was nevere yet Criseyde' (lines 1053–4; cf. lines 839–40), it is the almost insignificant qualifier 'yet' which stands out. The narrator employs the imagery of sight again at the end of the poem when Criseyde finally determines to transfer her love to Diomede:

> But syn I se ther is no bettre way,
> And that to late is now for me to rewe,
> To Diomede algate I wol be trewe. (v.1069–71)

Criseyde's attempt to excuse herself – she can *see* no other way to proceed – is undermined by the 'rewe'/'trewe' rhyme which has been associated with her love and fidelity to Troilus throughout the poem. The transfer of affections is too neat. In the following stanza Criseyde appears to abdicate responsibility for her actions when she comments: 'but al shal passe; and thus I take my leve' (line 1085). But Criseyde's resignation to what she sees as her fate ultimately cannot negate her active choice to forsake Troilus for Diomede.

At the heart of the consummation scene in Book III, Troilus compares Criseyde's visage to a text: 'Though ther be mercy writen in your cheere, / God woot the text ful hard is, soth, to fynde!' (lines 1356–7). Troilus's interpretative struggle is one which many, if not all, critics of the poem share. Chaucer's Criseyde is a far more complex and textured character than Boccaccio's Criseida, with a heightened awareness of her literary fame. Chaucer translates her from a lively, sensuous, but ultimately fickle woman into a character who is at once playful and reticent, fearful and calculating, faithful and tragically changeable. Unlike any medieval writer before him, he creates a semblance of psychological realism so compelling that some modern critics have even confessed themselves in love with her. But Chaucer also introduces a Boethian reading of her character through the use of vocabulary deliberately borrowed from the description of Fortune in *The Consolation of Philosophy* which prompts an assessment of her role in the poem in more philosophical terms. For all that she is 'tendre-herted', Criseyde is also 'slydyng of corage' (v.825). Her constancy, like Fortune's, is in her changeability, and we feel that she slides towards her betrayal of Troilus uncontrollably but inevitably: 'Troilus and Troie town / Shal knotteles thorughout hire herte slide' (v.768–9). The word 'slide' is associated with Fortune in the *Consolation* when Lady Philosophy persuades Boethius to forsake Fortune and her ways: 'Why suffrestow that slydynge Fortune turneth so grete enterchaungynges of thynges?' (*Boece* I, metrum 5, lines 35–6). The linguistic association between Criseyde and Fortune demonstrates Chaucer's immersion in the language and imagery of the *Consolation* when he was composing *Troilus* and, moreover, the sophistication of his interweaving of philosophy and narrative. Chaucer applies Boethius's discussion of free will to the dramatic situation of the love affair, but in the pagan context of Troy, the characters are necessarily limited in their understanding due to their lack of Christian revelation. This is most evident in Troilus's soliloquy in Book IV where, despite the references to 'God' in the singular, there is no Christian consolation to remedy his complaint. Unlike Boethius, Troilus is unable to reconcile the omniscience of God with the operation of free will by appealing to Providence, and he therefore reverts to his pagan fatalism, concluding that 'thus to be lorn, it is my destinee' (IV.959). This limited perspective is also evident in Troilus's attitude to Fortune:

> Fortune, allas the while!
> What have I don? What have I thus agylt?
> How myghtestow for rowthe me bigyle?
> Is ther no grace, and shal I thus be spilt?
> Shal thus Criseyde awey, for that thow wilt?
> Allas, how maistow in thyn herte fynde
> To ben to me thus cruwel and unkynde? (IV.260–6)

Troilus addresses Fortune as a goddess and his use of the word 'unkynde' demonstrates his fundamental misunderstanding of Fortune. While her behaviour seems cruel to Troilus, Fortune is not in fact being 'unkynde', that is, 'unnatural'. It is in her very nature to turn her wheel. Notions of grace and guilt do not apply to Fortune. But Troilus does not have Lady Philosophy to remind him that 'yif Fortune bygan to dwelle stable, she cessede thanne to be Fortune' (II Prosa 2). The narrator is complicit in Troilus's attitude, however, as he structures the poem on the turn of Fortune's wheel as a way of side-stepping Criseyde's betrayal. In the Proem to Book IV, the narrator attributes Troilus's impending sorrow to the actions of Fortune:

> From Troilus she gan hire brighte face
> Awey to writhe, and tok of hym non heede,
> But caste hym clene out of his lady grace,
> And on hire whiel she sette up Diomede. (IV.8–11)

In the Proem the narrator also links the fall of Troilus to the fall of Troy itself. He describes Fortune as a 'traitour comune' (IV.5), and 'comune' in Middle English means both common to all and pertaining to a whole community (cf. 'comune profyt', 'comune good'). This definition is pertinent because although the narrator claims that Fortune betrays everyone equally, his use of the word also reminds us that like Troilus, the city of Troy is also destined to fall from Fortune's wheel. Fortune has not only 'bigyled' Troilus ('little Troy'), she will be a 'traitour' to the community of Troy. The fate of Troilus and Criseyde is a metonym for the fate of Troy itself. In the opening stanzas of the poem the narrator reports Calkas's prophecy that 'Troie sholde destroied be' (I.68) and as Fortune's wheel begins to turn for Troilus at the beginning of Book IV, the destruction of Troy is similarly foregrounded with a description of the Greek host besieging the city and the capture of the Trojan prisoners which will lead to the exchanging of Criseyde (IV.29–56).

Whereas for Boccaccio the Trojan War was merely background material for the main plot, for Chaucer it provided both an additional poetic vocabulary and a contemporary political resonance. In the early part of the poem, Chaucer describes Troilus's wooing of Criseyde in military terms. When Criseyde sees Troilus from her window, for example, his 'manhod and his pyne / Made love withinne hire for to myne' (II.676–7). The verb 'mynen' means to undermine fortifications by tunnelling or to make entry into a besieged place, and here Criseyde's body becomes a battleground, a citadel under siege from Troilus. In the fourteenth century, the association between the besieged city and the female body had an additional political charge, however. By the time Chaucer was writing, the trope of London as New Troy was well established and in his *Vox Clamantis*, John Gower compared the city of London under siege from the 1381 rebels to a powerless widow, rather like Criseyde at the beginning of *Troilus*.[5] The image of London as New Troy was ambiguous. It was both a symbol of glorious empire, figuring London as 'þe metropol and þe mayster-toun' according to the contemporary hagiography *St Erkenwald*, and a sign of destruction, betrayal and internal divisions.[6] Chaucer's Troy with its 'noyse of peple . . . as breme as blase of strawe iset onfire' (IV.183–4) could not help but invoke contemporary London, besieged and burned by rebels, under threat from French invasion and with a king whose royal power had been fundamentally undermined, if not temporarily usurped, by the Lords Appellant. Fortune was not the only 'traitour commune' in the fourteenth-century city.

Chaucer frequently employs references to classical myths to enrich his narrative and create interpretative complexity. One of the symbols which he employs most effectively throughout his oeuvre is the nightingale, and at the beginning of Book II, Pandarus, in typical May morning fashion, is awoken by birdsong:

> The swalwe Proigne, with a sorowful lay,
> Whan morwen com, gan make hire waymentynge
> Whi she forshapen was; and evere lay
> Pandare abedde, half in a slomberynge,

> Til she so neigh hym made hire cheterynge
> How Tereus gan forth hire suster take,
> That with the noyse of hire he gan awake. (lines 64–70)

Procne and her sister refer to the legend in Ovid's *Metamorphoses*: Procne's husband Tereus raped and mutilated Philomela, cutting out her tongue, and the two sisters took their revenge by killing Procne's children and serving them to Tereus in a ghoulish cannibalistic feast. The three were then metamorphosed, Procne into a swallow, Tereus into a hoopoe and Philomela into that most courtly of birds, the nightingale. Procne sings to Pandarus: 'Remembryng hym his errand was to doone / From Troilus, and ek his grete emprise' (lines 72–3). That Procne's song should remind Pandarus of his promise to help Troilus by wooing Criseyde on his behalf is ominous. The tale behind her 'cheterynge' introduces a disturbing violence to the May morning scene but yet more portentous is the association which is established here, and later in Book II, of Criseyde with Philomela. Procne sings of how her sister 'forshapen was' and on more than one occasion in the poem, the verb 'shapen' is employed by Pandarus of his 'grete emprise' to bring the lovers together (e.g. II.1363). The word also collocates with destiny when Troilus sends his first letter to Criseyde: 'Lettre, a blisful destine / The shapyn is: my lady shal the see' (II.1091–2). Criseyde is malleable, pliable, she can be shaped to the destiny which Pandarus and Troilus have designed for her, but she could become 'forshapen', or misshapen, as a result. Indeed, in the *Ovide Moralisé* (a Christian moralisation of the *Metamorphoses*) Philomela transforms into precisely the same literary type as Criseyde herself: 'amour decevable et faillie' ('deceitful and failing love'). Symbol of 'li delit vain et muable' ('vain and changing delight'),[7] the nightingale sings Criseyde to sleep after she has experienced the first pangs of love for Troilus:

> A nyghtyngale, upon a cedre grene,
> Under the chambre wal ther as she ley,
> Ful loude song ayein the moone shene,
> Peraunter in his briddes wise a lay
> Of love, that made hire herte fressh and gay,
> That herkned she so longe in good entente,
> Til at the laste the dede slep hire hente. (II.918–24)

Chaucer does not make the Philomela reference explicit here (in fact the bird is a male nightingale) but the 'dede slep' which overtakes Criseyde as she listens to his lay inspires a vision of physical, Ovidian, violence:

And as she slep, anonright tho hire mette
How that an egle fethered whit as bon,
Under hire brest his longe clawes sette,
And out hire herte he rente, and that anon,
And did his herte into hire brest to gon –
Of which she nought agroos, ne nothyng smerte –
And forth he fleigh, with herte left for herte. (II. 925–31)

The dream, another of Chaucer's additions to the *Filostrato*, focuses on that key symbol of the poem, the heart. The eagle is a royal bird and thus represents Troilus, but it is also a bird of prey whose predatory power rips through the stanza and Criseyde's body. It rends out her heart with its long claws and although she 'nought agroos, ne nothyng smerte', the threat of pain remains and in the very moment of physical consummation in Book III, the birds of prey are again circling: 'What myghte or may the sely larke seye, / Whan that the sperhauk hath it in his foot?' (III.1191–2). The lark neither 'myghte or may' speak against the sparrowhawk; all possibility of future struggle is closed down by the alternative modalities of the rhetorical question. The cycle of Ovidian imagery is then completed immediately after the consummation, when Criseyde is directly compared to a nightingale:

And as the newe abaysed nyghtyngale,
That stynteth first whan she bygynnyth to synge,
Whan that she hereth any herde tale,
Or in the hegges any wyght stirynge,
And after siker doth hire vois out rynge,
Right so Criseyde, whan hire drede stente,
Opned hire herte and tolde hym hire entente. (III.1233–9)

Criseyde finally opens her heart to Troilus, but the sense of foreboding is heightened as the nightingale image places her in a forest, startled and fearful of figures stirring in the hedgerows, telling tales.

At the end of Chaucer's own tale, the narrator famously dismisses his book to pay homage at the steps of poetry:

Go, litel bok, go, litel myn tragedye,
Ther God thi makere yet, er that he dye,
So sende myght to make in som comedye!
But litel book, no makyng thow n'envie,
But subgit be to alle poesye;
And kis the steppes where thow seest pace
Virgile, Ovide, Omer, Lucan, and Stace. (V.1786–92)

The narrator's plea is both an example of the modesty topos – he is a 'makere' not an 'auctour' and his 'litel' book must pay homage to 'alle poesye' – and a sly hint that the story is not over until the Trojan sings, or in this case, laughs. The requested comedy duly arrives when Troilus is killed on the battlefield, ascends to the eighth sphere and laughs at 'this litel spot of erthe' and all its woe (line 1814). Yet there is something not entirely satisfactory about this sudden consolation and attempt to diminish the 'litel tragedye' of Criseyde's betrayal. Troilus's laugh conceals a pejorative rhetoric: he 'dampned al oure werk that foloweth so / The blynde lust, the which that may nat laste' (lines 1823–4). 'Blynde lust' is contrasted with the 'hevenyssh melodie' of the spheres (line 1813), but the reader, who like the narrator retains the image of Criseyde graven in his heart, will remember how she first appears in Book I, 'so aungelik' that

> lik a thing inmortal semed she,
> As doth an hevenyssh perfit creature,
> That down were sent in scornynge of nature. (lines 102–5)

Although by the end of the poem 'morwe' rhymes with 'sorowe', this does not negate the coupling of 'joie' and 'Troie' which formed the poem's heart.

In *Troilus and Criseyde*, Chaucer created characters, especially Criseyde, who would attract and provoke both readers and writers for years to come. The Middle Scots poet Robert Henryson, for example, penned *The Testament of Cresseid* (which for many years was often mistaken as Chaucer's sixth book of *Troilus*) in which the narrator attempts to further excuse the 'hevenyssh' heroine. He provocatively asks:

> Quha wait gif all that Chauceir wrait was trew?
> Nor I wait nocht gif this narratioun
> Be authoreist, or fenyeit of the new
> Be sum poeit, throw his inventioun
> Maid to report the lamentatioun
> And wofull end of this lustie Creisseid,
> And quhat distres scho thoillit, and quhat deid.[8]

Chaucer's achievement in *Troilus* was to enable this question to be asked. Where previously Criseyde had been a type of the faithless woman, now she was a locus for philosophical and moral debate. Questions had replaced assumptions, and in *Troilus*, affection and empathy had overcome accusation. Sympathy for Criseyde still weighed uncomfortably with the fact that we cannot wholly excuse her, but both narrator and reader are able to declare, nonetheless, that 'men seyn – *I not* – that she yaf him hir herte' (V.1050).

The Canterbury Tales

In *The Canterbury Tales*, Chaucer is the 'elvyssh' pilgrim at the edge of the picture who looks back to the Tabard Inn and forwards to Canterbury, the terrestrial Jerusalem (vii.704). His story collection is celebrated for its tellers and their tales, 'diverse folk, diversely they seyde'(i.3857). Chaucer embraces diversity of character, genre, theme and language, and it is this inclusivity and receptiveness to a variety of critical readings which ensures his continued place in the canon. Charles Muscatine characterised Chaucer's poetics in *The Canterbury Tales* as a 'mixed style': his ability to move freely between high rhetoric and proverbial wisdom, realistic portraiture and traditional iconography, and to allow such juxtapositions to coexist as a reflection upon the infinite variety which the world has to offer.[9] 'Here', as Dryden states, 'is God's plenty.'[10] Even The Knight's Tale, the most traditional of Chaucer's tales stylistically, has room for a variety of expression, from Arcite's rhetorical *exclamatio* 'allas, the deeth! allas, myn Emelye!' to his unpretentious image of their struggle like 'the houndes for the boon' (i.2773, 1177).

The use of such familiar or homely imagery is characteristic of Chaucer's lightness of touch in the *Tales*. The Wife of Bath is 'joly as a pye', the Cook's Perkyn Revelour is 'gaillard' as a 'goldfynch in the shawe', and the Summoner's Friar 'chirketh as a sparwe' (iii.456, i.4367, iii.1804). The Pardoner has little concern if his flock's 'soules goon a-blakeberyed' and the Host declares that Chaucer the pilgrim is 'a popet in an arm t'enbrace / For any womman, smal and fair of face' (vi.406, vii.701–2). But Chaucer is not afraid to confront the darker side of mankind, as witnessed by the Monk's tale of the starving Ugolino whose children urge him to 'ete the flessh upon us two' and the Knight's 'derke ymaginyng' of 'the smylere with the knyf under the cloke' in the Temple of Mars (vii.2450, i.1999). Chaucer also creates a more subtle tension in the *Tales* by employing language and imagery which, like Criseyde, encourages multiple interpretations. The portrait of the Prioress in the General Prologue, for example, combines the diction of the courtly lady with the iconography of the female religious, concluding with the ambiguous image of a brooch inscribed *amor vincit omnia* hanging from her rosary beads. The Prioress can 'countrefete cheere / Of court' but the reader is left wondering if this is the extent of her imitation (i.139–40).

In the tales themselves Chaucer creates a 'hochepot' of voices with their own individual styles (vii.1258): the Wife of Bath is characterised by her force of argument, the Canon's Yeoman by his 'termes' of alchemy, the Parson by his sober prose, and in the General Prologue the narrator declares his intention to 'reherce as ny as evere he kan / Everich a word' that the pilgrims speak (I.732–3). This assertion of verisimilitude gives the narrator a protean quality as he performs the various voices of the company. Even in the Prologue their voices filter through his ostensibly impartial portraits to create a multivocal narrative perspective. In his explanation of the Monk's refusal to stay in the cloister, for example, he adopts the Monk's own argument, concluding 'Let Austyn have his swynk to hym reserved!' (I.188). The portrait of the Monk is constructed out of anti-monastic discourses which satirised monks for their lavish lifestyles and refusal to remain enclosed, but by the late Middle Ages monasteries had become important economic centres and the divide between monks' secular and spiritual existences was no longer so rigid. When the narrator imitates the Monk's voice and asks 'How shal the world be served?' there is a recognition of the social reality behind the satire (I.187).

This layering of voices, progressing inwards from the narrator in the outer frame rather like a Chinese box, is the source of much of the complexity and multiplicity of the *Tales*, and the narrator's repeated 'ernest and game' (I.3186)/ 'sentence and solaas' (I.798) dyads invite, indeed insist upon, the reader's critical engagement in the tale-telling competition. Chaucer's juxtaposition of language from different registers and genres within the same tale also forces the reader to assess the validity of the narrator's claim in the General Prologue that 'the wordes moote be cosyn to the deede' (I.742). When the pilgrims violate this dictum, the result is often comic, Chauntecleer the cockerel in The Nun's Priest's Tale being described as 'roial, as a prince is in his halle', for example (VII.3184), but the statement also conceals a more tricksy intention. The word 'cosyn' is more than a signifier of familial relationship, it also relates to the verb 'cosyn': to cheat or defraud. If language has the potential to defraud its subject matter, poetry becomes implicated in matters of ethical choice, and the creation of 'sentence and solaas' is no longer a literary game without consequences. Chaucer's irreverence is never far away – he is after all a poet who rhymes 'word' with 'toord' (VII.929–30) – but the philosophical implications of his discussion of language are clear: poetic choice is always fraught with conflict and ambiguity and as the *House of Fame* testifies, there may be no 'man of gret auctorite' to provide a stable interpretation.

In the course of the tales Chaucer tests out the capabilities of the vernacular by re-registering words in different narrative contexts and destabilising the boundaries of genre. When the Miller bursts on to the scene at the end of The Knight's Tale he declares: 'I wol telle a legende and a lyf / Bothe of a carpenter and of his wyf' (I.3141–2). The juxtaposition of the genre markers 'legende and lyf' with 'carpenter and wyf' hoodwinks the reader into thinking that the

Miller is going to tell a religious tale (the most famous carpenter and wife being of course Mary and Joseph) but the fabliau which follows disrupts our horizon of expectations. It is, as Chaucer the pilgrim is quick to point out, a 'cherles tale' (I.3169). But in the hands of Chaucer the poet, the cuckolded husband and the adulterous lovers are still available for religious commentary. Nicholas, for example, sings a hymn on the annunciation (*angelus ad virginem*), introducing a profane association with the angel Gabriel (II.3216). In The Merchant's Tale, however, the conflation of secular and religious is less wholesome when decrepit husband January lures May into his lascivious garden of earthly pleasures with the poetry of the Song of Songs: 'The gardyn is enclosed al aboute; / Com forth, my white spouse!' (IV.2143–4) His 'lewed wordes' (IV.2149) also have the effect of stripping away the religious commentary with which the Song's sensuous imagery had been legitimised in the Middle Ages and again raising the question of what constitutes the right, or appropriate, reading of poetic texts.

Chaucer often juxtaposes images and lexis from different hermeneutic spheres in this way and allows them to speak to each other. The climax of Nicholas and Alisoun's affair in The Miller's Tale is a pertinent example:

> Ther was the revel and the melodye;
> And thus lith Alison and Nicholas,
> In bisynesse of myrthe and of solas,
> Til that the belle of laudes gan to rynge,
> And freres in the chauncel gone to synge. (I.3652–6)

The lovers' bedroom and the friars' chancel are not present as dialectical opposites; there is as much 'melodye' in the former as the latter. The activities of lovemaking and singing are contained within separate couplets but their proximity allows each to engage with and reflect upon the other, but without moral judgment. Chaucer's use of irony also operates in this passage. Nine lines earlier the cuckolded husband John has fallen asleep after hanging up the tubs which will ostensibly save them from the flood and here his 'wery bisynesse' (line 3643) makes way for the lovers' 'bisynesse of myrthe and of solas'. Chaucer often centres his irony upon a particular word which reappears throughout the tales and which functions as a nexus of competing interpretations. In The Second Nun's Tale, 'bisynesse' signifies spiritual virtue for both St Cecilia and the Second Nun, who declares in her prologue:

> And for to putte us fro swich ydelnesse,
> That cause is of so greet confusioun,
> I have heer doon my feithful bisynesse
> After the legende in translacioun. (VIII.22–5)

Here 'bisynesse' is a remedy for its rhyme-word 'ydelnesse', but as the Pardoner's Prologue demonstrates, not all 'bisynesse' is God's work:

> Myne handes and my tonge goon so yerne
> That it is joye to se my bisynesse.
> Of avarice and of swich cursednesse
> Is al my prechyng, for to make hem free
> To yeven hir pens, and namely unto me.
> For myn entente is nat but for to wynne,
> And nothyng for correccioun of synne. (VI.398–404)

The Pardoner's 'bisyness' will lead to his own 'cursednesse' and potentially to the damnation of his flock. He is the opposite of the Parson, who strives to 'drawen folk to hevene by his fairnesse, / By good ensample, this was his bisynesse' (I.519–20). Contemporary debates about the role of the clergy as a conduit to salvation centred upon the relationship between ecclesiastical office and personal virtue. 'For if a preest be foul, on whom we truste', the narrator declares in the General Prologue, 'no wonder is a lewed man to ruste' (I.501–2).

Free will, personal virtue and the efficacy of language are major themes throughout Chaucer's work and here they coalesce around another keyword of both the *Tales* and *Troilus*: 'entente'. The Pardoner's 'entente' is 'for to wynne'. His fellow pilgrim, the Wife of Bath, confesses that her 'entente' is 'for to pleye' (III.192). But lurking behind both declared intentions are far more complex relationships between the teller and the tale. When the Wife of Bath declares that she went on pilgrimage because she did not know 'wher my grace / Was shapen for to be, or in what place' (III.553–4), the reader is aware that her concept of 'grace' is inherently secular and that, as entertaining as her Prologue is, the place in which the Wife is destined to complete her life's journey might be a place of damnation. The Pardoner boasts that he can make 'oother folk . . . repente' despite it not being his 'principal entente' (VI.430–1) but he neglects to foresee that his confession of avarice will hinder the pilgrims' desire to buy his relics at the end of the tale. The rhyme of 'entente' and 'repente' strikes a discordant note coming from the Pardoner.

In *Troilus* Criseyde declared that 'th'entente is al' (V.1630), and through the repeated use of this word throughout the *Tales*, Chaucer foregrounds the effect of the teller upon the tale. In The Manciple's Tale, Chaucer takes this theme to its logical conclusion and calls into question the relationship between poetry and truth. In the tale, Apollo, the god of Poetry, is compared to Amphioun, who walled the city of Thebes with his song (IX.117). Poetry has the power to raise walls and encompass communities, but as Apollo discovers, language which is unregulated and uncontrolled also has the power to destroy. Apollo teaches his crow to 'countrefete the speche of every man' (line 134) and the violent outcome of this act is anticipated when the crow's song is compared to the nightingale (line 136). Apollo's wife commits adultery and so the crow addresses him: 'cokkow! cokkow! cokkow!' (line 243). The onomatopoeic quality of the word as an imitation of birdsong both conceals and heightens its double meaning: Apollo is a cuckold. The crow explains:

> 'Phebus', quod he, 'for al thy worthynesse,
> For al thy beautee and thy gentilesse,
> For al thy song and al thy mynstralcye,
> For al thy waityng, blered is thyn ye
> With oon of litel reputacioun
> Noght worth to thee, as in comparisoun,
> The montance of a gnat, so moote I thryve!
> For on thy bed thy wyf I saugh hym swyve.' (lines 248–55)

The crow's rhetoric, for one who is only able to 'countrefete' human speech, is masterful. In the first half of the speech he employs anaphora and the lexis of courtly virtue to contrast sharply with the fabliau's punchline: 'on thy bed thy wyf I saugh hym swyve'. The crow emphasises the fact that despite the wife and bed being Phebus's possessions, '*thy* bed *thy* wyf', he has been cuckolded, and the low-register verb 'swyve' is delayed to the end of the line for maximum impact. The use of this word is not a casual expletive, however, given the Manciple's earlier statement that 'the word moot nede accorde with the dede' (line 208). The crow follows this dictum to the letter when he chooses the appropriate verb for the wife's adulterous action. Apollo refuses to believe the crow, calling him a 'false theef' and a 'traytour' (lines 270, 92) but arguably it is the manner of the tale-telling rather than the tale itself that causes Apollo's violent reaction and murder of his wife. The importance of lexical choice could not be clearer. For the god of Poetry it is the difference between life and death, and as a logical extension of the cuckoldry of this literary figurehead, the Manciple ventriloquises his mother's advice to be 'noon auctour newe / Of tidynges, *wheither they been false or trewe*' (lines 359–60). Not only has the relationship between language and truth been called into question, but poetry itself has been accused of murder and silence is to be its punishment.

The rest of course was not silence. Chaucer's retraction (x.1081–92) expresses the desire to withdraw works such as *The Canterbury Tales* which 'sownen into synne' (x.1090), but this sudden confession of moral responsibility and the desire for penitence can scarcely be taken seriously, coming from a poet who has exploited the potential for language to 'cosyn' its readers.

Chaucer's legacy to English poetry is one of linguistic curiosity and a refusal of generic categorisation. With *Troilus and Criseyde* he heralded a new era of narrative poetry with the capacity to address philosophical questions and explore complex characterisations, and in *The Canterbury Tales* he created a diversity of genre, character and language which would only be matched by Shakespeare. Chaucer was the Canterbury pilgrim who not only fulfilled but surpassed Harry Bailey's criteria for story-telling success. He told tales of 'best sentence *and* moost solaas' (1.798).

Notes

1. All quotations refer to *The Riverside Chaucer*, ed. L. D. Benson (Oxford: Oxford University Press, 1988).
2. *The Complete Writings of William Blake*, ed. G. Keynes (London: Oxford University Press, 1966), p. 569.
3. *Ibid.*, p. 567.
4. D. Brewer, *Chaucer: The Critical Heritage*, 2 vols. (London: Routledge and Kegan Paul, 1978), vol. 1, p. 164; Macrobius, *Commentary on the Dream of Scipio*, ed. and trans. William Harris Stahl (New York: Columbia University Press, 1990).
5. *The Major Latin Works of John Gower*, ed. E. Stockton (Seattle: University of Washington Press), p. 69.
6. C. Peterson, *St Erkenwald* (Philadelphia: University of Pennsylvania Press, 1977), p. 73.
7. Quoted in Laura D. Kellogg, *Boccaccio's and Chaucer's Cressida* (New York: Peter Lang, 1995).
8. *The Poems of Robert Henryson*, ed. R. L. Kindrick (Kalamazoo, MI: Medieval Institute Publications, 1997), p. 158.
9. Charles Muscatine, *Medieval Literature, Style and Culture* (Columbia: University of South Carolina Press, 1999).
10. Brewer, *Critical Heritage*, p. 167.

Chapter 6

Late medieval literature in Scotland: Henryson, Dunbar and Douglas

FELICITY RIDDY

The writing lives of the Scottish poets Robert Henryson, William Dunbar and Gavin Douglas overlapped during a period of fifty years or so, from around 1460 to 1513, coinciding with the reigns of James III and IV of Scotland. The two younger poets – Dunbar was about fifteen years older than Douglas – came to maturity at the end of the fifteenth century in a literary milieu in which Henryson had been the great innovator of the previous generation, as they were to be the great innovators of theirs. They had all stopped writing by the end of 1513, it seems. By then Henryson had been dead for ten or twelve years; Dunbar simply drops from the records; while Douglas completed his translation of the *Aeneid* in July 1513 and wrote no more poetry.

Scottish literature – that is, writings in the variety of English spoken in the lowlands of Scotland – begins later than south of the border, or at least has a different pattern of survival. There is very little earlier than Barbour's *Bruce*, written in the 1370s, but a rapid flowering took place in the fifteenth century as knowledge of English writers – including Chaucer, Gower, Lydgate and the anonymous alliterative poets – spread into Scotland. *The Kingis Quair*, the first Scots philosophical dream-vision in the Chaucerian manner, was apparently composed in the late 1420s or 1430s by James I, who was held captive in England for eighteen years. Richard Holland's *Buke of the Howlat*, written around 1448, is the earliest long poem of the alliterative 'revival' in Scotland; it is a 'parliament of birds' fable cast in the form of a *chanson d'aventure*. Nevertheless, the originality of Henryson, Dunbar and Douglas is of a different order. They were all highly educated men who thought hard and came to different conclusions about what poetry is and does. Between them, they created Older Scots as a literary language.

Little is known about Robert Henryson. Dunbar's 'Lament for the Makaris', dated 1505, refers to the death in Dunfermline of 'maister Robert Henrisoun', so he must have been dead by then. 'Magister Robertus

Henrisone' is recorded as having been admitted to membership of Glasgow University in 1463, after apparently studying abroad. In 1477–8 a Robert Henryson was witness, as notary public, to three Dunfermline Abbey deeds. Since there is a sixteenth-century tradition that the poet was a schoolmaster in Dunfermline, and since other Dunfermline schoolmasters were notaries public, it is tempting to put these pieces of evidence together and trace the faint outlines of a biography. If all these references are to the same man, he was probably born in the later 1420s or early 1430s and may have lived till after 1500. Three major poems survive: *Orpheus and Eurydice*, which derives from Nicholas Trevet's fourteenth-century Latin commentary on Boethius's *Consolation of Philosophy*; *The Fables*, which also draws on academic tradition; and *The Testament of Cresseid*, written in response to Chaucer's *Troilus and Criseyde*. Their chronology is unknown. All three are evidence of Henryson's interest in the place of imaginative poetry in public culture, but for reasons of space the focus of this discussion is on his longest work, *The Fables*, and his masterpiece, *The Testament of Cresseid*.

The Fables, according to the Prologue, are 'ane maner of translatioun' (line 32) from the Latin of 'Esope' (line 27), made for 'ane lord' (line 34).[1] Nevertheless, Henryson did not work from a single source. His collection is eclectic and unparalleled: seven fables have analogues in a Latin Aesopic collection which, with commentaries, was used in late medieval schools. The other six derive from the 'beast-epic' tradition of Reynard the Fox. The Prologue invites readers to correct errors, but there is no single text to compare the 'translatioun' with and certainly not one by 'Esope', who is as fictive as the fables themselves. Nevertheless the figure of 'Esope' as ' My author' (line 43) holds together a disparate group of narratives, and provides a justification for interpreting the material world of everyday action as fraught with moral significance.

The Prologue raises the issue that goes back to Horace, of the relationship between pleasure and moral instruction in 'feinyeit fabils [simulated fictions] of ald poetre' (line 1), arguing that the fictions that follow are not only pleasurable but, understood figurally, will 'repreif' the reader of 'misleuing' (line 6). Later, in the dream dialogue between 'Esope' and the narrator that precedes 'The Lion and the Mouse', 'Esope', despairing of the present time, asks the question underlying the whole poem: 'quhat is it worth to tell ane fenyeit taill, / Quhen haly preiching may na thing auaill?' (lines 1389–90). The narrator persuades 'Esope' that poetry as 'morall fabill' – pleasurable, paradoxical, figural, truth-telling fiction – can impart 'sum thing' (line 1403) of value, and 'Esope' settles for the small gains possible in the modern world. He tells the central fable about governance, which is darkly, if unspecifically, critical of Scotland's leadership. An argument about the value of 'ald poetre' thus becomes one about how the modern poet can write for his own times 'in mother toung' (line 31), and effect change. The conventional protestation about his 'hamelie language' and 'termis rude' (line 36) does not disguise Henryson's ambition in turning the traditionally 'low' and brief Aesopic fable, with its pragmatic ethics, into a public poetry of high moral seriousness.

Henryson's choice of 'morall fabill' assumes that the ordinary behaviour of unexceptional people is worth both depicting and trying to change. It is the choice of the poet who, distanced from the metropolis, is unimpressed by power and whose conception of his public includes the 'freindis' (lines 365, 2969), 'worthie folk' (line 586) and 'gude folk' (lines 613, 789) who are his narratees. The stories are set in small towns and villages or the countryside and the animal characters are mocked, without being patronised, as they engage in familiar activities: they look for food and drink; they visit their relations; they quarrel with old enemies; they take each other to court. Chaucerian fabliaux had made a dazzling art out of the representation of stock characters in everyday actuality. Chaucer's own opulently digressive animal fable, The Nun's Priest's Tale, is more interested in parody, a different kind of mimesis. Henryson used it for his version of 'The Cock and the Fox', but he may have learned more from Chaucer's fabliaux about how to develop his skimpy analogues in the direction of the here and now. Even the shortest narrative, 'The Cock and the Jasp', about the cock who rejects the jewel he finds while scratching for food, is complicated by the realism of the jewel's back-story:

> As damisellis [servant girls] wantoun and insolent
> That fane wald play and on the streit be sene,
> To swoping of the hous thay tak na tent [pay no heed]
> Quhat be thairin, swa that [so long as] the flure be clene;
> Iowellis ar tint [lost], as oftymis hes bene sene,
> Vpon the flure, and swopit furth anone.
> Peraduenture, sa wes the samin stone. (lines 71–7)

This stanza conjures up a dense, interconnected, ordinary world: a street in which young working women parade themselves in their spare time; a house that needs to be looked after, which the servant girls sweep carelessly while ensuring that the floor is clean (because of the mistress's strict eye?); in which jewels (earrings? rings? removed to wash? to sleep?) are dropped on the floor, another of the inattentions that are the narrative's theme. The everyday involves complexities of representation that confound the simple drive to moralise.

The two-part structure dividing each of the 'morall fabills' into narrative and morality ensures that competing ways of representing human conduct are set off against each other. The narratives are governed by 'custum' and 'daylie rite' (common practice) (line 54): the ingrained habits of the world as it is. Their plots are unpredictable, not surprisingly, given the lability of fables. In some tales a last-minute trick rescues the victim; in others nothing can restrain the wolf's voracity or redirect the swoop of the kite. Arbitrariness is part of the fable world-view, the way things are, and the animal characters are presented as survivalists whose goal, often unsuccessful, is to keep alive. This is true even of 'The Preaching of the Swallow', the most ambitious narrative, which begins with a vision of the natural world as a means of understanding God's otherwise inscrutable providence:

> Yyt neuertheles we may haif knawlegeing
> Off God almychtie be his creatouris,
> That he is gude, fair, wyis and bening. (lines 1650–2)

This seems a risky claim to include in a collection of fables. For all the rhetorical power of the introductory vision of cosmic order, if we imagine that the narrative that follows will uncomplicatedly illustrate the fairness and benignity of God as seen through his creatures, we shall be wrong. It ends in the ugly brutality of the birds' deaths, while the industrious farmer protecting his crop turns out to represent the fiend.

The characters struggle to make sense of their world, using received wisdom – proverbs, *sententiae*, legal maxims. The cock justifies his rejection of the jasper, which he can only look at and not eat, with: 'wyfis say that lukand werk is licht' (line 102) and 'houngrie men may not weill leue on lukis' (line 104). The cock's wife, hearing he has been taken by the fox, comments that 'The prouerb sayis, "Als gude lufe cummis as gais." / I will put on my haly-dayis clais [Sunday best]' (lines 512–13). The lark silences the prudent swallow with a string of aphorisms, while the husbandman and the wolf conduct their quarrel over who owns the oxen through claim and counter-claim expressed in practical maxims. Narratives revolve round courts, parliaments, confessions, with their formalised judgments about right conduct, which rarely work and which are part of the world as it is. Such a superabundance of strategies for survival is available that the moralities risk being simply another voice in the cacophony, only overriding – if they do – because they have the last word. But their positioning means that readers have already made what they will of the narratives, and the moralities often clash alarmingly with this. They use a denunciatory preacher's rhetoric, rereading the animals not as survivalists but as creatures of appetite, and dissecting the everyday habits of the world in terms of the 'sins of aversion' that destroy community: pride, envy, anger, avarice and their many offshoots.[2] 'Esope' thought that the modern world was too sinful for 'morall fabills'. Another interpretation would be that in late fifteenth-century Scotland there were many competing ethical discourses and that poetry, as a kind of feigning or similitude, is answerable to them all.

In *The Testament of Cresseid*, Henryson experiments with a different poetic: here his focus is on 'tragedie'. Chaucer had called *Troilus and Criseyde* a 'tragedye' retrospectively; Henryson makes the genre clear from the start:

> Ane doolie [gloomy] sessoun to ane cairfull dyte [sad composition]
> Suld correspond, and be equiualent.
> Richt sa it wes quhen I began to wryte
> This tragedie . . . (lines 1–4)

The tragedy, moreover, is not Troilus's but Cresseid's. The poem arises out of a gap in *Troilus and Criseyde*, which created a much-loved but faithless woman and then abandoned her, as if her after-life were unrepresentable. Henryson follows Chaucer up to the moment at which Troilus realises that she will not return to Troy, and then turns to an 'vther quair [book]' (line 61) to fill in the blank that Criseyde has become. The sophisticated and fluent courtliness of *Troilus and Criseyde* becomes in *The Testament* a graver and terser mode in which the degradation of Cresseid is not flinched at. Chaucer had let Criseyde off apparently scot-free: the narrator's final comment on her is: 'Criseyde loveth the sone of Tideus, / And Troilus moot wepe in cares cold. / Swich is this world, whoso it kan byholde' (v.1746–8).[3] *The Testament* offers a different model of the world in which Criseyde does not escape suffering or guilt: her getting off scot-free is, for Henryson as a reader of Chaucer, not true to the way things are. That rigorous sense of the world as it is – the hallmark of *The Fables* – is also here in *The Testament*, which shares *The Fables'* focus on the unempowered.

At first *The Testament*'s model of the world looks much like *Troilus and Criseyde*'s. The Diomede who discards Cresseid is of a piece with the sexual opportunist whom Chaucer had depicted. Diomede sends her a bill of divorce ('ane lybell of repudie' (line 74)), implying that he no longer takes financial responsibility for her, after which, 'excludit fra his companie' (line 75), she drifts into promiscuity: 'Than desolait scho walkit vp and doun, / And sum men sayis, into the court, commoun' (lines 77–8). There is a compassionate realism in this brief record of a woman without a protector taking up with whoever will have her, which is what that powerfully positioned 'commoun' implies. No act of assent is involved, merely directionless movement. The debasing of Cresseid is understood at this moment in social terms, but the stanzas that follow take a different view:

> O fair Creisseid, the flour and A per se [paragon]
> Of Troy and Grece, how was thow fortunait [predestined]
> To change in filth all thy feminitie,
> And be with fleschelie lust sa maculait [defiled],
> And go amang the Greikis air [early] and lait,
> Sa giglotlike [wantonly] takand thy foull pleasance!
> I have pietie thow suld fall sic mischance! (lines 78–84)

There is on the one hand an appalled horror here at what is represented as sexual corruption: 'filth', 'maculait', 'giglotlike', 'foull pleasance'. Nevertheless, there is also an acknowledgment, more explicit in the next stanza, that fortune and not Cresseid herself is responsible for what is happening to her. These much-discussed contradictions can, perhaps, be linked to a duality in late medieval conceptions of tragedy, deriving on the one hand from Boethius, the philosopher of fortune, and on the other from the encyclopaedist, Isidore of Seville, whose definition of tragedy includes fault. Nicholas Trevet, for example, in his commentary on Boethius's *Consolation of Philosophy*, which Henryson knew, maintains both Isidore's tragedy of iniquity: 'According to Isidore ... tragedy is a poem about great crimes or iniquities beginning in prosperity and ending in adversity', and Boethius's tragedy of fortune: 'What else does the clamouring of tragedies bewail, except Fortune overturning happy kingdoms with an unforeseen blow?'[4] As the 'narratioun' unfolds it moves between the idea of the unforeseen blow and the idea of iniquity.

The planetary gods who appear in Cresseid's dream, after her return to her father's house, have 'power of all thing generabill' (line 148); they are the natural forces that govern the sublunary sphere, in accordance with orthodox late medieval thinking. They are the way the world works in this poem; the Christian scheme in which Chaucer's lovers are finally located is absent from *The Testament*. The gods, despite the studied balancing of benign against hostile powers as they process magisterially down from their spheres, are retributive and merciless. What they do to Cresseid is what happens to the promiscuous, according to some strands of late medieval thought; she contracts leprosy, believed to be a venereal disease and thus a natural result of her promiscuity as well as a natural judgment on it. Cresseid's magnificent complaint in response to her leprosy is marked out by a shift to the nine-line aabaabbab stanza of Chaucer's *Anelida and Arcite*, and by its dense alliteration. The *Anelida* stanza, where two rhymes constantly turn back on themselves, is more introverted than the rime royal of the rest of the poem, where the ababbcc scheme opens up in the final couplet. Cresseid speaks as the protagonist of a Boethian tragedy of fortune, an emblem and victim of change. The tragic dichotomy – prosperity and adversity – had structured the stark sentence of the gods: 'I change thy mirth into melancholy . . . Thyne insolence, thy play and wantones, / To greit diseis; thy pomp and thy riches / In mortall neid' (lines 316–21). It is also there in her complaint, which begins with an elegy for her own past that is at the same time an elegy for Troy. The gods' contempt for 'play and wantones' and 'pomp and riches' is flung back at them: the 'chalmer wantounlie besene [extravagantly arrayed]' (line 416), the 'cowpis of gold' (line 419), the 'gay garmentis' (line 422) summon up, with a defiant and nostalgic specificity, a dream of the vanished life of royal Troy. Finally, she addresses the 'ladyis fair of Troy and Grece':

> 'Nocht is your fairness bot ane faiding flour,
> . . .
> your roising reid [rosy red] to rotting sall retour [change];
> Exempill mak of me in your memour
> Quhilk [who] of sic [such] thingis wofull witness beiris.
> (lines 461, 464–6)

The image that has recurred in the poem of loveliness as a flower at this point signals the processes of decay: she is a speaking picture deliquescing before her own eyes.

The fact that the poem does not end here suggests not merely that the Boethian tragedy of fortune is conceptually inadequate in this instance but that it is also rhetorically unsatisfying. Some kind of resolution of the lovers' relationship is required after Chaucer had left it hanging, but the 'authoreist' (line 66) history does not allow a lovers' reunion. Instead, brilliantly, they meet but do not recognise each other, and in ignorance Troilus gives alms to Cresseid as a memorial to what she used to be. His action forces her to confront her own treachery for the first time: 'Fy, fals Cresseid; O trew knicht Troylus!' (line 553). She dies remorseful but with a steely dignity, neither asking forgiveness nor receiving it. Hers is in the end an Isidorean tragedy of iniquity; small-scale because it has a female protagonist who is the tool, not the agent, of public events, because it is located at the very margins of society, because its effects do not ramify beyond her own death and because its action is largely internal. The poem lies on the cusp of a new genre.

As with Henryson, we know little about William Dunbar. Born around 1460, he probably graduated from St Andrews in 1480. From 1500 until 1513, when he finally disappears from view, he received an annual pension from James IV and presumably had some clerkly function at court. In 1504 he became a priest and by 1509 was a chaplain, but although his income rose to £80 he never secured the benefice to which he believed he was entitled. Disappointment, anger and envy at the success of others nevertheless spurred him into song.

Dunbar's verse has a profligate verbal energy, channelled into a wider range of forms and modes than any of his predecessors, Scots or English. Over eighty poems survive. He is a master of the stanzaic short poem in many styles: courtly, devotional, comic, moralising, obscene. He can create at one moment a dazzling string of elevated Latinate nonce-words – 'hodiern', 'indeflore', 'habitakle' – and at another a string of obscene vernacular ones – 'quhillelille', 'slawsy', 'towdy'– with equal verve.[5] He refers to his poems as 'sangs' and 'ballattis' as if they are only a form of ephemeral light entertainment, calling their creation 'making', as Chaucer had done, and referring to himself as a 'makar' rather than a 'poeit' or 'rhetor'. Whereas Henryson and Douglas discuss theories of poetry, Dunbar records the struggle of the creative act itself (what Douglas hints at when he speaks of his 'lang disparyt wark').[6] In 'In to thir dirk and drublie dayis', creativity is a form of 'curage' [desire or inclination] (line 4), an internal activity that engages the 'spreit' (line 8) and the 'hairt' (line 9). It is a mysterious gift of 'Nature' (line 4) – as in *The Testament*, the dimension of time and change – that is inexplicably withheld in a dark season. The internal dialogue that follows, with Despair, Patience, Prudence, Age and Death, is about the forward movement of time, distractions that cannot distract, feelings of powerlessness and waste and the fear of death: the uncreative life. It can be read alongside 'My heid did yak (ache) yester nicht' – addressed, it seems, to the king – which also records the withdrawal of creativity. Although the speaker is kept awake because of a pounding headache, his 'curage sleipeing lyis' (line 12). The second stanza brilliantly catches the agony of being unable to write:

> To dyt [compose] thocht I begowthe [began] to dres [prepare],
> The sentence lay full evill till find,
> Vnsleipit [sleepless] in my heid behind,
> Dullit in dulness and distres. (lines 7–10)

The 'sentence' – what one is trying to say – is hidden in an unreachable space in the back of ('behind') his head, and the speaker, 'vnsleipit', is as a consequence in a state of utter inanition ('dullit'/'dulness' refer to melancholic torpor) and torment. It is typical of Dunbar's inventiveness that he should write poems about not writing poems.

On other occasions Dunbar seems to have written to order. 'The Thrissil and the Rose', for example, is an elegant allegory composed for James IV's wedding in 1503 to Henry VIII's sister, Margaret. Its beginning simultaneously echoes the lover's May awakening in the *Romaunt of the Rose*, and the grand opening of *The Canterbury Tales* ('Whan that Aprill with his shoures soote / The droghte of March hath perced to the roote'):[7]

> Quhen Merche wes with variand windis past,
> And Appryll had with hir siluer schouris
> Tane leif at [taken leave of] Nature with an orient blast,
> And lusty May, that mvddir [mother] is of flouris,
> Had maid the birdis to begyn thair houris
> Amang the tendir odouris reid and quhyt [white],
> Qhois [whose] harmony to heir it was delyt – (lines 1–7)

and so on. The elegance of this style lies in the way in which a relaxed and conversational mode of address is able to move so easily into a more formal or poetic register – 'variand', 'orient', 'odouris' – and out again; the dextrous accommodation of the suspended syntax (also part of the formal register) to the rime royal stanza; the playfulness of the image of the birds beginning 'thair houris', like small choristers singing lauds; and the overall lightness of touch.

Dunbar's longest poem, 'The Tretis of the Tua Mariit Wemen and the Wedo', seems to arise from the court's unofficial pastimes. Here the speaker eavesdrops on three richly dressed women discussing the sexual performances of their husbands and how badly they treat them. He ends by asking his readers the classic *demande d'amour*: 'Quhilk wald ye waill [choose] to your wif, gif ye suld wed one?' (line 530). Comic and obscene *demandes d'amour* had a long history in both French and English. Dunbar uses the unrhymed, alliterative long line that emerged in England in the fourteenth century and which is unprecedented in Scots, extravagantly expanding the *demande d'amour* in the direction of the ironic self-revelation of Chaucer's Wife of Bath's Prologue. The poem is a brilliant freak, positioned against Chaucer and yet also engaging with him. The form permits the poem's fluid structure and the virtuoso alliterative invective that is part of the comedy:

> I have a wallidrag [wastrel], ane worm, and auld wobat carle [hairy caterpillar of a man]
> A waistit wolroun [runt] na worth bot wourdis to clatter [babble],
> Ane bumbart [idler], ane dronbee [drone], ane bag full of flewme [phlegm],
> Ane scabbit skarth [cormorant], ane scorpioun, ane scutarde [squirter] behind
> (lines 89–92)

The selves that are revealed are paradigms of misogyny: loquacious, uncontrollable, deceiving, greedy, sexual. The first young wife's description of her old husband's lovemaking alludes to the wedding night of January and May in Chaucer's Merchant's Tale, where the perspectives of husband and wife are presented simultaneously. January's fantasy of May's pristineness ('fresshe', 'paradys', 'tender' (lines 1822, 1826)) collides with May's experience of the 'thikke brustles of his berd unsofte, / Lyk to the skyn of houndfish, sharp as brere' (lines 1824–5), scratching against her cheek.[8] In Dunbar's version there is only one perspective – the wife's – and the scene is wilder and grimmer. The old husband is depicted with the overheated grotesqueness of a satirical cartoon, as in this sudden close-up of his rheumy eyes, accumulating foul liquid like two blocked drains: 'With gor [slime] his tua grym ene are gladderit [smeared] all about / And gorgeit [choked] lyk tua guteris that war with glar [sludge] stoppit' (lines 98–9). The young wife goes on to describe her husband's embrace in terms that are similar to Chaucer's:

> Quhen schaiffyn [shaven] is that ald schaik [man] with a scharp rasour,
> He schowis [thrusts] on me his schewill [twisted] mouth and schendis [defiles] my lippis,
> And with his hard hurcheone [hedgehog] scyn sa heklis [scratches] he my chekis
> That as a glemand [gleaming] gled [ember] glowis my chaftis [jaws].
> (lines 105–8)

This husband does not fondle or kiss, as Chaucer's does, but 'schowis' and 'heklis' with repulsive urgency. His beard feels not just like dogfish skin but, with typical exaggeration, like the skin of a hedgehog. Indeed, he is something from another world – a 'glowrand gaist' (line 100), a 'hiddowus Mahowne' (line 101), 'auld Sathane' (line 102), a 'bogill' (line 111), 'Belzebub' (line 112).

The court, though, is also an imagined community produced by a long tradition of anti-curial satire that in English includes Chaucer's *Truth* and Caxton's translation of Alain Chartier's *Curial*. In this tradition it is a 'couente of peple that vnder fayntyse of Comyn wele assemble hem to gydre for to deceyue eche other', an uncertain and arbitrary zone where the talentless are rewarded and the virtuous despised.[9] For Dunbar, this precarious milieu stands in for the human predicament more generally and produces some of his finest lyrics. He frequently uses stanzaic forms with proverb-like refrains: 'All erdly joy returnis in pane'; 'A paralous seknes is vane prosperite'; 'Without glaidnes avalis no tresure'.[10] His greatest anti-curial poems discover, with deceptive simplicity, the truths that everyone already knows. 'Qhuom to sall I compleine my wo', with its refrain 'In to this warld may none assure', begins, characteristically, from an acute sense of isolation and anxiety:

Quhom to sall I compleine my wo
And kythe [make known] my cairis, ane or mo [to their full extent]?
I knaw not amang riche or pure,
Quha [who] is my freind, quha is my fo,
For in this warld may none assure. (lines 1–5)

As the poem proceeds the world becomes increasingly hallucinatory, inhabited by a sequence of vivid but disconnected personifications: 'Flattrie weiris ane furrit govn, / And Falsate with the lordis dois rovn [whisper], / And Trewthe standis barrit at the dure, / Exilit is Honour of the toun' (lines 36–9). By stanza 10 even this coherence has imploded into a bizarre vision of modern life in which other people are transmogrified into body parts:

Towngis now ar maid of quhite quhale bone,
And hartis ar maid of hard flynt stone,
And eyn are maid of blew asure,
And handis of adamant, laithe to dispone [unwilling to give] ...
(lines 46–9)

From here the perspective of the last third of the poem shifts unnervingly to Judgment Day when 'all ar deid or than de [die] sall' (line 54), and the damned 'Sall cry, allace, that women thame bure' (line 73). The final terrible question flung at the reader is:

Than quho shal wirk [strive] for warldis wrak [the world's goods],
Qhuone flude and fyre sall our [over] it frak [rush]
And frelie frustir [lay waste to] feild and fure [furrow],
With tempest keyne and thwndir crak?
In to this warld may none assure. (lines 76–80)

It is hard to read this apocalyptic vision of destruction, in which the disproportionate rage is barely contained by the pounding rhythm and alliteration, without sensing that the urgency and despair have, in the end, little to do with the neglect that set it all going and everything to do with the fear of death. The rage seems to arise from discovering that what seems merely a commonplace – 'In to this warld may none assure' – has nothing mere about it.

Fear of death provides the refrain – '*Timor mortis conturbat me*' ('the fear of death troubles me') – in 'Lament for the Makaris'. It comes from a responsory in the Office of the Dead and is accompanied by lessons from the book of Job, including: 'I go and return no more, to a land that is dark and covered with the mist of death: a land of misery and darkness, where the shadow of death and no order, but everlasting horror, dwells' (Job 10: 21–2). The poem has twenty-five stanzas aabB, in which the b rhymes throughout are, revealingly, on '*me*', and which shape an obsessive reverie on loss. The refrain is like some charm against dying that the speaker hopes will work through repetition. His own 'infermite' (line 3) undermines the stability of the whole world: 'As with the wind wavis the wicker, / So waueris this warldis vanite' (lines 14–15). Fear of his own death conjures up everyone else's:

> On to the ded [death] gois all estatis,
> Princis, prelotis and potestatis,
> Baith riche and pur of al degre:
> *Timor mortis conturbat me.* (lines 17–20)

The orderliness of this procession, which owes something to the late medieval dance of death, is, however, only momentary ('no order' dwells in Job's 'land of misery and darkness'). And so death – 'the ded' (line 17) – suddenly springs into parodic life, committing random acts of predation against which human powers, including the 'faculte [skill]' (line 47) of poets, are unavailing. In the second half of the poem the ghosts of the dead 'makaris' from Chaucer to 'Gud gentil Stobo and Quintyne Schaw' (line 86) – those great predecessors and 'brether' (line 93), English and Scots – are summoned back to the half-life of the necrology: this much the 'faculte' of the 'makar' can do for them. But commemorating them also evokes the terror of being the last poet left alive: 'On forse [inevitably] I man [must] his nyxt pray be' (line 95). In the final stanza the unchanged refrain and the repetition of 'ded'/'dede'/'deid' hold out small comfort.

In the context of these poems, Dunbar's magnificent 'Done is a battell on the dragon blak' can be read as a personal as well as a doctrinal triumph. It is written in the eight-line 'Monk's' stanza with the refrain '*Surrexit dominus de sepulcro*' (the Lord has risen from the tomb), from the Easter liturgy. Its subject is Christ's descent into hell after the crucifixion, his releasing the souls of the righteous, and his resurrection on the third day – but as if these had just taken place, and not there but here. Christ is 'our' champion (line 2); he endorses 'our' ransoms (line 7); he died for 'our' sake (line 17) and for 'our' quarrel (line 26). It seems that we are the 'borrowit' souls (line 6) retrieved from the devil; hell is not other people. The exultant first word, 'Done' – fought, accomplished, ended – fixes the tone of the whole poem: Look! We have come through! The powerfully assertive, repeatedly end-stopped lines of the first four stanzas break up into a more staccato pattern in the fifth, with the half-lines ending on past participles in a virtuoso grammatical riff that echoes the pastness of 'done':

> The fo is chasit, the battell is done ceis,
> The presone brokin, the jevellouris fleit and flemit,

> The weir is gon, confermit is the peis,
> The fetteris lowsit and the dungeon temit [brought under control],
> The ransoun maid, the presoneris redemit,
> The field is win, ourcumin is the fo,
> Dispulit of the tresur that he yemit [guarded]:
> *Surrexit dominus de sepulcro.* (line 33–40)

The refrain is in the past tense, too: it is done. This is unusual; Dunbar's refrains more commonly use the present tense – 'Timor mortis conturbat me', 'In this warld may none assure' – and evoke continuing states of anxiety, fear or uncertainty from which there is no release.

We know more about Gavin Douglas than the others. He was born in 1476[11] and, as the third son of Archibald, fifth Earl of Angus, was destined for an ecclesiastical career, graduating from St Andrews in 1494. Later in life he claimed he had 'passit . . . tyme' in France and Rome, and may have undertaken postgraduate study in Paris.[12] He dedicated his allegorical dream vision, *The Palice of Honour,* to James IV around 1501. By 1504 he was Provost of St Giles, Edinburgh. His translation of Virgil's *Aeneid* was completed in July 1513, seven weeks before the battle of Flodden at which James IV was killed. Under the new regime Douglas rapidly became enmeshed in politics as uncle of the widowed Queen's new husband. He became Bishop of Dunkeld in 1515 and died in London of the plague in 1522. Douglas had been urged to translate the *Aeneid* by his poetry-loving friend, Henry, Lord Sinclair, who died at Flodden along with the King and so may never have read it. Nevertheless, the *Eneados* was quickly copied: the six surviving manuscripts all predate the first publication by Copland in London in 1553. The Earl of Surrey used a manuscript version in working on his own translations of *Aeneid* II and IV into English blank verse, sometime between 1539 and his death in 1547.

Douglas must have known Dunbar in Edinburgh. The latter is mentioned in *The Palice of Honour* and was possibly a chaplain at St Giles.[13] Douglas was an intellectual in a way that Dunbar was not and his learning was, not surprisingly, more avant-garde than Henryson's. Well read in Latin and English, he had contacts among European humanists. For his translation he seems to have used the edition of the *Aeneid* produced in Paris in 1501 by the humanist printer Jodocus Badus Ascensius. This, like many other early editions, included the thirteenth book written by the Italian humanist Maphaeus Vegius in 1428, which includes Aeneas's marriage to Lavinia and his apotheosis.

Douglas explores his reasons for undertaking the translation in the prologues to each book, especially the first, as well as in an additional sequence of poems at the end of the translation.[14] One motive was his admiration for the

Aeneid, both its eloquence and its 'hie profund sentens [subject matter]' (Prol. I.71). As for many intellectuals of his generation, reconciling classical paganism with his own Christianity did not require the exercise of any great ingenuity. He was aware, though, of the contentiousness of his project. In the 'Directioun' appended to Book XIII, he foresees the backbiting that publication will provoke. His anxiety about the poem's reception stems partly from the fear that nitpickers will point out his mistakes, but also from his belief that the enterprise is already being disparaged by the conservatives:

Say thai nocht, I myne honeste [good name] have degraid [debased],
And at my self to schute a but [target] hes maid?
Nane other thing, thai threpe [insist], heir wrocht haue I
Bot fenyeit fabillys [false fictions] of idolatry. ('Directioun', lines 23–6)

The argument over 'fenyeit fabillys' has not gone away. Other detractors, he claims, are calling for the book to be burned ('Exclamatioun', lines 10–11). For his part, he wants the poem to move out of clerical into lay culture, to be known by 'euery gentill Scot' and read aloud to 'onletterit folk' ('Exclamatioun', lines 43–4). It delineates 'euery vertu belangand a nobill man' and 'euery bonte belangand a gentill wycht' (Prol. I.324 and 331), providing ethical models for contemporary laymen.

Linked to all this is another motive: his outrage at Caxton's travesty of the *Aeneid* in his *Eneydos*, printed around 1490. Not only did Caxton not know Latin (he translated the French prose *Livre des Eneydes*), but, to Douglas's contempt, his version extended 'the lufe and ded of Dido queyn' to take up half the work, skipped Book V, ignored Book VI because it presents a pagan view of the after-life and 'blaitly lattis ourslip' the last six books. Virgil's

ornate goldyn versis mair than gilt [gilded]
I spittit for dispyte [indignation] to see swa spilt [ruined]
With sych a wyght, quhilk [who] trewly be myne entent
Knew neuer thre wordis at all quhat Virgill ment. (Prol. I.149–52)

Douglas's contempt for 'Willyame Caxtoun, of Inglis natioun' (Prol. I.147), who writes in 'Inglys gros' (Prol.I.148), feeds his own pride in rendering Virgil for the first time 'in the langage of the Scottis natioun' (Prol. I.103) – and this on the eve of Flodden. His acknowledgment that he has been forced into 'Sum bastard Latyn, French or Inglys oyss [use] / Quhar scant was Scottis' (Prol. I.117–18), is in fact one of the earliest instances of the language of lowland Scotland being called 'Scottis' rather than 'Inglis'. The result is an exceptionally rich and eclectic diction that includes both neologisms and archaisms, and a range of registers. The original poems that form the prologues to each of the thirteen books are formally very varied, and the seasonal passages in Prologues VII, XII and XIII have been much discussed as early examples of the poetry of natural description.

Douglas's first principle as translator is fidelity to Virgil's meaning, making it 'braid and plane' (Prol. I.110). The explicitness that results is coupled with an expansiveness that derives, in part at least, from the fact that Douglas's unit is not Virgil's hexameter line but the five-stress couplet. This had come to Scots from Chaucer and was probably first used by Gilbert Hay around 1460 for his translation of the life of Alexander from French into Scots and then in the 1470s by 'Blind Harry' for his life of Wallace. These are both ambitious 'historical' works that engage, like the *Eneados*, with the making and breaking of nations; behind them lie Barbour's *Bruce* and the Scottish Troy fragments. Douglas is heir to a long Scottish tradition of heroic poetry. His expansiveness also derives, though, as Priscilla Bawcutt has shown, from his technique of incorporating into his translation material from the marginal commentaries in the early editions. Indeed, Douglas clearly intended to write his own commentary on the *Eneados*, although only a small part of this was completed or has survived, covering the first Prologue and three-quarters of Book I.[15]

The account of the death of Priam in Book II exemplifies some of Douglas's characteristics. In Troy's last hours, Achilles's son Pyrrhus (Neoptolemus) kills a son of Priam and Hecuba before their eyes. When Priam tells Pyrrhus that his father would not have behaved so, the latter jeers at him:

> Quod Pyrrus, 'Sen [since] always [in any case] thou saist swa [so],
> To Pellyus son, my fadir, thou most ga.
> Beir hym this message, ramembir weil thou tell
> Him al my warkis and dedis sa cruell –
> Schaw Neoptolemus is degenerit cleyn.
> Now salt thou de [die].' And with that word in teyn
> The ald [old man] trymlyng towart the altare he drew,
> That in the hait blude of his son, sched new,
> Fundrit [slipped]; and Pyrrus grippis hym by the hayr
> With his left hand, and with the tother al bayr
> Drew furth his schynand swerd, quhilk [which] in his syde
> Festynnyt, and onto the hyltis dyd he hyde. (II.ix.67–78)

The ratio here of twelve lines to Virgil's seven (*Aeneid* II.537–43) is more or less that for the whole work. Douglas is not peculiarly verbose: Dryden also takes twelve lines for this passage and Surrey ten. Douglas's 'Sen always thou saist swa' in the first line is a wobble; Surrey's 'Then thow shalt this thing report' (II.711)[16] better renders Virgil's '*Referes ergo haec*' (line 547).[17] Nevertheless,

Douglas's lines have a trenchant directness which derives from the repeated imperatives: 'Beir', 'ramembir', 'Schaw'; from the way the third line breaks into two halves, followed by the run-on from 'tell' to its forceful echo 'cruell'; from the powerful and economical 'Schaw Neoptolemus is degenerit cleyn', where the monosyllables at either end create a chiastic rhythmic structure that plays 'Neoptolemus' against 'degenerit' (the latter is the past participle of the rare verb 'degener' = 'to degenerate'). The sentence that follows overrides the couplets, with 'Fundrit' teetering at the end of a clause and the start of a line, and Pyrrhus's violent actions rushing one line on to the next. Douglas's 'gryppis hym by the hayr / With his left hand' is a cruder movement than Virgil's '*implicuitque comam laeua*' (line 552) (and wound his hair with his left hand), and 'dyd . . . hyde', a literal translation of '*abdidit*' (line 553), is – perhaps deliberately – unidiomatic: Surrey prefers 'thrust up to the hilts' (II.720). Nevertheless, the overall effect of this scene is one of swift and shocking inevitability. The elegy for Priam that follows has a McGonigall-ish moment in the first couplet ('Of Priamus thus was the finale fait – / Fortone heir endit his gloryus estait' (II.ix.79–80)), a reminder that Douglas sometimes has a bad ear. Nevertheless, it concludes strongly:

> That ryal prince, vmquhile [once] our [over] Asya
> Apon sa feil [many] pepil and realmys alswa
> Ryngnyt in welth, now by the cost lyis ded
> Bot as [no more than] a stok [trunk] and of hakkit his hed,
> A corps but [without] lyfe, renown or other fame,
> Onknawyn of ony wight quhat was his name. (II.ix.83–8)

The violence of Virgil's '*auulsumque umeris caput*' (and his head severed from his shoulders) (II.558) is caught in 'of hakkit his hed' in a way that Surrey's bland 'His hed and sholders parted ben in twaine' (line 728) fails to do. Douglas's last three and a half lines are characteristically wordy, compared with Virgil's '*Iacet ingens litore truncus, / auolsumque umeris caput, et sine nomine corpus*' (II.257–8). (A huge trunk lies on the shore, head severed from the shoulders, a corpse without a name.) Douglas's 'stok' and 'corps' – Virgil's '*truncus*' and '*corpus*' – make 'but lyfe' redundant, while the reduplicative 'renown' and 'fame' merely set up a rhyme for 'name'. On the other hand, there is a rhetorical purpose to this over-emphasis: the concluding couplet signals the end of one of Douglas's chapters. Douglas's syntax in line 88 has the curious and un-Virgilian effect of evoking the eerie non-presence of others: the 'feil pepil' of line 84 have dwindled to the 'ony wight' who does not know and is not there but who nevertheless haunts the line.

Eneas's meeting with Dido in the underworld in Book VI is a different kind of encounter. It is particularly important to Douglas because it provides the opportunity of rebutting medieval calumnies about Aeneas. In the Prologue to Book I, Douglas takes Chaucer to task for claiming in *The Legend of Good Women* that Aeneas broke his oath to Dido. Given that Virgil worked so hard 'Eneas for to loif [praise] and magnyfy' (Prol. I.419–21), if the latter were indeed 'maynsworn' (perjured) (Prol. I.422), it would mean that all Virgil's labours 'war nocht worth a myte' (Prol. I.424). Douglas argues that Virgil shows that Aeneas left Dido in Carthage at the gods' command. Oddly, at this point in the Prologue the marginal self-commentary on the text to which I have already referred remarks: 'This argument [i.e. Douglas's argument on behalf of Aeneas] excuses nocht the tratory of Eneas na his maynsweryng . . . Eneas vrought nocht be command of ony goddis, bot of his awyn fre wil, be the permission of God . . . He falit then gretly to the sueit Dido' (Prol. I, note to line 425). Bawcutt's view, surely correct, is that this comment is an interpolation, possibly by Matthew Geddes, the scribe of the Cambridge manuscript, which preserves the fullest version of the commentary. He, then, is one of those conservative readers whom Douglas had been nervous of, who cannot reconcile Virgil's world-view with Christianity.

Douglas's version of the meeting is, at over fifty lines, about twice as long as Virgil's. His Dido is introduced more sensationally than Virgil's; she is glimpsed with 'The greyn [fresh] wound gapand in hir breist al new' (VI.vii.57). This translates Virgil's chaste *'recens a volnere'* (VI.450) (literally, fresh from her wound): here there is no gaping, no breast and no repetition of 'greyn' and 'al new'. Douglas's version of Dido's wound seems to echo the metaphorical wound of the goddess Juno, early in Book I: 'The eterne wound hyd in hir breist ay greyn' (I.i.67). Juno's wound is partly caused by anger at the fate foretold of her beloved Carthage at the hands of the Trojans' Roman descendants; hence she summons up the storms that deflect Aeneas and his followers from Italy to the fatal meeting with Dido. The Dido–Juno parallel at this moment serves to strengthen Douglas's view that Aeneas is not 'maynsworn' but subject to a history greater than himself. Aeneas's words to Dido bring this out more emphatically than in the Latin: Virgil's *'inuitus, regina, tuo de litore cessi'* (VI.460), ('unwilling, queen, I departed from your shore'), is rendered as: 'Malgre [despite] my wyl, Prynces, sa mot I the [as I hope to thrive], / From thy costis depart I was constrenyt' (VI.vii.74–5). The sense of *'inuitus'* is conveyed twice, by 'Malgre my wil' and 'constrenyt'. 'Sa mot I the' is a standard line-filler; elsewhere in this passage, though, Douglas's expansiveness is less empty in its effects, as with the filling out of Aeneas's compassion for Dido:

With sik [such] wordis Eneas, full of wo,
Set him to meyss [appease] the sprete [spirit] of Queyn Dido,
Quhilk [who]
...
Maid him to weip and sched furth teris wak [watery].
(VI.vii.89–91, 93)

Virgil's '*lacrimasque ciebat*' (VI.468) (and [Aeneas] started to shed tears) expands to 'full of wo' (line 89) and 'Maid him to weip and sched furth teris wak' (line 93), while '*prosequitur lacrimis longe, et miseratur euntem*' (vi.476) ('pursues her at a distance with tears and pities her as she goes') becomes:

And weping gan hir follow a weil lang space,
Regratand [grieving] in his mynd, and had piete
Of the distress that movit hir so to fle. (VI.vii.106–8)

The heightened emotionalism of Douglas's lines shows Eneas to be a man of feeling, and counters the brutality of Chaucer's Eneas in the face of Dido's distress: 'Thus he hath laft Dido in wo and pyne, / And wedded ther a lady hyghte Lavyne.'[18]

In his 'Conclusio' Douglas says that he is making a votive offering to Virgil of his 'pen and instrumentis' (line 13) and that his muse from now on 'sal . . . be cleyn contemplatyve, / And solitar' (lines 14–15). It sounds as if the priest has decided that, for all the exhilaration of completing his hugely ambitious work, the cost of this foray into the active life led in the world – the focus of the *studia humanitatis* – has been too great. Recent discussions of the *Eneados* have emphasised the political aspects of Douglas's undertaking. Another approach is to suggest that the nascent humanism of the circles in which he moved offered a way out of the impasse of late medieval Scottish Catholicism. Set alongside Henryson's tragic sense of things, or the poetry of Dunbar, who writes so brilliantly of struggling to maintain an equilibrium in the face of failure or the passage of time or the prospect of dying, Douglas's *Eneados* offers a profound and optimistic vision of the end-directed life and gazes steadily on death.

Notes

1. All Henryson quotations are from *The Poems of Robert Henryson*, ed. Denton Fox (Oxford: Clarendon Press, 1981). The letter-form 'yogh' has been silently normalised to 'y'.
2. See John Bossy, *Christianity in the West 1400–1700* (Oxford: Oxford University Press, 1985), p. 35.

3. *The Riverside Chaucer*, ed. Larry D. Benson (Oxford: Oxford University Press, 1988), p. 583.
4. H. A. Kelly, *Ideas and Forms of Tragedy from Aristotle to the Middle Ages* (Cambridge: Cambridge University Press, 1993), p. 128.
5. All Dunbar quotations are from *The Poems of William Dunbar*, ed. Priscilla Bawcutt, 2 vols. (Glasgow: Association for Scottish Literary Studies, 1998); see 'Hale, sterne superne, hale, in eterne', lines 5, 14 and 55 and 'In secreit place this hyndeir nycht', lines 34, 39, 41 and 48. The letter-form 'yogh' has been silently normalised to 'y' or 'z'.
6. 'Ane exclamatioun aganyst detractouris', in *Virgil's Aeneid Translated into Scottish Verse by Gavin Douglas*, ed. David F. C. Coldwell, 4 vols., Scottish Text Society, third series, 25, 27, 28, 30 (Edinburgh: Blackwood, 1957–64), vol. IV, p. 193, line 2. All Douglas quotations are from this edition. The letter-form 'yogh' has been silently normalised to 'y'.
7. Benson (ed.), *Riverside Chaucer*, p. 23.
8. *Ibid.*, p. 161.
9. Alain Chartier, *Here foloweth the copye of a lettre whyche maistre Alayn Charetier wrote to hys brother . . . translated out of frensshe in to englysshe* (Westminster: William Caxton, 1483) fol. 80r.
10. See 'Off Lentren in the first mornyng', 'To speik of science, craft or sapience', 'Be mery, man, and tak nocht fer in mynd', in Bawcutt (ed.), *Poems of William Dunbar*, pp. 159, 266, 61.
11. Priscilla Bawcutt, 'New Light on Gavin Douglas', in A. A. MacDonald, M. Lynch and I. B. Cowan (eds.), *The Renaissance in Scotland: Studies in Religion, Literature and Culture Offered to John Durkan* (Leiden: E. J. Brill, 1994), pp. 95–106.
12. Biographical information is from Priscilla Bawcutt, *Gavin Douglas: A Critical Study* (Edinburgh: Edinburgh University Press, 1976).
13. *The Shorter Poems of Gavin Douglas*, ed. Priscilla Bawcutt (Edinburgh: Scottish Text Society, 2003), p. 63.
14. 'Conclusio'; 'Directioun' ('Heir the translator direkkis hys buke'); 'Exclamatioun' ('Ane exclamatioun against detractouris'); 'The tyme, space and date'; Virgil's epitaph; see Coldwell (ed.), *Virgil's Aeneid Translated . . . by Gavin Douglas*, vol. IV, pp. 188ff.
15. Bawcutt, *Gavin Douglas*, pp. 102–24.
16. 'They whisted all, with fixed face intent', in *Henry Howard, Earl of Surrey: Poems*, ed. Emrys Jones (Oxford: Clarendon Press, 1964), pp. 35–63. All Surrey quotations are from this edition.
17. All quotations from Virgil, *Aeneid*, are from *'Bucolics', 'Aeneid,' and 'Georgics' of Vergil*, ed. J. B. Greenough (Boston: Ginn & Co., 1900).
18. Benson (ed.), *Riverside Chaucer*, p. 613.

Chapter 7

Sixteenth-century poetry: Skelton, Wyatt and Surrey

ELIZABETH HEALE

The early Tudor poets John Skelton (*c*.1460–1529), Sir Thomas Wyatt (*c*.1503–42) and Thomas Howard, Earl of Surrey (1517–47) span a period of dramatic historical, social and cultural change. Skelton began his career in the service of Henry VII just after the Battle of Bosworth Field in 1485 and Surrey lost his head for treason days before the death of Henry VIII. Under these two centralising Tudor monarchs, policy, prosperity and the increasing influence of humanism caused major social changes. England became a significant European power, and, after Skelton's death, broke away from the Roman Catholic Church. The work of all three poets is marked by a sense of significant cultural change and the need to develop new poetic forms and voices. Above all, each poet's work is shaped by his uneasy relationship to a dominant, often tyrannical royal court.[1]

The careers of the three poets were very different. Skelton seems to have risen through his academic and rhetorical abilities, recognised in the academic title of laureate, to an early position as tutor to the infant Henry VIII. In 1503, however, he was pensioned off to the rectory of Diss in Norfolk, and spent much of the rest of his life trying, largely unsuccessfully, to regain an official post at court as poet and propagandist for the King.[2] Without a ready-made courtly audience, he made use of the new technology of printing. Wyatt was a courtier and diplomat who eschewed print publication, circulating his verse among an elite readership in manuscript.[3] Twice imprisoned by Henry VIII, he also served as the King's ambassador at foreign courts. Surrey was an aristocrat, the eldest son of the Duke of Norfolk, fatally conscious of his ancestry and its traditional privileges, but open, after a year spent at the dazzling court of France, to new Renaissance forms and models.[4]

To some extent we still view all three poets through Elizabethan eyes. The verse of Wyatt and Surrey was printed for the Elizabethans in the highly influential *Tottel's Miscellany* (first printed in 1557). For George Puttenham, writing in 1589, Wyatt and Surrey were worthy antecedents, 'courtly makers . . . who hauing trauailed into Italie, and there tast[ing] the sweete and stately measures and stile of the Italian Poesie . . . greatly pollished our rude & homely maner of vulgar [vernacular] Poesie, from that it had bene before'.[5] Skelton, however, seemed neither courtly nor polished, but either a kind of jester, following the publication of apocryphal *Merie Tales . . . Made by Master Skelton* in 1567, or as a proto-Protestant for his anti-ecclesiastical satire, *Collyn Clout*.[6] In Andrew Hadfield's words, Skelton is often seen as 'half medieval ape and half Renaissance man'.[7]

While there are undoubtedly significant differences between the three poets, they also have much in common. All three are experimental and innovative poets who ambitiously redefine and expand what can be written in English. All three create, or import from Latin and Continental models, new genres and verse forms. In particular, all three are interested in developing new kinds of verse in plainer styles that imitate in different ways the natural and dramatic emphases of speaking voices, and for all three, such voices characteristically articulate themes of alienation, opposition or disillusion. In the more ambitious work of all three, the role of the poet is a mark of a high calling, entailing the responsibility, and providing the rather slippery means, to expose vice and encourage virtue.

While the work of each poet stands out from that of their contemporaries in terms of range, innovation and ambition, none of the three writes in isolation and Wyatt's courtly verse in particular needs to be understood in terms of the wider practices of his courtly contemporaries. Wherever possible, I signal, within the constraints of space, the relationship of the work of the three authors to other contemporaneous writing.

Courtly verse

An elevated, 'aureate' style and idealising themes dominated complimentary courtly verse at the end of the fifteenth and early sixteenth centuries. Skelton's contemporary Stephen Hawes was a master of such verse and Skelton himself competently deploys this style, among others, in *The Garlande of Laurell* (printed in 1527 but containing verse from the mid 1490s).[8] The Countess of Surrey, for example, is addressed with aureate decorum: 'After all duly ordred obeisaunce, / In humble wyse as lowly as I may, / Unto you, madame, I make reconusaunce.'[9] That Skelton already found such a style potentially absurd is suggested by his burlesque poem, 'Th'auncient acquaintance', which begins by parodying aureate praise of a lady: 'Of all your feturs favorable to make tru discripcion, / I am insuffycyent to make such enterpryse . . .' The style changes radically in the third stanza, which develops a lewd parallel between women and horses:

> Wyth bound and rebound, bounsyngly take up
> Hys jentyll curtoyl, and set nowght by small naggys!
> Spur up at the hynder gyrth with, 'Gup, morell, gup!'
> With, 'Jayst ye, Jenet of Spayne, for your tayll waggys.'
>
> (IV[ii].8–9 and 15–18)

These lines are full of bestial puns and allusions: '*curtoyl* means both " a horse with a docked tail" and a "tunic"; *naggys* both "small horses" and (in slang) "the human testicles" '.[10] Morels and jennets are breeds of horse. Along with a rude, plain diction, and a strongly stressed style that imitates colloquial speech, comes a sardonic view of love and women.

The growing taste for plainer, less aureate styles, does not always take such rude form. Another of the complementary lyrics in *Garlande* praises 'maystres Margaret Hussey':

> Mirry Margaret,
> As mydsomer flowre,
> Jentill as fawcoun
> Or hawke of the towre;
>
> With solace and gladnes,
> Moche mirthe and no madnes,
> All good and no badnes,
> So joyously,
> So maydenly,
> So womanly
> Her demenyng (XXI.1004–14)

The short lines of five, six and four syllables, with two or three stresses, produce a playful song-like effect, increased by the repetition of the first four lines as a refrain.

A taste for such song-like rhythms and plainer diction, often joined with less idealising themes, is evident in manuscripts of elite verse from the late fifteenth century. One example, from the 'Findern' MS, is in the voice of a woman:

> Whatso men sayn,
> Love is no pain
> To them, certain,
> But varians:
> For they constrain

Ther hertes to fein,
Ther mouthes to plain,
Ther displesauns.[11]

Such 'balets' (song-like stanzaic poems, easily adapted for singing to popular dance tunes) became increasingly popular in courtly circles by the second decade of the sixteenth century.[12] An example from the 'Henry VIII' MS (compiled by someone close to the King *c.*1515), develops an aggressively masculine 'erotic hunter' theme: 'blow thi horne on hye! / There ys a do [doe] in yonder wode; in faith, she woll not dy'. The poem's 'wit' depends on double entendres on horns and arrows as well as on the deer/dear pun:

He to go and I to go,
    But he ran fast afore;
I bad hym shott and strik the do,
    For I myght shott no mere.

The penultimate stanza alerts the courtly audience, perhaps mixed, to the poem's lewd innuendo: 'Now the construccyon of the same – / What do yow meane or thynk?'[13]

Wyatt's balets clearly belong to this Tudor courtly genre. Their plain speaking and song-like effects are often used to voice scepticism about love and the trustworthiness of women. The balet 'Lo what it is to love!' is typical:

To love and to be wise!
To rage with good advice!
    Now thus, now then,
    Now off, now on,
Uncertain as the dice!
    There is no man
    At once that can
To love and to be wise.[14]

The varying three- and two-stress lines produce a more diverse and sophisticated song-like effect than either the Findern or erotic hunter balets and point to the great variety of Wyatt's lyric metres and his mastery of their light but often biting effects. Wyatt's balets are influenced by courtly Italian songs, such as the *frottola*, designed to be sung to a lute accompaniment, although it is unlikely Wyatt's were performed in this way. The *frottola* typically developed a witty and sardonic view of love and women.[15]

The insouciant brilliance of Wyatt's balets demonstrates the courtly ethos of *sprezzatura*, a display of excellence that appears effortless and natural, but is in fact carefully cultivated. In his highly influential *Libro del Cortegiano* (1528), Baldassare Castigilione describes the truly accomplished courtier as one who 'conceals all artistry and makes whatever [he] says or does seem uncontrived and effortless . . . true art is what does not seem to be art'.[16] The poetic forms which Wyatt introduces into English from Italy, such as the *frottola*, the eight-line *strambotto* and urbane Horatian verse satire, exemplify just such a combination of apparent spontaneity with subtle artifice. This is particularly the case with the Petrarchan sonnet, the most influential of Wyatt's introductions. The concentrated fourteen-line sonnet, with its intricate structure and rhyme scheme, is designed to voice, with passionate fluency, the intense thoughts and emotions of a first-person speaker/lover.

'Who list to hunt', an adaptation of Petrarch's *Rime* 190, demonstrates particularly clearly the power of the sonnet form and Wyatt's distinctive use of it. In Petrarch's original, the lover sees a tantalising vision of a pure white deer on which he gazes till, tired, he falls in the water and it disappears. Wyatt converts the sonnet into a version of the erotic hunt:

Whoso list to hunt, I know where is an hind,
But as for me, helas, I may no more.
The vain travail hath wearied me so sore,
I am of them that farthest cometh behind.
Yet may I by no means my wearied mind
Draw from the deer, but as she fleeth afore
Fainting I follow. I leave off therefore
Sithens in a net I seek to hold the wind.
Who list her hunt, I put him out of doubt,
As well as I may spend his time in vain.
And graven with diamonds in letters plain
There is written her fair neck round about:
'*Noli me tangere* for Caesar's I am,
And wild for to hold though I seem tame.' (XI)

Wyatt's 'major contribution' to the sonnet form which he imports into English is to break the final six lines, which in Petrarch usually rhyme cde, cde, into a quatrain and a couplet, allowing for a climactic ending, or, as is often the case with Wyatt's sonnets, a final sardonic comment.[17] This sonnet ends by quoting the enigmatic message written on a collar round the deer's neck. '*Noli me tangere*' alludes both to a supposed inscription round the necks of Caesar's deer, mentioned in the Petrarchan original, and, shockingly, to Christ's words after his resurrection in the Latin Vulgate Bible.[18] The lady is for a moment associated with something holy, but also, in the second half of the line, with the coins that in the Bible belong to Caesar, a worldly object owned.[19] In the final line the lady's disturbing otherness, beyond the desiring male grasp, is also a sign of a flirtatious and dangerous female duplicity.

Wyatt's sonnet focuses our attention not only on the tantalisingly desirable and despised object of the hunt, but also on the lover/hunter. The quatrains map his shifting moods: he is self-contradictory and ambivalent, aggressively masculine, peevish and plaintive. The poem dramatises a spontaneous and distinctive voice through plain diction and metrical irregularity. Such irregularity is a distinctive feature of Wyatt's sonnets and other short forms, such as *strambotti* and epigrams, and is used to dramatise the speaking voice, with stressed syllables and caesurae signalling emphases and changes in pace and tone.[20] In this sonnet, the extra metre of line 1 produces a confident opening invitation which then falters through the varying stress patterns and pauses of the next seven lines. Not until line 9 does the speaker resume the buoyant iambics of line 1, but this is again halted almost immediately by the ominous pace of line 11 with its extra syllable, before ending with the couplet, each of whose lines have only four stresses, causing their stark warnings to seem yet starker.

The lover/speaker of 'Whoso list to hunt' may be disempowered and self-contradictory, but his voice is expertly dramatised in a poem that announces its maker's mastery of a new, difficult and glamorous Continental form. Where the aureate verse of an earlier generation drew attention to its own artifice, the style of gentlemanly amateurism cultivated by Wyatt and his fellow courtier poets implies rather than displays its technical sophistication. Instead, the reader/listener's attention is drawn to the expressive fluency of the speaker, and the emotional drama. The form serves perfectly a competitive, courtly ethos of *sprezzatura*, self-assertion through the display of apparently spontaneous brilliance.

Few of Wyatt's contemporaries attempted the sonnet form, but Wyatt's balets were popular and influential. The 'Devonshire' and 'Blage' manuscripts, containing courtly verse of the 1530s and 1540s, make clear the role of verse such as Wyatt's balets and sonnets in social pastime.[21] The courtly women who used the Devonshire manuscript marked poems for copying or in some cases singing, and both manuscripts make clear that answering and adapting the verses of others was part of the fun. The evident popularity of Wyatt's verses is undoubtedly partly due to their wit and skill, but their vivid dramatisation of sceptical courtly speakers appears to be part of their appeal. They may be used as a provocative gambit in witty exchange between the sexes, but they may also figure a more general frustration and disillusion with the pursuit of favour and advancement at court. Wyatt's courtly poems negotiate, for himself and others, a conflict between gentlemanly self-assertion and courtly servility, between glamour and the danger of dependence on the great.

Thomas Howard, Earl of Surrey, found at the end of his life that he too, in spite of his aristocratic birth, had much to fear from those at the top of the greasy pole. Elegiac themes of loss, absence and betrayal recur throughout his poems. Surrey was a close reader and admirer of Wyatt's verse, but his poetry creates significantly different effects. Where Wyatt's lovers are self-divided and often disillusioned, Surrey's are grieving and faithful; their characteristic mode is that of complaint expressed in regular and musical metres.

Surrey followed Wyatt in translating Petrarchan sonnets, developing what became the dominant English form of three quatrains rhyming abab, cdcd, efef, with a final couplet. Where, however, Wyatt's couplets typically foreclose a fraught narrative with a final stinging comment on the pursuit of love and women ('Of such a root cometh fruit fruitless', xx), Surrey's lovers are faithful and enduring:

> For my swete thoughtes sometyme doe pleasure bring,
> But by and by the cause of my disease
> Geves me a pang that inwardly dothe sting,
> When that I thinke what griefe it is againe
> To live and lacke the thing should ridde my paine.[22]

The elegaic resignation produced by Surrey's implied narrative is complemented by the smooth rhythms of his verse, emphasised by the repetition of 'by and by' and the chiming of 'live and lacke' in the lines quoted above. The iambic metre is broken only in lines 12 and 13, which begin with stressed syllables. Surrey's lovers find sweetness in living and lacking.

It is perhaps Surrey's interest in the poetry of suffering that attracts him to women's voices in a number of his poems. Writing as his wife mourning the absence of her husband, Surrey develops his favourite themes of faithfulness and loss:

> Good ladies, you that have your pleasure in exyle,
> Stepp in your foote, come take a place, and mourne with me awhyle;
> And suche as by their lords do sett but lytle pryce,
> Lett them sitt still, it skills them not what chaunce come on the dyce.
> (no. 24, lines 1–4)

The first line hints that not only is the speaker's 'pleasure' absent, but that absence brings a kind of mournful sweetness. The pain of the virtuous wives elevates them above their insensible companions.

'Good ladies' is in poulter's measure, alternating rhyming iambic lines of fourteen and twelve syllables, a form that Wyatt had used for a complaint, 'So feeble is the thread' (LXXVI), but which Surrey made his own. Ungainly as the form seems to modern ears, used to the dominance of iambic pentameters, Surrey's poulter's measure complaints were highly influential on mid-Tudor poets. The form may derive from the ballad measure of fourteeners, and was certainly thought suitable for singing, adding to the plangency of the form.[23] A poem for which music survives, but which also demonstrates the potential of the form to dramatise the emphases and emotions of a speaking voice, is 'In winters just returne':

> And lowd (alas) he shryked oft, and 'Shepard', gan he call;
> 'Come, hie the[e] fast at ones, and print it in thy hart;
> So thou shalt know, and I shall tell the[e], giltlesse how I smart.'
> (no. 16, lines 38–40)

The lines maintain a balance between the emphases of a dramatised voice and the regular metre. We enter a stylised, literary world of a dying lover lamenting to a shepherd, a world of idealised, albeit tragic, emotions. The emotional pathos of Surrey's speakers is quite different from the sardonic intimacies of Wyatt's songs and sonnets.

Skelton, Wyatt and Surrey all respond to, and develop in innovative ways, the taste for plainer, less elaborately courtly styles in the early decades of the sixteenth century. Plain diction and a new metrical flexibility imitate the natural emphases of voices ranging from the rudeness of Skelton's 'Th'auncient acquaintaince' to the elegiac plangency of Surrey's poulter's measure complaints. Plain speakers and innovative metrical forms are also used by all three poets to construct powerful satires that exploit, or question, the relationship of plainness to truth.

Satires

Skelton's pre-1520 anti-courtly satires, *The Bowge of Court* (*c.*1498) and *Magnyfycence* (probably written *c.*1517), treat plain-style speakers with considerable suspicion. In *Bowge*, for example, the narrator Drede is beset by a group of false courtiers with names like Favel, Suspicion, Dyssymulation and Disceyte, who shift between different styles and idioms. Favel, or flattery, addresses Drede with sycophantic aureation:

> 'Noo thynge erthely that I wonder so sore
> As of your connynge, that is so excellent;
> Deynte to have with us suche one in store,
> So vertuously that hath his dayes spente.' (V.148–51)

The contorted syntax, and the refined vocabulary ('connynge' – learning; 'deynte' – pleasing), draw our attention to the artifice of Favel's rhetoric. When Favel is overheard talking about Drede to another false courtier, Suspect, he uses a quite different style:

> 'Twyste,' quod Suspecte, 'goo playe; hym I ne reke!'
> 'By Cryste,' quod Favell, 'Drede is soleyne freke!
> What, lete us holde him up, man, for a whyle.' (lines 186–8)

Favel's colloquial demotic ('soleyne freke' – unsociable fellow; 'holde . . . up' – leave him alone) adds coarseness to his untrustworthiness. The truth this plain speaking reveals is that courtiers are inherently duplicitous. A different kind of plainness is used by another courtier, Dyssymulation:

> I wolde eche man were as playne as I.
> It is a worlde, I saye, to here of some –
> I hate this faynynge, fye upon it, fye! (lines 463–5)

Dyssymulation's seemingly artless plainness is, of course, thoroughly artful; he mimics, in persuasive tones, the style of truth. Skelton associates rhetorical slipperiness with immorality, while demonstrating his own ability to dramatise, in rhyme royal stanzas, a range of spoken idioms.

It is not until the anti-Wolsey satires of 1522 and 1523, *Collyn Clout* and the Juvenalian 'Why Come Ye Nat to Courte?' that Skelton uses plain-speakers as honest truth-tellers. Even so, they adopt, like the scoundrel Counterfeit Countenance in *Magnyfycence*, a 'bastarde ryme, after the dogrell gyse' (xvi.408). The skeltonic line, with its two or three stresses, often using repeated rhymes over a number of lines, is Skelton's invention, adapting the short lines of two stresses and repeated rhymes that could be used for playful effect in 'To maystres Margaret Hussey' (see above), to produce an emphatic accusatory style.[24] The effect is of an energetic and seemingly spontaneous outpouring of blame and ridicule. In *Collyn Clout*, the speaker is a rustic figure in the tradition of Langland's Piers Plowman (Colin is derived from the Latin *colonus* – farmer, and a clout is a rag or a patch). Collyn claims to report, reluctantly, the overheard complaints of the common people directed against the hierarchy of the church, and particularly Cardinal Wolsey:

> Shall I tell you more? Ye, shall.
> I am lothe to tell all;
> But the communalte ye call
> Ydolles of Babylon,

> *De terra* Zabulon,
> *De terra* Neptalym;
> For you love to go trym,
> Brought up of poore estate,
> With pryde inordynate,
> Sodaynly upstarte
> From the donge carte,
> The mattocke and the shovll
> To reygne and to rule. (XIX.635–47)

The language and verse mimic a rude simplicity, but of course, the poem is an artful construct. The fragmentary biblical snippets are sufficient to associate the clergy with the paganism and idolatry of Babylon, Zabulon and Naphtali. Skelton keeps at two removes from the dangerous accusations voiced by the people and reported by the uneducated Collyn. The satire on Wolsey's prelatical and worldly pride that has forgotten its base origins is, however, unmistakable. The jeering chant of the short lines lends the demotic invective an energy and ferocity that makes Skelton's plain-speaking skeltonics a satirical weapon of great power.

The rhetoric of plain-speaking adopted by Wyatt in 'Mine owne John Poyntz', recalls that of Dyssymulation rather than Collyn:

> I am not he such eloquence to boast
> To make the crow singing as the swan,
> Nor make 'the lion' of coward beasts the most
> That cannot take a mouse as the cat can;
> . . .
> My wit is naught. I cannot learn the way.
> And much the less of things that greater be,
> That asken help of colours of device
> To join the mean with each extremity:
> With the nearest virtue to cloak alway the vice.
> (CXLIX.43–6, 57–61)

The 'colour of device' that the speaker is unable to learn is the quintessentially courtly figure of *paradistole*, the misnaming of virtues as vices and vices as virtues:

> As drunkenness good fellowship to call;
> The friendly foe with his double face
> Say he is gentle and courteous therewithal;

And say that Favel hath a goodly grace
In eloquence (lines 64–8)

The poem's speaker claims to quit the court of his own free will, disgusted by such duplicity, but it seems he has had little choice in the matter; he has 'a clog . . . at my heel' (line 86). The allusion seems to be to Wyatt's own rustication from the court in 1536 following his imprisonment for a supposed liaison with Queen Anne Boleyn.[25] The speaker is thus a version of Wyatt himself, but the poem is in fact a highly accomplished translation of a sophisticated Italian original, a satire by Luigi Alamanni, written in a difficult verse form of interlaced groups of three rhymes called *terza rima*, a form that Wyatt introduced into English. How much of a plain-speaker is this Wyatt persona? Is he really, as he claims, someone who cannot master the duplicitous arts of the court, or is the plain style a rhetorical costume shrugged on for protection, but with the art and irony visible to knowing friends? Like *Bowge*, Wyatt's satire undermines the very notion of plain-speaking.

Equally disconcerting is the satire, '"A spending hand"', addressed to a fellow diplomat, Sir Francis Brian. The speaker of this epistle is a friendly counsellor using down-to-earth proverbs and plain-speaking colloquialisms: 'Why dost thou wear thy body to the bones / And mightst at home sleep in thy bed of down'(CLI.14–15). Like Skelton's plain-speaking villains, this counsellor is a scoundrel, advocating venial flattery and self-serving duplicity:

Sometime also rich age beginneth to dote;
. . .
Stay him by the arm whereso he walk or go.
Be near alway and, if he cough too sore,
When he hath spit, tread out and please him so. (lines 51–6)

'Flee therefore truth' (line 34), the speaker advises in his truth-speaking plain style. To speak truth in a corrupt world is to counsel lying. But in a poem that acknowledges, as Skelton did in *Bowge*, that style is a mask to be adopted at will, who does speak the truth?

If Wyatt may have learned from Skelton's pre-1520 satires, it is possible the skeltonic satires may have influenced Surrey's 'London, hast thow' (1543). The poem was written to justify an escapade in which the aristocratic Surrey broke the expensive windows of the houses of city merchants with stones, by claiming it was done to warn the city of its ungodly vices. Instead of the rude skeltonic, Surrey uses short tetrameter lines:

Oh shamles hore! is dred then gone
By suche thy foes as ment thy weale?
Oh membre of false Babylon!
The shopp of craft! the denne of ire!
Thy dredfull dome drawes fast uppon.
Thy martyres blood, by swoord and fyre,
In Heaven and earth for justice call.
The Lord shall here their just desyre;
The flame of wrath shall on the[e] fall. (no. 33, lines 51–9)

Surrey uses the same *terza rima* rhyme scheme as Wyatt used in his satires, but his persona is quite unlike Wyatt's subtle and ironic plain-speakers. If skeltonic satire is an influence, it is synthesised with a prestigious new source, Petrarch's vituperative *Rime* 138, which attacks the papacy, and whose last line, '*Putta sfacciata: e dov'hai posto spene*?' is translated in Surrey's line 51. Surrey's voice, like Petrarch's, is that of a biblical prophet coruscating the vicious, rather than that of the lowly plain-speakers of Skelton's skeltonic satires. Both poets, however, use the angry tirade of plain-speaking to voice outrage at a modern world that radically violates their socially conservative values.

Poetic ambitions

Skelton, Wyatt and Surrey are, all three, serious and thoughtful about poetry and its role in articulating matters of the highest importance. In *The Garlande of Laurell*, added to over three decades, Skelton reflected on the roles of poetry and his own role as a poet. The poem was completed and printed in 1523 at the moment when Skelton, his satirical outspokenness curbed by the promise of lucrative patronage from Cardinal Wolsey, could once again claim to be *orator regius*.[26] The poem dramatises, by means of dream allegory, Skelton's claim to be awarded the laurel, the highest recognition, by Fame. The poem is both self-promotional and self-mocking.

It is not at all clear on what basis the laurel might be awarded, and by whose authority. Fame herself is accused by Pallas of being indiscriminate and of advancing the unworthy ('some sluggysh slovyns, that slepe day and nyght', XXI.191). Her court potentially offers a form of recognition independent of royal patronage, but it also seems to be a version of the royal court with its uncertain favours. While Skelton claims to be recognised as a brother by the great English poets, Gower, Chaucer and Lydgate, it is his delightfully embroidered laurel wreath, woven by his lady patrons, that wins the envy of other poets and catches Fame's eye (lines 1105–27). What it is to be a poet and what constitutes success is left uncertain or treated with irony in the poem: is it to be recognised by an undiscriminating fame in the new world of print, or to avoid offending a censorious royal court? Is it to write successful complimentary verses for aristocratic ladies, or to aspire to join the pantheon of his great English predecessors? In the end, Skelton awakes just as Fame is about to give her judgment.

In his final poem, a piece of hack work for Wolsey, Skelton nevertheless defiantly claims that the type of the true poet is the psalmist David, 'poete of poetes all' (XXIV.321), whose songs show that the source of true laureate authority is 'hevenly inspyracion', independent of either court patronage or the accidents of Fame:[27]

> there is a spyrituall,
> And a mysteriall,
> And a mysticall
> Effecte energiall,
> As Grekes do it call,
> Of suche an industry
> Of suche a pregnacy,
> Of hevenly inspyracion
> In laureate creacyon,
> Of poetes commendacion,
> That of divyne myseracion
> God maketh his habytacion
> In poetes which excelles,
> And sojourns with them and dwelles. (lines 365–78)

Not until Edmund Spenser in the later sixteenth century did an English poet make such claims for the inspired nature of laureate verse.[28]

Twenty years later, in 1542, Surrey cast Wyatt as the ideal poet/hero in a series of elegies (28, 29 and 30) that, in an unprecedented step for an aristocratic writer, he put into print. By so doing, Surrey implicitly appealed to a wider community of the virtuous over the heads of Wyatt's enemies – men, it is implied, with power at court. Wyatt is praised for wisdom, patriotism and skill:

> A hed, where wisdom misteries did frame;
> Whose hammers bet styll in that lively brayn
> As on a stithe, where that some work of fame
> Was dayly wrought to turne to Britaines gayn.
> ...
> A hand that taught what might be sayd in ryme;
> That reft Chaucer the glory of his wit (no. 28, lines 5–8, 13–14)

As an example of 'some work of fame ... wrought ... to Britaines gayn', Surrey may have had in mind Wyatt's psalms, where, he tells us in a separate sonnet, 'Rewlers may se in a myrrour clere / The bitter frewte of false concupiscense' (no. 31, lines 10–11). Surrey's Wyatt is clearly an idealised version of Surrey himself: a virtuous man, serving his country, who is threatened by those who use worldly power for corrupt ends. Surrey repeatedly appropriates eloquent models, Wyatt, Aeneas, Dido and David, through whom he articulates themes of isolated virtue, betrayal and loss.

Troy and its battles figure in some of Surrey's more youthful verse as a theme of romantic chivalry ('When ragying love') or as a nostalgic reminder of past glory ('So crewell prison'). In his translations of Virgil's poem of national celebration, the *Aeneid*, into a new English verse form, heroic blank verse, Surrey seems to embark on his own 'work of fame ... to turne to Britaines gayn' (no. 28, lines 7–8).[29] Surrey's choice of Books II and IV, however, focuses on narratives of loss rather than of 'imperial foundation'.[30] In Book II, Aeneas recounts the fall of Troy to Dido, and in Book IV we hear of Aeneas's betrayal of Dido, his departure from Carthage over which Dido rules as queen, and her suicide.

The unrhymed pentameter lines of heroic blank verse that Surrey adapted from Italian models and introduced into English are seen as his major contribution to English prosody, leading directly to Shakespeare's magnificent use of the form at the end of the century. Like classical verse forms, blank verse is unrhymed, but its ten-syllable, largely pentameter lines provide an accentual regularity that moves at a pace that suggests gravity without being ponderous. The form readily accommodates the natural stress patterns of English, producing powerful narrative sequences and the subtle, or dramatic, inflections of a speaking voice. In Book II, Aeneas recounts to Dido his attempts to help his family as Troy burns:

> guided by a god
> I passed through my foes and eke the flame:
> Their wepons and the fire eke gave me place.
> And when that I was come before the gates
> And auncient building of my fathers house,
> My father, whom I hoped to convey
> To the next hils, and did him thearto treat,
> Refused either to prolong his life
> Or bide exile ... (no. 41, lines 829–37)

The spare and rapid telling, with sentences often running over from one line to the next, suggests Aeneas's anxiety and haste. The repeated use of the word 'father' in lines 833–4 starts a sequence which is brought to a sudden halt by the verb 'Refused' at the beginning of line 836. Faced with his father's refusal to leave, Aeneas laments to his mother, the goddess Venus:

> Pyrrhus shall come besprent with Priams blood,
> That gored the son before the fathers face,
> And slew the father at the altar eke.
> O sacred mother, was it then for this
> That you me led through flame and wepons sharp,
> That I might in my secret chaumber see
> Mine enemies; and Ascanius my son,
> My father, with Creusa my swete wife
> Murdred, alas, the one in th'others blood? (lines 871–9)

The flexibility of Surrey's blank verse, its power to suggest Aeneas's anxious emotions and its narrative force, can be more plainly seen by comparing Surrey's lines with a major source, Gavin Douglas's translation in rhymed couplets:

> Is this the way, my haly moder, at thou
> Suld kepe me, fays and fyris passand throu,
> That I behald, within my chawmyr secrete,
> Myne ennemys, and se Ascanyus swete,
> My deir fader, and Crevsa my wyfe,
> Athir in otheris hait blude leys thar lyfe?[31]

Douglas repeatedly inverts natural word order to produce his rhymes, and the impetus of the narrative sequence 'I behald . . . Myne ennemys' is interrupted by what seems information of only marginal interest, 'within my chawmyr secrete'. In Surrey's version, 'my secret chaumber' (line 876) emphasises a moment of particular emotion. So horrific is the violation of this most intimate of spaces that it delays the main verb 'see', which then pauses at the end of line 876 before revealing its dreadful object. The final few lines of Surrey's version, emphasising the possessive 'my' that links all those most dear to Aeneas, culminates a sequence of 'm' sounds in the word 'Murdred', prominently placed at the beginning of line 879.

Both Books II and IV are about the destruction of a happy and glorious past. The elegiac dignity with which Surrey characteristically treats this favourite theme and its victims is exemplified in Dido's epitaph on herself before her suicide in Book IV:

> 'I lived and ranne the course fortune did graunt,
> And under earth my great gost now shall wende.

> A goodly town I built, and saw my walles,
> Happy, alas to happy, if these costes
> The Troyan shippes had never touched aye.'
>
> (no. 42, lines 873–7)

Line 873 strikingly recalls Surrey's elegy on Wyatt who 'Lived and ran the race that nature set' (no. 28, line 31). For Dido, it is 'fortune' that causes her tragedy, and Surrey, like Virgil, but unlike Douglas, allows her dignity and sympathy. Like Surrey's other female speakers, she articulates a position of passive but faithful suffering in the face of loss and deprivation. If the blank verse translation of *Aeneid* II and IV is Surrey's 'work of fame . . . to Britaines gayn', then it is no celebration of national glory, but a nostalgic narrative of the destruction of what is glorious and generous by the brutal exigencies of the present, and the noble suffering that entails.

In his final poems, psalm paraphrases written in late 1546 and early 1547, just before his execution for treason, Surrey again appropriated the voice of a past model of eloquence and suffering, the psalmist David. In these poems he presents himself, as he presented Wyatt, as an innocent man surrounded by enemies.[32] For Psalms 88 and 73, Surrey uses poulter's measure, giving David's voice a capacious but rhythmic line that may draw on the association of the form with song. With its rhymes and lengthy lines, poulter's measure draws our attention more insistently than blank verse to the artifice of the line, but it is also capable of suggesting the stresses and moods of a speaking voice, as in the following passage from Psalm 88:

> In terrour of the just thus raignes iniquitye,
> Armed with power, laden with gold, and dred for crueltye.
> Then vayne the warr might seme that I by faythe mayntayne
> Against the fleshe, whose false effects my pure hert wold distayne.
> For I am scourged still, that no offence have doon,
> By wrathes children; and from birth my chastesing begoon.
>
> (no. 49, lines 27–32)

'Thus' in line 27 invites an extra emphatic stress, producing three stressed syllables in a row, a pattern that is repeated with 'pure hert' in line 30, and 'wrathes children' in line 32, suggesting the anguished voice of the speaker.

For Surrey the vivid and personal voice of the psalmist/poet is not easily distinguishable from national or even divine themes. In Psalm 73, addressed to the Protestant courtier George Blage, Surrey claims for himself the psalmist's role as singer of God's truth: 'The livelye voyce of them that in thy word delight / Must be the trumppe that must resound the glorye of thy might' (no. 48, lines 29–30).[33] Surrey identifies himself with the elect and claims for his verse a role of spiritual witness in a time of corruption and godlessness.

In Surrey's final paraphrase, of Psalm 55, probably written after he knew of his own impending execution, he abandons poulter's measure for an unrhymed twelve-syllable line. The regular but emphatic rhythms of psalms 88 and 73 give way to a Wyatt-like dramatisation of a disturbed and colloquial speaker, surrounded by enemies, like a city betrayed from within:

> Rayne those unbrydled tungs! breake that conjured league!
> For I decyphred have amydd our towne the stryfe:
> Gyle and wrong kept the walles, they ward both day and night
> (no. 50, lines 13–15)

As Aeneas was most disturbed to find the enemy 'in my secret chaumber' (no. 41, line 876), and Dido was betrayed by the lover she trusted, the psalmist/Surrey finds his enemy in his 'bosom [where I] hyde my secret zeale to God' (line 25). Surrey's final elegy is for himself and a betrayal that undermines him from within. Unlike for Dido, there is no assuaging epitaph. Instead the poem concludes with an unresolved, colloquial anger: 'Such patching care I lothe as feeds the welth with lyes' (line 45).

Wyatt's own version of the penitential Psalms was undoubtedly in Surrey's thoughts when he began his own paraphrases, but the version of David and his songs produced by Wyatt is very different. Where Surrey uses the psalmist to articulate personal anguish and betrayal, Wyatt dramatises David in a carefully constructed work that resists any simple identification between Wyatt and psalmist – indeed, Surrey thought Wyatt's David was a model for concupiscent kings.[34] Wyatt follows an Italian model by Aretino that framed the five penitential Psalms within the story of David's penitence for his adultery with Bathsheba, prefacing each of the Psalms with linking narrative and commentary.[35] He thus dramatises the psalmist's voice within an artful framework. The use of *terza rima* for all five Psalms, a rhyme scheme which provides structure without drawing attention to its craft, creates an effect of continuity. The linking narratives, in *ottava rima*, suggest pauses before the psalmist continues his monologue to God.

In the early stages of his penitence, David's art as a singer and musician plays an important role. Before the first Psalm, the psalmist adjusts his deportment and calls on his skills to produce a moving performance:

> Dressed upright, seeking to counterpoise
> His song with sighs, and touching of the strings
> With tender heart, lo, thus to God he sings. (CLII.70–2)

Like Surrey in Psalm 88 (no. 48, lines 23–4), David suggests to God that his role as a poet is important enough to preserve him from death:

> Then if I die and go whereas I fear
> To think thereon, how shall thy great mercy
> Sound in my mouth unto the world's ear? (lines 134–6)

In Surrey's poem this claim goes uncritiqued, but in Wyatt's paraphrases, the psalmist gradually abandons his hubristic confidence in his own poetic skills. By the fifth Psalm, the narrator is uncertain whether 'he cries or sings' (line 26) and after the sixth, he becomes aware that his voice is merely an instrument for God:

> Because he knew he hath alone expressed
> These great things that greater sprite compiled,
> As shawm or pipe lets out the sound impressed,
> By music's art forged tofore and filed . . . (lines 634–7)

The analogy between God's art and man's implicitly relegates the forging and filing of the rough wind instrument of human song to a secondary craft. The seventh Psalm issues, apparently soundlessly, from a trance-like psalmist contemplating the word made flesh in Christ: 'he beholds the Word that should confound / The sword of death, by humble ear to be / In mortal maid' (lines 699–701).

God's act of creation silences David's craft; divine revelation puts 'forged and filed' art in its place. David performs his poems of penitence in a cave where he is unseen and inaudible to the outside world; divine inspiration does not authorise this poet. Of course, Wyatt's own art dramatises David's voice and tells his story, but we are reminded of the artifice and the fiction; the narrator/commentator somehow sees and overhears the silent and invisible psalmist in his cave. For Wyatt, rhetorical skill cannot escape an association with duplicity however skilfully it imitates truth and simplicity.

With Skelton, Surrey and Wyatt, the analogy of the poet's art with David's seems to bring us to the nub of each poet's understanding of poetry and its role. For Skelton, the divine inspiration of David's poetry potentially authorised his own poetic voice and affirmed the dignity and importance of the poetic calling. For Surrey, David gave the highest authorisation to the role of the poet as a personal and eloquent witness of the truth and a figure of noble suffering in a barbarous and faithless world. Wyatt's dramatisation of the penitential Psalms reflects on the limitations but also the power of poetry, able to create lifelike fictions, but unable to free itself from implication in a fallen and crafty world.

Skelton's claims for poetic authority and status can be understood in terms of his own dissatisfaction with the traditional forms and his failure to achieve the traditional roles that had given poets socially accepted significance and dignity. Wyatt's lively awareness of the duplicity of language and the power of rhetoric must have been sharpened by the need to succeed as both courtier and diplomat at the mercy of dangerous kings. Surrey, a privileged descendant of feudal aristocracy, embraces Renaissance models to create a powerful voice for the experience of personal alienation from the brutal *realpolitik* of a changing world.

All three turn their attention to finding new idioms and forms for their modern worlds. Alongside their interest in sophisticated experimentation and innovation in their craft comes a seemingly paradoxical interest in plain styles and the ways in which plainness can seem to give access to an authentic dramatised speaker. Forms such as the skeltonic, the sonnet and blank verse, deflect our attention from their artfulness to the speaking voice they articulate. Perhaps reflecting the conditions of the early Tudor court, these dramatised speakers are characteristically alienated or isolated, conscious of their own integrity in the face of the veniality and duplicity of powerful others. As the work of Skelton and Wyatt acknowledges, however, poets are themselves past masters of the sophisticated and duplicitous arts of language.

Notes

1. James Simpson, *Reform and Revolution*, vol. II, *1300–1547* of *The Oxford Literary History* (Oxford: Oxford University Press, 2004), p. 33. In his discussion of the complex cultural shifts of the period, Simpson identifies royal power as a significant factor.
2. See Greg Walker, *John Skelton and the Politics of the 1520s* (Cambridge: Cambridge University Press, 1988), especially chapter 2.
3. See K. Muir (ed.), *Life and Letters of Sir Thomas Wyatt* (Liverpool: Liverpool University Press, 1963).
4. See W. A. Sessions, *Henry Howard. The Poet Earl of Surrey: A Life* (Oxford: Oxford University Press, 1999).
5. *The Arte of English Poesie by George Puttenham* (1589), ed. Gladys Willcock and Alice Walker (Cambridge: Cambridge University Press, 1936), p. 60.
6. For Skelton's posthumous Elizabethan reputation, see Jane Griffiths, *John Skelton and Poetic Authority* (Oxford: Clarendon Press, 2006), pp. 158–84.
7. Andrew Hadfield, *Literature, Politics and National Identity: Reformation to Renaissance* (Cambridge: Cambridge University Press, 1994), p. 24.
8. For example, Hawes's *Pastime of Pleasure* printed in 1509. The continued popularity at court of aureate verse alongside plainer styles is evident in the 'Fayrfax' MS

of songs (*c.*1500), transcribed as Appendix A in John Stevens, *Music and Poetry in the Early Tudor Court* (London: Methuen, 1961), and the 'Welles' MS (late 1520s and early 1530s), printed in *The Welles Anthology: MS Rawlinson C.813*, ed. S. L. Jansen and K. Jordan (Binhampton, NY: Medieval and Renaissance Texts and Studies, 1991).

9. *John Skelton. The Complete Poems*, ed. John Scattergood (New Haven: Yale University Press, 1983), XXI.836–8. Future references to poem numbers and lines in this edition will be given in parentheses after quotations.
10. *Ibid.*, p. 394.
11. *Medieval English Lyrics. A Critical Anthology*, ed. R. T. Davies (London: Faber and Faber, 1963), p. 237, lines 1–8.
12. Stevens, *Music and Poetry*, pp. 127–32.
13. *Ibid.*, p. 400. See p. 222 for discussion of erotic hunter poems.
14. *Sir Thomas Wyatt. The Complete Poems*, ed. R. A. Rebholz (Harmondsworth: Penguin Books, 1978), CXXXII.17–24. Future references to poem numbers and lines from this edition will be given in parentheses after quotations.
15. Elizabeth Heale, *Wyatt, Surrey and Early Tudor Poetry* (London: Longman, 1998), pp. 78–83.
16. Baldassare Castiglione, *The Book of The Courtier*, translated by George Bull (Harmondsworth: Penguin, 1967), p. 67.
17. Michael R. G. Spiller, *The Development of the Sonnet. An Introduction* (London: Routledge, 1992), p. 85.
18. John 20:17.
19. Matthew 22:20–1. See discussion in Heale, *Wyatt*, pp. 57–8.
20. Wyatt's irregularity has caused difficulties to readers of his sonnets from their first printing in 1557 in *Tottel's Miscellany* (1557), where uneven lines and rhythms were editorially 'corrected'. See the helpful discussion in Suzanne Woods, *Natural Emphasis: English Versification from Chaucer to Dryden* (San Marino, CA: The Huntington Library, 1985), pp. 70–85.
21. Elizabeth Heale, 'Women and the Courtly Love Lyric: The Devonshire MS (BL Additional 17492)', *Modern Language Review*, 90 (1995), pp. 296–313. A number of poems from the 'Devonshire' and 'Blage' MSS are rather cavalierly ascribed to Wyatt and printed in *Collected Poems of Sir Thomas Wyatt*, ed. Kenneth Muir and Patricia Thomson (Liverpool: Liverpool University Press, 1969). The 'Blage' MS has been transcribed by S. O'Keefe, 'T.C.D. MS 160: A Tudor Miscellany', unpublished M.Litt. thesis, Trinity College, Dublin (1986).
22. *Henry Howard, Earl of Surrey: Poems*, ed. Emrys Jones (Oxford: Clarendon Press, 1964), no. 7, lines 10–14. Future references to poem numbers and lines in this edition will be given in parentheses after quotations.
23. I. L. Mumford, 'Musical Settings to the Poems of Henry Howard, Earl of Surrey', *English Miscellany*, 8 (1957), pp. 9–20. There is a useful but unsympathetic account of poulter's measure in John Thompson, *The Founding of English Metre* (London: Routledge and Kegan Paul, 1961), pp. 34–6.

24. For discussions of the origins of the skeltonic, see William Nelson, *John Skelton, Laureate* (New York: Columbia University Press, 1939), pp. 82–101, and John Norton-Smith, 'The Origin of the Skeltonic', *Essays in Criticism*, 23 (1973), pp. 57–62.
25. Muir (ed.) *Life and Letters*, pp. 27–37.
26. Walker, *John Skelton*, pp. 188–91.
27. Griffiths, *John Skelton*, p. 29.
28. Robert J. Meyer-Lee, *Poets and Power from Chaucer to Wyatt* (Cambridge: Cambridge University Press, 2007), pp. 220–32, contrasts Skelton's laureate ambitions with Wyatt, whom he dubs an anti-laureate.
29. See Sessions, *Henry Howard*, pp. 260–87, for a detailed discussion of the form.
30. Simpson, *Reform and Revolution*, p. 119. Simpson uses the phrase in his discussion of Gavin Douglas's and, briefly, Surrey's translations of the *Aeneid*.
31. *Virgil's Aeneid Translated into Scottish Verse by Gavin Douglas*, ed. David F. C. Coldwell, 4 vols., Scottish Text Society, third series 25, 27, 28, 30 (Edinburgh: Blackwood, 1957–64), vol. II, p. 98, lines 185–90.
32. Wyatt had presented himself in this way in 'Who list his wealth', written at the time of his imprisonment in 1536, which quotes Psalm 17 as a headnote: '*Circumdederunt me inimici mei*'.
33. For an account of Surrey's dedication to Blage and its significance in the context of Surrey's trial, see Sessions, *Henry Howard*, pp. 378–83.
34. Surrey is picking up a hint thrown out by Wyatt at line 18 of his Paraphrase of the Penitential Psalms (CLII).
35. Aretino, *I setti psalmi* (Venice: Francsco Marcolini da Forlì, 1536), uses prose narratives to link the psalms.

Chapter 8

Spenser

ANDREW HADFIELD

Edmund Spenser (1552?–99) may well have been the most influential and innovative poet who ever wrote in English. Just after Spenser published *The Shepheardes Calender* in 1579, Sir Philip Sidney, reflecting gloomily on the dearth of English poetry in the 1580s, thought that only the work of Chaucer, the lyrics of the Earl of Surrey, *A Mirror for Magistrates* and Spenser's poem were worth reading.[1] Sidney was exaggerating for polemical effect, of course. But in an astonishing publishing career of seventeen years Spenser transformed the range, nature and potential of English letters. He produced three new versions of the pastoral (*The Calender*, *Colin Clouts come home againe*, *Virgils Gnat*); published letters with a friend, Gabriel Harvey (*Three Proper, and wittie, familiar Letters*); a beast fable (*Mother Hubberds Tale*); a sequence of secular and sacred hymns (*The Fowre Hymns*); a sonnet sequence and other collections of sonnets (*The Amoretti*, *Visions of the Worlds Vanitie*, *The Ruins of Rome*, *The Visions of Petrarch*); a dream-vision (*The Ruines of Time*); elegies (*Daphnäda*, *Astrophel*); an epyllion or little epic (*Muiopotmos*); a lament (*Teares of the Muses*); a marriage hymn (*The Epithalamion*); an epideictic poem (*Prothalamion*); a collection of *Complaints*; and a new form of epic romance, *The Faerie Queene*. Ben Jonson famously commented to William Drummond that Spenser 'in affecting the Ancients, writ no Language', a comment which gives us an idea of what a dominant anomaly he seemed to his contemporaries, and that we should see him as a forcefully experimental poet eager to transform the landscape of English poetry.[2] It is more than a little ironic, then, that Spenser has most frequently been regarded as a conservative figure, a slavish adherent of the Queen's court, or as Karl Marx rather more colourfully put it, 'Elizabeth's arse-kissing poet'.[3]

Spenser obviously shared Sidney's analysis of the present state of English poetry and his career can be seen as a single-handed attempt to revitalise and rethink what could be done in English. In his early letters to Harvey (1580), published just after the *Calender* – probably by Harvey rather than Spenser – Spenser exclaims, 'Why a God's name may not we, as else the

Greeks, have the kingdom of our own language?'[4] The plea is that English might be able to plot its own destiny, just as Greek was able to seize the cultural agenda when establishing European culture. Spenser's hope is that English culture may now be able to rival that of ancient Greece, placing England in the vanguard of European letters as a rival to its pre-eminent contemporaries, Italy and France. He is confident that his poetry will transform the primitive state of English literature and produce work that is as epoch-making as that of Homer, Virgil, Dante and Petrarch, and which will eclipse that of Ronsard, Du Bellay, Tasso, Boiardo and Ariosto. In one of his published letters to Harvey, Spenser signals his intention to write English in quantitative rather than accentual metre, based on the length of syllables rather than stress patterns, in imitation of Latin verse, a further means of making English 'affect the ancients' and so establish its credentials as a serious literary language. Spenser refers with approval to the experiments of Sidney and Edward Dyer: 'they haue by authoritie of their whole Senate, prescribed certaine Lawes and rules of Quantities of English syllables, for English verse: hauing had thereof already greate practise, and drawen mee to their faction'.[5] For good measure, Spenser and Harvey attach a few of their works to the letters, but the experiment with quantitative metre was not a success and did not catch on, Spenser turning instead to the home-grown style in the array of metrical forms on display in the *Calender*.[6]

From the start of his literary career, Spenser looked back both to the ancients and native vernacular poets, principally Chaucer, but also to Langland and Gower, and across to Europe, combining forms, styles and registers as a means of establishing command over English. In the *Calender* Spenser imitates Virgil by beginning his literary career with a pastoral poem, signalling his eventual move towards the epic.[7] He also employs the forms and style of European writers, such as the neo-Latin eclogues of Mantuan and the pastorals and elegies of the French poet, Clément Marot, as the commentator, E. K. (perhaps another pseudonym of Spenser himself), acknowledges.[8] The series of poems employs a number of native models, literary and popular, principally the almanac/calendar that it imitates. The *Calender* also contains characters such as Diggon Davie and Piers, who come from a well-established English tradition of ploughman poetry written in the wake of *Piers Plowman*.[9] And, of course, Spenser's adoption of the name Colin Clout is borrowed from John Skelton's verse, establishing a link to a Henrician tradition.

The *Calender* is a showcase work. The book is produced as though it were a humanist edition of a major Latin writer, with commentary, woodcuts, dedications, and in a carefully chosen variety of fonts.[10] It also has a deliberately English style, with the use of a blunt and direct vernacular, rough rhythms that gesture towards the native alliterative style, harsh stress patterns and lines divided by a caesura; and the whole is characterised by a conspicuously Anglo-Saxon vocabulary. The opening of the April eclogue, a dialogue between the shepherds Thenot and Hobbinoll in praise of Elizabeth, is a good example of this aspect of the poem:

> THENOT
> Tell me good Hobbinoll, what garres thee greete?
> What? Hath some Wolfe thy tender Lambes ytorne?
> Or is thy Bagpipe broke, that soundes so sweete?
> Or art thou of thy loued lasse forlorne?
> Or bene thine eyes attempred to the yeare,
> Quenching the gasping furrowes thirst with rayne?
> Like April shoure, so stremes the trickling teares
> Adowne thy cheeke, to quenche thy thirstye payne
>
> HOBBINOLL
> Nor thys, nor that, so muche doeth make me mourne,
> But for the ladde, whome long I lovd so deare,
> Nowe loues a lasse, that all his loue doth scorne:
> He plonged in payne, his tressed locks doth teare.
>
> Shepheardes delights he dooth them all forsweare,
> Hys pleasaunt Pipe, which made vs merriment,
> Hy wilfully hath broke, and doth forbeare
> His wonted songs, wherein he all outwent.[11]

These lines exhibit many of the literary pyrotechnics that characterise the poem, a sign of Spenser's ambition and confidence that he alone had the ability to fundamentally alter the course of English poetry. The headnote informs the reader that 'This Aeclogue is purposely intended to the honour and prayse of our most gracious souereigne, Queene Elizabeth', but the poem starts with Hobbinoll (a figure of Gabriel Harvey, as the *Calender* itself makes clear) lamenting his thwarted passion for Colin (Spenser) who has left him for Rosalind. Moreover, as the opening lines indicate, the concerns of the shepherds are centred on their own lives, so that the relationship between the writers and the pastoral figures are rooted in their own worlds and not obviously connected to the ostensible subject of the poem. It is only when the subject turns to the songs that Colin composes for Rosalind that Thenot persuades Hobbinol to perform one, and he chooses to sing a complex 'laye' in her honour:

> Ye dayntye Nymphs, that in this blessed Brooke
> doe bathe your brest,

For sake your watry bowres, and hether looke,
    at my request:
And eke you Virgins, that on *Parnasse* dwell,
Whence floweth *Helicon* the learned well,
    Helpe me to blaze
    Her worthy praise,
Which in her sexe doth all excell. (lines 37–45)

There is a striking contrast between this hymn of praise, with its classical references (Helicon, Parnassus), register and diction (bowers, blaze, praise), elaborate rhyme scheme (ababccddc), which recalls the interlaced style of Italian poetry, varied line lengths (pentameters and dimeters) and metres (iambs and trochees), and the jog-trot of the quatrains produced by Hobbinol and Thenot. The notes to the poem encourage the reader to make this division between the types of poetry. E. K. glosses the phrase 'Colin thou kenst' in line 21, with a note about regional dialect: 'Seemeth hereby that Colin perteyneth to some Southern noble man, and perhaps in Surrye or Kent, the rather because he so often nameth the Kentish downes, and before, As lythe as lasse of Kent' (p. 66), which encourages speculation about Spenser's life and represents him – at least here – as rooted in the world of the shepherds. In contrast, the note to line 37, the first line of the song to Eliza, is in Latin: 'Ye daintie is, as it were an Exordium ad preparandos animos' (p. 67).

The poetry that has currency at court would appear to be in opposition to that produced by the shepherds, who are closer to a more popular understanding of literature, even though they can easily produce what is required by the Queen when necessary. Furthermore, the relationships between the figures in the poem are all at odds: Colin loves Rosalind and so does not produce any poetry, an inversion of the normal expectation that passion produces verse; Hobbinol loves Colin and so reads his verse to Eliza; Eliza is supposedly loved by her subjects but is given second-hand gifts. As Richard McCabe has pointed out, the eclogue undoubtedly criticises Elizabeth for her projected marriage with François, Duke of Alençon, showing that a union with a foreign prince would alienate her people.[12] It also indicates that writing the best poetry in English designed to make serious demands upon a sophisticated reader involves a whole host of allusions, styles, registers, perceptions and ambiguities that need to be pieced together. Not only must the reader be alert to the text of the poem itself, but he or she must think about the form of the printed book, the prefaces, layout, notes, pictures and paratexts that make up the work, as well as its relationship to external events of significance, usually through sly hints and references. In the *Calender* Spenser did more than simply write an important poem: he showed what could be done with a printed book and how writers and readers could establish a relationship that would change the ways in which the nation represented and thought about itself through its literature.

The range and diversity of the *Calender* was followed, after a hiatus of eleven years, by the innovative stanza form of *The Faerie Queene*, the first edition of which was published in 1590, although Spenser had been working on the poem for a long time. *The Faerie Queene* probably began life in a more Italianate version than its published form demonstrates, with parts of Books III and IV forming its initial core.[13] He developed a new poetic form, which now bears his name, the Spenserian stanza. This consists of a stanza of nine lines, the first eight lines being pentameters, and the last an alexandrine, with an interlaced rhyme scheme, ababbcbcc, a complex form which placed great demands on the poet, especially as he was writing in English (an analytic language which does not possess the range of word endings that a synthetic language, such as Italian, has). By simply trying to write a verse narrative using this stanza, Spenser was going beyond what his Italian predecessors had achieved using *ottava rima*. He was also placing greater demands on his technical competence as a poet than Chaucer had done in what was generally considered to be the greatest English poem before Spenser, *Troilus and Criseyde*, which had used rhyme royal, written in stanzas of seven iambic pentameters, with the rhyme scheme ababbcc. Chaucer's verse, also used in *The Parliament of Fowls*, which Spenser imitated in *Two Cantos of Mutabilitie*, had become the defining form for court poetry in English, and was employed by such diverse writers as John Lydgate, Robert Henryson, James I of Scotland, Thomas Wyatt and Thomas Sackville: in short, virtually every major poet writing in the British Isles, later including Spenser himself in *Fowre Hymns*. To produce a form that required more technical skill than his great English and Italian predecessors showed immense self-confidence and ambition, both for himself and English poetry.

The last two lines of the Spenserian stanza often work as a couplet, in some ways rather like the ending of the English sonnet, commenting on the previous lines but also, with their additional two syllables in the final line, slowing down the verse and forcing the reader to halt his or her progress through the narrative and reflect on what is taking place. The stanza is used to great effect by Despair, the demonic figure whose aim is to tempt the Red-Cross Knight to commit suicide as a means of ending his troublesome quest. Despair's duplicitous words and logic function as a commentary on the ways in which Spenser's verse works, tempting the reader to follow false reason and to desire, like Red-Cross, the painless state of endless sleep:

He there does now enioy eternall rest
And happie ease, which thou doest want and craue,
And further from it daily wanderest:
What if some litle paine the passage haue,
That makes fraile flesh to feare the bitter waue?
Is not short paine well borne, that brings long ease,
And layes the soule to sleepe in quiet graue?
Sleepe after toyle, port after stormie seas,
Ease after warre, death after life does greatly please. (I.ix.40)[14]

The spurious logic of the argument is not difficult for the alert reader to detect. What Despair claims would be true enough if the soul did indeed expire with the body and remain in the grave, but this was thought unlikely to be the case, and the suicide was singled out for particular punishment from God because he or she had desecrated what God had created and given the individual, which is, of course, why Despair appears at the knight's lowest point and provides him with this particularly dangerous temptation. Spenser later describes Red-Cross as 'charmed with inchaunted rimes' (I.ix.48.line 8), a highly self-conscious acknowledgment of the power of poetry, its pleasures and its dangers, ones that are especially relevant to a poem so concerned with the act of reading. Here we experience a verse that has to be read slowly if read aloud because of the large number of long vowel sounds, and which has a hypnotic effect through its repetitive structure, something the reader will either experience directly or at second hand through an appreciation of how such words would have seemed to the exhausted and morally bankrupt knight. 'Ease' is used three times (in lines 2, 6 and 9), and 'sleep' twice in succession (lines 7 and 8). The last two lines are worth particular attention. A sibilant 's' is used three times in line eight, as is an assonant 'o', and there is a link to the final line through the rhyme 'seas/Ease', which is then recalled through the final word, 'please'. Given the heavy pause demanded by the caesura in each line, and the naturally retarding effect of the final alexandrine, Spenser's lines imitate the process of falling asleep, the verse slowing down as it progresses, a bait that the Red-Cross Knight takes, showing that he no longer has the ability to control his destiny and is dangerously open to the power of suggestion.

Spenser's poetry always places heavy demands on readers. There is a particular obsession with the significance and range of meanings of individual words, both as semantic units within particular stanzas and in terms of etymology. The opening line of the poem, 'A Gentle Knight was pricking on the plaine', is a particularly witty and surprising pun designed to challenge the reader. Its wit is directly related to the fact that it is a straightforward double entendre, one that the reader is undoubtedly not expecting to encounter at the start of such an apparently exalted work. 'Pricking' here means both 'spurring', suggesting that the knight errant encourages his horse to gallop on rapidly, and, in a more lewd sense, and derived in part from the other, being led by his penis. Both senses of the word were in frequent use in early modern English, as the OED records, Philemon Holland, possibly with a hint of bawdy, stating that 'The Queene [was] ever at his elbow to pricke and proke him forward' (1609), and Robert Dallington using the word very definitely to mean 'penis' in 1592 ('The pissing Boye lift vp his pricke'). And, as we will learn through reading the opening book, the Red-Cross Knight's particular problem is his prick, something that does indeed lead him on, a flaw that might seem especially inappropriate in a knight who represents Holiness, but which also serves to remind readers how hard virginity is to achieve and how few were chosen to take this particular path of righteousness. If we also bear in mind that the use of the term in an epic romance reminds Spenser's readers that he demands they pay careful attention to their own native English traditions, as well as a European and classical heritage, we can understand how much information we can glean from this one line.

The opening canto serves as a reading lesson designed to give the reader the means to find a way through the labyrinth of the poem. The Red-Cross Knight, following his counterparts in medieval romance, wanders into the wood, along with Una and her dwarf, a familiar means of beginning an adventure. In describing a vast range of trees, all of which have a symbolic resonance, Spenser is not producing a series of allegorical triggers so much as alerting us to the symbolic import of the wood:

> And foorth they passe, with pleasure forward led,
> Ioying to heare the birdes sweete harmony,
> Which therein shrouded from the tempest dred,
> Seemd in their song to scorne the cruell sky.
> Much can they prayse the trees so straight and hy,
> The sayling Pine, the Cedar proud and tall,
> The vine-prop Elme, the Poplar neuer dry,
> The builder Oake, sole king of forrests all,
> The Aspine good for staues, the Cypresse funeral.
>
> The Laurell, meed of mightie Conquerors
> And Poets sage, the Firre that weepeth still,
> The Willow worne of forloren Paramours,
> The Eugh obedient to the benders will,

> The Birch for shaftes, the Sallow for the mill,
> The Mirrhe sweete bleeding in the bitter wound,
> The warlike Beech, the Ash for nothing ill,
> The Fruitfull Oliue, and the Plantane round,
> The caruer Holme, the Maple seldom inward sound. (1.i.8–9)

This looks like a moment overloaded with symbolism, but it isn't, at least not in the way that a reader might imagine symbolism to work. The trees do not, in fact, function as signs that carry useful and resonant information relevant to the narrative. Rather, in listing all these traditional symbols Spenser is drawing the reader's attention to the danger of the wood, in which everything is not quite what it seems, especially the apparent symbols.[15] The symbolic trees actually function as anti-symbols. They warn the reader to look elsewhere for meaning as they play no immediate role in the story apart from showing us that the Red-Cross Knight and Una are not very good readers themselves. The description also suggests that the text will provide two reading patterns layered on top of each other: one that looks as though it tells the truth, which actually misleads those who follow its path, and one that is harder to spot but which does actually lead the reader in the right direction. The opening line of the next verse, 'Led with delight, they thus beguile the way' (10, line 1) shows that the three travellers are not yet – and perhaps never will be – sophisticated readers who can find the true path. Instead, they take a sensuous enjoyment from the plethora of symbolic forms on offer, showing no ability to distinguish between what might really matter and what is inconsequential or misleading.

The Red-Cross Knight's first error is to imagine that in killing the half-serpent, half-woman monster whom he encounters immediately afterwards in Error's Den, he has destroyed error, a sign that he reads symbols too literally and that he is not alive to the nuances of appearance and the clues provided by descriptions. He makes this error, despite the warning contained in the line, 'Her vomit full of bookes and papers was' (20, line 6), an indication that the death of a beast named Error will not eliminate the possibility of errors and may, in fact, make them easier to disseminate when they are no longer contained within one overall symbolic form. Immediately after this event the dangers of the Red-Cross Knight's over-confidence become apparent when he encounters a figure of whom he should be suspicious, later revealed to us as Archimago, the evil magician who separates the knight and Una, initially by feeding his lustful fantasies (reminding us of the significance of the verb 'pricking'):

At length they chaunst to meet vpon the way
An aged Sire, in long black weedes yclad,
His feete all bare, his beard all hoarie gray,
And by his belt his booke he hanging had;
Sober he seemde, and very sagely sad,
And to the ground his eyes were lowly bent,
Simple in shew, and voyde of malice bad,
And all the way he prayd, as he went,
And often knockt his brest, as one that did repent. (1.i.29)

Unlike the apparently symbolic trees, which delight but do not signify, the description of Archimago is replete with clues that direct the reader's interpretation. He looks like a monk or hermit, with his black robes, grey beard and bare feet, which indicates that he probably belongs to a Catholic tradition. We do not know what book he carries. The initial assumption is that it is probably the Bible, but we learn a few stanzas later that he has a study full of magic books (36), so this may be one of them. As the stanza progresses, our suspicions, along with those of the travellers, should be aroused. Archimago seems sober and sad, which implies that he may not be, and the appearance without the reality of sanctity is confirmed in the last two lines when we learn that, although he appears modest, he prays ostentatiously and repents in public in lines that invert the sincere repentance of the publican in Luke 18:13 who 'would not lift up so much as his eyes to heauen, but smote his brest, saying, O God be mercifull to me a sinner'.[16] The Red-Cross Knight's grasp of allegorical reading is so primitive that he is able to understand the meaning of a monster that lives in Error's Den but not the effects of destroying the unified symbol, nor to be wary of the signs of religion without the substance. Spenser is showing us how superficial the Reformation has been in England, hardly surprisingly given its recent origin, and how its profound effects are yet to manifest themselves.

While the description of Archimago points us forward to the errors and trials of the Red-Cross Knight, it also refers us back to the description of Una near the start of the book. If we return and reread this stanza, we will notice connections with the later verse:

A louely Ladie rode him faire beside,
Vpon a lowly Asse more white then snow,
Yet she much whiter, but more the same did hide
Vnder a vele, that wimpled was full low,
And ouer all a blacke stole she did throw,
As one that inly mourned: so was she sad,

And heauie sat vpon her palfrey slow:
Seemed in heart some hidden care she had,
And by her in a line a milke white lambe she lad. (I.i.4)

Just as Archimago seems sober, so does Una seem as if she is hiding some cares; just as he looks as if he repents, so does she look as if she mourns. Several things should worry us about this description: Una is associated with and surrounded by symbols of traditional religion. There is an ass and a lamb, which may not connote anything especially troubling, but do indicate the need to hide behind symbols, especially given the description of the numerous trees in the wood five stanzas later. More pertinently, there is the description of her clothing, the black stole and the wimple, which make it obvious that she is dressed as a nun, linking her directly to Archimago and also indicating that she is not really a young woman ready for marriage, most especially to a knight who has been 'pricking on the plaine'. The fact that one cannot determine her thoughts and feelings, which are hidden away, is a further sign of her lack of openness to the prospect of marriage with the need for a declaration of mutual desire. The first two lines of the next stanza, 'So pure an innocent, as that same lambe, / She was in life and euery vertuous lore' (5, lines 1–2), confirm the suspicion that there may well be no easy relationship between the desire for purity and holiness, the subject of this book, and the desire for marriage, the subject of the third book, when Britomart takes over the narrative. It is embarrassingly easy for Archimago to part the Red-Cross Knight and Una, something he achieves through the creation of the false Una, who first tempts the knight and is then seen sporting with a squire, so that the lovers are parted by the start of the second canto. Moreover, the marriage is never consummated, as the knight is called away to serve Gloriana (I.xii. 42) (who, as the letter to Raleigh appended to the first edition of the poem informs us, was a version of Elizabeth, the Virgin Queen).[17] After he passes the quest on to Guyon, the Knight of Temperance, at the start of Book II, we only see the Red-Cross Knight one more time when he appears half-dressed in the Castle of the incontinent (lustful) Malecasta. The knight accompanies Britomart to the Castle, but when he becomes involved in the fray that develops, Spenser shows that we cannot be sure for whom his character fights, through one of his characteristic devices, the use of ambiguous pronouns. The line 'Her succourd eke the Champion of the bloudy Crosse' (III.i.64.l. 9) leaves us to decide whether he is trying to support Britomart or Malecasta.

The Faerie Queene is not a work that declares its hand in the first book. The truth is that the Book of Holiness needs to be read in terms of the inability of most people to live a chaste life, a recognition that was explicit within Christian teachings such as St Paul's letters to the Corinthians, in which he declared that if people felt they could not abstain from sexual intercourse, it was 'better to marrie then to burne' (I Cor. 7:9). This injunction formed one of the most powerful Protestant critiques of late medieval Christianity and led to the great emphasis placed on the need for marriage in general and married priests, and hostility to monastic institutions.[17] The Red-Cross Knight and Una are the first of a long line of dysfunctional lovers and ill-matched couples in the poem, looking forward to the elderly, jealous Malbecco and the lustful, easily seduced Hellenore, Florimell and her suitors, and the substantial list who populate Book VI: Crudor and Briana; Turpine and Blandina, Mirabella; and Coridon and Pastorella. What seems like the obvious allegory of Book I, that holiness is a virtue in itself that can be valued above all others, turns out to be anything but that, and the message that develops in *The Faerie Queene* is that the body is neglected at our peril. If the poem has an explicitly Protestant message this would appear to be it. Spenser's work always refuses easy judgments and makes the reader aware of moral complexity. It is, paradoxically enough, only through scrupulous attention to sexuality that chastity can be understood, and it is no accident that the quest of Britomart, the Knight of Chastity, begins with the revelations of her future marriage to Artegll, the Knight of Justice, in Merlin's magic mirror, a vision that takes place as a puberty rite administered by her nurse, Glaunce (Britomart refers to her 'bleeding bowels' (III.ii.39.line 2)).

Spenser's habitual mode is to complicate the allegory as the narrative progresses. The Garden of Adonis which stands at the epicentre of the six-book poem (III. vi) appears to be a representation of fecund self-reproduction that serves as an image of ideal nature. Yet its title should alert us to the fact that this perfect world is time-bound and is always on the cusp of destruction, just as the lovely young boy beloved by Venus is always about to die when his story is told. The image of the mons vereris in paradise, a 'stately Mount' (III.vi.43, line 2) that appears to organise and focus the natural fertility of the garden, also reminds us that this is a fiction within a fiction as reproduction is never so simple for men and women. Britomart's painful journey is a more accurate and trustworthy guide to what real people experience. This allegorical set-piece also forces the reader to look back and think about art and nature in Acrasia's bower, described in such intense, overpowering detail in the longest canto in the poem. There, Acrasia tries to seduce Guyon, the Knight of Temperance, with 'her false eyes', which are 'fast fixt in his sight, / As seeking medicine, whence she was strong, / Or greedily depasturing delight' (II.xii.73, lines 2–4). The last adjective compares her to a grazing cow and so links Acrasia to Grill, who is referred to at the end of the book (II.xii.86–7). Grill was the companion of Ulysses who was turned into a pig by Circe, an animal life he preferred to his former humanity. When a musician sings a version of the *carpe diem* motif derived from Tasso, the moral of Book II seems clear enough:

> So passeth, in the passing of a day,
> Of mortall life the leafe, the bud, the flowre,
> Ne more doth flourish after first decay,
> That earst was sought to decke both bed and bowre,
> Of many a Ladie, and many a Paramowre:
> Gather therefore the Rose, whilest yet is prime,
> For soone comes age, that will her pride deflower:
> Gather the Rose of loue, whilest yet is time,
> Whilest louing thou mayst loued be with equall crime. (II.xii.75)

Surrender to the dictates of the flesh, however appealingly this might be expressed and with whatever superficial logic the case might be made, and you risk losing your humanity. Guyon's destruction of the Bower of Bliss also appears to endorse this common moral message. But when we encounter the Garden of Adonis we surely cannot be so certain. There can be no future without sex, whatever we might want. Nature will grind to a halt, sustained only in fictional forms, if this stubborn reality is ignored. It is too simple to imagine that there is an easy answer to the problem of sexual behaviour, or that issues that are related to sex are simply sexual. The Garden of Adonis is a stark reminder to readers who have read the destruction of Acrasia's bower as an inevitable triumph that the world is too complex to entertain such one-sided solutions. That *locus amoenus* gestures towards a world beyond its confines, looking back to previous episodes which we now have to revisit and refigure. As we do so Spenser warns us that in fairyland readers need to be alert in order to sort out the fictional chaff from the real wheat, learning from the failures of the characters and the difficult process of the allegory.

Spenser does not simply force us to read carefully and scrupulously within one particular work, tracking back and rethinking what we have learned at any particular moment. He works inter-textually as well as intra-textually, making connections across his writing. The first edition of *The Faerie Queene* ends with Britomart staring at the lovers she has helped to unite, Scudamore and Amoret, as they combine to create a hermaphroditic form:

> Had ye them seene, ye would haue surely thought,
> That they had beene that faire *Hermaphrodite*,
> Which that rich *Romane* of white marble wrought,
> And in his costly Bath causd to bee site:

So seemd those two, as growne together quite,
That *Britomart* halfe enuying their blesse,
Was much empassiond in her gentle sprite,
And to her selfe oft wisht like happinesse,
In vaine she wisht, that fate n'ould let her yet possesse.
(III.xii.46 (1590 edn.))

This is a striking moment, one of the many set pieces in the poem that provoke and disturb, designed to stay in the memory, in line with the Horatian theory of poetry as *ut pictura poesis* whereby 'the poet and the painter both think in visual images which the one expresses in poetry, the other in pictures'.[18] No source for the description of the statue has ever been identified – assuming there is one – so we cannot know whether what the rich Roman saw from his bath was high art or base pornography. Probably, that is the point. We then follow Britomart's mixture of jealousy (the description, quite deliberately, has her as 'half enuying' their joy), passion (inspired by great art or provoking a desire for intercourse?) and isolation (wishing that she could be part of a similar fusion). In doing so, the reader experiences Britomart's feelings at one remove, with, surely, a certain amount of embarrassment, which is why the episode, tastefully but provocatively phrased, has a significant impact. Just as Britomart is confused as well as excited by what she sees, so are we troubled and interested by what we read. Even if Amoret and Scudamore are not physically making love, we are encouraged to imagine that they might be. Then we have to ask ourselves why we care about this issue: is it because we are sharing a tender moment of union that expresses the joys of marriage, or are we simply voyeurs, hoping to catch a glimpse of a couple going all the way? In framing this concluding vision as he does, Spenser is forcing his readers to think about what they value in poetry, and why they read it, bringing us back full circle to the issues raised at the start of Book I.

Perhaps the key word in the stanza is the penultimate, 'yet'. Britomart will have her day, even though it does not happen in the extant poem. She is a young, passionate woman who is on a quest that will lead her eventually to marriage. Seeing Amoret and Scudamore is simply part of the process of growing up, learning the mechanics of lovemaking as part-inspiration, part-horror. Spenser re-uses this scene in his marriage hymn, the *Epithalamion*, a great poetic tour de force, designed to celebrate his union with Elizabeth Boyle, his second wife, on 11 June 1594:

Who is the same, which at my window peepes?
Or whose is that faire face, that shines so bright?

Is it not Cinthia, she that neuer sleepes,
But walkes about high heauen al the night?
O fayreset goddesse, do thou not envy
My love with me to spy:
For thou likewise didst loue, though now vnthought,
And for a fleece of woll, which priuily,
The Latmian shephard once vnto thee brought,
His pleasures with thee wrought.
Therefore to vs be fauourable now;
And sith of wemens labours thou hast charge,
And generation goodly dost enlarge,
Encline thy will t'effect our wishfull vow.
And the chast wombe informe with timely seed,
That may our comfort breed:
Till which we cease our hopefull hap to sing,
Ne let the woods vs answere, nor our Eccho ring.

(lines 372–89; *Works*, vol. VIII, p. 251)

Instead of Britomart staring guiltily at Amoret and Scudamore, we have the unedifying scene of Cynthia, the goddess of chastity, and a form of Elizabeth throughout Spenser's works, looking through the window at Edmund and his Elizabeth. Read one way, this might seem innocent enough: the newlyweds live in Ireland and require particular protection from their monarch, and would surely welcome the knowledge that she will always be around to ensure their safety. Diana/Cynthia was chaste herself, but was the goddess of fertility and so was often asked to bless newlyweds with children. And, after all, the image is just that of the moon shining at night. But this would seem to be another example of deceptively easy symbolism that misleads the reader. As Spenser reminds us forcefully enough in another poem published in the same year as the *Epithalamion*, although dated four years earlier (27 December 1591), Elizabeth's shepherds had not fared especially well in her other island. *Colin Clouts come home againe* is another pastoral, one that looks back to the *Calender*, featuring many of the same shepherds – Colin, Cuddy, Hobbinol – and alluding to Virgil's eclogues in the opening lines, just as he had in the earlier poem. This time, however, the rustic Englishmen have been transported to Ireland and are eager to hear news of the homeland they have been forced to leave behind from Colin, who has just returned from a rare visit to Cynthia's land. Colin is vigorously questioned by Cuddy, who has difficulty understanding that there is land anywhere else:

Ah *Cuddy* (then quoth *Colin*) thous a fon [fool],
That hast not seene least part of natures worke:
Much more there is vnkend, then thou doest kon,
And much more that does from mens knowledge lurke.
For that same land much larger is then this,
And other men and beasts and birds doth feed:
There fruitfull corne, faire trees, fresh herbage is
And all things else that good liuing creatures need.

. . .

Both heauen and heauenly graces do much more
(Quoth he) abound in that same land, then this.
For there all happie peace and plenteous store
Conspire in one to make contented blisse:
No wayling there nor wretchednesse is heard,
No bloodie issues nor no leprosies,
No griesly famine, nor no raging sweard,
No nightly bodrags, nor no hue and cries;
The shepheardes there abroad may safely lie,
On hills and downes, withouten dread or daunger:
No ravenous wolues the good mans hope destroy,
Nor outlawes fell affray the forest raunger.

(lines 292–9, 308–19, *Works*, vol. VIII, pp. 156–7)

Rural England is an idyll where shepherds are properly protected and can flourish, whereas Ireland is a wasteland. The settlers are attacked day and night and there is constant violence and rebellion; there is also famine, not caused by the inadequacy of the farmland, but by the fractious body politic; and the danger from the wolves is both literal and metaphorical, wolves standing for Catholics, often disguised in sheep's clothing. *Colin Clout*, sixteen years on from his debut in the *Calender*, now has to face the harsh reality of life in Ireland. The shepherds are so alienated and remote from their rulers that they not only know nothing about conditions in rural England, but do not understand where or what England is. Their counterparts in the *Calender* sang songs in praise of the Queen, however barbed their undertone might have been. Here, they are so cut off from her that they have to establish their own version of Englishness in Ireland as they confront a ubiquitous and dangerous enemy determined to destroy their way of life.

Read against *Colin Clout*, the description of Cynthia in the *Epithalamion* as the goddess who never sleeps, always abroad protecting her flock, reads more like a pious hope than a description of reality. It draws attention to the vulnerable situation of the newlyweds in a remote corner of Elizabeth's dominions, soon after the start of the Nine Years' War, the most serious threat to Tudor rule in Ireland. Equally worrying for the couple is the pointed contrast between their hope for a life of married bliss, blessed with children, and the Queen's status as a virgin long past the age of reproduction with no heir apparent. Cynthia/Elizabeth has made their future uncertain through her inability to secure the succession, placing them in further danger. Any reader in 1596 would have been acutely aware of the chaos that a change of dynasty was likely to produce, witnessed most recently in England by the Wars of the Roses, which ended when Henry VII, Elizabeth's grandfather, became King. Indeed, in the chronicle history shown to Britomart in Merlin's magic mirror we learn of Henry's accession and the triumph of his descendant, 'a royall virgin' (*The Faerie Queene*, III.iii.49.line 6), who threatens Spanish rule and brings peace to the Low Countries ('which shall / Stretch her white rod ouer the *Belgicke* shore, / And the great Castle [i.e., Castile] smite so sore with all' [lines 6–8]). However, Merlin then has to stop, 'As ouercomen of the spirites powre, / Or other ghastly spectacle dismayd, / That secretly he saw, yet note discoure' (III.iii.50, lines 1–3), a hiatus that would have reminded any reader in 1590 that the future was uncertain and that Elizabeth's great triumphs might well count for nothing without a successor.

Most pointed of all is the contrast between the future that Edmund and Elizabeth can enjoy and the Queen's barren prospects. The stanza in *The Epithalamion* reads as a memento mori, like the more frequently cited stanza in 'Two Cantos of Mutabilitie', which reminds Elizabeth that she is ageing rapidly:

> And first, concerning her that is the first,
> Euen you faire *Cynthia*, whom so much ye make
> *Ioues* dearest darling, she was bred and nurst
> On *Cynthus* hill, whence she her name did take:
> Then is she mortall borne, how-so ye crake;
> Besides, her face and countenance euery day
> We changed see, and sundry forms partake,
> Now hornd, now round, now bright, now brown and gray:
> So that *as changefull as the Moone* men vse to say.
>
> (*Faerie Queene*, VII.vii.50)

In this stanza Elizabeth/Cynthia is reminded of her past youth in order to emphasise her decaying features. In the *Epithalamion* she is reminded of her past love for the 'Latmian shepherd', Endymion, who seduced her with the gift of a fleece, for which he was sent to sleep for ever. The reference looks back to John Lyly's play, the court allegory, *Endymion: the Man in the Moon* (1588), which quite clearly represented Endymion as Robert Dudley, Earl of

Leicester, the one Englishman whom Elizabeth might have married. Elizabeth had her chance and did not take it and now she looks down on Mr and Mrs Spenser with envy, the word reminding us of Britomart's reaction to Amoret and Scudamore's passionate embrace. Whereas Britomart would simply have to wait for her joy, however, the pleasures brought by the Latmian shepherd are long gone (Dudley died in 1588). There is a savage irony in Spenser asking Elizabeth to bless his marriage: one reason why she never sleeps is because she has no one to sleep with. Elizabeth has failed to provide a secure future for her subjects by neglecting her marital duties, which is why she is represented looking through the window. In effect, Spenser has modified or even reversed the myth of Actaeon, used frequently by Spenser in various ways in his poetry, a figure who was transformed into a stag and then torn to pieces by his hounds after he came across Diana bathing naked. Here the Queen is the voyeur. The myth of Diana's fierce self-protectiveness has also been transformed: she has turned herself into Actaeon and put her subjects in danger of being torn apart by the sort of civil war that could result from a contested succession. Spenser's lines may contain a certain sympathy for Elizabeth's splendid isolation as virgin queen, but they also remind readers that the bio-politics of the monarch generally determined the lives of his or her subjects.

Nevertheless, it is possible that recent readings have exaggerated the aggressive and oppositional nature of Spenser's poetry. After all, he was awarded a life pension of £50 by Elizabeth in 1591.[19] Perhaps the best way to read Spenser is to think more about the possibilities that he opened up for other writers, contemporaries and his successors, only part of which can be related to the political positions that his works adopted.[20] More significant still was Spenser's exploration of new forms of verse, his invention of the Spenserian stanza, which had such an impact on the subsequent history of English poetry, and his realisation of what could be done with, as well as through, the new medium of print.[21]

Notes

1. Sir Philip Sidney, *An Apology for Poetry*, ed. R. W. Maslen (Manchester: Manchester University Press, 2002), p. 110.
2. Cited in R. M. Cummings (ed.), *Spenser: The Critical Heritage* (London: Routledge, 1971), p. 294.
3. Cited in David Norbrook, *Poetry and Politics in the English Renaissance* (London: Routledge, 1984), p. 311.
4. *The Works of Edmund Spenser: A Variorum Edition*, ed. Edwin Greenlaw, 11 vols. (Baltimore: Johns Hopkins University Press, 1932–57), vol. x, p. 16 (hereafter referred to as *Works*, both in the notes and parenthetically in the text). For

commentary, see Richard Helgerson, *Forms of Nationhood: The Elizabethan Writing of England* (Chicago: University of Chicago Press, 1992), introduction.

5. *Works*, vol. x, p. 6.
6. See Derek Attridge, *Well-Weighed Syllables: Elizabethan Verse in Classical Metres* (Cambridge: Cambridge University Press, 1974), pp. 188–92.
7. See Patrick Cheney, *Spenser's Famous Flight: A Renaissance Idea of a Literary Career* (Toronto: University of Toronto Press, 1993).
8. Helen Cooper, 'Mantuan', in A. C. Hamilton (ed.), *The Spenser Encyclopedia* (London: Routledge, 1990), pp. 452–3; Anne Lake Prescott, *French Poets and the English Renaissance: Studies in Fame and Transformation* (New Haven: Yale University Press, 1978).
9. See Andrew Hadfield, 'Foresters, Ploughmen and Shepherds: Versions of Tudor Pastoral', in Michael Pincombe and Cathy Shrank (eds.), *The Oxford Handbook to Tudor Literature* (Oxford: Oxford University Press, 2009), pp. 537–53.
10. Michael McCanles, '*The Shepheardes Calender* as Document and Monument', *SEL*, 22 (1982), pp. 5–19.
11. *The Shepheardes Calender* in *The Shorter Poems*, ed. Richard A. McCabe (Harmondsworth: Penguin, 1999), April, lines 1–16. Subsequent references to this edition in parentheses in the text.
12. Richard A. McCabe, ' "Liitle booke, thy selfe present": The Politics of Presentation in *The Shepherdes Calender*', in Howard Erskine-Hill and Richard A. McCabe (eds.), *Presenting Poetry: Composition, Publication, Reception* (Cambridge: Cambridge University Press, 1995), pp. 1–40, at pp. 24–7.
13. The best account of what probably happened remains Josephine Waters Bennett, *The Evolution of 'The Faerie Queene'* (Chicago: University of Chicago Press, 1942).
14. All references in parentheses are to *The Faerie Queene*, ed. A. C. Hamilton, revised edition (London: Routledge, 2001).
15. See Helen Cooper, *The English Romance in Time: Transforming Motifs from Geoffrey of Monmouth to the Death of Shakespeare* (Oxford: Oxford University Press, 2004), p. 70.
16. This, and the quotation on page 146, are taken from the Geneva translation of the Bible (1560).
17. Diarmaid MacCulloch, *Reformation: Europe's House Divided, 1490–1700* (Harmondsworth: Penguin, 2003), chapters 15–16.
18. Frances A. Yates, *The Art of Memory* (Harmondsworth: Penguin, 1978, reprint of 1966), p. 43.
19. Willy Maley, *A Spenser Chronology* (Basingstoke: Macmillan, 1994), p. 56.
20. See Michelle O'Callaghan, *The 'Shepheardes Nation': Jacobean Spenserians and Early Stuart Political Culture, 1612–1625* (Oxford: Clarendon Press, 2000); William B. Hunter, Jr., *The English Spenserians: The Work of Giles Fletcher, George Wither, Michael Drayton, Phineas Fletcher and Henry More* (Salt Lake City: University of Utah Press, 1977).
21. For the history of Spenser's significance, see David Hill Radcliffe, *Edmund Spenser: A Reception History* (Columbia, SC: Camden House, 1996).

Chapter 9

Sidney, Shakespeare and the Elizabethan sonnet and lyric

KATHARINE A. CRAIK

In Shakespeare's early comedy *The Two Gentlemen of Verona*, Proteus offers Thurio, his rival for Silvia's favour, some advice on the art of seduction:

> You must lay lime to tangle her desires
> By wailful sonnets, whose composed rhymes
> Should be full-fraught with serviceable vows.[1]

There is no doubt the dullard Thurio needs a lesson or two in lovemaking. The above tutorial, however, is offered by one of Shakespeare's most perfidious lovers. Proteus has himself fallen in love with Silvia, whom he attempts to woo in Act 4 Scene 2. He is met with a frosty response: 'Thou subtile, perjur'd, false, disloyal man . . . I despise thee for thy wrongful suit' (4.2.95, 102). *The Two Gentlemen of Verona* was written in the 1590s when the vogue for sonnets in England was at its height, and Proteus's speech captures something of the energy, intensity and artfulness of this brief but important episode in the history of English poetry. Sonnets had developed by this time into a powerful vehicle for exploring the psyche, articulating inward experience and capturing the cadences of emotional turbulence. Usually written in the first person, they offered an opportunity for confessional utterance, each 'feeling line' promising to reveal what Proteus calls passionate 'integrity' (3.2.75–6). At the same time, however, and thanks to the demands posed by their inflexible form, Elizabethan sonnets are often astonishingly 'composed', or contrived, despite their appearance of spontaneity, and are always self-conscious about their mode of expression. They may be spoken by a Proteus whose very name declares his faithlessness; they may be fictionalised, ventriloquised, rehearsed, performed, studied or borrowed. The tensions Shakespeare sketches – between spontaneity and contrivance, between integrity and deceit – animate many Elizabethan sonnets and lyrics dealing with the subject of desire. They are indeed at the heart of Shakespeare's own *Sonnets*, published in 1609 but written in part in the 1590s.[2]

Early modern sonnet sequences comprise an unusually rich and vibrant body of work. Many of the men and women who wrote them lived at the centre of Renaissance intellectual and political culture, and their poems often expressed – and sometimes enacted – their public ambitions.[3] But these writers were exploring essentially private experiences as they revealed the self as an urgent and capacious subject for poetry. The Italian humanist scholar Petrarch (Francesco Petrarca, 1304–74) wrote his sonnets 'in sul mio primo giovenile errore' (during my first youthful error) and an imaginative preoccupation with the erotic was still associated in late sixteenth-century England with youthfulness and prodigality.[4] Many cultural commentators and moral philosophers, particularly Puritans, criticised lyric poetry as trifling and time-wasting; or, worse, as enervating, corrupting and dangerous. As John Harington wrote in 'A Briefe Apologie of Poetrie' (1591), sonnets were thought by many to 'sauour of wantonnes and loue and toying, and now and then breaking the rules of Poetry go into plaine scurrilitie'.[5] In *An Apology for Poetry* (1595), a treatise written partly in response to such objections, Sir Philip Sidney argued on the contrary that poetry, properly assimilated, encouraged men to aspire towards self-perfection. Recalling Plato's banishment of poets from his Republic, Sidney pointed out that Plato argued not 'that poetry abuseth man's wit, but that man's wit abuseth poetry'.[6] Whether or not love lyrics harmed the moral fibre of those who encountered them, or transgressed rules of decorum and usefulness, they were written and received with unprecedented enthusiasm between the years 1580 and 1610. Many readers and writers were taking poetry's delights remarkably seriously.

The first English anthology of poetry, *Songs and Sonnets*, was published by Richard Tottel in 1557. *Tottel's Miscellany*, as it became known, appeared in eight further editions before 1587. Lyric poetry dealing with the subject of courtly love had been flourishing on the Continent for some time. Dante Alighieri's *Vita Nuova* (1295) and Petrarch's *Canzoniere* or *Rime Sparse* (written over an extended period in the mid fourteenth century) became foundational texts for the development of European love poetry and song, influencing the Italian writers Pietro Bembo, Ludovico Ariosto and Torquato Tasso as well as the group of French poets known as the Pléiade, especially Pierre de Ronsard and Joachim Du Bellay.[7] Spiritual sonnet sequences began appearing in English in the 1560s, but the first sonnet sequence in the Italian and French tradition was Sidney's *Astrophil and Stella*, written by 1586 and published in 1591. In the seven years which followed, at least nineteen collections of amorous poems and sonnets were published, and others no doubt circulated in manuscript without ever reaching the press. Among the most important are Samuel Daniel's *Delia* (1592), Thomas Lodge's *Phillis* (1593), Henry Constable's *Diana* (1592; expanded 1594), Michael Drayton's *Ideas Mirror* (1594), Edmund Spenser's *Amoretti* (1595) and Richard Barnfield's *Cynthia* (1597).[8] Many aristocratic authors were, however, reluctant to allow their work to reach the wide, indiscriminate audience of print technology, preferring instead to circulate their verse privately in manuscript among a coterie readership made up predominantly of like-minded men.[9] Indeed, Renaissance lyric poets often reflect upon the nature of poetry and its methods of transmission. The sonnets of Sidney, Shakespeare and their contemporaries are freighted with the language of composition, penmanship, print and circulation and constantly explore the passionate engagement involved in experiences of literature.

Perhaps it was impossible to write sonnets in the 1590s without thinking deeply about the medium of verse, for, despite their seemingly simple form, they are among the most intricately worked examples of lyric poetry. The term 'sonnet' was used flexibly by early modern writers to denote a short song or lyric such as the three stanzas offered to Silvia in *The Two Gentlemen of Verona* ('Who is Silvia, what is she?', 4.2.39–53). The literary theorist George Gascoigne had indeed complained in 1575 that 'some thinke that all Poemes (being short) may be called Sonets'.[10] The sonnet proper, or poem in 'quatorzains', is a less flexible form, consisting of fourteen lines usually divided into an octave (subdivided into two quatrains) followed by a sestet. The Italian, or Petrarchan, sonnet form follows the rhyme scheme abba abba in the octave; and, in the sestet, a variety of schemes including cde cde; cdc dcd; or cde dce. This concise, tightly controlled structure was adopted by the early English sonneteers Thomas Wyatt (*c.*1503–42) and Henry Howard, Earl of Surrey (1516/17–47).[11] Usually separated by a decisive break known as the *volta* or 'turn', the two parts of the sonnet answer or complement each other. The use of alternate rhymes suggests narrative movement while the internal couplets inside each quatrain – and the couplet at lines four and five linking the two quatrains together – have a more static, contemplative effect. As J. W. Lever suggests, 'the effect is of exposition or narration constantly being impinged upon by lyric stress'.[12] The 'Shakespearean' sonnet form – which was in fact pioneered by earlier writers, including Surrey – consists of three quatrains rhyming abab cdcd efef which build upon one another before rounding off with a sententious couplet rhyming gg. The final couplet is a witty aphorism usually expressing paradox rather than simply clinching the preceding quatrains into a straightforward conclusion.

The exacting sonnet form required writers to articulate ideas and manipulate language with uncompromising economy. Himself an accomplished sonneteer, Daniel praised its formal strictures in his *Defence of Ryme* (*c*.1602). The poet works with a conceit by

> reducing it in *girum*, and a iust forme, neither too long for the shortest project, nor too short for the longest, being but only imploied for a present passion . . . is it not more pleasing to nature, that desires a certainty, & comports not with that which is infinit, to haue these clozes, rather than, not to know where to end, or how far to go, especially seeing our passions are often without measure.[13]

Sonnets are beautiful and useful precisely because of their concision and sense of proportion. Writing about lived experience ('present passion') risks producing poems which, in Proteus's words, are 'wailful' or 'full-fraught'. The solution lies in the sonnet's ingenious structure, the writer 'planting the sentence where it may best stand to hit'. Daniel's description of the sonnet form as a 'small room' hints at its incisive, epiphanic nature and its ability to present to the eye an impression of completeness no matter how overwhelming its emotional territory. Without diminishing measureless passion, sonnets make such passion civil or 'gallantly disposed' and their compressed architecture is uniquely suited to the candid nature of their subject matter.[14]

Sidney

The first English sonnet sequence, Sir Philip Sidney's *Astrophil and Stella*, exerted tremendous influence over those which followed. A courtier, scholar and statesman as well as a poet, Sidney was only thirty-one when he died on the battlefield at Zutphen in the Netherlands, and was rapidly elevated in the public imagination as a figure of ideal chivalric courtesy. His witty and brilliantly accomplished sequence was not published until 1591, but would already have been familiar to many readers in manuscript. *Astrophil and Stella* contains 108 sonnets interspersed with eleven songs, recalling Petrarch's mixing together of the *sonetto* (short song) and the *canzone* (long song). As C. S. Lewis wrote, 'the first thing to grasp about the sonnet sequence is that it is not a way of telling a story'.[15] It is nevertheless possible to discern various stages of a love affair in *Astrophil and Stella*: Stella spurns Astrophil's advances, then begins to waver, then confesses to reciprocating. Their affair is followed by a separation, and the closing sonnets chronicle Astrophil's dejection and the lovers' absence from one another. Sidney's Stella was Penelope Devereux, daughter of the first Earl of Essex, who had married Robert, Lord Rich on 1 November 1581. We know little more about the relationship between Sidney and Penelope Devereux than what Astrophil reveals, apart from the fact that her father had suggested on his deathbed a match between the two when his daughter was thirteen and Sidney was twenty-two. It is therefore impossible to determine the extent to which the startlingly intimate events described are based in fact, but the biographical contexts are less important than the poems themselves. Fast-paced and restless, *Astrophil and Stella* is a literary tour de force and was designed to convey the impression of virtuosic performance.

Sidney had earlier experimented with the sonnet form in the miscellaneous poems gathered together as *Certain Sonnets* and in the verse eclogues which separate the five books of his prose romance *The Arcadia*, but *Astrophil and Stella* confirmed his extraordinary originality and versatility as a lyricist. He marked his departure from the metrical norm established by Surrey and Wyatt by writing his famous first sonnet ('Loving in truth, and fain in verse my love to show') in twelve-syllable lines, or alexandrines, a form notoriously difficult to master. Part of Astrophil's arduous courtship of Stella involves the exacting labour of sonnet composition, for, as he admits, 'love doth hold my hand, and makes me write'.[16] The sequence explores the difficulty of separating the experience of desire from the experience of reading or writing about it. Love is like a pleasurable encounter with a book:

> In truth, O Love, with what boyish kind
> Thou dost proceed in thy most serious ways:
> That when the heaven to thee his best displays
> Yet of that best thou leav'st the best behind.
> For like a child, that some fair book doth find,
> With gilded leaves or coloured vellum plays,
> Or at the most, on some fine picture stays,
> But never heeds the fruit of writer's mind . . .
>
> (Sonnet 11, lines 1–8)

This opening octet gives the appearance of plain-speaking, thanks to its blunt opening phrase and direct apostrophic address. Love is 'boyish' despite its appearance of seriousness, skittishly inattentive and inclined to admire surface beauty rather than 'the best' qualities of the beloved – which, as the sonnet's final couplet makes clear, lie in her heart. Love is a childish reader charmed by the material trappings of a beautiful book but blind to its substance.

Sidney himself regarded *Astrophil and Stella* as a 'fair book' lacking fruitful matter and reportedly wished he had burnt it rather than merely withholding it from the press.[17] The central drama of *Astrophil and Stella*, indeed, lies in Astrophil's internal conflict between virtue and pleasure as Sidney explores the Neoplatonic idea that true goodness may be found in beauty.

According to Plato's philosophy in *Phaedrus*, beauty on earth was understood as a shadow of the ideal or absolute virtue found in celestial perfection. Depending on the beholder's perceptions, beauty inspires either sensual or spiritual love. Some readers have found Platonic notions of perfectibility encoded with the formal structure of the sequence. Songs 1–4 have a total of twenty-eight stanzas, a 'perfect' number suggesting virtue; Songs 5–9 have a total of sixty-three stanzas, signalling crisis and rupture; and Songs 10–11 have a total of seventeen stanzas, signifying discord.[18] If Sidney's own love sonnets were read for pleasure, he hoped – or at least professed to hope – that they would improve his readers rather than make them boyish.

Astrophil's description of love as a shamefully delightful reading experience sheds light on Sidney's own lifelong struggle to reconcile literary pursuits with a life of active service. There are many other similarities between author and character, and Sidney seems to have been fascinated by testing the boundaries between lived and represented experience. He had already created his own fictional double in *The Arcadia* in the form of the melancholy shepherd-lover Philisides, whose name suggests the Latin Philippus Sidneius.[19] Astrophil's name means 'lover of a Star' (Stella), and is again designed to invite comparison with Sidney's own. Like Sidney, Astrophil is a polished courtier, a knowledgeable politician, an accomplished tilter and, above all, a thoughtful writer. Astrophil often describes his melancholy (and joy) through metaphors of reading and writing: 'What ink is black enough to paint my woe'; 'all my hurts in my heart's wrack I read'; 'It is but love, which makes his paper perfect white / To write therein more fresh the story of delight' (Sonnet 93, lines 3, 13; Sonnet 102, lines 12–13).[22] In the first sonnet, he imagines Stella overcome with sympathy thanks to the pleasure his poems give her:

> Pleasure might cause her read, reading might make her know;
> Knowledge might pity win, and pity grace obtain. (lines 3–4)

Later, in sonnet 45, Astrophil jealously imagines Stella absorbed in a text which is not *Astrophil and Stella*. She remains untouched by Astrophil's 'beclouded' countenance, but reading about the 'grievous case' of lovers in a fable moves her to tears. Such a story may be untrue, but it draws her imagination – and inspires her favour – more readily than Astrophil's willingness to ruin himself in her service.[20] Here Sidney explores the Aristotelian paradox that art may stir up feelings which real life cannot. Astrophil's solution is flawlessly logical: he turns himself into a story in order that he might seduce Stella into feeling pity for him:

Then think, my dear, that you in me do read
Of lover's ruin some sad tragedy:
I am not I, pity the tale of me.[21] (lines 12–14)

The breezy simplicity of this remedy is belied, however, by its formal placement within the sonnet. Rather than positioning it as a pithy rhyming couplet, Sidney stretches it over three lines with a studiously awkward enjambment between lines twelve and thirteen.

This sonnet reveals the complexity of Sidney's ideas about authorship and the efforts of self-fictionalisation involved in writing poetry. The lyric voice of *Astrophil and Stella* is avowedly theatrical as Sidney repeatedly draws his imagined audience into dialogue, blending Astrophil's voice with his own. He is constantly turning over the question, raised by Proteus in *The Two Gentlemen of Verona*, of whether sonnets may discover the 'integrity' of those who write them. In *An Apology for Poetry*, Sidney had bemoaned the lack of sincerity found in most 'songs and sonnets':

> truly many of such writings as come under the banner of unresistible love, if I were a mistress, would never persuade me they were in love; so coldly they apply fiery speeches, as men that had rather read lovers' writings . . . than that in truth they feel those passions.[22]

To read love poetry is no substitute for falling in love, and Astrophil accordingly longs to abandon 'poor Petrarch's long-deceased woes' (Sonnet 15, line 7) and, with them, the effort of *imitatio* involved in assimilating the Italian tradition of sonneteering. Truthful passion nevertheless seems often to elude him, and he remains painfully aware of himself as a performer and a performance. As Michael Spiller has argued, 'Sidney created the first deconstructive lyric persona in the sonnet's history.'[23] Astrophil's polished utterances give an initial impression of cohesion, but they divide him too as the effort of writing becomes a source of excruciating shame:

My best wits still their own disgrace invent;
My very ink turns straight to Stella's name;
And yet my words, as them my pen doth frame,
Avise themselves that they are vainly spent.
(Sonnet 19, lines 5–8)

Writing involves embarrassing oneself, and then immediately regretting it. It is remarkable, given how painfully self-conscious Sidney makes Astrophil as a writer, that the sonnets in this sequence lose nothing of their emotional power as a result. Instead they capture the hazardously intricate behavioural protocols which governed the Elizabethan courtly milieu, while suggesting at the same time the disorientation and fragmentation of self which comes with infatuation with another.

Spenser, Drayton, Campion

The vogue for sonneteering took off after the publication of *Astrophil and Stella*. Edmund Spenser put to one side his epic romance *The Faerie Queene* (1590; 1596) in order to write *Amoretti*, published in 1595.[24] Unlike Sidney, who constructed elaborate self-fictions, Spenser presents himself candidly as the author of his sonnets. The sequence was written to celebrate his marriage to his second wife, Elizabeth Boyle, and although we do not know whether the poems were really presented to her, Spenser gives us the story of a private affair.[25] The conventions of courtly love are here revised in order to explore how virtuous courtship might lead to the mutual satisfaction of marriage.[26] *Amoretti* is followed in the 1595 volume by a wedding song, *Epithalamion*, and the two groups of poems are usually read as a pair. In *Amoretti* Spenser combined a local, temporal narrative with a broader ecclesiastical one, structuring his poems around the liturgical calendar leading from Ash Wednesday (Sonnet 22) to Easter Sunday (Sonnet 68).[27] The sequence therefore combines traditional Petrarchanism and Neoplatonism with 'Protestant matrimonial idealism', replacing unrequited love with ideals of mutuality, marital chastity and conjugal temperance.[28]

When he was seventeen Spenser had translated verses by Clément Marot and Joachim Du Bellay for a collection of spiritual epigrams, sonnets and prose entitled *A Theatre for Worldlings*, edited by the émigré Dutchman Jan van der Noot in 1569.[29] In *Amoretti* he developed a new and distinctive sonnet form whose diminutive title ('little love-offerings') belies the sonnets' technical complexity. Spenser's difficult rhyme scheme, abab bcbc cdcd ee, requires several interlinked rhymes to be sustained throughout each sonnet, linking the quatrains together to create a meditative, musically overlapping effect. This is illustrated in Sonnet 79, a beautiful love lyric, which echoes the Song of Solomon 4:1 ('Behold, thou art faire, my loue, behold, thou art faire'):[30]

> Men call you fayre, and you doe credit it,
> For that your selfe ye dayly such doe see:
> but the trew fayre, that is the gentle wit,
> and vertuous mind is much more praysd of me.
> For all the rest, how euer fayre it be,
> shall turne to nought and loose that glorious hew:

but onely that is permanent and free
from frayle corruption, that doth flesh ensew.
That is true beautie: that doth argue you
to be diuine and borne of heauenly seed:
deriu'd from that fayre Spirit, from whom al true
and perfect beauty did at first proceed.
He onely fayre, and what he fayre hath made,
all other fayre lyke flowres vntymely fade.

The speaker delays his own appearance until the end of line four, setting himself emphatically against general opinion which mistakes 'fayre lyke flowres' for true beauty. In a different use of the botanical metaphor, the beloved is born of 'heauenly seed', suggesting her divine ability to triumph over the 'frayle corruption' of the flesh. The word 'fayre' is used seven times in this sonnet, which returns to the Neoplatonic problem of celestial and sensual love. The beloved may 'credit' (believe, or perhaps prove) reports that she is fair, for physical beauty is easy to see. But 'trew fayre' resides in the invisible qualities of virtue and gentleness. The emphatic half-line 'That is true beautie' is prominently placed at the start of the third quatrain, the word 'true' picking up mid-line the c rhyme for further emphasis. The plain, monosyllabic rhyme of 'you' and 'true' at lines nine and eleven suggests that it may be possible for a time to sublimate desire by concentrating on the beloved's high spirituality. *Amoretti* nevertheless contains some remarkably sensuous lyrics, and the speaker often seems torn between spiritual aspiration and concupiscence. Sonnet 64 is one of the best poems ever written about kissing; and Sonnet 88, the penultimate of the sequence, points out the limits of Neoplatonic thought:

. . . beholding th'Idæa playne,
through contemplation of my purest part:
with light thereof I doe my selfe sustayne,
and thereon feed my loue-affamisht hart.
But with such brightnesse whylest I fill my mind,
I starue my body and mine eyes doe blynd.

Plato had argued that ideas are more 'real' than material objects since they are perceived by the intellect rather than by the unreliable physical senses. Forced into separation from the beloved, the speaker here attempts to find consolation in her abstract virtue. But contemplating 'th'Idæa playne' seems a poor substitution for physical union. Such contemplation may illuminate the mind, but the senses remain unfulfilled.

Michael Drayton's *Ideas Mirrour*, published in 1594, explores at length these same debates.[31] The sequence exists in several different versions published in the course of twenty-five years, and was retitled *Idea* in 1599. The title refers to the beloved herself, but also suggests Drayton's own imaginative ambition to contemplate, and to reflect in verse, her celestial beauty. [32] As he wrote in an address 'To the Reader of these Sonnets', 'My Verse is the true image of my Mind'.[33] Its inspiration is thought to have been Anne, daughter of Sir Henry Goodere who was for a time Drayton's patron. There is no reason to believe that Anne returned his devotions and, in 1595, the year of her father's death, she married Henry Rainsford.[34] Like Spenser, Drayton is not primarily remembered as a lyric poet and is better known for his verse histories and topographical writings. The sonnets in *Ideas Mirror* are indeed 'to Varietie inclin'd', reflecting his broad interests in cultural and political affairs, local history and popular science.[35]

Apart from his famous sixty-first sonnet about separation ('Since ther's no helpe, Come let us kisse and part') Drayton's lyrics remain unfamiliar to most readers. They are, however, much better than his description of them in the opening sonnet of *Ideas Mirror* as 'The drery abstracts of my endles cares' (line 2) might lead us to expect. 'Amour 32' in *Ideas Mirror* begins in alexandrines, like the first sonnet of *Astrophil and Stella*:

> Those teares which quench my hope, still kindle my desire,
> Those sighes which coole my hart, are coles unto my love,
> Disdayne Ice to my life, is to my soule a fire,
> With teares, sighes, & disdaine, thys contrary I prove.
> Quenchles desire, makes hope burne, dryes my teares,
> Love heats my hart, my hart-heat my sighes warmeth,
> With my soules fire, my life disdaine out-weares,
> Desire, my love, my soule, my hope, hart, & life charmeth.

This study of a lover's contrariness – and of sexual frustration – is realised through metrical pyrotechnics. The poem deals with opposites (quenching and kindling, cooling and warming, freezing and burning) and the regular iambic rhythm of the two opening, divided lines suggests balance and control. The tenor of the sonnet abruptly shifts in the fifth line, however, as the speaker approaches his complaint from a new perspective. Now hope burns instead of being quenched, tears dry up instead of flowing, and the heart is heated instead of cooled by sighs. The lover's fragmented state of mind is confirmed by the irregular, jarring tempo in the second quatrain which culminates in the crescendoing list of line eight. After the opening hexameter lines, the fifth begins with a trochee followed by an iamb, the deliberate awkwardness of the switch suggesting the lover's indecision. The momentary respite offered by two sets of three long-stressed syllables ('makes hope burne, dryes my teares') is abruptly curtailed in line six, whose brief attempted return to regular iambs is overturned again by the cumbersome hyphenated phrase 'hart-heat'. The studied chaos of this sonnet suggests the speaker's abandonment to passionate experience; and, in so doing, illustrates the difficulty of living one's life in obedience to theories of abstract beauty.

Drayton's contemporary Thomas Campion believed, by comparison, that poetry should raise the mind by first 'helping the ear with the acquaintance of sweet numbers'.[36] His commitment to melodious verse composition is evident in his songbooks, *A Book of Airs* (1601), *Two Books of Airs* and the *Third and Fourth Books of Airs*. Campion disliked excessive intricacy and syncopation in music, and his writing is likewise markedly unadorned. He would surely have agreed with Thomas Nashe's assessment in *The Unfortunate Traveller* (1594) that 'many become passionate louers onely to winne praise to theyr wits'.[37] His homophonic songs written for lute accompaniment are graceful lyrics:

> O what unhoped for sweet supply!
> O what joys exceeding!
> What an affecting charm feel I,
> From delight proceeding!
> That which I long despaired to be,
> To her I am, and she to me.[38]

The lovers' mutual satisfaction is reflected in the song's regularity, free from enjambment or metrical affectation, and the balanced final line of this first stanza suggests temperance and resolution. Campion's verse seems designed to reflect his belief that 'the world is made by symmetry and proportion' so that even when he deals with emotional upset, he does so with measured equanimity.[39]

Contemporary moral theorists believed that music's 'artificiall shaking, crispling, or tickling of the ayre' could inspire love, mercy, compassion and devotion by moving the passions in much the same way as poetry.[40] Lyric poetry originated in songs accompanied by the lyre (*lyra*), and, in the 1590s, music and poetry came together with a new sense of energy and creativity. English song reached maturity in the works of Campion and his close contemporaries Robert Southwell and John Dowland, whose *First Booke of Songes or Ayres* (1597) may have inspired Campion's. A renowned lutenist and composer, Dowland arranged many of his works so that they could be performed either as solo songs for lute accompaniment or as part songs for four voices. He probably wrote some of his own lyrics, and the frequent combination of Petrarchan courtly desire and spiritual melancholy indeed recalls the professional disappointments he suffered at Elizabeth's court thanks to his early Catholic sympathies. The Jesuit martyr Robert Southwell wrote devotional lyrics during his imprisonment for heresy, and these were published in 1595, the year of his execution. Southwell's ardour, like Campion's, is conveyed through rhythmic regularity and musical simplicity. His most famous lyric, 'The Burning Babe', applies the language of courtly love to the scene of Christ's nativity. Building upon the two-tier musical tradition of broadside ballads and devotional psalms, the sophisticated secular and sacred songs of Campion, Dowland and Southwell look forward to those of Suckling, Herrick, Jonson and Milton in the next century.

Shakespeare

Acquaintance with earlier lyrics and sonnets can scarcely prepare the reader for encountering Shakespeare's. This dazzling sequence explores how it feels passionately to love another person, delving with an unflinching gaze into the most intimate – and most unspeakable – aspects of emotional experience. The sequence contains powerful poems which articulate the jealousy, self-pity, resentment, grief, despair and occasional joy which accompany the experience of desire. At the same time, their subject matter extends far beyond the themes conventionally found in love lyrics. Shakespeare writes about some of the most fundamental aspects of life (youth and age, family, service, memory, ambition, solitude, death) with a voice remarkable for its candour and savage wit. Unlike Astrophil, the speaker of these sonnets does not imagine that virtue ideally attends the experience of love.[41] The bawdy cynicism of these poems could not have been imagined without the European tradition of sonneteering which preceded them, but *Shake-speares Sonnets* effectively overturned this tradition for ever.

Shakespeare's is the longest Renaissance sequence, with 154 sonnets. They remained unpublished until 1609, when they appeared in a volume alongside a beautiful and difficult narrative poem, *A Lover's Complaint*, written in the voice of a young woman abandoned by an unscrupulous seducer.[42] The sonnets are not formally experimental. Shakespeare captures the rhythms of speech using a predominantly iambic metre rhyming abab cdcd efef gg which almost always maintains a clear division between each quatrain, and between the octet and the sestet.[43] He departed radically from Petrarchan convention, however, when he addressed the first 126 sonnets to a beautiful young man. The remainder of the sequence concerns the poet's relationship with a dark-haired woman who could hardly be more different from the glacial, inscrutable lady of the Petrarchan tradition. The sonnets are often viciously cruel towards her, literalising the idea of lovesickness in Sonnet 144, for example, by replacing it with venereal disease, and the sequence draws to a close on a note of bitter reproach. The final two sonnets, whose relationship to the preceding sequence have provoked much debate, are dirty jokes about the love God Cupid.

The confessional tone of the sonnets seems to give unfettered access into the elusive territory of Shakespeare's consciousness, for the emotional turmoil they evoke with such clarity could hardly have been imagined by someone who had not experienced it. But as Lytton Strachey wrote in 1905, the sonnets 'lure the unwary traveller at every turn into paths already white with the bones of innumerable commentators' who have attempted to unravel their secrets by mapping them on to Shakespeare's biography.[44] Critics have been endlessly fascinated by the dedication of the sonnets to 'Mr W. H.', and by the identity of the dark lady. But the private affairs alluded to are impossible to guess at, and it is worth remembering that, as a dramatist, Shakespeare was an expert ventriloquist.

Whether or not the *Sonnets* deal with autobiographical material, Shakespeare's relationship with the literary craft was intensely self-reflective. His career was well advanced by 1609 for he had already written thirty plays and was known as the author of two narrative poems, *Venus and Adonis* and *The Rape of Lucrece*. Shakespeare wrote for the page as well as the stage, and the sonnets often reflect on poetry's ability to withstand the destructive force of time.[45] 'Time's injurious hand' may defile the beloved, but still 'His beauty shall in these black lines be seen'. The world is afflicted with 'sad mortality' but 'in black ink my love may still shine bright' (Sonnet 63, lines 2 and 13; Sonnet 65, lines 2 and 14). At the same time, however, the *Sonnets* explore the self-exposure involved in writing. The 'Rival Poet' sonnets (78–86) suggest the poet's prickly attitude towards his own craft, and the obsessions of the lover in Sonnet 76 are also those of the writer. This sonnet is an *apologia* summarising (in the octet) and then replying (in the sestet) to a complaint from the young man about the sonnets' inadequacies. They are so consistently 'barren of new pride' (line 1), and so cautiously lacking in ornament or ostentation, that their faults identify them instantly with their author. They are old-fashioned, lacking in 'variation' (line 2), and devoid of the 'new-found methods' (line 4) of more modern writers. As Helen Vendler has noted, 'Of all the indictments that could be made against these astonishingly inventive poems, monotony is the furthest off the mark.'[46] The complaint is nevertheless dignified with a graceful answer: if the sonnets seem monotonous, they are so because they describe faithful, constant devotion. The final two lines insist that beauty is found in routine and certainty, for the poet, like the sunrise, is forever 'still telling what is told' (line 14).

The subject of the poems offered to the beloved may never change ('I always write of you' (line 9)), but their innovation resides partly in stylistic elaboration ('dressing old words new' (line 11)). Shakespeare's relationship with old words is an important feature of his sequence. The fashion for Petrarchan versifying had faded, but the belatedness of Shakespeare's sonnets was an important part of their design. Shakespeare was reflecting – and sometimes parodying – the clichéd traditions of sonneteering, and was thinking critically about questions of influence and innovation. At times he appears hawkish towards earlier practitioners: in Sonnet 106, the authors of 'old rhyme' look with 'divining eyes' at Shakespeare's beloved, and would have written about him if only they could. Shakespeare's revision of tradition is radical and assertive enough to dismiss Petrarch's Laura, and all other earlier beloveds, as mere forethoughts of his own. Reading and writing are nevertheless crucial aspects of this love affair. The first seventeen sonnets urging the young man to marry and have a son are shot through with the language of writing, printing and copying as the sonneteer urges the young man that he 'shouldst print more, not let that copy die' (Sonnet 11, line 14). Reading and writing are active, transformative experiences rather than dry, abstract experiences of the mind as the sonnets set themselves the task of keeping the beloved alive and reproducing him for future generations.

Sonnet 15 engages in the labour of youth-making, waging war against the ravages of time. Working its way from the grandeur of the cosmos to the particularity of the beloved, this sonnet is both a philosophical reflection on life's impermanence and a spirited rebuttal of mortality in the young man's name. The rhyming monosyllables in the final couplet promise a heroic act of regeneration:

> And, all in war with Time for love of you,
> As he takes from you, I engraft you new.

To 'engraft' a tree is to renew it by replanting a small section upon a parent plant, but the word also puns on 'graphein', the Greek verb meaning 'to write'.[47] To think about the beloved is to think about writing about him so that love is not simply articulated but actually sustained through poetry. Writing indeed becomes a method of making 'increase' (line 5), cheating time as surely as any baby could. But the resolution offered by the clinching couplet is provisional; and this sonnet is bluntly answered by another which offers a bleaker, self-lacerating view of poetry:

> But wherefore do not you a mightier way
> Make war upon this bloody tyrant Time,
> And fortify yourself in your decay
> With means more blessèd than my barren rhyme?
>
> (Sonnet 16, lines 1–4)

The opening conceit returns to the image of waging war against time, now challenging the beloved with a direct question. Employing the *carpe diem* vocabulary familiarly used in Renaissance verse, the sonneteer claims that children would be both a 'mightier' and a 'more blessèd' method of fortifying himself against the decay of age. Continuing the botanical vocabulary, the speaker goes on to remind the beloved that there are 'maiden gardens' (line 6; unmarried women) who remain 'unset' (line 6) or unplanted. As 'living flowers' (line 7), children are more desirable to such maidens than any 'painted counterfeit' (line 8) or portrait of their lover. Collections of verse are also often described as posies or garlands, but literary imitation now looks 'barren' (line 4) whereas children are 'the lines of life that life repair' (line 9). The writer's humiliation becomes a failure of virility, his 'pupil pen' (line 10; punning on penis) incapable of proper reproduction.

The sonnets show keen awareness of the relationship between writing and remembrance, and are fiercely committed to recording the memory of the beloved even when they fail to do so. It is fitting, then, that the speaker's ultimate gesture of loving self-sacrifice (or, depending on one's point of view, his best weapon against the beloved's conscience) is the obliteration of his own memory. In Sonnets 71–4 he presses repeatedly upon the beloved the importance of forgetting him, even though the act of writing works expressly to counter such oblivion:

> No longer mourn for me when I am dead
> Than you shall hear the surly sullen bell
> Give warning to the world that I am fled
> From this vile world with vilest worms to dwell:
> Nay, if you read this line, remember not
> The hand that writ it, for I love you so
> That I in your sweet thoughts would be forgot,
> If thinking on me then should make you woe.
> O, if (I say) you look upon this verse
> When I (perhaps) compounded am with clay,
> Do not so much as my poor name rehearse;
> But let your love even with my life decay,
> Lest the wise world should look into your moan
> And mock you with me after I am gone. (Sonnet 71)

The crushing final couplet acts as a grim warning, but also as a challenge. Shakespeare's 'poor name' may not be worth mourning, but his voice in death is demonstrative, noisy and hyperbolic enough to make any such forgetfulness impossible. These sonnets on death have more in common with the impassioned devotional sonnets in John Donne's *Holy Sonnets* (1633) and *La Corona* (1635) than the amatory, Petrarchan tradition. The unforgettable concluding couplet of Shakespeare's Sonnet 146 is addressed to his own soul, advising it to turn inward, away from the body's impermanent raiment, and to look forward to the immortality conferred by salvation:

So shalt thou feed on Death, that feeds on men,
And Death once dead, there's no more dying then.

Samuel Daniel praised the harmony of sonnets with human nature 'that desires a certainty and comports not with that which is infinite'.[48] The radical simplicity of Shakespeare's final couplet is reassuring but also unsettling in its freewheeling reduction of spiritual doubt. The sonnet expresses an outraged resistance to death, but, at the same time, the brevity of its last two lines acknowledges that such resistance involves a tragedy of self-deceit. The constraints of the sonnet form work here to point out both the circumscribed nature of life, and the folly of our fleeting attempts to cheat it. Sonnet 146 brilliantly exemplifies the facility of early modern sonnets to combine a stringent adherence to form with the spontaneous expression of 'present passion'. The inflexibility of the sonnet form is perhaps its most powerful and moving feature.

Notes

1. *The Two Gentlemen of Verona*, 3.2.68–70. Quotations refer to *The Riverside Shakespeare*, second edition, ed. Herschel Baker *et al.* (Boston and New York: Houghton Mifflin, 1997).
2. The difficult question of the sonnets' dates, and their ordering within the 1609 volume *Shake-speares Sonnets*, is addressed in *Complete Sonnets and Poems*, ed. Colin Burrow (Oxford: Oxford University Press, 2002), pp. 103–11. All quotations from Shakespeare's Sonnets refer to this edition.
3. On the public ambitions of 'private' love poems, see Arthur F. Marotti, '"Love Is Not Love": Elizabethan Sonnet Sequences and the Social Order', *ELH*, 49 (1982), pp. 396–428.
4. For a discussion of this sonnet, and Petrarch's dismissal of his poetry as 'ineptiae' (follies) and 'nugellae' (trifles), see Michael R. G. Spiller, *The Development of the Sonnet: An Introduction* (London: Routledge, 1992), pp. 46–8.
5. John Harington, 'A Briefe Apologie of Poetrie' prefixed to *Orlando Furioso* (1591), sig. 5r. Harington's treatise is reprinted in Brian Vickers (ed.), *English Renaissance Literary Criticism* (Oxford: Oxford University Press, 1999), pp. 302–24 (p. 312).
6. Sir Philip Sidney, *An Apology for Poetry*, ed. Geoffrey Shepherd (Manchester: Manchester University Press, 1973), p. 125.

7. For a discussion of Renaissance reinterpretations of Petrarch in European lyric poetry of the fifteenth and sixteenth centuries, see William J. Kennedy, *Authorizing Petrarch* (Ithaca, NY: Cornell University Press, 1994). Petrarch's influence on English Renaissance lyric is the subject of Heather Dubrow's *Echoes of Desire: English Petrarchism and its Counterdiscourses* (Ithaca, NY: Cornell University Press, 1995).
8. Spiller includes a useful appendix of publication dates in *The Development of the Sonnet*, pp. 198–9. The majority cluster around the years between 1593 and 1597, following the publication of *Astrophil and Stella*.
9. See Harold Love, *Scribal Publication in Seventeenth-Century England* (Oxford: Clarendon Press, 1993). The Cambridge cleric Francis Meres famously wrote that Shakespeare shared his 'sugred sonnets among his private friends', in *Palladis Tamia. Wits Treasury. Being the Second Part of Wits Commonwealth* (1598), fol. 201v.
10. *Certayne Notes of Instruction*, in *The Posies of George Gascoigne* (1575), sig. U1v.
11. For a discussion of early English Petrarchan imitation, see Alistair Fox, *The English Renaissance: Identity and Representation in Elizabethan England* (Oxford: Blackwell, 1997), pp. 38–58.
12. J. W. Lever, *The Elizabethan Love Sonnet*, second edition (London: Methuen, 1966), p. 6.
13. Samuel Daniel, *A Defence of Ryme* (1602), sigs. F7v–F8r. A *girum* is a circle, regarded by Renaissance cosmologists as the perfect shape. Spiller describes the '"resistive" theory of art' which developed around the sonnet as writers worked with (and against) the confines of the form. See *The Development of the Sonnet*, p. 9.
14. Daniel, *A Defence of Ryme*, sig. F8r.
15. C. S. Lewis, *English Literature in the Sixteenth Century Excluding Drama* (Oxford: Clarendon Press, 1954), p. 128.
16. Sonnet 90, line 14. Quotations refer to *Sir Philip Sidney: A Critical Edition of the Major Works*, ed. Katherine Duncan-Jones (Oxford: Oxford University Press, 1989). On Sidney's 'highly metafictional interest' in *Astrophil and Stella*, see Spiller, *The Development of the Sonnet*, p. 111.
17. See Thomas Moffat's life of Sidney, *Nobilis or A View of the Life and Death of a Sidney and Lessus Lugubris*, ed. Virgil B. Heltzel and Hoyt H. Hudson (San Marino, CA: Huntington Library, 1940), p. 74.
18. Alastair Fowler provides a detailed 'numerological' reading in *Triumphal Forms: Structural Patterns in Elizabethan Poetry* (Cambridge: Cambridge University Press, 1970), pp. 174–80.
19. The complexity of Sidney's authorial persona is suggested by the Echo poem in hexameters spoken by Philisides in the Second Eclogues of *The Old Arcadia*, ed. Katherine Duncan-Jones (Oxford: Oxford University Press, 1985; repr. 1999), pp. 140–3.
20. For a discussion of Stella (and Penelope Rich) as Sidney's imagined reader, see Clark Hulse, 'Stella's Wit: Penelope Rich as Reader of Sidney's Sonnets', in Margaret W. Ferguson, Maureen Quilligan and Nancy J. Vickers (eds.),

Rewriting the Renaissance: the Discourses of Sexual Difference in Early Modern Europe (Chicago: University of Chicago Press, 1986), pp. 272–86.

21. Astrophil's self-fictionalisation continues in the eighth song, where Sidney introduces a narrator who tells the story of 'Astrophil' and 'Stella'. For a discussion of Sidney as a 'master of masking' see Dubrow, *Echoes of Desire*, p. 118.
22. Sidney, *An Apology for Poetry*, pp. 137–8.
23. Spiller, *The Development of the Sonnet*, p. 108.
24. The question of the date of *Amoretti* is addressed in *Edmund Spenser: The Shorter Poems*, ed. Colin McCabe (London: Penguin, 1999), p. 666. Quotations refer to this edition. Spenser berates himself in Sonnet 33 of *Amoretti* for leaving unfinished his 'Queene of faëry' (line 3).
25. Ilona Bell elaborates on this point in her chapter on *Amoretti* in *Elizabethan Women and the Poetry of Courtship* (Cambridge: Cambridge University Press, 1998), pp. 152–84 (p. 180). McCabe describes the autobiographical aspects of the sequence as 'curiously overt yet highly elusive', in *Shorter Poems*, p. 667.
26. Spenser nevertheless dealt with conventional Petrarchan themes in Sonnets 3, 8, 10 and 12. His Petrarchism is discussed in Kennedy, *Authorizing Petrarch*, pp. 195–280; and Bell, *Poetry of Courtship*, p. 174.
27. On the symmetrical structure of *Amoretti*, and its numerological design, see Alexander Dunlop, 'The Unity of Spenser's *Amoretti*', in Alastair Fowler (ed.), *Silent Poetry: Essays in Numerological Analysis* (London: Routledge and Kegan Paul, 1970), pp. 153–69.
28. The phrase is McCabe's from *The Shorter Poems*, p. 666. See also Lisa Klein, '"Let us love, dear love, lyk as we ought": Protestant Marriage and the Revision of Petrarchan Loving in Spenser's *Amoretti*', *Spenser Studies*, 10 (1992), pp. 109–37.
29. For a discussion of the place of this volume in the history of the English sonnet, see Lever, *The Elizabethan Love Sonnet*, p. 92; and McCabe, *The Shorter Poems*, p. 508.
30. See the 1611 King James Bible in the electronic database 'The Bible in English' (Chadwyck-Healey Ltd, 1996). The biblical reference is noted by William C. Johnson in *Spenser's Amoretti: Analogies of Love* (Lewisburg, PA: Bucknell University Press; London: Associated University Presses, 1990), p. 225.
31. The title of Samuel Daniel's sonnet sequence *Delia* (1592), an anagram of 'ideal', makes clear its Neoplatonic intent.
32. This point is made by Spiller, *The Development of the Sonnet*, p. 140. For the complex history of this sonnet sequence, see *The Works of Michael Drayton*, ed. J. William Hebel, 5 vols. (Oxford: Basil Blackwell, 1961), vol. v, pp. 137–9. Quotations refer to this edition.
33. *The Works of Michael Drayton*, vol. ii, p. 310. The address appears in later versions of the sequence.
34. The biographical background is outlined *ibid.*, vol. v, pp. 40–52.
35. The quotation appears in 'To the Reader of these Sonnets', line 11.
36. See the dedicatory epistle to Campion's *Observations in the Art of English Poesie*, in *Songs and Masques; with Observations in the Art of English Poesy*, ed. A. H. Bullen (London: A. H. Bullen, 1903), p. 231. Quotations refer to this edition.

37. *The Works of Thomas Nashe*, ed. Ronald B. McKerrow, 5 vols. (Oxford: Basil Blackwell, 1958), vol. II, p. 262.
38. This poem was published in the section entitled 'Light Conceits of Lovers' in *Two Bookes of Ayres* (*c*.1613). See *The Complete English Works of Thomas Campion*, ed. A. H. Bullen (London: Sidgwick & Jackson, 1909), pp. 67–8.
39. *Observations in the Art of English Poesie*, in Bullen (ed.), *Works*, p. 235.
40. This quotation is taken from Thomas Wright's treatise on the emotions, *The Passions of the Minde in Generall* (1601), ed. Thomas O. Sloan (Urbana: University of Illinois Press, 1971), sig. M5r.
41. The objects of the speaker's desire are not only idealised but also presented as flawed. See Paul Edmondson and Stanley Wells, *Shakespeare's Sonnets* (Oxford: Oxford University Press, 2004), pp. 42–3.
42. The relationship between *A Lover's Complaint* and the *Sonnets* has been much debated. See for example Wendy Wall, *The Imprint of Gender: Authorship and Publication in the English Renaissance* (Ithaca, NY: Cornell University Press, 1993), pp. 250–69.
43. The exception to these general rules is Sonnet 148, where the octet and sestet are linked with an enjambment; and Sonnet 145, which is written in iambic tetrameter. Shakespeare also occasionally varied his use of the sonnet form: Sonnet 99 has fifteen lines, and the twelve lines of Sonnet 126 are written in rhyming couplets.
44. *Spectatorial Essays by Lytton Strachey*, ed. James Strachey (London: Chatto and Windus, 1964), p. 71; repr. in Peter Jones (ed.), *Shakespeare: The Sonnets. A Casebook* (London: Macmillan, 1977), p. 52.
45. Recent critical work has explored Shakespeare's commitment to a career in print as well as in dramatic performance. See for example Lukas Erne, *Shakespeare as Literary Dramatist* (Cambridge: Cambridge University Press, 2003).
46. Helen Vendler, *The Art of Shakespeare's Sonnets* (Cambridge, MA: Harvard University Press, 1997), p. 344.
47. See Burrow's notes to Sonnet 15 in *Complete Sonnets and Poems*, p. 410.
48. Daniel, *Defence of Rime*, sig. F7v.

Chapter 10

The narrative poetry of Marlowe and Shakespeare

PAUL EDMONDSON

1599 was an important year in the after-life of Christopher Marlowe, as well as in the life of William Shakespeare. In *As You Like It* (probably written in 1599), the self-consciously Petrarchan Phoebe falls for Ganymede (Rosalind in disguise) and says: 'Dead shepherd, now I find thy saw of might: / "Whoever loved that loved not at first sight?"' (3. 5. 82–3).[1] Shakespeare, on whose writing thus far Marlowe had already had a considerable influence, here quotes directly from the erotic narrative poem, *Hero and Leander* (sestiad 1. 174–6),[2] published in 1598, probably for the first time. Why should Shakespeare have called Marlowe a 'shepherd' and what might this say about Marlowe's ongoing reputation as well as the relationship between the two poets?

1599 also saw the anonymous publication of Marlowe's poem, 'Come live with me, and be my love' in an anthology called *The Passionate Pilgrim*. It became one of the most famous and influential of all Elizabethan love lyrics, provoking responses from, among others, Sir Walter Raleigh and John Donne. The poem was first published without a title but became known as 'The Passionate Shepherd to His Love' in *England's Helicon*, published a year later. A generation of poets wrote lyrics inspired by it. Shakespeare, who had implicitly referred to Marlowe many times already, responded with a whole play rather than a poem. When Phoebe praises the 'dead shepherd', whose observations about love at first sight she is now experiencing at first hand, it is as if there is also a covert acknowledgment of the debt of gratitude Shakespeare owed his dead, and passionate, counterpart.

Marlowe was murdered at the age of twenty-nine in May 1593. 'Shepherd' seems a singularly inappropriate name for someone who was not only a scholar and an artist, but also a spy and a fraudster, a man who easily became angry and fought duels, a proactive and offensive atheist with a touch of the magician about him. As William Hazlitt observed: 'there is a lust of power in his writings, a hunger and thirst after unrighteousness, a glow of the imagination, unhallowed by anything but its own energies'.[3] But 'shepherd' does evoke the pastoral world of the Greek idyll and eclogue, and conjures up images of 'natural' poets (as well as poets of nature) competing on hillsides. Similarly, the classical tradition chimes most readily with Marlowe's sixteenth-century reputation as a writer. Michael Drayton imagined Marlowe 'bath [ing] . . . in the Thespian springs', possessing 'those brave translunary things, / That the first Poets had', as well as noticing Marlowe's 'fine madness' which 'rightly should possess a Poet's brain'.[4]

Marlowe has survived in both the study and the theatre as much for his own subjectivity as for his poetic achievement. No one thus far in English letters had celebrated and written about homosexual desire as Marlowe did, whether this was Edward II's love for Gaveston, the god Neptune's amorous and explicitly sensual desire for Leander, or Jupiter dandling the boy Ganymede in his lap at the beginning of *Dido, Queen of Carthage*. In *As You Like It*, Phoebe herself is desirous of another Ganymede (Rosalind in disguise), a relationship that is fraught with the tensions of same-sex desire. Shakespeare is, in a way, acknowledging Marlowe's sexuality by having Phoebe quote this particular line at this particular moment.

Another literary gloss on Shakespeare's 'dead shepherd' is Richard Barnfield's homoerotic 'The Tears of an Affectionate Shepherd Sick for Love; or The Complaint of Daphnis for the Love of Ganymede', published in 1594, the year after Marlowe died. Not only does Barnfield provide a third Ganymede to the dizzying possibilities of how Shakespeare's original audiences might have reacted to Rosalind, but the title of his poem also suggests a homoerotic connection with the title that was chosen for Marlowe's lyric 'Come live with me, and be my love'. Barnfield's shepherd was affectionate; Marlowe's would become passionate. When Shakespeare quotes *Hero and Leander* in *As You Like It*, he puts into circulation a series of cultural and poetic resonances. Between Barnfield, Marlowe and Shakespeare, passionate, affectionate and dead shepherds serve as useful pointers to sexually ambiguous Ganymedes who crackle with erotic tension.

Marlowe's poetic energies were drawn from his deep knowledge of classical texts. He translated Ovid and Lucan and, as he did so, helped to forge an English poetic rooted in the classical world. While appropriating, he innovated. Phoebe in *As You Like It* talks of Marlowe's 'saw of might'; in the First Folio of 1623 Ben Jonson praised 'Marlowe's mighty line' (which may or may not have been meant complimentarily). By the time he died, Marlowe had introduced and mastered the full rhetorical impact of the iambic line. He is also the poet of the rhyming couplet, and pushed it in new directions for the first time since Chaucer, finding within its intensity great wit and ironic tension. This prevails throughout his translation of Ovid's *Amores*, or *Elegies*, very likely Marlowe's first major poetic achievement. An appreciation of Marlowe's eroticism and use of the couplet in *Ovid's Elegies* provides a crucial context in which to appreciate *Hero and Leander*.

There were at least six editions of Marlowe's Ovidian translations before 1599, the year that saw Ovid's *Elegies* banned and burned as part of the Bishop of London's moral and literary clampdown. Ovid's *Elegies* were not as widely read as his other work in the Elizabethan period: Marlowe put them firmly on the literary map. 'Elegy', originally a Greek term for a poem of grief, came through Latin adaptations, especially Ovid's love elegies, to encompass poems on almost any kind of subject. In translating them, Marlowe also rewrote them, instigating a new kind of classical taste among his contemporaries. Stephen Orgel suggests that 'in a sense, this was Marlowe's sonnet sequence, the psychomachia of a poet-lover whose love is both his creation and his ultimate monomania, frustration and despair'.[5] In this context, Marlowe's achievement represents the most sexually frank sequence of poems in the period (until the appearance of Shakespeare's sonnets in 1609).

Marlowe sounds as though he is starting a new tradition when he writes the following at the beginning of the first book:

> We which were Ovid's five books now are three,
> For these before the rest preferreth he;
> If reading five thou plain'st of tediousness,
> Two ta'en away, thy labour will be less.
>
> With Muse prepared I meant to sing of arms,
> Choosing a subject fit for fierce alarms.
> Both verses were alike till Love (men say)
> Began to smile and took one foot away.
> Rash boy, who gave thee power to change a line?
> We are the Muses' prophets, none of thine. (1. 1. 5–10)

Echoing Virgil's 'of arms and the man I sing', Marlowe claims that classical battles are best avoided. Here is classical love instead, and a version condensed from five books to three. Already, there is wryness in the use of the couplet. Marlowe is in full control, able to involve hearsay – 'men say' – and call attention to his own use of metre – 'took one foot away' – and just at the moment when Love himself smiles. Here, too, is a good example of Marlowe's empowering ambiguity. 'Rash boy' is Cupid, but might also refer to Marlowe himself, reducing Ovid's five books to three and serving them up in witty, English iambic pentameter.

What kind of translation is Marlowe's? A comparison with Ben Jonson's translation of one of Ovid's *Elegies* makes clear Marlowe's sensual and aesthetic agenda. First, Marlowe on the immortality of verse:

> Therefore when flint and iron wear away,
> Verse is immortal, and shall ne'er decay. (1. 15. 31–2)

Jonson translates the same lines as:

> The suffering ploughshare or the flint may wear,
> But heavenly poesy no death can fear.

And at the end of the same elegy, Jonson has:

> Then when this body falls in funeral fire,
> My name shall live, and my best part aspire.[6]

Whereas Marlowe has:

> Then though death rakes my bones in funeral fire,
> I'll live, and as he pulls me down mount higher. (1. 15. 41–2)

In both examples, Marlowe's diction is tougher and more physical. His 'flint' and 'iron' stand in stark contrast to Jonson's 'ploughshare'. Jonson's body only falls (like Dido's) into 'funeral fire'; Marlowe's is raked (perhaps suggestive of 'wracked', too) by death himself. That last line is the most revealing of Marlowe's power for translation. Marlowe does not care about his 'name', like Jonson. Instead, he imagines his whole self, arising phoenix-like from the flames and, ever triumphantly, mounting (rather than merely aspiring) higher. It is Doctor Faustus's ambition that streams through this couplet: 'O, I'll leap up to my God! Who pulls me down?' (*Doctor Faustus*, scene 14, line 74).[7] Here indeed is Marlowe the over-reacher. There is, too, an echo of the end of this particular elegy in the death of Shakespeare's Richard II:

> Mount, mount, my soul; thy seat is up on high,
> Whilst my gross flesh sinks downward, here to die. (5. 5. 111–12)

As a translator, Marlowe works with an apparently simple, yet empowering verbal texture, rooted firmly in the physical and sensual world, making Jonson's pedantic literalism pale by comparison. Marlowe's translation of Ovid over-reaches itself into Shakespeare's English history play, where it becomes appropriated and subtly Christianised.

The muscular physicality of Marlowe's translation pervades the rest of *Ovid's Elegies*, relating most obviously to the language of sexual desire. For the most part *Ovid's Elegies* present a predominantly heterosexual gaze of desire, one primarily determined by the classical text itself. Having nothing better to do in the middle of a summer's day, the poet sees his beloved Corinna come into the room wearing 'a long loose gown'. The couplets here devour the beloved with an intensity of gazing which easily evokes the heat of passion with repetition and exclamation. The reader is defined by what the poet himself sees. He is totally in control of our point of view, manipulating our perspectives and feelings. He encourages us to gaze and then comically excludes us from the ensuing love bout.

> Stark naked as she stood before mine eye,
> Not one wen in her body could I spy.
> What arms and shoulders did I touch and see,
> How apt her breasts were to be pressed by me!
> How smooth a belly under her waist saw I,
> How large a leg and what a lusty thigh!
> To leave the rest, all liked me passing well;
> I clinged her naked body, down she fell.
> Judge you the rest: being tired she bade me kiss;
> Jove send me more such afternoons as this. (1. 5. 17–26)

Rhyming couplets might here have limited voyeurism with stiltedness, but Marlowe's achievement is instead one of engaging and inevitable flow. He asks us to follow him, but then playfully foreshortens the reader's own sense of climax by pushing us away from his own intimate pleasure: satisfied poet; tantalised reader.

At one point Marlowe's use of the couplet even evokes the sensation of kissing with tongues:

> 'Tis ill they pleased so much, for in my lips
> Lay her whole tongue hid, mine in hers she dips. (2. 5. 57–8)

At their wittiest Marlowe's couplets anticipate Lord Byron (who, like Leander, also swam the Hellespont) by 200 years:

> Thus I complained, but Love unlocked his quiver,
> Took out the shaft, ordained my heart to shiver. (1. 1. 25–6)

And later:

> Graecinus (well I wot) thou told'st me once
> I could not be in love with two at once.
> By thee deceived, by thee surprised am I,
> For now I love two women equally.

Both are well favoured, both in rich array,
Which is the loveliest it is hard to say.
This seems the fairest, so does that to me,
And this doth please me most, and so doth she. (2. 10. 1–8)

There is a balance in these lines which seeks no justification beyond the pleasure of itself, certainly no moral one. Couplets like these – apparently spontaneous, daring and confessional, yet finely tuned and self-ironic – represent Marlowe at his mischievous and Byronic best. In contrast stands Shakespeare's Sonnet 144 ('Two loves I have of comfort and despair'), which finds that two lovers present a complex moral dilemma, rather than an opportunity for Ovidian sexual pleasure. Marlowe shares with Ovid a liberating guiltlessness that never offers an apology.

Ovid's Elegies move beyond the mere erotic to a frankness about sex which might be more properly termed pornographic, a trait that Marlowe's translation clearly relishes. On occasion, nothing is left to the imagination. Here is the poet playfully describing and addressing his penis:

Yet notwithstanding, like one dead it lay,
Drooping more than a rose pulled yesterday.
Now, when he should not jet, he bolts upright,
And craves his task, and seeks to be at fight.
Lie down with shame, and see thou stir no more,
Seeing thou wouldst deceive me as before.

. . .

Nay more, the wench did not disdain a whit
To take it in her hand and play with it,
But when she saw it would by no means stand,
But still drooped down, regarding not her hand . . .
(3. 6. 65–70, 73–6)

And the poet, alas, cannot make a stand. This elegy ends with the disappointed mistress pouring water on the bedsheets to fool her maid into thinking she has had sex. Thomas Nashe would indulge in a more detailed description of erectile dysfunction in *The Choice of Valentines* or *Nashe His Dildo* (so pornographic that it was not published until 1899, and then only by private subscription), and the theme and tone would be taken up in the seventeenth century by the Earl of Rochester in poems such as 'The Imperfect Enjoyment', 'On his Prick', and 'A Curse on his Pintle'. By contrast, in Shakespeare's Sonnet 151 the poet has no problems experiencing an erection (at the *volta* or turning-point of the poem) and one which is happily, proudly, sustained in perfect relationship to his mistress until the end of the poem:

> No want of conscience hold it that I call
> Her 'love' for whose dear love I rise and fall.
>
> (Sonnet 151, lines 13–14)

Herein does Shakespeare combine sexual with poetic triumph over Ovid, Marlowe and Nashe, and establishes his anxiety of influence over Rochester.

Hero and Leander would have been impossible without Marlowe's translation of Ovid's *Elegies*, rooted as they are in an honest, yet ever playful eroticism. If one of the achievements of the couplet in translation was to intertwine the lovers, in *Hero and Leander*, the technique drives the reader inevitably forward, 395 times, like the strokes of a strong swimmer, to the moment when the couple lie 'both in each other's arms chained' (2. 306). The poem is an epyllion: a short, romantic epic. Leander is as heroic as the couplets which describe him.

The opening of the poem sets the scene in a tone of voice not dissimilar to the beginning of Shakespeare's *Romeo and Juliet*:

> On Hellespont, guilty of true love's blood,
> In view and opposite two cities stood (1. 1–2)

But, since 'Apollo courted Hero for her hair' (1. 6), we quickly understand that any tragic intonation is being thinly applied by Marlowe. Like the artificial flowers on Hero's veil which are overtaken by her own perfumed breath (1. 19–22), there is only the appearance of tragedy in Marlowe's poem. Its real essence is one of erotic, comic romance.

Like the beloved in 'Come live with me, and be my love', Hero is dressed in a 'kirtle' (1.15) with 'a myrtle wreath' (1. 17) for her head. Likewise, the coral around the tops of Hero's boots finds a counterpart in the 'coral clasps' on the 'belt of straw' that the poet promises his beloved. But Hero's kirtle is stained 'with the blood of wretched lovers slain' (1. 16). Marlowe's mock-heroic tone of voice helps to subvert the poem's status as an epic. Later, Hero is described in terms anticipative of Shakespeare's Cleopatra on her barge, who makes 'a gap in nature' (*Antony and Cleopatra*, 2. 2. 225):

> So lovely fair was Hero, Venus's nun,
> As Nature wept, thinking she was undone,
> Because she took more from her than she left,
> And of such wondrous beauty her bereft. (1. 45–8)

Just as the people rush to see Cleopatra, so they rush to see Hero. Marlowe describes the phenomenon with an extended simile which lavishes epic status on it, but at the same time he undercuts the effect with a humorous and archaic-sounding rhyme:

So ran the people forth to gaze upon her,
And all that viewed her were enamoured of her.
And as in fury of a dreadful fight,
Their fellows being slain or put to flight,
Poor soldiers stand with fear of death dead strooken,
So at her presence all surprised and tooken
Await the sentence of her scornful eyes;
He whom she favours lives, the other dies. (I. 117–24)

In line with epyllion tradition, Hero is presented as an archetypal Petrarchan female, whose fair skin makes pebbles look like diamonds (I. 25–6) and whose perfectly white hands would never burn in the sun (I. 27–30). She has not only blinded Cupid, he has also gone to her for nurture, mistaking her for his mother (I. 37–44). Hero is resolutely a virgin, at least for the first part of the poem. Like Phoebe in *As You Like It*, she can kill with looks and like Portia in *The Merchant of Venice*, 'many seeing great princes were denied, / Pined as they went, and thinking on her died' (I. 129–30). Hero is part of the tradition which Shakespeare debunks in Sonnets 127, 130, 131, 132 and 147: 'since Hero's time hath half the world been black' (I. 50). What Marlowe achieves is a depiction of Hero who breaks out of a tradition to become naked and vulnerable, and warm and sexy.

Similarly, Leander is presented within heroic and mythical terms. Like Hero, he too has impressive hair (I. 55). He is introduced with references to Musaeus (I. 52), Jason (I. 58) and Cynthia (I. 59). His body is like 'Circe's wand' (I. 61), and 'Jove might have sipped out nectar from his hand' (I. 62). Set against these highly artificial and hyperbolic comparisons is Marlowe's keenness for natural desire to be directed towards Leander:

Even as delicious meat is to the taste,
So was his neck in touching
. . . I could tell ye
How smooth his breast was, and how white his belly,
And whose immortal fingers did imprint
That heavenly path with many a curious dint
That runs along his back. (I. 63–9)

Having lured us intimately to touch and taste Leander's body, Marlowe changes direction:

But my rude pen
Can hardly blazon forth the loves of men,
Much less of powerful gods: let it suffice
That my slack muse sings of Leander's eyes. (I. 69–72)

The homoerotic gaze becomes self-conscious, and less erogenous parts of Leander's anatomy – his eyes – are noticed instead. Marlowe excuses himself by explaining that the chaste Hippolytus himself would have fallen for Leander (I. 77–8), and that:

> Some swore he was a maid in man's attire,
> For in his looks were all that men desire. (I. 83–4)

These lines recall Edward II's beloved Gaveston wanting to take the King in his arms 'like Leander gasped upon the sand', as well as his erotic fantasy of 'a lovely boy in Dian's shape' bathing in front of him, but using 'an olive tree / To hide those parts which men delight to see' (*Edward II*, scene I, lines 8–9 and 60–65).

Eyes are important in *Hero and Leander*. After gazing at Hero (whom Marlowe reads more like a figure in a book), and Leander (whom Marlowe touches and tastes), the eponymous heroes fall in love at first sight. Hero gets up from prayer and Love makes a direct hit at Leander with an unusually emphatic, quadruple rhyme:

> Thence flew Love's arrow with the golden head,
> And thus Leander was enamourèd.
> Stone still he stood, and evermore he gazèd,
> Till with the fire that from his count'nance blazèd
> Relenting Hero's gentle heart was strook:
> Such force and virtue hath an amorous look. (I. 161–6)

Like John Donne's lovers whose 'eye-beams twisted and did thread / Our eyes upon one double string' (in his poem 'The Ecstasy'),[8] Marlowe's couplets become like pairs of eyes watching, gazing, staring and crossing fateful beams with similar vowel sounds at the ends of the lines:

> It lies not in our power to love or hate,
> For will in us is overruled by fate.
> When two are stripped, long ere the course begin
> We wish that one should lose, the other win;
> And one especially do we affect
> Of two gold ingots like in each respect.
> The reason no man knows: let it suffice,
> What we behold is censured by our eyes.
> Where both deliberate, the love is slight;
> Who ever loved, that loved not at first sight? (I. 167–76)

If this is the epicentre of the poem, as far as the fate of the lovers is concerned, then from here onwards, the lovers and the mood gradually come further into a determinedly comic and even more erotic focus. Hero's tongue trips and she inadvertently invites Leander to 'come thither'; she blushes (1. 357–9). She weeps because of her vow of chastity, but Love turns her tears to pearls (1. 374–5). Between her accidental come-on and her subsequent faint (2. 1–2), Marlowe inserts a digression of ninety-eight lines about Mercury and a country maid. It is a characteristically erotic deferral. Georgia E. Brown observes that:

> The story of Mercury and the country maid links the rhetorical and the erotic, as the narrator's narrative accomplishments are recast as erotic arousal. The country maid puts Mercury off to bring him on, just as the narrator puts the reader off, by frustrating their desire to follow the main story of Hero and Leander, to bring them on.[9]

Mercury charms the maid with his 'snaky rod' (1. 398), they tumble on the grass (1. 406) and, like Gaveston, Mercury gazes 'on those parts which no eye should behold' (1. 408). At their first assignation, Marlowe's description of the 'greedy lovers' suggests a mutual devouring with comic relish:

> O who can tell the greeting
> These greedy lovers had at their first meeting?
> He asked, she gave, and nothing was denied. (2. 23–5)

Thereafter, the poem moves gradually – and tantalisingly (2. 75–8) – towards a fully realised sexual consummation for Hero and Leander. Hero places her myrtle wreath upon her lover's head (2. 105), and places her ring of solemn committal on his finger (2. 108–10). References to the four elements subtly surround Leander's return journey to Abydos (2. 115, 116, 118 and 124), suggesting that his identity and his physical relationship to Hero are being re-created and re-forged. Characteristically, any re-fashioning on Leander's part is comically undercut: 'His secret flame apparently was seen, / Leander's father knew where he had been' (2. 135–6). And then comes the glorious moment when Leander, unable to resist seeing Hero any longer, climbs a rock to stare at her tower across the river, strips off all of his clothes and leaps 'lively' into the Hellespont (2. 147–54). The god Neptune thinks he is Ganymede and starts making love to him (2. 157–68). There is something both liberating and oppressive about this extended homoerotic episode (2. 155–226). Marlowe is able leisurely to describe Leander's body and Neptune's embracing him, 'upon, his breast, his thighs, and every limb' (2. 189), but it all takes place during a strong current and partially underwater. Leander nearly drowns.

Panting and dripping with desire, Leander knocks on the door of Hero's tower. She does not wait to put on her robes and goes to answer the door immediately:

> Where seeing a naked man, she screeched for fear;
> Such sights as this to tender maids are rare. (2. 236–7)

Marlowe cannot resist interpolating his own narratorial voice here, characteristically comic in the way it helps to diffuse erotic tension. Then follows situation comedy pure and simple. Hero hides in the bed, and then allows Leander to move into 'her lukewarm place' (2. 254). Hero has changed from a nun sacrificing turtle doves to Venus into a lover who is able to arouse her beloved by the way she uses her bed linen. Just as Neptune oppressed Leander, so Leander finally must oppress Hero:

> Love is not full of pity (as men say)
> But deaf and cruel where he means to prey. (2. 287–8)

Hero finally gives in and together they enter a world of 'unknown joy' (2. 293). Leander, like Shakespeare's Biron in *Love's Labour's Lost*, finds love to be a Hercules in 'the orchard of the Hesperides' (2. 297–8). The classical references return, but Marlowe is achieving a new kind of comparison to celebrate a real and physical ecstasy, rather than to convey a literary trope.

Starting with George Chapman, whose continuation of Marlowe's poem runs for 1,638 lines (almost twice the length of Marlowe's original), critics over the centuries have worried about Marlowe's poem being unfinished. The idea especially impressed C. S. Lewis, who in 1952 tried to convince the British Academy of his argument that Marlowe's *Hero and Leander* should only be read in conjunction with Chapman's continuation. But Marlowe ends with an extended description of the dawn breaking through Hero's hair, who, siren-like, stands naked at the edge of the bed. This could well be Marlowe's new ending to the well-known tragic story. Doctor Faustus's tragic fate is recalled in the last lines, but here light triumphs over darkness, dawn overcomes the night:

> Till she, o'ercome with anguish, shame and rage,
> Danged down to hell her loathsome carriage. (2. 333–4)

Seeming to start with a tragedy, which is at best mock-heroic, Marlowe becomes utterly entranced by both Hero and Leander. For Marlowe, the narrative ends where an aubade should begin, a love poem which regrets the arrival of the dawn which separates the lovers. By fusing together Hero herself with the sunrise, Marlowe subverts another literary tradition. His gradual stripping away of literary tropes makes Hero and Leander's physical union quite literally a conclusion fit enough for the gods. As D. H. Lawrence said of the novel, in the context of *Lady Chatterley's Lover*, 'I always labour at the same thing, to make the sex relation valid and precious, instead of shameful. And the novel is the furthest I've gone. To me it is beautiful and tender and frail as the naked self is.'[10]

Venus and Adonis are depicted in the woven borders around Hero's sleeves (1. 11–14); Hero and Leander first see each other on a feast day for Adonis (1. 91–3). Spurred on by Marlowe's poetic achievements, Shakespeare explored love, sex and narrative style very differently. If Shakespeare knew Marlowe's poem before writing *Venus and Adonis*, it would have had to be through a manuscript version in private circulation. Or, he might even have discussed it with the author. *Venus and Adonis* was printed in or around June 1593, just a few weeks after Marlowe was murdered. Shakespeare's name first bursts into print as Marlowe himself is erased.

Venus and Adonis is Shakespeare's reply to *Hero and Leander*, and a response to Marlowe hovers with heightened self-consciousness over the gateway into Shakespeare's poem. The untranslated epigraph is from Ovid's *Amores*, which Marlowe had translated, in his version of Ovid's *Elegies*, as: 'Let base conceited wits admire vile things, / Fair Phoebus lead me to the Muses' springs' (1. 15. 35–6). Shakespeare is striving for new heights, carving out a place for himself above all other artistic endeavour. Ovid's account of Venus and Adonis takes up only about eighty lines in *Metamorphoses*, Book 10 (it is divided into two by Venus's story of Atalanta and Hippomenes). Shakespeare transforms this into a carefully sustained dramatic encounter of 1,194 lines. In Ovid, Adonis seems happily to requite Venus's attentions; they hunt hares, stags and deer together (she warns him about boars, lions, bears and wolves). Venus is on her way to Cyprus when Adonis is killed.

Shakespeare's account is much more driven than Ovid's by the erotics of male sexual fantasy. The tone of Shakespeare's version, like *Hero and Leander*, is predominantly comic, in spite of its definitely tragic ending. To have the goddess of love naked and begging for sex before you is the stuff of which some people's dreams are made. The voluptuous Venus throws herself at Adonis (lines 43–8), smothers him with kisses (lines 55–60), and openly invites him to have sex with her (lines 229–40). There are sweating palms (line 25) and a lustful stallion who, like the extended simile in *Hero and Leander* (2. 141–5), symbolises sexual passion and bolts in hot pursuit of a mare (lines 259–324). The overtly passionate expressions of complete adoration on Venus's part (lines 432–50), the wonderfully comic dialogue and direct descriptions of their physical positions: 'he on her belly falls, she on her back' (line 594), all contribute to the comic vision. Adonis is lazy and bashful. He covers his face with his bonnet (lines 339–40), and, like Leander, he is even a little effeminate (lines 216–17): a 'master mistress' (like the addressee of Sonnet 20) of Venus's passion.

There is comedy, too, in the exaggerated conflict between the two protagonists (lines 355–60, 769–80). Adonis resists Venus's advances, impressing upon her his naivety and youth, if not his ambiguous sexuality (lines 524–5). All of these effects are intensified by Venus and Adonis themselves being the only persons (one divine, one human) in the poem. There is no attempt to give the impression of the social world as Marlowe does, nor does Shakespeare involve other gods (like Neptune), nor classical references (unusually for Shakespeare). Instead, there is plenty of countryside and observation of the natural world. Adonis glances at Venus:

> Like a dive dapper peering though a wave
> Who, being looked on, ducks as quickly in. (lines 86–7)

The goddess and the young man are reclining on a bank of violets (lines 125–6), the approach of the fatal hunt brings mention of foxes, roes, conies (or rabbits), and there is the digression about the hare, 'poor Wat' (lines 672–702). For Shakespeare, these observations bring a gentleness of tone, a mutuality between the protagonists' images of themselves and the natural world which surrounds them. Venus's eulogy to Adonis is warm and couched in a pastoral world:

> To see his face the lion walked along
> Behind some hedge, because he would not fear him.
> To recreate himself when he hath sung,
> The tiger would be tame, and gently hear him.
> . . .
> When he was by, the birds such pleasure took
> That some would sing, some other in their bills
> Would bring him mulberries and ripe-red cherries.
> He fed them with his sight, they him with berries.
> (lines 1093–6 and 1101–4)

The best-loved books tend eventually to fall to pieces (only one copy of the first edition survives), and so popular was *Venus and Adonis* that at least sixteen editions were published by 1636 (ten of them in Shakespeare's lifetime). This means that it was more frequently reprinted that any other work by

Shakespeare during this period: such is the saleability of erotic literature. Certainly the poem was immensely popular among university undergraduates. In the second of the three anonymous *Parnassus* plays (written between 1598 and 1602, and performed by Cambridge students), for example, Gullio, in order to honour 'sweet Master Shakespeare' will sleep with a copy of *Venus and Adonis* under his pillow. In 1600, the poet and Cambridge academic Gabriel Harvey observed, 'the younger sort take much delight in Shakespeare's *Venus and Adonis*'.[11]

In contrast to Marlowe's depiction of sexuality, though, Shakespeare's poem is more directed by moral expectations. In his dedication to his patron, the nineteen-year-old Henry Wriothesley, Earl of Southampton, Shakespeare refers to *Venus and Adonis* as 'the first heir of my invention' and calls the Earl the poem's 'godfather'. This poem is like a child for which they are mutually responsible. Like some of the early printed sonnets, *Venus and Adonis* contains arguments in favour of procreation, the begetting of children. The rhetoric of paternal responsibility resonates through the poem with Venus's attempts to seduce Adonis. As the poet in several of the opening sonnets (especially numbers 1, 3, 6, 7, 9 and 13) urges a young man to stop being self-absorbed with his own beauty, and instead to reproduce his beauty by making children, so too does Venus urge Adonis:

> Things growing to themselves are growth's abuse;
> Seeds spring from seeds, and beauty breedeth beauty:
> Thou wast begot: to get it is thy duty. (lines 166–8)

Shakespeare's invitation to participate in erotic voyeurism contrasts strongly with Marlowe's, and includes a built-in reminder that real, physical love is more noble, more divine, than mere virtual, erotic indulgences. In this context, the message to beget might be paraphrased as: 'Stop reading erotic fiction and put your body to procreative use instead.' Lessons in life, as well as in erotic enjoyment, apply not only to the Earl but to Shakespeare's readers.

The sexual act is resolutely deferred and Venus and Adonis experience 'a war of looks' (lines 355–60), rather than love at first sight, like Hero and Leander. There is no sense of a moral grounding to Marlowe's erotic poetics. Moreover, there is no physical consummation in *Venus and Adonis*, except the brutal penetration of Adonis by the wild boar's tusk (lines 1051–6). Where Marlowe had his lovers being transfigured by the dawn, Shakespeare has Venus explain that Adonis's fatal wound will forever wound love itself (lines 1135–64). Adonis is turned into a purple and white flower and is already dying again, as Venus takes it away to dote upon with everlasting pain.

Tragedy visits the poet in Marlowe's version of Ovid's *Elegies* and complains that his work is not grave enough: 'She gave me leave, soft love in time makes haste, / Some greater work will urge me on at last' (3. 1. 69–70). Similarly, in his dedicatory epistle to *Venus and Adonis*, Shakespeare promises to honour his patron with 'some graver labour' to make up for so 'weak a burden'. He published *The Rape of Lucrece* the following year and also dedicated it to the Earl of Southampton. Whereas *Venus and Adonis* is comic and erotic, *The Rape of Lucrece* is defiantly tragic, and its erotic power might make the reader feel complicit in the crime it relates. Whereas *Venus and Adonis* depicts a struggle of love resisted and the pain of love unrequited between just two protagonists, *The Rape of Lucrece* is concerned with desire violently forced, the pains of guilt and shame which follow and the effect of the crime on a whole community.

Lucrece was raped in about 500 BC, an event which had long achieved mythical-historical status by the time Shakespeare came to write about it. Although Shakespeare found the story in Ovid's chronicles, Livy had recorded it in the *History of Rome*, and Chaucer also included it in his *Legend of Good Women*. The Argument which Shakespeare includes at the beginning of the poem (his longest surviving piece of non-dramatic prose) is based on Livy. There are interesting discrepancies in Shakespeare's retelling, suggesting perhaps that as he wrote the poem he diverged from his original plan. In the Argument, so moved are the people at Tarquin's crime that 'the state government changed from kings to consuls', that is from a monarchy to a republic. Lucrece's rape was a great political moment. Shakespeare knew this from both Ovid and Livy, but withholds this fact from the end of his poem. Instead, his emphasis is on the people gladly giving consent 'to Tarquin's everlasting banishment'. In the end, Shakespeare seems more concerned with personal punishment than state politics.

All of these earlier accounts are much shorter than Shakespeare's. From the major source, Ovid, we can see Shakespeare expanding a story of 132 lines into 1,855 (about the same length as *The Comedy of Errors*). His expansions include the journey of Tarquin to rape Lucrece (memorably recalled by Macbeth on his journey to kill King Duncan, 2. 1. 52–6). We see him making his way through a series of doors (lines 309); the wind blows out his torch, but his own lustful breath re-ignites it (lines 311–5). Interestingly, Shakespeare does not have Tarquin carry a sword, as Ovid, Livy and Chaucer do (this is not mentioned until he is with Lucrece at line 505). Tarquin's 'rolling greedy eye-balls' (line 368) prefigure those of Othello just moments before he kills Desdemona (*Othello* 5. 2. 40). Like Desdemona, Lucrece has 'alabaster skin' (*Othello* 5. 2. 5; *The Rape of Lucrece* line 419). Tarquin's careful observation of

Lucrece's body looks forward to another Tarquin, Giachimo, who visually rapes Innogen in *Cymbeline* (2. 2. 11–51). All this is couched in highly suspenseful verse written in the dramatic present tense. *The Rape of Lucrece* takes place in recognisably the same Roman world as *Titus Andronicus*, produced around the same time, and which includes the violent rape of Lavinia. Shakespeare was finding a new inflection for his tragic voice, which he would recall and re-invent throughout his career.

Other significant variations include Lucrece's behaviour before the rape and consciousness during it. Shakespeare has her arguing back strongly at Tarquin (lines 575–644). Ovid and Livy have her overcome by fear; in Chaucer's account she faints. After the rape (which is not described and takes place at some point between lines 680–6), Lucrece starts her 'living death' (lines 687 and 726), there is the self-disgust and guilt which overwhelm Tarquin (lines 688–718), and then come Lucrece's highly rhetorical apostrophes to Night, Honour, Opportunity and Time (lines 764–1036). Like Lavinia, she compares herself to the raped Philomel from Book Six of Ovid's *Metamorphoses* (*The Rape of Lucrece* lines 1079 and 1128; compare *Titus Andronicus* 4. 1. 30–62), and justifies suicide (lines 1158–211). Later comes an episode in which she reads carefully a painting of the destruction of Troy (lines 1366–568; earlier she saw herself as being like a sacked city, lines 722–3), identifying with the grief of Hecuba (lines 1447–91) and seeing Tarquin in the figure of Sinon (lines 1499–1561), whose image she tears (lines 1562–8).

Like *Venus and Adonis*, the poem represents a solitary and erotic artistic experience. But here the reader is drawn into something with which he or she should not want to be complicit. The claustrophobic moment during which Tarquin looks at Lucrece and gains his necessary erection is one of the most erotic passages in all of Shakespeare. The extra syllables at the end of each line imitate Tarquin's gradually stiffening tumescence:

> So o'er this sleeping soul doth Tarquin stay,
> His rage of lust by gazing qualified,
> Slaked not suppressed for standing by her side.
> His eye which late this mutiny restrains
> Unto a greater uproar tempts his veins,
>
> And they like straggling slaves for pillage fighting,
> Obdurate vassals fell exploits effecting,
> In bloody death and ravishment delighting,
> Nor children's tears nor mothers' groans respecting,
> Swell in their pride, the onset still expecting.

Anon his beating heart, alarum striking,
Gives the hot charge, and bids them do their liking.

His drumming heart cheers up his burning eye,
His eye commends the leading to his hand.
His hand, as proud of such a dignity,
Smoking with pride marched on to make his stand
On her bare breast, the heart of all her land,
Whose ranks of blue veins as his hand did scale
Left their round turrets destitute and pale. (lines 423–41)

'Standing by her side', 'proud of such a dignity', 'pride marched on to make his stand': in all, these lines represent as fine a description of male sexual arousal as you could hope to find anywhere in literature. But Shakespeare's depiction is alongside the violence of pillaging and the suffering of innocent mothers and children. Shakespeare erotically draws the reader in and supplies the potential for his reader's self-disgust.

There is no relief of metamorphoses for Lucrece at the end. Her husband Collatine, her father and others arrive (line 1584), hear her account of the rape (lines 1613–59 and 1676–717) and witness her suicide (lines 1721–33). Brutus takes out the knife from her breast and encourages Collatine that rational and legal revenge must be sought. Lucrece's 'bleeding body' is shown through Rome (lines 1850–2), apparently the most effective way of publishing Tarquin's crime. It is a grotesquely visual act and one determined by the historical sources rather than by Shakespeare. A spoilt and ruined body is now itself paraded with male authority before the common view. And Lucrece is raped a second time.

A distinctly moral imperative underpins Shakespeare's later narrative, *A Lover's Complaint*, a 329-line poem which was first published at the end of his collection of sonnets in 1609. Although printed under a separate headline which reiterates the attribution to Shakespeare, the authorship of *A Lover's Complaint* has long been questioned. In 2007, Brian Vickers tried to show that Sir John Davies of Hereford is the author, but Macdonald P. Jackson has thoroughly refuted Vickers's attempt.[12] From a Shakespearian's perspective, the sonnets themselves provide a creative context in which to read *A Lover's Complaint*, and to do so is to recognise the taste of sixteenth- and early seventeenth-century readers. Complaints could be a lament, a confrontation or an argument, and were not always about love. Samuel Daniel, Thomas Lodge and Richard Barnfield all include complaints at the end of their sonnet sequences, perhaps suggesting that such a sorry state of affairs is where love will lead.

A Lover's Complaint, produced sometime between 1599 and 1609, uses the same rhyme-royal, seven-lined stanzas as *The Rape of Lucrece*, heightening the effect of interiority and an almost claustrophobic morality. There is the repeated rhyme of one sound three times and the rhyming couplet at the end (for example 'inflame', 'fame', 'shame' and 'bears', 'fears', lines 268 and 270–273). We never learn whether the narrator of the poem is male or female. He or she imperfectly overhears (lines 1–7) the complaint of a young woman who has been thwarted in love by a universally adored young man (cross-reference Sonnet 20). She is pouring her heart out to a passing cattle grazer of dubious morals (lines 58–9).

Her complaint overtakes and submerges the framing device of the narrator, so the morality of *A Lover's Complaint* (in which all the persons involved remain firmly anonymous) is placed almost too firmly in our view; as Queen Gertrude says, 'The lady doth protest too much, methinks' (*Hamlet* 3. 2. 219). As readers, we never learn the effect that overhearing the complaint has had on the poem's narrator or the cattle grazer. Instead, the young woman takes full control of our moral focus. She details what the young man has said to her (lines 177–280). We only have access to her version of their love affair, and are compelled to feel her own sense of moral outrage at his 'all-hurting aim' (line 310). *A Lover's Complaint* is skilfully crafted and seeks to deny closure. There is only a resoundingly clear sense that the young man who has so wounded his former lover will 'new pervert a reconcilèd maid' (line 329).

Two poets, two perspectives, two dead shepherds. Clifford Leech, one of the scholars responsible for Marlowe's reappraisal in the second part of the twentieth century, commends his 'large-mindedness', notices Marlowe's 'double view of the aspiring mind' and admires his 'notion of the irresponsibility with which the universe functions'.[13] These are precisely the same kind of attributes which critics have long admired in Shakespeare: myriad-minded and able to hold complex perspectives in creative tension without offering any easy judgment. Great minds are thinking alike when Shakespeare cites *Hero and Leander* in *As You Like It*. For Ovid and his mistresses, Hero and Leander, Venus and Adonis, and Tarquin and Lucrece, both Marlowe and Shakespeare produce some of the finest comic, erotic and dramatic poetry in the language. But when their approaches to narrative and erotic verse are compared, it is Marlowe, rather than Shakespeare, who seems the most keen that his readers should enjoy the sex he is describing. It is as if Shakespeare is primarily interested in making us think, whereas Marlowe's thought is to make us laugh and feel. Although both poets present the sanctity of all flesh in their work, Shakespeare in *Venus and Adonis*, *The Rape of Lucrece*, and *A Lover's Complaint* presents flesh which is wounded. For Marlowe, flesh is to be unashamedly enjoyed, and can even amuse. Or, better still, as Marlowe says of his own Hero and Leander: 'Both might enjoy each other and be blessed'(I. 380).

Notes

1. William Shakespeare, *The Complete Works*, ed. Stanley Wells, Gary Taylor, John Jowett and William Montgomery, second edition (Oxford: Clarendon Press, 2005). All quotations from Shakespeare are cited from this edition unless otherwise stated.
2. Christopher Marlowe, *The Complete Poems and Translations*, ed. Stephen Orgel (Harmondsworth: Penguin, 1971). All quotations from Marlowe's poetry are cited from this edition unless otherwise stated.
3. Cited in Patrick Cheney, 'Introduction: Marlowe in the Twenty-First Century', in Patrick Cheney (ed.), *The Cambridge Companion to Christopher Marlowe* (Cambridge: Cambridge University Press, 2004), pp. 1–23 (p. 7).
4. *Ibid.*, p. 2.
5. Marlowe, *Poems and Translations*, p. 233.
6. Ben Jonson, translation of Ovid's *Elegies*, Book I, Elegy 15, quoted in *The Complete Poems of Christopher Marlowe*, ed. Orgel, p. 136.
7. Christopher Marlowe, *The Complete Plays*, ed. Frank Romany and Robert Lindsey (Harmondsworth: Penguin, 2003). All quotations from Marlowe's plays are cited from this edition unless otherwise stated.
8. *The Complete English Poems of John Donne*, ed. C. A. Patrides (London: J. M. Dent, 1985), p. 99.
9. Georgia E. Brown, 'Marlowe's Poems and Classicism', in Cheney (ed.), *The Cambridge Companion to Christopher Marlowe*, pp. 106–26 (p. 117).
10. D. H. Lawrence to Nancy Pearn, 12 April 1927, in *The Cambridge Edition of the Letters and Works of D. H. Lawrence*, ed. James T. Boulton and Margaret H. Boulton with Gerald M. Lacy (Cambridge: Cambridge University Press, 1991), vol. VI, p. 29.
11. Cited in Michael Dobson and Stanley Wells (eds.), *The Oxford Companion to Shakespeare* (Oxford: Oxford University Press, 2001; repr. 2005), p. 511.
12. Macdonald P. Jackson, 'Brian Vickers, *Shakespeare, "A Lover's Complaint"*, and John Davies of Hereford', *Review of English Studies*, 58 (2007), pp. 723–5.
13. Cheney, 'Introduction', p. 9.

Chapter 11

Seventeenth-century poetry 1: poetry in the age of Donne and Jonson

JONATHAN POST

By calling this chapter 'Poetry in the age of Donne and Jonson' rather than Jacobean or Stuart poetry, which might seem an appropriate sequel to what is often referred to as Elizabethan poetry, I mean to underscore a simple set of related literary observations: that John Donne and Ben Jonson were the two most original and influential poets writing in the earlier seventeenth century; that they were recognised as such by many, although not all, of their peers, which included other important poets of 'the age'; and that, as a sign of their significance, at least some of these poets gathered together to help form the sizeable outpouring of elegies that appeared in the immediate aftermath of each man's death: Donne's in 1631, and Jonson's in 1637.

Their impact was thus quickly recognised, their poetry much imitated, adapted and occasionally resisted. But in both cases, too, their achievement in verse, while differing significantly from each other in subject and manner – Donne is one of the great love poets in English, Jonson is England's first important neo-classicist – was only a part of their larger cultural and artistic legacy. Donne would eventually become one of the most recognised preachers of his era once he rose to the eminent position of Dean of St Paul's Cathedral in 1621; and the notoriety of his early erotic verse, which circulated widely in manuscript, would combine with his later fame as a preacher to create a unique place for him in English poetry – a sort of poet's corner of his own in St Paul's, where his statue still stands. Thomas Carew, the most astute reader of both men's verse, memorably captured Donne's double achievement at the end of his elegy to the poet:

Here lies a King, that rul'd as hee thought fit
The universall Monarchy of wit;
Here lie two Flamens, and both those, the best,
Apollo's first, at last, the true Gods Priest.[1]

Jonson, who revelled in nothing more than calling himself 'The Poet', as William Drummond recollected, was also much else besides.[2] To contemporaries he was – and still is – often regarded as Shakespeare's rival, not only in the theatre, where both men sought to earn a living on both sides of the Thames, but, as legend at least has it, in the tavern, where 'many were the wit-combats betwixt' the two. Jonson, like 'a Spanish great galleon . . . was built far higher in learning; solid, but slow in his performances. Shakespeare, with the English man-of-war, lesser in bulk, but lighter in sailing, could turn with all tides, tack about, and take advantage of all winds, by the quickness of his wit and invention.'[3] Spanish galleon or not, weighty Jonson somehow skilfully navigated his way from the raucous, masculine world of London's south bank to the more refined, sexually mixed world of the Jacobean court. When the Scottish King James came to the throne in 1603, Jonson, not Shakespeare, soon found a place there, and he became one of the key mythologisers of Jacobean rule. In collaboration with the stage designer, Inigo Jones, he served as the King's favourite writer of that most expensive of art forms enjoyed by aristocrats: the masque. A few years later, in 1616, the same Jonson would shock many contemporaries by bringing together a sizeable selection of his *own* plays, masques and poems, which he published in a large, carefully printed, handsomely designed folio called *The Works*. That was an honour usually accorded only to the great dead – like Homer or Virgil or, shortly, Shakespeare.

Samuel Johnson was the first critic to recognise that something new was afoot when, in his 'Life of Cowley', he noted that 'about the beginning of the seventeenth century appeared a race of writers that might be termed the metaphysical poets'.[4] Johnson's reference to 'a race of writers' suggests how alien these poets seemed to an Augustan sensibility nourished on classical standards of decorum, which, ironically, the earlier Jonson had helped to establish. But for later readers, Johnson's umbrella term, 'the metaphysical poets', created greater consternation. In an effort to show that 'metaphysical poetry' was not a 'quaint' byway, T. S. Eliot famously responded that poets like Donne, living before Milton and Dryden, somehow possessed, like Eden's Adam, perfectly unified sensibilities.[5] It wasn't true, of course, and Eliot would soon recant, although the ripple effect created by his initial enthusiasm would be felt throughout much of the twentieth century in the writings of poets and critics alike. It was also the case too that the rupture with the immediate past noted by Johnson included more than – to invoke Johnson's still valuable formulation – a sudden elevation of wit, in which 'the most heterogeneous ideas are yoked by violence together'.[6] The rupture involved something approaching a deliberate repudiation of the past altogether as a subject matter for poetry, and of those poets, Sidney and Spenser, who had been most associated with the dominant Elizabethan forms of pastoral romance and the Petrarchan love complaint, with their preferred emphasis on artifice and ornamentation.

In this regard, Donne and Jonson might well be counted England's first modern poets. They wrote about what they saw, thought, felt and desired with new, unprecedented directness. Here is a short poem by Jonson:

At court I met it, in clothes brave enough
  To be a courtier, and looks grave enough
To seem a statesman. As I near it came,
  It made me a great face; I asked the name;
A lord, it cried, buried in flesh and blood,
  And such from whom let no man hope least good,
For I will do none; and as little ill,
  For I will dare none. Good lord, walk dead still. (p. 225)

Although epigrams were hardly new, nothing quite like this had been written before in English: a simple but strange encounter, a courtier's befuddled outburst mimicked, and a definitive door-closing exit by the poet – all tidily accomplished in eight lines of plain speech, as if Jonson were telling a joke with a powerful punch line. Once done, it must have seemed easy thereafter. Nor had anything in the vast arsenal of Elizabethan love poetry quite anticipated the emotionally complex familiarity of the opening stanza of Donne's 'The Good Morrow', with its intimate intertwining of personal pronouns:

I wonder by my troth, what thou, and I
  Did, till we loved? were we not weaned till then,
But sucked on country pleasures, childishly?
  Or snorted we in the seven sleepers' den?
'Twas so; but this, all pleasures fancies be.
  If ever any beauty I did see,
Which I desired, and got, 'twas but a dream of thee.[7]

We seem suddenly in the midst of overhearing two people speaking to each other, even though, of course, in this dramatic monologue, only one person – 'Donne' – is doing the actual talking. And above all, it is alert talk. The amatory mood becomes more boisterously explicit with each question – three in four lines; then a further abrupt turn in the dismissive admission, ''Twas so', as Donne prepares to unfurl love's sentimental flag in the concluding tercet, except that the final sweep of the alexandrine includes the earthy aside, 'and got'. Take away that simple foot, smooth out the line into another pentameter, and Donne becomes something else: less immediately worldly and passionate, less psychologically complex, less triumphantly his own subject.

Donne and Jonson were born a generation after Sidney and Spenser but within a year of each other in 1572–3, and they differed from their notable Elizabethan predecessors by being Londoners both, deeply affected by the city's sudden growth, and by its newest art form in the 1590s – the theatre. Both poems cited above, for instance, could be snippets taken from the stage. And their preferred genres, at least initially, reflected their urban environment: Roman satire, as favoured by Horace, Juvenal and Martial; epigrams (like the one quoted above), which Jonson would elevate into a major genre; verse epistles of an Horatian town and country sort; and in Donne's case, the Ovidian love elegy, in all its spunky, racy particularity, in which the attention to a rhetoric of 'masculine persuasive force' (p. 57) would reappear, as we've just seen in 'The Good Morrow', in a more intimately dialogical form in the collection of love poetry known as *The Songs and Sonnets*.

They were also, in their individual ways, both outsiders in the often small world of London. In nervously Protestant England, Donne had been born into an ancient Catholic family, descended on his mother's side from Sir Thomas More, who had been executed in 1534 for refusing to subscribe to the Act of Supremacy declaring Henry VIII to be the true spiritual head of the Church of England; and for much of his life, Donne would be riddled with doubt over the true church and matters of personal salvation, topics that would be treated with unprecedented urgency in almost all his devotional poetry – the Holy Sonnets, occasional meditations and divine hymns – as well as the strenuous Third Satire, with its injunction to 'doubt wisely' (pp. 29–30). Donne's family would also be variously persecuted as Catholics in a Protestant state. In 1594, his brother Henry died from the plague in prison, where he had been committed for harbouring a Yorkshire priest. And Donne himself would seem to have thrown all caution to the wind when, in 1601, he determined to marry Anne More (a Protestant, no relation to Sir Thomas More), in a clandestine wedding that infuriated Anne's father and cost Donne his employment in the household of Sir Thomas Egerton, Lord Keeper of the Seal. The witticism, *'John Donne – Anne Donne – Undone'*, quickly emerged in the wake of these events, pointing to the financial and career downturn that suddenly put Donne on the periphery of London society and haunted him until he eventually settled on a career in the Church in 1615 at age forty-three. By this time, Donne had fathered eleven children and was soon to be a widower when Anne would die in giving birth to their twelfth child in 1617.

By contrast, and yet by the kind of parallel logic that could only happen in a nation that changed religions with each ruler in the sixteenth century, Jonson was born into impoverished circumstance as the posthumous son of an Anglican clergyman, who had earlier lost his estate under the Catholic Queen Mary. In poor straits until his mother married a bricklayer, Jonson, so the story goes, seems to have benefited from this new alliance in his later preference for remarkably sturdy verse, in his favoured mode of couplets, put together with greater attention to craftsmanship than inspiration. He was also soon to be taken under the wing of England's renowned historian and headmaster of the Westminster School, William Camden. Jonson was to thank Camden touchingly in Epigram 14, and the thorough education he received in classical languages, rhetoric and grammar did much to compensate for his own lack of a genteel birth in England's highly stratified society. Under Camden's tutelage, moreover, Jonson witnessed an ideal of surrogate paternal authority in learning that he would himself replicate among his own poetic 'sons'. Although he seems rarely to have been troubled by theological matters of the kind that afflicted Donne, he was converted to Catholicism while imprisoned in 1598 for having killed in a duel the actor Gabriel Spencer; and even if his rash actions in this instance had few long-term consequences, he was, like Donne, something of a loose cannon, especially when it came to other writers. His 'Conversations with Drummond' reads, at times, like a hit list: 'Daniel was at jealousies with him'; 'Drayton feared him, and he esteemed not of him'; 'He beat Marston, and took his pistol from him'; 'He cursed Petrarch for redacting verses to sonnets'. Jonson even thought that 'Donne, for not keeping of accent, deserved hanging' – and Donne was a friend, 'the first poet in the world in some things' (pp. 596–8). Admittedly, the phrasing in the 'Conversations' belongs to Drummond, who was himself the target of Jonson's criticism, but it supports what we know about Jonson: that his was not a serenely won neo-classicism, in spite of the elegant symmetries and clean diction he brought to English verse.

However much Jonson and Donne distanced themselves from their Elizabethan predecessors – 'Spenser, in affecting the ancients, writ no language', Jonson noted (p. 569) – the two poets differed significantly from each other in almost every way then imaginable in verse. As their contrasting portraits in the National Portrait Gallery suggest, it must have been a friendship based on opposites. Donne was primarily, indeed pre-eminently, a poet of relentless figuration, a 'master of metaphor' in Aristotle's sense. 'Emblems of more', in fact, a phrase from one of Donne's most conceited poems, 'A Valediction: Of Weeping', might serve as an emblem of Donne's restless desire to pursue an image or 'conceit' well beyond normal (one wants to say mortal) usage, whether in the many changes rung on the reference to 'Angels' – also the word for English coins – in the 110-line elegy 'Upon his Mistress's Lost Chain', which Jonson claimed to know by heart (p. 597), or in the manifestly witty concentration on tears found in the 'Valediction':

> Let me pour forth
> My tears before thy face, whilst I stay here,
> For thy face coins them, and thy stamp they bear,
> And by this mintage they are something worth,
> For thus they be
> Pregnant of thee;
> Fruits of much grief they are, emblems of more,
> When a tear falls, that thou falls which it bore,
> So thou and I are nothing then, when on a diverse shore. (p. 112)

This stanza possesses the meticulous, mysterious, microscopic intricacy of a Netherlandish painting by Jan van Eyck or Quentin Metsys, but, of course, none of painting's penchant for stasis. Indeed, Eliot's remark that the 'rapid association of thought' in this poem 'requires considerable agility on the part of the reader' is surely to the point, if somewhat understated.[8] As is, too, the purpose of the many conceits associated with tears. These draw the lovers together into an intimate knot, perhaps most suggestively rendered in the dimeter couplet nestled in the stanza's centre. But love knots in Donne, however tightly tied, also threaten to dissolve into nothingness, a problem of dissolution that Donne can also turn into a paradox of creation here, not only in the idea that grief can bear fruit (continuing the pregnancy metaphor) but in the fanciful sense that the individual stanzas might be thought of as tears in the shape they assume on the page, their accumulation productive of poetry itself. 'Fruits of much grief they are, emblems of more', including, perhaps, emblematically enshrouding the name of his lover, Anne More, in the pun on 'more', with an additional pun in the Latin for death.

If words for Donne are like coins, capable of endless minting and meanings, Jonson, for the most part, sought to resist or control this baroque play with language. 'A man coins not a new word without some peril, and less fruit', he noted (with perhaps a sideways glance at Donne's poem) in his commonplace book, *Timber: or Discoveries*, and then further observed: 'the chief virtue of a style is perspicuity, and nothing so vicious in it as to need an interpreter' (pp. 571–2). Taken to its extreme, Jonson's statement might be viewed as an argument for pure transparency of meaning, as if words could mirror things and syntax might perfectly reflect the disposition of thought – in effect even circumventing altogether the need or desire for poetry, as his contemporary Francis Bacon wished. But Jonson is also more forgiving and balanced in his attitude towards poetics, as in much else. In the same paragraph, he argues for a judicious moderation in the use of verbal ornamentation in poetry.

> Some words are to be culled out for ornament and colour, as we gather flowers to strew houses, or make garlands; but they are better when they grow to our style as in a meadow, where though the mere grass and greenness delights, yet the variety of flowers doth heighten and beautify. Marry, we must not play or riot too much with them, as in paronomasies, nor use too swelling or ill-sounding words, *quae per salebras altaque saxa cadunt* [which fall on rough places and steep rocks]. (p. 572)

'Paronomasia' is the rhetorical term for word-play or puns – the kind of heady activity that Donne could perform at the drop of a hat, even when addressing God in 'A Hymn to God the Father' on so serious a matter as his own salvation, punning all while on his name, especially in the refrain: 'When thou hast done, thou has not done, / For, I have more' (p. 333). Jonson could never be so playful – indeed not at all playful in his few religious poems, as a glance at his poem 'To Heaven' suggests. The poem is utterly and movingly devoid of pretence of any kind in addressing God on the subject of his own salvation. Jonson is more at ease, rather, with things in this world, even when the subjects involve personal grief, as in his famous epitaph 'On My First Son'. The poem, characteristically in couplets, is short enough to quote in full and illuminates his measured, subtle habits with language:

> Farewell, thou child of my right hand, and joy;
> My sin was too much hope of thee, loved boy.
> Seven years thou wert lent to me, and I thee pay,
> Exacted by thy fate, on the just day.
> Oh, could I lose all father now! For why
> Will man lament the state he should envy?
> To have so soon 'scaped world's and flesh's rage,
> And, if no other misery, yet age?
> Rest in soft peace, and, asked, say here doth lie
> Ben Jonson his best piece of poetry;
> For whose sake, henceforth, all his vows be such,
> As what he loves may never like too much. (pp. 236–7)

Few of Jonson's poems are as revealing as this one on so many fronts. Not only does it remind us of the significance of naming in all of his poetry – indeed of having a name and therefore a social identity. In this case, the name is one that links father with son, and, through the reference to the Bible (in Hebrew,

'Benjamin' means 'son of the right hand'), underscores the special pleasure Jonson felt towards his namesake, slightly amplified in the final foot, 'and joy', which in turn sets up the rhyme with 'loved boy' in the next line. But the bond between the two in life also extends into the realm of art, the one enriching the other. The poem is the 'child' of Jonson's right hand, and near the end, the son is imagined as a speaking epitaph testifying, in a complex self-reference, on behalf of the father's work as 'his best piece of poetry'. There is authorial ego here and paternal emotion – the father writes most lovingly of the son by praising him in the terms that mean most to an author – but no Donnean outpouring of tears: 'Oh, *could* I lose all father now!'(my italics). The poem is a mix of stoicism, borrowed from his classical source in Martial ('whatever you love, pray that it may not please you too much')[9] and tenderness, especially in the small addition of the adjective 'soft' to the formula 'rest in peace'. This is a poem where the play and placement of words are important, in fact crucial, in fathoming a father's sense of grief, right down to the last line, in which we are invited to distinguish between 'like' and 'love'. But the play is part of the poem's deep structure, grounded in the solemn occasion, and in the poem's biblical and classical past.

Donne's nose for the hyperbolic found expression early on in his experiments with the extremities of verse satire and the Ovidian elegy – poetic forms that, in the 1590s, begged trouble from the censors in what was an especially stressful decade in politics and religion. Anxieties about royal succession came increasingly to the fore, of which a crowning manifestation was the unsuccessful attempt by Essex to depose Elizabeth in 1601. Two years earlier, in 1599, the ecclesiastical authorities called in, to be burned, a number of erotic and satirical works by Thomas Nashe, Joseph Hall and John Marston, and including Marlowe's recent translation of Ovid's book of elegies. Still in manuscript, Donne's verse escaped the pyre, but portions of his satires were later censored and several of the elegies were suppressed in the posthumous 1633 printing of his *Poems*. It wasn't until the Restoration, in fact, that 'Love's Progress' – the most graphic of the elegies in its pursuit of woman's 'centrique part' (her 'v-ness' enhanced in the Variorium's old spelling text of the poem)[10] – would be published with Donne's name attached to it. In partial testimony to its popular underground reputation, it provided, in manuscript, a blueprint for Thomas Carew to model his ever more elaborate sexual fantasies in 'A Rapture'. The same publishing history is true with the infamous, often anthologised, elegy beginning 'Come, madam, come', including Carew's familiarity with it. Donne's highly dramatic adaptation (not translation) of Ovid's steamy elegy (I. 5) reveals the poet to be a singular and thoroughly

Renaissance man, updating his erotic source to fit the exploratory mentality of his New World age – 'O my America, my new found land' – including making a bawdy allusion to 'A heaven like Mahomet's paradise' and perhaps a sly reference to circumventing censorship itself when he begs his mistress to 'License my roving hands, and let them go / Behind, before, above, between, below', on his way to imagining 'Full nakedness' (p. 13).

There are significant differences in address between the elegies and the satires, but both are restless with energy – spontaneous overflows of outrageous wit. The longest satire, in fact, is a 244-line Dantesque cruise through London's underworld, replete with a descent into a hellish court, as Donne seems constantly tempted, here and elsewhere, to speak what has been often unsayable in verse, and sometimes paying a price for it. These lines from Satire II, for instance, were lopped off in 1633: 'And to every suitor lie in every thing, / Like a king's favourite, yea like a king', quickly followed by another pair of stricken lines:

> Bastardy abounds not in kings' titles, nor
> Simony and sodomy in churchmen's lives
> As these things do in him. (p. 23)[11]

The question is not so much *why* did these lines have to go as *where* did they come from? Or to phrase the matter with an eye towards decorum: if Jonson wanted to hang Donne for the liberties he took with his accents, it's also clear, as the censored lines indicate, that Donne's liberties didn't stop with his feet.

Here is a slightly longer view, not censored, on a topic he shared with Jonson (in Epigrams, 51, 56, 81 and 100) – contempt for plagiarists:

> But he is worst, who (beggarly) doth chaw
> Others' wits' fruits, and in his ravenous maw
> Rankly digested, doth those things out-spew,
> As his own things; and they are his own, 'tis truth,
> For if one eat my meat, though it be known
> The meat was mine, th'excrement is his own.
> (Satire II, lines 25–30)

One can only wince at the depiction here. These are pentameter couplets, we must remind ourselves, but of a deliberately 'unfit' kind, as if the speaker could whip or 'spue' corruption out of town by the sheer strength of expression. Variably enjambed, prosy with repetition ('things'/'things', 'own'/'own'), at times gnashingly overcrowded with stressed syllables ('Others' wits' fruits'), grotesquely or imperfectly rhymed ('chaw'/'maw'; 'out-spew'/'truth'), they eagerly forgo the niceties of verse in the name of exposing vice once and for all – not, in fact, at all like the polite outrage Alexander Pope fashioned when he rewrote these same lines as:

> Wretched indeed! but far more wretched yet
> Is he who makes his meal on others wit;
> 'Tis chang'd no doubt from what it was before,
> His rank digestion makes it wit no more:
> Sense, past thro' him, no longer is the same,
> For food digested takes another name.[12]

Pope's versified versions of two of Donne's Satires (II and IV) perform a fine gloss on these difficult originals, perhaps the best glosses we have, in fact. His 'sound' makes Donne's 'sense' more explicitly graspable – but also distinctly cleaner and less darkly threatening. Note how Donne's paragraph, a sentence of six lines, is calculated to land forcefully on the final scatological image, whereas Pope's same six lines function as three discretely witty couplets, with the last one urbanely turning away (utilising a phantom rhyme with 'it') from what Donne has so explicitly named.

As these lines suggest, and his contemporaries attested, Donne was a poet of excess, not just an explorer of potentially censorable subjects but a lyric poet of vertiginous heights – 'She'is all states, and all princes, I, / Nothing else is' ('The Sun Rising' (p. 93)) – and deep, melancholic troughs: 'Oh my black soul! Now thou art summoned / By sickness, death's herald, and champion' (Holy Sonnet 2 (p. 174)). 'Unfit' in love, he could be blasphemous to boot, as in 'The Canonization', but like Michelangelo when it came to imagining the terrible immediacy of Judgment Day:

> What if this present were the world's last night?
> Mark in my heart, O soul, where thou dost dwell,
> The picture of Christ crucified, and tell
> Whether that countenance can thee affright,
> Tears in his eyes quench the amazing light,
> Blood fills his frowns, which from his pierced head fell,
> And can that tongue adjudge thee unto hell,
> Which prayed forgiveness for his foes' fierce spite?
> (Holy Sonnet 9; p. 177)

Jonson, by contrast, is pre-eminently a poet of the middle way, even, it seems, of middle age. He once remarked, inaccurately, that Donne wrote 'all his best pieces ere he was twenty-five years old' (p. 597), that is, by 1598. (On the basis of those poems we can date with some certainty, we know this to be untrue.) But the comment points to an important truth about Jonson's own work.

Consciously or not, Jonson seems to have separated himself chronologically from Donne early on, since almost all his poems and plays that survive, indeed were collected by him in the 1616 *Works*, date from 1598 onwards. When Jonson finally tackled the Donnean topic of love, for instance, in the exquisite suite of poems called 'A Celebration of Charis' (after earlier explaining, rather truculently, in the prefatory poem to *The Forest* 'Why I write not of Love'), he did so from the comic perspective of a slightly ridiculous middle-aged wooer: 'Let it not your wonder move, / Less your laughter, that I love. / Though I now write fifty years / I have had, and have, my peers' (pp. 310–11). Indeed, even when he adopts some youthful Donnean language in the sequence, as happens in the lyric beginning 'For Love's sake, kiss me once again', it only further accentuates the fanciful posturing – as if he's gamely trying to put on tight jeans. Although Jonson could rise to moments of excess, these admitted 'fits' typically involved un-Donnean matters of art (in his 'A Fit of Rhyme against Rhyme' or 'An Expostulation with Inigo Jones'). Late in life, they took the form of the Horatian high road or a Pindaric 'leap' in the great odes he composed when his own authority as a poet was under fire.

For the more gravity-bound Jonson, not a series of poems on the 'Last Things' but a loose translation of Martial's popular epigram, 'The things that make the happier life are these' (p. 433), forms the fitting last word in *The Underwood*, the last volume Jonson put together for publication. The translation points to the deep wish for balance and civility at the heart of his verse. Jonson's poems are typically about this life, things that give pleasure, as he says, like inviting a friend to supper in the poem of that title, in which the guest's 'fair acceptance', not the food, is what matters; about good places to visit, like the Sidney estate; or about people worthy of praise, like Lucy Countess of Bedford:

> This morning, timely rapt with holy fire,
> I thought to form unto my zealous muse
> What kind of creature I could most desire
> To honour, serve and love, as poets use. (p. 247)

Jonson can be occasionally 'rapt' but rarely whimsical – that possibility will be explored later by Robert Herrick. He is more concerned with questions of authority and decorum, about using the medium of print, right down to the lowly comma, to establish a voice every bit equal in weight to the matter at hand, whether it is the lightly epitaphic touch needed to create a fable to 'explain' the death of a child actor, or the more extensive epistolary structure necessary to celebrate the Sidney family and their Penshurst estate, or the fine crafting required of his many songs, especially those translations from Catullus that elegantly dot *The Forest*. Here is Jonson praising Donne's employer in 'To Thomas, Lord Chancellor':

> Whilst thy weighed judgements, Egerton, I hear,
> And know thee then a judge not of one year;
> Whilst I behold thee live with purest hands;
> That no affection in thy voice commands;
> That still thou'rt present to the better cause,
> And no less wise than skilful in the laws;
> Whilst thou art certain to thy words, once gone,
> As is thy conscience, which is always one:
> The Virgin, long since fled from earth, I see,
> To our times returned, hath made her heaven in thee. (p. 247)

Who, we might ask, is the real judge here? Although Donne can often dazzle, he could never have written so settled and judicious an appraisal as this.

One can profitably develop further comparisons between Donne and Jonson, but these differences (and some similarities) are perhaps best illuminated by setting their poetry in a broader cultural and literary context. Jonson's interest in topographical poetry in 'To Penshurst', for instance, was notably continued in a number of country-house, or estate, poems by Carew, Herrick and Marvell, as well as perhaps anticipated by Aemelia Lanyer in her 'The Description of Cooke-ham'. The impulse behind these estate poems is primarily one of seeking patronage – then as now, poetry was a 'mean mistress', as Jonson observed. In the case of both Lanyer and Marvell, the praise of the estate was further motivated and complicated by their positions as tutors to the children of the elite: Lady Anne Clifford, in Lanyer's poem, the accomplished daughter of Sir George and Margaret Clifford, who spent much of her life attempting to recover property (including Cooke-ham) that had been bequeathed to her father's brother at the time of his death in 1605; and the young Maria Fairfax, sole daughter of Ann Vere and Sir Thomas Fairfax, the retired Lord General of the Parliamentary army, to whom the family estate of Appleton House was entailed. Although Marvell will be treated in another chapter in this volume, his profound talents benefited greatly by the examples of both Donne and Jonson, among others, in the century's extraordinary exfoliation of lyric possibilities.

Aemelia Lanyer (1569–1645) is an altogether different story. As the first Englishwoman to publish a substantial volume of original poems, *Salve Deus Rex Judaeorum* (1611), her poetry reflects these inaugural concerns, manifested in part simply by the extensive number of dedicatory poems to powerful women of the time, including Queen Elizabeth and Mary Sidney, the Countess of Pembroke (co-author with her brother, Philip, of a much celebrated translation of the psalms), with whom Lanyer claims poetic affiliation. The title poem, on Christ's Passion, likewise includes an 'apology' or defence of Eve, written in 'honour' of Queen Anne, and it, in turn, is followed by the estate poem on Cooke-ham, in which Lanyer describes herself as once belonging to an ideal sororal community, graced by Margaret Clifford herself.

The contrast with Jonson's 'Penshurst' could hardly be sharper, although whether it is deliberate or not may never be known. Neither poet ever mentions the other, nor does it seem possible, at the moment, to establish with certainty the priority of composition. Both poems, in fact, represent distinct and separate experiences, reflective of their author's different stations in life, their different audiences and their different literary 'sources': Jonson's from several epistles by Martial, and Lanyer's from Virgil's first eclogue. Jonson's descriptive celebration is formulated, moreover, entirely in the present tense, with an immediacy generated, it would seem, by a recent visit. It is also the fullest working out in his verse of the ideal mean as both a preferred literary and ethical model. As he noted in *Timber*, adapting Aristotle, 'we must express readily and fully, not profusely. There is a difference between a liberal and a prodigal hand' (pp. 572–3). The latter view informs the poem's famous opening, with its insistent differentiation of Penshurst from other 'prodigy' houses of the period being built – Hatfield House is often mentioned as an example of one such. 'Thou art not, Penshurst, built to envious show / Of touch or marble, nor canst boast a row / Of polished pillars' (p. 282); and the former ideal of expression is implicitly present throughout the poem in the ready and full, not profuse, descriptions of the estate that follow. Framed around the very concept of 'degree' that Lanyer will ruefully lament, it places Jonson, the poet, at the centre, in the house, partaking liberally in a feast and even fantasising that he is being treated like royalty.

Lanyer's poem, rather, is a 'Farewell'. As with Milton's later use of the topos in Eve's lament in *Paradise Lost*, but longer, it is throughout coloured by a melancholic sense of the speaker's expulsion from an Edenic landscape and community, in this case of women only. In the repeated figure of Philomela, the nightingale, it also includes elements of the female 'complaint' tradition, popular under Elizabeth and exploited more fully in Eve's apology in *Salve*, and thus decorously hints, as well, of Lanyer's critical attitude towards the established, male-centred Jacobean hierarchy, temporarily reversed or abated while 'Cooke-ham' was occupied by the Clifford ladies. The most visually triumphant moment in the poem, in fact, is reserved for Lady Margaret's monarchical – indeed, magical – view of the surrounding thirteen shires:

> A Prospect fit to please the eyes of Kings:
> And thirteen shires appear'd all in your sight,
> Europe could not affoard much more delight.[13]

And from this fancifully regal height (no such view is possible), parallel to Jonson's own fantasies of 'reigning' in 'Penshurst', Lanyer then continues to sustain the Countess's position of masculine authority by comparing her to the Old Testament Patriarchs: Moses, David and Joseph.

The appeal of the estate poem, as these two versions suggest, was its salient mix of flattery and geographical specificity. If Lanyer's poem had no discernible after-life, Jonson's topographical celebration allowed for considerable variation, both in the country-house poems already mentioned and in the subject of the 'good life' more generally. In this regard, Robert Herrick (1591–1674) is the most original of Jonson's many 'sons'.[14] A Londoner at heart and Anglican priest, he wrote about the English countryside from the perspective of a rusticated classicist with a keen sense of time passing. Often discontent in Devon, to cite the title of one of the eleven hundred or so poems that make up *Hesperides*, published with another sizeable bunch in *Noble Numbers* (1648), Herrick was also happiest when trusting to good verse, especially of a confessedly Jonsonian order:

> When I a Verse shall make,
> Know I have praied thee,
> For old *Religions* sake,
> Saint *Ben* to aide me.[15]

As this slight stanza hints, Herrick is mainly a poet of moods rather than statements, although bidding farewell to sack can require a pleasurably full, Falstaffian fifty-four lines of pentameter verse before the bottle is finally put down, and the always anthologised poem 'Corinna's going a Maying' is, along with Marvell's 'To His Coy Mistress', one of the century's most impressive *carpe diem* poems. Jonson might draw up a list of the 'things that make the happier life'. For the more delectably elegiac Herrick, such a list would have to include the names of the many mistresses he imagines having lost:

> Stately *Julia*, prime of all;
> *Sapho* next, a principall;
> Smooth *Anthea*, for a skin
> White and Heaven-like Chrystalline. (pp. 15–16)

Like Jonson, although for different reasons, Herrick has been read sometimes with suspicion or embarrassment. If the 'father's' adherence to hierarchy has drawn criticism for having produced a poetry of the same, not dynamic with change, the 'son's' particular brand of lyricism has sometimes seemed too promiscuous or 'peculiar' – to use a favourite word of his – especially to readers with strict consciences. Sociologically cruder but more revealing than Jonson (see 'The Hock-Cart'), Herrick is also sexually quirkier (see 'The Vine' or 'Upon the Nipples of Julia's Breast'), and whereas Jonson exhibited a distrust of the furtive eye in favour of the stolid mind or heart (as in the song 'Still to be Neat', in which he contrasts courtly artifice against the classical ideal of a 'sweet neglect'), Herrick was positively titillated by what he saw, especially if the subject involved clothes. 'Delight in Disorder', a take-off on Jonson's 'Still to be Neat', is all about the bewitchery – or animation – of surfaces, reflected in his own delightful play with rhyme, and (like Jonson's poem) slyly anti-Puritanical in its demurral against art that's 'too precise in every part' (p. 28).

Jonson's impact was felt down the century in the new prestige afforded to the couplet, pentameter, of course, but also tetrameter and trimeter, and in the authority the verse epistle assumed for enabling a sense of community, particularly through formulating individual judgments of a literary or commendatory kind. But some of the most interesting poets often managed a blend of Jonson and Donne. Both Thomas Carew (1595–1640) and Henry King (1592–1669), for instance, are almost unthinkable apart from their predecessors. I have already alluded to Carew's erotic, Donnean side in 'A Rapture'. That poem also possesses a Titian-like pictorial sensuousness reminiscent of a Venetian voluptuary like Jonson's Volpone – only Carew is more finely tuned to the social ironies and erotic play associated with a sexual Elysium that serves as a foil for the hypocrisies found in the dominant court culture. As a porn-utopia of sorts, 'A Rapture' may well reflect time Carew spent in Venice. The strong emphasis on the visual (although not its subject matter) – the poem might more profitably be read as an ecphrasis than a dramatic monologue – was also in keeping with a Caroline high culture that was itself becoming more pictorially sophisticated, as represented by the rich collection of paintings amassed by Charles I at Whitehall. Carew's best readers have always been attracted to his sharp, critical eye towards the poetry he inherited. Nowhere is this discernment more evident than in his different assessments of Donne and Jonson. Better than any contemporary, Carew was able to grasp, intellectually and emotionally, Donne's radical departure from previous poets; and no 'son' has more effectively escaped the shadow of a 'father' than Carew did in his criticism of Jonson's behaviour stemming from the failure of his late play, *The New Inn*, in 1629.

Like Carew, Henry King had poems on both Donne and Jonson, eulogies, in fact, to each, although neither shows Carew's cool intelligence. King was a churchman from a family of distinguished churchmen, and his own biography is significantly, even intimately, involved with Donne's later life as a preacher. Along with being entrusted with Donne's sermons in his final days, King delivered to the sculptor the drawing Donne made of himself for the effigy now in St Paul's. King had also been educated at Westminster School a generation after Jonson, a common experience perhaps recollected in the extended attention given to Jonson's rhetorical and grammatical skills in his elegy 'To my Dead Friend Ben: Jonson'. Although perfectly competent in these 'public' verses, King would remain largely a figure of historical curiosity today were it not for one poem, 'The Exequy', written on the occasion of his young wife's death in 1624, included in Grierson's ground-breaking 1921 anthology of *Metaphysical Lyrics and Poems of the Seventeenth Century*, and singled out by Eliot as 'one of the finest poems of the age', especially for its controlled use of extended simile.[16] Its 120 lines also continue to inspire modern poems like Peter Porter's 'An Exequy', in which, as a backdrop to his private misery, he reminds us, too, that 'Bishop King / Once hymned in tetrametric rhyme / His young wife, lost before her time'.[17]

Not every poet in the early seventeenth century came within Donne's or Jonson's compass, as the example of Aemelia Lanyer suggests; and, by way of closing, it should be noted that those most resistant remained largely committed to Elizabethan forms of verse. Sidney's legacy, for instance, was actively advanced in the writings of Mary Wroth (1587–1651?), brought up in the culturally rich environment of Penshurst, the daughter of Robert Sidney, himself a poet and brother to Sir Philip and Mary Sidney; and, after several centuries of neglect, she is now generally regarded as 'the most prolific, self-conscious, and impressive female author of the Jacobean era'.[18] The 100-plus sonnets (and several songs) that make up the sequence *Pamphilia to Amphilanthus* – the first such extended sequence by a female poet in English, but bolstered by European examples – speak not just from the subject position of a female wooer, in which the poet's task is to channel erotic desire into affirmations of constancy, but often with muted criticism of Jacobean court politics, as in the sonnets 'Like to the Indians, scorched with the sunne', based on Wroth's performance in Jonson's *Masque of Blackness* and 'When every one to pleasing pastime hies', in which Wroth exercises an aristocratic spirit at odds with the pleasures at court. Modern anthologists rarely agree over which of her poems to reprint (a challenge made more difficult by the many lyrics scattered throughout her gigantic prose romance, *The Countess of Montgomery's Urania*). But an often included sonnet like 'My pain, still smothered in my grieved breast', suggests the meditative, inward direction of her sufferings that readily distinguish her poems from her uncle's overtly dramatised addresses in *Astrophil and Stella*; and, of course, neither uncle, father nor daughter embark on the subtle intertwining of body and soul so evident, for instance, in Donne's 'The Ecstasy', a revision of Philip Sidney's eighth song in *Astrophil and Stella*.

Often nostalgic, Wroth's writings join company with pastoral verse by other poets on the fringes of court power, like the English 'Spenserians' William Browne and Michael Drayton, and the more geographically distant Scottish poet, William Drummond (1585–1649), the most talented of the Anglicised Scottish poets associated with James I, who chose, for the most part, to remain in Scotland, and whose poems, Jonson said, 'were not after the fancy of the time' (p. 597). A comparison of Drummond's 'The Happiness of a Flea' and 'Of that Same' from *Madrigals and Epigrams* (1616) with Donne's 'The Flea' quickly bears out the truth of Jonson's comment. Drummond's poems are very much, and quite deliberately, cut from Sidneyan and Continental cloth, especially of Italian fabric. His two 'Flea' poems, for instance, are direct imitations from Tasso, and in a letter to Arthur Johnson, one of Charles I's physicians, he spoke disdainfully of poetry abstracted to 'Metaphysicall Ideas, and Scholasticall Quiddityes', no doubt with Donne's example partly in mind.[19] Indeed, his first English (as distinguished from Scottish) publisher, Edward Phillips, declared with only some exaggeration in 1656:

> Never could any times afford a Story
> Of one so match'd unto great *Sidney's* glory,
> Or Fame so well divided, as between
> *Penshurst's* renowned shades, and *Hawthornden*.[20]

Not only did Drummond initiate his first volume of *Poems* (1616), published in Edinburgh, with a group of Petrarchan sonnets utilising many of Sidney's colloquialisms, but more unusual still in the seventeenth century, he tried his hand at continuing Sidney's Italianate experiments with that most 'doleful' of poetic forms, sestinas or 'Sextains', as Drummond calls them, often choosing some of the same terminal words as Sidney.

Still, a full 'story' must note, in closing, the significant variety of Drummond's verse, now being made more available in anthologies with a consciously less Anglo-centric focus. Drummond's fondness for Giambattista Marino, for instance, put him in the literary vanguard with regard to Mannerism, evident in elegant little poems like 'A Daedal of my death', based on Marino's 'Fabro dela mia morte'; and a religious poem, like the 'finely wrought'[21] sonnet on John the Baptist from *Flowers of Sion* (1623), can stand fully on its own, as is true with a number of the epigrams, especially those written late in life. Indeed, were it only in couplets, we might even imagine Jonson, in conversation with Drummond, nodding approvingly over the one on John Pym, the celebrated Parliamentarian who died in 1643:

> When Pym last night descended into hell,
> Ere he his cups of Lethe did carouse,
> 'What place is this', said he, 'I pray me tell?'
> To whom a devil: 'This is the lower house.'[22]

Notes

1. *The Poems of Thomas Carew*, ed. Rhodes Dunlap (Oxford: Clarendon Press, 1949), p. 74.
2. *Ben Jonson*, ed. Ian Donaldson (Oxford: Oxford University Press, 1985), p. 609. Further page references to Jonson will be included in the text.
3. From Thomas Fuller, *The Worthies of England*, in *Ben Jonson and the Cavalier Poets*, ed. Hugh MacClean (New York: W.W. Norton, 1974), p. 425.
4. *Samuel Johnson: Selected Poetry and Prose*, ed. Frank Brady and William Wimsatt (Berkeley: University of California Press, 1977), p. 347.
5. From T. S. Eliot, 'The Metaphysical Poets', *Selected Essays* (New York: Harcourt, Brace and World, 1964), p. 247.
6. Johnson, *Selected Poetry and Prose*, p. 348.
7. *John Donne: The Major Works*, ed. John Carey (Oxford: Oxford World's Classics, 1990), pp. 89–90. Further page references to Donne will be included in the text.
8. Eliot, 'The Metaphysical Poets', p. 242.
9. Quoted in Donaldson (ed.), *Ben Jonson*, p. 652.
10. *The Variorum Edition of the Poetry of John Donne: The Elegies*, ed. Gary A. Stringer (Bloomington: Indiana University Press, 2000), vol. II, p. 301 ('Perfection is in Vnity').
11. See the notes to these lines in *The Complete English Poems of John Donne*, ed. C. A. Patrides (London: J. M. Dent, 1985), p. 222.
12. Quoted from *The Complete English Poems of John Donne*, ed. Patrides, p. 501.
13. *The Poems of Aemilia Lanyer*, ed. Susanne Woods (New York: Oxford University Press, 1993), p. 133.
14. See *Ben Jonson and the Cavalier Poets* for more 'sons'.
15. *The Poetical Works of Robert Herrick*, ed. L. C. Martin (Oxford: Clarendon Press, 1956), p. 212 ('His *Prayer* to Ben. Johnson'). Further page references to Herrick will be included in the text.

16. Eliot, 'The Metaphysical Poets', p. 243.
17. Peter Porter, from *The Cost of Seriousness* (1978) in *Collected Poems*, 2 vols. (Oxford: Oxford University Press, 1999), vol. 1, pp. 328–31.
18. *Norton Anthology of English Literature*, gen. ed. Stephen Greenblatt, eighth edition, 2 vols. (New York: W. W. Norton, 2006), vol. 1, p. 1451.
19. *William Drummond of Hawthornden: Poems and Prose*, ed. Robert H. Macdonald (Edinburgh: Scottish Academic Press, 1976), p. 191.
20. *The Poetical Works of William Drummond*, ed. L. E. Kastner, 2 vols. (Edinburgh: William Blackwood and Sons, 1913), vol. 1, p. civ.
21. John Kerrigan, 'William Drummond and the British Problem', in *On Shakespeare and Early Modern Literature: Essays* (Oxford: Oxford University Press, 2001), p. 159.
22. *The New Oxford Book of Seventeenth-Century Verse*, ed. Alastair Fowler (Oxford: Oxford University Press, 1991), p. 221.

Chapter 12

Seventeenth-century poetry 2: Herbert, Vaughan, Philips, Cowley, Crashaw, Marvell

ALISON SHELL

Whether a lyric poem is addressed to a friend, to a lover or to God, its most intimate relationship of all is with the second person singular. It provides, or purports to provide, a privileged glimpse into the speaker's private thoughts, which are sometimes the writer's own; but its attention to personal address also has the effect of directing attention away from the poet. For this and other reasons, it defies easy distinctions between private and public. The following chapter will examine a number of issues arising from this continuum, each of which has a particular relevance to seventeenth-century conditions. What does it mean to write with God as your implied reader, in an age so conscious of the difference between religious denominations? How do coteries act to provide a halfway house between an audience of two and a wider, undifferentiated public, and how do the conditions of manuscript circulation reinforce this? How do writers of this era perform, celebrate and fictionalise relationships with their forebears, their contemporaries and their addressees? How did the Civil War inspire poets' injunctions towards public action, or celebrations of the retired life?

The career of the first poet to be considered, George Herbert, has often been read as epitomising a retreat from public to private. Beginning with Herbert's first biographer Izaak Walton, commentators on Herbert's life have noted a seeming imbalance between the glittering prizes of his early years – Public Orator at Cambridge, Member of Parliament – and his modest latter-day role as a parish priest. Walton, and some subsequent biographers, have seen this move towards religious retirement as prompted in the first instance by a failure of worldly hopes.[1] But looking at his English literary remains – the Latin ones tell a rather different story – Herbert's commitment to religious devotion and devotional writing does coexist with a certain intolerance of secular activity. What are probably his first surviving poems set the tone for what is to follow: two sonnets to his mother which lament the dominance of love poetry and ask for God to be more celebrated by poets. Walton identifies these as having been written when Herbert was not quite seventeen, which would date them during Herbert's undergraduate years, around 1609–10.[2] In them, Herbert asks God, 'Doth poetry / Wear Venus' livery, only serve her turn? / Why are not sonnets made of thee?' (sonnet 1, lines 3–5), and again, 'Why should I women's eyes for crystal take? / Such poor invention burns in their low mind, / Whose fire is wild, and doth not upward go / To praise, and on thee Lord, some ink bestow' (sonnet 2, lines 8–11).[3]

It is not to downplay Herbert's religious fervour to remark that these sonnets show the agonistic restlessness of a new literary generation. They would have been written around the same time as Shakespeare's were published, and like them, reflect the feeling that straightforward amatory sonnets are passé.[4] But whereas, in a sonnet such as 'My mistress' eyes are nothing like the sun', Shakespeare consciously looks back in parody, Herbert sets off in a God-ward direction that he claims has hardly been travelled. There is, it has to be said, some rhetorical exaggeration here. As far as Herbert's Elizabethan predecessors were concerned, the after-effects of the English Reformation did have a withering effect on non-Biblical religious verse, instilling widespread uneasiness about imaginative additions to scripture and prompting a move towards secular topics. But other English poets had written religious verse in the recent past, and the very poetic genre Herbert chooses, that of the sonnet, may be paying homage to John Donne's, Henry Lok's, Barnabe Barnes's or William Alabaster's previous efforts in that vein. As has been recognised ever since Louis Martz's pioneering study *The Poetry of Meditation*, there is also a very close relationship between Herbert's poetry and that of the Jesuit martyr Robert Southwell, which ran through a large number of editions after Southwell's execution in 1595.[5] It is not a debt which Herbert acknowledges – though Southwell was widely copied and borrowed from, his dissident's and martyr's status made it difficult for non-Catholics to cite him as an inspiration. Yet it is Southwell who provides the most obvious antecedent for two distinctive features of Herbert's poetic practice: his avowed distance from secular verse, and his advocacy of a plain style which is nevertheless consciously artful.

'Jordan (1)', one of the best-known poems in *The Temple*, provides a mature consideration of these issues. The poem has often, understandably, been read as a manifesto for Herbert's poetic philosophy, and it gives plenty of clues as to what Herbert is defining himself against. High on the list are pastorals, beloved of Elizabethan writers. But the speaker's questions, 'Is it no verse, except enchanted groves / And sudden arbours shadow coarse-spun lines?', 'Must all be veiled, while he that reads, divines, / Catching the sense at two removes?', combined with his later declaration 'Shepherds are honest people; let them sing' (lines 6–7, 9–11), betray a hostility not to the pastoral mode in itself, but to the way in which it was so often used as a vehicle for rustic diction and for commenting obliquely on current issues. In a poem which asks why poets have found it so difficult to 'plainly say, *My God, My King*' (line 15), the lines can be read as Herbert's dissociation from writers such as Edmund Spenser, whose *Shepheardes Calendar* used pastoral to engage with the religious climate of his time. Reacting against a period when, as commented above, it was difficult for poets to write about religion except at several removes, Herbert adopts a Neoplatonic distaste at second- or third-hand truth in order to condemn the indirect consideration of religious issues in poetry: 'Must no lines pass, except they do their duty / Not to a true, but painted chair?' (lines 4–5). Here, the Platonic prejudice against all poetry is recast to condemn poetry which, at best, praises God's creation rather than God himself.

Similar witty Christianisations of Neoplatonic commonplaces can be found in earlier religious poets: in Southwell's 'Man to the wound in Christs side', for instance, Christ's wound is seen as a cave which represents not the limitation of perception, as it does in *The Republic*, but the destination of choice for all seekers after heavenly bliss: 'O happy soule that flies so hie, / As to attaine this sacred cave' (lines 25–6).[6] The aspiration is one epitomised in the medieval prayer 'Anima Christi' – 'O good Jesu, hear me, / Within Thy wounds hide me' – and it was one which Herbert too utilised in his own poem to the wound in Christ's side, 'The Bag'.[7] Still, it is dissociation from a Southwellian trend in devotional poetry, and probably from Southwell himself, which initiates 'The Bag':

> Away despair; my gracious Lord doth hear.
> Though winds and waves assault my keel,
> He doth preserve it: he doth steer,
> Ev'n when the boat seems most to reel.
> Storms are the triumph of his art:
> Well may he close his eyes, but not his heart. (lines 1–6)

The storm was a fairly common metaphor at this date for the journey of the guilty soul towards repentance, and its most obvious poetic locus for anyone of Herbert's generation was likely to have been the beginning of Southwell's 'St Peter's Complaint': 'Launch foorth my Soule into a maine of teares, / Full fraught with griefe the traffick of thy mind: / Torne sayles will serve, thoughts rent with guilty feares: / Give care the sterne: use sighes in lieu of wind' (lines 1–4). Thus, in announcing 'Away despair', and proclaiming his trust in God, Herbert's speaker – and thus Herbert himself – is dissociating himself from the highly influential Southwellian poetic tradition of tears-poetry.[8] The emphasis is moved from the need to enact repentance by operatic emotional storminess, towards a calm affirmation of faith in Christ; depending on how far the critique is posed against Southwell himself rather than Southwell's Protestant followers, the shift could be read as having polemical undertones, commending Protestant notions of justification by faith rather than works. Nothing more is made of the storm-metaphor, and the poem's story only gets going in stanza two. In terms of the rest of the poem this beginning is somewhat gratuitous, but it jumps into relevance when one reads it as Herbert positioning himself against an earlier devotional tradition.

Stanza 2 begins in the interrogative mode that has been seen as typical of 'metaphysical' poetry: 'Hast thou not heard, that my Lord JESUS died? / Then let me tell thee a strange story' (lines 7–8).[9] The story proves to be that of Christ's incarnation and passion. When Christ is 'returning' to heaven upon the cross, 'there came one / That ran upon him with a spear' and, turning 'to his brethren', he asks them:

> If ye have any thing to send or write,
> (I have no bag, but here is room)
> Unto my father's hands and sight
> (Believe me) it shall safely come.
> That I shall mind, what you impart;
> Look, you may put it very near my heart.
>
> (lines 25, 26, 30, 31–6)

The notion of inserting a message to God in Christ's side refers to the carrying-pouches used by early modern couriers. But on one level, the thought of thrusting something into a bleeding stomach-wound is bound to engender a visceral disgust. Devout early modern readers, especially those influenced at any remove by the devotional traditions epitomised in Ignatius Loyola's Spiritual Exercises, would have alleviated this by meditating on the salvific quality of Christ's wounds, and Southwell's 'Man to the wound in Christs side' encourages this exemplary manner of reading: 'Heere would I view that bloudy sore, / Which dint of spitefull speare did breed, / The bloody wounds laid there in store / Would force a stony heart to bleede' (lines 17–20). Comparing this to Herbert's stanza forcibly presents one with a poet's main options when engaging with the topic: whether he should emphasise the affective impact of the wounds, or leave this up to the reader's imagination.

'The Bag' is one of the least Ignatian poems possible, with the carrying-pouch emblem directing the reader firmly away from the physicality of Christ. Perhaps this is Herbert's attempt to create a fully thought-through Protestant poetic praxis, happiest when picturing the divine by means of analogy – though, if so, it would pose an interesting tension with his evocation of a bloody Crucifixion in a poem like 'The Agony', and his declared preference for religious straightforwardness in 'Jordan (1)'. At the end of 'The Bag', Christ reiterates his intention to act as messenger between God the Father and man, returning to and confirming the injunctions at the beginning of the poem: 'what he sends / I will present, and somewhat more, / Not to his hurt. Sighs will convey / Any thing to me. Hark despair, away' (lines 39–42). The message here is that regret for sin is fitting, but that Christ cares too much about man's well-being to ask for anything more than 'sighs'; transports of repentance, we infer, are so nearly related to despair that they can only hinder salvation.

While some poems in *The Temple* convey a very different message about the efficacy of the emotions within repentance, Herbert's critique of the Southwellian tradition in this poem makes it necessary for him to advocate restraint, and this tells us something too about the emotional register that he made his own. Southwell, like many of the other religious poets addressed below – Vaughan and Crashaw come especially to mind – insistently pushes up against the limits of language, experience and perception; Herbert's distinctive genius is to convey the ineffability of the divine through understatement. This fondness for litotes is nowhere more obvious than in 'Love III', which consists of a dialogue between the soul and a personified divine Love, and sets out the moment of conversion. The soul realises his unworthiness for divine entertainment and demurs at the prospect of it, until Love assures him that he has paid the price already: 'And know you not, says Love, who bore the blame?' The soul's response, 'My dear, then I will serve', is intended to bear a double meaning: he is expressing delight that he is acceptable after all, and he is offering to serve at table (lines 15–16). Love's response is to remind him that he is a guest, not a servant – 'You must sit down, said Love, and taste my meat' – and the poem ends with a consummation intended to evoke the Christian sacrament of the eucharist: 'So I did sit and eat' (lines 17–18). It is a famously underplayed ending, one which has been read as epitomising low-key Anglican devotion. We are allowed to imagine raptures, but we are not actually told about them, and the poem folds itself away into repletion and silence. But this most fulfilling of endings should not prevent one noticing how 'Love III', the poem which ends *The Temple*, harks back to the collection's beginning. Both dramatise the notion of entering church, an immensely important one to Herbert. In 'Love III', the speaker is clearly in a space which he sees as designated for the regenerate, describing himself as growing 'slack' from his 'first entrance in' and as lacking a 'guest . . . worthy to be here' (lines 3, 4, 7). Similarly, *The Temple* is structured to evoke a Christian place of worship. While most of the poems are contained in a section named 'The Church', this is prefixed by one called 'The Church-Porch', which consists of one long and one short poem. The 'Perirrhanterium', called after the instrument used for sprinkling holy water, is the longer of the two. Reminding one that the water of baptism is the point of entry into the church, the poem's role is to instruct catechumens, those new to the Christian faith.

If 'Love III' is the poem of Herbert's most valued by critics and Christians alike, then in an age when overt didacticism is seen as aesthetically unappealing, 'Perirrhanterium' probably ranks among Herbert's least loved and read, even by his Anglican successors. Drawing on the Book of Proverbs and other Old Testament wisdom literature, and blending these with homely similitudes that would not have been out of place in a contemporary broadside ballad, it gives some ammunition to those who have dismissed Herbert as parochial and quaint: 'The way to make thy son rich, is to fill / His mind with rest, before his trunk with riches: / For wealth without contentment, climbs a hill / To feel those tempests, which fly over ditches' (lines 109–12). But Herbert, constantly aware of his pastoral role, would have responded to this criticism by asking how one could possibly separate mundane day-to-day moralism from heightened encounters with God. 'Superliminare', the short poem that acts as a stepping-stone between 'Perirrhanterium' and 'The Church', makes it clear that only 'Thou, whom the former precepts have / Sprinkled and taught, how to behave' can be invited to 'taste / The church's mystical repast': 'Avoid profaneness; come not here: / Nothing but holy, pure, and clear, / Or that which groaneth to be so, / May at his peril further go' (lines 1–8). As a poet, Herbert manifests the desire shared by his Laudian contemporaries for religious worship to be conducted decently and in order; but even viewed as the product of an age more tolerant of didacticism than our own, *The Temple* makes it very clear that its author sees poetic artistry as merely a means to an end: something to be taken or left, according to how the author can best point towards God in a particular context. Herbert figures in the literary canon for his artistic cleverness rather than the spiritual edification his verses were intended to give, but this state of affairs would have perplexed and saddened Herbert himself.[10]

Herbert could hardly have foreseen either how powerful an effect *The Temple* was to have on the generation of conformists who came after him, seeking a church of the mind in lieu of the physical buildings from which they had been alienated by the Civil Wars. Henry Vaughan, one of the most prominent of these, had – serendipitously enough – a common ancestry with Herbert as well as common literary aims, praising Herbert in his preface to *Silex Scintillans* (1650) as 'the first, that with any effectual success attempted a *diversion* of [the] foul and overflowing *stream*' of profane verse.[11] Several of Vaughan's verses are suggested by, or rewritings of, those in *The Temple*; but if Vaughan's debt to Herbert is often explicit, it is never slavish. The variations upon a theme in 'Praise', a poem which constantly alludes to Herbert's 'Praise (2)', illustrate how Vaughan uses Herbert as he does the Bible elsewhere, as a starting-point for creative meditation.[12] Herbert's verses 'Wherefore with my utmost art / I will sing thee, / And the cream of all my heart / I will bring thee . . . Sev'n whole days, not one in seven, / I will praise thee, / In my heart, though not in heaven, / I can raise thee' (lines 9–12, 17–20) become conflated by Vaughan: 'Wherefore with my utmost strength / I will praise thee, / And as thou giv'st line, and length, / I will raise thee' (lines 9–12). The rhymes to lines 1 and 3 are no gratuitous variation, but productive of an entirely new image: the speaker being granted 'line and length' by God in order to raise Him, which he will need his 'utmost strength' to do. The effect is parallelistic: as with a psalm-verse, the second half of the unit reiterates and confirms the first half without repeating it. Though the idea of man and God being connected by a pulley is fairly common in religious discourse of the seventeenth century, one may be intended to pick up an allusion to the title of another Herbert poem, 'The Pulley'. Herbert's poem, in which God heaves souls to heaven by denying them rest, makes orthodox use of the conceit. Vaughan, on the other hand, points towards a more reciprocal relationship between God and man: the speaker hauls up God, God pays out the rope. In the context of a religious poem, 'line' and 'length' also point towards the means employed by the poet to elevate God in verse.

But Vaughan's differences from Herbert are as suggestive as the similarities. He is a much more painterly poet than Herbert, and one reason why he has been read as foreshadowing the poets of the Romantic period is the close visual engagement of his speakers with the landscape that surrounds them. But compared to a poem like Wordsworth's *Prelude*, the focus of Vaughan's writing is less on the speaker's individual reactions to his surroundings, more on his delighted encounter with pre-existent figurations of divinity. Here, Vaughan is thoroughly of his time in thinking of the natural world as God's book, interpretable through a system of correspondences. Contemporary emblematics, to which Vaughan is everywhere indebted, depends on the idea that the natural world could yield objective meanings to the inquirer: some obvious, some less so. Paradoxically, emblems acted as a means both of revelation and of concealment, sweetening spiritual lessons by making them more accessible, but also testing the ingenuity of the *sunetoi*, elite readers able to appreciate the full resonance of an image.[13] Vaughan's preoccupation with hiding has invited exegesis in terms of his proven interest in hermetic philosophy and his position as a Royalist and an Anglican living through the Civil Wars and Interregnum, but it is also the formal consequence of his speakers' lived emblematics.[14] The narrative element in his religious poems invites comparison with the moral perambulations prescribed by the landscape gardeners of the next century, but also recalls the allegorical journeys of Spenser and his medieval forebears.

One of Vaughan's best-known poems, 'Regeneration', illustrates this well. The speaker begins in a vernal landscape, '*Primrosed*, and hung with shade' (line 4), which – as so often in spring – is unseasonably chilly: 'Yet, was it frost within, / And surly winds / Blasted my infant buds' (lines 5–7). Sin is to blame, and the speaker's growing consciousness of this triggers a change in his surroundings: 'I straight perceived my spring / Mere stage, and show, / My walk a monstrous, mountained thing / Rough-cast with rocks, and snow' (lines 9–12). Clambering to the mountain-top, he finds a pair of scales, in which he weighs pain against pleasure: the latter, surprisingly, proving heavier despite the intrinsic lightness of the contents. One way in which emblematists could rise above the predictable messages of broadside-ballad moralism, and indeed as good a test as any of poetic wit at this date, is the ability Vaughan shows here to fuse standard moral commonplaces in a way which both subverts and affirms them. Obeying the cry 'Away', the increasingly regenerate speaker enters a field of 'Virgin-soil, which no / Rude feet ere trod' (lines 25, 29–30), which is succeeded by a grove 'Of stately height, whose branches met / And mixed on every side' (lines 35–6). Vaughan's latter image is interpretable in several ways: as the temple of nature, a concept important within the hermetic world-view and exploited at a similar time by his brother Thomas Vaughan in *Lumen de Lumine* (1651); as the new home of the Church of England, whose worshippers were quite literally driven outdoors by the takeovers of the Civil War; and as an allusion to Vaughan's Welsh roots, since druids were traditionally supposed to worship in groves. Finally, the traveller arrives at a 'bank of flowers', hears a 'rushing wind' and experiences a theophany, with an effect quite literally breathtaking: 'Lord, then said I, *On me one breath, / And let me die before my death!*' (lines 65, 70, 81–2). But any easy assumptions that the speaker has had a foretaste of heaven are undercut by the other individuals resting on the bank: the spiritually slothful, 'fast asleep', are, for the moment, next to those who are 'broad-eyed / And taking in the ray' (lines 67–8). A similar message is purveyed by the fountain that features in the scene:

I drew her near, and found
The cistern full
Of divers stones, some bright, and round
Others ill-shaped, and dull.
The first (pray mark,) as quick as light
Danced through the flood,
But, the last more heavy than the night
Nailed to the centre stood. . . (lines 53–60)

Like the Duke in *As You Like It*, Vaughan is fond of looking for sermons in stones; perhaps this was partly a consolation for dispossession in both cases.[15] The heart of knapped flint, displayed in the frontispiece to his best-known poetic collection, *Silex Scintillans*, declares to the well-affected reader that the uses of adversity are sweet: a moral commonplace that demands to be read against Vaughan's own religious and political circumstances at the time. In 1650, Vaughan would still have been reeling from the execution of Charles I in 1649, which for him or any other Royalist would have given a topical cast to conventional emblems of ill-fortune.

Given the position of *Silex Scintillans* in Vaughan's career, after two earlier collections of secular poems, *Poems* (1646) and *Olor Iscanus* (1651), the volume might seem to announce both a religious conversion and a literary palinode.[16] Certainly Vaughan's turn to religion was noticed and praised by the next poet to be considered in this chapter, Katherine Philips, known to her contemporaries by the coterie name of 'The Matchless Orinda'. In a poem she wrote to him she expresses the hope that the 'disabused world' will, 'from the charming rigour thy muse brings, / Learn there's no pleasure but in serious things'.[17] It is a suggestive emphasis from a writer whose position in the republic of letters demanded that she cultivate a spotless reputation. As a member of the minor gentry whose poetic gifts gave her an entrée to exclusive social circles, and as a woman operating in a largely masculine, highly homosocial and sometimes misogynistic world, it is hardly surprising that Philips should display a mixture of caution and temerity both inside and outside her verse.[18] As Patrick Thomas points out, the precision and tact of Philips's self-positioning had enormous influence on succeeding generations of women poets.[19]

Like so many other women writers, Philips found manuscript circulation a more appropriate means than print of disseminating her writing because it gave her greater control over her audience, and the medium's connotations of intimacy were also highly appropriate for someone whose main subject matter was passionate friendship.[20] The highly charged verses which Philips addressed to various female confidantes, particularly her friend Anne Owen or 'Lucasia', are interpretable on a number of levels. They are a natural outworking of Philips's project to create a literary society founded on affection, and from the formal point of view, they also represent an opportunity for a woman poet to write love poetry without sacrificing modesty. How far they set out a sexual alternative is more controversial, though the poems have been subject to queering in recent years.[21] If this kind of reading is to be undertaken at all, it should be with appropriate sensitivity to notions that Philips herself would have endorsed: Neoplatonism, which saw all earthly love as pointing towards the divine, and emerging conventions of *honnêteté*, an intellectual fashion which set a high value on elevated and chaste affection. Writers could choose whether the divinity in question was pagan or Christian, and Philips, like many of Neoplatonism's more subtle devotees, invokes both. In one of her best-known poems to Lucasia, 'Friendship's Mysterys', 'Orinda' declares: 'To the dull, angry world let's prove / There's a religion in our Love' (lines 4–5), and later, 'Our hearts are doubled by their loss, / Here mixture is addition grown; / We both diffuse, and both engrosse, / And we, whose minds are so much one, / Never, yet ever, are alone' (lines 11–15). Even if the 'religion in our Love' celebrated here is the religion of Love itself, its debt to the Christian understanding of the Trinity is clear – especially once one factors in the audience.

Here, as elsewhere, the coterie quality of Philips's verse is both a proclamation of intimacy and a check upon it. So far from being a confidential missive from Philips to Anne Owen, 'Friendship's mysterys' was set to music by Philips's friend Henry Lawes and appears in his songbooks. Like her friendship with Vaughan, this suggests how wrong it would be to think of Philips as having no creative interaction with members of the opposite sex. *Honnêteté*, after all, allowed men and women to compliment each other on their beautiful minds, and in the 1650s, the time when Philips wrote much of her verse, had political connotations which transcended gender: popularised by Charles I's Queen Henrietta Maria, it could be a way of demonstrating cultural loyalty to the Stuart court during the Civil Wars.[22] From someone of Philips's known Royalist sympathies, the blend of amatory and political discourse in 'Friendship's mysterys' is startling: 'We are our selves but by rebound, / And all our titles shuffled so, / Both Princes, and both subjects too' (lines 23–5). But her consciousness of how both love and politics involve games with identity is mirrored in a creative habit she shared with other Royalists, the use of coterie names.[23] Often of a pastoral or emblematic nature, these had an element of disguise, or at least of masquerading. Capitalising on the pleasures of intimacy and revelation, they also gave poets the chance to embody an image, and their friends and correspondents a starting-point for compliment. One can see this happening in Vaughan's own testament to literary friendship, 'To the Most Excellently Accomplished, Mrs K. Philips': 'I might at distance worship you / A *Persian* votary, and say / *It was your light showed me the way*' (lines 28–30). As Alan Rudrum has pointed out, these lines show Vaughan comparing himself to a Zoroastrian sun-worshipper, perhaps alluding as well to the star from the east that led the wise men to Christ.[24] As well, these highly allusive lines suggest a triple macaronic pun: on 'Orinda', *orare*, the Latin for 'to pray', and *oriens*, the Latin for 'east'; on several counts, Philips's coterie name acts as a burning-glass to focalise Vaughan's imagination.

The next two poets to be considered, Richard Crashaw and Abraham Cowley, also set a high value on poetic interchange. 'Upon two greene Apricockes sent to Cowley by Sir Crashaw', upon first glance the most trivial of occasional verses, demonstrates the interpersonal utility of the conceit in exemplary manner.[25] This peculiar, seemingly ungenerous present is one that could only travel from one friend to another, and even then, only with some explanation. But justifying it gives Crashaw his rhetorical opportunity, and a gift which at first seems unusually deserving of a donor's conventional deprecation is transmuted into an exquisite demonstration of politeness. The unripeness of the apricots prompts Crashaw to reflect on productivity and precocity, and to compliment Cowley for a forwardness surpassing nature: 'How does thy April-Autumne mocke these cold / Progressions 'twixt whose termes poor time grows old? / With thee alone he weares no beard, thy braine / Gives him the morning worlds fresh gold againe' (lines 15–18).[26] The dialogue written jointly by Crashaw and Cowley, 'On Hope', gives equally potent, very different testimony to their friendship. Cowley is a worldly-wise philosopher who sees through hope, even while admitting its occult powers: 'Child of fond desire, / That blows the Chymicks, and the Lovers fire, / Still leading them insensibly on, / With the strange witchcraft of *Anon*' (lines 73–6). But it falls to Crashaw to advance the distinction between the false hopes of alchemists and lovers, and the Christian's hope: 'Though the vext Chymick vainly chases / His fugitive gold through all her faces, / And loves more fierce, more fruitlesse fires assay / One face more fugitive then all they, / True *Hope*'s a glorious Huntresse, and her chase / The God of Nature in the Field of Grace' (lines 85–90).

The honour of concluding the intercourse between the two poets was to fall to Cowley, in 'On the Death of Mr Crashaw'.

> Thou from low earth in nobler flames didst rise,
> And, like Elijah, mount alive the skies.
> Elisha-like (but with a wish much less,
> More fit thy greatness, and my littleness)
> Lo, here I beg – I whom thou once didst prove
> So humble to esteem, so good to love –
> Not that thy spirit might on me doubled be
> I ask, but half thy mighty spirit for me.[27]

Elegies and odes, where their addressee is a distinguished individual, manifest a distinctive combination of modesty and self-display. The poet is, as it were, obliged to rise to his subject matter, thus instigating a relay whereby other poets can celebrate him in turn. The Old Testament episode where Elisha inherits the prophet Elijah's mantle lends itself exceptionally well to shaping these patterns of literary inheritance, and was a powerful foundation myth for seventeenth-century poets: one reason why it was later satirised by Dryden at the end of *Mac Flecknoe*.[28] But given that Elisha was said to have inherited a 'double portion' of his father's spirit, it could potentially undermine the deference of poet to addressee: a danger of which Cowley shows himself impeccably aware in the extract above, asking for 'but half' Crashaw's abilities.[29]

Crashaw's taste, if not his poetic ability, has been called into question by subsequent generations of literary critics, many of whom have disliked the rhetoric of conscious excess so intrinsic to the baroque mode he adopted. The term 'baroque', its appropriateness for describing English writing and the nature of its relationship to Counter-Reformation devotional sensibility are all highly contested issues. But a preoccupation with ingenuity, movement and the limits of language have routinely been identified as central to its connotations, and all these features have a prominent place in verse such as 'The Weeper', Crashaw's celebration of the penitent Mary Magdalen: a subject which, in an English context, almost certainly harks back to Southwell, but may also have been suggested by one of Southwell's own models such as Giambattista Marino.[30]

> Upwards thou dost weep.
> Heavn's bosome drinks the gentle stream.
> Where th'milky rivers creep,
> Thine floates above; and is the cream.
> Waters above th'Heavns, what they be
> We'are taught best by thy TEARES and thee.

Every morn from hence
A brisk Cherub somthing sippes
Whose sacred influence
Addes sweetnes to his sweetest Lippes.
Then to his musick. And his song
Tasts of this Breakfast all day long. (stanzas 4–5)[31]

The passage begins with a counter-intuitive claim – that tears run 'upward' – which is then borne out. The reader's gaze follows them as they rise to the Milky Way, to heaven and above. Via an allusion to Psalm 148:4, 'Praise him, ye heavens of heavens, and ye waters that be above the heavens', they lap at the limits of religious perception. The passage includes, as so commonly in baroque religious sculpture, an anacreontic and calculatedly comic element: the 'brisk' and importunate cherub who breakfasts off Mary Magdalene's tears. In this and other ways, the stanzas show how fascinated Crashaw is by liquidity and deliquescence.[32] Over the course of 'The Weeper', Crashaw alludes to tears, streams, fountains, milk, cream, dew, balm and amber-drops. Mary Magdalene, on account of her exemplary weeping, was often used to embody the common imaginative link between liquefaction and repentance. While, as already suggested, this shows the influence of tears-poetry at one or more removes, it would be mistaken to assume that only Catholics were interested in writing this way. Like so much of Crashaw's verse, 'The Weeper' was written when he was still a member of the Church of England, and at all times he was conscious of his denominational forebears on both sides of the Catholic–Protestant divide: not least Herbert, to whom the title of 'Steps to the Temple' pays tribute.[33] In his poem 'On Mr G. Herberts booke, The Temple', this is enhanced by a delicate awareness of a book's physical qualities, comparing its covers to wings in a way that surely harks back to Herbert's own figured verse, 'Easter Wings': 'When your hands unty these strings, / Thinke you have an Angell by th'wings' (lines 5–6).

The devotional crossovers in Crashaw's verse do not end there. Much of what seems Catholic in it – devotion to the Virgin Mary, the saints and affective pictorial representations of Christ's body – was prevalent among High-Churchmen in 1630s and 1640s England, thanks to Archbishop Laud and his followers. The differences between Laudians and other members of the Church of England could, in this respect, be greater than those between Catholics and Laudians, an overlap which also characterises the publication history of Crashaw's verse. Much of this survives in two states: as first published in *Steps to the Temple* (first edition, 1646), and as altered in a later volume, *Carmen Deo Nostro* (1652). The first of these collections was published in England, the second on the Continent with engravings of religious subjects. Crashaw's two most recent editors have, rightly, been punctilious in printing them in parallel.[34] Yet if anything, this draws attention to how few differences there are between them, and how few of those are attributable to points at issue between Catholic and Protestant. The bibliographical differences, taken in tandem with the conceptual similarities, powerfully demonstrate how the history of English verse needs to encompass texts published outside England, especially in the case of writers who were driven into political and religious exile: on his conversion to Catholicism in the mid-1640s, Crashaw joined the court of Henrietta Maria on the Continent.

Crashaw's case gives one answer to the final question posed in the introduction to this chapter, that of how poets responded to the Civil Wars. Some others have been hinted at above: as a conformist exiled from religious centrality in his own country, Vaughan explores the poetics of secrecy; Philips sang the joys of intimacy as one whose engagement with public matters was problematic, because of her sex and her adherence to the Royalist cause. In an essay of limited length, Andrew Marvell's 'A Horatian Ode upon Cromwell's Return from Ireland' must epitomise the related tension between retirement and engagement – or, to use the Latin terms, *otium* and *negotium* – explored by so many other poets of the era.[35] The 'Ode' begins with an exhortation to action: 'The forward youth that would appear / Must now forsake his Muses dear, / Nor in the shadows sing / His numbers languishing: / 'Tis time to leave the books in dust, / And oil th'unusèd armour's rust' (lines 1–6). Yet even though engagement with the contemporary political scene is urged, it becomes clear that this need not mean coming down on one side or the other. The poem's speaker shuns partisanship in favour of a vision which is partly that of the historian, partly of the tragedian. For Marvell to call his poem a 'Horatian' ode is to claim both generic and tonal alignment with his classical predecessor.[36] Horace, who fought for republican causes at Philippi but came to be one of Augustus Caesar's most illustrious poetic advocates, had first-hand knowledge of political dubiety and conversion: one reason, perhaps, why some of his odes address the complexities of allegiance.[37] Written in the summer of 1650, a time when Cromwell had just returned from military success against Royalist forces in Ireland and was about to embark on a Scottish campaign, Marvell's ode exhibits a similar finesse, celebrating Cromwell's rising star but defying easy partisanship at a time when memories of Charles I's execution, which had taken place little more than a year before, were still fresh and painful to many.

Few seventeenth-century poems have been so much discussed, and debate has largely centred upon the question of how Marvell's own political sympathies inform the poem. So how does Marvell manage to affirm both Cromwell's unstoppability and Charles's sacrifice? Part of the answer lies in the poem's adoption of tragicomic structure. As many recent critics have explored, this was a time when the closure of the professional theatres resulted in a transposition of dramatic tropes and patterns into other genres.[38] For Royalists, Charles I's execution was readily classifiable as tragedy; those who thought like Marvell would have recognised its tragic overtones but wished to deny it full tragic status. One recognisable pattern within Renaissance tragicomedy is for deaths of subsidiary characters to occur halfway through the action, clearing the way for a happy ending while also powerfully qualifying it.[39] Accordingly, the description of Charles I's execution occupies the centre of Marvell's poem, and is explicitly depicted as a quasi-theatrical event: 'That thence the royal actor born / The tragic scaffold might adorn, / While round the armèd bands / Did clap their bloody hands' (lines 53–56).[40]

But if the poem has tragicomic features, it also resists closure in pointing towards future endeavour: 'The same arts that did gain / A pow'r must it maintain' (lines 119–20). Clearly, Cromwell's rule is dependent upon Cromwell's continued exertions and deserts. Yet it is also a providential dispensation to England. To call Marvell a Marxist would be anachronistic and violently unjust to his ability to empathise with both sides, as well as suggesting that the poem is more secular than it is. Nevertheless, 'A Horatian Ode' is fraught with the intuition of historical inevitability, which is placed on a level with natural law. 'Nature that hateth emptiness, / Allows of penetration less: / And therefore must make room / Where greater spirits come' (lines 41–4). The point being made here is that nature forbids the simultaneous occupation of the same space by two separate objects. It has the effect of endorsing *force majeure* in a way which renders questions of human culpability irrelevant; this tactfully directs attention away from embarrassing topics – whether Cromwell's military tactics in Ireland had been inappropriate, or whether Charles should have been executed – while suggesting that human beings do well to accept nature's and history's ordinances. Thus, though at opposite poles politically, both Cromwell and Charles I are praised because both have gracefully inhabited the roles assigned to them by greater forces than they.

'Upon Appleton House', Marvell's foray into the genre of country-house poem,[41] can be seen as in dialogue with the 'Horatian Ode'. The 'Ode' was written in June–July 1650, and 'Upon Appleton House' in the summer of 1651; at the time of writing, Marvell was acting as tutor to Maria, daughter or

Thomas, third Baron Fairfax, the owner of Appleton House. Looked at side by side, the poems complement each other in their exploration of *otium* and *negotium*. Where the 'Ode' calls its listeners out of the stately home to military action, 'Upon Appleton House' affirms retirement after exertion. But both poems align the status quo with providence's intention, and given Fairfax's career this would have been only tactful. Having served as chief commander of the Parliamentary forces towards the end of the First Civil War and during the Second Civil War, he forsook public life in the summer of 1650 and withdrew to his country estate.[42]

The poem, nevertheless, is fraught with reminders of military action. The garden of the estate emblematises war in a number of ways: it contains a fort – perhaps referring to a real-life garden building – while the flowers are on parade, 'Each regiment in order grows, / That of the tulip, pink, and rose' (lines 311–12). Gardens can enable the fallen world of 1650s England to hark back to an innocence evoking both the garden of Eden and of the classical golden age: 'Unhappy! Shall we never more / That sweet militia restore, / When gardens only had their towers, / And all the garrisons were flowers' (lines 329–32). Here as in his shorter poem, 'The Garden', Marvell rises to the opportunities for allusion and polysemy which a garden presents, and these have knock-on effects on genre. As country-house poems go, 'Upon Appleton House' is conspicuously short on hard description, but it compensates for this with a portmanteau quality. As Marvell and his readers stroll around the estate, he takes them on a guided tour through pastoral, piscatory and prospective poem: the latter a genre which used views as a starting-point for social and political reflection, made newly fashionable by Sir John Denham's *Coopers Hill* (1641/2). Thus, Fairfax's estate becomes a site of generic suggestiveness and convergence.

To these one can add anti-Catholic narrative, a genre made familiar by polemical pamphlets. The smaller house on the Nun Appleton estate was built from the remains of a convent that was dispossessed by one of Fairfax's ancestors, and Marvell, himself a convert from Catholicism, narrates the convent's demolition and presents it as entirely redemptive: 'Though many a nun there made her vow, / 'Twas no religious house till now' (lines 279–80). A similar dialogue with Catholicism – partly secularising, partly resacralising – can be seen in Marvell's imaginative tribute to his pupil Mary Fairfax. Her name, the sway she exercises over nature and her association with the colour blue, through her personification as a halcyon or kingfisher, all link her to poetic traditions of Marian veneration. The speaker compares the kingfisher's streak of blue to a comet, asserting that 'by her flames, in heaven tried, / Nature is wholly vitrified' (lines 687–8). Alluding to St John's vision of heaven as a sea of glass, this has apocalyptic overtones resonating with the traditional identification of Mary with the Book of Revelation's woman clothed with the sun and crowned with stars.[43] As the garden's tutelary spirit, Mary Fairfax is also a classical 'Nymph' (line 713), with a Diana-like modesty: 'But, since she would not have [her beauties] seen, / The wood about her draws a screen' (lines 703–4). This *hortus inclusus* has both pagan and sacred overtones, evoking the woman celebrated in the Song of Songs, who – in another turn to Marian imagery – was often identified with the Virgin Mary.[44]

In 'The Garden', as so often in poetry of this period, the line between secular and sacred is not easy to draw. Plainly this is not a religious poem, yet the biblical and devotional imagery is insistent: does this serve to sacralise the whole, or does it relegate Christian allusion to a merely ornamental status? Similar questions are raised by 'Eyes and Tears', Marvell's exercise in tears-poetry, a genre which we have already seen Southwell, Herbert and Crashaw explore. While the analogies with their efforts are obvious, Marvell's poem looks strikingly secular in comparison. True, Mary Magdalen makes an appearance: 'So Magdalen, in tears more wise / Dissolved those captivating eyes, / Whose liquid chains could flowing meet / To fetter her Redeemer's feet' (lines 29–32). But the contrast to a poem like Crashaw's 'The Weeper', discussed above, is instructive. Rather than being the exemplary subject whose consciousness shapes the poem, Mary Magdalen becomes one embellishment of the theme among many. Nigel Smith has suggested that the poem may have developed from the Latin epigram on Mary Magdalen which survives at its end, commenting on its abridged publication in the volume of secular verse *Poetical Recreations* (1688) that this 'confirms the transformation from sacred convention to secular lyric (a "deconversion", so to speak) that the poem's origins and method of composition embody'.[45] It is a transformation which incorporates several backward glances. The verse, 'I have through every garden been, / Amongst the white, the red, the green; / And yet, from all the flow'rs I saw, / No honey, but these tears could draw' (lines 17–20) is asking the reader to remember the generic connotations of these colours – red and white allude to the blazoning conventions of love poetry, green to pastoral – which draw on an implicit contrast between profane and sacred poetic endeavour.[46] But rather than a focus on repentance, the poem stresses the range of possible reasons why weeping should take place: complaint, grief, pity and, apparently, the need to prove one is human: 'Ope then mine eyes your double sluice, / And practise so your noblest use. / For others too can see, or sleep; / But only human eyes can weep' (lines 45–8).

Composed around half a century after Southwell's death, the poem demonstrates that drops could still be squeezed out of the lyric tradition he pioneered in England, and which was taken up by so many of the poets discussed above. But it also points towards a humanistic, secularised poetic melancholy which takes as its focus not God but the sensitivity of the poet, distinguished here from the 'others' who appear to be men rather than animals, but who can only 'see, or sleep'. The speaker exhorts his own eyes, literally staring into them, and looks forward to a time when 'eyes and tears [are] the same things: / And each the other's diff'rence bears; / These weeping eyes, those seeing tears' (lines 54–6): a narcissistic gambit, collapsing the distinction between first- and second-person addressees with which this chapter began, but also one which places huge exemplary demands on the speaker. The message, despite the usual contemporary connotations of weeping eyes, is not one of repentance before God but a more secularised self-scrutiny; only by the reflexive, unceasing interplay of 'weeping eyes' and 'seeing tears', the speaker argues, can humans be raised to their 'noblest' heights. In this as in other ways, Marvell's poem looks towards a more individualistic, less collaborative notion of the poetic role than this chapter has identified, with considerable implications for the poetry of succeeding eras. His speaker is most answerable not to God, his patrons or his peers, but to his own highest standards.

Notes

1. Izaak Walton, 'Life of Mr George Herbert', in George Saintsbury (ed.), *The Lives of John Donne, Sir Henry Wotton, Richard Hooker, George Herbert and Robert Sanderson* (London: Oxford University Press, 1927). For an up-to-date account of the issues, see Helen Wilcox's life of Herbert in the online *Oxford Dictionary of National Biography* (henceforth *ODNB*).
2. Walton, 'Life', ed. Saintsbury, pp. 268–9.
3. All quotations are from *George Herbert: The Complete English Poems*, ed. John Tobin (London: Penguin, 1994).
4. See the introduction to *Shakespeare's Sonnets*, ed. Katherine Duncan-Jones (London: Arden, 1997).
5. Louis L. Martz, *The Poetry of Meditation*, first edition (New Haven: Yale University Press, 1954).
6. All quotations from Southwell are taken from *St Robert Southwell: Collected Poems*, ed. Peter Davidson and Anne Sweeney (Manchester: Carcanet, 2007). For another storm-metaphor, cf. 'The prodigall chyldes soule wracke' (pp. 38–9).
7. See the entry for 'Anima Christi' in the online *Catholic Encyclopaedia*.
8. See Marjory E. Lange, *Telling Tears in the English Renaissance* (Leiden: Brill, 1996), and my *Catholicism, Controversy and the English Literary Imagination, 1558–1660* (Cambridge: Cambridge University Press, 1999), ch. 2.

9. See Jonathan Post's chapter in this volume.
10. On the debates over Herbert's complex religious stance, see Wilcox, 'Life'.
11. *Henry Vaughan: The Complete Poems*, ed. Alan Rudrum (Harmondsworth: Penguin, 1983), p. 142. All quotations are taken from this edition. On Vaughan's ancestry, see Alan Rudrum's 'Life' in the online *ODNB*. For another, ideologically comparable poetic admirer of Herbert's, see Judith Maltby, 'From *Temple* to *Synagogue*: "Old" Conformity in the 1640s-1650s and the Case of Christopher Harvey', in Peter Lake and Michael Questier (eds.), *Conformity and Orthodoxy in the English Church, c.1560–1660* (Woodbridge: Boydell, 2000), pp. 88–116.
12. Philip West, *Henry Vaughan's 'Silex Scintillans': Scripture Uses* (Oxford: Oxford University Press, 2001).
13. See Margery Corbett and Ronald Lightbown, *The Comely Frontispiece: The Emblematic Title-Page in England, 1550–1660* (London: Routledge and Kegan Paul, 1979), pp. 10–14, 18–19.
14. On the hermetic treatises composed by his brother Thomas Vaughan, see Jennifer Speake's 'Life' of the latter in the online *ODNB*.
15. William Shakespeare, *As You Like It*, ed. Juliet Dusinberre (London: Arden, 2006), Act 2 Scene 1, line 17.
16. Despite its publication date, *Olor Iscanus* has a preface dated December 1647.
17. Lines 33, 37–8, of 'To Mr Henry Vaughan, Silurist, upon his Poems', item 21 in *The Collected Works of Katherine Philips, The Matchless Orinda, Volume 1: The Poems*, ed. Patrick Thomas (Stump Cross: Stump Cross Books, 1990). All quotations are taken from this edition. On the hypothetical dating of the poem before the appearance of *Olor Iscanus* in 1651, see pp. 338–9.
18. See Warren Chernaik's 'Life' of Philips in the online *ODNB*.
19. *Collected Works*, ed. Thomas, introduction.
20. She appears to have been anxious to suppress the one collection of her poems to be printed during her lifetime; see Peter Beal, *In Praise of Scribes: Manuscripts and their Makers in 17th-Century England* (Oxford: Clarendon Press, 1998), ch. 5.
21. E.g. by Elaine Hobby, 'Katherine Philips: Seventeenth-Century Lesbian Poet', in Elaine Hobby and Chris White (eds.), *What Lesbians Do in Books* (London: The Women's Press, 1991), pp. 183–204.
22. See Erica Veevers, *Images of Love and Religion: Queen Henrietta Maria and Court Entertainments* (Cambridge: Cambridge University Press, 1989), esp. ch. 1, and Karen Britland, *Drama at the Courts of Queen Henrietta Maria* (Cambridge: Cambridge University Press, 2006), introduction.
23. On the connection between coterie names and royalism, see Lois Potter, *Secret Rites and Secret Writing: Royalist Literature, 1641–1660* (Cambridge: Cambridge University Press, 1989), ch. 3.
24. *Vaughan: Complete Poems*, ed. Rudrum, p. 500. If this poem, which appeared in *Olor Iscanus*, was written in reply to Philips's verse, it would have been added to the collection after the preface was written.
25. On the relationship between Cowley and Crashaw, see David Trotter, *The Poetry of Abraham Cowley* (London: Macmillan, 1979), ch. 4. On literary gift-giving,

see Jason Scott-Warren, *Sir John Harington and the Book as Gift* (Oxford: Oxford University Press, 2001).

26. *The Complete Poetry of Richard Crashaw*, ed. George Walton Williams (Garden City, NY: Anchor Books, 1974), pp. 494–5. All quotations from Crashaw's poems are taken from this edition. On Cowley's intellectual precocity, see Alexander Lindsay's 'Life' in the online *ODNB*.
27. 'On the Death of Mr Crashaw', in *Abraham Cowley: Selected Poems*, ed. David Hopkins and Tom Mason (Manchester: Fyfield, 1994), lines 65–72.
28. 2 Kings 2:9.
29. Cowley also wrote a Pindaric ode to Philips (*Poems*, ed. Thomas, pp. 20–1), while the two are praised as the greatest poets of their era by James Gardiner in a prefatory verse to Samuel Woodford's *A Paraphrase upon the Psalms of David* (1667), fol. d1v.
30. See Claes Schaar, *Marino and Crashaw, 'Sospetto d'Herode': A Commentary*, Lund Studies in English, 39 (Lund: Gleerup, 1971).
31. Quoted from the version in *Carmen Deo Nostro* (1652): for the earlier version, see *Complete Poetry*, ed. Walton Williams, p. 124.
32. For a reading of Crashaw which stresses the homoerotic implications of his verse, see Richard Rambuss, *Closet Devotions* (Durham, NC: Duke University Press, 1998).
33. However, this may have been supplied by the friend who published the poems: see *Complete Poetry*, ed. Walton Williams, p. xx.
34. Walton Williams; *The Poems, English, Latin and Greek, of Richard Crashaw*, ed. L. C. Martin (Oxford: Clarendon Press, 1957).
35. See Peter Davidson (ed.), *Poetry and Revolution: An Anthology of British and Irish Verse, 1625–1660* (Oxford: Clarendon Press, 1998).
36. All quotations are taken from *The Poems of Andrew Marvell*, ed. Nigel Smith (Harlow: Longman, 2007).
37. E.g. I.2, 35, 37; IV.4, 5, 14, 15. IV.iv is a prosphonetikon – celebration of a hero's return.
38. On Civil War drama, see Dale Randall, *Winter Fruit: English Drama, 1642–1660* (Lexington: Kentucky University Press, 1995) and Susan Wiseman, *Drama and Politics in the English Civil War* (Cambridge: Cambridge University Press, 1998).
39. Shakespeare's *The Winter's Tale* is a familiar example.
40. See Barbara Ravelhofer, 'News Drama: The Tragic Subject of Charles I', in Teresa Grant and Barbara Ravelhofer (eds.), *English Historical Drama, 1500–1660: Forms Outside the Canon* (Basingstoke: Palgrave, 2008).
41. On this genre, see Alastair Fowler, *The Country House Poem: A Cabinet of 17th-Century Estate Poems and Related Items* (Edinburgh: Edinburgh University Press, 1994).
42. For the question of which house the poem refers to, see *Poems*, ed. Smith, p. 210.
43. Revelation 12:1.
44. Song of Songs 4:12.
45. *Poems*, ed. Smith, pp. 50–1. Smith also discusses the poem's relationship to Counter-Reformation tears-poetry.
46. See the discussion of 'Jordan (1)' above.

Chapter 13
Milton's shorter poems

BARBARA K. LEWALSKI

The shorter poems of John Milton (1608–74) exhibit an extraordinary range of genres and topics. He took up genre after genre – verse letters, love elegies, hymns, odes, psalm translations, songs, epitaphs, funeral elegies, sonnets of many kinds, an entertainment, a masque and more. But his major poems transform those genres, opening them to new possibilities. Several early poems and prose works explore his anxieties and aspirations as a poet, providing the basis for the most complete self-portrait of the author as a young man before the nineteenth century. In a poem to his father he proclaimed more forcefully than had any English poet before him, that poetry was his vocation and at the core of his self-definition: 'it is my lot to have been born a poet'.[1] What that might mean he spelled out in 1642: worthy poetry is the product of inspiration, supplemented by intense study and broad experience; and its Horatian purpose, to teach and delight, should also involve being 'doctrinal and exemplary to a Nation'.[2]

In 1645 he published *Poems of Mr John Milton*, collecting most of his poetry from the previous twenty years or so. The volume is in two parts with separate title pages: a vernacular book of mostly English and a few Italian poems, and a classical book with mostly Latin and a few Greek poems. The poems are arranged chiefly by genre and (in the *Poemata*, by verse form), though with some attention to chronology. Only four had been previously published: an epitaph for Shakespeare, anonymously, in the Second Folio of his plays (1632);[3] the *Mask* known commonly as *Comus*, also anonymous (1637);[4] *Lycidas*, bearing only his initials, in a memorial collection (1638);[5] and *Epitaphium Damonis*, printed anonymously and privately, probably in 1640.[6] Humphrey Moseley published Milton's 1645 volume alongside several poetic collections by Cavalier poets: James Howell (1640), Edmund Waller (1645), James Shirley (1646), Sir John Suckling (1646), Abraham Cowley (1647), Robert Herrick (1648). But Milton, with poems in multiple languages, carefully organised to highlight his development as a serious reformist poet, separated himself decisively from Cavalier lyricists, court masque writers and Anglican devotional poets, offering to reform several genres dominated by them. He also claimed a kind shunned by them, prophecy.[7] In 1673, a year before his death, he published a second edition with a few additions but the same organisation.[8] Four sonnets – to Sir Thomas Fairfax, Oliver Cromwell, Sir Henry Vane, and Cyriack Skinner – could not be published until 1694, because of their political content.[9]

Few English poets had a more extensive or more fortunate preparation for that role.[10] His father, a scrivener by trade and an amateur musician of some reputation, encouraged his studies, his enduring passion for music and his poetic talents. Private tutors and schoolmasters at one of the finest grammar schools in the country, St Paul's, taught him languages and classical literature, praising his early poetic style as 'likely to live'.[11] Some of his early poetry reflects the widening political, religious and cultural strains in the national fabric: royal absolutism pitted against Parliament's rights; an extravagant court supposedly rife with Papists and licentious Cavaliers against a frugal London citizenry and the county aristocracy; and an established Church supposedly returning, under Archbishop Laud, to Roman Catholic liturgy, theology, ceremony and Church government, against reformist Protestants and Puritans. Within and among several of his early poems Milton staged a debate about alternative kinds of life and poetry – revelry and asceticism, light elegy and the higher poetic kinds, sensuous pleasure and labour, licentiousness and chastity, Mirth and Melancholy.

The earliest published examples of Milton's juvenalia are verse translations of Psalm 114 (in decasyllabic couplets) and Psalm 136 in iambic tetrameter, with the headnote 'done by the Author at fifteen years old'. At moments of personal and national crisis he produced other Psalm paraphrases (Psalms 80–8 in 1648 and Psalms 1–8 in 1653), identifying with the Davidic speaker. From 1625 to 1632 he completed his studies for the A.B. and A.M. degrees at Christ's College, Cambridge, intending at first to prepare for the ministry. His undergraduate poetry was mostly in Latin, often prompted by university occasions. The chief influence was Ovid, but he looked also to Virgil, Horace, Propertius, Tibullus, Catullus, Callimachus, Seneca, Lucan, Statius and such neo-Latin poets as George Buchanan and Marullo.[12] But Milton's Latin poems are not the usual collegiate poet's Latin exercises: Dr Johnson praised Milton as 'the first Englishman who, after the revival of letters, wrote Latin verse with classick elegance'.[13] Rather than imitating specific poems, he freely transforms Ovid and the others, often mixing classical and Christian allusions.[14]

He began with elegy – paired lines of alternating dactylic hexameter and pentameter – 'which in imitation I found most easie; and most agreeable to natures part in me'.[15] In that metre he wrote verse letters to his school friend and soul-mate Charles Diodati (Elegy I) and to his former (Puritan) tutor Thomas Young in Hamburg (Elegy IV), representing him as an exile from religious persecution in England. In 1626 he wrote two funeral elegies – for the university beadle (mace-bearer and crier), and for the eminent prelate Lancelot Andrewes – also obsequies in Horatian alcaic stanzas for the Vice-Chancellor Dr John Gostlin and in iambics for Nicholas Felton, Bishop of Ely. In 1626 also he wrote 'In quintum Novembris', a miniature epic in 226 hexameter lines on the thwarting of the Guy Fawkes Gunpowder Plot, the 1605 Roman Catholic conspiracy to blow up King and Parliament. With many echoes of Virgil, Tasso and Spenser, the poem exudes Protestant zeal and Virgilian aspiration, mixing the heroic and the grotesque, florid expressions of awe and horror with irony and mockery of the Pope and the conspirators. Four undated Latin epigrams on the Gunpowder Plot and another on the invention of gunpowder (all in elegiacs) may also be Guy Fawkes poems. His single love elegy (Elegy VII) rings comic changes on that common Ovidian topic, Cupid's vengeance on one who claims to be impervious to his arrows. Elegy V, 'On the Approach of Spring' (April 1629), his most creative and sensuous appropriation of Ovid, celebrates in lush, exuberant language within a classical hymnic structure the erotic desire pulsing through all nature, the pagan gods and the Miltonic poet.

The first original English poem Milton preserved was a funeral ode 'On the Death of a Fair Infant Dying of a Cough' (1627–8) about the two-year-old daughter of his sister Anne. Rather like Donne's Elizabeth Drury, this infant is made to embody the power of innocence to slake God's wrath for sin and drive off 'black perdition' and 'slaughtering pestilence'.[16] Indebted to Spenser for its archaisms and schemes of alliteration and assonance, the eleven seven-line stanzas meld Chaucerian rime royal with the Spenserian stanza ending with an alexandrine. 'At a Vacation Exercise in the Colledge', offered as a coda to the satiric and boisterous prose Latin prolusion he presented at the annual festival at Christ's (1628), is the first statement of Milton's poetic aspirations. With its graceful Jonsonian couplets and Spenserian imagery and sonorities, it apostrophises and celebrates the English language. Rejecting the 'new fangled toys' and 'trimming slight' that delight our 'late fantasticks' (the metaphysical style, perhaps) he seeks the 'richest Robes, and gay'st attire' English can provide for the 'graver' poems he hopes to write: hymns, sacred poems, and epic and romance in the vein of Homer and Spenser (lines 19–21, 30).

'On the Morning of Christ's Nativity' (December 1629) is Milton's first major poem, written in the month of his own important twenty-first birthday. He termed it his gift 'for the birthday of Christ' in a Latin verse letter to Diodati (Elegy VI) that playfully contrasts two lifestyles and the poetry appropriate to each. Identifying Diodati with the festive life and the light elegy, he locates himself with epic and hymnic poets – Homer, Tiresias, Linus, Orpheus – whose high subjects require an ascetic and chaste life. The Nativity poem already displays elements that remain constants in Milton's poetry: allusiveness, revisionism, mixture of genres, stunning originality, cosmic scope, reformist politics and prophetic voice. Unlike Christmas poems by his contemporaries Donne, Herbert and Crashaw, Milton's poem does not focus on the infant Jesus and the manger scene, but on the Incarnation and its meaning to humankind, nature and the entire cosmos. A four-stanza proem (six lines of iambic pentameter and a concluding alexandrine) imitates verse forms in Chaucer, Spenser and Milton's own 'Fair Infant'. Placing himself with the shepherds who came first to the Bethlehem stable, he describes the poem that follows as a 'humble ode', a pastoral, but also as a hymn, associating it with the angels' hymns at the Nativity and with Isaiah's prophecies (Isaiah 6:6–7): 'And join thy voice unto the Angel Quire, / From out his secret Altar toucht with hallow'd fire' (lines 27–8). With these lines Milton assumes the role of prophet-poet.

The 'Hymn' proper looks back to Homeric hymns and Pindaric odes and to the Christian literary hymns of Prudentius, Minturno, Mantuan and Spenser,[17] but it invents a strikingly original strophe: eight lines of varying lengths (6 6 10 6 6 10 8 12), culminating in a stately alexandrine and with an intricate, interlaced rhyme scheme (aabccbdd). There are many Spenserian elements: allegorical personifications (the masque-like descent of the 'meek-eyd Peace'), and onomatopoeia (at the Last Judgment 'The wakefull trump of doom must thunder through the deep' (lines 45, 156)). As a pastoral the poem revises Virgil's Fourth Eclogue, celebrating (probably) the birth of the Roman consul Pollio's son as the beginning of a new Golden Age and often read in Christian tradition as an unconscious prophecy of Christ's birth; Milton celebrates the birth of the Messiah who will restore the true Golden Age at the Millennium. This hymn offers a counter-statement to Milton's Elegy V: in that spring poem earth delights in the embraces of the Sun-God, and the poet urges the classical gods to remain in their forest homes; in this winter poem earth can no longer 'wanton with the Sun her lusty Paramour' (line 35) and the poet celebrates the expulsion of all the pagan gods from all their shrines. This poem re-views the classical ethos of Elegy V from a Christian perspective, presenting a complex interplay of classical and Christian myth: the pagan gods, understood literally, are conquered by Christ, but Christ is himself figured as the 'mighty *Pan*' (line 89) come to live among the shepherds, and as an infant Hercules strangling in his cradle the giant serpent Satan and all his monster crew.

The Nativity hymn centres on the uneasy encounter of the natural order with this supernatural event. Shifting focus continually from the morning of Christ's Nativity back to Creation and forward to Doomsday, and in cinematographic fashion from the Bethlehem scenes to the widest cosmic perspective, it encompasses all time and space. Nature is first personified as a wanton harlot camouflaging her guilt with a 'Saintly Vail' (line 41) of snow, and then as the awestruck natural order responding as if to the Second Coming not the first, as the sun supposes himself made superfluous by the greater Son. Then a homely scene of the shepherds chatting and tending their sheep opens out to the hymns of the angelic choir and the music of the spheres, described in wonderfully evocative lines, leading the poet to imagine the millennial Golden Age arriving. Then he is abruptly recalled to the Nativity moment – 'But wisest Fate sayes no' (line 149). The final section focuses on the immediate effects of the Nativity, beginning with the 'old Dragon' bound and continuing with the flight of all the pagan gods from all their shrines. Reproving easy speculation that the Millennium is imminent, the length of this catalogue of idols suggests, by a kind of formal mimesis, the long and difficult process that must precede it: ridding humankind of all its idols, as well lovely as hideous – from the utter blackness of Moloch to the shadowy 'Moon-lov'd maze' of the 'yellow-skirted *Fayes*' (lines 235–6). The passage also registers heightened concern in 1629 over the 'popish idolatry' which Laud's increasing power was seen to promote. The final stanza shifts the perspective back to the 'Courtly Stable' (line 243) – an oxymoron emblematic of the poem's paradoxical mode, but also one that transfers kingly power and state from earthly monarchs to their only proper locus, Christ.

During the next few years (1629–35) Milton wrote other brief lyrics on religious themes. 'The Passion' was designed to complement the Nativity Ode using the metrical stanza of its proem. But he chose to publish it as a fragment, explaining at the end that he found the subject 'to be above the yeers he had . . . and nothing satisfi'd with what was begun, left it unfinisht'. However, Milton's Protestant imagination was never stirred by Christ's passion, in youth or maturity. 'Upon the Circumcision', in two fourteen-line stanzas with a complex, interwoven rhyme pattern, is a competent but uninspired poem meant as a substitute for the failed 'Passion'. 'On Time' celebrates the victory of Eternity over Time, portraying Time in slow, ponderous rhythms and Eternity in swelling and soaring lines. The finest of these small religious odes, 'At a Solemn Musick', is an ecstatic celebration of sacred music and poetry, apostrophising those arts as sirens whose combined powers at a vocal concert seemed almost to restore the Platonic–Pythagorean–Biblical vision of universal harmony. The irregular line lengths and movement from alternating rhyme to couplets produce a mimesis of the musical subject.

Milton's secular lyrics of this period include a light-hearted English aubade, 'On May Morning', with close affinities to Elizabethan lyricists; some sonnets (discussed later); and a few epitaphs indebted to Ben Jonson. Two whimsical and irreverent epitaphs, 'On the University Carrier', were contributions to the spate of collegiate versifying about the death of Thomas Hobson, who hired out horses and transported students between London and Cambridge. Often anthologised anonymously in collections of witty verse, these poems develop the conceit that the inactivity forced on Hobson by the plague caused his death.[18] The seventy-six-line 'Epitaph on the Marchioness of Winchester', couched in octo- and heptasyllabic couplets, was probably intended for a university volume honouring Jane Paulet, a kinswoman of the university Chancellor. Emphasising the pathos of her early death and that of her stillborn infant, it begins conventionally by voicing the inscription on the tombstone, and ends by envisioning the Marchioness placed with Rachel in heaven – Milton's first poetic reference to Dante. His first published poem, the sixteen-line 'Epitaph on the Admirable Dramaticke Poet, W. Shakespeare', reworks the conventional conceit that a poet's best monument is his works, instead making Shakespeare's readers his true 'live-long Monument' (line 8) turned to marble by their wonder and astonishment. It is indebted to Jonson for style and tone – iambic pentameter couplets that combine formality with restrained feeling – and to an epitaph often attributed to Shakespeare for some elements of diction ('piled Stones', 'Star-ypointing *Pyramid*').[19] Explicitly claiming him as 'my *Shakespear*', Milton describes Shakespeare's poetry in terms that better describe his own: 'Delphick', inspired. But he also contrasts Shakespeare's 'easie numbers' with his own 'slow-endeavoring art' (lines 9–12).

The brilliantly inventive companion poems *L'Allegro* and *Il Penseroso* (*c.*1631) compare and evaluate the pleasures and the literary kinds appropriate to contrasting lifestyles – 'heart-easing Mirth', 'divinest Melancholy' – that a poet might choose, or might choose at different times, or in sequence. From these ideals any hint of cavalier licentiousness, or courtly Neoplatonism, or idolatry is excised. As celebrations of their respective deities – the Grace Euphrosyne (Youthful Mirth) and the allegorical figure Melancholy – both poems are modelled on the classical hymn: first, an exorcism or banishment of the opposing deity, then, an invocation to the deity celebrated, then a celebration of her qualities and activities, and finally a prayer to be admitted to her company. They also incorporate elements of the academic prolusion or debate, the Theocritan pastoral idyll of the ideal day and its festivals, the Theophrastian prose 'character' with such titles as 'The Happy Man' or 'The Melancholy Man', the encomium and the eulogistic oration. The final couplet of each poem echoes and answers the question posed in Marlowe's 'Come live with me and be my love' and its Elizabethan analogues. But despite the familiarity of these elements, Milton's paired poems have no close antecedents.

Metrically and rhythmically these poems are a tour de force. Both begin with a ten-line prelude, alternating lines of six and ten syllables in an intricate rhyme pattern, followed by octosyllabic couplets with seven-foot lines intermingled. Milton is now so skilful with metrics that from the same verse-form he can produce utterly different tonal effects. In *L'Allegro* the quick short vowels, the monosyllables, the liquid consonants and the frequent trochaic rhythms trip over the tongue in a mimesis of youthful frolic – an English version of anacreontic verse:

> Haste thee nymph, and bring with thee
> Jest and youthful jollity,
> Quips and Cranks, and wanton Wiles,
> Nods, and Becks, and Wreathed Smiles (lines 25–8)

In *Il Penseroso* polysyllables, clusters of consonants and a liberal use of spondaic feet produce a deliberate and sombre tone:

> Com pensive Nun, devout and pure,
> Sober, steadfast, and demure,
> All in a robe of darkest grain,
> Flowing with majestick train (lines 31–4)

L'Allegro's essence, youthful mirth, innocent joy, light-hearted pleasure, freedom from care, is chiefly displayed in the activities and values of the pastoral mode and literary genres harmonious with it: rural folk and fairy tales of Queen Mab and Goblin; court masques and pageants; Jonson's 'learned' comedy; romantic comedies in which 'sweetest *Shakespear*, fancies childe, / Warble[s] his native Wood-notes wilde' (lines 132–4); and love songs in the Greek Lydian mode. The poem shows the continuing influence of Jonson's lyric delicacy and grace, and it sometimes evokes the Shakespeare of *A Midsummer Night's Dream*. The prologue banishes *L'Allegro*'s conception of melancholy, 'loathed Melancholy' (line 1), the disease caused by an imbalance of black bile and associated with depression and madness. Then the speaker invites and praises youthful Mirth with her associates Jests, Sports and Laughter, identifying her special companion and defining quality as 'The Mountain Nymph, Sweet Liberty' (line 36). The sociable daytime pleasures of Mirth's devotee are portrayed in a series of delightful pastoral scenes that mix classical shepherds and shepherdesses – Corydon, Thyrsis, Phillis – with the sights and sounds, the sunshine holidays and the folk tales of rural England. His nocturnal pleasures are sought in 'Towred Cities' (line 17): festivals, knightly jousts, court masques, stage comedies. The poem ends by evoking in wonderfully mimetic lines soft and sweet (or as Plato thought, enervating) Lydian songs; they waken Orpheus, the figure of the poet, but do not rouse him to any activity. The life of mirth is not tainted, only limited, as the conditional terms of the final couplet also indicate: 'These delights, if thou canst give, / Mirth with thee, I mean to live' (lines 151–2).

Il Penseroso celebrates Melancholy as the saturnine temperament that seeks solitude, the scholarly life and religious contemplation.[20] Here the romance mode is employed to present the activities, pleasures and values of a solitary scholar-errant who wanders through a mysterious gothic landscape with a plaintive nightingale, a 'high lonely Towr' (line 86), a drowsy bellman, a cathedral cloister with 'high embowed Roof', stained-glass windows, 'dimm religious light' (lines 156–60) and a hermitage with mossy cells. This poem's prelude banishes the speaker's conception of Mirth – 'Vain deluding joys' (line 1) – then invites and praises Melancholy, who is sage and holy with a rapt soul and a visage saintly and black, 'staid Wisdoms hue' (line 16). Her companions are calm Peace and Quiet, Spare Fast and Silence, and her chief associate and defining characteristic is 'The Cherub Contemplation' (line 154). Reversing *L'Allegro*, this poem first describes the nocturnal pleasures of Melancholy's devotee – the esoteric philosophy of Plato and Hermes Trismegistus, romances like Chaucer's unfinished *Squire's Tale* for their marvels and their allegory, 'gorgeous' (line 97) Greek tragedies about Thebes and Troy, and Orphic hymns. During the day *Il Penseroso* enjoys 'twilight groves' and 'shadows brown' (lines 133–4), as well as sacred organ music and anthems that 'Dissolve me into extasies, / And bring all Heav'n before mine eyes' (lines 165–6).

The title personages of both poems are exaggerated types, often seen as perfectly parallel, though the poems' structure implies a progression. The first five sections of *Il Penseroso* are a little longer than those in *L'Allegro*, and *Il Penseroso*'s eight-line coda has no parallel. *L'Allegro* portrays the lifestyle of youth as a cyclic round, beginning with Mirth's man awakening from sleep and ending with the drowsing Orpheus. Melancholy's devotee begins with evening and ends in waking ecstasy and the vision of heaven. Also, the coda of *Il Penseroso* opens to the future, where age brings all-embracing scientific knowledge of nature and the ripening of 'old experience' into 'somthing like Prophetic strain' (lines 173–4) – prophetic poetry that can convey Il Penseroso's vision, knowledge and experience to others. Many later poets – among them Thomas Gray, James Thomson, and William Cowper – imitated the tetrameter couplets (known as Miltonicks) of these very popular poems, in lyrics filled with Miltonic allusions, poetic diction and syntax.

While living with his father (1632–8) and pursuing an arduous programme of self-education Milton was invited, probably through the musician Henry Lawes, to write two aristocratic entertainments, through which he took a public position in the culture wars then raging. The court was promoting a fashionable cult of platonic love and pastoralism as a benign representation and vindication of royal absolutism and the personal rule (1629–40), when Charles ruled without Parliament. In the very elaborate and prodigiously expensive court masques of the 1630s the King and Queen enacted under various mythological guises the union of heroic virtue (Charles) and divine beauty or love (Henrietta Maria).[21] Their dancing symbolised control of all the discordant elements represented in the anti-masques – unruly passions, discontented and mutinous elements in the populace and threats from abroad. In *Histrio-Mastix* (1632), a passionate tirade of over 1,000 pages, the Puritan William Prynne inveighed against court masques as well as stage plays, rural festivals and country sports on the Sabbath, Laudian ritual, stained-glass windows and much more, pointing to the Queen and King as participants in 'scurrilous amorous pastorals' and 'voluptuous, unchristian masque dancing'.[22] Prynne was placed in the pillory, had his ears cropped and was sentenced to life imprisonment.

In his entertainment *Arcades* (1632?)[23] and more completely in his *Mask* commonly called *Comus* (1634) Milton developed a stance towards art and recreation that repudiates both the court aesthetics and Prynne's wholesale prohibitions. *Arcades* comprised part of the festivities to honour seventy-three-year-old Alice Spencer, Dowager Countess of Derby, who had long been a patron of Protestant writers and poets, including Spenser. It was performed at her country seat, Harefield, by some of her grandchildren and others.[24] As an entertainment *Arcades* belongs to the genre usually employed to welcome and praise visiting royalty or their surrogates who bring the benefits and virtues of the court to a noble house. In Milton's reformed entertainment, the visitors, coming in pastoral guise from the 'Arcadian' court, pay homage to a far superior queen of a better Arcadia: 'Such a rural Queen / All *Arcadia* hath not seen' (lines 94–5, 108–9). Genius, the gardener/guardian who hears and seeks to imitate the music of the spheres, embodies the curative and harmony-producing powers of music and poetry, which, together with the ruling lady, sustain the virtues of Harefield. His last song calls on the visitors to leave their Arcadian court dances to serve this more excellent queen, a gesture that associates the better aesthetics he is promoting with the virtues of a soundly Protestant aristocracy.

Milton's *Mask Presented at Ludlow Castle* was performed on Michaelmas night (29 September 1634), to celebrate the Earl of Bridgewater's arrival as Lord President of the Council of Wales. Henry Lawes contributed the music. The principal characters were the Earl's children – Lady Alice, aged fifteen, the young heir John, Lord Brackley, aged eleven, and Thomas, aged nine – playing themselves, not masque figures. But their journey to their father's house for a celebration takes on overtones of the journey of life, with the children lost in the dark woods and the Lady confronting the seductions of Comus. Only Comus, Sabrina and the Attendant Spirit as the shepherd Thyrsis (played by Alice's music master, Lawes) are allegorical or mythic masque figures. Milton draws on Plato's *Phaedo*, Ovid, Spenser's *Faerie Queene*, Jonson's masque *Pleasure Reconciled to Virtue*, John Fletcher's *Faithful Shepherdess* and Shakespeare's *Midsummer Night's Dream*. He uses a mix of verse forms: iambic pentameter for most of the dialogue, octosyllabic couplets (echoing and perverting *L'Allegro*) for Comus's address to his rout and songs in a variety of intricate stanzas.

In all its versions,[25] this is a reformed masque in form, theme and spirit. It requires no expensive machinery or elaborate sets. Comus is a species of court masque enacting 'dazling Spells' and marvellous spectacles, but they only 'cheat the eye with blear illusion' (lines 154–5). He claims the world of pastoral by his shepherd disguise and his offer to guide the Lady to a 'low / But loyal cottage' (lines 319–20), but instead he leads her to a decadent court with an elaborate banquet and a beast-headed entourage. A masque audience would expect the court scene to be the main masque following the anti-masque of Comus's rout in the dark wood, but it is instead another anti-masque: the court is Comus's own residence. Instead, the main masque, the locus of virtue, is in Ludlow Castle and it is attained through pilgrimage; court figures do not, as is usual in masques, simply appear and dispel all dangers. The Platonism in this masque is a far cry from that of the Caroline court: external form does not reflect internal worth and at the end evil remains: the dark wood is still dangerous to pass through and Comus is neither conquered, nor transformed, nor reconciled.

Milton's masque again contrasts alternative styles of life and art, but now in terms of good and evil, as Comus's perversion of natural sensuality is opposed to the 'Sun-clad power of Chastity' (line 782) in the Lady. Milton's Comus is not the traditional belly god of drunkenness and gluttony but, as Cedric Brown notes, he presents these young aristocrats with the refined, dissolute, licentious Cavalier lifestyle they must learn to resist.[26] The ideal of chastity is clarified in two formal debates. In an exchange between the Lady's two brothers, the younger, a pessimistic realist, expects his exposed sister to suffer rape and worse in an evil world, while the elder, a Platonic idealist, believes that chastity alone will protect her from every evil – as if she were a Diana or a militant Britomart 'clad in compleat steele' (line 421). But in the Lady's sounder view, chastity is a principle of spiritual integrity, not a physical state or a magic charm; deceived, paralysed in Comus's chair and threatened with rape, she claims only the power of spiritual resistance: 'Thou canst not touch the freedom of my minde / With all charms, although this corporal rinde / Thou hast immanacl'd, while Heav'n sees good' (lines 663–5). Her debate with Comus concerns the nature of Nature, and the kinds of pleasure and art that accord with it. Comus offers his Circean cup of sensual pleasure, ease and joy as the true principle of nature, and in richly sensuous language, mesmerising in its sounds and rhythms but epitomising false rhetoric, he proposes a vision of Nature so prolific in its abundance and vitality that its bounty bids fair to strangle the world unless humans consume, consume, consume, with riotous abandon. Focusing the issue on the folly of virginity in such a nature, he echoes countless Cavalier seduction poems on the theme of *carpe diem* and *carpe floream*. In trenchant language with a satiric edge, the Lady denounces the profligate and wasteful consumption Comus promotes and court masques notoriously exhibit, as well as the 'dazling fence' of his 'deer Wit, and gay Rhetorick' (lines 790–1), describing nature in terms that square with common experience and ending with a remarkably egalitarian argument for the right of the worthy poor to share equitably in the earth's bounty. Her praises of virginity focus on the form of chastity (which in Milton's usage also includes marital fidelity) that is appropriate to her fifteen-year-old, as yet unmarried, self.

When her brothers' impetuous swordplay fails to rescue the Lady, the Attendant Spirit calls up in song a figure from a story by Spenser (*The Faerie Queene* II.x.19): Sabrina, an innocent virgin murdered and transformed into a nymph, whose lovely lyrics and rituals produce the masque transformations.

As agent of divine grace, Sabrina sprinkles water drops in a ceremony suggestive of baptism to free the Lady from Comus's chair, 'Smear'd with gumms of glutenous heat' (line 917): despite her virtue, she is subject to the unruly sensuality that results from original sin. As a personage in Spenser's poem and a singer herself, Sabrina is the good poet whose elegant songs and rituals free the Lady from the spells of the bad poet and debased rhetorician, Comus, and confirm her in the art she earlier manifested in her haunting Echo song.

Dance is at the heart of the masque genre and of this masque, further contrasting good and bad art. The anti-masques are antic dances of Comus's beast-headed rout – 'Tipsie dance, and Jollity' (line 104), 'Riot, and ill-manag'd Merriment' (line 172) – imaging the deformation of human nature when passions supplant reason, and evoking the depravities of court masques and feasts and rural holiday pastimes. The main masque scene at Ludlow Castle displays the pleasure, beauty and art that accord with the life of virtue, best nurtured in the households of the country aristocracy: the rustic dances of shepherds recuperate pastoral from Comus's deformation of it, the Attendant Spirit's song presents the children to their parents and the children's stately dances display their '*triumph in victorious dance / O're sensuall Folly, and Intemperance*' (lines 974–5). The Spirit's epilogue, in quick octosyllabic couplets, refers to an idyllic Garden of the Hesperides where Venus and Adonis are healing but not yet cured of the effects of the boar's wound (intemperance), and also to a higher realm where the cures and pleasures are perfect, where the celestial Cupid will at length welcome Psyche (a figure for the soul, the Lady and the Bride of Revelation) after her long journeys and trials. Milton's *Mask* conjoins and explores, as one subtle and complex ideal, chastity, true pleasure and good art.

Lycidas is the *chef d'oeuvre* of Milton's early poetry, and one of the greatest lyrics in the language. In it Milton confronts and works through his most profound personal concerns about vocation, early death, belatedness and unfulfilment, and the worth of poetry, achieving a stunning fusion of intense feeling and consummate art. He also sounds the leitmotifs of Reformist politics: the dangers posed by a corrupt clergy and church, the menace of Rome, the adumbrations of apocalypse, the call to prophecy. He wrote this funeral elegy for a Cambridge memorial volume, *Justa Edouardo King naufrago* (1638),[27] honouring his college classmate, Edward King, who died in a shipwreck off the coast of Cornwall at the age of twenty-five. The poem is not prompted by personal grief, as King was not a close friend. Its intense emotion arises from the fact that Milton takes this poet, scholar and ordained minister as an alter ego whose early death seems to display nature and human life subject to meaningless chaos, rendering exceptional talent, lofty ambition and noble ideals useless. Since Lycidas was cut off before his time the Miltonic 'uncouth Swain' (line 186) must sing an elegy before his poetic gifts are mature, plucking with 'forc'd fingers rude' (line 4) the unripe laurel and myrtle leaves.

The headnote identifies this poem as a monody, a song by a single singer,[28] though other speakers are quoted in the poem and the coda introduces another poetic voice. The conventional topics of funeral elegy – praise, lament, consolation – are present, though not as distinct parts of the poem, which also has affinities with Pindaric ode.[29] For the first time in English, Milton uses verse paragraphs of irregular length; the verse is chiefly iambic pentameter with occasional short lines and a very irregular rhyme scheme – a form that intensifies tensions, denies surface smoothness and prevents facile resolutions. The opening phrase, 'Yet once more', places *Lycidas* in the series of funeral poems Milton wrote for deceased Cantabridgians and others, in the long series of pastoral funeral elegies stretching back to Theocritus and in a series of biblical warnings and apocalyptic prophecies beginning with those words, especially Hebrews 12:26–8).

Virtually every line echoes other pastoral elegies by classical, neo-Latin and vernacular Renaissance poets – Theocritus, Moschus, Bion, Virgil, Petrarch, Castiglione, Mantuan, Joannes Secundus, Sannazaro, Spenser and many more[30] – and later elegies by Shelley, Tennyson and Arnold show its influence. Yet no previous, or I think subsequent, funeral poem has the scope, dimension, poignancy and power of *Lycidas*. It is, paradoxically, the most derivative and most original of elegies. Milton's choice of the pastoral mode, by then out of fashion for funeral elegies, might have surprised contemporaries: none of the other twenty-five contributions to *Justa* are pastorals. But that choice allowed him to call upon the rich symbolic resonances Renaissance pastoral had come to embrace. Imaging the harmony of nature and humankind in the Golden Age, pastoral traditionally portrays the rhythms of human life and death in harmony with the rhythms of the seasons. In classical tradition the shepherd is the poet, raising questions of the relation of art and nature. In Biblical tradition the shepherd is pastor of a flock, like Christ the Good Shepherd, and also a prophet, like the erstwhile shepherds Moses, Isaiah or David, associations that allow for moral and political comment, as in Spenser's *Shepheards Calender*.

Milton radically revises the genre by dramatising over and over, in relation to all the usual topics, the collapse of the pastoral vision. The dead and the living poets are first presented as youthful shepherds singing and tending sheep in a *locus amoenus*, an idealised Cambridge University characterised by *otium*, in which nature, humankind and poetic ambitions seem to be in harmony. Lycidas's death shatters this idyll, revealing in nature not the ordered seasonal processes of blossoming, mellowing, fruition and then death, but rather the wanton destruction of youth and beauty: the blighted rosebud, the taintworm destroying the weanling sheep and the frostbitten flowers in early spring. After the swain questions the pastoral nymphs and muses as to why they do not protect their bards, he recalls that even the muse Calliope could not save her son Orpheus, the archetypal poet, from horrific death and dismemberment by the Maenads, who embody the dark forces of savagery and mindless violence that so easily overcome the fragile civilising arts. So he demands, why not 'sport with *Amaryllis* in the shade, / Or with the tangles of Neaera's hair' instead of devoting 'laborious dayes' to 'the thankles Muse?' His anger and frustration are rendered in a graphic, appalling figure: 'Comes the blind *Fury* with th'abhorred shears, / And slits the thin-spun life' (lines 66–76). Some consolation is provided by Apollo, promising enduring fame in heaven from the best critic, 'all-judging *Jove*' (line 82). But that speech is in a 'higher mood' (line 87), requiring the swain to recall pastoral. He then questions the sea and wind deities but they deny all responsibility, ascribing the death to 'that fatall and perfidious Bark / Built in th'eclipse, and rigg'd with curses dark' (lines 100–1). That metaphor points beyond pastoral nature to the tragic human condition: sailing the sea of life in the frail ship of the body, bearing the curse of mortality due to the Fall.

A pastoral procession of mourners includes Camus, god of the River Cam, lamenting the loss of the university's 'dearest pledge' (line 107). But then Peter, 'Pilot of the *Galilean* Lake' (line 109), again silences the pastoral music with a fierce Jeremiad against the Laudian Church and clergy. His scornful paradox, 'Blind mouthes', brilliantly exposes the ignorance, ambition and greediness of those bad shepherds who seek only to feed their bellies, leaving the hungry sheep 'swoln with wind' and subject to the ravages of the Roman Catholic 'grim Woolf' (lines 119, 128). Yet there is a kind of consolation in this apocalyptic prophecy that some formidable if ambiguous 'two-handed engine' stands ready 'at the door' (line 130) to smite the guilty and cleanse the Church.[31] Then, again recalling the frightened pastoral river Alpheus and the Sicilian muse, the swain develops another topos of the genre, an exquisite flower passage in which he imagines Lycidas's funeral bier heaped with the various flowers into which classical figures were transformed, affording them a kind of immortality in nature. But that pastoral consolation soon collapses, based as it is on the 'false surmise' of nature's sympathy for humankind. Rather than receiving the tribute of nature's beauty, Lycidas's bones are hurled under the 'whelming tide', where he visits 'the bottom of the monstrous world' (lines 153–8).

From this nadir of 'bones hurld' the tone modulates to the peace of 'Sleep'st by the fable of Bellerus old' (lines 155–60), inviting recollection of earlier intimations of resurrection in the myths of Orpheus, Hyacinthus and Amaranthus. St Michael's Mount, off the Cornish coast where Lycidas drowned, now promises heavenly protection, as does the myth of the poet Orion saved by dolphins. The line, 'Weep no more, woful Shepherds weep no more' (line 165) – echoing the poem's first line – marks the decisive turn to true consolation. The swain reads nature's symbol of resurrection from the sea – the sun sinks into the ocean at night and rises at dawn – as a type of the divine Son who walked the waves and through whose power Peter, and now Lycidas, are 'mounted high' (line 172). In an ecstatic vision of a celestial pastoral scene the swain sees Lycidas enjoying true *otium* beside heavenly streams: as poet he takes part in the 'unexpressive nuptiall song' of the Lamb, and as pastor he is the 'Genius of the shore', a guide (by means of his exemplary story immortalised in this poem) to all who wander in the 'perilous flood' of human life (lines 176, 183–5). Pastoral has collapsed again, but now into the higher mode of prophetic vision.

In the eight-line coda a new voice speaks, suggesting that a more mature poetic self has been voicing the 'uncouth' swain's monody and presenting his hard-won progress from despair to affirmation. Having had his vision of the perfected pastoral in heaven, the swain can now take up his several pastoral roles in the world. He retains his shepherd's blue mantle (also suggestive of priestly and prophetic garb) and turns again to pastoral poetry – 'With eager thought warbling his *Dorick* lay' (line 189). He completes the daily cycle of pastoral – forth at dawn, home at evening – and prepares for new adventures, personal and literary: 'To morrow to fresh Woods, and Pastures new' (line 195).

These did not involve bidding a permanent farewell to his Latin muse. Sometime after leaving the university and probably around 1637 Milton wrote 'Ad Patrem', a verse epistle in dactylic hexameters that is in part a praise of his father for fostering his education and five years of self-education, in part a defence of poetry against his father's supposed disparagement of it and in part an implicit persuasion to his father to accept his vocation as a poet and continue to support him in it. As a defence of poetry, the poem sounds some familiar Renaissance themes: poetry's divine origins, the bard's heroic and divine subjects, Orpheus as a figure for the poet in that his song could move stones and trees and Hell itself, and the poet's priestly and prophetic roles. He wrote other impressive poems in Latin, dense with classical echoes and allusiveness, while on his 'Grand Tour' through France, Italy, and Switzerland in 1638–9. Among the plethora of new experiences and impressions was a concert by the much-praised singer and composer Leonora Baroni, to whom he paid hyperbolic tribute in three Latin epigrams. He presented some Latin poems to Florentine and Roman academies, and received from Italian friends some highly laudatory commendatory poems he later used to introduce his *Poemata*. His forty-one-line verse epistle to the Roman poet Salzilli appropriately laments his desperate illness in scazons, a halting or 'limping' metre with a spondee or trochee as the final foot in the iambic line.[32] To Manso, the patron of Tasso and Marino, he offered a 100-line verse letter in hexameters, to express gratitude for hospitality shown to him in Naples but also to assert his own worth and his aspiration to join a poetic line that includes Tasso and the English poets Chaucer, Spenser and the Druids. Reversing expectations, Milton does not exalt the patron, but emphasises rather the duty and high privilege of patrons to befriend and assist poets. The poem maintains a delicate balance between the decorum of gracious civility and Milton's bold revisionary claims.

Soon after he returned to England Milton composed *Epitaphium Damonis*[33] (219 lines in dactylic hexameter) for Charles Diodati, who had died while Milton was abroad. This pastoral elegy is his most autobiographical poem and arguably his most impressive achievement as a Latin poet. It probes the agonising question, how can Milton bear to go on with his life, his duty to God and country, and his new plans for epic, given the terrible loneliness caused by the loss of his most intimate companion. Even more than *Lycidas* this poem reverberates with echoes from the entire pastoral tradition, most insistently Virgil's *Eclogues* and *Georgics*;[34] it also challenges pastoral norms, though in quite different ways from *Lycidas*. There is no pathetic fallacy: the crops and the sheep do not suffer because of sorrow for Damon / Diodati but because Thrysis / Milton neglects them. The shepherds and shepherdesses do not form a procession of mourners for Damon, but try vainly to console Thrysis; nor do figures from the classical or Christian supernatural answer questions or offer consolation. Also, Thrysis reiterates seventeen times in the refrain his shocking refusal to fulfil his pastoral duties in the wake of Damon's loss: 'Go home unfed, your master has no time for you, my lambs' (line 18, etc.). But at length Thrysis sketches out plans for his projected Arthuriad and at the last occurrence of the refrain he dismisses his lambs in confidence of a new poetic direction. In contrast to the pastoral apotheosis and coda of *Lycidas*, *Epitaphium Damonis* concludes with an ecstatic vision of Damon enjoying sanctified bacchic revelries and festal orgies at the celestial marriage feast (lines 212–19).

Milton's last Latin poem, 'Ad Joannem Rousium' (1647), was sent with a replacement copy of his 1645 *Poems* to John Rouse, Librarian of the Bodleian. It is an experimental ode of consummate art and originality in which Milton sought to imitate the mixed formalism and freedom of Pindar while retaining the strophe–antistrophe–epode structure. Wittily imagining the travails of this once-lost book, he rejoices that it will be preserved for ever among the sublime Greek and Latin classics in the Bodleian.

Milton wrote only twenty-three sonnets over almost three decades, but he transformed the genre radically in regard to subjects, uses and tone – often by calling upon the resources of other genres. When the Romantic poets revived the sonnet Milton was a major influence. Milton's sonnets chiefly follow the octave / sestet structure and rhyme scheme of the Italian model (abba abba and often cdcdee), but increasingly Milton overlays that metrical pattern with insistent speech rhythms. His first sonnets date from the early 1630s. 'O Nightingale' has affinities with medieval debates between the nightingale as harbinger of love and the cuckoo as emblem of infidelity. A Petrarchan mini-sequence in Italian – two sonnets, a one-stanza canzone or song, then three more sonnets – stages a love experience, actual or wholly literary. Having mastered the Ovidian love elegy in Latin, Milton evidently decided to try out the other major mode of love poetry in the European tradition in *its* original language, with sonnets indebted to Petrarch, Tasso, Bembo and especially Giovanni della Casa.[35] Though he employs familiar Petrarchan topics, this speaker redefines conventional Petrarchan roles: his sonnet lady is not coy or forbidding but 'gentle' and gracious; her eyes and hair are black not blue and gold; she is no silent object of adoration but charms her lover with bilingual speech and enthralling songs. And, far from being his muse the Italian love poetry she inspires diverts him from greater poetic achievements.

Four sonnets deal with emotional and spiritual crises: two deal with his blindness, one with the death of his second wife, and the first of this group, 'How soon hath Time', is prompted by Milton's twenty-fourth birthday (9 December 1632).[36] It characterises Time as a thief stealing away his youth: his 'late spring' has brought no 'bud or blossom' of accomplishment and his external semblance belies his lack of 'inward ripenes' (lines 4, 7). The sestet offers a resolution in God's predestinating will: his lot is fixed, and Time is reimagined as a guide leading inexorably to it. The perfectly regular structure – a sharp turn between octave and sestet and strong end-stops at lines 2, 4, 8, 12 and 14 – offers a formal mimesis of that fixed course.

During the almost two decades while he wrote polemics defending the revolution and the cause of liberty and composed state papers for the Republic and Cromwell (1642–60), he had little time for poetry, but he did continue experimenting with the sonnet. He responded to fears of a Royalist attack on London in 1642 with a new kind of sonnet fusing personal experience with public event, 'On his dore when ye Citty expected an assault'.[37] The speaker offers to strike a bargain with a Royalist officer: poetic fame for him if he spares the poet and his house, as Alexander the Great spared Pindar's house and Lysander spared Athens, moved by verses from Euripides's *Electra*. But the speaker's tone is fraught with anxiety and self-irony: he is no Pindar or Euripides – at least not yet; and poetry in modern times may not have the power it once had.

In the years 1642–6 Milton wrote sonnets to or about friends. The three that praise women do so in terms of exemplary paradigms, not Petrarchan topics. The unknown subject of Sonnet IX, 'Lady that in the prime of earliest youth', is portrayed in quasi-allegorical terms as a young virgin who enacts biblical metaphors and reprises Biblical roles. Sonnet X, 'To ye Lady Margaret Ley', addresses a neighbour and friend, praising her as inheriting and so making manifest the nobility and virtues of her statesman father, Sir James Lee, a model (like Isocrates of old) of devotion to liberty.[38] The epitaph-sonnet 'On the religious memory of Mrs Catherine Thomason, my christian friend'[39] recasts the Everyman allegory in Protestant terms. Catherine is led to heaven by a series of allegorical personages validated only by Faith and Love. The sonnet to Henry Lawes[40] praises him, with some exaggeration, as the 'first' in England to set a poet's lyrics 'with just note & accent' (lines 1, 3), accommodating musical stress and quantity to verbal values.[41] In the final tercet Milton likens himself to Dante whose composer friend Casella in Purgatory sang one of Dante's poems; Lawes had set and sung Milton's songs in *A Mask*. A decade later (1655–6) two other friendship sonnets are set forth as invitations, importing features of Martial and Horace, as well as Ben Jonson's 'On Inviting a Friend to Dinner'. In them Milton begins by praising the distinguished ancestors of his young friends, Edward Lawrence and Cyriack Skinner, then extends invitations of hospitality and urbane companionship, urging occasional respite from intellectual labour through refined and temperate pleasure.

Milton turned the sonnet to the purposes of satire in 1646. 'I did but prompt the age to quit their cloggs' uses the hissing of sibilants to characterise the Presbyterian clergy and pamphleteers who vilified Milton for his divorce tracts as animals – 'Owls and Cuckoes, Asses, Apes, and Dogs' (line 4). By contrast, Milton presents himself as a classical republican orator and a Christian prophet recalling free-born citizens to their 'ancient liberty' of free speech and divorce.

'A Book was writ of late call'd *Tetrachordon*', complains in a tone that is sometimes irritated, sometimes self-deprecating, that his most scholarly and densely argued divorce tract is being scorned by ignorant stall-readers put off by its Greek title. A *sonetto caudato*, 'On the Forcers of Conscience', is perhaps the first use in English of that Italian form whose 'tails' of two and a half lines added to the usual fourteen were meant to sting or lash the subject. Milton chastises the Presbyterians for venality, Pharisaical hypocrisy, ambition, corruption and power-grabbing, challenging those would-be persecutors in powerful, prophetic terms and identifying these new persecutors with old, in nature as in name: '*New Presbyter* is but *Old Priest* writ Large' (line 20).

His next three sonnets are addressed to great men in the exalted encomiastic manner of Tasso's 'Heroic Sonnets', but Milton mixes his high praise with urgent advice.[42] Exalting the 'firm unshak'n vertue' and Herculean military exploits of the army's Commander-in-Chief Thomas Fairfax (1648), he then urges Fairfax to take on the 'nobler task' of cleansing greed, corruption and religious repression from civil government, the English Augean stables (lines 5, 9). 'To the Lord Generall Cromwell May 1652 On the proposalls of certaine ministers at ye Commtee for Propagation of the Gospell' urges Cromwell to resist proposals by conservative Independents to define doctrinal fundamentals, retain a state-supported Church and suppress heresies. The couplet ending, unique among Milton's English sonnets, uses the contemptuous end rhyme to characterise their persecutions and their appetite for public funds as bestial: 'Helpe us to save free Conscience from the paw / Of hireling wolves whose Gospell is their maw' (lines 13–14). On the same occasion Milton addressed his statesman friend 'Sir Henry Vane the younger'[43] with a sonnet almost wholly in the panegyric mode though its implicit plea is as powerful, lauding his exceptional understanding of the proper bounds of the two swords, 'spirituall powre & civill' (line 10) and identifying the 'young' Vane as, paradoxically, religion's eldest son and protector.

'When I consider how my light is spent' (1652) responds to the crisis of total blindness. This sonnet, like that on the slaughter of the Waldensians and on the loss of his wife, brings the genre to new heights of emotional intensity, formal complexity and art. In the octave Milton represents himself as a helpless wanderer groping over vast spaces in utter darkness with an extinguished lantern. He sees himself as servant to a harsh divine taskmaster, the pitiless moneylender of the parable of the talents (Matthew 25:14–30), ready to cast into outer darkness an unprofitable servant who fails to use his talent. The sestet diffuses the crisis by offering a more gracious paradigm: God is a king of royal state, needing no servants yet served by myriads in their several stations;

the courtly metaphor even implies that waiting upon the King in his glory may be the most worthy role. This sonnet displays Milton's consummate skill in setting speech rhythms against the formal metrical pattern: the pauses dictated by meaning and syntax come in the middle of lines, as does the *volta*. He also varies the tempo to striking effect: short, discrete monosyllables and alliteration on the plosive consonant 'd' seem almost to spit out his bitter question to the universe: 'Doth God exact day-labour, light deny'd' (line 7). The pseudo-onomatopoeia of 'Thousands at his bidding speed . . .' mimics that haste. Then the last line achieves a stately dignity as its perfect iambics produce a solemn drumbeat: 'They also serve who only stand and waite' (lines 12–14)[44]. Form is emblematic of meaning: an agonised rebellion that challenges providential order but is yet contained within it is mirrored by the disruptions in rhythm and tempo that are yet contained within the perfect metrical pattern of a Petrarchan sonnet. Three years later, in a sonnet to his friend Cyriack Skinner, Milton revisits this crisis in a more cheerful mood. Through regretting that he can no longer see 'Sun or Moon or Starre', or 'man or woman', he insists that he can 'bear up & steer / Right onward' (lines 5–9) as a pilot boldly steering a ship into the wind – a sharp contrast to his earlier location with those who 'only stand and waite'. The sestet declares the grounds for his cheerfulness: pride that he has willingly sacrificed his vision 'in libertyes defence' (line 11), and confidence in God's guidance.

The slaughter of the Waldensians by the Roman Catholic Duke of Savoy, a notorious event in the annals of Protestant martyrology, prompted 'On the late Massacher in Piemont' (1655), which combines horrific details and graphic images of burning, pillaging and savage butchery from contemporary news reports with echoes of prophetic denunciation from Lamentations, Psalms, Isaiah and the Book of Revelation.[45] It is unique among Milton's sonnets and in the entire repertoire of the genre, forcing that lyric kind to deal with a contemporary event of tragic or epic proportions and taking on the tonalities and topics of the Jeremiad. A denunciatory voice calls down God's vengeance – 'Avenge O Lord thy slaughter'd Saints' (line 1) – apparently seeking immediate divine retribution for these martyrs who retained their gospel purity of worship while Europe was sunk in pagan or Roman Catholic idolatry. But the cry in the next segment – 'Forget not' – urges rather that their 'groanes' (line 5) be recorded in the book by which humankind will be judged on the Last Day (Revelation 20:12). After the *volta* within line 10, allusion to the parable of the sower (Matthew 13:3) suggests another response: widespread conversions to Protestantism resulting from the 'seed' sown by the Waldensians' slaughter. But allusion to the Cadmus myth intimates that, like the dragons' teeth, the massacre might produce armed Protestant warriors. The final line urges flight from the Roman Babylon, doomed to destruction now or later, by whatever means. Rove-over lines and strong syntactic breaks within the lines again set speech rhythms against formal elements, and the long 'o' sounds – 'bones', 'cold', 'old', 'Stones', 'groanes', 'Fold', 'roll'd', 'moans', 'sow', 'grow' and 'wo' – seem to echo the martyrs' cries.

'Mee thought I saw my late espoused Saint' is one of the great love poems in the language, occasioned by the death of Milton's second wife Katharine (1658) after two years of marriage. This poem merges the sonnet with the dream vision: there are precedents in the Petrarchan tradition,[46] but none that strike so intense a note of love, grief, pain and loss. The first twelve lines narrate the dream vision, pointing first to a classical analogue: like Alcestis brought back to her husband Admetus from the underworld, Katharine comes veiled, pale and faint. She is dressed all in white like one purified after childbirth in the Old Testament (Leviticus 12:2–5) – but her garments symbolise rather the purity of mind of one saved by grace. The dreamer's 'fancied sight' now perceives her 'love, sweetness, goodness' shining 'clear' (lines 10–12) through the veil, and he expects in heaven the 'full sight' of her that his blind eyes never enjoyed on earth. The turn comes in the final two lines, arguably the most poignant in all Milton's poetry, underscoring profound ironies. After his nocturnal vision, the new day brings back Milton's dark night of blindness, absence, grief and desolation: 'But O as to embrace me she enclin'd, / I wak't, she fled, and day brought back my night' (lines 13–14).

Notes

1. 'Nunc tibi quid mirum, si me genuisse poetam', 'Ad Patrem', line 61, quoted from *Poems of Mr John Milton, Both English and Latin. Compos'd at Several Times* (1645), in *John Milton: Complete Shorter Poems*, ed. Stella P. Revard (Oxford: Wiley-Blackwell, 2009). Unless otherwise noted, Milton's poems are quoted from this edition.
2. Preface to Book II, *Reason of Church Government*, in *Complete Prose Works of John Milton*, ed. Don. M. Wolfe *et al.*, 8 vols. (New Haven: Yale University Press, 1953–82), vol. I, p. 815. Milton's prose tracts are quoted from this edition, hereafter *CPW*.
3. 'An Epitaph on the admirable Dramaticke Poet, W. Shakespeare', in *Mr William Shakespeares Comedies, Histories, and Tragedies* (London, 1632), sig. A5.
4. *A Maske Presented at Ludlow Castle, 1634. On Michaelmas night, before the Right Honorable John Earle of Bridgewater* (London, 1637).
5. *Justa Edouardo King naufrago, ab Amicis moerentibus* (Cambridge, 1638).
6. An apparently unique copy of the private printing, undated, without author's or printer's names, is in the British Library (C 57.d.48).

7. In his title-page epigraph from Virgil's Eclogue VII Milton presents himself as predestined bard (*vati . . . futuro*).
8. *Poems, &c.. Upon Several Occasons. By Mr John Milton: Both English and Latin, &c. Composed at Several Times* (London, 1673).
9. In *Letters of State, Written by Mr John Milton . . . To which is added an Account of his Life. Together with several of his Poems* (London, 1694). Milton's nephew Edward Phillips edited these materials and wrote the brief Life.
10. For details of Milton's life, see Barbara K. Lewalski, *The Life of John Milton: A Critical Biography*, revised edition (Oxford: Blackwell, 2003).
11. *Reason of Church Government*, *CPW* 1.809.
12. See Douglas Bush *et al.* (eds.), *A Variorum Commentary on the Poems of John Milton*, 3 vols. (New York: Columbia University Press, 1970–5), pp. 3–24; and Stella P. Revard, *Milton and the Tangles of Neaera's Hair* (Columbia: University of Missouri Press, 1997).
13. Samuel Johnson, *Lives of the English Poets*, ed. G. B. Hill, 3 vols. (Oxford: Oxford University Press, 1905), vol. 1, p. 87.
14. John K. Hale, 'Milton Playing with Ovid', *Milton Studies*, 25 (1989), pp. 3–20.
15. *An Apology against a Pamphlet*, *CPW* 1.889.
16. This poem and the 'Vacation Exercise' were first printed in *Poems* (1673), and are quoted from the Revard edition.
17. See Phillip Rollinson, 'Milton's Nativity Ode and the Decorum of Genre', *Milton Studies*, 7 (1975), pp. 165–84; Revard, *Tangles of Neaera's Hair*, pp. 64–90, and *Reason of Church Government* (*CPW* 1.815).
18. John T. Shawcross, *A Bibliography for the Years 1624–1700* (Binghamton, NY: Medieval and Renaissance Text Society, 1984), pp. 3–5, lists some twenty-five manuscript versions of one or both of Milton's Hobson poems.
19. This epitaph on Sir Edward Standly begins, 'Not monumentall stones preserves our Fame; / Nor sky-aspiring Piramides our name'. See E. K. Chambers, *William Shakespeare: A Study of Facts and Problems*, 2 vols. (Oxford: Clarendon Press, 1988), vol. 1, p. 551.
20. See Raymond Klibansky, Erwin Panofsky and Fritz Saxl, *Saturn and Melancholy* (London: Nelson, 1964); also Robert Burton, *The Anatomy of Melancholy* (London, 1621).
21. The principal masques, most of them mounted by Inigo Jones, were: Ben Jonson, *Love's Triumph through Callipolis* (9 January 1631); Jonson, *Chloridia* (22 February 1631); Aurelian Townshend, *Tempe Restored* (14 February 1632); James Shirley, *The Triumph of Peace* (3 February 1634); Thomas Carew, *Coelum Britannicum* (18 February 1634).
22. William Prynne, *Histrio-mastix: or, The Players Scourge and Actors Tragedy* (London, 1633 [1632]), pp. 225, 236.
23. The full title in the 1645 *Poems* is: '*Arcades*. Part of an Entertainment presented to the Countess Dowager of *Derby* at *Harefield*, by some Noble persons of her Family, who appear on the Scene in pastoral habit, moving toward the seat of State'.

24. For her support of family members, including the wife and daughter of the Earl of Castlehaven, executed in May 1631 for outrageous sexual abuse of them, see Barbara Breasted, 'Comus and the Castlehaven Scandal', *Milton Studies*, 3 (1971), pp. 201–24.
25. These include the Bridgewater manuscript, probably close to the acting version, a longer text in Milton's Trinity manuscript (in which several of his early poems are inscribed, some in his hand) and published editions in 1637, 1645 and 1673.
26. Cedric C. Brown, *Milton's Aristocratic Entertainments* (Cambridge: Cambridge University Press, 1985), pp. 57–77.
27. The first section of Latin and Greek poems is followed by an English section with separate title page and pagination, *Obsequies to the Memorie of Mr Edward King*, sometimes printed and bound separately. *Lycidas* appears last, on pp. 20–5. The autograph version in the Trinity manuscript is heavily revised.
28. [George] Puttenham, *The Arte of English Poesie* (London, 1589), p. 39, identifies two classical varieties of funeral song: '*Epicedia* ... sung by many, and *Monodia* ... uttered by one alone'.
29. See O. B. Hardison, *The Enduring Monument* (Chapel Hill: University of North Carolina Press, 1962) and Revard, *Tangles of Neaera's Hair*, pp. 165–79.
30. See *Variorum Commentary*, vol. II, Part 2, pp. 544–734, for allusions and a résumé of criticism.
31. See *ibid.*, pp. 686–704 for a survey of interpretations of this image, the poem's most-debated crux.
32. See Estelle Haan, *From Academia to Amicitia: Milton's Latin Writings and the Italian Academies* (Philadelphia: American Philosophical Society, 1998), pp. 81–98.
33. The title aligns the poem with the Greek *epitaphios*, a generic label that often designates laments expressing a strong sense of personal loss.
34. The *Variorum Commentary* records some seventy citations of Virgil's *Eclogues* (especially nos. 5 and 10), thirty-five to the *Georgics* and forty to the *Aeneid*.
35. He bought Giovanni della Casa's *Rime & Prose* (Venice, 1563) for ten pence and inscribed his name and date on the title page.
36. Milton included this sonnet in a 1633 letter to an unidentified older friend, almost certainly a clergyman.
37. The first title in the Trinity manuscript imagines the sonnet as a paper pinned to his door; a less specific title is substituted below it, 'When the assault was intended to ye City'. In the editions of 1645 and 1673 it simply bears the number VIII. See Janet Mueller, 'On Genesis in Genre: Milton's Politicizing of the Sonnet in "Captain and Colonel"', in Barbara K. Lewalski (ed.), *Renaissance Genres* (Cambridge, MA: Harvard University Press, 1986), pp. 213–40.
38. Milton portrays Lee as brought to his death by the dissolution of Parliament (4 March 1629) that began Charles I's eleven-year arbitrary rule. Isocrates was thought to have starved himself to death after Philip of Macedon conquered Athens and Thebes in 338 BC. See Annabel Patterson, 'That Old Man Eloquent', in Diana Trevino Benet and Michael Lieb (eds.), *Literary Milton: Text, Pretext, Context* (Pittsburgh, PA: Pittsburgh University Press, 1994), pp. 36–44.

39. Catherine was the wife of the bookseller George Thomason.
40. It was published in *Choice Psalmes put into Musick, for Three Voices* (1648) under the title 'To My Friend Mr. *Henry Lawes*'.
41. Other song writers who allowed the melodic line to follow the pace of the verse were William Lawes, John Wilson, Simon Ives, Charles Coleman, John Gamble and earlier, Thomas Campion. See Willa M. Evans, *Henry Lawes* (New York: Modern Language Association, 1941).
42. Quotations from these sonnets, omitted in the 1673 edition, are from the Trinity manuscript of Milton's poetry (R. 3.4.) at Trinity College, Cambridge.
43. The sonnet was first printed anonymously in [George Sikes], *The Life and Death of Sir Henry Vane* (London, 1662), pp. 93–4, just after Vane's execution.
44. Cf. Spenser's 'Hymne of Heavenly Love' (lines 64–9) for a parallel: 'There they ... / About him wait, and on his will depend, / Wither with nimble wings to cut the skies, / When he them on his messages doth send, / Or on his owne dread presence to attend' (cited in *Variorum Commentary*, vol. II, Part 2, 466–7).
45. In April 1655 Carlo Emanuele II, Duke of Savoy, for reasons not fully understood, ordered his army to root out and destroy the Waldensians, or Vaudois, who for centuries had lived in the mountainous regions of Piedmont practising what contemporary Protestants saw as a survival of primitive Christianity uncontaminated by Rome. News reports told of women ripped open or impaled on spikes; men nailed upside down to trees; many hacked, tortured and roasted alive; fugitives huddled high in the mountains freezing and starving; men, women and children flung from precipices.
46. Cf. Sidney, *Astrophil*, 38; Desportes, *Diane*, 35; Drayton's 'The Vision of Matilda'.

Chapter 14

Milton: *Paradise Lost, Paradise Regained, Samson Agonistes*

BARBARA K. LEWALSKI

When the Restoration of Charles II in May 1660 crushed Milton's political hopes – pursued for twenty years in polemic tracts and service to the English Republic – he did not, as is sometimes supposed, abandon his Reformist ideals for a purely spiritual or aesthetic 'paradise within'. *Paradise Lost, Paradise Regained* and *Samson Agonistes*[1] are superlative artistic achievements addressed to the ages, but as well, they undertake a strenuous project of educating readers in the virtues, values and attitudes that make a people worthy of liberty, exercising them in rigorous judgment, imaginative apprehension and choice. They also encourage Milton's countrymen to think again and think better about the ideological and polemic controversies of the English Civil War and its aftermath. Milton's example of artistic excellence coupled with Reformist political engagement was a profound influence on the Romantic poets – Blake, the young Wordsworth, Byron and Shelley – prompting Wordsworth's apostrophe, 'Milton! thou should'st be living at this hour: / England hath need of thee.'[2]

Milton poured into his last three poems all that he had learned and thought and experienced about life, love, artistic creativity, religious faith, work, history, politics, man and woman, God and nature, liberty and tyranny, monarchy and republicanism, learning and wisdom. Also, some of the heterodox theological doctrines he worked out in his *De Doctrina Christiana* (a Latin manifesto still in preparation while he was composing his last poems)[3] brought distinct literary benefits. For one thing, he could escape the Biblical literalism common among Puritans because he gave the indwelling spirit of God priority over the letter of scripture, insisting from the time of his divorce tracts (1643–5) that every scripture text must be understood so as to accord with the principles of reason, charity and the good of humankind. The bardic speaker, Adam, Abdiel, Jesus in *Paradise Regained* and Samson all appeal to reason, experience and inspiration to interpret God's words and works. In *Paradise*

Lost Milton presents the Genesis creation account in terms that make place for contemporary and future science. The angel Raphael explicitly terms the six-day creation story an accommodation, 'So told as earthly notion can receave' (7.179). Also, by refusing Adam's urgent plea to resolve the problem of planetary motion and inviting him to consider Ptolemaic, Copernican and far more radical concepts, Raphael removes astronomy from the sphere of revelation and leaves it open to scientific inquiry – though he insists that Adam give primary attention to the human world. And unlike most poets treating Biblical subjects Milton freely devises scenes and stories that have no textual basis in the Bible.

As well, Milton's theology allowed him to portray God the Father as an epic character, a literary choice often thought impossible and probably sacrilegious. Milton held that all ideas or images of the incomprehensible God are necessarily metaphoric, but that they should correspond to the way God is represented in scripture, so his epics can and do present God displaying fear, wrath, scorn, dismay and love – partial reflections only, seen from particular perspectives.[4] Also, in Milton's distinctive version of the Arian heresy, the Son of God is a subordinate deity, not omniscient or omnipotent or eternal or immutable but produced by an act of God's will and enjoying divine attributes only as God devolves them upon him.[5] So Milton can portray the Son of God in both epics as genuinely heroic, acting freely, in a state of incomplete knowledge. Central to all three poems and to much else that Milton wrote is Arminianism, a belief in free will as opposed to Calvinist divine predestination to election or reprobation.[6] In *Paradise Lost*, the Father in dialogue with his Son explains that his 'high Decree' (3.128) from all eternity mandates freedom of choice for both angels and humans, choices he foresees but does not predetermine: they were made 'just and right, / Sufficient to have stood, though free to fall' (3.98–9). In that dialogue, the Father foreknew but did not determine the Son's choice to die to save humankind; he also foreknew the victory over Satan Jesus won in *Paradise Regained* – by his own right choices.

Milton may have begun writing *Paradise Lost* around 1658 and completed it in 1665.[7] In the proem to Book 9 he states that he had thought long and hard about the right epic subject, 'Since first this Subject for Heroic Song / Pleas'd me long choosing, and beginning late' (9.25–6). As early as 1628, as an undergraduate student at Cambridge, he declared his desire to write epic and romance in English in the vein of Homer and Spenser, and for some time supposed he would write an Arthuriad. He thought of the Fall as a subject for tragedy, including in his Trinity manuscript four brief sketches for a tragedy on that topic.[8] Milton's nephew and sometime amanuensis Edward Phillips claimed that Milton used lines from one such tragedy in Satan's soliloquy on Mount Niphates (4.32–41).[9] The dramatic scenes of Adam and Eve's marital dispute, temptation, fall and mental anguish in Books 9 and 10 are presented as an embedded tragedy, signalled by the phrase, 'I now must change these notes to tragic' (9.5–6). But at some point Milton decided that the Fall and its consequences for humankind, 'all our woe' (1.3), was the great epic subject for his times.

The proem to Book 7 (lines 1–39) alludes to the circumstances in which Milton wrote much of *Paradise Lost*, 'On evil dayes though fall'n, and evil tongues, / In darkness, and with dangers compast round' (7.26–7). The 'darkness' of blindness forced him to rely on ad hoc arrangements with students and friends to transcribe his dictated lines, and the dangers were very real. After the Restoration Puritan dissenters were severely repressed, and several of Milton's regicide friends and associates were executed by the horrific method of hanging, drawing off the blood, disembowelling and quartering, prompting Milton's fear that the 'barbarous dissonance' of Restoration court revellers (7.32) might drown out his poetic song and, like the Bacchantes with the archetypal bard Orpheus, might kill and dismember him. In 1665 he fled London to escape a particularly lethal visitation of plague and the next year lived through the terror of the Great Fire, which came within a quarter-mile of his house. But in 1667 the epic was published by Samuel Simmons, under the first recorded contract assuring an author of intellectual property rights and royalties.[10]

Milton's allusions continually acknowledge structural and verbal debts to the great classical models for epic or epic-like poems – Homer, Virgil, Hesiod, Ovid, Lucan, Lucretius – and to such moderns as Ariosto, Tasso, Du Bartas, Camöens and Spenser. He incorporates topics and conventions from the Homeric and Virgilian epic tradition: statement of theme, invocations to the Muse, an epic question, a beginning *in medias res*, a classical epic hero in Satan, a Homeric catalogue of Satan's generals, councils in Hell and in Heaven, epic pageants and games and supernatural powers – God, the Son, good and evil angels. Also, a fierce battle in Heaven replete with chariot clashes, taunts and vaunts, and hill-hurlings; single combats of heroes, most notably the Son of God as a lone warrior overcoming the entire Satanic force; narratives of past actions in Raphael's narratives of the war in heaven and the Creation; and prophecies of the hero's descendants in Michael's Biblical history of humankind. Yet the bard claims in the opening proem that he intends to surpass all those earlier epics, that his 'adventrous Song' will soar 'Above th'*Aeonian* Mount' (1.13–15).

At some point Milton decided on a ten-book format, thereby distinguishing his poem from the more usual twelve-book Virgilian model and the Virgilianism appropriated by English Royalists before and especially after the Restoration to celebrate that era as a Golden Age restored, with Charles II as a new Augustus.[11] Milton's opening lines point instead to the true restoration that must await a divine hero: 'Till one greater Man / Restore us, and regain the blissful Seat' (1.5–6). The ten-book format associates *Paradise Lost* with Lucan's unfinished epic, *Pharsalia*, or *The Civil War*, the font of a counter-tradition to Virgil, treating the failed resistance of the Roman republic and its heroes Pompey and Cato to Caesar's empire.[12] In 1674, when Royalist Virgilianism had abated, Milton recast his poem into twelve books by splitting Books 7 and 10 and adding a few lines, placing it in the central epic tradition.

Tasso's prescriptions in two essays on the heroic poem and the model offered by his *Gerusalemme Liberata* had perhaps the largest influence on aspiring epic poets in the Renaissance. Tasso held that the heroic poem should have some foundation in history, should concern notable martial deeds by Christian heroes, should take place in an age far enough distant to allow for fiction and poetic licence and should draw marvellous events and supernatural agents from Christian story.[13] Several of Milton's English Royalist contemporaries also undertook to write and theorise the modern epic poem. They agreed that the subject should treat warriors and battles, at least in part, and that couplets or rhymed stanzas should be used, but disagreed on other matters. In the preface to his projected five-book epic *Gondibert* (1651), only half finished, William Davenant and his laudatory commentator Hobbes defended its wholly fictional plot, its characters from a foreign country and earlier times and its entire elimination of supernatural personages, wonders and 'enthusiastic' bardic claims of inspiration.[14] Richard Fanshawe translated and defended Camöens's *Os Lusiadas* (1572, 1655) as 'of *mixt nature* between *Fable* and *History*',[15] praising its nationalist subject in the vein of Virgil and Tasso, its employment of classical gods acting in and on a Christian world and its abundance of wonders and invocations. In his unfinished *Davideis, Or, A Sacred Poem of the Troubles of David* (1655), Abraham Cowley urged use of true Biblical stories and the full Christian supernatural as offering to epic the most heroic deeds and wonders, though he also emphasised the difficulty of treating such subjects worthily.[16] A few months before *Paradise Lost* appeared Dryden published *Annus Mirabilis: The Year of Wonders, 1666*, a heroic poem on contemporary history – the Dutch Wars and the Great Fire – designed to recoup Charles

II's tottering reputation in the wake of many scandals and disasters, claiming it as 'the most heroick Subject' possible, and indebted to Virgil 'every where'.[17]

In the proems to Books 1, 3, 7 and 9 Milton treats his own conception of epic and his experience in writing this epic.[18] In no other formal epic does the poet insert himself so directly and extensively into his work, making his daring authorial undertaking an analogue to his epic story. He everywhere signals his debts to literary tradition, but he also makes bold claims both to originality and to bardic inspiration. In the first proem (1.1–26) he alludes to Homer and Virgil in his thematic statement and highlights the problematics of derivation and originality by claiming originality in Ariosto's very words: '*Cosa non detta in prosa mai ne in rima*', 'Things unattempted yet in Prose or Rhime' (1.16).[19] Also, echoing the first words of Genesis – 'In the Beginning' – he places himself in the line of Moses who 'first taught' the matter his poem now teaches.[20] He can hope to surpass other great epic poets since his subject is both truer and more heroic than theirs, and since he looks for illumination and collaboration to the Heavenly Muse who formerly inspired Moses, David and other prophet-poets, as well as to the great creating Spirit of God who must illumine his darkness, raise his fallenness, instruct him and re-create him so he can create his poetic universe.

In the proem to Book 3, 'Hail holy Light' (3.1–55), a literary hymn to Light as a primary manifestation of God, the Miltonic bard associates himself with, but also departs from, the experience of Orpheus, Dante and Satan in his poetic journey through Chaos and Hell. Then he describes a psychological journey through changing emotional states. His poignant complaint that the light of God 'Revisit'st not these eyes' (3.23) is followed by a hauntingly evocative pastoral description of classical and Biblical sites of poetic and prophetic inspiration where he hears the nightingale sing 'darkling' (3.39) and imagines himself among the great blind bards and prophets of Greece. He laments his own paradise lost – the light and beauty of the natural world and the wisdom and human companionship it provides – ending with a plea for the Celestial Light essential to treat his next subjects: heaven, unfallen Eden and the Godhead, 'things invisible to mortal sight' (3.55). In the proem to Book 7 (7.1–39) he apostrophises his heavenly muse by the name Urania, creating a myth based on Proverbs 8 to identify her with the creation of sacred poetry in heaven and earth. He presents himself as a Bellerophon who ascended to the heavens on the winged horse Pegasus (a figure for inspiration), but who, as he shifts to earthly subjects, risks Bellerophon's ultimate fate – falling to earth and wandering blind. Recalling that Calliope, the muse of epic poetry, could not save her son, the archetypal poet Orpheus, Milton hopes that his heavenly Urania can better protect him from the Restoration worshippers of Bacchus, as he implores her to 'govern' his song and 'fit audience find, though few' (7.30–1).

In the proem to Book 9 Milton offers his own defence of his epic (9.1–47). His 'higher Argument' – Man's disobedience and its tragic consequences – is 'Not less but more Heroic' (9.14) than the wrath of Achilles or Turnus. He flatly denies that epics require a martial subject, 'hitherto the onely Argument / Heroic deem'd'; he makes scornful reference to the 'tedious' romance matter characteristic of most modern heroic poems – 'fabl'd Knights' 'Races and Games, / Or tilting Furniture' – and he asserts a new heroic standard, 'the better fortitude / Of Patience and Heroic Martyrdom' (9.28–33). He has indeed given over the traditional epic subject, wars and empire, and the traditional epic hero as the epitome of courage and battle prowess. His protagonists are a domestic pair, the scene of their action is a pastoral garden and their primary challenge is, 'under long obedience tri'd' (7.159), to make themselves, their marital relationship and their garden – the nucleus of the human world – ever more perfect. Though they fail, they learn at length to understand and identify with the new heroic standard exemplified in the 'greater Man', Christ, who will redeem humankind. Claiming continued inspiration, the bard describes Urania's 'nightly' visits 'unimplor'd', in which she 'dictates to me slumbring, or inspires / Easie my unpremeditated Verse' (9.22–4). These lines point to the inexplicable and subconscious element in poetic creation as well as to Milton's nocturnal habits of composition. But they do not imply divine ventriloquism, given the bard's claim in this same proem that he has long considered and evaluated various epic subjects, topics and styles, making complex literary decisions. Rather, Urania's divine illumination informs his poetic dreams with a true understanding of the sacred history that is his subject, so he can experience his magnificent lines cascading forth as a divine gift. That version of poetic inspiration was profoundly influential for Romantic poets like Blake and Wordsworth.

Milton continued his defence in the paragraph solicited by the printer in 1668 for new issues of the poem, to address the expectation of rhyme fostered by the other modern heroic poems as well as by Dryden's essay *Of Dramatick Poesie*, also published in 1667.[21] Milton placed his poem in the proper company: 'The Measure is *English* Heroic Verse without Rime, as that of *Homer* in *Greek*, and *Virgil* in *Latin*', identifying rhyme with the barbarous gothic age and the vulgar taste of the present and also, as several critics have observed,[22] with debased Stuart culture and Stuart tyranny. The resonances of his language make Milton's choice of blank verse a liberating act and an aesthetic compliment to republican politics and culture, 'an example set, the first in *English*, of ancient liberty recover'd to Heroic Poem from the troublesom and modern bondage of Rimeing'.

To create for his great Argument an 'answerable style' (9.20) Milton produced rushing, enjambed, blank-verse lines that propel the reader through verse paragraphs of varying length, with few pauses for line-endings or full stops. This energetic, sublime high style is marked by elevated diction, complex syntax and sound patternings that make a magnificent music. Dense allusiveness to classical myths, to biblical, historical and literary names and stories, and to geographical places, ancient and contemporary, import all those associations into the poem. Sometimes, classical allusions are organised into a series couched in negatives, so as to call up the suggestiveness of those myths while redefining them as false or imperfect versions of Milton's true stories: 'Not that faire field / Of *Enna*, where *Proserpin* gathering flours / Her self a fairer Floure by gloomie *Dis* / Was gatherd, which cost *Ceres* all that pain / To seek her through the world; nor that sweet Grove / Of *Daphne* by *Orontes*, and th'inspir'd / *Castalian* Spring, might with this Paradise / Of *Eden* strive' (4.268–75). The euphonious names in such passages echo in pervasive sound patterns of assonance, consonance and repetition. Also, unusual grammatical constructions such as 'palpable obscure' (2.406) prevent visualisation but produce an evocative, almost synaesthetic, sense of that indescribable place, Chaos. This style is estranged from English syntactic norms by a freedom of word order common to inflected languages, and dense layers of meaning are embedded in particular words by exploiting their Latin or Greek etymological senses.

While Milton's diction is often polysyllabic and ornamental, he also uses simple Anglo-Saxon words, as in this list of Hell's geographical features: 'Rocks, Caves, Lakes, Fens, Bogs, Dens, and shades of death' (2.621). And he can employ simple diction and syntax to poignant emotional effect, as in this account of what he has lost by blindness: 'Thus with the Year / Seasons return, but not to me returns / Day, or the sweet approach of Ev'n or Morn, / Or sight of vernal bloom, or Summers Rose, / Or flocks, or heards, or human face divine' (3.40–4). His many epic similes often develop a little story or description from nature or folklore that invite associations beyond the specific comparison. In the best-known example, Satan is explicitly compared to the Biblical Leviathan in terms of great size (1.200–9), but the incorporated mariners' tale of the whale mistaken for a sheltering island foreshadows the deceptions of Satan, who attracts but then destroys the unwary.

Milton's epic incorporates a wide range of other genres with their appropriate styles. There are several lyrics, the loveliest of which is Eve's sonnet-like love song to Adam, a sixteen-line epanalepsis that begins 'Sweet is the breath of morn' and ends with the same word, 'without thee is sweet' (4.641–56). The many hymns include the angels' celebrations of God and the Son in Book 3 and of each day of creation in Book 7, as well as the extended morning hymn of Adam and Eve beginning 'These are thy glorious works, Parent of good' (5.153–208). Moloch, Belial, Mammon and Beelzebub deliver speeches of formal deliberative oratory in the parliament in Hell, God gives a forensic oration in Book 3 setting forth the case against fallen humankind, Satan and Abdiel engage in a formal debate in Book 5 and Satan tempts Eve with an impassioned deliberative speech in the manner of 'som Orator renound / In *Athens* or free *Rome*' (9.670–731). Sin, Eve and Adam report their earliest life experiences in autobiographical narratives, and Satan contrives a false life story for the snake he inhabits. The Battle in Heaven contains several mock-heroic passages filled with scatological imagery and double entendres. Satan's encounter at Hell's Gate with his daughter-wife Sin and the product of their incestuous union, Death, has elements of allegory but also of black comedy as Satan fails to recognise his own offspring. Satan delivers an intensely dramatic, emotion-filled soliloquy as he confronts his guilt on Mount Niphates, Adam utters an extended, passionate complaint beginning 'O miserable of happie' (10.720) and Eve delivers an elegiac lament upon learning that she must leave the garden. If the Miltonic style is an organ sound, it is produced from a multitude of stops, even as Milton's epic incorporates, in accordance with Renaissance theory, a veritable encyclopaedia of genres.[23]

In many areas Milton's poem challenges readers' expectations, then and now. His splendid Satan, taken by many critics from the Romantic period to the mid twentieth century as the intended or unintended hero of the poem, is presented, especially in Books 1 and 2, as a figure of power, awesome size, proud and courageous bearing, regal authority and above all, magnificent rhetoric: this is no grotesque medieval devil with a tail. His stirring language of defiance against tyranny and laments for loss are powerfully attractive, challenging readers to discern the discrepancies between Satan's noble words and his motives and actions. Constant allusions compare him to the greatest heroes – Achilles, Odysseus, Aeneas, Prometheus and others – in regard to the usual epic traits: physical prowess, battle courage, anger, fortitude, determination, endurance, leadership, *aristeia* or battle glory. Such comparisons do not condemn these heroes, nor do they exalt Satan as hero of this poem;

rather, they engage readers in a poem-long re-definition of heroes and heroism, prompting them to discover how Satan sometimes exemplifies but in essence perverts the classical exemplars, and to measure all other versions of the heroic against the self-sacrificing love of the Son of God and the moral courage of Abdiel, who alone opposed the mass rebellion incited by Satan. The Battle in Heaven, with its grotesque scenes of cannon shot and hill-hurling and its near-destruction of Heaven's lovely landscape, together with Michael's denunciation of the Giants who sought glory in battle and conquest, have suggested to some that Milton had repudiated warfare and the English revolution.[24] But these scenes, rather, undermine epic *aristeia*, battle glory, by portraying warfare in its essence and its effects as tragic, not glorious – however divinely authorised and necessary as a response to blatant evil as the Battle in Heaven clearly was and Milton thought the English revolution had been.

Surprisingly, Milton represents Hell, Heaven and Eden as regions in process: their physical conditions are fitted to the beings that inhabit them, but these inhabitants interact with and shape their environments, creating societies in their own image. Hell is first presented in traditional terms, with the fallen angels chained on a lake of fire. But unlike Dante's *Inferno*, where the damned are confined within distinct circles to endure eternally repeated punishments, Milton presents a damned society in the making, with Royalist politics, perverted language, perverse rhetoric, political manipulation and demagoguery. His fallen angels mine gold and gems, build a government centre (Pandaemonium), hold a parliament, send Satan on a mission of exploration and conquest, investigate their spacious and varied though sterile landscape, engage in martial games and parades, perform music, compose epic poems about their own deeds and argue (without resolving) hard philosophical questions about fate and free will. Their parliament in Book 2 presents an archetype of debased political assemblies and rhetoric. In this House of Lords the 'great Seraphic Lords and Cherubim' (2.794) debate issues of war and peace in secret conclave while the common angels, reduced to pygmy size, swarm without. Moloch, the quintessential hawk, urges perpetual war at any cost; Beliel counsels peace through ignominious inaction; Mammon would build up a rival empire in Hell founded on riches and magnificence but describes it, ironically, in terms of republican virtue: 'Hard liberty before the easie yoke / Of servile Pomp' (2.256–7). Then the monarch, Satan, sways the council to his will through the agency of his chief minister, Beelzebub, and is at length accorded divine honours – an exaggerated version of the idolatry Milton had long associated with the Stuart ideology of the divine right of kings.

Heaven combines courtly magnificence with pastoral nature. It provides an image of wholeness for human society through the mixture of heroic, georgic and pastoral modes and activities: elegant hymns suited to various occasions, martial parades, warfare, pageantry, masque dancing, feasting, lovemaking, political debate, the protection of Eden. Milton's Heaven is also a place of process, not stasis, complexity not simplicity, and the continuous and active choice of good rather than the absence of evil, as Raphael explains to Adam: 'My self and all th' Angelic Host that stand / In sight of God enthron'd, our happie state / Hold, as you yours, while our obedience holds' (5.535–7). This representation seems to imply an affirmative answer to Raphael's suggestive question, 'what if Earth / Be but the shaddow of Heav'n, and things therein / Each to other like, more then on earth is thought?' (5.574–6). Underlying this conception is the monist ontology, best characterised as 'animist materialism', that Milton set forth in his *Christian Doctrine*; like Hobbes and some other contemporaries, he rejected traditional dualism, which takes God and the angels to be pure spirit while humans are a mixture of spirit (soul) and matter (body).[25] In *Paradise Lost* Raphael tells Adam and Eve that 'one first matter' is the substance of all beings, who can by degrees develop towards greater ('more spiritous, and pure') refinement or towards grosser corporeality (5.469–500). Angels and humans share proportionally in intuitive and discursive reasoning, which differ 'but in degree, of kind the same' (5.490) – making for an unusually fluid conception of hierarchy. As a corollary, creation for Milton is not *ex nihilo* (out of nothing) as in most orthodox formulations, but *ex Deo* (out of God), who withdrew from the matter issuing from him so it could become mutable and subject to the will of other beings.[26] So in *Paradise Lost* Milton portrays Chaos as a region of inchoate matter comprised of constantly warring elements, out of which the Son of God creates the universe and through which Sin and Death construct a bridge linking Hell to earth.

Most Christian commentators on the Genesis story portrayed Eden as a garden replete with all the beauties of nature held in perfection. Adam and Eve's serene life was free from passion or anxiety, the gardening required of them was only to keep them from idleness and they did not remain in Eden long enough to have sex.[27] Milton, uniquely, undertook to imagine what an extended life in innocence might be like. His Eden is a lush and lovely enclosed garden with a superabundance of natural delights and a myriad of frolicking animals, but it would revert to wilderness unless Adam and Eve continually prop and prune the burgeoning vegetation. Their labour is pleasant but absolutely necessary: Milton's ecological insight is that humans had responsibility from the very beginning to care for and maintain the natural world.[28] In Milton's version of an ideal companionate marriage, Adam and Eve share gardening tasks in their world, as well as the duty to prune their own sometimes wayward impulses and passions. Both have also to negotiate the complexities of pre-lapsarian love, sex, gender hierarchy and domestic society,[29] as well as the inevitable but potentially creative tension in any love relationship between autonomy and interdependence. Both learn from Raphael, who at once assuages and stimulates their intellectual curiosity; and both must resist temptation. All these challenges are components of an ideal human life in innocence, which is never childlike ignorance of evil or static perfection, but rather a condition of challenge, choice and growth, in preparation for a more exalted state.

Eve's story of her first day of life is in some ways a version of the Narcissus myth, suggesting her potential for self-love, but she also defines herself against that myth. She did not remain fixed for ever, enamoured of her watery image, but accepted the arguments of God and Adam to share love and companionship with Adam in marriage and create human society – living images. Eve's Satan-inspired dream and Adam's analysis of it underscore the poem's fundamental assumption that impulses, passions and desires are not sinful unless the will consents to the evil they may promote. Adam's admission of passion sparked by Eve's beauty and seeming absolute perfection earns the angel Raphael's stern rebuke, but Adam resists his apparent disparagement of human sex, leading him to acknowledge that happiness for angels as for humans must involve some kind of physical union in love. In the marital dispute (9.205–386), without precedent in other literary versions of the Genesis story, Milton dramatises brilliantly how Adam and Eve enmesh themselves in ever greater misunderstandings – an archetype of those all-too-familiar situations in which lovers or friends, by no one's design, exacerbate slight disagreements into great divides, leading to unwise decisions and dire results. Eve is right to insist that both are sufficient to stand, but wrong to infer that 'exterior help' (9.336) should therefore be shunned, or that reasonable precautions in the presence of danger violate Edenic happiness. Adam is right not to prohibit Eve from gardening alone and thereby control her free choice, but wrong to give over his proper leadership role by providing a better rationale for separation than any she had thought of, and by unwittingly intensifying the psychological pressure she feels with repeated imperatives – 'Go . . . Go . . . relie . . . do' (9.372–4). Neither has sinned in this dispute: Adam and Eve remain innocent until they deliberately decide to eat the fruit. But their imperfectly controlled emotions sabotage dialogue for the first time in Eden, creating the mounting sense of inevitability proper to tragedy.

Early modern notions of male superiority are voiced by Adam, Eve and Raphael, but they strain against Milton's representation of Adam and Eve's shared activities and abilities and Adam's emotional neediness: the profound sense of incompleteness that underlies his argument with God for an 'equal' mate, and the dread of loneliness that prompts his instant choice to fall with Eve. Milton's literary strategies also trouble gender hierarchy. Eve is as much a lyric poet as Adam, perhaps more so: she creates the first love lyric in Eden, the delicate, rhetorically artful, sonnet-like pastoral that begins 'Sweet is the breath of morn' (4.641–56). In the Fall sequence and its aftermath Milton's epic almost turns into an Eviad: she initiates the marital colloquy about gardening separately, she engages in a lengthy and highly dramatic dialogue with Satan embodied in the serpent, she analyses her motives and emotions in probing soliloquies and after the Fall she responds first to prevenient grace, breaking what would otherwise be an endless cycle of accusations and recriminations. Her poignant lament, 'Forsake me not thus, Adam' (10.914–36), becomes the human means to lead Adam back from the paralysis of despair to love, repentance and reconciliation, first with her and then with God. Her offer to take all God's anger on herself echoes the Son's offer in the Council in Heaven, and while Eve cannot play the Son's redemptive role she becomes the first human to reach towards that new standard of heroism. Hers is the last speech of the poem, and in it she casts herself as central protagonist in both the Fall and the Redemption: 'though all by mee is lost, / Such favour I unworthie am voutsaft, / By mee the Promis'd Seed shall all restore' (12.621–3).

Some acute critics find ambiguous political messages in the fact that the poem represents both God and Satan as monarchs and presents Satan as a self-styled grand rebel, marshalling Milton's own republican rhetoric from *The Tenure of Kings and Magistrates* against what Satan terms God's tyranny.[30] But the Abdiel–Satan debates of Books 5 and 6 underscore the Miltonic principle that there can be no possible parallel between the monarchy proper to God as creator and any other king, challenging readers to refuse Royalist analogies between God and King Charles, Satan and the Puritan rebels, and to recognise as idolatry any earthly monarch's appropriation of the imagery and accoutrements of absolute kingship. The Nimrod passage in Michael's prophecy presents republicanism as humankind's proper natural state, as Adam castigates that first king for usurping over his equals the dominion proper only to God. Michael's prophecy also incorporates other topics central to Milton's polemics: the corruption of the Christian Church by Roman Catholic 'wolves', the misuse of civil power to force consciences and the gift of the Spirit to all believers. *Paradise Lost* also alludes to contemporary issues of exploration and colonisation, with Satan undertaking the discovery and colonisation of Eden.

The last segment of the poem presents the post-lapsarian education of Adam and Eve, who must learn how to read unfolding Biblical history, and specifically, how to interpret the metaphor of the woman's seed bruising the serpent's head as a promise of redemption through Christ. For Adam, that meaning is progressively clarified as his faulty interpretations of several pageants and narratives from his own age to the Apocalypse are corrected by the angel Michael. Eve also learns something of this history through dreams sent from God – a recognised vehicle of prophecy, though inferior to vision (cf. Joel 2:28). Michael sums up human history as tragic: 'so shall the World goe on, / To good malignant, to bad men benigne, / Under her own waight groaning' (12.537–9) until the Millennium, but he promises Adam 'A paradise within thee, happier farr' (12.587) if he learns to live in faith and charity. This has seemed to some a recipe for quietism and retreat from the political arena, but Michael's prophetic history testifies against any kind of passivity, spiritual, moral or political. It emphasises the responsibility of the few just men in every age to oppose, if God calls them to do so, Nimrods, or Pharaohs or tyrannous kings, even though they will likely be overcome by the many wicked and, like the loyal angels in the Battle in Heaven, must await the arrival of the Son to win lasting victories.

Milton offers *Paradise Lost* as a theodicy, an effort to 'justifie the wayes of God to men' (1.26). But this theodicy is less a matter of theological argument than of poetic vision, presenting human life, human love and the human condition as good, despite the tragedy of the Fall and all our woe. That vision arises from the concepts of human freedom, moral responsibility and capacity for growth and change celebrated throughout the entire poem. Milton's poignant, quiet, wonderfully evocative final lines are elegiac in substance and tone, conjoining loss and consolation. Prophecy and providence provide part of that consolation, but the emphasis falls upon the comforts and challenges of Adam and Eve's loving union as they go forth 'hand in hand' to live out all that has been foreseen:

> Som natural tears they drop'd, but wip'd them soon;
> The World was all before them, where to choose

Thir place of rest, and Providence thir guide:
They hand in hand with wandring steps and slow,
Through Eden took thir solitarie way. (12. 645–9).

In 1671 Milton published two remarkable new poems together: *Paradise Regain'd. A Poem. In IV Books. To which is added Samson Agonistes*. The first is a brief epic, a counterpart to *Paradise Lost*, the second a biblical tragedy. Edward Phillips thought that *Paradise Regained* 'doubtless was begun and finisht and Printed' after *Paradise Lost* was published.[31] Much if not all of *Samson Agonistes* was probably written after *Paradise Regained*, during the years 1667–70, as the political and religious issues faced by the defeated and imprisoned Samson resonate strongly with the situation of the defeated Puritans.[32] The joint publication has invited much critical debate as to whether the model of heroism exemplified by Jesus discredits the militant and violent deeds of Samson.

The poems invite comparison and contrast. Both continue the educational project of *Paradise Lost*: to create imaginative experiences that will help readers advance in moral and political understanding and virtue. In both, isolated heroes engage in hard intellectual struggles with challengers, thereby gaining further understanding of themselves and their different missions; and both heroes see themselves responding to divine illumination. *Paradise Regained* offers in Jesus a model of non-violent yet forceful resistance to, and denunciation of, all versions of the sinful or disordered life, and all faulty and false models of church and state.[33] Jesus takes as his immediate role 'to guide Nations in the way of truth' (2.473), insisting that it would be futile to free by force the 'unrepentant, unreform'd' Israelites who worship idols along with God; but he holds out the Millennial hope that God 'by some wond'rous call / May bring them back repentant and sincere' (3.427–35). In contrast, *Samson Agonistes* presents a warrior hero whose martial victories and final catastrophic act gives the Israelites an opportunity to free themselves from Philistine domination, if they have the necessary political understanding, virtue and will. As well, both poems carry forward Milton's effort to redefine the heroic for the modern age. They challenge the aesthetics and cultural politics of the contemporary heroic drama: its pentameter couplets and what Steven Zwicker terms 'its bombast and cant, its aristocratic code of virtue and honour, its spectacle and rhetoric . . . its warring heroes and virgin queens, its exaltation of passion and elevation of empire'.[34] Milton's largely dialogic brief epic celebrates in blank verse the heroism of intellectual and moral struggle and entirely redefines the nature of empire and glory. And his severe classical tragedy, written in a species of free verse, eschews every vestige of exotic spectacle, links erotic passion with idolatry and constructs a tragic hero whose intense mental suffering leads to spiritual growth. Milton's 'Preface' to *Samson Agonistes* makes the contrast explicit, describing his tragedy as 'coming forth after the antient manner, much different from what among us passes for best'.[35]

The only major sources for *Paradise Regained* are the Biblical accounts of the three temptations of Jesus in the Wilderness (Luke 4:1–13 and Matthew 4:1–11) and the pertinent exegetical tradition. Readers are often surprised by Milton's choice of this subject rather than the Passion–Crucifixion narrative, and by his portrait of an austere, nay-saying Jesus who disparages and refuses all worldly pleasures and goods.[36] But this subject allows Milton to present Jesus's moral and intellectual trials as a higher epic heroism, a model for right knowing and choosing and a challenge to think rightly about kingship, prophecy, idolatry, millenarian zeal, church and state, the place of secular learning and the abuses of pleasure, glory and power.

In the epic proposition and invocation the Miltonic bard, who in *Paradise Lost* had often voiced his authorial anxieties and difficulties, says very little of himself. He now invokes the Spirit in an easy, confident tone arising from his experience of the Spirit's aid with *Paradise Lost*: 'inspire, / As thou art wont' (1.21–2). His epic proposition makes the rather startling claim that this poem's subject is much more heroic than that of *Paradise Lost*, since this hero conquers his enemy, regains the regions lost to Satan and establishes his own kingdom. The opening lines – 'I who e're while the happy Garden sung . . . now sing' – allude to the supposedly genuine opening verses in most Renaissance editions of the *Aeneid*, announcing Virgil's movement from pastoral and georgic to an epic subject.[37] That echo suggests, with witty audacity, that Milton has also graduated from pastoral apprentice-work about a happy garden to the true epic subject, the spiritual warfare and victory of Jesus. Several allusions to the Book of Job, including the frame episode of Satan as 'Adversary' hearing another superlative hero exalted by God, associate this poem with a poetic project Milton considered a quarter of a century earlier when he identified the Book of Job as a 'brief model' for epic.[38]

Milton transformed the episode central to epic, the single combat of hero and antagonist, into a three-day verbal battle. He also incorporated several epic conventions and topics: an *in medias res* beginning with Christ's Baptism, two Councils of Satan and his followers, a Council in Heaven in which God foretells his Son's immediate and ultimate victory over Satan and two transformed epic recitals – Jesus's meditation about his youthful experiences and aspirations, and Mary's reminiscences about the prophecies she received. Also, an epic catalogue of the kingdoms of the world, a martial pageant of Parthian warriors and a prophetic vision in which the hero does not, like Aeneas, view his *own* destined kingdom but sees and rejects kingdoms that are not his. Like *Paradise Lost*, this poem also incorporates other genres: dialogue in which Satan's inflated rhetoric is met by Jesus's spare answers; pastoral groves where Jesus is presented with a sensuous banquet and with classical learning; and angelic hymns that begin and end the Temptation. There are a few striking epic similes: Jesus assaulted by Satan is compared to a wine-press vainly attacked by buzzing bees and to a solid rock against which waves ineffectually beat. But much of the poem eschews the soaring eloquence of *Paradise Lost* for a restrained dialogic style, tense with the parry and thrust of intellectual exchange.

The question of identity is the primary focus for the poem's drama, centring on the title 'Son of God' bestowed in a special way upon Jesus at his Baptism. Neither Satan nor Jesus realises that he is one with the Son in Heaven. Satan indicates that one purpose of his temptations is to discover 'In what degree or meaning thou art call'd / The Son of God' (4.516–17). And Jesus, as he enters the desert, states that he knows something of himself and his messianic role from his mother's testimony and from reading the prophets but he does not yet understand the full meaning of the prophetic metaphors or of his 'God-like office' (1.188). He is led by the Spirit 'to what intent / I learn not yet', but is confident of on-going illumination (1.291–3). The poem's action turns on a central paradox: Satan dances around Jesus in a fever of motion, trying one approach and one argument after another while Jesus remains impassive and unmoved, yet it is in Jesus's consciousness that real change takes place. He progresses by somewhat uneven stages to full understanding, whereas realisation is forced upon Satan only by his utter defeat and fall from the Tower.

Milton creates epic scope by making the temptation episode encapsulate past and future history through typological reference and allusion. God describes Jesus as an 'abler' Job and a second Adam who will win 'by Conquest what the first man lost / By fallacy surpriz'd' (1.151–5) and also as a young champion who will lay down in the Wilderness the 'rudiments' (l. 157) of his great warfare and office throughout history. The debates between Jesus and Satan make continual reference to commonly accepted Biblical and classical types of Jesus and his office of prophet, king and priest: Moses, Elijah, Gideon, David, Job, Socrates. Satan proposes counter-models – Balaam, Antipater, Caesar, Alexander, the schools of Greek philosophy – or else insists that Jesus must follow his types exactly. Satan's temptations presume the classical idea of history as cyclical repetition – what has been must be again – whereas Jesus must learn to fulfil and subsume those types so as to redefine history as progress and re-creation.

The poem's complex structure develops several interrelated paradigms. In one, Jesus is the 'second Adam' withstanding the temptations to which Adam and Eve succumbed, which in the exegetical tradition of the 'triple equation' were identified as sensuality (in Protestant versions, distrust), avarice or ambition, and vainglory.[39] That paradigm is explored in the Stones into Bread temptation and that part of the Kingdoms temptation dealing with kingship over self. Also, temptations are addressed to the three functions of Christ's office: Prophet or Teacher; King, not of the literal Israel but of the invisible church; and Priest, i.e. redemptive sacrifice and mediator.[40] In the extended Kingdoms temptation (Books 2, 3 and part of 4) Satan offers Jesus the literal Israel and urges him to claim it immediately, forcing time; then he offers Parthian armies – state power, the wrong means to establish his true kingdom, the Church; and at length he offers Rome, the great kingdom of this world incorporating all the goods offered before, as well as the Roman Catholic Church. As a climax Satan presents Athens, the zenith of classical learning, poetry and oratory, describing it in lines of mesmerising beauty:

> See there the Olive Grove of *Academe*,
> *Plato's* retirement, where the *Attic* Bird
> Trills her thick-warbl'd notes the summer long,
> There flowrie hill *Hymettus* with the sound
> Of Bees industrious murmur oft invites
> To studious musing; there *Ilissus* rouls
> His whispering stream . . . (4.244–50)

The harshness of Jesus's responses seems shocking but he is forcing discriminations. Satan is here an arch-Sophist, proposing universal knowledge not as a way to truth but as a means to power, glory and pleasure: 'Be famous . . . / By wisdom; As thy Empire must extend, / So let extend thy mind o'er all the world' (4.221–3). He also seeks to undermine Jesus's unique role as spiritual teacher by insisting on the *necessity* of classical learning for the attainment of his own defined goals: the kingdom within – 'These rules will render thee a King compleat / Within thy self' (4.283–4) – and his office of teaching and ruling by persuasion. Jesus does not repudiate learning as such, but he flatly denies that it is *necessary* to virtue, salvation or the accomplishment of God's work in the world: 'Think not but that I know these things, or think / I know them not; not therefore am I short / Of knowing what I aught: he who receives / Light from above, from the fountain of light, / No other doctrine needs' (4.286–90).

Jesus's victory is celebrated with an angelic banquet and a long hymn of praise that makes explicit his identity with the Son in Heaven, indicating by shifts in tense that his victory is now complete but that it is only just beginning. Then, quietly, like Adam and Eve wandering forth to begin the history whose end Adam has foreseen, Jesus returns from the angelic celebration of the prophesied end to his human beginnings: 'hee unobserv'd / Home to his Mothers house private return'd' (4.638–9).

The separate title page of *Samson Agonistes* terms it 'A Dramatic Poem', not a drama. It could not be presented on the Restoration stage alongside Wycherley's bawdy comedies and Dryden's exotic tragedies, but it did provide a model for later poetic closet dramas such as Shelley's *Prometheus Unbound* and Eliot's *Murder in the Cathedral*. Milton made large alterations in the Samson narrative from Judges 13–16, all but eliminating stories of the trickster who tied fiery brands to foxes' tales and set riddles for wedding guests; he also changed the harlot Dalila into Samson's wife, grounding their relationship in marital love and duty. Most important, he conflated the Biblical strong man with Job and the Psalmist complaining of God's ways, and so created a hero capable of self-analysis, intellectual struggle, tragic suffering and bitter self-castigation.

Samson Agonistes has elicited a cacophony of interpretations. Some see Samson enacting a paradigm of fall and regeneration; others think he remains tragically flawed in his vindictiveness, despair, self-concern and suicidal revenge; and still others find Samson's character undecidable, given the contradictory contemporary uses of the Samson story and the absence of any authoritative vantage point.[41] The poem has been read as a near-allegory of the English revolution and its aftermath, or as a covert call to English Puritans to rise again, or as a repudiation of the English revolution and all military action, or as figuring the situation of the Puritan dissenters in the Restoration, or as projecting Puritan radicals' expectation of God's destruction of the wicked by means of his Saints.[42] In the wake of 9/11 John Carey argued that Samson is a terrorist[43] – but of course one person's terrorist is another's freedom fighter. Milton indeed emphasises the ambiguous signs and events of the Samson story – the wonders surrounding his birth, his extraordinary strength and awesome deeds, his claims to 'intimate impulse' (line 223) and 'rouzing motions' (line 382), and his final, violent destruction of the Philistines and himself – which, along with such prominent stylistic features as antitheses and either/or constructions, require readers to choose among interpretative possibilities. Though it is not a political allegory, the work invites application to the post-Restoration ethos, achieving a brilliant mimesis of the confusions attending moments of political crisis. It challenges Milton's contemporaries to think through the hard questions raised by the revolution and its failure: how is a nation to know the liberators raised up by God to promote change? Are military victories or defeats reliable indices of God's favour to or God's rejection of leaders or nations? How can would-be liberators know when they are led by God and when by their own desires? When if ever may they act outside the law and outside God's law? And if they appeal to 'rouzing motions', what standards can be invoked to judge their actions?

The preface, 'Of that sort of Dramatic Poem which is call'd Tragedy', is Milton's only extended commentary on a poem of his own. He begins by paraphrasing Aristotle's famous definition of tragedy but in terms tailored to this work.[44] Unlike Aristotle, Milton emphasises the moral profit of tragedy and glosses catharsis as a purging or tempering of the passions by aesthetic delight – a concept encapsulated in the poem's final line: 'calm of mind, all passion spent' (line 223). He also changes the object of imitation: for Aristotle it is 'an action', the plot or mythos; for Milton, it is the tragic passions, 'pity or fear and terror', that are to be 'well imitated' – here, the pain-wracked struggles, passionate speeches and violent death of Samson. In Aristotle's paradigmatic tragedy, Sophocles's *Oedipus Rex*, the hero falls from prosperity into misery through an error or fault (*hamartia*) that enmeshes him in the toils of Fate; Milton's tragedy begins with Samson already fallen, like the heroes of Aeschylus's *Prometheus Bound* or Sophocles's *Oedipus at Colonus*, though Samson plunges deeper into despair during his encounter with his father Manoa. The preface also reports the drama's adherence to the neo-classical unities of time and place: the action takes only a few hours, and the single locale is a shady bank in front of Samson's prison, with a messenger reporting all action elsewhere. The Chorus is said to be designed 'after the Greek manner', but Milton's Chorus of Danites do not simply voice community mores; they are challenged both to interpretation and responsive action by Samson's extraordinary deeds. The preface also points to the Book of Revelation as a Biblical model of tragedy.[45]

Milton's style is boldly experimental: on a ground of blank verse he overlays passages that look forward to modernist free verse, marked by irregular line lengths, broken rhythms, a striking use of imagery and sound effects, and very occasional rhyme.[46] In Samson's opening lament, the blind and defeated

Milton's identification with his hero produces lines of great poignancy and power, rendered with consummate metrical art:

> O dark, dark, dark, amid the blaze of noon,
> Irrecoverably dark, total Eclipse
> Without all hope of day!
> O first created Beam, and thou great Word,
> Let there be light, and light was over all;
> Why am I thus bereav'd thy prime decree?
> The Sun to me is dark
> And silent as the Moon,
> When she deserts the night
> Hid in her vacant interlunar cave. (lines 80–9)

This style challenges the heroic couplets that had become normative for Restoration tragedy, and also marks the culmination of Milton's lifelong experimentation with verse forms. There is nothing like this in Milton's earlier poetry, nor in any previous English verse.

Milton follows the structure of Greek tragedy closely.[47] The Prologue spoken by Samson reveals his physical and psychological anguish, bitterness and despondency. The Parados or entry song of the Chorus of Danites, Samson's tribesmen, proclaims their shock and bafflement over the contrast between his former great exploits and his present bondage and blindness. Their later odes follow the five agons or dialogic struggles with visitors through which Samson, like Oedipus in *Oedipus Rex*, gains self-knowledge, in part by overcoming versions of his former self. In the first agon with the Danites he moves beyond the tribe and its legalistic mores, defending his Gentile marriages on the ground of 'intimate impulse', and refusing blame for his failure to free Israel, redirecting it to Israel's cowardly governors who betrayed him amidst his victories. A parallel with England is reinforced as Samson voices the Miltonic principle that inner servitude leads to political bondage in every country. In the second agon Samson resists definition by family; recoiling viscerally from the prospect of becoming an idol of his past glory on the family hearth, he refuses his father Manoa's proposals to ransom him, sensing that he should not retreat into privateness and passivity. That decision leaves him poised to respond to future possibilities.

In the agon with Dalila Samson shows that he is no longer the sensualist enslaved by passion who succumbed to her pleas to reveal the secret of his strength; his resistance to her now enables him to spring back from despair.

He refuses Dalila's sexually charged offer to take him home and care for him, and implacably rebuffs her pleas for forgiveness, her constant rhetoric of self-exculpation and her shifting excuses based on female stereotypes: woman's curiosity to know and tell secrets, woman's frailty and woman's domestic love that seeks to keep a husband safe at home. He meets her final excuse, that she betrayed him in obedience to the Philistine magistrates and priests and the 'grounded maxim' of *salus populi*, by citing the law of nature and nations that privileges the marriage bond above the claims of the state – recalling appeals to natural law against civil and ecclesiastical authority during the revolution. Dalila's acts for her gods and country in many ways parallel Samson's, inviting the question whether there are overarching moral principles that reach beyond cultural relativism. Samson's agon with the swaggering giant Harapha leads him beyond his former identity as a strong-man. His renewed confidence in God's pardon prompts him to reclaim his vocation as divinely appointed liberator, offering it to the trial of battle but also defending it by reasoned political argument. When Harapha declares Samson a covenant-breaker and murderous rebel against his rulers – echoing Royalist denunciations of the Puritans before and after the Restoration – Samson reprises Milton's justifications of the revolution in terms of natural law, which always allows armed resistance to the oppressed.[48]

The final agon between Samson, the Philistine Officer and the Chorus explores the claims of several kinds of authority: civil power, religious law, conscience and inward illumination. When the Officer directs Samson to perform feats of strength at an idolatrous feast honouring Dagon – a parallel to the Test Act requiring dissenters to participate in the liturgy of an 'idolatrous' Anglican church –[49] the fearful Danite Chorus justifies yielding to civil power as a gesture of outward conformity: 'Where the heart joins not, outward acts defile not' (line 1368). Samson, however, appeals to religious law and his own conscience in refusing to prostitute his divinely restored strength to idols, distinguishing clearly between submitting to overwhelming force and obeying commands. He locates the highest authority in divine illumination as he claims to experience 'rouzing motions' that dispose 'To something extraordinary my thoughts' (lines 1382–3). But he qualifies this Antinomian stance by insisting three times to his countrymen that his actions will fulfil the spirit of the law and the moral norms of the community: 'of me expect to hear / Nothing dishonorable, impure, unworthy / Our God, our Law, my Nation, or myself' (lines 1423–5).[50] Like Jesus walking on to the desert, Samson goes to the theatre expecting further clarification of what he should do.

The Exode – comprising nearly one-fifth of the poem – contains the distraught Messenger's report of Samson's death and the responses of Manoa and the Chorus. None of them have direct access to Samson's motives or spiritual state, but must make what they can of the external signs: Samson patiently performing feats of 'incredible, stupendious force' (line 1627) culminating in destruction of the theatre and the Philistine nobility – though Milton adds the extra-Biblical detail that the 'vulgar' outside the walls escaped (line 1659). He also omits the Biblical Samson's prayer for vengeance 'for my two eyes' (Judges 16:28). The episode has apocalyptic overtones evoking the final destruction of Antichrist's forces as well as many Biblical stories of a wrathful God taking revenge on his enemies.[51] Wrath is an aspect of Milton's God as of the Biblical deity, and Samson might be seen as his agent, since God is evidently the source of his restored strength. But Samson cannot stand in for Christ at the apocalypse, and his victory in death is very partial, evoking confused responses. Manoa is all too ready to dismiss the tragedy occasioned by the guilt of Samson and Israel – 'Nothing is here for tears' (line 1721) – and to make an idol of Samson's tomb, but he also recognises that Samson has provided Israel a chance for liberation: 'To *Israel* / Honour hath left, and freedom, let but them / Find courage to lay hold on this occasion' (lines 1714–16). In the Kommos – the funeral dirge and consolations – the Danite Chorus displays some change from their earlier tendency to interpret what is happening in terms of maxims, proverbs and exemplary histories, resisting the extraordinary challenge presented by Samson. Their final ode, with its richly evocative imagery of eagle and phoenix representing Samson's restored vision in blindness, indicates some new openness to illumination. But they fall back on sententious maxims again in the rhymed sonnet that ends the work, observing that 'All is best' and that 'in the close' we can best know the champions to whom God and history bear witness. That comfortable formula ignores the tragedy's demonstration that actions must be taken *in medias res*, in circumstances always characterised by imperfect knowledge and conflicting testimony. Though choices are still possible as the poem ends,[52] further tragedy looms: Samson's countrymen (like Milton's Englishmen) will probably be too servile to grasp their new chance for liberty. Nor did they, as the Biblical record shows. The Samson paradigm indicates that all human heroes are flawed, that the signs of God's action in history are inordinately hard to read and that Israelites and Englishmen are more disposed to choose 'Bondage with ease then strenuous liberty' (line 271). Yet the Chorus's final lines also suggest that Samson's story might offer the Danites (and Milton's countrymen) some 'new acquist / Of true experience' (lines 1755–6) – perhaps the recognition that any successful action against oppression requires a virtuous citizenry that understands the political stakes and values liberty. *Samson Agonistes*, with its complex ways with language and its imaginative power, is a fit poetic climax to Milton's lifelong effort to help create such citizens in his own time – and beyond.

Notes

1. Citations in text and notes to *Paradise Lost* are to the 1674 second edition, ed. Barbara K. Lewalski (Oxford: Blackwell, 2007); citations of *Paradise Regained* and *Samson Agonistes* are to vol. II, ed. Laura Lunger Knoppers (Oxford: Oxford University Press, 2008), of *The Complete Poems of John Milton*.
2. William Wordsworth, 'London. 1802', in *Poems in Two Volumes* (London, 1807).
3. The manuscript, *Joannis Miltoni Angli De Doctrina Christiana*, is at the Public Record Office, Kew, SP 9/61; it is being edited anew by a consortium of scholars. Citations are to the translation, *The Christian Doctrine*, ed. Maurice Kelley, trans. John Carey, *The Complete Prose Works of John Milton*, 8 vols. (New Haven: Yale University Press, 1953–82), vol. VI. Milton's other prose tracts are also cited from this edition, hereafter *CPW*.
4. *Christian Doctrine*, chapter 2. *CPW* VI.133–7.
5. *Ibid.*, chapter 5, *CPW* VI.204–12, 259–64. See Stephen Dobranski and John P. Rumich (eds.), *Milton and Heresy* (Cambridge: Cambridge University Press, 1998).
6. *Christian Doctrine*, chapters 3–4, *CPW* VI.153–202.
7. For biographical details relating to these last poems, see Barbara K. Lewalski, *The Life of John Milton*, revised edition (Oxford: Blackwell, 2003), pp. 398–538.
8. The sketches appear in a list, probably dating from 1639–41, containing almost 100 possible tragic subjects from the Bible and British history, Trinity manuscript, Trinity College, Cambridge (R. 3.4); facsimile reproduction (Menston: Scolar Press, 1972).
9. John Aubrey, *Minutes of the Life of Mr John Milton*, in Helen Darbishire (ed.), *The Early Lives of Milton* (London: Constable, 1932), p. 13.
10. *Paradise lost. A Poem Written in Ten Books* (London, 1667); Michael Lieb and John Shawcross (eds.), *'Paradise Lost: A Poem Written in Ten Books': An Authoritative Text of the 1667 First Edition* (Pittsburgh, PA: Duquesne University Press, 2006). See Peter Lindenbaum, 'The Poet in the Marketplace: Milton and Samuel Simmons', in Paul G. Stanwood (ed.), *Of Poetry and Politics: New Essays on Milton and His World* (Binghamton, NY: Medieval and Renaissance Text Society, 1955), pp. 249–62.
11. Laura Lunger Knoppers, *Historicizing Milton* (Athens: University of Georgia Press, 1994), pp. 67–122.
12. Lucan, *Pharsalia*, trans. J. D. Duff (Cambridge, MA: Harvard University Press, 1928); see David Norbrook, 'Lucan, Thomas May, and the Creation of a

Republican Literary Culture', in Kevin Sharpe and Peter Lake (eds.), *Culture and Politics in Early Stuart England* (Stanford, CA: Stanford University Press, 1993), pp. 45–66.

13. Tasso, *Discorsi del Poema Eroico* (Naples, 1594); *Discorsi dell'Arte Poetica e del Poema Eroico*, ed. Luigi Poma (Bari: Laterza, 1964); *La Gerusalemme Liberata* (Ferrara, 1581).
14. William Davenant, *Gondibert: An Heroick Poem*. (London, 1651), Preface; 'The Answer of Mr Hobbes to Sr Will. Davanant's Preface before *Gondibert*'.
15. Richard Fanshawe, *The Lusiad, or Portugals Historicall Poem* (London, 1655), sig. A2v.
16. Abraham Cowley, *Davideis* (London, 1656), Preface.
17. John Dryden, *Annus Mirabilis: The Year of Wonders, 1666. An Historical Poem: Containing the Progress and various Successes of our Naval War with Holland . . . And Describing* THE FIRE OF LONDON (London, 1667), sigs. A 5v–A 6v (dated 10 November 1666).
18. Barbara K. Lewalski, 'Milton's Idea of Authorship', in Michael Lieb and Albert C. Labriola (eds.), *Milton in the Age of Fish: Essays on Authorship, Text, and Terrorism* (Pittsburgh, PA: Duquesne University Press, 206), pp. 53–79.
19. Ariosto, *Orlando Furioso*, I.2.2 (Ferrara, 1516), p. 2.
20. *Paradise Lost*, Book 1, lines 8–9. See Jason Rosenblatt, 'The Mosaic Voice in *Paradise Lost*', *Milton Studies*, 7 (1975), pp. 107–32.
21. John Dryden, *Of Dramatick Poesie, An Essay* (London, 1668) [1667].
22. See e.g. Steven Zwicker, 'Lines of Authority', in Kevin Sharpe and Steven Zwicker (eds.), *Politics of Discourse: The Literature and History of Seventeenth-Century England* (Berkeley: University of California Press, 1987), 249.
23. See Barbara K. Lewalski, *Paradise Lost and the Rhetoric of Literary Forms* (Princeton, NJ: Princeton University Press, 1985).
24. See Blair Worden, 'Milton's Republicanism and the Tyranny of Heaven', in Gisela Bok, Quintin Skinner and Maurizio Viroli (eds.), *Machiavelli and Republicanism* (Cambridge: Cambridge University Press, 1990), pp. 242–4.
25. See Stephen M. Fallon, *Milton among the Philosophers: Poetry and Materialism in Seventeenth-Century England* (Ithaca, NY: Cornell University Press, 1991).
26. See *Christian Doctrine*, chapter 7, *CPW* VI.299–325 and *Paradise Lost*, Book 7, lines 163–73.
27. See J. M. Evans, *Paradise Lost and the Genesis Tradition* (Oxford: Clarendon Press, 1968).
28. See Diane McColley, *Poetry and Ecology in the Age of Milton and Marvell* (Aldershot: Ashgate, 2007), pp. 197–228; Ken Hiltner, *Milton and Ecology* (Cambridge: Cambridge University Press, 2003).
29. See Diane McColley, *Milton's Eve* (Urbana: University of Illinois Press, 1983); Christine Fruola, 'When Eve Reads Milton: Undoing the Canonical Economy', *Criticial Enquiry*, 10 (1983), pp. 321–47, and essays in Julia Walker (ed.), *Milton and the Idea of Woman* (Urbana: University of Illinois Press, 1988).
30. Compare *Tenure*, *CPW* III.198–202 and *Paradise Lost*, Book 5, lines 787–802.

31. Edward Phillips, *The Life of Mr John Milton*, in Darbishire (ed.), *Early Lives*, p. 75.
32. See Mary Ann Radzinowicz, *Toward Samson Agonistes: The Growth of Milton's Mind* (Princeton, NJ: Princeton University Press, 1978), pp. 387–407; Sharon Achinstein, '*Samson Agonistes* and the Drama of Dissent', in *The Miltonic Samson, Milton Studies*, 33 (1996), pp. 133–58. Efforts to place this work in the 1640s and 1650s on metrical and biographical grounds have not proved persuasive.
33. David Loewenstein finds a contemporary analogue in the much-persecuted Quakers who vehemently denounced the Restoration church and state in testimony and tracts. 'The Kingdom Within: Radical Religious Culture and the Politics of *Paradise Regained*', *Literature and History*, 3 (1994), pp. 63–89.
34. Steven N. Zwicker, 'Milton, Dryden, and the Politics of Literary Controversy', in Gerald Maclean (ed.), *Culture and Society in the Stuart Restoration* (Cambridge: Cambridge University Press, 1995), pp. 139–40, 151.
35. *Samson Agonistes*, ed. Knoppers, p. 67.
36. See e.g. Alan Fisher, 'Why is *Paradise Regained* So Cold?', *Milton Studies*, 14 (1980), pp. 195–217.
37. *Virgil*, ed. H. Rushton Fairclough (Cambridge, MA: Harvard University Press, 1960), vol. I, pp. 240–1: *Paradise Regained*, lines 1–7.
38. See *The Reason of Church Government, CPW* I.813, and Job 1:6–12. See Barbara K. Lewalski, *Milton's Brief Epic: The Genre, Meaning, and Art of Paradise Regained* (London: Methuen, 1996), pp. 3–129.
39. Elizabeth M. Pope, *Paradise Regained: The Tradition and the Poem* (Baltimore: Johns Hopkins University Press, 1947).
40. See *De Doctrina Christiana (CPW* VI.430–7).
41. See e.g. John H. Steadman, '"Faithful Champion": The Theological Basis of Milton's Hero of Faith', *Anglia*, 77 (1959), pp. 12–28; Joseph A. Wittreich, Jr., *Interpreting Samson Agonistes* (Princeton: Princeton University Press, 1986).
42. See e.g. Christopher Hill, *Milton and the English Revolution* (London: Faber and Faber, 1977), pp. 428–48; and essays in Albert C. Labriola and Michael Lieb (eds.), *The Miltonic Samson, Milton Studies*, 33 (1996), pp. 159–80.
43. John Carey, 'A Work in Praise of Terrorism? September 11 and *Samson Agonistes*', *TLS*, 6 September 2002, p. 15. See also Feisal G. Mohamed, 'Confronting Religious Violence: Milton's *Samson Agonistes*', *PMLA*, 120 (March 2005), pp. 327–40.
44. *Samson Agonistes*, ed. Knoppers, pp. 66–8. The title page quotes the first several words, in Latin translation; see *The Poetics* 6.1, trans. W. Hamilton Fyfe, *Aristotle*, vol. XXIII (Cambridge, MA: Harvard University Press, 1973), pp. 24–5.
45. Milton cites David Pareus (*A Commentary upon the Divine Revelation of the Apostle and Evangelist John*, trans. Elias Arnold, Amsterdam, 1644) as he did also in *The Reason of Church Government (CPW* I.815).
46. Among the 1,758 lines about 150 rhyme.

47. See W. R. Parker, *Milton's Debt to Greek Tragedy in Samson Agonistes* (Baltimore: Johns Hopkins University Press, 1937) and Anthony Low, *The Blaze of Noon: A Reading of Samson Agonistes* (New York: Columbia University Press, 1974).
48. 'They who seek nothing but thir own just libertie, have alwaies right to winn it and to keep it, when ever they have power, be the voices never so numerous that oppose it', *The Readie & Easie Way to Establish a Free Commonwealth*, 1660 (*CPW* VII.455).
49. See Achinstein in '*Samson Agonistes* and the Drama of Dissent', pp. 133–58.
50. See also lines 1385–6 and 1408–9.
51. See e.g. Michael Lieb, '"Our Living Dread": The God of *Samson Agonistes*', and David Loewenstein, 'The Revenge of the Saint', in *The Miltonic Samson*, *Milton Studies*, 33 (1996), pp. 3–23, 159–80.
52. As first printed, the poem had ten lines added at the end, marked as '*Omissa*', with directions to insert as lines 1527–35 and line 1537. I cite line numbers based on this correction, though Knoppers's edition places them at the end, as in the 1671 publication. In these lines the Chorus imagines Samson with his sight restored destroying his enemies – leaving readers, perhaps, with a different final impression than does the corrected text.

Chapter 15

Restoration poetry: Behn, Dryden and their contemporaries

HESTER JONES

Jane Spencer, citing Dustin Griffin, has observed that the period following the interregnum 'was a transitional one between a court-based literary culture and a market-based print culture'. Aphra Behn, like Milton and Dryden, belonged 'to both cultures – the old world of patronage and the new world of booksellers'.[1] Whereas the next chapter focuses in detail on three of Dryden's major poems (discussed more briefly and with different emphases, here), this chapter places Dryden alongside his fellow writers, in particular Aphra Behn, in order to explore the nature of Restoration poetry. It sees Behn and Dryden as occupying a liminal relation to previous and subsequent writing, as well as arising out of a larger context of contemporary poetry, including Rochester, Oldham, Killigrew and Philips, and looking towards Pope and Swift. In particular, areas of continuity between their poetry can be found in their responses to the heterogeneous diversity of nature, their representations of sexuality and forms of engagement with contemporary religious debate. Above all, perhaps, traditional in the broadest sense of the word, but emerging from a context of courtly libertinism, the poetry of both is engaged with the nature of individual freedom.

Critical and biographical commentary has often identified troubling contradictions and silences in the life and work of both artists: Dryden's timely conversion to Roman Catholicism is sometimes seen as existing in tension with his assertions of poetic integrity, Behn's political conservatism with the liberal probing of the boundaries of sexuality and gender in her poetry. Literary tradition has sometimes also oversimplified the work of both, contrasting Behn unfavourably with Philips or Finch, Dryden with Pope and Rochester, and underestimating the scope for complexity and ambiguity within their apparently transparent styles.

The question of authorship is vexed in relation to Behn's poetry: some of her best-known works also appeared first in volumes edited by other authors and were wrongly attributed. Indeed, 'The Disappointment', originally attributed to Rochester, ends with an image of female flight that might be read as a self-reflexive gesture on the author's part, a contrived elusiveness that is partly a consequence of gendered production, partly a feature of writing in this period. The similarity with Rochester makes the confusion of authorship understandable, but Rochester's characteristic attitude in poems such as 'Imperfect Enjoyment' is both more preoccupied with the body's indignities, as David Farley-Hills has pointed out, and, in the 'reversed idealism' that arises from such outrage, more enduringly committed to a gravely sustained embodiment of its own hollowness.[2]

Rochester's fascination with finding a form for the void is held in common with another contemporary, Samuel Butler, whose ebullient and unsettling *Hudibras* was published in three parts in 1663, 1664 and 1678. A well-known example of burlesque poetry, characterised by disruptive discontinuities and a violent comic energy somehow without humour, this poem delights in repeatedly and haphazardly disrupting its own form, in particular by breaking down the distinction between poet and protagonist, the contemptuous railer. And, as Farley-Hills has observed, many of Rochester's libertine poems, including 'Imperfect Enjoyment', retain burlesque's denigrating and self-denigrating vigour but subject both to a more stringent and consistently elegant poetic treatment.[3]

Condemnation is not so central to Behn, and she often also undercuts any pretence to immortal fame: the first published female poet to make an income from her writing, she instead projects a provisional, ludic and performative persona of the poet. Thus she takes this period's ambiguity surrounding textual embodiedness as her starting-point and discovers in it a source of delight and richness. Far from being spiritedly feminist, however, such a gesture can be seen as a challenge to all attempts to read the body into the text of a poem.

Janet Todd suggests that a volume published in 1672, *The Covent Garden Drolery*, was probably compiled by Behn, and contained some of her earlier poems. She also circulated other poems in manuscript as 'coterie verse', but subsequently collected and published them for money with Jacob Tonson as *Poems upon Several Occasions*, together with *A Voyage to the Island of Love*, a version of the Abbé Paul Tallemant's *Voyages de L'isle Amour*. These included a range of genres; indeed, Janet Todd has described Behn as a 'ventriloquist, dissolving herself into the variety of genres, styles and modes of her age'.[4] However, among these the courtly pastoral lyric is predominant, and, published in 1684, soon after the Exclusion Crisis of 1679–1681, many are in tune with a revival of Stuart celebration and evoke the Golden Age in imagery and theme.

This volume was followed a year later by *Miscellany, being a collection of poems by several Hands*, many translations; and then *Lycidus, or the lover in fashion*. Other poems also appeared in collections, and some were initially misattributed. *Poems*, however, contains the poetic work for which Behn is remembered, expressing Behn's political sympathies more overtly, Melinda Zook has argued, than her drama or fiction.[5] Here we see voiced the disillusionment and bitterness experienced by the Cavalier party that followed the Restoration of Charles II in 1660, a bitterness possibly felt with particular intensity by Behn herself, refused reward after her espionage in Holland in 1666. Behn idealises therefore the figure of the libertine Cavalier, unconfined by need and expansively cultivated, focusing this figure on that of the Duke of Monmouth, who appears in several poems. But her attachment to the Golden Age as a trope and theme carries significance that extends beyond contemporary political allegiances alone. Perhaps above all, it signifies a freedom that, as critics and biographers remind us, Behn saw as the frequent prerogative of aristocratic men and denied to women of any class, though often presented with compelling power in relation to female subjectivity.

In the first poem in *Poems upon Several Occasions*, 'The Golden Age. A Paraphrase on a Translation out of French', in fact a version of the prologue to the Italian Tasso's *Aminta* (1573), many of these concerns may be seen. Here Behn lyrically invokes and disturbs the peaceful waters of pastoral innocence. The title, indeed, ironically reminds us of its own distanced and shimmering perspective on the 'undisturbed and clear' (line 12) water of pastoral lyric poetry: using alternating strophes and antistrophes, the poem works around 'evocations of the golden past and denunciations of the corrupted present', as Jessica Munns observes,[6] before turning sharply in its final stanza to the *carpe diem* motif with its use of explicitly gendered motifs and voices and its situating itself in the bounded world of time. But the poem also through many devices alerts its contemporary reader to the mythical and performed nature of 'origins': the golden world is not only framed by references to the modern social world, characterised in the poem by violence, sexual and cultural mastery and enmity between the sexes, but is inaccessible other than through such polluted and ambivalent means.

Alexander Pope mocked the first stanza of this poem in *Peri Bathous or, The Art of Sinking in Poetry* on account of its florid – and by implication, weakly feminine – style, remarking acerbically that such linguistic flowers 'do many times grow in great plenty at the bottom of ponds and ditches'.[7] But this is to overlook Behn's considerable, if sometimes decadent, sophistication here and elsewhere in her poetry. While the first two lines present an image of clarity, the second two negate this: 'when no scorn'd Shepherds on your Banks were seen, / Tortur'd by Love, by Jelousie, or Fear' (lines 3–4), while the third present a time 'When an Eternal Spring drest evr'y Bough, / And Blossoms fell, by new ones dispossest' (lines 5–6), where eternity is assumed as a garment and the Fall leads to dispossession and exile. This Golden Age is commercialised and sexualised from the start, its pastoral plenitude defined through negatives – no 'rude Rapes' had been made, snakes were 'Not doing harm', 'Ambition was not known' (lines 32, 45, 55) and its 'Shade' (line 7) a covert place, exposed therefore to loss and semantic change. Such openness is epitomised in Behn's use of the word 'affording' (line 7), a word containing both the sense of 'to bear the expense' (*OED* 3) or 'to yield naturally' (*OED* 7), the latter particularly frequent in literature of this time, and clearly the predominant meaning at this point in the poem. The shade's beneficence accommodates all who seek it; but the poem hints that it also can be bought or sold; its 'kindness' – 'Kind increase' (line 63), 'Kind Resistance' (line 99) – as often thus coloured with sexual innuendo.

Before the 'rude Rapes' of civilisation reduces it to phallic singularity, the earth teems with life. Throughout the poem, order and abandon are opposed but also shown to be aspects of the same process. For example, in Stanza v, 'Power taught Mankind to invade' (line 66); in stanza vi the word 'invade' recurs in its idealised context: 'And now the woods, and now the streames invade, / And where they came all things were gay and glad' (lines 87–8), with the imperfect rhyme and the alternation of past and present tenses pointing up the subtle interrelation of life and loss. The command in the final stanza to 'let the Golden Age again, / Assume its Glorious Reign' (lines 166–7) is therefore compromised on many grounds: by the monarchical metaphor rejected in earlier stanzas, the uncertainty of 'assume', the pause after 'again'; all challenge the claim for the *carpe diem* mode as a smooth recapitulation of Golden Age idealism. The Golden Age, as the poem has demonstrated throughout, cannot come 'again' without alteration.

Jessica Munns follows Carol Barash in understanding Behn's relation to Golden Age mythology uncritically, a 'time prior to both monarchy and commerce' and therefore available to 'revisionary poetics',[8] but, as I have suggested, the depiction of such landscape as naively 'open' perhaps overlooks the sophisticated and persistent use of aesthetic distancing and artful concealment, which Behn inscribes on the pastoral and Edenic landscape, one which 'appear'd all drest' (line 9), and is concealed and conveyed through the effortful contrivance of bosky and imaginary umbrage: 'as if the willing Branches strove' (line 13). Within such imaginary space, the spiritual and sexual unite and interfuse in 'Mystick Twines' (line 11): Behn mixes high and low, idyllic and bathetic, lyrical and polemic modes in a manner which leaves the reader at once tantalised and alienated. Barash and Munns point out that Behn's attempt in this poem to accommodate Golden Age freedom, with its potential for varied and textured versions of the self, to her contemporary context of male dominance and royal authority, founders in its 'strenuous but imperfect conclusion'.[9] Dominant in this section is, indeed, a masculine sun ('He rises from his Watry Bed' (line 182)), the singular swain, encouraged to 'love on' (line 175), and the conventional indication of female beauty's transient power, in contrast to the blossoms that were restored in the 'kind Shade' (line 7) of the Golden Age.

But while near-contemporary *carpe diem* poems such as Marvell's 'To His Coy Mistress' urge immediate pleasure, this concludes 'Then let us *Sylvia* yet be wise, / And the Gay hasty minutes prize' (lines 195–6). Sexual power is contrasted here with lasting wisdom that will survive the 'Night', and the speaker includes herself in 'our short Light' (lines 197–8). Behn's literary pseudonym Astraea, derived from the contemporary romance *L'astrée*, allied Behn with the night and not with the phallic sun, and the gender of the speaker here is unclear. 'The Golden Age' ends therefore with an emphasis on the value of reflection, gained not through the hungry possessing of time but through the considered 'prizing' of it. This is a poised and skilful resolution of the polarities of restraint and pleasure offered by the poem.

Behn's erotic poems continue in this way 'espousing and protesting libertinism', as Joshua Scodel puts it,[10] and consequently refine and complicate the tradition of sexual explicitness developed most flamboyantly by Rochester, making this available for the morally more reflective period of writing that follows. Behn's poem 'The Disappointment' is generically parallel to Rochester's 'Imperfect Enjoyment' published four years earlier in 1680. Its focus, as Munns says, is not 'the absence of climax'[11] but rather climax reached and deepened through voyeuristic fantasy. The poem's French source by de Cantenac helps to redirect Behn's focus from male frustration to female disappointment, channelled through the pastoral figure of Cloris. Authenticity, expressed as desire – 'love' – and the honour code of 'shame', vie for prominence and their conflict is figured, as Barash observes, once again through shifting tenses, as the narrative past strives to contain present desire.[12] Shame and honour, products of post-lapsarian dualism, are expressed through 'vain' oppositions (between ceasing and calling out, between 'retiring' (line 28) and the murder of a life already 'given' through 'conquest' (line 30)). In the final stanzas, Behn uses Ovidian myths of transformation to indicate the necessary use of allusive fictive personae for female authorship. As

S.J. Wiseman and Ros Ballaster have pointed out, 'sexual and rhetorical potency are set against each other' often in Behn's work, and in this poem both male and female figures are undone by desire but reconstituted by their ability to see and imagine the loss of power anew.[13]

The poem 'To the fair Clarinda, who made love to me, imagin'd more than Woman' has generated much debate, on account of its provocative ambiguity and refusal to disclose an 'easy solution' to the 'riddle' posed by the poem.[14] Some read it as biographically inspired, some as an expression of lesbian identity.[15] Ballaster suggests the subject may be a transvestite figure, but then concludes that the poem is best viewed 'within the context of Behn's narcissistic contemplation of her own poetic practice'[16] and as a reflection of the poet's own play of sexual and poetic subjectivity. Also important, however, as in 'The Disappointment' and in 'The Golden Age', is the manner in which disguise is offered as a counter to the less visible protection of the neutral and assertive first-person plural pronoun. A malleable 'form', projected by the speaking voice on page or stage, offers material for the imagination which 'acts upon and is also created by the lover/speaker'.[17] This is a moment where Behn draws attention to and so challenges the 'spectatorial economy' of Restoration culture, and shows it in tension with the capacity of speech to denote subjectivity and therefore autonomy.[18] As Barash observes, the poem 'moves from name to form to body', and it is as 'textual body that the women's relationship is finally resolved'.[19]

A continued preoccupation with the rich potential of textual sexuality can be seen in Behn's political poetry, in that on the Duke of Monmouth ('Song to a New Scotch Tune', which laments the decline of Cavalier hopes, 'Silvio's Complaint: A song: to a fine Scotch tune', 'A voyage to the Isle of love') and that on royal Queens, Catherine of Braganza, the widow of Charles II, and Mary of Modena; and, thirdly, in that on James II's coronation, 'her longest and most ambitious Pindaric poem'.[20] Following the Revolution of 1688, Gilbert Burnet asked Behn to write in support of William and Mary, but she refused, despite the acquiescence of other contemporary Tory and Stuart supporters. It is not clear why Behn reacted in this way, but she did produce a celebratory poem addressed to 'Her Sacred Majesty QUEEN MARY, UPON HER ARRIVAL IN ENGLAND', a poem which deplores William's arrival but does manage to praise Mary, the 'Illustrious Daughter of a King' (line 62). Behn's poetry, therefore, achieves a sophisticated and often ambiguous relation to modes of writing that are distinctively 'male' or 'female', sometimes challenging male assumptions and sometimes seeming to adopt them.

Such ambivalence concerning tradition can be seen also to a greater or lesser extent in other of Behn's contemporary female poets. Jane Barker, for example, who in this period published *Poetical Recreations* (1688) and 'A Collection of Poems referring to the times' (1701), has been contrasted by Kathryn R. King with Mary Astell, and described as enacting 'compensatory exceptionalism' in her relation to female writing and eschewing Behn's 'sensuous luxuriousness', engaging rather with the cooler mode of retreat poetry so fashionable in the 1670s and 1680s.[21] Poems such as 'A Virgin Life' uphold singleness as a choice of life – in comparison with those poems to become popular a little later, as King points out, which use singleness to point up the 'slavery' of the marriage contract. Barker, rather, develops the focus on solitude's advantages, using the persona Fidelia to trace the process of spiritual growth that had led to her conversion to Catholicism. But as Jeslyn Medoff points out, Behn in particular left little room for other women poets, though as virtue became an asset to publication her star waned.[22] Anne Killigrew is chiefly remembered on account of Dryden's ode on her death, containing such faint praise as 'Art she had none, yet wanted none: / For nature did that want supply',[23] and by claims of plagiarism, indignantly refuted as deriving from envy in 'Upon the saying that my verses were made by another',[24] though 'On the birth-day of Queen Katherine' contains a memorable dream sequence.

Dryden's poem responds to his subject's bridging of disciplines, perhaps inspired by 'a picture painted by herself', and such an openness to contrasting points of view or those not shared by the poet himself characterises his work. But, like Behn, he is also a master of transition, who distrusted the instability of English as a medium and looked to the solidity and impervious strength of Latin to 'clear my doubts'.[25] The early poetry, panegyric and perhaps expedient in purpose, contains what David Hopkins has described as poetry 'of general speculation', but nonetheless remarkable for its imaginative vitality. *Annus Mirabilis*, written in 1666, the year of sea-battles against the Dutch, the Fire of London and the Plague, is long and diverse in its content. David Hopkins comments, however, on the balance between 'sympathetic involvement and distanced amusement' even in this early poem; the energy of turmoil overflows political allegory or religious typology.[26] Here we see already the combining of panegyric and satire characteristic of Dryden's work, used as a focus to explore the relation between individual freedom and moral or cultural constraint.

Freedom versus constraint, latitude versus strictness, are key concerns for Dryden that unite his career as both poet and translator. The distinctions he makes between different kinds of translation in his 'Preface to Ovid's Epistles' control his stylistic choices throughout his poetry and they run in parallel with his ethics as a satirist. In his preface, Dryden outlines three approaches: metaphrase, or literal translation; paraphrase, or 'translation with latitude'; and imitation, where the translator 'assumes the liberty' to wander from the original. The first is, in fact, unattainable, 'like dancing on ropes with fettered legs'. Imitation shows the translator most favourably, but at the expense of the 'memory and reputation of the dead'; paraphrase, 'translation with latitude', is in Dryden's view the 'reasonable' middle path, tempering fidelity with freedom, for 'I suppose he may stretch his chain to such a latitude, but by innovation of thoughts, methinks he breaks it.'[27] The consistency between Dryden's view of translation and the rest of his work can be seen from his first ventures into directly satirical poetry, in which (as in Behn's writing) political and literary targets are frequently found together.

From the heroic and panegyric tendencies of his earlier poetry, with its breezy energy and vitality, *Mac Flecknoe* (first circulated in manuscript 1676, published in an unauthorised text in October 1682) signals a darker tone and direction. It is densely resonant of contemporary literary dispute, here the work of minor dramatist Thomas Shadwell, attached to a rival theatre, and that of the Catholic priest, poet and playwright, Richard Flecknoe, alluded to also by Andrew Marvell in 'Flecknoe, an English priest at Rome'. However, Howard Erskine-Hill has also suggested further, both personal and literary, influences, including Marvell's 'Tom May's Death' (which he describes as possibly 'the first Augustan satire') and Rochester's 'An Allusion to Horace' (1675), containing hard-hitting gestures towards Dryden. Donne's Satire IV and Horace's *Satires* I ix as well as Virgilian echoes underlie the mock-heroic vision.[28]

Central to the poem are questions about literary succession and the nature of true creativity that recur in different forms throughout Dryden's writing career. Shadwell had challenged Dryden's pension as laureate and historiographer royal. Dryden had also put considerable energy into securing patronage, approaching Rochester, whose aristocratic wit and prestige he perhaps sought to emulate as well as to engage to his own advantage. Rochester, however, seems to have slighted this advance, and so Dryden focused his attempts at securing favour on Rochester's enemy the Earl of Mulgrave, who supported the Duke of York, Rochester himself supporting Monmouth. Personal satire therefore, from both Shadwell and Rochester, combined with Dryden's own investment in the Duke of York's cause, contributed to the poem's satiric momentum, and its desire to recover through mock-heroic writing the high ground of wit from the Whigs.

Mac Flecknoe is constructed around character portraits, a form practised by Halifax, Burnet and Clarendon and looking back to earlier character writing by Hall and Overbury and, before these, to Plutarch's *Lives*, and it might seem distant from the playful writing that we have considered by Aphra Behn. However, as many readers have noticed with delight and surprise, commitment to moral and social order is undercut in many ways by a dazzling, and sometimes destabilising, openness to imaginative possibility. Compassionate, sometimes hilarious, transformations are used implicitly as a defence for vitriolic satire on poor literary judgment. Shadwell had been rewarded by his predecessor on the grounds that he 'Should only rule, who most resembles me'. The rhyme points up this cultural and personal narcissism, 'only' adding petulance to tyranny: Shadwell follows and fulfils through repetition rather than creative development the work of minor dramatists Heywood and Shirley, 'but types of thee, / Thou last great prophet of tautology' (lines 30, 13–14). This is a striking line, and Dryden uses the critical term 'tautology' only twice in his poetry, both in this poem. Flecknoe and Shadwell were criticised for literary repetition; prophecy and tautology are incongruous terms, and Dryden implies that without such creative originality they cannot participate in literary tradition nor be regarded as of moment. They look neither forward nor backward and so fail meaningfully to inhabit time, embodying a prophecy that only looks to itself.

The depiction of Shadwell in the opening sections of the poem, whose ironies and ambiguities David Hopkins and other readers have appreciated, comes to a triumphant climax in the lines 'Besides his goodly fabric fills the eye, / And seems designed for thoughtless majesty: / Thoughtless as Monarch Oaks, that shade the plain, / And, spread in solemn state, supinely reign' (lines 25–8). This invokes the Royal Oak in which Charles II was reputed to have sheltered after the Battle of Worcester, and hence also confirms the disturbing association in the passage between tediously unimaginative art and the monarchy made accessible, decadent and dull through promiscuity, vitiating the line of succession. In her writing on 'hylozoic poetry', Diane Kelsey McColley makes a strong case for the presence of Royalist tendencies in writing of the seventeenth century that extends imaginative sympathy towards trees, on the grounds that 'forest' denotes a royal preserve 'for the recreation of princes'.[29] McColley suggests that the vitalist movement, expressed in such 'hylozoic poetry', locating spirit throughout natural life, was brought to an end largely by means of a language fashioned by Dryden. The lines I have quoted here from *Mac Flecknoe* seem to confirm this judgment about nature's lack of consciousness. But McColley notes passages, such as the translation of Ovid's *Metamorphoses* xv, where Dryden invests life and spirit in animal creation with sensitivity; she cites 'if men with fleshly morsels must be fed, / And chew with bloody teeth the breathing bread', to suggest that Dryden at points displays more in common with this understanding of nature's inherently spiritual life than with a rationalistic and anthropomorphic one.[30] Dryden is, of course, using such references to imply the wider and more far-ranging consequences of what may seem to be a relatively small-scale literary and even personal dispute, and justifying his deployment of considerable linguistic elegance and skill to this end: he is suggesting that the death of culture and the death of nature – of hylozoic poetry – are linked. Furthermore, the misapplication of prophetic utterance in the literature he satirises – for Shadwell is no John the Baptist – is a religious as well as a cultural and political offence. This ability to use lucid language, at first sight lacking in shadow or nuance, to connect delightfully mundane detail with movements and concerns of the highest importance, is characteristic of Dryden, and a bridge with the satiric poetry of both Donne and Pope.

Mac Flecknoe was followed by the further satire, *Absalom and Achitophel*, published on 17 November 1681. This came amidst the plethora of pamphlets accompanying the Exclusion Crisis of 1679–1681, the attempts to prevent the Roman Catholic Duke of York from succeeding Charles II to the throne and instate James, Duke of Monmouth in his stead. Dryden may have been yielding to royal pressure in producing his satirical defence of the throne; indeed, Paul Hammond has remarked that it is highly 'atypical' of his work in its direct engagement with current political controversy.[31] In applying the account of Absalom's rebellion against David to contemporary events, Dryden was sure to engage a curious, not to say, prurient, readership, offering a personally inflected satirical reading of an unfolding situation. At its best, though, the poem unites the creation of imaginary characters with contemporary reference; and its sharpest satire is reserved for those characters whose restlessness and lack of perspective obscure understanding of history's ultimate pattern. Representing this long view is the character of David, the persona for Charles II, whom Dryden represents initially as physically frail but in his final speech as spiritually infallible. Dryden singled out the portrait of Zimri, corresponding to the Duke of Buckingham, as being of lasting worth. It is certainly the most assured and polished section of the poem; lines such as 'Was every thing by starts, and nothing long' (line 458) both capture the restless transience of history, and also reach out most securely to later poetic character writing – its trenchant wit anticipates Pope at his best – and also backwards to Shakespearean eulogy and Juvenalian satire.[32] But the poem is not just a matter of isolated character studies: Paul Hammond also indicates the significant use of diverse but coexisting time frames in the poem – Biblical, mythical, Edenic, recent historical, contemporary historical, eternal – and points out that, unlike the Elizabethan and more viscerally punitive approach of his contemporary John Oldham in *Satyres upon the Jesuits* (1680), Dryden avoids much contemporary historical reference, using the myth of kingly divinity to accommodate contemporary events and participants within a 'complex narrative of rebellion', in which the King is immutably allied with eternal and divine decree.[33] Against this eternal right the efforts of those such as Shaftesbury are doomed to fail.

In these two major satires, Dryden employs what Ronald Paulson calls a 'normative poet's voice', of the kind Pope comes to imitate, and following him, Samuel Johnson. *Absalom* was followed by the relatively minor *The Medal* (1682), which, as Paulson points out, mediates mock-heroic with 'Juvenalian denunciation' to confirm the rebels of *Absalom* as successfully contained and the new order proclaimed and established.[34] After these, satire is used as a subsidiary device, sometimes in Horatian Epistles at which Dryden excelled. In the tender and moving 'To my dear friend Mr Congreve', composed following the loss of the Laureateship in 1688, Dryden 'rewrites his own Mac Flecknoe', alongside echoes of Thomas Southerne's commendatory poem 'To Mr *Congreve*'.[35] Southerne's poem also employs images of succession and patrilineal inheritance, but Dryden's enriches and complicates both earlier poems with a vein of complicated personal feeling. Lineal narratives, containing underlying themes of competition and usurpation, are offset by Horatian claims to generosity and irony. The motif of succession is undercut by the knowledge that Congreve is neither son nor heir to any substantial literary throne.[36] Dryden addresses the young dramatist in terms reminiscent of Marvell's address to Cromwell, the 'forward youth' in the Horatian Ode, a poem also ending with an unsettling reflection on the difficulties of 'maintaining' early and precarious success; the speaker is 'just abandoning th' ungrateful stage' (line 67) as Charles I in the earlier poem left his; though Dryden perhaps dignifies his loss of status with his dramatic verb. Thomas Rymer has followed Thomas Shadwell; 'Tom the Second reigns like Tom the First' (line 48), they are 'like' in non-entity. Congreve and Dryden are unalike in significant ways, old and young, deposed and successful, and their relationship is defined through negation: 'Not mine (that's little) but thy laurel wear' (line 54): the angularity of the sentence, reminiscent of Jonsonian eulogy, strains to point up the distinctions between the men: he, 'just abandoning', Congreve, long awaited (the poem repeats 'at length' (lines 11 and 15, both times rhymed with 'strength') and begins 'at last' (line 1) to heighten the contrast between occasional merit amidst a background of mediocrity). As Jennifer Brady says, the poem transforms Southerne's conventional account of Dryden, subtly alternating eulogy with elegy on the poet himself;[37] by implication, it leads us to question the value of praise that issues from a figure himself in need of support and patronage. Bereft of public recognition, private acknowledgment through such epistolary writing must suffice; but 'You merit more', and here Dryden is as much speaking to himself as to his elective laureate. The negative on which the poem ends, 'nor could my love do less' (line 77), reads as a despondent afterthought, relying on the value of private feeling despite so much in the poem to suggest otherwise.

The poem's careful attention to the difference in fortune and age between the poets offers points of contact with Dryden's earlier elegy, 'To the Memory of Mr Oldham'. John Oldham died prematurely at the age of thirty in 1683, but had already begun to explore the potential of satire and to make translations of Horace and Juvenal. He looked to Abraham Cowley, whose epic *Davideis* underlies Dryden's *Mac Flecknoe*. Paul Hammond has indicated Oldham's originality and his importance for Dryden and subsequent translators: his confident freedom from his originals laid the ground for later critical scholarship.[38] Dryden's tribute to Oldham points up the irony of youthful friendship, in which common goals and gifts 'To the same goal did both our studies drive' (line 7), by invoking Virgil's episode of Nisus and Euryalus. In this incident in the *Aeneid*, the victorious one is 'conquered through his friend' ('Nisus and Eurylus', line 68), rather than poignantly coexisting with him in disappointment: mishap is turned into glorious success, yet success remains tainted by 'the treacherous puddle' where Nisus 'Slipped first, and slipping, fell' (lines 54 and 58). The convention of heroic friendship does not obscure the cost of sacrifice; rather, generous praise and request for help coexist. Public rejection and betrayal become the opportunity for private celebration, and thus make a claim for praise that is unsullied by political or other considerations.

Dryden's nuanced, ironic and sometimes self-undercutting perspective continues in *Religio Laici or A Layman's Faith: A Poem* (1682) and *The Hind and the Panther* (1687), poems engaged with vexed questions of religious allegiance. The first begins with an assurance that its narrator stands 'at a distance' (The Preface, line 15) and makes 'only a Confession of my own' (lines 13–14). But despite its 'plain and natural style' (lines 441–2), of course this is no mere 'poetry of statement', rather a Horatian epistolary poem containing a range of voices. Dryden may earlier have aligned himself with the Latitudinarians, a grouping associated with the Cambridge Platonists and affirming the role of human reason in the path to salvation. Latitudinarianism became increasingly established after 1688 and sought to moderate between a commercial, secular culture, open to deist rationalism, and the Reformed religion of the earlier period. The beginning of *Religio Laici*, however, makes it clear that this no longer represents Dryden's understanding of Christian faith since 'reason's glimmering ray / Was lent, not to assure our doubtful way, / But guide us upward to a better day' (lines 5–7).

With hindsight, the metaphors of openness and journeying in the poem seem prophetic, since soon afterwards Dryden had converted to Roman Catholicism, perhaps opportunistically, but for reasons that, like Dryden's view of scripture, remain not wholly clear. George Douglas Atkins has suggested that Roman Catholicism offered 'ecclesiastical analogy to his royalism'[39] and its opposition to individual interpretation of the Bible was also important. More so, also, was the greater freedom among Catholic clergy from political involvement – something Dryden continues to chastise with particular vigour. *The Hind and the Panther*, despite the earlier poem's opposition to the Catholic position, seeks to establish connection, tolerance and 'breadth' by seeing the Anglicans as the Moon to the Catholic Sun: 'Big with the beams which from her mother flow / And reigning o'er the rising tides below' (lines 501–2). When it was composed in 1687, King James II was by means of Indulgences endeavouring to remove penalties issued against Roman Catholics by Parliament; the poem is therefore in part confessional, but also much more than this – timely and engaged. Dividing into three parts, it is what Annabel Patterson has described as an 'overgrown Aesopian fable',[40] figuring the Hind, as the Church of Rome (pure, a peacemaker), and the Panther (corrupt and quixotic) as the Church of England. Between these moral poles and within the genre of the fable, many forms of religious writing are employed; the speaker, moreover, acknowledges a youth 'winged with vain desires, / My manhood, long misled by wandering fires . . . Such was I, such by nature still I am, / Be thine the glory, and be mine the shame' (Part 1, lines 72–3, 76–7). As often, verbs such as 'winged' and 'wandering' seem to elevate the error also regretted, leading some readers to question the poet's claim to rest and finality.

As *Mac Flecknoe* satirised contemporary literary sterility and *Absalom* the seductive allure of change, *The Hind*, despite its formal expansiveness, explores the dangers of religious 'breadth'. In Dryden's view of translation, latitude may be a virtue in relation to the original text. Here, though, breadth is associated with excessive freedom, changeability made superficially attractive through 'ease': 'Your sons of breadth at home, are much like these, / Their soft and yielding metals run with ease' (Part III, lines 187–8). Once again, though here in a context of religious dispute, Dryden can be seen to be working with a tension between creative generosity – which can become lax 'breadth' – and fidelity to the given – which can become sterile aridity.[41]

A similar opposition, this time couched in terms of a tension between cloistered virtue and embodied generosity, can be found in Dryden's panegyric poem *Eleonora* (1692). This was written probably for commission on the death of the Countess of Abingdon, a friend of John Aubrey, known to Dryden, and celebrates exceptional virtue in a world regarded as debased and disappointing. What saves the poem from stiltedness is the incorporation into its language of praise of the very elements that threaten the poem's values of integrity and generosity. Like the Good Parson in Dryden's *Fables*, the virtuous lady has invested her talents wisely, repaying divine bounty with interest: 'Heaven, that had largely given, was largely paid', giving all, or, as the poem corrects itself, 'if a bribe appear, / No less than heaven, to heap huge treasures there' (lines 25, 30–1). Her spiritual business is cannily conducted: 'was she not profuse; but feared to waste, / And wisely managed, that the stock might last' (lines 65–6). Dryden's mercenary language boldly presents the poem as the expression of spiritual interest after a life whose treasures are in heaven; God, he argues, demonstrates such creative economy in a solar system powered by reflection, where one source of light is made generally available through the mediating effect of the planets. Neither profuse nor avaricious, Eleonora knows how to give and how to withhold. She is, in short, comparable in her combination of bounty and purity to the bride of the Song of Songs, invoked, as Anne Barbieu Gardiner and others have noticed, also in the figure of the Hind.[42] 'She did but dream of heaven, and she was there' (line 316), perhaps alluding to Aeneas's ascent from the underworld, conveys with its mid-line caesura both solemnity and ease – the poem consoles by reminding how common her fate is, while at the same time acknowledging, in the half-rhyme of 'there' and 'her' (lines 315–16), the dreadful gap between warm flesh and cold philosophy. Similarly, the motifs of conventional eulogy are used to explore the interchange between confinement and release: 'this full soul, in narrow limits pent, / Unable to contain her, sought a vent / To issue out, and in some friendly breast / Discharge her treasures, and securely rest' (lines 244–7); and 'Thus her friend's heart her country dwelling was, / A sweet retirement to a coarser place' (lines 259–60). Friendship conceits (friendship as a 'vent' for the heart and a 'retirement' from courtly deceit and pretence) are the location for divine encounter, where friends are able 'to mix their minds, and to communicate' (line 251), punning with a sacramental nuance on this last word. Eleonora demonstrates her idealised quality as much in her 'unbosomed' release as in cloistered virtue, her engagement with commercial exchange as with a life of prayer, and therefore serves as a figure of the poet himself.

Whether Dryden's conversion to Catholicism brought a diminution of his creative gift, or, conversely, liberated within him and perfected a particular genius for 'translation with latitude', the last decade of the century, following the 1688 Revolution and Act of Settlement, brought with it once again, but in a modulated key, questions of validity and power. This period of Dryden's life is taken up with works of translation, including Virgil's *Georgics* and his *Aeneid*, published in 1697, and *Fables ancient and modern,* published in March 1700, including translations from Ovid and Homer, Boccaccio and Chaucer. The Virgil translation, epic in its size and content, continued and made perhaps more explicit an engagement with the Roman poet present throughout Dryden's life, whether in the earlier satires or in *Sylvae*. It heralded a period in which classical poetry, the *Aeneid* in particular, was to take over from the Bible as a source of uncontested authority.

We have observed that the shift from *Religio* to *The Hind* saw the diminishing of the role of scripture and Dryden's increased acceptance of ecclesiastical authority. This shift is accompanied also by a sustained growth of interest in the works of the Roman poets, in particular of Virgil, presented with particular beauty and elegance through the collaborations of Dryden and Tonson. Full as it is of images of displacement, exile, the ravages of fortune and, finally, the steady dutifulness that will lead in the end to restitution and return, Virgilian epic seemed to speak with particular effect to a culture recoiling from decades of political unrest and instability. The *Fables* also continue this naturalising of classics which Dryden seems to have seen increasingly as his poetic vocation, mediating a wide range of cultural material through a continuous idiom. Dryden also created a national language, accessible and elegant, for writing that had previously been available only to the very few, and for some, a means of comparison and contrast between cultures, at a time when culture, following the century's civil war and its several changes of monarchic dynasty, was itself in turmoil and could be redefined and reoriented. He also, as Charles Tomlinson has put it, 'set the standard' for subsequent translators, Alexander Pope among them.[43] But while stylistically these poems crystallised a form of speech for a nation, and while the religious poems seemed to have declared a rest from strife and a world of Lucretian randomness and materialism, the translations are surprisingly, perhaps, full still of images of flux and metamorphosis, of change and doubleness. Paul Hammond has described the translations as 'a double-faced but not duplicitous commentary', one inscribed always with what is absent and lacking.[44] Perhaps it was only once Dryden had committed himself to an image of order and absolute perpetuity that he could fully accommodate and give voice to the sceptical anxieties also present in his mind. Yet, as Dryden writes in the Preface to the *Fables*, as if in consolatory manner: 'Mankind is ever the same, and nothing is lost out of Nature, though everything is alter'd.' In the course of producing a voice and language which could, over time, be moulded into a 'tradition', as T. S. Eliot saw it, Dryden considers all that detracts from or impacts on such attempts at cultural continuity and at accommodating the fluctuations of individual existence within such a common tradition.

Notes

1. Jane Spencer, *Aphra Behn's Afterlife* (Oxford: Oxford University Press, 2000), p. 22, quoting Dustin Griffin, 'The Beginnings of Modern Authorship: Milton and Dryden', *Milton Quarterly*, 24:1 (1990), pp. 2, 5.
2. See David Farley-Hills, *Rochester's Poetry* (London: Bell and Hyman, 1978), p. 114, and Barbara Everett, 'Rochester: The Sense of Nothing', in *Poets in their Time* (Oxford: Clarendon Press, 1991), p. 115.
3. Farley-Hills, *Rochester's Poetry*, p. 8.
4. *The Works of Aphra Behn: Volume 1*, ed. Janet Todd (London: Pickering, 1992), p. xxxix. All quotations from Behn's poetry are from this edition.
5. See Melinda S. Zook, 'The Political Poetry of Aphra Behn', in Derek Hughes and Janet Todd (eds.), *The Cambridge Companion to Aphra Behn* (Cambridge: Cambridge University Press, 2004), pp. 46–67.
6. Jessica Munns, 'Pastoral and Lyric: Astraea in Arcadia', in Derek Hughes and Janet Todd (eds.), *The Cambridge Companion to Aphra Behn* (Cambridge: Cambridge University Press, 2004), pp. 48, 217.
7. Alexander Pope, *Peri Bathous or, The Art of Sinking in Poetry* (1727). See Todd (ed.), *Works*, p. 385.
8. Carol Barash, *English Women's Poetry: 1649–1714: Politics, Community and Linguistic Authority* (Oxford: Clarendon Press, 1996), p. 108.
9. *Ibid.*, p. 218.
10. Joshua Scodel, 'Lyric Forms', in Steven N. Zwicker (ed.), *Cambridge Companion to English Literature 1650–1740* (Cambridge: Cambridge University Press, 1998), p. 130.
11. Munns, 'Pastoral and Lyric', p. 213.
12. Barash, *English Women's Poetry*, p. 120.
13. S. J. Wiseman, *Aphra Behn* (Plymouth: Northcote House, 1996), p. 22; Ros Ballaster, *Seductive Forms: Women's Amatory Fiction from 1684–1740* (Oxford: Oxford University Press, 1992).
14. Ballaster, *Seductive Forms*, p. 76.
15. See Angeline Goreau, *Reconstructing Aphra: A Social Biography of Aphra Behn* (Oxford: Oxford University Press, 1980), p. 206.

16. Ballaster, *Seductive Forms*, p. 76.
17. Wiseman, *Aphra Behn*, p. 23.
18. See Bridget Orr, 'The Feminine in Restoration Erotica', in Clare Brant and Diane Purkiss (eds.), *Women, Texts and Histories 1575–1760* (London: Routledge, 1992), p. 199.
19. Barash, *English Women's Poetry*, p. 128.
20. Janet Todd, quoted by Melinda Zook, 'The Political Poetry', in Hughes and Todd (eds.), *Cambridge Companion to Aphra Behn*, p. 57.
21. Kathryn R. King, *Jane Barker, Exile: A Literary Career, 1675–1725* (Oxford: Clarendon Press, 2000), pp. 55–7.
22. Jeslyn Medoff, 'The Daughters of Behn and the Problem of Reputation', in Isobel Grundy and Susan Wiseman (eds.), *Women, Writing, History 1640–1740* (London: B. T. Batsford, 1992), p. 34.
23. John Dryden, 'To the Pious Memory of the Accomplished Young Lady Mrs Anne Killigrew, Excellent in the Two Sister-Arts of Poesy and Painting', in *The Poems of John Dryden*, ed. Paul Hammond and David Hopkins, 5 vols. (London and New York: Longman / Pearson Education Limited, 1995–2005), lines 71–2. All quotations from Dryden's poetry come from this five-volume edition, and line references will be given to the poems.
24. Anne Killigrew, *Poems 1686*, ed. Richard Morton (Gainesville, FL: Facsimile Reprint, 1967), p. 47.
25. Paul Hammond, *John Dryden: A Literary Life* (Basingstoke: Macmillan, 1991), p. 7.
26. David Hopkins, *John Dryden* (Cambridge: Cambridge University Press, 1986), p. 50.
27. *Works of John Dryden: Poems 1649–1680*, eds. Edward Niles Hooker and H. T. Swedenberg (Berkeley: University of California Press, 1956), p. 114.
28. Howard Erskine-Hill, 'Mac Flecknoe, Heir of Augustus', in Paul Hammond and David Hopkins (eds.), *John Dryden: Tercentenary Essays* (Oxford: Oxford University Press, 2000), pp. 17–19.
29. Diane Kelsey McColley, *Poetry and Ecology in the Age of Milton and Marvell* (Aldershot: Ashgate, 2007), pp. 102, 143.
30. *Ibid.*, p. 176.
31. Hammond, *John Dryden*, p. 96.
32. See Hopkins, *John Dryden* p. 82.
33. Hammond, *John Dryden*, p. 108.
34. Ronald Paulson, 'Dryden and the Energies of Satire', in Steven N. Zwicker (ed.), *The Cambridge Companion to John Dryden* (Cambridge: Cambridge University Press, 2004), p. 52.
35. Jennifer Brady, 'Dryden and Congreve's Collaboration in *The Double Dealer*', in Hammond and Hopkins (eds.), *Tercentenary Essays*, p. 130; see also Earl Miner, *Literary Transmission and Authority: Dryden and Other Writers* (Cambridge: Cambridge University Press, 1993), p. 17.
36. John Mullan has rightly observed the nuances in the opening lines of the poem; see 'Dryden's Anonymity', in Zwicker (ed.), *Cambridge Companion to John Dryden*, p. 175.

37. See Brady, 'Dryden and Congreve's Collaboration', p. 130.
38. See Paul Hammond, *John Oldham and the Renewal of Classical Culture* (Cambridge: Cambridge University Press, 1983), p. 3.
39. See George Douglas Atkins, *The Faith of John Dryden: Change and Continuity* (Lexington: University Press of Kentucky, 1980), p. 123.
40. Annabel Patterson, 'Dryden and Political Allegiance', in Zwicker (ed.), *Cambridge Companion to John Dryden*, p. 233.
41. Felicity Rosslyn considers this issue in relation to the poem's 'thin apologetics' in 'Dryden: Poet or Translator?', in Stuart Gillespie (ed.), *John Dryden: Classicist and Translator* (Edinburgh: Edinburgh University Press, 2001), p. 26.
42. Anne Barbieu Gardiner, *Ancient Faith and Modern Freedom in John Dryden's 'The Hind and the Panther'* (Washington, DC: Catholic University of America Press, 1998).
43. Charles Tomlinson, 'Why Dryden's Translations Matter', in Gillespie (ed.), *Classicist and Translator*, p. 10.
44. Paul Hammond, *Dryden and the Traces of Classical Rome* (Oxford: Oxford University Press, 1999), p. 146.

Chapter 16

Dryden: major poems

STEVEN N. ZWICKER

John Dryden came into his own as a poet during the Exclusion Crisis (1679–81) and he maintained a superb pace of verse writing over the next several years. *Absalom and Achitophel* was published in November of 1681, *The Medal* in March of 1682, *Religio Laici* in November of that year; in 1684 and 1685 Dryden produced translations, miscellanies and occasional pieces; and in the early spring of 1687 he finished his longest poem, *The Hind and the Panther*. These works stand at the centre of Dryden's contribution to English poetry and they display the ways in which politics engaged his imagination and emboldened his art; but they do not stand alone. The energy, refinements and ironies that characterise these works light up a number of other poems that continue to offer pleasure: his commemorative pieces on John Oldham and Henry Purcell, his send-up of literary rivals in *Mac Flecknoe*, his verse epistle to the young Congreve, his translations of Ovid, Horace and Virgil, and the country-life piece, *To my Honour'd Kinsman*, with its alluring touches of self-reflection.

What defines Dryden's poetry and his poetic achievement and how might we best situate his work in a history of English poetry? To Dryden's place in that history, we shall come at the end of this chapter. To matters of definition there are at least two approaches: the more obvious is in relation to his learning – his erudition, his technical knowledge, his capacity to act at once as disinterested historian and confident advocate. But Dryden's poetry must also be defined by temperament, by Dryden's uses of irony as a force-field within which he came to discover himself and to fashion a way of handling the world. Of course irony is a device for attacking enemies and humiliating rivals; it proved as well, for Dryden, a way of embracing contingency, of forestalling commitments and of keeping some distance on those forces – the political turmoil and confessional tensions; the patrons, rivals and enmities – that shaped Restoration letters.

As to Dryden's learning: he is the most self-aware, critically articulate and theoretically sophisticated of all the early modern poets. He displayed that self-consciousness from the beginning to the end of his career in the creation of an unprecedented field of literary criticism in English. Not even Ben Jonson, surely his rival as man of letters in the early modern period, comes close to Dryden's accomplishments together as poet, practising critic and theorist of the aesthetic. Though Dryden's criticism is not often free-standing, the *Essay of Dramatic Poesy* (1667) is exactly that, an independent exercise in literary criticism and history that reviews the aesthetics and practices of ancients and moderns, juxtaposes national styles and surveys dramatic forms and techniques, and all in a way that allows the simultaneous display of idea and character. The *Essay* is both symposium and theatre – an effort to lay out contrasting principles of dramatic writing and at the same time to set in play the voices and gestures of his contemporaries: Charles, Lord Buckhurst (Eugenius), Sir Robert Howard (Crites), Sir Charles Sedley (Lisideius) and the poet himself in the person of Neander. In the *Essay* Dryden also began to think about the style and conditions for a new theatre, epic dramas (here called 'serious Playes') wrought from rhyming couplets, exotic costumes, exalted scenes and heightened expressions of love and honour.[1] Beyond theorising the heroic drama, Dryden used his critical writing to explore a variety of literary modes and practices, to articulate aesthetic ideals and shape literary taste, and repeatedly to imagine and engage, and to provoke and abrade, his reading public.

Surrounding his poetry and drama then, interpolated into the spaces of preface, epistle and dedication, is a body of criticism that acts as the foundation and rationale and a kind of advance press for Dryden's own creation of a modern vernacular literature. This criticism was shaped by Dryden's deep appreciation of the ancients, but it was also driven by the need to rationalise particular pieces of his writing as he anticipated their appearance before patrons, on stage and in the marketplace of print. He creates a defence of the heroic drama even as he establishes his dominance over the Restoration stage; he treads carefully between epic and history as he discovers a place for the ambitious quatrains of *Annus Mirabilis*; he studies the varieties, traditions and social power of satire as he introduces his translations of Juvenal and Persius; and in the 1690s he reflects on the tensions and strains within his own literary career even as he fashions a portrait of Virgil caught in similar cross-currents of complaisance and statecraft. In the midst of writing literary theory and history, of appreciating the past and explaining the present, Dryden was also busy caressing the great, complimenting the young and commending himself. These varied drives do not always lead in the same direction; indeed, there are plenty of contradictions in Dryden's criticism, even a sense that the criticism is a kind of bricolage of occasioned opinion. He was of course writing from the workshop and often in a hurry or in the midst of other projects and problems. Yet there are recurrent, if at times paradoxical, themes and ideals: he prized heightened realism as well as fancy and informality; he admired regularity and decorum but he also defends and indulges the pleasures of digression; he celebrates the new even as he writes on behalf of antiquity; and he is absorbed in the creation of his own literary authority even as he borrows from ancients and moderns. Dryden translated, and knew intimately, the poetry of Homer and Virgil, Ovid and Lucretius, Horace, Juvenal and Persius; he adapted Boccaccio and read carefully in Ariosto and Tasso; he versified Boileau, admired Rapin and studied Corneille, Racine and Molière; and yet he is ever the busy advocate of modern English letters. Even as he perfected the arts of allusion and imitation, he was intent on fashioning his own voice, on creating the idioms of his own art.[2]

Granted Dryden's work on behalf of the forms that he invented or half-invented, his learning and his skilled negotiation of literary history, we still have only identified part of his literary character. What also defines Dryden's poetry is his inimitable – because it is in his very condition of being, not a technique or posture but a way of seeing the world – sense of and uses for irony. Irony is where Dryden located himself and his verse; it is the space that he opened for his poetry and from which he launched his most telling satiric effects; it is the shifting, uncertain field where he formed and reformulated his political and religious identities; and ironic self-hood is the achievement both of his first exercise in self-fashioning and of his late reflections on his own person and career.

The figure of Neander in the *Essay of Dramatic Poesy* is a wonderful rendering of Dryden as diffident enthusiast, deferential mediator, even as the poet – mimicking and managing all the voices in the *Essay* – arranges the triumph of English over French theatre, the moderns over the ancients, and indulges in a witty and aggressive send-up of his brother-in-law, sometime collaborator and social superior, Sir Robert Howard. At the end of his life a deeply ironic sense of self allowed Dryden to dismiss his critics, to refute the moralism of the 1690s and to glance disparagingly once more at the Duke of Buckingham, his old antagonist who had made a mockery of him in *The Rehearsal*. Between the *Essay* and the Preface to *Fables* there is a striking array of ironies on display, from the comic rendering of literary rivals in *Mac Flecknoe* to the nervous admiration of Rochester, the hedging appreciation of Milton and the delicate, perhaps slightly embarrassed competitiveness with John Oldham. Irony inflects Dryden's funny and morally equivocal portrait of Charles II at the opening of *Absalom and Achitophel*, his careless disregard for Catherine of Braganza – 'A Soyl ungratefull to the Tiller's care' (line 12) – his brutal and brilliant jokes on Catholic ceremonial – 'Where Gods were recommended by their Tast' (line 119) – and his daring conflation of Stuart courts and brothels, both apparently exactly the right place, indeed perhaps the same place, to 'rake' for converts to Roman Catholicism. The slighting of popery is one thing – and no doubt the ironic diminution aims, by ridicule, to take the danger out of this religion at a high-tide of fears of popery and absolutism – but the insult also reaches surprisingly close to the Duke of York, perhaps the most famous devotee, *c.*1682, of both brothels and the Catholic confessional. It is surely not the case that Dryden's ironies and ironic self-understanding precluded other modes of literary consciousness and self-consciousness; a touch of self-pity can be gleaned from his late writing; and at moments he can play the straight man as he does superbly in the *Essay of Dramatic Poesy*. Further, a sufficient number of Dryden's contemporaries (not least the Duke of Buckingham) remarked his self-regard for us to be aware of this aspect of his literary personality, though what Dryden says directly of himself can be disarmingly modest, and irony must have provided shelter for uncertain self-esteem in the very competitive world of Restoration poetry, patronage and social climbing. But irony was also for Dryden a staging area for aggression, a way of holding in tension conflicting arguments and ideals, a device that allowed equivocation and delay and at times a way of simply disappearing under the cloud cover of scepticism and uncertainty. Such disappearing acts seem more characteristic of the late than of the early writing, but in the 1680s there was no mistaking the force of Dryden's ironies or the damaging effects that this mode of consciousness and self-consciousness was intended to have.

Absalom and Achitophel

Absalom and Achitophel (1681) is bound together by rhyme and rhythm, by the cross-currents of argument and imagery, by repeated figures, keen juxtapositions and of course throughout by an allegorical scheme that layers Biblical characters over Restoration figures and scriptural history over contemporary politics. But we must also allow that the poem is made up of scattered bits and pieces. It is a wonderful miscellany, equally on terms with parody and praise – a deft mixture of pamphlet scurrility and Virgilian commemoration, of sexual slander and Miltonic allusion, of town gossip and scriptural allegory. The texture of the poem is pointedly, argumentatively varied, and perhaps – to thematise mixture and miscellany – we might see some congruence, some collusion between the patchwork character of the body politic that Dryden conjures up in 1681 and the instrument that he fashions to analyse and ameliorate its condition. The figure of the body politic from the preface to *Absalom and Achitophel* speaks to an ideal of organic wholeness and a tradition of civic harmonies and reciprocities; yet the poem dwells on heats and distempers, plots and pretended frights, on the busy stirrings of faction and dissent. Indeed, the poem conveys a strong sense that its ideals and its energies move in contradictory directions, and at every level. On the one hand the heroic couplets tightly bind the verse, on the other hand the couplets shine disparately – so many glittering points strung nervously together. Even a thematic understanding of the poem's mixed modes does not resolve the tension between the poem as something like an organic whole and its memorable qualities as a scattering of buzzes and stings.[3] This is not true, or at least not as true, of *Religio Laici* or of *The Hind and the Panther*, both of which display a strong sense of design and of individual parts subdued to design, and yet *Absalom and Achitophel* is the poem to which we turn first for evidence – and perhaps the strongest evidence – of Dryden's literary manners and mastery, and it is worth pausing over this problem of parts and whole to ask what holds the poem together, what aligns its energies and arguments.

The preface to *Absalom and Achitophel* suggests Dryden's strong sense of the aesthetic. Here he celebrates poetry and genius, the seductive power of language and the poetic line, and he writes in the idioms of pleasure, authority and judgment. Even as he prefaces a work that is everywhere and keenly partisan, a poem whose occasion and most telling gestures are designed by patronage and interest, Dryden urges the aesthetic as a value independent of politics. As a polemicist he appreciated the rhetorical value of opening a space above the partisan, but as a poet Dryden understood the tensions between aesthetics and partisanship, the ways in which the aesthetic was always in debt to honesty, that is, disinterestedness. Hence his care to delineate the ideal reader as the 'honest Party', for those 'least concern'd, are commonly the least Corrupt' (II:3). Of course 'honesty' and 'corruption' are terms that belong not only to aesthetics; perhaps Dryden chose this language because it negotiates between aesthetics and politics – central domains in this verse. Yet the claim of disinterestedness itself is subject to partisan review, and Dryden allows as much when he acknowledges that his plea for impartiality might be misread – 'And now, if you are a Malitious Reader, I expect you should return upon me, that I affect to be thought more Impartial than I am. But, if men are not to be judg'd by their Professions, God forgive you Common-wealths-men, for professing so plausibly for the Government' (II:3–4). Even as he attempts to retain some value for the impartial designs of his art, Dryden wearily acknowledges the pressure that politics exerts on poetry. And yet from the abundant evidence of his poetry, such pressure was not difficult for Dryden to convert into poetic energy. Perhaps even to suggest equation, to suggest that politics and poetry were simply fungible accounts, is to underestimate the authority that political crisis and polemical warfare lent to Dryden's art. Not only was political crisis often the occasion and driving force of his writing, but a sense of danger and defensiveness – the need to manoeuvre and to recoup – invariably pushed Dryden's writing to interesting places. *Absalom and Achitophel* is a wonderful demonstration of that.

The central device of the poem, the counterpointing of contemporary events with sacred history, was of course hardly original to Dryden, and hardly new to the 1680s. The heyday of such applications had been the time of civil war, and though scriptural allegory was often used to vindicate Puritan righteousness, neither the solace nor the arguments of scripture belonged to any one party. Perhaps Dryden's turn to sacred history was merely a bit of Royalist payback, a reading of late seventeenth-century politics in the idiom most favoured by those whom Dryden hoped to smear as the sanctimonious progenitors of Whiggery and Exclusion. Certainly he made a point in this poem of linking political radicalism and social experimentation in the 1640s with the efforts of Exclusionists to tamper with the sacred properties of the crown and lineal descent. But scriptural allegory also seems a particularly effective way – even in the half-light of irony – to excite memories of the divisive and disastrous past while recovering the idioms of sacred history for the crown, and refashioning them in the midst of a crisis that many thought had been brought about less by an excess of piety than by the unbridled lust and fornication of the King. Yet if the nimble interweaving of sacred history and topical matter were the only attraction of *Absalom and Achitophel*, it would not have outlived the urgencies of Exclusion. The poem was an immediate success, spawning imitations, adaptations and keys, but it also became a late seventeenth-century touchstone of Tory poetics and a lightning rod for attacks on the crown and no less on its laureate whose hand, despite the ruse of anonymity, was easily discerned behind its programme and portraiture. Indeed, *Absalom and Achitophel* remains the poem for which Dryden is best known, even when we no longer much care who were friends or enemies of the late Stuart crown.

That said, the gallery of rogues that Dryden fashions out of the band of Exclusionists is superb; the figure of the Duke of Buckingham (Zimri), or the likes of Titus Oates (Corah) and Slingsby Bethel (Shimei) are unmatched by any of the character literature in this age of 'characters'. The poet got exactly right the proportions of his satiric art: he mixes diminution, ridicule and insult with an occasional touch of 'honest' praise, and he modulates his voice seamlessly from contempt and indignation to pity and scorn.

The pleasures of such satire can be felt throughout the poem: in the soft condescension with which Dryden treats the dim but charismatic Duke of Monmouth (Absalom), in the excoriation of Shaftesbury (Achitophel) and brusque handling of his deformed 'body politic'; in the reduction of Whig policy to thuggery and faction, and of dissenting spirituality to cheating and praying. But Dryden also heightens the entire project by imagining and personating civic ideals, giving character and literary depth to concepts which in the abstract only name categories of the good but in poetic form lend an affecting life to such notions as patriarchy, political loyalty and civic generosity. As Dryden mingles caricature with portraiture and balances ironic subversion with the articulation of high ideals, the poem emerges from the buzz of satire into a fuller, more complex music. He had made a point – and on the title page – of identifying *Absalom and Achitophel* as poetry, and as he shades irony into admiration and elegy Dryden moves the arguments of the poem beyond any single mode, beyond either satire or panegyric. From the beginning, the initial and somewhat boisterous (if not altogether good-natured) joking over paternity, what Dryden aims to figure in the poem are the sinews of a patriarchal world – the deep ties of honour and affect that define fatherhood and bind the commonweal.

This is exactly the elevating and elegiac aim of Dryden's twinned portrait of the Duke of Ormond and his recently deceased son, the Earl of Ossory. As Dryden celebrates aristocratic honour and mourns a father's, and a patron's, loss, he recalls passages in *Aeneid* v (lines 49–50) where Aeneas prepares the funeral games in memory of his father, and in *Aeneid* vi (lines 860–6) where Anchises shows to Aeneas a vision of the elder and younger Marcellus, and of the youth's early death. Dryden was to use this Virgilian moment on other occasions – the commemoration of Oldham with its beautiful drift of downward cadences: 'Once more, hail and farewel; farewel, thou young, / But ah too short, Marcellus of our Tongue' (ii:175, lines 22–3), the Dedication of *Fables* and the verse epistle to the second Duchess of Ormond opening that collection – but nowhere is the allusive and argumentative power of his poetry stronger than in this scene from *Absalom and Achitophel* where so many different kinds of argument are at stake. Here Dryden uses Virgil to unfold patronage relations, literary affiliation and contemporary politics into a claim for political authority and cultural pre-eminence.[4]

A number of gifts, various kinds of erudition and an extraordinary facility with generic mixture are evident in *Absalom and Achitophel*; what needs to be emphasised is the way in which they are articulated together, articulated in the voices that the poet mimics and assumes – satirist and tempter; Virgilian poet and character assassin; elegist and architect of praise; political theorist and tender father; king and common man. And even as Dryden displays a mastery of the poem's many tongues and literary kinds, his own voice – its gait, his exacting diction, the argumentative force and fluency – is audible everywhere. *Absalom and Achitophel* was published anonymously, but Dryden's contemporaries had no trouble discerning his presence in its couplets and commemoration or in the edgy prose that introduces the poem and so deftly navigates the shoals of party formation and partisan reading. We began by asking what holds this poem together. Of course, the arguments and moves on behalf of lineal descent and the sanctity of the crown are fashioned as a coherent political programme for *Absalom and Achitophel*, but the poem's disparate energies are also aligned by a sensibility, by the voice of the poet that inhabits all of its modes and animates both its learning and its buoyant partisanship: 'If a Poem have a Genius, it will force its own reception in the World' (II:3).

Religio Laici

After the striking characters and caricatures, the intricate topicality, the aggressive baiting and of course and above all the wit of *Absalom and Achitophel*, *Religio Laici* seems surprisingly cool, indeed rather dismissive of wit itself. At the opening of the Preface to *Religio Laici* Dryden is all demurral and defence: he protests 'weakness and want of Learning' (II:98), politely refuses to make himself 'a Judge of Faith, in others' (II:98) and ingenuously confesses the pious and unimpeachable 'helps' that he has used in making his 'small Treatise' (II:98). There was nothing scandalous about a layman writing on religion, and earlier in his career Dryden had used the stage to reflect on ethical conflict and spiritual dilemmas.[5] But a 'Confession' of faith does suggest some intimacy with the spiritual, surely an integrity of conviction, and these qualities may have seemed at odds with the poet's recent and quite worldly, indeed scandalous, mockery of priests and priestcraft in *Absalom and Achitophel*. There he had not only abused Roman Catholic ceremonial and sectarian self-interest but had argued that 'Priests of all Religions are the same: / Of whatsoe'r descent their Godhead be . . . For 'twas their duty, all the Learned think, / T'espouse his Cause by whom they eat and drink' (II:8, lines 99–107). Perhaps this and similar passages had poisoned the air for spiritual confession by the 'Play-maker', but it still seems surprising that one of Dryden's contemporaries – the collector and parliamentary diarist Narcissus Luttrell – should have written 'Atheisticall' on the title page of his copy of *Religio Laici*.[6]

When Dryden published his conversion to Rome in *The Hind and the Panther* (1687), the Anglicanism (if it was that) of *Religio Laici* was made an embarrassment.[7] But in 1682, after the defeat of Exclusion and the humiliation of dissenting and sectarian interests, it could hardly have been embarrassing for the laureate to outline a vision of the Anglican *via media*. And yet, as Dryden backs into his confession of faith, he seems hesitant and cautious. Was he anticipating the charge that Luttrell would make? The soft-spined and repeated claims of charity in the Preface and poem and the ameliorative treatment of pagans and heathens – they are allowed (perhaps more than 'Rubrick-Martyrs', II:115, line 211) the gift of eternal life, and that without knowledge of the incarnation – might have seemed surprisingly latitudinarian (perhaps even unchristian). And the poem's supposed origins as a commendation of the English translation and publication of Richard Simon's *Histoire Critique du Vieux Testament* might have raised suspicions about the religion of *Religio Laici* since Simon's book – a critique of the textual integrity of the Old Testament – upset both Anglican and Catholic officialdom. But Dryden corrects for these problems; he carefully surrounds his declarations of charity and heathen salvation with invocations of Anglican piety, and his opinion of Simon's *Critical History* is difficult exactly to discern – an evasiveness that may itself have been an attempt to avoid scandal.

The real provocation of *Religio Laici* was yet to come. It awaited the reader near the end of a poem in which Dryden maps a middle way between the arrogance of Rome and the scurrility of dissent. Here, at the summit of spiritual quest – after he has reviewed and dismissed the spiritual claims of ancient philosophers, deists, papists and a swarming variety of sects – Dryden discovers that 'Common quiet is Mankind's concern' (II:122, line 250). This declaration of civil religion stands as the structural and spiritual climax of the pilgrimage that begins with 'lonely, weary, wandring Travellers' seeking a certain guide to salvation (II:109, line 2). To what extent, Dryden's readers might have wondered, was 'Common quiet' the fulfilment of the incarnation and crucifixion: 'God descending in thy Humane Frame; / Th' offended, suff'ring in th' Offenders Name' (II:12, lines 107–8)? Indeed, 'Common quiet' might rather have conjured up the spirit of Hobbes than the resurrection. And along with the ghost of Hobbes's civil religion, 'Common quiet' might also have raised the spectre of atheism, a charge repeatedly brought against the philosopher of *Leviathan*. As well, 'Common quiet' might have suggested the civic interest of Dryden's master and patron, Charles II, whose theology was best expressed by the doctrinal indifference of a politic toleration.

With the invocation of 'Common quiet' we are near the end of *Religio Laici* – line 450 of 456 lines – but not quite there. Following the invocation of civil religion, Dryden makes another surprising move by claiming Thomas Sternhold and Thomas Shadwell as something like exemplars for the style of *Religio Laici*:

> Thus have I made my own Opinions clear:
> Yet neither Praise expect, nor Censure fear:
> And this unpolish'd, rugged Verse, I chose;
> As fittest for Discourse, and nearest Prose:
> For, while from Sacred Truth I do not swerve,
> Tom Sternhold's, or Tom Shadwell's Rhimes will serve.
>
> (II:122, lines 451–6)

By the late seventeenth century, the Sternhold and Hopkins Psalter was proverbial for dullness, and, at least for Dryden, Shadwell was the very type of the bad poet, an object of Dryden's contempt at least from the time of his writing *Mac Flecknoe* (1676). Sternhold and Shadwell make their joint appearance in the very last line of *Religio Laici* where they seem an abrasion, a forceful and mocking assertion of stylistic choice, an ironic evocation of the plain style and a telling reminder of this poet's varied powers. With the appearance of Sternhold and Shadwell Dryden seems to say that he could have written either with more elevation or more satiric edge, but he has chosen another manner, even against his literary self-interest. He is fully and aggressively aware of what he is doing, nor was there any missing Dryden's self-consciousness about style altogether in this piece.

Indeed, there is no poem to whose style Dryden draws more attention, or any poem more attentive to the meanings of style than *Religio Laici*, where the poet repeatedly avers his plainness. In the Preface he cuts short expectations of lyric grace or the elevation of epic poetry, and at the close of *Religio Laici* Dryden suggests that he has edged his verse as near to prose as he can; elsewhere in both preface and poem he variously urges the virtues of clarity and plainness, though he is also careful not to go too far down-market: limpid is one thing, scurrilous quite another. There is throughout a studied effort to claim and to effect a style that occupies the middle ground, and the connection between style and confessional identity is everywhere evident. The *via media* is both the manner of the poem and the traditional position of the Anglican confession, midway between extremes: between the spiritual absolutism of the Roman Church and the bedlam of dissent, between infallibility and the railing of the sects. That much about the meaning of style is clear. But there is a separate though related set of assertions and associations to be unfolded from Dryden's argument about style and theology in *Religio Laici*. These concern scriptural exegesis, the way in which the Bible is to be read, understood and expounded. Here again Dryden aims to discover a middle ground, to hew between a reading of scripture too exclusive and authoritarian – too dependent on claims of priestly wit and eloquence – and the distortions of individual inspiration, the fanatic's spiritual discipline in which, Dryden contemptuously remarks, texts are expounded 'by Fasting, and by Prayer' (II:121, line 414).

The subject of scriptural exegesis is introduced by way of Father Simon's *Critical History*, a work of scholarship that disclosed the textual corruptions of the Old Testament, presumably a blow to Reformed religion, which so exalted the authenticity and authority of the sacred text, but a fright to Catholic officialdom as well. From there, Dryden leads the argument about textual uncertainty towards the modesty and safety of the middle ground, an acceptance of textual contingencies and corruptions and of interpretative hazards and puzzles, but as well an assertion of the essential clarity and explanatory self-sufficiency of scripture. We can hear of course an alliance between the exegetical position and Dryden's arguments on behalf of a middle style: the poem floats upon plain numbers because it makes a plea for intellectual and interpretative modesty and minimalism. One position emerges from the other, and both are premised on the Protestant commonplace that in all things necessary for salvation the scriptures are plain and clear.

There is one further issue folded into the matter of scriptural exegesis: who gets to determine meaning? The question is posed in relation to scripture, but housed within the exegetical issue is a broader, more pervasive anxiety about control over interpretation and the uncertain capacity of language to declare its own meaning. Once you acknowledge the corruption of the written word, and indeed of the oral tradition, you must then ask: how is meaning determined and to be determined? The Catholic Church had long answered these questions with assertions of its own infallible interpretative authority, its privilege over and ownership of the scriptures, or so Dryden, in his Anglican confession, charges. Possession of the scriptures meant possessing salvation: the Catholic Church had 'parcel'd out the Bible by retail: / But still expounded what She sold or gave; / To keep it in her Power to Damn and Save' (II:120, lines 377–9). The politics of interpretation could not be clearer nor the charge of venality harsher: the power of the Catholic Church depended on claims of infallible interpretative authority; under such a regime, interest and greed determined salvation. Textual corruption might seem a relatively minor problem in the face of the self-perpetuating institutional corruption of such a church.

Nor does the fanatic Church offer better guidance. Though wresting the Book from Catholic interest and claims of infallibility freed the common legacy of mankind, this reformation had an unintended consequence, a cascading debasement of scriptural interpretation. False authority now removed, the 'right t' interpret' (II:120, line 362) became the property of everyman – the dialectical movement of history had swung the interpretation of scripture from the intellectual arrogance of Rome to the free-for-all of sectarian zeal and ignorance. Without a middle way, without modesty and a certain reverence for tradition, an honest layman might be forever buffeted between omniscience and ignorance. The resolution, the synthesis, is, of course, the Anglican confession, the *via media*, which made an ethic of intellectual style and a style of its ethic – it is the style of *Religio Laici* – plain and natural, limpid and clear. After all, like the scriptures, this poem 'speaks it Self, and what it does contain, / In all things needfull to be known, is plain' (II:120, lines 368–9). That much could be said for *Religio Laici*; how the dictum might be applied to Dryden's next exercise in the confessional mode poses something of a problem. No one reading *The Hind and the Panther*, then or now, has ever thought the poem too simple or too plain.

The Hind and the Panther

What greeted Dryden's confession of Catholic faith were howls of derision and confusion. And howling is what Dryden might have anticipated for a poem that translated the discourse of religion into the language of beasts, and not a simple beast fable but fables within fables, a bestiary of literary kinds, a virtual zoo in which apes and boars, bears and wolves, foxes and lions, swallows and martins, buzzards and pigeons – to say nothing of a hind and a panther – do the talking and stalking. Swift mocked *The Hind and the Panther* as 'a complete abstract of sixteen thousand school-men, from Scotus to Bellarmin', but others were not so confident either of its design or its content.[8] For sure, everyone understood that the poem was intended to announce Dryden's new religion. And the poet tells us in his preface that he intended at least part of the poem (though exactly which passages has remained unclear for the past 320 years) to support James II's design to remove the Test Act and to promote religious toleration.[9] But why should a poem about the removal of the Test Act and the declaring of a religious toleration; or the efficacy of the Real Presence and the distinction between signs and things; or the character of infallibility and the nature of the private spirit – why should such a poem be cast in the idiom of Aesop and Mother Hubbard? In antiquity and early modernity fables were associated with the instruction of children, but Dryden aimed at something far more learned and challenging in the 2,392 lines of *The Hind and the Panther*.[10] By the time we get to the programme in part 3, where beasts themselves are telling beast fables – the Hind's story of the flight of the Swallows with its allusions to internecine warfare among the English Catholics and its prophecies of impending doom; or the Panther's barnyard tale which begins with a simple farmer coming into possession of his estate but evolves into a fable that features doves, pigeons, roosters and a buzzard boasting a lifeguard that bear on their breastplates the letter 'B' (a hit at Gilbert Burnet? III:195, line 1138) – we seem very far removed from instruction of any kind, indeed from persuasion, or from any other recognisable rhetorical acts, though perhaps mystification belongs to the arts of rhetoric.[11] And once we attempt to solve local puzzles, we are inevitably caught up in the poem's tangled skeins of allegory and enigma. So inwardly turned is the mysterious writ of this poem that the California Dryden needs 133 pages of densely packed commentary to gloss the 77 pages of text. The poet did not intend for his readers easily to penetrate the mysteries of this poem of personal confession and programmatic apology; there is indeed every indication that the poem's patches of near unintelligibility are quite calculated. Dryden was aware that contemporaries would look for the road from *Religio Laici* to *The Hind and the Panther* and that they would discover exactly what they sought – a trail of crumbs, convenience and self-interest marking the way from Lambeth to Rome. A Catholic King had come to the throne in 1685; the laureate's conversion could not be very far behind.

And conversion – its motives, its character, the poet's changing spirituality, indeed his spirituality altogether – has remained the centre of interest for those trying to parse and puzzle their way through this text and to figure its relation to *Religio Laici*. In his time, Dryden's conversion was read almost wholly in political terms, if we understand politics to include patronage and favour, and Dryden built into his poem a defence of the purity of his motives by denying the relation between conversion and privilege, displaying – at the cost of humiliation (though humiliation had its own rewards in spiritual warfare) – his failure to obtain favour from the hands of a Catholic king:

> Now for my converts, who you say unfed
> Have follow'd me for miracles of bread,
> Judge not by hear-say, but observe at least,
> If since their change, their loaves have been increast.
> The Lyon buys no Converts, if he did,
> Beasts would be sold as fast as he cou'd bid. (III:167, lines 221–6)

There had been no miracles of bread for the laureate who aimed, more than once in the months following James's accession, at sinecure.[12] The acknowledgment of such failure must have been a costly way for Dryden to vindicate the purity of his spirit, but his contemporaries would have none of it, and their attacks on *The Hind and the Panther* were uniformly sceptical of the laureate's integrity and spirituality.

In our own time it is spirituality rather than politics and patronage that has dominated the efforts to understand *The Hind and the Panther*; modern scholarship has sought to trace the steps from sceptical Anglicanism to the embrace of mystery and, failing that, to restore to Dryden his spiritual integrity and to rationalise the relationship between his two confessions of faith. Of course politics and spirituality provide the most telling, the most obvious points of contact between the poems, but the deepest intellectual, psychological and literary relations between *Religio Laici* and *The Hind and the Panther* derive from Dryden's address to scriptural exegesis and, more generally, to the problem of interpretation: how are words to be understood and who gets to determine and declare meaning? These questions represent Dryden's most probing address to the philosophy of language and they excited in him a deep and productive anxiety. They explain the choice of literary modes in *The Hind and the Panther* – the uses of and fascination with fable and mysterious writ – and they point to the creative turn that defines much of the rest of Dryden's career: the choice of translation as the predominant expressive mode in the last decade of his life.

In *Religio Laici* Dryden still had the linguistic and philosophical confidence to suppose that texts, or at least the scriptures, spoke their own meaning; he had aimed to achieve just such a poetics of the plainness and clarity of necessary things in his Anglican confession. With *The Hind and the Panther* Dryden knew that he was engaged in a struggle to control the meaning of his words, that his poem was written from a combat zone and would not be allowed to declare its own meaning. He did not expect 'either fair War, or even so much as fair Quarter from a Reader of the opposite Party'; he knew that he would be 'knock'd down before the Reasons of his own are heard', that the conventional work of a preface – a 'bespeaking of Favour' (III.119) – was hopeless. The answers to *The Hind and the Panther*, the mocking imitations and ridiculing transversions, give evidence of just the kind of oppositional reading that he anticipated and feared. Though perhaps fear is not exactly the mood in which Dryden wrote *The Hind and the Panther*. He knew that the poem's mysteries, its beasts discoursing of religion, its bold inversion of positions he had taken in *Religio Laici*, its threatening applications of Virgil, its eerie omens, dreams and signs would confuse and offend. In that regard, at least, he must have seen the initial responses to *The Hind and the Panther* as a sign of success: he had forced the opposition on to his own ground where he would attempt to control meaning or at least to baffle the efforts of others to wrest and distort the sense of his words.

For nearly all his literary life Dryden had been engaged – willingly or not – in an effort to stabilise and control the meanings of his words. Of course he had himself long practised transformations and transversions – the taking by allusion and adaptation of others' language – and he knew that this was one of his deepest linguistic and literary skills, and it was often an act of literary homage. But the reconfiguring of prophecy and the repossession of scripture that began as early as *Annus Mirabilis* and culminated in the brilliant seizure of 2 Samuel in *Absalom and Achitophel* represented something other and more aggressive than homage; it represented a kind of triumphant imposition of his will to meaning. But along with his practices and stratagems to fix the meaning of others' language within the frame of his own art, Dryden began in the late 1660s to experience a hermeneutic backwash, to experience the impositions, distortions and reassignments of the meaning of his words by others. It took place in the art of ridicule that the Duke of Buckingham and his collaborators practised in *The Rehearsal*, in the Rota pamphlets that lavishly quoted from and laughed at his plays, in the reflections on *Absalom and Achitophel*, in the aggressive re-titling of his poems, in derisions, imitations and mock panegyrics – that is, repeatedly and altogether in the aggressive pamphlet warfare that attacked, after the early 1670s, nearly everything Dryden wrote. No wonder, on the occasion of declaring his Roman Catholic faith and defending James II's programme to establish toleration, Dryden would seek shelter; he knew that his poem would be combated and contested, combed and parsed, with great malice and care.

He would mystify and obfuscate, he would rhyme the opposition to death. But beyond the challenges of literary strategy, Dryden must also have felt that he now faced a hermeneutic crisis; repeatedly in *The Hind and the Panther* he argued that words were unstable and insecure signs: 'The word's a weather-cock to ev'ry wind' (III:136, line 465); scripture could be used to defend all positions; malice and wit could obscure any meaning; all knowledge would be reduced to an endless wrangling over sense for only the constituent elements of words – only the vowels and consonants – are ever clear: '*He darkly writ* is true applied to all' (III:149, line 345). This was not a productive position for a poet to occupy – too much conviction in that direction would mean an end to writing altogether. But *The Hind and the Panther* did not signal the end of Dryden's career; he not only returned to the stage in the late 1680s, he turned full time to translating the ancients, and in one regard – in a philosophical respect – we might think that adopting the language of others was a response to the hermeneutic dilemma he had faced in *The Hind and the Panther*. The great project of his last decade was a complete translation of Virgil. Of course Dryden had long been preoccupied with Virgil, and in that regard the translation was the culmination of the deepest of his literary kinships. But we might also understand the position of translator as the ultimate logic of the knowledge he had been forced – by ridicule, transversion and imitation – to accept. In all the contingencies and uncertainties of this world, the text would never be allowed to declare its own meaning. The poet could not speak *ex cathedra* the meaning of his poems; he would have to allow them to float out to the sea of interpretation where they would be tossed on waves of misunderstanding and distortion beyond his control. At least the shelter of another's text – of Virgil's text – would provide some arms against that sea of troubles. And Dryden made a wonderful use, a brilliant consolation out of translation; it was the place he had arrived at, the philosophical, literary and linguistic position which, by way of revolution and misfortune, triumph and humiliation, he had embraced by the end of his life.

Where does Dryden belong in a history of English poetry? Of course he had himself answered this question – he was the heir of Virgil, the intimate of Chaucer, the close kin of Fairfax and Waller, of Spenser and Milton, the descendant of Shakespeare, Jonson and Fletcher, secure in the family of poetry, fast among its 'Lineal Descents and Clans' (VII:25). Late in his life Dryden thought of himself as father to the next generation of poets, and he had long figured literary relations in this way, long meditated on kinship and inheritance, on fathers and sons. One of his most affecting and affectionate poems is in commendation of the young Congreve, 'lineal to the Throne' (IV:433, line 44), and charged, as heir, not only with preserving a literary inheritance but with protecting Dryden's name, defending his reputation, though Dryden was not, as perhaps he feared, in immediate danger from rivals or critics; he had achieved the greatness that he had often wished and proclaimed for himself. But in the late 1690s Swift was hard at work – even while busily disguising his own debts to Dryden as a master of ironies – undermining 'cousin Dryden', maliciously thrusting him among the ignorant moderns, ridiculing his claims of kinship with antiquity, mocking his translation of Virgil, laughing at his spirituality, his self-promotion, his political service and pliancy, and others in the eighteenth century and beyond would join in the demolition of his character – a project that would not have surprised Dryden. But the idea that his poetry itself would one day be thought of merely, or at best, as prose, such an idea of what constituted poetry and his removal from among the company of poets would have been a shocking turn for Dryden. Of course, as a 'classic of our prose' Dryden had the good company of Pope, but Matthew Arnold would surely have denied him the kinship of Virgil, of Chaucer, of Shakespeare and Milton, and it is in that family, among those poets, that Dryden thought to have made his home.[13] He was flattened into prose by nineteenth-century critics and historians, but in the early and middle decades of the twentieth century and among such poets and critics as T. S. Eliot, W. H. Auden, William Empson and, more recently, Geoffrey Hill and Christopher Ricks, Dryden has been returned to the family of poets, to a notion of what poetry might do, and – especially by Empson, Hill and Ricks – to an understanding that the quirky and surprising nature of his intelligence and his luminous capacity for irony might just evidence a quality of mind and provide a music that conforms very well to our notion of poetry.[14] Among such readers, Dryden's position in a history of English poetry seems prominent and secure.

For others he is in danger not of becoming prose, but of becoming invisible. Dryden's literary career almost exactly spans his age and, together with the Restoration, he seems in danger of vanishing in that ever-diminishing space between early modernity and the long eighteenth century. But perhaps Dryden is also in danger of disappearing within the Restoration itself because he is in so many ways difficult to distinguish from the Restoration, a chameleon who both invented and became his age, complicit with its morals and manners, a keen operative, an eager servant of the great, dismissive of rivals, energetic, ironic, by turns contemptuous of priest-craft and absorbed by religion. Rather more than any of his contemporaries – surely more than Milton who is so often writing against the grain, or Marvell who excoriates his time but is impervious either to its corruptions or its allure, or Rochester, whose obscenities and intelligence shine so brightly out of his age – Dryden seems to have become merely a synonym for the Restoration. He seems, that is, in danger of simply disappearing into his age and becoming the most distinguished of our unread poets – a fate that would mean, I think, a great diminution of our literary pleasures.

Notes

1. *The Works of John Dryden*, ed. E. N. Hooker and H. T. Swedenberg, Jr. *et al.*, 20 vols. (Berkeley: University of California Press, 1956–2002), vol. XVII, p. 68, line 24, and see discussion also in vol. XVII, p. 74; future citations will be to this edition and given parenthetically in the text by volume, page and, for verse, line numbers. See also Robert Hume, *Dryden's Criticism* (Ithaca, NY: Cornell University Press, 1970), p. 204.
2. On Dryden and allusion see, especially, Reuben Brower, *Alexander Pope and the Poetry of Allusion* (Oxford: Oxford University Press, 1963), pp. 1–14, and Christopher Ricks, *Allusion to the Poets* (Oxford: Oxford University Press, 2002), pp. 9–42.
3. The phrase is from Bacon's essay 31, 'Of Suspicion', in *The Essays and Councels, Civill and Morall*, ed. Michael Kiernan (Cambridge, MA: Harvard University Press, 1985), p. 103.
4. On this scene, see Jane Ohlmeyer and Steven Zwicker, 'John Dryden, the House of Ormond, and the Politics of Anglo-Irish Patronage', *Historical Journal*, 49:3 (2006), pp. 688–9.
5. For precedents to *Religio Laici*, see *The Poems of John Dryden*, ed. James Kinsley, 4 vols. (Oxford: Oxford University Press, 1956), vol. IV, p. 1933.
6. Luttrell's copy of *Religio Laici* is now part of the John Dryden Collection formed by Percy J. Dobell, Folger Shakespeare Library. Luttrell was not alone in the accusation of atheism; see also *The Weekly Pacquet of Advice from Rome* (London, 12 January 1682–3), vol. 21, pp. 165–6, with its reference to *Religio Laici* as Dryden's 'Obscure and Atheistical Sheets'.
7. See e.g. *The Revolter: A Trage-Comedy acted between the Hind and Panther, and Religio Laici* (London, 1687).
8. 'The Tale of a Tub', in *Jonathan Swift*, ed. Angus Ross and David Woolley (Oxford: Oxford University Press, 1984), p. 93.
9. 'To the Reader', III:121, lines 5–13. Neither Dryden's editors nor other students of this poem have been able to agree on what these 'many things' in part 3 might have been.
10. See Jayne Lewis, *The English Fable: Aesop and Literary Culture, 1651–1740* (Cambridge: Cambridge University Press, 1996), pp. 11–12, 195, footnote 37.
11. On the rhetoric of paradox and on mystification in *The Hind and the Panther*, see Steven N. Zwicker, 'The Paradoxes of Tender Conscience', *ELH*, 63 (1996), pp. 851–69.
12. See James A. Winn, *John Dryden and his World* (New Haven: Yale University Press, 1987), p. 613, footnote 90. The rumours of Dryden's quests turn up in a number of places, including the 'Entering Books' of Roger Morrice, and in manuscript verse, including several pieces in BL, MS 38671. My thanks to

Andrew Carpenter for this reference; one example, 'On Doctor Dryden's Coming over to the Provost of Trinity College', is published in *Verse in English from Tudor and Stuart Ireland*, ed. Andrew Carpenter (Cork: Cork University Press, 2003), pp. 502–3. See also Hugh Macdonald, *John Dryden: A Bibliography of Early Editions and of Drydeniana* (Oxford: Clarendon Press, 1939), p. 138, note 2 and p. 265.

13. Arnold first made this assessment in 1880 in 'The Study of Poetry'; see *The Complete Prose Works of Matthew Arnold*, ed. R. H. Super, 11 vols. (Ann Arbor: University of Michigan Press, 1960–77), vol. IX, p. 181.
14. William Empson's work on Dryden has been collected in *Using Biography* (Cambridge, MA: Harvard University Press, 1984), pp. 99–127; for Geoffrey Hill on Dryden, see *The Enemy's Country* (Stanford, CA: Stanford University Press, 1991), pp. 63–82; Christopher Ricks has written most recently on Dryden in *Allusion to the Poets* and in 'Dryden's Triplets', in Steven N. Zwicker (ed.), *The Cambridge Companion to John Dryden* (Cambridge: Cambridge University Press, 2004), pp. 92–112.

Chapter 17
Swift

CLAUDE RAWSON

Swift claimed, late in life, to have been 'only a Man of Rhimes, and that upon Trifles, never having written serious Couplets in my Life, yet never without a moral View'.[1] There are many subtexts to this statement, one of which is that he was a prolific poet, almost as prolific as his friend Pope, whose 'serious Couplets' he admired but thought himself unfitted for. Swift bowed before the mastery of Pope in the higher discursive styles, content perhaps with his own standing as the greatest prose author of his time. But his autobiographical poems show that he thought of himself, and was thought of by others, as a poet. Swift wrote almost as much verse as Pope, if we exclude Pope's Homer translation, and he has always been admired (and sometimes preferred to Pope) by poets, including Byron, Yeats, Eliot, Auden, Geoffrey Hill, Derek Mahon and Ted Hughes. Swift's regard for the couplet which Pope perfected and which became the dominant mode of serious poetic expression in his day, was as genuine as his reluctance to use it himself.

'Only a Man of Rhimes' is Swift's acknowledgment of the supremacy of 'serious Couplets' and of Pope. It may also be seen as a refusal to compete. The hegemony Pope exercised over poetic standards, though Swift was happy to accept it, cannot be said to have determined his choices. Well before he knew Pope or Pope was known as a poet, Swift had developed his comic tetrameter style with such poems as 'Verses Wrote in a Lady's Ivory Table-Book' (1698), and 'Baucis and Philemon' (1709). His poetic career began with a handful of odes in the wedding-cake stanzas of which Cowley's 'Pindariques' were the famous English example, and one or two poems wholly or mostly in 'serious Couplets', in honour of Congreve and Swift's patron Sir William Temple. A possibly apocryphal story that Dryden told Swift 'Cousin Swift, you will never be a poet' (or a 'Pindaric poet', versions differ) may be responsible, as Samuel Johnson reported, for Swift's hatred of Dryden, and perhaps also, if true, for his almost total retreat from high styles throughout the rest of his writing career.

So complete was his shrinking from any form of high manner that, although almost all his poems are in some sense parodic, he never attempted in his verse the style of mock-epic of which Pope's *Rape of the Lock* and *Dunciad* became the culminating exemplars, as though Swift feared that some of the majesties of the heroic original might rub off on the parody (an effect aimed at by both Dryden and Pope). The single exception, the *Battle of the Books*, a brilliant mock-Virgilian narrative allegorising the Battle of the Ancients and Moderns, seems to want to divert readers from the fact that it is travestying an epic by simultaneously being in the flattening medium of prose, and offering competing layers of less exalted mimicry, mock-scholarly and mock-journalese.[2]

When, in his late poem *The Legion Club* (1736; lines 83ff.), Swift allowed himself an extended allusion to Virgil's underworld (*Aeneid*, VI. 264–94), showing Irish politicians as denizens of a vicious and demented inferno, he used the low 'burlesque' style repudiated by Boileau and Pope, in which high evocations are expressed in low demotic terms, as though Aeneas and Dido, in Boileau's classic definition of burlesque, were speaking like 'fishwives and porters' instead of the other way round.[3] In other words, he declined the elevation implicit in the low being raised to majestic heights. In the early 1690s, at the time of the Pindaric Odes, Swift himself apparently was translating from a passage from the *Aeneid*, while conceding to his cousin Thomas Swift (3 May 1692) that he could not 'write anything easy to be understood thô it were but in the praise of an old Shooe'.[4] The late style of the *Legion Club* is an angry version of the 'light' verse of Cotton's *Virgile Travesty*, not the majestic elevation of Pope's mock-heroic style.

In so far as the two manners were rivals, it was Pope's which established itself as the dominant voice of serious English poetry in the time Swift was writing. Swift's excellence was deemed to be in his prose, and Swift was willing to acknowledge Pope's supremacy in poetry:

In Pope, I cannot read a Line,
But with a Sigh, I wish it mine;
When he can in one Couplet fix
More Sense than I can do in Six:
It gives me such a jealous Fit,
I cry, Pox take him, and his Wit.
(*Verses on the Death of Dr Swift* (1731–9), lines 47–52)[5]

The lines pretend to illustrate the maxim that everyone envies the success of their friends and takes pleasure in their distresses, and they characteristically implicate himself in his own satire. The gesture is playful, and its 'envy' is turned into a compliment to his rival, showing Swift as after all not envious but warmly admiring, an arch intimation that he is 'not like that, really'. There was a habit of jokey self-disparagement and reciprocal compliment between the two poets. Swift wrote a poem saying Pope wrote the *Dunciad* (which is dedicated to Swift) only because Swift was too deaf to maintain conversation with him, and Pope maintained the fiction, also reporting in the *Dunciad Variorum* (1729) that 'Dr *Swift* ... may be said ... to be the Author of the Poem',[6] since he had snatched a first sketch of it from the fire. The respectful camaraderie shows a touch of narcissistic spikiness on both sides. In the lines from the *Verses on the Death*, the Shandean simper may be a natural hazard of writing one's own obituary, but it is found in some other poems, including *Cadenus and Vanessa* (1713), where self-accusation is even more elaborately self-exculpatory, and may reflect an element of subtle bad faith in otherwise attractive poems.

The loose playful informality of Swift's lines about Pope's couplet are in his favourite four-stress metre, a sophisticated adaptation of the rhythms of popular balladry somewhat removed from demotic culture. The manner derives from Samuel Butler's *Hudibras* (1663–80) and Charles Cotton's *Scarronides* (1663–5), an adaptation of Scarron's *Virgile Travesti*, in which the Virgilian story is told in low language. The tetrameter announces itself as loose, rambling, not suited to the disciplined ordering of argument or theme, and free of the structural symmetries and oppositions encouraged by the heroic couplet. Swift's verse does not aim at the tightly definitional containment of unruly forces, but at looser, more unstructured energies.

Swift's poems are the most overtly self-revealing of all his writings, and activate a deep temperamental resistance to making himself vulnerable by solemn or grandiloquent expression. 'I the lofty Stile decline', he writes in *An Epistle to a Lady* (1733, possibly written 1728) to the lady who desired him 'to make Verses on Her, in the Heroick Stile', adding that in such a style 'I Shou'd make a Figure scurvy' (lines 218–19). This ostensibly light-hearted poem offers intimate insights into his idea of himself as a poet, and contains perhaps the fullest statement of his temperamental shyness of grand poetic gestures. It also expresses an embattled and high-spirited commitment to his satirical purposes, which he saw (contrary to the stereotype) as Horatian rather than Juvenalian.

In the *Epistle*, 'Heroick' stands for the excessive compliments to ladies found in romances and love poems. Swift had already, in *Cadenus and Vanessa*, linked the 'lofty Style' with a 'high romantick Strain' (lines 796, 821), a mingling of epic pretension and erotic extravagance exploited in Pope's *Rape of the Lock*, and amicably parodied in Fielding's descriptions of heroines, where exaggerated gallantries take on a 'Homerican' blowsiness.[7] Swift, unlike Pope, could never use the idiom of 'fair-sexing' without parody or stylistic subversion, even when, as in some poems to Stella, he was expressing unqualified affection.

Swift had a profound sense of the damaging absurdity of the excessive compliments made fashionable by love poems and romances, which had passed into, and corrupted, the language of social and sexual relations. The harshest of a group of poems about women satirising this phenomenon is the *Beautiful Young Nymph Going to Bed* (1734), about a whore getting undressed. The formulaic 'horror' of this poem is its revelation that every part of the beautiful woman (teeth, hair, breasts, eye) is what we would now call prosthetic, and that their dismantling reveals a syphilitic body covered in 'Shankers, Issues, running Sores' (line 30). Part of the idea goes back to the *Battle of the Books*'s Goddess Criticism, whose filthy parts, impregnated with 'Black Juice', disintegrate and then reconstitute themselves into the writings of Bentley and his ilk, like the Nymph reassembled for the next day's work, except that the characters of the *Battle* are books and not persons.[8]

The poem follows a generic formula which goes back to classical times. The usual irony is of a good-looking woman or man whose beauty turns out to depend on an assembly of mechanical parts.[9] A variant, anthologised in W. H. Auden's *Oxford Book of Light Verse* (1938), is about a dying airman who asks his mechanics to take the cylinders out of his kidneys, the connecting-rod out of his brain, 'And assemble the engine again'.[10] The gruesomely particularised disclosures of Swift's poem may deliberately be outplaying the other writers who have toyed with this formulaic convention. Swift's horrific deadpan particularity may be a nudge and wink to the reader, implying some jokey undercutting, as in some poems where an excess of hyperbolic invective disarms itself by the exuberance of the excess itself. The poem's tone may, however, seem unrelenting, and its concluding outburst of unprocessed feeling is not easy to account for:

> *Corinna* in the Morning dizen'd,
> Who sees, will spew; who smells, be poison'd. (lines 73–4)

The irony of the subtitle, 'Written for the Honour of the Fair Sex', may or may not imply misogyny and body-hatred, but it is also concerned with the social assumptions behind 'fair sex' language. Its demonstration that women are not angels contains an element of overkill, whose character is perhaps best defined as a form of black humour. The accompanying poems in the group, *The Lady's Dressing Room* (1730), 'Strephon and Chloe' and 'Cassinus and Peter' (both written in 1731 and published with the *Beautiful Young Nymph* in 1734), each portray a young swain's dismay at the discovery that Celia shits and Chloe pisses. Since they ridicule traditions of literary expression and social outlook which pretend otherwise, much of the satire is at the expense of the discountenanced young men. The tone has a light-hearted sharpness, later imitated by Byron, and this portrait of modern courtship from 'Strephon and Chloe' has some of the easy-going geniality of *Beppo* or *Don Juan*:

> Think what a Case all Men are now in,
> What ogling, sighing, toasting, vowing!
> What powder'd Wigs! What Flames and Darts!
> What Hampers full of bleeding Hearts! (lines 33–6)

These poems have been taken, by Lawrence, Aldous Huxley and others, to express an extreme misogyny and body-hatred, and have acquired a reputation which may be as excessive as the feelings it attributes to Swift. Their emotional temperature is difficult to gauge with exactness. Their comedy is often confident and unfraught, though the *Beautiful Young Nymph* may not reflect a relaxed view of sexual issues. A concern underlying the poems is that women should receive an education which would enable them to share the same interests as men, and be taken seriously as intelligent beings on terms of mutual respect. This rational perspective did not extend to believing women were actually equal to men or could ever achieve the same level. Its objective was to provide a sounder basis for a durable friendship or marriage than the customary affectations of mindless gallantry or the seduction of impermanent physical charms.

Swift's views fall short of some wishful claims by his feminist admirers, but they do not support the imputations of radical misogyny frequently levelled at him. Their fullest expression is the prose 'Letter to a Young Lady, on her Marriage' (1723) and the poems addressed to Vanessa and Stella, his two closest female friends. Both were younger than himself, and his not fully understood relationship with them included a tutorial element. The self-exculpating and disagreeable poem *Cadenus and Vanessa* (1713–26) has found friends in some circles in the teeth of a coyly self-righteous boastfulness of its report of a young woman's passion for him. But it is Stella, rather than the vivacious Vanessa, who remained his steadiest and closest woman friend, as well as the most cherished product of his teaching. His poems to Stella on her birthday and other occasions between 1719 and her death in 1728 are a serious and deeply felt complement to the views underlying the satirical poems about Celia, Chloe and Corinna.

It is interesting to see how in these poems Swift himself slips into the conventional language of amorous compliment, as though Stella were deserving of it in a uniquely literal way. The fact reveals how deeply, as Swift himself complained, the vocabulary of fair-sexing had permeated everyday usage, but it also shows him speaking with a profound tenderness not found elsewhere in his work. Almost every poem takes up an affectionately ironic position on this stylistic matter, which was much more than merely stylistic. In the first poem, 'Stella's Birthday' (1718–19), when Stella was thirty-four, he remembered her 'at Sixteen / The brightest Virgin on the Green' (lines 5–6), and still very beautiful. Although Swift self-consciously claims, in 'To Stella, Who Collected and Transcribed his Poems', that he sang of his lady 'Without one Word of *Cupid*'s Darts, / Of killing Eyes, or bleeding Hearts' (lines 11–12), he continued to invoke with affectionate variations some of the poetic commonplaces of poetical angel worship, especially in several poignant poems describing Stella's ageing:

> Now, this is Stella's Case in Fact;
> An Angel's Face, a little crack't;
> (Could Poets or could Painters fix
> How Angels look at thirty six)
> This drew us in at first to find
> In such a Form an Angel's Mind
> And ev'ry Virtue now supplyes
> The fainting Rays of Stella's Eyes . . .
> ('Stella's Birthday' (1721), lines 15–22)

The playful but compulsive involvement with the idiom he repudiates elsewhere is parodied upwards, to a plane of higher seriousness in which the hyperbolic celebration is diverted to Stella's intellect, virtue and devotion to Swift. In his broken-hearted memoir of Stella written on the night of her death, he reported that she '. . . was looked upon as one of the most beautiful, graceful, and agreeable young women in London, only a little too fat. Her hair was blacker than a raven, and every feature of her face in perfection.'[11] This highly personal memoir was written under the stress of immediate grief, and not for publication. It is remarkable to see how, where Stella is concerned, Swift remains unable to abandon the mannerisms used, in writings he despised, for praising mistresses or describing romance heroines, while at the same time feeling compelled to deflate them without subverting his own affection. The firmness of the self-deflation is itself an index of the depth of feeling that made him adopt the language in the first place.

Swift's poems to Vanessa and Stella are more informal and more autobiographical than Pope's major poem about women, the epistle *To a Lady*. Pope's poem addressed to his friend Martha Blount and published two years after Swift's poem of the same title (1735) was subtitled *Of the Characters of Women*. For all its definitional pyrotechnics and its allure of philosophic assurance, Pope's poem concludes in precisely the mode of fair-sexing compliment Swift despised. The back-handed gallantry of Pope's argument that his addressee combines all the perfections of both sexes ('Heav'n, when it strives to polish all it can / Its last best work, but forms a softer Man')[12] might have struck Swift as a preposterous foolery if his opinion of Pope had been unfriendly or disrespectful, and if Swift hadn't himself concocted an embarrassed fiction employing this conceit on the subject of Vanessa, shown as having been created by Venus and Pallas with the virtues of both sexes. Swift offered the clarification that 'Knowledge, Judgment, Wit', bestowed on Vanessa by divine deceit, were manly virtues 'long unknown to Womankind' (*Cadenus and Vanessa*, lines 198 ff., 203–5). He said similar things about Stella without the flustered elaboration.

The discountenanced awkwardness of Swift's fable in *Cadenus and Vanessa* contrasts revealingly with the cheeky aplomb which Swift admired in Pope and avoided himself. Swift's own *Epistle to a Lady* begins, as we have seen, by dissociating Swift from the styles of exaggerated compliment supposedly desired by modern ladies. It is as though, as in the poems to Stella, Swift could only liberate himself from a style he despised by engaging with it in an ironic or critical mode. The critique embodied in Swift's *Epistle* makes it his most important statement in verse about his poetic manner and aims. It is also a political diatribe against Walpole's government, for which Swift himself was nearly arrested, and it offers an insight into the Juvenalian intensities sometimes imputed to him, which the poem itself disavows.

The mock-gallant levity with which he refuses the lady her gallant compliments, declining lofty styles and professing a laughing Horatian style, goes on to say, in an unusually abrupt transition, that his laughter at 'the Nation's Representers' is hardly amicable, and that 'I would hang them if I cou'd' (lines 156, 170):

> Let me, tho' the Smell be Noisome,
> Strip their Bums; let CALEB hoyse 'em;
> Then, apply ALECTO's Whip,
> Till they wriggle, howl, and skip. (lines 177–80)

This vitriolic escalation is remarkably lacking in the traditional majesties of satiric denunciation. It expresses not a righteous rage from on high, but lowers the satirist to the level of his victims, in an aggressive and scatological intimacy. Swift's agenda is not to crush the objects of his ire, but to torment and unnerve them from close up, setting their 'Spirits all a working' (line 206). The disclosure tells us much about the manner of *Gulliver's Travels* (1726) and its quarrelsome and somewhat panic-inducing closeness not only to its satiric victims but to a more or less victimised reader.

The lines are a true Swiftian signature, but their intensity may also be in part a joke with a straight face. His invectives of the 1730s against Irish politicians show a variant of this phenomenon:

> Traulus of amphibious Breed,
> Motly Fruit of Mungril Seed:
> By the *Dam* from Lordlings sprung,
> By the *Sire* exhal'd from Dung.
> (*Traulus: The Second Part* (1730), lines 1–4)

The *Traulus* poems (1730) and the *Legion Club* (1736) recall the drumming incantation of tribal curses, often self-consciously used by poets in purported invocations of the primitive origins of satire, designed, as Ben Jonson said, at the end of the *Poetaster*, to make the victims 'hang themselues', and to 'Rime 'hem to death, as they doe *Irish* rats / In drumming tunes'.[13] The death-dealing routines with which Irish bards killed rats or caused blisters ('blistering attacks'?) are almost certainly being remembered in Swift's attack on Traulus (the Irish politician Lord Allen), with an exuberant excess which is partly a playful surrender to the genre, and to this extent self-distancing if not self-disarming.

These extreme outbursts are in any case rare, and are as close as Swift's poems get to that 'savage indignation' which, as he claimed in the privacy of the Latin epitaph he dictated in his will in 1740, 'lacerated his heart'. He also described himself there as 'Libertatis Vindicator', the champion of liberty,[14] which W. B. Yeats, in his English poem, 'Swift's Epitaph', rendered as 'he / Served human liberty'.[15] Swift himself would never have gone public with such grandeur. The ringing lines in the *Verses on the Death of Dr Swift* are very oblique:

> Fair LIBERTY was all his Cry;
> For her he stood prepared to die;
> For her he boldly stood alone;
> For her he oft expos'd his own. (lines 347–50)

Unlike comparable self-celebrations by Pope or Yeats, this boast is spoken not by Swift but by an invented 'impartial' obituarist, and variously hedged against grandeur by levities and coded jokes that obstruct an over-solemn reading. The poem as a whole is full of genial banter about how others will react to his death: 'The Dean is dead, (*and What is Trumps*?)' (line 228). It is only in the impersonal gravity of a posthumous Latin monument, erected in St Patrick's Cathedral, Dublin, that Swift was able to claim in his own name the character of a noble defender of freedom. The epitaph shows how seriously he cared for this reputation and his reluctance to indulge the boast.

The *Verses on the Death* not only avoid the self-mythologising rhetoric of the *Epistle to Dr Arbuthnot* but shrink from the comic psychodrama with which Pope stages himself as the centre-piece of a malign confederacy of dunces (discussed in the next chapter). Such humorous grandstanding was no more Swift's style than ringing declarations, and Swift would have felt it gave him as much of a 'Figure scurvy' (*An Epistle to a Lady*, line 219) as lofty styles themselves. There is no reason to think he did not admire such things in Pope, whom, as we have seen, he regarded as a superior poetic master. Since the early days of the Scriblerus Club, of which they were the most distinguished founder members, Swift and Pope had been friends and allies in the culture wars of the time, with close personal bonds and an even closer writerly complicity. They had radically different temperaments, and indeed represent divergent types of satire, Swift's uncompromising in its portrayal of depravity and folly, rejectionist, disposed to 'vex' the reader, Pope's more confident in a notional order and addressing the reader as an accomplice rather than adversary.

Swift's relatively infrequent use of the couplet is an outward sign of such differences, but he did write some significant poems in that medium. Two of his best-known couplet poems, the 'Description of the Morning' (1709) and the 'Description of a City-Shower' (1710), were written before Pope's example had established its hegemony. The first is a mock-description of dawn parodying Virgil's *Georgics* in a 'low' urban-pastoral mode which Swift's Scriblerian associate John Gay was to make his own. The deadpan flatness of its social notation ('Duns at his Lordships Gate began to meet, / And Brickdust *Moll* had Scream'd through half the Street' (lines 13–14)) has left its mark on the early poems of T. S. Eliot, whose work as a whole has deep roots in Swift's poems. The 'City Shower', another mock-Georgic, works up to an extraordinary animation:

> Sweepings from Butchers Stalls, Dung, Guts, and Blood,
> Drown'd Puppies, stinking Sprats, all drench'd in Mud,
> Dead Cats and Turnip-Tops come tumbling down the Flood
>
> (lines 61–3)

This triplet (a couplet rounded off with an alexandrine), a form 'wholly avoided by the best Poets, since these Verses were written', parodies

'DRYDEN, and other Poets in the reign of CHARLES II'.[16] Swift's first two lines show a couplet's ability to represent an animated tumble-down disorder which is the antithesis of the orderly containments of Dryden and especially Pope, an effect accentuated by the metrical overflow of the longer third line. The alexandrine was sometimes used by seventeenth-century poets to round off a portentous point, as in Pope's parody, published the year after Swift's:

> A *needless Alexandrine* ends the Song,
> That like a wounded Snake, drags its slow length along.[17]

Swift's alexandrine was headlong, not slow, and Swift himself used the form occasionally to comic or familiar effect. But for both poets, it was an unserious metre. Though it was, in Adam Smith's words, 'the heroic verse in French', the alexandrine tended in English to the burlesque: 'Nothing would appear more absurd in English, than a tragedy written in the Alexandrine verses of the French; or in French, than a work of the same kind in verses of ten syllables.'[18]

In a sense, Swift's various experiments with longer and shorter lines were informal ways of circumventing the couplet.[19] Swift did write significant poems in couplets, but they usually avoid the definitional allure, the metrical ordering of the cæsura, the reciprocal patterning of half-lines and the tightly structured closures of rhyme, which, though not invented by Pope, became the stamp of Popeian style. When these poems were written, Pope was about to enter the limelight (the *Pastorals* appeared in 1709, and the *Essay on Criticism* in 1711). But even as Swift acknowledged Pope's mastery of the couplet's packed concentration, he would imitate neither its grandeurs nor its symmetries. Even when he does practise it, as in 'The Author upon Himself' (1714, published 1735), the tone is low-key and professes a downbeat modesty: '*S* — had the Sin of Wit, no venial Crime; / Nay, 'twas affirm'd, he sometimes dealt in Rhime' (lines 9–10), one of several revelations that he perceived his reputation as being that of a poet, though this poem's concerns are mostly with his political fortunes. A poem of vehement resentments which was not published until 1735, 'The Author upon Himself' remains one of the most interesting of his couplet poems, espousing at times a homespun narrative mode, without metrical brio, but always with a powerful, but un-Popeian, command of the form.

It contains some unprocessed self-exposure, and has an air of paying off scores. Like the *Verses on the Death of Dr. Swift*, it refers, with a somewhat mincing boastfulness, to his favour with ministers during Harley's Prime Ministership: 'And, *Harley*, not asham'd his Choice to own, / Takes him to *Windsor* in his Coach, alone' (lines 31–2). Samuel Johnson remarked on the element of abasement in Swift's pleasure at the importance conferred on him by his political masters.[20] Such sentiments appear in their most uncensored form in the intimately playful letters he wrote to Esther Johnson which are known as the *Journal to Stella*. Swift had a proudly defensive temperament, and his unguarded self-exposure in the poem can only be satisfactorily explained as a misjudgment of tone. The poem may have contained more of the vulnerable intimacy of the Stella correspondence than Swift intended. Swift clearly desired to establish that he was favoured by the nation's leaders, but the effort to avoid the risks of lofty self-celebration through a series of low-key details sometimes comes over as embarrassed. There is none of the aplomb of Pope's '*Envy* must own, I live among the Great, / No Pimp of Pleasure, and no Spy of State.'[21]

Swift was more successful in the lines spoken by an 'impartial' obituarist in the *Verses on the Death*, where he can put a more declarative stamp on some of the potentially demeaning details of his satisfaction at petty triumphs: Harley taking him in his coach, his path being cleared as if he were a duke ('The Author upan Himself', lines 27–36). Through a proxy speaker, and in cadences that continue to guard against lofty accents, he could recycle the same details into a proud refusal to be awed by titles, though even here the Popeian superbia of 'I live among the Great' is trumped by homelier preferences:

> He never thought an Honour done him,
> Because a Duke was proud to own him:
> Would rather slip aside, and chuse
> To talk with Wits in dirty Shoes.
>
> (*Verses on the Death*, lines 319–22)

The greater assurance of the *Verses* may be due to the fact that they are not in heroic couplets but in a metre paradoxically less designed to display assurance, though the earlier poem's couplets have a raw un-Popeian power of their own. A poem of the same date as the *Verses* which offers particular opportunities of observing an individual Swiftian stamp in a metre Swift preferred to leave to Pope, is 'To Mr Gay, on his Being Steward to the Duke of Queensberry' (1731), published in *Works*, 1735. Although Swift's biographer Irvin Ehrenpreis opines that it 'abounds in weaknesses', perhaps because 'the form was unsympathetic', it is one of the most substantial of Swift's couplet poems, in both length and stature.[22] Gay was (mistakenly) reported to have been offered the appointment after he had turned down a court appointment which he considered demeaning. The topic of preferment, always a touchy one with Swift, was a recurrent theme in his transactions with and writings about Gay.

The poem quickly turns into a diatribe against Walpole, which includes a set-piece portrait of the Prime Minister:

And first: To make my Observation right,
I place a ST *****AN full before my Sight.
A bloated *M——r* in all his Geer,
With shameless Visage and perfidious Leer,
Two Rows of Teeth arm each devouring Jaw;
And, *Ostrich*-like, his all-digesting Maw.
My Fancy drags this *Monster* to my View,
To show the World his chief Reverse in you.
Of loud un-meaning Sounds, a rapid Flood
Rolls from his Mouth in plenteous Streams of Mud;
With these, the Court and Senate-house he plies,
Made up of Noise, and Impudence, and Lies. (lines 31–42)

Compared with the characters of disreputable public figures in Pope's *Moral Essays* and Horatian imitations, which mostly belong to the years between the writing and publication of Swift's poem (1731–5), Swift's lines are closer to a form of demonising invective than to the rounded portraiture of the Popeian couplet. They have none of the definitional brio of Pope's portrait of Wharton or the mocking Virgilian elevation ('alas! how chang'd') of the account of the death of Buckingham,[23] discussed in the next chapter, and none of that upward contamination of loftiness pursued by Dryden and Pope through parody.

Pope's feats of summation have 'heroic' pretensions of fearless sword-wielding, more Juvenalian than Horatian, for which Swift, for all his professed *saeva indignatio*, had no appetite, just as Swift had no predilection for cameo portraiture, with its implication that depravity was amenable to easy definition. Even when apparently adopting the paired arrangements characteristic of contemporary coupleteering, Swift's gives a sense of overspilling energies rather than containment:

Two Rows of Teeth arm each devouring Jaw;
And, *Ostrich*-like, his all-digesting Maw.

Deformity and viciousness, in Pope or the prose of Fielding, appear in defiled simulation of symmetry, as when we read in Pope's *Iliad* (1715) of Thersites, whom Homer had merely described as bandy-legged and lame, that 'One Eye was blinking, and one Leg was lame',[24] Pope adding the eye to create a paired deformity. The definitional allure, and the sense of naturally ordered symmetry even in conditions of betrayal, which Pope's manner is straining after, is wholly absent in Swift, who shows in Walpole's features only a brutal chaos of menacing ugliness.

Similar things might be said about Walpole's oratory, which may again be set against that of Pope's Thersites:

> Loquacious, loud, and turbulent of Tongue:
> Aw'd by no Shame, by no Respect controul'd,
> In Scandal busie, in Reproaches bold.[25]

Again, Pope superimposes an elaborate metrical architecture, a kind of disfigured Palladian montage, on Homer's account of a garrulous malcontent, disorderly and disrespectful of speech. Swift has no Homeric model to rearrange, but, by contrast with Pope's regulated and 'heightened' sketch of the foul-mouthed barrack orator, attributes to Walpole's speech-making a fantasticating runaway grotesquerie:

> Of loud un-meaning Sounds, a rapid Flood
> Rolls from his Mouth in plenteous Streams of Mud.

Though without a Homeric original to rearrange, the passage harks back to Swift's only mock-epic work, the prose *Battle of the Books*, where the scholar Bentley's bad breath acquires, under provocation, an 'atramentous Quality, of most malignant Nature, [which] was seen to distil from his Lips'.[26] A little earlier the Goddess Criticism's effluvia of 'Black Juice' dissolve, as we have seen, in the 'Letters' of print through which Bentley and his friend express themselves. The cascading grotesquerie of the streams of mud rolling from Walpole's mouth is in vivid contrast to the measured stateliness of the *Dunciad*'s Fleet Ditch, an actual filthy stream that 'Rolls the large tribute of dead dogs to Thames'.[27] It seems possible that Swift was half-remembering Pope's line, from a poem actually dedicated to himself, in which case the difference between the two poets appears even more striking. It is conversely likely that the lurid pathos of Pope's death of Buckingham owes something to Swift, as Pope's darker grotesqueries tend to do, borrowing and transforming something of Swift's register into a shabby but orderly grandeur outside Swift's ambition or scope.

It would be interesting to know who was remembering whom, since the poets were seeing each other's work, in the cadence and thrust of Swift's:

> With these, the Court and Senate-house he plies,
> Made up of Noise, and Impudence, and Lies.

whose second line seems in dialogue with Pope's

> Poor *Cornus* sees his frantic Wife elope,
> And curses Wit, and Poetry, and Pope . . .[28]

Pope's *Epistle* was published in January of the year 'To Mr Gay' appeared in the Faulkner edition of Swift's *Works* (1735). Swift's poem, though written in 1731, had been almost certainly the subject of correspondence between Pope, Swift and Gay at the time. Either way, Swift is practising a Popeian measure without the Popeian allure of conclusive metrical domination, and his couplet almost tends to the garrulous, informal manner of his tetrameter style, where headlong rush is more evident than tight measure. While Swift writes couplets that want to be tetrameters, Pope can convey a comic hint of tripping animation ('I nod in Company, I wake at Night')[29] whose natural home might be the Swiftian tetrameter, but on to which Pope has by contrast stamped the couplet's disciplined march.

'To Mr Gay' closes with potential candidates for Walpole's job (on the accession of George II in 1727) being put off by the smell of corruption, leaving Walpole in place:

> Thus, when a greedy Sloven once has thrown
> His *Snot* into the *Mess; 'tis all his own.* (lines 161–2)

The enjambed line would be uncharacteristic in Pope (except when Pope is parodying Milton), as would the brutally laconic pay-off, which resembles that of *A Beautiful Young Nymph Going to Bed*. These abrupt accesses of seemingly unprocessed spite are not altogether characteristic of Swift either. They suggest a loss of cool, and it may be that they are unusually unguarded moments, unlikely in a writer so guarded. In view of Swift's habitual renunciation of hectoring invective, it is possible that Swift's virulent denunciation of Walpole was intended as to some extent a self-disarming rant, signalling its own excess without abandoning the animus, and that its temperature, like that of the poems about Corinna and Celia, is similarly hard to gauge.

Notes

1. Swift to Charles Wogan, July–2 August 1732 in *The Correspondence of Jonathan Swift, D. D.*, ed. David Woolley, 4 vols. to date (Frankfurt am Main: Lang, 1999–), vol. III, p. 515.
2. Claude Rawson, *Satire and Sentiment 1660–1830* (Cambridge: Cambridge University Press, 1994), pp. 74–97.
3. Nicolas Boileau, *Le Lutrin* (Paris, 1674), 'Au lecteur'.
4. *Correspondence*, ed. Woolley, vol. I, p. 111.
5. All quotations are from *Poems*, ed. Harold Williams, 3 vols., second edition (Oxford: Clarendon Press, 1958), with line numbers in parentheses.
6. 'Dr SW–– to Mr P––', pp. 405–6, *ibid.*; Alexander Pope, Appendix to *Dunciad Valiorum* (1729), in *The Dunciad (1728) and The Dunciad Valiorum (1729)*, ed. Valerie Rumbold (Harlow: Longman, 2007), p. 321.

7. Book IV, Chapter VIII of Fielding's *Tom Jones* is subtitled, 'A battle sung by the Muse in the Homerican stile . . .'
8. Jonathan Swift, *Battle of the Books* (1704), in *A Tale of a Tub*, ed. Herbert Davis (Oxford: Blackwell, 1957), p. 155.
9. Irvin Ehrenpreis, *The Personality of Jonathan Swift* (London: Methuen, 1958), pp. 43–6; Claude Rawson, *Order from Confusion Sprung: Studies in Eighteenth-Century Literature from Swift to Cowper* (London: Allen and Unwin, 1985), pp. 162–3.
10. Anon., 'The Dying Airman', in *The Oxford Book of Light Verse*, chosen by W. H. Auden (London: Oxford Clarendon Press, 1938), p. 521.
11. Jonathan Swift, 'On the Death of Mrs Johnson [Stella]' (1728), in *Miscellaneous and Autobiographical Pieces*, ed. Herbert Davis (Oxford: Blackwell, 1969), p. 227.
12. *An Epistle to a Lady*, lines 271–2, in *The Poems of Alexander Pope: A One-volume Edition of the Twickenham Text*, ed. John Butt (London: Methuen, 1963). (Henceforth *Poems*, ed. Butt.)
13. See Robert C. Elliott, *The Power of Satire: Magic, Ritual, Art* (Princeton: Princeton University Press, 1960), pp. 3–48.
14. *Jonathan Swift: A Critical Edition of the Major Works*, ed. Angus Ross and David Woolley (Oxford: Oxford University Press, 1984), pp. 603–4.
15. W. B. Yeats, 'Swift's Epitaph', in *The Major Works*, ed. Edward Larrissy (Oxford: Oxford University Press, 1997), p. 129.
16. Swift's note, quoted in *Poems*, ed. Williams, vol. I, pp. 139–40.
17. Pope, *Essay on Criticism*, lines 356–7, in *Poems*, ed. Butt, p. 155.
18. Adam Smith, *Theory of Moral Sentiments* (1759), V.i.6, ed. D. D. Raphael and A. L. Macafie (Indianapolis, IN: Liberty Fund, 1982).
19. On Swift's varied metrical forms, see Pat Rogers's introduction to *Complete Poems* (Harmondsworth: Penguin, and New Haven: Yale University Press, 1983), pp. 37–40.
20. Samuel Johnson, 'Swift', in *Lives of the Most Eminent English Poets* (1779–81), ed. Roger Lonsdale, 4 vols. (Oxford: Clarendon Press, 2006), vol. II, p. 197 (§ 52).
21. Pope, *The First Satire of the Second Book of Horace Imitated*, lines 133–4, in *Poems*, ed. Butt, p. 618.
22. Irvin Ehrenpreis, *Swift: The Man, His Works, and the Age*, 3 vols. (London: Methuen, 1962–83), vol. III, p. 701.
23. Pope, *Epistle to Allen Lord Bathurst*, line 305, in *Poems*, ed. Butt, p. 583.
24. Pope, *The Iliad*, ed. Maynard Mack (London: Methuen, 1967), Book II, line 264 (II. 217 in Homer), vol. VII, p. 140, of *The Twickenham Edition of the Poems of Alexander Pope*, gen. ed. John Butt.
25. *Ibid.*, lines 256–8.
26. Swift, *Battle of the Books*, p. 160.
27. Pope, *Dunciad*, Book II, line 272 (260 in 1729).
28. Pope, *Epistle to Arbuthnot*, lines 25–6, in *Poems*, ed. Butt, p. 598.
29. Pope, *The First Satire of the Second Book of Horace Imitated*, line 13, in *Poems*, ed. Butt, p. 614.

Chapter 18

Poetry of the first half of the eighteenth century: Pope, Johnson and the couplet

CLAUDE RAWSON

When Voltaire asked Pope why Milton had not written in rhyme, Pope replied, '*Because he could not*'.[1] The arrogance seems striking, but Dryden, who, like Pope himself, revered *Paradise Lost*, also thought Milton 'plainly' wrote it in blank verse because 'Rhyme was not his Talent'.[2] The official French assumption that the twelve-syllable alexandrine couplet was the appropriate measure for serious poems was mirrored by the status, for Dryden's or Pope's generation, of its English cultural analogue, the pentameter couplet. Pope 'translated' or 'versify'd' Chaucer or Donne, almost in the spirit in which Voltaire translated Shakespeare and Milton into rhymed alexandrines. Samuel Wesley wrote in 1700 that Chaucer's 'lines' were '*rough and unequal*' for 'our Augustan days'.[3] Pope believed that he was bringing to these unpolished English writers (who themselves wrote in couplets) some of the structural symmetry and 'correctness' which he considered the achievement of a politer age, and to which Milton sourly attributed a possibly Frenchified trendiness. There were no French poets among those Milton praised for '*Heroic Verse without Rime*', who included '*some both* Italian and Spanish *Poets of prime* note', along with classical masters.[4]

Both the alexandrine and the English heroic couplet are medieval forms, the former named after the twelfth-century *Roman d'Alexandre* (which it predates) and the latter much used by Chaucer. They were, however, seen as having been through an analogous process of refinement (which Boileau described as 'Just Weight and Measure', easy grace of diction, clarity, order and no enjambment), as the poetic currency of a 'polite' culture.[5] François de Malherbe (1555–1628), the French poet credited with the transformation, belonged to an earlier age, but Boileau's declaration of his transfiguring influence, 'Enfin Malherbe vint' (*Art Poétique*, I.131), appeared in 1674, the year of the final version of *Paradise Lost*. The more recent polishing of the English couplet by John Denham and Edmund Waller was quickly understood as a comparable breakthrough, and Waller replaces Malherbe in the adaptation by Dryden and Sir William Soames, but without the ban on enjambment (*The Art of Poetry*, I.111–46, 131).

George Puttenham, unusually, thought in 1589 that the alexandrine was 'with our moderne rimers most vsuall', and most fit 'for graue and stately matters', though not before saying first that 'The meeter of ten sillables is very stately and Heroicall'.[6] Roger Ascham said the alexandrine 'doth rather trotte and hoble than run smoothly in our English tong'.[7] On the eve of Pope's poetic career Samuel Wesley declared: 'More *num'rous* the *Pentameter* and *strong*'.[8] Adam Smith made the interesting point that the comparable status of the two metres as the standard measure for dignified verse in their respective languages also meant that each metre would be equally aberrant in the other language, tending in an equal and opposite way to the burlesque.[9] The clumsy alexandrines of the Thames-side scenes in Michael Drayton's *Poly-Olbion* lend support to Smith's point, when compared with corresponding couplets of Denham's *Cooper's Hill*, or Pope's *Windsor-Forest*, or the satirical scenes of Pope's 'silver *Thames*' in the *Rape of the Lock*, for example, or the grandly scabrous riverine purlieus of the *Dunciad*.

Pope spoke of the '*Easie Vigor* of a Line, / Where *Denham*'s Strength, and *Waller*'s Sweetness join', adding:

True Ease in Writing comes from Art, not Chance,
As those move easiest who have learn'd to dance.

(*Essay on Criticism*, lines 360–4)[10]

which evokes his sense of the urbanity and craftsmanship of the couplet form. Dryden had compared it to 'a Dance which is well-contriv'd', not a linkage which would appeal to Milton.[11]

Milton also thought rhyme an affront to English liberty, a bondage in verse that mirrored political tyranny. The contrast between English freedoms and French despotism was a national myth to which Pope subscribed in his way when he spoke with ambiguous admiration of French classical discipline:

But *Critic Learning* flourish'd most in *France*.
The *Rules*, a Nation born to serve, obeys,
And *Boileau* still in Right of *Horace* sways.
But *we*, brave *Britons, Foreign Laws* despis'd,
And kept *unconquer'd*, and *unciviliz'd*,
Fierce for the *Liberties of Wit*, and bold,
We still defy'd the *Romans*, as *of old*.

(*Essay on Criticism*, lines 712–18)

William Empson was true to the nuances when he said Pope despised the British for breaking the rules and the French even more for obeying them.[12] But the main thrust of Pope's argument proposes an unservile retention of ancient models, and approves Boileau's Horatian authority. Boileau's *Art Poétique* was a highly respected model for Pope's *Essay*, and his *Le Lutrin* (1674–83) was a generic and metrical model for the *Rape of the Lock*, even helping to shape some of the cadences of Pope's couplets. Boileau's transmission of Horatian standards implied a polite and easy correctness, paradoxically achieved by Milton's '*troublesom and modern bondage of Rimeing*', which was itself neither Horatian nor classical.[13]

Pope's remark to Voltaire expressed his sense of proprietorship over an idiom he felt he had perfected, and consolidated as the chief 'serious' style, as he became the commanding authority on poetry of his age, a role he nurtured early. The four 'Pastorals' with which he made his debut in 1709 were a way of saying 'watch this space', signposting a Virgilian progress from humble pastoral to the crowning achievement of an epic, which had become a model of lifetime achievement for important poets, including Milton. When Pope gave the name of Lycidas to the first speaker of 'Winter', an afterthought, replacing the manuscript's 'Melibœus',[14] he was probably evoking Milton's famous pastoral elegy, though both names occur in Virgil. The young Pope was positioning himself as the heir of both Virgil and Milton, the only English poet who rated as an honorary classic, and who was appropriated, with Homer and Virgil, into the great epic triad out of which Pope forged the intricate orchestrations of the *Rape of the Lock* and the urgent despondent accents of the *Dunciad*.

When Pope reprinted the Pastorals in his collected *Works* (1717), itself a mark of early prestige, he exhibited his critical authority by prefixing 'A Discourse on Pastoral Poetry', in which he took issue with the great English prototype, Spenser's *Shephearde's Calender*, though it was, 'in Mr. *Dryden*'s opinion . . . the most complete work of [the pastoral] kind which any Nation has produc'd since the time of Virgil'. He variously found Spenser wanting in classical 'simplicity' (as opposed to 'rusticity'), and objected among other things that 'the old *English* and country phrases of *Spenser* were either entirely obsolete, or spoken only by people of the lowest condition'. One of the underlying points is that 'country phrases' suggest an attempt at realistic portraiture which Pope considers inappropriate to the genre, an issue which surfaced obliquely in a recent controversy concerning the pastorals of Pope's rival Ambrose Philips, whose 'Spenserian' use of English rustics, in place of what Addison called 'antiquated fables', Pope ridiculed in an essay in 1713.[15]

Philips was promoting indigenous English settings rather than 'realism'. But Pope emphasises in the 'Discourse' that 'if we would copy Nature, it may be useful to take this Idea along with us', that in a pastoral 'we are not to describe our shepherds as shepherds at this day really are, but as they may be conceiv'd then to have been; when the best of men follow'd the employment', i.e. an Arcadian 'Golden age', free of the reek of country toil.[16] Pope's Scriblerian allies wrote parodies in which, instead of 'idly piping on oaten Reeds', the shepherds and shepherdesses milk cows, drive hogs to the sty, and weed and cut roots.[17] When Wordsworth later said that among the occupations 'dictated' and 'adorned' by 'sovereign Nature', 'Shepherds were the men that pleased me first', he explained that his shepherds lived in an exacting landscape, not 'Arcadian fastnesses' of 'Grecian song'. In saying this, however, he was taking the debate beyond realism to an alternative sense of what constitutes elevated seriousness in poetry. His shepherds were 'real', in the sense Pope disapproved, but were ennobled, not reduced, by the suffering and toil of country life, a mark of dignity and decency rather than rustic squalor.[18]

Pope's phrasing, that to 'copy Nature' expressly implies the opposite of 'naturalistic' description, presupposes a conception of Nature not as everyday reality, but as an ideal order of things, embodied in the poetic genres themselves (pastoral, as it might be, or epic, or tragedy). Defending rhyme against the charge of being unnatural, because 'no man . . . speaks in Rhyme', Dryden's Neander said that, on the contrary, rhyme was actually 'nearest the Nature of a serious Play', which 'is indeed the representation of Nature, but . . . wrought up to an higher pitch'. In this sense, 'to be like Nature, is to be set above it', by the very criterion which justifies the use of verse in plays at all. Dryden adds that if this is true of Tragedy, it is also true of Epic, and thus that 'Heroick Rhime is nearest Nature, as being the noblest kind of modern verse' (*DP*, pp. 65, 74–5, 79). This may sound sophistical as a defence of the couplet. But the fact that Dryden chose to vindicate the couplet as an illustration of the order of art brings home how much seemed at stake behind his and Pope's remarks about Milton's alleged inability to rhyme. These had as much to do with defending cultural territory as did Milton's own distaste for couplets, though Dryden was also continuing a posthumous personal debate about his 'tagging' of *Paradise Lost* in a rhymed opera.[19]

The tension, even friction, between higher and lower uses of 'nature', is much exploited in the writing of Pope's day, notably in *Gulliver's Travels*.[20] It survives in modern usage when we speak of an 'unnatural crime', even if the act was 'natural' or instinctive on the perpetrator's part. Pope's view of art as offering a higher reality than that of the visible world (more beautiful, or elevated, or of higher moral worth, or, as in comedy and satire, viewed realistically in the corrective framework of a higher standard) was generally taken for granted. The values of 'realism' and particularity, to which the novel form was beginning to give expression, were often contested in Pope's lifetime and indeed after.

The 'nature' proper to art was typically deemed to be embodied in the great classical masterworks, the creative and allusively versatile imitation of which became a standard of Augustan writing. Two years after the *Pastorals*, in *An Essay on Criticism* (1711), itself a loose imitation of Horace's *Ars Poetica* and Boileau's *Art Poétique* (1674), Pope returned to the idea of Nature, of how poems are to 'draw' on or 'copy' it, and of the role of art and its 'rules' in the process. The most telling illustration centres on the epic masterpieces, on Virgil, his dependence on his predecessor Homer, and the latter's role in the formation of rules. Pope imagines the poetic evolution of the young Virgil, drawing only 'from *Nature's Fountains*' and seeming '*above* the Critick's Law':

> But when t' examine ev'ry Part he came,
> *Nature* and *Homer* were, he found, the *same*:
> Convinc'd, amaz'd, he checks the bold Design,
> And Rules as strict his labour'd Work confine,
> As if the *Stagyrite* o'erlook'd each Line.
> Learn hence for Ancient *Rules* a just Esteem;
> To copy *Nature* is to copy *Them*. (lines 130–40)

'*Nature* and *Homer* were, he found, the *same*': the line is an early example of the elated conclusiveness which is a signature of Pope's mastery of the couplet. The emphasis here is less on definitional bravura than on the exhilaration of discovery, as though, in an old truth suddenly become vivid, a whole culture of classical loyalty had come to life. In a poem of precepts, arguing the primacy of poetry, it is one of several points where the precept becomes poetry, and where Pope's idea of 'What oft was *Thought*, but ne'er so well *Exprest*' (*Essay on Criticism*, line 298), approaches a Keatsian feeling of 'fine suddenness'. Both poets, in a way not replicated in the analogues cited by Pope's editors, are concerned with a deep instinctual return of the familiar, '*Something*, whose Truth convinc'd at Sight we find, / That gives us back the Image of our Mind' (lines 299–300), Keats's 'repetition of its own silent Working coming continually on the spirit' of the 'imaginative Mind'.[21]

After discovering that Nature and Homer were the same, however, Virgil starts writing, not like Homer, but 'As if the *Stagyrite* o'erlook'd each Line', a remarkable transition which ostensibly equates or even subordinates the poetic model to the critic's teaching. The reasoning behind this startling upward slippage of 'the Critick's Law' is that, as the embodiment of primary poetic principles, it takes you straight to the heart of the poetry, which is in turn presumed to be the foundation of traditional canons of taste. Aristotle acquires this authority because he had, in the first place, codified his 'rules' from the poet's example, not the other way round ('Those RULES of old *discover'd*, not *devis'd*, / Are *Nature* still, but *Nature Methodiz'd*', lines 88–9). Pope is not exposing Virgil's pedantic subservience, but expressing the writerly concern that made Ben Jonson remark that Aristotle had 'not only found out the way not to erre, but the short way we should take not to erre'. Jonson copied the remark from the Latin of the Dutch humanist Heinsius ('neque viam tantum ne aberret, sed & habeat compendium qua eat'), adding to it a flavour of working applicability, which illustrates how, in a culture of consensual reverence for ancient masters and their later disciples, an established idea, even a truism, might have a fresh and renewable vitality.[22]

It was not because of Homer's lifelikeness that Pope found that '*Nature* and *Homer* were . . . the *same*'. The Homeric realism about bloody battles was a feature of ancient epic which made Pope and others uneasy. Pope was at pains to distinguish Homer from his brutal subject matter, partly on the grounds that the poetry transposed it to a higher plane. Aristotle's critical certification of the Homeric model, by a remarkable upward slippage, is redefined as a summary version of the poet's creative act. Elevated expression, for which epic poetry was the highest model, is one aspect of 'methodising' Nature in which poet and critic, in those mighty prototypes, were collaboratively engaged. Pope doubtless felt that he was adding the civilising properties of rhyme to this process.

Copying nature, then, is what epic poets do when, like pastoral poets, they are being the opposite of naturalistic. In this sense also, Pope's 'Pastorals' are in active, though modest, relationship with the epic aspiration. Their methodising consists of removing roughness and rusticity, streamlining the structure, prettification. Their charm resides in an exquisite slightness, and indeed in their interest in the exquisiteness of nature's own processes. Delicate motions of winds and trees, quiverings of light and shadow contending for dominion, are presented as an elegant ballet of unruly forces, subordinated or amenable to an ordering which partly evokes old notions of harmony in discord (*discordia concors rerum*), but whose satisfactions are still, at this early stage, somewhat ornamental.

This ordering self-consciously grows in substance in *Windsor-Forest* (1713), set in the same lightly mythologised Thames-side landscape:

> Here Hills and Vales, the Woodland and the Plain,
> Here Earth and Water seem to strive again,

> Not *Chaos*-like together crush'd and bruis'd,
> But as the World, harmoniously confus'd:
> Where Order in Variety we see,
> And where, tho' all things differ, all agree.
> Here waving Groves a checquer'd Scene display,
> And part admit and part exclude the Day;
> As some coy Nymph her Lover's warm Address
> Nor quite indulges, nor can quite repress. (lines 11–20)

The natural landscape of the 'Pastorals', with similar tensions and contrarieties, is more grandly reformulated as 'Order in Variety', but remains a slenderly apprehended harmony which, in reality, projects a poetic predilection for containment more than an active faith in the substantive coherence of things. The perceived tensions remain slight, a regulated and stylised to-ing and fro-ing rather than large centrifugal energies brought under control. The nymph's coy treatment of the lover, nor quite indulging nor quite repressing, looks forward to *The Rape of the Lock*, much as the dance of the waving groves looks back to the 'Pastorals'. The composition, in which horizontals and verticals (lawns and trees, plains and hills) alternate in a lavish orchestration of colours, reflects a painterly disposition which led Pope, soon after, to take painting lessons from his friend and portraitist, the painter Charles Jervas. Getting himself painted was a lifetime enterprise for Pope, who became the most painted poet of his day.[23]

Windsor-Forest, however, also gives notice of a more substantial perspective:

> Here *Ceres'* Gifts in waving Prospect stand,
> And nodding tempt the joyful Reaper's Hand,
> Rich Industry sits smiling on the Plains,
> And Peace and Plenty tell, a STUART reigns. (lines 39–42)

The poem incorporates a history of English valour, liberty and prosperity, and a defence of the imminent Peace of Utrecht (which ended the War of the Spanish Succession), denounced by opponents of Oxford's Tory administration, but here presented as a glorious climax, emblematic of the (actually nearly extinct) Stuart succession. It was also an expression of solidarity with the Prime Minister, a member of the Scriblerus coterie, whose other members included Swift, Gay, Arbuthnot and Thomas Parnell, all of whom also wrote in defence of the Peace.

Windsor-Forest marks Pope's first prominent move beyond a poetry where, as he was to say in the *Epistle to Dr Arbuthnot*, 'pure Description held the place of Sense' (line 148, and see lines 339–40), to the weightier moral and political concerns which Pope thought were 'the very distinguishing Excellence' of *Cooper's-Hill* (1642), Sir John Denham's influential historical landscape poem and Pope's analogue to Virgil's *Georgics* in his progress from pastoral to epic.[24]

This reminder of self-development is part of a crafted self-image, also retrospectively registered in the later poems. While the grand narrative is Virgilian, several apologias for Pope's poetic career broadly derive from the first satire of Horace's second book, a generic ancestor of the *Epilogue to the Satires* (1738), and the specific original of Pope's *First Satire of the Second Book of Horace, Imitated* (1733), the first poem in his Horatian series. 'Autobiography' is here limited by a traditional rhetoric of self-portrayal, at a distance from confessional intimacy, and specifically authorised by the Horatian example. Such cover was built into 'poetical imitation', in which the ancient model purportedly supplied the substantial framework, removing responsibility (e.g. for any appearance of arrogance) from the imitator's shoulders, while at the same time providing the basis for ironic variations and arresting parallels between the old poem and the new.

In the first satire of the second book, Horace's lawyer friend Trebatius advises him to curtail his satiric activity, which may, for example, offend the powerful. He tells him, in a single word, to keep quiet ('quiescas'), and the poet asks if that means not writing poems, to which the lawyer replies yes ('Aio'). Horace says he can't sleep ('verum nequeo dormire', Satires II.I.4–7),[25] three words for which Pope takes more than three lines:

> Not write? but then I *think*,
> And for my Soul I cannot sleep a wink.
> I nod in Company, I wake at Night,
> Fools rush into my Head, and so I write. (lines 11–14)

Pope's imitations were printed with the original Latin on the facing page, to enable the reader to spot additions, variations and parallels. Insomnia is sometimes invoked by satirists to show how the foolishness and wickedness of the world or even its noise keep them or others awake.[26] Horace may be implying this, but he does not say it, only that he writes to pass away the night. Pope, however, says it for him, while freely showing the reader that Horace didn't. Where Horace holds back from self-mythologising, Pope adds a billowing psychodrama of comic discomfiture. Although Pope sometimes elaborates on his classical originals with grandiose or mock-pompous periphrases, the effect here is not inflation or ornament, but additional matter and a new affect.

Pope may have got the idea of the swarming fools from Juvenal's first satire, also in its way a response to Horace's poem. Describing the proliferation of bad poets infesting Rome ('cum tot ubique / vatibus'), Juvenal says it's a false kindness not to write (Satire I, lines 17–18). His irritation with the invasive confederacy of dunces has something of the same pantomime of embattled helplessness. Pope exhibits an even more literal self-centredness, however, placing himself (or the inside of his head) in the middle of a vast massing of fools, an overheated comedy somewhat different from Juvenal's mighty indignations or self-mocking irritabilities. Both poets become the victimised magnets of the world's fools and knaves, but Pope's insomnia is his own, foreshadowing the self-cherishing fuss we sometimes call Shandean.

The opening of the *Epistle to Dr. Arbuthnot* also recalls Juvenal's swarms of poets. A throng of would-be poets and poetical groupies are besieging Pope's villa, clamouring for the master's attention or support. Pope addresses his servant:

> Shut, shut the door, good *John!* fatigu'd I said,
> Tye up the knocker, say I'm sick, I'm dead,
> The Dog-star rages! nay 'tis past a doubt,
> All *Bedlam*, or *Parnassus*, is let out:
> Fire in each eye, and Papers in each hand,
> They rave, recite, and madden round the land ... (lines I–6)

This time, the fools are rushing into the poet's house instead of his head, but their wild vitality is similar. The scene is broadly reminiscent of Horace besieged by importunate suitors (*Satires* II.vi), where he appears exposed to unwelcome solicitations for influence or information because of his perceived influence in high places, which he professes to minimise while making sure we know about it. It also recalls Juvenal's hyperactive poetasters 'reciting in ... August' (Satire I, line Iff.; Satire 3, line 9), the dog days, *canicula*, being a time for poetry recitations in Rome, a theme taken up by Dryden and Byron as well as Pope, which calls to mind the lunacy of Noel Coward's mad dogs and Englishmen going out in the midday sun.[27]

But neither Roman poet places these nuisances at or near the poet's own residence, with himself as a beleaguered celebrity. Pope's opening, 'Shut, shut the door, good *John!*', has the same cantankerous theatricality as the lines on insomnia. It might almost be said to be playing with a specifically theatrical issue raised by Dryden's Crites, who says that it is impossible, 'with any grace', 'to call a Servant, or bid a door be shut in Rhime'. Dryden's spokesman Neander retorted that Seneca (*Hippolytus*, line 863) could make opening a door 'sound high and lofty' by saying what Dryden translates as 'Set wide the Palace gates' (*DP*, pp. 67, 78). Pope's stylisation works through wit and rhyme rather than heroic elevation, the 'heightening' proper to a 'middle style', imposing an order of art on the idiom of daily life. But it places the opening spotlight on a dramatically personalised discomfiture, organised to display Pope's super-celebrity status. The fluster is never allowed to suggest that the poet is deriding himself, and the Shandean self-regard merges with a bid for attention of a more majestic order, characteristically Popeian.

The imitator of Horace, as has often been remarked, is here writing with a fervour closer to and perhaps exceeding Juvenal's, while the reputedly Juvenalian Swift actually favoured a low-key Horatian informality. In his fight for virtue, Pope wields a quill which recalls the swords (*stilus, ensis*) of both Horace and Juvenal,[28] but omits to say that these poets were referring not to themselves, but to the fearless Lucilius. Pope's exclamation, 'Satire's my Weapon' (*First Satire of the Second Book of Horace*, line 69), for once briefer than Horace, is completely disencumbered from the competing evocation of a satirical ancestor whom Roman satirists looked up to as a model. Describing himself, in small capitals, as being 'TO VIRTUE ONLY AND HER FRIENDS, A FRIEND' (line 121), with the Latin, this time in full capitals, on the facing page: 'UNI ÆQUUS VIRTUTI ATQUÆ EJUS AMICIS' (Horace, line 70), Pope again transfers to himself words that Horace had applied to Lucilius, reinforcing the non-parallel typographically. Though he is a looming presence in both Roman poets, Lucilius is not named at all in Pope's poem. A little later, Pope uses the facing page to bring out another non-parallel:

And who unknown defame me, let them be
Scriblers or Peers, alike are *Mob* to me

(*First Satire*, lines 139–40)

This stinging orchestration of lordly accents putting down lords is an English 'Augustan' hauteur, neither Horatian nor Juvenalian, with the Latin counterpart visibly missing.

In a late poem, *One Thousand Seven Hundred and Thirty Eight* (1738, better known as the *Epilogue to the Satires*), also modelled on the same Horatian original, a Friend attempts to moderate the satirist's aggressive self-righteousness, calling him 'strangely proud' (II.197–205). Pope's reply has a more self-affirming grandiloquence even than Juvenal's:[29]

So proud, I am no Slave:
So impudent, I own myself no Knave:
So odd, My Country's Ruin makes me grave.

Yes, I am proud; I must be proud to see
Men not afraid of God, afraid of me. (II.205–9)

Pope renamed this poem *Epilogue to the Satires* in his collected *Works* of 1740, designing it as the conclusion of a definitive ordering of his Imitations of the 'SATIRES and EPISTLES of *Horace*'. The cycle thus ends, as it began, with a glowing self-exaltation. Although such accents are not to everyone's taste, they belong to a received style, and did not seem improper even to Swift, though he shrank from them in his own name, as he shrank from the heroic couplets he unreservedly admired in Pope. Pope would expect to be understood as affirming his public character as a poet rather than describing his private self. These displays of the poet's high calling not only have longstanding classical precedents. They survive in writers less attuned to traditionally prescribed rhetorical roles. Yeats, who disliked Pope, held the view that poets who shrank from high talk were underselling poetry, and the arrogant sweep of some of his poems has Popeian cadences, with lofty accents to match.

This poetic chutzpah, partly side-stepped by Horace though implicit in Juvenal, is an affirmation of command, also manifested in Pope's case in the definitional triumphalism of the *Moral Essays* and *Essay on Man*, where turbulent and conflicting energies of personality and circumstance are submitted to a display of explanatory power: 'And, spite of Pride, in erring Reason's spite, / One truth is clear, "Whatever is, is RIGHT"' (I.293–4). Such hammer-blow affirmations, which close each section of the *Essay on Man*, can be grating. They are not intended to imply that the world is a happy place, but that there is an order which ensures that ostensible evils have a purpose, often invisible, but reflecting the omnipotent beneficence of the Deity. The claim is circular and self-validating. Such theodicies were satirised by Voltaire in *Candide* and Samuel Johnson in *Rasselas*, where any suggestion that we live in the best of all possible worlds is subjected to ridicule by the realities of catastrophe or misery, however much the technical argument can be logically defended. The poem was a self-imposed exercise to explain the universal order without support from any scriptural or Church teaching, and shows little philosophical engagement. It did not appeal to orthodox religious thinkers of either the Protestant or Catholic faiths any more than to irreverent rationalists like Voltaire, and Pope was subjected to some vociferous theological belabouring.

The poem is nevertheless impressive for the gusto and virtuosity with which Pope takes on the issues of evil, disaster and confused and dissatisfied mental states, and brings them within the scope of his system, as in these replies to those who complain of shortcomings of the human body:

Why has not Man a microscopic Eye?
For this plain reason, Man is not a Fly.
Say what the use, were finer optics giv'n,
T'inspect a mite, not comprehend the heav'n?
Or touch, if tremblingly alive all o'er,
To smart and agonize at ev'ry pore?
Or quick effluvia darting thro' the brain,
Die of a rose in aromatic pain? (I.193–200)

The breathless slapping down ('For this plain reason, Man is not a Fly') has a triumphalist vitality which makes it more than a series of easy rebuttals. The description of exquisitely refined torments ('To smart and agonize at ev'ry pore', 'quick effluvia darting thro' the brain'), goes beyond Pope's early delicate capturing of evanescent movement. The half-jeering 'Die of a rose in aromatic pain' shows the debating point transfigured into poetry of a high order, in a different class from its supposed verbal sources in Dryden and Lady Winchilsea.[30]

These spurts of conclusiveness are more important for Pope than the 'philosophy' they are meant to support. The opening of Epistle II (lines 1–18) revels in the contradictions of the human animal, traditionally positioned on the Great Chain of Being between the bestial and the divine. The declamatory superbia of the concluding judgment, that the human cauldron of paradoxes is 'The glory, jest, and riddle of the world!', is locally or rhetorically triumphal, even as it seems to intimate defeat. The bravura exposition of contending forces in this poem and the associated *Moral Essays* (1731–5) is remarkable. The complexity of the universe, the differing perspectives of observers, the variability and evanescence of the phenomena needing to be captured as they fly, are enumerated with such gusto that they seem set up for resolution, as surely as a mock-heroic crescendo is programmed for deflation. The obstacles to definition have a definitional allure in themselves.

The *Moral Essays* are concerned with human behaviour in a narrower psychological or social frame. In the opening *Epistle to Cobham* (1733), 'Of the Characters of Men', Pope's priority is again to describe the intractability of his topic:

That each from other differs, first confess;
Next, that he varies from himself no less . . . (lines 19–20)

The passage quickens with every example, from the first condensed listing, through an escalation that takes in the subjectivity of the viewer, the gap between 'the optics seeing' and 'the object seen', and finally the depths and shallows, 'Quick whirls, and shifting eddies, of our minds' (lines 21–30). *Windsor-Forest*'s modest centrifugal energies, and the reassurances of a 'World, harmoniously confus'd' (lines 13–19), give way to a chaos that is darker and more painfully turbulent, but where a notional order remains a *donnée*, if only as an act of poetic aplomb. Confronting the wayward complexity of human beings, Pope offers, in place of theodicy, a psychological concept known as the Ruling Passion, already outlined in *Essay on Man*, II.123–44, and partly derived from the old humoural psychology.[31] Each person has a ruling passion which determines all their behaviour. If a person's ruling passion is greed, this might equally explain an act of aggression at one time, and of passive acquiescence at another. Other persons might be motivated by a different passion to commit the same acts. The trick is to discover the key:

> Search then the Ruling Passion: There, alone,
> The Wild are constant, and the Cunning known. (lines 174–5)

The psychology is threadbare. Its application to the poem's noble dedicatee, whose ruling passion is love of his country (lines 262–5), is predictable dedicationese, reappearing in another form in the complementary *Epistle to a Lady*. The assertions of psychological infallibility, 'This clue once found, unravels all the rest, / The prospect clears, and Wharton stands confest' (lines 178–9), play a similar role to the assertive abstractions of the *Essay on Man* ('All Discord, Harmony, not understood', I.291). But the stinging power of the portrait of the vain and unstable Duke of Wharton is fuelled by Pope's mixture of explanatory certainty and driven triumphalism (lines 174–209).

Wharton's portrait is partly modelled on Dryden's Zimri, one of the great prototypes in English of the satirical verse portrait. Zimri's original, the Duke of Buckingham, reappears in a lurid (but unhistorical) death-scene in Pope's *Epistle to Bathurst* (1733):

> In the worst inn's worst room, with mat half-hung,
> The floors of plaister, and the walls of dung,
> On once a flock-bed, but repair'd with straw,
> With tape-ty'd curtains, never meant to draw,
> The George and Garter dangling from that bed
> Where tawdry yellow strove with dirty red,
> Great Villiers lies – alas! how chang'd from him
> That life of pleasure, and that soul of whim! (lines 299–306)

This extraordinary account of a degraded and undignified end, its shabby grandeur accentuated by the Virgilian and Miltonic resonances of 'alas! how chang'd from him', is a distillation of mock-heroic style which looks forward to Johnson's account of the death of Charles XII.

Pope's virtuosity is thus more strikingly on display in individual portraiture than in the unfolding of grand designs, necessary as these seem as fuel for exhilarated summations. The opening of the *Essay on Man* tells us that, although the 'mighty maze' of his subject matter is 'not without a plan' (line 6), it is in the first place a maze, and a mighty one. The 'plan' is the poet's pay-off, but the exercise depends not on systems of cosmology or psychology, but on specific poetic containments, in individual lines, couplets, paragraphs and character sketches, whose validations are local and cumulative. They thrive on a sense of strenuously recalcitrant material and reside more in the penetrating paradoxes of the portraits than in the declarative abstractions which frame them.

These make a particularly giddy appearance in *To a Lady: Of the Characters of Women* (1735):

> Nothing so true as what you once let fall,
> 'Most Women have no Characters at all.' (lines 1–2)

This provocative outburst contradicts from the start the entire system of psychology proposed in the preceding *Epistle to Cobham*. It is itself variously contradicted, by successive statements that women ('like variegated Tulips') are changeable (lines 41–2); that 'In Men, we various Ruling Passions find, / In Women, two almost divide the kind' (lines 207–8); that 'Men, some to Bus'ness, some to Pleasure take; / But ev'ry Woman is at heart a Rake' (lines 215–16); that 'Woman's at best a Contradiction still' (line 270); and finally, in a compliment to the addressee, which takes her altogether outside the system, and, in another flourish of dedicationese, makes of her Heaven's 'last best work . . . a softer Man', a distillation of all the best qualities of both men and women (lines 271–80).

The encompassing formula of the ruling passion here dissolves in a philosophic incoherence which nevertheless manages to provide a frame for remarkable accesses of perception. The portrait of Atossa (lines 115–50) ranks with the account of Wharton, or of Atticus and Sporus in the *Epistle to Dr Arbuthnot*, in its vivid apprehension of contradictory and perverse personalities. Another example is Narcissa, whose benign 'nature' conceals a callousness on which the poet descends with feline ferocity:

> Narcissa's nature, tolerably mild,
> To make a wash, would hardly stew a child;
> Has ev'n been prov'd to grant a Lover's pray'r,
> And paid a Tradesman once to make him stare. (lines 53–6)

Shorter portraits also deal, in a series of cameo triumphs, with people who, like Flavia, 'purchase Pain with all that Joy can give, / And die of nothing but a Rage to live' (lines 99–100), or who otherwise operate outside the expected laws of nature. Play is made of 'natural' arrangements gone into reverse, as often in Swift or Fielding, though the downbeat acerbities of Swift's prose contrast sharply with Pope's definitional elations.

A shallower play of female contradiction is the contrast of Sappho 'at her toilet's greasy task' with her social appearance, 'fragrant at an ev'ning Mask' (lines 25–6), its brio fuelled by the poet's hostility to his one-time friend, Lady Mary Wortley Montagu (1689–1762), a distinguished woman of letters better remembered for her correspondence than for her own poetical works, which include squibs against Pope, Swift and their circle, where she might have thought she was giving as good as she got.[32]

The *Essay on Man* and *Moral Essays* were conceived as portions of a comprehensive philosophical poem Pope thought of as his 'opus magnum', a work of Lucretian scope which, like Pope's planned epic on Brutus, remained unconsummated.[33] The word 'Essay' points in two directions. It suggests an informal sketch, as in the free-ranging pieces of Montaigne or Bacon, who called them 'dispersed Meditacions'.[34] But by the time of Locke's *Essay Concerning Human Understanding* (1689), the term could assume the connotations of a major treatise. Pope's *Essay on Criticism*, loosely modelled on Horace's epistolary *Ars Poetica*, already combined an air of law-giving authority with an element of conversational discursiveness. In the *Essay on Man*, Pope refers self-consciously to his adoption of 'the Epistolary Way of Writing . . . notwithstanding his Subject was high and of dignity' ('To the Reader'). The *Essay* is divided into 'Epistles', not 'Books', which were collected in 1734 as 'The First Book of Ethic Epistles', as though simultaneously affirming and shrinking from its pretensions to comprehensive coverage. The *Moral Essays* were once labelled 'Ethic Epistles, the Second Book', but in 1739 Pope preferred to group them with other epistles as 'Epistles to Several Persons'.[35]

The fact that the 'opus magnum' was never completed was doubtless attributable to the large cultural changes which made comprehensive philosophical poems on the scale of Lucretius virtually impossible for good poets to write, as the epic had become impossible to write. A loosening sense of universal coherence, however emphatically asserted, a progressive fragmentation of faiths, vast accretions of knowledge in the particulars of the universe, could not be expected to sustain confident or consensual articulations of a universal vision, in much the same way as the evolution of bourgeois society and the growth of anti-war sentiment made it harder for good poets to write epics. That Pope attempted both is a reflection of his poetic ambition, but that he failed to complete either reflects the sureness of his talent.

The epic aspiration survived to the end with a heroic poem on Brutus, the founder of Britain, an ambitious project of which only a few lines survive. They are in blank verse, with Miltonising aspirations, but otherwise conditioned by the end-stopped couplet.[36] On the available evidence, this would have been more concerned with didactic discourses than heroic action, and was variously bound up with the 'opus magnum'. The overtly discursive *Essay on Man* opens with Miltonic evocations. Pope's ambition to 'vindicate the ways of God to Man' (I.16), alludes to Milton's claim to 'justifie the wayes of God to men'.[37] Pope's use of 'vindicate', and 'Man' rather than 'men', strikes a militant note, perhaps reflecting poetic and doctrinal edginess, and a provocative feeling of 'tagging' Milton into couplets. But the words put down an epic marker, while pursuing the epic ambition by discursive rather than narrative means. The *Essay*'s closing boast of having progressed as a poet 'From sounds to things, from fancy to the heart' (IV.392) is another reminder of that developmental self-consciousness already evident in the early poems.

This Virgilian conception of a 'progress' differs from the model of poetic maturing and change found in Romantic and later poets, in Wordsworth's 'Immortality Ode', Coleridge's 'Dejection' and several poems by Wallace Stevens and Yeats, where self-renewal rather than 'progression' is presupposed. The change from child to man, or from one state of mind to another, called for a new style to reflect an altered being. The older scenario of self-development still envisaged by Pope was not a transformative one, but 'progressive' through broadly prescribed stages, from slighter to weightier undertakings. The path prescribed by a pastoral debut was foreseeable from the start, laid down by centuries of cultural consensus rather than determined by particularities of personal change.

That he discarded his youthful attempts, and did not execute his mature plan for an epic, testifies to the fact, as previously mentioned, that, after *Paradise Lost*, for reasons deeply embedded in the changing culture, epics were no longer possible for good poets. It was bad poets, like the Biblical and patriotic epic writers derided by Boileau in France, or like Sir Richard Blackmore in England, who wrote epics, while good poets, like Dryden or Pope, were clear-sighted enough to know they could not. They saw the recent attempts as an expression of 'modern' arrogance, and Blackmore as an example of what to avoid. The lag between a passionately retained conviction that epic was the highest genre, and the sense that a good epic was no longer achievable, is an animating fact of Pope's career. The aspiration was never abandoned, but Pope could only realise it by proxy, by a translation of Homer, or through a protective filter of irony, in the recently developed genre of mock-heroic, which Pope perfected in *The Rape of the Lock* (1712–17) and *The Dunciad* (1728–43).

Pope had attempted and destroyed a youthful epic, 'Alcander, Prince of Rhodes'. Even in this he followed the example of Virgil, who was said to have begun 'writing a poem of the *Alban* and *Roman* affairs; which he found above his years', before 'descending' to pastoral.[38] By the time of *Windsor-Forest*, Pope had already begun the two epic-related enterprises which were to take the place, in his poetic progress as in Dryden's before him, of an epic of his own. One was translation. As Dryden completed his career with a great translation of Virgil, in addition to the first book of the *Iliad*, Pope had, at the beginning of his career, modelled himself on the mature Dryden, translating episodes from Homer and Statius, and preparing the ground for his translations of both the *Iliad* (1715–20) and *Odyssey* (1725–6), which are distinguished expressions by proxy of a heroic voice he could not achieve in his own name.

At the same time, his first exercise in mock-heroic, 'The Rape of the Locke' (with an 'e'), a two-canto version, had appeared in a miscellany in 1712, and the five-canto *The Rape of the Lock* in 1714. The story revolves around a real-life incident of the cutting off ('rape') of a lock of the heroine's hair, which triggered a disproportionate social imbroglio. The title was suggested by Tassoni's *La Secchia Rapita* ('stolen bucket', 1622), subtitled *Poema eroicomico*, and sometimes considered the first real mock-heroic. 'Rape' principally means 'theft' or 'abduction', though Pope exploits a jokey sexual charge in keeping with a sustained atmosphere of double entendre in the poem as a whole. Pope's most important model, however, was Boileau's *Le Lutrin* (1674–83), which recounts an epic dispute over the positioning of a church pulpit. Boileau claimed to introduce a 'new burlesque', in which high language is used by and about low people, instead of the other way round, as in Paul Scarron's popular *Virgile Travesti* (1648–53), adapted into English by Charles Cotton as *Scarronides* (1664–5).

Dryden explained the significance of Boileau's distinction by arguing that the parody in which low people talked high allowed the 'the Majesty of the Heroique' to rub off on the parody, giving it something of the elevation of heroic poetry itself, thus approximating to the genre it parodied.[39] The older burlesque, on the other hand, in which Dido and Aeneas are made to speak like fishwives and porters, merely brought the level down.[40] An example from the English *Scarronides* shows how the majestic opening of the *Aeneid* ('Arma virumque cano', or 'Arms, and the Man I sing')[41] is reduced to the demotic coarseness of:

> *I Sing the Man*, (read it who list,
> A *Trojan*, true, as ever pist).[42]

By contrast, *The Rape of the Lock* inflates rather than deflates:

> What dire Offence from am'rous Causes springs,
> What mighty Contests rise from trivial Things,
> I sing. (I.I–3)

For Dryden, as for Boileau and Pope, the object was to find an idiom in which the epic aspiration could be entertained even when it seemed no longer possible to write straight epic. A style which ironically misapplied grandiloquent speech to a lowered modern reality offered the protections of irony, and made possible a form of parody that did not mock the original so much as pay tribute to it.

Pope's *Rape of the Lock* concludes with a battle of the beaux and belles, a comic enactment of the war of the sexes whose notional prototype is a lost epic of a war between Amazons and heroes. It is announced that no blood will be shed:

> No common Weapons in their Hands are found,
> Like Gods they fight, nor dread a mortal Wound. (V.43–4)

The reassurance mimics Milton's declaration that the combatants in the War in Heaven are 'Incapable of mortal injurie',[43] since all are celestial beings, whose wounds, as in Homer's gods, are quickly repairable. The Sylph in the *Rape*, cut 'in twain' between the fatal shears that severed Belinda's lock, is instantly reconstituted because 'Airy Substance soon unites again' (III.151–2). Milton, who had, within his own poem, deplored the epic's implication in the disasters of war, managed to retain the epic subject while preserving himself from the heroic taint of human carnage. Pope, and others who picked up Milton's trick, were, on the other hand, minimising the reminder of carnage, and more protective of the epic than of themselves. Mock-heroic is a loyalist form.

The engagements, sieges, conquests and deaths in Pope's poem are erotic rather than military. No one dies except in the sexual sense, or when suitors are killed by a mistress's look or frown (V.64, 68). Thalestris of the Amazon name 'scatters Deaths around from both her Eyes' (V.58). The traditional military metaphors of love poetry are wittily appropriated in a mock-literal sense, so that an erotic conquest or death is described as though it were an epic combat: 'She smil'd to see the doughty Hero slain / But at her Smile, the Beau reviv'd again' (v.67–70). The continuous double entendre which derives from the comic splicing of two poetic genres is complemented by another received double entendre in which those who die in love can rise again in resurrection.

The battle which, in more than one sense, is the climax of the story, is manifestly stripped of bodily harm. It jokily allegorises that war of the sexes whose essential rhythms of resistance and attraction were sketched in *Windsor-Forest*'s 'coy Nymph', exposing through these transgressive pranks the sexual reality beneath the elegant social forms. The satire is essentially loyalist, however, sizing up both silliness and sin, but responsive to the 'graceful Ease, and Sweetness void of Pride' (I.15) in which social elegance merges into a kind of moral grace.

The poem offers a textbook application of high language to low subject, with a programmed deflation. Protracted rants, for example, are set up for a fall, as when 'Not youthful Kings in Battel seiz'd alive, / Not scornful Virgins who their Charms survive', nor a further series of similarly distressed persons,

> E'er felt such Rage, Resentment and Despair,
> As thou, sad Virgin! for thy ravish'd Hair, (IV.1–10)

A project in which mock-heroic was to elevate satire into a species of heroic poetry is not, however, mainly defined by deflation, as *The Dunciad* shows, though even that poem has its genial relaxations. Its main point is often not the insignificance of an ignoble subject matter but its enormity. Dryden described his knaves and dunces as bloated monsters, 'Monumental Brass',[44] a phrase Pope appropriated in *The Dunciad* II.313, along with *Mac Flecknoe*'s 'dunces' (line 31), who have a commanding monumentality 'Through all the Realms of *Non-sense*, absolute' (line 6), seemingly capable of dominating the culture. The resonances of epic are used in a negative rather than diminished way, claiming not disproportion but an obscene simulacrum. The vision of cultural break-down at the end of *The Dunciad* brings the Miltonic inferno to London in order to suggest that the modern reality has comparable dimensions of evil, helping to inaugurate through epic imitation an image of the great city as hell that reverberates in the poetry of Shelley, Baudelaire and T. S. Eliot.

Like the *Rape*, *The Dunciad* plays with the customary generic episodes of epic (heroic games for example, or the replay of Aeneas's westward voyage), and has every stylistic routine or mannerism, though unlike the *Rape* it altogether omits any suggestion of combat, the principal epic subject. There are no mock-battles, however slight, and no bloodshed. Although it has none of the *Rape*'s playful deflations, the poem also accommodates remarkable accesses of geniality towards the enemy: the surreal beauty of bad poems (I.72–8), the boyish pranks of the Games in Book II, the busy and not ungenial vacuousness emanating intermittently from the prose subplot about Cibber in Pope's notes. These sometimes point towards an embryonic novelistic subtext, in which subheroic figures become in their way attractive as well as stupid or bad, and the comparison with heroes not only carries the sense of a lowered modern life, but subversively intimates that the failure to be heroic may be not unattractive in its own right.

The derision showered on the dunces in countless satirical sequences, the comedy of disproportion which shows the dunces at childish play or in ignoble postures, coexists with a dominant note of polluted grandeurs that go beyond the joke. An example is the scene in which the dunces 'descend' past Bridewell,

> To where Fleet-ditch with disemboguing streams
> Rolls the large tribute of dead dogs to Thames. (II.271–2)

The processional grandeur is disgusting but hardly 'reduced'. The majestic degradation contrasts sharply with Swift's animated focus on the low vitality of a similar set of phenomena: 'Drown'd Puppies, stinking Sprats, all drench'd in Mud, / Dead Cats and Turnip-Tops come tumbling down the Flood'.[45]

It is in the doom-laden finale that *The Dunciad* achieves its most sustained piece of mirthless enormity, as the culture reverts (literally) to Milton's primal Chaos:

> Lo! thy dread Empire, CHAOS! is restor'd;
> Light dies before thy uncreating Word:
> Thy hand, great Anarch! lets the curtain fall,
> And Universal Darkness buries All. (IV.653–6)

The heroic couplet has seldom been brought to such a pitch of elevated gravity and urgency in a satirical context. But in the progress towards making mock-heroic a species of heroic poetry itself, the poem's evident impulse to go beyond the mock-heroic joke is frustrated by the assumption that a heroic voice can only be achieved by a form that parodies it.

The possibility of underisive elevation in high satire was perhaps opened up by Samuel Johnson, whose *London*, an imitation of Juvenal's Third Satire, appeared in May 1738, as Boswell reports, 'on the same morning with Pope's satire, entitled "1738"; so that England had at once its Juvenal and Horace'. Boswell added that on learning that the author 'was some obscure man, Pope said, "he will soon be *deterré*" '.[46] But it is in the *Vanity of Human Wishes* (1749), Johnson's imitation of Juvenal's Tenth Satire, that the quest for an elevated style which is neither epic nor ironically dependent on the epic relationship finds an important new voice.

Although Johnson's poem follows the contours of its Juvenalian original, including, among other satirical themes, the vanity of high office or military glory, the corrupt depredations of tyrants and conquerors, the bloodshed of war, his tone is of melancholy gravity, largely eschewing indignation or mockery (whether of himself or others), and without the sting of Juvenal's jeering at human unreason. A passage on the futility of military triumphs,

> The festal blazes, the triumphal show,
> The ravish'd standard, and the captive foe . . .
> . . .
> For such the steady Romans shook the world;
> For such in distant lands the Britons shine,
> And stain with blood the Danube or the Rhine;[47]

omits Juvenal's references to 'trophies of war, – the breastplate fastened to a bare tree trunk, a cheekpiece hanging from a shattered helmet' (Juvenal, Satire 10, lines 134–6).

Johnson's accounts even of battle tend to rise above the battle. The air of weighty sadness, the compassionate and largely unaggressive way of pointing out human unreason but withholding the satirical kill, is deeply Johnsonian. It is most evidently displayed in the account of Charles XII (lines 191–222), a figure much attacked by satirists including Swift and Fielding as well as Pope, and here the counterpart to Juvenal's Hannibal and Alexander as an example of the futility of conquest. The King, who liked to be called the Alexander of the North, exercised considerable fascination, partly through Voltaire's *History of Charles XII*, over both Fielding and Johnson, who planned to write a play about him. While Voltaire had treated Charles as a proud and inflexible military hero who instinctively reached for his sword at the moment of death, and Fielding saw him as a ruthless thug, Johnson offers an uncastigating reflection on the ultimate pointlessness of conquest:

> His fall was destin'd to a barren strand,
> A petty fortress, and a dubious hand;
> He left the name, at which the world grew pale,
> To point a moral, or adorn a tale. (lines 219–22)

The bleak unglamorous death corresponds to those of Juvenal's Hannibal, who poisoned himself, and Alexander, whose conquered worlds had shrunk to a coffin (after a fever, with rumours of poisoning – Juvenal, Satire 10, lines 163–72). Johnson's 'dubious hand' refers to rumours that Charles was assassinated by one of his own men, though by most accounts Charles was hit in the face by an enemy cannon-ball. Johnson's decision to evoke the conspiracy theory may have been due to a wish to stay close to the letter of Juvenalian scenarios of petty death, although Johnson is usually willing to jettison Juvenalian elements which challenge the composure and dignity of his own poem. But it is the pathos, not the ignominy, of Charles's death that Johnson brings out, with a stark eloquence and sense of lonely grandeur, very different from the shabby degradation of the Juvenalian counterparts. The account is remarkable for the way Johnson uses the resources of the tight, end-stopped Augustan couplet, normally the instrument of choice for definitional summations, satirical portraiture and witty exposition, to achieve a sombre and majestic meditation which is none of these things.

The *Vanity of Human Wishes* moves beyond satire not only in the sense of holding back from the satirical kill, but in seeking a register which altogether transcends castigation or derision. Charles's downfall, like that of Pope's Buckingham, expresses the sentiment of 'alas! how chang'd from him', without Pope's contempt, but also without the evocation of Virgilian phrasing. It achieves heroic accents without the support of an epic original, or the crutch of satiric indignation, or even the epic gesturing with which Juvenal makes claims of heroic stature for his satiric enterprise even as he insults epic writers. Unimpeded, as Pope was not, by the formal obligations of parody or the *pudeur* of epic ambitions, Johnson achieves that retreat from the joke which mock-heroic, however serious, could not achieve because of its irreducible parodic character. Johnson's poem might be said to fulfil the ambition, inherent in the finale of *The Dunciad*, of opening a path to the ironic, allusive but essentially unsatiric majestic degradations of *The Waste Land*, a poem which took part of its inspiration and style from Pope, by a poet who was a great admirer of Johnson's poem.

Notes

1. See Voltaire, *Questions sur l'Encyclopédie*, second edition, 9 vols. (London, 1771), vol. v, p. 223 (article 'Epopée'), and see p. 127 ('Eglogue').
2. Dryden, *Discourse Concerning Satire* (1693), *Works of John Dryden*, ed. E. N. Hooker, J. T. Swedenberg *et al.*, 20 vols. (Berkeley: University of California Press, 1956–2000), vol. iv, p. 15.
3. Samuel Wesley, *An Epistle to a Friend Concerning Poetry* (London, 1700), pp. 446–17, 621.
4. John Milton, *Paradise Lost*, 'The Verse'.

5. See Nicolas Boileau-Despréaux, *Art Poétique* (1674), I.112–46; quotation from canto I, line 132, in *The art of poetry, written in French by the Sieur de Boileau. In four canto's. Made English, by Sir William Soames. Since revis'd by John Dryden, Esq.* (London, 1710; first published anonymously in 1683).
6. George Puttenham, *The Arte of English Poesie* (London, 1589), ed. Gladys Doidge Willcox and Alice Walker (Cambridge: Cambridge University Press, 1936), II.iii [iv], p. 72.
7. Roger Ascham, *The Schoolmaster* (1563–9), cited in Richard Bradford, *Augustan Measures: Restoration and Eighteenth-Century Writings on Prosody and Metre* (Aldershot: Ashgate, 2002), p. 7.
8. Wesley, *An Epistle to a Friend*, line 466.
9. Adam Smith, *Theory of Moral Sentiments* (1759), v.i.6, ed. D. D. Raphael and A. L. Macafie (1976; Indianapolis, IN: Liberty Fund, 1982), pp. 196–7.
10. Vol. I of *The Twickenham Edition of the Poems of Alexander Pope*, ed. John Butt, Maynard Mack *et al.*, 11 vols. in 12 (London: Methuen, 1939–69). Henceforth *TE*.
11. Pope recycled these lines over two decades later (*Second Epistle of the Second Book of Horace, Imitated*, lines 178–9); Dryden, *Of Dramatick Poesie* (1668), in *Works*, vol. XVII, p. 76 (hereafter identified as *DP* and by page). For the dance analogy, see Claude Rawson, *Henry Fielding and the Augustan Ideal under Stress* (London: Routledge, 1972), chapters 1–3.
12. William Empson,*The Structure of Complex Words* (London: Chatto, 1951), p. 98.
13. Milton, *Paradise Lost*, 'The Verse', in *The Riverside Milton*, ed. Roy Flannagan (Boston: Houghton Mifflin, 1998), p. 352. This edition is used for all quotations from Milton.
14. *TE* vol. I, pp. 46–7n.
15. *TE* vol. I, pp. 17–20; Joseph Addison, *Spectator*, 523, 30 October 1712; Pope, *Guardian*, 40, 27 April 1713 (*The Prose Works of Alexander Pope*, ed. Norman Ault and Rosemary Cowler, 2 vols. (Oxford: Blackwell, 1936–86), vol. I, pp. 97–106).
16. 'A Discourse on Pastoral Poetry', in *TE* vol. I, p. 25.
17. John Gay, *Shepherd's Week* (1714), 'Proeme'; Jonathan Swift, 'A Pastoral Dialogue' (1729); see J. E. Congleton, *Theories of Pastoral Poetry in England, 1684–1798* (Gainesville: University of Florida Press, 1952), esp. pp. 75–95.
18. Quoted from William Wordsworth, *The Prelude 1799, 1805, 1850*, ed. Jonathan Wordsworth, M. H. Abrams, Stephen Gill (New York: Norton, 1979), VIII.121ff.
19. See Andrew Marvell, 'On *Paradise Lost*', prefixed to 1674 edition of *Paradise Lost*, lines 45–54. For the biographical facts on this much-discussed story, see Barbara Lewalski, *Life of John Milton*, revised edition (Oxford: Blackwell, 2003), pp. 508–10; James A. Winn, *John Dryden and His World* (New Haven: Yale University Press, 1987), pp. 264–5, 584nn.
20. See A. O. Lovejoy, 'Nature as Aesthetic Norm', *Modern Language Notes*, 42:7 (November 1927), pp. 444–50.

21. John Keats, letter to Benjamin Bailey, 22 November 1817, *Letters of John Keats, 1814–1821*, ed. H. E. Rollins, 2 vols. (Cambridge, MA: Harvard University Press, 1958), vol. I, p. 185.
22. Ben Jonson, *Timber: or, Discoveries* (1641) and Daniel Heinsius, *De Tragediae Constitutione* (Leyden, 1611), both in *Critical Essays of the Seventeenth Century*, ed. J. E. Spingarn, 3 vols. (Oxford: Clarendon, 1908–9), vol. I, pp. 56, 229 n.
23. W. K. Wimsatt, *The Portraits of Alexander Pope* (New Haven: Yale University Press, 1965), p. xv, and throughout.
24. Pope's note to *Iliad* translation, XVI.466, *TE* vol. VIII, p. 261, and see *TE* vol. I, p. 134.
25. See also Frank Stack, *Pope and Horace: Studies in Imitation* (Cambridge: Cambridge University Press, 1985), pp. 29–59, and James McLaverty, *Pope, Print and Meaning* (Oxford: Oxford University Press, 2001), pp. 147–68.
26. See Juvenal, Satire 1, line 77; Satire 3, lines 54ff., 232ff.
27. See *The Dunciad*, iv.9; Dryden, *Absalom and Achitophel*, line 334; Byron, 'Dedication', *Don Juan*, Stanza 4, line 30, quoted from *Lord Byron: The Major Works*, ed. Jerome J. McGann (Oxford: Oxford University Press, 2000). On Roman recitations, see the commentaries on Juvenal, Satire 3, line 9 by J. E. B Mayor: *Mayor's Juvenal: Thirteen Satires: Introduction, Complete Text, and Commentary on Satires I–XVI*, ed. John Henderson, 2 vols. (Bristol: Bristol Phoenix Press, 2007); and E. Courtney, *Commentary on the 'Satires' of Juvenal* (London: Continuum, 1980).
28. Horace, *Satires* II.i.39–40; Juvenal Satire 1, line 165. Horace uses both terms, Juvenal only 'ensis' (sword). 'Stilus' means a pointed instrument, a dagger (as in *stiletto*) or pen, as well as 'style', though the form 'stylus', is a corruption, reproduced in the Latin of Pope's facing page.
29. See G. K. Hunter, 'The "Romanticism" of Pope's Horace (1960)', in Maynard Mack, (ed.) *Essential Articles for the Study of Alexander Pope*, revised and enlarged edition (Hamden, CT: Archon, 1968), pp. 591–606.
30. *TE* vol. III. i, p. 40 n. 199–200.
31. See Maynard Mack's discussion of the ruling passion, in his introduction to the *Essay on Man*, *TE* vol. III. i, pp. xxxvi–xxxix.
32. For Pope's attacks on Sappho, see *TE* vol. III. ii, pp. 51–2 n. 24. Lady Mary's miscellaneous writings are collected in *Essays and Poems*, ed. Robert Halsband and Isobel Grundy (Oxford: Clarendon Press, 1977). For her letters, see the *Complete Letters*, ed. Robert Halsband, 3 vols. (Oxford: Clarendon Press, 1965–7).
33. On this, see Miriam Leranbaum, *Alexander Pope's 'Opus Magnum', 1729–1744* (Oxford: Clarendon Press, 1977).
34. Francis Bacon, unpublished dedication *c.*1612 to Prince Henry for second edition of *Essaies*: 'The word is late, but the thing is auncient.'
35. The title under which they now appear in *TE* vol. III. ii (see Introduction, Section III, pp. xxxvii–xxxviii, xlix–l); Leranbaum, *Alexander Pope's 'Opus Magnum'*, pp. 137–40.
36. Maynard Mack, *Alexander Pope: A Life* (London: Yale University Press, 1985), pp. 773–4.

37. Milton, *Paradise Lost*, Book 1, line 26.
38. Pope's note (1744) to *Essay on Criticism*, 130–1, *TE* vol. I, p. 254.
39. Dryden, 'Discourse Concerning Satire' (1693), *Works*, vol. IV, p. 84.
40. Boileau, *Le Lutrin*, 'Au lecteur', prefixed to first edition (Paris, 1674).
41. Dryden's translation of *Aeneid*, I.1.
42. *Scarronides: or, Virgile Travesti* (1664–5), I.1–2.
43. Milton, *Paradise Lost*, Book 6, line 434.
44. Dryden, *Absalom and Achitophel*, line 633.
45. 'Description of a City Shower', lines 62–3, in *The Poems of Jonathan Swift*, ed. Harold Williams, 3 vols. (second edition, Oxford: Clarendon Press, 1958), vol. I, p. 139.
46. James Boswell, *Life of Johnson* (1791), ed. G. B. Hill and L. F. Powell, revised edition, 6 vols. (Oxford: Clarendon, 1971), vol. I, p. 139; vol. II, p. 85.
47. Lines 175–82; Samuel Johnson, *Poems*, Yale Edition of the Works of Samuel Johnson, vol. VI, ed. E. L. McAdam (New Haven: Yale University Press, 1964), p. 100.

Chapter 19

Eighteenth-century women poets

CHRISTINE GERRARD

The rediscovery of women's poetry has transformed the literary landscape of the eighteenth century. As recently as the early 1980s, students and general readers confronted a canon far narrower and almost exclusively male. Although so-called 'Augustan' verse had always offered more generic and stylistic diversity than the social and political satire by which the age is often stereotyped, very few poems by women appeared in anthologies or on university syllabuses. Of the several hundred items in Geoffrey Tillotson, Paul Fussell and Marshall Waingrow's compendious *Eighteenth-Century English Literature* (1969) there are only four poems by women – three by Anne Finch, Countess of Winchilsea, and one short lyric by Lady Mary Wortley Montagu. Charles Peake's *Poetry of the Landscape and the Night* (1967), a kind of 'alternative' eighteenth-century verse anthology, included only one piece by a woman, Finch's 'Nocturnal Reverie'. Yet by the mid 1980s much had changed. Feminist criticism and scholarship had invested heavily in rediscovering literary 'mothers';[1] and a wide range of textual scholars had started to undertake the challenge of editing some of the many coterie manuscript poems by women which represented a significant facet of female writing of the period.[2] Roger Lonsdale's ground-breaking *Eighteenth-Century Women Poets* (1989) helped place in the public domain unfamiliar women poets, some published and popular in their own time, who had since disappeared from view. Eighteenth-century women's poetry is now widely accessible in both anthologies and individual scholarly editions, and numerous names have now augmented literary syllabuses – the outspoken teenage poetess Sarah Fyge Egerton; the labouring poets Mary Leapor, Mary Collier and Ann Yearsley; middle-class admirers and followers of Pope and Swift, such as Mary Jones and Mary Barber; those who courted scandal for their unconventional lives and autobiographical self-disclosure, such as Laetitia Pilkington and Martha Fowke Sansom.

The enrichment of the canon stems not only from the increased accessibility of female voices, but from the restored interplay between male and female poetic voices.[3] Eighteenth-century women's poetry can never be ghettoised or segregated from eighteenth-century male poetry. Aspiring female poets may have lacked access to the classical education bestowed on their brothers or husbands, but a burgeoning print culture made printed poetic texts increasingly available to women readers. It is no coincidence that many women poets, at least in the first half of the eighteenth century, modelled their verses on Pope, the most widely published and accessible poetic role-model of the day. Yet if women poets acquired prosodic techniques from their male counterparts, they did not slavishly imitate their verse. Alert to the distinctions of their own gender, they admired, borrowed, adapted, parodied and attacked, but never passively absorbed. At one extreme are the 'occasional' poems, ripostes to specific individuals and events – Lady Mary Wortley Montagu's attack on Pope in *Verses Address'd to the Imitator of Horace*, Mary Collier's *The Woman's Labour*, a rebuttal of Stephen Duck's *The Thresher's Labour*, or Martha Fowke's *Innocent Inconstant*, a libertine reply to Richard Savage's 'Unconstant'. But everywhere in women's verse we recognise thoughtful, inflected, sometimes humorous reworking of themes, genres, poetic lines, metaphors. The story of eighteenth-century women's poetry is inseparable from the story of eighteenth-century men's poetry.

Many poets of both sexes writing around 1700 had come to poetic maturity during a time of unprecedented civic and political upheaval. Poets such as Jane Barker, Mary, Lady Chudleigh, and Anne Finch, Countess of Winchilsea, shared with Dryden, Pope and Swift a personal experience of the Civil War's aftermath, living through a sequence of upheavals including the bloodless 'revolution' of 1688 which ended a short-lived Stuart Restoration and placed Dutch William on the throne. Women's poetry was more politically engaged around the turn of the century than in the later decades under Hanoverian rule despite the steady growth of party-political writing which peaked in the late 1730s under the Walpole regime. Women poets of the 1690s absorbed and mobilised the language of political theory drawn from Hobbes, Filmer and Locke, concerned with definitions of civic rights and responsibilities, and extended these into the sphere of women's marital duty and education. The 1690s witnessed the emergence of the so-called 'advocacy' texts which raised, among other issues, women's rights to education and to divorce. Mary, Lady Chudleigh, author of the 'Ladies' Defence' (1701), a plea for female education, had corresponded with the early feminist Mary Astell. The teenage Sarah Fyge Egerton, author of *The Female Advocate* (1686), a spirited poetic response to Robert Gould's misogynistic *Love Given O'er* (1682), was banished to the countryside by her father, an exile that prompted her embittered diatribe against paternal tyranny, 'On my leaving London, June the 29'. Her polemic, rooted in a personal experience of being silenced and shut away, gains impetus from its dynamic end-stopped couplets which harness strong emotion within a prosodic re-enactment of the 'Gyves and Manacles' and 'Fetters of Formality' that represented women's lot in life. Her voice is instantly memorable: 'Say Tyrant Custom, why must we obey / The impositions of thy haughty Sway? / From the first dawn of Life, unto the Grave, / Poor Womankind's in every State, a Slave' ('The Emulation', lines 1–4).[4]

Egerton's one-note militant feminism is very different from the flexible and generically wide-ranging verse of her more famous contemporary, Anne Finch, Countess of Winchilsea: yet both mobilise a politicised language to articulate a sense of female constriction. Finch's 'A Nocturnal Reverie' reads initially as a sensitive evocation of the natural world after dark, in which sounds and sights register themselves on the reader's senses through one sinuous and fluid unbroken syntactic unit. 'In such a *Night*', opens the poem, echoing Shakespeare's Jessica, the liberated soul achieves a sublime apotheosis, 'Something, too high for Syllables to speak' (line 42, FG). That this sense of expansion, a democracy of the soul shared with other oppressed life forms – beasts of burden, hunted animals – should occur at night 'whilst *Tyrant-Man* do's sleep' (line 38) – is telling. Although Finch's 'Reverie' has been anthologised alongside other nocturnal poems, such as Thomas Parnell's 'Night-Piece on Death' (1721), it is very different from Parnell's Augustan moralising. Finch's nocturnal retreat, located in the beautiful Eastwell Park in Kent, where she and her husband lived out their later years, belongs to a Royalist tradition of retirement verse going back to Lovelace and Jonson. Finch spent much of her own life in exile: married to the successful courtier Heneage Finch, she had been a Maid of Honour to Mary of Modena, James II's wife, until the revolution of 1688 ended their careers and forced them into flight. Although subsequently recuperated by her entrance into literary society and a friendship with Jonathan Swift, Finch and her husband remained non-jurors, refusing to swear allegiance to George I.

The political tumults of Finch's life find their 'objective correlative' in the great storm of November 1703 which devastated the southern coast of England. 'Upon the Hurricane', the ambitious Pindaric ode Finch wrote in the storm's immediate aftermath, draws on a wide range of literary models – Biblical, classical and contemporary – to shape its narrative of devastation.[5] At one level the poem is an inversion or deconstruction of the seventeenth-century loco-descriptive poem derived from Jonson's 'To Penshurst' via Marvell's 'Appleton House' through to Denham's *Coopers-Hill* and Pope's

Windsor-Forest, in which the rural landscape becomes both backdrop and metaphor for events of national significance. The hunted stag, a familiar Royalist topos from Denham's poem, appears here as a symptom of wide-ranging natural and civic disorder:

Free as the Men, who wild Confusion love
  And lawless Liberty approve,
Their Fellow-Brutes pursue their way
To their own Loss, and disadvantage stray,
As wretched in their Choice, as unadvis'd as They.
The tim'rous *Deer*, whilst he forsakes the Park,
And wanders on, in the misguiding Dark,
Believes, a Foe from ev'ry unknown Bush
  Will on his trembling Body rush. (lines 204–12, FG)

Finch echoes Dryden's account of the Civil War in *Astraea Redux* ('they own'd a lawless salvage Libertie')[6] and the Hobbesian language of Rochester's *Satire against Reason* to present man in a state of nature. The poem upends the royal oak trees which Pope celebrates in *Windsor-Forest*, a poem published (though not composed) in the same year as Finch's. Whereas Pope's oaks joyfully 'rush into [the] floods' to join the British navy,[7] Finch's oaks are ripped untimely from their roots. 'In vain the *Oak* (so often storm'd) / Rely'd upon that native Force.'

The strait and ornamental *Pine*
Did in the like Ambition joyn,
And thought his Fame shou'd ever last,
When in some Royal Ship he stood the planted Mast.
(lines 15–16, 23–6, FG)

Finch is careful to veil her political stance. There is a small speculative satisfaction in the death of Richard Kidder, recently appointed Bishop of Bath and Wells, and his wife, killed by a chimney stack falling through the roof of the palace formerly occupied by the popular but now displaced non-juring Bishop Thomas Ken. 'But let no daring Thought presume / To point a Cause for that oppressive Doom. / Yet strictly pious *KEN!* Had'st Thou been there, / This Fate, we think, had not become thy share' (lines 98–101). But although the poem draws heavily on the providentialist rhetoric of the mid 1660s, which interpreted natural disasters such as the Great Fire as God's punishment for the nation's 'Secret sins', it is hard to align Finch's 'Great disposer's Righteous Will' (line 188) with a partisan allegiance. The hurricane is no respecter of political parties: 'Nor WHIG, nor TORY now the rash

Contender calls' (line 177). Its sublime annihilation of human endeavour transcends all politics.

Women's poetry of the early Hanoverian period lacks the same sense of imaginative political engagement. The Stuart court and its coterie writing centred on female monarchs – Mary of Modena, Queen Anne, even, to a lesser extent, Williams's consort Queen Mary (celebrated by Elizabeth Singer Rowe) – fostered a community of women writers who found authority for their own expression in the figure of a female monarch.[8] Sarah Fyge Egerton's 'The Emulation' (line 33, FG) proclaims that 'Wits Empire, now, shall know a Female Reign'. Following Anne's death in 1714 very few women poets remained as personally involved in the new political scene. The less active role taken by the new German-speaking Hanoverian monarch in practical politics or English literary culture seems to have deflected female poetic interest. Protestant Whig women poets such as Jane Brereton or Susanna Centlivre greeted the new regime with patriotic odes rehearsing the standard topoi of Whig panegyric – liberty, commerce, empire, the security of Protestantism – but such poems are public and often impersonal.[9]

Yet it was in this initially unpromising new territory that Lady Mary Wortley Montagu first made a name for herself. George I's daughter-in-law Caroline of Anspach, the future Queen Caroline, was an intellectual and unorthodox woman. More a patron of theologians than poets (though the thresher poet Stephen Duck, Richard Savage and Milton's elderly daughter were publicised beneficiaries), Caroline cultivated a racy 'set' with a literary fringe. Among her celebrated ladies-in-waiting was the beautiful Mary Leppell, wife of the notoriously bisexual courtier, Lord Hervey. The tone of this 'alternative' Hanoverian court was very different from the decorous feminine piety of Queen Mary and Queen Anne's reigns. Rumours of sexual scandals and affairs fuelled court gossip and fed the Grub Street press. This was the young Lady Mary's literary milieu: her good looks, talent and birth rapidly made her popular with Caroline and Prince George.[10] Lady Mary's posthumous reputation rested for many years on her *Persian Letters*, the only one of her numerous works that she herself prepared for publication. Her sense of aristocratic decorum inhibited her from publishing her poems or acknowledging their pirated printings. Robert Halsband and Isobel Grundy's scholarly edition of her essays and poems, first published in 1977, revealed an adroit and sophisticated poetic talent.[11]

Lady Mary's relationship with the Scriblerian circle of Gay, Parnell, Bolingbroke and especially Pope – first as friend, then as an enemy – has often overshadowed the real qualities of her work. Despite a formally limited education, she was a precocious reader in her father's extensive library and was producing sophisticated poems by the age of twelve. Her witty poem 'Roxana', written in February or March 1715, may have recommended her to Pope as a literary collaborator and socially desirable ally. 'Roxana' was retitled 'Monday' and became the first of six so-called 'Town Eclogues', recruited into the Scriblerian genre-parody project which had created Swift's urban pastorals ('A Description of the Morning' and 'A Description of a City Shower') and Gay's *The Shepherd's Week* and *The Beggar's Opera*. The 'Town Eclogues' may have been the product of collaboration with Gay and Pope, though Isobel Grundy has convincingly argued for Lady Mary's main authorship.[12] Although they bear a superficial resemblance in theme and setting to other Scriblerian poems such as *The Shepherd's Week* (in their burlesque of the formal pastoral singing match) and *Trivia* and *The Rape of the Lock* in their urban and beau-monde settings, they are otherwise quite distinct. Some of the fictional characters were modelled on real-life court counterparts (Lydia, in 'Friday, The Toilette,' was inspired by Mary Coke, wife of the Vice-Chamberlain). Edmund Curll immediately saw their potential as marketable commodities and published a pirated edition, *Court Poems*.[13] Appropriately, the poems themselves fetishise consumer commodities. Material objects acquire an independent identity as objective correlatives for repressed sexual desire. The ageing Lydia of 'Friday, The Toilette' defiantly rejects the prospect of a life of self-denial, praying in chapel with 'grey Religious maids':

> Straight then I'll dress and take my wonted Range,
> Through India shops, to Motteaux's, or the Change,
> Where the Tall Jar erects his stately Pride
> With Antick Shapes in China's Azure dy'd,
> There careless lyes a rich Brocard unroll'd,
> Here shines a Cabinet with burnish'd Gold. (lines 26–31)

The 'Tall Jar' which 'erects his stately Pride' is the masculine counterpart to the feminised 'rich Brocard unroll'd'. The words 'careless' and 'unroll'd' hint at a kind of erotic negligence and the 'rich Brocard' recalls Pope's Belinda, who, it is feared, might simultaneously 'stain her honour, or her new Brocade'.[14] The sexual innuendo of 'Tuesday, St James's Coffee-house', is more overt. Two young blades around town, Patch and Silliander, boasting of their rival conquests among society women, describe a peep-show world of disclosures – an upmarket version of Gay's shepherds peering at a country-wench's stockings. 'Her Grace' gives Silliander a hidden glimpse. While she 'Lean'd cross two chairs to whisper to a Freind', the 'stiff whalebone with the motion rose /

And thousand Beauties to my sight expose' (lines 65–7). The juxtaposition of the mechanical and the amatory is funny but erotically charged. The 'Town Eclogues' established some of the dominant themes of Lady Mary's verse. No other woman poet of the century wrote so directly, satirically and dryly about sexuality.

> The Lover starts from his unfinish'd Loves,
> To snatch his Hat, and seek his scatter'd Gloves,
> The sighing Dame to meet her Dear prepares;
> While Strephon cursing slips down the back Stairs.
> ('Wednesday, The Tête à Tête', lines 89–92)

Her poetry reflects an aristocratic world free from bourgeois sentimentality in which marriages were made for convenience, ambition or, in her own case, compromise; and where infidelity, while not officially sanctioned, was widely acknowledged and the source of much gossip. The vestiges of Restoration libertine culture shot through with Hobbesian self-interest form the poems' backdrop. Society world is for women a battleground. Loss of one's looks through age or disease means loss of power and status, as the next 'reigning beauty' takes pleasure in her rival's discomfiture. There is little sense of female community. As the wretched Flavia acknowledges in 'Satturday, The Small Pox', 'Monarchs, and Beauties rule with equal sway, / All strive to serve, and Glory to obey, / Alike unpity'd when depos'd they grow, / Men mock the Idol of their Former vow' (lines 85–8). Yet Flavia is scarcely a sympathetic character: her equation of lost beauty and lost 'Empire' fails to lead to any self-knowledge: like the poem, she deals only in surfaces.

A worldly cynicism about human relationships permeates Lady Mary's poems: happiness is rarely found within marriage and those who die young escape a lifetime of marital acrimony. The extempore lines on the fifteen-year-old heiress Eleanor Bowes, who died soon after marriage, celebrate her three months of rapture before her husband had the chance to substitute 'the tender Lover, for th'imperious Lord' ('On the Death of Mrs Bowes', line 8). Her impromptu on John Hughes and Sarah Drew, the rustic lovers struck down by lightning near Stanton Harcourt in 1718 and memorialised as icons of domestic bliss by Thomson and Pope, follows a similar theme.

> Who knows if 'twas not kindly done?
> For had they seen the next Year's Sun
> A Beaten Wife and Cuckold Swain
> Had jointly curs'd the marriage chain.

Now they are happy in their Doom
For P. has wrote upon their Tomb.
('Here lies John Hughes and Sarah Drew', lines 15–20)

The final trite couplet parodies Pope's easy sentimentalism and authorial self-regard. But there is an underlying tension within Lady Mary's poems between desire and repression, between idealism and cynicism. Her earliest surviving poem, 'Julia to Ovid', is a dramatic monologue in which Julia, like Pope's Eloisa, burns with desire for her banished lover. Impossible, obsessive love is also the subject of her later, more contentious Ovidian (mock?) heroic epistle, the 'Epistle from Arthur Gray to Mrs Murray'. Griselda Murray, friend of Lady Mary, separated from her husband, was reported to have suffered an attempted rape at the hands of her lovesick footman Arthur Gray. Following wide-scale publicity, Gray was tried and found guilty of felony, sentenced to death but subsequently transported. Lady Mary wrote two poems on the subject, the bawdy broadside ballad 'Virtue in Danger', punning on Gray's secret 'weapon', and the longer 'Epistle from Arthur Gray', a first-person account written by a fictionalised and romanticised Gray. Recent scholarship has established that Gray had either a voyeuristic or a blackmailer's interest in Griselda Murray's extra-marital affairs and that the fiction of the 'passionate servant' was put about as a convenient cover-up for a less romantic truth.[15] In this context the 'Epistle from Arthur Gray' could be read as an entirely ironic fiction – yet the intensity of feeling which the poem's speaker projects cannot be lightly brushed away.

But when I saw! (oh had I never seen
That wounding softness, that engaging Mien!)
The mist of wretched Education flys,
Shame, Fear, Desire, Despair, and Love arise. (lines 15–18)

The desperate urge to break through the 'mist of wretched Education' must have been shared by many female writers; and the breathless, conflicted last line of this passage echoes Pope's Eloisa in her struggles between duty and passion: 'How often, hope, despair, resent, regret, / Conceal, disdain – do all things but forget.'[16]

In the closing lines of 'Eloisa to Abelard' Pope had adopted the voice of the tortured, confessional lover pining for an absent Lady Mary: 'Condemn'd whole years in absence to deplore, / And image charms he must behold no more'.[17] But any intensity of feeling between Pope and Lady Mary soon turned to hatred. Whatever the cause of the quarrel, by the 1730s they belonged to opposing literary and political camps. Pope's personal attacks on 'Sappho', archetype of the emotionally intense, promiscuous intellectual woman, provoked her counter-attack written with Lord Hervey, the controversial *Verses Address'd to the Imitator of Horace* (1733). This poem's uncharacteristically crude assault links Pope's physical deformity with the mark of Cain: the 'Emblem of thy crooked mind, / Mark'd on thy Back, like *Cain*, by God's own Hand; / Wander like him, accursed through the Land' (lines 110–12). The scabrous imagery of the *Verses* was far more like acerbic Juvenal than genial Horace. Lady Mary persistently played on Pope's low birth to puncture his social pretensions. Her unpublished satire of 1734–5, 'Pope to Bolingbroke', brilliantly parodies the social deference bordering on obsequiousness embedded in Pope's recent addresses to Bolingbroke in the *Essay on Man* and the *Second Satire of the Second Book of Horace*. 'Permit me too, a small attendant Star, / To twinkle, tho' in a more distant Sphere' (lines 9–10). The unfinished poem known as 'Her Palace Plac'd beneath a muddy Road', an ambitious reworking of Pope's *Dunciad*, raises the political stakes by its clever tactical inversion of Pope's topography of Dulness. Whereas Pope had linked Dulness with the decline of learning associated with Whig 'moderns', Lady Mary equates Dulness with Catholic superstition and Tory nostalgia and defends the clarity of modern court Whig writing. Lady Mary's most genuinely Horatian epistle, the 'Epistle to Lord Bathurst' (*c.*1725), addressed to her friend Ralph Allen, captures the conversational tone of its model in its teasing account of Allen's volatile tastes in love, art and gardening – 'The Spring beheld you warm in this Design, / But scarce the cold attacks your favourite Trees, / Your Inclinations fail, and wishes freeze, / You quit the Grove, so lately so admir'd, / With other views your eager Hopes are fir'd' (lines 18–22). Written several years before Pope himself attempted to imitate Horace, the poem seems to have inspired Pope's *Epistle to Burlington* and *To a Lady* (Papilla's passion for, then detestation of, those 'odious, odious Trees').[18] In Pope, capriciousness becomes, ironically, a defining female trait.

Pope's imitations of Horace's epistles may have turned Lady Mary away from the form, but they inspired numerous other women poets to address in verse their social circles and poetic ambitions. The conversational epistle was a form ideally suited to the expression of female friendship and this is the mode we encounter in Mary Leapor's poems to her friend Bridget Freemantle or Mary Jones's 'Epistle to Lady Bower'. The ethical dimension of Pope's Horatian persona, expatiating on the characters of men and women, the uses of riches, taste and so forth, enabled women writers to address major issues, including gender, in an informal mode: and the *Epistle to Arbuthnot*, perhaps the single most important Popeian model for women poets, allowed them to explore and project their own identities as writers. In this intensely self-protective but self-aggrandising poem, Pope oscillates between modesty and aggression as he defends his own writing career. Playing on his physical vulnerability (weakness and small stature) and his domestic piety (nursing his mother in poor health and rocking 'the cradle of reposing Age'[19]), he figuratively disarms his critics from the 'lash' of his satire. Pope's autobiographical projection of multiple identities was ideally suited to women writers seeking to accommodate, if not reconcile, their public and private selves, their necessary modesty and their latent ambition, including their need for financial support and patronage.

Mary Jones (1707–78), sister of a Christ Church don, was taken up by female members of the Lovelace family, including Martha Lovelace, lady-in-waiting to Queen Caroline, and Lady Bower. They were determined to put her into print and her *Miscellanies in Verse and Prose* (1750) gained over 1,400 subscribers. Yet being cast into the glare of publicity was alien to her nature and the preface self-effacingly claims that 'the poetry she can say nothing to; it being quite accidental, that her thoughts ever rambled into rhyme'.[20] There is an echo here of Pope's profession in the *Epistle to Arbuthnot* that 'he lisped in numbers, for the numbers came'.[21] Like Pope, Jones claims a preference for obscurity: but her friends push her into print in order that she may 'get a name'.

> Well, but the joy to see my works in print!
> My self too pictur'd in a Mezzo-Tint!
> The Preface done, the Dedication fram'd,
> With lies enough to make a Lord asham'd!
> Thus I step forth; an Auth'ress in some sort.
> My Patron's name? 'O choose some Lord at Court'.
>
> (lines 29–34, FG)

In the *Epistle to Arbuthnot* Pope carefully effaces details of his own real-life relationship to the mechanics of print culture and the literary marketplace. Jones, however, goes into considerable, often comic detail, about the struggles and humiliations of getting into print – often a problematic process for the aspiring female writer. Pope had borrowed Horace's half-humorous, half-irritated account of his attempts to flee from would-be poets and literary hangers-on, including a 'maudlin Poetess',[22] anxious to get themselves into print. Jones conversely depicts herself as one of the literary hangers-on, questing for patronage, waiting at a levee for a word with 'his lordship' and encountering instead his philistine butler, who professes taste and authority in poetry. She dramatises with exquisite irony the humiliation of having to court the favours of an uneducated servant with his own literary aspirations, who takes her manuscripts and claims (in an ironic echo of Horace's dictum '*poeta non fit, nascitur*') that he

> Was born a poet, tho' no poet bred:
> And if I find they'll bear my nicer view,
> I'll recommend your poetry – and you. (lines 77–9, FG)

In her closing lines Jones elides her identity with Pope's as she describes her humble parentage, desire for a decent modest life and care of an ageing mother. Yet if Jones is comfortable with this 'feminised' Pope self-projection she is less secure in conceptualising her literary relationship with Pope. The poem opens with a 'modesty topos'. Only once in an age can a great literary genius arise, who by necessity must overshadow all other lesser talents. Pope becomes a masculine 'lofty oak'.

> No lays, like mine, can live beneath his shade.
> Nothing but weeds, and moss, and shrubs are found.
> Cut, cut them down, why cumber they the ground?
> (lines 10–12, FG)

The half-line act of repetitive self-erasure – 'Cut, cut them down' – echoes, almost unconsciously, the opening line of *Arbuthnot* – 'Shut, shut the door, good John!'[23]

Pope's disclosure of his physical frailty led other female poets to identify with him, none more closely than Mary Chandler, proprietor of a millinery shop near the Bath pump rooms, who shared the same short stature and spinal curvature as her favourite poet. Her 'Letter to the Right Honourable the Lady Russell' goes even further than Pope's *Arbuthnot* in making comic capital out of disability. Pope humours his male friends and admirers who try to persuade him to marry, or who gloss over his physical inadequacies by comparing him to the classical greats: 'I cough like Horace, and though lean, am short.'[24] Chandler describes her friends' well-meaning but insensitive attempts to marry her off to a similarly hunchbacked male farmer acquaintance ('Two Bodies so exactly pair'd!) and, like Pope, takes refuge in a single life dedicated to friendship, conversation and poetry.[25]

Mary Leapor (1722–46), one of the most interesting of the eighteenth-century women poets rediscovered in the late twentieth century, shared the same high estimation of Pope, 'the author she most admired . . . whom she chiefly endeavoured to imitate'.[26] Though Leapor died when only twenty-four, her sparkling, accomplished but quirky poems are a remarkable testament to intellectual vivacity overcoming personal difficulties.[27] A gardener's daughter who subsequently worked as a kitchen maid, she broadened the reading gained from free school through access to the library at Weston Hall, where she was employed by Susanna Jennens. Leapor wrote fluently and voluminously in her spare time, encouraged by female friends, especially Bridget Freemantle, a local vicar's daughter, who was responsible for bringing Leapor's work to posthumous publication in 1751. In her own 'take' on Pope's *Epistle to Arbuthnot*, 'An Epistle to Artemisia. On Fame', Leapor, under her nom-de-plume 'Mira', reworks Pope's experience of the downside of local fame by depicting the endless intrusions into her domestic space made by admirers, critics and literary tourists. The most irritating is the brainless Cressida, who pays a visit to Mira's 'fame' ('My Fame's obliged', she replies) and insists on wasting four hours in empty chit-chat until she finally leaves.

> I wish, alas! But Wishes are in vain.
> I like your Garden; and I'll come again.
> Dear, how I wish! – I do, or let me die,
> That we liv'd near"
> – Thinks *Mira*, 'So don't I'. (lines 113–17, FG)

Leapor shares with Rochester and Pope the knack of running dialogue across rhyming couplets. For all her comic self-deprecation in this poem, Leapor's social satire is needle-sharp in its puncturing of female 'Impertinence'. She has a 'stubborn Will' (line 148) and, like her model Pope, does not suffer fools gladly.

Leapor's assimilation of a wide range of poetic forms and modes is all the more remarkable given her youth. 'Man the Monarch', an acerbic rewriting of the Genesis myth, recalls the feminist 'advocacy' poems of the 1690s with its grim acknowledgment that 'ev'ry Cottage brings / A long succession of Domestic Kings' (lines 64–5). *Crumble-Hall*, her most debated poem, appropriates the 'country house' mode stretching back via Pope's recent *Epistle to Burlington* to Marvell's 'Appleton House' and Jonson's 'To Penshurst', a series of odd, servant's eye perspectives shaping her quirky descriptions of Edgcote, the country house in which she herself had been employed.[28] 'Mira's Picture: A Pastoral' belongs to the burlesque pastoral mode of Gay's *Shepherd's Week* in which 'Philario' and 'Corydon' vie with each other not to praise a mistress but to denigrate Mira's outlandishly unfeminine appearance. Gay's 'Tuesday: Or, the Ditty' directly influenced the below-stairs scenes in *Crumble-Hall*, where Urs'la bewails the indifference of Roger, slumped snoring over the table after beef and dumplings. Leapor's reading in satirical verse extended beyond Pope to Gay, Swift and Parnell.

Even women writers like Leapor, Barber and Chandler, who professed admiration for Pope and his circle, often took issue with their now notorious encapsulations of female character, female appearance and female vanity. As Kathryn King has argued, much of the poetry of the second three decades of the century reflects the view that 'woman is an assemblage of looks, gestures and physical contrivances; a creature of masquerade and performance'. 'Woman's beauty in particular is a pernicious artifice; female identity a dissemblance and outward show.'[29] Women poets themselves are particularly sensitive to the pervasive idea that female beauty is the currency, capital or stock-in-trade upon which female value is constructed: loss of beauty through age or disfigurement entails loss of identity and status. Early to mid eighteenth-century verse abounds with specular images of women peering anxiously in the mirror, seeking affirmation from their reflections and encountering alienation and horror instead.[30] Leapor's 'Dorinda at her Glass', a close encounter between Dorinda and her ageing image, is partly inspired by Pope's *Rape of the Lock*. Dorinda seems an older version of Pope's Belinda: she 'slights her Form, no more by Youth inspir'd / And loaths that Idol which she once admire'd' (lines 29–30, FG). Yet in this poem Leapor also reprises Parnell's 'Elegy to An Old Beauty' (1721), which depicts a fifty-five-year-old woman behaving 'age-inappropriately' – refusing to hand over the dance floor and the family pearls to her fifteen-year-old granddaughter Fanny. Whereas the speaker of Parnell's 'Elegy, To an Old Beauty' sternly upbraids the middle-aged coquette, 'Henceforth retire, reduce your roving Airs, / Haunt less the Plays, and more the publick Pray'rs' (lines 43–4, FG), Leapor's Dorinda is allowed to speak for herself. While acknowledging the loss of beauty as an inevitable part of the natural cycle, she recommends the comforts of 'letting it go':

> Let *Isabel* unload her aking Head
> Of twisted Papers, and of binding Lead;
> Let sage *Augusta* now, without a Frown,
> Strip those gay Ribbands from her aged Crown.
>
> (lines 88–91, FG)

This last line – 'strip those gay Ribbands' – catches an echo of Parnell's metaphor for an ageing woman's face when 'with'ring Seasons in Succession, here, / Strip the gay Gardens, and deform the Year' ('Elegy', lines 18–19, FG), yet the action here is upbeat and self-willed. Similarly, Parnell's ageing beauty is warned that 'If Truth in spite of Manners must be told, / Why really *Fifty Five* is something old' (lines 5–6, FG) – the insistent rhyme of 'told' (with a pun on 'tolled') and 'old' sounds a death knell. Leapor's Dorinda warns her friend

Sempronia, 'Dear Nymph believe – 'tis true, as you're alive, / Those Temples show the Marks of Fifty-five' ('Dorinda at Her Glass', lines 86–7, FG) – yet how much more positive is the rhyme 'Alive/fifty-five' than 'old/told'. Leapor's poem advances the compensations of common sense and female friendship, and celebrates a life beyond the mirror.

Women poets often presented themselves and their physical appearance self-deprecatingly, comically or obliquely as if to avert the voyeuristic scrutiny of male readers. Leapor's 'caricatura' of her self in 'Mira's picture' as scrawny, brown-skinned and dirty, seems almost unconsciously to echo Martha Fowke's self-portrayal in 'Clio's Picture', first published in Anthony Hammond's *New Miscellany* (1720), an anthology which also contained early verses by Lady Mary Wortley Montagu. Although Fowke submits her 'form' to the 'kind' eyes of the male reader, she subverts convention by depicting herself as big-boned (with a 'Large' but 'not wond'rous Fair' forehead), and brown-skinned. 'Easy my Neck, but of no darling White' (p. 209, FG). In her *Epistles of Clio and Strephon* (1720), a popular sequence of verse epistles co-authored with William Bond (Lady Mary owned a copy), Fowke adopts the persona of a woman scarred by smallpox, whose true inner beauty is fully revealed only through her passionate letters. 'But Heav'n forbid that you should ever see / That *Outside*, which the *Vulgar* World calls me'.[31] Strephon never meets Clio, and thus Fowke bypasses the issue of physical appearance altogether. Mary Jones's 'After the Small Pox', modelled on Swift's 1721 birthday poem to Stella with its metaphor of woman as commercial commodity, briskly tackles the fact that beauty is 'but a Sign', the stock-in-trade of female identity. Stella has had to take down her sign now that 'all her stock of beauty's gone', but she has not become bankrupt. Her credit intact, she will erect a new 'sign', revealing the beauties of her mind, not just her body (pp. 307–8, FG).

Pope's death in 1744 and Swift's the following year did not have an immediate impact on women's poetry. While new modes began to transform the poetic landscape of the 1740s and 1750s – the visionary Pindaric ode of Gray, Collins and the Whartons, the long blank-verse meditative/philosophical poem such as Akenside's *Pleasures of Imagination* or Young's *Night Thoughts* – many women poets, at least until the 1770s, clung to an innate conservatism of form and continued to model themselves on Pope and Swift. Mary Robinson's 'London's Summer's Morning' and 'The Poet's Garret', inspired by Swift's urban pastorals and Pope's *Dunciad*, first appeared in print in 1800 and 1804 respectively, some years after Wordsworth and Coleridge's ground-breaking *Lyrical Ballads*. Yet the *Lyrical Ballads*' project to make poetry out of authentic feeling derived from common experience, especially of suffering, had already had its avatars in women poets such as the washerwoman Mary Collier and especially the milkseller Anne Yearsley. Collier's *The Woman's Labour* (1739), an indignant riposte to Duck's *The Thresher's Labour*, took its title, inspiration and publicity from its relationship to that poem. Collier protested at Duck's dismissive treatment of women, passive onlookers in a masculine and heroised world of sweaty toil. Collier counters Duck's patronising account of women's 'tattling' and 'prattling' with a robust defence of what we would now call female multi-tasking. Childless herself, she recognised the daily heroism of mothers gleaning in the fields all day then doing all the family's domestic duties, often on little sleep. Collier's blunt, end-stopped rhyming couplets capture the inescapable grind of the labouring woman's lot, as does the visceral image of hands rubbed raw from pan scouring:

> Until with Heat and Work, 'tis often known,
> Not only Sweat, but Blood runs trickling down
> Our Wrists and Fingers; still our Work demands
> The constant Action of our lab'ring Hands.
>
> (*The Woman's Labour*, lines 184–7, FG)

By the time Ann Yearsley, an impoverished labouring-class mother of six, was writing in the 1780s, the literature of sensibility had heightened reader responses to images of poverty and deprivation, particular if the sufferer was female. Just as Stephen Duck had been placed in the public domain by middle- or upper-class patrons anxious to discover untaught genius, so Yearsley was taken up by the evangelical writer Hannah More and the painful circumstances of her poverty paraded before the public eye. As More recounts in her prefatory letter to Yearsley's *Poems on Several Occasions* (1785), during the winter of 1783–4 Yearsley and her family were in acute distress and close to starvation, having resigned themselves to die in a barn. Relief came too late for Yearsley's mother, who died soon after. More and the bluestocking writer Elizabeth Montague enlisted support nationally for a subscription edition of Yearsley's poems and gave her grammar books to help her correct her language. *Poems on Several Occasions* attracted over a thousand subscribers. More's preface, which included a ten-page letter introducing the milkwoman's story and her work, attempted to place 'the wild genius of her rustic muse' within a literary context which valued wildness, originality and native vigour.[32] Yearsley refused, however, to be tamed. Unlike Collier and Duck, grateful recipients of the patronage system, Yearsley bit the hand that fed her. Resenting More's preface and her insistence on placing the extensive profits from the edition in trust for Yearsley's family lest sudden fame should turn their mother's head, Yearsley fought back, exploiting the media and the law to regain control of her own property.[33] As she proudly asserted in 'An Epistle to Stella', 'For mine's a stubborn and a savage will' (line 8) – itself an echo of the earlier labouring poet Mary Leapor's account of her own 'stubborn Will' ('Epistle to Artemisia', line 148, FG).

The attraction of Yearsley's verse comes from its refusal to kowtow, compromise or apologise for its lack of sophistication, correctness or learning. 'No customs, manners, or soft arts I boast, / On my rough soul your nicest rules are lost' ('An Epistle to Stella', lines 9–10). Yearsley's long prospect poem *Clifton Hill* shows evidence of far wider reading than More claimed for her – there are echoes of Thomson, Pope, Cowper, Collins, Akenside and Gray – and indeed, as her unpublished poem 'Addressed to Ignorance' shows, she resented any patronising aspersions of her ignorance. But central to Yearsley's poetic pitch is the argument that formal education alone does not make a great poet. Yearsley harnesses the idea prevalent in much writing of the 1750s and beyond (a path that led to the Preface to the *Lyrical Ballads*) that too many literary rules stifled poetic creativity. In 'To Mr **** An Unletter'd Poet, on Genius Unimproved', Yearsley develops the argument that the untrained mind is more receptive to moments of inspiration and intuition than the trained one: 'Deep in the soul live ever tuneful springs, / Waiting the touch of Ecstacy, which strikes / Most pow'rful on defenceless, untaught Minds' (lines 49–51). She boldly argues for her own poetic independence:

> . . . Dauntless Thought
> I eager seiz'd, no formal Rules e'er aw'd;
> No Precedent controul'd; no Custom fix'd
> My independent spirit: on the wing
> She still shall guideless soar. (lines 37–41, FG)

In the first decade of the century the non-conformist Isaac Watts had sent his 'Adventurous Muse' over similarly uncharted water. 'Impatient of the Reins', she 'Pursues an unattempted Course, / Breaks all the Criticks Iron Chains' ('The Adventurous Muse', lines 32–3, FG). Yet Yearsley speaks for herself, not through an impersonal muse. Few women poets of the century are so self-reflexive, so prepared to grapple with and lay bare the sources of, and barriers to, their own literary creativity.

> Oft as I trod my native wilds alone,
> Strong gusts of thought wou'd rise, but rise to die;

> The portals of the swelling soul, ne'er op'd
> By liberal converse, rude ideas strove
> Awhile for vent, but found it not, and died.
> Thus rust the Mind's best powers.
>
> ('On Mrs Montagu', p. 482, FG)

Hannah More framed Yearsley within a recognised discourse of rural obscurity and buried talent, as Thomas Gray might have seen her. In her Introduction to the *Poems* she adapts and quotes lines 51–2 of Gray's *Elegy*: 'Chill Penury repress'd her noble rage / And froze the genial current of her soul.'[34] Yearsley transcends this framework by vocalising her own frustrations. As David Fairer notes, moments of compression and entanglement represent Yearsley at her best, as a poet of struggle and difficulty.[35]

The last monosyllabic half line – 'Thus rust the Mind's best powers' – shows an almost metaphysical compression. More perceptively claimed that Yearsley's verse was sometimes 'obscure from brevity' and at other times 'diffuse from redundancy'. This unevenness of texture, ranging from rhetorical floridity to a kind of minimalist imagism, characterises her long and unusual topographical poem *Clifton Hill*, first published in *Poems on Several Occasions*.[36] In the 'tangled wood' deep in Clifton Gorge, lower animal life forms competing for food 'Chew the wash'd weed driven by the beating wave' – the alliterative 'wash'd', 'weed', 'wave' driving the line along (line 180). *Clifton Hill* draws on the tradition of topographical and 'prospect' poems such as Denham's *Cooper's Hill* and Pope's *Windsor-Forest* but offers no sweeping vistas or views in which the eye 'commands' the landscape. The reader's eye is drawn to the minutiae of flora and fauna competing for survival in the valley – the snail, the timid rabbit, the sightless mole, the sheep struggling to gain 'a meal penurious from the barren plain' – 'Ye bleating innocents! Dispel your fears, / My woe-struck soul in all your troubles shares' (lines 106–8). Like Finch's 'Nocturnal Reverie', *Clifton Hill* describes a feminised landscape in which both woman and animal share a sense of vulnerability to human activity. But Yearsley seeks a closer identification with oppressed nature, finding within it, almost like the seventeenth-century poets Lovelace and Marvell, emblems of the self. The 'harmless' snail which 'shuns the bolder day' becomes a type for the poet '(Alas! If transmigration should prevail, / I fear LACTILLA's soul must house in snail', lines 1701–1, 172–3, FG). So too does 'the toad envenom'd, hating human eyes, / [which] Here springs to light, lives long, and aged dies' (lines 166–7, FG) – in some ways a far more appropriate natural emblem of Yearsley's prickly, self-defensive solitariness.

Although recent critics, notably Donna Landry and David Fairer, have recuperated *Clifton Hill*, it is important to acknowledge that it is a poem of very variable quality.[37] Like the work of many autodidacts it wears its sources on its sleeve, and there are lapses in taste and unintentional stylistic incongruities, such as the application of Thomson's description of a bull in 'Winter' – 'The conscious Heifer snuffs the stormy Gale'[38] – to a lovesick young swain who 'stalks along the vale, / And snuffs fresh ardour from the flying gale' (Yearsley, *Clifton Hill*, lines 45–6, FG). Like other eighteenth-century georgics such as *The Seasons* and Cowper's *The Task*, it is a poem of striking thematic juxtapositions and sudden tonal shifts, where public-spirited diatribes against 'Indolence' and 'Fashion' give way to personal meditation or landscape description. Such juxtapositions are brought into even sharper relief by the relentless drive of the rhyming couplets, an oddly constricting choice of form given the poem's mainly blank-verse models. Yet *Clifton Hill* remains one of the most memorable of eighteenth-century women's poems. For all her snail-like shyness, Yearsley has the confidence to use the landscape as a projection of the poet's mind, either in moments of ecstasy, or in recoiling from personal trauma such as her mother's death. Whereas poets such as Thomson and Cowper had incorporated within their georgic poems 'interpolated narratives' such as the tales of the lightning-struck Celadon and Amelia or the story of poor crazy Kate, Yearsley's tale of Louisa, the traumatised German refugee haunting the Clifton Hills, takes over the narrative. Nature mirrors mind:

> O'erwhelm'd, thou dy'st amid the wilder roar
> Of lawless anarchy, which sweeps the soul,
> While her drown'd faculties like pebbles roll,
> Unloos'd, uptorn, by whirlwinds of despair. (lines 282–5, FG)

Yearsley's Louisa, who 'once confessed, in a lucid interval, that she had escaped from a Convent, in which she had been confin'd by her father, on refusing a marriage of his proposing, her affections being engaged to another man', recalls Pope's Eloisa, an earlier victim of illicit passion incarcerated within convent walls.[39] But unlike Pope, who ends 'Eloisa to Abelard' by affirming the poet's immortality as one who transforms suffering into art ('He best can paint 'em, who shall feel 'em most),[40] Yearsley rejects such consolations. Her identification with Louisa's broken mind and disconnected thoughts makes the process too painful.

> Ill starr'd LOUISA! Memory, 'tis a strain,
> Which fills my soul with sympathetic pain.
> Remembrance, hence, give thy vain struggles o'er,
> Nor swell the line with forms that live no more.
> (lines 293–6, FG)

It is a gesture characteristic of eighteenth-century women poets, who refuse to construct their own poetic immortality out of the sufferings of others.

Notes

1. See Isobel Grundy, '(Re)discovering Women's Texts', in Vivien Jones (ed.), *Women and Literature in Britain 1700–1800* (Cambridge: Cambridge University Press, 2000), pp. 179–96.
2. See Margaret Ezell, *Writing Women's Literary History* (Baltimore: Johns Hopkins University Press, 1993) and *Social Authorship and the Advent of Print* (Baltimore: Johns Hopkins University Press, 1999).
3. As Margaret Doody notes, 'The study of women's poetry has yet to be fully integrated with the study of our poetry in general.' See 'Women Poets of the Eighteenth Century', in Jones (ed.), *Women and Literature in Britain*, p. 218.
4. In Sarah Fyge Egerton, *Poems on Several Occasions* (London: J. Nutt, 1703), pp. 23–4, and David Fairer and Christine Gerrard (eds.), *Eighteenth-Century Poetry: An Annotated Anthology*, second revised edition (Oxford: Blackwell, 2004). Further quotations from the Fairer and Gerrard edition will be indicated as FG, preceded by line numbers or page numbers.
5. First published in *Miscellany Poems* (1713), pp. 230–47, reprinted in FG, pp. 26–33.
6. *Astraea Redux*, line 46, in *The Poems of John Dryden*, ed. James Kinsley (Oxford: Oxford University Press, 1962), p. 17.
7. *Windsor-Forest*, line 386, in *Alexander Pope: A Critical Edition of the Major Works*, ed. Pat Rogers (Oxford: Oxford University Press, 1993).
8. See esp. Carol Barash, *English Women's Poetry, 1649–1714: Politics, Community and Linguistic Authority* (Oxford: Clarendon Press, 1996).
9. See Susanna Centlivre, *A Poem. Humbly Presented to His Most Sacred Majesty George, King of Great Britain, France and Ireland* (London, 1714) and Kathryn King, 'Political Verse and Satire: Monarchy, Party and Female Political Agency', in Sarah Prescott and David E. Shuttleton (eds.), *Women and Poetry 1660–1750* (Basingstoke: Palgrave Macmillan, 2003), pp. 203–22.
10. See Isobel Grundy, *Lady Mary Wortley Montagu: Comet of the Enlightenment* (Oxford: Oxford University Press, 1999), pp. 89–93; David Fairer, *English Poetry of the Eighteenth Century* (London: Longman, 2003), pp. 12–13.
11. Lady Mary Wortley Montagu, *Essays and Poems, and 'Simplicity, a Comedy'*, ed. Robert Halsband and Isobel Grundy (Oxford: Clarendon Press, 1977, revised edition 1993). All further quotations from Montagu's poetry, unless otherwise stated, are from this edition, and cited by line number.
12. Isobel Grundy, 'Lady Mary Wortley Montagu and the Theatrical Eclogue', *Lumen*, 17 (1998), pp. 63–75. See also her 'Lady Mary Wortley Montagu, *Six Town Eclogues* and other Poems' in Christine Gerrard (ed.), *A Companion to Eighteenth-Century Poetry* (Oxford: Blackwell, 2006), pp. 184–96.
13. See Fairer, *English Poetry of the Eighteenth Century*, pp. 12–13.
14. Pope, *The Rape of the Lock*, i.107, *Major Works*.

15. See Grundy, 'Lady Mary Wortley Montagu, *Six Town Eclogues*', pp. 192–4.
16. Pope, 'Eloisa to Abelard', lines 199–200. *Major Works*.
17. *Ibid.*, lines 363–4.
18. Pope, *An Epistle to a Lady*, line 40, *Major Works*.
19. Pope, *An Epistle to Dr Arbuthnot*, line 409, *Major Works*.
20. Mary Jones, *Miscellanies in Prose and Verse* (Oxford, 1760), p. vi.
21. Pope, *An Epistle to Dr Arbuthnot*, line 303, *Major Works*.
22. *Ibid.*, line 16.
23. *Ibid.*, line 1.
24. *Ibid.*, line 116.
25. Mary Chandler, 'A Letter to the Right Honourable the Lady Russell', in *The Description of Bath, a Poem* (London, 1738).
26. Mary Leapor, *Poems on Several Occasions* (1748), 'To the Reader'.
27. See esp. Richard Greene, *Mary Leapor: A Study in Eighteenth-Century Women's Poetry* (Oxford: Clarendon Press, 1993).
28. See esp. Valerie Rumbold, 'The Alienated Insider: Mary Leapor in "Crumble-Hall"', *British Journal for Eighteenth-Century Studies*, 19 (1996), pp. 63–76, and David Fairer, 'Mary Leapor, "Crumble-Hall"', in Gerrard (ed.), *A Companion to Eighteenth-Century Poetry*, pp. 223–36.
29. Kathryn R. King, 'The Constructions of Femininity', in Gerrard (ed.), *A Companion to Eighteenth-Century Poetry*, p. 432.
30. For a comprehensive discussion of this trope, see Margaret Anne Doody, 'Women Poets of the Eighteenth Century', in Vivien Jones (ed.), *Women and Literature in Britain 1700–1800* (Cambridge: Cambridge University Press, 2000), pp. 225–6, and King, 'The Constructions of Femininity', pp. 434–7.
31. Martha Fowke, *The Epistles of Clio and Strephon* (London, 1720), p. xxix
32. Ann Yearsley, *Poems on Several Occasions* (London, 1785), p. vii. Subsequent quotations from Yearsley's poetry are from this edition, unless otherwise stated.
33. See Donna Landry, *The Muses of Resistance: Labouring-Class Women's Poetry in Britain, 1739–1796* (Cambridge: Cambridge University Press, 1990), pp. 120–65, and Moira Ferguson, *Eighteenth-Century Women Poets: Nation, Class, and Gender* (Albany: State University of New York Press, 1995), pp. 45–89.
34. See Introduction to Yearsley, *Poems on Several Occasions*, p. viii.
35. FG, p. 498, headnote.
36. More, Introduction to Yearsley, *Poems on Several Occasions*, p. viii; and see FG, pp. 483–9.
37. See Landry, *The Muses of Resistance*, pp. 130–43, and Fairer, *English Poetry of the Eighteenth Century*, pp. 207–9.
38. James Thomson, 'Winter', in *The Seasons* (London, 1748), line 133.
39. FG, p. 488, n. 206.
40. Pope, 'Eloisa to Abelard', lines 367–8, FG.

Chapter 20

Longer eighteenth-century poems (Akenside, Thomson, Young, Cowper and others)

RICHARD TERRY

The opening of 'Summer' in James Thomson's *The Seasons* (1730) finds the narrator hastening into the umbrageous depths of 'the mid-wood Shade' in order to sing 'the Glories of the circling Year'.[1] Embosomed in darkness, he petitions the spirit of '*Inspiration*' to infuse him with creative ecstasy. The effect of the passage is to announce a new manifesto for poetry, sharply at odds with the aesthetic principles upheld by most major poets of Thomson's day.[2] Pope, for example, in his *Epistle to Arbuthnot* (1735) justifies his own compositional practices on the grounds

> That not in Fancy's Maze he wander'd long,
> But stoop'd to Truth, and moraliz'd his song.[3]

Pope portrays 'Fancy' (or imagination) as a treacherous labyrinth into which any poet who forsakes truth and morality is all too easily lured, there to be undone. Not for him Thomson's heady description of creativity in terms of heightened emotions and mental entrancement.

From 'Summer', the poem returns to the narrator in his nocturnal wanderings: 'STILL let me pierce into the midnight Depth' (line 516). It is only now that he enters the haunts, and feels the dusky presence, of 'antient Bards' (line 523), with whom he inwardly communes. These bards are not named, but may well be intended as Druids, who, in the terms of one popular poetic myth, had become identified as founding fathers of the British poetic tradition. This idea that poetic self-realisation has got something to do with understanding one's filiation to an antecedent tradition is also evident in Mark Akenside's *The Pleasures of Imagination* (1744), in a section discussing the futility of trying to scale 'the severe ascent / Of high Parnassus' through toil alone. Instead, the aspiring poet must be touched by 'Nature's kindling breath' if he is to frequent the company of 'bards and sages old' (*TPoI*, 1.36–7, 42).[4] In a later passage, startlingly reminiscent of *The Seasons*, the narrator wanders in the 'windings' of an ancient wood and encounters a being 'more than human' who tutors him on the subject of universal benevolence as expressed through nature (*TPoI*, II.187, 226).

The removal to these dim-lit wooded settings suggests a poetry that arises from retreat or social withdrawal, from the idealised 'loneliness' that John Sitter has found to be a feature of many poems of the mid eighteenth century.[5] In all the poems discussed here, *The Seasons* and *The Pleasures of Imagination* as well as Edward Young's *Night Thoughts* (1742–5) and William Cowper's *The Task* (1785), some tension is felt between engagement with the world and withdrawal from it. In Cowper, for example, the depiction of a debased and oppressive outside world is always balanced against the harmonious domesticity that the poet enjoyed with Mary Unwin; in Young's career, if not in his major poem itself, an uneasy paradox exists, cruelly pointed out by George Eliot, between the other-worldly piety of which the poet became a public proponent and the cringing worldliness of his practical attempts to gain preferment.[6]

It is at the level of thematic consistencies of this kind, rather than in terms of any formalised set of generic prescripts, that this chapter will try to make sense of the 'longer poem' as a coherent entity. These are poems indeed whose family resemblance derives in good part from their very defiance of genre. Perhaps the best we can conclude is that these are verse works of notable length, which dispense, other than in the most desultory way, with narrative as an organisational principle. The matter that they accommodate can be variously descriptive, reflective, philosophical, didactic, panegyric or comic, or indeed all of these within a single work. What else helps nowadays to corral these works into a unified grouping is that they all alike could be seen as challenging or muddying the literary historical categories within which modern critics have tended to work. These are poems to which the term 'pre-Romantic' has been seen as having particular relevance.[7] In their championing of imagination as the prime source of creativity, reverence for nature, sentimental acknowledgment of suffering and politics of emancipation, they all could be viewed as prefiguring a Romantic aesthetic, or, perhaps more convincingly, as enlarging the rival conception of the 'Augustan'.

Another stream of literary-historical development within which these poems float is the slow modulation of English blank verse poetry that could be seen as connecting Milton and Wordsworth as unrivalled, though very different, practitioners of the form.[8] In the early eighteenth century, the heroic couplet, with its poised and stately certitudes, remains the dominant verse-form, though also prevalent, in writers like Swift and Prior, is the more rollicking octosyllabic or Hudibrastic couplet, with its rattling monosyllables and comic rhymes. Joined with these, however, is a species of blank verse poetry, inherited from Milton's *Paradise Lost* (1667). Milton bequeathed to eighteenth-century poets a repertoire of verse and stylistic techniques: sprawling verse paragraphs, convolved syntax, a powerfully sonorous sublimity, alliterative and mellifluous techniques and the use of verse to convey often quite scholarly and technical matter.[9] In an influential essay written in 1930, T. S. Eliot suggested that a distinctive dreariness pervades much eighteenth-century blank verse as a result of weaker poets being smothered by Milton's influence.[10] No poet before Cowper, a supreme admirer of Milton, is able to compose in a blank verse style that sufficiently resists Milton's influence as to seem fully relaxed and conversational.

While the Miltonic grand style exercised pressure on eighteenth-century blank verse writing from one side, the heroic couplet did so from another. Take some lines from Young's *Night Thoughts*:

> Our dying Friends come o'er us like a Cloud,
> To damp our brainless Ardors; and abate
> That Glare of Life, which often blinds the Wise.
> Our dying Friends are Pioneers, to smooth
> Our rugged Pass to Death; to break those Bars
> Of Terror, and Abhorrence, Nature throws
> Cross our obstructed way; and, thus, to make
> Wellcome, as Safe, our Port from every Storm.
> Each Friend by Fate snatcht from us, is a Plume
> Pluckt from the wing of human Vanity,
> Which makes us stoop from our aërial Heights,
> And dampt with Omen of our own Decease. (III.277–88)[11]

There is a good deal here that typifies the poem as a whole, in particular its ceaseless spiritual blackmailing of the reader, here invoked and included in an envisioned common destiny through the repeated use of the pronoun 'our'. The passage (as I have excerpted it) rounds off with a premonition of death, just as death itself, as the poem relentlessly assures us, will supply its own inevitable rounding off. In one sense, the lines quoted are not entirely representative of Young's verse style. The passage above contains six run-on lines, an unusually high ratio in relation to Young's general preference for heavy end-stopping. The overspill at the line-ending, however, is compensated by frequent obstructive punctuation in the mid-line, so that the general feel remains one of restraint and boundedness. Young's blank verse is invariably touched by the ghostly lineaments of the couplet: even if the sense-units and line-units are not everywhere closely married, the poem constantly strives to deliver its exhortations in the form of apothegm. Dying friends are 'Pioneers' and the deaths of those close to us are, as it were, feathers 'Pluckt from the wing of human Vanity'. The very texture of Young's poem is epigrammatic, an unstinting flow of highly chiselled and arresting formulations of Christian responsibility out of which its huge length is generated.

Young's blank verse, bearing as it does the faint impression of residual couplets, can be contrasted with the much more Miltonic style of Akenside:

> For as old Memnon's image, long renown'd
> By fabling Nilus, to the quiv'ring touch
> Of Titan's ray, with each repulsive string
> Consenting, sound thro' the warbling air
> Unbidden strains; even so did nature's hand
> To certain species of external things,
> Attune the finer organs of the mind:
> So the glad impulse of congenial pow'rs,
> Or of sweet sound, or fair proportion'd form,
> The grace of motion, or the bloom of light,
> Thrills thro' imagination's tender frame,
> From nerve to nerve: all naked and alive
> They catch the spreading rays: till now the soul
> At length discloses every tuneful spring,
> To that harmonious movement from without
> Responsive. (*TPoI*, I.109–24)

Akenside's two poems are an exploration of the nature of human sensory experience and its relation to pleasure and morality, the more daring for attempting to dissect these elusive concepts in the windy and grandiloquent style of *Paradise Lost*. The passage above is made up of a number of trademark Miltonic ingredients: mythological references, the tolling of proper nouns, a tendency to listing or itemisation and the inversion of natural syntactical order, as in 'To that harmonious movement . . . / Responsive'. Unlike Young's, Akenside's blank verse generates a strong forward momentum: no halting punctuation mark occurs until the sixth line of the passage above. The lines themselves constantly tumble forward over the line-ending, simply not acknowledging it.

What too often vitiates Akenside's poetry is its determined poeticality, its occasional dustiness of phrasing, tendency for anthropomorphosis and habit of word clustering. In the quotation above, 'sound', 'warbling' and 'strains' (lines 112–13) trip over each other semantically, as do 'glad' and 'congenial' lower down. For a blank verse fashioned in Milton's shadow, and yet denuded of poeticalities of this sort, we have to wait until Cowper's *The Task*:

God made the country, and man made the town.
What wonder then, that health and virtue, gifts
That can alone make sweet the bitter draught
That life holds out to all, should most abound
And least be threatened in the fields and groves?
Possess ye therefore, ye who borne about
In chariots and sedans, know no fatigue
But that of idleness, and taste no scenes
But such as art contrives, possess ye still
Your element; there only, ye can shine,
There only minds like yours can do no harm.

(*The Task*, I.749–59)[12]

What distinguishes Cowper's lines is their ease of transition, from the sharply apothegmatic to relaxed exposition, and finally, and undemonstratively, into the vocative case. Verbal modification is much less in evidence here than, for example, in Akenside's lines, in which the adjectives virtually crowd each other out. Perhaps what chiefly distinguishes the unrhymed verse of *The Task*, marking it out as perhaps the finest written in the eighteenth century up until that point, is its proximity to prose, or prose invested with the subtlest sense of measure and cadence.

When Thomson's narrator implores the coming of '*Inspiration*' in 'Summer' (lines 15–20), he envisages her arrival as leading to his own self-invention as a poet. He hopes to 'steal one Look / Creative of the Poet' from the deity's 'fix'd serious Eye, and raptur'd Glance' (lines 17–19). These lines associate inspiration to a striking degree with vision, with seeing things truly and proportionately and deriving pleasure from viewing them. The idea that inspiration equates to a refined way of seeing is prominent in all the poems discussed in this chapter. Take these lines from *The Task*:

And witness, dear companion of my walks,
Whose arm this twentieth winter I perceive
Fast lock'd in mine, with pleasure such as love,
Confirm'd by long experience of thy worth
And well-tried virtues could alone inspire –
Witness a joy that thou hast doubled long.
Thou know'st my praise of nature most sincere,
And that my raptures are not conjured up
To serve occasions of poetic pomp,
But genuine, and art partner of them all.
How oft upon yon eminence, our pace

Has slacken'd to a pause, and we have borne
The ruffling wind scarce conscious that it blew,
While admiration feeding at the eye,
And still unsated, dwelt upon the scene. (1.144–58)

Cowper's close companionship with Mary Unwin, begun in 1765, was only broken by her death in 1796, a trauma from which he never recovered. In the lines above, she appears as both a partner in the poet's adoration of nature but also as a witness of it, of its artistic authenticity. Cowper's raptures are characteristically those of the gaze, his 'admiration feeding at the eye, / And still unsated'. The lines cited are notable for the way that sight is unobtrusively lent primacy over the other senses. The pressure of Mary's arm, linked securely in his own, is not here felt but 'perceived', and the wind that ruffles their countenances, far from being a Wordsworthian 'correspondent breeze' bringing joy as it fans the poet's cheek, is simply dismissed as a distraction to the serenity of the gaze.

Having gained the 'eminence', Cowper and his companion are able to survey the snaking Ouse valley, their eyes being conducted to the square tower of Clifton church and to distant villages wreathed in smoke. What the passage unfolds is a poetic prospect, a description of a terrain, generally as perceived from an elevated vantage point, that visually imparts a sense of compositional harmony. The idea of the visual prospect is an important organisational principle throughout Thomson's and Cowper's poems, but the prospect does not in itself explain the extraordinary ascendancy of the eye in their poems. What perhaps helps rather more to understand this are the new theories of imagination that became current in the early eighteenth century, such as the one advanced in Joseph Addison's influential *Spectator* papers on the pleasures of the imagination.

Spectator 411 (21 June 1712) begins by setting out Addison's conviction of the superiority of the sight over its fellow senses, especially the touch: 'OUR Sight is the most perfect and most delightful of all our Senses.' Its superiority lies in its ability to commune with its objects of stimulation from much further afield than any of the other senses: it diffuses outwards, spreading itself over 'an infinite Multitude of Bodies'.[13] It is sight moreover that furnishes the 'imagination', a faculty that Addison associates with the apprehension of objects actually present to the eye as well as those existing only in the mind's eye. The overall effect of Addison's theory was to blur the point at which vision stops and imagination begins. Between the passive reception of visual data, on the one hand, and the coining of the entirely fictitious, on the other, lay a mental process to which both sight and imagination might lay equal claim. This was the activity through which the mind assimilates, and in doing so helps to mould, what has been received by the eye. It is what Young refers to when he states that the senses 'half create the wondrous World, they see' (*Night Thoughts*, VI. 427). The idea that sight actively creates its own objects accounts in good measure for the exaltation of the poetic gaze that we find in Thomson and Cowper.

Thomson's *The Seasons* is perhaps the earliest major poem written in illustration of Addison's ideas about imagination. Take the following lines:

> Oft let me wander o'er the dewy Fields
> Where Freshness breathes, and dash the trembling Drops
> From the bent Bush, as thro' the verdant Maze
> Of Sweet-briar Hedges I pursue my Walk;
> Or taste the Smell of Dairy; or ascend
> Some Eminence, AUGUSTA, in thy Plains,
> And see the Country, far-diffus'd around,
> One boundless Blush, one white-empurpled Shower
> Of mingled Blossoms; where the raptur'd Eye
> Hurries from Joy to Joy, and, hid beneath
> The fair Profusion, yellow Autumn spies. ('Spring', lines 103–13)

Wandering through the 'Plains', the narrator's sensory experiences are tactile and olfactory, and only when he surmounts the 'Eminence' are these senses usurped by that of sight. Only when this happens, moreover, do the lines burst into rapture and a nearly religious affirmation of nature. The countryside viewed by the poet lies 'far-diffus'd around', this being an expression Thomson uses regularly to describe a panoramic view sweeping around a full 360 degrees. What exists in the poet's field of vision and what is actually created by his gaze is confused. The land is 'diffus'd around' as if the whole countryside has been poured out or dispersed from the fixed position from which the poet views it, but the term also invokes Addison's notion that sight is itself a sort of distant or 'diffusive kind of Touch'.[14] The land itself and the poet's visual apprehension of it become almost as one.

Thomson's descriptions of nature are composed of a complex natural iconography. The panorama described here is 'boundless', one of his favourite words for representing a prospect of a particular sort. In 'Summer', for example, he recounts climbing Richmond Hill and, having reached the top, surveying with 'raptur'd Eye' the 'boundless Landskip' beneath ('Summer', line 1409): 'boundless', here, means that the gaze can advance without impediment to the horizon. Thomson's boundless prospects, however, provoke not just rapture but also poignancy, for they put the reader in mind that the human condition, as that of all creatures, is to be metaphysically limited and bounded. Only God, 'The sun of being, boundless, unimpair'd' (*TPoI*, II.356), in Akenside's words, and God's infinite love for humanity, can ever truly partake of boundlessness. All other life falls under the condition of impairment, the relative privation of any creature in the hierarchical order being determined by its negative differentiation from God. Of all creaturely limitations, the greatest is supplied, of course, by the universal subjection to death. For this reason, Thomson's epiphanies of enraptured, unbounded vision always seem chimerical, or at least as merely presentiments of something belonging not to this world but to another one.

Another reason why sight was considered superior to the other senses was its near-alliance with the understanding. Whereas knowledge enters at the eye, the other senses could be seen instead as conduits to indulgence and luxury. This is what Akenside has in mind when he notes that the 'beams of truth' can gratify 'understanding's eye' more 'Than all the blandishments of sound his ear, / Than all of taste his tongue' (*TPoI*, II.100–3). What ravishes the gazing eye in these poems is not the harmony of the landscape so much as its profuseness, the sheer copiousness of the created world. Nature's bounty, however, is to be found not just in the visible world but also the microscopic one by which early eighteenth-century writers were particularly fascinated:

> GRADUAL . . . what numerous Kinds descend,
> Evading even the microscopic Eye!
> Full Nature swarms with Life; one wondrous Mass
> Of Animals, or Atoms organiz'd,
> Waiting the *vital Breath*, when PARENT-HEAVEN
> Shall bid his Spirit blow. The hoary Fen
> In putrid Steams, emits the living Cloud
> Of Pestilence. Thro' subterranean Cells,
> Where searching Sun-beams scarce can find a Way,
> Earth animated heaves
>
> . . .
>
> Nor is the Stream
> Of purest Crystal, nor the lucid Air,
> Tho' one transparent Vacancy it seems,
> Void of their unseen People. These, conceal'd
> By the kind Art of forming HEAVEN, escape
> The grosser Eye of Man. ('Summer', lines 287–96, 308–13)

The passage draws upon the observations of micro-organisms made since their original discovery by the Belgian natural historian Antony van

Leeuwenhoek in 1674.[15] Typically of Thomson, however, a plethora of different discourses encroaches upon the act of description, of which science is only one. What the passage details, in fact, is not what you might see through a microscope but rather what you can't see, what evades 'even the microscopic Eye'. The inner recesses of the invisible are accessible not to magnification but to imagination. The invisibility of much of what God has created could seem to constitute an anomaly: why should God divorce us from a full appreciation of his handiwork? But Thomson explains the mystery by arguing that even in this detail God takes pains to provide for us, for if humans became sensible of the 'Worlds / In Worlds inclos'd', they would be overwhelmed and 'stun'd' by sensory overload ('Summer', lines 313–17).

From microbes to insects, birds and the higher mammals, Thomson depicts nature heaving and teeming with created life. Nor does such a generality exclude man himself: 'Now swarms the Village o'er the jovial Mead' ('Summer', line 352). Such abundance is connected with Thomson's boundless God, a God who invests himself in nature through an outpouring of his creativity, 'Whose single Smile has, from the first of Time, / Fill'd, overflowing, all those Lamps of Heaven' ('Summer', lines 179–80). Images of overflow and inundation are particularly frequent and graphic in *The Seasons*, exemplifying the sublimity of the natural world but also the dangers it inherently presents to humankind. What is most to be feared is invariably shown as something that descends from above. In 'Summer', 'potent Heat and Floods' are described as 'Prone-rushing from the Clouds' (lines 654–5) and, later in the poem, winter and its harbinger, frost, are depicted as dropping from the sky ('Winter', line 742). Images of a world in which divine creativity has run to an overwhelming excess can be found in other long poems. Akenside, for example, describes the sun as 'pouring' out a 'redundant stream / Of light' (*TPoI*, I.192–3).

Thomson's vision of a natural abundance that can ravish but also engulf humankind is nowhere expressed so poignantly as in the description of the shepherd perishing in the snow:

> As thus the Snows arise; and foul, and fierce,
> All Winter drives along the darken'd Air;
> In his own loose-revolving Fields the Swain
> Disaster'd stands; sees other Hills ascend,
> Of unknown joyless Brow; and other Scenes,
> Of horrid Prospect, shag the trackless Plain:
> Nor finds the River, nor the Forest, hid
> Beneath the formless Wild; but wanders on
> From Hill to Dale, still more and more astray;

Impatient flouncing thro' the drifted Heaps,
Stung with the Thoughts of Home; the Thoughts of Home
Rush on his Nerves and call their Vigour forth
In many a vain Attempt. How sinks his Soul!

. . .

In vain for him th'officious Wife prepares
The Fire fair-blazing and the Vestment warm;
In vain his little Children, peeping out
Into the mingling Storm, demand their Sire,
With Tears of artless Innocence. Alas!
Nor Wife, nor Children, more shall he behold,
Nor Friends, nor sacred Home. On every Nerve
The deadly Winter seizes; shuts up Sense;
And, o'er his inmost Vitals creeping cold,
Lays him along the Snows, a stiffen'd Corse,
Stretch'd out and bleaching in the northern Blast.

('Winter', lines 276–88, 311–21)

What slays the shepherd is 'deadly Winter', the human plight of subjection to seasonality. Although, by this point, the poem has described, or at least attested to, numerous animal deaths, this scene is climactic in terms of recording the first death of a human being, occurring in the season in which the year itself succumbs to its own death.

Just as elsewhere the ecstasies of sensory experience are shown as pertaining uniquely to the eye, so here does the agony of death. Oddly, the 'creeping cold' only registers once the shepherd's senses have already begun to 'shut up'. Instead, it is his eye that undergoes the ultimate dismay. As he searches the circle of his vision, surveying the 'loose-revolving Fields', the prospect that he meets is 'horrid'. In its own grimly ironic way, this is another of Thomson's 'boundless' landscapes, except boundless in the sense of having all its features obliterated by the white blanket. As the shepherd flails around, he feels the bitterness of disappointed sight, 'His Wife, his Children, and his Friends unseen' (line 310), and, as he perishes, fixed on his mind's eye is the image of their defeated anticipation of his return, as they wait 'peeping out / Into the mingling Storm'. The thick canopy of snow that, having killed the man, will in time bury him, is just one of those inundations in the poem that stem from Thomson's 'overflowing' God, whose wanton plenitude can both amaze and destroy.

While Thomson's *The Seasons* and Cowper's *The Task* are rightly enough poems about nature, the poet's communion with nature is invariably informed, or even interrupted, by a range of encroaching discourses. We can think of the brute economic realities that are brought home to Cowper when he finds the path of his ramble barred by a landowner's gates, and the landscapes pictured by both poets draw on contemporary ideas about vision, including microscopic vision.[16] Yet what also encroach on descriptions of nature in the long poems are theological issues concerning the exact relation between God and the created world. Thomson's and Cowper's poems are informed by a strong sense of God's immanence within nature: 'Nature is but a name for an effect / Whose cause is God' (*The Task*, VI.223–4). For Akenside and Young, however, nature is characteristically seen as a harmonious volume inviting the perusal of the godly, a set text for those wishing to receive demonstration of God's purposes. All the poets assume that the true constitution of the natural world is to be understood as much by faith and theological doctrine as by observation.

The natural plenitude that both Thomson's and Cowper's descriptions so frequently discover is perhaps less something that is viewed than something that is dictated by theology. Plenitude provided a precise theological justification, a theodicy, accounting for what otherwise could seem undisguised flaws in the created world. Both Thomson and Cowper were men of strongly humanitarian sympathies and acutely attuned to the sufferings incident to animals. Cowper kept domesticated hares as a statement of his compassion, and Thomson envisages the possibility of animals moving up a staircase of vertical reincarnations until they eventually become no longer subject to maltreatment by humans.[17] The visibility of animal suffering, however, was something that could only lead to reflections about the relative privations of animals, the limitation of their capacities in comparison with humans and their depressed status in the hierarchy of creation.

The fact of widespread animal suffering might be put down to the cruelty of individual human beings, but could also be seen as pointing to something remiss and inequitable in creation as a whole. One purpose served by the theory of plenitude was accordingly to provide a very particular exculpation of God in the face of such a charge, by alleging such privation to be necessary and unavoidable since God fell under an ethical imperative to confer life on all creatures who could possibly receive it: the strong and the weak, the fast and the slow, the fierce and the defenceless. Akenside explicitly reflects this doctrine when describing how God infuses life into 'endless forms of being', endowing with life all creatures 'thro the sum / Of possible existence' (*TPoI*, II.318, 326–7). Such a belief led directly to the further one that the chain of being was unbroken, with each link filled by some creature nearly allied to, but minutely differentiated from, those above and beneath it. This is what

Thomson is reasoning when in 'Spring' (line 545), he records of a riot of floral colour that 'No gradual Bloom is wanting'; and the same idea is evident in various passages in Young's *Night Thoughts*. 'By what minute degrees her [Nature's] Scale ascends', wonders Young, and elsewhere salutes mankind as a 'Distinguisht *Link* in Being's endless Chain!' (*Night Thoughts*, VI.715, I.73) For the mid-century poets to paint nature was for them to see it as God's handiwork, made by Him and justifying Him.[18]

Eighteenth-century long poems describe, reflect, digress, moralise and rhapsodise but do not, in any consistent way, narrate. Indeed, all the major poems seem highly conscious of the need to manage length, to create principles of articulation, in the absence of any sustaining narrative thread. Of course, such issues were also presenting themselves to prose writers of the same era. Fielding and Smollett are the earliest English fictional writers self-consciously to carve up their fictional material into chapters. In Fielding's novels, the artifice gives rise to comic intrusions by the narrator as well as telegraphed modulations of tone and genre. In Sterne's *Tristram Shandy*, the arrangement of the novel into books and chapters only serves to highlight the narrator's unflappable indirectness.

One model of how a non-narrative poem might unfold itself was provided by the theory of mental association, pioneered by Locke but also addressed by Hartley and Hume.[19] Alexander Knox even claimed that mental association provides a key to understanding the very essence of poetic composition: 'poetry owes its very existence to that natural exercise of the human mind which is usually termed the association of ideas'.[20] Thought association as a poetic technique or, more probably, as a retrospective defence of works that might otherwise seem disjointed and formless, is integral to long eighteenth-century poems. Young, for example, begins *Night Thoughts* with the following plea on behalf of the work: '*AS the Occasion of this Poem was* Real, *not* Fictitious; *so the Method pursued in it, was rather* imposed, *by what spontaneously arose in the Author's Mind, on that Occasion, than* meditated, *or* designed.' The poet feels liberated in not needing consciously to impart form to the work, but at the same time he is depicted as more the servant than the master of his own thought processes. The order of the poem was 'imposed', as he puts it, by the course of his own spontaneity. Later he notes that the 'Facts mentioned' in the poem, chiefly the deaths recorded in Books I–III, '*did naturally pour these moral Reflections on the Thought of the Writer*', as if he were powerless to stop the visitation of the solemn ideas arising in his head.[21] The poem gathers length through the continuous unfurling of moral reflections from the sparse incidents of the narrative.

In the 'Advertisement' to *The Task*, Cowper describes the genesis of that poem in terms similar to the 'Method' pursued in *Night Thoughts*. The poem had arisen when the subject of a sofa had been suggested to him, and the poet 'having much leisure, connected another subject with it; and pursuing the train of thought to which his situation and turn of mind led him, brought forth at length . . . a serious affair – a Volume'. *The Task* starts out as a comic eulogy on the humble but serviceable sofa, but through a chain of imaginative synapses it eventually builds to a volume of substance and gravity. The opening focus on the sofa provides a strong poetic mooring that then leads to imaginative embarkation and travel through the rest of the poem.

Unlike the other works discussed in this essay, Cowper's sallies of the imagination are always set in relation to the stasis and snugness of home. The imagination streams out to encounter the crowded, dangerous external world, but the poet can retreat back at will into the tranquillising cosiness of his fireside: it is like a dream from which he can easily shake himself awake. In 'The Winter Evening', Cowper contemplates himself 'sitting and surveying thus at ease / The globe and its concerns' (*The Task*, IV.94–5), where there is a stress on the insulated repose from which imagination emanates. Imagining a sea voyager traversing the oceans, Cowper muses that

> He travels and I too. I tread his deck,
> Ascend his topmast, through his peering eyes
> Discover countries, with a kindred heart
> Suffer his woes and share in his escapes,
> While fancy, like the finger of a clock,
> Runs the great circuit, and is still at home.
>
> (*The Task*, IV.114–19)

What is distinctive here is not imagination conceived as travel, but the domestic intimacy to which the imagination can always return once it has run its course: 'fancy . . . / Runs the great circuit, and is still at home'.[22] The main term through which Cowper here conveys a sense of the rambling nature of imagination is 'roving'. To rove is to wander, if not aimlessly, then with a measure of disregard for any predetermined itinerary or destination: 'Roving as I rove / Where shall I find an end, or how proceed?' (*The Task*, IV.232–3). At the end of his poem, Cowper justifies his poetic labour in terms of having 'roved for fruit', having 'Roved far and gather'd much' (*The Task*, VI.1011–12). 'Roving' encapsulates the view so powerful in both Thomson's and Cowper's long poems that imagination is essentially an itinerant activity, an excursion of the mind.

The absence of narrative thread led many eighteenth-century long poems to assume the form of a medley, a work composed of a heterogeneous mixture of parts. The management of the constituent elements of a long work was identified as a key skill that developing poets needed to master, one that eighteenth-century critics associated with the term 'contexture', defined by Dr Johnson as 'The disposition of parts one amongst others; the composition of any thing out of separate parts . . . the manner in which any thing is woven and formed'.[23] Long poems were in effect exercises in poetic contexture. The fact that Thomson's *The Seasons* and Akenside's *The Pleasures of Imagination* were so extensively rewritten also suggests that the particular assemblage of materials that constituted any one version of a poem was seen as essentially provisional and impermanent. A poem like *The Seasons* is accordingly not so much a verbal artefact as a verbal process.[24]

Long poems sought to diversify themselves through incorporating a range of generic or conventional forms: sublime or rhapsodic passages; eulogiums on individuals, modern inventions or on national advancement in general; passages of mock-heroic inflation or georgic instruction; and comic or pathetic vignettes. However, the structural rhythm of such poems is in the main established by the interspersing of passages of description and reflection. This can be seen in Book I of *The Task* and in the 'Argument' affixed to it, of which I cite the opening part:

> *Historical deduction of seats, from the stool to the Sofa. – A School-boy's ramble. – A walk in the country. – The scene described. – Rural sounds as well as sights delightful. – Another walk. – Mistake concerning the charms of solitude, corrected. – Colonnades commended. – Alcove and the view from it. – The Wilderness. – The Grove. – The Thresher. – The necessity and the benefits of exercise.*

The contents of the first book are rendered as a series of described events, surveyed landscapes or wholesome reflections. As announced in the 'Argument', these appear as a breathless train, with no clarification as to the logic by which one topic succeeds from another. The '*School-boy's ramble*' follows inscrutably from a passage about the aetiology of seating, and it is only in the poem itself that the logic of the link, that exercise provides an antidote to the luxury epitomised by the modern sofa, divulges itself. Reading a poem such as *The Task* is a process of deciphering the occult argumentative links or transitions of thought through which such ostensibly discrete subjects are combined.

That a poem should be composed of parts entailed that it should also employ transitions from one part to another. The best kind of transitions were ones that provoked some measure of surprise but that at the same time disclosed to the reader the nature of their own internal logic. The need was always to balance the diversification brought by digression outwards from a particular topic against the competing claim of thematic coherence. Several long poems betray a degree of uneasiness or at least delicacy around the issue of their own ostensible digressiveness. Thomson, in the Argument of 'Spring', speaks of his own '*Digressions arising from the Subject*' (so hardly digressive at all), as Richard Jago does in the Preface to his *Edge Hill*: 'Digressions, and Episodes belonging to, or easily deducible from the Subject'.[25] The aesthetic of the long poem was always one that involved having it both ways, benefiting from the eclecticism of being essentially a compendium of topics while still laying claim to the integrity of a single work.

Eighteenth-century long poems are characterised by their substitution of narrative drive with complex internal mechanisms of self-articulation. Thomson's and Cowper's poems are carried along by the nimble, roving imaginative eye. In *Night Thoughts*, length is guaranteed through Young's windy rhetorical temporising, his unflagging generation of moral reflections based on the limited human incidents portrayed in the poem. Yet paradoxically, these are poems that are all alike obsessed with the very thing that their indirect and procrastinatory techniques might seem most determined to stave off: that is, the End. Their poetic resistance to closure understands only too well the irresistibility of the individual end to which all of us must eventually succumb, as well as the judgment to be handed out on the Last Day.[26]

Young's *Night Thoughts*, over its huge sprawling length, is a meditation on the inevitability of death, and an exhortation to the Christian to lead a life unremittingly informed by death's proximity. As Young says in a letter to the Duchess of Portland: 'The shortness, & Casualty of Life, & ye Certainty of Death, are such obvious, & quite Indisputable Points' that people ought really to 'think of little else'.[27] Of all the visual or imaginative prospects from which these long poems are to a significant extent constructed, death itself is the most sublimely foreboding. The sense of a grim countdown is evident also in *The Task*, Book II of which, 'The Time-Piece', was intended to document the social evils that gave notice of approaching judgment. The clock of time, both human and eschatological, ticks audibly in the background of each poem.

Much as the significant internal motion of each poem is a sinuous and open-ended transition from one topic to another, this pattern is arrested by a competing rhythm of closure or at least circularity. Young's poem is a sequence of nocturnal reveries, each night constituting the death of the previous day's life, as well as figuring the death to which all of our indirections must eventually lead us. Thomson's *The Seasons* is also haunted by its own recurring intimations of mortality. The fall of evening brings to a close 'the long vernal Day of Life'

('Spring', line 1171) in the same way that the onset of winter figuratively pre-enacts human decay and death. In both *The Seasons* and *The Task*, the rhythm of the seasons invests each poem with a rudimentary shape. Thomson's poem darkens discernibly, its contemplation of human mortality becoming keener and more absorbed, as it progresses through the seasonal year, while *The Task* itself draws to a close with three books set in winter and with its own strong envisagement of death. It is *The Seasons* that spells out most explicitly the symbolic correlation between seasonality and the human life-cycle:

> Behold, fond Man!
> See here thy pictur'd Life; pass some few Years,
> Thy flowering Spring, thy Summer's ardent strength,
> Thy sober Autumn fading into Age,
> And pale concluding Winter comes at last,
> And shuts the Scene. ('Winter', lines 1028–33)

While the poem as a whole resists being reduced to such a tidy encapsulation, an awareness of the allegoric dimension adds complexity to some of its main episodes, such as the death of the shepherd. What kills him is winter, the very season that allegorises human death in general. The agent of his death is at the same time the symbol of his mortality.

The end to which all four poems tend is foreseen in remarkably similar ways. What is promised the Christian is a final dissolution of the cloud of unknowing, and an entrance into a state of unhindered vision and understanding. What Cowper awaits, as 'heav'n-ward all things tend', is 'A sight to which our eyes are strangers yet' (*The Task*, VI.818, 825). Typical of these poems, the ultimate gratification will be accorded to the eye, which will feast on 'Scenes of unaccomplish'd bliss', previously intuited only 'in distant prospect' (*The Task*, VI.760–1). For Thomson, the moment at which human vision finally clarifies itself will be identical with the point at which we first comprehend the wisdom and completeness of God's benison. Only then will human vision fully coalesce with the viewpoint of God:

> *The great eternal Scheme,*
> Involving All, and in a *perfect Whole*
> Uniting, as the Prospect wider spreads,
> To Reason's Eye refin'd clears up apace.
> ('Winter', lines 1046–9)

What follows death is an unhindered understanding of the role that suffering, partial evil, plays within a created order that in its totality tends towards ultimate good. We see at this point, as it were, through God's 'boundless eye', which, connecting all aspects of the creation in its unhindered sweep, 'Beholds the perfect beauty' (*TPotI*, II.200–02).

Young's poem is, of course, the one that most ardently yearns and prepares for 'the blessed Day of our Discharge', and the visual banquet laid out for us on the other side of death's curtain:

> *There*, not the *Moral* World alone unfolds;
> The World *Material* lately seen in Shades,
> And in those Shades, by Fragments, only seen,
> And seen those Fragments by the *labouring* Eye,
> Unbroken, then, illustrious, and entire,
> Its ample Sphere, its universal Frame,
> In full Dimensions, swells to the Survey;
> And enters, at one Glance, the ravisht Sight.
> From some superior Point (where, who can tell?
> Suffice it, 'tis a Point where Gods reside)
> How shall the stranger Man's illumin'd Eye,
> In the vast Ocean of unbounded Space,
> Behold an Infinite of floating Worlds
> Divide the Crystal Waves of Ether pure,
> In endless Voyage, without Port? (*Night Thoughts*, VI.166–80)

Once more the after-life is imagined as a spectacle, an overarching prospect. The beauty and harmony of the universe, and the moral logic of God's purposes, are finally unfolded before the ravished gaze, the particular vantage point from which the prospect is apprehended being identical with the viewpoint of God. In fairness to Young, it should be said that he is troubled by the contradiction that nestles at the heart of all this. Given that human beings in life must resign themselves to only an impaired vision, how can the poet know with such certainty the nature of the spectacle that will be unfolded to us after death? The answer is perhaps that he does not know it as such, but that these long poems themselves, intent as they are on roving through and surveying God's handiwork, are offered to us as premonitions and pre-enactments of that boundlessness to which (they promise us) we all will eventually accede. As Young says, as he takes a final parting from his own poem, 'My Song the Midnight Raven has outwing'd . . . ambitious of unbounded Scenes' (*Night Thoughts*, IX, 2414–15).

Notes

1. 'Summer', lines 9, 14; cited from *The Seasons*, ed. James Sambrook (Oxford: Clarendon Press, 1981). Further quotations are from this edition. The poem appeared in sections from 1726 onwards. Sambrook reproduces the 1746 text.

2. For a discussion of developments in aesthetic taste around this time, see David Fairer, *English Poetry of the Eighteenth Century 1700–1789* (London: Longman, 2003), pp. 102–21.
3. *Twickenham Edition of the Poems of Alexander Pope*, general editor John Butt, 11 vols. (London: Methuen, 1939–69), vol. IV, ed. J. Butt, p. 120 (lines 340–1).
4. Akenside's two related but different poems, *The Pleasures of Imagination* (*TPoI*) and *The Pleasures of the Imagination* (*TPotI*), appeared in 1744 and 1772 respectively, the latter following Akenside's death. Cited from *The Poetical Works of Mark Akenside*, ed. Robin Dix (London: Associated University Presses, 1996). Further quotations are from this edition.
5. John E. Sitter, *Literary Loneliness in Mid-Eighteenth Century England* (Ithaca, NY: Cornell University Press, 1982). See also William C. Dowling, 'Ideology and the Flight from History in Eighteenth-Century Poetry', in Leo Damrosch (ed.), *The Profession of Eighteenth-Century Literature* (Madison: University of Wisconsin Press, 1992), pp. 135–53.
6. See 'Worldliness and Other-Worldliness: The Poet Young', in *The Essays of George Eliot*, ed. Thomas Pinney (London: Routledge and Kegan Paul, 1963), pp. 335–85.
7. See Marshall Brown, *Preromanticism* (Stanford, CA: Stanford University Press, 1991).
8. For a general discussion of Thomson, Akenside and Cowper as precursors of Wordsworth, see Mary Jacobus, *Tradition and Experiment in Wordsworth's Lyrical Ballads 1798* (Oxford: Oxford University Press, 1976), pp. 38–58.
9. For the influence of Milton on eighteenth-century verse, see R. D. Havens, *Milton's Influence on English Poetry* (Cambridge, MA: Harvard University Press, 1922); and Dustin Griffin, *Regaining Paradise: Milton and the Eighteenth Century* (Cambridge: Cambridge University Press, 1986).
10. T. S. Eliot, 'Poetry in the Eighteenth Century', in Boris Ford (ed.), *The New Pelican Guide to English Literature Vol. 4: From Dryden to Johnson* (Harmondsworth: Pelican, 1982), pp. 228–34.
11. The poem is cited from Edward Young, *Night Thoughts*, ed. Stephen Cornford (Cambridge: Cambridge University Press, 1989). Further quotations are from this edition. Young probably began the poem in 1741 with 'Night the First' being published in 1742. The first complete edition came out in 1750, but Young tinkered with the poem up until the final lifetime edition in 1762.
12. *The Task* is cited from *The Poems of William Cowper*, ed. John D. Baird and Charles Ryskamp, 3 vols. (Oxford: Clarendon Press, 1980–95), vol. II. Further quotations are from this edition.
13. *Spectator* 411 (21 June 1712), in *The Spectator*, ed. Donald F. Bond, 5 vols. (Oxford: Clarendon Press, 1965), vol. III, pp. 535–6.
14. *Ibid.*, vol. III, p. 536.
15. See Marjorie Hope Nicolson, 'The Microscope and English Imagination', in her *Science and Imagination* (Ithaca, NY: Cornell University Press, 1956), pp. 155–234, 164–9.

16. See *The Task*, 1.330–3: 'The folded gates would bar my progress now . . . '
17. See, amongst other similar passages, 'Spring', lines 374–8.
18. See John Sitter, 'Theodicy at Mid-Century: Young, Akenside, and Hume', *Eighteenth-Century Studies*, 12 (1978), pp. 90–106; and my ' "Through Nature shedding influence malign": Thomson's *The Seasons* as a Theodicy', *Durham University Journal*, 87 (1995), pp. 257–68.
19. On the architectonics of long poems, see my 'Transitions and Digressions in the Eighteenth-Century Long Poem', *Studies in English Literature*, 32 (1992), pp. 495–510.
20. Alexander Knox, in *The Flapper*, no. 38 (11 June 1796); cited from Ralph Cohen, *The Art of Discrimination: Thomson's 'The Seasons' and the Language of Criticism* (London: Routledge and Kegan Paul, 1964), p. 180.
21. Young, *Night Thoughts*, p. 35.
22. The larger passage from which the excerpt comes is discussed in Karen O'Brien, '"Still at Home": Cowper's Domestic Empires', in Thomas Woodman (ed.), *Early Romantics: Perspectives in British Poetry from Pope to Wordsworth* (Basingstoke: Macmillan, 1998), pp. 134–47, 139–40.
23. *Dictionary of the English Language* (1755), 'contexture'.
24. See T. E. Blom, 'Eighteenth-Century Reflexive Process Poetry', *Eighteenth-Century Studies*, 10 (1976), pp. 52–72.
25. Richard Jago, *Edge-Hill, or the Rural Prospect Delineated and Moralized* (London, 1767), p. vii.
26. For comments on poetic closure and death in eighteenth-century poems, see Margaret Doody, *The Daring Muse: Augustan Poetry Reconsidered* (Cambridge: Cambridge University Press, 1985), pp. 183–9.
27. Letter of 23 November 1746, in Edward Young, *Correspondence*, ed. H. Pettit (Oxford: Clarendon Press, 1971), p. 249.

Chapter 21

Lyric poetry: 1740–1790

DAVID FAIRER

The lyric poetry of the mid eighteenth century has traditionally been hard to locate in literary history as anything other than transitional, as 'post-Augustan' or 'pre-Romantic', as decline or anticipation. It has struggled to establish a critical vocabulary in which it can be judged on its own terms. Pinned between the canonical achievements of Dryden–Pope on the one side and Wordsworth–Coleridge on the other, this poetry has often been used to further other agendas, to play a 'minor' role in reinforcing 'major' achievements, or to exemplify an individual eccentricity. But such tired 'survey course' arguments have now begun to look very limited. The old categories need to be set aside, and these poets be allowed to set their own agenda. The challenge is to find critical perspectives that will do justice to them as individual poets while acknowledging their contemporaneity and suggesting lines of connection between them. It should also be possible, through them, to question some of the traditional criteria for literary judgment. These two trajectories will help to guide the discussion that follows.

Thomas Gray (1716–71), William Collins (1721–59), the Warton brothers, Thomas (1728–90) and Joseph (1722–1800), Christopher Smart (1722–71), James Macpherson (1736–96), Thomas Chatterton (1752–70) and Robert Burns (1759–96) offer as wide a range of voices as any group of poets in history; but there are ways in which they can gain from being discussed together. To take one extreme example: the lyric lamentations of Macpherson's Ossian, the third-century bard who sings in his melancholy rhythmical prose of fallen heroes and a doomed race, could not be more different from Burns's catchy rhymes, satirically edged and interspersed with responsive tavern laughter or drawing-room applause. Yet each is capturing a mood and is conscious of projecting an expressive, strongly characterised voice that carries the poem so as to reach the heart of the listener. Both are in their very different ways, lyric performances. The 'now' of the poem is a helpful concept here, with its emphasis on a performative element within the text. Hence the frequent use of a persona or an imagined poet-speaker who is ostensibly delivering the words (Ossian, the Psalmist, Thomas Rowley). An element of ventriloquism, of conscious voice-projection, is often assumed.

Certainly, much of this verse benefits from being read aloud, and a silent reader has to work harder for the text's aural qualities to come across. The reader's imaginative and emotional engagement is in different ways assumed by the poet, who is often consciously exploiting the mechanisms of feeling. But this does not diminish the formal qualities of the verse. Leaving the couplet behind, with its associations of wit, satire and social polish, these poets find new challenges for their craftsmanship. Many varieties of lyric form are on display, each unlocking fresh potential from the English language.

To approach the work of these highly individual poets as a group helps us appreciate the range encompassed by the concept of 'lyric', a term that takes in the solemn sounds of the ancient Celtic bard, the divine hymning of the Hebrew Psalmist, the romance balladry of the medieval minstrel and the refined raptures of the Greek lyric singer (literally lyre-accompanied). In the eighteenth century these exotic elements were being accommodated to the tastes of a modern sophisticated audience who were asking poetry to recapture its powers as an inspired art. In the preface to *Winter* (1726), James Thomson had issued a call: 'let POETRY, once more, be restored to her antient Truth, and Purity; let Her be inspired from Heaven, and, in Return, her Incense ascend thither'; and he expressed the hope that poets would again 'become the Delight and Wonder, of Mankind'.[1] By mid-century, the concept of a lost 'genuine poetry' (true to its inspirational origins) was encouraging people to look beyond a modern verse of ethics, argument and observation, to that of expressive vision and feeling. William Duff in his *Essay on Original Genius* (1767) concluded that 'the early and uncultivated periods of society are peculiarly favourable to the display of original Poetic Genius, and that this quality will seldom appear in a very high degree in cultivated life'.[2] Modern taste sought out elements of primitive simplicity. Critics began to stress the aural qualities of poetry, and Milton became increasingly the champion of those who found the heroic couplet of Dryden and Pope too limited in range. Pope's translation of Homer into rhymed pentameters was, for Edward Young, 'to put Achilles in petticoats a second time'. For Young, Homer's verse required a different register that would allow his full power to be heard: 'How much nobler had it been', he wrote, 'if his numbers had rolled on in full flow, through the various modulations of masculine melody, into those grandeurs of solemn sound, which are indispensably demanded by the native dignity of Heroick song?'[3] As Young declares this we can hear him becoming conscious of his own reverberating phrases ('modulations of masculine melody').

If we bring together these elements of vocal performance and historical curiosity we can discern a connective thread through the poets. Smart was interested in how ancient Hebrew poetry was performed; Chatterton's head rang with the cadences of medieval words; Macpherson collected bardic remains; Gray was immersed in musical history, metre and Old Icelandic and Welsh poetry; the Warton brothers were literary historians and Thomas spent a lifetime researching his *History of English Poetry* (1774–90); their friend Collins's interests ranged from ancient Greek literature and music to the superstitions of the Scottish Highlands; Burns became preoccupied with collecting old songs and writing new lyrics to traditional tunes. In other words, all these poets had a degree of historical curiosity and a specific interest in the vocal elements of older poetry: each seems to have had not only a visual but also a strong aural imagination. In their different ways, this remarkable group was fascinated by the possibility of recovering the genuine remains of the past. But in the cases of Macpherson and Chatterton, they were so anxious to recapture the authentic sound of old poetry that they helped create it themselves through their surrogates of Ossian and Rowley. Ironically, it was their pursuit of the 'genuine' that led to their fabrications.

At the heart of this lyric poetry is not just the sound and meaning of the individual words, but the echoes created between them. All these poets write with powerful simplicity at times, but they also enrich their language by linking words with associative or metaphorical potential in a lexis that differs from that of everyday prose. We encounter here the concept of 'poetic diction', a term often used to denigrate any writers, like Gray and Collins, who might be suspected of 'decorating' their poetry with 'fine' words and phrases.[4] Every age has its bland poets who try to heighten their verse in this way (not least our own), but the term presupposes an unhelpful equation of the 'poetic' with the 'artificial' or 'false'. The best artful eighteenth-century poets, like those of other ages, worked with a rich historical vocabulary; they were conscious of a word's hinterland of suggestion, its historic etymology, its use by previous poets, its often complex field of association and context. Words became multi-faceted, coloured or charged with potential meanings that other words would help to draw out. In prose, language tends not to work under such pressure, so the possibilities for lexical reaction are fewer.

The *cause célèbre* for the accusation of artificial 'poetic diction' is Wordsworth's attack, in his preface to *Lyrical Ballads* (1800), on Gray's 'Sonnet on the Death of Richard West' (1742). Wordsworth is aiming to press home his point that 'there neither is nor can be any essential difference' between 'the language of prose and metrical composition'. This disingenuous idea is alien to the lyric poets discussed in this chapter, all of whom were conscious of how poetry worked under heightened pressure, and that when compressed into metre, language was being intensified in a way that prose seldom achieved. Gray, says Wordsworth, was 'curiously elaborate in the structure of his own poetic diction'; and in illustration he prints the West sonnet in full, italicising lines 6–8 and 13–14, with the comment: 'It will easily be perceived that the only part of this Sonnet which is of any value is the lines printed in Italics.'[5] Wordsworth was confident, for example, that the poem's opening quatrain was valueless:

> In vain to me the smileing Mornings shine,
> And redning Phœbus lifts his golden Fire:
> The Birds in vain their amorous Descant joyn;
> Or chearful Fields resume their green Attire . . .[6]

Wordsworth does not explain what he dislikes, but the obvious bugbears would seem to be the image of the sun as 'redning Phœbus' and the 'amorous Descant' of the birds. 'The sun rises' could be a neat prose paraphrase of Gray's second line, but it drains all the poetic meaning away (i.e. the meaning that comes from words working creatively together under formal pressure). This elegiac sonnet on Gray's school friend works by contrasting the activity of nature's returning life with the pointless emptiness of his own. This means that Gray is selecting a plain and simple, almost naked, language for his own inner world ('A different Object do these Eyes require. / My lonely Anguish melts no Heart, but mine' and 'I . . . weep the more, because I weep in vain'); in contrast, the natural world is given a vocabulary that is rich with implication, with 'poetic' meanings. The blank left by his dead friend is filled by the image of the young blushing god, Phoebus Apollo, who presides over youth and beauty, and over the world of poetry that he and West had shared. This makes the emotional void emptier. The 'red' and 'gold' add their blazing colours as the life force returns to the sky and lights up the world. Gray is drawing on a celebratory solar iconography that has existed for thousands of years, but which for him has now lost its power. The reader can hear the words 'in vain' as they chime three times through the text like the passing bell (they form the poem's opening and closing words), a melancholy note that is contrasted not with the birds' 'song', but with their 'amorous descant', a phrase that links feelings of love to the descant in choral singing when a soaring accompaniment embroiders the melody with fresh harmonies. This is another 'poetic' idea that draws on a wealth of association. By denying its value Wordsworth has missed the very thing that gives Gray's lyric voice its power, and which helps unlock the sonnet's suppressed emotion and project it into our imaginations as we read.

The mechanisms of the mid-century lyric unashamedly engage the associative responses of the reader in ways like this; but the effect, as in Gray's sonnet, is also ironically placed, so that the result is intelligent feeling. Eighteenth-century 'sensibility' was able to negotiate both together, to enter a situation and a feeling while being aware of positioning them ironically too. This connotative aspect of Gray's language is evident in his stanzaic 'Ode on the Spring' (1742), where he catches the atmosphere of the scene and imbues it with suggestions and potential ironies. It is a simple scene of insects swarming over a stream, yet he turns it into a teasing performance for his readers. We register the airiness, but also sense that something is 'in the air': an idea is being hinted at and made almost tangible:

> . . . hark, how thro' the peopled air
> The busy murmur glows!
> The insect youth are on the wing,
> Eager to taste the honied spring,
> And float amid the liquid noon:
> Some lightly o'er the current skim,
> Some shew their gayly-gilded trim
> Quick-glancing to the sun. (lines 23–30)

Youth is having its moment of delight, its time in the sun, and the words reflect and colour each other, underlining the euphoric effect. There is continual play between literal and metaphorical meanings. 'On the wing' also implies that time is flying by; 'insect youth' hovers between 'young insects' and 'insect-like youth'. The word 'glows' catches all the senses of the Latin *fervere*: to be agitated, to glow with passion, to bustle, to swarm. Each fits Gray's passage, so that the word 'busy' takes on the extra meaning of 'fervid'. The spring is 'honied' in its promise of sweetness, and the word adds a bee-like activity to the scene. 'Liquid' picks up the image, drawing also on the Latin *liquidus* (meaning 'bright and clear') to create a sensuous idea, 'float amid the liquid noon', which links the current of air to the 'current' below, where many of these flies will die when evening comes. 'Light' is another key idea throughout the stanza, which plays with lightness, with things being 'on the wing', 'lightly' anticipating the light effects of the final line, where 'glancing' catches the light from an oblique angle (as in a 'glancing blow'). Similarly, 'Quick' conveys the rapidity and also the sense of living (as in 'the quick and the dead'), an idea that introduces associations of mortality that the poem will confront ('Brush'd by the hand of rough Mischance, / Or chill'd by age, their airy dance / They leave, in dust to rest', lines 38–40). Behind the whole intricate word-picture, however, is another scene conjured by the phrase 'eager to taste', which for many eighteenth-century readers would recall Milton's description of the temptation in the Garden of Eden where Eve's 'eager appetite' causes her to 'taste' the forbidden fruit.[7] We realise that Gray's scene has a darker context of lost innocence, an idea confirmed when the poet loses his own moralising innocence at the end. He imagines the insects' mocking answer, so that the light lyric poem is finally an elegy on himself: 'On hasty wings thy youth is flown; / Thy sun is set, thy spring is gone – / We frolick, while 'tis May' (lines 48–50).

The elegiac elements in Gray's poetry are more powerful because they are complicated by an ironic intelligence. An expressive lyricism is combined with something we can call a 'reflective' quality in various senses of that term. An emotion will be expressed, reflected upon and then reflected from another angle as the perspective changes. This happens at the end of 'Ode on the Spring', and Gray uses a similar technique in his two best-known lyric poems, *Ode on a Distant Prospect of Eton College* (1742) and *Elegy Written in a Country Churchyard* (1750). In the ode, the poet who watches the schoolchildren at play runs through a succession of emotions: the language begins in sentimental recollection ('Ah happy hills, ah pleasing shade'), then moves into playful, mock-heroic tones ('cleave / With pliant arm thy glassy wave'); then it becomes philosophically moralising ('Gay hope is theirs by fancy fed, / Less pleasing when possest'); it then darkens into a hellish allegorical vision ('Jealousy with rankling tooth, / That inly gnaws the secret heart'); until finally the poet, in another 'glancing' moment, turns round on himself:

> Yet ah! why should they know their fate?
> Since sorrow never comes too late,
> And happiness too swiftly flies.
> Thought would destroy their paradise.
> No more; where ignorance is bliss,
> 'Tis folly to be wise. (lines 95–100)

The cumulatively *wise* tone and structure of the text seems to be undercut in the last line, until we recognise that this final insight reflects the poem's deepest wisdom of all: its ability to reflect on itself, and encourage us to engage with the performance from different angles.

Gray's *Elegy* is another powerful lyric performance where the text itself effectively loses its innocence as we read. The poem opens conventionally enough as an evening meditation, with the solitary poet seated in a graveyard and contemplating the generations of buried villagers. Their undistinguished lives appear to tell a story of humility, obscurity, neglect and limitation ('But Knowledge to their eyes her ample page / Rich with the spoils of time did ne'er unroll', lines 49–50). But we begin to realise that underneath the quiet elegy there are expressive sounds and vocal outpourings being held in check. We hear them break through the stillness from time to time: the morning notes of the countryside: the 'breezy call' (line 17), 'the cock's shrill clarion' (line 19) and 'the ecchoing horn' (line 19); the sung anthem that 'swells the note of praise' (line 40) echoing 'thro' the long-drawn isle and fretted vault' (line 39) of the church; the musician who might have 'wak'd to extasy the living lyre' (line 48); and the cry of the dead themselves: 'Ev'n from the tomb the voice of Nature cries' (line 91). For a poem that is conscious of the 'noiseless tenor' (line 76) of these villagers' lives, it is remarkable for repeatedly evoking the idea of musical performance, as if the poet's imagination has caught these sounds and given them lyric expression. By stanza 23 he has become not only their spokesman, but almost a sacramental presence ('On some fond breast the parting soul relies, / Some pious drops the closing eye requires', lines 89–90). It is therefore a surprise when in the next stanza, at a point where we expect a return to the poet himself, the text makes an unexpected twist:

> For thee, who mindful of th'unhonoured Dead
> Dost in these lines their artless tale relate;
> If chance, by lonely contemplation led,
> Some kindred Spirit shall inquire thy fate . . . (lines 93–6)

The poet imagines another contemplative 'kindred Spirit' who might perform the lyric obsequies for him. And this role the reader is invited to fill. An old countryman recalls the poet and points to his gravestone, inviting us to read the inscription aloud: 'Approach and read (for thou can'st read) the lay, / Grav'd on the stone' (lines 115–16). We 'readers' bring the poem to a close by speaking the poet's epitaph as the old man listens. It is a remarkable poetic structure, in which the idea of lyric expression and performance is handled with great subtlety.

In this elegy Gray consciously holds in check the dynamic potential of classical lyric, its inspired fervour and metrical daring. Although possibilities of release are occasionally hinted at, the poem gains from the sense of energies being suppressed and voices muffled ('Some mute inglorious Milton here may rest', line 59). But it is clear that Gray was fascinated by the outpourings of the Greek lyric ode, of which Pindar was the master, and like other mid-century poets he experimented with reproducing the formal 'Pindaric' in English. Many earlier ode-writers thought they had a licence to write with bold abandon in an irregular metre, but classically trained poets like Gray and Collins understood the structural sophistication of Pindar's forms (he never employed the same metre twice). Gray's ode, 'The Progress of Poesy', was originally entitled simply 'Ode in the Greek Manner', a sign that he was consciously adopting the inspirational adventurousness, combined with formal discipline, of his model.[8] Appropriately enough, both Gray and Collins used the lyric ode to celebrate the origins of poetry:

Awake, Æolian lyre, awake,
And give to rapture all thy trembling strings.
From Helicon's harmonious springs
A thousand rills their mazy progress take
. . .
Now the rich stream of music winds along
Deep, majestic, smooth, and strong . . . (lines 1–8)

Here at the opening of 'The Progress of Poesy' (1757), Gray 'wakes to extasy the living lyre' (to use the words of his *Elegy*), exploiting the idea of the lyric poem as a natural outpouring that flows unstoppably from a divine source. This is Mount Helicon, home of the Greek Muses led by Apollo, from whose springs all *poesis* (poetry as a creative art) has emanated, striking out in many directions. But in his footnote on the passage Gray makes it clear that he is acknowledging another genealogy too: '*Awake, my glory: awake, lute and harp. David's Psalms*'.[9] The note alludes to Psalm 57, verse 8, and the lyric poetry of the Hebrew Bible. Earlier critics, notably John Dennis (1657–1734), had argued that 'by the Institution of their Order' the Biblical prophets were the original poets ('Poetry was one of the Prophetick Functions'),[10] but the question of priority was seen as less important than the fact that the two traditions drew from an essential life-source. Gray's poem happily subsumes both within his celebration of the power of harmony:

Oh! Sovereign of the willing soul,
Parent of sweet and solemn-breathing airs,
Enchanting shell! the sullen Cares,
And frantic Passions hear thy soft controul. (lines 13–16)

The claim for poetry's power goes beyond the level of verbal skill and taps into a deeper seam of magic and healing. This Orphic tradition of 'genuine' poetry could directly touch the soul and influence behaviour.

Collins's 'Ode on the Poetical Character' (1746) celebrates this same mystical dimension, taking the image of Venus's belt, or 'cestus', from Spenser's *Faerie Queene* and interpreting it as the symbol of poetic power. It is a 'God-like Gift' (line 20) awarded only to the chosen few 'to gird their blest prophetic Loins' (line 21). The high claim entails a serious responsibility, and Collins builds the difficulty into his text. He alternates between complex interlocking rhymed paragraphs, and regular octosyllabic couplets of a more incantatory character, as if he is moving in and out of a dance. The mystical element of choral chanting is distinct from a more personal voice that captures the individual poet's struggle. Collins gives poetry its own creation myth, and we enter the mystical tent for the moment of divine insemination when 'Fancy', or the Imagination (the 'lov'd *Enthusiast*'), is impregnated by the divine Idea and Poetry is conceived:

> The Band, as Fairy Legends say,
> Was wove on that creating Day,
> When He, who call'd with Thought to Birth
> Yon tented Sky, this laughing Earth,
> And drest with Springs, and Forests tall,
> And pour'd the Main engirting all,
> Long by the lov'd *Enthusiast* woo'd,
> Himself in some Diviner Mood,
> Retiring, sate with her alone,
> And plac'd her on his Saphire Throne,
> The whiles, the vaulted Shrine around,
> Seraphic Wires were heard to sound
>
> . . .
>
> And she, from out the veiling Cloud,
> Breath'd her magic Notes aloud:
> And Thou, Thou rich-hair'd Youth of Morn,
> And all thy subject Life was born! (lines 23–40)

It is also the moment of the birth of Apollo, and of the creation of the sun and the planets. Collins daringly brings *poesis* and *logos* together into a single creative act, the primal scene of the earth itself. But if this regular lyric measure seems too easy, Collins takes us out into the personal struggle of the poet, where the vision of poetic greatness remains inaccessible. The metrical feet no longer dance, but tread more circumspectly as the path ahead becomes difficult:

> My trembling Feet his guiding Steps pursue;
> In vain – Such Bliss to One alone,

Of all the Sons of Soul was known,
And Heav'n, and *Fancy*, kindred Pow'rs,
Have now o'erturn'd th'inspiring Bow'rs,
Or curtain'd close such Scene from ev'ry future View.
(lines 71–6)

These lines, with their reference to Milton's epic achievement, are often used to suggest that Collins and his contemporaries were inhibited by their great predecessor, paralysed by 'the anxiety of influence'.[11] But in some ways these eighteenth-century lyric voices claim an absolute authority, their visions being placed beyond question. If Collins concludes that poetry's divine power is tantalisingly out of reach, 'curtain'd close . . . from ev'ry future View', we are also being encouraged to feel that in this poem the youthful Collins has been allowed to penetrate further into the sacred mysteries than anyone else.

It is not inhibition, but youthful presumption that tends to characterise this mid-century lyric verse. In 1746 Collins and his school friend Joseph Warton, both in their mid twenties, were planning to publish their odes together, but in the end the volumes appeared separately. There is, however, no reason to believe that Collins did not enthusiastically assent to Warton's provocative 'Advertisement', in which he made the most ambitious claims for his verse:

> The Public has been so much accustom'd of late to didactic Poetry alone, and Essays on moral Subjects, that any work where the imagination is much indulged, will perhaps not be relished or regarded. The author therefore of these pieces . . . as he is convinced that the fashion for moralizing in verse has been carried too far, and as he looks upon Invention and Imagination to be the chief faculties of a Poet, so he will be happy if the following Odes may be look'd upon as an attempt to bring back Poetry into its right channel.[12]

Warton appropriately opens his volume with its presiding figure, 'Fancy' (from the Greek *phantasia*), who in Collins's ode gave birth to poetry through immaculate conception. Warton's 'Ode to Fancy', in octosyllabic couplets throughout, is a lyric of the simplest kind; but its tutelary goddess is clearly the same as Collins's:

O warm, enthusiastic maid,
Without thy powerful, vital aid,
That breathes an energy divine,
That gives a soul to every line,

Ne'er may I strive with lips profane
To utter an unhallow'd strain,
Nor dare to touch the sacred string,
Save when with smiles thou bid'st me sing. (lines 89–96)

Warton's Imagination is a more humanised concept, a woman who is passionate, even flirtatious, and who will occasionally smile sweetly and invite him to 'touch' the instrument of poetry. She is a sentimental figure who likes to spend the evening sitting by her 'darling' Shakespeare's grave. In his ode, Warton lures her away with the picture of a youthful living poet who scorns 'frigid art' and looks to her for inspiration: 'Like light'ning, let his mighty verse / The bosom's inmost foldings pierce' (lines 115–16). Warton has no inhibitions about being that potential suitor.

Of course, such poetry-about-poetry runs the risk of enacting promises rather than producing achievements, of allowing its own dedications and performative ambitions to become gestural. Much of the poetry discussed in this chapter is about the concept of the poetic itself, its character, vocation, inspiration, powers. This need not be a limitation, but can be seen as exploratory, moving beyond the descriptive towards elements of the performative, enacting its own potential to create or embody an idea. We can see this at work in Joseph Warton's *The Enthusiast: Or The Lover of Nature* (1744), when he pictures the infant Shakespeare being reared by Fancy in her cave. She had discovered him by the River Avon,

And bore the smiling babe
To a close cavern: (still the shepherds shew
The sacred place, whence with religious awe
They hear, returning from the field at eve,
Strange whisp'ring of sweet musick thro' the air)
Here, as with honey gather'd from the rock,
She fed the little prattler, and with songs
Oft' sooth'd his wondering ears, with deep delight
On her soft lap he sat, and caught the sounds. (lines 171–9)

It is a loving, almost a domestic scene; and its effectiveness lies in capturing elements of wonder, sweetness, musicality, mimicry and responsiveness, not by any kind of imitative onomatopoeia, but by expressing them through the care of the language itself. The extended parenthesis encloses the moment of awe, and gently prolongs the whisper. It goes beyond the description of a scene and becomes a means of conveying the 'inmost foldings' of an idea.

This kind of writing is simultaneously evocative and elusive, hard to pin down because it has no ulterior motive. Its means are effectively its end. Paraphrase could easily destroy it. In Collins's 'Ode to Evening', as the poet traces the twilight through a succession of scenes, the tonal brushwork begins to form an aural/visual mood-picture:

> Then lead, calm Vot'ress, where some sheety lake
> Cheers the lone heath, or some time-hallow'd pile,
> Or up-land fallows grey
> Reflect its last cool gleam. (lines 29–32)

The effect is almost Whistlerian: the elements of the scene (lake, heathland, building, fields) remain subdued by the light, not individualised but brought into atmospheric composition. The Idea is leading him and is simultaneously being realised.

In the poetry of Thomas Warton these reflective techniques are harnessed to another medium, that of time and the receding perspectives of history. His 'Ode written at Vale-Royal Abbey in Cheshire' (1777), for example, opens with the grey cloak of evening spreading over the scene ('As Evening slowly spreads his mantle hoar', line 1), and seems to recall Gray's 'Elegy' in its location, mood and verse-form. But unlike Gray's text, Warton's is concerned with recovering the past and finding continuities. As the ruinous monastic site composes itself, the gothic details that Warton loved come into focus. Images of past and present alternate through the poem, with the effect that the vanished living scene begins to overlay the dereliction and bring it to life:

> The prickly thistle sheds its plumy crest,
> And matted nettles shade the crumbling mass,
> Where shone the pavement's surface smooth, impress
> With rich reflection of the storied glass. (lines 13–16)

Past and present are both equally alive in the poetry. Warton is alert to the irony by which the reflections are 'imprest' on the active imagination, so that the abbey ruins are reconstituted with some of their old symbolic meanings. He plays with the idea of the heraldic *impresa*, or emblem, and the 'stories' told in glass are recalled by the 'plumy crest' of the thistle. There are hints at the language of chivalry here. As elsewhere in his work, Warton reanimates history, not by returning to an imagined past but by bringing the past imaginatively into the present. It is thus the opposite of nostalgia:

High o'er the trackless heath at midnight seen,
No more the windows, rang'd in long array,
Where the tall shaft and fretted nook between
Thick ivy twines, the taper'd rites betray. (lines 29–32)

The syntax is also entwined, and there are two strands: the medieval traveller approaching the abbey at midnight had glimpsed the candlelit ('taper'd') chancel in the distance; and the eighteenth-century visitor is intrigued by the way the ivy curves round the carved stonework to become part of the gothic effect. In Warton's poem, one scene is enfolded in the other, so that together they produce a picturesque double perspective. For the reader the experiences are simultaneous.

Past and present are overlaid in an uncanny way in the poetry of Thomas Chatterton, who died at seventeen, leaving behind an extraordinary archive of texts in which he had created an imagined medieval world. Casting himself as 'Thomas Rowley', a fifteenth-century 'secular priest' of Bristol, Chatterton is able to project a lyric voice that flows with a rhythmical ease that seems entirely natural. In the opening stanza of 'An Excelente Balade of Charitie' (1770) he sets the scene with a style that matches Chaucer's most sweet-tongued manner:

In Virgyne the sweltrie sun gan sheene,
And hotte upon the mees did caste his raie;
The apple rodded from its palie greene,
And the mole peare did bende the leafy spraie;
The peede chelandri sunge the livelong daie;
'Twas nowe the pride, the manhode of the yeare,
And eke the grounde was dighte in its mose defte aumere.
(lines 1–7)

What is surprising is how fresh this language sounds, as if newly minted (as indeed it was). It asks to be read aloud. Somehow Chatterton has succeeded, out of his cod-medieval vocabulary accumulated from glossaries, deeds and old black-letter editions, to forge a lyric instrument for himself. The 'peede chelandri' and the 'defte aumere' (respectively the 'pied goldfinch' and 'ornamental robe', according to Chatterton's notes) sound just right, as if they really meant what he thought or wished them to mean.

'Rowley' is setting the scene for an encounter between a starving pilgrim and a wealthy abbot in what will be his version of the Good Samaritan story, and this opening stanza establishes a background of simple nature. Only in its last line do we hear the hint of excess and finery that will be picked up again when the richly accoutred Abbot of St Godwin's enters with his 'gold button fasten'd neere his chynne' (line 51). The 'Balade' is strengthened by the satiric edge given the language when Chatterton sets a Frenchified vocabulary against plain and honest Anglo-Saxon. The abbot's ecclesiastical garments of 'chapournette' (line 45) and 'autremete' (line 52) contrast starkly with those of the poor charitable friar, who is described in simple monosyllables: 'His cope and jape were graie, and eke were clene' (line 74). John Keats was alert to this etymological scrupulosity when he declared that 'Chatterton . . . is the purest writer in the English Language. He has no French idiom, or particles like Chaucer – 'tis genuine English Idiom in English Words.'[13] One of the strengths of Chatterton's ballad is its avoidance of lame phrases like 'friar grey', a staple of ballad writing where a French word-order prevails and adjectives are tagged on loosely for the rhyme. Chatterton's lyrics have more rhythmic energy; and it is clear that he could create a powerful image without using a single adjective, as he does here in the 'Mynstrelles Song' from his verse tragedy *Ælla*:

> Comme, wythe acorne-coppe and thorne,
> Drayne mie hartys blodde awaie;
> Lyfe and all yttes goode I scorne,
> Daunce bie nete, or feaste by daie.
> Mie love ys dedde,
> Gon to hys death-bedde,
> Al under the wyllowe tree. (lines 50–6)

These were favourite lines of Keats, and his friend Benjamin Bailey vividly recalled how the poet would speak them aloud: 'Methinks I now hear him recite, or *chant*, in his peculiar manner, the following stanza . . . The first line to his ear possessed the great charm. Indeed his sense of melody was quite exquisite.'[14] Bailey's remarks are a reminder that this lyric poetry is not meant to lie flat on the page, but is waiting to shape itself to the palate of the speaker, to the tones of human speech, and we can perhaps imagine the sound Keats made: 'Comme, wythe acorne-coppe and thorne'. The poet, who was writing *Endymion* at this time (1817), evidently relished the line's sharp-edged assonance and its miniaturised picture compressed to the fairy scale.

We have lost the art of 'chanting' poetry, which in old voice recordings often sounds ridiculous; but in lyric a degree of weighted delivery and melodious tonal projection can be appropriate. One area where chanting is still permissible is in religious ritual, and the lyric poet who most exploited this was Christopher Smart. In his long poem *Jubilate Agno* ('Rejoice in the Lamb'), produced methodically day by day during his years in a Bethnal Green madhouse, he is consciously offering what he called his 'MAGNIFICAT', a canticle of praise performed at evensong. It seems to have been modelled on the antiphonal singing of the Psalms, a topic opened up by Smart's friend Robert Lowth (later Bishop of London) in his scholarly study of Hebrew verse, *De sacra poesi Hebraeorum* (1753). In the parts where both 'Let' and 'For' passages survive, it seems we are meant to hear the pair of alternating voices:

> *Let* Hobab rejoice with Necydalus, who is the Greek of a Grub. *For* I have glorified God in GREEK and LATIN, the consecrated languages spoken by the Lord on earth. (B6)

The connection between Moses' father-in-law and a silk-worm larva remains unclear; but this verse like the others puts exotic names and alliteration on display in a vocal offering to God. Personal comments and details from Smart's life are paired with Biblical characters and creatures from the natural world in what becomes a capacious Noah's ark of a poem. The most memorable creature of all is Smart's cat Jeoffry:

For he is a mixture of gravity and waggery.
For he knows that God is his Saviour.
For there is nothing sweeter than his peace when at rest.
For there is nothing brisker than his life when in motion.
For he is of the Lord's poor and so indeed is he called by benevolence perpetually –
Poor Jeoffry! poor Jeoffry! the rat has bit thy throat.
For I bless the name of the Lord Jesus that Jeoffry is better.
For the divine spirit comes about his body to sustain it in compleat cat.
(lines 42–8)

Once again, this is much more than description. The aim is to capture the essence of Jeoffry through characteristic moments and gestures. It is not a composed picture but a repeated imprinting of him on our minds. Smart himself puts this idea well elsewhere in the poem: 'For my talent is to give an impression upon words by punching, that when the reader casts his eye upon 'em, he takes up the image from the mould which I have made' (B404).

Jubilate Agno remains baffling in its purpose, but perhaps Smart was intending no more than to 'make a joyful noise unto God' (Psalm 66:1), combining adoration and gratitude for life itself in all its variety. The language of the Psalms was ingrained in him, and his translation of them into stanzaic verse was printed in 1765 for use by congregations. Smart thought of himself as 'the Reviver of ADORATION amongst ENGLISH-MEN' (*Jubilate Agno*, B332), and a prolonged and vocal adoration is the keynote of his most brilliant long poem, *A Song to David* (1763), which compresses into itself the rich and various life of nature, vegetable, animal, and mineral:

> Of fishes – ev'ry size and shape,
> Which nature frames of light escape,
> Devouring man to shun:
> The shells are in the wealthy deep,
> The shoals upon the surface leap,
> And love the glancing sun. (lines 139–44)

At every point creation seems to stretch to its full extent, here reaching from the 'shells' on the ocean bed to the leaping 'shoals' that break the surface; the most passive and the most active are equally expressing the divine; there is weight and depth, lightness and play together. Throughout the poem, qualities and attributes are being celebrated as much as things. Needless to say, the character of sound features strongly, here in the idea of the Aeolian harp playing in the wind:

> For ADORATION on the strings
> The western breezes work their wings,
> The captive ear to sooth. –
> Hark! 'tis a voice – how still, and small –
> That makes the cataracts to fall,
> Or bids the sea be smooth. (lines 397–402)

The most powerful song can be wordless and without a human voice to shape it. We are reminded of the 'still, small voice' alongside the sounding cataract. The essence of lyric is caught in this idea of a primal natural music, which prompted humans into their first spontaneous expressive speech. The critic Charles Gildon considered that poetry had begun in the Garden of Eden itself: 'poetry', he wrote in 1721, 'is as old as mankind, coeval with [the] human race, and was invented as soon as man thought of addressing either his prayers or his praise to heaven'.[15] In these primal scenes poetry takes the form of spontaneous 'genuine' feeling that pours out in response to the beauty or sublimity of nature.

This essential, disembodied quality of lyric *poesis* has haunted much of the material discussed so far. In the poetry of the Wartons it repeatedly appears in the imagery of springs, caves, echoes and whispers; genuine poetry, it is suggested, is something distant, time-hallow'd, caught from the air itself and mediated by it, as when Thomas Warton delights in 'the sacred sounds, / Which, as they lengthen thro' the Gothic vaults, / In hollow murmurs reach my ravish'd ear'.[16] Gray imagines that the Eton boys at play 'hear a voice in every wind' (line 39); and Collins's Evening will teach him 'to breathe some soften'd strain, / Whose numbers stealing thro' thy darkning vale, / May not unseemly with its stillness suit' (lines 16–18). Such immaterial aspects of lyric are taken to their ultimate in Macpherson's *Ossian*, where the melodious bardic language is consistently filtered through the moods of the landscape, as in this extract from *Temora* (1763):

> The voice of music came. It seemed, at first, the noise of a stream, far-distant on its rocks. Slow it rolled along the hill like the ruffled wing of a breeze, when it takes the tufted beard of the rocks, in the still season of night. – It was the voice of Condan, mixed with Carril's trembling harp.[17]

The source of the song may be the human voice accompanied by the harp, but it takes on the tones and timbre of nature; it follows the contours of the landscape, is filtered through the breeze and sweeps across the overgrown rocks. Nature, like an instrument itself, is moulding the sound.

At moments like this (and there are many in the Ossianic texts) the music takes over, and words themselves begin to register merely as sounds and images. The result may be frustratingly elusive, but this is appropriate. Macpherson's whole Ossian project is based on attempting to capture lost words; it is driven by the frustration of no longer possessing the thing itself, but only memories and overheard fragments of it. The Ossianic text is a sensorium registering its own echoes. Without the constraint of metre, the language is continually modulating like a sensitised emotional medium. After experimenting with 'translating' into verse, and finding the results lame and unpoetic, Macpherson settled on a rhythmical prose that is sinuous, buoyant, and always elusive, as if we are hearing a melody whose paraphrasable meaning is less important than the act of singing itself. As Macpherson gives it to us, the Ossian voice is hardly discernible from the wind that carries it, and the language comes close to sheer process; it is almost, to use a musical analogy, a *vocalise* (or wordless song). The poems are about the voice: its emotive content, its persistence, its survival:

> Farewel, thou bravest of men! Thou conqueror in the field! But the field shall see thee no more; nor the dark wood be lightened with the splendor of thy steel. Thou hast left no son. But the song shall preserve thy name. Future times shall hear of thee; they shall hear of the fallen Morar . . . The song

comes, with its music, to melt and please the soul. It is like soft mist, that, rising from a lake, pours on the silent vale.[18]

Elegy is Macpherson's mode, and he understands the irony of its farewells: that there are few things less terminal than the elegiac. What is not there is always potentially here in the song, and lyric works by offering its words for us to realise. Because lyric is disembodied it is capable of being repeatedly reclaimed by future readers, listeners and singers.

Robert Burns felt the force of this, and he played games with the idea. In his comic-satiric vein he enjoys offering his poetry as a running celebration of the embodied quality of his inspiration, and the humour frequently depends on his refusing to leave poetry hanging in the air:

The sky was blue, the wind was still,
　　The moon was shining clearly;
I set her down, wi' right good will,
　　Amang the rigs o'barley:
I ken't her heart was a' my ain;
　　I lov'd her most sincerely;
I kiss'd her owre and owre again,
　　Amang the rigs o'barley.[19] (lines 9–16)

This conqueror in the field is victorious each time the song is sung. The relish, the joy, the ecstasy, are waiting to be re-enacted at every performance.

Burns knows that he is an unconventional bard, but it is a role he insists on claiming. In his long early poem, 'The Vision', he dedicates himself to the role of '*rustic Bard*' (line 216), a more localised version of the singers of old. Coila, the spirit of Kyle (Burns's Ayrshire district), appears before him, and appoints him her official laureate, crowning him with a bough of the local holly. She hails him as '*my own* inspired Bard!' (line 97). She has watched him develop since the days of his earliest 'uncouth rhymes' (line 160) and has secretly been his teacher. Through her, Burns is able to characterise his own poetic character as a mixture of inspired spirit and the distracting 'pulse' of the body. She tells him:

I saw thy pulse's maddening play,
Wild-send thee Pleasure's devious way,
Misled by Fancy's *meteor-ray*,
　　By Passion driven;
But yet the *light* that led astray,
　　Was *light* from Heaven. (lines 187–92)

Sometimes behind Burns the poet-entertainer there lurks this melancholy bardic figure who is consciously not Ossian. Burns's almost manic geniality, his insistence on incorporating a responsive, even drunken, sociability into his performances, suggests that outside the tavern door (as Tam O'Shanter found) dangerous spirits, echoes from the past, are lurking. Conversely, we might think of Ossian's voice of exile and loss as possessing certain sentimental tones and gestures which seem to come from the seductive spaces where Burns's lyrics operate, but which have become isolated in a primal, dark and instinctive world. In their different ways both Macpherson and Burns challenged the decorums of the 'polite', but together they succeeded in conquering the drawing rooms and charming the ladies. In the words of Ossian: 'The song comes, with its music, to melt and please the soul.'[20]

Burns's love songs are especially effective in releasing the lyric spirit from the confines of his own experience. They are not personalised in this way. But the term 'universal' (with its suggestion of generality) is not quite right either. The key to Burns's songs instead lies in the way the lyric seems to be offered individually to us, so that we can make the voice our own:

> Till a' the seas gang dry, my dear,
> And the rocks melt wi' the sun!
> And I will luve thee still, my dear,
> While the sands o' life shall run.
> And fare thee weel, my only luve,
> And fare thee weel a while!
> And I will come again my luve,
> Tho' it were ten thousand mile![21]

This is not a song about love, but a love song. As such it permits what I have referred to elsewhere as 'lyric appropriation', where the reader or singer makes the words his/her own and becomes the medium for the experience.[22] The words are always potentially fresh and living, repeatedly being embodied and claimed by future lovers. Nor do time and space impose any limit: in the song the sands are always running, and the imagination can travel a million miles per second.

Much has been written about eighteenth-century poetry in terms of the visual, but the key to the lyric poetry of 1740–90 lies in this move from representation to expression. Through its explicit connections with music the mid-century lyric broke away from the Lockean concept of words as arbitrary 'sensible Signs' for our ideas,[23] and embraced the possibility of coming closer to music itself, by being, as Paul Barry argues, 'an empty sign' freed from representation.[24] In 1744, James Harris, in discussing the relationship between music and poetry, described words as 'the *compact Symbols* of all kinds of Ideas'. The move from 'sensible Signs' to '*compact Symbols*' leads Harris to conclude that, thanks to this freedom from representation, poetry 'is able to find Sounds expressive of *every* Idea',[25] and it suggests how a lyric like Coleridge's 'Kubla Khan' from the 1790s will find kinship with the poetry discussed in this chapter.

Notes

1. James Thomson, *Winter. A Poem*, second edition (London, 1726), p. 12.
2. William Duff, *Essay on Original Genius* (London, 1767), pp. viii–ix.
3. Edward Young, *Conjectures on Original Composition* (London, 1759), p. 59.
4. See Shakespeare, *Twelfth Night*, I.v.195–6 (*Viola*: ''tis poetical', *Olivia*: 'It is the more like to be feigned).
5. *Lyrical Ballads, with Other Poems. In Two Volumes. By W. Wordsworth* (London: Longman; Bristol: Cottle, 1800), vol. I, pp. xxiv–xxv.
6. Unless otherwise stated, all texts are quoted from *Eighteenth-Century Poetry: An Annotated Anthology*, eds. David Fairer and Christine Gerrard, second edition (Oxford: Blackwell, 2004).
7. Milton, *Paradise Lost*, IX.739–43.
8. The ode adopts the triadic structure of Greek lyric, in which two symmetrical stanzas ('strophe' and 'antistrophe') – so called from the chorus dancing to right and left in turn as they sang – are followed by the 'epode' in a different metrical form. Gray's ode has three sets of this triad.
9. For his *Poems* (1768) Gray added explanatory notes to his two odes, 'The Progress of Poesy' and 'The Bard'. They were first published in *Odes, by Mr Gray* (London, 1757).
10. John Dennis, *The Grounds of Criticism in Poetry* (London, 1704), chapter 5.
11. See Harold Bloom, *The Anxiety of Influence* (New York: Oxford University Press, 1973). Also influential has been W. J. Bate, *The Burden of the Past and the English Poet* (Cambridge, MA: Belknap, 1970).
12. Joseph Warton, *Odes on Various Subjects* (London, 1746), p. 3.
13. Keats to Reynolds, 21 September 1819, in *The Letters of John Keats: 1814–1821*, ed. H. E. Rollins, 2 vols. (Cambridge, MA: Harvard University Press, 1958), vol. II, p. 167.
14. Benjamin Bailey to R. M. Milnes, 7 May 1849, in H. E. Rollins (ed.) *The Keats Circle*, ed. H. E. Rollins, 2 vols. (Cambridge, MA: Harvard University Press, 1965), vol. II, pp. 276–7.
15. Charles Gildon, *The Laws of Poetry* (London, 1721), p. 14.
16. Thomas Warton, *The Pleasures of Melancholy* (1747), lines 203–5.
17. 'Temora', Book VIII in *The Poems of Ossian*, ed. Howard Gaskill (Edinburgh: Edinburgh University Press, 1996), p. 292.
18. 'The Songs of Selma' (*The Poems of Ossian*, pp. 168–9).

19. 'Song', in *Poems, Chiefly in the Scottish Dialect, by Robert Burns* (Kilmarnock, 1786), p. 223.
20. 'The Songs of Selma' (*The Poems of Ossian*, p. 168).
21. 'A red red Rose' (1794), first printed in *The Scots Musical Museum* (Edinburgh, 1796). The text was reconstructed from oral tradition; but see *Poems and Songs of Robert Burns*, ed. James Kinsley (Oxford: Clarendon Press, 1968), p. 1455.
22. David Fairer, *English Poetry of the Eighteenth Century* (Harlow: Longman, 2003), pp. 179–85.
23. John Locke, *An Essay Concerning Human Understanding*, III.ii.1.
24. See Paul Barry, *Language, Music and the Sign: A Study in Aesthetics, Poetics and Poetic Practice from Collins to Coleridge* (Cambridge: Cambridge University Press, 1987), pp. 1–18.
25. James Harris, *Three Treatises* (London: H. Woodfall, 1744), pp. 75–6.

Chapter 22

Romantic poetry: an overview

SEAMUS PERRY

'We live in mental representations of the past', said Wallace Stevens, which might itself appear a very 'Romantic' way of looking at things;[1] and 'Romanticism' is one of those representations. We live in mental representations of the present too of course, though, as it happens 'Romantic' was not a representation that would have seemed important to the 'Romantics' themselves: in English letters it is a retrospective category. 'Wordsworth, Byron, Shelley, and Keats did not regard themselves as writing "romantic" poems', Ian Jack observes, 'and would not – in fact – have been particularly flattered if they had been told that that was what they were doing.'[2] The word is current within the period, as it still is, in the sense that Johnson's *Dictionary* offers ('resembling the tales of romances') before moving on to more judgmental uses, both negative ('Improbable; false') and more positive ('Fanciful; full of wild scenery')[3] – as in the 'deep romantic chasm which slanted / Down the green hill athwart a cedarn cover' from 'Kubla Khan' (lines 12–13). Jack judiciously omits Coleridge from his list of authors for Coleridge *did* think of some of his poems as 'romantic', and not without pride: he recollected his planned contribution to *Lyrical Ballads* as poems 'directed to persons and characters supernatural, or at least romantic'.[4] But the word as used at the time is hardly a key to the intricacies of the age: it lacks the implicit 'structure of dogma' that William Empson identifies as the heart of a 'complex word'.[5] Its one possible intricacy is an ability to express correct disapproval for something sneakingly regarded: 'Wrong but Wromantic';[6] or as *OED* quotes Trench (1854), 'A romantic scheme is one which is wild, impracticable, and yet contains something which captivates the fancy.' The word appears with that spin in eighteenth- and nineteenth-century writing when an enlightened judgment regards the irregular achievements of a less polished age – what Thomas Warton calls 'the beautiful extravagancies of romantic fabling'.[7] Such a sentiment was not unusual in an age that thrilled to Macpherson's *Ossian*, its 'scenery throughout, wild and romantic' (as Hugh Blair, Professor of Rhetoric and Belles Lettres at Edinburgh, enthused in his 'Critical Dissertation of the Poems of Ossian'), and which found a kindred excitement in the rude primitivism of Bishop Percy's *Reliques of Ancient English Poetry* (1765), the third volume of which was '*chiefly devoted to Romantic Subjects*'.[8] The North Country, only latterly civilised according to Percy, was home, he said, to the best of the old ballads, full of 'a romantic wildness'.[9] (The word has much the same resonance, then, as 'gothic' – as when Pope praises Shakespeare as 'an ancient majestic piece of *Gothick* Architecture compar'd with a Modern building'.)[10] The romantic spirit had survived in some modern productions: in his essay on Pope, Warton quotes some fairy-filled lines from James Thomson's *Castle of Indolence* – 'I cannot at present recollect any solitude so romantic, or peopled with beings so proper to the place, and the spectator.'[11] The word used indulgently, thus, is always conscious of its vulnerability to a more hard-headed view, such as that of John Foster, for whom 'romantic' had come to mean but the pejorative associate of 'wild, extravagant, and visionary'.[12]

The currency of 'Romantic' might imply a special interest in the relationship between modern literature and native (as opposed to classical) antiquity; and such a relationship is indeed a key characteristic of much later eighteenth- and early nineteenth-century writing. A broadly historicist literary temper was fostered, not only by the presentation of 'folk' poetry in Percy's *Reliques* and John Aikin's *Essays on Song Writing* (1772) and other volumes, but by great works of archival scholarship, pre-eminently Warton's *History of English Poetry* (1774–81), and by some heroic anthologising, by Robert Anderson (*Works of the British Poets*, 1792–5) and others, all of which helped extend well beyond the range of Johnson's *Lives of the Poets* the sense of the English literary tradition, back to the Renaissance and beyond. 'The paradox of British Romanticism', as Stuart Curran puts it, 'is that its revolution came about through an intense and largely isolated engagement with its own past';[13] and one obvious exemplification of that 'engagement' (as Curran handsomely demonstrates) is the immense energy that writers devoted to the re-discovery and re-invention of older forms and modes, from sonnet and hymn to pastoral and epic and, of course, romance too.

But the terms 'Romantic' and 'Romanticism' were not used at the time with any of Curran's generalising purpose to characterise the contemporary scene. When Coleridge refers to 'Romantic writers' he means just 'writers of romances';[14] and when a reviewer describes *Christabel* as a 'romantic fragment' it is clear that he is thinking about the romance worlds of old poems, in which (as that disenchanted reviewer observed) 'the absurd trammels of mere physical possibility are . . . thrown aside'.[15] William Maginn called Coleridge 'the founder of the romantic school in poetry';[16] but, as the context makes clear, this is principally as the author of *Christabel* – just as, when Henry Nelson Coleridge praised the 'romantic witchery of the "Christabel" and "Ancient Mariner" ' he did so to draw a contrast with the qualities of Coleridge's other poems.[17]

To modern readers, of course, it is the innovation of *Christabel* that seems more striking than any kinship with the old literature. The way the poem explores the haunting and uncanny feels wholly modern: at once an evocation of supernatural powers and an exploration of the mind's dark creativity, the poem anticipates a work such as Henry James's *Turn of the Screw* much more than it looks back to the ballads. The poetry is, as Henry Nelson Coleridge asserts, 'the most difficult of execution in the whole field of romance – witchery by daylight':[18] while appearing straightforwardly to set goodness against evil, Coleridge's poem actually works to unsettle any such stability, half-implying that the psychic energies which animate our moral categories are in truth disturbingly fluid. And the form that Coleridge finds can appear quite as novel. As a matter of structure, he brilliantly exploits as a source of endless suggestion what might otherwise seem the mere contingency of the poem's incompleteness; while at a more local level, the life that Coleridge imagines is acted out in the brilliantly inventive accentual waywardness of the verse. Coleridge himself seems to have thought this the greatest achievement of the poem, and it certainly affected his contemporaries Scott and Byron powerfully, though to lesser effect: the versification of *Christabel*, Coleridge claimed in the preface he supplied in 1816, obeys a 'new principle: namely, that of counting in each line the accents, not the syllables'. Each line has (he says) four accents, but the number of syllables 'may vary from seven to twelve', an 'occasional variation in the number of syllables' which 'is not introduced wantonly, or for the mere ends of convenience, but in correspondence with some transition in the nature of the imagery or passion'.[19] Whether Coleridge's practice was actually as novel as he claims has been a matter of dispute among the critics; but in the self-conscious experimentation with which he approached the matter, his anticipation of the modern metrics of Hopkins, especially, feels very clear.

Making notes on 'Modern Taste' in 1820, Coleridge attributes 'the re-establishment of the Romantic & Italian School in Germany & G. Britain' to 'the genius of Wieland, Goethe, Tieck, Southey, Scott & Byron among the Poets, and the Lectures of Coleridge, Schlegel, Campbell & others among the Critics':[20] the word 'Romantic' is being used, not to nominate what distinguished his contemporaries from their predecessors, but to label a certain style or idiom – what W. P. Ker was later to call 'the fairy way of writing'.[21] Almost alone of his contemporaries, Coleridge knew of the more ambitious classificatory work being done with the word in Germany, and he borrowed Schlegel's distinction between 'Classic' and 'Romantic' in some of his literary lectures; but there his point is chiefly to characterise Shakespeare as originator of the 'Romantic' (as opposed to 'Ancient') drama:[22] 'the true genuine modern Poetry [is] the romantic – & the works of Shakespere are romantic Poetry revealing itself in the drama'.[23] Coleridge does not seem to have thought the antithesis of 'Romantic' and 'classic' especially momentous, as George Whalley remarks;[24] and, more generally, the distinction, although advertised by de Staël in *De l'Allemagne* (1813), did not really catch on in Britain until much later.[25]

The term took its place within a group of vigorous but informal literary labels: the 'Lake School' was probably the most tenacious, and 'Romantic' qualities are usually defined in opposition to it. Francis Jeffrey invented the Lake School in 1802, identifying as its principal dogma a 'great love of nature': 'a new school of poetry', as he later put it, 'outrageous for simplicity'.[26] The implications of 'Romantic', typically, were quite to the contrary: a cultivation of wildness and exotic differentness; and Scott (as poet, but also as collector of the *Minstrelsy of the Scottish Border: Consisting of Historical and Romantic Ballads*) and Byron (as author of the Oriental tales and *Childe Harold*) appeared repeatedly as its exempla: Scott found his materials in 'the fabric of our old romances', Jeffrey explained, and Byron in foreign tales and places – 'romantic climes', as Scott called them.[27] The authors helped to establish their own characterisation: Scott, in his 'General Preface' of 1829, described his progress towards 'romantic composition';[28] Byron subtitled *Childe Harold* 'A Romaunt'; and later literary historians took them at their word. Thomas Shaw's *Outlines of English Literature* (1849) nominates Scott as the 'romantic poet and novelist of Scotland' and as 'the type, sign, or measure of the first step in literature towards romanticism'; Byron appears as 'the greatest of the romanticists'; and contrasted with them both are 'Wordsworth, Coleridge, and the New Poetry'.[29] The leader of the 'purely romantic school' for David Macbeth Moir in 1851 was 'Monk' Lewis, with Scott, Southey, Coleridge, Hogg and others coming behind. (The Lake School, 'one of the most brilliant constellations of genius that ever illustrated our literature', was something quite different.)[30] And in 1862, Thomas Arnold is explicit: 'By *romantic poems* . . . we mean, poems in which heroic subjects are epically treated, after the manner of the old romances of chivalry': so for him, the exemplary figure is Scott, alongside Byron's Oriental tales – which are really, says Arnold, 'imitations, with changed scenery and accessories, of Scott's romantic poems' (a good piece of criticism).[31] W. L. Phelps, in 1893, was still identifying Romanticism in 'full maturity' in Scott and Byron;[32] at the turn of the century, Henry A. Beers similarly took 'Romanticism' to mean writing shaped by 'the life and thought of the Middle Ages';[33] and when, in a sequel volume, Beers sought to defend the narrowness of his usage he did so by asking, rhetorically, 'what Englishman will be satisfied with a definition of *romantic* which excludes Scott?'[34]

In a letter of 1881, Gerard Manley Hopkins improvised a dazzling piece of literary history. There was, he explained, 'the Romantic school (Romantic is a bad word) of Keats, Leigh Hunt, Hood, indeed of Scott early in the century', whose writings had led to Victorian medievalism; there was the 'school' of 'Lake poets, and also of Shelley and Landor'; and there was a third, 'sentimental school, of Byron, Moore, Mrs Hemans, and Haynes Bailey'.[35] Hopkins plays his own variations, but that poetry of the early century in general might usefully be gathered under the title 'Romantic' evidently does not occur to him. And this is entirely typical: the Victorians repeatedly looked back to the poetic achievements of the early years of their century; but, as David Perkins observes, not one of them seems to have thought it worth characterising that literature as 'Romantic' or as part of a 'Romantic movement', let alone as the local version of a more widely experienced 'Romanticism'.[36] The idea of a more inclusive English 'Romantic School' seems to have first appeared in the *History* by H. A. Taine (1863): 'Now [i.e. 1793–4] appeared the English romantic school, closely resembling the French in its doctrines, origins, and alliances' – principally for Taine, a distasteful mishmash of Rousseauism and social protest.[37] But whether the analogy with France works very well is doubtful – as is the case with the German parallel made by Alois Brandl a few years later in his *Samuel Taylor Coleridge and the English Romantic School* (1886), where the heart of the English Romantic school (Wordsworth, Coleridge and Scott) is said to have drawn 'endless inspiration from the Middle Ages'.[38] It is a peculiar way of thinking about Wordsworth, and odd for much of Coleridge; but Heine had characterised the German 'Romantic school' in such terms:[39] you feel the mismatch between the imported paradigm and the native material it is trying to organise. Beers sturdily criticised Brandl's attempt at re-branding: Wordsworth was 'absolutely unromantic in contrast with Scott and Coleridge': 'I prefer to think of Cowper as a naturalist, of Shelley as an idealist, and of Wordsworth as a transcendental realist, and to reserve the name "romanticist" for writers like Scott, Coleridge, and Keats' – that is, authors of medievalist pieces.[40]

Beers felt moved to self-defence because his understanding of the word 'Romantic', restricted and coherent, was coming to seem outmoded. The meaning of the word begins to shift in English usage around the turn of the century: Walter Raleigh is one good place to see it happening. In the old style, he puts forward Percy's *Reliques* as particularly important in a romantic revival, and singles out Scott, Coleridge and Keats as creating 'an original literature, suggested by the old'.[41] But there are other senses hovering too: he speaks in a lecture of 1904, for example, of '[t]he romantic apotheosis of individual feeling, this impatience of the discipline of fact', neither of which are very obviously connected with medievalism. 'The thesis', as he wrote, 'is that the seeds of subsequent extravagance and decay were in the early poets – indeed, the purpose is mainly anti-Romantic.'[42] He sounds curiously like Eliot there, tarnishing the 'Romantic' with what's egotistical, introverted, excessively self-willed. Raleigh hardly initiated such an expansion in the range of the word: one of the voguish definitions that Beers tried to fight off had been Brunetière's, 'the emancipation of the ego';[43] and Phelps had included 'Subjectivity' amongst the attributes all Romantics shared.[44] Describing the egotism of Kantian philosophy in a book of 1916, George Santayana makes very clear this newly important cluster of notions: 'The direction in which German philosophy is profound is the direction of inwardness'; and the consequence of this is that, 'Rather than religious . . . this philosophy is romantic', which is to say: 'It cannot take outer facts very seriously; they are at best symbols of its own unfathomable impulses.'[45] Lascelles Abercrombie, in a book published in 1926, marks the trend. Apologising for introducing 'those dreadful words, "romanticism" and "classicism" ', Abercrombie defines as the 'true antithesis' that 'between romanticism and realism': Romanticism, in this reading, is defined by '*a tendency away from actuality*': 'We see the spirit of the mind withdrawing more and more from commerce with the outer world, and endeavouring, or at least desiring, to rely more and more on the things it finds within itself.' Romanticism, he says, in tune with Santayana, 'takes its most obvious form in *egoism*'.[46] Humbert Wolfe, in a sprightly lecture of 1933, makes the same link with a sort of innate idealism: 'It was the belief that not only we but the objective [*sic*] about us are such stuff as dreams are made of, and that one dream may assume dominion upon another.'[47]

The establishment of T. S. Eliot in the early 1920s as an important presence on the literary scene marks an episode in the history of the term: Eliot later recalled 'my recurrent theme of Classicism versus Romanticism', a theme especially evident in the arguments with Middleton Murry conducted in *The Criterion* and *Adelphi*.[48] Wolfe saw the 'dim, if unrecognized, guidance of the austere figure of Professor Irving Babbitt', who had been one of Eliot's professors at Harvard;[49] but just as relevant, if more obscured, is the figure of Matthew Arnold: the charges of disabling subjectivism and dreamy irreality which are the bad hallmarks of Romanticism in early Eliot are very close to the defining characteristics of Arnold's famous portrait of Shelley, 'beautiful and ineffectual angel, beating in the void his luminous wings in vain'.[50] Eliot prized what he called 'the sense of fact';[51] and he enjoyed expressing his bewilderment at Shelley's language ('I should be grateful for any explanation of this stanza') when it seemed to him to leave behind the recognisable world for the charm of its own expression: 'For the first time perhaps in verse of such eminence, sound exists without sense.'[52] But Shelley is not the only introverted consciousness on offer within the period: Hazlitt's powerful myth of Wordsworth ('The power of his mind preys upon itself . . . He lives in the busy solitude of his own heart; in the deep silence of thought') makes him one of the same visionary company.[53] Coleridge, too, appears repeatedly in memoirs and appreciations as a person locked within the private space of his own consciousness: 'The self-created sustenance of a mind / Debarred from nature's living images, / Compelled to be a life unto itself', as Wordsworth pictured him in *The Prelude* (VI, lines 312–14).[54] Similar versions of the Coleridgean type, kindly or satirical, appear in De Quincey, Lamb, Carlyle and others; and they draw on the self-mythologised inward existence that features in, say, the 'Preface' to 'Kubla Khan', where Coleridge recalls 'a profound sleep, at least of the external senses' (during which the vision of the poem occurred) before the person from Porlock drew the poet back to the daylight. It is Coleridge's achievement to make the poem itself, at once incantatory and deeply conditional, an adequate symbol of his own poetic self-mythologising, both vatic and defeatist. Swinburne found in this 'aversion to externals' (as Coleridge said of Hamlet)[55] a most thrilling case: 'Coleridge was the reverse of Antæus; the contact of earth took all strength out of him.'[56] Clough found in Wordsworth a similar sort of profound inwardness, which he regarded, characteristically, with a wry but admiring indulgence:

> instead of looking directly at an object, and considering it as a thing in itself, and allowing it to operate upon him as a fact in itself, he takes the sentiment produced by it in his own mind as the thing, as the important and really real fact. The real things cease to be real; the world no longer exists; all that exists is the feeling, somehow generated in the poet's sensibility.[57]

The great myth of the 'Romantic' artist, which such accounts help to establish – that he is, in Frank Kermode's formulation, 'different, isolated'[58] –

persists influentially through to the modern period and helps to confirm a new sense of 'Romantic' as inward, self-involved, egotistical, unreal, subjectivist. '[W]e cannot believe', remarks the young Eliot in his essay 'A Romantic Aristocrat', 'that George Wyndham lived in the real world':[59] Eliot was prompted by Charles Whibley's deathly remark that Wyndham, 'by character and training a romantic . . . looked with wonder upon the world as upon a fairyland'.[60] 'Romanticism is a short cut to the strangeness without the reality, and it leads its disciples only back upon themselves. George Wyndham had curiosity, but he employed it romantically, not to penetrate the real world, but to complete the varied features of the world he made for himself.'[61] Elsewhere Eliot holds Coleridge the critic prone to an analogous fault, 'apt to take leave of the data of criticism, and arouse the suspicion that he has been diverted into a metaphysical hare-and-hounds'.[62] That was what everyone had been saying about Coleridge ever since Hazlitt; but by Eliot's time it has become a definition of what made him *Romantic*. 'Romantic' and 'Romanticism' become more meaningful – useful – terms, once they define something against which to react; and such a phenomenon is entirely normal. 'The naming of a period, or if I can call it so the –isming of a period', says Kermode, 'always entails the construction of . . . a myth, which simplifies history and makes valuation of the work of one period easier by devaluing another period (usually the one that comes immediately before).'[63] The older notion of what's 'Romantic' persists; but in the word's most tendentious and vigorous appearances, what makes Romantic poetry 'romantic' has shifted.

'The essence of the mood', said Irving Babbitt, 'is always the straining of the imagination away from the here and now, from an actuality that seems paltry and faded compared to the radiant hues of one's dream.'[64] In a properly classical poem, thought T. E. Hulme, such as he preferred, 'it is always the light of ordinary day, never the light that never was on land or sea'.[65] Hulme has dreamed up there his own version of some beautiful lines from Wordsworth's 'Elegiac Stanzas', which describe the poet's task – to

> add the gleam,
> The light that never was, on sea or land,
> The consecration, and the Poet's dream . . . (lines 14–16)

Coleridge thought those lines 'at once an instance and an illustration' of imaginative power:[66] poetry, in such a view, is something that happens when imagination does something transformative and improving to the merely ordinary world, turning 'Bodies to spirit by sublimation strange'.[67] Shakespeare is one exemplary genius: his characters, said Coleridge, 'from

Othello or Macbeth down to Dogberry are ideal: they are not <the> things but the abstracts of the things which a great mind may take into itself and naturalize to its own heaven'.[68] Shelley saw a similar kind of transmuting power in Wordsworth, and articulated what he saw in a paused moment of wonder amid the satirical ebullience of *Peter Bell the Third*:

> Yet his was individual mind,
> And new created all he saw
> In a new manner, and refined
> Those new creations, and combined
> Them, by a master-spirit's law.[69] (lines 303–7)

The ordinary world – Coleridge's 'inanimate cold world' ('Dejection: An Ode', line 51) – is not all it might be: 'High poetry', as Coleridge said wonderingly, thinking of Milton, 'is the translation of reality into the ideal.'[70]

Babbitt's reference to 'the radiant hues of one's dream' is arch but astute: the dream is a natural metaphor for what poets might do within the private space of their own consciousness; and for any anti-Romantic polemic, the shortcomings of living in a dream are not hard to point out – as, it should at once be said, Wordsworth himself does, bravely and sadly, in his 'Elegiac Stanzas' ('Farewell, farewell, the Heart that lives alone, / Housed in a dream, at distance from the Kind!', lines 54–5). F. R. Leavis was one of the most influential mediators of Eliot's thought, and that included Eliot's early insistence on the lingering presence of 'romanticism', a term which (Eliot said in 1933) 'in its more comprehensive significance . . . comes to include nearly everything that distinguishes the last two hundred and fifty years'.[71] In *New Bearings in English Poetry*, Leavis tells us that nineteenth-century poetry, written within preconceptions formed by the 'great Romantics', 'was characteristically preoccupied with the creation of a dream-world', something of which Leavis disapproves, echoing Eliot: 'The effort to construct a dream world . . . alters English poetry so greatly in the nineteenth century.'[72] (Shelley is foremost among the offenders for Leavis, his 'essential trait' – concurring with Arnold's view – a 'weak grasp upon the actual'.)[73] F. L. Lucas was no admirer of Eliot, yet offered as 'an Aristotelian definition of Romanticism' the same sort of formula: 'a dream-picture of life'. ('Classicism' is, by contrast, 'wide awake and strictly sober'.) Coleridge, says Lucas, is the figure behind whom follows 'the long pageant of Romantic dreamers': he is 'the master-critic of Romanticism'; and 'Imagination' is its 'master-spirit'.[74] 'Imagination', understood as a special kind of subjectivity or visionary idealism, becomes the major hallmark of Romanticism: in his Norton lectures for 1948–9, Maurice

Bowra takes 'the importance which they attached to the imagination' as the defining characteristic of the English Romantics, 'part of the contemporary belief in the individual self'.[75]

Such a characterisation encourages Bowra to put Blake centre-stage, 'the most rigorous in his conception of the imagination': 'Coleridge does not go so far as Blake in the claims which he makes for the imagination', writes Bowra, delightfully. 'He is still a little hampered by the presence of an external world and feels that in some way he must conform to it.'[76] Bowra is not odd in clearing central space for Blake: the triumphant entrance of Blake into the new Romantic canon in the middle part of the twentieth century is very striking. In Harold Bloom's *The Visionary Company* (1971 (1962)), Blake has become exemplarily romantic, 'an absolute norm by means of which all other romantic poets are to be understood and measured', as Paul de Man noticed.[77] By the measure of Blake's fierce anti-naturalism and anti-materialism ('Natural Objects always did & now do weaken, deaden & obliterate Imagination in Me') truly 'Romantic' poetry becomes really 'an antinature poetry', in Bloom's charismatic phrase.[78] Idealism is its obvious metaphysical corollary: 'Mental things are alone Real; what is call'd Corporeal, Nobody Knows of its Dwelling Place; it is in Fallacy, & its Existence an Imposture', says Blake.[79] 'I confess that I am one of those who am unable to refuse my assent to the conclusions of those philosophers who assert that nothing exists but as it is perceived', says Shelley, tip-toeing up to a Berkeleian position.[80] This was the Shelley who appealed so strongly to Yeats, a man who refused to distinguish in kind between dreams and the 'thoughts, which are called *real, or external objects*':[81] when Denis Donoghue wishes to place Yeats's own work within the context of 'European Romanticism', he naturally chooses 'idealism as its philosophical companion'.[82] This whole aspect of 'Romantic' thought, in John Bayley's formulation, 'stresses the sublime and vital function of man's imagination, which gives order and meaning to his surroundings, and of poetry, the imagination's chief instrument of expression'.[83] It is the understanding of what's Romantic that shaped the Yale School of Romanticists in the 1970s, drawn as they were to the thought of a poetry marked (as Bloom said Wordsworth's was) 'by the evanescence of any subject but subjectivity, the loss of what a poem is "about" ': Bloom describes that as Wordsworth's 'Copernican revolution in poetry', by purposeful analogy with the 'Copernican revolution' that Kant's idealism sought to effect in metaphysics.[84] (Bloom follows in the footsteps of Clough, who noted Wordsworth's 'sentimentalising over sentiment, this sensibility about sensibility'.)[85] As Romantic criticism took its revisionary, 'materialist' turn in the 1980s, it did not refute that characterisation of 'Romantic poetry' so much as re-confirm it: 'The idea that poetry, or even consciousness, can set one free of the ruins of history and culture is the grand illusion of every Romantic poet', announced Jerome McGann, sounding not so unlike T. E. Hulme.[86] As Susan Wolfson observed, 'transcendent idealism has been dubbed by McGann as "*the* Romantic Ideology" '.[87]

Any literary classification, says David Perkins, comprises the mutually interfering activity of three elements: 'a name . . . a concept, and a canon of works subsumed under the concept. Reasoning goes from the concept to the canon, from the canon to the concept.' What happens in the course of the twentieth century is a change in the canon of early nineteenth-century works that habitually fall under the term 'Romantic', which in turn effects a change in the concept of 'Romanticism' that promises to organise them: 'The "romantic ideology" was formed at this time and not in the romantic period itself.'[88] Beers might rhetorically question who could consider 'Arnold's clean-cut, reserved, delicately intellectual work as romantic';[89] but a modern critic would have no problem identifying Arnold as 'a very influential transmitter of Romantic thought'.[90] It is not that we have come to understand Arnold's 'Romanticism' better or more fully; nor that our knowledge of him has changed through new discoveries in his oeuvre or biography. But what feels critically pertinent about him *has* changed: the features by which he has come to be recognised and placed within the continuities and discontinuities of nineteenth-century literary history have become different. That 'Romantic' was the name to hand to articulate those new senses of literary relationship is one of the contingencies of the story (and one of its possible confusions).

But the establishment of the 'Romantic ideology' is not as single-minded a story as I have been making it seem. For Bloom was being agreeably tendentious when he said that the Romantics wrote 'antinature' poetry, especially with Wordsworth in mind: Wordsworth's reputation, or notoriety, as a 'poet of nature' was already well established during his lifetime. Blake's belated arrival within the Romantic canon is one startling feature of mid twentieth-century literary criticism; but the establishment, some time earlier, of Wordsworth as a central figure is another, and complicates the picture. By the end of the nineteenth century, for most literary historians the convenient starting date for the 'Romantic' movement had settled at 1798, the year of the first edition of *Lyrical Ballads*: a 'first generation' of poets (Wordsworth, Coleridge, Southey) was succeeded by a second (Byron, Shelley, Keats) in indebted reaction to their precursors. A modern critic such as McGann can take it for granted that the 'Romantic ideology' *is* the 'Wordsworthian–Coleridgean ideology';[91] but the revision of the old canon here is very striking. During his lifetime, and for several decades after his death, Wordsworth had typically been taken for something definitively other than 'Romantic', or included within the 'Romantic' grouping only at a stretch. Now he becomes a central figure: by 1897, C. H. Herford's comprehensive (and still impressive) overview had settled on 1798–1832 as 'The Age of Wordsworth'.[92] Beers had once rejected a definition of 'Romantic' because it would not fit the qualities of Scott; but medievalism is rejected as a definition of Romanticism by H. J. C. Grierson in 1923 because it will not fit the new test-case, Wordsworth.[93]

The example of Wordsworth encourages the idea, commonly found in literary histories from the later nineteenth century onward, that 'Romantic poetry' involves crucially a 'return to nature' – not that Wordsworth himself needed to return, as Raleigh said gallantly, since he 'had never deserted her'.[94] Idealist passages are hardly difficult to locate within Wordsworth, it is true; but other passages, including many of his most polemical, point in quite a different direction – not towards the separateness and elevation of the artist and his works over the ordinary world, but, quite to the contrary, towards the rediscovery of the ordinary world as an object of imaginative interest in its own right. Blake's stress upon the wonderful supremacy of the creative mind leads him to place a corresponding emphasis upon the sovereignty of art: 'I wish to live for art', Henry Crabb Robinson recalled him saying, as though anticipating the rhetoric of a later nineteenth-century *symbolisme*.[95] Wordsworth could strike the same lofty note: 'High is our calling, Friend! – Creative Art' ('To B. R. Haydon, Esq.', line 1); but his more provocative, and certainly his most widely noticed remarks, especially the 'Preface' to *Lyrical Ballads* (1800; 1802), gave the impression, in Jeffrey's dismayed phrase, of 'the positive and *bona fide* rejection of art altogether'.[96] Imprecisely but emotively attuned to an enlightened and democratic ethos, the heroic principles of Wordsworth's 'Preface' are 'nature', the 'human', the 'common', the 'ordinary': the poems are said to turn about 'incidents and situations from common life', and be couched in an idiom that aspires to 'the language really used by men'; and Wordsworth goes out of his way to disclaim for his verse any special differentness – 'Poetry sheds no tears "such as Angels weep," but natural and human tears; she can boast of no celestial Ichor that distinguishes her vital juices from those of prose; the same human blood circulates through the veins of them both.'[97] These ambitions diversely articulate a fundamental Wordsworthian belief in what he called, in the 'Essays on Epitaphs', 'the rights and dignity of Nature'.[98] The political rhetoric of 'rights' is a characteristic provocation: Jeffrey was not alone in regarding the gestures of *Lyrical Ballads* with acute mistrust, as though the poetry were enacting in its way the egalitarianism fomented by the ideals of the revolution in France – 'the master-theme of our epoch', as Shelley said.[99] 'Nature' is a term of almost endless polysemy, to be sure, and Wordsworth himself was capable of using it with judicious imprecision.[100] It could sponsor a poetry based on the quiet realities of the domestic routine, as in Cowper's best-selling *The Task*; but, equally, it might sponsor Burns's dazzling experiments in vernacular, or Coleridge's cultivation of a 'conversational' mode; or Clare's poems of natural sightings – testimony to 'the infinite variety of natural appearances', as Wordsworth said in old age, describing the object of his life work, that had hitherto been 'unnoticed by the poets of any age or country'.[101]

McGann's epithet for the 'ideology' that he discerns, 'Wordsworthian–Coleridgean', nominates a disagreement as much as an alliance. When Coleridge takes Wordsworth to task in *Biographia*, it is in large part for the '*matter-of-factness*' that marks and (in Coleridge's view) mars his verse – for 'the feeling of incongruity' that arises when Wordsworth descends from high poetry to something lower and more prosaic, as though the proper 'sublimation strange' of imagination had been incompletely or imperfectly achieved.[102] 'Assuredly we seem to sink most abruptly, not to say burlesquely, and almost as in a *medly* from this couplet ['They flash upon that inward eye, / Which is the bliss of solitude'] to – 'And then my heart with pleasure fills, / And dances with the *daffodils*.'[103] In that respect Coleridge shared the judgment of many contemporaries, who agreed that the stubborn ordinariness of Wordsworth's subject matter often exceeded his capacity to transform it into art: 'It is the vice of Wordsworth's intellect to be always upon the stretch and strain', Southey complained, 'to look at pile-worts and daffodowndillies through the same telescope which he applies to the moon and stars.'[104] Keats, too, learning that Wordsworth was about to publish a poem entitled 'Peter Bell', wondered at the odd belligerence of this genius: 'what a perverse fellow it is! Why wilt he talk about Peter Bells.'[105] So, when Wordsworth criticised Crabbe's poems as 'mere matters of fact' it was with the sensitivity of a man who had faced much the same criticism himself.[106] Crabbe wrote in heroic couplets, as Pope had, though the movement of his verse and the homely unhappiness that it typically narrates are both a world away from Pope:

> Blaney, a wealthy heir at twenty-one,
> At twenty-five was ruin'd and undone:
> These years with grievous crimes we need not load,
> He found his ruin in the common road . . .[107]

The matter-of-fact art of 'the common road' was often stigmatised within the period as 'Dutch', by analogy with Dutch still-life painting, which specialised in scenes of ordinary and low life and was travestied as slavishly in hock to the merely mundane: for Hazlitt, Crabbe was the drab poet of choice for 'the adept in Dutch interiors'.[108] Contrariwise, McGann praises Crabbe for escaping 'Idealistic traditions of poetry and criticism', a firmly anti-Romantic writer whose work exhibits 'matter-of-fact and anti-imaginative qualities' and shows that 'no subject lies outside the province of verse'.[109] In one sense of the word, McGann is obviously right, and Crabbe as un-'Romantic' as can be; but 'Dutch' ordinariness has its own claim to be a 'Romantic' phenomenon too: for Wordsworth, Coleridge, Keats, Clare and others, knew too that no subject lay outside the province of verse, and that the humdrum and familiar could serve not as a constraint upon imagination but as the occasion for it. Later in the nineteenth century, George Eliot would turn the disparagement of 'Dutch' art on its head, praising 'the faithful representing of commonplace things' as a true aim for the author;[110] and she wrote fully conscious of Wordsworth's declared ambition for poetry, 'whereby ordinary things should be presented to the mind in an unusual way'.[111] Coleridge could be as rude about Dutch painters as anyone, but (with Wordsworth in mind) he nevertheless found in the illumination of the commonplace the hallmark of poetic genius: it is, he says in *Biographia*, the distinction of great poets '[t]o carry on the feelings of childhood into the powers of manhood; to combine the child's sense of wonder and novelty with the appearances, which every day for perhaps forty years had rendered familiar';[112] and his own verse bears repeated witness to that principle:

> All this long eve, so balmy and serene,
> Have I been gazing on the western sky,
> And its peculiar tint of yellow green . . .
>
> ('Dejection: An Ode', lines 27–9)

The lines matter, not because they are evidence of the transformative power of the poetic mind, but because of their fidelity to the truth, as though perceived for the first time, of reiterated experience. In a letter to his friend Woodhouse, Keats worked out his opposition to idealism in his own terms, contrasting the 'wordsworthian or egotistical sublime; which is a thing per se and stands alone' with his own 'poetical Character', empowered with a genius for empathetic impersonation, 'continually in for – and filling some other Body':[113] in reaction to the 'solitary, isolated' Romantic genius, as Bayley puts it, Keats celebrates 'the ability to enter into all modes of being, animate and inanimate, and to understand and express their nature as it were from the inside'.[114] That puts the point at its most magical; but within the world of Keats's poems, less mysteriously, ordinariness repeatedly appears in a flash amid the literariness of old romance, creating its own version of the 'incongruity' that Coleridge noted (but to deplore) in Wordsworth:

> Madeline, St Agnes' charmèd maid,
> Rose, like a missioned spirit, unaware.
> With silver taper's light, and pious care,
> She turned, and down the agèd gossip led
> To a safe level matting . . .[115]

'The last word drags a weight of the commonplace that is almost sublime', remarks Bayley, sublimely.[116]

This literature of the commonplace and humanly ordinary has sometimes been characterised as an especially female kind of Romantic writing, a domestically scaled alternative to more visionary masculine flights: Stuart Curran, for instance, finds 'an investment in quotidian tones and details' exemplified in the work of Anna Barbauld, Mary Russell Mitford, Mary Robinson, Hannah More and others;[117] and when Anne Mellor praises Dorothy Wordsworth's descriptive writing for teaching us *'how to see'* she invokes a conception of the 'Romantic' starkly opposed to the egotistical sublime.[118] But really, the matter subsumes questions of gender within a much broader set of concerns. The Romantic discovery, or the invention, of the ordinary has been placed in a philosophical context by Stanley Cavell, who sees the poets 'bringing the world back, as to life' in reaction to the perceptual constraints of Kant's scepticism.[119] Wordsworth's German contemporary Hölderlin put that epochal perplexity into the mouth of his Empedokles: 'And what indeed would Heaven be and Ocean / And islands and the stars . . . what would it mean or be, / This dead stringed instrument, did I not lend it / A resonance, a language and a soul?';[120] and though Kant can't have mattered to most of the English poets, for few of them really knew much about him, still the power of Cavell's general case is nevertheless striking. Romantic egotism isolates as much as it empowers, and the resort to a reality outside the self holds out a saving hope, as Coleridge put it, of 'that freshness of sensation which is the constant accompaniment of mental, no less than of bodily, convalescence'.[121] Quite apart from Cavell's specific philosophical bearings, one can intuitively grasp the moral wisdom involved in freshly appreciating the value of the ordinary world, 'the very world', in Wordsworth's resonant words, 'which is the world / Of all of us, the place in which, in the end, / We find our happiness, or not at all' (*Prelude* x, lines 726–8); and appreciating the autonomy of that world, the way that its life is ultimately quite distinct from the claims of human consciousness, brings its own kind of illumination, even a political one: a buzzing fly would drive the despotic Czar Nicholas I to distraction, the Marquis de Custine reported, 'The independence of nature seems to him a bad example.'[122] Hegel, for one, thought Dutch paintings celebratory rather than slavish, the expression of a 'freshly awakened spiritual freedom and vitality': his praise closely resembles Coleridge's admiration for an art that throws off the deadening weight of familiarity for the new-found perceptual liberation of 'wonder and novelty'.[123]

That contradictory elements were abroad and sometimes coincided was not lost on writers at the time: 'a Dutch attempt at German sublimity' was Southey's snooty response to the challenge of 'The Ancient Mariner'.[124] 'Romanticism', said Eliot over a century later, 'splits up into two directions: escape from the world of fact, and devotion to brute fact':[125] this puts the dualism in 'Romantic' with a bracing lack of sympathy. Paul de Man leaves us with a good poser recognising the same dichotomy: 'For what are we to believe? Is romanticism a subjective idealism, open to all the attacks of solipsism . . . Or is it instead a return to a certain form of naturalism after the forced abstraction of the Enlightenment . . . ?'[126] There is no right answer to the question: it depends on the version of 'Romantic' you have in mind, each of which has a protracted history of definition and use that might be traced. Wordsworth's peculiar centrality to the discussion lies not so much in the consistency or assurance with which he assumes one of the positions, as in the way that he encompasses them – not in any magisterial act of synthesis, but rather through a thoroughly enabling lack of self-acquaintance, so exemplifying one of Wordsworth's own credentials for poetic genius: a 'comprehensive soul'.[127]

Notes

1. *The Letters of Wallace Stevens*, ed. Holly Stevens (London: Faber, 1967), p. 722.
2. Ian Jack, *English Literature 1815–1832* (Oxford: Clarendon Press, 1963), p. 410.
3. 'Romantick' §§1, 2, 3: Samuel Johnson, *A Dictionary of the English Language*, 2 vols. (London, 1755).
4. Samuel Taylor Coleridge, *Poems*, ed. John Beer (London: Everyman, 1999). Further quotations from Coleridge's poems are taken from this edition, unless otherwise stated. Samuel Taylor Coleridge, *Biographia Literaria*, ed. James Engell and W. Jackson Bate, 2 vols. (Princeton: Princeton University Press, 1982), vol. II, p. 6.

5. William Empson, *The Structure of Complex Words*, repr. with additions (London: Chatto and Windus, 1952), p. xii.
6. The account of the Cavaliers in W. C. Sellar and R. J. Yeatman, *1066 and All That* (London: Methuen, 1930), p. 63.
7. 'Dissertation II': *Thomas Warton's History of English Poetry*, intro. David Fairer, 4 vols. (London: Routledge, 1998), vol. I [n.p.].
8. Quoted in James Macpherson, *The Poems of Ossian and Related Works*, ed. Howard Gaskill (Edinburgh: Edinburgh University Press, 1996), p. 356.
9. Thomas Percy, *Reliques of Ancient English Poetry*, ed. Henry B. Wheatley, 3 vols. (1876–7), vol. I, p. xxii.
10. *Prose Works of Alexander Pope*, ed. Norman Ault and Rosemary Cowler, 2 vols. (Oxford: Blackwell, 1936–86), vol. II, p. 25.
11. Joseph Warton, *Essay on the Genius and Writings of Pope*, fourth edition, 2 vols. (1782), vol. I, p. 366.
12. John Foster, *Essays in a Series of Letters to a Friend*, 2 vols. (London: Longman Hurst, 1805), vol. II, p. 10.
13. Stuart Curran, *Poetic Form and British Romanticism* (New York: Oxford University Press, 1986), p. 24.
14. Coleridge, *Biographia*, vol. II, p. 212.
15. *Coleridge: The Critical Heritage*, ed. J. R. de J. Jackson, 2 vols. (London: Routledge and Kegan Paul, 1970–92) vol. I, p. 200; George Whalley, 'England/Romantic-Romanticism', in Hans Eichner (ed.), *'Romantic' and Its Cognates/The European History of a Word* (Toronto: University of Toronto Press, 1972), p. 159. Whalley's historical survey is invaluable. I also draw here on some examples from my 'Romanticism: The Brief History of a Concept'; in Duncan Wu (ed.), *A Companion to Romanticism* (Oxford: Blackwell, 1998), pp. 3–11.
16. *Fraser's Magazine*, 8 (1833), p. 64.
17. *Coleridge: Critical Heritage*, vol. I, p. 647.
18. *Ibid.*, p. 645.
19. Samuel Taylor Coleridge, *Christabel, Kubla Khan, a Vision; The Pains of Sleep* (London, 1816), p. vii.
20. Samuel Taylor Coleridge, *Shorter Works and Fragments*, ed. H. J. Jackson and J. R. de J. Jackson, 2 vols. (Princeton: Princeton University Press, 1995), vol. II, p. 858.
21. W. P. Ker, *The Art of Poetry. Seven Lectures 1920–1922* (Oxford: Clarendon Press, 1923), p. 79.
22. See Samuel Taylor Coleridge, *Lectures 1808–1819 on Literature*, ed. R. A. Foakes, 2 vols. (Princeton: Princeton University Press, 1987), vol. I, p. xlix; pp. 419, 481.
23. *Ibid.*, p. 466.
24. Whalley, 'England/Romantic-Romanticism', pp. 208–9.
25. See *ibid.*, p. 160.
26. *Edinburgh Review*, 1 (1802), p. 64; 13 (1809), p. 276.
27. *Byron: The Critical Heritage*, ed. Andrew Rutherford (London: Routledge and Kegan Paul, 1970), pp. 57, 88.

28. Walter Scott, *Waverley*, ed. Claire Lamont (Oxford: Oxford University Press, 1981), p. 353.
29. Thomas Shaw, *Outlines of English Literature* (London, 1849), pp. 390, 423, 432, 518.
30. David Macbeth Moir, *Sketches of the Poetical Literature of the Past Half-Century, in Six Lectures* (Edinburgh, 1851), pp. 17, 59.
31. Thomas Arnold, *A Manual of English Literature, Historical and Critical, with an Appendix of English Metres* (London, 1862), pp. 285, 286.
32. William Lyon Phelps, *The Beginnings of the English Romantic Movement. A Study in Eighteenth Century Literature* (Boston, 1893; repr. Boston: Ginn, 1902), p. vi.
33. Henry A. Beers, *A History of English Romanticism in the Eighteenth Century* (London: Kegan Paul, 1899), p. 2.
34. Henry A. Beers, *A History of English Romanticism in the Nineteenth Century* (London: Kegan Paul, 1902), p. vi.
35. *The Correspondence of Gerard Manley Hopkins and Richard Watson Dixon*, ed. Claude Colleer Abbott (London: Oxford University Press, 1935), p. 98.
36. David Perkins, *Is Literary History Possible?* (Baltimore: Johns Hopkins University Press, 1992), p. 97.
37. H. A. Taine, *History of English Literature*, trans. H. Van Laun, 2 vols. (Edinburgh: Edmonston and Douglas, 1871), vol. II, p. 247.
38. Alois Brandl, *Samuel Taylor Coleridge and the English Romantic School*, trans. Lady Eastlake (London: John Murray, 1887), pp. 221–2.
39. 'But what was the Romantic School in Germany? It was nothing other than the revival of the poetry of the Middle Ages. . .': Heinrich Heine, *Selected Works*, trans. Helen M. Mustard (New York: Random House, 1973), p. 131.
40. Beers, *History of English Romanticism in the Nineteenth Century*, pp. 51, 49.
41. Walter Raleigh, *Wordsworth* (London: Edward Arnold, 1903), pp. 43–4; *Romance. Two Lectures* (Princeton: Princeton University Press, 1916), p. 7.
42. Walter Raleigh, *On Writing and Writers. Being Extracts from his Notebooks*, ed. George Gordon (London: Arnold, 1926), pp. 202; 7.
43. Beers, *History of English Romanticism in the Nineteenth Century*, p. vi.
44. Phelps, *Beginnings of the English Romantic Movement*, p. 4.
45. George Santayana, *Egotism in German Philosophy* (London: J. M. Dent, 1916), pp. 12–14.
46. Lascelles Abercrombie, *Romanticism* (London: Martin Secker, 1926), pp. 7, 33, 49, 135.
47. Humbert Wolfe, *Romantic and Unromantic Poetry* (Bristol: University of Bristol Press, 1933), p. 8.
48. T. S. Eliot, *To Criticize the Critic and Other Writings* (London: Faber and Faber, 1965), p. 17.
49. Wolfe, *Romantic and Unromantic Poetry*, p. 7. For Babbitt and Eliot see George Bornstein, *Transformations of Romanticism in Yeats, Eliot, and Stevens* (Chicago: University of Chicago Press, 1976), pp. 101–4.
50. Matthew Arnold, *Essays on English Literature*, ed. F. W. Bateson (London: University of London Press, 1965), p. 183.
51. T. S. Eliot, *Selected Essays* (London: Faber, 1932; third edition 1951, 1980), p. 31.

52. T. S. Eliot, *For Lancelot Andrewes: Essays on Style and Order* (London: Faber, 1928; 1970), pp. 96–7.
53. *Complete Works of William Hazlitt*, ed. P. P. Howe, 21 vols. (London: J. M. Dent, 1930–4), vol. IV, p. 113.
54. William Wordsworth, *The Major Works*, ed. Stephen Gill (Oxford: Oxford University Press, 2000). Further quotations from Wordsworth's poems are taken from this edition.
55. Samuel Taylor Coleridge, *Lectures 1808–1819 on Literature*, ed. R. A. Foakes, vol. I, p. 540.
56. *Swinburne as Critic*, ed. Clyde K. Hyder (London: Routledge and Kegan Paul, 1972), p. 137.
57. *Prose Remains of Arthur Hugh Clough [. . .], edited by his wife* (London: Macmillan, 1888), p. 315.
58. Frank Kermode, *Romantic Image* (London: Routledge and Kegan Paul, 1957), p. 3.
59. T. S. Eliot, *The Sacred Wood. Essays on Poetry and Criticism* (London: Methuen, 1920; third edition 1932), p. 26.
60. Quoted in George Wyndham, *Essays in Romantic Literature* (London: Macmillan, 1919), p. xv.
61. Eliot, *Sacred Wood*, pp. 31–2.
62. *Ibid.*, p. 13.
63. Frank Kermode, *History and Value: The Clarendon Lectures and the Northcliffe Lectures 1987* (Oxford: Clarendon Press, 1988), p. 143.
64. Irving Babbitt, *Rousseau and Romanticism* (Boston: Houghton Mifflin, 1919; 1935), p. 92.
65. *The Collected Writings of T. E. Hulme*, ed. Karen Csengeri (Oxford: Clarendon Press, 1994), pp. 59–73, 66.
66. Coleridge, *Biographia*, vol. II, p. 151.
67. *Ibid.*, p. 17; quoting Sir John Davies's 'Nosce Teipsum'.
68. Coleridge, *Lectures*, vol. I, p. 351.
69. Percy Bysshe Shelley, *The Major Works*, ed. Zachary Leader and Michael O'Neill (Oxford: Oxford University Press, 2003).
70. Coleridge, *Lectures*, vol. II, p. 426.
71. T. S. Eliot, *The Use of Poetry and the Use of Criticism: Studies in the Relation of Criticism to Poetry in England* (London: Faber and Faber, 1933), p. 128.
72. F. R. Leavis, *New Bearings in English Poetry. A Study of the Contemporary Situation* (London: Chatto and Windus, 1932; revised edition 1950; repr. 1971), p. 10; Eliot, *Selected Essays*, p. 301.
73. F. R. Leavis, *Revaluation: Tradition and Development in English Poetry* (London: Chatto and Windus, 1936), p. 206.
74. F. L. Lucas, *The Decline and Fall of the Romantic Ideal* (Cambridge: Cambridge University Press, 1936), pp. 35–6, 38, 157. Babbitt also says that the 'cult of intoxication' is a characteristic of romanticism (Babbitt, *Rousseau and Romanticism*, p. 181) – both must have in mind Baudelaire's prose poem 'Enivrez-vous'.

75. C. M. Bowra, *The Romantic Imagination* (London: Oxford University Press, 1950; repr. 1961), p. 1.
76. *Ibid.*, pp. 14, 17.
77. Paul de Man, *Critical Writings, 1953–1978*, ed. Lindsay Waters (Minneapolis: University of Minnesota Press, 1989) pp. 90–6, 94.
78. William Blake, *Complete Writings with Variant Readings*, ed. Geoffrey Keynes (London: Oxford University Press, 1966), p. 783; Harold Bloom, *The Ringers in the Tower: Studies in Romantic Tradition* (Chicago: University of Chicago Press, 1971), p. 19.
79. Blake, *Complete Writings*, p. 617.
80. Percy Bysshe Shelley, *Shelley's Prose, or, The Trumpet of a Prophecy*, ed. David Lee Clark (Albuquerque: University of New Mexico Press, 1954; corrected edition, 1988), p. 173.
81. *Ibid.*, p. 182. Quoted in W. B. Yeats, *Selected Criticism and Prose*, ed. A. N. Jeffares (London: Pan Macmillan, 1976, 1980), p. 63.
82. Denis Donoghue, *Yeats* (London: Fontana, 1971; repr. 1982), p. 18.
83. John Bayley, *The Romantic Survival: A Study in Poetic Evolution* (London: Constable, 1957), p. 8.
84. Bloom, *Ringers in the Tower*, p. 18. Cf. Immanuel Kant, *Critique of Pure Reason*, trans. Norman Kemp Smith (London: Macmillan, 1929; corrected repr. 1933, 1990), p. 25.
85. Clough, *Prose Remains*, p. 315.
86. Jerome McGann, *The Romantic Ideology: A Critical Investigation* (Chicago: University of Chicago Press, 1983), p. 91.
87. Susan Wolfson, 'Questioning "The Romantic Ideology": Wordsworth', *Revue Internationale de Philosophie*, 44 (1990), pp. 429–47, 430.
88. Perkins, *Literary History*, pp. 73, 104.
89. Beers, *History of English Romanticism in the Nineteenth Century*, p. 278.
90. Kermode, *Romantic Image*, p. 12.
91. McGann, *Romantic Ideology*, p. 38. It might be noted that, after a long dip in his fortunes, Southey, the subject of recent major editorial work, is beginning to enjoy serious critical attention. In truth, he always had his admirers: for example (and within limits) Geoffrey Grigson, whose *Choice of Southey's Verse* (London: Faber, 1970) remains the best starting-point.
92. C. H. Herford, *The Age of Wordsworth* (London, 1897; rev. edn 1899; repr. 1908), pp. xiii–xiv.
93. H. J. C. Grierson, *Classical and Romantic* (Cambridge: Cambridge University Press, 1923), p. 8.
94. Raleigh, *Wordsworth*, p. 45.
95. Quoted in *Blake Records. Second Edition*, ed. G. E. Bentley, Jr. (New Haven: Yale University Press, 2004), p. 422.
96. *Edinburgh Review*, 1 (1802), p. 65.
97. *Wordsworth's Literary Criticism*, ed. W. J. B. Owen (London: Routledge and Kegan Paul, 1974), pp. 69–90, 71, 76.

98. *Ibid.*, p. 150.
99. *The Letters of Percy Bysshe Shelley*, ed. Frederick L. Jones, 2 vols. (Oxford: Clarendon, 1964), vol. I, p. 504.
100. The classic account of the term's variety remains A. O. Lovejoy, ' "Nature" as Aesthetic Norm', in *Essays in the History of Ideas* (Baltimore: Johns Hopkins University Press, 1948, 1960), pp. 69–77.
101. *The Fenwick Notes of William Wordsworth*, ed. Jared Curtis (London: Bristol Classical, 1993), p. 7.
102. Coleridge, *Biographia*, vol. II, p. 126.
103. *Ibid.*, p. 137.
104. Quoted in *William Wordsworth: A Critical Anthology*, ed. Graham McMaster (Harmondsworth: Penguin, 1972), p. 112.
105. *The Letters of John Keats, 1814–1821*, ed. Hyder Edward Rollins, 2 vols. (Cambridge, MA: Harvard University Press, 1958), vol. II, p. 83.
106. Quoted in *Crabbe: The Critical Heritage*, ed. Arthur Pollard (London: Routledge and Kegan Paul, 1972, 1985), p. 290.
107. George Crabbe, *The Borough*: 'Inhabitants of the Alms-House: Blaney', lines 13–16, in *George Crabbe, Tales, 1812 and Other Selected Poems*, ed. Howard Mills (Cambridge: Cambridge University Press, 1967), p. 95.
108. Hazlitt, *Complete Works*, vol. XI, p. 166.
109. Jerome McGann, *The Beauty of Inflections: Literary Investigations in Historical Method and Theory* (Oxford: Clarendon Press, 1985), pp. 295, 306.
110. George Eliot, *Adam Bede* (London: Everyman, 1992), p. 201.
111. *Wordsworth's Literary Criticism*, p. 71.
112. Coleridge, *Biographia*, vol. I, pp. 80–1.
113. Keats, *Letters*, vol. I, pp. 387, 386, 387. See Frederick Garber, 'Nature and the Romantic Mind: Egotism, Empathy, Irony', *Comparative Literature*, 29 (1977), pp. 193–212, 199–204.
114. Bayley, *Romantic Survival*, p. 8.
115. John Keats, *The Eve of St Agnes*, lines 192–6, in *The Poems of John Keats*, ed. Miriam Allott (London: Longman, 1970; corrected imprint, 1972).
116. John Bayley, 'Keats and Reality': *Proceedings of the British Academy*, 48 (1962), pp. 91–125, 121.
117. Stuart Curran, 'Romantic Poetry: The I Altered', in Anne K. Mellor (ed.), *Romanticism and Feminism* (Bloomington: Indiana University Press, 1988), pp. 185–203.
118. Anne K. Mellor, *Romanticism and Gender* (New York: Routledge, 1993), p. 163.
119. Stanley Cavell, *In Quest of the Ordinary: Lines of Skepticism and Romanticism* (Chicago: University of Chicago Press, 1988), p. 53.
120. Friedrich Hölderlin, *Poems and Fragments*, trans. Michael Hamburger, fourth edition (London: Anvil Press Poetry; 2004), p. 383.
121. Coleridge, *Biographia*, vol. I, p. 81.
122. *La Russie en 1839* (1843); quoted in Theodore Dalrymple, *Our Culture, What's Left of It: The Mandarins and the Masses* (Chicago: Ivan R. Dee, 2005), p. 171.

123. G. W. F. Hegel, *Aesthetics: Lectures on Fine Art*, trans. T. M. Knox, 2 vols. (Oxford: Clarendon Press, 1975), vol. 1, p. 170.
124. *Coleridge: Critical Heritage*, vol. 1, p. 53.
125. T. S. Eliot, *Syllabus of a Course of Six Lectures on Modern French Literature* (1916); quoted in J. D. Margolis, *T. S. Eliot's Intellectual Development 1922–1939* (Chicago: University of Chicago Press, 1972), p. 10. Cf. Babbitt, *Rousseau and Romanticism*, pp. 4, 103, 104.
126. Paul de Man, *Blindness and Insight: Essays in the Rhetoric of Contemporary Criticism*, second edition (London: Methuen, 1983), p. 198.
127. *Wordsworth's Literary Criticism*, p. 77.

Chapter 23

Blake's poetry and prophecies

JOHN BEER

From an early age William Blake showed a determination to make his mark in the contemporary scene, though it was not at first clear which field would claim his attention. He had some musical talent, and accompanied some of his early poems on the harp; he studied at the Royal Academy and his training was as an engraver. Had he lived a century later he might indeed have become an advocate of the 'gesamtkunstwerke' ('total work of art') as did Richard Wagner; but as it was, the possibility of combining the poetic and visual arts fascinated him particularly. In his time poetry found a ready audience, but the literary world in which he grew up produced very little in the way of new lyrical poetry – a fact which he lamented in fitting verse:

TO THE MUSES

Whether on Ida's shady brow,
  Or in the chambers of the East,
The chambers of the sun, that now
  From antient melody have ceas'd;

Whether in Heav'n ye wander fair,
  Or the green corners of the earth,
Or the blue regions of the air
  Where the melodious winds have birth;

Whether on chrystal rocks ye rove,
  Beneath the bosom of the sea,
Wand'ring in many a coral grove;
  Fair Nine, forsaking Poetry!

How have you left the antient love
  That bards of old enjoy'd in you!
The languid strings do scarcely move!
  The sound is forc'd, the notes are few![1]

Another piece in the collection demonstrates the degree to which Blake himself conceived his own mission as a lyric poet:

How sweet I roam'd from field to field,
    And tasted all the summer's pride,
'Till I the prince of love beheld,
    Who in the sunny beams did glide!

. . .

With sweet May dews my wings were wet,
    And Phoebus fir'd my vocal rage;
He caught me in his silken net,
    And shut me in his golden cage.

He loves to sit and hear me sing,
    Then, laughing, sports and plays with me;
Then stretches out my golden wing,
    And mocks my loss of liberty.
('How sweet I roam'd', lines 1–4, 9–16)

Had Blake left nothing but the *Poetical Sketches* behind him, he might well be remembered still for a lyric such as this, and the absence of any further writing from him be mourned as a substantial loss. It is unlikely, however, that the developments that were to come could have been predicted in detail – even if the last line, with its passing reference to the 'loss of liberty' might have suggested something of his rebellious future.

The possible veiled sting in that last phrase might also alert an astute reader to the presence of dialectic in the arrangement of his poems. One could for example read the love poetry of the first of two 'Songs' and its description of an idealised young woman with little more than simple enjoyment:

Fresh from the dewy hill, the merry year
Smiles on my head and mounts his flaming car;
Round my young brows the laurel wreathes a shade,
And rising glories beam around my head

. . .

So when she speaks, the voice of Heaven I hear
So when we walk, nothing impure comes near;
Each field seems Eden, and each calm retreat;
Each village seems the haunt of holy feet.

But that sweet village where my black-ey'd maid
Closes her eyes in sleep beneath night's shade,
Whene'er I enter, more than mortal fire
Burns in my soul, and does my song inspire. (lines 1–4, 13–20)

This looks back to the evocation of the earthly paradise by Milton and a line of poets devoted to the pastoral ideal, and one simply notes how the picturing of the young woman as angelic is accompanied by aspirations towards immortality, and even claims to divine status, on the part of the poet himself.

If one proceeds to the next 'Song', however, it is to discover that the atmosphere has changed abruptly as human failings emerge:

When early morn walks forth in sober grey;
Then to my black-ey'd maid I haste away;
When evening sits beneath her dusky bow'r,
And gently sighs away the silent hour;
The village bell alarms, away I go;
And the vale darkens at my pensive woe.

To that sweet village, where my black-ey'd maid
Doth drop a tear beneath the silent shade,
I turn my eyes; and, pensive as I go,
Curse my black stars and bless my pleasing woe.

Oft when the summer sleeps among the trees,
Whisp'ring faint murmurs to the scanty breeze,
I walk the village round; if at her side
A youth doth walk in stolen joy and pride,
I curse my stars in bitter grief and woe,
That made my love so high, and me so low.

O should she e'er prove false, his limbs I'd tear,
And throw all pity on the burning air;
I'd curse bright fortune for my mixed lot,
And then I'd die in peace, and be forgot. (lines 1–20)

Does that phrase 'bless my pleasing woe' carry a touch of self-satire? It is hard to judge the level of poetic intelligence at which Blake is writing here. What is evident, however, is that his ambitions were increasingly Shakespearean. The lyrics inserted into his predecessor's plays were a ready sign of his lyric gifts when he chose to bring them into play; yet his equally superb achievements in drama might suggest to a younger poet better ways to develop. Blake evidently took the hint, since *Poetical Sketches* concludes with a dramatic fragment entitled 'Edward the Third' that clearly looks back to the Elizabethans. In this work, however, he also shows his developing devotion to rhythmic force, as when the Minstrel describes the arrival in Britain of the Trojans and the resistance from the indigenous inhabitants: 'wild men, / Naked and roaring like lions, hurling rocks, / And wielding knotty clubs, like oaks entangled / Thick as a forest, ready for the axe' (lines 6–9). Finally

Brutus proclaims his vision of the future: 'Liberty shall stand upon the cliffs of Albion, / Casting her blue eyes over the green ocean' (lines 55–6). There is little sign of Blake's nascent radical views, however: such political passion as he can muster is directed rather towards the realisation of Liberty and the defeat of Tyranny, in any of their various manifestations.

In the next important work he produced, 'An Island in the Moon', the running together of words and music was still a major preoccupation, the Islanders entertaining themselves with songs, the words of which might be relevant to contemporary poetical debate, though they also included skits on current intellectual fashions. Although the predominant note is one of cynicism, however, two of the songs, 'Upon a holy thursday' and 'When the tongues of children are heard on the green', indicate that Blake was moving away from mere cynicism, so that, with no more than a few alterations, they could reappear in his *Songs of Innocence*.

As the Shakespearean ending of *Poetical Sketches* – and indeed the diversity of stance in some of the other poems – suggested, however, an impulse towards dramatisation was evidently characterising much of his poetical endeavour during this period of his life, his succeeding work 'Tiriel' betraying his debt to that writer along with many other exponents of the sublime. Where Lear addresses his daughters as 'Tigers, not daughters', for example, Blake's baffled tyrant cries out to his progeny that they are 'Serpents, not sons' (line 21).

When Blake turned to more meditative work, on the other hand, his aims were different. Gray, Collins, Chatterton and Ossian were his likely models. The first two, particularly, were drawn to the concept of the poet as divine figure, re-creating in his verse the original act of creation by God himself. When it came to the details of writing, moreover, the mode of James Macpherson attracted them. Johnson might thunder, concerning 'Ossian', 'Sir, a man might write such stuff for ever, if he would *abandon* his mind to it',[2] but a new class of poetic writer had arisen, who responded readily to such verse, finding it, in James Sutherland's phrasing, 'vague, infinitely sad, full of regret for vanished splendours, wild and exclamatory, mysterious, visionary'.[3] Just such a series of characteristics might be traced, for example, in *The Book of Thel*, engraved in 1789, where Thel complains

> Ah! Thel is like a watry bow, and like a parting cloud,
> Like a reflection in a glass. like shadows in the water.
> Like dreams of infants, like a smile upon an infants face,
> Like the doves voice, like transient day. like music in the air . . .[4]

In this case, however, other powers are at work. Thel has at least spirit enough to wish to break out of the state in which she feels herself imprisoned, though when she enters the 'land unknown' that invites her she finds to her dismay that what she has entered is the human condition, with its own law-bound restrictions – more unwelcome than those of the innocent condition she left behind her – so that her verse turns to questioning and implicit protest, concluding

> Why a Tongue impress'd with honey from every wind?
> Why an Ear, a whirlpool fierce to draw creations in?
> Why a Nostril wide inhaling terror trembling & affright
> Why a tender curb upon the youthful burning boy!
> Why a little curtain of flesh on the bed of our desire?[5]

The differing voices of *The Book of Thel* are expressive of the varying states that continued to stir Blake's mind. On the one hand the lyrical impulse that had wakened in him as a young man attracted him to everything that spoke of human innocence, on the other his own dealings with the factual world, dealings that had brought him up against the violence of the Gordon Riots, or – at one remove at least – the ferocity of the French Revolution, warned him that the world he had been brought into was very different. He could no longer hope for a single-minded attitude of his own; on occasion he adopted the expedient of initiating his work with lines (rhyming or otherwise) that were deliberately enigmatic:

> Does the Eagle know what is in the pit?
> Or wilt thou go ask the Mole:
> Can Wisdom be put in a silver rod?
> Or Love in a golden bowl? ('Thel's Motto', lines 1–4)

or

> I loved Theotormon
> And I was not ashamed
> I trembled in my virgin fears
> And I hid in Leutha's Vale!
>
> I plucked Leutha's flower,
> And I rose up from the vale;
> But the terrible thunders tore
> My virgin mantle in twain.
> ('Visions of the Daughters of Albion', lines 1–8)

These were years of experiment, of *The Marriage of Heaven and Hell*, where dramatic prose was interspersed with poetic as he groped his way towards an adequate prophetic style, or where he simply explored the poetic possibilities of simple innocence, which might be conveyed by process of echoed words and self-reinforcing imagery. A good example can be found in the first of the poems devoted to 'Holy Thursday', where the narrator expresses himself as being overcome by the sheer beauty of the setting and the music:

> O what a multitude they seemd these flowers of London town
> Seated in companies they sit with radiance all their own
> The hum of multitudes was there but multitudes of lambs
> Thousands of little girls & boys raising their innocent hands
>
> Now like a mighty wind they raise to heaven the voice of song
> Or like harmonious thunderings the seats of heavn among
> Beneath them sit the aged men the wise guardians of the poor
> Then cherish pity, lest you drive an angel from your door (lines 1–12)

In what sense can the narrator here be identified with the poet himself? If there is any such relationship it must be between opposing moods: only a total variation could be thought to account for such an extraordinary difference within the same person. And if this is another example of the tendency towards dialectic in Blake's mind it is dramatically illustrated further as one turns to the equivalent 'Holy Thursday' in *Songs of Experience*, where the note of pleasure changes into one of indignation at the state that is sensed as underlying the tradition described:

> Is this a holy thing to see
> In a rich and fruitful land,
> Babes reducd to misery,
> Fed with cold and usurous hand?
>
> Is that trembling cry a song?
> Can it be a song of joy?
> And so many children poor?
> It is a land of poverty!
>
> And their sun does never shine,
> And their fields are bleak & bare,
> And their ways are fill'd with thorns.
> It is eternal winter there.
>
> For where-e'er the sun does shine,
> And where-e'er the rain does fall:
> Babe can never hunger there,
> Nor poverty the mind appall. (lines 1–16)

The shift of stance here makes room for the voice of honest indignation, the alternative to simple indulgence in delight. It also allows for the possibilities of a warm human response of the kind expressed in 'The Little Vagabond':

Dear Mother, dear Mother, the Church is cold,
But the Ale-house is healthy & pleasant & warm;
Besides I can tell where I am use'd well,
Such usage in heaven will never do well.

But if at the Church they would give us some Ale.
And a pleasant fire, our souls to regale;
We'd sing and we'd pray, all the live-long day;
Nor ever once wish from the Church to stray . . . (lines 1–8)

One notices how Blake is prepared to give precedence to the rhythm of ordinary speech where necessary; even more significant is the scope afforded in such verses for the exploration of language in word-play and ambiguity. 'London', one of his best poems, begins

I wander thro' each charter'd street,
Near where the charter'd Thames does flow.
And mark in every face I meet
Marks of weakness, marks of woe.

In every cry of every Man,
In every Infants cry of fear,
In every voice: in every ban,
The mind-forg'd manacles I hear (lines 1–8)

One of Blake's greatest poems, this has the quality, which shapes his most characteristic utterances, of describing the world as if one were looking at it for the first time. There is nothing naive about the vision, moreover; we need only turn back to the first stanza to see complex effects at work. 'And mark in every face I meet / Marks of weakness, marks of woe': there is something awkward in the repetition of the word 'mark'. The observer 'marks', but what he marks are 'marks'. Yet the awkwardness is in no way inept; by that dulling repetition Blake reinforces the effect of being dragged into an imprisoned world, where nothing radiates from the faces he sees: he marks them, but they do not seem to mark him in return. The arrow of his perception finds its mark, but finds itself fixed there, no longer at liberty.[6]

The word 'charter'd', repeated in the second line, also draws the reader's attention by its suggestion of irony. The word was originally associated with liberty. Magna Carta, signed by King John in 1215, was traditionally one of the foundations of British liberty, and one of many such charters over the centuries. But these charters were freedoms granted to particular classes of people: they automatically involved a loss of liberty for others who did not belong; and by Blake's time it was hard to walk around London without feeling that the whole city had been parcelled out among different groups of this kind, leaving no freedom for the individual human beings who were excluded. 'It is a perversion of terms to say that a charter gives rights', wrote Thomas Paine in *The Rights of Man*; 'it operates by a contrary effect – that of taking rights away.'[7] Even the Thames, which might be thought by definition to be free, was so given over to the uses of commerce as to lose all identity except as a trade route. One of Shakespeare's characters describes the air as a 'chartered libertine';[8] used in connection with the Thames, the word would read more like 'shackled' – looking forward to the 'mind-forg'd manacles' of the second stanza. The poetic compression which first brings together the words 'mind-forged' and 'manacles', then makes the manacles what is *heard* in the cries about him, is masterly.

A rare glimpse into the process of his composition is afforded by the existence of a notebook fragment which formed one of the building-blocks for the finished lyrics. It was presented as 'An ancient Proverb' and – including deletions – runs

Remove away that blackning church
Remove away that marriage hearse
Remove away that ——— of blood
Youll quite remove the ancient curse[9]

The most striking elements in this were then taken into the still more finished concluding stanzas of his lyric:

How the Chimney-sweeper's cry
Every blackning Church appalls;
And the hapless Soldiers sigh
Runs in blood down Palace walls

But most thro' midnight streets I hear
How the youthful Harlots curse
Blasts the new-born Infants tear,
And blights with plagues the Marriage hearse (lines 9–16)

The verse here is not only complex in its effects but unusually straightforward. There is a sense of accumulating power, gathering strength from the dramatic use of certain words, such as 'appalls' (which draws into itself the sense of 'pall'), and culminating in the 'Marriage hearse' of the ending. And the lines are once again packed with meaning. It has been pointed out that the 'new-born infant's tear' may well carry a reference to the effects of venereal disease – which in turn may be condemning to death not only the new-born babe that inherits it but also those victims who attempt to escape into lawful wedlock and who in the process transform a human bed into a hearse. In this way

Blake's poetic language can not only produce a triumph of compressed meaning, but in doing so reinforce the underlying emotions into greater intensity.

A similar effect can be found in the process by which his various working on the draft of 'The Tyger' eventually produced the spareness of the question 'What dread hand? & what dread feet?' (line 12) This appeals directly to the subconscious, evoking collocations of images that can work closely with one another towards an effect of awe coupled with attraction that would have been the envy of any gothic literary writer.

The sense here that Blake is writing at the height of his powers is confirmed by the full effect of 'The Tyger', where he manages to combine the sense of Promethean daring ('What the hand, dare seize the fire?' (line 8)) with a science that acknowledges the power, yet also the limitations, of industrialism ('In what furnace was thy brain?' (line 2)). In the same way 'The Fly' proves deceptively brief, as Blake manages to twist his poetic syntax until readers are not sure whether they are reading about an insect or a human being.

Blake's fascination with the potentialities of compressed meaning was also driving another enterprise at this time: the urge to prophecy. In his contemporary world, things were changing so much that it was natural to look for the patterns underlying events. In a series of 'illuminated' texts, which he termed his 'Prophetic Books', he offered visionary presentations and commentary on events in the troubled world following the French Revolution, accompanied in each case by an introductory segment of what might be thought of as a mythology that better suited his contemporaries than the Biblical and subdued Christian theology too often offered them. In line with this programme he produced poems with titles such as 'America', 'Europe', 'Asia' and 'Africa'. Central to the mythology underlying his interpretation of events is the sense of an increasing confrontation between Urizen, the static and conservative divine power who seems to be in charge of eighteenth-century culture, and Orc, his fiery revolutionary son, who refuses to be bound by the constraints of the contemporary world, taking as his theme the motif of energetic fruitfulness:

> For every thing that lives is holy, life delights in life;
> Because the soul of sweet delight can never be defil'd.
>
> (*America*, Plate 8, lines 13–14)

The culmination of this stage of his development was the construction of the poem 'Vala', later renamed *The Four Zoas*, in which he aimed at a full epic poem that would subsume various of the incidents in previous books, such as that of the binding of Urizen in *The Book of Urizen* – a passage which could now be taken into the full text word for word. The 'Nights' that constituted this new work also contained passages of extraordinary originality and power: one thinks, for example, of the account of the armies of Urizen and their mathematical organisation,

Travelling in silent majesty along their orderd ways
In right lined paths outmeasurd by proportions of number weight
And measure. mathematic motion wondrous. along the deep
In fiery pyramid. or Cube. or unornamented pillar
Of fire far shining. travelling along even to its destind end
Then falling down. a terrible space recovring in winter dire
Its wasted strength. it back returns upon a nether course
Till fired with ardour fresh recruited in its humble season
It rises up on high all summer till its wearied course
Turns into autumn. such the period of many worlds
Others triangular right angled course maintain. others obtuse
Acute Scalene, in simple paths. but others move
In intricate ways biquadrate. Trapeziums Rhombs Rhomboids
Paralellograms. triple & quadruple. polygonic
In their amazing hard subdued course in the vast deep . . .
(page 33, lines 22–36)

Few writers would have thought it possible to indicate the poetic sublime in terms of geometric diagrams; it is a sign of Blake's intellectual generosity towards the Urizenic vision that he could at one and the same time assert his hostility to it yet also give it its due. The extraordinary virtuosity by which this mathematical organisation is mustered and operated is matched yet set in a totally different key by the emotional cry that breaks in after it as Enion, in the 'dark deep', bewails the state of her loneliness:

What is the price of Experience do men buy it for a song
Or wisdom for a dance in the street? No it is bought with the price
Of all that a man hath his house his wife his children
Wisdom is sold in the desolate market where none come to buy
And in the witherd field where the farmer plows for bread in vain . . .
(page 35, lines 11–15)

It is an easy thing to laugh at wrathful elements
To hear the dog howl at the wintry door, the ox in the slaughter house moan
To see a god on every wind & a blessing on every blast
To hear sounds of love in the thunder storm that destroys our enemies house
To rejoice in the blight that covers his field, & the sickness that cuts off his children
While our olive & vine sing & laugh round our door & our children bring
fruits & flowers . . . (page 36, lines 3–8)

> It is an easy thing to rejoice in the tents of prosperity
> Thus could I sing & thus rejoice, but it is not so with me!
>
> (page 36, lines 12–13)

The bleakness of this utterance establishes the full range of Blake's poetic powers.

The length of the manuscript of 'Vala' suggests that Blake went a long way towards completing it as a kind of sequel to *Paradise Lost*; and indeed there are whole stretches of it, such as the ones cited earlier, which strike the reader as notably successful. Yet there are also passages, particularly in the later Nights, where he seems to be running out of inspiration, and where he seems to have encountered insuperable problems of construction. Further investigation suggests the degree to which Milton's achievement should have been viewed not as a halfway house to something which might have proved more successful, but as a clever weaving together of various available traditions, the existing structure of the English Bible, the Romantic potentialities of the English literary tradition and the Puritan drive towards cultivation of political freedom and the independent intellect. By trying to develop further certain factors of this kind at the expense of others, Blake was setting himself not an achievable goal but an ultimately impossible task, the strains entailed becoming evident in the efforts at rewriting and reconstructing which result in the longueurs of some later passages. Finally, in the Ninth Night, he brought things to a telling consummation by producing a concluding Apocalypse; however, the links between the intricate workings and conflicts described in the earlier Nights and the devices that might produce the triumphant volte-face of the conclusion escaped him. Reading and admiring the last pages we yet feel not the working out of an elaborate mechanism but something more like the operation of a clever conjuring trick – good enough for a literary tour de force, but not convincing as a true successor or adequate substitute for Milton's poetic achievement.

One of the things Blake had increasingly realised was that, as he had shown in the two 'Songs' quoted above from *Poetical Sketches*, his own nature was divided, and even at times contradictory. He expressed this in various ways, as in the well-known letter of 22 November 1802:

> . . . double the vision my Eyes do see
> And a double vision is always with me
> With my inward Eye 'tis an old Man grey
> With my outward a Thistle across my way (lines 27–30)

Nor was it enough to think simply of two levels of vision:

> . . . I a fourfold vision see
> And a fourfold vision is given to me
> Tis fourfold in my supreme delight
> And threefold in soft Beulahs night
> And twofold Always. May God us keep
> From Single vision & Newtons sleep! (lines 83–8)

The power of twofold vision continued to dominate, however, and in the latter part of his career he became accustomed to writing in two modes, each reflecting an element in what had come earlier. The prophetic mode was not unlike that of the earlier book, but the effort at producing a supreme myth, a long book to rival *Paradise Lost*, was left aside in favour of a looser organisation that allowed him to devote a single plate (text and illustration), or run of plates, to a leading insight of the moment that could be related to his larger themes – which had now resolved themselves into those of true inspiration (as envisaged in *Milton*) or the ideal human society (as explored in *Jerusalem*).

There was no sharp break of continuity, however: indeed, as, already pointed out, phrases and ideas from the earlier prophetic books recurred in the two later works – and at one point a whole passage from a version of Night Seven is repeated word for word in the new text. Although these later works were largely written in the earlier style, heavily influenced by the Old Testament and Milton, Blake moreover could at times remind his reader of his sensuous powers. One can cite for example two passages in *Milton* where he describes delights of the physical world: first the wonder of the lark's song, then the mysteriously evocative power of flowers and their scents:

> First eer the morning breaks joy opens in the flowery bosoms
> Joy even to tears, which the Sun rising dries; first the Wild Thyme
> And Meadow-sweet downy & soft waving among the reeds.
> Light spring on the air lead the sweet Dance: they wake
> The Honeysuckle sleeping on the Oak: the flaunting beauty
> Revels along upon the wind; the White-thorn lovely May
> Opens her many lovely eyes: listening the Rose still sleeps
> None dare to wake her. soon she bursts her crimson curtaind bed
> And comes forth in the majesty of beauty; every Flower:
> The Pink, the Jessamine, the Wall-flower, the Carnation
> The Jonquil, the mild Lilly opes her heavens! every Tree
> And Flower & Herb soon fill the air with an innumerable Dance
> Yet all in order sweet & lovely, Men are sick with Love!
> (*Milton*, Plate 31, lines 50–62)

One notes in passing how the placing of the words 'Revels' and 'Opens' at the beginning of a line displays Blake's mastery of maximum poetic effect.

In the same way Blake can find opportunities in the wide scope of *Jerusalem* to insert lyrics that will prove equally memorable, like the one that begins

> The fields from Islington to Marybone,
> To Primrose Hill and Saint Johns Wood:
> Were builded over with pillars of gold,
> And there Jerusalems pillars stood . . . (Plate 27, lines 1–4)

Although rhyming verses are not common in Blake's later verse – and indeed he wrote of them as a form of 'bondage' – rhyme itself could readily be called to his service when more informal verse was to be entered into his notebook. This could range from the gross,

> When a Man has Married a Wife
> he finds out whether
> Her knees & elbows are only
> glued together
> ('When a Man has Married a Wife', lines 1–4)

to the scornful:

> He has observd the Golden Rule
> Till hes become the Golden Fool
> ('He has observd the Golden Rule')

and

> Thus, Hayley on his Toilette seeing the sope,
> Cries Homer is very much improvd by Pope.
> ('Blakes apology for his Catalogue', lines 9–10)

Yet in his later writing he could find a place for long stretches of writing that would consist entirely of rhyming couplets, which enable him to bind together larger themes with a series of pithy comments, as with some of those in 'The Everlasting Gospel':

> If he had been Antichrist Creeping Jesus
> Hed have done any thing to please us
> ('The Everlasting Gospel', lines 55–6)

or

> Thou art a Man God is no more
> Thy own humanity learn to adore (lines 75–6)

The other long poem of this kind, entitled 'Auguries of Innocence', also begins with four lines of rhymed verse:

To see a World in a Grain of Sand
And a Heaven in a Wild Flower
Hold Infinity in the palm of your hand
And Eternity in an hour (lines 1–4)

In this case, the dominance of individual lines over total form is such that it has been possible for editors to differ about the overall shape of the poem and propose what each one feels to be the best organisation of it. But beyond straightforward (and highly quotable) couplets such as 'A Robin Red breast in a cage / Puts all Heaven in a Rage' (lines 5–6), the composition is notable also for its pregnant sayings, some of which make it clear that the real enemy being addressed is the analytic reason – 'The Questioner who sits so sly' (line 93). Throughout, cautious doubting is trumped by vehement faith:

A Riddle or the Crickets Cry
Is to Doubt a fit Reply
The Emmets Inch & Eagles Mile
Make Lame Philosophy to smile
He who doubts from what he sees
Will neer Believe do what you Please
If the Sun & Moon should Doubt
Theyd immediately Go out (lines 103–10)

What is being invoked as the object of true belief, however, can also be expressed here in simple couplets:

God Appears & God is Light
To those poor Souls who dwell in Night
But does a Human Form Display
To those who Dwell in Realms of day (lines 129–32)

The correlative message to humankind is as simple, and already expressed:

Thou art a Man God is no more
Thy own humanity learn to adore (lines 59–60)

Dr Johnson would not have agreed, but he could hardly have put it more lucidly.

At the same time Blake also showed himself eager to court a certain formality, and even symmetry, in his larger works, so that when he produced his finished version of *Jerusalem* he did so by reducing what might have been a somewhat shapeless construction to four sections of exactly twenty-five plates, each opening with a passage addressed to some part of his potential audience. The first of these, moreover, included a passage of polemic in which he claimed that his poetry now followed new and original principles:

> When this Verse was first dictated to me I consider'd a Monotonous Cadence like that used by Milton & Shakspeare & all writers of English Blank Verse, derived from the modern bondage of Rhyming; to be a necessary and indispensible part of Verse. But I soon found that in the mouth of a true Orator such monotony was not only awkward, but as much a bondage as rhyme itself. I therefore have produced a variety in every line, both of cadences & number of syllables. Every word and every letter is studied and put into its fit place: the terrific numbers are reserved for the terrific parts – the mild & gentle, for the mild & gentle parts, and the prosaic, for inferior parts: all are necessary to each other. Poetry Fetter'd, Fetters the Human Race! Nations are Destroy'd, or Flourish, in proportion as Their Poetry Painting and Music, are Destroy'd or Flourish! The Primeval State of Man, was Wisdom, Art, and Science.[10]

The reader is left to make of such assertions what he or she will; but a more crucial need for the purposes of understanding is to respond to the general tone rather than to individual points. It would be all too easy to become bogged down in matters of individual interpretation, such as the identification and significance of every place name; but the important thing for the reader must be to pick up by degrees the tone of the whole: to respond adequately to a vision based on the confidence that the cities and areas of England are potentially as sublime to a modern human being as those of Israel were to the prophet and Psalmist of ancient times.

In his last years, Blake remained deeply wedded to important visionary texts, which he was often drawn to illustrate. Significant designs of this kind that he undertook related to Bunyan, Dante and Biblical works such as the Book of Job. His most important influence during the last years, meanwhile, was on younger painters, the main group – which included Samuel Palmer, George Richmond, Frederick Tatham and Edward Calvert – calling themselves the 'Ancients'. His impact on contemporary poets was less marked, since there was no one who wished to continue in the vein of visionary writing that he had opened up. It was not, in fact, until a generation later, when the first biography (by Alexander Gilchrist) appeared, to be followed by Rossetti's editorial work and Swinburne's 1868 *Critical Essay*, that the situation changed. Despite the subsequent enthusiasm of Yeats and others, however, Blake's reputation as a poet still did not grow to its later stature until the new century, when a critic such as John Middleton Murry could identify the essentially 'poetic' nature of the writing as a 'passing and repassing into clarity' (while warning his readers, rather blinkeredly, against 'those learned and well-meaning persons who would systematize Blake's symbols').[11] Numerous other writers and critics, likewise, have found it a source of value in the writing that at some point it contains an incomplete or enigmatic element, which only adds to its gnomic quality as true poetry.

Notes

1. *Poetry and Prose of William Blake*, ed. David V. Erdman (New York: Doubleday, 1965). All further quotations from Blake's poetry are from this edition.
2. *C.*1783: James Boswell, *The Life of Samuel Johnson*, ed. Arnold Glover, 3 vols. (London: Dent, 1901)', vol. III, p. 225.
3. James R. Sutherland, *A Preface to Eighteenth Century Poetry* (Oxford: Clarendon Press, 1948) p. 161.
4. Plate 1, lines 8–11, *The Book of Thel* (London, 1789).
5. Plate 6, lines 16–20, *ibid.*
6. See Heather Glen, *Vision and Disenchantment: Blake's 'Songs' and Wordsworth's 'Lyrical Ballads'* (Cambridge: Cambridge University Press, 1983), pp. 210–12, for further discussion of 'mark'. I am not sure how far the discussion can be pressed, given the common use of the word in Shakespeare and poetic usage following him, but her invocation of the appearance of the word in Revelation is telling, given Blake's fondness for that Biblical book.
7. Thomas Paine, *The Rights of Man* (1791–2), cited by E. P. Thompson, *Witness against the Beast* (Cambridge: Cambridge University Press, 1993), p. 179.
8. Archbishop of Canterbury, in *Henry V* I.I.48.
9. Erdman (ed.), *Poetry and Prose*, p. 466.
10. *Ibid.*, p. 144.
11. William Blake, *Visions of the Daughters of Albion*, note by John Middleton Murry (London: Dent, 1932), p. 14.

Chapter 24

Wordsworth and Coleridge: *Lyrical Ballads* and other poems

TIMOTHY WEBB

It is widely believed that *Lyrical Ballads* by Wordsworth and Coleridge was one of those rare books which was a significant publishing event in itself and which also changed the course of English poetry. Penguin Books have reinforced this general belief by issuing the 1798 edition in the same series as Burns's *Poems, Chiefly in the Scottish Dialect*, Housman's *A Shropshire Lad* and Yeats's *The Tower*. Another recent reprint adopts a similar perspective and insists on the volume's innovative and radical credentials by prefacing the introduction with two strongly expressed quotations: first an apparently unqualified endorsement by an unidentified critic in *The Guardian*: '[it] must have come on like punk rock to a public groaning under the weight of over-cooked Augustanisms'; and, secondly, a description from the *Courier Mail*: 'a grenade hurled against the Establishment'.[1] Yet a third publisher compromises the latest edition of a judicious, scholarly and carefully balanced book by printing on its cover, without explanation or apparent reservation, exactly the same passage from *The Guardian*.[2]

While all three publishers are justified in recognising the special force of *Lyrical Ballads* (which in its way was a great deal more innovative and revolutionary than any of its companions in the Penguin list), the implications of such apparently unqualified endorsements could easily be deceptive. To begin with, the collection's title was a great deal less daring and original than most readers assume. As early as 1954 Robert Mayo reported rather different findings:

> The more one reads the minor poetry of the magazines from 1788 to 1798, the more it is impossible to escape the impression that the concept of the 'lyrical ballad' does not represent a significant innovation in 1798, nor as a term is it peculiarly appropriate to the contents of this volume of poems . . . Certainly as titles went in the years before 1798, this one was likely to surprise nobody.[3]

By a similar process of misunderstanding, the generic diversity of the *Ballads* may have been assumed to have had some connection with its shock effect, but this assumption is easily undermined by a glance at Robert Southey's *Annual Anthology* (editions in 1799 and 1800), whose printer was also responsible for *Lyrical Ballads*.

A further, and inescapable, complication involves the very identity of *Lyrical Ballads*. Many publishing choices and critical assessments seem to suggest that the significant edition of *Lyrical Ballads* was the first edition, which came out in 1798. Yet, for all its innovative force, this version only included twenty-three poems, whereas the second edition of 1800 ran to sixty-one poems and included Wordsworth's essential and surprising 'Preface' in place of the relatively short 'Advertisement' of 1798 (this 'Preface' was itself extended in 1802, when it carried an 'Appendix' on poetic diction). While publication in 1798 was certainly an important event in the history of English poetry, much discussion of *Lyrical Ballads* tends to elide the differences between the editions and the progressive force of the book's example. Although the first edition carried particular force, it is probably fanciful to think of it in terms of irreparable explosive effects. *Lyrical Ballads*, in fact, is perhaps most accurately regarded as a continuum rather than as a single publishing event. As Michael Mason has acutely noted, it 'was not a single phenomenon but a sequence of four editions spread over seven years; its appearance in English literature was not a historical moment but a sequence of moments – 1798, 1800, 1802, 1805'.[4]

The superficially arresting comparisons carry other possibilities which may seem attractive but which could be dangerously misleading. For example, 'a grenade hurled against the Establishment' suggests a simple revolutionary act which is hard to relate to the complexities and variations of the poetry. Does this image of revolutionary protest find room for poems such as 'Tintern Abbey'? And what, precisely, constituted 'the Establishment' which Wordsworth and Coleridge planned to discomfort and perhaps destroy? Likewise, there is no easy fit in references to punk rock, apart from an obvious distaste with prevailing poetical systems. With a very few exceptions, *Lyrical Ballads* was not designed to outrage traditional readers rather than those who were inattentive or lazy. The very image of punk rock implies an antagonism between the young and the old, with Wordsworth and Coleridge being identified (rather improbably) with the strident protests of the younger generation against the complacent harmonies of their parents. Although *Lyrical Ballads* expresses its dissatisfaction, both explicitly and implicitly, with the prevailing poetic conventions, there is little sense that this is a revolution of seemingly outrageous youth against the restrictive solidities of an older order. In his Preface to the second edition, Wordsworth does recognise that the old metrical contract which bound together reader and poet is being rewritten;[5] but the rational and measured prose in which this innovation is explained is closer to the philosophical discourse of Jean-Jacques Rousseau than to the calculated, and offensive, licences of Sid Vicious.

The comparison might also seem to suggest the adulation of a mass audience, yet Wordsworth complained that taste could not be changed without difficulty and persistent effort, and he claimed, perhaps with some exaggeration, that sales of his own books proceeded all too slowly. What he interpreted as the relative failure of Milton, compared to the commercial success of contemporaries, caused him to reflect, not without personal satisfaction, how 'strange are the obliquities of admiration'.[6] This unfortunate sluggishness in sales was almost a required justification of his methods; yet, as he well knew, there were also readers who purchased his poems for the wrong reasons and failed to exert themselves sufficiently. In March 1801, for instance, John Wordsworth predicted that his brother's poetry would not become popular for some time since 'it certainly does not suit the present taste'. He reported a meeting with 'a gentleman' who admired 'The Old Cumberland Beggar' (which first appeared in the 1800 edition, though it may have been written in 1798) but disappointingly declared: 'Why . . . this is very pretty but you may call it any but poetry.' With a diagnostic acumen and an acute sensitivity to the difficult status of poetry in polite society which matched that of the poet himself, John Wordsworth concluded: 'the truth is there are few people that like, or read, poetry many who buy it – buy it for the name – read about twenty [lines] . . . Most of Ws poetry improves upon 2d 3 or 4th reading now people in general are not sufficiently interested with the first reading to induce them to try a 2d.'[7]

William Wordsworth himself was well aware of these obstacles and the challenges involved in changing poetic taste and reading habits. In letters written about the time of the *Ballads*, he is bluntly insistent on the inadequacies of polite readers and the consequent need to appeal to a different kind of readership. For example, in a letter of June 1802 to John Wilson, a great admirer of his early work but still only a teenage student, he responds to Wilson's anxieties about 'The Idiot Boy' by questioning the very premises of his critical stance: 'You begin what you say upon the Idiot Boy with this observation, that nothing is a fit subject for poetry which does not please. But here follows a question, Does not please whom?'

Wordsworth answers his own question by providing a list of possible objectors, which is detailed, extensive, not always predictable and (it would seem) the product of authentic authorial experience:

> Some have little knowledge of natural imagery of any kind, and, of course, little relish for it, some are disgusted with the very mention of the words pastoral poetry, sheep or shepherds, some cannot tolerate a poem with a ghost or any supernatural agency in it, others would shrink from an animated description of the pleasures of love, as from a thing carnal and libidinous some cannot bear to see delicate and refined feelings ascribed to men in low conditions of society, because their vanity and self-love tell them that these belong only to themselves and men like themselves in dress, station, and way of life: others are disgusted with the naked language of some of the most interesting passions of men, because either it is indelicate, or gross, or [vu]lgar, as many fine ladies could not bear certain expressions in The [Mad] Mother and the Thorn [both printed in the first edition of *Lyrical Ballads*], and, as in the instance of Adam Smith, who, we [are] told, could not endure the Ballad of Clym of the Clough [a sixteenth-century ballad included in Percy's *Reliques*], because the [au]thor had not written like a gentleman; then there are professional[, loca]l and national prejudices forevermore some take no interest in the [descri]ption of a particular passion or quality, as love of solitariness, we will say, [gen]ial activity of fancy, love of nature, religion, and so forth, because they have [little or?] nothing of it in themselves, and so on without end.[8]

The list covers no fewer than eight categories of those who are not qualified to pass judgment on a poem like 'The Idiot Boy', although both 'forevermore' and 'without end' suggest that some of these categories are almost infinitely, and terrifyingly, subject to further extension. As Wordsworth's listing proceeds, he becomes more censorious and less merely notational – his contempt for the self-protecting vanities of 'polite' readers is evident as the descriptions lengthen and can hardly be missed in references to 'vanity and self-love', and to disgust with 'the naked language of some of the most interesting passions of men'. Throughout this account, Wordsworth emphasises a selfishness or an unconsidered privileging of personal preferences (or even 'prejudices'), which can impede serious engagement with the instructive otherness of the poetry.

This detailed and passionate analysis of the limitations of readers is primarily a defence of the innovations of 'The Idiot Boy' but more widely includes the *Lyrical Ballads* and even the genre of ballad itself. Wordsworth deplores the snobbish instincts which animate so many readers: 'some cannot bear to see delicate and refined feelings ascribed to men in low conditions of society'. This characterisation pinpoints a reaction which can be identified in many of Wordsworth's early critics and reminds one what forces he was combating when writing his contributions to *Lyrical Ballads* and the poems which appeared as late as 1807. In a letter to the Whig politician Charles James Fox in which he explained 'The Brothers' and 'Michael' (both of which were introduced in 1800 to *Lyrical Ballads*, in which the final poem was not 'Tintern Abbey' but 'Michael'), Wordsworth declared: 'our best qualities are possessed by men whom we are too apt to consider, not with reference to the points in which they resemble us, but to those in which they manifestly differ from us'. Elsewhere in the letter, he put the case plainly: 'The two poems . . . were written with a view to shew that men who do not wear fine cloaths can feel deeply.'[9] Even the unreconstructed spelling of 'cloaths' (also used by Coleridge) seems, though perhaps by accident, to underline the importance of acknowledging the otherness and the emotional significance of those who lead their lives outside the confines of societies which consider themselves superior in their polite exclusiveness.

Many of these factors can be seen at work in 'Simon Lee'. With its conventional references to 'pleasant Ivor Hall' and Simon's cheek 'like a cherry' (lines 2, 16), this poem begins by briefly invoking the tradition of ballads whose narrative structure it will soon teasingly subvert: 'My gentle reader, I perceive / How patiently you've waited, / And I'm afraid that you expect / Some tale will be related' (lines 69–72). Not only does Wordsworth's poem fail to satisfy a conventional craving for tangible, or extraordinary, incident; its address to the 'gentle reader' (pointedly repeated in the next stanza) also indicates that he has planned an uncomfortable collision between the cosy gentilities of his presumed readership and the disconcerting social realities familiar to a 'lower' class, though seldom mentioned in polite poetry. The directness and simplicity of the language unmistakably enforce the point: 'the more he works, the more / His poor old ancles swell' (lines 67–8). Here, as so often, Wordsworth's rejection of the distancing periphrases of poetic diction achieves a social point as much as a literary one. Uncompromisingly and uncomfortably, the poet is 'a man speaking to men'. In this case, the 'gentle reader' is required to engage imaginatively with the humiliating physical impotence of the elderly huntsman much as elsewhere she/he is expected to recognise the social significance of the mentally handicapped or the facts of death in the unsentimental attitude of a child. In all these cases, as in a number of other poems in *Lyrical Ballads*, the reader is challenged to understand the importance of an alternative system of values which seems to be at odds with the insulated certainties of ladies and gentlemen in their comfortable drawing rooms. In this poem, too, Wordsworth is explicit about the significance of a reading which is properly engaged: instead of satisfying her/himself with predictable narrative gratifications, the reader must approach the text reflectively with the result that she/he will find 'A tale in every thing' (line 76). Through a functional repetition, Wordsworth insists on the responsibility of the reader, who is required to avoid conventional indifference: 'It is no tale; but should you think, / Perhaps a tale you'll make it' (lines 79–80). The concluding stanza might seem to suggest a conventional morality but, like Blake, Wordsworth employs unthreatening rhyme schemes and energetic metre to discomforting, even shocking, effect.

The letter to John Wilson has much more to say about perspectives, unthinking habituations, class and an appreciation of poetry which is genuine rather than culturally 'expected':

> People in our rank in life are perpetually falling into one sad mistake, namely, that of supposing that human nature and the persons they associate with are one and the same thing ... few ever consider books but with reference to their power of pleasing these persons and men of a higher rank few descend lower, among cottages and fields and among children. A man must have done this habitually before his judgment upon the Idiot Boy would be in any way decisive with me.[10]

As so often in Wordsworth's prose, there is here a certain defensiveness, even a telltale asperity. In the downrightness of the final sentence there is also a glimpse of Wordsworth's stubborn insistence on his own rightness. In an extraordinary letter to Sara Hutchinson dating from the same month as his letter to Wilson, he defended at some length 'Resolution and Independence' (which was written *after* the first two editions of *Lyrical Ballads* but which has much in common with some of those earlier poems): 'You speak of his speech as tedious: everything is tedious when one does not read with the feelings of the Author – "*The Thorn*" is tedious to hundreds; and so is the *Idiot Boy* to hundreds.'[11] This letter may demonstrate that Wordsworth regarded his poetic contributions to *Lyrical Ballads* and his other poems from this period as a continuum; but it also reveals a symptomatic, sometimes risky, insistence on the dominant centrality of the poet's own perspective. Not even the most selfless and dedicated reader can always be expected to accept the poet's perspective unconditionally or always to 'read with the feelings of the Author'.

Something of this asperity and this sense of his own rightness can be found in a letter to Lady Beaumont which dates from 21 May 1807. Wordsworth's indignation with inattentive reading is not only generated by his valuation of poetry in general and his own poetry in particular, but informed by a distinction between those who have time to cultivate a wise passiveness and those who live in the all-consuming world of 'routs, dinners, morning calls, hurry from door to door, from street to street, on foot or in Carriage'. He concludes this fierce but revealing analysis with a declaration which remains arresting in its wider implications:

> It is an awful truth, that there neither is, nor can be, any genuine enjoyment of Poetry among nineteen out of twenty of those persons who live, or wish to live, in the broad light of the world – among those who either are, or are striving to make themselves, people of consideration in society. This is a truth, and an awful one, because to be incapable of a feeling of Poetry in my sense of the word is to be without love of human nature and reverence for God.[12]

The solemnity of this conclusion must be observed, no less than Wordsworth's claim that poetry (or Poetry, since the dignifying capital is significant and deliberate) is a religious force: the final conjunction ('love of human nature and reverence for God') expresses a view which was not shared by all his contemporaries but is central to his poetics. In the 'Preface' he had claimed a status for the poet which might be surprising to some of his readers: 'He is the rock of defence of human nature; an upholder and preserver, carrying everywhere with him relationship and love' (p. 77). These were the qualities which were precluded by the feverish momentum of a public life which was deprived of 'thought' and 'love'. Such a choice of emphasis seems far removed from the tactics of the punk rocker or the terrorist, or even from Hazlitt's claim that Wordsworth's poetics were as revolutionary as some of the politics of his day. Wordsworth may have been uncomfortable with the poetic status quo but his temperament was conservative as well as non-conforming and for the 'wearisome unintelligible obliquities of city life' (*Prose Works*, I.255) he chose to substitute the security of values which were traditional.

As Byron acutely but selfishly recognised, such a choice involved a rejection of the polite values of a public world. In *Beppo*[13] and later in *Don Juan*, he was to find fault with authors who were not men of the world – in particular, the 'Lake Poets' were condemned for their 'tadpole' loyalties and their geographical timidity – but, as one of his letters shows more explicitly than the poetry, Wordsworth for one renounced 'the world' and the 'worldlings' who chose to inhabit it with a dedicated severity which was almost monastic. In the letter to Wilson he admitted that 'These persons are, it is true, a part of human nature' (I.355), but he made a distinction between human nature in that limited sense and the human nature which he investigates in the letter to Lady Beaumont and in poems such as 'The Idiot Boy'.

As he told Coleridge, in a letter which predated *Lyrical Ballads* and which partly anticipated the letter to Lady Beaumont, Wordsworth rejected 'transitory manners reflecting the wearisome unintelligible obliquities of city life' and preferred 'manners connected with the permanent objects of nature and partaking of the simplicity of those objects'.[14] Much of his poetic output was oppositional or adversarial, in the sense that it diagnosed a dangerous limitation in contemporary urban culture and attempted to find an alternative in the traditional simplicities of country life. Such a conflict animates those parts of *The Prelude* which engage with city life and makes a striking appearance in the 'Preface' to *Lyrical Ballads* with a dismissive account of urban culture and its 'degrading thirst after outrageous stimulation': Wordsworth attributes this cultural decline to ' the great national events which are daily taking place, and the increasing accumulation of men in cities, where the uniformity of their occupations produces a craving for extraordinary incident, which the rapid communication of intelligence hourly gratifies'.[15] Although he was writing in 1800, and although he may have been unduly influenced by the city-hating polemics of Cowper and Rousseau, much of this analysis is still frighteningly recognisable.

The unhealthy and uncreative 'hurry of images'[16] which Wordsworth identified in the streets of London and in the public world as characterised to Lady Beaumont represented a contrast to that fruitful singularity, that steady and stabilising focus on the individual or the single object which marks much of his best poetry; who but Wordsworth would have ignored the poetic tradition and complimented the dead and unobtrusive Lucy by noting that she was 'Fair as a star, when only one / Is shining in the sky'? ('She dwelt among th' untrodden ways', lines 7–8; first published in *Lyrical Ballads* (1800)).[17] Such alternative perspectives allow Wordsworth to shift the focus of his own poetry, not only socially but also geographically. Both *Lyrical Ballads*, in its various editions, and *Poems* (1807) owe much of their revolutionary force to the fact that they concentrate on the natural world rather than on urban society or urban myths about the countryside ('pastoral' was an urban invention, so that Wordsworth's decision to subtitle 'Michael' as 'A pastoral poem' involves not only a precise definition but a determined attempt to claim back the term from those who had used it from a distance and misunderstood its implications). Poetry could now be proudly 'provincial', in that it asserted the central significance of those parts of Britain which had previously been regarded as outside the scope of London culture and therefore merely 'provincial'. It is not an accident that *Lyrical Ballads* was first planned when Wordsworth and Coleridge were living in the West Country (before they moved to the Lake District, which may have been marginally more fashionable but was still artistically 'marginal'); nor is it insignificant that the first imprint bore the name of a Bristol publisher.

The name of Wordsworth is often linked with that of Coleridge but, although they were (at one time) friends, collaborators and neighbours, and although *The Prelude* (1805) could even be read as an extended verse epistle addressed to Coleridge in Malta, apparent conjunction between the two poets can easily be misleading. Coleridge had contributed only five poems to the first edition of *Lyrical Ballads* but his contribution did not increase in the second edition, although the total number of poems nearly tripled. Yet Coleridge was reluctant to concede he was a victim and the weaker partner in this triumphalist collaboration. As late as 1800, he admitted to an admiration for Wordsworth's poetry (not least, the 'divine Poem called Michael') which suggests that it overrode any anxiety about being marginalised or realising his own comparative deficiency: 'I should judge of a man's Heart, and Intellect precisely according to the degree & intensity of the admiration, with which he read those poems.'[18] There were growing differences between the stubborn collaborators but his own private account insists that in its origins the book was the product of intellectual intimacy: 'Wordsworth's Preface [which had first appeared in 1800] is half a child of my own Brain'; its first passages 'were ... partly taken from notes of mine'; and it 'arose out of Conversations, so frequent, that with few exceptions we could scarcely either of us perhaps positively say, which first started any particular Thought'.[19]

For all the force of these retrospective claims, the Preface was actually written by, and publicly attributed to, William Wordsworth, who had overwhelmingly increased his stake in the enterprise of *Lyrical Ballads* by contributing fifty-six poems out of sixty-one. 'The Rime of the Ancyent Marinere' had been the first poem of the 1798 edition, balanced at the end of the book by Wordsworth's 'Tintern Abbey', a very different and subjective poem in blank verse. In the 1800 edition, Coleridge acknowledged a change in feeling by altering his poem's title to 'The Ancient Mariner: A Poet's Reverie' (which was more in keeping with Wordsworth's poem and with the collection's emphasis on personal experience, perhaps indicated by '*Lyrical*'); he also reduced the more superficial medieval elements, such as the diction. An even more significant change was effected by Wordsworth, who placed his own 'Expostulation and Reply' (which had not appeared in the first edition) at the beginning of the first volume of the second edition, while he removed Coleridge's narrative from its position of initiatory privilege so that it now featured near the end of the volume just before his own 'Tintern Abbey'. Such significant alterations indicate that the dynamics of collaboration were far from comfortable and that Coleridge's critique of *Lyrical Ballads* in the pages of *Biographia Literaria* is not, as it might appear, an eccentric example of self-indulgence but a recognition of an inescapable publishing reality (and, at the same time, a serious act of critical appraisal).

In its original location, Coleridge's poem was in some ways an ideal introduction to *Lyrical Ballads* because at the outset it engaged with the ballad inheritance which Wordsworth was to interrogate in so many of the other poems. On the surface, too, Coleridge seemed to be more interested than Wordsworth in traditional narrative, an interest which may have been stimulated by his capacity to absorb and redeploy phrases and imagery from a wide range of nautical adventures and maritime texts.[20] Yet, as many readers have awkwardly sensed and puzzled critics have been forced to admit, the causalities of this poem are hard to follow and do not make obvious sense. One consequence was the introduction of a simplistic morality which seemed to elucidate the mysterious. Coleridge himself recognised the problem since in later life he admitted that 'the chief fault of the poem was that it had too much moral, and that too openly obtruded on the reader'. He would have preferred the apparently random sequences of *The Arabian Nights*: 'It ought to have had no more moral than the story of the merchant sitting down to eat dates by the side of a well and throwing the shells aside, and the Genii starting up and saying he must kill the merchant, because a date shell had put out the eye of the Genii's son.'[21] Nor, might Coleridge have said, could the teasing sequence of events be explained (or explained away) in rational terms such as those suggested, jokingly perhaps, by William Empson: the albatross is a good source of nourishing soup which might have protected sailors from scurvy or malnutrition (hinted at by the mention of 'biscuit-worms').

Such confusions should not be lightly dismissed since they represent crucial category errors for which Coleridge, as he conceded, may have been partly to blame. The poem displays extraordinary narrative momentum and a capacity to record marine adventures with memorable simplicity ('We were the first that ever burst / Into that silent Sea' (lines 101–2); 'And Ice mast-high came floating by / As green as Emerauld' (lines 51–2); 'The moving Moon went up the sky / And no where did abide: / Softly she was going up / And a star or two beside –' (lines 255–8; text from 1798)). Yet, as the altered title may indicate, Coleridge's central concern was more obviously psychological (or spiritual) than in the telling, with whatever vivid immediacy or imaginative displacement or gothic embellishment, of a ballad which was essentially centred on action and on nautical discovery. If intelligent and experienced readers were (and still are) mistaken, such misreadings are not surprising since 'The Rime' simulates the traditional ballad while questioning and rewriting the very tradition from which it draws strength.

Coleridge's other notable poem in *Lyrical Ballads* is 'The Nightingale' (which was printed, though in different groupings, in 1798 and 1800). This is a very different kind of poem from 'The Rime' or (to take another example) from 'The Foster-mother's Tale', a fragment in dramatic blank verse which belonged to *Osorio* and which Robert Mayo has described as combining 'sensibility, sentimental primitivism, and Gothic mystery'.[22] Both of these poems show Coleridge's capacity to dramatise while 'The Nightingale' is more obviously centred on his own life (though, as always, the life is poetically transformed). But 'The Nightingale' is also corrective. Coleridge insisted that poetic tradition (which even included Milton) had associated the nightingale with melancholy whereas its effect on listeners was entirely different. 'In nature', he claimed, substituting one subjectivity for another, 'there is nothing melancholy' (line 15); 'Nature's sweet voices [are] always full of love and joyance!' His poem offers a description which controverts tradition: ''Tis the merry Nightingale / That crowds, and hurries and precipitates / With fast thick warble his delicious notes' (lines 43–5); later, he records how the nightingales in wood and thicket 'answer and provoke each other's songs – / With skirmish and capricious passagings / And murmurs musical and swift jug jug / And one low piping sound more sweet than all' (lines 58–61). Although even this passage is not without its debts to literary predecessors, it seems much closer to natural reality than most of its poetic predecessors and has something in common with the results of painting *en plein air* in its attempts to find a more appropriate linguistic and metrical register and to notate ornithological observations with responsive directness. In his different way, Wordsworth too was affected since he specifically endorsed Coleridge's poem in his 1802 letter to Wilson[23] and, in 1807, followed Coleridge's lead in celebrating the 'fiery heart' of the Nightingale: 'Thou sings't as if the God of wine / Had help'd thee to a Valentine.'[24] In its seemingly unobtrusive way, then, Coleridge's unassuming poem enacts its own quiet (if many-voiced) poetic revolution.

In at least two other ways, 'The Nightingale' initiates innovation. In the first place, it is a conversational poem which follows but happily complicates the example of William Cowper since it is not a poem of retreat or escape or displaced anxiety, but finds a positive force in the natural world which connects with the Wordsworth of, say, 'Tintern Abbey', or 'Michael', or 'Nutting', or 'There was a Boy' or of many other poems – though it remains distinctly different. This difference is partly a matter of tone, and this tone achieves an alert informality which is the product of a distinctly Coleridgean poetics. Coleridge's apparent simplicities can easily be distinguished from those of his slightly older contemporary. It can be regretted that Coleridge did not achieve more in this vein, which seems to have suited his temperament, but 'Frost at Midnight' and 'This Lime-Tree Bower My Prison' are uniquely memorable examples of what he could manage in such a relaxed poetic mode.

The second innovation may be related to the first since it concerns the way in which personal experience can be written into the poem and become central to its imaginative existence. In 'The Nightingale', Coleridge remembers the behaviour of young Hartley (who is not named in the poetic text): 'How he would place his hand beside his ear, / His little hand, the small forefinger up, / And bid us listen!' (lines 89–91). After a brief connecting passage on the 'dear babe's' close connection with nature (or 'Nature'), Coleridge continues with a reminiscence which is highly specific:

> once when he awoke
> In most distressful mood (some inward pain
> Had made up that strange thing, an infant's dream)
> I hurried with him to our orchard plot,
> And he beholds the moon, and hushed at once
> Suspends his sobs, and laughs most silently,
> While his fair eyes that swam with undropt tears
> Did glitter in the yellow moon-beam! (lines 93–100)

The originating episode is related in one of Coleridge's notebooks[25] but a close examination would show that it has been rewritten, or reimagined, for the purposes of the poem; in particular, Coleridge's switching of tenses and his use of the historic present to dramatise the magical silence at the centre of the episode has no equivalent in the notebook entry.

The example is instructive since it shows that poetic texts cannot be searched for biographical actualities without the greatest caution (predictably, the same conclusion can be reached by comparing Wordsworth's 'Resolution and Independence' to Dorothy's notebook entry or to Wordsworth's own earlier drafts).[26] Poetic truth should not be confused with biographical truth even in poetry which seems to draw its strength from a grounding in realities which are directly personal. And yet, to use Robert Langbaum's label, much of the earlier poetry of Coleridge is the poetry of experience.[27] More than one of his most effective poems can be related to prose passages in his letters and therefore to identifiable episodes in his life: for example, 'This Lime-Tree Bower My Prison' and especially 'Dejection: An Ode'.[28] Of course, even the accounts in letters (or notebooks or diaries) are at some remove from raw reality or unmediated experience; yet, not least in the case of Coleridge's two poems, one can follow a process whereby poetic conventions and the supposed requirements of a reading public transform the relative immediacies of the epistolary version. This is particularly clear in the case of 'Dejection: An Ode'. In that case, the poem as originally presented in the body of a letter becomes more structured and more public at the cost of its personal utterance: as it becomes an 'Ode', it is, at least partly, separated from the source of its vitality. Yet, the alteration cannot be seriously regretted, except perhaps by biographers: the poem may lose some of its original energy but it also loses much of its frenetic self-pity and it becomes a work of art for public consumption.

This paradox can certainly be applied to much of Wordsworth's poetry, especially in *Lyrical Ballads* and *Poems* and even the earlier versions of *The Prelude*. A comparison between Dorothy's notebooks and William's poetic representations of the same events would reveal William's recurrent dependence on his sister's individuality of vision; but it would also demonstrate his functional belief that poetry had its own value-system and its own, superior, version of 'truth'. The evidence of the Wordsworth notebooks indicates that he was highly conscious of the demands of poetic art. 'Michael' would not be the same poem if it were framed in ballad form (as he had once intended) rather than blank verse; nor would it have achieved the same memorable austerity had he included in it the beautiful, if slightly self-indulgent, passage on the delights of winter mornings.[29] For Wordsworth as for Coleridge, the process of revision was more often affected by considerations which were purely aesthetic than by those which were merely tactical. *Lyrical Ballads* and the poems of much the same creative period may present themselves as guileless alternatives to etiolated and decadent artificialities but their innocent simplicities are the sophisticated products of a carefully considered poetics.

Notes

1. *Lyrical Ballads*, ed. R. L. Brett and A. R. Jones, second edition, Routledge Classics (London: Routledge, 2005).
2. *Lyrical Ballads*, ed. Michael Mason, second edition (1992; London: Pearson Longman, 2007). All subsequent quotations will be taken from this edition.
3. Robert Mayo, 'The Contemporaneity of the *Lyrical Ballads*', *PMLA*, 69 (1954), pp. 486–522.
4. *Lyrical Ballads*, ed. Mason, p. 1.
5. *Ibid.*, pp. 58–9.
6. *The Prose Works of William Wordsworth*, ed. W. J. B. Owen and Jane Worthington Smyser, 3 vols. (Oxford: Clarendon Press, 1974), vol. III, pp. 70–1.
7. *William Wordsworth: The Critical Heritage,* vol. 1., *1793–820*, ed. Robert Woof (London and New York: Routledge and Kegan Paul, 2001), p. 98.

8. *The Letters of William and Dorothy Wordsworth 1787–1805*, ed. Ernest de Selincourt, 2nd edn, revised by Chester L. Shaver (Oxford: Clarendon Press, 1967), vol. I, pp. 352–8 (whole letter).
9. *Ibid.*, p. 315.
10. *Ibid.*, p. 355.
11. *Ibid.*, p. 367.
12. *The Letters of William and Dorothy Wordsworth*, ed. Ernest de Selincourt, 2nd edn, revised by Mary Moorman (Oxford: Clarendon Press, 1969), vol. II, pp. 145–6.
13. See 'twenty score / Of well-bred persons, called *'the World'* (lines 470–1) and 'Men of the world, who know the world like men' (line 602).
14. *Letters . . . 1787–1805*, p. 255.
15. *Lyrical Ballads*, ed. Mason, pp. 64–65.
16. *The Letters of William and Dorothy Wordsworth*, ed. Ernest de Selincourt, 2nd edn, revised by Mary Moorman, vol. II, p. 146.
17. For details, see Introduction to *Lyrical Ballads*, ed. Mason, and Timothy Webb, 'The Stiff Collar and the Mysteries of the Human Heart: The Younger Romantics and *Lyrical Ballads*', in C. C. Barfoot (ed.), *'A Natural Delineation of Human Passions': The Historic Moment of 'Lyrical Ballads'* (Amsterdam: Rodopi, 2004), pp. 209–14.
18. *Collected Letters of Samuel Taylor Coleridge*, ed. Earl Leslie Griggs, 6 vols. (Oxford: Clarendon Press, 1956), vol. II, pp. 707, 714.
19. *Ibid.*, pp. 830, 812, 830.
20. For details, see John Livingston Lowes, *The Road to Xanadu: A Study in the Ways of the Imagination*, revised edition (London: Constable, 1930).
21. Samuel Taylor Coleridge, *Table Talk*, ed. Carl Woodring, 2 vols. (London and Princeton: Routledge and Princeton University Press, 1990), vol. I, pp. 272–3.
22. Cited in *Lyrical Ballads*, ed. Mason, p. 115.
23. *Letters . . . 1787–1805*, p. 356.
24. 'O Nightingale! thou surely art', lines 5–6 (cited from *Wordsworth's Poems of 1807*, ed. Alun R. Jones (Basingstoke and London: Macmillan, 1987), p. 89.
25. *The Notebooks of Samuel Taylor Coleridge*, ed. Kathleen Coburn *et al.*, 2 vols. (London: Routledge and Kegan Paul, 1957), vol. I, p. 219.
26. For some details, see *Wordsworth's Poems of 1807*, ed. Alun R. Jones (Basingstoke: Macmillan, 1987), pp. 157–8.
27. Robert A. Langbaum, *The Poetry of Experience: The Dramatic Monologue in Modern Literary Tradition* (New York: Norton, 1963).
28. *Coleridge, Collected Letters*, vol. II, pp. 790–8 ('Dejection'), vol. I, pp. 334–6 ('This Lime-Tree'). See also *Coleridge's 'Dejection': The Earliest Manuscripts and the Earliest Printings*, ed. Stephen Maxfield Parrish (Ithaca, NY: Cornell University Press, 1988).
29. See *Lyrical Ballads and Other Poems, 1797–1800*, ed. James Butler and Karen Green (Ithaca, NY: Cornell University Press, 1992), pp. 598–601 (ballad version), pp. 649–61 (discarded passage), pp. 603–709 (fragments and discarded attempts).

Chapter 25

Wordsworth's *The Prelude* and *The Excursion*

ALISON HICKEY

Wordsworth's autobiographical *Prelude* traces 'the growth of the poet's mind' from infancy to adulthood. Fuelling this growth in its various phases is an energy that Wordsworth most often calls 'passion', beginning with the infant's attachment to the intertwined figures of mother and nature and taking other forms over the course of his life: the 'troubled pleasure'[1] of the boy who intrudes upon nature's quietness, the thrill of fear or conquest when he ventures to new heights or pushes beyond familiar boundaries. Passion drives the youth to depredations of nature and is redoubled by the sublime power with which nature's reaction works on his imagination afterwards. Intense, unnameable passion also attends traumatic experiences such as the death of parents, the bewildering entanglements of sexual desire and revolutionary enthusiasm, the fear of betrayal. In these seemingly diverse realms of experience, passion is the energy that animates the dynamic interchange between the developing consciousness and the world. In the Preface to *Lyrical Ballads*, Wordsworth connects passion to 'the pleasure which the mind derives from the perception of similitude in dissimilitude and dissimilitude in similitude'.[2] Pleasure feeds passions as diverse as sexual appetite and metrical language, a complex, sensitive instrument that not only expresses passion and registers its effects but also reacts to it, influences its direction and regulates its intensity. Metre is (to adapt Keats's notion of the 'pleasure thermometer') a passion thermostat.

Tracing the path of passion, measuring its rise and fall and flow, can deepen our understanding of a poem's workings. Closely tied to imagination, passion in *The Prelude* frequently appears as a sublime power that rises up, interrupts, overthrows or overwhelms – actions that are doubled or thrown back by the action of the verse. One such uprising follows upon the poet's learning, in the Simplon Pass episode of Book VI, that he has crossed the Alps unawares. He is baffled, his expectation short-circuited – and here ('from the mind's abyss', in the 1850 version, VI. 594) imagination 'lift[s] up itself' 'like an unfathered vapour' (VI.525, 527).

The spontaneous outpouring at this climatic moment in *The Prelude* puts Wordsworth in mind of 'the overflowing Nile' (vi.549). In *The Excursion*, by contrast, imagination is a scarce resource, like 'cool refreshing water, by the care / Of the industrious husbandman, diffused / Through a parched meadow-ground, in time of drought'.[3] An industrious husbandman seems the proper sort of figure to tread the 'tamer ground / Of these our unimaginative days' (*Excursion* ii.25–6), post-Romantic both in relation to the roving minstrels of yore and the more recent tumultuous romance of the French Revolution. The Wanderer traverses this tamer ground, dispensing words of feeling, 'pure discourse' (ii.77), touching on such matters as joy and sorrow, love, duty, science, natural and moral law, philanthropy and 'central peace, subsisting at the heart / Of endless agitation' (iv.1140–1). These 'eloquent harangue[s]' (iv.1272) are usually of general human import, although his peroration in Book ix culminates in a topical call for universal education (ix.352–418), and the text as a whole is coloured by its post-revolutionary contexts and rooted in England's historical discourse of revolution, reform and restoration. Book i combines the Wanderer's narration of Margaret's story, a revised version of *The Ruined Cottage* (composed 1797–8; revised 1802, 1804),[4] with framing material from *The Pedlar*, whose eponymous main character was an early version of the Wanderer. At the heart of the poem are further '[n]arratives of calm and humble life' (viii.6) exhumed by the Pastor, an offshoot of the Wanderer whose 'authentic epitaphs' (v.653) perpetuate the memory of deceased local inhabitants.

Both the interconnection of Wordsworth's two major poems and their important differences can be better understood if each is considered as part of *The Recluse*, the massively ambitious poetic project conceived for Wordsworth largely by his friend and fellow poet Coleridge (thereby hangs a tale – one mostly beyond the scope of this chapter). As Wordsworth explains in the 1814 Preface to *The Excursion*, *The Recluse* was to be a 'long and labourious Work', a tripartite 'philosophical Poem, containing views of Man, Nature, and Society' and 'having for its principal subject the sensations and opinions of a poet living in retirement'. *The Excursion* 'belongs to the second part' of the planned Work, the only part completed (*Excursion*, p. 38).

Understandably daunted by the task before him, Wordsworth had first undertaken a 'review of his own mind' in order to 'examine how far Nature and Education had qualified him for such employment' (*Excursion*, p. 38). This became the book-length poem we now know as *The Prelude*, composed largely between 1798 and 1805, revisited and revised over several decades, and finally published shortly after Wordsworth's death in 1850.[5] *The Prelude*'s 'preparatory' relation to the *Recluse*, Wordsworth observed, was like the relation of 'the Anti-chapel . . . to the body of a gothic Church' (*Excursion*, p. 38). Ironically, it was *The Prelude* that literary history would deem the essential part of the project, though in recent decades *The Excursion* has garnered an increased share of scholarly attention, culminating in the magnificent new Cornell edition of the poem.

While textual study and analysis of the political and personal history and the cultural discourse shared by the poems illuminate the substantial connections between them, comparing them as poetry continues to pose difficulties. *The Excursion* has been stereotyped as the work of an ageing poet, his imagination dry as the summer dust of the poem's desiccated landscape, his former passionate self buried in the graveyard of his long epitaphic poem like the erring characters whose stories the poem relates. If we apply Wordsworth's own declaration that 'all good poetry is the spontaneous overflow of powerful feelings' (*WW*, p. 598), we must conclude that *The Excursion* is not 'good poetry'. But Wordsworth immediately qualifies: the feelings must belong to a man of 'organic sensibility' who has 'thought long and deeply'. The long thinking gradually tames and assimilates the original emotion until it hardly seems to be an emotion at all; thoughts are tranquillised feelings or 'representatives' of past feelings. To recollect emotion in tranquillity involves contemplating its 'representative', thought, 'till by a species of reaction the tranquillity gradually disappears, and an emotion, kindred to that which was before the subject of contemplation, is gradually produced, and does itself actually exist in the mind' (p. 611). It is this 'kindred' emotion, reawakened from tranquillity, that spontaneously overflows. This is a familiar recurrent dynamic in *The Prelude*, which recounts emotionally charged scenes and incidents that persist in memory after the feeling has subsided; the former emotion is contemplated 'till' a reaction 'is produced', and 'kindred' feelings arise. In *The Excursion*, the same forces interact, but long and deep thought – the Wanderer's forte – steadily prevails. So 'long and deeply' has he thought, in fact, that he anticipates and neutralises potential overflows in advance. Spontaneous overflow of feelings lies on a continuum with thoughts as representatives of past feelings and participates in the same cycle. *The Prelude*, which features spontaneous overflow, and *The Excursion*,which gravitates toward representative thoughts, are 'kindred' poems.

The Prelude's full-length (and best-known) versions, the manuscript version of 1805 and the posthumously published 1850 version, begin with a 'glad preamble' (VII.4) in which the poet rejoices that the 'earth is all before' him (I.15), as full of possibility as the world that lay before Adam and Eve. But glad preamble soon lapses into anxious post-preamble as, having run through and rejected several potential themes, he realises that his direction remains uncertain. Whither shall he turn? Long before, finding himself in a similar predicament, Milton had taken as his great argument the Fall of man (interwoven with the British theme of revolution and restoration), shifting the epic realm from the battlefields of classical epic to the heights and depths of heaven and hell and the whole of human history. After *Paradise Lost*, any other British theme or romantic tale seems uninspiring, minor. Searching his mind to discover where he has gone astray, Wordsworth finds himself in *media res*: his theme *is* the mind, a vast untrodden region 'by Milton left unsung' (I.180), though Satan conceived of it, influentially, as a place. 'No realm', writes Wordsworth in what was conceived as a Prospectus to *The Recluse*,

> can breed such fear and awe
> As fall upon us often when we look
> Into our Minds, into the Mind of Man –
> My haunt, and the main region of my Song.
> (*The Excursion*, Preface, lines 38–41)

Still, the earth is all before him, and his 'high argument' is not the mind or nature in isolation but the exquisite mutual 'fitt[ing]' of the two (lines 65, 67, 71). They are brought together in the opening lines of the preamble to *The Prelude*: the poet senses a blessing in the breeze and feels within himself 'a corresponding mild creative breeze' (I.43). The internal breeze does not merely respond to the breath of inspiration in the natural breeze; already 'creative', it co-responds, as if the two have already been conversing. It also co-responds with itself, working itself up into a 'tempest, a redundant energy, / Vexing its owncreation' (I.46–7). The phrasing suggests the ambivalence of creative energy: close kin to self-thwarting authorial anxiety, it is potentially redundant not just in the ordinary sense but also in an etymological sense that harbours more possible sublimity: 'redundant' like a wave thrown back on its 'own creation'.

The preamble leads to, or is interrupted by, this crucial question:

> Was it for this
> That one, the fairest of all rivers, loved
> To blend his murmurs with my nurse's song,
> And from his alder shades and rocky falls,
> And from his fords and shallows, sent a voice
> That flowed along my dreams? (I.271–6)

From 1805 on, these lines are preceded by the preamble, but they are among the earliest composed passages associated with *The Prelude*, and they serve as the opening lines of the earliest text generally counted as a version of the poem, the 1799 *Two-Part Prelude*. When preceded by nothing but a blank, the question – simply worded but inscrutable – seems to arise spontaneously like an interrogative version of such foundational beginnings as 'There was a boy' or 'Let there be light'.[6] These clauses combine the most rudimentary of verbs – 'was', 'is' – with a noun or pronoun to represent nothing more or less than being, issuing from the void at the origin of a world of words.

Wordsworth's interrogative fiat suspends us in a question that remains open and generates further questions: was what for what? What is 'this'? What 'was' 'it'? What is meant by the ambiguous 'for'? Consciousness emerges in the articulation of time, as we become aware of a complex mind reflecting, in the here and now of the verse, on the uncertain relation between 'this' present moment and a past ('it') that exists in memory. The action of the poem is the movement of this consciousness in the shifting temporal landscape of memory.

Another passage captures the poet's uncanny sense, when pondering his former self, that the mind is inhabited by multiple 'consciousnesses':

so wide appears
The vacancy between me and those days,
Which yet have such self-presence in my mind
That sometimes when I think of them I seem
Two consciousnesses, conscious of myself,
And of some other being. (II.28–33)

Past days, though separated by a 'vacancy' from the present, have an ambiguous 'self-presence': they are present in the mind of the present self, while retaining their own self-presence or identity as past. The odd plural 'consciousnesses' multiplies ambiguities about the operations and objects of consciousness. How many consciousnesses are there? What is conscious of what? If consciousness becomes the object of one's own consciousness, is it still 'conscious'? Would present consciousness not supersede past consciousness, so that the 'other being' would remain no more than a shadowy intimation? Or would past consciousness, once conjured up, usurp – and thus become – present consciousness? Like emotion, past consciousness can be recollected in tranquillity, but, whereas the recollection of emotion produces a kindred emotion that displaces tranquillity, the recollection of consciousness produces a redundancy of consciousnesses.

The question 'was it for this?' opens the floodgate to a stream of recollections of the influences that flowed into – and 'along' – the emerging consciousness of the poet in infancy. The Derwent blends his murmurs of nature with the nurse's song, as nature and humanity, interflowing tributaries, supplement the mother's role. As the poet grows in awareness and begins to differentiate himself from both nature and other human beings, the harmony will be disrupted – by revolutions internal and external, by disappointment, loss, betrayal and other traumas – but the music that has been interfused along his veins is a part of him, and the initial composing harmony, having passed into his mind, remains a steadying undersong, at once fluid and 'gravitational' (II.263), that increases the mind's resilience and capacity to absorb shocks, integrate accidents and negotiate the passages 'of danger or desire' (I.498) by which the boy's passions gain maturity and passionate love of nature passes into love of mankind.

Book I moves from depictions of infancy to vivid evocations of the child's growing closeness with nature. He is '[f]ostered alike by beauty and by fear' (I.306): by nature's gentle influence and by its severe interventions. The most powerful episodes recount moments when the boy first became terrifyingly aware of nature's sublime power:

> Oh, when I have hung
> Above the raven's nest, by knots of grass
> And half-inch fissures in the slippery rock
> But ill sustained, and almost, as it seemed,
> Suspended by the blast which blew amain,
> Shouldering the naked crag, oh, at that time
> While on the perilous ridge I hung alone,
> With what strange utterance did the loud dry wind
> Blow through my ears! the sky seemed not a sky
> Of earth – and with what motion moved the clouds! (I.341–50)

He hangs suspended between earth and sky, clinging with all his might, seemingly held up by that which should make him fall. The feeling of 'that time' is contemplated in the verse, which, 'by a species of reaction', re-enacts the suspension, producing a kindred feeling: the lines 'hung . . . / Suspended', their syntax 'slippery' and 'ill sustained' across repeated subordinate clauses and prepositional phrases, momentary slips of metrical footing and multiple enjambments (including one that hangs, in characteristic Miltonic–Wordsworthian style, on 'hung' and one 'almost, as it seemed, / Suspended' between enjambed and end-stopped). Whenever the sentence seems about to find purchase in a grammatical subject introducing a main clause, the hanging is still further, breath-suspendingly, prolonged; instead of a straightforward 'when . . . then' culminating in a completed indicative statement, we have a 'when' repeatedly dislodged by ambiguous, incompatible temporal indicators.

The arrival of the main clause fails to resolve the suspension: the sentence blows off its own would-be subject, 'I', substituting 'wind' and 'motion' that ought to increase his peril but that instead, somehow, suspend him, neither rescuing him and his pronoun from their perilous ridge nor leaving them entirely alone and unhelped. What could have been an indicative statement is suspended in exclamation, and the exclamation is on the verge of slipping into an interrogative: with what strange utterance *did* the loud dry wind blow through his ears? And with what motion did the clouds move? The sky seems 'not a sky of earth' (of what strange place is it!), the sentence is ungrounded and time is unmoored: the mixture of perfect and imperfect tenses keeps the contours of the past unsettled, the recollected moments at once singular, habitual, ever-present and shifting in memory.

This passage exemplifies Wordsworth's genius for making emotion present. Instead of reporting, for example, that he 'thought' a particular thought or 'felt' a particular feeling, he presents thoughts and feelings in physical terms of action and reaction: the boy commits an 'act of stealth and troubled pleasure' (I.388–9), striking out from shore in a purloined boat; seemingly in reaction, a huge peak rears up 'like a living thing' (I.411), and for days afterwards 'huge and mighty forms . . . / . . . Moved slowly through [his] mind' (I.424–5):

my brain
Worked with a dim and undetermined sense
Of unknown modes of being. In my thoughts
There was a darkness – call it solitude
Or blank desertion. (I.418–22)

The use of ordinary words in estranging ways conveys the dim and undetermined sense of a mind deserted by familiar sights and traversed instead by 'forms' that intimate unknown modes of being.

Such spectacles and the workings they set in motion are generally included under the heading of 'spots of time'. In the 1799 text this important phrase emerges as the poet reflects on the way in which the acute feelings of a particular moment become attached to spots and images that 'impress' the mind (I.283):

There are in our existence spots of time
That with distinct preeminence retain
A fructifying virtue, whence, depressed
By trivial occupations and the round
Of ordinary intercourse, our minds –

Especially the imaginative power –
Are nourished and invisibly repaired. (1799, I.288–94)

Here as elsewhere in *The Prelude*, a 'philosophical' meditation shares with the adjacent episodes a 'language of the sense' (*WW*; 'Tintern Abbey', line 109): 'there are' literal eminences, copses, crags and other physical presences in a remembered landscape – and 'there are' spots that have 'distinct preeminence' in the landscape of our existence. The intriguing phrase 'spots of time' blends place and time, creating a sense of temporal–spatial depth. As the growing mind is impressed by the forms and images of nature, topographical pre-eminence and the pre-eminence of certain recollections become vitally conjoined in imagination.

The rumination on 'spots of time' is followed by two especially stark examples. In the first, the young boy out riding on the moor loses his guide and stumbles on the site where a murderer's body had been hung in chains; nearby appear some 'monumental' letters that he takes to be the murderer's name, carved into the turf by an 'unknown hand' (XI.293). Fleeing, he comes upon this cluster of figures in the otherwise bare landscape:

A naked pool that lay beneath the hills,
The beacon on the summit, and more near,
A girl who bore a pitcher on her head,
And seemed with difficult steps to force her way
Against the blowing wind. It was, in truth,
An ordinary sight, but I should need
Colours and words that are unknown to man,
To paint the visionary dreariness
Which, while I looked all round for my lost guide,
Did at that time invest the naked pool,
The beacon on the lonely eminence,
The woman, and her garments vexed and tossed
By the strong wind. (XI.303–15)

The second 'spot' is another scene of visionary dreariness, this time associated with his feeling of impatient anticipation as he awaited the arrival of the horses that would transport him and his brothers home from school for Christmas. '[U]ncertain on which road to fix / [His] expectation', he climbed a 'crag, / An eminence' (XI.349–50) overlooking both. The day, he recalls, was

Stormy, and rough, and wild, and on the grass
I sate half sheltered by a naked wall.
Upon my right hand was a single sheep,

Upon my left a blasted hawthorn stood;
With those companions at my side, I watched,
Straining my eyes intensely, as the mist
Gave intermitting prospect of the wood
And plain beneath. Ere I to school returned
That dreary time, ere I had been ten days
A dweller in my father's house, he died. (XI.356–65)

The father's death becomes associated in the boy's mind with the tempestuous scene of anticipation. He feels it as a 'chastisement' for his desires, as if his own impatience and 'anxiety of hope' (XI.369, 371) had caused the death or as if by straining for certainty he had overreached the proper bounds of human knowledge. Afterwards, he recognises the spot as a crossroads in his existence and often returns to it in memory.

Both spots reward sustained attention. In the first, the garments 'vexed and tossed' recall the 'tempest, [the] redundant energy / Vexing its own creation' in the preamble. Here the agitation affects the garments but not the 'naked' image; by making visible the otherwise unseen force against which the girl wins her way, the garments also reveal her countering strength, steady and unflappable. Such moments, Wordsworth elaborates in *1805*, lurk among those passages of life that give 'Profoundest knowledge to what point, and how / The mind is lord and master – outward sense / The obedient servant of her will' (XI.221–3). Rather than declare *that* the mind is lord and master, he matches force against force in isometric contest, concentrating strength and will in one 'point' of stillness. The sense of the mind's power lies partly in the use of the feminine possessive pronoun in support of 'her' will. The female embodies, emblematises and feeds the will. The feminine possessive pronoun lends the whole image a source from which he can drink 'virtue' – an androgynous noun – and recognise his own role in investing it with sublimity. The virtue he drinks there is his own imagination, its power springing from contending and mutually strengthening male and female forces.

The male–female dynamic is crucial at every stage of the mind's growth. In the early phases of *The Prelude*, it is manifested in the fostering of the child by both maternal and paternal powers; the youthful passion for nature and the taming of that passion into love; and the mutual 'fitting' of the mind and the external world. At the other end of the poem, multiplied male and female influences come together in the spectacular climax of imagination atop Snowdon: a glorious, moving symphony of contending powers – male and female; sublime and beautiful; human, divine and natural: the 'perfect image of a mighty Mind' (XIII.69) that is at once of and 'from the Deity' (XIII.196), with a chasm right in the midst: a 'dark deep thoroughfare' where Nature has 'lodged / The soul, the imagination of the whole' (XIII.64–5). Contrast the exhilaratingly dreary evocation of the singular, opaque 'female' figure, sublime not despite but because of its ordinariness. Charged with the energy of stilled time and motion, the 'female' is an emblem of perseverance, strength and endurance. The wind brings her to this still-moving impasse, but the image, preserved by imagination, also illustrates, as both an example and an analogy, imagination's power, as 'lord and master', to invest the ordinary with sublimity.

Although Wordsworth recognises that the sight was 'ordinary', he still feels he needs 'Colours and words that are unknown to man, / To paint the visionary dreariness' (XI.308–10). Yet he does 'paint' it – not with 'colours and words unknown to man', but with ordinary words in unexpected combinations, such as 'visionary dreariness' itself, a black hole and a fountain of a phrase that absorbs and generates interpretations. In the transformative reordering of words resides the 'Visionary power' (V.619) that makes ordinary things appear 'as objects recognised, / In flashes, and with a glory scarce their own' (V.648–9). The 'as' and 'and' highlight the close connection of recognition and 're-cognition', actions of a mind that is 'creator and receiver both, / Working but in alliance with the works / Which it beholds' (II.273–5). This 'first poetic spirit of our human life', ordinarily lost when the child becomes a man, in some remains '[p]reeminent till death' (II.265).

Like the first spot of time, the second is made up of 'elements' (XI.376) that solicit yet baffle interpretation. A sheep, a tree (iconic images, iconically situated 'upon' the poet's right and left hands). Roads diverging, the 'choice uncertain'. That the objects are so 'elemental' makes them seem all the more likely bearers of symbolic meaning, but the Christian meanings commonly borne by these images do not take hold. The 'elements' of an Oedipal reading are here, too: the boy's desires troublingly linked with desire for his father's death, so that the actual death seems like a severe intervention by the father of all father figures, God, who 'thus corrected [his] desires' (XI.375). The image of the two roads suggests the crossroads at which Oedipus unknowingly killed his father. The 'questionable shape' of Hamlet's ghost also haunts these 'indisputable shapes' (XI. 381). But to bind the powerfully multivalent images to any single interpretation would be misguided. The interpreter is like the expectant boy, suspended in such 'anxiety of hope', uncertain which road to watch, straining his eyes to make out forms in the mist. Pointing in more than one direction, the image of the two roads is itself an image for interpretative choices, a signifier of multivalence.

Such spots, Wordsworth tells us, are 'scattered everywhere' (like seeds) in our existence; they are often sown during the seed-time of childhood. The spatialisation of time means that, through all our 'passages of life', they are never irrevocably past, but rather always 'there' to be revisited (XI.274, 269). This point helps to explain the importance of one of the salient strange facts of *The Prelude*'s textual history: in *1805*, the 'spots' sequence does not appear until Book XI. Nine additional books (ten in *1850*, which splits what was Book X into two parts) interpose between the clustered recollections of the boy's early encounters with nature and the (re)turn to the source of renovating virtue, and they are books that depict especially difficult and treacherous phases of the passage from boyhood to manhood. The son's passage into adulthood involves his recognition of his own power of imagination, thrillingly and terrifyingly 'unfathered' – or unfathering itself.

As Keats recognised (from 'Tintern Abbey'), Wordsworth's imagination was 'explorative of . . . dark passages'.[7] Among Wordsworth's darkest 'passages of life' are those haunted by the waking nightmare of violence into which the French Revolution had devolved. What Wordsworth had deemed a noble passion for reform to advance the causes of liberty and social justice – a passion that he shared and acted upon in ways that have occasioned much speculation[8] – had became uncontrollable and turned to terror. With 'a heart confounded . . . / Misguided, and misguiding', and 'turned aside / From Nature's way', he 'lost / All feeling of conviction' and 'yielded up moral questions in despair' (X.887–900).

At the beginning of Book IX, finally on the verge of pursuing his story into these dark passages of memory, he admits that his trepidation about revisiting that time has led him to postpone, with 'motions retrograde' (IX.8), his arrival at this crisis in his mental history. In *1805*, he surrounds the books devoted to the revolution (Books IX and X) with passages that affirm the capacity of his imagination to recover, and even to gain strength, from the experience of being overpowered. Before the revolution books come the uprising of imagination in the Alps episode (the crossing that sets him on the path towards the encounter with his revolutionary past) and the restoration of imagination and nature (Book VIII) after the cognitive overload of London (Book VII). Afterwards, in a different place but still 'there', are the spots of time. Even when he almost allowed himself to be seduced away from the paths of nature and could find no guide or moral compass, they were 'there' in the mi(d)st, like beacons marking the spot to which he could 'repair', as they had been all along and were from the beginning.

The Prelude offers numerous instances of emotion recollected in tranquillity and contemplated until a new emotion, kindred to the original, is produced. Kindred emotion is central to *The Excursion*, too – but the important kinship in the later poem is not the likeness of the reproduced feeling to the original but the feeling of kinship itself. *The Excursion* focuses on the flow of sympathies to the far reaches and recesses of the 'community of the living and the dead'. The phrase is from Edmund Burke, whose influence Wordsworth acknowledges most famously in his paean to the 'Genius of Burke' in Book VII of *The Prelude* from 1832 on, a passage commonly cited as evidence of the poet's renunciation of revolutionary enthusiasm. In *The Excursion*, too (in which it is more integrated) this Burkean mode of imagination is best understood in its particular context in the wake of the French Revolution and the continuing pressures of the Napoleonic Wars during the chief years of poem's composition.

Coleridge had urged Wordsworth to 'write a poem, in blank verse, addressed to those, who, in consequence of the complete failure of the French Revolution, have thrown up all hopes of the amelioration of mankind, and are sinking into an almost epicurean selfishness'.[9] Although Coleridge specified a poem written in Wordsworth's 'own Person', Wordsworth instead adopts 'something of a dramatic form' and speaks 'through the intervention of characters' (*Excursion*, p. 39): the Wanderer, a venerable retired peddler whose mind is richly informed by nature and humankind and who continues to make his rounds, delivering cheerfulness, nurturing sympathies and strengthening bonds of community; the Poet, his eager apprentice; and the Solitary, a melancholy sceptic whose hopes have been wrecked twice – by the failure of the Revolution and by the untimely death of his young family. These characters are later joined by the Pastor, a non-wandering Wanderer in churchman's garb.

The poem with 'something of a dramatic form' has something of a dramatic action in the Wanderer's endeavour to teach both the Poet and the Solitary the proper cultivation, management and purpose of feelings. The Poet's feelings are mostly expressed as spontaneous overflow, which he must learn to direct towards the cultivation of a more mature sympathy; the remains of the Solitary's blasted hopes have gone deep underground, but some roots remain and may perhaps be nurtured back to health. Such agricultural metaphors, connected to the central purpose of sympathetic education, pervade *The Excursion*, a poem with roots in the georgic tradition, including the didactic loco-descriptive poems of the eighteenth century. The Wanderer's two pupils (one eager, one resistant) represent two aspects of the same project. The Poet's developing mind must continue to be 'formed' and informed. The Solitary's, having been de-formed, must be re-formed.

The Wanderer assumes the task of fostering these two minds, educating them in his own patient, philosophical ways. The Wanderer has cultivated such a tranquillity through years of rounds as a peddler – a trade that was, in turn, a regularised version of his childhood wanderings – and now he retreads the same paths in retirement. Every emotion that the poem associates with him is couched in the mediating language of thought. He 'kept . . . / His mind in a just equipoise of love', 'unclouded by the cares / Of ordinary life; unvexed, unwarped' (I.382–4, 385–6) (the insistent prefix pre-emptively negates all possibility of disturbance). So encompassing is his serenity that even the fraught word 'revolutions' can be hazarded, as if it could pass unnoticed: 'No piteous revolutions had he felt, / No wild varieties of joy and grief' (I.388–9). The plural denies the allusion to one particular revolution, while the adjective 'piteous' suggests a spectatorial relation to tragedy, and, by evoking the reaction before naming the action, mitigates the shock in advance. 'He was alive', we are told in language that evokes vital, active participation: 'alive / To all that was enjoyed . . . / And all that was endured' (I.364–6). The energy of 'was alive', momentarily liberated at the end of the line, is redirected to the next line, where, after another burst of energy ('alive / To all'), it sinks into vagueness and passivity. Such 'skilful distribution' (I.72) of sound and sense over the lines works continually to maintain equipoise: in general, *The Excursion*'s enjambments feel less like hanging on for dear life (as in *The Prelude*) than like careful balancing of a scale, collaborating with the generally even metre to neutralise 'wild varieties' of feeling that would vex, warp, bind or overthrow. Without 'the co-presence of something regular' to restrain and temper excitement, 'there is some danger', as Wordsworth remarks in the Preface to *Lyrical Ballads*, 'that the excitement may be carried beyond its proper bounds' (*WW*, p. 609) – overflow is just a step or two from overthrow.

A happy husbandman of feelings, the Wanderer stores them within himself as 'empassioned thoughts' (II.20) and distributes them, in measured amounts, as sympathy. Being rich, he can '*afford* to suffer / With those whom he saw suffer' (I.329–30). He has provided for the occasional expense of sympathy, expressed in the doubled word 'suffer', an extravagance redoubled by the doubled feminine ending. (The Wanderer can 'afford' hints of feminine weakness, along with all the other subversions.) The Poet's observation about the Wanderer of course echoes the spontaneous exclamation of Shakespeare's Miranda, whose innate sympathy and wonder know no bounds. Sharing Miranda's uncalculating responsiveness, he overflows in tears upon hearing the sad story of Margaret and 'blesse[s] her in the impotence of grief' – whereupon the Wanderer informs him that he has now given 'enough to sorrow' (I.968). Sympathy is warranted, but only in moderation, lest it become a wasteful expense of spirit, fertilising nothing. The Wanderer is a pedestrian Prospero who exerts his influence not by magic but by careful use of his resources.

The stories told by the Wanderer and, later in the poem, the Pastor, depict the disintegration of relationship and love, the betrayals, the passions run wild with disastrous consequences, the accidents, trauma, reversals of fortune, purposes gone astray – with occasional happier tales and with both hopeful and sceptical commentary. An extract from the 'argument' of Book VI summarises a typical sequence:

> an instance of unrequited Love. – Anguish of mind subdued, and how. – The lonely Miner. – An instance of perseverance. – Which leads by contrast to an example of abused talents, irresolution, and weakness. – Solitary, appl[ies] this covertly to his own case . . . The rule by which Peace may be obtained . . . – Solitary hints at an overpowering Fatality. – Answer of the Pastor. –

The stories are framed as instances of a particular passion, behaviour or situation. Rather than imposing a moral, however, they cultivate 'moral feeling' (I.329) and a long perspective from which even extremes of emotion are seen as a part of the rhythms of human life. The larger perspective can be and often is read as specifically Christian, but Wordsworth seems to be most interested in a habitual state of mind, a 'philosophic' emotional imperturbability.

The prevailing mode of *The Excursion* is incorporation – of 'revolutions', of errant characters such as 'the Prodigal', of solitaries, unkind hearts, inhabitants of remote mountain reaches, workers in mines, abandoned or 'ruined' women, the 'Deaf Dalesman' and other hard-to-reach individuals, including the dead whose 'lives' make up the poem's central material. The Wanderer praises the faculty that 'with interpositions, which would hide / And darken, so can deal that they become / Contingencies of pomp', like the moon whose brightness transforms the dark trees 'Into a substance glorious as her own, / Yea with her own incorporated' (IV.1056–8; 1065–6). The Solitary is powerfully drawn to such visions, but sceptical about the possibility of communion and wary of the threat it poses to individuality and particularity. His ambivalence is audible in his blazing description, in Book II of the poem, of the 'gorgeous spectacle' of a 'mighty City' (II. 866, 870). The passage – which De Quincey incorporated in his *Confessions* – vividly evokes a 'marvellous array / of temple, palace, citadel, and huge / Fantastic pomp of structure without name' (II.892–4). The memory stirs the Solitary's emotion, but it is held in check by two counter-recollections of the ties that bind him to other human beings and to the earth. He first recalls his humanitarian 'Charge' (II.913) – the old man he had set out to rescue from the storm – and then explains the glorious vision as an 'effect . . . wrought / Upon the dark materials of the storm' by 'earthly nature' (II.881–2): the rising sun inflaming the dissipating storm clouds. Far from denying the visionary power and mystery, he marvels at what nature has 'wrought' from 'dark materials': the Miltonic phrase evokes the sublime supernatural naturalism that interfuses natural processes, divine creation, and human imagination. The perception of dark materials as essential elements of sublimity is distinct from the assumption that darkness is an 'interposition' to be 'dealt' with as a mere 'contingency'. The Solitary is the chief representative of the irreducible particularity of dark materials – both his own and nature's – as a source of sublimity. His relationship to nature is more intense and specific than the Wanderer's or anyone else's in the poem. To the Solitary are attributed sublime descriptions of nature, the passionate evocations of the storm's 'wild concert', the 'roaring sound' of winds, the 'mighty current', the 'headlong flood' (II. 727, 729, 731, 732). The tumult finds expression in a rhythmic turbulence that is rare in the poem as a whole but that not infrequently ruffles the Solitary's speech. Nature at once reflects his 'troubled mind' and lets him look beyond its confines to contemplate things external to himself, as in this stirring description of twin peaks in view of his dwelling:

– between those heights
And on the top of either pinnacle,
More keenly than elsewhere in night's blue vault,
Sparkle the Stars as of their station proud.
Thoughts are not busier in the mind of man
Than the mute Agents stirring there: – alone
Here do I sit and watch. (II.746–52)

The 'mute agents stirring there', the 'I' sitting 'Here' and 'Thoughts . . . in the mind of man' (themselves 'mute Agents') ply a busy trade between the twinned points 'there' and 'Here'. The dynamic interchange of connection and disjunction is reflected in frequent shifts between regular and irregular metrical feet, especially when stressed syllables come up against each other across an enjambment: 'vault, / Sparkle', 'proud / Thoughts', 'alone / Here'.

None of this motion is visible or audible to the external senses; it is all in the silent-speaking words, the metre and 'in the mind of man'. There in the midst, the phrase emanates a Wordsworthian glory and depth that connect *The*

Excursion's relatively untrodden ways (where there have been few to praise or love it) with the main region of his song. It has a distinct pre-eminence in the three major poetic expressions of Wordsworth's philosophy of mind and nature – interfused with 'the light of setting suns' and 'all the mighty world of eye and ear' (*WW*; 'Tintern Abbey', lines 98, 106–7), deemed more beautiful than the earth and of fabric more divine (*Prelude* XIII.6), more sublime than chaos or the darkest pit of Erebus ('Prospectus' to *The Recluse*, line 36, in Preface to *The Excursion*). The phrase appears nowhere else in *The Excursion*. And, although *The Excursion*'s other characters refer to the mind in many and varied ways, only the Solitary looks into it (with sidelong eye, to be sure) and 'watch[es]' its motions, 'alone', yet conscious of himself and of some other being.

It is hard not to feel that Wordsworth is of the Solitary's party at such moments – as, according to Blake's pronouncement, Milton was of the Devil's. Of course, one of the Solitary's chief attractions is that (as his somewhat of a name indicates) he is a party of one. But his solitude also represents the points 'within our soul', where 'all of us . . . stand single' (*Prelude* III.186–7) – the parts that Wordsworth had claimed as the main region of his song. The Solitary's experience closely resembles Wordsworth's, particularly during the revolutionary years, when both let abstract speculation seduce them away from fostering nature. The Solitary is the 'other being' that may also be the poet's past self – and if the child is father of the man, the poet who denies his character's vital connection to his earlier self not only cuts himself off from his best work as a father of poems but also unfathers himself.

The Solitary's resistance to incorporation by the party of Wordsworths talking to Wordsworths is a reminder that, alongside the assimilating faculty that 'abides' within the soul (IV.1055) there is a darkness. Darkness is the main region of much of *The Prelude* – 'darkness makes abode' in the visionary power of words (V.622); 'the soul, the imagination of the whole' inhabits 'the dark, deep thoroughfare' (XIII.64–5) of a chasm (of nature, mind, both). Without the impenetrable, inexhaustible thereness of dark materials, the glory would be unimaginable. Perhaps this is one aspect of Prospero's recognition of Caliban near the close of *The Tempest*: 'This thing of darkness I / Acknowledge mine.'[10] Although the drama of *The Excursion* is framed most obviously around the question of whether (or to what degree and how) the Solitary will be enlightened, the dark mirror image of that question persists alongside the positive one: can the party of Wordsworth(s) acknowledge him as an essential member, not just in spite of but because of his darkness? Wordsworth's 'future Labours' left the continuation of the story 'untold' (IX.795), the question just open enough to allow some room for imagination.

Notes

1. *The Prelude, 1799, 1805, 1850*, ed. Jonathan Wordsworth, M. H. Abrams and Stephen Gill (New York: Norton, 1979), Book 1, line 389. Hereafter cited by book and line number, in the 1805 version, unless otherwise noted.
2. Preface to *Lyrical Ballads* (1802), in *William Wordsworth*, ed. Stephen Gill (Oxford: Oxford University Press, 1984), p. 610. Subsequent references to Wordsworth's prose and to poems other than *The Prelude* and *The Excursion* are to this edition, hereafter cited as *WW*.
3. *The Excursion*, ed. Sally Bushell, James A. Butler and Michael C. Jaye (Ithaca, NY: Cornell University Press, 2007), Book 1, lines 73–5. Hereafter cited parenthetically by book and line number.
4. The relative merits of 'The Ruined Cottage' and Book 1 have been much debated. Christian pieties inserted awkwardly into the latter in 1845 have not helped its case. See Jonathan Wordsworth, *The Music of Humanity* (New York: Harper and Row, 1969). For composition history, see *Excursion*, pp. 17–19, 429–77.
5. For a cogent survey of the composition history, see Stephen Gill (ed.), *William Wordsworth's The Prelude: A Casebook* (Oxford: Oxford University Press, 2006), pp. 4–20.
6. That 'was it for this?' in classical elegy is a lament for youthful promise is also pertinent.
7. *The Letters of John Keats, 1814–21*, ed. Hyder E. Rollins, 2 vols. (Cambridge, MA: Harvard University Press, 1958), vol. 1, p. 280.
8. See especially Alan Liu, Kenneth R. Johnston and David Bromwich (Bibliography).
9. *Collected Letters of Samuel Taylor Coleridge*, ed. Earl Leslie Griggs, 6 vols. (1956–71; Oxford: Oxford University Press, 2000), vol. 1, p. 527.
10. Act 5, Scene 1, lines 275–6, in *The Arden Shakespeare*, revised edition, ed. Richard Proudfoot, Ann Thompson, David Scott Kastan and H. R. Woudhuysen (London: Cengage, 2001).

Chapter 26

Second-generation Romantic poetry I: Hunt, Byron, Moore

JANE STABLER

In 1818 Byron was discomforted to find himself grouped by the *Quarterly Review* with 'men of the most opposite habits, tastes, and opinions in life and poetry . . . Moore, Byron, Shelley, Hazlitt, Haydon, Leigh Hunt, Lamb – what resemblance do ye find among all or any of these men?' Byron asked John Murray, 'and how could any sort of system or plan be carried on, or attempted amongst them?'[1] Byron's outrage was, as usual, slightly disingenuous. His own youthful poetic career had been inspired by reading Thomas Moore and Leigh Hunt and his friendship with them both meant that not only had he been trusted to make editorial suggestions on the manuscript of Hunt's *The Story of Rimini* in 1813 (which was dedicated to him), but also that by 1818 he had already contemplated several collaborative writing enterprises with Thomas Moore. In 1812, Moore had written to Byron: 'I have a most immortalizing scheme to propose to you . . . You & I shall write Epistles to each other – in all measures and all styles upon all possible subjects . . . in short do every thing that the mixture of fun & philosophy there is in both of us can inspire.'[2] In 1815, Byron proposed a trip to Italy and Greece with Moore and in 1817 suggested that they compose 'canticles' together.[3] Byron dedicated *The Corsair* (1814) to Moore; Moore dedicated *Fables for the Holy Alliance* (1823) to Byron. In 1822 Byron would join the production of the *Liberal* with Shelley, Hazlitt and Hunt after floating vague earlier schemes of a newspaper with Moore.[4] Byron remained reluctant, however, to commit himself to any joint venture in the long term and the Tory press was gleefully aware that both Hunt and Moore viewed Byron's literary relationships with each other as undesirable. Moore advised Byron to steer clear of the *Liberal* partnership; Byron said that he remained in it only to help Hunt out of a corner, but Moore did not quite trust Byron not to drag him in too and wrote to John Hunt specifically to request that any satirical poems that might have been included in letters from Moore to Byron should not find their way into the new journal through Byron's sense of '*fun*'.[5]

The jealousy of Hunt and Moore over Byron's friendship, which erupted into open war over ownership of his biography, alerts us to ground which is common and contested between all three writers. Hazlitt – elsewhere ever keen to divide his contemporaries – acknowledged in his *Spirit of the Age* essay that Hunt 'bears no very remote resemblance to the patriot and wit' Thomas Moore; later in the same essay he observed that if 'Lord Byron is a sublime coxcomb . . . Mr Hunt is a delightful one'.[6] Byron, Hunt and Moore existed in a triangular relationship, meeting each other at points (for example, in Hunt's prison cell in 1813), but also holding each other apart. This chapter will assess what was always an uneasy triumvirate in relation to the literary tradition.

The 'Epicurean system' invented by the *Quarterly* was part of a naming and shaming of contemporary 'schools' which grew out of attacks on the Della Crusucans in the 1790s and resurged in the first issue of the *Edinburgh Review* (October 1802) when Francis Jeffrey attacked the new poetic 'school' of Southey, Wordsworth and Coleridge in his review of Southey's *Thalaba*. The collective notion of a school was, of course, hotly denied by Coleridge in *Biographia Literaria*,[7] but the name stuck and Hunt referred to 'the Lake Poets' in the book publication of his literary satire *The Feast of the Poets* (1814), unaware at that point that he would be excoriated as founder member of the Cockney School by *Blackwood's* as it sought to establish its own cultural credentials by opposing a freshly manufactured school in 1817.[8]

Recent scholarly interest in group biography, circles of writers and the co-productions of coteries has given fresh credence to the paranoid claims of the *Quarterly* and *Blackwood's* about the existence of organised poetic groups. Jeffrey Cox proposes that 'the second generation of romantic poets is not merely a temporal gathering of distinct voices but a self-consciously defined group'.[9] The freely associating group was, he claims 'a cultural, social and political project', that provided 'the best vehicle for cultural and political reform'. Cox centres the Cockney School group on Leigh Hunt and he sees Moore and Byron as affiliated members. His scholarship has rescued the Cockney School from the realms of satiric caricature: if we look beyond the enemies these writers had in common, however, we often find divergences of style and opinions about the role of poetry which undermine their temporary alliances and accidental convergences.

They were all precocious at a time when poets were expected to be child prodigies: Hunt's *Juvenilia* was published in 1801 when he was just sixteen; Moore's *Poetical Works of Thomas Little* (also 1801), was supposedly the production of a poet who died in his 'one-and-twentieth year', written at 'an age when the passions very often give a colouring too warm to the imagination';[10]

Byron unwisely drew attention to his minority on the title page of *Hours of Idleness* (1807). It was to compete with these writers that Coleridge claimed at the start of *Biographia* that his *Poems on Various Subjects* (1796) had been published 'when I had barely passed the verge of manhood'.[11] Their various developments of a schoolboy's classical education tell us a great deal about what they shared and where they diverged. Moore's translations from Anacreon (1800) were dedicated to the Regent and suggest that Moore was aspiring to the connoisseurship exemplified by the Prince who commissioned Canova's *Ninfa della fontana*.[12]

Anacreon's repertoire of drinking, garlands of roses and love might seem to represent an inherently conservative subject matter but, as Patricia Rosenmeyer points out, Anacreon's *recusatio* paradigm (a rhetorical refusal) enabled young poets to explore the possibility of invoking and rejecting models from the poetic tradition in order to carve out new areas for themselves.[13] Anacreon's turning away from poetry that glorifies martial prowess in the 'first' Ode anticipates the stance of satiric anti-war writing exemplified in Byron's unfinished 'The Devil's Drive' (1813), the siege cantos of *Don Juan* (1823) and Hunt's *Captain Sword and Captain Pen* (1835). Celebration of luxury becomes a more subversive choice of form when Moore pointedly places 'Anacreontic to a Plumassier' after a satire on the Prince Regent in *Trifles* (1814):

> Now you have the triple feather,
> Bind the kindred stems together
> With a silken tie, whose hue
> Once was brilliant Buff and Blue.[14]

In this context, Anacreontics become an ironic commentary on the Regent's determined quest for pleasure, which did not look quite as emancipatory when he was in his fifties as it had done when he was in his thirties, though it was the cultural cachet of the Prince's dandy set that inspired the cultivated mannerism of Moore, Hunt and Byron.

As Hazlitt remarked in his essay 'On manner': 'Nothing can frequently be more striking than the difference of style or manner, when the *matter* remains the same, as in paraphrases and translations.'[15] Byron also translated Anacreon between 1805 and 1806 and published the results in his *Hours of Idleness*. Byron's rendition of the so-called first Ode in iambic tetrameter stresses Anacreon's habits of anaphora and refrain.

> Adieu ye chiefs, renown'd in arms,
> Adieu the clang of war's alarms.
> To other deeds my soul is strung,

And sweeter notes shall now be sung;
My harp shall all its powers reveal,
To tell the tale my heart must feel,
Love, love alone, my lyre shall claim,
In songs of bliss, and sighs of flame.[16]

We can see here Byron's tendencies to end the line on a strong verb that requires emphatic utterance; Moore's version, by contrast, is smoother and his line endings are often on weaker nouns that glide into the following line. These habits of elision are part of Moore's polished lyricism and a voice that maintains a courteous, level mode of address even when the addressee is being spurned:

Then fare thee well, seductive dream,
That mad'st me follow Glory's theme;
For thou my lyre, and thou my heart,
Shall never more in spirit part;
And all that one has felt so well
The other shall as sweetly tell! (lines 17–22)

Leigh Hunt's first publication was a verse translation of Horace and his translations of Anacreon feature in his *Juvenilia*; he would later claim to have no knowledge of the Greek tragedians – 'With the Greek dramatists I am ashamed to say I am unacquainted' – although this pretension was part of an assault on literary tradition in the Preface to *The Story of Rimini* (1816).[17] Hunt's teenage version of Anancreon distilled the original to an even greater degree, but kept the iteration of the refrain:

Ah then adieu, ye heroes! To our song,
No themes so lofty, and so loud belong;
For, as my fingers sweep the warbling lyre,
The Loves alone the tender chords inspire![18]

Hunt's inversions and caesurae accentuate rhyme and there is an intimation of his defiantly jaunty cockney rhymes in the concluding '-ing lyre' / 'inspire' chime of this ode. Moore commented elsewhere on the 'gratuitous R of the cocknies after words ending in A' that would make 'desire' rhyme with 'Maria'.[19]

It is worth pausing over their imagination of sound: Byron never imagined that his own poetry 'warbled' – he usually reserved this word in its literal sense for birdsong – whereas both Hunt and Moore were happy to identify theirs with choral display: 'there is nothing so delightful as those alternate sinkings & risings, both of feeling & style, which you have exhibited', Moore wrote to Hunt in 1811.[20] Moore was, of course, known for his fine singing voice (as was

Hunt) and the occasion of the public aria with musical accompaniment allowed him to extract great pathos from even flat description. Jeffrey Vail quotes a first-hand account of Moore's performance: 'every shade of thought is syllabled and dwelt upon, and the sentiment of the song goes through your blood, warming you to the very eyelids, and starting you to tears, if you have soul or sense in you'.[21] Hunt's musical soirées were associated with his literary appreciation and his musical sensibility is evident in a remark he made in the Preface to *Works* (1832): 'I confess I like the very bracket that marks out the triplet to the reader's eye, and prepares him for the music of it. It has a look like the bridge of a lute.'[22]

Songs about drinking and vignettes about Venus and Cupid were predictable lyric apprentice pieces, but Anacreon's depiction of love as an overpowering force involving loss of control and dissolution of identity was one of the more disturbing features of his verse that attracted the younger poets. A great deal of 'commingling' goes on in Moore's verse. This aesthetic of hybridity was developed in different ways by Hunt, whose verse forwarded the dissolution of social boundaries, and by Byron, who created a more existential dissolution through his 'inexplicably mix'd' heroes (*Lara*, Canto I, line 290).[23] Mixtures could be comic as when Moore writes of his flirtatious collisions with a young lady in a carriage 'as we mingled our legs and our feet' ('Fanny of Timmol', line 13), but more often, it captured the threatened obliteration of identity Byron describes with Juan and Haidee, 'Mix'd in each other's arms' (*Don Juan*, Canto IV, stanza 27).

Between the anguished refrains of Anacreon's love poetry a precocious disenchantment comes into being, and a bleak message about male inconstancy. The focus of the poet's affections changes from poem to poem – only Byron's poetry has the distinction of being sometimes addressed to a boy (a fact to which select readers were attuned) – but the language remains predictable. Boundless desire generates an energy that the young male contenders for poetic fame found irresistible, but across a collection, the transient nature of romantic love threatens to tarnish lyric intensity. The Anacreontic tracks of inevitable disappointment allowed a rehearsal of bitterness and regret that was easily converted into satiric spleen. Inconstancy is matter for stock misogynistic mirth in Moore's *The Poetical Works of Thomas Little*:

> And do I then wonder that Julia deceives me,
> When surely there's nothing in nature more common;
> She vows to be true, and while vowing she leaves me –
> But could I expect any more from a woman?
>
> ('Inconstancy', lines 1–4)

The liquid anapaestic tetrameter creates a delicate suspension in each concluding dactyl so that listeners anticipate the metrical shortcoming of 'woman'. It is teasingly glib, but when Moore turns lovers' laments to evoke the forlorn condition of Ireland in his *Irish Melodies*, we hear a more plangent music. In songs like 'When I First Met Thee', 'The Time I've Lost in Wooing' and 'She Sung of Love', personal and local pain ripples out to stir listeners into sympathy with the suggestion of a national abandonment and betrayal.

Moore's *Irish Melodies* began the popular Irish nineteenth-century tradition of songs to or about Cathleen Ni Houlihan, refracted in the late twentieth-century envois of Paul Muldoon. Moore's broken-heartedness is lilting and consolatory, and it binds a community together. There is nothing consolatory in Byron's evocation of cosmic perfidy. 'Again Deceived! Again Betrayed!' carries an epigraph from *Macbeth*: 'I pull in resolution and begin / To doubt the equivocation of the fiend / That lies like truth.' The poem turns from bitter accusations of 'every smiling maid / That ever "lied like truth" ' (lines 3–4) to an acknowledgment of the diffuse capriciousness that characterises human life:

> In turn deceiving or deceived
> The wayward Passion roves,
> Beguiled by her we most believed,
> Or leaving her who loves. (lines 9–12)

In the pendulum swing of rhyming quatrains, Byron's ballad predicts a recurrent human failure to resist alteration: his agonised scrutiny of the erasure of identity that accompanies infidelity anticipates the intermittent meditation on constancy in *Don Juan*, whose wandering hero suggests that faith should only be placed in the present moment. 'But Juan! had he quite forgotten Julia?' (Canto II, stanza 208), *Don Juan*'s narrator prompts the reader, who has necessarily forgotten her as well in order to keep up with the poem. Faithlessness is a central preoccupation of Byron's verse both thematically and in the sense that verse form becomes a necessary counter to the slippages of personal biography and human history. It was when Byron's verses turned from stock complaints about female inconstancy to more topical satire on political mutability that he incurred the wrath of the Tory reviewers.

One of Byron's most controversial lyrics, 'Lines to a Lady Weeping', inverts the familiar complaint of feminine frailty to indict the Prince Regent's desertion of the Whigs in 1812. The poem was published anonymously in the *Morning Chronicle* and then in the second edition of *The Corsair*. In attacking the

Prince Regent, Byron was openly joining forces with Moore's presentation of the Regent as a fashion victim:

> A new era's arrived – though you'd hardly believe it
> And all things, of course, must be new to receive it.
> New villas, new fêtes (which e'en Waitham attends) –
> New saddles, new helmets, and – why not *new friends?*
> ('Parody of a Celebrated Letter', lines 57–60)

Most critics agree that Byron's interest in satirical writing was spurred by his friendship with Moore (dating from November 1811), although it must be remembered that the manuscript of *Childe Harold's Pilgrimage*, Cantos I and II, contained several satirical animadversions which elicited the stern disapproval of the Tory reviewers when the poem was published in 1812. Byron's comments on the likelihood of Catholic relief 'under a less bigoted government', for example, were drafted during his stay in Athens in January 1811.[24]

Vail claims that Moore's topical political satire is Byron's most important model and that his *ottava rima* poems represent the eventual successful incorporation of Moore's 'colloquial, Horatian, sociopolitical approach'.[25] But this is not to say that either poet eschewed Juvenalian satire entirely. 'Windsor Poetics', which Byron circulated in manuscript, commemorated the Prince Regent's presence at the disinterment of the remains of Henry VIII and Charles I from the vaults of Windsor Castle in 1813:

> Famed for their civil and domestic quarrels,
> See heartless Henry lies by headless Charles;
> Between them stands another sceptred thing,
> It lives, it reigns – 'aye, every inch a king'.
> . . .
> Justice and Death have mix'd their dust in vain,
> The royal Vampires join and rise again.
> What now can tombs avail, since these disgorge
> The blood and dirt of both to mould a George!
> (lines 1–4, 7–10)

The curdling contempt of 'sceptred thing', Byron's use of the pronoun 'it' and the fragment of King Lear's speech from the scene where he conducts an imaginary trial for adultery measures the corpulent, philandering Regent in a merciless heroic couplet. The bodily corruption of dead monarchs is worked to full advantage, reinforcing, in Jacobin style, the gothic horror of hereditary tyranny. Like the image of the blood-sucking rulers which Percy Shelley uses in 'England in 1819', Byron probably draws his image from Moore's satire *Corruption* (1808), where 'Treasury leeches' on the civil list are described as:

That greedy vampire, which from Freedom's tomb
Comes forth with all the mimicry of bloom
Upon its lifeless cheek, and sucks and drains
A people's blood to feed its putrid veins! (lines 141–4)

As with Byron's heroic couplets, the enjambment and obliteration of the mid-line caesura reveal the difference between Moore's and Pope's heroic couplets. Whereas Pope controls his readers' expectations, allowing us to pause and applaud each perfectly achieved couplet, Byron's iambic pentameter rushes headlong; Pope would not have allowed the rhyme 'quarrels/ Charles' which Byron relishes.

Although Pope spent most of his life in opposition, by the late eighteenth century Popeian heroic couplets were received as the voice of Establishment censure. Gary Dyer has suggested that radical satirists in nineteenth-century England had to develop a pluralistic playfulness to avoid prosecution and to separate themselves from this authoritarian traditional Tory mode.[26] Describing himself as the poetical son of William Gifford, Byron (unlike Hunt) was not discomforted by any proximity to traditional forms and returned to Juvenalian heroic couplets for *The Age of Bronze* (1823). Moore's Regency satires, *The Twopenny Post Bag* (1814) and *The Fudge Family in Paris* (1818), blend radical critique with parlour game in supplying a plethora of dashes which his readers have to substitute for proper nouns. Dyer suggests that this reticence is part of the satiric attack as it dramatises the need to circumvent authoritarian surveillance but is also part of Moore's habitual lightness of touch. His *Fables for the Holy Alliance* pokes fun at the abuses of arbitrary kingship with a shortened tetrameter measure and alternating couplets and quatrains. Juvenalian satire only occasionally disturbs an instinctively accommodating manner.

While defending his *Irish Melodies* from the charge of inflammatory nationalism, Moore repudiated 'any appeal to the passions of an ignorant and angry multitude': his work, he said, 'looks much higher for its audience and readers – it is found upon the piano fortes of the rich and the educated – of those who can afford to have their national zeal a little stimulated without exciting much dread of the excesses into which it may hurry them'.[27] Byron and Hunt were more concerned to unsettle readerly complacency but like Moore, Hunt's companionable editorial stance is ill suited to the savagery of traditional Juvenalian verse satire. Except for *The Feast of the Poets* (which is only mildly satirical) and *Ultra-Crepidarius* (1823), which is a retaliatory strike at Gifford's career, Hunt avoided satiric couplets. Instead, as Steven Jones observes, the 'banter' of his newspaper columns was a vital combative milieu that stimulated and informed the satirical energies of his contemporaries, including Shelley and Byron.[28]

Hunt's addition of extensive notes to later editions of *The Feast of the Poets* suggests that prose was the medium he felt most appropriate for the discussion of topical issues. In other verse, his satiric insights are often delivered in prefatory remarks and throwaway comparisons that invite the reader to realise the nature of the present times in a glancing, confidential manner. The 'mute anguish' (Canto IV, line 396) of the people at the end of *The Story of Rimini*, for example, conveys the bleak political climate of 1813 by talking about that most English of topics, the weather, 'at close of autumn, – still, / A little rainy, and toward nightfall chill' (Canto IV, lines 121–2). With understated ease, this recalls to the reader Hunt's immediate circumstances 'while rains autumnal, as I sing, / Wash the dull bars, chilling my sicklied wing, / And all the climate presses on my senses' (Canto III, lines 5–7). Hunt's journalism made him one of the most powerful satirists of the Regency period, but his prime satiric influence at that time was through prose or in skilful editing rather than verse. For example, his decision to re-print Coleridge's 'Fear, Famine and Slaughter' in the *Examiner* in 1816 worked brilliantly to highlight the older poet's change of political allegiance, but did so simply by an act of attention that anticipated what would happen to Southey in February 1817 when *Wat Tyler* made its embarrassing reappearance in print. Much later in 1835, Hunt published his mordant anti-war satire, *Captain Sword and Captain Pen*, in the decade that also saw the first appearance of Shelley's *The Masque of Anarchy* (1832), deemed too dangerous to publish when first sent to Hunt in 1819. As Hunt knew after his time in gaol, direct attacks on Establishment figures were hazardous: during the Regency period, Hunt's revolutionary politics were forwarded by stylistic means.

Captain Sword and Captain Pen is prefaced by Hunt's comments on the form of the poem and signals his continuing preference for what is 'irregular'.[29] Hunt described Pope's Homer as an 'elegant mistake' in *Foliage* and felt that with the 'French School', English poetry had lost its way.[30] This had been the opinion of the Warton brothers, who influenced William Lisle Bowles's presentation of Pope; the same impulse led William Cowper in 1791 to prefer 'a manly, rough line, with a deal of meaning in it, rather than a whole poem full of musical periods, that have nothing but their oily smoothness to recommend them'.[31] For the best English heroic couplets, Hunt advocated a mixture of the 'vigour' of Dryden, 'the ready and easy variety of pause' in

Crabbe and the 'poetic consciousness' of Keats's *Lamia*, 'in which the lines seem to take pleasure in the progress of their own beauty'; Hunt insisted that the real harmonies of the English heroic were inseparable from the principle of variety.[32] The Preface to *Rimini* asserts that Pope and his followers 'have mistaken mere smoothness for harmony'[33] and in the poem itself we can see how ready Hunt was to introduce pauses to accentuate the drama of the moment:

> With various earnstness the crowd admire
> Horsemen and horse, the motion and the attire.
> Some watch, as they go by, the riders' faces
> Looking composure, and their knightly graces;
> The life, the carelessness, the sudden heed,
> The body curving to the rearing steed,
> The patting hand, that best persuades the check,
> And makes the quarrel up with a proud neck,
> The thigh broad pressed, the spanning palm upon it,
> And the jerked feather swaling in the bonnet.
>
> (Canto I, lines 199–208)

There is limited enjambment in this passage, but it is remarkable for its metrical variety and the improvisatory trochaic rhythm created by tumbling participles. The last line would be an example of what Michael O'Neill calls Hunt's 'dissonant registers' or what Moore called 'some unusual words in which you appear inclined to indulge'.[34] Hunt set out to avoid 'phrases of common property' but his word choice is both demotically inclusive and defiantly recherché.[35] The *Quarterly* picked on this as an example of Hunt's jargon: 'swaling' is a new word dated by the *OED* to 1820–2 when *Blackwood's* used it as part of an attack on cockney poetics. It is associated with costume and mannerism: 'swaling with his coat-tails . . . goes the kind Cockney King'. The ugliness of the word with its yawning vowel sound is satiric and derogatory in *Blackwood's*; in Hunt's poem, it collides with 'knightly graces'.[36]

Richard Cronin suggests that Hunt's admiration of the troop of knights creates a kind of Cockney 'simper' that 'superimpose[s] Hampstead on Rimini', but what Orwell might have called an 'upper-lower-middle-class' perspective is triumphantly achieved:[37] Hunt foregrounds the way in which spectators look at different things and details the 'variousness' of the crowd, fragmenting the picture into disembodied particulars. A restless attention to the interaction of details animates what might otherwise be merely pictorial as Hunt creates an elliptical narrative from the details of human contact with things. Readers are invited to follow the dispersed traces of human relationship, but these points of contact are sporadic and local; the narrative focalisation remains one that darts among the whole crowd rather than identifying with a single figure. In this way, Hunt represents the democratic alternative to Byron's verse narratives. For his attention to things and experiments with register Hunt was attacked as a suburban poet, but he levelled the same accusation at Moore when he quoted Hazlitt's *Spirit of the Age* verdict on Moore's achievement: 'Mr Moore', wrote Hazlitt,

> has a little mistaken the art of poetry for the *cosmetic art* . . . He gets together a number of fine things and fine names, and thinks that, flung on heaps, they make up a fine poem. This dissipated, fulsome, painted, patch-work style may succeed in the levity and languor of the *boudoir*, or it might have been adapted to the Pavilions of royalty, but it is not the style of Parnassus . . .[38]

This demolishes the exquisite poetic fabric of *Lalla Rookh* (1817), where Moore is a dream-weaver of sustained hypnotic power. Cataloguing was a feature of Anacreon's verse and it is used by Byron, Hunt and Moore in different ways that reveal their varying philosophic and aesthetic allegiances. When Moore describes a tented city in *Lalla Rookh*, the distance from the spectacle is emphasised by the scholarly footnotes which (like his translation work) imply that every detail has been excavated from antiquarian research. The luxury and exoticism of the picture came to its early readers filtered through the plates Richard Westall engraved to accompany the volume, and the elements of self-indulgence or escapism are tethered to a serious effort of historical reconstruction:

> Far as the eye can see,
> This world of tents, and domes, and sun-bright armoury: –
> Princely pavilions, screen'd by many a fold
> Of crimson cloth, and topp'd with balls of gold: –
> Steeds, with their housings of rich silver spun,
> Their chains and poitrels glittering in the sun;
> And camels, tufted o'er with Yemen's shells,
> Shaking in every breeze their light-ton'd bells!
> ('The Veiled Prophet of Khorassan', lines 1415–22)

Moore always remains at the same remove from his subject, which is presumably why he was never mistaken for a fire-worshipper himself, as Byron remarked when complaining of the tendency of readers to confuse him with his heroes.[39] Moore's careful research shines through the carefully planted 'poitrels' and a note with his source for the camel bells/shells. Metrically, Moore is the smoothest of the three writers and the regular iambic pentameter line introduces hardly any significant mid-line breaks. Byron's *Giaour* sounds quite different. Parodying the antiquarians (and contrary to Hunt's practice[40]), there is a palaver of notes: in the passage below it is the word 'jerreed' that warrants substantial comment:

> Jerreed, or Djerrid, a blunted Turkish javelin, which is darted from horseback with great force and precision. It is a favourite exercise of the Mussulmans; but I know not if it can be called a *manly* one, since the most expert in the art are the Black Eunuchs of Constantinople. – I think, next to these, a Mamlouk at Smyrna was the most skilful that came within my own observation.[41]

The laconic pace of this note is in marked contrast to the feverish pace of the poetry. Byron's self-indulgent trail of association permits a degree of sexual suggestiveness and personal recollection that keeps the personality of the poet and his itinerary hovering behind the narrative:

> Impatient of his flight delayed
> Here loud his raven charger neighed –
> Down glanced that hand, and grasped his blade –
> That sound had burst his waking dream,
> As slumber starts at owlet's scream. –
> The spur hath lanced his courser's sides –
> Away – away – for life he rides –
> Swift as the hurled on high jerreed,
> Springs to the touch his startled steed. (lines 244–52)

'Impatience' might define Byron's poetic attitude: instead of the coy narrative pace of Hunt's *Story of Rimini* or the dreamy lilt of *Lalla Rookh*, Byron pushes on with fervent verbs and dashes that sustain a race towards the end of the line even when the line describes arrested motion. Beating alliteration and the uneven pulse of dactylic feet inject urgency into the iambic tetrameter; simile rather than Huntian synecdoche enlarges the sphere of the poem. *The Giaour* was a fragment, 'very indistinctly told',[42] in which readers had to leap across gulphs in the narrative: as it passed rapidly through thirteen lengthening editions this scramble to keep hold of the plot added infinitely to the sense of mystery and excitement. Byron's phenomenal success was always associated rhythmically with speed and thematically with secrets: the sensation of high velocity is given additional impetus by the frequent pauses and changes of direction.

Moments of departure and disclosure energise the first two cantos of *Childe Harold's Pilgrimage* as Harold and Byron bid adieu to their homelands and then roam around the eastern Mediterranean, taking leave of a succession of places and people: 'he quits, forever quits / A scene of peace' (Canto I, stanza 28), we are told about Harold, with a repetition that allows him to linger in the act of bidding farewell. Detained only by and for the duration of the adieu, the narrator and Harold are then impelled onward to the next location. The poem's stops and starts create a peculiar kind of momentum that draws all landscape and human history into its power. This applies not only to the terrain about to be traversed, but also to the structures encountered on the way, which are defined in terms of what has swept over or through them: 'Fair Greece! sad relic of departed worth!' (Canto II, stanza 73). The same force of change hollows out the poet himself; he treats the human skull as any other ruin:

> Look on its broken arch, its ruin'd wall,
> Its chambers desolate, and portals foul:
> Yes, this was once Ambition's airy hall,
> The dome of Thought, the palace of the Soul:
> The gay recess of Wisdom and of Wit
> And Passion's host, that never brook'd control:
> Can all, saint, sage, or sophist ever writ,
> People this lonely tower, this tenement refit?
>
> (Canto II, stanza 6)

That Byron was thinking of Hamlet's address to Yorick is here indicated by the aside to a 'churlish Priest' in the variants to the next stanza but one. The catalogue of what was 'once' is weighed against present vacancy. Byron momentarily re-peoples this dwelling place with teeming life, only to empty it again in the final couplet. The wind whistles through another shell of human existence just as the breaths enforced by frequent pauses sigh through the eye sockets of the stanza. Readers are invited to take a tour through their own ephemerality led by a poet whose identity is magisterially present, but also poised on the brink of extinction.

The Spenserian romaunt had always enabled a turning away from social reality into inner space, a move that was emphasised – as Greg Kucich has pointed out – by the incorporation of the personality of the poet in James Beattie's *The Minstrel*.[43] Byron augmented still further the confessional, autobiographical aspect of the poet's persona. He emphasised his privileged access to the topography he described: 'Oh, thou Parnassus!' he addresses the mountain, 'whom I now survey, / Not in the phrenzy of a dreamer's eye, / Not in the fabled landscape of a lay' (Canto I, stanza 60). And, just in case his readers had missed his genuine traveller's credentials: 'Shall I unmov'd behold the hallow'd scene, / Which others rave of, though they know it not?' (Canto I, stanza 62). Not only was *Childe Harold's Pilgrimage* 'written . . . amidst the scenes which it attempts to describe', it coaxed its readers into curiosity about an alluring mental geography too.[44]

By dramatising the expressive moments when utterance 'bursts from my heart' (*Childe Harold*, Canto I, stanza 91) but also bidding readers not to ask 'what secret woe / I bear' ('To Inez', lines 5–6), Byron created a tantalising enigma to which critics such as Tom Mole have recently attributed his commercial success.[45] As with the dynamic of departure, the charm of partial disclosure was that it merged presence and absence, allowing readers to half create what they saw. The revelation of secrets in the first cantos of *Childe Harold's Pilgrimage* anticipated Byron's use of the fragment form in *The Giaour* and a series of rapid verse narratives that skimmed the Eastern territory others had painstakingly itemised. Nameless sin allowed every reader to project his or her own fantasy on to the infamous cipher that was Byron while the fragment form evolved across the rhyming Turkish tales into the suggestive use of hemistich and dashes in the dramatic blank verse of *Manfred*: Manfred's repeated pledges of non-allegiance develop Byron's preoccupation with faithlessness just as *The Giaour* works out the same theme in the character of the professional infidel. But while they glamorised the radical dislocation of their hero, the Spenserian stanzas of *Childe Harold's Pilgrimage* were deeply entwined with an appreciation for what Gray called the 'Second Italian School'.[46] In Cantos III (1816) and IV (1818), Byron's reaching through time and space extends in the breath-denying enjambments between lines and across stanzas: 'And thus the heart will break, yet brokenly live on: // Even as a broken mirror' (Canto III, stanzas 32–3).

Byron's grammar of desolation, 'break . . . brokenly . . . broken', recites a painful lesson, memorising the unforgettable, endlessly refracted agonies of the heart which 'not forsakes'. Each line bears and intensifies unbearable reflection, 'The same, and still the more, the more it breaks' where Byron's shattered but encased world of 'sleepless sorrow aches, / Yet withers on' (stanza 33), possibly moving Keats to imagine how numbed life 'may ache' underneath the cold of 'The Eve of St Agnes'. In these late, great Cantos, Byron flexes to breaking-point the form that has become the mirror of his poetic consciousness. The closing lines of the last Canto buckle to contain the sea as the image of Eternity: 'Dark-heaving; – boundless, endless, and sublime –' (Canto IV, stanza 183); the farewell 'sound which makes us linger' in the last stanza (186) is an aural recognition that both form and theme have been exhausted.

'The Spenserian stanza is . . . almost insurmountably difficult', Wordsworth wrote to the aspiring poet Catherine Godwin in 1829,

> You have succeeded in the broken and more impassioned movement – of which Lord Byron has given good instances – but it is a form of verse ill adapted to conflicting passion; and it is not injustice to say that the stanza is spoiled in Lord Byron's hands; his own strong and ungovernable passions blinded him to its character . . . observe that Spenser never gives way to violent and conflicting passion, and that his narrative is bare of circumstances, slow in movement, and (for modern relish) too much clogged with description.[47]

Wordsworth objects to the misappropriation of form by an undisciplined poetic personality. To an extent, Byron agreed with him. He told Moore that he loved the Spenserian measure, but found it 'too slow and dignified for narrative'.[48] His own wildness, however, seemed a form of laxity, and in 1817 Byron told his publisher, 'I certainly am a devil of a mannerist – & must leave off'.[49] The term 'mannerist' in the sense of 'a person who exhibits mannerisms of speech, behaviour, gesture . . . a person who adopts a mannered style of writing' (*OED*) dates from 1813, and is linked with Byron's creation of a style so distinctive that it was copied by half of Europe.

But this, to Byron, was a problem. His resistance to the idea of a shared set of poetic principles was linked with his scepticism about 'systems' of poetry among contemporary poets especially when manifest in the coterie cultivation of a 'strange style'.[50] In his *Observations* he points out that while Pope could be seen as heading a school of worthy imitators, the problem with the present day (in Byron's eyes) was that poets had no proper connection with poetic forefathers, only a trail of self-indulgent and inferior imitators. Byron needed a stanzaic form that would socialise mannerism by curbing its excesses: he found it in a return to the Italian School.

In the Preface to *Childe Harold's Pilgrimage*, Byron mentioned 'the example of some in the highest order of Italian poets'.[51] Ariosto is mentioned by name and his *Orlando Furioso* is an acknowledged forerunner of the Spenserian stanza. Byron's first use of *ottava rima* was in the 'Epistle to Augusta', which was written in 1816 but not published until 1830. Byron uses the stanza as a version of the Spenserian stanza (as suggested by the differently aligned last line in E. H. Coleridge's edition) and the ghost of a pause between lines 4 and 5. Introduced by the 'c' rhyme in line 5, the Spenserian couplet is less of a single unit than it often sounds in *ottava rima*:

> Oh that thou wert but with me! – but I grow
>   The fool of my own wishes – and forget
> The solitude which I have vaunted so
>   Has lost its praise in this but one regret –
> There may be others which I less may show –

I am not of the plaintive mood – and yet
I feel an ebb in my philosophy,
And the tide rising in my altered eye. (lines 65–72)

Ottava rima here follows the fluxes and refluxes of the speaker's voice. The hint of regrets which may not be shown demonstrates continuity with the confessional mode of the pilgrimage; Byron's ' – and yet' prepares us for the shift to the couplet, where '-phy' and 'eye' chime in a way that skirmishes on the threshold of comical self-deprecation. *Ottava rima* allows the poet to track changes both with and against the resolutions of rhyme. The shift between the Spenserian and Ariosto's octave tilts the rhyming balance from a self-inwoven to an outward-looking character. In the Epistle's dialogue with Wordsworth's 'Tintern Abbey', the poet's sister is not present and the poet produces a catalogue of accidents that might account for his 'strange quiet':

Perhaps – the workings of defiance stir
    Within me, – or perhaps a cold despair –
Brought on when ills habitually recur, –
    Perhaps a harder clime – or purer air . . . (lines 41–4)

Whatever the cause, the stanza form charts the poet's survival of 'wordly shocks' (line 20); and the regular return of the rhyme becomes one with the 'spirit of slight patience' (line 39), which upholds him. Ariosto's bracing medium holds without attempting to heal the treachery of laureates and lovers. In *Beppo* (1818) and then *Don Juan* (1819–24), rhyme joins the memory of the past with the necessity of moving on. This formal change enables a new attitude to the vagaries of human relationship – one in which the 'and yet' reflex of Byron's verse might imagine the pain of betrayal from a female perspective:

yet as real
Torture is theirs, what they inflict they feel.

They are right; for man, to man so oft unjust,
    Is always so to women; one sole bond
Awaits them, treachery is all their trust;
    Taught to conceal, their bursting hearts despond
Over their idol, till some wealthier lust
    Buys them in marriage – and what rests beyond?
A thankless husband, next a faithless lover,
Then dressing, nursing, praying, and all's over.
(*Don Juan*, Canto II, stanzas 199–200)

Byron is the only canonical male romantic poet to imagine the numbing catalogue of a woman's existence when emptied of happiness in marriage.

At the end of *Persuasion* Jane Austen gives Anne Elliot a steadfast defence of female constancy: ' "All the privilege I claim for my own sex (it is not a very enviable one, you need not covet it) is that of loving longest, when existence or when hope is gone." '[52] She speaks for her own endurance and for art's ability to outlast human mutability and to hold true against the overwhelming odds of indifference or outright cruelty. There is a strong chance that Byron read Anne Elliot's speech, but unlike Austen's knowingly compassionate gift to her heroine in *Persuasion* there are no second chances for the abandoned women in *Don Juan*. Byron never got over the infidelity of his readers, although by enshrining changeability as an art form, he found a way to survive it. His faith in the permanence of human art as opposed to human promises is conveyed most memorably in his conviction that the poetry of Pope would be snatched by the survivors of apocalypse.[53] Byron's defence of Pope's formal perfection, like Shelley's of Keats, reinforces a belief not just in a single poet, but also in the possibility of unsullied commitment itself.

When Shelley's *Adonais* assembled Byron, Moore and Hunt as the Pilgrim of Eternity, the sweetest lyricist of Ierne and the gentlest of the wise, the sequential presentation conjoined separate talents. The worth of Keats was one of many things on which they disagreed, but Shelley's Spenserian form mantles aesthetic differences in the service of high art – the realm that Shelley believed would place all of them beyond the stain of critical schools and political parties.

Notes

1. *Byron's Letters and Journals*, ed. Leslie A. Marchand, 13 vols. (London: John Murray, 1973–94), vol. VI, p. 83.
2. *The Letters of Thomas Moore*, ed. Wilfred S. Dowden, 2 vols. (Oxford: Clarendon Press, 1964), vol. I, p. 176.
3. *Byron's Letters and Journals*, vol. IV, p. 269; vol. V, p. 165.
4. *Ibid.*, vol. VIII, pp. 55, 140, 166.
5. *Letters of Moore*, vol. II, p. 508.
6. *The Complete Works of William Hazlitt*, ed. P. P. Howe, 21 vols. (Tokyo: Yushodo, 1967), vol. XI, pp. 176–7.
7. Samuel Taylor Coleridge, *Biographia Literaria* (London: J. M. Dent, 1997), p. 34.
8. Leigh Hunt, *The Feast of the Poets with Other Pieces in Verse* (London: Gale, Curtis and Fenner, 1815), pp. 78, 81.
9. Jeffrey N. Cox, *Poetry and Politics in the Cockney School: Keats, Shelley, Hunt and their Circle* (Cambridge: Cambridge University Press, 1998), p. 4.
10. Thomas Moore, *The Poetical Works of Thomas Little* (Oxford: Woodstock, 1990), pp. iv-v.

11. Coleridge, *Biographia Literaria*, p. 3.
12. Thomas Moore, *Odes of Anacreon, Translated into English Verse*, 2 vols. (London: J. and T. Carpenter, 1802), vol. I, p. 24.
13. Patricia A. Rosenmeyer, *The Poetics of Imitation: Anacreon and the Anacreontic Tradition* (Cambridge: Cambridge University Press, 1992), pp. 99–102.
14. Lines 36–9. Unless otherwise stated, quotations from Moore are from *The Poetical Works of Thomas Moore*, 10 vols. (London: Longman, Orme, Brown, Green, and Longmans, 1840). Compare with Byron's 'I still retain my "buff and blue" ' in the Dedication to *Don Juan*, stanza 17.
15. *Complete Works of Hazlitt*, vol. xx, p. 53.
16. Lines 19–26, in Byron, *The Complete Poetical Works*, ed. Jerome J. McGann, 7 vols. (Oxford: Clarendon Press, 1980–93). All quotations from Byron's poetry are from this edition.
17. Leigh Hunt, The *Story of Rimini*, third edition (London: C. and J. Ollier, 1819), p. xvii.
18. Lines 9–12. Leigh Hunt, *Juvenilia; or, a Collection of Poems*, second edition (London: J. Whiting, 1801).
19. *Letters of Moore*, vol. I, p. 274.
20. *Ibid*., p. 157.
21. Jeffrey W. Vail, *The Literary Relationship of Lord Byron and Thomas Moore* (Baltimore: Johns Hopkins University Press, 2001), p. 85.
22. Leigh Hunt, *The Poetical Works of Leigh Hunt* (London: Edward Moxon, 1832), p. xxiii.
23. Richard Cronin discusses Hunt's stylistic challenge to social order in *The Politics of Romantic Poetry: In Search of the Pure Commonwealth* (Basingstoke: Macmillan, 2000), pp. 182–8.
24. Byron, *Complete Poetical Works*, vol. II, p. 202.
25. Vail, *Literary Relationship*, p. 43.
26. Gary Dyer, *British Satire and the Politics of Style, 1789–1832* (Cambridge: Cambridge University Press, 1997), pp. 67–84.
27. *The Poetical Works of Thomas Moore* (London: Frederick Warne, not dated), p. 194.
28. Steven Jones, *Shelley's Satire: Violence, Exhortation, and Authority* (DeKalb: Northern Illinois University Press, 1994), pp. 53–6. See also Jones's discussion of Hunt and 'pantomimic satire' in *Satire and Romanticism* (New York: St Martin's Press, 2000), pp. 169–85.
29. Leigh Hunt, *Captain Sword and Captain Pen* (London: Charles Knight, 1835), p. viii.
30. Leigh Hunt, *Foliage; or Poems Original and Translated* (London: C. and J. Ollier, 1818), p. 31.
31. *The Life and Works of William Cowper*, ed. Robert Southey, 9 vols. (London: Henry G. Bohn, 1854), vol. IV, pp. 159–60.
32. Hunt, *Works*, pp. xxxvi–xxxvii; *Feast of the Poets*, p. 32.
33. Hunt, *Rimini*, p. xiv.
34. Michael O'Neill, 'Leigh Hunt and Romantic Spontaneity', in Nicholas Roe (ed.), *Leigh Hunt: Life, Poetics, Politics* (London: Routledge, 2003), p. 139; *Letters of Moore*, vol. I, p. 274.

35. Hunt, *Feast of the Poets*, p. 129. Hunt later referred to 'occasional quaintnesses and neologisms, which formerly disfigured the *Story of Rimini*' (*Works*, pp. xv–xvi).
36. Hunt later substituted 'flowing' for 'swaling'.
37. Cronin, *The Politics of Romantic Poetry*, p. 187.
38. *Complete Works of Hazlitt*, vol. XI, pp. 171–7. Hunt quotes extensively from this criticism in his review of Moore's *Life* of Byron in *The Tatler*, No. 114, 14 January 1831, before aligning Moore with 'the very perfection of Della Cruscan sentiment'. In the Preface to *Foliage*, Hunt had praised *Lalla Rookh*'s 'new-modelled heroic numbers' (p. 14).
39. Lord Byron, *The Complete Miscellaneous Prose*, ed. Andrew Nicholson (Oxford: Clarendon Press, 1991), p. 90.
40. In the Preface to *Rimini* Hunt declares himself content that the reader 'not be quite sensible of the mighty extent of my information' (p. xii).
41. Byron, *Complete Poetical Works*, vol. III, p. 417.
42. John Watkins, *Memoirs of the Life and Writings of the Right Honourable Lord Byron, with Anecdotes of Some of His Contemporaries* (London: Henry Colburn & Co., 1822), p. 180.
43. Greg Kucich, *Keats, Shelley, and Romantic Spenserianism* (University Park: Pennsylvania State University Press, 1991), p. 71.
44. Byron, *Complete Poetical Works*, vol. II, p. 3.
45. Tom Mole, *Byron's Romantic Celebrity: Industrial Culture and the Hermeneutic of Intimacy* (Basingstoke: Palgrave, 2007).
46. See David Fairer, *English Poetry of the Eighteenth Century 1700–1789* (London: Longman, 2003), p. 157.
47. *The Letters of William and Dorothy Wordsworth. The Later Years Part* II *1829–1834*, ed. Ernest de Selincourt, revised by Alan G. Hill, second edition, vol. V (Oxford: Clarendon Press, 1979), p. 58.
48. *Byron's Letters and Journals*, vol. IV, p. 13.
49. *Ibid.*, vol. V, p. 185.
50. Referring to Hunt's *Rimini*; *Byron's Letters and Journals*, vol. VI, p. 46.
51. Byron, *Complete Poetical Works*, vol. II, p. 5.
52. *The Novels of Jane Austen*, ed. R. W. Chapman, third edition, 5 vols. (Oxford: Oxford University Press, 1953), vol. V, p. 235.
53. Byron, *Complete Miscellaneous Prose*, p. 150.

Chapter 27
Byron's *Don Juan*

BERNARD BEATTY

Byron's *Don Juan* begins with disarming directness: 'I want a hero' (I.1) and, a few lines later, names this hero as 'our ancient friend Don Juan' (I.1). Such a Chaucerian opening is unlike that of any of the great Romantic long poems and, critically, it has never sat easily alongside them.

Don Juan is direct and it does disarm but it relies on multiple indirectnesses to achieve this sustained candour. The relation between directness and indirectness, and between declared improvisation and declared planning, forms the art and life of the poem. In its first published version, the briefest of epigraphical overtures tells us that the poem takes such relationships as its Horatian foundation: 'difficile est proprie communia dicere', which Byron himself translated as ''Tis no slight task to write on common things.'[1]

That is not how the present reader encounters the poem. Depending on the edition, we will find a series of competing overtures before we reach the main text. Some of these were withdrawn by Byron with or against his better judgment; one was unwittingly omitted. Taken together, they invite the reader to make certain helpful presumptions both in what they say, and in the reasons for their omission. We can begin with them.

The Horatian tag, for instance, is balanced by the later epigraph to Canto III:

> Di Sopra vi contai questa novella
> Quando................
> ....
> Credo che fu de l'altro libro al fine

which is elaborately referenced to 'Berni. *Orlando Inamorato*. Canto 67. Libro Terzo. stanza 14'. Jerome McGann translates it 'Earlier I told you this story when ... I think that was at the end of another book.'[2] The translation is accurate but McGann's compression of the missing lines to three points, though understandable, misleads, for the calculated extent of the gap is part of the communication. The epigraph from Horace tells us, correctly, that *Don*

Juan is to continue Horace's conducting of poetry as 'sermo' or discourse. The epigraph from Berni tells us that *Don Juan* will be also a comic, satiric, burlesque transformation of an inherited story through which, in Stuart Curran's phrase, 'romance' will be 'at once demystified and reified'.[3] This story will be self-consciously put aside and resumed through the manipulation of gaps, sometimes through digressions and sometimes through jumps in narrative which are accommodated through the spacing of digressions and canto endings. The effect is often more dramatic than epic and, of course, resembles the pattern of the original Don Juan story.

There was to have been a different initial epigraph from the same Horatian poem: 'domestica facta'. This was omitted because John Cam Hobhouse, mindful of the stir caused by the publication of 'Poems on Domestic Circumstances' just after Byron's separation from his wife, wisely counselled that the epigraph would over-foreground the obvious references to Byron's wife in the first Canto. Horace's phrase refers to affairs in general rather than sexual or domestic ones.[4] Byron is therefore wittily inviting us to misunderstand the Latin whilst also telling us that *Don Juan* is to be about domestic life (i.e. sex and marriage, which Byron calls 'domestic doings', III.57), public life (i.e. war and politics) and common things (i.e. matters both universal and interim). This is its object; its method is 'To build up common things with common places' (XIV.56). Byron finds, but does not continually seek, fine phrases, nor does he evade known truths, much to Hazlitt's horror at Byron's 'tissue of commonplaces'.[5] Hazlitt is right about the commonplaces but wrong about the tissue. Byron's phrase is 'build up', and what Byron builds up is what we must always attend to. Hazlitt has a romantic preference for the strange and unexpected but Byron's poetry deliberately oscillates and mediates between common things and unknowable things, received language and unexpected language. This is what his artistry 'builds up', for he wishes his readers both to lose direction and yet recognise everything that they see.

Byron readily accepted Hobhouse's criticism of the phrase 'domestica facta' and first suggested one of his favourite quotations as a replacement: 'No hopes for them as laughs', which he claimed to be the warning issued by a Methodist preacher to someone who laughed whilst he preached.[6] In the end he settled for the existing epigraph but he did not forget or forgo 'them as laughs' since he chose a parallel Shakespearian epigraph for the preface to Cantos VI, VII and VIII: 'Dost thou think because thou art virtuous, there shall be no more Cakes and Ale? Yes, by St Anne; and Ginger shall be hot i' the mouth.'[7] The words could be used as justification by the irreverent bystander to the preacher who rebuked him. In both cases, we are told that the immediacy of laughter and of the senses is central to the poem and that it will not be understood or enjoyed by anyone who belittles either of them.

The other paratexts – a verse dedication and two prose prefaces – are on a larger scale. The dedication reluctantly, and the initial preface deliberately, were withdrawn by Byron. Only the preface to Cantos VI, VII and VIII was originally published. It was designed to tell us a fact about the poem's composition. Juan's career is continuous but narrated through closely detailed sequences, jumps, gaps and résumés, but the poem, though published serially (Cantos I–II, III–V, VI–VIII, IX–XI, XII–XIV, XV–XVI), was continuously written. Except, that is, for the gap between V and VI, which is glossed over as narrative ('We left our hero and third heroine in / A kind of state more awkward than uncommon', VI.49) but real both in Byron's life and the momentarily external attention of the reader. Byron obscured and exaggerated the extent of this gap[8] – it was some twelve rather than eighteen months – but it is certainly significant. This preface could, and sometimes has, been read as signifying a change of direction in the poem to a new kind of seriousness which, in effect, means privileging political seriousness. Doubtless this is partly true; Byron knew that he was going to take Juan from domestic harem to public affairs. The siege cantos, even more than the shipwreck, interpose a huge question mark into the poem's confidence in itself and in life. The turn away from sexual love in differing social contexts as subject seems to me primarily, nevertheless, to be a matter of maintaining balance in the poem, for it is always about both senses of 'domestica facta' and neither has a monopoly of seriousness. Seriousness is everywhere and nowhere in *Don Juan*. The poem refuses to circumscribe it in customary ways.

I am more interested in the poem's publicised alignment between poetry and 'life' (one of Byron's favourite and insisted upon words), for 'life' here never means or could mean that which can be uncovered by socio-cultural inquiry or presumption. *Don Juan* tracks political events closely once we have, via the siege cantos, a date (1790) as marker, but the poem has its own marking and occupancy of time. Juan is sixteen when his adventures first begin. He is, like Lady Adeline, twenty-one at the end of the poem. This five-year period corresponds more or less exactly to the writing time of the poem and Byron's own life. The contrast with Wordsworth's *The Prelude* is instructive. That poem advertises the relationship between its growth and that of the author's mind but does so by retrospection and editing, which allows the imagination to create and re-create memory. *Don Juan* proceeds by a sustained act of daring in relation to that mediation between past and future which is always its present genesis.[9] 'HAIL, Muse! *et cetera*' (III.1) is its guiding formula, which blends bravura and risk but serves the purposes of interweaving meditative commentary and narrative. This is the basic structure of both Wordsworth's poem and Byron's.

The preface to the poem as a whole is, indeed, an elaborate guying of Wordsworth's Preface to *Lyrical Ballads* and, in particular, Wordsworth's note on the speaker in 'The Thorn'. It shows us that Byron wants *Don Juan* to be a restorative displacement of Wordsworth's new ordering of the relation between poetry and common life, poetry and common language and the relation of poet to dramatised speaker. If Byron is right about these things, then Wordsworth is wrong. The proof of the pudding is in the reading.

The Dedication to Southey is far more direct but confirms the manifesto character of Byron's enterprise. By attacking the poet laureate's experimental poetics and reactionary politics, which, in turn, is here associated with Castlereagh's repressive politics and 'set trash of phrase' (line 97), Byron deliberately picks up Pope's mantle in *The Dunciad*. For Pope's attack on his poet laureates combines satire on bad speech writing and official taste with an attack on the entire cultural and political shallowness of the mid eighteenth century. *Don Juan* is to be a comparable corrective – both aesthetic and moral – to the alliance, as Byron saw it, between political reaction and cultural experiment in the early nineteenth century. Nevertheless the epigraphs to the poem are from Horace's epistles, *Twelfth Night* and Berni's burlesque romance, not from Juvenal's satires. *Don Juan* is to be satirical but it is more *satura* (i.e. medley) than *satira* (satire).

If we ask what the poem is, the best place to start is structure. Byron as narrator[10] often implies that his poem has no structure, for his poetry is simply:

> A paper kite, which flies 'twixt life and death,
> A shadow which the onward Soul behind throws (xiv.61–2)

The implication is that the kite is at the mercy of 'the way the wind blows' (xiv.58). The only ordering which it might reflect is that of the melancholy thrower. He resembles Rousseau in Shelley's *The Triumph of Life*, whose onward life continually erases the present tense, of which it leaves only scattered shadowy traces. But, whereas Shelley's poem confirms the explicit viewpoints reiterated within it, Byron's does not support his strange image. The image implicitly conflates the kite, which we deliberately pull behind us to get it upward, with the shadow, which our physical forward progress involuntarily throws (usually) behind and downwards. Writing, which uses matter but is an activity of the soul, is both playful and a compelled representation of the life which, in producing it, moves away from it. Yet *Don Juan* has a remarkably lucid and controlled forward structure of which anticipation and repetition with difference are intrinsic parts and in which the narrator's wholly mental world corresponds to the sky world of epic machinery, whereas Juan's world of heart and instinct belongs, like that of Fielding's Tom Jones, to the sub-lunar world of vital temporal life. Only once does Juan 'concern / His brain about the action of the sky' and we are instantly informed that 'puberty assisted' (1.741–2; 744).

The first canto of *Don Juan* is self-contained, like *Beppo*. Doubtless, Byron was experimenting (as he often did) with formal possibilities and did not have a fully worked-out scheme or scale for his new poem. *Ottava rima*, as the epigraph from Berni suggests, has nevertheless been primarily used for complex sustained narratives, and the traditional story of Don Juan – which Byron inverts by making Juan seduced rather than seducing but clearly has in mind – is inherently episodic, unlike that of Beppo, which – a miniature Odyssey in this – is based on the single and permanent return of its hero. The original Don Juan will return to Seville but Byron's clearly will not. Peter Vassallo has plausibly suggested that the kernel episode in Canto 1 of Juan's upbringing, the affair with Julia and the farcical discovery and escape, was to have been a closed episode in the manner of one of Casti's *Novelle*, which Byron admired.[11] The episode would have been an equivalent poem to *Beppo*. Certainly, the Italian influence is extremely important. When Byron imitates Pope's satirical couplets directly in *English Bards and Scotch Reviewers* etc., he does so with accuracy and panache but the tradition stays where it was. When he does so via Casti's *ottava rima*, the tradition that he so much admired takes on a new lease of life in him. Yet Byron must have realised whilst fashioning this shape that the escape rather than return motif which concludes this episode is inherently open-ended and the motif of escape provides the continuing structure of the original Don Juan story. Byron had just published the final canto of *Childe Harold's Pilgrimage* in April 1818 and began to write *Don Juan* five weeks later. The *Beppo* manner, and the motif of escape mirrored in separate cantos, would make possible a new kind of long poem based not on images of pilgrimage and flight but on contingency and escape. *Ottava rima* poems usually have a number of narrative strands whereas the original Don Juan story has a single story in diverse settings. Byron takes the latter but uses this diversity to examine different kinds of love conventions within different societies. He does this systematically in what, in other respects, seems the most casually spacious of his poems. The single, though episodic, story is deliberately complicated by tangential digression and the creation of parallels between scenes which initially are set up as antitheses. We learn to read forwards but also across. In both activities we are increasingly aware of the past of the poem gathering into its present shaping. This simultaneously gives us the formal satisfactions of art whilst mimicking the strange conjunction of predictable pattern and outright accident which we recognise as our own life. Michael O'Neill thoughtfully suggests that the story here 'has the logic and inconsequence of existential event'.[12] Byron's formal distance from his own creation as narrative and as ironised narration is directly linked with his reckless self-exposure caught between memory, thought and instinct.

The poem traverses five cultures (Spanish, Greek, Turkish, Russian, English) in which Juan, correspondingly, sleeps with five women (Julia, Haidee, Dudù, Catharine, Fitz-Fulke) though he is the object of attention of two others (Gulbeyaz and Lady Adeline) and is himself attracted in parallel but different ways to a further two (Leila, Aurora Raby). Byron's general purpose is clear: 'I meant to have made him a Cavalier Servente in Italy and a cause for a divorce in England – and a Sentimental "Werther-faced man" in Germany – so as to show the different ridicules of the society in each of those countries.'[13] There is an obvious contrast between love in a strait-laced city (Seville) and free love on an island, which is followed in turn by forced, and then accidental, love in the Seraglio. What is resisted there is submitted to in Catharine's Russia, but the move to England is to a society in which eros has little public authorisation. These five contrasting love sections are themselves contrasted with two episodes of destruction and death (shipwreck and siege) in Cantos II, and VII–VIII, which intersect them. This large structure can be carried in the head. It is no accident that Byron's plays and poems have been set to music by great composers or that he spent much time in the theatre and, at the time of writing *Don Juan*, in the opera house listening to Rossini's multi-voiced, lightly energetic, ensembles.[14] As in music, what is set apart converges and what seems wholly different may be a variation on a theme.

Love, for instance, however carefully differentiated, is always set in motion by a woman, not by Juan. If Juan loves Haidee freely, he is, according to the accusing voice of 'The Isles of Greece' poet, a slave of passion in a world of slaves. Thus, when he becomes a literal slave of the Sultana's passion, there is repetition as well as contrast. Byron was going to make Leila, the girl whom he rescues during the Siege, into a woman with whom he would be in love, but she would not love him.[15] He rightly rejected this obvious novelty partly because Byron, unlike sonnet tradition, is only interested in reciprocated love,[16] but mainly because the poem depends upon repetition in different circumstances. Instead he makes her a parallel to, and harbinger of, Aurora Raby, who will not initiate love with him either but does not altogether refuse it. Aurora checks and alters him but, in doing so through her being rather than through speech or action, re-asserts the life of poetry rather than that of a novel. In the latter, we would primarily be interested in Juan's character and its development, and confidently interpret romantic disillusion as maturity. Byron had probably read more novels than any of his major poetic contemporaries and *Don Juan* is clearly influenced by them.[17] So Byron changes Leila into the first intimation of what will become a major presence. She is written out as soon as Aurora appears. The Duchess of Fitz-Fulke, similarly, is a comic reprise of Catharine the Great whose sexual energies are discharged through play rather than war, but, in playfully dressing as the Black Friar in order to gain access to Juan's bed, the Duchess is associated both with Aurora's Catholic spirituality and with the insistences of the flesh. If war seems wholly different from love, specifically virile energies are expended in both, and the war is between the two court societies (Ottoman Turkey and Russia) which the poem has visited. Both of these are dominated by eros (the Sultan's harem and Catharine's taste for well-made soldiers). Byron thinks structurally and musically in what Jerome McGann calls 'the interface' between these criss-crossing parallels and antitheses.[18] John Jump's question about the poem – is it poem or hold-all? – seems pertinent but the 'or' ought to be 'and'.[19] It is a poem that holds together 'all'.

Structures are still and spatial, whereas music is a temporal art. Byron writes frequently and well about great buildings[20] – often as models of consciousness – and he prefers stanzas (literally 'rooms') to blank verse, but *Don Juan* has a diachronic as well as a synchronic shaping. It repeats, balances and contrasts yet it also develops.[21] The poem is not in the same literal, poetic, moral and spiritual place in its last cantos as in its opening ones. This is not primarily because Juan changes (he does and he does not) but because the poem is 'life' as well as poem and because it puts its own presumption that the constant renewal of life through sexual love is a good thing to prolonged and sometimes bitter testing.

An instance of this is the Juan and Haidee episode. It has three sections: the detailed sequence of Juan's arrival, recovery and first lovemaking with Haidee; the representative sequence of the banquet over which Juan and Haidee preside; and Lambro's disruption of their idyll. The structure is clear-cut and emphasised brilliantly (again the musical comparison is helpful) by Haidee's dream in Canto IV. This repeats in minor key the sequence of Juan's arrival and her discovery of his body. Against this strong forward ordering,

Byron insists that their love as such has no development but is a permanent state into which they step.[22]

Their social state, however, has changed. In Canto I, Byron has shown us adulterous secret love in a city where, as in Pope's 'Eloisa to Abelard' (which is the formal model for Julia's famous letter to Juan), 'glowing guilt excites the keen delight!'[23] The poem invites us to contrast the delights of guilty sex with Juan and Haidee's 'indulgence of their innocent desires' (III.98) in an island society which they completely control and re-order. As always Byron both gives us this simple opposition but then complicates it. I have missed out the word 'illicit' which he puts before 'indulgence of their innocent desires'. We are meant to be intelligently puzzled in the midst of the very simplification which we have been invited to sustain and our puzzlement is intensified by the presence of dwarfs, eunuchs, slaves, elaborate clothes, objects and foods in this supposedly natural idyll, which, here, seems to be very like the court world of Constantinople in the next episode. Romance here borders upon satire, but not sufficiently to undo the value placed upon the 'innocence' of Juan and Haidee's desires nor does the poetry undermine Haidee's status as one of the greatest love heroines in poetry. Rather it is a matter of continual readjustments as we read through the poem.

We have to make the same continual readjustments in miniature as we read each stanza. I said earlier that seriousness is everywhere and nowhere in *Don Juan*. The following stanza makes the point:

> There were four Honourable Misters, whose
> Honour was more before their names than after;
> There was the preux Chevalier de la Ruse,
> Whom France and Fortune lately deign'd to waft here,
> Whose chiefly harmless talent was to amuse;
> But the clubs found it rather serious laughter,
> Because – such was his magic power to please –
> The dice seem'd charm'd too with his repartees. (XIII.86)

Byron is the acknowledged master of *ottava rima*, a difficult form in English. His syntax, though often complex, is transparent. Here the sense is governed by the explicit sequence 'There were . . . whose / There was . . . whom . . . Whose / But / Because'. Each of these directing formulas is at the beginning of a line, so there is congruence between grammatical and metrical orderings as there usually is in Pope or Dryden. The exception is the first 'whose', which occurs at the end of the first line and is the only example of enjambment in the stanza. The rhyme thus caused, characteristically, is both necessary ('whose', 'Ruse', 'amuse') and daring beyond anything that Pope would countenance. But the rhetoric clearly derives from Pope, who is the model for Byron's zeugma which allows two very different entities ('France' and 'Fortune') to share the same verb ('waft'). Fortuna is often represented with wings and thus could 'waft' chevaliers much as the sylphs 'waft on the breeze' above Belinda's boat in *The Rape of the Lock* (II.60) but France cannot waft.[24] If we laugh at this, and we should, then the rhyme of 'waft here' and 'laughter' will reinforce the point. Both activities depend up the movement of air. The connection is serious and hidden. Laughter, like channel breezes, moves us into a new place whether we like it or not. The comic juxtaposition, on the other hand, is evident and surprising. We register first the one and then the other. Later, we can hold the two things together.

Similarly, if we trace the sequence from Mister to Chevalier, we will notice the local play on titles of different register which pronounce and stress the 'er' endings differently to comic effect. The previous stanza moves from 'the Duke of Dash' to 'the six Miss Rawbolds'. Hence, across the two stanzas, the sequence of common and aristocrat titles is wittily chiasmic (Duke, Miss, Mister, Chevalier). In both stanzas, the subject matter is partly the distinction between 'peers' and 'commoners' (XI.675, 677) so the change of voice tone is itself emblematic of the class shifts under discussion, but it is also the comedian's (especially the English comedian's) stock-in-trade. As with the comedian, there is a slight suggestive pause before the change of voice.

It is impossible to overestimate the importance of attending to changes of voice in *Don Juan*. Everything depends upon what Matthew Bevis calls 'talk transcribed, transfigured, and finessed'.[25] Final couplets are often a case in point. In this one, the pause occurs after the initiating 'Because' and produces the change of tone to knowing aside in 'such was his magic power to please', which then allows the delayed major clause to fill out the whole final line as a ringing conclusion to the stanza. Byron's alertness of ear to all kinds of speech vindicates his epigraph's claim to speak of common things rather more accurately than any speech to be found in *Lyrical Ballads*, but it is musical as well as prosaic, an operatic feast of artfully balanced voices as well as 'the very language of men'. Thus the prosaically iambic 'before their names than after', or the barely metrical 'But the clubs found it' are balanced by the loftily iambic 'Whom France and Fortune lately deign'd to waft here' with its superb pivot on 'lately deign'd'. The play on sound is obvious enough. Less obvious is the way Byron sets balanced trochaic cadences against his normal speech pattern ('lately deign'd to'; 'chiefly harmless talent') which is, perhaps, a trick that he learned from Gray. Byron's manuscript alterations to his text suggest a preference for apparently casual formulations but are, in their way, a sign of his often overlooked fastidiousness.

We do not turn from the style to the sense of the stanza as to some separate territory. Everything is incongruous in *Don Juan* (that is why we laugh but could weep), yet everything hangs together or is transformed into its opposite here, too (that is why to read the poem is 'to ponder deeply', IV.16). For instance, the play on meanings in 'magic power to please' and 'The dice seem'd charm'd too with his repartees' where 'charm'd' means by magic and by wit (it is an implicit zeugma again) charms the reader. The placing, cadence and force of the word 'seem'd' convey an inexplicably witty grace to the reader who, thereby, encounters directly both the charm of the Chevalier and the superintending intelligent zest of Byron's voice and spirit. The Hebrew Bible makes God's breath (*ruach*) the source of energy and form in all creation. Milton invokes the same breath as 'Spirit' to form *Paradise Lost* and Shelley diverts it into the Wild West Wind which drives his ode and the breath that terminates *Adonais*. A 'keel-compelling gale' (II.172) hurtles Childe Harold across the Mediterranean. It is a magnificent phrase[26] which catches the co-operation and tension between wayward storm energies and dark purposes sustained in hidden depths. The boat of *Don Juan*'s author, however, is a 'slight, trim, / But *still* sea-worthy skiff' (X.31) which draws less depth and is more modestly propelled.[27] Byron suggests that the poem's 'real qualities are not on the *surface* – but still if people will dive a little – I think it will reward them for their trouble'.[28] The poem is wafted by laughter, its muse is a butterfly which 'hath but her wings' (XIII.709) and even these accept their limitations: 'March, my Muse! If you cannot fly, yet flutter' (XV.210). Auden was right to note that Byron was 'the master of the airy manner'.[29] But his comment needs this corrective: concealed but operative within the aerial playfulness and beauty of 'flutter' is the purposeful groundedness of 'March'. Most early reviewers wholly misread the poem, but Lockhart beautifully caught its forwards and sideways motion, slight but real depth and aerial energy when he praised its mixture of 'the sweep, the pith, the soaring pinion'.[30]

For all this, the congruence of Chevalier and poet in this stanza raises a problem for us. He is the Chevalier de la Ruse. The real referent is usually thought to be the Comte de Montrond, who was a successful gambler wit, and a stylish but less successful diplomat. The way that this section of the poem both invites but also resists full identification of its many satirised characters again reminds us of Horace and Pope. Byron invests him with a name ('the Knight of Trickery') that recalls the title of the first Don Juan (*El Burlador de Sevilla*, 'The Prankster of Seville') and links forward to the great trick of Fitz-Fulke, who, like the original Don Juan, adopts a disguise in order to seduce, and seems to be motivated as much by delight in trickery as in sex. She is exactly characterised as 'her frolic Grace' (XVI.1031).

But if this is so, and the poet has just exercised a kindred magic charm in the act of writing and talking to us, then the congruence of style and sentiment in poem and poet may seem diverting but simply shallow. The butterfly's flight delights in the surfaces upon which it barely and fitfully alights. It has often been the fate of the poem to be admired and dismissed thus, from Hazlitt to Auden. Fortunately the stanza itself hinges on the issue of where seriousness is to be found.

Byron says that his 'desultory rhyme . . . rings what's uppermost of new or hoary, / Just as I feel the "Improvisatore"'(XV.154, 159–60) but he remembers what he has written and shapes his poem backwards as well as forwards (we recall the paper kite and shadow which his 'onward soul behind throws'). Thus the 'hoary' as well as the 'new' may be 'uppermost'. Stanza 86's discussion of serious laughter picks up the direction announced in the opening lines of Canto XIII:

> I now mean to be serious; it is time,
> Since laughter now-a-days is deemed too serious.

We know that 'I now mean to be serious' must be a joke, but then the joke turns round on us twice in the next three lines:

> A jest at Vice by Virtue's call'd a crime,
> And critically held as deleterious:
> Besides, the sad's a source of the sublime . . .

The initial explanation is familiar. Vice is tamed by ridicule. That is a position which Horace, Ben Jonson, Dryden, Pope, Swift, Churchill and Crabbe – whom Byron much admired – all agreed upon. But 'now-a-days' such ridicule is disliked by people at large and by critics, for people in general do not want their hypocrisy disturbed and misread the pillorying of vice as an enticement to it (hence 'a crime'), and Byron's contemporary critics were busy deriding the notion that satire could be great poetry (hence 'deleterious'). The reception of *Don Juan* by English people and by English critics revealed exactly this double tendency. Hence we must have misread the first line for he does mean to be serious after all, and indeed the Norman abbey cantos which begin here are the most obviously satirical section of the poem. But then the next line stymies this understanding. It is governed by that most camply prosaic of openings – 'Besides' – which we know is going to add a comically alternative reason for the turn to seriousness. In itself 'the sad's a source of the sublime' is perfectly plausible. It is the throwaway 'Besides' that makes us distrust it and this is confirmed by the next line, which is another instance of Byron's sotto voce asides: 'Although when long a little apt to weary us'.

If we put these contrary indications together and then match them to the canto which follows we will find the following. Byron certainly means to be 'serious' in the sense that he intends to construct, for the first time in the poem, a fully peopled world which will be presented openly in the tradition of Popeian satire as a riposte to bad English taste and morals. But this world of would-be serious people who are seriously satirised is set in an ancient ruined abbey turned into a country house which will be described in some of the most obviously sublime and wholly unironised stanzas in the poem (xiii.56–63). This is the setting not only of caricatures like those in Peacock's *Nightmare Abbey* but of Aurora Raby, whose eyes, which shine 'like seraphs', are described specifically as both 'sublime' and 'sad' (xv.354, 55). She was correctly identified by T. S. Eliot as 'the most serious character of Byron's invention',[31] and she certainly introduces a wholly new kind of seriousness in Don Juan himself and in *Don Juan*. Attention to verbal detail and local effect like this clearly connects with the strange thrusts and turns of the poem as a whole, for Byron thinks through connections in much the same way on a small scale as on a vast one.

Hence when, eighty-five stanzas later, we have encountered first the sublime ruined abbey and then its imperfect satirised inhabitants, Byron reminds us of his earlier association of seriousness and laughter and invites us to reconsider it. It means something rather different in its new setting. Although '*preux*' chevalier is a standard phrase for a valiant knight since knights are bound to honour and to the fight, the Chevalier's 'chiefly harmless talent is to amuse'. He belongs in an interior world of play and laughter conducted round the mock-combats of the gaming table just as Pope's Sir Plume and Baron are to be found playing ombre. He is, however, a successful knight in this harmless jousting, either through the good 'Fortune' that has wafted him to England or through cheating (the word 'seem'd' may suggest the latter). The gambling clubs therefore, which lose money through him, find it 'rather serious laughter', which means that they do not find anything funny about it at all. Seriousness and laughter do not coincide. The sequence is that aphorised in *Beppo*, where 'laughter / Leaves us so doubly serious shortly after' (line 79). This is in contrast to the dice themselves, which, though 'which' deftly doubles as 'who', are 'charmed' not by some hidden manipulation but by the wit of his repartees, which is here identical with the wit of poet and poem. The charm of graceful speech is itself a form of action which alters the game of chance which is gambling, life and poem. The world of satiric laughter at the canto's opening 'is deemed too serious' nowadays and is thus ignored; it now seems less powerful here than the world of amusement, repartee and charm which in fact has real and 'serious' consequences. Pope said that he 'stoop'd to Truth and moraliz'd his song'.[32] Byron, his pupil in 'ethical' poetry,[33] charms us into truth and morality. The poem is a triumph of lightness of touch but it is not light. Within its 'flutter' is the pulse of a 'march'. This brings us to present attitudes to the poem which part company on this issue.

Don Juan has never been more widely read or highly regarded than it has in the last fifty years.[34] Excellent books and articles, and wonderful editions, have transformed the landscape in myriad ways. Moreover, the indebtedness of such different poets as T. S. Eliot, W. H. Auden and Paul Muldoon to *Don Juan* has become increasingly apparent. Despite this welcome diversity of approach to a diverse poem, two dominant schools of thought have claimed the clue to its unravelling. The first is new or old historicism, which founds the poem's coherence and 'seriousness' in extra-literary contexts. The second is postmodernism, which stitches up the poem in advance as knowingly incoherent, beyond good and evil, seriousness and non-seriousness. Neither of these emphases is wholly new, both work up to a point, but both are incomplete, and incompleteness misleads. One thing that *Don Juan* consistently demonstrates is that to know we must strive to include as much as possible and be aware that there could always be more. In this respect, its closest parallels are Proust's *A la Recherche* and Dante's *Divina Commedia*, for these works seem both interested in everything which is knowable in their worlds and yet press into the immediate unknown which girds what they can discern and represent. Byron's suggestion that art is a plaything 'which flies 'twixt life and death, / A shadow which the onward Soul behind throws' is apposite for both works. Dante as pilgrim moves forward into vivid worlds twixt life and death, which have been fixed by the shadows of the past, and Proust necessarily moves forwards in a second surrogate life of writing which recreates a past world of ideas, feelings and events that can be represented but never recovered. Byron's remark (originally about *Childe Harold's Pilgrimage*) that he had created 'a *Human*' poem as opposed to a divine one, and that this is no mean achievement, is apposite here.[35] *Don Juan*, however modest in mode,[36] is undeniably comparable to works by Dante and Proust in the audacity, penetration and scope through which we receive 'the anatomy of a culture'.[37] It is hard to think of any other English poem, except *The Canterbury Tales*, which could stand the comparison.

Jerome McGann in *Don Juan in Context* used 'Ordinary Language Philosophy' to ground a materialist reading of the poem. Wittgenstein might be more helpful still. As I understand it, the Wittgenstein of the *Tractatus* wished, like Bertrand Russell, to remodel language so that it would not mislead clear thought, but the Wittgenstein of *Philosophical Investigations* thought the exact opposite. It is only by inhabiting and paying close attention to the instructive vagaries of actual language use that we can learn about reality but, importantly, the relationship of language and reality can never itself be pictured or stated. This is because there is no vantage point, philosophical or otherwise, that enables us to stand outside this relationship though we stand within it all the time. All historicisms imply that the relationship can be pictured and post-modernism denies the relationship. The poem, even in its own time, both straddles and undermines these hermeneutic options. Byron knew and practised what Wittgenstein came to recognise. We misread it if we see it as a world on its own set against chaotic reality, as G. M. Ridenour was the first explicitly to do,[38] and we misread it if we see it as somehow subordinated to or simply part of 'reality', as those who have seen it primarily as a satire have done. Byron said that

> . . . words are things, and a small drop of ink,
> Falling like dew, upon a thought, produces
> That which makes thousands, perhaps millions, think . . .
>
> (IV.793–5)

It is one of many times in the poem where Byron castigates human pretensions and reminds us of the mutable materialities which found our loftiest pretensions. 'Words' and 'thinks' are 'things'. But the opposite is just as true. A 'small drop of ink' is dew which generates a million thoughts. Byron is always a dualist. No single system will explain everything. But he is a dualist who rhymes. Logic distinguishes but counter-logical rhyme connects and thus, whilst dependent on more than one, it brings two incongruous things together as indissolubly congruent just as 'ink' and 'think' are here. Arbitrary fact (the accidents of rhyme) discloses connections in life and language. Laughter wafts. So too does sexual love, for Venus is the mother of laughter even though, in the guise of Catharine the Great, she is perilously close to being the mother of slaughter. Every stanza of the poem reveals such connections, but so too do the vast structural juxtapositions, incongruous and varied but always unexpectedly congruous, which are its life and form. In this way, rhyme in *Don Juan* is simultaneously life and art. It exists – to use Byron's phrases again – as both 'plaything' and mirror ''twixt life and death'. As with Wittgenstein, this insight where observant scepticism presses directly into what exceeds human grasping is not religiously formulated but increasingly knows itself to be close to religious perspectives.[39] This is why Aurora Raby appears at the end of the poem with her 'depth of feeling' which embraces boundlessness and space (XVI. 48). She takes the reader completely by surprise both because she seems to have an existence not simply conferred by the poem but also because she is a necessary bastion of the comic end-play of the poem, in which the space ''twixt life and death' is comically, but only temporarily, occupied by Fitz-Fulke's transformation from dead monk into living flesh. Fitz-Fulke's transformation of seriousness into laughter will be followed by the contrary movement 'shortly after'. For the reader, too, the transition between the end of Canto XVI and the opening of Canto XVII (which follows shortly after) is into the 'serious' deflation of 'breakfast, tea, and toast / Of which most men partake, but no one sings' (XVII.99). But Aurora permanently occupies this space, for her smile (Byron insists that it is her hallmark at XV.45, 55, 78, 80 and XVI.92) mediates between flesh and spirit, seriousness and laughter, in a poise of rest which the poem has constantly traversed but never previously attained as distinctive presence. The clash and congruence of rhyme in *Don Juan* ceaselessly mimics and embodies that traversal. In it we find the interplay of the familiar and already formulated with the ever-present intrusion of the 'voiceless thought' which rushes across strange seas, like the lightning which refuses but grants articulacy to the poet in the great storm in Canto III of *Childe Harold's Pilgrimage*. The great torrent of language which makes up *Don Juan* is more humanly and humanely situated than that of the earlier poem, for it 'seeks to speak' 'of common things', but it has the same elemental force.

Notes

1. 'Hints from Horace' (1821) in *Lord Byron. The Complete Poetical Works*, ed. Jerome J. McGann and Barry Weller, 7 vols. (Oxford: Clarendon Press, 1980–93), vol. I, p. 296. Hereafter *CPW*. All quotations from Byron's poetry are taken from this edition. References to *Don Juan* are to canto and stanza number. See Stephen Cheeke's informed discussion of the epigraph and the relation of *Don Juan* to commonplace in 'Byron and the Horatian Commonplace', *The Byron Journal*, 36:1 (2008), pp. 5–18.
2. *CPW*, vol. V, p. 670.
3. Stuart Curran, *Poetic Form and British Romanticism* (New York: Oxford University Press, 1986), p. 192.
4. *CPW*, vol. V, p. 670.
5. William Hazlitt, 'Lord Byron', in *The Complete Works of William Hazlitt*, ed. P. P. Howe, 21 vols. (London: Dent, 1932), vol. XI, p. 68. T. S. Eliot repeats exactly the same charge: 'sonorous affirmations of the commonplace with no

depth of significance' and adduces the last stanza of Canto xv as an instance: 'Byron' (*On Poetry and Poets*) reprinted in M. H. Abrams (ed.), *English Romantic Poets: Modern Essays in Criticism* (Oxford: Oxford University Press, 1975), p. 263.

6. See note 4 above.
7. *CPW*, vol. v, p. 293.
8. See commentary at *CPW*, vol. v, pp. 714–15.
9. In this way, *Don Juan* is a vindication and commentary on Byron's aphorism in the Ravenna Journal: 'What is Poetry? – The Feeling of a Former world and Future.' *Byron's Letters and Journals*, ed. Leslie A. Marchand, 13 vols. (London: John Murray, 1973–94), vol. VIII, p. 37. Hereafter *BLJ*.
10. I use this phrase 'Byron as narrator', in future simplified to 'Byron', for occasions when it would be misleading to imply that the narrator is simply a constructed presence wholly separate from the living author, though there is a sense in which this is always true and there are occasions when the narrator is foregrounded as such a construction.
11. Peter Vassallo, *Byron: The Italian Literary Influence* (London: Macmillan, 1984), p. 67. *CPW*, vol. v, p. 667, makes the same point and suggests September 1818 as the time when the larger concept emerged.
12. Michael O'Neill, *The All-Sustaining Air* (Oxford: Oxford University Press, 2007), p. 119.
13. *BLJ*, vol. VIII, p. 78.
14. Byron declared that his story of opera singers sold into slavery in Canto IV was based on a story that he had heard, and that he had seen one of the women, returned from captivity, singing at a performance of *L'Italiana in Algeri* in La Fenice (v.704, note 640).
15. 'In his suite he shall have a girl whom he shall have rescued during one of his northern campaigns, who shall be in love with him, and he not with her.' Medwin's *Conversations of Lord Byron*, ed. Ernest J. Lovell (Princeton: Princeton University Press, 1966), p. 165.
16. Byron's unreturned and unrequited love for Loukas Chalandritsanos in his last days in Greece, which provoked a series of poems, is the only exception to this.
17. See for instance A. B. England's excellent account of the influence of Fielding on the poem in his *Byron's Don Juan and Eighteenth-Century Literature* (London: Associated University Presses, 1975).
18. Jerome J. McGann, *Don Juan in Context* (London: John Murray, 1976), p. 95.
19. J. D. Jump, *Byron's 'Don Juan': Poem or Hold-All?* (Swansea: University of Swansea Press, 1968).
20. The ruined Parthenon, the ruined castles of the Rhine, the Colosseum and St Peter's are all explicitly associated with consciousness in *Childe Harold's Pilgrimage*. Norman Abbey 'moans' and has ' a voice to charm' in Canto XIII, stanza 63.
21. See my discussion in Bernard Beatty, *Byron's Don Juan* (London: Croom Helm, 1985).

22. Byron says that moons have changed but Juan and Haidee's love remains 'changeless' (IV.121).
23. Alexander Pope 'Eloisa to Abelard', line 230. The line echoes Ovid's *Amores*, XIX.ii.3. *The Poems of Alexander Pope*, ed. John Butt (London: Methuen, 1963), p. 258.
24. Byron had a retentive memory and he may just be recalling *Henry VI*, Part 3, 5.7.41: 'Away with her, and waft her hence to France', where 'waft' retained its original sense of 'convey safely over water'. A wafter was an armed vessel protecting a convoy. *William Shakespeare: The Complete Works*, ed. Stanley Wells and Gary Taylor (Oxford: Clarendon Press, 1988), p. 123. It is more likely that Pope's phrase 'The Adriatic main / Wafts the smooth eunuch' (*The Dunciad*, IV. 309–10) is the main source.
25. Matthew Bevis, *The Art of Eloquence: Byron, Dickens, Joyce* (Oxford: Oxford University Press, 2007), p. 62.
26. The phrase is presumably modelled on Pope's Homeric formula 'cloud-compelling Zeus'.
27. Shelley attempts a parallel modesty in such late poems as 'The Witch of Atlas', where his witch sails in 'the lightest boat / Which ever upon mortal stream did float' (lines 295–6). *Shelley's Poetry and Prose* ed. Donald Reiman and Sharon B. Powers (London: Norton, 1977), p. 356.
28. *BLJ*, vol. IX, p. 55.
29. 'Letter to Lord Byron', III.7, in W. H. Auden, *Collected Longer Poems* (London: Faber and Faber, 1968), p. 59.
30. Letter to 'Christopher North' signed M. O'DOHERTY, concerning *Don Juan* Cantos IX–XI, printed in *Blackwood's Edinburgh Magazine*, September 1823. The author is usually thought to have been John Gibson Lockhart. In Theodore Redpath, *The Young Romantics and Critical Opinion 1807–1824* (London: Harrap, 1973), p. 298.
31. T. S. Eliot, 'Byron', p. 272.
32. Alexander Pope, *Epistle to Dr. Arbuthnot*, line 341, in *The Poems of Alexander Pope*, p. 608.
33. 'I take him on his strong ground – as an *Ethical* poet. . .the latter is the highest of all poetry.' *Letter to John Murray Esq.*, in Lord Byron, *The Complete Miscellaneous Prose*, ed. Andrew Nicholson (Oxford: Clarendon Press, 1991), p. 148.
34. William St Clair's, *The Reading Nation in the Romantic Period* (Cambridge: Cambridge University Press, 2004) has altered our sense that *Don Juan* found comparatively few sympathetic readers in the early nineteenth century by demonstrating how very widely it was read in cheap pirated editions to which John Hunt responded by printing his own cheap editions.
35. 'You have so many "divine" poems, is it nothing to have written a *Human* one?' *BLJ*, vol. VI, p. 105.
36. *Don Juan* is modestly presented in comparison with Southey's and Wordsworth's major poems yet, of course, there is a sense that this modesty, though real, is calculated and flaunted.

37. Drummond Bone, '*Childe Harold's Pilgrimage* IV, *Don Juan* and *Beppo*', in Drummond Bone (ed.), *The Cambridge Companion to Byron* (Cambridge: Cambridge University Press, 2004), p. 157.
38. *Don Juan* is 'an attempt to give color, form, and warmth to a world naturally colorless, indefinite and chill'. G. M. Ridenour, *The Style of Don Juan* (New Haven: Yale University Press, 1960), p. 33. I disagree wholly with this but, in its time, this book stood alone as a brilliantly serious account of a then largely unregarded poem.
39. In Byron's case the criss-crossing of flesh and spirit in Catholic worship is one of the main reasons for his attraction to it (see *BLJ*, vol. IX, p. 122). Transubstantiation in practice, if not in theory, works like rhyme.

Chapter 28

Second-generation Romantic poetry 2: Shelley and Keats

MICHAEL O'NEILL

The two poets treated in this chapter, Percy Bysshe Shelley and John Keats, have entered the cultural imagination as a fused type of the inspired Romantic poet who burns with self-consuming lyric ardour and dies young. Even before Arthur Hallam grouped them together as 'poets of sensation' in his review of Tennyson's 1832 volume, *Poems, Chiefly Lyrical*, they both enjoyed the editorial championship of Leigh Hunt, who fêted them, with John Hamilton Reynolds, a close friend of Keats, in his 'Young Poets' *Examiner* article of December 1816.[1] Time meant Shelley and Keats to be allied, poetic incarnations of the same second-generation British Romantic *Zeitgeist*. Born three years apart, Shelley in August 1792, Keats in October 1795, they died in consecutive years, Keats in February 1821 and Shelley in July 1822. And yet the two poets were never exactly friends, and their work is fascinatingly different as well as alike.

Indeed, they can be and have been set against one another in credible if at times too sharply opposed ways: Shelley as a poet of intellectual beauty, Keats of the physical; Shelley of radical aspiration, Keats of liberal realism; Shelley of belief in Godwinian perfectibility, Keats of scepticism about 'Godwin-methodist' approaches to life, as demonstrated by his friend Dilke.[2] Shelley may appear more mistrustful of language's adequacy than Keats, more inclined to use similes that concede their final lack of correspondence with non-verbal reality: 'What thou art we know not; / What is most like thee?' – these lines, addressed to the skylark, embody Shelley's grasp of language's inability fully to embody and yet point towards its resourcefulness in his hands.[3] Keats can seem a more metaphorically confident poet than Shelley, able through a humanising verb and bunching, chiastic clusters of assonance to animate the inanimate in a line such as 'A shielded scutcheon blushed with blood of queens and kings'.[4] Provisionally useful, however, such antitheses can and should also be interrogated, even as value remains in juxtaposing the poets.

Before exploring their separate achievements, then, the chapter will sketch ways in which the poets influenced or responded to or connect with one another. A. C. Bradley argued that 'It seems almost beyond doubt that the story of Cynthia and Endymion would not have taken' the form it did take in Keats's *Endymion* (published in 1817) 'but for *Alastor*', Shelley's tragic romance of 1816.[5] Shelley's poem drives towards its ineluctable climax, in which the Poet, pursuing an elusive *anima* figure, dies, seemingly at one with, even as he is let down by, the natural world. Its blank verse, steeped in Wordsworthian cadences and phrasing, enacts something close to an anti-Wordsworthian message as the poem's Narrator comes to a stoic, heartbroken close:

> It is a woe too 'deep for tears,' when all
> Is reft at once, when some surpassing Spirit,
> Whose light adorned the world around it, leaves
> Those who remain behind, not sobs or groans,
> The passionate tumult of a clinging hope;
> But pale despair and cold tranquillity,
> Nature's vast frame, the web of human things,
> Birth and the grave, that are not as they were. (lines 713–20)

The first line's acknowledged allusion to the final words of Wordsworth's 'Ode: Intimations of Immortality' sees in a depth beyond tears merely 'woe' where Wordsworth senses an ennobling wisdom. The lines also refer to the same ode's intuition of 'Strength in what remains behind' (line 183) and opening conviction that 'It is not now as it has been of yore' (line 6).[6] But Shelley, involved in a critique of Wordsworth's moments of natural piety, suggests, through his allusive art, that the older poet is no longer what he was. He is alert, too, to stress-points in Wordsworth's by no means uncomplicated vision of nature's trustworthiness, in, say, 'Lines Written above Tintern Abbey'.

The passage's wording points to a sad divorce between 'some surpassing Spirit' and 'Nature's vast frame', a divorce which underpins Shelley's idealising and often frustrated quests for a redefined marriage between self and transformed world. The passage, like the poem, suggests poetic traits which run though Shelley's work: his practice of dialogue with precursor texts and poets; his command of a rhetoric capable of a tragic inflection born out of disappointed hope; and his control of a rhythmic power resonant with strong feeling. Above all, the passage reveals, in context, the co-presence of seemingly single-minded intensity and alertness to the importance of perspectives. As suggested above, the poem is shaped as a narrative, in which the Poet's life is told to us by a highly subjective Narrator. In addition, we reach the poem proper via a preface that adds interpretative complexities, praising the Poet as 'a youth of uncorrupted feelings and adventurous genius' but finding him guilty of 'self-centred seclusion' (p. 92). Shelley's interest in perspectival instability matches the movement between hope and despair in his poetry. It is as though to mention one of these loaded nouns, each with a political flavour in the post-Waterloo period when revolutionary desire seemed to have foundered, is to generate a sharpened awareness of the other.

Keats, too, unmoors us from any single perspective in *Endymion*. The poem's use of loosely enjambed couplets encourages a rebellious wandering from a controlling plot design. It is a tribute to Keats's success in this respect that the reader may feel doubt about the poem's final assertion of union between the real and the ideal when Indian maid and moon-goddess miraculously turn out to be one. Douglas Bush sees the poem as involving, in contrast to the Poet's 'vain quest' for 'realization of his ideal vision' in Shelley's *Alastor*, 'the Keatsian discovery that the way to the ideal lies through the actual', and views the 'contrast' as 'characteristic of their authors'.[7] Certainly Keats makes space for Endymion to realise the error of his idealising ways: 'I have clung / To nothing, loved a nothing, nothing seen / Or felt but a great dream!' (IV.636–8), he says. As the beautifully enacted tension between verb and object in 'clung / To nothing' shows, Keats's 'poetic romance', to quote its subtitle, is prodigal in poetic invention, as Shelley half-indicates when he refers to its 'treasures poured forth with indistinct profusion'.[8] It pursues, with metapoetic, indefatigable relish, a line-by-line rendering of imagined experience.

Wordsworth described the 'Hymn to Pan' from Book I as 'a very pretty piece of Paganism' when Keats recited it in his presence. The painter, Benjamin Robert Haydon, recalls the older poet as speaking 'drily' and says that Keats 'felt it *deeply*',[9] but Wordsworth's account of mythology in Book IV of *The Excursion* (much admired by the younger poet) sponsors the inset poem. Whereas Wordsworth rehearses what once happened, Keats reinvents for the present. His Pan, 'Dread opener of the mysterious doors / Leading to universal knowledge' (I.288–9), is not, despite that last phrase, an enthusiast for Enlightenment rationalism. Rather, and Keats's bardic rhythms and phrasing affirm as much, he is the begetter of an inspired and inspiring kind of poetry, in touch with the 'dull and clodded earth' (I.297) and able to give it 'a touch ethereal, a new birth' (I.298). In *Endymion* Keats seeks 'Richer entanglements, enthralments far / More self-destroying' (I.798–9), not merely to mirror or render the real, but to recreate and re-experience it, 'repeated in a finer tone' (*LettersJK*, I.186). 'Entanglements' that are also 'enthralments' seek to 'destroy' self-concern as Keats practises '*Negative Capability*' (*LettersJK*, I.193), or imaginative identification through language.

The experience of the vanishing goddess in *Endymion* differs from the impact in *Alastor* of the dissolving 'veilèd maid' (line 151). In *Endymion*, Book II, for example, the disappearance ushers in a medley of inflections. Keats makes physical Endymion's bemused amazement, his apparently improvised couplets equal to the task of imagining 'The wanderer, / Holding his forehead, to keep off the burr / Of smothering fancies' (lines 137–9). The positioning of 'burr' permits the musculature of the verse to support the meaning. Keats may recall 'the seventeenth-century use of the word meaning a nebulous dish of light around the moon',[10] or, indeed, as the *OED* itself suggests (n.6.2), he may mean 'whirr, vibratory or rushing noise'. Yet the word also stays in touch with its more familiar sense, a prickly seed-head that clings. As the passage progresses, it presents the hero's disappointment as typical of 'human life' (line 153), defined further as 'The disappointment, the anxiety, / Imagination's struggles, far and nigh' (lines 154–5), a free-flowing if arduous couplet that brings in its train the gloss 'All human' (line 156), Keats alighting on an adjective of great significance for him. One thinks, in 'Ode on a Grecian Urn', of the love depicted on the urn, said to be, with calibrated lack of certainty, 'All breathing human passion far above' (line 28).

In the passage from *Endymion*, the reader encounters both 'disappointment' and the conviction that such experiences 'make us feel existence' (line 158). Keats's capacity to 'make us feel existence' shows when in the same book he compares Endymion's posture while he implores the goddess with 'old Deucalion mountained o'er the flood, / Or blind Orion hungry for the morn' (lines 197–8). These painterly lines probably recall Poussin's *Landscape with Orion*, yet appeal to senses other than the visual; the word 'hungry', for instance, imbues the line about Orion with an appetitive urgency. That second line is possibly a source for one of Shelley's most majestic lines in *Prometheus Unbound*, when Ocean tells Apollo, as a renovated universe dawns after Jupiter has fallen, that 'It is the unpastured sea hungering for calm' (III.2.49): a line augustly jubilant at conflict's imminent resolution.

Whereas, in *Endymion*, Keats keeps in play jostling possibilities, Shelley takes us to the centre of a deeply ambiguous experience before allowing his narrative to be haunted by unsureness about the dream's significance. Projection and otherness twine round the use of 'like' in this line and a half, in which dreamed audibility melts into a far-extending psychic inwardness: 'Her voice was like the voice of his own soul / Heard in the calm of thought' (*Alastor*, lines 153–4). Again, the post-dream sense of loss finds expression through images that return thought and feeling back on themselves as reflected vacancies: 'His wan eyes / Gaze on the empty scene as vacantly / As ocean's moon looks on the moon in heaven' (lines 200–2). Rhythm and phrasing convey a state of 'vacant' gazing, even as the wording challenges our expectations; the Poet gazes on the 'empty scene' in the way that the moon's reflection looks at the real moon, which suggests his experience of being emptied out by the dream-vision's vanishing.

Attuned to idealism's longings and failures, Shelley is a poet of becoming, hope and aspiration. 'Ode to the West Wind' is probably his greatest and most expressive shorter poem. The resonant sweep of its five sonnet-sections, each composed of four *terza rima* tercets concluding with a couplet, reflects and inflects the poet's invocation of a natural force ('breath of Autumn's being', line 1) that serves as a secular version of the Holy Spirit and metaphorical equivalent of revolutionary power. At its heart is a poet's crisis about his own capabilities and function, and it is fascinating that Shelley's echoic radar picks up a pivotal moment in Keats's early evocation of poetry's purposes in *Sleep and Poetry*. There, Keats attacks the Popeian tradition in couplets that move with enjambed and exhilarating freshness between description and forward-looking dedication to 'the agonies, the strife / Of human hearts' (lines 124–5). At one stage, he is critical of contemporary poetry that

> feeds upon the burrs
> And thorns of life, forgetting the great end
> Of Poesy, that it should be a friend
> To soothe the cares and lift the thoughts of man. (lines 244–7)

In section IV of 'Ode to the West Wind', at the nadir of his spirits and poetic confidence, Shelley, recognising his exclusion from the natural cycle of leaf, wave and cloud, exclaims, 'I fall upon the thorns of life! I bleed!' (line 54). The echo of Keats is complex in effect, but it acknowledges a shared awareness of all that opposes poetic desire. Keats proposes a role for art that is ennobling in its vision of comfort, but his own poetry affects us more powerfully for wanting poetry to 'soothe the cares and lift the thoughts of man' than for proffering any care-soothing or thought-elevating wisdom.

Shelley in his last poem *The Triumph of Life* recasts Dante's *Commedia* for his own Romantic purposes. Keats's career as a poet effectively comes to a close in 1819 when he tinkers with a Dantescan poem, in his case *The Fall of Hyperion*, a reworking of his earlier Miltonic epic torso, *Hyperion*. Shelley's poem seems fiercely to question the nature of 'life', shaping a poetry of endlessly streaming figures and images as it reworks Dante for an age dominated by the apparent failure of revolutionary ideals: in place of 'the rhyme // Of him who from the lowest depths of Hell / Through every Paradise and through all glory / Love led serene, and who returned to tell // In words of hate and awe the wondrous story / How all things are transfigured, except Love' (lines 471–6), Shelley narrates, in a *terza rima* that frequently impels itself past the barriers posed by tercets, the story of reiterated disfigurations. From the opening lines, which seem both to identify and residually hold back from identifying the sun with 'a spirit hastening to his task / Of glory and of good' (lines 1–2), Shelley deploys the full resources of his mature figurative art to perplex, test, destabilise. That Rousseau, prophet of nature, brings to mind 'an old root which grew / To strange distortion out of the hillside' (lines 182–3) shows that the law of *contra-passo* which rules Dante's *Inferno* is at work in the Romantic poet's vision.

Lucidity coexists with enigma. Visionary events fall on one another's heels with a teasing appearance of logic and causality, but Shelley refuses to supply explanations: Rousseau's line, 'Why this should be my mind can compass not' (line 303) might also be the poem's epigraph. Shelley conveys this inability fully to comprehend in verse of pellucid, harrowing elegance, grace and power. This is most easily demonstrated at the climax of Rousseau's encounter with a bewitching, alluring, somehow dangerous 'shape all light' (line 352) whose 'feet' (line 382)

seemed as they moved, to blot
The thoughts of him who gazed on them, and soon

All that was seemed as if it had been not,
As if the gazer's mind was strewn beneath
Her feet like embers, and she, thought by thought,

Trampled its fires into the dust of death . . . (lines 383–8)

The shape, mesmeric in her dance-like motions, is yet another agent in the poem of the extinction of light, or here 'fires', as that strong stress on 'Trampled' suggests. Rousseau is so hypnotised by the experience that he seems other to himself, referring to himself in the third person, 'The thoughts of him'. Shelley gives us the experience, but denies us any simple allegorical meaning. Hauntingly, the shape is herself supplanted by a new vision, and just as she has appeared to Rousseau like day supplanting the stars, so, when in her turn, she is replaced by a new vision, she appears as a star extinguished by the day. Nothing more graphically demonstrates the art of Shelley's figurative mobility. The shape attracts to herself images that are in conflict in the poem, because the poem's view of her is itself unstable, riddled with doubts.

Keats, in *The Fall of Hyperion*, also stages an encounter with a poet-surrogate and a muse-figure when the poet-dreamer meets Moneta, who, after a scene involving severe rebuke of him as 'a dreaming thing, / A fever of thyself' (1.168–9), softens in her attitude, and allows him to see her face. As with much of the austerely purgatorial verse of *The Fall of Hyperion*, the writing shows the influence of Keats's study of Dante, especially as mediated through Henry Cary's translation, and the pilgrim's initially lacerating re-encounter with Beatrice in the later cantos of the *Purgatorio* is reworked in intensely tragic lines:

> Then saw I a wan face,
> Not pined by human sorrows, but bright blanched
> By an immortal sickness which kills not.
> It works a constant change, which happy death
> Can put no end to; deathwards progressing
> To no death was that visage . . . (I.256–61)

Deeply, even agonisingly personal, the verse also attunes itself, with steadfast attentiveness, to a vision that lies outside the self. As always, Keats's imaginative instinct and gift to us are to make his vision of enduring sorrow one that can be located in a physical body. Moneta's 'immortal sickness which kills not' might be a Christ-like awareness, albeit secularised for a humanist poet; Keats might even be gazing into the countenance of poetry itself. But the poetry embodies its paradoxical suggestion of 'a constant change' in 'a wan face'; this 'constant change' takes place in an eternal now, at once arrested and ongoing. All Keats's efforts to spur poetry into a fuller knowledge of reality find their focus here. The result is a potent sense of poetry's possibilities and burdens. A little later, the poet-dreamer experiences 'A power within me of enormous ken / To see as a god sees' (I.303–4), where the 'power' emerges, in the strongly stressed use of 'see' and 'sees', as a visionary capacity. But in a subsequent passage, as he seeks to restage scenarios from the original *Hyperion*, such a claim seems hollow: 'Without stay or prop / But my own weak mortality', asserts the poet-dreamer, 'I bore / The load of this eternal quietude' (I.388–90). Keats's predilection for states of imagined stillness takes him here to the bourn of a frozen 'quietude'.

Shelley's poetry is remarkable for its swiftness of thought and feeling, and for its readiness to challenge the reader. In the unfinished lyric poem 'The Two Spirits – An Allegory', the poet's art shows in a tough delicacy of conception and execution. The voices of the spirits express opposed yet related feelings about aspiration. The first spirit warns, but his invocations and vowel music express latent admiration for the second spirit's daring: 'O Thou who plumed with strong desire / Would float above the Earth – beware! / A shadow tracks thy flight of fire – / Night is coming!' (lines 1–4). The second spirit spurns the fear-ridden admonitions of the first: 'Within my heart', he asserts, 'is the lamp of love / Which makes night day' (lines 11–12), and the poem reveals how each spirit constructs reality in the light of its own deepest convictions. Its coda – two stanzas introduced by 'Some say' and offering contrasting figurative scenarios – shows Shelley's fascination with the subjective nature of desire, its possible illusoriness and its unquenchable persistence. Subtleties include the use in both stanzas of the word 'shape' (lines 38, 45) for the object of imagining: Shelley suggests that each of the groups intimated by 'Some say' beholds the 'shape' projected by its essential outlook. They include, too, the nuanced suggestions of the close. Hopeful intimations inhere in the 'Sweet whispers' 'heard by the traveller' (line 43) who, on awakening, 'finds night day' (line 48). But 'day' and 'night' generate one another in a dance of tropes, fears and hopes that the poem only briefly brings to a halt. Though 'day' is what is desired, it is at 'night' that 'a shape like his early love doth pass / Upborne by her wild and glittering hair' (lines 45–6). If 'pass' hints at that impermanence contained in the word's use by Rousseau in *The Triumph of Life*, where he pleads achingly with the shape all light that she should not 'Pass away upon the passing stream' (line 399), 'Upborne' arrests the image of the traveller's 'early love' for an instant.

It is characteristic of Shelley to give full weight to the impulses of the moment, yet not always wholly to endorse such impulses. *Julian and Maddalo*, written in a conversational idiom that questions the limits of the conversational mode, is a dialogue poem that thrives on perspectival challenges. Julian, optimistic if 'rather serious', according to the Preface's slyly ironic jab (p. 213), is a lover of the sublime and the beauty of Venice. His evocation of sunset over the lagoon and city, colouring and recomposing mountains and sky, is Turneresque in its delight in metamorphic incandescence; he captures how it seems 'as if the Earth and Sea had been / Dissolved into one lake of fire' (lines 80–1). The Byronic Maddalo, possessed of 'the most consummate genius' but tormented by 'an intense apprehension of the nothingness of human life' (p. 212), provides a counter-voice, offering what for him is a fitter emblem of the human condition: a 'madhouse and its belfry tower' (line 107), which he allegorises as typifying the thwarted nature of 'soul' (line 123) and 'rent heart' (line 126). The fineness of the writing allows for our twin sense that each man's view is partial and that an account of life that ignored either would be deficient.

Matters come to a head, even as they are left in the air, when Julian and Maddalo visit a madman. Trapped in his own isolated cell of self-loathing, desperate survival and pathos-ridden, tortuous self-defence, the Maniac refuses to serve as a test-case; his impassioned words check and challenge the assumptions of his visitors, who find that their 'argument was quite forgot' (line 520) after overhearing an anguished soliloquy in which the psychic hurts suffered by a self-idealising figure subjected to mockery, scorn and detestation by a loved woman are to the fore. Maddalo wins from the encounter the following aphorism about 'suffering' and 'song': 'Most wretched men / Are cradled into poetry by wrong, / They learn in suffering what they teach in song' (lines 544–6). The irony of being 'cradled into poetry by wrong' is typical of Maddalo, but the switchbacks that run between 'learning' and 'teaching', 'suffering' and 'song' place Shelley's more idealistic conceptions of poetry – such as will be articulated in *A Defence of Poetry* – under stress. The poem concludes with a final enigma, the reader shut out from knowledge of 'how / All happened' (lines 616–17) between the Maniac and his lady, as though to suggest our own membership of the 'cold world' (line 617) unable to respond appropriately to the display of distress; as though, too, to imply a final equivocalness about the merits of disclosure.

Yet any pre-Freudian doubt about talking cures cannot disguise Shelley's capacity for dramatic inquiry. *The Cenci* is among the finest plays meant for the theatre of the period. It was not staged, in part because of its shocking subject matter (Beatrice has her tyrannical father, Count Cenci, murdered, after he has incestuously raped her). But it develops a dramatic style remarkable for its economy ('That matter of the murder is hushed up' is its compelling first line), its psychological acuteness (Orsino's analytical 'Such self-anatomy shall teach the will / Dangerous secrets' (2.2, lines 110–11) is an illustration) and its self-reflexive concern with speech and silence. In his lyrical drama, *Prometheus Unbound*, Shelley puts into practice his assertion, in the Preface to the work, that 'Didactic poetry is my abhorrence', as he seeks to work on the imagination of his readers, acquainting them with 'beautiful idealisms of moral excellence' (p. 232). Contesting Aeschylean and Miltonic notions of epic and heroism, Shelley's hero successfully battles against adversaries who, the poem strongly hints, are often internal. Shelley uses an array of arresting and thought-provoking devices in Act 1 to underscore these hints. Corrective allusions to an earlier work are frequent. Satan is the subject of ambivalent admiration in Shelley's Preface, where he explains that he chose Prometheus rather than Satan as his hero because 'The character of Satan engenders in the mind a pernicious casuistry which leads us to weigh his faults with his wrongs, and to excuse the former because the latter exceed all measure' (p. 230). But Satan's scorn for 'Knee-worship yet unpaid' (*Paradise Lost*, Book 5, line 782)[11] to the Messiah finds a resolute yet provisional endorsement in Shelley's text, when Prometheus speaks with disdain of Jupiter's 'slaves, whom thou / Requitest for knee-worship, prayer, and praise . . . With fear and self-contempt and barren hope' (I.5–6, 8). The endorsement is 'provisional' because Prometheus needs to advance beyond disdain if he is to ensure that hope becomes creative rather than barren.

Shelley's allusions can involve larger-scale reconfigurations of earlier ways of reading the world. From Aeschylus's *Oresteia*, he takes the Furies attendant upon remorse and guilt, and makes them voice the doubts that assail Prometheus and liberal intellectuals, especially the fear that 'those who do endure / Deep wrongs for man, and scorn, and chains, but heap / Thousandfold torment on themselves and him' (I.594–6). These Furies seem to voice Prometheus's own self-doubts. They offer exempla of the historical damage caused by well-meaning idealism, both in the form of Christ's teaching that results, against the intentions of its formulator, in wars of religion, and in the Janus-faced phenomenon of the French Revolution. In depicting the trajectory of the latter, a semi-choral lyric turns in the middle of a line from dreams of fraternity to nightmares of terror and a return to absolutist rule. At the same time, the Furies 'can obscure not / The soul which burns within' (I.484–5), and illustrate Shelley's capacity to adapt mythology to his own contemporary concerns.

Other devices used in Act I, and typifying the conceptual and imaginative inventiveness of the lyrical drama, include the strategy of having Prometheus hear his former curse against Jupiter repeated by the tyrant's ghostly Phantasm, called up from an underworld evoked with grave authority. Haunting Earth's evocation of this underworld are ideas of separation and ultimate reunion. Immediately, the speaking of the curse by Jupiter's Phantasm expresses deftly the sense that the unregenerate Prometheus was in some ways the mirror-image of the tyrant against whom he rebelled; moreover, it allows us to hear his defiance as both necessary and partial. More generally, the depiction of a place 'underneath the grave, where do inhabit / The shadows of all forms that think and live / Till death unite them and they part no more; / Dreams and the light imaginings of men, / And all that faith creates or love desires' (I.197–201) speaks resonantly to the play's overall concerns. Plato's language of 'shadows' and 'forms' turns out to serve a turbulent, restlessly ironising yet longing vision, one in which the seemingly slight 'Dreams' and 'light imaginings of men' convert themselves across a line-break into close kin to 'all that faith creates or love desires'. This underworld may be a repository of worn-out ideologies; it may be a kind of *spiritus mundi* from which future possibilities can be born. Certainly the lyrical drama seeks a language for all that 'love desires', even as it stays alert to the 'miscreative' (I.448) as well as the creative powers of mind. That language, as manifest in the 'Life of Life' lyric (II.5, 48–71) addressed to the transfigured Asia, mimics a mistrust of the codified, the final, the fixed; in this urbane, ecstatic lyric, the poem dances angelically on the pin of Asia's non-definability, thriving on paradox in an iridescent display of Romantic and Shelleyan wit:

Fair are others; none beholds thee,
  But thy voice sounds low and tender
Like the fairest, for it folds thee
  From the sight, that liquid splendour,
And all feel, yet see thee never,
As I feel now, lost for ever! (II.5, 60–5)

All, as so often in Shelley, tends towards a condition of lyric encounter between self and idealised other: an encounter that acts, in miniature, as an emblem of the lyrical drama's progressive re-imagining of human potential. This process culminates in the cosmic masque of the final act, in which Shelley gives the renovated universe a poetic voice. He recasts precursor visions, notably Milton's account of 'The chariot of paternal deity'.[12] In a blank verse instinct with a forward-moving yet intricate energy, Asia's sister Panthea describes the earth as 'A sphere, which is as many thousand spheres' (iv.238). Milton's chariot 'forth rushed with whirlwind sound';[13] Shelley's 'multitudinous Orb' (IV.253), the all-inclusive object into which Panthea's vision resolves itself, 'Rushes, with loud and whirlwind harmony' (IV.237). Milton's verb 'rushed' becomes 'Rushes' in Shelley's reworking, a detail illustrative of the present-tense transformation being wrought by the very poem we are reading, the guarantor of whose value is its 'harmony', and whose engagement in the process of subduing reality to its own utopian purposes finds an echo in the way in which the 'Orb' 'Grinds the bright brook into an azure mist / Of elemental subtlety, like light' (IV.254–5). That formulation typifies Shelley's thought and style. A strongly physical verb 'Grinds' results in a barely graspable and highly protean outcome, 'an azure mist / Of elemental subtlety, like light'. The 'elemental subtlety' is itself a near-oxymoron; reduced to the basic forms out of which life is compounded, the subtlety is 'subtle' in the sense of 'pervasive or elusive, out of tenuity' (*OED*). The *OED*'s 'or' is one that Shelley shifts to 'and'; the Orb participates in a poetic 'subtlety' that is both 'pervasive' and 'elusive', but serves to bring together, through 'the intense yet self-conflicting speed' (IV.259) of the writing, past, present and future.

That a transformed future may lie beyond our grasp is conceded at the end of Act III, where the Spirit of the Hour offers a 'self-conflicted' image of aspiration in its glimpse of 'The loftiest star of unascended Heaven, / Pinnacled dim in the intense inane' (III.4.203–4). 'Unascended' is a typical negative epithet.[14] Here the device places 'The loftiest star' within the reach of imagined ascensions, before the last line, quickened by its short 'i' sounds, reminds us of its inaccessibility in an 'intense inane', where the Latinate noun 'inane' refers to the empty void of space. Elsewhere, the final two acts balance jubilation and a more sobered recognition of 'sad reality', to use Shelley's phrase from his dedicatory letter to Hunt at the head of *The Cenci* (p. 314). So, for example, the Spirit of the Hour reports that, in the transformed world,

> None talked that common, false, cold, hollow talk
> Which makes the heart deny the *yes* it breathes,
> Yet question that unmeant hypocrisy
> With such a self-mistrust as has no name. (III.4.149–52)

The writing illuminates vividly the falsity of everyday communication, even as it announces the end of 'unmeant hypocrisy', a phrase which may derive from Coleridge's account of a father's 'words of unmeant bitterness' in the Conclusion to Part II of *Christabel*.[15] Shelley's ability to understand such 'self-mistrust' from the inside shows in his words and even his sounds: from the disappointment registered in the first line's dispiriting procession of adjectives and its slumped repetition of 'talked' and 'talk', to the finely adjusting connections made through variations on a 'common' sound in '*yes*', 'question', 'unmeant' and, most pointedly, 'self'.

Alert to the utopian status of its discourse, *Prometheus Unbound* closes with Demogorgon's advice to the assembled *dramatis personae* about what to do if tyranny returns, advice that is also an injunction to Shelley's contemporary readership in the present. All must 'hope, till Hope creates / From its own wreck the thing it contemplates' (IV.573–4), where rhyme crystallises our grasp of a vertiginously self-reflexive process by which Hope gazes at its own wreck, and in so doing reaffirms its capacity to generate fresh ideals. Yet in *Adonais*, Shelley's elegy for Keats, hope is itself a source of danger towards the close: in stanza 47 the poet warns an addressee virtually indistinguishable from himself to 'keep thy heart light lest it make thee sink / When hope has kindled hope, and lured thee to the brink' (lines 422–3). Shelley uses the Spenserian stanza's alexandrine to enact the lure of the 'brink'.

Indeed, the final third of his elegy engages in continual brinkmanship as, driven by the desire to reject a poetry-hating culture held responsible for Adonais's death, Shelley seeks answers to his desolate questions in stanza 21: 'Whence are we, and why are we? of what scene / The actors or spectators?' (lines 184–5). These lines, in which the very rhythm's initial departure from an iambic norm mimes a sense of crisis, find a tumult of answers in the conclusion. Shelley here rejects 'the contagion of the world's slow stain' (line 356) and, arguably if implicitly, his this-worldly political hopes, and sets his gaze on a variety of brilliantly evoked and yet seemingly fictive absolutes, all associated with Adonais's outsoaring of 'the shadow of our night' (line 352): the 'One' (line 460), 'the white radiance of Eternity' (line 463) and, finally, 'the abode where the Eternal are' (line 495). And yet, for all the drive towards transcendence, the poem does not wholly leave this world behind. The 'white radiance of Eternity' does not annul the counter-attractions of the 'Life' which, 'like a dome of many-coloured glass, / Stains' (lines 462–3) it. Shelley speaks as much of transforming as of transcending life, invoking a 'sustaining Love' (line 481) at work in the 'web of being' (line 482), and depicts himself at the end as a voyager, 'borne darkly, fearfully, afar' (line 492). The stance is an appropriate one for a poet fascinated by process and an imaginative 'going out of our own nature' (*A Defence of Poetry*, p. 682).

In his major poems, many of which are collected in his 1820 volume, Keats explores vividly yet vigilantly a series of interrelated concerns, including the tensions between imagination and reality, enchantment and disillusion, and sensations and thought. His letters are often full of notions that are prophetic of later thematic obsessions in the poetry. One such idea is the 1817 pronouncement: 'What the imagination seizes as Beauty must be truth – whether it existed before or not', a declaration whose seeming whole-hearted fervour is qualified by the subsequent expression, in the same letter, of admiration for 'a complex Mind – one that is imaginative and at the same time careful of its fruits – who would exist partly on sensation partly on thought' (*LettersJK*, I.184, 186). The poetry both trusts in 'imagination' and seeks to preside over the emergence within itself of 'a complex Mind'.

'Imagination's struggles', to borrow an already quoted phrase from *Endymion* (II.155), are sometimes explicitly dramatised in Keats's work, sometime implicitly. Of the major narrative poems, *The Eve of St Agnes* is an example of the latter, *Isabella* an example of the former. *Isabella*, using a variously melodic and jaunty *ottava rima* to retell a story from Boccaccio, shuttles between cinematic close-ups and defamiliarising attention to its status as narrative. In stanza 47, for example, the heroine digs up the body of her murdered lover, Lorenzo, 'nor stayed her care, / But to throw back at times her veiling hair' (lines 375–6), where her busy endeavour, in all its frantic pathos, is caught in a touchingly quotidian gesture.[16] Two stanzas later, the narrator seems out of sorts with the story he is telling, ruefully asking 'wherefore all this wormy circumstance' (line 385), and expressing a mock-longing for 'the gentleness of old romance' (line 387). The effect is 'complex', reflective of the 'Mind' at work in the poem. In one way, we are invited to lose ourselves in 'romance', to accept its conventions as having living contact with central experiences of love and loss; in another way, we are reminded that 'romance' is an artifice. But in a third way, the narrative interpolations underscore the fact that Keats is unable to sustain the original 'music' (line 392) of romance, which must compete with the strain of realism evident in 'wormy circumstance' and, more profoundly, in the simultaneously tender and dry-eyed depiction of Isabella's fetishistic, deranged obsession with the pot of basil in which she hides Lorenzo's skull.

The Eve of St Agnes brings a different kind of modernising consciousness to bear on the conventions of romance. Here the narrator remains scrupulously withdrawn from proceedings as, in richly slow-paced Spenserian stanzas, Keats lavishes the resources of his verbal alchemy on the tale of Madeline dreaming of her lover, the appearance of Porphyro in her bedroom, their lovemaking and their departure from the castle. Backdrops sumptuously take over the poem's foreground, and questions of individual motive retire in the face of conjurations of perennial contraries: cold and warmth; secular love and religion; youth and age; sex and death. Keats breathes a creaturely kinship into his accounts of the 'hare' that 'limped trembling through the frozen grass' (line 3), where the rhythm limps in empathetic accord; of the coldly glamorous sound of 'The silver, snarling trumpets' (line 31) greeting the 'argent revelry' (line 37); of Porphyro, struck by 'a thought' that 'came like a full-blown rose, / Flushing his brow' (line 136–7); of 'A casement high and triple-arched' (line 208); and of Madeline 'trembling in her soft and chilly nest' (line 235). Despite critical attempts to present Madeline as a hoodwinked dreamer or Porphyro as a voyeuristic date-rapist, the poem in its published version locates its deepest sources of interest elsewhere: in the idea that dream and reality might converge, as is suggested by the near-but-not-quite mawkish and suggestive phrase 'Into her dream he entered' (line 320) to describe the lovemaking, and in the awareness that the poem coaxing us into acceptance of such a convergence is only a poem, a fiction. This awareness shows, in particular, in the transition from the present tense of 'The key turns, and the door upon its hinges groans' (line 369) as the lovers creep out of the castle, to the final stanza's immediate and haunting concession that 'ages long ago, / These lovers fled away into the storm' (lines 370–1).

Keats himself, in some proposed coarsening revisions, rejected by his publishers, seemed to have second thoughts about the nature of the poem, and *Lamia* is the narrative poem in which qualifying doubts about the imagination assume their most reductively ironic form in his work. Drydenesque couplets mediate a breezy knowingness, as when Hermes's masculine self-love is punctured by and after the turn of a line: 'Ah, what a world of love was at her feet! / So Hermes thought' (I.21–2). Lamia receives a set-piece description that turns her into a dazzlingly oxymoronic menagerie, 'Striped like a zebra, freckled like a pard' (I.49), the very epitome of enigma who initially reduces the narrator to a state of multiple-choice bewilderment: 'some penanced lady elf, / Some demon's mistress, or the demon's self' (I.55–6). But, as the story progresses, Keats's sympathies seem covertly to proclaim themselves for her. The falling-in-love of Lamia and Lycius is precisely that: a fall – and yet the long trajectory of narrative lyricism that describes it traces its path through notes other than, though as well as, ironic detachment at the young man's surrender to delusion. By the poem's close, when Apollonius's pitiless stare uncovers the snake beneath the skin, Keats appears to set head and heart in irremediable conflict: reason cannot but applaud the philosopher's determination to ward off the perils of seductive enchantment, but the heart may sense that a stake has been driven by Keats through one of his deepest convictions. In this poem, what the imagination seizes as beauty turns out to have 'charms' that 'fly / At the mere touch of cold philosophy' (II.229–30), even if Lamia resists being regarded as solely hollow and delusory, any more than the Belle Dame of Keats's limpid, etymologically close-grained, and enigmatic ballad will wholly yield up a simple secret about the menace of enchantment; it is, after all, in a 'dream' (line 35) that the 'knight-at arms' (line 1) is warned of an enthralment that, on closer inspection, seems inseparable from poetic imagination.

Keats's Odes owe much of their power to their treatment of the poet's struggle towards a 'complex Mind' at once aware of and inextricable from the poetry's associative imaginative processes. Characteristic of the unpredictable and rich transitions made by the poems is the movement in the final stanza of 'Ode on Grecian Urn', where the writing begins by capturing disillusion with the artwork, now seen as merely an 'Attic shape' (line 41) and provoking the cry, 'Cold pastoral!' (line 45), before it signs a truce of sorts with the Urn, finally a 'friend to man' (line 48). This truce concedes nothing to mere aestheticism ('old age shall', Keats says with emphasis, 'this generation waste', line 46), but it tolerantly permits art's message of an identification between Beauty and Truth to proclaim itself. Again, in stanza VII of 'Ode to a Nightingale', Keats seems to be intent on praising the symbolic bird's freedom from mortality, but, as he traces its imagined audiences – from those in 'ancient days' (line 64), to 'the sad heart of Ruth' (line 66), to dwellers behind 'magic casements' (line 69) – he reminds us, with intensified force, of the permanence of sorrow and of the human longing to escape it. Ruth, presented as 'sick for home' (line 69), is turned by phrasing of great gestural resonance into an archetype of homelessness. Where 'home' might be found is a question the poem merely raises: 'fairy lands forlorn' (line 70) offer only a flickering respite from the 'sole self' (line 72), while 'The fancy cannot cheat so well / As she is famed to do, deceiving elf' (lines 73–4). The very poverty of the rhyme between 'self' and 'elf' serves to expose 'fancy's' capacity to 'cheat'. Yet whether 'fancy' has simply flattered to deceive is an open question, since it has permitted the imaginative voyage of the poem. Its stanzas, derived from Keats's experimentation with the sonnet, are so many rooms in what is as near to a 'home' – so the poem's final interrogations concede – as the poet is likely to find.

The Odes as a group take their point of departure from and travel a long way beyond the heady discovery of 'some untrodden region of my mind' (line 51) that the final stanza of 'Ode to Psyche' proclaims. That stanza may represent the high point of the Odes' affirmations about the 'gardener Fancy' (line 62), and yet, for all its delight in unrestricted invention, it is not without misgivings about 'shadowy thought' (line 65). The adjective takes a marked emphasis and sends us back, by contrast, to the less self-reflexive imaginative activity described in the poem's opening when the poet 'wandered in a forest thoughtlessly' (line 7). The poem describes a journey from 'thoughtless' reverie, a state in which mythology still has the force of actual experience, to a reworking of myth through 'thought', in which Keats's true subject becomes his mind. So, the final stanza, for all its descriptive details, describes a mindscape. Yet the fact that 'those dark-clustered trees' (line 54) seem to forget that they are metaphors of thought, and send us back to a real landscape, supplies an implicit recognition on Keats's part that triumphs of poetic inwardness come at a high cost. This recognition explains the fine movement of feeling at the close, when the poem imagines 'a casement ope at night, / To let the warm Love in!' (lines 65–6). Cupid is readmitted, but also 'Love'; the poem opens its own casement as though to ward off the imagination's self-asphyxiation.

What makes the Odes remarkable as poems is Keats's ability to dramatise contentions of feeling and thought, all the developments described by Douglas Bush as the poetry's 'elevations and depressions and contradictions'.[17] 'Ode on Melancholy' turns these 'contradictions' into an ethos and a poetic. Its three compact stanzas mix the zestfully jaunty and the exuberantly near-tragic as they recommend no dulling of 'the wakeful anguish of the soul' (line 10), a phrase all the more memorably potent for rhyming with the comparatively flippant 'downy owl' (line 7), symbol of a rejected gothic morbidity. The final figurative scenario, in which an imagined quester finds the 'sovran shrine' (line 26) of Melancholy, 'Veiled' (line 26) as though she were her own high priestess, compounds tones and mimes its difficult blend of discovery and succumbing through an expressive syntax.[18] Only the person who 'Can burst Joy's grape against his palate fine' (line 28) will see Melancholy's 'shrine', yet this active pursuit of experience will result in his passive submission, when he is 'among her cloudy trophies hung' (line 30).

In 'To Autumn', Keats affectingly stills but he does not erase the expression of inner drama. The poem avoids the first person or direct reflections on the human condition. Quietly hinted connections between the natural and the human occur, as when we are told of bees who are beguiled into thinking 'warm days will never cease' (line 10), as that misleading warmth spills over into the plenitude- and loss-laden extra stanzaic line that Keats uses in this ode. Keats distils a wealth of suggestions through a way of reporting on the natural that does not force points. So, at the very close, 'gathering swallows twitter in the skies' (line 33); the swallows are not harbingers of doom, merely birds 'gathering' for their annual migration in 'skies' that soften the verb 'dies' (line 29) with which they rhyme. At the same time a sense of temporality, even mortality, laps round the line, giving it a braced yet not inhumanly suppressed pathos. Keats brings to his absorption in a transitional season a new capacity to 'Think of the earth' (*The Fall of Hyperion*, I.169), in Moneta's phrase. The result is a poem as finely balanced as any in the language between the impulse to celebrate or elegise, and the knowledge of the need to accept, even to acquiesce in, what it means to dwell in the natural world as any. When Shelley thinks of the earth in the figures and metaphysics of 'Mont Blanc', he questions, at the poem's close, what meanings would attach to it without the 'human mind's imaginings' (line 143), the final word rhyming and vying with 'things' (line 139). But if Shelley's 'imaginings' in his near-ode are typically metapoetic, Keats's in 'To Autumn' are no less powerful for their intent reticence.[19]

Notes

1. Quoted from *Tennyson's Poetry*, ed. Robert W. Hill Jr., second edition (New York: Norton, 1999), p. 582.
2. *The Letters of John Keats 1814–1821*, ed. Hyder E. Rollins, 2 vols. (Cambridge, MA: Harvard University Press, 1958), vol. II, p. 213; hereafter *LettersJK*.

3. 'To a Skylark', lines 31–2. Shelley's poetry and prose are quoted from *Percy Bysshe Shelley: The Major Works*, ed. Zachary Leader and Michael O'Neill (Oxford: Oxford University Press, 2003). See also 'Hymn to Intellectual Beauty' for a use of simile that concedes the difficulty of definition (as in stanza 1), but also deepens the poem's experience, as in stanza 3, where the invocation of 'Thy light alone' (line 32) points up the poet's underlying anxieties and his visionary excitement through its association with images such as 'mist o'er mountains driven' (line 32). For further discussion, see Judith Chernaik, *The Lyrics of Shelley* (Cleveland, OH and London: The Press of Case Western Reserve University, 1972).
4. *The Eve of St Agnes*, line 216. Keats's poetry is quoted from *The Poems of John Keats*, ed. Miriam Allott (London: Longman, 1970).
5. A. C. Bradley, *Oxford Lectures on Poetry*, intro. M. R. Ridley (1909; London: Macmillan, 1965), p. 241. See also ch. 3 of Mark Sandy, *Poetics of Form and Self in Keats and Shelley: Nietzschean Subjectivity and Genre* (Aldershot: Ashgate, 2005).
6. Wordsworth and Coleridge are quoted from Michael O'Neill and Charles Mahoney (eds.), *Romantic Poetry: An Annotated Anthology* (Malden, MA: Blackwell, 2007).
7. Douglas Bush, *John Keats: His Life and Writings* (London: Weidenfeld and Nicolson, 1966), p. 57.
8. *The Letters of Percy Bysshe Shelley*, ed. F. L. Jones (Oxford: Clarendon Press, 1964), vol. II, p. 220.
9. Quoted in *The Poems of John Keats*, ed. Allott, p. 130.
10. *Ibid.*, p. 130.
11. Quoted from *The Poems of John Milton*, ed. John Carey and Alastair Fowler (London: Longmans, 1968). All further Milton quotations are from this edition.
12. *Paradise Lost*, Book 6, line 750.
13. *Ibid.*, line 749.
14. See Timothy Webb, 'The Unascended Heaven: Negatives in *Prometheus Unbound*', in *Shelley Revalued*, ed. Kelvin Everest (Leicester: Leicester University Press, 1983), pp. 37–62.
15. Line 653, in O'Neill and Mahoney (eds.), *Romantic Poetry*.
16. See John Jones, *John Keats's Dream of Truth* (London: Chatto, 1969), p. 19.
17. Bush, *John Keats*, p. 136.
18. See Helen Vendler, *The Odes of John Keats* (Cambridge, MA: Harvard University Press, 1983), p. 179.
19. For further discussion of 'Mont Blanc', see William Keach, *Shelley's Style* (New York: Methuen, 1984).

Chapter 29

Third-generation Romantic poetry: Beddoes, Clare, Darley, Hemans, Landon

MICHAEL BRADSHAW

It is a melancholy thought that poets of the 1820s and 1830s have often been defined by what they were not, by what they almost were, but failed to be. Keats died in 1821, Percy Shelley in 1822 and Byron in 1824 – and what then? Well, then of course there was a gap, before the early work of Tennyson. Arnold's image of 'Wandering between two worlds, one dead, / The other powerless to be born' now seems perfect for the strained, stranded sensibilities of a poet like George Darley.[1] The poets themselves could sometimes be gloomy about the prospects for their generation:

> The disappearance of Shelley from the world seems, like the tropical setting of that luminary (*aside*, I hate that word) to which his poetical genius alone can be compared with reference to the companions of his day, to have been followed by instant darkness and owl-season: whether the vociferous Darley is to be the comet, or tender, fullfaced L. E. L. the milk-and watery moon of our darkness, are questions for the astrologers: if I were the literary weather-guesser for 1825 I would safely prognosticate fog, rain, blight in due succession for it's [*sic*] dullard months.[2]

Beddoes is a harsh judge of the work of nearly all his contemporaries, and he does not spare himself. And yet, leaving England in 1825 for a lifetime of wandering in Europe, he gradually lost his feel for the contemporary literary scene, continuing to imagine English poetry in this post-Shelleyan limbo of the early 1820s, and mourning the absence of revolutionary prophecy well into the reign of Victoria. Beddoes always had a talent for anachronism. Yet his letters somehow make a 'true' epitaph for his generation, as the sensuous idioms of Romanticism reverberated into modernity. It is true that if this generation continues to be defined only against greater neighbours, it will continue to be found wanting – depressive and anxious in comparison with the exuberance of the Romantic generations who preceded, narrow and introspective in comparison with the fully formed Victorians who followed.

Ironically, one of the defining features that does make the Romantic third generation a coherent grouping is the fact that it is beset by problems of classification. The accepted, too-comfortable formula of a 'transitional' phase between 'Romantic' and 'Victorian' has been rightly questioned by recent scholarship, which draws attention to the suspicious tidiness of thinking which can smooth over chronological complications, the conservative periodisation that expects to find its assumptions confirmed rather than challenged by rereading.[3] In Hemans's and Darley's poetry, for instance, there is much of the moralism and lyrical smoothness of Victorian post-Romantic styling, and yet also a confident engagement with themes of nationality that runs counter to their twentieth-century reputations for domesticity and sentiment.

And yet, as Beddoes demonstrates, 1820s and 1830s poetry was affected by literary belatedness, the poets' awareness of suffering in comparison with their over-shadowing forebears, in the style made famous by Harold Bloom's psychoanalytic myth of influence. They sometimes convey a sense of watching a modern canon take shape and being excluded from it, a sense of awkwardness and failure to fit in. This finds expression in the grotesque comedy with which Beddoes cocks a snook at the smooth niceties of the poetry establishment, as if he wouldn't want to be in their club anyway:

DUKE And what's your tune?
...
ISBRAND What's the lobster's tune when he is boiled?
I hate your ballads that are made to come
Round like a squirrel's cage, and round again.
We nightingales sing boldly from our hearts:
So listen to us ... (*Death's Jest-Book*, III.iii, lines 310–20)

But the poetry of exclusion is tragic as well as comic, having perhaps its strongest expression in John Clare's meditations on the social and economic class issues that kept him always at one remove from the poetic academy, even in his days as a celebrated writer for a fashionable London publishing house. For a time, following the publication of his first collection in 1820, Clare attracted more notice than Keats, his stable-mate with Taylor and Hessey; but when the two poets' posthumous reputations were fashioned in Victorian reading and writing, it was Keats who rose, as Clare sank.

Imaginative themes such as exclusion, marginality and defeat may have deterred some generations of readers and critics, but in the twenty-first century should be found much more congenial, with our postmodern attraction to misfits and margins. One of the reasons why it is important that we reread poets like Beddoes, Clare, Darley, Hemans and Landon is that they interrogate the comfortable assumptions of the Romantic; they make visible the frustrations that may be concealed by the ecstatic apocalypse of Romantic greatness. These poets still require and attract interventions from contemporary scholarship interested in re-evaluating the assumptions of the 'Romantic', and should be considered especially useful if they help us to understand its boundaries. Related to this sense of exclusion is a highly developed and self-conscious literariness. These later poets followed the Keats–Shelley generation's rediscovery of disciplined formal experimentation into an increasing mellifluousness – a mannered sweetness, with an underswell of political anxiety about the role and social relevance of the poet. Their poetic careers were shaped by the keenly felt pressures of an increasingly professionalised literary marketplace. . . Beddoes's career was impelled by early acclaim which he avidly watched unfold in the pages of *Blackwood's* and *The London Magazine*, but which he could never replicate with his mature writing. Clare became well known in a London literary scene that both venerated and patronised him as 'peasant poet', a designation which he was never able to escape. Darley's career was shaped by an expatriate's enthusiasm for literary London and his agonising failure to convert a potential for poetic fame into its fulfilment, often venting his frustration with a ruthless reviewer's pen. On the other hand, Hemans and Landon (as 'L. E. L.'), made expert use of ephemeral periodical genres to build flourishing commercial publishing careers and personal celebrity – in Hemans's case, to the eventual detriment of her reputation as a serious writer (in the twentieth century, at least), and in Landon's case, at the cost of vicious slander and personal tragedy.

In their critical reception, these poets have been affected by the definition of literary periods and categories. The general category of Romanticism has proved to be both enduring and limiting as a way of accounting for the flamboyant macabre of Beddoes, or the impassioned natural observation of Clare. Modern criticism of Beddoes has been characterised by its attempts to draw the poet towards major critical paradigms, and although Romanticism is still the most persistent of these – in contradistinction to gothic, say, or proto-Modernism – it still seems a very partial way of defining the lurid intensity of his writing;[4] and Beddoes's use of dramatic form also sidelined him from the lyrical and epic agenda of Romantic verse, until the theatrical legacy of Romanticism began to be reclaimed and re-asserted in the 1990s. John Clare's whole writing career and posthumous reputation also make us aware of the discontents of Romanticism, in the class-based assumptions about poetic authorship that excluded him from the canonical mainstream for so long; as Roger Sales argues, 'Clare has not been well served...by literary histories that privilege Romanticism as the key term, particularly Wordsworthian or visionary Romanticism.'[5] Feminist re-appraisals of Romanticism by Anne K. Mellor, Anne Janowitz, Stuart Curran and others also assert that this whole aesthetic/ideological category has been based on assumptions that can be characterised as masculine. Darley too struggles against his appointed home in literary periodisation, in terms of a lyricism that apparently refuses to play along to the appropriate philosophical tune of Wordsworth or Keats.

Related to their literary and canonical self-consciousness is a consistent attraction to mortality, morbidity and melancholy among 'third-generation Romantic' poets. Beddoes and Darley, painfully aware of their belated relationship with great forebears and of their potential 'minor' status, gave expression to the period of depression and deflation – political and personal – that seemed to follow the Romantic ecstasy of the recent past. Beddoes is well known for his consistent, highly evolved lifelong obsession with death. 'Death' in Beddoes's poetry and drama has so many moods and manifestations that it is hardly proper to call it a theme at all, but more the intellectual and aesthetic universe in which Beddoes always operates. Clare's confession of anguished mental states, not by any sensible criteria 'mad' poetry, but often shockingly calm and rational, represents an alienated and isolated self who can find the prospect of final disappearance enticing and seductive.

Long considered a morbid misfit on the margins of late Romanticism, Thomas Lovell Beddoes (1803–49) has nevertheless fascinated many generations of readers, with his disturbingly beautiful poetry of death, and his trademark grotesque comedy. But in recent years, Beddoes's writing – and his Renaissance-styled revenge tragedy *Death's Jest-Book* in particular – has attracted international scholarly attention, and he is now regarded as a major Romantic writer. After achieving early acclaim as a dramatist, Beddoes travelled to Göttingen to study medicine in 1825, and lived most of the rest of his life in the German states and in Switzerland, where he was as committed to radical political causes and to medical science as he was to writing verse dramas.[6] It is thought that Beddoes was gay, and that this was probably an important aspect of his decision to live on the Continent; theories of sexuality have sometimes influenced the interpretation of his writings, especially in their alienated spectral eroticism and plots based on male friendship.

As an undergraduate student Beddoes published *The Improvisatore* (1821), a series of verse horror stories held together in a loose narrative; growing quickly as a poet, and embarrassed by this juvenile poem, Beddoes attempted to track down and destroy all remaining copies. Shortly after this, he published *The Brides' Tragedy* (1822), a sporadically brilliant pastiche Renaissance tragedy about a young aristocrat who murders his secret bride in order to make an advantageous marriage, and becomes consumed by evil: *The Brides' Tragedy* attracted some highly complimentary reviews, including one by Darley in *The London Magazine*: the play seemed likely to make Beddoes's reputation, and – clearly excited by the praise he was winning – Beddoes began work on several new tragedies in 1823–4. Then he travelled to Germany to study medicine, and never published another book in his lifetime.

Death's Jest-Book, Beddoes's signature work, was substantially written between his arrival in Germany in the summer of 1825 and late 1828, when he sent a draft to his friends in England; their apparently negative reaction to this most intense and uncompromising of great works, caused Beddoes to delay publication indefinitely and revise the work over most of the rest of his life. Following Beddoes's suicide in Basel in 1849, Thomas Forbes Kelsall, the poet's friend and literary executor, had *Death's Jest-Book* published in 1850. Huge, sprawling and digressive, inexhaustibly preoccupied with treachery, murder, death and decay, resurrection and haunting, *Death's Jest-Book* is a work that may well have alienated its earliest readers. Beddoes modelled it on the Shakespearean five-act tragedy in blank verse, which was actually quite a conventional decision in the 1820s, but embellished this form with a large number of lyrics, especially in the later revised versions. Beddoes conjured up the inception of his great work for his friend Bryan Waller Procter in a verse letter: taking time out from his medical studies ('Freed from the slavery of my ruling spright / Anatomy the grim'), he says, he has been devoting the stolen nocturnal hours to a grandiose new satirical project:

In it Despair has married wildest Mirth
And to their wedding-banquet all the earth
Is bade to bring its enmities and loves
Triumphs and horrors. . .

. . .

But he who fills the cups and makes the jest
Pipes to the dancers, is the fool o' the feast.
Who's he? I've dug him up and decked him trim
And made a mock, a fool, a slave of him
Who was the planet's tyrant: dotard Death. . .

. . .

For death is more 'a jest' than Life: you see
Contempt grows quick from familiarity.
I owe this wisdom to Anatomy. . .[7]

This 'jest-book' is to be the literary counterpart to a philosophical mission to defeat the supremacy of death over the human, located in the scientific study of anatomy; and the joke of course backfires. Thus the identity of Fool, symbolised by the jester's coxcomb, is passed around between a professional clown, a revenger and political over-reacher, a risen ghost and Death itself. The play is set in Silesia in the fourteenth century, and concerns two brothers – the noble knight Wolfram and the revenger Isbrand, who has disguised himself as a fool – and their feud with the corrupt duke, Melveric. Wolfram's forgiveness of and friendship with Melveric is repaid with treachery when the duke murders him just after he has saved his life on a crusade. Wolfram is resurrected by a necromancer, and haunts the duke for the rest of the action. Isbrand leads a successful coup against Melveric, only to replace him as a new tyrant ripe for overthrow.

Death's Jest-Book was Beddoes's culminating work, into which he not only fitted most of his new writings, but also poured a back-catalogue of recycled matter from earlier texts, such as 'Dream of Dying', a blank-verse fragment originally written for inclusion in one of Beddoes's plays-in-progress around 1823:

> Shivering in fever, weak, and parched to sand,
> My ears, those entrances of word-dressed thoughts,
> My pictured eyes, and my assuring touch,
> Fell from me, and my body turned me forth
> From its beloved abode: then was I dead;
> And in my grave beside my corpse I sat,
> In vain attempting to return: meantime
> There came the untimely spectres of two babes,
> And played in my abandoned body's ruins;
> They went away; and, one by one, by snakes
> My limbs were swallowed; and, at last, I sat
> With only one, blue-eyed, curled round my ribs,
> Eating the last remainder of my heart,
> And hissing to himself. O sleep, thou fiend!
> Thou blackness of the night! how sad and frightful
> Are these thy dreams! (lines 1–16)

The passage is reworked and shortened to make a speech for the resurrected Wolfram in the final scene of *Death's Jest-Book* (v.iv, lines 198–202), an example of Beddoes's fragmenting method of composition, cannibalising drafts of earlier works. The speaker is both sardonic and touchingly melancholy on his post-mortem fate, as he considers the disintegration of the subject. Beddoes uses blank verse here as a site for philosophical inquiry into the human being – separating soul as well as body from the speaking self, combining this with a provocative mixture of anatomical science and gothic horror. The political and supernatural plots of *Death's Jest-Book* provided Beddoes with ample opportunity to experiment with verse drama as a medium for this kind of ironically defended philosophical inquiry.

As sudden thunder
  Pierces night;
As magic wonder,
  Mad affright
Rives asunder
  Men's delight:
Our ghost, our corpse and we
  Rise to be

As flies the lizard
  Serpent fell;
As goblin vizard,
  At the spell
Of pale wizard,
  Sinks to hell;
Our life, our laugh, our lay.
  Pass away.

As wake the morning
  Trumpets bright;
As snowdrop, scorning
  Winter's might,
Rises warning
  Like a sprite:
The buried, dead and slain
  Rise again. (I.iv, lines 204–27, 'γ' text)[8]

This haunting lyric was inserted into the expanded first act. Beddoes's gift for smooth and arresting lyrical music, familiar to many readers from the celebrated anthology piece 'Dream Pedlary', is at its most complex when he places a lyric, as here, in a very exact dramatic context: on the murder of Wolfram, disembodied voices 'from the waters' (line 203) warn the duke that his wronged blood-brother will return, and that debts may be paid from beyond the grave. By expanding the *Jest-Book* as a psychic drama of 'voices' as well as characters, Beddoes can be seen to adapt the influence of his poetic hero Percy Shelley.[9] Yet recent assessments of the *Jest-Book* have moved decisively away from an emphasis on the psychic, the mental and the subjective, and resituated

Beddoes in the theatre history of the Romantic age: having often been assumed unperformable – a 'closet drama' or dramatic poem – the *Jest-Book* is now once again a *play*, and interpreted in ways that accept much more literally the author's interest in stage performance.[10]

As the duke exclaims in horror when confronted with the accusing ghost of the friend he has murdered, 'Then there is rebellion / Against all kings, even Death' (III.iii, lines 688–9): the play turns on this analogy between supernatural resurrection and political insurrection, and it is important to be aware of Beddoes's reimagining of the French Revolution within the carefully woven web of his anachronistic medievalesque plot.

> A king's a man, and I will be no man
> Unless I am a king. Why, where's the difference?
> Throne steps divide us: they're soon climbed perhaps:
> I have a bit of FIAT in my soul,
> And can myself create my little world.
>
> . . .
>
> How I despise
> All you men of mere muscle! It was ever
> My study to find out a way to godhead,
> And on reflection soon I found that first
> I was but half created; that a power
> Was wanting in my soul to be its soul,
> And this was mine to make. . . (V.i, lines 35–52)

Beddoes uses the revenge tragedy form to interrogate the glory and disgrace of the Revolution, experimenting with the fate of the politician Isbrand, here glimpsed as Renaissance-style over-reacher dragged into the libertarian nineteenth century, a mixture of Tamburlaine, Napoleon, radical biological scientist and Nietzschean superman. The will to political power appears as a revolving cycle of solipsism and atrocity.

One of the things this *Jest-Book* laughs at is the literary culture that, Frankenstein-like, both created and rejected it. Beddoes also called it 'my unhappy devil of a tragedy';[11] in the twenty-first century, its power to bedevil and provoke is still formidable.

John Clare (1793–1864) was born, lived, worked, loved and wrote in the village of Helpston, Northamptonshire; another man of his class and circumstances might well have died there too. Clare began working as an agricultural labourer while still a boy.[12] Poetry took him away from his native environment, physically in his journeys to visit London publishers, and in a sense mentally too, in opening a subtle but irreparable distance between

Clare's new life of literature and the rural oral culture which had nurtured him and those close to him – as he records in the January eclogue of the *The Shepherd's Calendar*:

> The fairey feats that once prevald
> Told to delight & never faild
> Were are they now their fears & sighs
> & tears from founts of happy eyes
> Breathless suspense & all their crew
> To what wild dwelling have they flew
> I read in books but find them not
> For poesy hath its youth forgot
> I hear them told to children still
> But fear near numbs my spirit chill
> I still see faces pale wi dread
> While mine coud laugh at what is said (lines 247–58)[13]

The passage expresses a nostalgic longing not only for an edenic childhood, but also for the unity of imagination and speech from which the self-conscious world of print and fame has separated him. This poem also illustrates one of the complications of reading Clare in the twentieth and twenty-first centuries, for here it has been edited with fidelity to the manuscript. Alternative methodologies exist for editing Clare's texts. A purist approach preserves the inviolate manuscript at all cost, and therefore strips away the editorial interventions of Clare's early editors, who had cleansed the syntax, spelling and dialect usage, and inserted conventional punctuation. Other practices prefer to leave in place much of this editorial regularisation, as more consistent with the poems' original publications, and also with Clare's expectations for a printed text. As Jonathan Bate summarises: 'Is justice done to Clare by the presentation of his manuscripts in the raw, free from the shackles of prescriptive grammar? Or does the reproduction of their idiosyncrasies unintentionally perpetuate the image of him as a semi-literate primitive, an eternal child?'[14] The tendency in recent editions of Clare is to restore most of the unevenness of the poet's original drafts, even though it is also acknowledged that Clare did not necessarily envisage them being printed in this form, being well used to the interventions of copy-editors. The quotations discussed here are taken from original-spelling editions of Clare's work. One reason for prizing the unevenness of Clare's verse is that it seems to catch the immediacy of his response to the natural world; as in this often-quoted moment from 'The Mores', when a rare incidence of punctuation seems almost to mimic the intrusive appearance of the fences and signs of ownership:

On paths to freedom and to childhood dear
A board sticks up to notice 'no road here'
And on the tree with ivy overhung
The hated sign by vulgar taste is hung (lines 69–72)[15]

The poem makes a stand against those who would arrogantly interrupt the freedom of living creatures to roam, the pen of the poet to represent them, the eye and ear of the reader to respond and empathise. It was John Barrell who established the importance of the 'agricultural revolution' and the Enclosure Acts to Clare's writing; all interpretation of Clare's poetry which finds connections between its stylistic qualities and a historically specific view of Clare's relationship with the land he worked on is following Barrell's lead.[16] 'The Mores' is one of the most celebrated 'Enclosure elegies', and a good example of what Hugh Haughton calls Clare's 'open field poetics':[17] the metrical, syntactical and imaginative openness of the text, as it mimics and follows the eye of the observer tracking across the landscape, unopposed by the 'fence of ownership' (line 8) imposed by the new privatisation.

It was the local businessman Edward Drury who first put Clare in touch with John Taylor, the London publisher of Keats, who was shortly to assume control of the *London Magazine*. And Taylor, although he has sometimes been harshly criticised for his influence on Clare's writing, was a believer in the importance of Clare's talent, and an active promoter of his works.[18] Taylor and Hessey were a modern business partnership, who employed lawyers and were dedicated to turning an honest profit. And yet Clare was simultaneously introduced to the more antiquated world of aristocratic patronage, and throughout the rest of his life benefited from the sometimes conditional generosity of patrons such as the Marquis of Exeter, Earl Fitzwilliam and Lord Radstock, who provided financial support, and took an active interest in his affairs.

Poems, Descriptive of Rural Life and Scenery was published to immediate acclaim in 1820; Clare was celebrated as 'the Northamptonshire Peasant Poet', and visited London with Taylor to make the acquaintance of a new literary peer group that included Lamb, Hazlitt and De Quincey. *Poems, Descriptive* sold fast and well, caused a steady procession of literary pilgrims and well-wishers to Clare's reluctant door, and was immediately reprinted. *The Village Minstrel* (1821) achieved modest sales by comparison. In 1827 *The Shepherd's Calendar* followed, an ambitious volume of twelve descriptive eclogues and four tales; and then *The Rural Muse* (1835). No further collections were published, despite Clare's prolific writing in the years when he was confined in mental hospitals.

In 1831 Clare had moved from Helpston to Northborough, intending to become established as an independent smallholder, but became physically ill, and increasingly subject to bouts of mental and emotional distress. This short but poignantly disruptive journey is commemorated in 'The Flitting' (1832), Clare's great poem of displacement, in which he evokes the vital importance of the specific, the material here-and-now in the make-up of human identity and experience. From a modern perspective, there is much in Clare's poetry which problematises the connection between habitation and ownership. The theme of dwelling in Clare's poetry, from the fragile nesting sites of birds and animals to his cottage next to the pub in Helpston and his own broken relationship with locations, is often connected with the ability to sing and bear witness. Here, in 'The nightingales nest', Clare's speaker plays the intruder who comes perilously close to disturbing the origin of the bird's song:

> The timid bird had left the hazel bush
> And at a distance hid to sing again
> Lost in a wilderness of listening leaves
> Rich extacy would pour its luscious strain (lines 30–3)

In 1837 Taylor arranged for Clare to be committed to High Beech, Matthew Allen's private asylum in Essex. In 1841 Clare discharged himself, and walked home in the tragic expectation of finding his childhood love Mary Joyce waiting for him, recording the experience in the extraordinary travelogue now known as the 'Journey from Essex'. He was later taken to the Northamptonshire General Lunatic Asylum, with fees paid on his behalf by patrons, and lived there until his death in 1864.

Clare's biographers and critics have attempted various explanations of the circumstances that led to his residence in mental institutions; and these theories have certainly been affected by changing trends in the sense of what is ethically acceptable in describing mental illness. The Tibbles changed their verdict from 'schizophrenia' to 'manic depression' between first and second editions of their life of Clare.[19] Roy Porter contextualises Clare's treatment at High Beech and Northampton very thoroughly in terms of nineteenth-century psychiatric practices, but also warns of the futility of forensic diagnosis.[20] What can and should be said is that it is a mistake to divide Clare's poetry into consecutive rural and asylum phases and expect these categories to remain stable and discrete. Clare's body of work must be interpreted as a continuous whole: a coherent interpretation of Clare's prolific output, with its profusion of generic voices and detailed lyrical observation, must engage with the central theme of endangered and fractured identity, a capacity for self-formation in language that is intimately connected to the contours of the land it inhabits.

To a winter scene
Hail scenes of Desolation and despair
Keen Winters over bearing sport and scorn
Torn by his Rage in ruins you are
To me more pleasing then a summers morn
Your shatter'd scenes appear – despoild and bare
Stript of your clothing naked and forlorn
– Yes Winters havoc wretched as you shine
Dismal to others as your fate may seem
Your fate is pleasing to this heart of mine
Your wildest horrors I the most esteem. –
The ice-bound floods that still with rigour freeze
The snow clothd valley and the naked tree
These sympathising scenes my heart can please
Distress is theirs – and they resemble me (lines 1–14)

In this poem – not from the asylum years, but from Clare's successful first collection – external and internal nature are represented as a continuous theme: this is a reckless statement of a distressed state of mind that welcomes the ravages of winter on the external landscape. 'Nature' is not merely invoked in order to provide a language for the poet's state of mind; even while linking the sense of self so strongly to the details of the natural landscape, the lyrical voice also seems to defer to it, acknowledging the power and integrity of the non-human. Here again, in the opening stanza of a 'Song', Clare is preoccupied with the textures of the natural world even while trying to consider his love and speak of himself: the pain in these lines lies in his inability to escape the specificity of a nature that just might be other than, and greater than, his love for Mary and his need to confess it:

I hid my love when young while I
Couldn't bear the buzzing of a flye
I hid my love to my despite
Till I could not bear to look at light
I dare not gaze upon her face
But left her memory in each place
Where ere I saw a wild flower lye
I kissed and bade my love goodbye (lines 1–8)

The poem addresses the interaction between the mind and the natural world. Here the external landscape is not the peaceful, centred foundation of his identity, but rather that which provokes and antagonises it into being.

Clare's marginalisation from society as a rural labourer was reflected and extended by his life as an inmate of mental asyla. In the twin roles of 'peasant poet' and 'mad poet' he was simultaneously disempowered, denied agency as a writer in command of his tradition and craft, and yet also venerated as a manifestation of natural genius. 'He was first marketed in 1820 as a Northamptonshire Peasant and could never shake off this label or brandname despite the quality and quantity of his work: that is the literary life in a nutshell', writes Roger Sales.[21] And yet Clare's writing consistently shows awareness both of his poetic heritage, and of how his rural working background gave him a sharp personal insight into the great Romantic theme – 'nature' – when more gentrified poets were compelled to rhapsodise from a slightly embarrassed distance (as Wordsworth arguably does in 'The Solitary Reaper', for example). Clare's brilliant meditation on his role as rural poet in 'The Progress of Rhyme' articulates not only the diffidence of a naive newcomer in the exclusive terrain of 'poesy', but also a sense of entitlement and gentle assertiveness in the authenticity he commands:

> To think that I in humble dress
> Might have a right to happiness
> And sing as well as greater men... (lines 107–9)

The poem critiques the cult of immortal fame, by closing with an address to the mythic presence of his childhood love Mary Joyce, in which success and fame as a poet become merged with his goal of finding favour in Mary's eyes.

It has been the work of much twentieth-century criticism to free Clare from the misleading comparison with Wordsworth, whose philosophical nature poetry was always incommensurable with Clare's poetry of intimate, accurate observation – much as Clare admired the older poet. Clare the working man, the naturalist and the ecologist have prevailed instead. But contemporary criticism is now establishing more strongly than before just how literary a poet Clare is. The following stanza is from his Byronic satire 'Don Juan', in which Clare mimics Byron's comic *ottava rima* brilliantly, exercising all his flourishes, vulgar insults, asides and parentheses, while also representing natural detail. The combination is a subtly woven intertextuality that completely belies the myth of uneducated genius, as the Byronic masquerade becomes a consciously deployed vehicle for his view of the world:

> These batch of toadstools on this rotten tree
> Shall be the cabinet of any queen
> Though not such cobblers as her servants be
> They're of Gods making – that is plainly seen

Nor red nor green nor orange – they are free
To thrive and flourish as the Whigs have been
But come tomorrow – like the Whigs forgotten
You'll find them withered stinking dead and rotten (lines 121–8)

The poetry of George Darley (1795–1846) has yet to benefit extensively from the ongoing work of revising the canons of Romantic poetry that has had such a profound effect on the reputations of Beddoes and Clare. Still a marginal figure as both poet and critic, Darley has been of most interest to writers who find an allegorical significance in the career of a 'minor poet'. Darley was born in Dublin, raised a Protestant and studied at Trinity College; in 1822 he moved to London where he began writing for John Taylor's *London Magazine*, contributing poems and reviews, quickly acquiring a reputation for scathing criticism in his evaluation of contemporary drama. Darley's publications included *The Errors of Ecstasie* (1822), an allegorical meditation on poetic withdrawal from the world, and *Sylvia* (1827), an idyllic pastoral drama. He also published two full-length stage plays and several mathematical textbooks. Despite a certain amount of success, Darley always felt he had been overlooked as a poet, and the sting of personal failure may well have added to the critical rigour he applied to others' works. Certainly, he did not easily make his peace with this label of 'minor': 'Why have a score of years not established my title with the world? Why did not "Sylvia," with all its faults, ten years since? It ranked me among the *small* poets. I had as soon be ranked among the piping bullfinches.'[22] *Nepenthe*, which is now considered his most substantial poetic work, was privately printed and circulated among a limited readership in 1835: it is the one work in which his undoubted gifts as a writer of metrical verse are matched with a complex and sustainable theme: in *Nepenthe*, Darley's alter-ego the 'Wanderer' is impelled by the desire for ever-greater imaginative excitement, only to discover that his egotistical ambition is the source of his discontent; the long visionary narrative, teeming with mythic allusion and startling imagery, breaks off after two cantos. The phoenix stands for ecstatic egotism, the unicorn for seductive melancholy, both of which must be conquered and transcended by the ideal – and unwritten – final canto.

Mute as I gaze my feet below,
By times the silvery ashes glow
Under me, where the Bird of Fire
In her own flames seemed to expire,
Chanting her odorous monody;
Methought in each faint glow, again
I saw her last dim glance at me,

Languid with hope akin to pain.
. . .
I sprinkled on the embers white,
Few drops; they curdle – close – unite,
Each with his orb of atomies,
Till in firm corporation these
Leaguing again by law occult,
Shapening and shapening by degrees
Develop fair the full result;
And like the sun in giant mould
Cast of unnumbered stars, behold
The Phenix with her crest of gold,
Her silver wings, her starry eyes,
The Phenix from her ashes rise! (I, lines 267–94)[23]

There follows a long sequence in which the Wanderer falls in with revelling Maenads and ranges all around eastern Europe and Asia Minor: this includes some passages of shrill and bathetic lyricism, studded with exclamation marks. In passages like these Darley is at the mercy of modern taste, and has often been found naive and excessive.[24] Throughout both completed cantos, Darley's marginal notes keep a running commentary on the adventures of the Wanderer: the tone is frosty, and often scathing: '*Voluptuous emotions begin*' (I, 375). At the end of Canto I when the visionary 'I' of the poem eventually succumbs to a series of increasing stimuli and crashes into the ocean, sharing the fate of Icarus, the final marginal comment reads, '*Swept into ocean – Fate of the Extravagator*' (I, 849); this seems a harsh summary after we have lived with the Wanderer for the best part of 1,000 lines and shared his admittedly impetuous enthusiasms. The main verse text and the marginal gloss can be seen to constitute a kind of dialogue of parodic types, with a balanced and compassionate account of things presumably to be found by exploring the space between them – which is actually an extension and a deepening of Darley's pseudo-medical theme of the quest for a panacea of healthy equilibrium.

For all its faults, *Nepenthe* is a significant Romantic vision poem in the tradition of *Alastor* and *Endymion*. It will go on waiting for a full critical re-assessment as long as scholarship remains more interested in Darley as an exemplary literary figure than in what he actually wrote.

Felicia Hemans (1793–1835) was among the most widely read of all poets of the nineteenth century: in her book and magazine sales and the money they made her, in the adoring enthusiasm of her readers and in terms of her general celebrity, she even offered some competition to Byron.[25] *Poems*, the first collection of the teenage Felicia Dorothea Browne, was published in 1808; it was followed by *The Domestic Affections* (1812), and a new volume appeared almost every year until her death. Her poems were often first printed in literary periodicals such as *The New Monthly Magazine* or *Blackwood's Magazine*, before being supplemented with more material and collected into books, which in turn would be reprinted, increasing profits. Remaining popular throughout the later nineteenth century, Hemans's fortunes nevertheless fell with the turn of the twentieth; Ian Jack's reference to 'her refusal to affront conventional morality' is an example of a more disparaging reaction to her poetry of patriotism and sentiment.[26]

> **The return to poetry**
> Once more the eternal melodies from far,
> Woo me like songs of home: once more discerning
> Through fitful clouds the pure majestic star,
> Above the poet's world serenely burning,
> Thither my soul, fresh-winged by love, is turning,
> As o'er the waves the wood-bird seeks her nest,
> For those green heights of dewy stillness yearning,
> Whence glorious minds o'erlook the earth's unrest.
> – Now be the spirit of Heaven's truth my guide
> Through the bright land! – that no brief gladness, found
> In passing bloom, rich odour, or sweet sound,
> May lure my footsteps from their aim aside:
> Their true, high quest – to seek, if ne'er to gain,
> The inmost, purest shrine of that august domain. (lines 1–14)[27]

The poem is from one of Hemans's several autobiographical sonnet sequences, and marks the resumption of poetic vocation. Although this renewed purpose is said to be 'fresh-winged by love', Hemans is at pains to claim an idealistic moral purpose for her writing that will cause her to turn away from any pleasing distractions afforded by aesthetic style. In this combination of sentimental moral purpose with the promise of a sensual pleasure just out of reach, and in the way the persona of the 'poetess' herself is commodified in self-aware exploitation of the literary marketplace, Hemans finds an obvious counterpart in Letitia Landon.

The career of Letitia Landon (1802–38) was fashioned, flourished and fell in the commodity culture of the British periodical press. Her lyrics printed in William Jerdan's *Literary Gazette* (to which she first contributed when only thirteen years old) attracted such excited interest that her writing persona became a mysterious fantasy figure for a generation of young male readers.[28]

Landon became the foremost of the so-called 'initial school' of lyrical and occasional poets, as expensively produced, cherishable poetry gift-books and annuals became objects of sentimental exchange in an expanding literary marketplace. Dominating the market in annuals and keepsake books, Landon also published many volumes, including *The Improvisatrice* (1824), *The Golden Violet* (1827) and *The Venetian Bracelet* (1828), which defends a woman's choice of love as a poetic theme.

> When should lovers breathe their vows?
> When should ladies hear them?
> When the dew is on the boughs,
> When none else are near them;
> When the moon shines cold and pale,
> When the birds are sleeping,
> When no voice is on the gale,
> When the rose is weeping;
> When the stars are bright on high,
> Like hopes in young Love's dreaming,
> And glancing round the light clouds fly,
> Like soft fears to shade their beaming. (lines 1–12)[29]

This lyric develops a theme of private sincerity, which associates authentic subjective speech with a flight into seclusion. The poem figures its own theme, in terms of lovers' confidences: the listening ladies can only trust what is declared to them at night, without any eavesdropping audience. The reader of the lyric and of the collection is therefore constructed as a private auditor of erotic promises, the experience of poetry as something delicate, shy and fugitive.

The writings, careers and reputations of Hemans and Landon at once call into question the traditional assumptions of Romanticism, and transcend it as a useful literary period or category. The significance of their writing and the celebrity they attained among nineteenth-century readerships is felt more strongly in the history of women's writing and the relationship between gender and canonicity, than in the intellectual or imaginative patterns that characterise Romantic poetry.

Although this group of poets is disparate in many ways, they may be usefully considered as a 'third generation' of British Romantics. They used highly wrought literary languages to express the various alienations of the self, including poetic and authorial self-identity. If sometimes their writings can seem eager to please aesthetically, with their intricate forms and sensuous images, on closer inspection they are temperamentally drawn to silence, disappearance, defeat and extinction; and in this, they gesture towards modernity.

Notes

1. 'Stanzas from the Grande Chartreuse' (*c.*1852), in *The Poems of Matthew Arnold*, second edition, ed. Kenneth Allott and Miriam Allott (London: Longman, 1979), lines 85–6.
2. Thomas Lovell Beddoes, letter to Thomas Forbes Kelsall, 1824, in *The Works of Thomas Lovell Beddoes*, ed. H. W. Donner (New York: AMS Press, 1978), p. 589: all quotations from Beddoes are taken from this edition.
3. See e.g. C. C. Barfoot (ed.), *Victorian Keats and Romantic Carlyle: The Fusions and Confusions of Literary Periods* (Amsterdam: Rodopi, 1999).
4. For classic instances of the Romantic and proto-Modernist Beddoes respectively, see e.g. Harold Bloom, *The Visionary Company: A Reading of English Romantic Poetry* (London: Faber and Faber, 1962); and Northrop Frye, *A Study of English Romanticism* (New York: Random House, 1968).
5. Roger Sales, *John Clare: A Literary Life* (Basingstoke: Palgrave, 2002), p. xiii.
6. There are two full-length biographies of Beddoes: Royall H. Snow, *Thomas Lovell Beddoes, Eccentric and Poet* (New York: Covici-Friede, 1928); and H. W. Donner, *Thomas Lovell Beddoes: The Making of a Poet* (Oxford: Blackwell, 1935). Edmund Gosse's entry on Beddoes in the *Dictionary of National Biography* (1885–1900) perpetuated a falsified account of accidental death; the recently updated *DNB* (2004) includes a new life of Beddoes by Alan Halsey, with an accurate account of his suicide.
7. Unpublished letter to Bryan Waller Procter, in *The Works of Thomas Lovell Beddoes*, pp. 614–15.
8. The [γ] text is the term used by H. W. Donner, editor of the definitive *Works*, for the accumulation of Beddoes's later revisions to the drama, made between 1830 and about 1844.
9. For an example of the play read as monodramatic meditation on consciousness, see e.g. Alan Richardson, '*Death's Jest-Book*: "shadows of words" ', in *A Mental Theater: Poetic Drama and Consciousness in the Romantic Age* (University Park: Pennsylvania State University Press, 1988), pp. 154–73; for Beddoes's intertextual relationship with Shelley, see e.g. Michael O'Neill, ' "A storm of ghosts": Beddoes, Shelley, Death and Reputation', *Cambridge Quarterly*, 28.2 (1999), pp. 102–15.
10. See e.g. essays by Ute Berns and Nat Leach in Ute Berns and Michael Bradshaw (eds.), *The Ashgate Research Companion to Thomas Lovell Beddoes* (Aldershot: Ashgate, 2007).
11. *The Works of Thomas Lovell Beddoes*, p. 620.
12. Two biographies of Clare have been published recently: Jonathan Bate, *John Clare: A Biography* (London: Picador, 2003) is the new definitive life, and involves a re-evaluation of all the key sources; Sales, *John Clare* (cited above) takes a complementary historical approach, narrating Clare's life alongside those of a number of his contemporaries, whether autodidact writers or inmates of mental asyla.

13. From 'January: a cottage evening', John Clare, *Poems of the Middle Period, 1822–1837*, ed. Eric Robinson, David Powell and P. M. S. Dawson (Oxford: Clarendon Press, 1996), vol. I.
14. Bate, *John Clare*, p. xix.
15. This and subsequent quotations from Clare's poetry are taken from *The Oxford Authors: John Clare: A Critical Edition of the Major Works*, ed. Eric Robinson and David Powell (Oxford: Oxford University Press, 1984).
16. See John Barrell, *The Idea of Landscape and the Sense of Place, 1730–1840: An Approach to the Poetry of John Clare* (Cambridge: Cambridge University Press, 1972).
17. Hugh Haughton, 'Progress and Rhyme: "The Nightingale's Nest" and Romantic Poetry', in Hugh Haughton, Adam Phillips and Geoffrey Summerfield (eds.), *John Clare in Context* (Cambridge: Cambridge University Press, 1994), pp. 51–86 (p. 66).
18. For varying views of Clare's relationship with Taylor, see Tim Chilcott, *A Publisher and his Circle: The Life and Work of John Taylor* (London: Routledge and Kegan Paul, 1972); Eric Robinson and Geoffrey Summerfield, 'John Taylor's Editing of John Clare's *The Shepherd's Calendar*', *The Review of English Studies*, 14:56 (1963), pp. 359–69; and Zachary Leader, 'John Taylor and the Poems of John Clare', in *Revision and Romantic Authorship* (Oxford: Clarendon Press, 1996), pp. 206–61.
19. J. W. and Anne Tibble, *John Clare: A Life* (London: Cobden-Sanderson, 1932; second edition 1972).
20. See Roy Porter, ' "All madness for writing": John Clare and the Asylum', in Haughton, Phillips and Summerfield (eds.), *John Clare in Context*, pp. 259–78.
21. Sales, *John Clare*, p. xv.
22. Letter to Bryan Waller Procter, 1840, quoted in Leslie Brisman, 'George Darley: The Poet as Pigmy', *Studies in Romanticism*, 15 (1976), pp. 119–41 (p. 119).
23. The text is taken from *Selected Poems of George Darley*, ed. Anne Ridler (London: Merrion, 1979).
24. See e.g. Ian Jack: 'The author of *Hudibras* would have enjoyed this poem, which is none the less nonsense for being the nonsense of a poet.' *English Literature 1815–32: Scott, Byron and Keats* (Oxford: Clarendon Press, 1963), p. 145.
25. Hemans and Landon, discussed briefly here in the context of a Romantic 'third generation', are considered more extensively in chapter 30.
26. Jack, *English Literature 1815–32*, p. 168.
27. The text is taken from Felicia Hemans, *Selected Poems, Prose, and Letters*, ed. Gary Kelly (Peterborough, Ontario: Broadview, 2002); this poem was first published in 'Records of the Autumn of 1834' in *Blackwood's Magazine* (1834).
28. See e.g. Edward Bulwer-Lytton, quoted in Anne K. Mellor, *Romanticism and Gender* (New York: Routledge, 1993), p. 110.
29. The first stanza of 'When should lovers breathe their vows?' is taken from Letitia Elizabeth Landon, *Selected Writings*, ed. Jerome McGann and Daniel Riess (Peterborough, Ontario: Broadview, 1997); this poem concluded the volume *The Improvisatrice and Other Poems* (1824).

Chapter 30

Women poets of the Romantic period (Barbauld to Landon)

HEIDI THOMSON

The last twenty years have been marked by a surge of access to writings by and about Romantic women poets. Specialised anthologies, starting with Roger Lonsdale's 1989 *Eighteenth Century Women Poets: An Oxford Anthology*, have followed each other in quick succession, while the more general anthologies have greatly increased their intake of Romantic women poets. The Brown University Women Writers project textbase and databases such as *Eighteenth Century Collections Online*, *Literature Online*, and others, have facilitated access to texts in ways which were barely conceivable thirty years ago. With the availability of primary texts we have also seen an increase in scholarly editions, well-annotated selections, critical studies and major new biographies. Greatly expanded bibliographical tools (*Literature Online*, the MLA Database) are useful aids for surveying the field. All of these materials, the improved methods of access and the myriad possibilities of specialised searches highlight the quantity, quality and versatility of women poets of the Romantic period. Technological and editorial enhancements have made it possible to study women poets alongside or in dialogue with male poets, and to think about them in their contemporary literary, cultural and political contexts, thereby integrating them into the larger world of letters.

A major reason for the neglect of Romantic women poets in the twentieth century may be attributed to a radical shift of sensibility in the arts towards a more elitist, Modernist aesthetic. A female sensibility which centred on extended professions of grief became over time associated with over-indulgence in unearned emotion. The over-exposure, the surfeit of similar poems and by contrast, the masculinist, more minimalist aesthetic of Modernism with its self-consciously iconoclastic experimentation, all contributed to the waning of interest in the Romantic women poets. Their rediscovery was initially propelled by the feminist revaluation of women writers; they have now again become part of the Romantic canon, which is, at the moment at least, characterised by an avid interest in political, commercial and cultural contexts.

Romantic women poets write, naturally enough, about gender-specific concerns such as motherhood, access to education and an income, but they also share with the male poets a prominent interest in the idea of Sensibility. Many poems explore the tenuous connections between thinking and feeling, common sense and impulse, reason and passion. Moreover, many women poets write against the popular stereotype of women's supposed lack of reason and excess of feeling by submitting their passions to unflinching intellectual scrutiny. The contemporary construction of women in terms of their marriage and family also led them to explore the demands of life as an individual artist and the heavy burdens of a conventional domestic life.

A great many of the Romantic women's poems are characterised by a humanitarian, meliorist and sometimes evangelical vision; hence the poems against slave trading, slavery and the loss of individual identity, against complacent consumption of products of luxury derived from slavery, against warfare and its concomitant injustices and disrespect for nature and human life. Those issues are often expressed with a female sensibility of loss which is informed by a poignant awareness of the particular restrictions which women faced in their own lives. Conduct-book notions of female propriety complicated women poets' endeavours, publications and subject matter. The expectations and concurrent thwarting of women's personal or domestic happiness, artistic and professional ambitions were often the subject matter itself.

The era provided plenty of opportunity for elegiac verse. In addition to the hazards of childbirth and early childhood, the Romantic women poets lived with an awareness of relentless wars which, although waged abroad, had a devastating economic and social impact on the British population. Apart from the brief window of the fragile Peace of Amiens (1802–3), Britain was continually at war with France from 1793 until the defeat of Napoleon at Waterloo in 1815. While it would be reductive to extrapolate a distinct female tradition from these writings, it could be suggested that the biology of motherhood puts a particular slant on how women wrote about war: every soldier was, after all, born of a mother who is programmed to fervently desire the survival of her child. Anti-war poetry during the wars with France also ran the risk of association with unpatriotic Jacobinism. In the wake of Waterloo, Britain emerged as a colonial superpower, a status which was achieved and maintained at the cost of much bloodshed, as Hemans's 'England's Graves' sombrely illustrates.

Anna Laetitia Barbauld (1743–1825)

In a letter Coleridge praises Barbauld for her '*Propriety* of Mind' and 'great *acuteness*' which she managed to keep within 'the bounds of practical Reason'.[1] Barbauld's correctness of language and her sensitive, didactic intelligence are associated with a rational sensibility and a public moral vision. Her own blank-verse address 'To Mr. Coleridge' (1797) warns with alarming foresight against what became Coleridge's curse, an inability to move beyond midway on so many projects. Barbauld is brilliant when she exposes insubstantiality, be it poetical, philosophical, political or emotional. Losing oneself in idle speculation leads to 'cheated sense' (line 9); confusing indolence with 'deep philosophy' (line 21) leaves the mind 'pampered with most unsubstantial food' (line 30).[2] Moreover, Barbauld emphasises a moral obligation in him who is a 'Youth belov'd, / Of Science – of the Muse belov'd' (lines 32–3) to translate his individual talent into a 'generous enterprise' (line 16) which will reach an audience of both friends and country. The mixture of praise and admonition in the concluding lines ('Now Heaven conduct thee with a parent's love!', line 43) reflects Barbauld's pedagogical strain. The rejection of solipsism and the moral necessity of connecting with others are equally visible in the heroic stanzas of 'The Rights of Woman'. Mary Wollstonecraft's singling out of Barbauld's 'To a Lady, with some painted flowers' for criticism in the *Vindication of the Rights of Woman* led to a subtle response. Barbauld's counter-argument, encased in crisp quatrains but expressed in discursive iambic pentameters, both praises and corrects Wollstonecraft by cataloguing and paraphrasing Wollstonecraft's ideas in exhortative imperatives, only to do away with single-minded ideology at the end. The penultimate stanza carries a preliminary warning ('But hope not', line 25) which is finally put to an insistent, spondaic stop in 'Then, then abandon each ambitious thought' (line 29) (of separatist female rights). Barbauld invokes Milton to advocate reciprocity and mutual love between the sexes as the way forward, a conclusion which advocates her conciliatory social vision.

Barbauld translated her principles and convictions about collective responsibility and individual accountability into overtly political poems. Her 1791 satiric verse 'Epistle to Wilberforce, Esq., on the Rejection of the Bill for Abolishing the Slave Trade' warns against the demands of indolently tyrannical 'pale Beauty' (line 57), expresses sympathy with Wilberforce's thwarted efforts and lashes Britain for knowing collusion with the slave trade from the very first couplet: 'Cease, Wilberforce, to urge thy generous aim! / Thy Country knows the sin, and stands the shame!' In the concluding couplet of

'To the Poor' (1795) she comes close to the message of Blake's *Songs of Experience* when she addresses the harassment of the poor in sermons: 'Prepare to meet a father undismayed, / Nor fear the God whom priests and kings have made' (lines 21–2). Barbauld's most famous poem, *Eighteen Hundred and Eleven, A Poem* (1812), published at a time of xenophobic patriotism, was savaged in patronising terms by John Wilson Croker in the Tory *Quarterly Review*. Its heroic couplets chillingly formalise Barbauld's apocalyptic anti-war message. The measured use of classical form highlights the counter-natural state of Britain. The country may have been untouched by the war itself, but nature is 'bounteous in vain' (line 11) through the gratuitous destruction of harvests, and women are 'fruitful in vain' (line 23) because their sons die in foreign lands and their daughters remain unmarried. The paucity of substantial signs which articulate incomprehensible loss is captured in the following domestic scene:

> Oft o'er the daily page some soft-one bends,
> To learn the fate of husband, brothers, friends,
> Or the spread map with anxious eye explores,
> Its dotted boundaries and penciled shores,
> Asks *where* the spot that wrecked her bliss is found,
> And learns its name but to detest its sound. (lines 33–8)

The future lies with America, and in the cultural pilgrimage of a young traveller to the 'faded glories' of London, Barbauld evokes the ruins of Britain among which 'Egyptian granites' from the British Museum are mentioned concurrently with Joshua Reynolds. The overall 'Spirit' (lines 215ff.) which she invokes is reminiscent of Shelley's spirits but with a more indeterminate twist: 'Moody and viewless as the changing wind, / No force arrests his foot, no chains can bind' (lines 217–18).

Barbauld's poetry observes the world with a fresh curiosity in conservative forms. Her interest in natural phenomena is obvious in a wide range of poems, from 'The Mouse's Petition [to Dr. Priestley]' to the 'Inscription for an Ice-House'. The latter poem, written in the year of Keats's birth (1795), anticipates that poet's delight in oxymoronic sense impressions in the evocation of fruit ices: 'Congeals the melting peach, the nectarine smooth, / Burnished and glowing from the sunny wall: / Darts sudden frost into the crimson veins / Of the moist berry; moulds the sugared hail' (lines 22–5). In a proto-ecologist fashion, Barbauld explores the tensions between the practical uses of imprisoned winter in the form of ice blocks which arrest nature in the preservation of fruit, and the counter-natural interruption of a seasonal cycle. The emasculation of winter, suggested in the allusions to Samson and Hercules, for the purpose of luxurious living is associated with the tyranny over a natural phenomenon which must necessarily come to an end: the propulsion of the whirlwinds (line 31) announces the approaching liberation of the imprisoned force. 'Washing Day' (1797), usually referred to for its mock epic treatment of the travails of washing day, transcends the mundane by its reference to the surprising delights of childhood. The literally transcendent image of Montgolfier's sky balloon unites childhood's play and adulthood's chores as the soap bubble, a fortunate if ephemeral by-product of the washing suds, imaginatively transforms into a silken sky balloon and the gentle all-embracing mockery of life and verse itself.

Barbauld's interest in ontological questions emerges from the title and the surprisingly tender quatrains of 'To a little invisible being who is expected soon to become visible'. The well-founded fears about the dangers of giving birth connect this poem with 'On the Death of Princess Charlotte', who died hours after her stillborn baby. What makes Barbauld's poem different from the many elegies which were produced on the occasion is her sympathetic portrayal of those whose inability to mourn separates them from the human community ('spare one tear / For him who does not weep', lines 34–5). Finally, 'Life', a keenly curious poem, reflects on the separation of body and soul after death in alternating pentameters and rollicking tetrameters: 'And in this strange divorce, / Ah tell where I must seek this compound I?' (lines 11–12).

Charlotte Turner Smith (1749–1806)

Mary Robinson, Wordsworth, Coleridge and Keats learned a great deal from Smith's experimentation with the, at that stage neglected, sonnet form. In her popular *Elegiac Sonnets*, first published in 1784, Smith broadcast her domestic troubles as part and parcel of her identity as poet, insisting in a footnote to Sonnet 79 about Rousseau that he may well have been 'heavily taxed with that excessive irritability, too often if not always attendant on genius', but that her own readers should take note that she has more pressing problems to deal with: 'it has been my misfortune to have endured real calamities that disqualified me for finding any enjoyment in the pleasures and pursuits which occupy the generality of the world'.[3] The double-edged subject of Smith's sonnets is the infinity of her suffering, all the more poignant because its intensity produces the quality of her work: 'How dear the Muse's favours cost, / *If those paint sorrow best – who feel it most!*' (Sonnet 1, lines 13–14; Smith's emphasis). The self-professed excellence of her art is predicated upon the repeated insistence of an unhappiness which cannot be alleviated.

This could easily be a hollow claim, but Smith's masterly use of the sonnet cycle makes it a convincing one. Each sonnet crystallises a moment of sadness, expressed through a range of characters, from her own autobiographical persona, to characters from her own novels, to characters derived from Petrarch, or Goethe. While each sonnet displays its individual beauty, the succession of them, like beads in a necklace, reveals their collective purpose, the dark infinity of private suffering, with Smith engaged in a creative but ultimately Sisyphean effort. There is no promise of a cure (Sonnet 14, 'From Petrarch': 'Nor cure for me in time or change be found: / The shaft extracted does not cure the wound!' (lines 13–14)), only a more articulate and therefore more painful affirmation of her ongoing misery, and in her articulation of that suspended state Smith anticipates Byron, who also insists on dissociating diagnosis from cure. A concluding couplet does not turn us away from the grief; instead it is usually a resounding translation of the natural awareness of the landscape into a personal profession of despair. While one sonnet by itself could be perceived as an evocation of a transient moment, the cumulative cataloguing of them creates a DNA-like string which captures a state of being beyond the single moment. The instance of sorrow is transformed into a permanent state of despair, a condition which cannot be equated with a temporarily fashionable pose. The absence of a solution to this state is captured even at the structural level of the sonnet itself; Smith gives Sonnet 44, 'Written in the church-yard at Middleton in Sussex', for instance, a bifocal twist by having a Petrarchan rhyme scheme even though it also makes sense to read it as if it is a Shakespearean sonnet with a concluding couplet which returns the focus to the private sorrow of the speaker. That particular sonnet also illustrates Smith's ability to substantiate an indistinct atmosphere with a perceptible form. In contrast with the commonplace image of the pastoral graveyard, Smith offers us a churchyard which has been swept away by the sea, where the wild blast '[d]rives the huge billows from their heaving bed; / Tears from their grassy tombs the village dead, / And breaks the silent sabbath of the grave!' (lines 6–8). In the intermingling of the bones with the shingle on the shore, subject to the relentless rhythm of the tides, this merging of human remains with a cosmic landscape constitutes an enviable image for the speaker who is doomed 'by life's long storm opprest, / To gaze with envy on their gloomy rest' (lines 13–14).

The coast, her beloved Sussex Downs landscape and the natural world as a whole, is a source of endless inspiration for Smith and it figures in many of her poems, including *The Emigrants* (1793), and the unfinished *Beachy Head* (1807). The dangers of shipwreck and drowning, but also the many attractions associated with this liminal setting of sea and shore, relate directly to the fate of the characters who are suspended in a state over which they have no control and which, for all its natural variation, is infinite. Sonnet 66, 'Written in a tempestuous night, on the coast of Sussex' has a sea which 'rakes upon the stony shore' (line 1) and rock which is 'mined by corrosive tides' (line 5), suggesting the hypnotically dull drone in the head of the sleepless speaker. Sonnet 71, 'Written at Weymouth in winter', first associates whiteness with bleak cold ('The chill waves whiten in the sharp North-east; / Cold, cold the night-blast comes, with sullen sound' (lines 1–2)) followed by the sunny vista of sails which 'whiten all the summer bay' (line 8). The repetition of 'whiteness' highlights the fact that neither impression affects the speaker who is locked in a permanently mournful state. Smith's love of birds connects her with John Clare; in her loco-descriptive meditative poem *Beachy Head* she captures the lark in a synesthesia of sound, movement and glistening appearance: 'The lark sings matins; and above the clouds / Floating, embathes his spotted breast in dew' (lines 477–8). An accomplished botanist and natural historian, Smith's uncanny ability to associate a character's morbid sensibility with precise descriptions of fossils, of birds both dead and alive, of flowers in all stages of development, anticipates the images of Sylvia Plath and Ted Hughes. Smith uses footnotes not merely as an authoritative display of her vast store of knowledge; she makes them part of the rhetorical effect of her writing. The juxtaposition of a botanical note about the manifestations of bindweed with notes about Otway and Collins in Sonnet 30 'To the River Arun' establishes natural observation and poetry reading as associated sensibilities. Both plants and poets share a connection with the beloved river which ran its course through her father's estate in Sussex. Sonnet 42 'Composed during a walk on the Downs, in November 1787' ends on an image of 'vulture Care – that feeds upon the heart' (line 14), preceded by a description of the night-jar. The strictly factual footnote, 'As I have never seen it dead, I know not to what species it belongs', casts an aura of mental precision over the emotional turmoil conveyed in the poem and enhances the reader's awareness of the poet's reference to the vulture in the body of the poem.

Smith's speaker, in the tradition of Gray's innocents, envies the shepherd for his ability to live for the moment, '[n]o pangs of sorrow past, or coming dread' (line 10; Sonnet 31, 'Written in Farm Wood, South Down, in May 1784). More radically, Smith does not distance herself from the crazed man in Sonnet 70, 'On being cautioned against walking on a headland overlooking the sea, because it was frequented by a lunatic'; she sees 'him more with envy than with fear' because he does not know 'the depth or the duration of his woe' (line 14). The curse of having seen better times also lies at the heart of her political blank-verse poem, *The Emigrants* (1793), which focuses on the bewilderment of the French émigrés who are arriving on the British shores and who have had to abandon their past privileges in exchange for an exiled existence where they depend on the kindness of strangers. Both in this poem and in the unfinished *Beachy Head*, Smith juxtaposes social and national constructions of identity with her own isolated and formerly privileged self. Like Barbauld, Smith portrays war as a global destructive leveller, affecting all nations and above all its most vulnerable inhabitants: 'while War, wide-ravaging annihilates / The hope of cultivation' (*The Emigrants*, Book the Second, lines 73–4).

Mary Robinson (1758–1800)

'[T]hat Woman has an Ear',[4] Coleridge wrote to Southey in a commentary about Mary Robinson's 'The Haunted Beach', the poem in which the 'green billows' (line 9) play in tetrameters, mocking the guilt-ridden fisherman who murdered when he should have saved a shipwrecked mariner.[5] *Lyrical Tales* (1800) invites comparison with Wordsworth's *Lyrical Ballads* because many of the poems share social and historical conditions. But Robinson differs from Wordsworth, as Stuart Curran has pointed out, in that her characters are portrayed without the self-reflexive intrusion of the poem's narrator.[6] Yet, against the grain of the simple ballad-like lyrics they inhabit, the poems' characters reveal themselves to be psychologically and emotionally complex despite the absence of a poetic speaker who controls the narrative. Robinson's conscious use of simple forms (tetrameters, ballad stanzas) to reveal the contradictory impulses of her characters produces both a comic and tragic effect. The authorial detachment associated with the absence of a synthesising narrative voice highlights the existential loneliness of her characters and the moral ambiguity of each simple tale. In contrast with Wordsworth's 'We Are Seven', in which the little girl insists on her community of siblings, dead and alive, the boy in Robinson's title poem 'All Alone' rejects the meaningless comfort of the sympathetic traveller because he knows that he will have no mourner after his death. The comic verse tales expose the characters' pathetic attempts to gratify their sexual desires with an amused detachment. No-nonsense tetrameters create a stage for punitive outcomes in gossipy village settings. All characters, virtuous and vile, young and old, male and female, high and low, are at the mercy of the unpredictability of their passions.

Robinson's sensibility is devoid of moralising sentimentality. Over and over again her poetry explores the conundrum of sensibility itself, the precarious balance between the inevitable abandonment of oneself to emotion and the rational knowledge of its seductive dangers. In 'To Apathy', for instance, Robinson anticipates Letitia Landon's retreat into a pose of cultivated indifference.

That resolution, however, is tragically doomed, as *Sappho and Phaon: In a Series of Legitimate Sonnets* demonstrates in a cycle of forty-four Petrarchan sonnets delineating Sappho's infatuation with the unworthy Phaon. Robinson explores Sappho's self-destructive sensibility in conjunction with her poetic genius. The deliberate choice of the more challenging Petrarchan, or legitimate, sonnet over the Shakespearean model sets Robinson apart in the fashionable era of the sonnet. Unlike Charlotte Smith, who considered the Petrarchan sonnet too confining, Robinson defines herself as a more experimental poet and situates herself in a solid, male tradition. Robinson emphasises in her introduction that Sappho's own passionate lyrics transcended the confines of gender and that, when the Greeks paid tribute to her, 'they idolized the muse, and not the woman'. Unlike Smith, Robinson stays clear of any references to her own financially precarious, unhappy domestic state; instead she refers to a general lack of patronage and in a final paragraph pays tribute to her 'illustrious countrywomen; who, unpatronized by courts, and unprotected by the powerful, persevere in the paths of literature, and ennoble themselves by the unperishable lustre of mental pre-eminence!'[7] The assertion of intellectual and professional independence, the insistence on the quality of poetic genius, transcend gender, but the subject matter is infused with a characteristic female sensibility of the incompatibility of the heart and the mind. Sappho's suicidal leap into the waves in the final sonnet comes after an extended exploration of her infatuation, her thwarted expectations and her attempt to redefine herself after her abandonment.

Felicia Hemans (1793–1835)

Hemans's poetry provides the contemporary reader with a challenge, because her polished verse can be mistaken for polite obtuseness. Yet, simply considering the subject matter of her verse makes one aware that she does not shrink from the horrors of natural and wilful destruction which have characterised humanity across the ages and across continents. A catalogue of horrors could easily amount to mere gothic excess, but Hemans translated unspeakable events into socially acceptable verse by focusing on the psychology of her subjects and by using highly effective distancing strategies. The repetitive simplicity of her style with its conservative tenor, as in 'The Homes of England', 'England's Dead' or 'The Graves of a Household', heightens the ambiguity of her message. As in Blake's 'Holy Thursday' poems, in which the sheer number of charity children underlines the nefarious state of Britain, the number of graves in 'England's Dead' (1822) and the geographical spread of them – 'Wave may not foam, nor wild wind weep / Where rest not England's dead' (lines 55–6) – not only affirm the extent of Britain as a colonial power but mourn the human cost of imperial expansion.[8]

Not surprisingly, Hemans's poetry is primarily elegiac even when it celebrates. Women are trapped in sacrificial suffering and mourn not only the loss of their men and children but also the loss of their own identity through their deaths and departures. Women stay when men flee across the seas, as in stanzas 32 and 33 of the Second Part of 'The Forest Sanctuary' (1825): 'Not thus is woman. Closely *her* still heart / Doth twine itself with ev'n each lifeless thing, / Which, long remember'd, seem'd to bear its part / In her calm joys' (lines 289–92). Women choose death over life so as not to be separated from their children, as in 'The Image in Lava', which immortalises a mother protectively clasping her infant to her breast at the moment of being engulfed.

Even though their techniques are very different, Barbauld and Hemans both write in disciplined forms against the monomaniacal pursuits of military conquests and ideologies. They both emphasise an ideal of harmonious living in which a conciliatory dynamic between men and women is a paramount foundation for good citizenship. Hemans was only too aware that harmony under the banner of country and God was a good idea rather than a reality. Her celebrated 'The Homes of England', with its rallying call from Walter Scott's *Marmion* ('Where's the coward that would not dare / To fight for such a land?'), is the first of the 'Miscellaneous Pieces' in *Records of Woman* (1828); as such it follows the poetic records of individual women experiencing horrific ordeals. In the wake of the palpable flesh and blood suffering of the women, the harmonious homes, which are disembodied apart from the references to the 'woman's voice' (line 13) and the 'child's glad spirit' (line 39), feel rather empty: they are ideals rather than realities.

Hemans draws her examples of female heroic suffering from a huge range of historical, cultural and geographical contexts. The speaker in 'The Widow of Crescentius', from *Tales and Historic Scenes* (1819), channels all her creative energy into avenging her husband's murder by posing as a minstrel who 'breathes each wounded feeling's tone / In music's eloquence alone' (lines 169–70). Clearly Byronic in origin but with a focused sense of purpose and in the socially acceptable guise of a bereft wife, the poem has the young widow assert that her 'life has been a lingering death' (line 266). Her statement of a woman's unfulfilled and rudderless life applies to many of Hemans's female characters: 'he died, and I was changed – my soul, / A lonely wanderer, spurn'd control' (lines 281–2).

By portraying legitimate widowed heroism, Hemans usually avoids the more scandalous erotic implications of male–female relationships which both Robinson and Landon addressed at the expense of their own reputations. She does, however, address unrequited love in 'Properzia Rossi', which, as a poem inspired by a contemporary French painting by Louis Ducis featuring a sixteenth-century Italian sculptor who is inspired by a Greek myth, serves as a fine example of Hemans's intricate technique. A dramatic monologue in predominantly iambic pentameters with highly effective use of enjambments, 'Properzia Rossi' (*Records of Woman*, 1828) celebrates and mourns the artistic vigour and emotional vulnerability of the sculptor who, according to Hemans's own headnote, 'died in consequence of an unrequited attachment' (p. 352). As in the other 'Records of Woman' Hemans frames Properzia's monologue with a factual headnote which sets up a Chinese box effect, in this case not only doubling the artistic medium (painting and sculpture) but also the stories of romantic abandonment (Properzia's own and Ariadne's abandonment by Theseus): 'A painting by Ducis represents her showing her last work, a basso-relievo of Ariadne, to a Roman knight, the object of her affection, who regards it with indifference' (p. 352). Ekphrasis, in this case interpreting and elucidating visual art in writing, allowed Hemans to write decorously and dispassionately about strong emotions which could not possibly be identified with Hemans herself. By framing the poem as a mental interpretation she also claims an intellectual authority which distances the poem from mere emotional effusion. In her monologue Rossi identifies her final sculpture as 'one dream of passion and of beauty more!' (line 1), an image which is reminiscent of Keats's Grecian Urn which immortalises passion for the interpretation of future generations as well. Rossi's bitter-sweet address to her artistic subject, Ariadne, captures both the identification with her fate of unrequited love, but also the very artistic shape, transcending reality in beauty, which Rossi's genius bestows on her.

Tellingly, Hemans not only celebrates art as a socially sanctioned way of asserting mental control over one's passions, she also champions the spirit of artistic genius as an enduring public record of human achievement in the face of tyranny and useless destruction. Her celebration of the artist's interpretative and intellectual genius resembles Shelley's characterisation of the sculptor in 'Ozymandias' who 'well those passions read / Which yet survive'.[9] In 'The Statue of the Dying Gladiator' (*The Domestic Affections*, 1812), Hemans's couplets affirm the connection between 'divine control' (line 47) and 'soul' (line 48). In *The Restoration of the Works of Art to Italy: A Poem* (1816), a public poem about the return of Napoleon's loot to Italy, Hemans emphasises, in the wake of so much destruction, the immortality of art – 'to deathless fame consign'd' (line 99) – as well as the spiritual power of the artist – 'Oh! Who can tell what beams of heavenly light / Flash'd o'er the sculptor's intellectual sight' (lines 191–2). For Hemans, art has a salutary value: as an interpretation of the past it conveys the relevance of an artistic historic record to the present. While art objects may be claimed by hostile forces, Hemans's poem also argues that the artistic spirit itself is indomitable.

Hemans's formal control harnesses the inexorable human capacity for destruction which defies words; in 'Casabianca' (1829), moments after the 'wreathing fires' (line 28) take on the horrifically beautiful form of 'banners in the sky' (line 32) on the burning ship, a child is blown to bits. By focusing on the filial moral sense of duty of the child Hemans wisely stays clear of the contentious moral issue of warfare with its potentially simplistic debate about winners and losers. Her art affirms that, when it comes to the insanity of warfare, we are all losers at heart.

Letitia Landon (L. E. L.) (1802–38)

Letitia Landon started publishing her poems in William Jerdan's *The Literary Gazette* in 1820, signing herself L. E. L. She was a prolific contributor to and editor of the annuals that were so popular in the 1820s and 1830s. Like Hemans's, much of Landon's work is ekphrastic: they are companion pieces to the engravings and prints in the annuals. She became famous with *The Improvisatrice and Other Poems* (1824) and *The Troubadour, Catalogue of Pictures and Historical Sketches* (1825), which together also made her £900. Landon's successful poetic formula revolves around the 'improvisatrice', the performing female poet who is inspired by Madame de Staël's *Corinne* (1807). Landon created an autobiographical connection between herself and her poetic persona, inviting regard both for herself and her poetry, an identification which also caused inevitable damage to her reputation given the cynical, erotic charge in much of her work.

While Hemans attributes a morally transcendental value to art as a preserver of what is best in life, Landon is more of a blues singer, cynically confirming her art in the very collapse of her personal life. Her blank-verse meditation 'Erinna' (*The Golden Violet*, 1826) highlights the prostitution of the poet's gifts and talents to fame, 'the destroyer of life's calm content' (line 216), and the desperate need for connection with others: 'Ay, fair as are / The visions of a poet's solitude, / There must be something more for happiness; / They seek communion'(lines 247–50).[10] 'Lines of Life' (*The Venetian Bracelet*, 1829) epitomises the best features of Landon's work. The title itself suggests an encasing of life within an artistic delineation, and the epigraph which precedes the poem encapsulates Landon's main themes: the disenchanted loneliness in the absence of any meaningful connection with other human beings which leads the subject to the doomed resolution to seek sympathy in herself: 'Orphan in my first year's, I early learnt / To make my heart suffice itself, and seek / Support and sympathy in its own depths.' Her nihilistic introspection resembles Byron's Childe Harold's in Canto 3 as she describes the loss of herself into a hardening pose. Turning herself into an ekphrastic subject of sorts, Landon offers herself as an inscrutable, fragmented spectacle which she has learned to control by copying the mannerisms of others: 'I live among the cold, the false, / And I must seem like them; / And such I am, for I am false / As those I most condemn' (lines 9–12). This guardedness is the key to social survival even though it comes at the cost of an emotional identity by suppressing her own feelings 'like wrecks / In the unfathom'd main' (line 25). Unlike Coleridge, who in 'Dejection: An Ode' (1802), blames habitual suppression for the stifling of his artistic sensibility, Landon affirms her art at the expense of her heart. Landon's use of quatrains with iambic tetrameters and trimeters gives her work both an intense and deadpan quality. The disconcerting juxtaposition of cloying sentimentality and detached cynicism teases and repels at the same time, leaving the reader at a loss about the tonal register, particularly when Landon echoes other poets, Byron in particular. Like Keats she associates beauty with death, revelling in both voluptuous surrender and ominous destruction, as in 'The Fairy of the Fountains' (1835). 'When Should Lovers Breathe Their Vows?' (*The Improvisatrice*, 1824) also echoes Keats's 'La Belle Dame Sans Merci'; for while the breathless anaphoric catalogue of 'When' questions provides stereotypically sentimental answers, the overall atmosphere is ominously chilling: 'the moon shines cold and pale' (line 5) and 'the rose is weeping' (line 8). Landon exploits the sentimental connotations of a love letter in 'Lines written under a picture of a girl burning a love-letter' (*The Improvisatrice*, 1824) by opening with a laborious epigraph: 'The lines were filled with many a tender thing, / All the impassioned heart's fond communing.' While the focus in the epigraph is on the material sentimental value of the keepsake, the short, stark lines of the poem itself revolve around the opposition of 'I' and 'thy', a confirmation of separation. The destruction of the letter, for the reason that the speaker cannot bear someone else reading it, confirms that, while the letter may be a testimony of tenderness, the experience of love itself is all-consuming. Instead of celebrating the union of one person with another, Landon always points to the availability of a predator for every victim. In 'A Child Screening a Dove from a Hawk. By Stewardson' (*The Troubadour*, 1825) she gently but unflinchingly exposes the futility of the vulnerable trying to protect the vulnerable: 'Alas! there's tears for every eye, / A hawk for every dove!' (lines 11–12).

Towards the end of her essay 'On the Character of Mrs Hemans's Writings' (1835), Landon exposes yet again the dangers of making one's art public: 'What is poetry, and what is a poetical career? The first is to have an organization of extreme sensibility, which the second exposes bare-headed to the rudest weather' (p. 184). In her two poetic tributes to Hemans she emphasises both the skill and the soul, the reward and the cost. In the incantatory 'Stanzas on the Death of Mrs Hemans' (1835), she praises Hemans by invoking 'Properzia Rossi'. Finally, the strong enjambment and the strategically ambiguous position of the word 'never' in 'Felicia Hemans' (1838) summarise the strength and plight of many Romantic women poets:

> Was not this purchased all too dearly? – never
> Can fame atone for all that fame hath cost. (lines 33–4)

Notes

1. *Collected Letters of Samuel Taylor Coleridge, vol. 1, 1785–1800*, ed. Earl Leslie Griggs (Oxford: Clarendon Press, 1966), p. 578.
2. In Anna Laetitia Barbauld, *Selected Poetry and Prose*, ed. William McCarthy and Elizabeth Kraft (Peterborough, ONT: Broadview Press, 2002), p. 143. All references to Barbauld's works are from this edition.
3. *The Poems of Charlotte Smith*, ed. Stuart Curran (Oxford and New York: Oxford University Press, 1993), p. 68. All references to Smith's work are from this edition.
4. Coleridge, *Collected Letters*, p. 576.
5. All references to Mary Robinson's work are from *Mary Robinson: Selected Poems*, ed. Judith Pascoe (Peterborough, Ontario: Broadview Press, 2000).
6. See Stuart Curran's excellent essay 'Mary Robinson's *Lyrical Tales* in Context', in Carol Shiner Wilson and Joel Haefner (eds.), *Re-Visioning Romanticism: British Women Writers, 1776–1837* (Philadelphia: University of Pennsylvania Press, 1994), pp. 17–35.
7. Robinson, *Selected Poems*, pp. 153, 149.

8. All references to Felicia Hemans's work are from *Felicia Hemans: Selected Poems, Letters, Reception Materials*, ed. Susan J. Wolfson (Princeton: Princeton University Press, 2000).
9. 'Ozymandias', in *Shelley's Poetry and Prose*, ed. Donald H. Reiman and Sharon B. Powers (New York and London: Norton, 1977), lines 6–7.
10. All references to Letitia Landon's work are from *Letitia Elizabeth Landon: Selected Writings*, ed. Jerome J. McGann and Daniel Riess (Peterborough, Ontario: Broadview Press, 1997).

Chapter 31
Victorian poetry: an overview

RICHARD CRONIN

The Victorian poetry fair

There is no style that Victorian poets share. One reason for this is that they had too many styles to choose from. Every Victorian poet was something like Tennyson's 'Soul' wandering through the palace of art: to assimilate Victorian culture was to be presented with a compendium so extensive and so miscellaneous that it resembled a curiosity shop rather than a museum:

> Isaïah with fierce Ezekiel,
>   Swarth Moses by the Coptic sea,
> Plato, Petrarca, Livy, and Raphaël,
>   And eastern Confutzee.
>
> ('The Palace of Art,' 1832 text)[1]

As a consequence, Victorian poetry, like Victorian architecture, was characteristically eclectic: it borrowed promiscuously from different historical periods and different poetic traditions. Victorian poets thought of themselves as 'modern' – the love they experienced was, in the title of Meredith's great poem, *Modern Love*, the ill from which they suffered was what Arnold called 'this strange disease of modern life' ('The Scholar-Gipsy,' line 203) – but their modernity was of a special kind. It did not release them into a new life: rather they were modern in their awareness of themselves as experiencing an almost posthumous existence. As Isobel Armstrong notices, Victorian poetry was 'overwhelmingly secondary'.[2]

Its secondary character was somewhat paradoxical because amongst the tenets inherited by the Victorian poets from their Romantic predecessors was the very high value attached to originality, and the notion that style should express the individual personality of the poet. Victorian poets needed to find a style of their own, and they set about it rather in the manner of Browning's Sordello when he 'slow re-wrought' the language of poetry, 'welding words into the crude / Mass from the new speech round him, till a rude / Armour was hammered out' (*Sordello* (1840), 2, lines 574–7). Browning and his hero come very close together here, because the lines describing how Sordello re-made the language of Italian poetry also serve to exemplify the style that Browning was himself developing just as self-consciously. Browning, like other Victorian poets, like Swinburne, Christina Rossetti and Hopkins, cultivated a pointedly individualised poetic manner, but, like the style hammered out by Sordello, it was a manner that was forged rather than found. The result is that the poetic styles so energetically developed often seem like performances, as if poets had found their own voices when they had shown themselves to be their own best impersonators. When Everard Hall, the poet of Tennyson's *Morte d'Arthur* reads, 'mouthing out his hollow oes and aes' ('The Epic,' line 50), Tennyson, although he probably wrote the poem in 1837–8, before he was thirty, was already so aware of himself as a Tennysonian poet that he could make a quiet joke of it. Swinburne more flamboyantly ended his volume of parodies, *The Heptalogia* (1880), with 'Nephelidia', in which he contrives the most accomplished Victorian parody of the Swinburnian, singing from 'the depth of the dreamy decline of the dawn through a notable nimbus of nebulous moonshine' (line 1).

Keats had insisted that the poet's nature can never be identical with itself: 'Not one word I ever utter can be taken for granted as an opinion growing out of my identical nature.'[3] That seemed the case to Tennyson as he wrote *Morte d'Arthur* at the very beginning of the Victorian period, and it still seemed so to Arthur Symons a few years before its close. For Symons, the poet is the detached spectator of his own performance:

Chained by enchantment to my stall,
  I see myself upon the stage
Dance to amuse a music-hall.
  ('Prologue' (1895), lines 3–5)

In the act of writing, Victorian poets experience and often explore a sense of being divided from themselves. In Augusta Webster's 'Faded' (1870, first published 1893), a woman contemplates a youthful portrait of herself, and finds, instead of a Wordsworthian confidence that the days of her life are 'bound each to each', only a bleak confirmation that she is separated from her youthful self as abruptly as the dead are from the living. She can bring herself to gaze at her youthful portrait only at dusk, in the 'hushed, hueless light' when 'we two a little time are one' (lines 10 and 17). The poem is a dramatic monologue in which Webster, who was in her early thirties, married and mother to a young daughter, speaks as a woman who, in remaining single, has missed 'a woman's destiny and sole hope' (line 103). Such women are 'irretrievable bankrupts of [their] very selves' (line 70), their fate predicted in a dream that the speaker remembers, a nightmare in which she found herself with her family, speaking to them, hugging them, but all unnoticed, because, as a voice explains to her, she is dead. Webster was a supporter of the women's suffrage movement and an acquaintance of Frances Power Cobbe and John Stuart Mill. In 'Faded' she is addressing her interest in the lot of Victorian women, and also, if less evidently, in the lot of Victorian poets. Aged speakers, and characters like Tennyson's *Enoch Arden*, condemned to a posthumous life, proved oddly congenial even to youthful Victorian poets, presumably because they allowed them to express a sense that they were practising an art of the past, an art that in the modern world might soon become obsolete. In 'Faded' the portrait, unlike its subject, does not age, but this does not figure for Webster the power of art to transcend time. The portrait like the sitter will be superseded, consigned to the attic, its place usurped by some newer model. Only then will the woman and her portrait become 'one again', reunited in neglect.

The significance of Webster's title, 'Faded', might be extended to the genre within which she worked. Few Victorian poets, even poets as self-consciously modern as the Brownings, seem entirely free from the suspicion that their work was only a supplement to the achievement of the English poets who had preceded them. Victorian poets seem always aware of the gulf that separates them from their readership, their poems from the times in which they were being written and poetry-making from the real business of life. They are more modest in the claims they are prepared to make for their art than their Romantic predecessors. They often favour the enclosed space rather than those landscapes 'boundless, as we wish our souls to be' (*Julian and Maddalo*, line 17)[4] favoured by Shelley. Matthew Arnold's 'Lines Written in Kensington Gardens' is written from a place that is within the great city of London and yet secluded from it. The place may remind him that even in his 'helpless cradle' he was 'breathed on by the rural Pan' (lines 23–4), and yet all through the poem he registers the traffic noises, the 'girdling city's hum' (line 6) and 'jar' (line 38) audible even as he lies beneath the trees. Arnold entertains the illusion that he writes from a place where the birds, the daisies and the 'air-stirred forest' (line 16) enjoy an 'endless, active life' (line 14) that exposes the urgent bustle of the city streets as no more than an 'impious uproar' (line 25). But the poem exposes that illusion as much as entertains it. The only human presence that intrudes on Arnold's solitude, the child carrying his broken toy to his nurse, reveals that the place that Arnold associates with the 'calm soul of all things' (line 37) is only an urban park and cannot offer a true alternative to metropolitan London, because it was planned, planted and is maintained by the city that surrounds it. It is London that grants Arnold and the other visitors to the park the experience that the poem celebrates, the illusion that they have escaped the city. In 'Lines Written in Kensington Gardens' Arnold makes poetry out of his own bad faith, the bad faith of being a man of leisure, a man without gainful occupation, and, which Arnold half suspects may amount to the same thing, the bad faith of being a poet in such a busy, prosaic age as the nineteenth century.

Victorian poets seem not to feel at one with themselves, and they are equally likely to write poems that signal a sense that they feel displaced from the time in which they live. Or it may be that they live not so much at a particular time as inhabit a vacant in-between space, 'Wandering between two worlds, one dead, / The other powerless to be born' (Arnold, 'Stanzas from the Grande Chartreuse', lines 85–6). Browning's poems often focus on transitional figures, Paracelsus (1835), Sordello (1840), 'Pictor Ignotus' (1845), in a way that reflects, surely, Browning's sense that he too was living through a transitional time. Another group of poems are set, in the phrase that haunted Tennyson, 'far – far – away', but include a frame that attaches them to the modern world. In Tennyson's *Morte d'Arthur*, the poet Everard Hall reads his poem, and then the narrator goes to bed to dream of Arthur returned, dressed no longer in battle armour but 'like a modern gentleman / Of stateliest port' (lines 294–5). He does not so much dream of the poem as of the long lapse of years that separates him from it.

In D. G. Rossetti's 'The Burden of Nineveh' (1856, revised 1870), the speaker stares at the 'Great Bull' that Layard had excavated, the relic of a culture so strange that it seems scarcely imaginable. But the speaker encounters the city sacked in 612 BC from within an aggressively modern space. As he leaves the British Museum making the 'swing-door spin' (line 8; the first phase of the building was not completed until 1852), the colossal statue is being hoisted in. It had arrived in London in the autumn of 1850. Rossetti has a sardonic sense of the distance that separates the culture that produced the statue from the culture within which it is displayed. In the one he imagines 'brown maidens' singing from 'purple mouths' (lines 23–4): in the other 'school-foundations' (line 76) rigidly arranged in crocodiles three abreast survey the beast and vaguely connect it with 'that zealous tract: / "Rome, – Babylon, and Nineveh" ' (lines 79–80). Only the shadow that the beast throws, the same in London as it was in Nineveh, seems to connect it with what it had been all those centuries before. Rossetti's cadences echo Keats's 'Ode on a Grecian Urn':

> What vows, what rites, what prayers preferr'd
> What songs has the strange image heard?
> In what blind vigil stood interr'd
> For ages, till an English word
> Broke silence first at Nineveh? (lines 26–30)

But the Keatsian confidence that Rossetti feels when he looks at Greek sculpture – 'Her Art for ever in fresh wise / From hour to hour rejoicing me' (lines 4–5) – does not survive the encounter with the Assyrian statue, the remnant of a culture that remains unknown and unknowable. London and Assyria seem quite disconnected until Rossetti imagines London itself become, like Nineveh, an archaeological site, and the Great Bull disinterred by Australasian excavators who will view it as 'a relic now / of London, not of Nineveh!' (lines 179–80) At once the statue, its flanks fretted with 'dark runes' (line 13) that had resisted Rossetti's best attempts to read them, becomes all too legible:

> Those heavy wings spread high,
> So sure of flight, which do not fly;
> That set gaze never on the sky . . . (lines 192–4)

The statue becomes fraught with meaning, but only when Rossetti stops looking at it as a work of art and agrees to understand it simply as a symptom of the society that produced it, as a commodity rather like the 'corpulent, straggling epergne' that graces Mr Podsnap's dining table in Dickens's *Our Mutual Friend*, and so perfectly embodies Mr Podsnap's philosophy of life that all his dinner guests feel as if it is being thrust down their throat with every morsel they eat.[5]

There was good reason why a poet such as Rossetti should have defined works of art as the antitheses of commodities, for by mid century it was the novel rather than poetry that dominated the literary marketplace. Economically, too, poetry had become secondary. At the beginning of the Victorian period that subordinate position is best indicated by the Annuals, lavishly produced volumes published each year to meet the Christmas gift book market, in which the poems were subordinated to the engravings on which the bulk of the production costs was spent. Poets were often supplied with an engraving and expected to write verse in illustration of it. In the decade from 1825 to 1835 the poetry market was so dominated by the Annuals that most publishers gave up publishing new volumes by single poets. One publisher, Edward Moxon, continued to do so, but he published only on the basis that the poets themselves shared the publishing risks, which he minimised by publishing small first editions, usually of 500 copies. Because he had scarcely any competitors, Moxon published almost all the leading early Victorian poets, including Elizabeth Barrett, Tennyson and Robert Browning, but he would publish any volume of poems whatever if the author were prepared to underwrite the full production cost. The chief reason for the collapse of the poetry market was certainly the failure of poetry to match the appeal of the novel, for readers and also for publishers, who had a significant guaranteed sale of any novel to circulating libraries. As A. H. Clough noted, readers preferred *Vanity Fair* and *Bleak House* to any modern poetry.[6] In 1848, when Clough published *The Bothie of Toper-na-fuosich* (subsequently entitled *The Bothie of Tober-na-vuolich* after Clough discovered that his first title was improper), he chose to have his poem printed at the Chiswick Press, owned by Charles Whittingham, the finest printer of the mid nineteenth century. It was the decision of a man who recognised that publication was an extravagant self-indulgence, not an attempt to secure a living. Poets with the determination and the financial resources to persist in their profession might eventually make money. The turning-point for Tennyson came with the publication of *In Memoriam* (1850), which went through five editions in eighteen months, and *Enoch Arden* (1864) was published in a first edition of 60,000. But this was exceptional. Robert Browning's experience was more typical. The volume for which he is now best known, *Men and Women* (1855), did not go into a second edition. He did not begin to sell well until Chapman and Hall brought out a collected edition of his poems in 1863.[7]

These economic circumstances are a crucial context for the understanding of Victorian poetry, as Browning suggests with typical indirection in one of his best-known monologues, 'Fra Lippo Lippi'. Lippo Lippi is a street child who has joined the Carmelite convent to avoid starvation. It is the monks who discover his artistic talent. But the Prior disapproves of Lippo Lippi's habit of painting 'Faces, arms, legs and bodies like the true / As much as pea and pea' (lines 177–8), holding rather that the painter's task is to make his audience 'forget there's such a thing as flesh' (line 182) by giving them 'no more of body than shows soul' (line 188). This stimulates the painter to develop his own, radical naturalistic aesthetic that, as all the poem's readers have noted, has a close affinity with Browning's own. But Browning places Lippo Lippi at a historical pivot, at the point when patronage of the arts was passing from the Church to the great families such as the Medici whose power was based on wealth derived from their banking and mercantile interests. Lippo Lippi may still be a friar but, as he assures the guard who apprehends him as he slips away from a brothel, he is currently

lodging with a friend
Three streets off – he's a certain . . . how d'ye call?
Master – a . . . Cosimo of the Medici. (lines 15–17)

Because he no longer paints for the Church but for the private rooms of the new mercantile nobility of Florence, Lippo Lippi has secured his artistic freedom: 'I'm my own master, paint now as I please – / Having a friend, you see, in the Corner-house' (lines 226–7). In Browning's own day the Pre-Raphaelites were able to assert their independence of the Royal Academy because they found patrons amongst the rich manufacturers of the Midlands and the North of England, but, as Browning must have been only too glumly aware, this was not the case for Victorian poets. They enjoyed an almost unqualified freedom to write as they would, but they enjoyed that freedom only because almost all of them published their volumes at their own expense, or, as in the case of G. M. Hopkins, scarcely published at all.

A poem written after Victoria's death, John Davidson's 'The Crystal Palace' (1908–9), offers a useful retrospect on the whole period. Like 'The Palace of Art' and 'The Burden of Nineveh' the poem is set in an exhibition space. Sir Joseph Paxton's masterpiece of glass and iron had been built to house the Great Exhibition. After the exhibition closed in 1851 the building was re-erected in South London, where it became the centre of the nation's first theme park. Davidson's poem records his visit to the Palace in 1905, accompanied by Max Beerbohm. The poet-narrator expresses throughout a scornful detachment from this 'Victorian temple of commercialism' (line 14), maintaining the scorn of commerce so general amongst Victorian poets anxious to offer the weak market for poetry as an indication of its cultural value, and he maintains, too, like most Victorian poets, a strong sense of his distance from the crowd. But for Davidson the crowd has become 'Mob', the word and the refusal of a dignifying article suggesting that by 1908 Victorian aloofness is sharpening into a proto-Modernist disdain. His hauteur is most zealously announced by his use of a bizarrely eclectic diction: 'magnific rotatory engine' (line 9), 'the Tartar's Volant oratory' (line 67), 'solemn youths / Sustaining ravished donahs' (lines 87–8), a slice of lemon as a 'starred bisection' (line 194). The diction seems designed to mock the Palace, the 'glass and iron' (line 30) modernity of which is seen as an unnatural attempt to deny time by producing a kind of architecture that can never 'mellow or decay' (line 35), and hence an architecture that has, as its only proper counterpart, the prehistoric: it is compared to the 'fossil of a giant myriapod' (line 23). The story of the poem is the story of how all Davidson's attempts to elevate himself above the other visitors to the Palace fail, so that the Palace that he tries so carefully to establish as the antithesis of the culture to which he is devoted becomes, despite his best efforts, its type. It is a culture in which Cellini's *Perseus* coexists in stucco replica with a 'stupid thing' (line 260) by Canova. The prime business of the visitors is not with the exhibits but with the eating and the drinking, done on a new system, not by paying for the food directly, but by purchasing tokens that can be exchanged for it. This, quite literally, is a society of consumers, and the poet, although he eats his sole more daintily, savouring the 'delicate texture of the foam-white fish' (line 198) which, with the addition of lemon, evolves a 'palatable harmony / That music might by better chance express' (lines 199–200), is just as much a consumer as all the other visitors, except that he has the funds to be more choosy. Arnold had urged on poets the ambition to become the secular priests of the nineteenth century. Davidson meets, in the billiard room, a curate who 'tells two funny stories' and 'talks about the stage' (lines 237–8). His business is

> To entertain and not to preach: you see,
> It's with the theatre and the music-hall,
> Actor and artists, the parson must compete. (lines 240–2)

It was a competition in which, like it or not, the poet too was entered.

Voice in Victorian poetry

The bizarre diction of 'The Crystal Palace' strikingly underwrites the proposition that every Victorian poet had to forge rather than find a voice. The most important consequence is that in almost all Victorian poems the voice is dramatic even if it only dramatises, like 'The Crystal Palace', the voice of the poet himself. The voice that Davidson forges in that poem is strikingly divergent from the voice of the Cockney clerk that he deploys in his best-known poem, 'Thirty Bob a Week' (1894), and yet both voices are, quite evidently, performed. The voices of the poets of the 1890s veer erratically between the demotic of 'Thirty Bob a Week' or Kipling's *Barrack-Room Ballads* (1892) and poems that seem affectedly precious in their diction. But the difference appears less extreme if both styles are recognised as performances. Kipling is clearly inventing the voice of the British Tommy who pays his tribute to 'Fuzzy-Wuzzy' (1892) – 'Then 'ere's *to* you, Fuzzy-Wuzzy, an' the missis and the kid' (line 21) – but Wilde is just as clearly inventing the voice of the exquisite *flâneur* who watches balloons float over the city:

Against these turbid, turquoise skies
 The light and luminous balloons
 Dip and drift like satin moons,
Drift like silken butterflies.

('Les Ballons' (1887), lines 1–4)

The speaker looks at the balloons very knowingly, aware that they are gorgeous, and hollow, held up only by a breath, and that they have all this in common with the poem that celebrates them. But Wilde's poem performs the affectations of its speaker just as flamboyantly as Kipling performs his speaker's gruff sincerity.

Such self-consciousness, predictable in the poets of the 1890s, is evident already in early Victorian poets, and in the least expected poems. The afterlife of Macaulay's 'Horatius' (1842) was as a stirring recitation piece: it was once much favoured by histrionic schoolmasters. The poem takes its story from the Roman historian Livy. It is, as Macaulay puts it in his subtitle, 'A Lay made about the Year of the City CCCLX'. The date suggests that the poem is designed to meet a taste in Victorian men formed by the Latin lessons of the schoolroom, but Macaulay is anxious to widen the appeal of his material. The word 'Lay' associates the poem with Walter Scott's medievalising ballads, *The Lay of the Last Minstrel* and its successors, a suggestion confirmed by the poem's metre and by its manner. Romans and Etruscans do battle as, in Scott's poems, the English and the Scots wage war, each side ever willing to act as the admiring audience of the other's valour. When Horatius displays his heroism 'even the ranks of Tuscany / Could scarce forbear to cheer' (lines 508–9). It is an ethics of the playing field, common to Scott, to the Kipling of 'Fuzzy-Wuzzy' and to Macaulay here, except that he prefaced his poem with a dry note suggesting that its author seems to have been 'much given to pining after good old times which had never really existed'. Macaulay was a Whig, of course, and anxious no doubt to dissociate himself from the Tory assumptions embedded in Walter Scott's variety of medievalism, and so he offers his poem as dramatic. But the crucial point is that Macaulay was choosing an option always available within a literary culture in which the salient fact about each and every poetic style was that it was assumed.

This is the context in which the most distinctive generic innovation of Victorian poets, the dramatic monologue, should be understood. If to speak in one's own voice involves an act of impersonation, frankly to assume the voice of another amounts to a paradoxical kind of sincerity. But the Victorian dramatic monologue is not only characterised by the use of an assumed voice. The strongest examples choose speakers who live on the margins, which is why so many dramatic monologues express the sense common to the poets of the period that they were writing at a distance from the centre of Victorian society. In 'Faded', for example, the speaker, ageing and unmarried, feels that she no longer has an identity, and has become a 'shadow and an echo – one that was' (line 140). Fra Lippo Lippi, on the other hand, has an irrepressible sense of self. He speaks from the margins of respectability, apprehended by the watch in a red-light area. Dramatic monologues may be spoken by a prostitute (Webster's 'A Castaway'), her customer (D. G. Rossetti's 'Jenny'), a murderer (Robert Browning's 'Porphyria's Lover'), an escaped slave (Elizabeth Barrett Browning's 'The Runaway Slave at Pilgrim's Point'). Often the speaker is distanced from the poet in time or in space, or both, as when Robert Browning speaks as Karshish, an Arab physician of the first century, but the more distant the setting the more local and contemporary the theme: the Arab scientist present at the dawning of the Christian era is offered as a mirror image of all those British scientists of the nineteenth century who feared they might be witnessing its end.

Amy Levy's 'Xantippe: A Fragment' (1880) is representative. Amy Levy speaks as the widow of Sokrates, a woman who has been deprived of her identity by history, flattened into a common noun signifying any shrewish wife. Told when she was just seventeen that she was to marry a man 'all ungainly and uncouth' (line 57), she put aside her youthful dream of a husband whose 'perfect body matched the perfect soul' (line 78), and set herself diligently to the task of finding out the soul of the man to whom she had been given 'athwart the grosser flesh' (line 87), only to find that Sokrates is blind to her best efforts. He remains confident that, except in the case of rare exceptions such as Aspasia, the foreign-born consort of Perikles, women have bodies too frail to stand 'the test of soul' (line 173). When Xantippe protests, she finds herself mocked by Sokrates's disciples, by the beautiful Alkibiades, by Plato with his 'narrow eyes and niggard mouth' (line 197) and by Sokrates himself. Her husband does not even invite her to join his friends to witness how nobly a philosopher can die. She speaks in her old age, long after she has become the woman that her husband took her for: her days are spent in spinning rather than needlework, but she delights just as much as her modern-day counterparts in gossip, and in spreading scandal.

Amy Levy was Cambridge-educated, the first Jewish student to be admitted to Newnham College. In 'Xantippe' she speaks not for herself but for her sex, tracing the exclusion of women from the life of the mind to the point at which that life was born, in Athens of the fifth century BC. Arthur Hugh Clough is glumly aware that too much education can be as debilitating as too little. In *Amours de Voyage* (1858), his hero, the Oxford-educated Claude, is so conscious that truth is 'Flexible, changeable, vague, and multiform, and doubtful' (Canto 5, line 102) that he is unable to commit himself to a political cause, to a woman, or even, without misgivings, to a work of art. 'Michael Angelo's dome, that had hung the Pantheon in heaven' (Canto 1, line 113), is spoiled for Claude, who cannot forget his disapproval of the 'metallic beliefs and regimental devotions' (Canto 1, line 111) of the Catholic worshippers. He finds it just as hard to forget Mrs Trevellyn long enough to fall in love with her daughter. Mrs Trevellyn is an intellectual, and yet, even when she 'adventures on Schiller' (Canto 1, line 210) she manages still to grate 'the fastidious ear with the slightly mercantile accent' (Canto 1, line 212). Claude's sensitivity to Mrs Trevellyn's voice trains the reader to be equally sensitive to his own, alert to the callowness that he masks as sophistication, to the facetiousness with which he disguises his fear of making a fool of himself and to the cynicism in which he cloaks his sentimentality. Claude is most fully revealed in Clough's metre, the hexameters that keep him at a remove from the life that he records by revealing that, even though he is so far away from Oxford, he remains enclosed within a cloistered life. Clough's example suggests one reason why so much Victorian poetry is in some sense dramatic. It is an all but inevitable consequence for poets who have inherited the notion that poets most completely express themselves in their styles, but have added to it a new suspicion that style might itself be pathological, a symptom of the disease of its exponent rather than the medium that communicates a uniquely valuable vision of the world.

Victorian poetry and the world

Wordsworth represented his poetry as a 'spousal verse' celebrating the marriage of the human mind with 'this goodly universe'. Unlike Wordsworth, Hopkins was committed to the notion that the natural world, properly read, might figure spiritual truths, and yet Hopkins lacked Wordsworth's happy sense of 'how exquisitely' the 'individual Mind' and the 'external world' are fitted to each other.[8] 'When I compare myself, my being-myself', he noted, 'with anything else whatever, all things alike, all in the same degree, rebuff me with blank unlikeness.'[9] But Hopkins continued to study the natural world, intent on locating within it the truths, human and spiritual, which alone could justify the attention he paid it. In consequence, many of his sonnets share a common pattern. The octave pays its tribute to some instance of natural beauty, and the sestet insists that it figures a divine truth, but octave and sestet are divided by a *volta* that is always threatening to become a volte-face.

In 'The Windhover' (1877) the octave ends with what Hopkins elsewhere ('Henry Purcell', line 13) calls 'a colossal smile', as Hopkins exclaims at 'the achieve of, the mastery of the thing!' (line 8). His tribute seems to extend from the mastery displayed by the bird in flight to the mastery of the octave in which Hopkins has so deftly captured it. But that leaves him in the sestet with the hard task of explaining why it is appropriate that he should be so 'Stirred for a bird' (line 8). The bird stirs his 'heart in hiding' (line 7). 'Hide' might already signify the covert in which birdwatchers concealed themselves, but the notion of a life spent in hiding was of more central importance to Hopkins. Ignatius Loyola, the founder of his order, had himself chosen to live an obscure life, and that was the life he enjoined on all Jesuits, which is why, as Hopkins explained in a letter, the part of Christ's life that Jesuits find most consoling is what he calls 'the hidden life in Galilee',[10] the years before he embarked on his mission in which Jesus lived as an obscure, unknown individual. In 'The Windhover', the priestly observer lives a life in hiding, and when he watches the falcon, he is so stirred, surely, because the falcon's life is so different from his own. His life is given over to self-restraint, whereas the kestrel's life is wholly given over to self-display. The kestrel in flight flamboyantly, wonderfully, proclaims itself. It cries, '*What I do is me, for that I came*' ('As kingfishers catch fire', line 8). The sestet begins by acknowledging that the beauty of Christ in his crucifixion, atoning for the sins of mankind, is 'a billion / Times told lovelier' (lines 10–11) than the merely 'Brute beauty' (line 9) of the bird, and ends by celebrating the life of 'sheer plod' (line 12), the life given over to the humdrum and the mundane, which is the life Hopkins himself has chosen. Hopkins was moved by just-fallen conkers, 'Fresh-firecoal chestnut-falls' ('Pied Beauty', line 4), the dull green husk split to reveal a nut that, before the air dulls it, is momentarily lustrous as flame. He ends this sonnet with a similar image, 'blue-bleak' (line 13) ashes slipping to reveal as they fall the red coals beneath. The hidden life, he wants to say, has its own beauty, which seems wholly unlike the beauty of a kestrel in flight, except that, rightly understood, the two apparently quite different kinds of beauty cannot be quite unlike one another, because nothing can be beautiful except in so far as it resembles Christ. The poem begins with a gasp of awe at the beauty of a bird: it ends when it has shown that gasp to be in the service of Christ. But the reader is left with a sharp awareness of the force needed to 'buckle' (line 10) the two parts of the poem together.

Hopkins was untypical in continuing in the nineteenth century to attempt a typological reading of the natural world (though Christina Rossetti did the same), but he was entirely representative in finding the passage between natural appearance and human meaning so difficult. There were Victorian poets who maintained a Romantic faith that there might be a deep correspondence between nature and the mind, between, for example, the natural wind and poetic inspiration. Several of Emily Brontë's poems turn on the possibility. In 'The Night-Wind' (1840) she may deny that the wind's music has 'power to reach [her] mind' (line 20), but she represents the wind as an importunate suitor who insists that his proper place is as her consort. When the wind makes the leaves rustle they seem 'instinct with spirit' (line 16): when the night wind blows it carries the message that 'Heaven' is 'glorious' and the 'sleeping Earth' is 'fair' (lines 7–8). And yet even this poem ends when the wind recognises that the marriage he proposes does not, any more than marriage between a man and a woman, have the power to survive death:

> 'And when thy heart is laid at rest
>   Beneath the church-yard stone
> I shall have time enough to mourn
>   And thou to be alone' – (lines 33–6)

More usually, Victorian poets assume a condition that their Romantic predecessors associated with dejection or with a state of imaginative loss, a condition in which the mind seems dissevered from the world in which it has its being. Romantic poets had celebrated those moments when the world within and the world without seemed fused, but for Tennyson such experiences are infantile:

> The baby new to earth and sky,
> What time his tender palm is prest
> Against the circle of the breast,
> Has never thought that 'this is I:'
>
> But as he grows he gathers much,
> And learns the use of 'I', and 'me,'
> And finds 'I am not what I see,
> And other than the things I touch.'
>
> (*In Memoriam*, XLV.1–8)

Many Victorian poets cultivated what Carol Christ has termed an 'aesthetics of particularity',[11] issuing in descriptions of the natural world that aspire to the kind of minute accuracy that one associates with Pre-Raphaelite painting. The effect is usually in the poems as in the paintings to distance the world described from the observer.

Most critics account for this by referring to nineteenth-century intellectual developments, in particular to the higher status of 'scientific' accounts of the world, 'scientific' signifying here the practice of describing the world as subject to physical laws which are assumed to be independent of human psychology. In *In Memoriam* (1850) Tennyson's Christian faith that 'not a worm is cloven in vain' (LIV.9) collides with the grim truth known to all Victorian naturalists that nature is quite 'careless of the single life' (LV.8), and careful only of the type, and the geologist's discovery in 'scarpèd cliff and quarried stone' (LVI.2) of the still bleaker truth that nature regards the disappearance even of species with indifference. But it still needs to be explained why this scientific way of looking at the world seems to have impacted in the nineteenth century on poets so much more forcefully than on novelists. Explanations offer themselves. Victorian poets were the inheritors of a Romanticism that celebrated the 'one life' at once 'within us and abroad'[12] (Coleridge, 'The Eolian Harp', line 26) and so may have been more sensitive to ways of thinking that insisted that the life within had come to seem quite severed from the life without. But it may also be that a forlorn sense of disconnection from the world is a more resonant experience for those practising an art in which the reading public often seemed to take so little interest.

For whatever reason, many Victorian poems hinge on the difficulty of forging any connection between the world of fact and the world of value. In D. G. Rossetti's 'The Woodspurge' (1870) the grief-stricken speaker experiences a state of raw disseverance from the world. In Romantic poems such as Shelley's 'Ode to the West Wind' the wind often merges with the breath of the poet, but Rossetti's wind remains quite alien: 'The wind flapped loose, the wind was still' (line 1). The noise of everyday life intrudes like an outrage on his 'naked ears' (line 8). As he slumps, his head bent over the grass, a single plant impresses itself on his memory, the woodspurge with its 'three cups in one' (line 12). The experience offers no consolation: it remains quite arbitrary, a version of the Trinity for a wholly deconsecrated world. Rossetti, it may be suspected, is making a polemical point of his disenchantment, but in 'Cyclamens' (1893) by Michael Field (the name under which Katherine Bradley and Edith Cooper published their jointly written poems) there seems no such intention. The poem constructs a landscape 'terribly white' (line 1) in which the cyclamens outdo the whiteness of the snow-covered, moonlit landscape, and it ends when the speaker acknowledges the power of the 'chiselled white' (line 6) of the flowers to strike her to the heart. But the pang remains quite contentless, delivered by the 'handful of cyclamen' (line 7) like the stroke of a calmly indifferent sculptor. Both poems share a characteristic Victorian preoccupation with the enigmatic relationship between the world observed with such sharp precision and the feelings of the observer.

Victorian poets often seem to be subject to contradictory impulses, either acknowledging, usually sadly, that poetry can only survive by retreating from 'the world' as the nineteenth century understands it, or insisting, usually robustly, that poems must be made out of an energetic engagement with that world. Arnold's 'The Scholar-Gipsy' (1853) treats the legend of a youth who, because he is too poor to support his studies at Oxford, leaves the university and joins the gypsies. This figure, found in a little-known seventeenth-century text by Joseph Glanvill, enables him to associate the poetic impulse with the pre-industrial past, with youthful potential that can never be fulfilled, and with a disposition so shy that the scholar-gipsy can be seen only 'by rare glimpses' (line 54), only out of the corner of the eye. The poem ends enigmatically, with a Tyrian trader who escapes the competition of a 'merry Grecian coaster' (line 237) by searching out new custom amongst 'the dark Iberians', 'shy traffickers' (line 249) who will examine his goods only if he leaves them on the shore and retires. Only in transactions so delicate, Arnold implies, can the poet have dealings with the public world. W. E. Henley's *In Hospital* (1875, revised in 1888), a poem based on Henley's experience as a long-term patient in Edinburgh Infirmary, seems to embrace exactly the kind of modern realities that Arnold in the person of the scholar-gipsy repudiates. But the hospital patient just as much as Arnold's retiring scholar is a kind of recluse, and hospital experience still more emphatically confirms the sense that dominates Arnold's poem of the mind being out of harmony with the world in which it finds itself. The patient who sees his foot 'Swaddled in wet, white lint / Brilliantly hideous with red' (lines 224–5) becomes aware of a world in which even his own body has become blankly, disturbingly unfamiliar.

In 'The Buried Life' (1852) Arnold represents the poet as speaking into a 'world-deafened air' (line 82): poetry is what, in the ordinary business of life, gets drowned out. In Christina Rossetti the notion generates a desire to protect her privacy so intense that it results in poems that might best be described as anti-lyrics. In 'Winter: My Secret' (1862) the speaker never reveals what her secret might be. She even accommodates the playful suggestion that 'there is no secret after all' (line 8), so that its only function is to produce the illusion of psychological depth that distinguishes the lyric subject. It might seem to follow that public poetry is a contradiction in terms, but, if so, it was a contradiction that fascinated poets throughout the century. Elizabeth Barrett

Browning's 'The Runaway Slave at Pilgrim's Point' (1848), first published in the Philadelphia journal, *The Liberty Bell*, was her contribution to the abolitionist campaign, and yet the poem remains suspicious of the public voice that such campaigns demand. The horror of slavery is articulated through the voice of a mother who can love the child that she has borne only when it is dead, a perverse emotion that issues directly from the perverse society of which the mother, raped by white men, is a victim. The woman can accept her role as the child's mother only when differences of colour disappear, 'in the death-dark where we may kiss and agree' (line 251). Only when the child is in its grave is she free to sing to the child the only song she knows, a song that she learned in her 'maidenhood' (line 189). The song has the power to 'join the souls of both of us' (line 196), the power to transcend difference that poets had once claimed for their own songs, but Barrett Browning's poem is a monologue spoken precisely because such a song seems to the speaker still unsingable, a memorial to a poem that cannot be written.

'The Runaway Slave at Pilgrim's Point' directly addresses a central Victorian value, motherhood, but it is informed by Barrett Browning's awareness that even private values cannot preserve their independence from the public world. The most vivid of all poetic accounts of marriage in the verse of the period, Meredith's *Modern Love* (1862), approaches its topic through infidelity, separation and suicide. Meredith chooses an appropriately perverse verse form, a sixteen-line stanza made up of two Petrarchan octaves, to recount the story of a marriage in which the partners manage to cleave to one another no more successfully than the two stiffly symmetrical parts of Meredith's 'sonnet'. The husband is achingly aware of his wife's body, of the curve of her eyelid 'Full-sloping like the breasts beneath' (Sonnet 15, line 8), but it is a sensitivity sharpened by his knowledge of his wife's adultery. Their marriage is the envy of friends quite unaware that theirs is a complicity of guilt. At the dinner table they even become 'enamoured' (Sonnet 17, line 10) each of the other's acting, but it is a feeling that cannot survive in the most intimate of all domestic spaces, the bedroom:

> I think she sleeps: it must be sleep, when low
> Hangs that abandoned arm toward the floor;
> The face turned with it. (Sonnet 15, lines 1–3)

Meredith understands that marriage is at once a private bond and a social institution, and his sequence explores the complications that arise from this double identity.

As in the case of love poetry, it is the perverse religious poetry, poems that arrive at a kind of inverse piety through the intensity with which they express their disbelief, rather than, for example, Keble's phenomenally popular *Christian Year* (1827), that still seem vital. In *In Memoriam* (1850) Tennyson develops a rhetoric in which scepticism, what Tennyson terms 'honest doubt' (XCVI.11), becomes the indispensable badge of authentic religious feeling. The poem moves towards faith in a progress that wins the reader's confidence only because it is faltering, lame and faint (lyric lv). Victorian poets more confident in their faithlessness can at times achieve a kind of liturgical authority through the powerfully ecclesiastical rhythms in which they record their disbelief. Clough's 'Easter Day. Naples, 1849' (not published until 1951) is best understood as an inverted hymn:

> Eat, drink and die, for we are souls bereaved,
> Of all the creatures under this broad sky
> We are most hopeless, that had hoped most high,
> And most beliefless, that had most believed.
>   Ashes to ashes, dust to dust;
>   As of the unjust, also of the just –
>   Yea, of that Just One too.
> It is the one sad Gospel that is true,
>   Christ is not risen. (lines 86–94)

Unlike Tennyson's modest faith, Clough's unbelief demands the grandly assertive rhythms of the ode. The effect is at its most extreme in James Thomson's *The City of Dreadful Night* (1874) at the centre of which is a sermon spoken from a 'dark pulpit' (line 702) by a preacher who bids the congregation rejoice because humanity is the product of impersonal natural laws, because 'this little life is all we must endure' (line 734) and because those who find their brief life too long may 'end it' when they will 'without the fear of waking after death' (lines 768–9). It is the most eloquent verse sermon of the century. Hopkins's Terrible Sonnets are entirely characteristic of the poetry of the period in their recognition that the most profound religious experience available to nineteenth-century poets was the experience of the absence of God.

On his tombstone in Glasgow's Necropolis William Miller, author of 'Wee Willie Winkie', is celebrated as the 'Laureate of the Nursery'. There were many competitors for the title, amongst them Edward Lear, Lewis Carroll, Robert Louis Stevenson and W. B. Rands. The nursery is the room in which the infant of the middle-class house is safely enclosed, a place where the child is at once pampered and confined. In a much-ridiculed poem included in *Poems Chiefly Lyrical* (1830) Tennyson comes close to identifying the child's nursery with the poet's study:

O darling room, my heart's delight,
Dear room, the apple of my sight,
With thy two couches soft and white,
There is no room so exquisite,
No little room so warm and bright,
Wherein to read, wherein to write.
('O Darling Room,' lines 1–6)

It seemed to some of Tennyson's readers that the productions of the nation's laureate and the laureates of the nursery were not so unlike as might have been expected. In *Through the Looking Glass*, Lewis Carroll turned the garden lyrics in *Maud* into Nonsense, and Lear even subjected Tennyson's verse compliment to him to the process. Tennyson had written:

Illyrian woodlands, echoing falls
Of water, sheets of summer glass,
The long divine Peneïan pass,
The vast Akrokeraunian walls.
('To E. L., on His Travels in Greece', lines 1–4)

This becomes:

Delirious Bulldogs; – echoing calls
My daughter, – green as summer grass; –
The long supine Plebeian ass,
The nasty crockery boring falls; –[13]

Lear's parody does not so much travesty Tennyson's lines as release a nonsensicality that is already implicit in the Tennysonian original. There is a close affinity between Nonsense poems and some of the most representative nineteenth-century poetry. The characters in Lear's limericks compulsively repeating the same action are oddly similar to characters such as Tennyson's 'Mariana'. Tennyson's Ulysses is so nearly absurd that it seems quite natural to compare his heroism with that of Lear's Jumblies who go to sea in a sieve. Lear's limerick stanza even has formal similarities with Tennyson's *In Memoriam* stanza. Both end by looking back to their beginning, and this is appropriate because Nonsense behaviour, like grief, is characterised by a refusal to move forward, an impulse towards repetition and a rigidly maintained exclusion of other people.

In the nineteenth century elegy has a special tendency to verge on Nonsense. In 'Ave atque Vale' (1867), his richly elaborate elegy to Baudelaire, Swinburne insists throughout on the absurdity of his poem. The fact that he wrote it in response to a false rumour of Baudelaire's death has an odd appropriateness, for the whole poem consistently exposes itself as an empty charade, an offering made to gods in whose existence Swinburne firmly disbelieves. The poem builds its rich funeral music out of negatives: 'Thee not Orestes nor Electra mourns' (line 129). It is a poem fully conscious of its own futility, always aware that it is addressed to someone who is 'far too far for wings of words to follow' (line 89), that poetry is helpless in the face of death and just as helpless in the face of life: 'not all our songs, O friend, / Will make death clear or make life durable' (lines 171–2).

In 'Stanzas from the Grande Chartreuse' (1855) Arnold surveys the poetry of the early nineteenth century:

> What helps it now, that Byron bore,
> With haughty scorn which mocked the smart,
> Through Europe to the Aetolian shore
> The pageant of his bleeding heart? (lines 133–6)

Byron's case is that of all the moderns: 'What boots it, Shelley! that the breeze / Carried thy lovely wail away?' (lines 139–40). Arnold represents his poem as written on a visit to the chief Carthusian monastery, a monument that resembles 'some fallen Runic stone' (line 83), because it commemorates a faith that is no longer comprehensible. All modern poetry seems to him a song of despair wrung from those who have lost their faith, and hence, for all its charm, such poetry is only a symptom of spiritual weakness. By contrast, 'the best are silent now' (line 114), the 'kings of modern thought are dumb' (line 116). The poem ends when Arnold figures his own generation as children brought up in a secluded forest glade in the shelter of a ruined abbey, who have become far too used to their surroundings to respond to the future when it calls them. In 'Stanzas from the Grande Chartreuse' Arnold forges once more the 'tremulous cadence slow', the 'melancholy, long, withdrawing' music ('Dover Beach', lines 13, 25), which, as he well knew, gave his poems their distinctive, Arnoldian character, and yet he is not entirely unpersuasive in his claim to speak for his whole generation. Not all Victorian poets had lost their faith, and of those who had, not all were left feeling bereft, and yet they all needed to come to terms with a cultural circumstance that crucially distinguished them from their predecessors. In some way the most pressing knowledge that Victorian poets share, and that a rather large number of Victorian poems address, almost always indirectly, is the knowledge that poetry had lost the cultural centrality that earlier poets could take for granted.

Notes

1. Quotations are taken from *Victorian Poetry: An Annotated Anthology*, ed. Francis O'Gorman (Oxford; Blackwell, 2004), except from Robert Browning, *Sordello*, which is taken from Robert Browning, *The Poems*, vol. 1, ed. John Pettigrew and Thomas J. Collins (London: Penguin, 1981) and Tennyson's 'The Palace of Art' (1832 text) and 'To E. L., on His Travels in Greece,' which are taken from *Tennyson: A Selected Edition*, ed. Christopher Ricks (London: Longman, 1989).
2. Isobel Armstrong, *Victorian Poetry: Poetry, Poetics and Politics* (London: Routledge, 1993), p. 3.
3. *The Letters of John Keats*, ed. Hyder Edward Rollins, 2 vols. (Cambridge: Cambridge University Press, 1958), vol. 1, p. 387.
4. *Shelley's Poetry and Prose*, ed. Donald H. Reiman and Neil Fraistat (New York: Norton, 2002).
5. Charles Dickens, *Our Mutual Friend* (London: Oxford University Press, 1952), p. 131.
6. *Prose Remains of Arthur Hugh Clough*, ed. Blanche Clough (London: Macmillan, 1888), pp. 356–7.
7. See Lee Erickson, 'The Market', in Richard Cronin, Alison Chapman and Antony H. Harrison (eds.), *A Companion to Victorian Poetry* (Oxford: Blackwell, 2002), pp. 345–60.
8. Lines from *The Recluse* prefixed to *The Excursion*, in William Wordsworth, *The Poems*, ed. John O. Hayden, 2 vols. (New Haven and London: Yale University Press, 1981).
9. *The Sermons and Devotional Writings of Gerard Manley Hopkins*, ed. Christopher Devlin, SJ (London: Oxford University Press, 1959), p. 123.
10. *The Correspondence of Gerard Manley Hopkins and Richard Watson Dixon*, ed. C. C. Abbott (London: Oxford University Press, 1935), p. 96.
11. Carol T. Christ, *The Finer Optic: The Aesthetic of Particularity in Victorian Poetry* (New Haven: Yale University Press, 1975).
12. 'The Eolian Harp', line 26, in Samuel Taylor Coleridge, *Poetical Works*, ed. J. C. C. Mays (Princeton: Princeton University Press, 2001).
13. *The Later Letters of Edward Lear*, ed. Lady Strachey (London: T. Fisher Unwin, 1911), p. 140.

Chapter 32
Tennyson

ROBERT DOUGLAS-FAIRHURST

'Still life'

'In poetry', Matthew Arnold announced in 1880, 'the spirit of our race will find . . . its consolation and stay.'[1] It is a reassuring idea, but as Arnold had already pointed out in the Preface to his 1853 *Poems*, the hope that poetry would provide a cultural 'stay' (a device for supporting or steadying a structure) was all too often hampered in the period by writing which seemed to be suffering from a different form of 'stay': 'a stoppage, arrest, or suspension of action; a check, set-back'.[2] Consider W. H. Mallock's pamphlet *Every Man His Own Poet: Or, The Inspired Singer's Recipe Book* (1872), which offered tongue-in-cheek advice on 'How To Write A Poem Like Mr Tennyson'. To produce an epic like *Idylls of the King*, for example, take 'one blameless prig', add 'a beautiful wife' and 'one married goodly man', tie them together in a bundle 'with a link or two of Destiny', and surround them by 'a large number of men and women of the nineteenth century, in fairy-ball costume, flavoured with a great many possible vices, and a few impossible virtues'.

> Stir these briskly about for two volumes, to the great annoyance of the blameless prig, who is, however, to be kept carefully below swearing-point, for the whole time. If he once boils over into any natural action or exclamation, he is forthwith worthless, and you must get another. Next break the wife's reputation into small pieces, and dust them well over the blameless prig. Then take a few vials of tribulation, and wrath, and empty these generally over the whole ingredients of your poem, and, taking the sword of the heathen, cut into small pieces the greater part of your minor characters. Then wound slightly the head of the blameless prig, remove him suddenly from the table, and keep him in a cool barge for future use.[3]

Tennyson is not the only target of Mallock's satire – his pamphlet also includes 'recipes' for Swinburne, Arnold, 'How To Make An Ordinary Love Poem', and more – but this spoof is unusually sharp-eared in highlighting features which made the *Idylls* so vulnerable to parody: clumsy narrative links ('Next . . . and . . . Then . . . and . . . and . . . Then . . . and'), endlessly self-propelling rhythms ('and keep him in a cool barge for future use' is a line of blank verse perfectly skewered by 'cool') and the suspicion that Tennyson describes the virtues of his passive hero ('the blameless prig') with a vehemence that betrays his own doubts over whether they are solid enough to act in or on the real world.

It is no coincidence that all three of these implicit criticisms revolve around Tennyson's habit of repeating himself, from the smallest details of his verse to imaginative preoccupations that span his career. Even Tennyson's keenest contemporary admirers sometimes wondered how much of their pleasure in his verse arose from its cosseting sameness, how far familiarity bred content. The hero of Charles Kingsley's *Alton Locke*, praising Tennyson's ability to reveal 'the poetry which lies in everyday things', is especially enthusiastic about his defamiliarising of the natural world: 'The descriptions of the desolate pools and creeks where the dying swan floated, the hint of the silvery marsh mosses by Mariana's moat, came to me like revelations.'[4] Suddenly he finds himself returning with fresh eyes to everything he thought he knew, but his account also hints at how easily this wonder might be directed complacently inwards, at his own renovated powers of observation, as those internal chimes ('floated . . . moat') and ripples of alliteration ('descriptions . . . desolate . . . dying . . . marsh mosses . . . Mariana's moat') threaten to bring his voice stammering to a halt.

The seductive aural pleasures of Tennyson's verse were brilliantly described by Walt Whitman: 'There is such a latent charm in mere words, cunning collocutions, and in the voice ringing them, which he has caught and brought out, beyond all others – as in the line, "And hollow, hollow, hollow, all delight," in "The Passing of Arthur."'[5] Like all good criticism, this is intimate with its subject, as the self-affirming chime of 'caught and brought out' attunes itself to the echo-chamber of Tennyson's verse, and in particular to a line like 'And hollow, hollow, hollow, all delight', which reveals the ability of art to celebrate itself even as it is lamenting other losses. It is a common pattern in Tennyson's writing, which frequently braces itself against the unpredictable flux of experience in verse which 'loiters, slowly drawn' ('Œnone', line 5).[6] Lines such as 'Here rests the sap within the leaf, / Here stays the blood along the veins' ('The Day-Dream: The Sleeping Palace', lines 3–4) may describe an unnatural arrest of life's processes, but they also reflect self-consciously on the competing tugs of movement and stasis in the verse itself, as each line struggles towards a correspondence of word unit and rhythmical unit (the iambic pulse which flutters briefly in 'within' and 'along') before it is clogged up by further monosyllables. Even the simplest form of lyrical repetition can carry a similar resistance to change in Tennyson, as we hear in 'the days that are no more' (line 5) in 'Tears, idle tears', a refrain which is doubly a time-beater in its ability to measure out time while revealing the irrelevance of mere chronology to someone caught in the coils of an obsession.

The danger with such lyrical patterns, of course, is that they risk offering readers aesthetic pleasures that are hollow of anything other than delight. According to W. F. Rawnsley, 'In speaking of Browning, [Tennyson] once said to me: "I don't think that poetry should be *all thought*: there should be some melody." '[7] The possibility that thought and melody were separate categories for Tennyson is a stick that hostile critics have often used to beat him with, from G. K. Chesterton's argument that 'he had much more power of expression than was wanted for anything he had to express',[8] to Robert Graves's impatience with the refrain in 'The Ballad of Oriana', which he claimed would make just as much sense if it were replaced by the phrase 'bottom upwards':[9]

They should have stabbed me where I lay,
    Oriana!
How could I rise and come away,
    Oriana?
How could I look upon the day?
They should have stabbed me where I lay,
    Oriana –
They should have trod me into clay,
    Oriana. (lines 55–63)

The most acute contemporary criticism came from Alfred Austin, in an essay which saw Tennyson as the central impediment to progress in an 'unpoetical' age:

> What is one of the chief marks of great poetry? Surely, action. Indeed, we may say of great poetry, what Demosthenes said of great oratory, that the soul of it is – action, action, action. The 'Iliad' is all action. So, almost all, is the 'Aeneid'. Look at the action in 'Paradise Lost'! To name the poetry of Shakespeare is to name the poetry of action. . . . Turn to Mr Tennyson, and what do we see? Still life – almost uniform still life.[10]

There is a good joke in that last sentence, as it reaches out and collapses back on itself in a way that mimics Tennyson's own habits in poems like *Maud*, where a speaker who is suffering from the failure of a 'vast speculation' (I.9) finds his voice shrinking from the future in his own syntax: 'If I be dear. / If I be dear to some one else' (I.535–6), 'Let all be well, be well' (I.683). But the line which Austin goes on to choose as the key to Tennyson's writing, 'A perfect form in perfect rest' ('The Day-Dream: The Sleeping Beauty', line 24), does not seem altogether true to the experience of reading poems which, while often revolving around stilled lives like the lurking Kraken or the sense-numbed Lotos-Eaters, tend to depict this state as more fraught than restful. Indeed, what animates individual poems – even 'The Day-Dream', where the description of the enchanted Princess being revived by her suitor comes close to being an allegory of reading – is an ongoing struggle between the desire for rest and a nagging restlessness:

A touch, a kiss! the charm was snapt.
    There rose a noise of striking clocks,
And feet that ran, and doors that clapt,
    And barking dogs, and crowing cocks;
A fuller light illumined all,
    A breeze through all the garden swept,
A sudden hubbub shook the hall,
    And sixty feet the fountain leapt.
        ('The Day-Dream: The Revival', lines 1–8)

The more tightly organised Tennyson's stanzas – as here, where each line is riveted in place with a perfect rhyme and terminal punctuation – the more they start to resemble coiled springs, in which nouns and verbs seem to be pulling in different directions. Naturally, any poet's work might thrive on a similar tension between movement and stasis, given that all printed verse exists as both an unfolding process and a fixed set of relations. But Tennyson was unusual in the extent to which he drew on this double life of poetry as an imaginative resource. When he came to write 'Verse-Memoranda' during his travels, he was instinctively drawn to fragments which described different kinds of repression, and on several occasions used the form of his writing to suggest the force required to keep life's restive energies in check:

(*Torquay.*)   As the little thrift
  Trembles in perilous places o'er the deep

– where the gulf into which the fragile sea-plant may be dragged is suggested in the space opened up on the page between 'thrift' and 'Trembles'; or:

(*From the Old Red Sandstone.*)   As a strong spring
  Blocks its own issue (tho' it makes a fresh one of course)[11]

– where the flow of the sentence over the line-break is baulked by the unexpected stress on 'Blocks', like a cartoon figure opening a door and walking straight into a wall. Completed poems, similarly, emerge from the reciprocal pressures exercised by the thrust of individual lines and the structure which is attempting to contain them:

The air is damp, and hushed, and close,
As a sick man's room when he taketh repose
    An hour before death;
My very heart faints and my whole soul grieves
At the moist rich smell of the rotting leaves,
    And the breath
    Of the fading edges of box beneath,
And the year's last rose.
  Heavily hangs the broad sunflower
    Over its grave i' the earth so chilly;
  Heavily hangs the hollyhock,
    Heavily hangs the tiger-lily.
        ('A Spirit Haunts the Year's Last Hours', lines 13–24)

The year is dying, and the speaker longs for death, yet as so often in Tennyson the poem pauses on the brink of a final outcome,[12] and even hints at an alternative to the speaker's downward longings in its own imaginative life. 'Heavily hangs the hollyhock, / Heavily hangs the tiger-lily': the lines have a dying fall, sinking under the weight of that extra syllable in 'Heavily', yet after eight lines which conclude with terminal stresses, the drift towards words which end on an offbeat ('sunflower', 'chilly', 'hollyhock', 'tiger-lily') produces a series of small protests against finality. And just as the suspended animation of these line-endings celebrates the tenacious hold on life exhibited by every form, flowers as well as poems, so the references to rotting leaves and drooping blossoms come within a stanza that reminds us of the seasonal rhythms underlying such natural processes. Verse and nature find themselves moving in harmony, local fluctuations of tempo being underwritten by larger periodicities, and the result is a Beckett-like sense of endurance (what is, still) emerging from descriptions which on first hearing seem to be absolute for death (what is still).

'As he exulted in the wilder aspects of Nature', Hallam Tennyson recalled, 'so he felt a joy in her orderliness; he felt a rest in her steadfastness, patient progress and hopefulness; the same seasons ever returned; the same stars wheeled in their courses; the flowers and trees blossomed and the birds sang yearly in their appointed months; and he had a triumphant appreciation of her ever-renewed revelations of beauty.'[13] Poems such as 'Early Spring' echo this pleasure in nature's orderly patterns:

Hearing thy chuckled note,
  O twinkling bird,

My tricksy fancies range,
    And, lightly stirred,
Ring little bells of change
    From word to word. (lines 25–30)

It is a slight poem, but like the 'twinkling bird' it resonates beyond itself, in part because the construction 'from x to x' is one that Tennyson often returned to in his search for a grammatical form that would carry his sense of 'patient progress', and in part because of the rhyme of 'range' with 'change'. This too offers a model of 'ever-renewed revelations', not only in the way that all rhymes work by turning one word into another through a form of linguistic alchemy, but also because of the regularity with which Tennyson used it to set descriptions of change against reassuring evidence of his own constancy:

The quick-wing'd gnat doth make a boat
Of his old husk wherewith to float
To a new life! All low things range
To higher! but I cannot change.[14]

Forward, forward let us range,
Let the great world spin for ever down the ringing grooves of change.
('Locksley Hall', lines 181–2)

Our voices took a higher range;
    Once more we sang: 'They do not die
    Nor lose their mortal sympathy,
Nor change to us, although they change . . .
(*In Memoriam*, XXX. 21–4)

The hope that human creativity might work along the same lines as the 'ever-renewed revelations' of the natural world is one that underlies some of Tennyson's most distinctive literary habits: tinkering with old poems; borrowing from his own earlier work; writing alternatives to poems which continued to present themselves as questions rather than answers – 'Locksley Hall Sixty Years After' as a querulous reply to 'Locksley Hall', 'Nothing Will Die' as a faith-saving counter-argument to 'All Things Will Die'. Tennyson's imagination, too, often finds itself conjuring up worrying alternatives to its own eloquence: empty chatter, silence, 'the sound of a voice that is still' ('Break, break, break', line 12). As early as *The Devil and the Lady* he sets out to describe what a tapestry usually conceals: 'The dark reverse of it, / The intertwining and rough wanderings / Of random threads and wayward colourings' (I.iii.40–2). If this draws attention to Tennyson's wide-ranging interest in the hidden and occult, from *Maud*'s line about the 'rosy' undersides of daisies (1.435) to the corruption which spreads through Camelot like a stain, it is also a good analogy for his later poetry, in which beautiful designs always contain the possibility of a dark reverse.

Sometimes this is restricted to isolated lines and images, as individual poems glance suspiciously at their own rhetoric, like someone catching sight of him- or herself in the mirror. For example, Tennyson's stress on the importance of 'melody' did not prevent him from introducing wincing discords where the verse speaks of events which disrupt the natural order of things:

Oh! that 'twere possible,
After long grief and pain,
To find the arms of my true-love
Round me once again!
('Oh! that 'twere possible', lines 1–4)

Such lines register the impossibility of this reunion as well as the desire for it in their anguished near-overlaps of 'tha**t** **'t**were' and 'lon**g** **g**rief', just as Tennyson could ignore his own insistence on reducing sibilance (a process he described as 'kicking the geese out of the boat')[15] when he came to explain how Arthur Hallam's death had caused a collapse of the order normally upheld by grammatical tense: 'But all he *was is* overworn' (*In Memoriam*, 1.17; my emphases). Even when they are at their most assured, Tennyson's poems find themselves being threatened by the fate which haunts 'The Day-Dream': 'The rhymes are dazzled from their place, / And ordered words asunder fly' (lines 19–20). It is not just that Tennyson is attracted to thresholds, such as windows, seashores or 'the quiet limit of the world' ('Tithonus', line 7); his poems are themselves thresholds, in which 'eloquent shapes' (*The Devil and the Lady*) are forever confronting their shadowy twins.

Break, break, break,
On thy cold gray stones, O Sea!
And I would that my tongue could utter
The thoughts that arise in me.
('Break, break, break', lines 1–4)

Wishing that more could be said, or that words could say more of what is felt, the poem confesses its inadequacy with an 'O' that starts off as a public address ('O Sea!') before rounding on itself to form a private sigh: 'But O for the touch of a vanished hand' (line 11). The same impulses are closely entwined from the opening line, where the relentlessly pounding rhythms of nature both shape the verse and threaten to swamp it (a poem in which every word was stressed would no longer be a poem), just as the words themselves reveal the uncomfortable proximity of eloquent speech and meaningless babble. Not until we cross the threatening blank space between the first and second lines do we realise that the speaker is appealing to the sea rather than to his own heart or voice, as if tempted into a response like Kent's to the death of King Lear, 'Breake heart, I prythee breake',[16] before using the momentum of the line to escape death's gravitational pull. The stanza thus offers a perfect illustration of a feature of Tennyson's verse recognised by R. H. Hutton: 'it is not want of motion, but rather excessive compression, which gives to so many of Tennyson's poems the air of moving through a resisting medium'.[17] These acts of resistance take many forms, as Tennyson sets out to create a poetry capable of responding to the coercive pressures of public speech, the noisy accretions of literary history and the deepening grooves of his own style, and it is through their ability to attend to such obstacles without being subdued by them that his poems achieve their distinctive life: 'We live but by *resistance*' ('Conrad! Why call thy life monotonous?', line 9).

'my sole self'

If Tennyson's poems live by resistance, one might legitimately ask how far they are merely local ambushes on a rival – the novel – that had already won the battle for cultural dominance. An elegiac poet, it is tempting to read his career as one long elegy for poetry itself, and especially for a Romantic faith in the power of poetry to reform the world. Even some of his most virtuosic lines from *The Princess* (1847) might be read as evidence that, by this stage of his career, full-throated Romanticism had shrunk to nothing more than 'An echo from a measured strain' ('The Miller's Daughter', line 66):

> The moan of doves in immemorial elms,
> And murmuring of innumerable bees. (VII.206–7)

Far from seeing this as evidence of poetry's delight in a world which includes itself, with those interlaced 'm's and 'n's mimicking the overlaid sounds of the landscape, Peter Conrad reads it as nostalgically harking back to a time before the poet's voice was reduced, like the shipwrecked Enoch Arden, to mere 'muttering and mumbling' (*Enoch Arden*, line 639). A word like 'murmur' may capture the endless buzzing of the bees in its self-echoing form, but it also hints at writing that has retreated from the real world, or been banished from it, into a private soundscape: 'The elms are memorials to a dead time, the song of the doves is a moan, and by the second line there is nothing left but muted, unspecific buzzing, not lyricism but the elegiac echo of it.'[18] It is a persuasive argument, especially given the imaginative association elsewhere in Tennyson's work between human impotence and the drone of insects (if everything ends in death, 'Vastness' reasons, what is life 'but a murmur of gnats in the gloom, / Or a moment's anger of bees in the hive'?, lines 34–5), and it looks even stronger when the narrator of *The Princess* goes on to report that Ida reads this poem 'low-toned' and speaks 'brokenly' (lines 208, 213). 'I saw the forms: I knew not where I was: / They did but look like hollow shows' (lines 118–19) is how the narrator describes his earlier feverish symptoms, but the narrative context does not altogether remove a note of nervous self-banter in Tennyson as well.

However, although Tennyson never quite resolves on the right balance of style and substance in *The Princess* – an experimental poem which is largely written about itself – his writing is not merely post-Romantic in the sense of being belated or unachieved; it is also post-Romantic in continuing a strand of self-doubt that is at the heart of some of the greatest Romantic poems. William Allingham recalled Tennyson's special fondness for Keats's 'Ode to a Nightingale':

> T. – 'The last perfection is the wild and wonderful
>
> Charm'd magic casements, opening on the foam
> Of perilous seas, in faery lands forlorn.'[19]

Keats's lines are themselves a 'magic casement', a textual frame that opens on to a parallel world of the imagination, and Tennyson's quotation of them goes even further by turning them into a window on to a world of romance that was lost along with Keats. (There is a curious mixture of admiration and mourning in that phrase 'last perfection'.) As Herbert Tucker has pointed out,[20] in order to make Keats's ode fit this idea Tennyson has to employ a grammatical sleight which turns 'Charm'd' from a verb into a past participle by lopping off the preceding lines: 'The same that oft-times hath / Charm'd magic casements'. What seems equally important, though, is Tennyson's decision to cut the next lines of the ode, in which Keats makes a sudden retreat from the realm of enchantment: 'Forlorn! The very word is like a bell / To toll me back from thee to my sole self!'[21] Writing of the movement from 'faery lands forlorn' to 'Forlorn!' Geoffrey Hill suggests that 'The echo is not so much a recollection as a revocation; and what is revoked is an attitude towards art and within art. The menace that is flinched from is certainly mortality ("Where youth grows pale, and spectre-thin, and dies") but it is also the menace of the high claims of poetry', particularly the looming presence of

Milton at the moment Keats's ode turns back on itself: 'Stygian cave forlorn' (*L'Allegro*, line 3); 'these wilde Woods forlorn' (*Paradise Lost*, Book 9, line 910).[22] This is brilliantly observed, but one might also observe that Keats's flinching is central to the poem's overall shape; his anxieties about the reach of art are mastered by the same piece of art they put at risk. A similar pattern can be detected in Tennyson's early poems, which frequently entertain fears about the poet becoming an isolated and marginal figure, but do so in a way that manages these fears in the very act of articulating them. Take Mariana in her moated grange:[23]

> All day within the dreamy house,
>   The doors upon their hinges creaked;
> The blue fly sung in the pane; the mouse
>   Behind the mouldering wainscot shrieked,
> Or from the crevice peered about.
>   Old faces glimmered through the doors,
>   Old footsteps trod the upper floors,
> Old voices called her from without.
>   She only said, 'My life is dreary,
>   He cometh not,' she said;
>   She said, 'I am aweary, aweary,
>   I would that I were dead!'   ('Mariana', lines 61–72)

Here the setting is not just a context for the action; to a large extent it *is* the action, as Mariana's melancholy is displaced on to her surroundings. Each stanza zooms in on different details with an eye that makes them seem both familiar and strange, like a morbid version of the way that someone in love might look at the world, but the end is always the same: 'I would that I were dead.' Like the rhymes in the first stanza, the conjunction of 'grange' and 'strange' refuses to produce change. To some extent Mariana is another of Tennyson's poet-surrogates, whose powers of perception produce sharp close-ups which appear to be isolated from each other, like an album of photographs, but start to blur together over time ('dreamy . . . dreary'): a good demonstration of what Arthur Hallam meant when he praised Tennyson's 'vivid, picturesque delineation of objects' and 'the peculiar skill with which he holds all of them *fused* . . . in a medium of strong emotion'.[24] At the same time, the flat sameness of 'aweary, aweary' shows how easily a poem expressing suicidal wishes could become something more like a suicidal poem, which by sympathetically echoing the mood of its characters starts to talk itself out of existence. As the poem continues, and as the situation continues to stay the same, each stanza – literally a standing or stopping place[25] – comes to resemble what *The Princess* describes as a 'muffled cage of life' (VII.47), its lines working like prison bars to trap Mariana in this arrested version of her story. But then, as so often in Tennyson's writing, what saves 'Mariana' from collapse is his ability to create suggestions of freedom even within a structure that seems determined to keep everything in its place. 'The blue fly sung in the pane' offers a frail counter-voice to the general drive doomwards: trapped, certainly, but – it is delicately suggested – still singing through its pain, and still willing, in the shift from regular iambics to jerky monosyllables, to assert its voice against its surroundings. It is a futile gesture, perhaps, but also a concentrated image of the writer's ability to carve out a private space within a public language as he transforms suffering into art. And in this sense 'Mariana' is not only a poem *about* Mariana; it also suggests the sort of poem that might be written *by* Mariana if only she could break out from the holding pattern of her refrain.

The image of a fly buzzing against a window is not an altogether positive metaphor for the situation of the Victorian poet, even if Tennyson's line reminds us that there are benefits as well as drawbacks to being cut off in this way. Windows can present themselves as obstacles rather than openings, but the same material which prevents a voice from reaching the outside world can also amplify it. This was Arthur Hallam's argument in his influential review of the volume which first contained 'Mariana': *Poems, Chiefly Lyrical* (1830). As one of the 'poets of sensation rather than reflection', among whom he numbered Shelley and Keats, what distinguishes Tennyson's poetry, he suggests, is its ability to seduce readers into perceiving the world through senses that are more sensitive than their own. The danger with this approach, as Hallam is quick to recognise, is that the poems might end up abandoning ideas and feelings which once circulated as common currency between poets and their readers: a poet who detaches himself from his society risks finding himself with an audience of one. 'Hence the melancholy, which so evidently characterises the spirit of modern poetry; hence that return of the mind upon itself, and the habit of seeking relief in idiosyncrasies rather than community of interest.'[26] Hallam's diagnosis of the contemporary cultural scene includes a strand of nostalgia that does not altogether fit the facts: one wonders how far a satirist like Pope or Dryden would agree that 'In the old times the poetic impulse went along with the general impulse of the nation', and only now is it 'a reaction against it'.[27] However, his review is still a valuable summary of the period's increasing doubts over who the poet is talking to or for, and a suggestive account of Tennyson's skill at making poems out of these very doubts.

A common tactic in the early poems is to describe locations such as gardens, or palaces of art, or other kinds of 'lonely place' ('The Poet's Song', line 5) which are left tellingly unspecified, in which more abstract ideas about the place of poetry can be explored. Few of these poems are anything more than literary exercises, the sound of a young poet clearing his throat, even if some images neatly concentrate Tennyson's uncertainty over what he is up to and whether or not he is up to it. 'Not wholly in the busy world, nor quite / Beyond it, blooms the garden that I love' ('The Gardener's Daughter', lines 33–4) is hardly a helpful set of directions, while 'wingèd shafts of truth' ('The Poet', line 26) sound suitably impressive as a metaphor for poems until one recalls that they are actually 'arrow-seeds of the field flower' (line 19), i.e. dandelion seeds, which makes poetry sound about as threatening as a powder-puff. More often, though, it is the form of Tennyson's poems which stages his ambivalence over their scope and reach. In part this is because 'form' could refer either to what is most distinctive about an individual, such as Aphrodite's 'rounded form' in 'Œnone' (line 180), or to shared social values ('he had sympathy with those who feel that faith is larger and nobler than form', Tennyson's son recalled, and 'at the same time he had tenderness and appreciation for those who find their faith helped by form'),[28] so that Tennyson's use of the word can refer both to the shape of private thoughts and to the social structures against which these thoughts might strain and chafe. And his poems do more than merely play on this ambivalence; they also embody it, by using their own forms to investigate the period's troubled relationship between private impulses and 'general impulse'.

This can provide material for comedy, as when Simeon Stylites speaks in blank verse that shows how easily an individual line of thought can find itself drifting into bland pieties, and the poem's form is used to both stage and stooge his desire to be 'Example, pattern' ('St Simeon Stylites', line 220) to his followers. It can equally produce moments of genuine anguish, as when the speaker of 'Supposed Confessions of a Second-Rate Sensitive Mind' shows how at odds with his fellow men he is in the rhythmically jerky way he describes how 'Men pass me by; / Christians with happy countenances' (lines 19–20). ('The Two Voices' offers a more cheering alternative in the description of a man walking to church 'With measured footfall firm and mild' (line 413) – a line which practises what it preaches in its own measured rhythmical tread and, usually a good clue to conservative thinking in Tennyson, the abba structure of '**m**easured **f**ootfall **f**irm and **m**ild'.) The same tussle between private and public 'impulses' can also be used to reflect on political questions. For T. S. Eliot, Tennyson was 'the most instinctive rebel against the society in which he was the most perfect conformist',[29] and Tennyson's political poems eloquently demonstrate these mixed feelings, as they endeavour to reflect his trust in 'a power to make / This ever-changing world of circumstance, / In changing, chime with never-changing Law' ('To the Duke of Argyll', lines 9–11), while also revealing the struggle to fit the power of circumstance to poetry's more obdurate structures. However, where Tennyson's poems are at their most successful, the form of his writing reflects back on itself to stage questions about the poet's engagement with the world which cannot be reduced to politics, any more than they can be wholly divorced from politics.

'The Lady of Shalott' is probably the best-known example by Tennyson of a poem which in part offers itself as a fable of writing. Perhaps it is for this reason that changing responses to 'The Lady of Shalott' also form something like a potted history of literary criticism since the poem's first publication in 1832. 'A small vessel, built on fine lines, is likely to float further down the stream of time than a big raft',[30] Tennyson claimed, and to a large extent this poem has proven him right. From New Critical readings, in which the Lady's fate represents the life of the imagination being destroyed by a desire to enter active public life, to the playful poststructuralism of Geoffrey Hartman, for whom the Lady's barge is a 'floating signifier' forever slipping beyond our interpretative grasp, Tennyson's poem has acted as a barometer to chart the changing cultural pressures which have acted on it at different times.[31] In some ways this is a natural response to its own mixture of the straightforward and the furtive; to borrow a Tennysonian turn of phrase, it is a poem which delights in half-revealing and half-concealing. For example, Lancelot's response to the appearance of her corpse may seem inadequate ('She has a lovely face', line 169), but none of the other things he might have said, such as 'Can I watch the autopsy?' or 'Do you think I could have the boat after we bury her?'[32] are likely to strike us as any better; the poem confesses the inadequacy of our drive to make sense of the world even as it is laying tempting clues for us to follow. But the central reason for our feeling that the poem is at once complete in itself and provocatively open-ended lies in the form, which carries the sound of tragic inevitability in the way that 'Camelot', 'Lancelot' and 'Shalott' seem bound to involve each other, but also hints at the main character's efforts to tell her story in her own way:

> She left the web, she left the loom,
> She made three paces through the room,
> She saw the water-lily bloom,

She saw the helmet and the plume,
    She looked down to Camelot.
Out flew the web and floated wide;
The mirror cracked from side to side;
'The curse is come upon me,' cried
    The Lady of Shalott. (lines 109–17)

Six times in five lines the stanza describes actions she chooses to take, using rhyme-words that weave a set of variations on a single theme, like a linguistic echo of her work at the loom. Only when the rhyme-word 'Camelot' is reached does individual agency succumb to the force of destiny: the web flies out and the mirror cracks as impersonal consequences rather than deliberate choices. But the final two lines show how in the act of admitting her fate the Lady also starts to reassert some control over it: for the first time in the stanza, a line-ending does not correspond with the end of a grammatical clause, and as a result the word 'cried' rebels against the constraints of the story in which she finds herself. It is a perfect miniature of the way that the poem sets biography against autobiography, 'The Lady of Shalott' as a tomb-stone inscription against 'The Lady of Shalott' as a signature. Like any good story-teller, Tennyson suggests, her voice must reach a compromise between entering the world and keeping itself in check if it is to transform itself into a lasting work of art.

'Is this the end?'

'The Lady of Shalott' establishes a key pattern for Tennyson's writing, in which lines of verse repeatedly reach out into the margin that separates art from the world of their readers, before nervously recoiling back on themselves. Put another way, his work is shaped by rival centrifugal and centripetal forces, the desire to expand into public life and the desire to retreat into something more 'self-involved' (itself a Tennysonian coinage).[33] For much of the twentieth century, the standard model of his career was that of the 'two voices': a shift from private brooding to public declamation which can be dated to his elevation to the Laureateship in 1850. Actually, the relationship between these two voices remained unstable throughout his career, and can often be found squaring up to one another within the same poem. Perhaps this is not surprising from the man known informally as 'The Poet of the People',[34] because in seeking to speak with a public voice Tennyson often found himself having to register its self-divisions in his own voice, to take the measure of social differences in his own literary measures.[35] Hence his knack of writing lines that can resemble both bridges and barriers; hence a poem such as 'The Charge of the Light Brigade', which ripples with nervous self-qualifications even where it appears to be at its most unselfconsciously jingoistic:

> 'Forward, the Light Brigade!'
> Was there a man dismayed?
> Not though the soldier knew
>   Some one had blundered:
> Their's not to make reply,
> Their's not to reason why,
> Their's but to do and die:
> Into the valley of Death
>   Rode the six hundred. (lines 9–17)

Like most anthology pieces, this has been blunted by repetition, but it is a poem which achieves its most powerful ends by the most delicate means: flattening the gung-ho cry 'do or die' into the tragic inevitability of 'do and die'; self-consciously using the resources of verse (literally 'a turning', from the Latin 'vertere', to turn) to dramatise the cavalry's refusal to turn back; singling out the guilty commander ('some one') in a way that 'someone' would pass over too quickly. And then there are the dactylic rhythms, which first inspired Tennyson when he read about 'some hideous blunder' in *The Times*'s report of the charge, and which multiply on the page to bring together the cavalry, their helpless observers in the Crimea and eventually Tennyson's readers ('All the world wondered' (line 31)) in a single pulse of doom. It is through this interplay of narrative and form that Tennyson implicates us in a set of events which shows what can happen when loyalty or patriotism harden into rigid patterns, just as Tennyson's deliberately neutral tone reminds us of the many different ways in which one might 'wonder' at such behaviour. Outspoken confidence is laced with *sotto voce* caution; 'the voice of the people' includes a heckler who recognises that, even if the cavalry made no reply to their orders, a range of replies, from retort to reproof, may be necessary to make sense of what happened next.

Similar tussles between public and private speech underlie a poem which was first published in the same collection as 'The Charge of the Light Brigade', but which at first sight might appear to be its mirror-opposite: *Maud*. It is one of Tennyson's most disturbing poems, largely because it features his most disturbed speaker, whose erotic obsession with Maud repeatedly frays his speech – and the narrative thread of the poem – into lines that do not always seem to connect either to the real world or to each other. Tennyson was proud of his attempts to dramatise an unstable character in an equally unstable form: 'No other poem (a monotone with plenty of change and no weariness) has been made into a drama where successive phases of passion in one person take the place of successive persons.'[36] The number and length of the occasions upon which he insisted on reading *Maud* aloud to his guests, interrupting himself with wounded explanations and self-justifications, might suggest that his intentions were not fully realised in the writing itself, but that does not seriously detract from the achievement of a poem which brilliantly stages these 'phases of passion' by making them at once insistent and resistant. Each section registers the brooding certainty of a lover that he alone sees the world clearly, here and now, even as his inability to stick to a single way of speaking (each section is written in a different verse form) carries his nagging worry that nothing and nobody can be relied upon in a world of chance and change. 'There is none like her, none' (I.xviii) is the climax of his wooing – whether real or imagined we cannot be sure – but it is noticeable that even in confirming Maud's uniqueness the speaker cannot prevent himself from circling back over his words, as if nervously aware that they may turn out to be no more reliable than most of the people who use them.

The original title in the 1855 volume was *Maud, or the Madness*, which accurately indicates the off-kilter nature of the speaker's voice, even if many of his speech-tics, such as brooding repetitions, lilting rhythms and syntactic delays, also come close to being morbid exaggerations of Tennyson's own creative habits. (The idea that *Maud*'s speaker is a frustrated artist is dazzlingly brought to life in the garden scene, where the birds cawing 'Maud, Maud, Maud' (I.438) are like a sad parody of the Shelleyan poet who 'sits in darkness, and sings to soothe its own solitude with sweet sounds'.)[37] Even the poem's imaginative co-ordinates, the slippery relations between 'Maud', 'made' and 'mad', have awkward affinities with Tennyson's pleasure elsewhere in the way that poetry can blur the boundaries of words to expose some of the world's hidden connections: 'Listen! bells in yonder town, / Lin, lan, lone' ('New Year's Eve', lines 1–2). And yet, to a large extent these overlaps between Tennyson and his speaker are inevitable. This is not because, as some of the poem's first reviewers assumed, Tennyson was simply using a mouthpiece to disguise his own ranting and raving, but because he takes care to suggest that his speaker, who ends up claiming that 'I am one with my kind' (III.58), has actually been one with his kind all along. After all, 'the Madness' of the title could refer to a condition rather than an individual (the speaker is, significantly, anonymous), and the poem gives good grounds for thinking that this is also the condition of England, in which madness is spreading like a contagion.[38] What is a little erotic obsession, Tennyson seems to be asking, compared to bakers who adulterate their bread, mothers who poison their own children and Quakers who do not know peace from war? Read in this way, the ending of the poem, in which the speaker sets off for the organised slaughter of the Crimea, is not a recantation of Britain's collective madness but its confirmation.

The question of where one voice ends and another one begins – a question that is central to the act of reading as well as to many of Tennyson's compositional habits (allusion, revision, self-borrowing) – is most delicately explored in a poem which is in some ways a more optimistic version of *Maud*: *In Memoriam*. Both poems are monodramas which would much prefer to be dramatic monologues, if only they could restore the sympathetic listener who seems to have abandoned them. ('Come into the garden, Maud' is like a sad, mad attempt to reproduce the successful communion described in section XCV of *In Memoriam*.) Both involve a struggle between Tennyson's narrative ambitions and his fundamentally lyrical impulses. And in both it is poetic form which dramatises the urge to make coherent sense of the world straining against the competing forces of fragmentation and dispersal. ('Fragments of an Elegy', one of Tennyson's draft titles for *In Memoriam*, could apply equally well to *Maud*, a poem in which the elegiac mood is generated by a death even more far-reaching than Arthur Hallam's: the death of possibility.) But whereas the speaker of *Maud* never repeats the same verse form twice, unable to find any correspondence between shared structures of feeling and his own fluctuating moods, *In Memoriam* is built on an abba stanza that is perfectly suited to a speaker caught between the desire to burrow inwards and the desire to expand the circumference of the self. In particular, it is through the movement of this stanza that *In Memoriam* measures abstract human responses to loss – such as recognising the need to go on while repeatedly being drawn back, like shale by the tide – against the moment-by-moment experience of a single bereaved speaker.

'So careful of the type she seems, / So careless of the single life' (LV.7–8) is Tennyson's complaint about nature, and his poem recognises how easily an elegy, similarly, might find itself idealising the dead or turning the experience of grief into an all-too-compliant model of mourning. This is something the poem discusses out loud and at length, but it is also articulated more restrainedly in its form – 'form' being one of *In Memoriam*'s key words, appearing on over twenty occasions, in addition to painful near-relations such as 'former' and 'forlorn'. In particular, the word provides a crucial point of intersection between worries about the fate of individual bodies ('changes wrought on form and face', LXXXII.2), the questionable consolation offered by shared social structures ('For who would keep an ancient form / Through which the spirit breathes no more?', CV.19–20) and a language that is as open to corruption as the people who speak it ('matter-moulded forms of speech', XCV.46). Even when not referred to explicitly, the network of ideas associated with 'form' continues to spread deep into Tennyson's verse. Section XLV describes the baby's growing sense of separateness from his mother as an analogy for the way that the dead may wake up to a new form of life:

So rounds he to a separate mind
  From whence clear memory may begin,
  As through the frame that binds him in
His isolation grows defined. (lines 9–12)

Across the line-break separating 'binds him in' and 'His isolation' there is a sudden dawning of self-consciousness, as the baby realises that the body embracing him is no longer his mother but his own flesh. But even as this section is affirming our absolute isolation from each other it is gesturing towards a more generous alternative, because it is paraphrasing a section from Arthur Hallam's essay 'On Sympathy' which describes the same phenomenon in a similar – but, importantly, not an identical – way. The binding power of the stanza works simultaneously to connect and to differentiate; it recalls the lasting ties of friendship even as it is rehearsing an after-life where 'Eternal form shall still divide / The eternal soul from all beside' (XLVII.6–7). This may or may not be convincing as theology, but as poetry it is a fine example of Tennyson's ability to use literary form, as T. S. Eliot pointed out, to 'turn his limitations to good purpose'.[39]

The idea that a poem's limitations are compactly achieved rather than impotently suffered is one that resonates through *In Memoriam*. The poem's repeated images of closed doors, for instance, accurately sketch out the speaker's sense of a world in which many of life's openings have been shut off, but the poem cannot resist keeping its own doorways ajar. Even the description of bells which 'Swell out and fail, as if a door / Were shut between me and the sound' (XXVIII.7–8) places 'door' so that it is followed by a space on the page in which imaginative possibilities reverberate beyond the grammatical fact of the door itself being closed. But then throughout his career Tennyson succeeded in writing poetry that was the work of a consummate escape-artist, forever slipping the leash of the constraints he imposed on himself. 'The Dreamer' was, according to his son, 'the last poem he finished',[40] but even this poem puts up some resistance to finishing in its refrain: 'And all's well that ends well, / Whirl, and follow the Sun!' (lines 19–20). The echo of 'well' in 'Whirl' may be a literary in-joke, but it is also a serious reflection on Tennyson's reluctance to be done with things, his skill at transforming a possible breakdown into an imaginative breakthrough. It is this skill that sustains *In Memoriam* at the moments it seems closest to collapse, so that when the moaning voice calls out 'Is this the end? is this the end?' (XII.16) one notices how carefully 'the end', that most traditional of formulas for signing off a literary work, is twice evoked and twice evaded, first by being placed in the middle of a line, and then by being followed by a question-mark. And like most of Tennyson's compositional habits, his ability to write lines that reach beyond themselves was maintained to the last. *Morte d'Arthur* ends with Arthur drifting past the horizon of the poem's final line, as the speaker of 'The Epic' imagines how modern voices might greet his return:

> 'Arthur is come again: he cannot die.'
> Then those that stood upon the hills behind
> Repeated – 'Come again, and thrice as fair;'
> And, further inland, voices echoed – 'Come
> With all good things, and war shall be no more.'
>
> (lines 296–300)

How moving is that double repetition of 'Come', especially as it reappears at the end of a line, taking on an edge of yearning as it is released into the open space of the future: 'Come / With all good things'. And how much more moving that Tennyson should echo the phrase 'Come again', an invitation that lies at the heart of all poems that last, when he felt that he was close to his own end: 'He spoke of the next world as assuredly accomplishing the beginnings of this. And whether he had any presage of death I know not, but as he said, "Farewell", he said, "Come again, my time cannot be long."'[41]

Notes

1. 'The Study of Poetry' (1880), reprinted in *The Complete Prose Works of Matthew Arnold*, ed. R. H. Super, 11 vols. (Ann Arbor: University of Michigan Press, 1960–77), vol. IX, p. 163.
2. *OED*, 'stay'.
3. Reprinted in Joseph Bristow (ed.), *The Victorian Poet: Poetics and Persona* (London: Croom Helm, 1987), p. 129.
4. Charles Kingsley, *Alton Locke* (London, 1850), chapter 9.
5. Walt Whitman, 'A Word about Tennyson' (1887), reprinted in John D. Jump (ed.), *Tennyson: The Critical Heritage* (London: Routledge, 1967), pp. 349–50.

6. All quotations from Tennyson's poetry are taken from *The Poems of Tennyson*, ed. Christopher Ricks, 3 vols. (Harlow: Longman, 1987).
7. 'Personal Recollections of Tennyson' (1925), reprinted in Norman Page (ed.), *Tennyson: Interviews and Recollections* (London: Macmillan, 1983), p. 21.
8. G. K. Chesterton, *The Victorian Age in Literature* (London: Oxford University Press, 1913), p. 101.
9. Robert Graves, *The Crowning Privilege* (London: Cassell, 1955), pp. 110–11. I owe this reference to Seamus Perry's excellent *Alfred Tennyson* (Tavistock: Northcote, 2005), p. 27.
10. Alfred Austin, 'Mr Tennyson', *The Poetry of the Period* (1870), reprinted in Bristow (ed.), *The Victorian Poet*, p. 124.
11. Repr. in Hallam Tennyson, *Alfred, Lord Tennyson: A Memoir by his Son*, 2 vols. (London: Macmillan, 1897), vol. I, pp. 465–6.
12. See Christopher Ricks, *Tennyson* (New York: Macmillan, 1972), p. 19.
13. Hallam Tennyson, *Tennyson: A Memoir*, vol. I, pp. 312–13.
14. *Ibid.*, vol I, p. 18.
15. *Ibid.*, vol. II, p. 14.
16. *King Lear*, 5.3. I quote from the 1623 Folio text, reprinted in *The Tragedie of King Lear*, ed. Nick de Somogyi (London: Nick Hern Books, 2004), p. 199.
17. R. H. Hutton, 'Tennyson', *Literary Essays* (1888), repr. in Jump (ed.), *Tennyson: The Critical Heritage*, p. 365.
18. Peter Conrad, *Cassell's History of English Literature* (London: Cassell, 2003), p. 524.
19. *William Allingham: A Diary* (1907), reprinted in Page (ed.), *Tennyson: Interviews and Recollections*, p. 145.
20. Herbert Tucker, *Tennyson and the Doom of Romanticism* (Cambridge, MA: Harvard University Press, 1988), p. 27.
21. 'Ode to a Nightingale' (1820) lines 68–9, 71–2, reprinted in *Keats: The Complete Poems*, ed. Miriam Allott (Harlow: Longman, 1970), p. 532.
22. Geoffrey Hill, *The Lords of Limit: Essays on Literature and Ideas* (New York: Oxford University Press, 1984), p. 5.
23. The following discussions of 'Mariana' and 'The Lady of Shalott' adapt material previously published in the introduction to Robert Douglas-Fairhurst and Seamus Perry (eds.), *Tennyson among the Poets: Bicentenary Essays* (Oxford: Oxford University Press, 2009).
24. Arthur Hallam, Review of *Poems, Chiefly Lyrical* (1830), reprinted in Jump (ed.), *Tennyson: The Critical Heritage*, p. 42.
25. *OED*, 'stanza'.
26. Jump (ed.), *Tennyson: The Critical Heritage*, p. 41.
27. *Ibid.*
28. Hallam Tennyson, *Tennyson: A Memoir*, vol. I, p. 310.
29. 'In Memoriam' (1936), reprinted in *Selected Prose of T. S. Eliot*, ed. Frank Kermode (London: Faber, 1975), p. 246.
30. Hallam Tennyson, *Tennyson: A Memoir*, vol. II, p. 230.

31. See Gerhard Joseph, *Tennyson and the Text: The Weaver's Shuttle* (Cambridge: Cambridge University Press, 1992).
32. I borrow these sample questions from Kathy Alexis Psomiades, ' "The Lady of Shalott" and the Critical Fortunes of Victorian Poetry', in Joseph Bristow (ed.), *The Cambridge Companion to Victorian Poetry* (Cambridge: Cambridge University Press, 2000), p. 29.
33. *OED* cites 'The Day-Dream' (1842) as the first recorded use: 'The pensive mind . . . all too dearly self-involved' (line 261).
34. Hallam Tennyson, *Tennyson: A Memoir*, vol. II, p. 6.
35. See Eric Griffiths, *The Printed Voice of Victorian Poetry* (Oxford: Clarendon Press, 1989), pp. 97–170, and Matthew Bevis, *The Art of Eloquence: Byron, Dickens, Tennyson, Joyce* (Oxford: Oxford University Press, 2007), pp. 145–203.
36. Tennyson to Knowles in 1870–1, cited in Gordon N. Ray, *Tennyson Reads 'Maud'* (Vancouver: Publications Centre, University of British Columbia, 1968), p. 43.
37. 'A Defence of Poetry' (1821), reprinted in *Shelley's Prose*, ed. David Lee Clark (London: Fourth Estate, 1988), p. 282.
38. See A. Dwight Culler, *The Poetry of Tennyson* (New Haven: Yale University Press, 1977), p. 207.
39. *Ibid.*, p. 242.
40. Hallam Tennyson, *Tennyson: A Memoir*, vol. II, p. 419.
41. Reported by H. D. Rawnsley, 'Memories of Farringford' (1900), reprinted in Page (ed.), *Tennyson: Interviews and Recollections*, p. 66.

Chapter 33

Elizabeth Barrett and Robert Browning

HERBERT F. TUCKER

The clandestine marriage and elopement of Elizabeth Barrett Moulton Barrett (1806–61) with Robert Browning (1812–89) – hereafter for convenience EBB and RB – has mated them for ever in the popular imagination. They go together here for that reason, and also because one strong force behind their artistic development, not to mention marital compatibility, was the stake each held in the cultural formation of evangelical dissent that did so much to create the modern world. This was the insurgent interest that in the crisis of early Victorian Reform assumed control of the long-standing Anglican state and made it over, in modern non-sectarian terms, between the founding of the University of London (1826) and the Great Exhibition (1851). The dissenting ascendancy represented a convergence of commercial, engineering, banking and legal concerns to which both the Barrett and the Browning family belonged; and its Whiggish patriotism meant business. In the name of a newly self-conscious middle class, Reform MPs enacted measures enfranchising Britons to worship without penalty outside the Established Church and to sell their goods and labour on the laissez-faire principles of contractual individualism. Reviving the suspended momentum of revolutionary zeal from the latter eighteenth century, they aimed to extirpate slavery, prostitution and child labour, to reshape national education and to loosen the privileged bond between Church and state by combating the prejudices on which both ancient bulwarks rested. To these aims both Brownings made their poetry, in the largest sense, an accessory.

Our tendency nowadays to condescend to the industrious first Victorians results, ironically, from their success. Because of the very singleness of purpose with which they linked economic and technological transformation at home to imperial expansion abroad, we at the receiving end of all they wrought find much in it to blame, with environmental and imperial devastation standing high in the bill. Moreover, the default frames of reference whereby we assess the Brownings' generation derive from precisely those contemporaries – Carlyle and Newman, Engels and Marx, Ruskin and Morris – who were most appalled by what they saw. For each of the quite diverse writers just named depicted the reforming mind as radically unimaginative. Dickens's fact-besotted Gradgrind and Arnold's culture-snubbing Philistine were caricatures cut from the same cloth: professionally blinkered half-men whose positivist cheapening of the human prospect found its complement in a religion that dieted the soul on raw self-interest and the thin gruel of Calvinist logic. The spirit of dissent was noisy, it was tireless and it was effective; but elegance and fancy did not rank among its virtues. It was not, in a word, poetic.

Appreciation of the place EBB and RB jointly hold in literary history may begin by noting that just such a failure to be poetic is what their detractors have always resented. Typically the charge is couched in formal terms – faults of accent, breaches of decorum – which open out through the poets' indiscriminate diction and embrace of objectionable subjects to imply that in EBB the affronted reader meets a bluestocking virago who has lost her compass, in RB a clever upstart who is not quite a gentleman. Was he perhaps Jewish? Had her family's Jamaican ventures contracted a Creole stain? Such persistent conjectures racialise what was at bottom a *class* offence. It was the smell of new money that wrinkled noses over the Brownings' relish for slang and inkhorn terms, far-fetched high-compression images and aggressively sweeping way with metre. These innovations have so far prevailed in the poetry of their successors that it is well to recall how pointed a challenge the original prototypes could, and still can, present:

Polypheme's white tooth
Slips on the nut if, after frequent showers,
The shell is over-smooth.
(EBB, *Sonnets from the Portuguese* (1850), no. 40, lines 7–9)[1]

Nokes outdares Stokes in azure feats, –
Both gorge. Who fished the murex up?
What porridge had John Keats?
(RB, 'Popularity' (1855), lines 63–5)

On which, without pause, up the telegraph-line
Swept smoothly the next news from Gaeta: – *Shot.*
Tell his mother. Ah, ah, 'his,' 'their' mother – not 'mine,'
No voice says 'My mother' again to me. What?
You think Guido forgot?
(EBB, 'Mother and Poet' (1862), lines 56–60)

pavements, as with teeth,
Griped huge weed widening crack and split
In squares and circles stone-work erst.
Oh, Nature – good! Oh, Art – no whit
Less worthy! Both in one – accurst!
(RB, 'Bad Dreams' (1889), lines 32–6)

In their day, verses like these elicited so unwonted a mixture of bodily sensation with strenuous thought that it is no surprise their flexing of muscle and brain struck Victorians as excessive. What was wrong with poetry like this, critics grumbled, was the same thing that was wrong with the forward meritocracy that was pressing its advantage on old English ways too hard and too fast. 'The poetry of barbarism': George Santayana's phrase for RB at the turn of the twentieth century merely flushed out into the open what conservatives had been implying about both our poets for decades.[2]

Not that the Brownings' mature manner won universal favour from their own class constituency. Among the prerogatives at which Victorian arrivistes were pleased to arrive was that of imitating their established betters; and one habit easy to imitate was a taste for literary gentility whose acme was the melodious lyricism of Tennysonian cliché that RB and EBB flouted. That such obstinate nonconformity proved more galling to their classmates' dissenting Podsnappery than to thoroughgoing conservatism was due to the stinging rebuke the Brownings' twinned oeuvre delivered to smugness. The Protestant work of protest was never done, they implied; the good news of salvation obliged a full look at the bad news of backsliding; and the duty of saying so was discharged, as a matter of poetic form, in the nigh-puritanical self-scrutiny that crackles across the passages just quoted. Summoning minds and hearts to service, EBB and RB may have wielded a keener goad within the fold of triumphant dissent than outside it. There come times when preaching to the choir is the thing most needful, and arguably one such time was the mid-Victorian ascendancy of the spirit of Reform. If the nation's new rulers succumbed to the order of things they had commodified, or let a monetised, automated abstraction usurp their birthright of joy in the glory of creation, it was not for want of the explicit warning and, more important, the imaginative callisthenics that were provided by the Brownings' art.

Before young poets can reform their traditions they have to possess them – a process that transpires with great clarity where such possession is not an entailment but must be earned. The barring of early nineteenth-century dissenters from higher education had results that were compounded for

EBB by reason of her sex, for RB of a restive curiosity parentally indulged. That both poets were first children educated at home and thus, given their precocity, in effect self-taught, is a circumstance their work routinely attests. Sometimes it emerges in zeal to prove they knew the things conventionally educated readers did (ancient Greek), sometimes in wildly wrong guesses about what such readers might be counted on to know (the intricacies of Italian politics whether from the nineteenth century or the thirteenth). At all events home schooling encouraged both poets to recapitulate within their own development that of modern poetry at large. At fourteen each produced a viable pastiche of eighteenth-century style: EBB's *The Battle of Marathon* (1820, privately published) sustained an epic action over a thousand lines of heroic couplets in the manner of Pope's Homer, while RB's unpublished 'The Dance of Death', like other fugitives from his unpublished *Incondita*, would not be out of place among the irregular odes of the Sensibility era.

To these adolescent imitations of their parents' taste there soon succeeded works decisively original, marked moreover by the poets' awareness that the Romantic revolution in poetry had made originality harder to come by than formerly. First, in *An Essay on Mind* (1826), EBB stayed with neo-classicism but moved beyond narrative into the more exacting discursive mode of Pope's maturity; this poem was worthiest of its high model in several passages where, chafing at the point of her own wit, EBB twisted the couplet against itself to express impatience with neo-classical poise as such. A decade later *The Seraphim* (1838) was a visionary play script that leapt right out of the human condition, into an operatic dialogue of angels hovering on high as they ponder the Crucifixion occurring at Calvary miles below. Here airswept spirituality, ballasted by compassion, set the options for a mixture of mood that would characterise EBB's writing across the decades. Still missing, however, from *The Seraphim* and the unworldly poems that adjoined it is that deft and sudden embodiment of material reality which habitually grounds EBB's developed imagination. If the undisguised topic in 1838 was evangelical redemption, the poetic modality drew hard on Romanticism, especially Shelley's, whose lead in the hybrid genre of lyrical drama EBB had already followed in a translation of Aeschylus's *Prometheus Bound* (1833).

How to incorporate Shelleyan Romanticism – atheistic, radical – within an orientation that was progressive-Christian, and eventually Victorian-liberal, formed the insoluble, unshirkable problem that made RB an original poet in the 1830s and kept him one for half a century. The anonymously published *Pauline* (1833) is a vividly irresolute 'fragment of a confession', wherein a nameless poet struggles to recoup the faith he lost after falling for a utopianism that he now half-heartedly repudiates. This double apostasy was recapitulated in the way RB kept disowning and reclaiming *Pauline* for decades, even to the point of revising it in detail the year before he died; in a more extended sense, we find rehearsed in it the patterns of aspiration, disillusion and ambivalence that characterise his most engaging psychological studies. For the 'morbid and intense self-consciousness' that John Stuart Mill noted at once in a review of *Pauline*[3] was in effect this poet's inspiration – indeed, it was his dissenting endowment – and his career is legible as a series of experiments with techniques for expressing it.

Two large experiments that soon ensued, *Paracelsus* (1835) and *Sordello* (1840), carried RB's psychological curiosity into the thick of history. The former, a Faustian drama of broken genius and hope resurgent that divided the honours of heroic failure between the eponymous doctor and a poet named Aprile (rhymes with Shelley), not only won the elder Wordsworth's praise but earned RB engagements to write half a dozen more or less stage-worthy scripts between 1836 and 1845 for London's best actor-managers. The latter experiment, *Sordello*, was a venture in avant-garde literary and political historiography so uncompromising that readers across the board pronounced it unintelligible. Although in time this ambitious effort would attract the regard of an eminent posterity including Morris, Swinburne and Pound, it had the immediate effect of sabotaging his reputation for the next quarter-century. If *Paracelsus* sparkled with learned imagery and the exuberant beauty of late Romantic verse, *Sordello* felt more like homework, even as it broke new stylistic ground into the staccato, elliptical manner we now hail as Browningesque.

EBB, meanwhile, numbered among her talents the one RB conspicuously lacked: an accurate estimate of what the inchoate early Victorian poetry public were looking for. The death of Felicia Hemans and Letitia Landon, who *circa* 1830 had been the most popular living poets, cleared EBB's way to assume their laurels on the terms of marketable domesticity which they had pioneered within the flourishing trade in albums and gift book annuals. EBB wrote for these feminised venues often, trimming her craft from the world-historical scope at which we have seen her labouring thus far, in order to produce scaled-down tales, laments and meditations in easy-reading ballad stanzas. These poems squarely met the public taste for a melancholy that was exotically dispersed across ages ('The Romaunt of Margret') and climes ('A Romance of the Ganges', both 1838) where the familiar and the lovely might certify each other, under the additional dispensation of a piety that sprang from stainless disappointment at an unfeeling world. Rooted in Christian convictions to which EBB habitually gave the last word, the range of her lyrical sentiment gained extra cogency from the dash of intellect that never left her art for long, and also from a circumstance with which readers became rapidly acquainted: by 1830 or so she was effectively a housebound invalid. Her actual complaint was one that modern medicine can only conjecture about, but beyond question it had the effect of dovetailing the figure of the invalid poetess with a cherished nineteenth-century ideal of helpless sensitivity. For this central-casting windfall of womanly disability EBB found thematic applications too. She affirmed the female power that dwelt in tenderness with poems on Hemans and Landon, the Virgin Mary and the lately crowned teenager Victoria; childlike candour's title to freshness of outlook validated her poetic revisionism in Wordsworthian mnemonic pieces like 'The Deserted Garden' and 'A Sea-Side Walk'.

Thus while RB, free to tour Europe from Italy to Russia, came before the world to small avail in works of large ambit, the literary public beat a path to EBB's door – not in Wimpole Street, of course, but in the periodical venues where Victorian Britain increasingly did its reading, and in the lesser poetic forms these venues rewarded. On this paradoxical symmetry there now supervened a chiasmus: during the early 1840s, just before they momentously met, the two poets began poaching on each other's territory. In 1842 RB floated in the cheap double-columned format of *Dramatic Lyrics* a booklet of short poems that, while it made no dent in market share, owns a permanent place within literary history for having debuted the genre we now call the dramatic monologue. This impersonative variation on Romanticism's lyrical norm arguably ranks as the signal Victorian contribution to the resources of modern poetry, and it is one that remains indissolubly linked to RB's name. As exemplified in an 1842 classic like 'My Last Duchess', the genre set sympathetic intimacy in tension with ironic distance to provoke, within brief compass, a remarkably complex moral valuation of imaginary speakers apprehended in dense historical and cultural particularity. The very restriction of compass indemnified RB's vivid intelligence against the liability to digress, and the compensatory hurry to condense, that had made such rough going of *Sordello*; and it constrained him to refine that poem's new, nervously energetic style to advantage. RB framed the sequence of monologues, furthermore, with genres aimed to please current poetic taste: a brace of good-humoured song lyrics and a picturesque narrative parable, 'The Pied Piper of Hamelin', that has held young readers' attention ever since.

EBB for her part stepped in 1844 into the male world of culture critique as an anonymous contributor of major-author overviews to R. H. Horne's landmark *A New Spirit of the Age*. More important, and under her own name, she issued in *Poems* (1844) a collection whose lasting importance springs from the versatility with which she added to her often occasion-bound 1830s lyricism forms that were ampler, and louder. New poems held forth on topics distinctly more broad, and certainly less polite, than the esteemed poetess had thus far handled, among them factory labour ('The Cry of the Children'), class prejudice and sexual politics ('Lady Geraldine's Courtship'), cultural myth and world history ('The Dead Pan'). EBB entered on such topics with a resolution to distend the limits of womanliness she had formerly obeyed, claiming a place instead within the western canon that she rehearsed at times with due reverence ('A Vision of Poets'), at times with a *sprezzatura* more impressive still ('Wine of Cyprus'). We can measure the assertiveness of 1844 by comparing her new *Drama of Exile* with *The Seraphim*. Both are biblical Christian closet-dramas, but to the antiphonal oratorio of six years ago there now succeeded an archetypal moral conflict, played out within the guilty soul of Eve, and an engaging human interest, even (or especially) in the fallen, affective hunger of Lucifer. What was properly dramatic about *A Drama of Exile* charged EBB's 1844 sequence of archly pivoting sonnets as well. And, signally for our story here, in 'Bertha in the Lane' she produced a full-blown dramatic monologue whose ironies, worthy of RB's at this time, quiz the very ideology of feminine self-denial on which her career to date had been grounded.

The mid-1840s consilience between these two poised, self-critically self-confident children of poetic Romanticism and evangelical dissent looks in hindsight like a prediction of their fateful meeting in person. In 1845 RB obtained an invitation to write a letter to EBB, whose reply set into motion a two-year correspondence that the London post office facilitated at virtually the speed of e-mail, and that ripened before long into regular visits at Wimpole Street. The RB/EBB letters – preserved in near entirety on both sides and in our time scrupulously edited more than once – form a joint text that is not only legendary in the annals of true romance, but independently valuable for the reflections on poetry that it contains, and that quickly bore fruit in RB's 1845 *Dramatic Romances and Lyrics*, to which the letters show EBB serving as a kind of coach. The correspondence stopped, at once and for ever, with the improbable yet successful elopement to Florence that dislodged a bride of forty from the bosom of her implacable father and a groom of thirty-four from his familial roof and network of London literary relations. Thrown into one another's arms, into parenthood a few years later, and at Florence into a new and often colourfully eccentric Anglo-American community, the Brownings spent the next fifteen years at Casa Guidi in modest expatriate comfort on EBB's income, and on the diet of fresh impressions with which an Italian life and a Continental viewpoint nourished their inquiring minds. Their major writing henceforth wears the stamp of this chosen and shared exile, which constituted a large act of dissent in itself – and was received as such, at times indignantly, by the home readership to whom they sent the extraordinary works composed in each other's physical and imaginative orbit.

First among these works, and still foremost in literate pop culture, was the booklet of *Sonnets from the Portuguese* that EBB gave her husband a year after marriage and published in 1850 – in proper acknowledgement that this intimate act of connubial endearment was also a work of public literary importance. The conversional pattern executed in each of the more than forty sonnets is for good measure writ large in the sonnet-like proportions of the sequence taken whole, as long deliberative reluctance yields around the two-thirds mark to passionate joy. This development not only repudiated the melancholy with which EBB was widely identified, and thanks to which she rivalled Tennyson at mid-century for the poet laureateship; it also sloughed off the poetess role that female sonneteers since Charlotte Smith and Mary Robinson had been cultivating for half a century. The slowly won commitment, self-acceptance and unmasked erotic fulfilment that EBB's *Sonnets* perform essentially repositioned Petrarch's genre for all subsequent aspirants, who across the nineteenth century and into the twentieth were numerous and of both sexes. Reclaiming the lyric sequence in the heyday of the novel, EBB planted married love at its centre of narrative concern: a social ideal, to be sure, but also a proving ground for the confessional self.

The personal disclosure of EBB's autobiographically grounded testimony was a gift that RB, at least the poet in him, could never requite. Although acts of homage to EBB became a new and lifelong strain within his repertoire, the dramatic poet's reticence about disclosure emerges in these acts as an oddity, something like an over-exposure in photography, dark with excess of light. This blinding effect he eventually put to noteworthy artistic purposes; but the first attempt he made, *Christmas-Eve and Easter-Day* (also 1850), remains one of his least satisfactory. EBB's *Sonnets* made a present of herself, no longer aloof with her 'lost saints' (sonnet 43) but open to the world that he had mixed with and called her to; his tributary answer was a pair of confessions of faith, and doubt, expressly couched in the terms of Christian practice that had formerly been her element. In the joco-serious dream-vision *Christmas-Eve* the poetic 'I' rides the hem of the Lord's garment on a sectarian tour of Victorian religious options, from dingy chapel to Vatican pomp to German Higher-Critical scripture analytics. Awake at last in the chapel at sermon's end, RB's proxy affirms in compromise a position that seems very like his own customised evangelicalism; yet this position is neither sufficiently disowned by the poet, nor sufficiently embraced, to create much light or heat. *Easter-Day*, a long thought-experiment in the shape of interior dialogue, poses with some acuteness (if a knowingly tinsel apocalypticism) the question whether a worldly or an otherworldly Christianity better meets the needs of the hopeful spirit.

Implicitly this question lay at the heart of *Sonnets from the Portuguese*, as of several other 1850 additions to EBB's reissued *Poems*, a two-volume summation of work to date that formulated the relation between this world and the next by celebrating a bodily world made meaningful through the sacrament of love. This both/and resolution of EBB's is counterpoised by RB in *Easter-Day*, characteristically, by the either/or of poise itself. Where she adds and synthetically merges, he divides and alternates, with much the same investigative energy we also find at this time in his most important prose statement: an introductory 'Essay on Shelley' that he was invited to contribute to what later emerged as a spurious edition (1852) of newly found letters by his favourite poet. Here RB draws a distinction between 'subjective' poetry (lyrical, Shelleyan) and 'objective' poetry (dramatic, Shakespearean), only to blur the line with interlacing qualifications about how the one imaginative faculty runs in on the other and an admission that, although it has not happened yet, in principle nothing forbids the same poet from excelling in both modes simultaneously. This concession calls to mind, of course, certain lately published dramatic romances and lyrics wherein the two modes had focalised each other in a concurrence of sympathetic intimacy with ironising distance. The concurrence cannot have been lost on RB, who at the time of writing his Shelley essay was at work on a two-volume collection of fifty poems, *Men and Women*, which would set the high-water mark for dramatic monologue as a genre subjective and objective at once.

Meanwhile in 1851 EBB had broken new ground with *Casa Guidi Windows*, a poem that shares with her husband's *Sordello* a nobly incautious depth of engagement in Italian politics, a rhetorical turbidity to match and, notwithstanding its flaws, the distinction of having enabled major breakthroughs lying just ahead. This is the first of EBB's works that reads as if the poetic object in view – freeing her beloved adoptive country from a foreign occupation whose worst oppression has been to blunt the national mind – matters so much that the poetic object in hand, the mere poem, must take its chances of giving offence. EBB's prophetic outlook from a Florentine apartment falls into a breathless, interlockingly Dantesque rhyme scheme bent on soldering bright image to radical idea, and speeding motivated thought towards political action. The entire poem exhales her faith that from the domestic workshop of nursery and writing desk above the piazza a world-historical panorama is unrolling that summons her as not a spectator but an engaged witness. To rear and deliver the prostrated land and to own as civic the moral force of womanhood form one and the same project – a project that becomes frankly visionary once the practical hopes of the poem's first part (written 1848) are disappointed by events and the second part faces up to a tougher prospect involving longer scope and wilder ideas. 'Salt, and bitter, and good' were the qualities EBB would vest at decade's end in a woman's curse ('A Curse for a Nation', line 48), and these virtues are present in force within *Casa Guidi Windows*. They season the poet's angry flirtation with what it tempts retrospect to call fascist thinking, and they pungently bespeak the circumstances that hemmed in any nineteenth-century woman who so much as presumed to discuss matters of state. That women were disfranchised exiles all, at home no less than abroad, was the scandal simmering just outside this indecorous text's allegories. The poem served notice that giving voice to her sisters' silence, and awakening their tribune conscience at the heart of male power, would furnish EBB's maturity with a secular mission sanctified by the tradition of dissent.

Differences of degree rather than kind distinguish the sophistication of RB's monologues in *Men and Women* (1855) from their 1840s prototypes. The same dialectical axes of history and desire stake out the imaginative space, the latter now being more fully textured, and as it were personalised, by a redoubled density of circumstance. The ideal and the real – what we may want and what we must endure – are at odds within these poems. Yet in another sense they are reciprocally constitutive; and it is this radically unbalanced ratio between heart and mind, in manifold gradation, that diversifies RB's gallery of the human condition in polymorphous self-articulation. Thus 'Pictor Ignotus' from a decade before yields to 'Andrea del Sarto', another avatar of 'the faultless painter' but now equipped with a theory of moral-aesthetic imperfection that feeds, and with subtle perversity eats, into the fabric of his marital and artisanal husbandry. Thus instead of the comparatively easy mark offered by 'The Bishop Orders His Tomb at St Praxed's Church' (1845) we encounter 'Bishop Blougram's Apology' and learn, with our modern cosmopolitan stand-in Gigadibs, that modernity and cosmopolitanism are not all they seemed, and are indeed partaken with gusto by a Victorian prelate whose worldly acumen stands in exact proportion to his supermundane will to belief. Thus

'Cleon' supervenes on 'My Last Duchess' as RB's mature representation of a culture magnate whose power has cost him his hope, and who knows it – a magnate here directly descended from Shelley's compromised sculptor in 'Ozymandias', whose artistic and political components RB writes into fresh mutual relation.

Keeping pace with the evolution of the novel since 1840, RB made the heightened local colour of these new poems an instrument for depicting human experience dynamically. With Balzac and Trollope, that is, he updated the literary devices whereby Scott had grasped the inexorably changing constraints that history sets on our motives and behaviour. This nineteenth-century lesson RB applied not only to the past but also to contemporary settings, whether strewn with goods like Bishop Blougram's tablecloth, intimately implicit in the apparel of 'A Woman's Last Word', or swept clean for the musical performance of a fantasy past in the conservatory of 'A Toccata of Galuppi's', where the keyboard traveller into vanished Venetian indulgences can but return to confront the ashen intellection he has thought, by playing the time-tourist, to escape. Throughout this 1855 collection an irrepressible self-consciousness drives speaker after speaker – Karshish, Childe Roland, the busybodies who speak 'How It Strikes a Contemporary' and ' "Transcendentalism: A Poem in Twelve Books" ' – into theorising his life as if it were an ascetic spiritual or artistic practice. Which it is, of course, in culmination of RB's lifelong project to construct on paper an array of lives that are launched on constructive projects fractally homologous with his own, in which self-fashioning and construing the things of this world are sides of one endless activity. Each speaker might say with Fra Lippo Lippi, 'This world's no blot . . . / Nor blank; it means intensely, and means good: / To find its meaning is my meat and drink' (lines 48–50).

How individual temperaments reveal themselves by the way they find meaning, which is to say the way they make meaning, is RB's meat and drink too; and he metabolises it in *Men and Women* through the enzyme of verse-form. Most of the poems just named come in blank-verse pentameter. But within this most elastic of traditional measures RB had learned from the tradition, pre-eminently from Shakespeare, to temper metres to temperaments. With the prosodic equivalent of biorhythmic voiceprints, a habit of idiosyncratic outburst or mellowing diffusion will often suffice to distinguish Lippo from Andrea, or Karshish from Cleon, on the basis of passages chosen at random. To this instrumentation RB added lexical and grammatical profiling that drew on the widest vocabulary sported in any British poet's oeuvre, and on syntactic patterns of aggregation or subordination that show monologists organising particulars into a subjectively characteristic whole. Comparable effects also appear in a number of fine stanzaic monologues, where rhyme's insistence frames forth a humoresque ('Up at a Villa – Down in the City'), or an obsession ('Mesmerism', 'The Last Ride Together'), or the banter of sex play ('Another Way of Love'), or the bitten-back reticence of shocked betrayal ('In a Year').

It is with the theme of love between men and women, appropriately, that this collection rings its richest changes on the human condition, and nearly always in stanzaic verse where the sweetness of rhyme figures, in the imperfection of its fit, love's differential drive towards a unison never consummated, ever desired (see 'Two in the Campagna'). Here lay RB's profoundest bequest to modern poetry: in the individuating correlation of verbal with psychic structure, through gesturally performative voice. The personal type that emerges from the text leaves an exact and persistent impression, even as it remains uncannily hard to memorise and often a little embarrassing to recite. This is because for all his realism RB wrote not to the specification of a mimetic transcript but in an endo-vernacular that, seemingly colloquial, speaks in fact to the hearing eye or reading ear. His curtain-call in 'One Word More' to hand a lover's postscript to EBB offers another case in point: there, with a small hint that reverberates back across the entire collection, he cites as unique his own employment of trochaic pentameter, 'Lines I write the first time and the last time' (line 120), as the way to fold into song all that he cannot speak out.

RB thus scored for many voices his 1850s proof of the constitutive paradox that underlay the culture of dissent for his generation and inhabited the democratising capitalist culture of his day. His choice of representative epochs exposed modernity's long roots: first within the Renaissance or early-modern period that he foremost among the Victorians hailed as the nursery of individualism; then, yet further down, within the Roman Imperial or early-Christian period, when the soul of the West had arguably learned to thirst for the same kind of personal salvation that persisted through the Protestant's ethical calling into the Romantic ideology of elected poetic genius.

What *Men and Women* by its very conception forbade was to treat this theme sustainedly from a single point of view. Just such a treatment formed the core idea for EBB's masterpiece of the next year. *Aurora Leigh* was, and is, a verse novel in the eyes of some readers – it sold like one, in contrast to the *succès d'estime* that remained her husband's lot even with *Men and Women* – and in others' eyes an epic summa for the High Victorian years. Under either generic description, EBB's poem followed out the logic linking individualist premises to autobiographic forms centred on an actual or fictional self's narrative of its own becoming in the modern world. In obvious ways this scheme brought to fruition the narrative potential that had flowered in *Sonnets from the Portuguese* from the lyric seed of the 1830s. Equally true to those beginnings, if a degree harder to see, is the faith *Aurora Leigh*'s plot of *Bildung* keeps with the puritan-confessional pattern of self-surveillance, modulated here into a series of falls into unwitting small-mindedness, and then recuperative saves that attest the healing grace of love.

A fictive autobiography is by nature a self-consciousness machine. The self transpires diegetically, in retrospect, from the fortunes it gradually narrates and also exegetically, on the narratorial spot, in self-interrupting, self-interpreting commentary delivered from the superior vantage on youthful error that is afforded by the very lessons error has taught. (Witness Wordsworth's *Prelude* or Dickens's *David Copperfield*, two *Künstlerroman* prototypes published a few years before.) In *Aurora Leigh* EBB capitalised on this generic self-consciousness by making it the keynote of her eponymous heroine's character. Orphan, bookworm, poet, independent woman-of-letters-about-London, unattached tourist in Paris, domestic freeholder of a Florentine villa, Aurora is composed in equal parts of a tenderly overflowing susceptibility to life's beauty and squalor, and of a prickliness that makes her peremptory judgments often wittily brilliant, and sometimes badly wrong. The exegetic faculty that pronounces on her own and others' mistakes, in other words, is more than once itself mistaken.

By a further twist EBB converted this generic involution of the autobiographical self into a plot device: she contrived her long poem as a cross between a standard fixed-point memoir and an effusively serial diary. More than once the bedrock of certitude on which Aurora's opinions have been founded in a previous book of the poem is seen to have shifted, without notice, as a new book gets underway from a narrative point in time months later. By this means the poem effects an irony that exposes the heroine not just to her own advancing judgment but to ours. The effect is comparable to the operation of dramatic irony in sophisticated monologues from *Men and Women*, in that it does not cancel our bond with the protagonist but texturally complicates it instead. Readers love Aurora, as does her steadfast if hapless cousin and eventual mate Romney, for the very headstrong impulsiveness that repeatedly lands her in trouble.

For if Aurora's verve leads her wrong, it no less leads her right – right into Romney's battered but true heart; right into a chastened, forgiving if also envious attitude towards the unwed mother she befriends; right into the metaphysicalised poetics, utopian idealism and trenchant societal satire that make the central book 5 so remarkable a Victorian showcase. Above all, and with great inventive brio across this long poem, the heroine's impulsiveness leads right into the thick of a flexible blank verse that is now arch and now solemn, now grand and now conspiratorially fine-tuned. Credit for this sustained versatility goes first to Aurora herself, in *prima facie* evidence of her poetic gift. But of course the real credit is EBB's, who crowned here a lifetime's exercise in a tonal range, and a topical variety, to which no woman's poem of the century, and very few poems by men, will stand comparison. The fertile precipitation of styles in *Aurora Leigh* meets a crossroads of poetic kinds including satire, ekphrasis, *ars poetica*, landscape and domestic genre scenes, devotional meditation, love song, urban phantasmagoria. To compass this subgeneric plenitude it is natural to invoke the dialogic powers of the novel; yet to make that assignment of genre is to miss the critique of fiction's conventionality that EBB's choice of verse implies and that her mimetically implausible plot outcome all but trumpets. At last all things come to Aurora: her brilliant career, her faith, her protégée and infant ward, her adoring man, her home, her city – and, at the horizon of vision, her resurgent motherland – in a blissful convergence that more than one canon of realist fiction should censure, but that in epic terms shines as an ideal of order disclosed at the far edge of the real.

All EBB's work hereafter subsided to lyric forms, which fill the last collection she assembled, *Poems before Congress* (1860), and the posthumous *Last Poems* that RB saw through the press in 1862. While everything in the first collection was forthrightly political, and much in the second was too, after *Aurora Leigh*'s comprehensiveness their partisan lyric interventions feel partial. The ardent, often eccentric bias of the new poems elicited angry dismissal on their publication, and the depth of their absorption in specific occasions long out of mind relegates many of them now to the care of specialists. Nevertheless, there is good reason to suppose that EBB wrote them firmly convinced that more than passing interests lay at stake, and that the Risorgimento, however halting or thwarted, presented the chance of her lifetime to advance the causes of liberation and redress to which she held poetry was divinely called. 'Napoleon III in Italy' is unpalatably strident – any straight-faced civic ode risks striking a modern taste that way – and yet without appreciating its urgent 'voice and verse, / Which God set in me to acclaim and sing / Conviction, exaltation, aspiration', we can hardly appreciate what, and how much, the fistful of strenuously vital lyric complaints that do survive from EBB's last phase are disappointed by.

The best of these complaints lament, beyond their precipitating occasion, the power of poetry itself. Not its impotence, which EBB was less apt to concede than any Victorian poet of consequence; but its price, its misdirection, the unintended collateral damage it wreaks. These themes are almost geometrically worked out in 'A Musical Instrument', where the earth-renewing thrill of inspiration exacts in sacrifice the very pith of human nature; and in 'Mother and Poet', where the warrior ethos that Laura Savio once ecstatically chanted brings ideology home by robbing the poetess of both her sons. The themes of these two lyrics combine in the two halves of 'A Curse for a Nation'. Here against her will the poet is forced to prophesy against the slaveholding United States, not so much decrying slavery ('The Runaway Slave at Pilgrim's Point' had done that in 1848) as anatomising the moral bondage – a self-imposed gag order within the parliament of nations – that America's complicity with slavery places on an allegedly free people. Likewise the nonce elegy that EBB curtly entitled ' "Died . . ." ' mourns less at getting news of a death than at how the debasement of language has cheapened what can be said about the deceased, or anybody else for that matter. Poetry hurts, in the best of EBB's last poems; and precisely that was her final proof that it counts.

RB's widowed return to London, with a teenage son still to raise and a substantial public yet to cultivate, found him on elegiac ground with *Dramatis Personae* (1864). A mourner's economy of regret and resignation now tinged his portraits of familiar types like the artist ('Abt Vogler', 'Youth and Art'), the lover ('James Lee's Wife', 'Too Late') and the believer ('A Death in the Desert', 'Caliban upon Setebos'). It was chiefly religion that grounded this volume, in response not just to the poet's late tribulation but to the shock that Darwin and the Higher Criticism of scripture had administered to the nation's believers. In fact *The Origin of Species* (1859) and *Essays and Reviews* (1860) inducted a new generation of readers onto the historicist and contextualist terrain that RB's art, like his liberal evangelicalism, had occupied for decades. (Reception of this, his first book to need a second edition, portended his eventual promotion to Victorian sagedom with the founding of the London Browning Society in 1881.) *Dramatis Personae* offered to the perplexed 1860s a characteristic mix of good cheer with chilly but still Christian comfort: to accept creatureliness was to know oneself the creature of circumstances, and was thus to behold Caliban blinking back from the glass, darkly. The epiphanic moment of privileged insight was authentic, all right ('Epilogue'), but its privilege had to be paid for on life-long instalment in the currency of opportunities squandered, misprised, rued. The imaginative temptation to beat these tough odds and game God's system forms a chastening subtext for the longest piece of 1864, 'Mr Sludge, "The Medium"', which may be RB's bitterest exercise in self-caricature. Here an upstart séance impersonator, caught in the act of channelling the dead by throwing his voice and rigging special effects, bears discomfiting likeness to the dramatic poet who has ventriloquised him alongside St John and Rabbi Ben Ezra. The *coup de grâce* comes with Sludge's bewildering confession 'I don't know, can't be sure / But there was something in it, tricks and all! / Really, I want to light up my own mind' (lines 809–11).

Lighting up the modern mind meant putting it on stage, where it could be seen objectively at a distance. The group corollary of this individualist-dramatic theorem provided the fulcrum on which RB went on to leverage a flea-market bargain into his *opus maximum*, the twelve-book epic *The Ring and the Book* (1868–9). The obscure bundle of Roman trial documents from 1698 that RB had picked up on a Florentine bookstall proved to be a veritable time capsule, its patriarchal, bourgeois, courtly, commercial, ecclesiastic and legal contents all massed at a tipping point between authoritarian and liberal dispensations. Whether and when a dishonoured husband might kill his wife was a question shedding Grand Guignol limelight on a subtler issue – the contest between traditional customs and individual rights – that in myriad forms had defined the Victorian middle-class ethos of dissent since the inaugural Victorian epoch of Reform. At the 1867 crisis of Second Reform this unresolved issue constituted, RB saw, a theme of solidly epic proportions. Its details moreover held personal resonance for him: the death of a martyred young mother appealed to his chivalry, while the recrimination of the knightly priest who had loved but could not save her drew on the mature emotional register of a man bereaved.

Best of all, the clash of depositions and pleadings bound up in the Old Yellow Book suggested a multi-perspectival experiment in narrative that transported RB's dramatic principles to a new level. *The Ring and the Book* rehearses the story of the Franceschini murder trial at exhaustive length from the perspective of nine contemporaries, in a series of dramatic monologues that advances from ideologically embroiled bystanders towards the central triangle of husband, lover, wife, then out again via the trial lawyers, the Pope on final appeal and at last the condemned husband, so transformed by his imminent execution as to speak in effect from a fresh, tenth viewpoint. This crowd of testimony is further framed in books 1 and 12 by the testimony of RB *in propria persona*: how he acquired and studied the documents, in a flash of inspiration seized their truth and then elaborated a narrative plan to convey that truth not in spite of perspectival bias but by means of it. It is the beauty of this plan to let RB have his words and eat them too. Endorsing the Pope's judgment against Guido's villainy and for the robustly self-mythologising virtue of Pompilia and Caponsacchi, he all the while represents his own conviction as no different in kind from the rest of the convictions his epic strategy submits to ironising reduction. That RB may have got things wrong – subsequent scholarship shows he probably did – is a liability that he invites, and indeed indemnifies his poem against. For it is an integral structural property of *The Ring and the Book* to dissent from itself: a capstone to the poet's career, and a resounding affirmation of the tradition that produced him.

From this high point the two decades that lay ahead of RB remain problematic, not because he failed to produce some superb poetry all the way to *Asolando* (1889), his final book of lyrics, but because in the process he produced so much that was merely curious – at a phase in his career too late for the charm of promise that graces a quirky early work like *Pippa Passes* (1841). Mega-monologues on sex (*Fifine at the Fair*, 1871) and politics (*Prince Hohenstiehl-Schwangau*, 1871), verse novels (*The Inn Album*, 1875), translations of Greek tragedy (the perverse literality of *Agamemnon*, 1877, is notorious), the *sui generis* disquisitiveness of *Ferishtah's Fancies* (1884) and *Parleyings with Certain People of Importance in Their Day* (1887): the sheer volume of RB's later books will daunt even intrepid seekers. An unflagging resiliency of mind defies dismissal on intellectual grounds; yet just when pages of toilsome discourse have made a poem seem intellectual and nothing but, there can emerge a passage of sudden, stunning beauty like the glorious *terza rima* lyric on Thamuris's contest with the Muses that erupts several thousand lines into *Aristophanes' Apology* (1875). To say that criticism has not yet taken the late RB's measure is safe yet also a little embarrassing, since the poetry so frequently meets whatever standards for linguistic and formal creativity may be derived from the much better-studied work of his middle years.

Here let us side-step the question by returning to one special thread in the fabric of RB's late poetry, the role EBB plays there as ghostly collaborator. We could call her a muse, although he does not, and although a vein of humour that ripples across her appearances keeps the whole phenomenon well on the human side of divination. Admittedly, sheer earnestness prevails in RB's evocations of the *Ewig-Weibliche* spirit who embodies male strife's reward at journey's end in 'Prospice' (1864) and again in the thunderingly hearty credo RB designated his last poem, the 'Epilogue' to *Asolando*. The prismatical ice queen of 'Numpholeptos' belongs with the spookery of 'Saint Martin's Summer' (both 1876), 'Never the Time and the Place' and 'Adam, Lilith, and Eve' (both 1883), as expressions of a haunted paranoia that cast long shadows across RB's marital memory. There is gallantly compounded tribute in the fiction-embedded Euripidean translation *Balaustion's Adventure* (1871) and its sequel *Aristophanes' Apology*, which recreated in the rhapsode Balaustion a younger and healthier EBB than he had been able to know. Something more poignant than gallantry speaks through the needy invocative eloquence that closes book 1 of *The Ring and the Book*: 'O lyric Love, half angel and half bird / And all a wonder and a wild desire' (book 1, lines 1391–2).

Still and all, the edge that must have nerved this remarkable marriage between high-strung poets of genius comes out most richly in RB's late imagination as an irony made gentle by having been lived with, and lived into. Out of nowhere yet also on cue, like a lucky rhyme, the revenant EBB comes to RB as an apparition blithely gratuitous, teasingly near. In 'The Householder' (1871) his sputtering incredulity elicits rejoinders that are so credible because so down-to-earth: 'I again, what else did you expect?' (line 8), 'And was I so better off up there?' (line 24). In 'Amphibian' (1871), where he is the swimmer in the bay and she the butterfly visiting him overhead, they are each locked in elementally separate spheres: his and hers, this world and the next. Yet together they yearn across the mortal bar by the power they have honoured in each other and hallowed with the gift of both their lives (*amphi bioi*): the power that can, when the weather lightens and the play of voice lightens with it, 'substitute, in a fashion, / For heaven – poetry' (lines 55–6).

Notes

1. I cite throughout Elizabeth Barrett Browning, *The Poetical Works* (Boston: Houghton Mifflin, 1974); Robert Browning, *The Poems*, ed. John Pettigrew and Thomas J. Collins, 2 vols. (New Haven and London: Yale University Press, 1981) and *The Ring and the Book*, ed. Thomas J. Collins and Richard D. Altick (Peterborough, Ontario: Broadview Press, 2001).
2. George Santayana, 'The Poetry of Barbarism', in *Interpretations of Poetry and Religion* (New York: Scribner, 1905), pp. 166–216.
3. Quoted in *The Poetical Works of Robert Browning*, ed. Ian Jack and Margaret Smith (Oxford: Clarendon Press, 1983), p. 11. For Mill's manuscript review and its context see William S. Peterson and Fred L. Standley, 'The J. S. Mill Marginalia in Robert Browning's *Pauline*: A History and Transcription', *Papers of the Bibliographical Society of America*, 66 (1972), pp. 135–70.

Chapter 34

Emily Brontë, Arnold, Clough

MICHAEL O'NEILL

This chapter focuses on the works of three post-Romantic poets who present, in their poetry, markedly individual responses to and versions of crises troubling Victorian culture. Emily Brontë appears in Arnold's 'Haworth Churchyard' as one of a band of 'Unquiet souls' (line 134), an elegiac salute to the famous close of *Wuthering Heights*.[1] Writing in free 'pindarics', that is, lines that are unrhymed, varying in their number of stresses and arranged in verse paragraphs of differing lengths, Arnold conveys a knotty admiration for the deceased Emily Brontë. '(How shall I sing her?)', his tribute begins in puzzled parentheses, 'whose soul / Knew no fellow for might, / Passion, vehemence, grief, / Daring, since Byron died' (lines 93–6). The swaying enjambments and piled-up nouns suggest that Arnold is pulled towards a force from which he seeks to protect himself. Brontë, for Arnold, might be an example of the fate of genius in a 'Baffled' culture which had lost its bearings, as she 'sank / Baffled, unknown, self-consumed; / Whose too bold dying song / Stirred, like a clarion-blast, my soul' (lines 97–100). The male poet's soul answers Brontë's soul at the ends of respective lines across this passage, which alludes to the dead poet's 'No Coward Soul is Mine', a poem which shares with Arnold's and Clough's work a sense of disillusion with the 'thousand creeds / That move men's hearts' (lines 9–10), dismissed as 'unutterably vain' (line 10).[2]

No doubt, Arnold found 'too bold' Brontë's remarkable invoking of the 'God within my breast' (line 5), an address that flowers out of the pantheism of Wordsworth and the atheism of Shelley, even though, as published in 1850, the boldness of her poem was toned down by the editing of her sister Charlotte.[3] For Brontë's exultant visionary inwardness, Arnold – also slipping the moorings of traditional belief – substitutes a sense of living through a cultural malaise, reproaching himself and his generation, in 'The Scholar-Gipsy', as 'Light half-believers of our casual creeds' (line 172). The phrase reveals Arnold's gift for acutely diagnostic indictment, and in turn allows us to contrast and compare his poetic inflections with those of Clough, some of whose most compelling utterances come from the dramatised figure of Claude, both ineffectual bystander and wincingly honest homespun philosopher, in *Amours de Voyage*. Claude tries for the note of self-dependence struck in 'No Coward Soul', only, with characteristic wryness and irony, to find it, for himself, a 'factitious' pose. In the poem's hexameters, a metre that, in Clough's hands, is as alert as a compass needle to every alteration of irresolute mood, Claude speaks of having 'Found in my own poor soul a great moral basis to rest on' (v.v.97).[4] But his threadbare, self-mocking adjectives place any such discovery firmly in an unreliable past, as the next lines make clear: 'Ah, but indeed, I see, I feel it factitious entirely; / I refuse, reject, and put it utterly from me' (v.v.98–9). Even there, the language, again consciously, risks overstatement (as its absolute adverbs and use of the hexametrical strong closing foot indicate), and the subsequent trust in 'Truth' (v.v.101) must admit, straightway, that, for this speaker and, indeed, for Clough himself, truth will be 'Flexible, changeable, vague, and multiform, and doubtful' (v.v.102). The variety of styles, modes, moods and inflections offered by these three poets, as they give the reader their poetic versions of 'Truth', will be the central theme of this chapter.

Emily Brontë, who published only twenty-one poems in her lifetime, all in *Poems* (1846) by herself, and her sisters Charlotte and Anne, the three sisters appearing under the male pseudonyms, Currer, Ellis and Acton Bell, is a poet who brings together opposites in fascinating ways. Even as some of her poems exist within the narrative framework of her imaginary world of Gondal, their lyric autonomy makes them much more than footnotes to a larger story. And yet though narrative often lyricises itself in Brontë's work, the poetry does not draw its meanings or power from some supposedly autobiographical revelation; the lyric experience it communicates has a sinuous inseparability from larger cultural significances and shared, subterranean human desires. Again, though it gives the sense, for all its frequent use of common ballad metre, of a strongly individual voice, the poetry has productive commerce with Brontë's Romantic forebears.

Wordsworth and Shelley frequently appear as vitalising presences. The Shelleyan image of the superiority of stars to the sun, repeated throughout his work and dominant in *Adonais* and *The Triumph of Life*, underpins 'Stars', a poem published in 1846. Felicia Hemans, too, in 'The Lost Pleiad' with its praise of 'starry myriads burning' (line 11) and lament for glory from the heavens departed' (line 1) may also be a precursor of Brontë's opening elegiac question,

'Have you departed, every one, / And left a desert sky?' (lines 3–4).[5] Brontë, as often in her work, plays a longing for 'boundless regions' (line 14) against an awareness of restriction; her tightly disciplined stanza form accommodates both the longing and the awareness. The fourth stanza identifies full mental freedom with the stellar world, under interdiction after the sun's return:

> Thought followed thought, star followed star,
>   Through boundless regions, on;
> While one sweet influence, near and far,
>   Thrilled through, and proved us one! (lines 13–16)

Brontë's verbs do justice to the sense that 'we' (presumably self and stars) are 'one', but 'proved' itself proves to be premature in the face of the sun's 'hostile light, / That does not warm, but burn' (lines 43–4). Hemans's 'starry myriads burning' generate a majestic rather than a 'hostile' radiance; Brontë's sun emblematises separateness, conflict and a counter-force to the poet's imagination. It is nature as Blake and Shelley fear it, determined to trample the onlooker's thoughts into the dust of death. Brontë evokes the fearful dazzle of the sun's power through an accelerating run of vibrant verbs: 'I saw him, blazing, still, / And steep in gold the misty dale, / And flash upon the hill' (lines 26–8). 'Saw' sets itself with stoic resolve against the unstoppable force of 'steep' and 'flash', and looks ahead to the poem's final prayer to 'sleep through his blinding reign, / And only wake with you!' (lines 47–8).

The poem illustrates Brontë's ability to use the lyric self to enact a drama of visionary desire in the face of what are felt to be near-insuperable obstacles. In 'The Prisoner (A Fragment)', a poem excerpted from and reworking a longer Gondal piece, 'Julian M. and A. G. Rochelle', she stages an encounter between three characters: a 'jailer grim' (line 21); the Julian figure, in the published version a tyrannical yet empathising captor; and a female prisoner, who speaks of nightly visitings from a 'A messenger of Hope' (line 35). These visitings offer 'eternal liberty' (line 36), but though the poem, first published two years before the 1848 revolutions throughout Europe, may have a latent political subtext, its alexandrines, marked by heavy caesural pauses that create double effects (sometimes of calm amidst storm, sometimes of a check when freedom had beckoned), speak most eloquently of near-mystical experience:[6]

> He comes with western winds, with evening's wandering airs,
> With that clear dusk of heaven that brings the thickest stars.
> Winds take a pensive tone, and stars a tender fire,
> And visions rise, and change, that kill me with desire. (lines 37–40)

Alliteration weaves an alluring web that catches within it the promise of rising and changing 'visions', visions 'that kill me', writes Brontë at her most Shelleyan, 'with desire'. Shelley's *Epipsychidion* uses the murderous verb 'kill' (see line 85) with a similar sense of ecstatic delight at the prospect of ordinary selfhood's loss. As Brontë depicts a multiply epiphanic and an almost oxymoronically 'clear dusk' when 'He comes', all is liminal, swaying, 'wandering' and unfixable. The passage sustains its evocation for a further five stanzas, its abstractions – 'Then dawns the Invisible; the Unseen its truth reveals' (line 49) – emerging convincingly from the intricate changes that have been recorded.

Nothing is as affecting or as typical of Brontë's readiness unflinchingly to accommodate opposite sides of experience, however, as the return to habitual self: 'Oh, dreadful is the check – intense the agony – / When the ear begins to hear, and the eye begins to see' (lines 53–4). Repetition, as often in Brontë, locates us in a place of struggle, often a failed struggle, for freedom from oppressive feeling. Here, the echoic sound in '*dread*ful', '*check*', and 'in*tense*' (emphases added) reinforces a stifling impression, while the two uses of 'begins' suggest the winding up, once more, of the clock of the quotidian. Rhyme supports paradox: the physical ability to 'see' explains the experience of 'agony'. The final stanza leaves the captive still imprisoned, but indomitably free from the cruelty of her captors. In the poem's final appeal to 'Heaven' (line 64), Brontë allows the speaker, the master, to fall back on a seemingly conventional religious idiom, yet, as Gezari points out, 'the feminine endings in the last couplet [given/Heaven], the only feminine endings in the poem, have a destabilizing effect'.[7] Certainly the power of its central passage derives from a language that is intransigently at a remove from the traditional Christian mysticism which it recalls.[8] The 'He' who 'comes' might be simply a 'messenger of Hope', or a male muse, or a secularised Christ.

Beneath a tone that seems ardently unswerving, Brontë often conveys doubleness of feeling. In 'Remembrance' the speaker questions in self-reproachful terms whether she has forgotten her 'only Love' (line 3) and expresses a fierce pride at her ability to 'check the tears of useless passion' (line 25). Even as she lingers with barely analysable feelings over thoughts of her beloved as 'Cold in the earth – and the deep snow piled above thee' (line 1), she recognises that 'fifteen wild Decembers / . . . have melted into spring' (lines 9–10). The first line expresses pity, loss and an implicit sense that the speaker's own feelings have been in cold storage, with the further, barely consoling suggestion that they have been so in order not to alter their condition of profound grief. The third stanza invokes a natural cycle and spurs the speaker to assert, 'Faithful, indeed, is the spirit that remembers / After such years of change and suffering' (lines 11–12). In so doing, it readmits time and process, 'change and suffering' (the last word rhyming ironically with the returning 'spring'), but it half-claims that the speaker possesses such an unalterable 'spirit'. If the speaker confesses that she has verged on forgetting the beloved, she claims that any such forgetting is momentary, that the abiding reality has been the stoic endurance of total loss, and that such endurance has been punctuated intermittently by passionate longing for union with the dead. 'Remembrance' represents obsession with the dead beloved as a pervasively unavoidable state that sharpens, when the speaker lowers her guard, into 'memory's rapturous pain' (line 30). Expressing compounded feelings through a rhythm and syntax that work through slowings, doublings, pauses and elongations, it shapes an austerely haunting blend of stern denial with 'divinest anguish' (line 31). The poem, like the best of Brontë's work, shows her to be a technical master, capable of mingling emotional depth and bare restraint.

That Matthew Arnold should have written a memorable poem in response to the legacy of the Brontë sisters should not surprise, since his poetry is often at its finest when expressing elegiac feeling, often feeling that succeeds in assuming a larger cultural resonance. In *Empedocles on Etna*, which pits the hero's disillusioned accents against the joyfully accepting strains of Callicles, his young disciple, Empedocles voices a post-Romantic angst. He speaks for a generation who 'feel, day and night, / The burden of ourselves' (1.ii.127–8). The long chant of which these lines are part, made up of five-line stanzas, each with four alternately rhyming trimeters followed by an alexandrine that is normally exhausted outcry or noose-tightening summary as it clinches a rhyme with its confrère in the previous stanza, articulates a powerful sense that 'Limits we did not set / Condition all we do' (lines 184–5). Rather like the Fury who tempts Shelley's Prometheus in Act 1 (lines 618–31) with a vision of human contradictoriness, Empedocles deploys in his chant a language that delights unsimply in sardonically bare contests between simple words: 'We do not what we ought, / What we ought not, we do' (lines 237–8), he says, remodelling the General Confession from *The Book of Common Prayer* but with no hope of absolution beyond the stoic self-command with which the speech closes, 'Because thou must not dream, thou need'st not then despair!' (line 426).[9]

Stoicism does not have the last ideological word, however, since Empedocles, echoing various Romantic forebears, speaks, before he leaps into the volcanic crater, of how human beings will always feel 'The ineffable longing for the life of life, / Baffled for ever' (II.357–8). Such a 'longing' is often voiced in Arnold's poetry, and lends his rhythms an individual lilt as they manage to speak with affecting power about that 'unspeakable desire / After the knowledge of our buried life' (lines 47–8) which is the subject of 'The Buried Life'. Arnold often displays the mixture of inwardness with feeling and simultaneous ability to analyse it exhibited by 'The Buried Life'; much of his work's affective capacity derives from this blend. So, in 'The Buried Life', he at once allows for and sorrows over feelings that 'convey / A melancholy into all our day' (lines 75–6), where much work is done, as Swinburne noted in a review, by the Wordsworthian 'use of words usually kept back for prose (such as "convey")'.[10] This is a lyricism that understands that the heart has its reasons which reason does not know, and yet stays in touch with the rational. Few poets understand more deeply than Arnold does the power of restraint, of the withheld, of the marshalling and disciplined mind bringing its will to bear on emotion. *Empedocles on Etna* follows Empedocles's final post-Romantic agonies and ecstasies with a Winckelmann-like neo-classicism as Callicles sings of Apollo and the muses. Hymning the contraries of existence with a limpid clarity that judges yet is judged by Empedocles's desolate insights and feverish longings, Callicles brings the poem to a close by invoking 'The day in his hotness, / The strife with the palm; / The night in her silence, / The stars in their calm' (II.465–8). The two-stressed lines plait opposites – night and day, hotness and silence, strife and calm – in such a way that they evoke and elegise an Olympian, classical stance, even if Callicles's utterance seems like a beautiful exercise in a manner that has at best only an uncertain authority.

To create this effect is central to the poem's dramatic achievement. Arnold's love of comparable moments of distancing and calming shows in the concluding description of the 'majestic river' (line 875) at the close of the tragic narrative of 'Sohrab and Rustum'. A single sentence mimes, in its caesurae and rhythmic halting and ongoings, the river's journey until it arrives at 'The longed-for dash of waves' (line 889) and finds its 'luminous home of waters' (line 890). The passage contrasts with human misery and gives suppressed expression to the longing for a 'luminous home' where conflict is resolved. Elsewhere, a more caustic accent twines round Arnold's suffering voice. At the close of 'To Marguerite – Continued', in which a suite of love poems takes on an enlarged significance, Arnold, brooding on loneliness and its consequential 'longing like despair' (line 13), asks, 'Who ordered, that their longing's fire / Should be, as soon as kindled, cooled?' (lines 19–20). The collocation of the verbs captures the cold water poured on longing, while the question sees human beings as the playthings of some power over which they have no control. The answer is akin to a mockery of Victorian theodicy: 'A God, a God their severance ruled! / And bade betwixt their shores to be / The unplumbed, salt, estranging sea' (lines 22–4). The decree of this fictive 'God' expresses itself in a ponderable couplet weighed down by an estrangement embodied in and inflicted by the sea, a sea that is necessarily metaphorical after its earlier appearance as 'the sea of life' in which we are 'enisled' (line 1). A possible debt to Coleridge's image for estranged friends in *Christabel*, that of 'A dreary sea' (line 423), declares itself,[11] and yet Arnold's originality shows in the last line's run of connected, mutually inflecting adjectives. The icy precision of the writing enacts control, even as the wording concedes that the sea is at once dominant, unfathomable and the source of pain.

Arnold's gift for seeming to plumb the 'unplumbed', through the crafted precision of his language, is evident in 'Stanzas from the Grande Chartreuse', a lyric meditation on the fate of the Victorian poet. 'Wandering between two worlds, one dead, / The other powerless to be born' (lines 85–6), it is Arnold's destiny to discover a mode of desolate freedom in his 'Wandering' state; powerlessness empowers his lyric voice. The Carthusian monastery is emblem of a lost 'faith' (line 68) and of a 'cloistral round' (line 205) with which Arnold ambiguously identifies: ambiguously since his revision in the final line of 'forest' (1855) to 'desert' (1867) suggests that he can at best raise only two cheers for 'The House, the Brotherhood austere' (line 65). But the poem's six-line, octosyllabic stanzas roomily accommodate shifts of perspective, even as they pointedly encourage a consistent sharpness of phrasing. Arnold arrests with his self-questioning 'And what am I, that I am here?' (line 66), where 'I' is at once conscious of futility and of its own unsponsored freedom; he then holds the reader's attention with his assertion of secularised, noticeably uninspired aspiration towards 'the high, white star of Truth' (line 69), and with his evocative lament for the Romantics (especially Shelley and Byron); and he rounds out his poem with a powerfully troubled balancing of the claims of 'Action and pleasure' (line 194) against those of the elegist's need to mourn for what he no longer believes.

Arnold addresses comparable themes in 'Dover Beach', though here his mode – as he arranges his reflection into four verse paragraphs of varying lengths with cunningly unpredictable rhymes – draws on, yet reworks, the conversation poem as practised by Romantic poets such as Coleridge.[12] The poem begins with a seeming celebration of some blend of human feeling and natural beauty. Yet the poem places us in a border zone – of 'straits' (line 3) – for a purpose. The poem does not locate Arnold and his partner in a space to be imaginatively connected with 'animated nature' (Coleridge, 'The Eolian Harp', line 44). Rather, despite the initial note of delight ('Come to the window, sweet is the night-air!', line 6), they exist in a treacherously beguiling and fitfully 'Glimmering' (line 5) state. Their window opens up, not even on to Keatsian 'perilous seas, in faery lands forlorn' ('Ode to a Nightingale', line 70),[13] but on to a 'sea' (line 8) whose 'grating roar' (line 9) provokes thoughts of a comfortless falling away from a time when 'The Sea of Faith / Was once, too, at the full' (lines 21–2).

There is much imaginative skill at work as Arnold manages his transition from the actual scene to a non-literal seascape. He contrives to make the 'long, withdrawing roar, / Retreating, to the breath / Of the night-wind' (lines 25–7) at once literal and symbolic, even as the off-rhyme between 'faith' and 'breath' marks the disruption which is Arnold's theme. The poem regretfully lays by the enchanting delusion that 'the world' (line 30) is 'a land of dreams, / So various, so beautiful, so new' (lines 31–2), its regret caught in the lingering 'so's. The best that can be salvaged is private fidelity, as Arnold enjoins, 'let us be true / To one another' (lines 29–30), where the enjambment enforces the sudden sense of closed-down possibilities. Yet the poem concludes with a brave, unconsoling public gesture: 'And we are here as on a darkling plain / Swept with confused alarms of struggle and flight, / Where ignorant armies clash by night' (lines 35–7). Remodelling Keats's 'Darkling' attention ('Ode to a Nightingale', line 51) to the nightingale's song, as well as Thucydides's description of Peloponnesian battle,[14] Arnold, abandoning mellifluous vowel music for a more percussive, braced and dissonant music, gazes outwards to a world which resists pathetic fallacy and tempts to 'flight' more than 'fight'. But the poet's own 'struggle' to see life steadily and see it whole in the poem accounts, in part, for its hauntingly near-tragic lyricism.

As with the best of Arnold's work, 'Dover Beach' involves the reader in a drama involving the divided self and a fractured world, and a cause of his success emerges from the wording of the following lines from the poem: 'we / Find also in the sound a thought, / Hearing it by this distant northern sea' (lines 18–20). The poem is the place where the poet is able to 'find' in a 'sound', the sonic echo supporting the linkage, a 'thought'. Arnold is capable of the large gesture, but he grounds it in authenticating subjective experience. And yet he does not cosset or 'privilege' such experience. If 'we are here', our presence situates itself 'as on a darkling plain' and is buffeted by 'confused alarms' and the 'clashing' of 'ignorant armies'. Any wisdom superior to such 'ignorance' must take it into account and often, for Arnold, offers only tempered relief from it. As a result, his work allows us to trace what in his Preface to the first edition of *Poems* Arnold calls 'the dialogue of the mind with itself'. '[M]odern problems have presented themselves',[15] he continues, with late classical Greek culture in mind, but he might have been discussing the predicament that his own poetry addresses. In 'The Scholar-Gipsy', possibly his finest poem, he follows unexpected and sharply delineated trajectories of feeling. The poem opens with a sensuously post-Keatsian celebration of the seventeenth-century scholar-gipsy, depicted as a representative of some simpler, less divided mode of life. This part of the poem culminates in a questioningly imagined encounter with the scholar-gipsy 'on the wooden bridge, / Wrapped in thy cloak and battling with the snow, / Thy face tow'rd Hinksey and its wintry ridge' (lines 123–5), where pastoral fantasy deepens into a more urgently fashioned strange meeting. Although Arnold's intent wording and rhythms make substantial the ghostly figure, the moment induces an immediate recoil, and sparks off the counter-exclamation, 'But what – I dream!' (line 131). Deploying a 'Keatsian technique',[16] the poet backs away from his imagining, and sets out, in stanzas that abandon evocation and adopt a keenly analytical idiom, the ills of a present characterised by 'sick fatigue' and 'languid doubt' (line 164). Arnold's remedy may seem to be escapism when he instructs the scholar-gipsy to 'Fly hence, our contact fear!' (line 206), but the same stanza's comparison between the scholar-gipsy with Dido means that the poet of the present is given the role of Aeneas, his role to endure, to follow a complex destiny. The final two stanzas of the poem involve an elaborately extended simile, in which the scholar-gipsy is this time compared to a 'grave Tyrian trader' (line 232) who flees 'the merry Grecian coaster' (line 237). The comparison is by no means straightforward, endowing the scholar-gipsy with a gravity which seems more the property of the poet himself, and the implicit merging of the two figures which occurs here recasts the poem's previous divisions in modifying and characteristically thought-expanding ways.

Clough and Arnold share a clear-sighted sense of the gulf between the self and the world, an awareness that 'The world is what it is, for all our dust and din' (I.ii.206), as Arnold puts it in *Empedocles on Etna*. Yet they are aware, too, with post-Romantic irony, that, from the perspective of human subjectivity, the world is what it seems to be. Both these awarenesses inform Clough's measured if less than generous reproof of Arnold's *Empedocles on Etna* volume: 'Not by turning and twisting his eyes, in the hope of seeing things as Homer, Sophocles, Virgil, or Milton saw them; but by seeing them, by accepting them as he sees them, and faithfully depicting accordingly, will he attain the object he desires.'[17] This criticism underplays the degree to which Arnold's poetry represents controlled experiments in ways of 'seeing things'. But its sinuous wording allows for the twinned but jostling goals of fidelity to things as they are and to the way they are seen. Clough's poetry frequently dramatises gaps and contradictions. It ruefully acknowledges that it is caught in the very traps which it exposes to view. In particular, it makes clear that the mode of non-subjective vision which it often suggests is desirable may be beyond the capacity of human beings who must see subjectively.

The consequence is a poetry of subtle irresolution, tugged between impulse and doubt, visions and revisions. In *Dipsychus and The Spirit*, unpublished in his lifetime and bequeathing tricky editorial problems of arrangement, Clough daringly and Byronically sets serious and satirical voices against one another. One voice, that of Dipsychus, is itself double-minded in its tormented sense of the easy passage from 'our better into our worst selves' (I.3.6), a passage which centres on the temptations offered by prostitution, temptation taken in its stride by the Mephistophelean Spirit. His frivolous cynicism provides the poem with its other voice, one that pours scorn on his companion's 'high moral way of talking' (I.3.97), and delights in an altogether slangier, mocking mode, drawing on the language of the street and the tavern: so of prostitutes he exclaims cheerily, 'Fiddle di daddle, fal lal lal! / By candlelight they are *pas mal*' (I.3.114–15). Elsewhere, Dipsychus expresses his lacerated state of mind in a tortured blank verse, while the Spirit jokes in doggerel-tending couplets. So, the Spirit's, 'What we all love is good touched up with evil, / Religion's self must have a spice of devil' (I.4.58–59), meets as its counterpart Dipsychus's sense that the look of 'Some vague miscreant' 'for a whole sick day / Lepers me' (I.4.67, 68–9), the chillingly striking verb expressing a *Hamlet*-like mixture of disgust and self-loathing. The overall result is among the most daring examples of Clough's compulsion and ability to interweave idioms, view-points, and voices.

One of his most famous short poems, 'The Struggle', wrenches a painfully hard-won and densely inspiriting lyricism out of conflicting mental attitudes. 'Say not the struggle nought availeth' (line 1), the poem starts, its tongue-twisting syntax seeming to ward off, but only just to ward off, a pessimistic assertion that might spring easily to the speaker's lips. The rest of the stanza articulates what the opening line says should not be said. When the turnabout comes in line 5, its basis turns out to be a near-sophistical piece of word-play, 'If hopes were dupes, fears may be liars' (line 5), and in the next line that word 'may' sustains the attack on 'fears' with a crooked, even slightly crocked, courage. If optimism wins out, it is because Clough finds a path towards it through images that expose their constructed nature with cunningly dogged, disarming candour: 'In front the sun climbs slow, how slowly, / But westward, look! the land is bright' (lines 15–16).

The image works like a paradox or a riddle, identifying radiance with the quarter where the sun sets. Courage, one might wish to gloss the poem, driven to do so through its rhythmic enactments, flames the more brightly when it is aware of near-insuperable obstacles. Again, Clough likes to pair poems, as in his two 'Easter Day' poems, the first expressing the stark agnostic view that 'Christ is not risen' (line 156), the second articulating a more hopeful sense that, in some way, 'In the great Gospel and true Creed,' 'Christ is yet risen' (lines 49, 51). That 'yet' acts as a stay against Clough's own deep religious doubts, and emerges, typically, from a dialogue of his mind with itself: 'I with my secret self held communing of mine own' (line 12). The line shows Clough's predilection for the longer line (in this lyric counterpoised against shorter lines), and among his enduring legacies is a metrical and rhythmic mastery which shows itself most fully in his handling of the hexameter, a form which he uses to entertaining and moving effect in his masterpiece, the epistolary *Amours de Voyage*.

J. P. Phelan comments wittily that the poem is 'an introspective and solipsistic critique of introspection and solipsism'.[18] It is also, such is its self-pivoting agility of mind, a critique of the fact that it is such a critique. Claude's visit to Rome during a period of political turbulence, as Mazzini's fledgling Republic is invaded by the French the year after the momentous revolutionary events of 1848, involves the criss-crossing of public events and private crisis. We see matters mainly from Claude's perspective, though there are letters from others, notably Mary Trevellyn, with whom he develops a relationship that comes to nothing after she departs with her family. Clough manages to create our interest in, and sympathy for, Claude, despite, yet in many ways because of, his fastidious detachment from life (he is, initially, patronising about the Trevellyns as 'not wholly / Pure of the taint of the shop', I.VI.125–6) and air of world-weariness ('Rome disappoints me much; I hardly as yet understand, but / *Rubbishy* seems the word that most exactly would suit it', I.I.19–20). A key to this interest and sympathy is the impression we gain, through the poetry's expertly handled rhythms, of listening to a voice that is intent on a peculiar exactness, a nuanced honesty. So, in the lines about the Trevellyns just quoted, Claude seems engagingly to send up his own upper-class phrasing, proffering his words as if holding them out on self-mockingly silvered tongs, even as he invites Eustace to share his prejudice against the family. And in the confession that he 'hardly as yet' understands his disappointment with Rome, the poetry moves across the line-ending into the unexpected '*Rubbishy*', a word that is wittily singled out as though it were a specialist aesthetic term.

Such writing makes available to us a highly self-aware, proto-Jamesian consciousness that relishes and is perplexed by 'juxtaposition' (III.VI.107), the poem's chief narrative principle and one of its main thematic concerns. While it would devalue Clough's dramatic achievement to identify him simply or solely with Claude, the character licenses some of the poet's most persuasive social, psychological, moral and existential explorations. Alert to his own snobbery, Claude is capable of more unaffected yet always self-watchful feelings. As he begins to be drawn towards Mary, 'entering into all sorts of relations', he describes himself in a series of images as having 'Quitted the sea and the shore, passed into the magical island' (I.XII.229, 235) to enter an erotic, sexual and always social 'labyrinth' which 'closes around me, / Path into path rounding slyly' (I.XII.237–8). Claude's verbs, transferring agency from his quitting and passing to the labyrinth's closing round him, skilfully express one aspect of his condition, the possibility of a gradual loss of control. Even more subtly, as the passage continues, it conveys his sense that he will always be saved by 'the great massy strengths of abstraction' (I.XII.251) that will winch him to contemplative safety.

It is as though, in this passage, Claude has foresuffered all, and yet the poem's development fascinatingly shows him experiencing chinks in his armour of ironic detachment, an armour which he seems half-weary of knowing will protect him from involvement with others. The question of participation in the political struggle around him is aired, dismissed and half-resuscitated: Claude feels a spasm of libertarian regret at the fate of 'thee, thou poor little Roman Republic' (II.I.22), yet he is no warrior, with at best an uncertain willingness to 'incarnadine ever this inky pacifical finger' (II.IV.72), where the hexameter accommodates a polysyllabic grimace, and where the echo of *Macbeth* only points up Claude's 'pacifical' distaste for bloodshed. Georgina Trevellyn reports Mary owning that he 'was *most* useful and kind on the terrible thirtieth of April' (II.VIII.227), and the narrative shifts at this stage into the tortuous nature of Claude's and Mary's relationship. Clough captures the accents of Claude's wry wish to hold the conventional labels at arm's length in a line concluding a letter to his friend Eustace, 'I am in love, you say; I do not think so exactly' (II.X.263), where 'exactly' falls with hesitantly precise recognition of the difficulty that Claude finds in naming and acknowledging his feelings.

As in much Victorian literature, the question of love raises larger questions of will, choice, purpose, destiny, chance and nature. Hamlet-like, Claude exclaims '*HANG* this thinking at last! what good is it? oh, and what evil!' (III.x.207), a line that sways between doubt whether 'thinking' can lead to 'good' and certainty that it does produce 'evil'. But no more than Shakespeare's hero can Clough's abandon thought, and in an unwritten letter, composed in the depths of the loss he feels over his unfulfilled relationship with Mary, he affectingly compares his need for another to the human need for 'a Being / In a conception of whom there is freedom from all limitation' (V.V.73–4). It is characteristic of Clough, as of the other two poets discussed in this chapter, to evoke such a 'conception' of 'freedom from all limitation' in a way that makes us see it as both necessary and, almost definitely, unrealisable.

Notes

1. Arnold's poetry is quoted from *The Poems of Matthew Arnold*, ed. Kenneth Allott, second edition ed. Miriam Allott (London: Longman, 1979). *Wuthering Heights* concludes with Lockwood wondering how 'anyone could ever imagine unquiet slumbers, for the sleepers in that quiet earth'. *Wuthering Heights*, ed. David Daiches (Harmondsworth: Penguin, 1965), p. 367.
2. Emily Brontë's poetry is quoted from Emily Jane Brontë, *The Complete Poems*, ed. Janet Gezari (London: Penguin, 1992).
3. Charlotte rewrote 'earth and moon' (line 21) as 'earth and man', deleted 'Since' from the penultimate line and capitalised 'thou' in the last two lines, all changes that tilt the poem away from its refusal to locate 'its authority outside the self', as Janet Gezari observes in her *Last Things: Emily Bronte's Poems* (Oxford: Oxford University Press, 2007), p. 134.
4. Clough's poetry is quoted from *Clough: Selected Poems*, ed. J. P. Phelan (London: Longman, 1995).
5. Hemans is quoted from *Romantic Poetry: An Annotated Anthology*, ed. Michael O'Neill and Charles Mahoney (Malden, MA: Blackwell, 2007).
6. See Francis O'Gorman (ed.), *Victorian Poetry: An Annotated Anthology* (Malden, MA: Blackwell, 2004) for commentary on the way in which this feature of the poem intensifies its 'formal poise', p. 223.
7. Gezari, *Last Things*, p. 74.
8. O'Gorman notes that the poem 'mimics elements of Christian vocabulary, but only to keep a guarded distance from the religious', *Victorian Poetry*, p. 223.
9. See Allott (ed.), *Poems of Matthew Arnold*, p. 175n.
10. See *Matthew Arnold: The Poetry: The Critical Heritage*, ed. Carl Dawson (London: Routledge, 1973), p. 176.
11. See Allott (ed.), *Poems of Matthew Arnold*, p. 129, referring to Kathleen Tillotson, 'Yes: in the Sea of Life', *Review of English Studies*, n.s. 3 (1952), pp. 346–64.
12. See Nils Clausson, 'Arnold's Coleridgean Conversation Poem: "Dover Beach" and "The Eolian Harp"', *Papers on Language and Literature* (2008). Available via FindArticles.com.

13. Coleridge and Keats are quoted from *Romantic Poetry: An Annotated Anthology*, ed. Michael O'Neill and Charles Mahoney (Malden, MA: Blackwell, 2007).
14. See Allott (ed.), *Poems of Matthew Arnold*, p. 257n.
15. *Ibid.*, p. 654.
16. *Ibid.*, p. 363n.
17. Quoted in Phelan (ed.), *Clough: Selected Poems*, p. 28.
18. *Ibid.*, p. 29.

Chapter 35

Dante Gabriel Rossetti and Swinburne

DAVID G. RIEDE

When Arthur Henry Hallam introduced the poetry of his friend Tennyson to the Victorian reading public in 1831, he introduced him as a poet of 'sensation' in the school of Keats and Shelley as opposed to 'reflection' in the school of Wordsworth. In introducing Tennyson as a poet who does not suffer his mind 'to be occupied during its creation by any other predominant motive than the desire of beauty',[1] Hallam was perhaps premature in heralding the advent of a genuinely aesthetic school of British poetry, but he seems almost prophetically to have introduced the later generation of great Victorian poets of what Walter Pater called the ' "aesthetic" poetry': Dante Gabriel Rossetti, Algernon Swinburne and William Morris. Pater introduced the term 'aesthetic poetry' in his review of Morris's *The Earthly Paradise* in 1868, but he dated the origin of such poetry to Morris's earlier volume, *The Defence of Guenevere and Other Poems* (1858), and he defined it as a poetry 'tormented and awry with passion, like the body of Guenevere defending herself from the charge of adultery', poetry characterised by 'the strange suggestion of a deliberate choice between Christ and a rival lover'.[2] Pater was primarily interested in the way in which these poets, like the poets of the late Middle Ages, expressed the 'composite experiences of all the ages'[3] as transmitted in art and incorporated in the body and mind of the poet. His use of the term 'aesthetic' was undoubtedly intended to suggest the intellectual apprehension of past artistic achievements, but it also very explicitly and aptly returns to the root meaning of 'aesthetic' in sensation and the body. Pater did not use the loaded term 'sensational', which had recently been associated with novels widely considered as dangerously immoral, but Hallam's term was used in this newly moralised sense to attack the aesthetic poetry: attacks on Swinburne's sensual *Poem and Ballads* were about to explode into an all-out critical barrage on Swinburne, Rossetti and Morris as poets of the morally degrading 'sensational school of literature', which 'delight[s] in extreme physical experiences – ecstasies and horrors – for their own sake, or rather for the sake of the morbid appetite they create and for the moment help to satisfy'.[4]

Pater's assessment was particularly apt not only because it helped to buffer Morris, Rossetti and Swinburne from attacks on them as a merely sensual, morbid, 'fleshly school' of poetry without denying their genuine delight in bodily beauty and passion, but also because it correctly recognised the beginnings of 'aesthetic poetry' in the first book to emerge from the close association of the three poets that had begun in 1857 when Rossetti agreed to paint murals for the Oxford Union and had been joined by Morris, Ned Jones (later Edward Coley Burne-Jones) and, as an engaged onlooker, the undergraduate Swinburne. The murals were all on Arthurian themes, and all the artists agreed that, as Rossetti put it in a different context, in contrast to Tennyson's Christian moralising of the legends, the treatment of Malory's tales would be conducted in a way 'wherein God and Guenevere will be weighed against each other by another table of weights and measures' and would 'emphasise the marked superiority of Guenevere over God'.[5] Morris's poem is not quite so bold, since the work, influenced in form by Browning, is a dramatic monologue spoken by Guenevere. Nevertheless Guenevere's defence against charges of adultery amounts to little more than the claim that her physical beauty and passion outweigh mere moral, Christian considerations, and the implied poet intervenes in his own voice to praise her for her beauty and passion, if not her arguments:

> still she stood right up, and never shrunk,
> But spoke on bravely, glorious lady fair!
> Whatever tears her full lips may have drunk,
>
> She stood, and seemed to think and wrung her hair,
> Spoke out at last with no more trace of shame,
> With passionate twisting of her body there . . .[6]

Though Morris's was the first true volume of 'aesthetic poetry', the origins of the style are to be found in the early works of the group's acknowledged leader, Rossetti.

By the time of the Oxford murals project Rossetti was already a famous and influential artist, primarily as a painter and a founding member and leader of the Pre-Raphaelite Brotherhood, which had begun to revolutionise British painting in 1849 with its conflicted returns 'to nature' and to early Italian devotional forms of painting in defiance of the formal rules of the Royal Academy. Though he was best known at this time as a painter, Rossetti already had a considerable reputation as a poet based on his translations of Dante and the early Italian poets and occasional publications in small avant-garde journals that he and Morris had been instrumental in creating. Rossetti, however, had not started out as conspicuously a poet of the bodily senses, but rather as a disciple of the Christian poetry of Dante and the *stilnovisti*: he had even collected much of his own poetry in a manuscript entitled 'Songs of the Art-Catholic' and sent it to the surviving friend of Keats and Shelley, Leigh Hunt, who had particular praise for the 'Dantesque heavens' of the precocious 'The Blessed Damozel', the poem that more than any other helped to establish and sustain Rossetti's fame. The interest in Catholic spirituality came naturally to Rossetti as the son of an Italian expatriate scholar of Dante and a devoutly Anglo-Catholic mother, and was even more conspicuously present in Rossetti's early paintings, *The Girlhood of Mary Virgin* (1849), and *Ecce Ancilla Domini!* (1850), in their accompanying sonnets and in such poems as 'Ave' and 'My Sister's Sleep'. Nevertheless, as his militantly agnostic brother William liked to point out, Rossetti was never a true believer in Catholic or even Christian dogma, and the emphasis in the term 'Art-Catholic' always fell, for him, on the first word: he was, that is, always an 'aesthetic' poet. Certainly his early poetry and painting do not seem strikingly sensual and scarcely hint at bodies tormented and awry with passion, but even as Rossetti drew on medieval Catholicism for spiritually suggestive imagery, he was also deploying more concretely sensual imagery. Most notoriously, in the dramatic poem 'Jenny' Rossetti's speaker contemplates the sleeping body of a prostitute and ponders the wide gap between the sensual truths of the body and the moral idealisms of Christianity, more or less explicitly juxtaposing Christ with a rival lover, and even parodying and replacing the ascetic ideal of the Virgin Mary with the bodily charms of the sleeping whore: 'Poor shameful Jenny, full of grace'.[7] 'Jenny' is of course a dramatic poem, and it is a mistake to identify the speaker with Rossetti himself, but it is difficult to judge just how much ironic distance Rossetti puts between himself and the speaker. For modern readers it is easy to condemn the sexism of the speaker when his sympathy for Jenny is mixed with contemptuous comments on her status as a commodity and on her defiled mind, or when he regards her as an enigma to be gazed at but not spoken to. Rossetti, however, sympathetically described the speaker as a 'young and thoughtful man of the world' and insisted that the only way to come to terms with the pressing problem of prostitution was to approach it from the '*inner* standing point' of such a man.[8] Consequently the poem is probably best seen as a serious effort to examine a major social problem of the day even as it simultaneously reflected Rossetti's own position as a painter and poet dealing in representations of female beauty as a commodity.

Even in his Art-Catholic poems, Rossetti's 'Dantesque heavens' had always been aesthetic, even 'sensational', representations of bodily beauty, as in the very first stanzas of his most celebrated poem, 'The Blessed Damozel':

> The Blessed damozel leaned out
> 	From the gold bar of Heaven;
> Her eyes were deeper than the depth
> 	Of waters stilled at even;
> She had three lilies in her hand,
> 	And the stars in her hair were seven.
>
> Her robe, ungirt from clasp to hem,
> 	No wrought flowers did adorn,
> But a white rose of Mary's gift,
> 	For service meetly worn;
> Her hair that lay along her back
> 	Was yellow like ripe corn.

If the open robe of the damozel does not sufficiently call attention to the flesh and blood materiality of this angelic vision, Rossetti's emphasis on the female body becomes explicit in the later speculation that 'her bosom must have made / The bar she leaned on warm' (lines 45–6).

Similar effects are evident in 'My Sister's Sleep', an obviously 'Art-Catholic' poem in its invocation of 'Christ's blessing on the newly born' (line 60) as the speaker's sister dies on Christmas morn. As Jerome McGann has pointed out, however, the poem is best understood as a dramatic utterance in which belief in the 'religious ideas and forms' is not crucially linked to moral feeling. McGann's point is, perhaps, most forcefully made in his reading of stanza four:

> Without there was a cold moon up,
> Of winter radiance sheer and thin;
> The hollow halo it was in
> Was like an icy crystal cup.

> These tropes have an inherent religious urgency which is only increased by the context, by the religious motif present from the first line. The stanza is an artistic triumph because it succeeds in sterilizing completely the religious potency of the images. Rossetti's art here is highly self-conscious; he wants us to seek and fail to find the religious 'meaning' in his stanza, and failing to find it, to recognize the purely sensational value of the lines.[9]

As McGann's argument illustrates, Rossetti was a poet of sensation from the start, though the quotation is from the version of the poem published in the 1870 *Poems* and had been revised, in Rossetti's words, to 'eliminate the Christian element altogether'[10] partly by substituting the 'icy crystal cup' for the 'altar-cup' of the 1848 and 1850 versions. Even in the earliest version, though, Rossetti had deliberately emptied the poem of Christian presence by emptying the chalice: the moon's light 'Seemed hollow like an altar-cup' (line 16).

Rossetti did not fully expunge the religious element from his poetry until his revisions for the publication of *Poems* in 1870, but by the time of his close association with Morris and Swinburne he was explicitly refusing to link physical imagery or bodily experience to religious or spiritual meaning, and he had become emphatically a poet of bodily sensation, deploying imagery that appealed directly to the physical senses, with no necessary referent beyond. The point is made almost programmatically in 'The Woodspurge', in which the speaker submits so completely to a sensation of grief that consciousness, as McGann points out, is extinguished and nothing remains but the sensation of 'environmental stimuli'.[11] The famous closing image of the woodspurge flower might have been used to suggest a theological or spiritual meaning, but is instead emptied out to suggest nothing more than its own 'enormous relevance' as a 'non-symbolic fact':

> From perfect grief there need not be
> Wisdom or even memory:
> One thing then learnt remains to me, –
> The woodspurge has a cup of three. (lines 13–16)

McGann aptly points out that this extreme version of 'Keatsian' insistence on the material image, this truth 'first of all to experience, not ideas' is the 'basis of Rossetti's notorious aestheticism'.[12]

Of course the blossom of the woodspurge is still a far cry from the body of Guenevere twisted and awry with passion, but beginning from the mid 1850s Rossetti did devote his art increasingly and almost exclusively not only to the representation of the impassioned body, but even to the 'deliberate choice between Christ and a rival lover'. By the time he met Morris and Swinburne, Rossetti had devoted himself almost exclusively to painting enigmatically symbolic and often erotic scenes from medieval legend. The complete shift from spiritual, Dantean themes in Rossetti's art, however, appears most dramatically in 1859 when he left behind his characteristic drawings and paintings of his deceased wife Elizabeth Siddall as Beatrice and other chaste damozels for the lushly sensual painting of his mistress Fanny Cornforth, as *Bocca Baciata*. In his poetry, the shift to frankly sensual representation of the physical, impassioned body is most obvious in the 1860 'Song of the Bower', which describes the erotic ideal and the bodily type of female beauty that preoccupied Rossetti as a painter and poet for the rest of his life:

> What were my prize, could I enter thy bower,
> This day, to-morrow, at eve or at morn?
> Large lovely arms and a neck like a tower,
> Bosom then heaving that now lies forlorn.
> Deep in warm pillows, (the sun's kiss is colder!)
> Thy sweetness all near me, so distant to-day;
> My hand round thy head and thy hand on my shoulder,
> My mouth to thy neck as the world melts away.[13]

Once he had dedicated himself to an aestheticist, 'sensational' commitment to art and beauty, the crowning achievement of Rossetti's poetic career was the sonnet sequence *The House of Life*, consisting of 102 miscellaneous sonnets, many of which celebrate erotic love and its representation in art as the highest form of genius. Rossetti did continue to insist upon the morally and spiritually redemptive power of love, but in such sonnets as 'Genius in Beauty', his emphasis falls on female beauty enshrined in art:

> Beauty like hers is genius. Not the call
> Of Homer's or of Dante's heart sublime, –
> Not Michael's hand furrowing the zones of time, –
> Is more with compassed mysteries musical;
> Nay, not in Spring's or Summer's sweet footfall
> More gathered gifts exuberant life bequeaths
> Than doth this sovereign face, whose love-spell breathes
> Even from its shadowed contour on the wall. (lines 1–8)

Rossetti's contemporary admirers, such as F. W. H. Myers, praised him and defended the seeming amorality of his aestheticism on the moral grounds that for

> The worshipper of Beauty . . . the highest things are also the loveliest, and . . . the strongest of moral agencies is also the most pervading and keenest joy. Art and Religion, which no compression could amalgamate, may by Love be expanded and interfused; and thus the poet may not err so wholly who seeks in a woman's eyes 'the meaning of all things that are'; and 'the soul's sphere of infinite images' may not be a mere prismatic fringe to reality, but rather those images may be as dark rays made visible by passing through the medium of a mind which is fitted to refract and reflect them.[14]

Rossetti certainly did endow erotic love with such idealism, and as his use of the Petrarchan sonnet form suggests, he was drawing on the neo-Platonism of the courtly love tradition, but Myers's elaborate defences would not have been necessary if what he called Rossetti's 'Religion of Art' and 'Worship of Beauty' had not been presented in terms that shocked contemporary morality by displacing the Christian God with an altogether different deity: the personified 'Love' of the *The House of Life* may be in part Platonic, but Plato was a pagan, and 'Love' more closely resembles Venus than Christ. Further, the erotic evocation of soul is more carnal than Victorian morality would characteristically approve, as in the evocation of deity in 'The Kiss':

I was a child beneath her touch, – a man
    When breast to breast we clung, even I and she, –
    A spirit when her spirit looked through me, –
A god when all our life-breath met to fan
Our life-blood, till love's emulous ardours ran,
    Fire within fire, desire in deity. (lines 9–14)

Love is also meant to be redemptive in the poem that Rossetti eventually suppressed because of the harsh criticism of its eroticism, 'Nuptial Sleep':

Sleep sank them lower than the tide of dreams,
    And their dreams watched them sink, and slid away.
Slowly their souls swam up again, through gleams
    Of watered light and dull drowned waifs of day;
Till from some wonder of new woods and streams
    He woke, and wondered more: for there she lay. (lines 9–14)

These lines have an impeccable pedigree in their clear allusion to Milton's account of Adam's dream and the creation of Eve, and also to Keats's comment on Adam's dream as a proof of the 'holiness of the Heart's affections and the truth of Imagination',[15] but as the octave of the sonnet graphically relates, the path to this redemptive notion of Love is emphatically carnal:

At length their long kiss severed, with sweet smart:
    And as the last slow sudden drops are shed
    From sparkling eaves when all the storm has fled,
So singly flagged the pulses of each heart.
Their bosoms sundered, with the opening start
    Of married flowers to either side outspread
    From the knit stem; yet still their mouths, burnt red,
Fawned on each other where they lay apart. (lines 1–8)

Eventually voices of shocked indignation would be raised against this carnality, but not before being provoked by Swinburne's much more shockingly sensational and genuinely blasphemous poetry.

The young Swinburne was well on his way towards a frankly pagan 'Worship of Beauty' of his own when he met Rossetti at Oxford. Like Rossetti, he had been raised in an Anglo-Catholic home, but he seems to have retained his faith until his enrolment at Oxford and he was only beginning his fierce reaction against the faith of his youth in 1857. At the tender age of twenty, Swinburne had long been practising his craft, had written great quantities of precocious juvenilia and was at work on two tragedies, *The Queen Mother* and *Rosamund* (published together in 1860), which already reflected his interest in unorthodox, sadistic and masochistic expressions of passionate sexuality and especially in the destructive power of passionate women. Under the influence of Rossetti and Morris, he wrote various medievalist poems, including *Queen Yseult* which, like 'The Defence of Guenevere', sided with beauty and passion as opposed to the orthodox morality of Tennyson's *Idylls*.

Swinburne left Oxford to settle in London near Rossetti, Morris and Jones in 1860 and throughout the early 1860s established himself as the *enfant terrible* of English letters. During these years he wrote in a remarkable variety of forms, from French burlesques of Victor Hugo and hoax reviews of obscene French poets to serious and important literary criticism, an impressive epistolary novel (serialised in 1877 as *A Year's Letters*, and published in book form as *Love's Cross-Currents* in 1901) and, most significantly, the plays and poems that were to make him famous and kick up a storm of controversy with their publications in the mid 1860s: *Atalanta in Calydon* (1865), *Chastelard* (1865) and *Poems and Ballads* (1866).

Atalanta in Calydon, still justly acknowledged as one of Swinburne's greatest works, showcased his extraordinary learning and critical tact in its compelling reproduction of Aeschylean tragedy, his astonishing lyrical gifts in the famous choruses and his favourite themes of the fatal power and passion of women in the legend of Atalanta the huntress and Althaea, the fatal mother who slew her own son, Meleager. In addition, the pagan setting enabled him to express his anti-theism and genuinely pagan belief in the beauty of the cyclical pattern of generation and destruction in nature; and the very form of the work, echoing Aeschylus, enabled him to represent his aesthetic faith that great art endures, that art alone survives the fatal cycles of nature. Like Rossetti's Petrarchan sonnets and the Dantean *terza rima* of Morris's 'Defence of Guenevere', the characteristically 'aesthetic' use of traditional form brought the nineteenth century into contact with the remote past, enabling the poet to represent the 'composite experience of all the ages' formally as well as thematically.

In addition, the play situates Swinburne as a poet of sensation, the lushness and sensuality recalling Keats, and the rush of images and ideas recalling Shelley. The characteristically rapid anapaestic verse is perhaps most evident in the famous first chorus:

When the hounds of spring are on winter's traces,
    The mother of months in meadow or plain
Fills the shadows and windy places
    With lisp of leaves and ripple of rain;
And the brown bright nightingale amorous
Is half assuaged for Itylus,
For the Thracian ships and the foreign faces,
    The tongueless vigil and all the pain.[16]

These famous lines have been much derided for their supposed Swinburnean tendency to substitute a rush of sound for meaning and to sweep the reader away in a haze of words, and it is true that the rapidity of the metre and the sonorous effects of the assonance and alliteration may sweep readers beyond the full implications of the lines. The difficulty, however, is caused less by the rush of sound than by a rush of meaning: there is almost too much meaning, especially for readers not trained in the classics. Swinburne uses the choruses to draw in the entire context of Greek mythology, here alluding particularly to the goddess Artemis in all of her aspects as goddess of the hunt and therefore of death and destruction, chaste goddess of the moon and the months, and goddess of fertility and the seasons: the point, economically made by allusion to the body of Greek myth, is that chastity and fertility, life and death, generation and destruction, idealism and actuality, are so inextricably mixed as to be represented in one personification, the presiding deity of the tragedy. The further allusions, to the myth of Itylus, draw in the sadism and violence of Greek myth with the story, parallel to Althaea's tale, of Procne's murder of her son Itylus in revenge against her husband Tereus, who had raped her sister Philomela and cut out her tongue. Because the legend includes the metamorphosis of Philomela into a nightingale, who sings her grief for all eternity, Swinburne's allusion also contributes to the play's meaning in its suggestion that song, poetry, is the product of passion and violence, and survives to transcend the cycles of death and rebirth presided over by Artemis. This is not the place to explicate the stanza fully, let alone to provide a full reading of the play, but even this brief glance at the stanza's breadth and depth of allusion should illustrate that Swinburne does not substitute sound for sense as his detractors have traditionally claimed. Catherine Maxwell convincingly argues that his metres ideally 'help dramatize the meaning of the verse':

> Yeats's proposition that 'the purpose of rhythm . . . is to prolong the moment of contemplation . . . to keep us in that state of perhaps real trance in which the mind liberated from the pressure of the will is unfolded in symbols' is a good description of the way in which Swinburne's often mesmerizing metres can lull readers into acquiescence so that they absorb through the poem's imagery controversial or disturbing ideas they might otherwise not tolerate.[17]

Certainly the linking of motherhood and murder, essential to the myths Swinburne is dramatising, might be hard to tolerate, but even harder for Victorian audiences to tolerate was the overt anti-theism later voiced in the chorus's denunciation of 'the supreme evil, God' (line 1151).

Because of its obvious poetic brilliance but probably even more because of its pre-Christian setting, *Atalanta in Calydon* was well received and the paganism, sensuality and anti-theism went largely uncensored. The Christian British setting of his next publication, the tragedy *Chastelard*, however, offered no such excuse, and even when reviewers admired the mastery of Swinburne's poetic expression they noted with disapproval that 'passionate burning kisses meet us on every page'[18] or objected to the representation of Mary Stuart as 'morally repulsive'.[19] The obvious talent and learning exhibited in *Atalanta in Calydon* and even in *Chastelard* had inhibited any extreme statements of moral outrage against his pagan sensuality, but the dam burst upon the publication of *Poems and Ballads*, which established the poet's reputation as the 'libidinous laureate of a pack of satyrs' and 'an unclean fiery imp from the pit'.[20]

Swinburne delighted in outraging the virtuous decorum of Victorian society, and undoubtedly many of his poems were designed to do just that. He himself described 'Dolores', for example, as 'boiling and gushing infamy',[21] and he might have added blasphemy, since the poem not only celebrates sado-masochistic sexuality but also parodies hymns to the virgin: the subtitle, '*Notre Dame des Sept Douleurs*', alludes to 'our Lady of the seven sorrows', the Virgin Mary, but in context must be understood as 'our lady of the seven pains', the dominatrix, Dolores, a 'mystical rose', but a 'mystical rose of the mire' (line 21). Dolores is a love goddess of the gutter, a purely carnal icon of sado-masochistic lust, and she is invoked accordingly:

> Ah, beautiful passionate body
>   That never has ached with a heart!
> On thy mouth though the kisses are bloody,
>   Though they sting till it shudder and smart,

More kind than the love they adore is,
They hurt not the heart or the brain,
O bitter and tender Dolores,
Our Lady of Pain. (lines 81–8)

Shocking as 'Dolores' is, many other poems in the volume were equally or more appalling to Victorian moral sensibilities. 'Faustine', for example, is a kind of hymn to the fierce loves and sadistic pleasures of the empress who revelled in the slaughter of Christians. Worse, Swinburne favourably compares the pagan pleasures of ancient Rome with his own time

of famished hours,
Maimed loves and mean,
This ghastly thin-faced time of ours. (lines 137–9).

Even worse is 'The Leper', a dramatic monologue based on a supposed French chronicle history of a sinful lady whose many knightly lovers abandoned her when she contracted leprosy, but who retained the love of a poor scribe who continued to love her even as the leprosy ate away her features, ultimately continuing to make love to the corpse. The graphic representation of the Lady's loves and of the scribe's passionate necrophilia was only apparently justified by an excerpt from the medieval French chronicle, since the excerpt was actually a hoax devised and written by Swinburne, and once again the poem's sins against decorum are exacerbated by an attack on the Christian God who 'makes time and ruins it' and who wantonly 'Changed with disease her body sweet, / The body of love wherein she abode' (lines 45, 47–8). Swinburne undoubtedly intended all of these poems to shock his contemporaries, but they all also paradigmatically embody the characteristic aesthetic substitution of the physical for the metaphysical, and they all juxtapose present sensibilities with the past to represent something like the composite experience of all the ages.

For Swinburne, ascetic Christianity constituted an unremitting attack on the body of love, Christ's rival lover. For all of its outrageous libidinousness and blasphemy, *Poems and Ballads* was a serious effort to challenge and extend the moral limits placed upon art. Underlying the volume's nihilistic attack on Christian morality is a defiant aestheticism complete with a genuine paganism. In his pioneering critical essay on William Blake, Swinburne had argued for an aestheticism that would see Christian asceticism as the antithesis of beauty, and would celebrate a belief that the sensual apprehension of beauty is superior to mere morality or delusional belief in the immortal soul. Like Pater, he saw the art of the Middle Ages as a 'pagan revival' pitting Christ against some rival lover as in the legend of Venus and Tannhäuser, which, he argued, implied a sympathetic feeling 'for the pagan side of things, revealing in the tradition the presence and touch of some poet'.[22] At about the same time he was writing his essay on Blake, he was also writing his own version of the Tannhäuser legend, 'Laus Veneris', which became the title poem of the American edition of *Poems and Ballads*. The legend of Tannhäuser involves precisely the knight's choice between Christ and his pagan rival Venus. Swinburne's version makes it clear that if the choice comes down to a question of beauty, as it always must in Swinburne's aestheticism, it must fall to Venus:

> Alas, Lord, surely thou art great and fair.
> But lo her wonderfully woven hair!
> And thou didst heal us with thy piteous kiss,
> But see now, Lord; her mouth is lovelier. (lines 17–20)

Tannhäuser's choice of Venus could be excused in Victorian eyes because the poem, like Rossetti's 'Jenny' and Morris's 'The Defence of Guenevere', is a dramatic monologue and cannot be simply understood as the poet's own expression of his views. Tannhäuser's views do, however, correspond with Swinburne's aestheticism as expressed in the study of Blake, and the same choice of the pagan gods and the senses is expressed by speaker after speaker in *Poems and Ballads*, nowhere more clearly than in the words of one of the last remaining pagans of the early Christian era: 'Thou hast conquered, O pale Galilean; the world has grown grey from thy breath; / We have drunken of things Lethean, and fed on the fullness of death' ('Hymn to Proserpine', lines 35–6). As in 'Dolores' and 'Laus Veneris', the 'rival lover' is pitted even more explicitly against the Virgin mother than against Christ, as the speaker pits Venus against her:

> Not as thine, not as thine, was our mother, a blossom of flowering seas,
> Clothed round with the world's desire as with raiment, and fair as the foam,
>
> . . .
>
> For thine came weeping, a slave among slaves, and rejected; but she
> Came flushed with the full-flushed wave, and imperial, her foot on the sea.
> And the wonderful waters knew her, the winds and the viewless ways,
> And the rose grew rosier, and bluer the sea-blue stream of the bays.
> ('Anactoria', lines 78–88)

However shocking, this paganism offers an alternative to Christianity that is not actually far from even Matthew Arnold's arguments in the contemporaneous *Culture and Anarchy* that an overzealous devotion to Biblical morality, 'Hebraism', was in need of correction by a renewed emphasis on the pagan ideal of beauty, 'Hellenism'. Further, as is generally true of Swinburne's and Rossetti's aesthetic poetry, the claim is not only made discursively but embodied in the dramatised speaker's desire, in the pulsations of the verse and the appeal to the senses of the imagery, which enriches the world with colour and endows it even with a tactile sense of weight and power, merging the natural force of the sea with the impassioned beauty of the female body.

Swinburne's aestheticism, of course, is far more extreme than Arnold's Hellenism, mostly because it is more boldly sensual and far more critical of Christianity, but also because it makes an argument that only poetry and art, not any ideal of God, transcend the limits of mortality. Swinburne's pagan aesthetic idealism is most obviously manifested in the magnificent elegy for Charles Baudelaire, 'Ave atque Vale', written shortly after the publication of *Poems and Ballads*, and in the equally magisterial dramatic monologue spoken by Sappho to her lover, 'Anactoria'. Although it is a dramatic monologue expressing sentiments entirely appropriate to Sappho and even in part appropriated from her surviving poetry, 'Anactoria' was among the poems most savagely attacked by censorious reviewers of *Poems and Ballads*. The abuse of the poem is not surprising considering its representations of the 'amorous agonies' (line 29) of sadistic lesbian love. The eroticism includes a great deal of characteristically Swinburnean biting and even eating, which may suggest less about Swinburne's understanding of lesbian practices than about his interest in a kind of parodic, eroticised Eucharist:

> Ah, that my lips were tuneless lips, but pressed
> To the bruised blossom of thy scourged white breast!
> Ah that thy mouth for Muses' milk were fed
> On the sweet blood thy sweet small wounds had bled!
> That with my tongue I felt them, and could taste
> The faint flakes from thy bosom to the waist!
> That I could drink thy veins as wine, and eat
> Thy breasts like honey! that from face to feet
> Thy body were abolished and consumed,
> And in my flesh thy very flesh entombed! (lines 105–14)

The sensual imagery, appealing less to sight and sound than to the more primal senses of taste and hunger, exaggerates, but epitomises Swinburne's (and Rossetti's and Morris's) substitution of body for soul, sensation for reflection. Further, nothing could more emphatically express Swinburne's notion of the all-consuming nature of desire than Sappho's apparent willingness to sacrifice her poetic gift for the erotic satisfaction of complete union with the beloved, but the yet more important point made in Sappho's speech is that from the power of this passion comes the more enduring power of poetic song. Once again, as in 'Dolores' and, far more compellingly, in *Atalanta in Calydon*, the sadistic violence of passion put into song is presented as the only way to harmonise human emotion with a world apparently created by a sadistic God, with 'The mystery of the cruelty of things' (line 154). As Keats had recognised, the law of nature is 'an eternal fierce destruction',[23] or as Swinburne's Sappho puts it, 'the earth, / Filled full with deadly works of life and birth, / Sore spent with hungry lusts of birth and death, / Has pain like mine' (lines 233–6). The expression of Sappho's own cruel and hungry lusts is in perfect harmony with the spirit of nature, so that even if she can't fuse her body wholly with her beloved's, she can fuse her soul wholly with nature, become a part of nature and, like Keats's nightingale, live long beyond the 'hungry generations' of mere mortality. In the best early expression of the aestheticist myth that characterised Swinburne's later poetry, Sappho insists late in the poem that her music so harmonises the human spirit with the natural that until the end of human history,

> Men shall not see bright fire nor hear the sea,
> Nor mix their hearts with music
> ...
> But in the light and laughter, in the moan
> And music, and in grasp of lip and hand
> And shudder of water that makes felt on land
> The immeasurable tremor of all the sea,
> Memories shall mix and metaphors of me.
> (lines 204–5, 210–14)

Sappho's passionate song, reincarnated in the bodies and senses of all who read it will live as long as poetry is read – longer, certainly, than the gods of her time were to be worshipped.

Declining, or unable, to see Swinburne's real intentions and achievements, the most damaging of his critics, John Morley, simply reviled 'the spurious passions of a putrescent imagination'.[24] Prompting a deluge of outraged criticism, *Poems and Ballads* initiated a culture war over the acceptable and proper role of art in society that reverberated throughout the rest of the century and extended beyond the questions of decency in art and the creed of 'art for art's sake' into clinical and legal debate over not only the representation but the practice of sexual 'perversities'. Then as now, culture wars shed more heat than light, and in the heat of this war Swinburne was accused by Robert Buchanan of revelling in filth 'for the mere sake of uncleanness'[25] and by the *London Review* of familiarising himself with the 'worst circles of Parisian life' and 'drenching himself in the worst creations of Parisian literature' to pollute English life and letters with 'lust, bitterness, and despair'.[26] Still eager to shock, Swinburne himself did little to raise the tone of the discussion in his response to the attacks as 'the virulent virtue of pressmen and prostitutes'.[27] All in all, the effect on Victorian society was, as Thomas Hardy later put it, 'as though a garland of red roses / Had fallen about the hood of some smug nun' (lines 6–7).[28] Written at a time when the 'sensation novel' was under virulent attack for its shocking and unnerving content, and was condemned particularly for 'preaching to the nerves',[29] Swinburne's contributions to the school of sensation were clearly intended as an attack on certain smug Victorian attitudes, and they were sure to invite critical hostility. Catherine Maxwell concisely describes the apparent intent of such poetry and provides perhaps the best justification yet offered for the poet's prurient excess, suggesting that he was indeed appealing to readers' 'physical as well as intellectual beings as the verse communicates simultaneously to the mind and senses, predominantly through that psychologically charged bodily element, the nerves'.[30] It is not of profound interest that in Swinburne's actual sexual life he could not be taught that 'biting's no use',[31] but Maxwell's account of the embodiment of Swinburnean desire in verse is crucial to understanding his poetry: 'with regard to literary creativity Swinburne sees the transmutative activity of form as a liberating violence, binding and disciplining language and yet releasing its energy. Form gives language its teeth so that the finished poem is itself a pleasurable violence on the sensibility of the reader.'[32] Undoubtedly Swinburne's attack on certain smug moral attitudes was salutary, but his real purpose, beyond simply creating beautiful poems, was to advance the aestheticism that he had gleaned largely from Théophile Gautier and Charles Baudelaire and had developed in his study of William Blake, particularly the idea that art cannot strive to be the 'handmaid of morality' or even to advance moral ideas, but must be concerned solely with 'mere excellence of verse or colour': 'Art for art's sake, first of all, and afterwards we may suppose all the rest shall be added to her.'[33] Further, as he made clear in his elegy to Baudelaire and in 'Anactoria', the transformation of even the most violent and messy passions into the perfect form of art may indeed constitute an attack on the reader, but it is a violence essential to break down resistance and to fuse the reader's sensibility to the poet's own. Swinburne's contemporaries rarely doubted his mastery of poetic form, but they were, for the most part, incapable of the kind of response to his violent sexual themes that Catherine Maxwell has said the poems call for. They were certainly incapable of appreciating his poetry the way he appreciated the poetry of John Ford:

> No poet is less forgetable [*sic*] than Ford, none fastens (as it were) the fangs of his genius and his will more deeply in your memory. You cannot shake hands with him and pass by . . . if he touch you once he takes you, and what he takes he keeps his hold of; his work becomes part of your thought and part of your spiritual furniture for ever.[34]

It is in just this way that Sappho's stinging and biting sensibility becomes all but immortal, a part of the minds of readers across indefinite generations.

Especially since Swinburne was too confident of his own powers to be a casualty, his opening salvo in the culture war was undoubtedly beneficial in beginning a necessary discussion, but it unfortunately set the stage for a devastating effect on Rossetti, who was less confident and less capable of withstanding the assault. Rossetti, forebodingly anxious about his reputation when he finally published his collected *Poems* in 1870, had attempted to circumvent hostile criticism by arranging for many of his closest friends and admirers to review the volume in the leading journals. Swinburne, Morris and others obligingly heaped praises on the volume, saluting Rossetti as one of the greatest poets in the history of English literature, but eventually one of Swinburne's fiercest detractors, Robert Buchanan, was able to find an outlet for a virulent attack on both Rossetti and Swinburne and indeed on the entire group of what he called 'The Fleshly School of Poetry'. Enraged by the praises heaped on Rossetti as well as by a literary feud with William Rossetti, Buchanan's personal animus was so great that he almost dismissed the charge against Swinburne by comparison to the offences of the acknowledged master of the 'fleshly school': the younger Swinburne was 'only a little mad boy letting off squibs; no great strong man, who might be really dangerous to society'. Buchanan's attack, moreover, was more personal than literary:

> Mr. Rossetti is never dramatic, never impersonal, – always attitudinizing, posturing, and describing his own exquisite emotions. He is the 'Blessed Damozel,' leaning over the 'gold bar of heaven' . . . he is 'heaven-born Helen, Sparta's queen,' whose 'each twin breast is an apple sweet'; he is Lilith the first wife of Adam; he is the rosy Virgin of the poem called 'Ave,' and the Queen in the 'Staff and Scrip'; he is 'Sister Helen' melting her waxen man; he is all these, just as surely as he is Mr Rossetti soliloquizing over Jenny in her London lodging, or the very nuptial person writing erotic sonnets to his wife . . . he is just Mr Rossetti, a fleshly person, with nothing particular to tell us or teach us.[35]

Rossetti replied to this obtuse reading by insisting that the poems were, in fact, dramatic, but the attack rankled because a great deal of highly personal material did inform the sonnets of *The House of Life*. When Buchanan amplified the assault in a pamphlet, Rossetti feared the exposure of his darkest secrets: many of his sonnets commemorated his ongoing affair with Jane Morris, the wife of his best friend, and worse, he suspected that Buchanan knew of his exhumation of his wife to recover the poems he had buried with her in a grandly romantic gesture. Already failing in health, Rossetti had a major nervous breakdown that left him incapacitated for poetry until the last years of his life, 1879–81, when he wrote two lengthy ballads and added enough sonnets to *The House of Life* to expand it from 50 to 102 sonnets, despite dropping 'Nuptial Sleep'.

Swinburne was easily able to defy the critical attacks on himself, but he was already turning his attention away from erotic poetry to the radical political concerns that had long preoccupied him and had already found expression in a number of early poems. As he became increasingly a political poet he conceded privately to William Rossetti that 'It was only Gabriel and his followers in art (l'art pour l'art) who for a time frightened me from speaking out' politically.[36] Without actually disowning his aestheticism, Swinburne did speak out his politics over a series of volumes in the next decade: *A Song of Italy* (1867), *Songs before Sunrise* (1871) and *Songs of Two Nations* (1875). These poems, inspired by the efforts to unite Italy as a republic and by the charismatic Italian leader, Mazzini, contained too much blasphemy and too much of the 'reddest of red republicanism'[37] to placate his critics, but Swinburne regarded *Songs before Sunrise*, in particular, as his greatest work, and it does contain many lyrics of great poetic as well as political power. His next true masterpiece, however, is his return to the form of Greek tragedy, with *Erechtheus* (1876), which forsook the eroticism and explicit blasphemies of *Atalanta* for the sake of a quieter political engagement. *Erechtheus* was a tour de force in the manner of *Atalanta*, only more so. *Atalanta*, like 'Anactoria', had been concerned with the 'mystery of the cruelty of things', but like the political poetry, *Erechtheus*, dramatising the founding of Athens as the ideal republic, was more optimistically concerned to represent the benefits of harmonising human institutions with the everlasting laws of the cosmos. The theme, transcending the merely human, led Swinburne, as McGann has pointed out, to attempt to suggest 'the existence of universal law' without representing particular manifestations of law. The effect is a paucity of characterisation and particularisation, an abstractness that leads Swinburne to rely more than ever on the verbal pyrotechnics and rushes of metaphor and allusion that are sometimes described as 'a diffuseness, a fuzz of words and linguistic forms which become an incantation or a monotone . . . echoes [that] are thrown entirely back on themselves. Atmospheric nourishment, uprooted language, elaborate unmeaning.'[38] The objection must be taken seriously because it continues to represent widespread responses not only to *Erechtheus*, but to all of Swinburne's still under-appreciated late poetry. The only way to refute the objection is by extended close reading of the poetry, and such readings, especially those of McGann and Margot Louis, have done much to substantiate McGann's argument that the effect of Swinburne's difficult but mesmerising late poetry can be much like the effect of the celebrated Marabar Caves in Forster's *A Passage to India*: 'A sound of complex reverberations which have been somehow completely harmonized. In both we encounter not the reality of correspondence and harmony, the maya of its truth, but its law, the transcendent content we sometimes call its form.'[39] Probably few readers will be willing to grant quite so much to Swinburne's aestheticism, or to believe he achieves the perfection of form that reveals the inner workings of the universe, but the aspiration and, to an extent, the achievement, are to be found in such memorable late works as 'By the North Sea' (1881), 'The Lake of Gaube' (1904) and 'On the Cliffs' (1879), which reprises his myth of the nightingale's song as the transmuted song of Sappho and the symbol of poetry through the ages. Perhaps the greatest work of his later period, however; is the magisterial epic-length *Tristram of Lyonesse* (1882), a poetic tour de force that also brought Swinburne full circle back to the early Arthurian interests that he shared with Morris, Rossetti and Burne-Jones and to the defence of the rival lover, sexual passion, over Christian morality. *Tristram of Lyonesse*, moreover, combined Swinburne's later style, his elaborate but to some extent disembodied and abstract harmonies, with the sensual imagery of nature and especially of the impassioned and beautiful body that was the hallmark of his aesthetic poetry, as well as that of Morris and Rossetti.

Notes

1. Arthur Henry Hallam, 'On Some Characteristics of Modern Poetry and on the Lyrical Poems of Alfred Tennyson', in *The Writings of Arthur Hallam*, ed. T. H. Vail Motter (London: Oxford University Press, 1943), pp. 182–98 (p. 184).
2. Walter Pater, 'Poems by William Morris', *Westminster Review* (October 1868), p. 301.
3. *Ibid.*, p. 307.
4. Clyde K. Hyde (ed.), *Swinburne: The Critical Heritage* (New York: Barnes and Noble, 1970), p. 133.

5. *The Correspondence of Dante Gabriel Rossetti*, ed. William E. Fredeman, 9 vols. (Cambridge: D. S. Brewer, 2002–8), vol. IV, pp. 339, 394.
6. Lines 55–60, in William Morris, *The Defence of Guenevere, and Other Poems*, ed. Margaret Lourie (New York: Garland Publishers, 1981).
7. Dante Gabriel Rossetti, *The Collected Poetry and Prose* (New Haven: Yale University Press, 2003). All quotations from Rossetti's poetry are from this edition.
8. Dante Gabriel Rossetti, 'The Stealthy School of Criticism', in *Collected Poetry and Prose*, ed. Jerome McGann (New Haven: Yale University Press, 2003), pp. 337–8.
9. Jerome McGann, 'Rossetti's Significant Details', *Victorian Poetry*, 7 (1969), p. 44.
10. Rossetti, *Correspondence*, vol. II, p. 731.
11. Jerome J. McGann, 'Rossetti's Significant Details', *Victorian Poetry*, 7 (1969), p. 46.
12. *Ibid.*, pp. 47–8.
13. Quoted from the manuscript version in the Fitzwilliam Museum, Cambridge.
14. F. W. H. Myers, 'Rossetti and the Religion of Beauty', in *Essays: Modern* (London: Macmillan, 1885).
15. John Keats, *Letters*, ed. Hyder Edward Rollins, 2 vols. (Cambridge, MA: Harvard University Press, 1958), vol. I, p. 184.
16. Algernon Charles Swinburne, *Major Poems and Selected Prose*, ed. Jerome McGann and Charles L. Sligh (New Haven: Yale University Press, 2004). Unless otherwise noted, all quotations from Swinburne are from this edition.
17. Catherine Maxwell, *Swinburne* (Tavistock, Devon: Northcote Publishers, 2006), p. 20.
18. Hyder (ed.), *Swinburne: The Critical Heritage*, p. xvii.
19. *Ibid.*, p. 17.
20. *Ibid.*, p. 29.
21. Algernon Swinburne, *Letters*, ed. Cecil Y. Lang, 6 vols. (New Haven: Yale University Press, 1959–62), vol. I, p. 122.
22. Algernon Swinburne, *William Blake: A Critical Essay*, ed. Hugh J. Luke (Lincoln: University of Nebraska Press, 1970), p. 89n.
23. Keats, *Letters*, vol. I, p. 97
24. Hyder, *Swinburne: The Critical Heritage*, pp. 24–5.
25. *Ibid.*, p. 31.
26. *Ibid.*, p. 35.
27. *Ibid.*, p. 51.
28. 'A Singer Asleep', *The Complete Poems of Thomas Hardy*, ed. James Gibson (London: Macmillan, 1976), p. 265.
29. H. L. Mansel, 'Sensation Novels', *Quarterly Review* (April 1863), p. 482.
30. Maxwell, *Swinburne*, p. 21.
31. Philip Henderson, *Swinburne: Portrait of a Poet* (New York: Macmillan, 1974), p. 131.
32. Maxwell, *Swinburne*, p. 21.
33. Swinburne, *William Blake*, pp. 91–2.

34. Quoted by Maxwell, *Swinburne*, p. 24
35. Robert Buchanan, 'The Fleshly School of Poetry: Mr D. G. Rossetti', *Contemporary Review*, 18 (1871), pp. 334–50, reprinted in David G. Riede (ed.), *Critical Essays on Dante Gabriel Rossetti* (New York: G. K. Hall, 1992), p. 29.
36. Swinburne, *Letters*, vol. 1, p. 195.
37. Hyder (ed.), *Swinburne: The Critical Heritage*, p. 129.
38. Jerome J. McGann, *Swinburne: An Experiment in Criticism* (Chicago: University of Chicago Press, 1972), p. 132.
39. Maxwell, *Swinburne*, p. 133.

Chapter 36
Christina Rossetti and Hopkins

CATHERINE PHILLIPS

Writing one of his characteristically bubbling letters to William Mowbray Baillie in July 1864, Gerard Manley Hopkins told him that, 'I have now a more rational hope than before of doing something – in poetry and painting. About the first I have said all there is to say in a letter; about the latter I have no more room to speak, but when next I see you I have great things to tell. I have been introduced to Miss and Miss Christina Rossetti. I met them and Holman Hunt and George Macdonald and Peter Cun[n]ingham and Jenny Lind at the Gurneys'.'[1] Clearly Christina was something of a celebrity and the undergraduate Hopkins was at the height of his ambitions of belonging to the artistic avant-garde as he knew of it in London. He had, he told Baillie, 'nearly finished an answer to Miss Rossetti's *Convent Threshold*, to be called *A voice from the world*, or something like that, with which I am at present in the fatal condition of satisfaction'.[2] Rossetti's 'Convent Threshold' is not an account of demure spiritual yearnings but depicts the turmoil of a woman caught between forbidden love and a petrifying fear of damnation, a fear of the sort engendered at Christ Church, Albany Street where Christina worshipped; critics have pointed to Pope's 'Eloisa to Abelard' as a literary precedent.[3] Hopkins's 'answer' reveals both the strengths and weaknesses of his immature verse. The initial paragraph contains vibrant natural description, including the extended metaphor of cuckoos calling, with the precise observation that the call varies between five notes and seven and that it can be heard earlier in some years than in others, but Hopkins had not the range of human experience to convey with conviction the pain of losing a lover.[4]

More convincing is the passage following the lovers' attempts to save each other at the Last Judgment. Ironically, Hopkins's narrator finds that, unlike his lover, whose womanly love he had wrongly dismissed as 'not strong' (line 48) because female, he cannot give up his chance of salvation for her. Conveniently, in the poem such price is not exacted; instead the young man concludes that he had been 'ignorantly bold' (line 126) even to dream that he had been asked to make such a sacrifice and in thinking through the episode he records:

> My hopes and my unworthiness,
> At once perceivèd, with excess
> Of burden came and bow'd my head,
> Yea, crush'd my heart, and made me dumb . . .
> . . .
> O hideous vice to haggle yet
> For more with Him who gives thee all,
> Freely forgives the monstrous debt!
> Having the infinitely great
> Therewith to hanker for the small!
> ('A voice from the world', lines 130–3, 162–6)

It is worth asking in what way Hopkins's poem constitutes an answer to Christina Rossetti's. Hopkins's protagonist rejects earthly love, for which the speaker of 'The Convent Threshold' still yearns, as 'ways sown with salt' (line 168) and he seeks instead for the means by which to 'turn my passion-pastured thought / To gentle manna and simple bread' (lines 187–8). The difficulty of conveying religious humility without appearing to pose is evident, and the satisfaction he mentioned to Baillie may in part be that of 'correcting' what he saw as a spiritually erroneous attitude. He remained interested in the poem for some years, composing elegiacs in Latin ('Fraterna nobis') in 1867(?) based on the opening and closing sections. In 1872 he compared Christina's work with that of her brother: 'From the little I have seen and gathered of it [Dante Gabriel Rossetti's *Poems*, 1870] I daresay he has more range, force, and interest, and then there is the difference between a man and a woman, but for pathos and pure beauty of art I do not think he is her equal: in fact the simple beauty of her work cannot be matched.'[5] Betty Flowers rightly praises 'the perfect pitch and clarity of her line, the subtle effects of rhyme and rhythm [that] owe much to the nakedness of feeling and simplicity of form to be found in the hymns she knew so well'.[6] In her recent biography of Christina Rossetti, Jan Marsh gathers evidence to suggest that although Christina undoubtedly drew on her experience in her writing, she also consciously belonged to the tradition of women's poetry that concentrated on the themes of 'nature, domestic affection, deathbeds and devotional religion'.[7] Christina's mature verse with its apparent simplicity has a distilled essence that is haunting, sometimes excoriating. Whether or not she experienced its full bitterness, she gives voice to loneliness, lost hope and frustrated love as effectively as Tennyson spoke of troubled faith and grief. A narrowing but intensifying of her range of tone and subject was further increased by criticisms made by her brother, Dante Gabriel Rossetti, to whom she showed most of what she published during his lifetime. He counselled her to cut her more outspoken and 'feminist' verse on such subjects as illegitimate children and women abandoned by faithless lovers, some of which, such as 'Cousin Kate', she purged from her later collections.[8]

Christina was born in London in 1830 and remained contentedly urban. Her father was Italian, exiled from the kingdom of Naples. He taught Italian at the University of London until Christina was in her teens, when severe eye problems forced him to retire, leaving him reluctantly dependent on the other members of the family. The house was a meeting place for Italian political exiles and all the children had to come to terms with their father's eccentric interpretations of Dante. Christina's mother, Frances, was English and Christina was devoted to her, looking after her and two of her aunts till their deaths, by which time she was herself terminally ill with cancer. Frances encouraged the intellectual achievement of her four children, who grew up assisting each other's artistic efforts; Christina modelled for Dante Gabriel's paintings and the siblings exchanged *bouts rimés* over many years; Christina frequently knocking them off in less than ten minutes.[9]

Although Christina's grandfather privately printed a collection of her verse when she was only sixteen, and she had two poems printed by the prestigious *Athenaeum* when she was just seventeen,[10] her first volume to attract public attention was *Goblin Market* (1862). She had by then published individual poems in *Macmillan's* and various other journals and contributed pseudonymously to *The Germ*. 'Goblin Market' seems, in a number of respects, to link to the work of the Pre-Raphaelites, particularly that of Dante Gabriel Rossetti. By the 1860s he was producing his morally ambiguous 'Venetian' pictures with their voluptuous women framed by lush flora.[11] 'Goblin Market' shares this sexually charged lushness, but Christina brings to it an agile imagination that produces nightmarish characters with the hands of men and the faces of cats and vermin. Confronted by images of bodily attack, exotic fruit with fatal overpowering effects and cautions about pre-marital sex, it is little wonder that so many modern interpretations are gender-political: variations on the theme of young women entering a male economic sphere with only their bodies for barter.[12] But, as with many of Christina's most well-known poems, moving from a sense of general meaning of temptation and exploitation to precise, allegorical decoding soon leads to inconsistency and a sexual explicitness that seems biographically unconvincing. Part of the fascination with 'Goblin Market' is the richness of the paradigms and sources to which it suggests allusion. Laura reacts to the goblins and their fruit like a modern-day Eve, and her eating of it recalls Proserpine. However, her decline becomes an examination of the psychology of sin; the mechanism of the lifting of the curse brings 'The Rime of the Ancient Mariner' to mind, and Laura's respite is purchased by Lizzie's 'martyrdom'. The story is told with romping free verse, opening with split pairs of tetrameter lines but considerable variety in pacing. The second line's opening spondee might suggest Hopkins's sprung rhythm: 'Maids heard the goblins cry'. The diction similarly ranges from the isocolonic, childlike cautions, 'We must not look at goblin men, / We must not buy their fruits' (lines 42–3) to absorbing the polysyllabic 'obstreperously' and the colloquial 'mad to tug her standard down' (line 421) when describing Lizzie's withstanding the goblins' assault. The sensuous delights of the fruit are mouthed by the reader through the articulation required by 'Plump unpecked cherries, / Melons and raspberries, / Bloom-down-cheeked peaches' (lines 7–9). Resolving the poem into a set of familial values (asserting that 'there is no friend like a sister' (line 562) while the two mothers caution their children to value their family ties) was both highly acceptable to contemporary audiences and in keeping with Christina's lifelong practice.

The volume included religious poems that such critics as Nilda Jiménez, Jerome McGann and Betty Flowers point out evince complexity in verses that may appear to secular readers to be only unexceptionably pious. Flowers cites 'I Will Lift up Mine Eyes unto the Hills', in which verses from Psalms, Revelation, Ecclesiastes, Proverbs, Isaiah and 1 John are interwoven, each bringing contexts that colour the quotations, combining them into a 'richly shaded emotional journey'.[13] McGann gestures towards what he sees as Christina's attempts to convey emotion that is beyond human experience and expression. He says of 'A better resurrection' and poems like it that 'until we understand how fiercely the poem is trying to annihilate all ordinary and personal attachments' we will not understand its 'disturbing brilliance':[14]

> I have no wit, no words, no tears;
> My heart within me like a stone
> Is numbed too much for hopes or fears;
> Look right, look left, I dwell alone;
> I lift mine eyes, but dimmed with grief
> No everlasting hills I see;
> My life is in the falling leaf:
> O Jesus, quicken me. (lines 1–8)

The diction has an unadorned simplicity that conveys absolute sincerity, the large number of monosyllables worthy of stress weighing down the rhythm in sombre contrast to the final line's iambic plea, whose syntax breaks the metrical foot ('us, quick') with sudden trochaic effect: 'O Jesus, qúicken me'. These 'everlasting hills' are indescribable through worldly existence and their Biblical connotation is used to indicate yearning for immortal life beyond death and human comprehension. Christina was to go on to write *Annus Domini: A Prayer for Each Day of the Year, Founded on a Text of Holy Scripture* (1874) and, ultimately, five volumes of religious verse and commentary for publication by the Society for Promoting Christian Knowledge.[15]

Many of Christina's poems in *Goblin Market and Other Poems* concern love: tales of broken relationships, generally through duplicitous behaviour ('Cousin Kate', 'After Death', 'The Hour and the Ghost', 'An Apple-Gathering', 'Maude Clare', 'Noble Sisters'), indirect mourning of lost love, such as 'Shut Out' and 'May', in which the indirection includes the titles, and 'A Pause for Thought' in which what is longed for is both unnamed and easy to guess. By way of contrast, 'No, thank you, John' is a rather brutal rejection of courtship[16] and 'A Triad' an unsentimental analysis of married love. 'Song: . . .' with its three shifts in perspective similarly treats the happiness of couples within a religious context that limits its value; such awareness of tension between love for the human and divine seems to have been fundamental to Christina's mature sensibility and may also partly explain the number of poems that place the speaker either beyond death, looking back to a lover, or dying, as in 'Wife to Husband'. Such perspective invites nightmare. 'My Dream', with its voracious crocodile who prudently begs for forgiveness when a ghostly ship arrives to avenge the crocodile relatives it has devoured, is a child's allegorical poem of sin and retribution, but 'The Convent Threshold' and 'From House to Home' suggest eerie symbolism on 'primeval levels of consciousness';[17] in the latter the vision of a woman suspended by chains of light from above is weird and powerful. The figure, with eyes 'like some fire-enshrining gem' (line 121), 'stately' yet 'tender . . . stood on inner ground that budded flowers' (lines 122, 126). But 'every flower was lifted on a thorn, / And every thorn shot upright from its sands / To gall her feet; hoarse laughter pealed in scorn / With cruel clapping hands' (lines 129–32). Her taste for such resonant visions was developed by gothic novels of the sort written by Charles Maturin – she liked *Melmoth the Wanderer* best[18] – that mediate imagery from Revelation.

'The Prince's Progress', the title poem to her second volume (1866), is, like 'Goblin Market', similarly difficult to interpret more than very loosely. The story is of a fairytale prince who is deflected so often and for so long in his journey to claim his affianced princess that when he eventually arrives, it is to be greeted by her funeral cortège. Readers have seen the influence of Bunyan's *Pilgrim's Progress* and experimented with suggesting that, inverting the roles, the prince represents the human soul, cautioned that it may lose its place in heaven (the bride) if it dallies with the lures of the world too long.[19] But questions arise as to whether the princess can convincingly be seen to fit such a scheme. Lines 511–40 describing her enduring her lonely wait were written before the first part of the poem and retain differences in tone and use of symbolism. Joan Rees suggests that the poem gives us 'a picture of two kinds of spiritual testing, side by side: one test consists of a call to effort and the test is failed; one is a call to suppress normal human yearning and to live and die in hard-won patience'.[20] Antony Harrison further points out that Rossetti reworks echoes from such poets as Keats ('La Belle Dame Sans Merci') for the Prince's delay with the milkmaid, from Tennyson ('Tristram' from the *Idylls*) and Browning's 'Childe Roland' for the nightmarish landscape the Prince traverses.[21] These, he claims persuasively, suggest

> a highly self-conscious poet appropriating the work of her precursors in revisionist ways that create a tension in the reader between on the one hand sympathetic involvement with the characters and events of her poem and on the other an intellectual detachment compelled by an awareness of specific literary precedents and traditions that have helped to generate the poem.[22]

Christina's Italian was fluent and she wrote poems in Italian, including ones perhaps written about her deep friendship with Charles Cayley, a shy scholar and former pupil of her father's, thought to be the principal love of her life. Like her siblings, Dante Gabriel and Maria, she made translations of Dante, and later wrote a review article on contemporary translations of his works.[23] Her knowledge of Italian literature may also have affected the tone of some of her English poems, such as 'The Convent Threshold', which describe violent passions belonging more to the poems she and Dante Gabriel translated than to English precedents. Cayley is also thought to be the lover who inspired Christina's 'Mona Innominata', a sequence of sonnets by a 'lady troubadour' published in her collection *A Pageant and Other Poems* (1881). Each sonnet has two epigraphs, one by Dante and one by Petrarch. Christina's headnote to the sequence explains that Beatrice and Laura lack tenderness because we do not see their feelings. She suggests that Elizabeth Barrett Browning might have constructed a series with a speaker comparable to Beatrice and Laura but more attractively tender had she been unhappy, rather than in her contentment producing her *Sonnets from the Portuguese*. The impression created by

'Mona Innominata' is described by Antony Harrison as a Pre-Raphaelite 'aesthetic withdrawal', an 'ethereal final effect' created by 'the dialectic of desire and renunciation'.[24] But this would imply a certain detachment from experience that does not seem to me to have been attained; the power of the poems lies in the strength of the feelings they convey, whatever their origins. Rossetti insisted that none of the poems be printed singly, a contextualising that emphasises the poetic persona. Jan Marsh suggests that into this sequence, intended for publication, Christina articulated 'love in all its aspects – romantic, wistful, steadfast, self-denying, painful, heroic, serene', informed in some places by her love 'but not defined or limited by that and certainly not meant to describe or disclose its details'.[25]

Like many women of the middle class, Christina's involvement with her church led her to carry out charitable work. However, Christina was somewhat unusual in that her work was preaching to prostitutes and abandoned mothers and children at St Mary Magdalen Home for Fallen Women and later at Highgate Penitentiary. That she reacted sympathetically to the plight of single mothers and abandoned lovers is suggested by such poems as 'Light Love', 'Cousin Kate' and 'An Apple Gathering'.

In the early 1860s Christina was a 'corresponding member' of the Portfolio, a group of women writers and artists including Jean Ingelow, Adelaide Proctor and Barbara Bodichon, who regularly set a theme on which all the members were to produce work either literary or artistic. Christina protested, as she often did, that she could not produce poems to order, and she rifled her considerable store of old or unpublished poems of the 1850s to find something that might fit rather than writing something new. 'Reflections' (originally titled 'Day Dreams'), 'A Study' (originally 'A Soul'), 'My Old Friends' (originally 'A Burthen'), 'Rivals' (originally 'A Shadow of Dorothea'), 'A Coast' (originally 'Nightmare') were all such contributions. Certain themes may have propelled her into writing from unusual perspectives: 'A Bird's Eye View', for example, which Marsh suggests might have been a subject set by the Portfolio, tells the story of a bride forgotten except by the birds.[26]

Unlike Hopkins, Christina had a gift for story-telling and she made use of the ballad form in poems such as 'Jessie Cameron' and 'Songs in a Cornfield', both tales of marriage. Although she was close to her brothers and had several long friendships with men, in her verse, men are not usually seen except as lost lovers, their inconstancy highlighted by comparison with Christ's enduring care. She also wrote poems in which a reader senses that rather than choosing a spiritual life of chastity, the higher love has been invoked in order to repress perversely a human longing for a loving companion. 'Repining' is of this sort, where the human desires seem wrongfully crushed. In others a desire for death seems stronger than that for eternal life, as in 'Life and Death', for example.

Although romantic and religious subjects dominate Christina Rossetti's work, she also wrote a volume of verse for children and included in her other volumes a few poems on contemporary issues, such as 'In the Round Tower at Jhansi, 8 June 1857', based on a mistaken newspaper account of the final moments of Captain Skene and his wife,[27] and 'A Royal Princess', which she donated to a fund-raising anthology for Lancashire textile workers affected by the trade embargo against Southern 'slave' cotton.[28] While her most constant social participation in contemporary political movements was the campaign to make vivisection illegal, her verse reveals her disdain for the burgeoning materialism of the period and her scrupulous perception of hypocrisy that also gives an incisive wit to some of her letters. Her contemporary stature as a poet is suggested by the fact that when Tennyson died in 1892, Christina was mentioned as a potential candidate to succeed him as Poet Laureate. The rise of Modernism had the inverse effect on Christina's posthumous reputation from that of Hopkins, and it has only been in recent decades that estimation of her achievement has begun to regain the level that made her the celebrity whom Hopkins met in 1864.

Gerard Manley Hopkins was born on 28 July 1844, the eldest of eight children. His father, Manley, was a marine insurance adjuster who had been unable to go to university because of the disarray in which his own father had left his financial affairs. However, Manley not only became the director of his own insurance firm; he also wrote poetry, articles on a variety of topics from Hawaii to fossils, published two well-regarded handbooks for shipmasters in marine disaster, composed songs and drew in pen and ink and painted in watercolours. He was thoughtful, devout, sensitive to the beauty and fragility of nature and conventionally upstanding. Many of his attitudes can be seen expressed more strikingly in his son's work. Gerard grew up on the outskirts of London with the attitude to the country of those whose livelihood is not furnished by it, loving its beauty, imbuing all with a Romantic sense of being. Of his extant works it is his drawings that are the earliest examples we have of his vision. In 1862–3, when he would seem to have been following Ruskin's advice as set out in his *Elements of Drawing*, he made delicate studies of hedgerow plants, trees blowing in the wind and flowing water. These are subjects that are found vividly described throughout his poetry. It was his aesthetic sensibility, not his poetry, that was mentioned in the newspaper notices of his death in 1889.[29]

The two clearest turning-points in Hopkins's work occur in 1866, when he converted to the Roman Catholic Church, and in 1875–6, when he wrote 'The Wreck of the Deutschland'. His early poetry was influenced by Herbert, who was becoming popular in the nineteenth century, by Tennyson and by Keats. His gift for precise observation and unusual phrasing is sometimes evident but the descriptions lack purpose. He experimented with using them as metaphors in plays modelled on Elizabethan dramas of crossed lovers but his lack of human experience and lifelong inability to complete extensive projects – 'The Wreck of the Deutschland', his first major poem, was to remain his longest completed one – make the works primarily interesting because they are the youthful experiments of the later accomplished artist, and express many of the subjects to which he was later to return: the nature of perception, natural beauty, a personal sense of lack of accomplishment, religious observance, shipwreck. His early work also includes conventional poems of frustrated love, 'Troubadour' sonnets of admiration to Oxford, eighteenth-century pastorals and the religious poems that have received most attention: 'Heaven-Haven' and 'Easter Communion'.

When Hopkins was an undergraduate at Oxford he experienced the university at a time of intellectual turmoil. On the one hand there were the agnostic Fellows, such as Jowett and W. H. Green, who were aware of new-historical analyses that cast straightforward belief in the Bible in doubt and the rapid development and organisation of science at the university under such figures as Henry Acland, evident in the building of the Oxford Museum, designed to bring together the nascent science departments. On the other hand, a second phase of the Oxford Movement was pushing various students beyond the High-Church preaching and practice of W. H. Liddon and Edward Pusey into following J. H. Newman in his conversion to Catholicism. The education of the day equipped Hopkins with a knowledge of Greek and Latin literature, rather precise religious doctrine, a general ability to engage in ethical philosophical debate and an interest in etymology. To these he added extensive reading of journals, following up throughout his life contemporary literature, religious debate and ideas about architecture. He read Walt Whitman, George Eliot, Thomas Hardy's novels, Mrs Gaskell, and classed contemporary poets such as his former schoolmaster Richard Watson Dixon and Dante Gabriel Rossetti into 'schools' that he traced loosely from the Renaissance and Romantic traditions.

In July 1866 he decided to enter the Roman Catholic communion and was received by Newman on 21 October. When Hopkins converted to the Catholic Church, he removed himself from the Anglican artistic circles of his childhood, placing himself instead within the social subset of middle-class converts, landed Catholic families and the swelling numbers of impoverished Catholic immigrants. Graduating from Oxford with a First, he was to spend the rest of his life in extended training for the priesthood and in teaching at secondary and tertiary level combined with parish work. After a spell of teaching at Newman's Oratory school in Birmingham from September 1867 to April 1868, he resolved to enter a religious order, burning copies of his poems as a symbolic turning away from his earlier artistic ambitions; he had sent Robert Bridges the latest versions of any he already had. His initial training from 1868 to 1870 was in London, at Manresa House, Roehampton, a stately home modified to accommodate novices, lay brothers and priests. From there he went to St Mary's Hall for three years of philosophy. St Mary's Hall was built in the grounds of Stonyhurst, a long-established Catholic school in Lancashire that was at the time the headquarters of the Jesuit order in Britain. It also provided tuition for undergraduates, generally Catholics, taking extension degrees from the University of London. Hopkins was to spend three periods here before being moved to Ireland. From St Mary's Hall one looked across to bare rounded hills on the far side of the Ribble valley; the bleak simplicity of the landscape drew attention to the variety of the skyscapes. Although he wrote no poetry at St Mary's Hall, Hopkins was refining his descriptive skills in his diary entries, and in 1872 the discovery of the thought of Duns Scotus gave religious authority to his Romantic sense of the individual identity of all things. These were important preparatory stages for his mature poems.

From Lancashire, he moved back to Roehampton to teach rhetoric for a year. His lecture notes on verse show the long gestation of his style. They include his statement that 'poetry is speech framed for contemplation of the mind by the way of hearing or speech framed to be heard for its own sake and interest even over and above its interest of meaning. Some matter and meaning is essential to it but only as an element necessary to support and employ the shape which is contemplated for its own sake.'[30] The writing of 'The Wreck of the Deutschland' was over twelve months away, composed among the Welsh hills, where for three years he studied theology at St Beuno's College near St Asaphs. 'The Wreck', a Pindaric ode 'To the happy memory of five Franciscan nuns, exiles by the Falck Laws, drowned between midnight and morning of December 7' (1875), broke with his previous verse in a number of ways. The unit is here not the line but the stanza, whose flowing stream of sound engages and projects the excitement within the descriptions. He used for it what he called sprung rhythm, which required one stress a foot but allowed a variable number of unstressed syllables, from none to three. Examples of such verse he cited in Shakespeare, nursery rhymes and music, but he claimed to be the first poet to make the rhythm the ruling metre. The stanzas of 'The Wreck' are set out to show the different lengths of the lines within the stanzaic unit: 2, 3, 4, 3, 5, 5, 4, 6 with an extra stress in the first lines of the stanzas of Part the Second. The poem's first part is discursive, informed by a distillation of the theological and philosophical training Hopkins had been receiving, but the ideas are grasped in such a way that they become visceral experience:

> Thou hast bound bones and veins in me, fastened me flesh,
> And after it álmost únmade, what with dread,
> Thy doing: and dost thou touch me afresh?
> Over again I feel thy finger and find thée . . . (stanza 1, lines 5–8)

> We lash with the best or worst
> Word last! How a lush-kept plush-capped sloe
> Will, mouthed to flesh-burst,
> Gush! – flush the man, the being with it, sour or sweet
> Brim, in a flash, full! (stanza 8, lines 2–6)

The poem sets out the relation Hopkins knows and feels between the world and a God who brings his people to him, those susceptible to influence with overwhelming sweetness, the recalcitrant through terror. He is the creator and mover of all under the heavens, hidden yet on occasion perceptible through nature, his Being to be stressed, instressed: perceived by a ready heart and acknowledged (stanza 5). The poem develops more complex ideas of the history of Christ's continuing influence within the world since his crucifixion in the continuing strain of redemptive grace (stanza 7). The second and more accessible part (stanzas 11–34) introduces elements of Christian elegy and Miltonic epic, explaining the possible salvation of souls from the *Deutschland*, which was wrecked on a sandbank near the mouth of the Thames. It was carrying, among others, five nuns expelled from their German convent to new lives of hospital service in America. The question of how Christ's influence is exerted within the modern world is in this instance shown to come from public witness, something which has a strong tradition in America and of which English Roman Catholicism might be a bit wary. The tall nun becomes a modern-day Mary, bringing knowledge of Christ into the world through her witness – as Mary gave him physical presence – reminding the passengers of their Christian belief in their crucial last moments. When read well aloud, as Hopkins wished all his verse to be, the second part is highly dramatic, the flexibility of the rhythm and the compressed description bringing the scene alive:

> They fought with God's cold –
> And they could not, and fell to the deck
> (Crushed them) or water (and drowned them) or rolled
> With the searomp over the wreck.
> Night roared, with the heartbreak hearing a heartbroke rabble,
> The woman's wailing, the crying of child without check – (stanza 17)

Both parts end with invocations that together ask God to work on the hearts and minds of the English people to bring them back gently to the Catholic communion. The poem was much longer and far more complex than the few published by the public Jesuit journal, the *Month*, and it was perhaps predictably rejected. Hopkins was not to write many more such openly public poems, and turned to the sonnet form, which he developed and used almost exclusively for the rest of his life. Sonnets were, he told Canon Dixon, one of the most perfect of poetic forms;[31] it may also have suited his short but intense spurts of inspiration, his infrequent spare time and psychological need to exercise his brilliant idiosyncrasy within boundaries set by authority; for example, as late as 1887 he pestered Robert Bridges for information about Milton's use of codas for his poem 'Tom's Garland', preferring to follow precedent rather than simply fulfilling his poem's needs.[32]

Starting with 'The Wreck of the Deutschland', Hopkins embarked on numerous experiments in rhythm and rhyme, influenced by Greek compound words and patterns of Welsh *cynghangedd* (patterns of alliteration and assonance he deduced in Welsh poems he learned to read). The year 1877 was particularly fruitful, producing such favourites as 'Spring', 'God's Grandeur', 'Pied Beauty', 'The Starlight Night', 'The Windhover', 'Hurrahing in Harvest' and 'The Lantern out of doors'. In these an octave of freshly observed natural description is often followed by a sestet that uncovers its religious dimension. Not all critics find the latter amenable but the Christocentric vision gives significance to the natural elements, binding them into a large, metaphysical scheme that takes them beyond the fragmentary experiments of his apprentice verse. The pattern has some similarity to the Ignatian Spiritual Exercises that bid the exercitant to imagine a scene of importance in Christ's life, or a concept such as Hell, by imagining its effect on each of the senses, then thinking through its religious significance. The sonnet that has attracted most attention, 'The Windhover', is a bravura exercise in which every line of the octave ends in 'ing', the 'a' and 'b' rhymes differentiated by the double rhyming 'b's ('iding'). Yet the lines are so enjambed that the reader or listener is generally unaware of its tight rhyme scheme. Within the smaller compass of the sonnet Hopkins sets out to establish the 'inscape', visible essence, of the kestrel, identifiable not by his colouring alone but by his unique ability to hold his position through flying into the wind, matching the wind's speed with the variable beating of his wings. Such a phrase as 'his riding / Of the rolling level underneath him steady air' (lines 2–3) provokes the reader into vocalising the bird's suspension within the air. Lines 9–10 may be interpreted as the coming together within the observer's mind of the characteristics of shape and behaviour that identify the bird: 'Brute beauty and valour and act, oh, air, pride, plume, here / Buckle'. The early versions of the poem (and many others) were lifted into more striking individuality later when Hopkins revised the transcriptions Bridges had made for him in 1883–4. For example, so flexible is the rhythm of the poem that Hopkins was able to add syllables that mimicked the bird's movement more closely, such as adding the second 'off' to the phrase, 'then off / off, forth on swing, / As a skate's heel sweeps smooth on a bow-bend' (lines 5–6) that imitates (in 'off, off') that second push most people require to begin moving across ice and the movement of the bird as it manoeuvres to change direction. He also modified the early version's opening lines from 'I caught this morning morning's minion, king / Of daylight's dauphin' to 'king-dom of daylight's dauphin' (lines 1–2), which clarified the bird's royal position.

Among Hopkins's technical innovations of this period was his use of 'outrides', loops strategically placed below a few syllables that allowed him to swell the length of lines while notionally still adhering to their metre. He explained to Dixon that outrides were a mechanical means of increasing the absolute size and weightiness of English sonnets so that they more nearly matched the perfection of Italian Petrarchan sonnets spoken with the caressing of vowel sounds he identified as natural to Italian speech.[33] They were not to count in the calculating of the metre although they were spoken. 'God's Grandeur', written like 'The Starlight Night' when he was supposed to be revising for an examination, shows another of his innovations of the period: counterpoint. Taking the term from music, he used it to suggest that after establishing one rhythm, generally iambic, a poet can introduce a second one by placing two inverted feet sequentially, especially if the feet chosen are third and fourth in the line so that a reader hears the trochaic rhythm without losing the dominant iambic one. The effect on the meaning of the opening assertion in 'God's Grandeur' is subtle: 'The wórld / is chárged / wíth the / grándeur / of Gód'. The inversion placing a stress on 'wíth' and 'gránd', signalled to the reader by figures of eight placed sideways above the vowels, emphasises not where the grandeur is, nor that it is charged but what is to be found. It also allows greater stress to be placed on 'grándeur' by preparing the reader for its full weight. Although counterpoint would seem incompatible with sprung rhythm, Hopkins did later write poems that combined them. As with musical analysis, it is sometimes clear that he wrote relying on his naturally good ear, trying to capture in verse identifying movement of things or people he was describing, and then concocted a formal analysis. For example, he described the lurch of the Eurydice as it sank in the line: 'Then a lurch forward, frigate and men' ('The Loss of the Eurydice', line 41), analysing it to Robert Bridges as: 'imitative as usual – an anapaest, followed by a trochee, a dactyl, and a syllable, so that the rhythm is anacrustic, or, as I should call it, "encountering" '.[34] The interest in using poetry to capture things is at its most extreme in 'Harry Ploughman', which he told Bridges was the 'direct picture of a ploughman, without afterthought'.[35] The octave describes the ploughman as he stands, almost a nude statue, but the sestet is more experimental. If one follows the plethora of marks Hopkins had devised by 1887, the verse teeters between having meaning and a flow of sound that conveys the movement of the ploughman as he follows his plough through tough soil, counterbalancing its movement, and lurching forward as it cuts through softer ground. The effect is amongst the most daring of the century.

The interest in etymology that Hopkins developed in his early years at Oxford has its most striking poetic result in the opening lines of his late poem, 'Spelt from Sibyl's Leaves' (1884–6), whose eight-foot lines he described as 'the longest sonnet ever made' and probably, given that it had taken him two years, 'the longest making'.[36] Imagining that he is witnessing the last evening when nature is dissolved before the Day of Judgment, the speaker's words evolve through cognate words that Hopkins believed were etymologically linked in chains of adjectives embellishing the statement that 'evening strains to be night':

> Earnest, earthless, equal, attuneable, | vaulty, voluminous . . . stupendous
> Evening strains to be tíme's vást, | womb-of-all, home-of-all, hearse-of-all night.
> ('Spelt from Sibyl's Leaves', lines 1–2)

He is unlikely to have expected that his own end would occur within less than three years. In 1889 he fell ill with what was eventually diagnosed as typhoid, from which, some weeks later on 8 June, he died. Many of his papers were sent to Robert Bridges, among them a group of sonnets now known as the dark sonnets, or sonnets of desolation, which were probably the ones

Hopkins had described to Bridges in 1885 as coming unbidden, one of them 'written in blood', generally thought to be 'I wake and feel the fell of dark, not day'.[37] Here the psychological loneliness of the speaker is amplified by his physical situation, waking in the middle of the night to find himself in a darkness so dense it is like being smothered by the thick pelt of an animal ('the fell of dark'); his disappointment at not finding the release of daylight is caught by the stark, elliptical phrase, 'not day'. Cut off from the world and unable to communicate with God ('dearest him that lives alas! away' (line 8)), he turns inward, dwelling on his incomprehensible and irrevocable lack of success ('God's most deep decree' (line 9)) until he feels reduced to bitter gall and heartburn, tormentedly imprisoned within himself, as Hopkins believed those condemned to hell were. The final lines that seem to see into hell mirror desperation by how close they come to saying that this torment is 'worse' than that experienced by the lost: 'The lost are like this, and their scourge to be / As I am mine, their sweating selves; but worse' (lines 13–14). Part of the poignancy of the poem arises from its dialogic structure, conveying both the intensity of emotion as gall and heartburn and a clear-headed diagnosis of its causes – the mind ('stomach') gnawing on itself – culminating in the final ambiguity ('but worse') that either confirms the loss of perspective in self-pitying despair, or provides a *volta* that turns away in objective recognition that others are in a worse state. The sonnets of desolation have contributed greatly to Hopkins's posthumous reputation. Bridges, perhaps their first reader, was deeply impressed. The feelings of isolation, despair, an ennui so intense it seems to pervade the world, fitted well into the bleakness of the two decades following World War I. Bridges prepared the first edition of Hopkins's poems for publication in 1918, but it was not until over a decade later, with the availability of a second edition of his poems and the spread of Modernism, that there was a wider audience appreciative of his verbal music. Since then many poets have gone through a 'Hopkins' phase, their ear caught by his alliterative compounds, abrupt phrases or concision and attracted by the bleak, honest view of mankind and his own human failings or his concern for a beautiful natural world threatened by man. Although he would have wished the proportions reversed, Hopkins has made many more literary than religious converts. The slightly built Jesuit, convinced of what he wanted to express, knowing that he was ahead of his time, miserable at the anti-British feeling around him in Dublin, left a small body of work that 'exploded' more effectively into the Modern world than that of any other Victorian literary figure, and his popularity has continued to grow into the twenty-first century.

Notes

1. 20 July–14 August 1864, *Further Letters of Gerard Manley Hopkins Including His Correspondence with Coventry Patmore*, ed. Claude Colleer Abbott, second edition, revised and enlarged (London: Oxford University Press, 1938, 1956), p. 214. Hereafter cited as *Further Letters*.
2. 20 July–1 August 1864, *Further Letters*, p. 213.
3. The connection was made by William Michael Rossetti in his edition of Christina's poems (*The Poetical Works of Christina Georgina Rossetti, with Memoir and Notes* (London: Macmillan, 1904), p. 482) and has been repeated frequently since. See *Christina Rossetti: The Complete Poems*, text by R. W. Crump, notes and introduction by Betty S. Flowers (Harmondsworth: Penguin Books, 2001), p. 899. All further quotations from Christina Rossetti's poetry are from this edition.
4. *The Poetical Works of Gerard Manley Hopkins*, ed. Norman H. MacKenzie (Oxford: Clarendon Press, 1990), p. 49, lines 64–70. All further quotations from Hopkins's poetry are from this edition.
5. 5 March 1872, *Further Letters*, p. 119.
6. Flowers, in *Christina Rossetti: The Complete Poems*, p. xl.
7. Jan Marsh, *Christina Rossetti: A Literary Biography* (Harmondsworth: Penguin, 1994), pp. 68–9.
8. See *ibid.*, pp. 226–8, 328–32, 428.
9. *Ibid.*, p. 84.
10. *Ibid.*, pp. 74–5, 88. The poems were 'Death's Chill Between' and 'Heart's Chill Between'.
11. See for example *The Blue Bower*, *Bocca Baciata*, *Fair Rosamund*, *Regina Cordium*, *Lady Lilith*, *Venus Verticordia*.
12. See for example the essays by Catherine Maxwell, Richard Menke, Lorraine Janzen Kooistra, in Mary Arseneau, Antony H. Harrison and Lorraine Janzen Kooistra (eds.), *The Culture of Christina Rossetti: Female Poetics and Victorian Contexts* (Athens: Ohio University Press, 1999).
13. Flowers, in *Christina Rossetti: The Complete Poems*, p. xl.
14. Jerome McGann, 'Introduction', in David A. Kent (ed.), *The Achievement of Christina Rossetti* (Ithaca, NY: Cornell University Press, 1987), pp. 1–19, 5–7.
15. *Seek and Find: A Double Series of Short Studies of the Benedicite* (1879), *Called to be Saints: The Minor Festivals Devotionally Studied* (1881), *Letter and Spirit: Notes on the Commandments* (1883), *Time Flies: A Reading Diary (1885)*, *The Face of the Deep: A Devotional Commentary on the Apocalypse* (1892).
16. Jan Marsh notes in her biography of Christina Rossetti that Christina told Dante Gabriel Rossetti that 'there was no risk of emotional exposure, because "no such person exists or existed"'. But in 1890, making notes on a new edition of her works, she pencilled in: 'The original John was obnoxious because he never gave scope for "No thank you"!', p. 203. Marsh speculates that the original was John Brett.

17. Antony A. Harrison, *Christina Rossetti in Context* (Brighton: Harvester Press, 1988), p. 118.
18. Marsh, *Christina Rossetti*, p. 44.
19. See Joan Rees, 'Christina Rossetti: Poet', *Critical Quarterly*, 26:3 (1984), pp. 59–72; Mary Arsenau, 'Pilgrimage and Postponement: Christina Rossetti's The Prince's Progress', *Victorian Poetry*, 32:3–4 (1994), pp. 279–98, esp. note 4, and Diane D'Amico, *Christina Rossetti: Faith, Gender, and Time* (Baton Rouge: Louisiana State University Press, 1999), especially chapter 3.
20. Rees, 'Christina Rossetti: Poet', p. 69.
21. Harrison, *Christina Rossetti in Context*, p. 118.
22. *Ibid.*, p. 117.
23. Marsh, *Christina Rossetti*, pp. 508–9.
24. Harrison, *Christina Rossetti in Context*, p. 95.
25. Marsh, *Christina Rossetti*, p. 475.
26. *Ibid.*, p. 297.
27. *Ibid.*, pp. 194–6.
28. *Ibid.*, p. 276.
29. *The Nation*, 15 June 1889, cited in Norman White, *Gerard Manley Hopkins: A Literary Biography* (Oxford: Clarendon Press, 1992), p. 457.
30. 'Poetry and Verse', in *The Journals and Papers of Gerard Manley Hopkins*, ed. H. House and Graham Storey (London: Oxford University Press, 1959), p. 289.
31. 29 October 1881, *The Correspondence of Gerard Manley Hopkins and Richard Watson Dixon*, ed. C. C. Abbott, second revised edition (Oxford: Oxford University Press, 1955), pp. 85–7. Hereafter cited as *Correspondence*.
32. 'Next please tell me how correctly to make codas to sonnets; with the most approved order of rhymes and so on . . . a sonnet is hot on the anvil and wants the coda', 2 November 1887, *The Letters of Gerard Manley Hopkins to Robert Bridges*, ed. C. C. Abbott (London: Oxford University Press, 1955), p. 263. Hereafter cited as *Letters to Bridges*.
33. 29 October 1881, *Correspondence*, pp. 86–7.
34. 30 May 1878, *Letters to Bridges*, pp. 52–3.
35. 28 September 1887, *ibid.*, p. 262.
36. 26 November 1886, *ibid.*, p. 245.
37. 17 May 1885, *ibid.*, p. 219.

Chapter 37

Later Victorian voices 1: James Thomson, Symons, Dowson, Lionel Johnson, Housman

NICHOLAS SHRIMPTON

The best-known poets of the late Victorian period were quick to mythologise themselves. 'Go from me: I am one of those, who fall', Lionel Johnson wrote in his poem 'Mystic and Cavalier' of 1889.[1] 'The day is overworn', Ernest Dowson declared ten years later, 'And we have reaped the crops the gods have sown; / Despair and death.'[2] W. B. Yeats, encouraged by such utterances, would commemorate his literary friends of the 1890s as a 'Tragic Generation'.[3] Drink, drugs, sexual misadventure, melancholy and self-neglect did indeed bring some writers to early deaths or breakdowns, and experiences of this kind were often the topics of their poetry. 'I think', Yeats speculated, 'that perhaps our form of lyric, our insistence upon emotion which has no relation to any public interest, gathered together overwrought, unstable men.'[4] An ageing monarch and a century approaching its end intensified this sensation of decay. After the title of a play by the French dramatists F. de Jouvenot and H. Micard had made the phrase *fin de siècle* familiar in 1888, it was eagerly adopted as the label for a variety of contemporary assumptions, all of them in one way or another pessimistic, disillusioned or morally antinomian.[5]

The consequence has been a tendency to see the poetry of this period, either as a sinister dead-end, or as a mere 'transition' between the more significant achievements of the High Victorian and Modernist eras. At the time many writers understood it rather differently. Ernest Rhys, for example, one of the supposedly 'overwrought, unstable men' whom Yeats met at the Rhymers' Club in the Cheshire Cheese pub off Fleet Street in London, wrote a poem which celebrated the activities of that Club, not as an indulgence in decay, but as a much-needed reinvention of the manner and technique of English poetry:

As once Rare Ben and Herrick
  Set older Fleet Street mad,
With wit, not esoteric,

And laughter that was lyric,
 And roystering rhymes and glad

As they, we drink defiance
 Tonight to all but Rhyme,
And most of all to Science,
And all such skins of lions
 That hide the ass of time.

Tonight, to rhyme as they did
 Were well, – ah, were it ours,
Who find the Muse degraded,
And changed, I fear, and faded,
 Her laurel crown and flowers.[6]

The Parnassian formal intricacy of this cheerful toast (with its conspicuously ingenious rhymes), and the Symbolist quality of its hostility to empirical science, make it very clearly a poem of the late nineteenth century. Yet its wish to re-make English poetry on the model of the 'witty' writing of the School of Ben anticipates T. S. Eliot's agenda for Modernist verse by more than twenty years. Holbrook Jackson, in his celebrated survey *The Eighteen Nineties* (1913), described the 'restless, inquisitive, impudent mood of the Nineties' and talked of it as 'the decade of a thousand "movements"'. This was the era of the New Drama, the New Journalism, the New Woman and, in the field of furniture and interior decoration, Art Nouveau. Even the movement which we have come to call 'decadence' was, Jackson argued, an expression of 'the liveliness of the times',[7] a liveliness which generated poetry of many different kinds, from the rumbustuous imperialism of Kipling and Henley, to the melancholy Celtic Revival verse of Yeats, William Sharp and Katherine Tynan, or the delicate late Aestheticism of women poets like Amy Levy, 'Michael Field' (the joint pseudonym of Katherine Bradley and Edith Cooper), Alice Meynell and Rosamund Marriott Watson.

English poetic practice in the last decades of the nineteenth century was, in other words, complex and various, and much of it had no significant connection, either to a notion of 'decadence' or to a consciousness of living in a '*fin de siècle*'. But a good deal of the best verse of the period did, nonetheless, have meaningful links to those concepts. Looking back at such writing, in 1936, and thinking especially of the work of the Rhymers' Club, of Ernest Dowson and Lionel Johnson, of 'Michael Field', of his own poetry, of Housman, of some of Kipling's verse and of 'certain poems by Hardy', Yeats would shift his attention from tragic lives to artistic achievement. The period, he observed, 'has, it seems, more good lyric poets than any similar period since the seventeenth century – no great overpowering figures, but many poets who have written some three or four lyrics apiece which may be permanent in our literature'.[8] This poetry was, interestingly, itself of more than one kind.

One relatively straightforward poetic response to the mood of termination and decay was an expression of anxiety about cultural deterioration, in a tone of indignation or regret. Anticipating by more than twenty years the spirit of Max Nordau's *Degeneration* (1892; translated into English in 1895), Tennyson denounced Aestheticism in an epigram probably written in the early 1870s but first published in his son's *Memoir* of 1897: 'Art for Art's sake! Hail . . . / Hail Genius, blaster of the Moral Will! / . . . / So prone are we toward that broad way to Hell'.[9] Gerard Manley Hopkins took the same strenuously moral view in 1889 when he contrasted his own poetic impotence with the artistic success of his Decadent contemporaries in his 'Thou art indeed just, Lord' sonnet:

Oh, the sots and thralls of lust
Do in spare hours more thrive than I that spend,
Sir, life upon thy cause.[10]

As this movingly suggests, the imitators of Baudelaire and Gautier, and of the English 'Fleshly School of Poetry' (Rossetti, Swinburne and their followers), played a more prominent and prolific role in contemporary verse than Hopkins's idiosyncratic development of the Tractarian poetics of Keble and Newman.

Tennyson had made the case more publicly in 1873 in 'To the Queen', the much-reprinted epilogue to *Idylls of the King*. Here an attack on the fashion for 'Art with poisonous honey stolen from France' was linked with an early expression of what would soon become a widespread anxiety about national decline in the closing years of the nineteenth century:

Is this the tone of empire? here the faith
That made us rulers? this, indeed, her voice
And meaning, whom the roar of Hougoumont
Left mightiest of all peoples under heaven?
What shock has fooled her since, that she should speak
So feebly? wealthier – wealthier – hour by hour!
The voice of Britain, or a sinking land,
Some third-rate isle half-lost among her seas?[11]

Anxieties about Empire were easily stirred, and the high point of British imperial power was readily, if rather prematurely, identified with the threatened Roman imperium of the fifth century AD, on the basis of a moralistic analysis which saw deteriorating ethical and cultural standards as the cause of geopolitical weakness. Rudyard Kipling expressed similar concerns in his great 'Recessional' of 1897. These writers did not sympathise with, or enjoy, a contemporary sense of decline. They did, none the less, register it vividly in their verse.

Much of the best poetry of the late Victorian period responded to this 'spirit of the age' in a very different way. Pessimists, like James Thomson, Thomas Hardy and A. E. Housman, and Decadents (or 'Symbolists') like Ernest Dowson, Lionel Johnson, Oscar Wilde, W. B. Yeats and Arthur Symons, sought to describe from within those aspects of contemporary consciousness which Tennyson, Hopkins and Kipling regretted or resisted. Their poems are, accordingly, less criticisms of the dark or degenerate mood of the late century than deliberate articulations of it.

James Thomson (who used the pseudonym 'B. V.') was born in 1834, thirty years before most of the poets we consider to be 'late Victorian'. But his disadvantaged background meant that he established himself as a writer only after a long delay. His best poem, *The City of Dreadful Night*, composed between 1870 and 1873, was serialised in Charles Bradlaugh's secularist newspaper *The National Reformer* in 1874 but not published in book form until 1880. Thomson's juvenilia include a poem 'Suggested by Matthew Arnold's "Stanzas from the Grande Chartreuse" ' and the formal roots of his verse are often assumed to lie in Arnold's reflective manner. He certainly sought to write an Arnoldian poetry of statement, 'adequate' to contemporary thought in the way which Arnold had first recommended in his 'On the Modern Element in Literature' lecture of 1857. By the 1870s the views with which a 'modern' poetry needed to be thus 'adequately' engaged included not just the scientific and textual challenges to faith but philosophical pessimism.

An idea already current in the ancient world (the Chorus in Sophocles's *Oedipus at Colonus* had suggested that 'Not to be born at all / Is best'), pessimism stands at the opposite pole from optimism in a metaphysical debate about whether the universe is, at root, a good thing or a bad one. Eclipsed by Christianity, by the optimistic views of Leibniz and by the Romantic belief in the transformative power of the imagination, it was restated by Byron, Leopardi, Heine and Schopenhauer. The attitudes expressed by the poets (the purpose of Byron's poem *Don Juan* was, he declared, 'holding up the nothingness of life')[12] had a more immediate effect than those of the philosopher, whose work, first published in 1819, was largely forgotten until the mid-1850s. But, once he had been rediscovered, Schopenhauer gave this rapidly spreading opinion an academic authority. Unlike other Idealists, Schopenhauer argued that the world of things-as-in-themselves-they-really-were was worse, not better, than the phenomenal world of appearances. The underlying reality was the 'will', a 'blind force' which senselessly drove an intolerable universe to perpetuate itself. Like Arnold (though with fewer reservations), Thomson was drawn to the melancholy of Leopardi and the cynicism of Heine. The Byronic gloom of Arnold's 'Dover Beach' (first published in 1867) provides a direct, though partial, precedent for Thomson's more systematic despair.

Thomson did not, on the other hand, admire Tennyson. 'He is certainly an exquisite carver of luxuries in ivory', he dismissively observed in 1866, 'but we must be content to admire the caskets, for there are no jewels inside.'[13] In practice, however, the manner of Thomson's poetry bears a closer resemblance to the narrative and discursive styles which Tennyson developed in the 1840s, after his turn away from the poetry of sensation, than it does to the austerity of Arnold's later technique. His minor poems are picturesque and rhetorical in ways which Arnold would have shunned. His one great work is perhaps best understood as a poem in the tradition of Tennyson's *Maud: A Monodrama*.

Thomson's *The City of Dreadful Night* has less plot than *Maud* and lacks the optimistic (though suicidal) conclusion which Tennyson insisted on providing for his dark tale of violence, insanity and thwarted love. But it is a long poem made up of short lyrics in the manner which Tennyson had distinctively established for *In Memoriam* and *Maud*, relies throughout on a profoundly Tennysonian use of symbolic landscape and uses the monodrama format in which successive or prolonged phases of passion are traced in the mind of a dramatic speaker.

The narrator of *The City of Dreadful Night* explores an environment which is urban and nocturnal in ways which anticipate the landscapes of Decadent poetry, though without the relish which a Baudelairean *flâneur* like Arthur Symons would later bring to them. Like him, Thomson describes his city with a high degree of specific detail, so much so that his poem seems at times to be an almost literal account of walking the streets of a modern metropolis in the middle of the night:

> Although lamps burn along the silent streets,
>   Even when moonlight silvers empty squares
> The dark holds countless lanes and close retreats;
>   But when the night its sphereless mantle wears
> The open spaces yawn with gloom abysmal,
> The sombre mansions loom immense and dismal,
>   The lanes are black as subterranean lairs.[14]

But, as the epigraph from Dante's *Inferno* makes clear ('Through me you pass into the city of woe'), this place is also hell, or, more precisely, a grim form of limbo, and the descriptive or meditative lyrics alternate with a series of nightmarish encounters with its inhabitants. Wandering 'in a suburb of the north' (18.1), the speaker comes upon 'something crawling in the lane below' (18.14), a 'befouled' (18.24) old man seeking desperately to return to childhood innocence. In the City's spectral cathedral, he attends a desolating pessimist sermon:

> Good tidings of great joy for you, for all:
> There is no God; no Fiend with names divine
> Made us and tortures us, if we must pine,
> It is to satiate no Being's gall
>
> . . .
>
> I find no hint throughout the Universe
> Of good or ill, of blessing or of curse;
> I find alone Necessity Supreme (14.39–75)

Contemplating the heavens, the narrator himself observes that 'The empyréan is a void abyss' (17.28), and the whole sequence of twenty-two linked lyrics concludes with a vision of Dürer's *Melancholia* as a gigantic statue and a 'confirmation of the old despair' (21.84).

The City of Dreadful Night can be read either as a psychological poem about clinical depression (a condition which provoked the alcoholism from which Thomson died in 1882), or as a more general statement about the human condition in the aftermath of what Nietzsche would call the death of God. Its power as poetry arises partly from the haunting imagery of its imagined landscapes, partly from what Anne Ridler called 'the terrible reiterations' of its phrasing, and above all from the rhythmic intensity of its individual lyrics:[15]

> As I came through the desert thus it was,
> As I came through the desert: All was black,
> In heaven no single star, on earth no track;
> A brooding hush without a stir or note,
> The air so thick it clotted in my throat;
> And this for hours; then some enormous things
> Swooped past with savage cries and clanking wings:
> But I strode on austere;
> No hope could have no fear. (4.7–15)

Similar views informed the early poetry of Thomas Hardy, who began writing verse in the 1860s but did not publish his first volume of it, *Wessex Poems*, until 1898. Though Hardy's personality was (relatively) less gloomy than Thomson's, and he usually preferred grim humour to denunciation or lament, he was in philosophical terms a better-informed pessimist since he certainly read both Schopenhauer and von Hartmann. Even in very early poems like 'Hap' (1866) and 'Neutral Tones' (1867), which predate such reading, he can strike a chilling note of cosmic despair:

> How arrives it joy lies slain,
> And why unblooms the best hope ever sown?
> – Crass Casualty obstructs the sun and rain,
> And dicing Time for gladness casts a moan . . .
> These purblind Doomsters had as readily strown
> Blisses about my pilgrimage as pain.[16] (lines 9–14)

Hardy's arguments are illustrated, not by the construction of an imagined landscape, but by the close observation of a real one, and his lyrical forms are tighter than Thomson's. By the time of his second volume, *Poems of the Past and the Present* in 1901, indeed, Hardy was combining his pessimistic view of the world with the Parnassian taste for ingenious stanza forms more usually associated with Decadent writers. 'The Caged Thrush Freed and Home Again', with its dark observation that men have no more power to make their lives happy than birds do, is a villanelle. 'Birds at Winter Nightfall', 'The Puzzled Game-Birds' and 'Winter in Durnover Field' are all written as triolets.

The best-known poem in Hardy's 1901 volume, 'The Darkling Thrush', engages directly with the concept of *fin de siècle*. Originally titled 'By the Century's Deathbed', and first published in the *Graphic* on 29 December 1900, it seeks to find a parallel between the historical occasion and the simple natural circumstance of a thrush singing in the dusk of a winter's day. By implication we are invited to remember that this dying century was one in which many of the ideas from which human beings had traditionally derived comfort had themselves died. Assaulted by the successive challenges of Malthusian economics, geology, the 'higher criticism' of the Bible and Darwinian biology, the consolations of religion had become ever more elusive. Even Positivism, the optimistic belief in scientific progress to which many intellectuals had turned after their loss of faith, was itself undermined by the discovery, in the field of thermodynamics, of the principle of entropy. In 1900, the economic difficulties created by the agricultural depression of the 1870s and 1880s were still a recent memory and Britain was fighting a costly and controversial war in South Africa. In this 'darkling' landscape (Hardy's second title allusively involves both Keats's 'Ode to a Nightingale' and the 'darkling plain' of Arnold's 'Dover

Beach'), the speaker hears 'a full-hearted evensong / Of joy illimited' (lines 19–20). The thrush is singing with such 'ecstatic sound' (line 26),

> That I could think there trembled through
> His happy good-night air
> Some blessed Hope, whereof he knew
> And I was unaware. (lines 29–32)

Hardy's awkwardly mixed diction, with its curious neologisms ('outleant', 'illimited') reminds us that he, like Thomson, was largely self-educated. But its oddly tentative or experimental quality here helps to enact the sense of scrupulous uncertainty ('could . . . trembled . . . some . . . he knew . . . I was unaware') with which the poem ventures its positive assertion.

A. E. Housman was very far from being an autodidact. By the time he published *A Shropshire Lad* in 1896 he was Professor of Latin at University College London, and his relationship to the Shropshire he described was scarcely closer than that of Theocritus, writing in ancient Alexandria, to rural Sicily. But, like Hardy in his villanelle and triolets, Housman combined the expression of profoundly pessimistic views with the use of tersely exquisite lyric form.

Both Hardy and Housman denied that they were, in the full or technical sense, pessimists. Hardy claimed to be a meliorist (believing, that is, that the universe was bad but capable of getting better). Housman told R. H. Goodale that he had 'not read Schopenhauer' and stated, in a letter to Maurice Pollet, that he was 'not a pessimist but a pejorist'.[17] Schopenhauer believed that the universe was already as bad as it could be. Housman, as a pejorist, believed that the universe was both bad and getting worse. If such a view seems scarcely less gloomy than the Schopenhauerian one which Housman repudiated, the narrative form of *A Shropshire Lad* further blurs the boundary between them. Housman originally wished to call his volume 'Poems by Terence Hearsay'. Though a friend persuaded him to change the title, the lines continue to be spoken by the 'Terence' referred to in Poems 8 ('Farewell to barn and stack and tree') and 62 ('"Terence, this is stupid stuff"'). Unlike Housman, who grew up in the Birmingham suburb of Bromsgrove, Terence is a Shropshire countryman who knows at first hand about ploughing and fighting and playing village football. His dark view of the world must therefore be presented as an immemorial folk wisdom rather than a particular modern philosophy. Despite that fictive circumstance, the ideas expressed in *A Shropshire Lad* are as characteristic of late Victorian despair as those articulated by Thomson and Hardy.

The opening poems of this sequence of sixty-three short lyrics seem at first sight to be straightforwardly patriotic and pastoral. 'From Clee to heaven the beacon burns' is a celebration of Queen Victoria's Golden Jubilee in 1887. 'Loveliest of trees, the cherry now' is a delighted description of spring blossom. But both poems are preoccupied with death, and with the significance of death in a godless universe. To mark the Jubilee, the Shropshire villagers sing the national anthem, 'God save the Queen'. But there is no God, and what saves the Queen is, in this disillusioned, late nineteenth-century understanding, not divine power but a material circumstance: the self-sacrifice of her soldiers.[18] In the second poem the reason why it is important to enjoy the cherry blossom is the dreadful brevity of human life:

Now, of my threescore years and ten,
Twenty will not come again,
And take from seventy springs a score,
It only leaves me fifty more. (lines 5–8)

This anxious calculation of the limited span of sensory experience might seem to be counteracted by the mention of 'Eastertide' in the first stanza. But the reference proves to be a merely chronological marker, without religious significance or implications of resurrection, and the poem ends with a visual image which is at the same time beautiful and morbidly chilly:

And since to look at things in bloom
Fifty springs are little room,
About the woodlands I will go
To see the cherry hung with snow. (lines 9–12)

An innocently pastoral lyric turns out, in practice, to be an encapsulation of Pater's notorious insistence, in the 'Conclusion' to *The Renaissance*, that a failure to 'burn always with this hard, gem-like flame, to maintain this ecstasy, is . . . on this short day of frost and sun, to sleep before evening'.[19]

Like Pater, Housman was a self-declared Cyrenaic, a version of Epicureanism which argued that only immediate sensations could be known, and which identified good with the pleasure of the moment. Where he went beyond Pater was in his pessimistic (or pejoristic) stress on the thought that death could be preferable to the pain of life in an indifferent universe. When 'ecstasy' was not possible, in other words, unconsciousness might be better. In Poem 7 ('When smoke stood up from Ludlow'), Terence Hearsay hears a blackbird singing in the hedge. Housman's blackbird is both more explicit and more gloomy than Hardy's thrush:

'Lie down, lie down, young yeoman;
The sun moves always west;
The road one treads to labour
Will lead one home to rest,
And that will be the best.' (lines 26–30)

Poem after poem gives lyric expression to feelings of loss and failure, with the grave as the only consolation, and a haunting sense of the gap between aspiration and experience. In Poem 40 ('Into my heart an air that kills') what seems, momentarily, to be a literal view of the distant Shropshire hills is actually an allegorical landscape which represents the human condition as a state of necessary disappointment.

In a lecture given in 1933, *The Name and Nature of Poetry*, Housman articulated a distinctive theory of poetic creation as a 'morbid secretion' – the process by which the irritating presence of a grain of sand causes an oyster, self-protectively, to produce a pearl.[20] *A Shropshire Lad* can certainly be read as a disguised response to painful personal experience. As an undergraduate Housman had fallen deeply, though hopelessly, in love with his friend Moses Jackson; he may subsequently have had a happier relationship with Jackson's brother Adalbert. Moses Jackson married in 1889. Adalbert died suddenly in the autumn of 1892. If Housman was reflecting in 1895 on the passions and losses of his earlier life, the trials of Oscar Wilde in April and May, and the suicide of a cadet at Woolwich Military Academy in August (referred to in Poem 44, 'Shot! so quick, so clean an ending') made this a particularly stressful time at which to consider the topic of homosexual love.

But the disguise is very thorough and the volume as a whole remains a generalised, though deeply felt, expression of the pessimistic understanding of the human condition which was so persistent a characteristic of the poetry of the *fin de siècle*. The penultimate poem of the collection, ' "Terence, this is stupid stuff" ', actually questions the utility of a poetry of despair. In response to a complaint that this is 'Moping melancholy mad', Terence Hearsay provides another of Housman's robustly commonsensical explanations of the nature of poetry. The gloom of these verses, he explains, functions as an inoculation or homeopathic treatment. Having encountered pessimism in this extreme form, we are better equipped to cope with the relatively minor pains of everyday life.[21]

By 1896, when *A Shropshire Lad* appeared, the self-consciously 'decadent' poetry of the period was already well established. Arthur Symons's *Days and Nights* volume appeared in 1889 and his *Silhouettes* in 1892. Ernest Dowson's 'Non sum qualis eram bonae sub regno Cynarae' was first published in the

Century Guild Hobby Horse in April 1891. 1892 saw the appearance of the first *Book of the Rhymers' Club*, with a second volume following in 1894. 1893 brought John Gray's *Silverpoints*, 1894 Oscar Wilde's *The Sphinx*. Lionel Johnson's *Poems* and Symons's *London Nights* were published in 1895. Dowson's *Verses* appeared in 1896. Housman refused to be associated with such writing. When asked in 1928 for permission to include some of his poems in A. J. A. Symons's pioneering *Anthology of 'Nineties' Verse*, he responded with the acerbic (if self-mocking) observation that, 'to include me in an anthology of the Nineties would be just as technically correct, and just as essentially inappropriate, as to include Lot in a book on Sodomites'.[22]

Since then he has, for the most part, been taken at his word. But the formal elegance of his technique makes him a bridge between the philosophical poetry of Thomson and Hardy and the Decadent verse of Symons, Dowson and Johnson. His models are not the Old French ones chosen by most Parnassian poets: the roundel, or triolet or villanelle. Instead, he turns to eighteenth-century English precedents: the short iambic quatrains of the common-metre hymn and popular ballad or, most distinctively, the 'Laura Matilda' stanza used by Dr Johnson in his 'A Short Song of Congratulation' ('Long-expected one and twenty / Ling'ring year, at last is flown')[23] and by James and Horace Smith in their parody of Hannah Cowley. In its pure form this is a quatrain of trochaic tetrameters, rhymed abab, with the second and fourth lines truncated to give masculine rhymes:

> Wake: the silver dusk returning
>   Up the beach of darkness brims,
> And the ship of sunrise burning
>   Strands upon the eastern rims. ('Reveille', lines 1–4)

Housman often uses iambs, not trochees, and sometimes supplies only the 'b' rhymes. In either version, his most brilliant technical achievement is to use his jaunty stanza forms paradoxically. They naturally enact an optimistic sense that life is comfortable, comic and controllable. Housman uses them, instead, as the vehicle of a despairingly pessimistic vision, counterpointing positive rhythm and negative statement in ways which ensure complexity of tone. His weakness as a poet is his diction, which lies at the opposite end of the verbal spectrum from the eccentricity of Hardy and can sometimes sink from the orthodox to the commonplace. His strength is the strictness and precision of his stanzaic patterns – which put him, like the Decadents, in the strenuous tradition of Théophile Gautier's *Emaux et camées*.

Decadence, as a literary category, was first significantly invoked in the 1830s by the French critic Désiré Nisard. In his book *Etudes de moeurs et de critique sur les poètes latins de la décadence* (1834), Nisard attacked the poetry of the Romantic school by suggesting that it resembled, not the Latin literature of the 'Golden Age' (Virgil, Horace and Ovid), but the 'Silver Age' writing of the late first and early second centuries AD (Statius, Martial and Apuleius). The poems of Nisard's contemporaries displayed, in his opinion, the same exaggeration, excessive subtlety and taste for the ugly.[24] At this stage decadence was chiefly a stylistic notion and it retained that quality when Gautier began, gradually, to give it a positive implication in his 'Preface' to Baudelaire's *Les Fleurs du mal* of 1868:

> The style of decadence . . . is nothing else than art arrived at that extreme point of maturity produced by . . . old civilizations . . . a style that is ingenious, complicated, learned, full of shades of meaning and research, always pushing further the limits of language . . . The style of decadence is the last effort of the Word, called upon to express everything, and pushed to the utmost extremity. We may remind ourselves, in connection with it, of the language of the later Roman Empire, already mottled with the greenness of decomposition, and, as it were, gamy, and of the complicated refinements of the Byzantine school, the last form of Greek art fallen into deliquescence.[25]

Pater brought the concept into English, by now in a wholly positive sense, in the 'Preface' to *The Renaissance* in 1873. Explaining his unusual conception of a long Renaissance, not confined to fourteenth- and fifteenth-century Italy but stretching from the late twelfth century to the sixteenth-century writing of Joachim du Bellay, Pater suggested that 'the Renaissance . . . [put] forth in France an aftermath, a wonderful later growth, the products of which have to the full the subtle and delicate sweetness which belong to a refined and comely decadence'.[26] Belatedness, Pater is arguing, has its charms. Sophistication, refinement and elaboration are valid artistic criteria.

Ten years later, in 1883, the French poet Paul Verlaine chose to celebrate, not the 'refined and comely' decadence of Joachim du Bellay, but the late Roman culture which Nisard had condemned and Gautier ambiguously recommended. 'I am', he declared in his sonnet 'Langueur', 'the Empire at the time of the decadence.'[27] Verlaine's creative identity is presented in the poem as that of a fifth-century patrician, indolently preoccupied with the composition of 'acrostics' while the invading barbarians march into the streets of Rome. He is the learned but over-refined inheritor of hundreds of years of intellectual and artistic achievement, afflicted by a mysterious 'ennui' (boredom) whose causes he is unable to identify. Perhaps the culture of late nineteenth-century Europe, with its pessimism, its sophistication and its world-weariness, resembled that of the Roman Empire in its era of decline and fall? Arthur Symons, considering what he called 'The Decadent Movement in Literature', in 1893, certainly made that assumption. The movement has, he said, 'all the qualities that mark the end of great periods, the qualities that we find in the Greek, the Latin decadence: an intense self-consciousness, a restless curiosity in research, an over-subtilizing refinement upon refinement, a spiritual and moral perversity'.[28] Symons's final phrase makes it clear that these are now both qualities of style and the expression of a more comprehensive artistic creed.

By 1880 the theoretical assumptions of the Aesthetic Movement had been current for more than sixty years, and had been conspicuously demonstrated in the poetic practice of Rossetti, Swinburne and William Morris. Swinburne, in his *William Blake, A Critical Essay* in 1868, had memorably restated the case for the independence of art from moral constraints: to be a successful work of art a text needed only to be beautiful, not ethically or politically correct. Pater did the same for the belief in the priority of form over content in his 1877 essay 'The School of Giorgione'. Now, in the 1880s, the idea that art did not have to be morally good began to shift into the rather different notion that art needed to be morally bad.

In its simplest form this proposition consisted merely of the view that texts demonstrated their effectiveness by their ability to *épater le bourgeois*. At a deeper level it involved the notion that originality was inseparable from transgression. 'What is termed Sin', Wilde wrote in the first of his 'The Critic as Artist' dialogues, published in July 1890, 'is an essential element of progress. Without it the world would stagnate, or grow old, or become colourless. By its curiosity, Sin increases the experience of the race.'[29] The sestet of Arthur Symons's sonnet 'The Opium-Smoker', published in his *Days and Nights* volume of 1889, described the degrading circumstances of the addict's life with the specificity of a Realist novel. It concluded, not with condemnation, but with celebration of the transformative effects of his intoxication. Symons's next collection, *Silhouettes* (1892), provided an 'Absinthe-Drinker' ('Gently I wave the visible world away' (line 1)) to set beside his opium-smoker.[30] His third volume, *London Nights* in 1895, was notoriously full of poems about casual sex with prostitutes or chorus girls. The thoughts in the second of the two poems 'To One in Alienation', for example, are spoken as the poet 'clasped the stranger-woman I had hired' (line 2). Still more shockingly, 'Stella Maris' uses a traditional term for the Virgin Mary as the title of a poem about a street-walking prostitute who is then figured as the heroine of Shakespeare's most celebrated treatment of romantic love, 'The Juliet of a night' (line 5). The parodist Owen Seaman mocked Symons's writing as tactless erotic boasting ('Yes I am, I know, / The devil of a Romeo!').[31] Less subtly, the *Pall Mall Gazette* declared, in September 1895, that 'Mr Arthur Symons is a dirty-minded man, and his mind is reflected in the puddle of his bad verses.'[32]

Bad verse is not, however, the appropriate term for a poem like 'White Heliotrope' where Symons (naughtily) uses Tennyson's *In Memoriam* stanza to create a vivid impression of the morning after an improper night before. The low-life scene is presented with a Pope-like catalogue of domestic detail:

> The feverish room and that white bed,
> The tumbled skirts upon a chair,
> The novel flung half-open, where
> Hat, hair-pins, puffs, and paints, are spread . . . (lines 1–4)

But this lurid confession turns, unexpectedly, into a Proustian account of the power of the sense of smell over the involuntary memory – the smell in this case being the vulgar one of a cheap perfume.

The supreme example of this poetry of 'Sin' is Ernest Dowson's 'Non sum qualis eram bonae sub regno Cynarae', originally printed in 1891 and collected in the first of the two slim volumes, *Verses* (1896) and *Decorations* (1899), which he published before his early death in 1900:

> All night upon mine heart I felt her warm heart beat,
> Night-long within mine arms in love and sleep she lay;
> Surely the kisses of her bought red mouth were sweet;
> But I was desolate and sick of an old passion,
> When I awoke and found the dawn was gray:
> I have been faithful to thee, Cynara! in my fashion. (lines 7–12)

The use of a line from a Horace ode for the title might seem to create an incongruous link to the Latin literature of the Golden Age, rather than the Silver Age poetry with which Decadent poets naturally associated themselves. But the body of the poem is written in that very French verse form, the alexandrine (varied with a single pentameter in the fifth line of each stanza), and in a complex stanzaic form, rhymed abacbc, where the c rhymes are the same words ('passion', 'fashion') throughout the poem, operating as an interrupted refrain. The effect is to create a sense of belatedness, as if an ingenious late Latin poet (with a taste perhaps for acrostics) were revisiting an ancient predecessor to recast his topic into the idiom of another age. The diction is a deliberately curious mixture of colloquial monosyllables ('warm', 'sleep', 'bought', 'sick'), with the archaic ('mine heart'), the neologistic ('night-long') and the elegantly Latinate ('desolate'). The Latin 'desolatus', with its specific sense of being left 'solus' or alone, lurks here behind the customary English meaning to produce, in Gautier's phrase, 'a style that is ingenious, complicated, learned, full of shades of meaning and research'. At the same time, in Symons's terms, the poem displays a 'spiritual and moral perversity'. Going to bed with other women demonstrates, we are told, not unfaithfulness, but its contrary – the profound commitment of the speaker to his previous lover. Familiarity with the poem dulls, but cannot entirely eliminate, the shock of the phrase 'I have been faithful to thee' at the end of stanza after stanza of frankly stated infidelity.

The poem's topic is not, however, just sleeping with a prostitute. Rather, it is the gulf between the ideal and the actual. The perfect love, figured here as Cynara, is lost or unavailable or impossible. But, dismayingly, it continues to haunt us, however much we may try to distract ourselves from it by immersion in physical pleasure. This is, in other words, both a poem about erotic experience and, more profoundly, an account of our relationship with the ideal or spiritual in an age of materialism and unbelief.

Lionel Johnson's poetry differs from that of Symons and Dowson because it is conceived in the spirit of Pater's 'refined and comely decadence', rather than the seamy ancient Rome of Gautier. The verse of sixteenth-century France, in Pater's view, was a poetry

> not for the people, but for a confined circle, for . . . erudite persons . . . a party who in an age of great troubles, losses, anxieties, amuse themselves with art . . . Its charm is that of a thing not vigorous or original, but full of the grace that comes of long study and reiterated refinements . . . with an exquisite faintness, a *fadeur exquise*, a certain tenuity and caducity, as for those who can bear nothing vehement or strong.[33]

When Johnson wishes to bring the ideal and the actual into contact with one another he does it, not by a description of a night with a prostitute, but by an account of reading Plato in a London garret:

> Thou hast held converse with things rare:
> Look now upon another sight!
> The calm stars, in their living skies:
> And then, these surging cries,
> This restless glare! ('Plato in London', lines 24–8)

Yet even Johnson achieves some of his most memorable effects with disturbing accounts of moral failure. 'Vinum Daemonum' is a dramatic description of his alcoholism. In 'Mystic and Cavalier', in 1889, he presents himself as an example of what Verlaine, five years previously, had termed a *poète maudit*. In 'The Dark Angel', first published in 1894, he describes the satanic other-self of his pious, scholarly and fastidious personality. Johnson's greatest poem, 'By the Statue of King Charles at Charing Cross', is, however, marked by the milder 'tenuity and caducity' which Pater had identified with the decadence of the sixteenth century. Written in 1889 and published in the *Book of the Rhymers' Club* in 1892, this is a product of that nocturnal wandering of the streets of London which was so often the business of his debauched or dandified contemporaries. The speaker of Johnson's poem, more innocently, contemplates the equestrian statue of King Charles I which stands at the end of Pall Mall looking towards Charing Cross Station:

> Comely and calm, he rides
> Hard by his own Whitehall:
> Only the night wind glides:
> No crowds, nor rebels, brawl.
>
> Gone, too, his Court: and yet,
> The stars his courtiers are:
> Stars in their stations set;
> And every wandering star. (lines 9–16)

Johnson identifies with King Charles because he was deposed and executed, and finds in the destruction of Stuart culture both a native analogy for the fall of Rome and a precedent for the doomed mood of the *fin de siècle*.

Writing in terse iambic trimeters, with frequent trochaic substitutions in the first foot, Johnson uses subtle variations of rhythm to produce complex effects of tone and meaning. At first sight the 'Stars in their stations set' are a comforting reassertion of the justice and order of the universe: though Charles may have lost his literal court, he has a better and more permanent one in the heavens. But, as the next line unexpectedly and movingly reminds us, not all the stars are 'set'. Some 'wander' (like fecklessly self-destructive Decadent poets, perhaps) and, as we are told this, the metre wanders correspondingly into the two anapaestic feet with which the line concludes.

Symons, writing about 'The Decadent Movement in Literature' in 1893, was not sure that 'Decadent' was the right word for the phenomenon which he was describing. 'The latest movement in European literature', he observed, 'has been called by many names, none of them quite exact or comprehensive – Decadence, Symbolism, Impressionism, for instance.'[34] His own poetry was often concerned with the fixing of momentary impressions, in the manner of contemporary painters like Whistler, Monet or Sickert. The 'Décor de Théâtre' sequence in his *London Nights* volume offers six vivid glimpses of music hall performers, a topic which recommended itself to Decadent poets not just because it was urban, nocturnal and improper, but because it reflected so directly their rejection of nature in favour of the artificial. In the fifth poem, 'La Mélinite: Moulin Rouge', Symons observes the dancer Jane Avril:

> Down the long hall the dance returning
> Rounds the full circle, rounds
> The perfect rose of lights and sounds,
> The rose returning
> Into the circle of its rounds.
>
> Alone, apart, one dancer watches
> Her mirrored, morbid grace;
> Before the mirror, face to face,
> Alone she watches
> Her morbid, vague, ambiguous grace. (lines 6–15)

Written in an exceptionally intricate verse form (six five-line stanzas of 4, 3, 4, 2 and 4 iambs, rhymed abbab, with the a rhymes and the first and last b rhymes using the same word), it is none the less an impression of a single moment. Within this momentary experience, Symons is able to suggest the 'ambiguous' qualities of the word 'grace'. The term's double reference, both sensual and religious, is developed instantaneously by the repetition intrinsic to this ingeniously repetitious stanza form. Yeats thought this 'one of the most perfect lyrics of our time'.[35]

Oscar Wilde's early verse was often derivative, and his most self-consciously Decadent poem, *The Sphinx* (1894), suffers from an overstated straining for effect. But he too produced some striking 'impressions', using Whistler's synaesthetic mixing of terms from different arts in titles like 'In the Gold Room: A Harmony' (1881), or 'Symphony in Yellow' (1889). His best-known poem *The Ballad of Reading Gaol* (1898) represents a turn away from art for art's sake assumptions towards the didacticism and rhetoric which Decadent poets had meticulously avoided. Its most powerful moments tend, none the less, to involve impressionistic effects, such as the vivid account of the landscape of the prison's exercise yard as 'that little tent of blue / Which prisoners call the sky'.[36]

In France Symbolism had effectively superseded Decadence by the late 1880s (the literary review *Le Décadent*, founded in 1886, closed in 1889) and when, in 1899, Symons returned to his attempt to characterise the art of his era, Yeats persuaded him to call his book *The Symbolist Movement in Literature*. Yeats's own poetry in this period was certainly Symbolist rather than Decadent, seeking to suggest or evoke a deeper reality of which physical objects and experiences were merely 'symbols'. The rose in his poem 'The Secret Rose' (1896) is the emblem of a profound meaning in the universe, not found by those who had previously sought it 'in the Holy Sepulchre, / Or in the wine-vat' (in conventional religion, that is, or in physical pleasure). In the past its 'leaves' enfolded those who came close to the heart of the mystery: the Magi and a series of figures from ancient Irish mythology. Now, Yeats waits impatiently for the end of the era of scientific materialism:

> When shall the stars be blown about the sky,
> Like the sparks blown out of a smithy, and die?[37]

The abrupt change of metaphor (from rose to wind), and the conventional iambic pentameter couplets, suggest that Yeats has not yet found his distinctive poetic voice. His work does, however, make very clear the growing importance of Symbolist assumptions in the later 1890s.

Decadence remains the best term for the poetry of Symons, Dowson and Johnson, if only because it is so much more inclusive than the 'Impressionist' or 'Symbolist' alternatives. The pessimistic gloom, the identification with eras of failure and decline, the learned sophistication, the interest in momentary sensation, the immoralism and the rejection of the Romantic cult of nature in favour of artifice or spirituality (poems like Dowson's 'Benedictio Domini' or Johnson's 'The Church of a Dream' remind one that supernatural religion was as significantly 'unnatural' as music halls or cosmetics), combined to produce that rare and elusive thing – a fresh mood or flavour for the familiar mode of lyric. This was not a remarkable era for narrative, discursive or satirical poetry, for odes, epics or elegies. But it was, as Yeats rightly suggested, a great age of lyrical verse.

Notes

1. Line 1; *Complete Poems of Lionel Johnson*, ed. Iain Fletcher (London: Unicorn Press, 1953). Further quotations from Johnson's poetry are from this edition.
2. Lines 2–3, 'A Last Word', in *Poems of Ernest Dowson*, ed. Mark Longaker (Philadephia: University of Pennsylvania Press, 1968), p. 138. Further quotations from Dowson's poetry are from this edition.
3. 'The Tragic Generation' is the title of Book 4 of Yeats's *The Trembling of the Veil* (1922), here quoted from W. B. Yeats, *Autobiographies* (London: Macmillan, 1980).
4. *Ibid.*, p. 300.
5. *Fin-de-siècle* (Paris, 1888) by Micard, Jouvenot and Cohen (whose name was subsequently deleted) opened at the Théâtre du Château d'Eau in April 1888. In England the first citation in *OED* is the *Daily News*, 29 December 1890, on the 'fin de siècle' quality of the year's financial events.

6. Lines 1–15, 'At the Rhymers' Club, 1. The Toast,' published in the *Book of the Rhymers' Club* (1892), here quoted from *Writing of the 'Nineties*, ed. Derek Stanford (London: Dent, 1971).
7. Holbrook Jackson, *The Eighteen Nineties* (Harmondsworth: Penguin, 1950), pp. 103, 29, 68.
8. Printed as 'Modern Poetry: A Broadcast' in W. B. Yeats, *Essays and Introductions* (London: Macmillan, 1989), p. 491.
9. *The Poems of Tennyson*, ed. Christopher Ricks (London: Longmans, 1969), p. 1229.
10. Lines 7–9; *The Poetical Works of Gerard Manley Hopkins*, ed. Norman H. Mackenzie (Oxford: Clarendon Press, 1990).
11. Lines 56, 18–25; Tennyson, *Poems*.
12. Byron, *Don Juan* VII.6; *Poetical Works of Lord Byron*, ed. Humphrey Milford (London: Oxford University Press, 1921), p. 731.
13. 'The Poems of William Blake', in *The Speedy Extinction of Evil and Misery: Selected Prose of James Thomson (B. V.)*, ed. W. D. Schaefer (Berkeley: University of California Press, 1967), p. 232.
14. 3.1–7; references are to stanzas and line numbers. *Poems and Some Letters of James Thomson*, ed. Anne Ridler (London: Centaur Press, 1963). Further quotations from Thomson's poetry are from this edition.
15. Quoted in Thomson, *Poems*, p. xxxix.
16. 'Hap'; *Complete Poetical Works of Thomas Hardy*, ed. Samuel Hynes (Oxford: Clarendon Press, 1982). Further quotations from Hardy's poetry are from this edition. Hardy's 1886 *Notebooks* record reading Schopenhauer in James Sully's *Pessimism* (1877).
17. R. H. Goodale, 'Schopenhauer and Pessimism in Nineteenth-Century English Literature', *PMLA*, 47:1 (1932), p. 260; *The Letters of A. E. Housman*, ed. Henry Maas (London: Rupert Hart Davis, 1971), p. 329.
18. *The Poems of A. E. Housman*, ed. Archie Burnett (Oxford: Clarendon Press, 1997), pp. 3–4. Further quotations from Housman's poetry are from this edition.
19. Walter H. Pater, *Studies in the History of the Renaissance* (London: Macmillan, 1873), pp. 210–11.
20. A. E. Housman, *The Name and Nature of Poetry* (Cambridge: Cambridge University Press, 1945), p. 48.
21. Housman, *Poems*, pp. 63–5.
22. Letter to Grant Richards, 9 October 1928, in *A. E. Housman: Collected Poems & Selected Prose*, ed. C. Ricks (London: Penguin, 1989), p. 466.
23. Lines 1–2; *The Poems of Samuel Johnson*, ed. Nichol Smith and E. L. McAdam (Oxford: Clarendon Press, 1974).
24. Désiré Nisard, *Etudes de moeurs et de critique sur les poètes latins de la décadence* (Brussels: L. Hauman, 1834).
25. This was the preface to vol. 1 of the immediately posthumous edition of Charles Baudelaire's *Oeuvres Complètes* (Paris: Lévy, 1868).
26. Pater, *The Renaissance*, p. xii.

27. 'Langueur' was first published in *Le Chat Noir* on 26 May 1883 and reprinted in Verlaine's *Jadis et naguère* volume of 1884.
28. Arthur Symons, 'The Decadent Movement in Literature', originally published in *Harper's New Monthly Magazine*, November 1893, reprinted in K. Beckson (ed.), *Aesthetes and Decadents of the 1890s*, revised edition (Chicago: Academy Chicago, 1981), p. 135.
29. Oscar Wilde, *Criticism*, ed. Josephine M. Guy, vol. IV of *The Complete Works of Oscar Wilde*, general editor, Ian Small (Oxford: Oxford University Press, 2007), p. 148.
30. *Poems by Arthur Symons* (London: Heinemann, 1916). Further quotations from Symons's poetry are from this edition.
31. Owen Seaman, 'A Vigo-Street Eclogue', in *The Battle of the Bays* (London: John Lane, 1896), p. 29.
32. *Pall Mall Gazette*, 2 September 1895, p. 4.
33. Pater, *The Renaissance*, pp. 136–9.
34. Symons, 'Decadent Movement', quoted in Beckson, *Aesthetes and Decadents*, p. 135.
35. Review of Symons's *Amoris Victima*, *Bookman*, April 1897, reprinted in *Uncollected Prose by W. B. Yeats*, ed. J. P. Frayne and C. Johnson, 2 vols. (London: Macmillan, 1970), vol. II, p. 40.
36. Lines 15–16; Oscar Wilde, *Poems & Poems in Prose*, ed. B. Fong and K. Beckson, vol. I of *The Complete Works of Oscar Wilde* (Oxford: Oxford University Press, 2007).
37. First published as 'O'Sullivan Rua to the Secret Rose', in *The Savoy*, September 1896, then as 'To the Secret Rose', in Yeats's *The Secret Rose* (1897), and as 'The Secret Rose' in *The Wind among the Reeds* (1899); lines 3–4, 29–30; *The Collected Poems of W. B. Yeats* (London: Macmillan, 1967).

Chapter 38

Later Victorian voices 2: Davidson, Kipling, 'Michael Field' (Bradley and Cooper), Lee-Hamilton, Kendall, Webster

FRANCIS O'GORMAN

Looking back from between the two world wars, it might have been easy to forget that any of the poets considered in this chapter had existed. John Drinkwater omitted them all from his introductory study *Victorian Poetry* (1923). F. R. Leavis's *New Bearings in English Poetry* (1932) regarded no late Victorian except Gerard Manley Hopkins. *Revaluation* (1936) did not go any further. 'A study of the latter end of *The Oxford Book of Victorian Verse*', Leavis said, suggests 'the conclusion that something has been wrong for forty or fifty years at the least.'[1] Browning and Tennyson dominated Drinkwater's conception of the period and he admitted he was sorry only to have missed Thomas Hardy. But Hardy was 'post-Victorian in character'[2] anyway. That idea would become a category which would do criticism some service: turned the other way around, it gave to later twentieth-century writers a useful reason for rereading some late Victorian poets that the earlier period had set aside or explicitly disliked. It is true that Isobel Armstrong's influential study *Victorian Poetry: Poetry, Poetics and Politics* (1993) was nearly as silent on the poets in this chapter as her predecessors *entre deux guerres*. But, for others, John Davidson (1857–1909) and Michael Field (Katherine Bradley (1846–1914) and Edith Cooper (1862–1913)) were particular beneficiaries of the 'post-Victorian' argument. Or rather, not as 'post-Victorian' but as 'pre-Modernist', they could be integrated into a larger cluster of late nineteenth-century writers – George Gissing, Gerard Manley Hopkins, Vernon Lee, Francis Thompson, even John Ruskin among them – and read as precursors of Modernist themes and literary practices.

That sense of the late nineteenth century as precursory has been valuable. No one would want to forget it, even if the retrospective imposition of 'foreseeing' is always a kind of historical confusion. This aside, 'foreseeing'

Modernism is not by definition a criterion for significance. Such privileging of the Modernists easily encourages readers to miss the Victorianness of the Victorians. This matters more than for local arguments about periodisation: it matters for comprehending the ethical temper, the aesthetic climate, the terms of debate, amid which later Victorian dramatic verse belonged. Various and new, the poets considered here faced their own challenges and explored their own possibilities in their own age. Involved in debates transmitted from the mid nineteenth century, they asked about who could be represented – and opened up questions about the limits of representation, the relationship between voice and personality, between what was said and what was intended. They sketched how hard it could be to understand the viewpoints of others. They inquired about the possibilities of discerning collective opinions among diverse speakers, and looked at the temptations to simplify human lives and desires, to make reductive moral judgments in the face of human complexity. Such matters were part of the ancient concerns of poetry, but, highly visible in the post-Romantic environment of Victorian dramatic verse (not just of the 'dramatic monologue'), they took new energy from issues inseparable from the nineteenth-century liberal state. Diversely, this was poetry musing on the implications of a changing national sense of the democratic. In the fullness of its implications, such poetry invited thought about the political structures of representative government with its moral and philosophical problems. Here was writing in fresh dialogue with the age of the growing franchise.

Playwright, poet, translator, feminist public speaker and essayist, Augusta Webster (1837–94) found in the dramatic monologue a genre suitable for opinions: forceful, dissenting, unexpectedly sympathetic. Webster was not a dramatic writer only – her uncompleted sonnet sequence *Mother and Daughter* (1895) has recently returned to the canon. But her career grew through her lively extension of the scope of the monologue, and her negotiation of the Tennyson/Browning inheritance. Portraits, to use the title of her 1870 volume, mattered. To social questions, Webster's contribution through verse embraced women's education, domestic sexual politics and prostitution. The 'silly rules this silly world / Makes about women!' (lines 377–8)[3] irritated the speaker of 'A Castaway' (1870/93). That poem was one of the most firm-minded confutations of easy clichés about Victorian views of prostitution – and a challenge to D. G. Rossetti's 'Jenny' (1870), which Webster may have seen in manuscript. A more general malaise about a 'rare century' with 'rotten depths [that] grow rottener' (lines 238–40) drove the speaker of 'Tired' (1870/93). Identity politics *avant la lettre* were at stake in Webster's representations of mythic figures too: in enabling them to 'speak for themselves', she could claim, as Amy Levy could, to be imagining the private mental histories of the marginalised in a redemptory way. In his early monologues, Robert Browning had imagined murderers speaking for themselves: he made them disconcertingly plausible. But he was not the only one so to trouble a reader's moral co-ordinates. Webster proposed understandings of the emotional life and motivations of killers too: 'Medea in Athens' (1870/93) records Medea's dispirited life after she has slain her children, challenging how one might relate emotionally to infanticide. Another sorceress, in 'Circe' (1870/93), is given probing but not unsympathetic treatment. Posing counter-narratives to more familiar representations of figures from the Western corpus of myth, these were refusals of what was implicitly coded as history's forgetfulness: they were attempts to imagine the 'lost' viewpoints of the maligned.

The more conspicuous social interventions made by Webster's modern speakers – 'A Castaway' is the obvious example, a monologue spoken by a high-class prostitute – invited the reader to consider political convictions, and to wonder whose they were. 'A Castaway' had much to say about wrong-headed attempts to reclaim prostitutes (about the 'Coarse pittance, prison rules' of the reformatory (lines 238–40) the speaker is scornful), on women's education and on the tedium of middle-class women's lives. Yet the monologue teased with uncertainties. Did the poet speak through Eulalie's voice? What was the relationship between the 'spoken' words and the authorial mind behind them? Was the speaker's social protest being made available for critique or did it come with authorial blessing? How could the reader be sure?

Webster's portraits required the reader to think about where Webster was. At a broader level, they forced him or her to sense how difficult it could be in human communication to distinguish what was really intended, what was sincere, let alone coherent or convincing. This figuring of the vulnerability of utterance, its liability to misconception, the difficulty of articulating and of receiving testimonies, was implicit in the dramatic monologue as a form. But the uncertainty of interpretation was apparent with a particular force when Webster seemed to put the dramatic monologue to the explicit purpose of view-taking. And in other ways, Webster's verse asked the reader to meditate on the problems of hearing human meanings. Her writing, at its charismatic best, evidenced a fascination with human testimonies that were limited in audience, even as it sought to recover imaginatively, sometimes as part of a feminist project, the witness of those whom history and mythology had misconstrued. Webster's monologues went often unheard. I do not mean simply that she was unread, but rather that her speakers were talking to themselves. Like Dostoevsky's Raskolnikov, whose private monologues at the beginning of *Crime and Punishment* (1866) declared his radical social alienation,[4] Webster's speakers were solitary confessors to the air, detached from community and audience, freed from the responsibility of having to censor their thoughts. But Webster also disclosed another attraction to forms of human witness that were hard to receive. 'Medea in Athens', 'Tired', 'A Castaway', 'An Inventor' (1870/93) were glimpses of human individualities out of earshot, figures whose self-representations were untroubled by impediments to their communication. Other speakers, more obviously, were caught up with the impeded reception of testimonies: they were the ones simply forgotten. 'I rave in vain' (line 33), declared the monologist of 'With the Dead' (1866), for his unheard words could not change his fate, doomed to haunt the tomb of his beloved in perpetuity. 'Coming Home' (1870/93) was predicated on the expectation – about which the reader grows more anxious through the text – that the speaker has not been forgotten: Medea was certain she had been. 'I am forgotten. / Forgotten', she says: 'something goes from life in that' (lines 156–7).

Developing queries pertinent to the dramatic monologue *qua* dramatic monologue, Webster's texts suggested dubieties about the reception of human viewpoints, about the relationship between voice and meaning, about how to hear all that was intended. These were dubieties about the voices of dramatic poetry and what forms of knowledge they offered. But they were also, displaced, among the implicit challenges of a state changing its understanding of what representation meant. Given distinctive momentum by electoral debates that were considering afresh the notion of representative government, the matters of how to take into account a range of human views and respond to them, were topics freshly energised by the contentious issue of the franchise across Victoria's reign. Ruminating on scenes in which human meanings were hard to lay hold of and confidently to represent to others, Webster searched issues apposite for a nation, in a period of three Reform Acts, which was extending the borders of who, in a parliamentary sense, was represented. The hidden political musing of the dramatic monologue in a democratic age – a genre which came into being almost simultaneously with the Great Reform Act in 1832[5] – involved the testing, as the period developed, of efforts to represent the lives or views of another. And that testing occurred in a remarkable number of ways, constituting the key feature of the political engagement of late Victorian dramatic writing. Probing the margins of respectable society and fashioning simulacra of voices struggling to be heard, John Davidson posed similar questions to Webster – and then challenged their foundations. But Rudyard Kipling (1865–1936), who established his place among readers at the end of the century with the volume of monologues, *Barrack-Room Ballads: First Series* (1892), looked more plainly at matters of human representation. No democrat, Kipling was nonetheless concerned with poetry as a vibrant way of imagining voices that were easily ignored even as he recognised the power of Empire to occupy regions beyond British shores and to influence the nature of others' self-representation. His were speakers, however involved in imperial projects, with a case to make against a society in which they did not feel recognised.

Barrack-Room Ballads was addressed with 'my best respects'[6] to Thomas Atkins, a formal version of the generic name for a British private soldier. Proposing the recovery of the viewpoints of ordinary combat troops, the volume offered itself as recuperating narratives easily lost sight of amid official histories of wars, shaped by officers' perceptions. Describing the poor treatment of British troops at home and envisaging the obstructions in a soldier's efforts to buy beer, visit the theatre or live an acceptable domestic life, 'Tommy' was the most impatient of the monologues. 'For it's Tommy this an' Tommy that', the speaker complains, 'an' "Chuck him out, the brute!" / But it's "Saviour of 'is country" when the guns begin to shoot' (lines 37–8). This was a shocked voice, asking to be heard. 'The Widow at Windsor', 'Fuzzy-Wuzzy', 'Gunga Din', 'Screw-Guns' were differently engaged with a fantasy of the demotic, the voice of the marginalised men claiming to be at the foundation of the Empire's success. Men in action dominated the volume as if in a more assertively masculinist rebuke to the dreamy feyness of other forms of *fin de siècle* manliness but also in a vocally colourful challenge to the notion that only the voices of the privileged might be heard.

Kipling's acts of recuperation were conscious of the borders that were hard to cross, even as they suggested that readers crossed them in recognising subjectivities habitually misapprehended. His dedication in *Barrack-Room Ballads* separated the authorial view from the speakers' and in doing so reminded the reader of the central democratic problem in the text. 'I have made for you a song', he wrote to 'Thomas Atkins': 'And it may be right or wrong, But only you can tell me if it's true' ('To Thomas Atkins', lines 12–13). The short poem took up the unmistakeable (abba) rhyme scheme of Tennyson's *In Memoriam* stanza: perhaps it was coyly hinting that recollecting the obscured was as worthy an undertaking as the Laureate's remembrance of the noble dead. The lack of congruence between writer and subject invited more obtrusive questions about the ways in which an individual could indeed represent another and speak for him. How, the dedication implied, might a man represent another when he could not know if what he was representing was the other's authentic experiences? Kipling's speakers made their community allegiances clear as if they were implying that none but their own could undertake properly to represent them. The brave but ordinary soldiers, speaking non-standard English, with understandings of local circumstances but little of the broader international dramas in which they played: these were social groups with obvious commonalities and equally obvious divisions from other classes. Speaking from their decentred spaces in the social hierarchy, they were asking for recognition while remaining in Kipling's figuration as part of a distinctive social group with plain limitations to their view.

Jethro Brown, in *The New Democracy* (1899), thought that representative government should ideally consist of a 'political system under which the people rule through chosen deputies over whom they exercise a real and constant control.'[7] But what was such control? And what philosophical and psychological issues were involved in the notion that a man could rule through another? Could one, at any rate, speak for another, especially when not part of the same group? *Barrack-Room Ballads* shaped the question of a representative democracy as it was absorbed into a structure of power – the British Army – where democracy could have little place. But Kipling was concerned with the poet's capacity to speak for others all the same: and his preoccupation determined imagined scenes even to the point where he obliquely seemed to dramatise the representative intentions of the volume as a whole. Easily seen crudely as evidence of the embeddedness of late nineteenth-century racism, 'Gunga Din' more subtly mapped out the business and problems of recovering someone else's lost history, which was Kipling's task in the collection as a whole. Told from the point of view of another Tommy Atkins, 'Gunga Din' recalls the heroism and death of an Indian water-bearer during the siege of Delhi, ending with the British soldier's admission that, despite his failings, the water-carrier deserved respect. 'By the livin' Gawd that made you,' he declares, with words that have become proverbial, 'You're a better man than I am, Gunga Din!' (lines 84–5). The poem celebrated a marginalised man celebrating a marginalised man, and through that it reminded the reader of the alleged purposes of the volume as a whole and its troubles. Kipling's dedication had asked about the reliability of one man's account of, and belief about, another. Listening to the speaker of 'Gunga Din' retelling an obscure history of an individual nearly lost to human records, the monologue was an emblem of *Barrack-Room Ballads* and a distinctive, quiet, but self-conscious invitation to think about what verity was possible in speaking for someone else.

Vocal colour, the lively demotic of Kipling's speakers, inscribed individuality with the contours of colloquial and regional speech. But even as that discourse proposed spoken language as a personal possession, it offered at the same time *types* of human being where language was not personal but a common signifier of specific classes and groups. Challenges of representation; of attending to nearly lost voices; of adjudicating between the individual and the collective through the shape of poetic language; of discerning what was meant in human testimonies as they were mediated through voices: the late Victorian dramatic monologue transacted, in imaginative form, with some of the implications of John Stuart Mill's influential belief in representative government before the Second Reform Act. In the age of electoral transformation, such government was, as Mill put it in *Considerations on Representative Government* (1861), the only acceptable manner of national administration. '[Completely] popular government', Mill said, 'is the only polity which can make out any claim' to be 'practicable or eligible', and to be attended by 'the greatest [number] of beneficial consequences, immediate and prospective'.[8] But whether one person could represent another or speak for them, what 'completely popular government' meant in philosophical (to say nothing of practical) terms, were not questions easy to answer. In decades distinctive in the accelerating pace of electoral change, ideas about how to speak for those not oneself – about how to represent their views, how to bear the moral responsibility of so doing, how to resist oversimplifying, how to discern some form of majority opinion among diversity – mattered not only for the arguments about the nature of nineteenth-century polity. Reconceived in the domain of the aesthetic, they mattered for the verse which contemplated human testimonies mediated through the words of others.

Michael Field's first volume of poetry, *Long Ago* (1889), attended to precarious, mediated voices too. And it extended Kipling's anxiety about fidelity to those represented by allowing the reader to observe candidly the fiction involved in imagining the voices of others. The ventriloquisation, on this occasion, happened across time. *Long Ago*, a succession of poems as if spoken by Sappho, did not disguise the provisional nature of its fabrication of the ancient Greek poetess, even as it cherished the imagined presence it created. Real fragments of Sappho's verse headed the brief lyrics, reminding the reader that she survived in ruins, and that she was re-invented as a fantasy predicated on the smallest of empirical remnants. 'Though in unfathomed seas I sink',

Long Ago ended, with a dream of Sappho's final death song before she plunged suicidal into the sea:

> Men will remember me, I think,
> Remember me, my King, as thine;
> And must I take a shape divine
> As thine immortal, let me be
> A dumb sea-bird with breast love-free,
> And feel the waves fall over me.[9]

The Ovidian lines yearned for remembrance, but, so doing, they shyly pointed to *Long Ago*'s inability assuredly to recollect Sappho, to 'represent' her properly. Contemplating her transformation into a 'dumb sea-bird', Sappho signalled that she would always be known to futurity under conditions of alteration, oddly inaudible for a poet. With mysterious strength and grace, it may be, she would live into the modern world. But she would always be as broken as 'love' was broken across 'fall over' (line 21) and, forever half a myth, a figure whose life could be imagined not ascertained.

A volume in part about distant testimonies, and implicitly about the distance between testimony and testifier, *Long Ago* attempted to reach back chronologically through time as the new technologies of sound (the telegraph, radio and telephone) reached across space, to catch something of the presence of the far-removed. Written in English, *Long Ago* endeavoured to project a new voice for the Greek Sappho as if, in this act of cultural transfer, the extent of her distance from the present day was marked even in the words she 'spoke'. Hailing the 'recovery' of the nearly absent history of a woman artist, *Long Ago* suggested a genealogy of poetic predecessors whom Michael Field implicitly hailed as their own. But precious recoveries depended on the plausibility of fiction. Representing someone else's view was a matter of illusion, a well-meaning deception. Musing on the task of speaking for someone in these problematic terms, *Long Ago* still celebrated the redemptory purposes of giving Sappho a new voice even as it was self-evidently an invented one. But others elsewhere tested and ironised the capacity of the monologue to speak up for the unrepresented in devastating ways. Recounting voices of exceptional unpleasantness, fashioning dramatic writing to repudiate the views and lives of others, John Davidson's verse made plain the limits of the democratic in the discomfort of the reading experience. Deriving energy from an ironisation of writing that endeavoured to return the neglected to literary consciousness, Davidson's ventriloquisations defied their readers, in the emotional force of the verse, and asked them to be discriminating about who, exactly, might be given a hearing. 'If all mankind minus one, were of one opinion', J. S. Mill said in *On Liberty* (1859), 'and only one person were of the contrary opinion, mankind would be no more justified in silencing that one person, than he, if he had the power, would be justified in silencing mankind.'[10] Yet, in the dim afterglow of Mill's optimism, Davidson allowed the reader to feel, however faintly, what the desire to silence might feel like. Sometimes Davidson represented simply the unadmirable, the life destroyers. 'A Woman and Her Son', playing with Browning's resurrectionist poetics, posed a narrow-minded Christian mother with her hard son – 'Hard as the nether millstone'[11] – who admonishes his mother's ungenerous faith even on her deathbed. Both 'were bigots', this account of impoverished human relations concluded, with a candid intervention Browning's monologues never used: 'fateful souls that plague / The gentle world' (lines 249–50). What was 'gentle' about it, the text did not say. Neither speaker was edifying, neither redeemed by sympathy; but they were of a different order from the speaker of 'The Testament of a Vivisector' (1901), a monologue glancing at another feature of Browning's work in the form of his appalled horror at vivisection.[12] Davidson figured the thoughts of a man experimenting on a living horse. But could such a matter really be admitted to verse? Did such lives deserve a hearing? Raskolnikov's dream of a mare savagely beaten to death in *Crime and Punishment* was the closest the nineteenth century came elsewhere to Davidson's breathtakingly awful scene. 'I ransomed Dobbin', the speaker remarks seemingly without moral consciousness, searching the living body for an understanding of the springs of vitality,

> pitying his case,
> He seemed so cheerful maugre destiny.
> Enfranchised in my meadow, all his hours
> Were golden, till the end with autumn came,
> Even while my impulse sundered husk and shell
> Of habit and utility. Two days
> He lay a-dying, and could not die. Endowed
> With strength, affection, blood, nerve, hearing, sight;
> Laden with lust of life for the behoof
> Of Matter; gelded, bitted, scourged, starved, dying –
> Where could the meaning of the riddle lie? (lines 131–41)

Here was a robust defiance of the tragic, a refusal to allow poetry to be in any way ennobling of suffering, or to recover even the dimmest of moral rewards in the aesthetic representation of pain. Urging the reader to wonder what the moral identity of such a speaker could be, Davidson experimented with his audience's patience – as the speaker brutally prolonged the horse's anguish – to hear out the voice of a man who tested tolerance. The vivisector's language, with its syntax crumpled like a ruined body across the lines, fittingly pulls out the stark ugliness of verbal forms ('gelded, bitted, scourged, starved') even as elsewhere words encapsulate with compact precision the alienation of the speaker and his gross business. That carefully placed, ungainly, obtrusive anti-pun on 'behoof' was evidence, even at the most local level, of an insensitivity that pointed to the alien, out-of-place, radically desensitised nature not merely of the speaker's use of words but of his moral identity, his use of life.

Conceptually, 'The Testament of a Vivisector' made the limits of the democratic felt, posing a moral challenge to Mill's antagonism to censorship, to the silencing of witnesses. But the democratic was assailed more openly. About the business of depriving others of their voices, 'The Testament of an Empire-Builder' sketched the mental landscape of human dominance. Proposing a Nietzschean form of heroism, it offered a salute to individual self-assertion and a faith in 'chosen ones' (line 689) possessed of the right of conquest that was bewilderingly innocent of collective moral parameters. 'Some half million of capable persons', a *Times* leader in 1885 regretted after the Third Reform Act, 'who looked to be enfranchised under the Act . . . have been disappointed in their hopes.' The list of ordinary workers, 'Shopmen, shop managers, warehousemen, farm managers, warders, and others, all included under the class of resident employés',[13] which the leader found omitted, belonged to the class of clerks and 'blue collar' workers whom Davidson treated both sympathetically ('Thirty Bob a Week') but also with disdain. 'The Crystal Palace' dramatised a slur on the rights of the suburban classes to gain a hearing, presenting a scene of moral distaste tapped out in language aloof from, and mocking of, the verbal repertoire of the clerk classes. Yet it was 'The Testament of Sir Simon Simplex Concerning Automobilism' that ironised most effectively the democratic, representational promise of dramatic writing. Prophetic concerning the coming of the motor car and its potential to render the train redundant, the monologue described a seemingly democratic form of transport (the railway) against the assertive individualism permitted by the automobile. An injury to hierarchy, the railway was (supposedly) democracy embodied and it was the car that alone spoke of the real truth of inequality. 'Men are not equal', Sir Simon announces, celebrating driving as self-determination:

no two intellects
Are of a calibre; desires, defects,
Powers, aptitudes are never on a par,
No more than fingerprints and noses are.

And on my soul and conscience I maintain
Political equality's as vain
As personal. (lines 191–7)

The words demurely figure what is not 'on a par' by pushing out the symmetry of the next line so that the rhyme word 'are' lies untidily away from it. Denouncing the latent politics of the railway carriage, the speaker is an anti-democrat in a conflictual relationship with the implicit purposes of Webster and Kipling's dramatic writing. He turns the dramatic monologue inside out – and his self-assurance in doing so is awkwardly captivating, glamorously modern. What had for others been bound up with rescuing the marginalised – from Browning's Caliban to Amy Levy's Xantippe – became a depiction of selection, a spectacle of the restoration of hierarchies among those who could or should find a hearing, a case for censorship.

Late Victorian poetry's investment in the potential of recuperated voices could be otherwise challenged. May Kendall (1861–*c.*1931), not engaged with dramatic writing in the form of monologues or dramas, was, nevertheless, attracted by questions of representation and the implications of recovering unexpected voices speaking in their own fantasised words. Kendall lingers now, as she always has, on the outer edge of Victorian verse. Her output was small, her life obscure, even her death date unknown. But her poetry, before she abandoned it for work with the poor, presents in places unusual and comic instances of a late Victorian engagement with lost perspectives and re-imagined viewpoints. Hers was a satiric voice, intrigued most by the humorous possibilities of Darwinian evolution in relation to humanity's claims for development. And, in that, she found opportunity for explorations of unrepresented speakers in a manner caught between serious satire and wry amusement. The jelly-fish in 'The Philanthropist and the Jelly-fish' offers, for example, what now seems like a mock-Hardyesque view of the advantages of not being able to feel pleasure or pain against humanity's perpetual capacity to suffer. This is a lament for the sensitivity of humanity cast into different shape by Hardy's 'Before Life and After' (*Time's Laughingstocks*, 1909). More extensively, the speaker of Kendall's most often-reprinted poem, the 'Lay of the Trilobite', posed the voice of a mountain climber against the recovered, imagined voice of an ancient fossil to produce a different form of evaluation of the human. Discerning a trilobite fossil, the speaker is surprised to hear the creature speak, narrating a life of calm simplicity which is a rebuke to the divided, unhappy existence of modern men and women. The innocence of the fossil – its remembrance of life 'gentle, stupid, free from woe' – precipitates a realisation of the difference. 'I wish', the man concludes, with the obvious moral,

our brains were not so good,
I wish our skulls were thicker,
I wish that Evolution could
Have stopped a little quicker;
For oh, it was a happy plight,
Of liberty and ease
To be a simple Trilobite
In the Silurian seas!'[14]

The poem had few claims to make beyond its satiric ambitions. Yet its comic exploration of the witness of a curious voice suggested how the potentially democratic legacy of ventriloquisation, through an act of aesthetic franchising, could test not simply the boundaries between different groups of men and women, but the borders of the human itself.

Aesthetic franchising, the project of imagining voices-not-one's-own through ventriloquising verse, described an implicit field that was alive with political significance. Acts of imagining created versions of alternative societies where the barriers of who could be represented, of who was entitled to be heard, were potentially in a provocative relationship with the world beyond the page. In those imagined figures, hard political questions about democracy, the debates surrounding representative government and the worth of views alternative from the collective were breathed into verse of individual deposition. The poetry of Eugene Lee-Hamilton (1845–1907) continued to suggest perspectives on the question of perspectives. With bravura historical imagination *Imaginary Sonnets* (1888) – dramatic pieces throughout – figured experiences of the celebrated and notorious whose private thoughts were to the modern world unknown. They changed the sonnet's long history – from thirteenth-century Italy – as a form for personal representation into one apt for imagined ventriloquisation, and posed inquiries about the limitations of individual views in the sweep of history. Lee-Hamilton offered the *condottiere* Carmagnola in 1432, for instance, speaking to the republic of Venice just before his execution; the anatomist Gabriello Fallopius in 1550 on his way to experiment with living human beings provided by the Duke of Tuscany; the last Grand Master of the Templars Jacques de Molay in 1314 speaking to his dead comrades as the flames of execution rose round his feet. Lee-Hamilton's purposes were, like those of the new phonograph, a saving of sounds. '*My spirit stood and listened in its awe*', he said in his prefatory poem:

Beside the great abyss where seethes the Past,
And caught the voices that were upward cast
By those whom Fate whirled on like floatingstraw . . .[15]

What could be vaguely seen could, it seems, be more clearly heard: like a new Dante, Lee-Hamilton proposed to recover from the depths the sounds of the doomed. Yet individual witnesses were interrogated as much as they were proposed, as much as they were imaginarily reconstructed. Offering historical moments perceived from the viewpoint of single men and women, Lee-Hamilton's sonnets elevated individual experience over the grand narratives of history. Yet the testimonies could only be understood, despite that, with that ampler narrative somewhere in mind. Without knowledge of the circumstances of Carmagnola or the final defeat of the Templars, local, personal perspectives missed their significance.

Suggesting what was needed before individual witness made sense, Lee-Hamilton's quirky, scholarly verse saluted personal views and recognised they could hardly be sufficient. Sufficiency: the matter of the adequacy of individual witness lingered in Lee-Hamilton's writing. And the question of the partiality of knowledge which could be derived from individual perspectives was present in his longer dramatic writing too. Here was the most morally uncomfortable interrogation among late Victorian imaginative explorations of the extending franchise and the responsibilities one man might have in accounting for the lives and views of others. Dramatic verse could, symptomatically, pose the reader with the most puzzling of moral conundrums. This is to offer, at one level, merely a cliché about (Victorian) dramatic writing. Yet it is easy to forget that nineteenth-century dramatic verse could peculiarly tempt its readers to make moral choices about those conundrums and to fail to embrace ambivalences. The difficult ethical balance, the tension, as Robert Langbaum famously put it, between sympathy and judgment,[16] had a clear inheritance from Robert Browning and Alfred Tennyson and it survived after them. But the temptation to decide between sympathy and judgment, to make the moral decision, was a distinctive lure of Victorian dramatic writing all the same, as it tried the reader's moral fabric with the seductive tug of belief over knowledge.

Browning's late volumes investigated the reader's inclination to give in to judgment despite facing evidence that seemed to constitute an Empsonian ambiguity of the seventh type. The reconciliation of radically conflicting views was not possible except by ignoring the claims of one side or the other. What, the monologues silently asked, was a reader's capacity for taking the easier route of moral judgment instead of admitting to uncertainties? What, indeed, were readers' capacities for prejudice? In 'Ivàn Ivànovitch', from *Dramatic Idyls 1* (1879), a difficult moral tale exemplified Browning's interest in silently exposing how easily a reader could be tempted to make a decision, to take the less demanding option of deciding one way or another, despite evidential ambivalence. *The Ring and the Book* (1868–9) had been the longest of Browning's essays in the confuting of easy judgments in a narrative which, nonetheless, sustained the desire to make a judgment. Set in Russia, 'Ivàn Ivànovitch' pursued the same preoccupation more succinctly internalised in the reader's ethical speculations. The monologue describes how a woman is savagely slain by a villager as a penalty for allowing her children to die in circumstances of desperation. Is that penalty, the poem implicitly inquires, justified? 'Ivàn Ivànovitch' traps the unwary reader – and many of its first readers succumbed to the trap – into believing rather than knowing, into deciding on the woman's guilt and trying not to hear the counter-claims. Allowing, potentially, the mental process of moral decision to be sensed, 'Ivàn Ivànovitch' offered the chance to the reader of observing what such decisions involved, how far they could be from a stable basis of certainty, how oppositional to other beliefs derived from the same suggestible data. Browning's poem uncomfortably allowed readers to infer how easy it was to oversimplify; how easy, in the context of debates about one man representing another, it was to (mis)judge.

The consequences of conviction, of facing divergent evidence with a will to choose one way or the other, reached provocative form in Lee-Hamilton's most celebrated poem, 'The New Medusa'. Among the most disturbing of late Victorian inquiries into what evidence a person might need to make ethical judgments, the monologue narrates the tale of a man who comes to believe that the woman he loves is a new Medusa, a mass of writhing vipers beneath a human form. As he meditates on this suspicion, the speaker's anxiety mounts: does he hallucinate or is he truly the victim of a lamia-like creature? The poem never allows the reader to know – but it reveals the penalties of thinking one does. In the final moments, the speaker wakes beside his partner for the last time and sees – or the reader is told he sees – 'All round the face, convulsed in sleep and white, / Innumerable snakes'.[17] His response, slaying her with a sword, is violent and unalterable. But it cannot cast out the dubiety that has dogged him throughout the poem. Overwhelmed, the speaker flees the scene to the moonlit rocks above, allowing his monologue to end only with the confirmation of persistent uncertainty: 'Doubt, with his tormentors, came and racked' (line 376). The matter of the speaker's sanity is unresolved. Yet what the reader has witnessed is a matter beyond a local inquiry into an individual's mental stability. In creating the conditions which permit that reader to reflect on decisions made in the starkest of circumstances with uncertain facts, 'The New Medusa' plays out a cautionary tale about its genre: ventriloquising verse, like the 'New Medusa', tempts one to make decisions – to choose between sympathy and judgment – but then to see that such decisions come at the expense of a redemptory acceptance of uncertainty.

The speaker of Lee-Hamilton's gothic tale may act on the basis of a fiction, a delusion; his action, predicated so uncertainly, poses questions about the errors that may lurk in one person's understanding of another. But the dramatic poem, endeavouring to make voices heard, summoned all voices from fictions. Ventriloquising arts invoked the illusion of presence, the phantoms of what Matthew Campbell calls the 'rhythm of will'[18] which, if convincing, were nevertheless conjured, fantasised, *willed*. Browning's trope for his art was that of the resurrectionist, calling up the simulacra of the dead. But the sense of dramatic verse's transactions with the insubstantial, the imagined, was not limited to such claims of authority over the departed. How to imagine someone else's life was a central problem of ventriloquising poetics. And its basis in illusions of other human beings was but one aspect of its complicated, many-sided engagement with the aesthetic and political difficulties of speaking on behalf of someone else, of trying to judge them adequately. Victorian writers' habits of publishing collections of dramatic verse – Browning's *Men and Women* (1855), *Dramatis Personae* (1864) and many others afterwards; Webster's *Portraits*; Lee-Hamilton's *Imaginary Sonnets* – offered a final perspective on verse's imaginative settlement with implications of the democratic: in this case, a shaping of questions about representation en masse. Reading Victorian dramatic verse in its original form was often to read it in groups: to follow one dramatic piece by another, to 'hear' different speakers in sequence or rather seemingly contingently arranged, placed side by side. Collections bade readers feel, in their effort to grasp and recall speakers, a democratic problem: the volumes confronted them with an ample cast which could not easily be kept in the memory or, more importantly, seen as wholes with manageably collective viewpoints.

Browning's late volumes and *Imaginary Sonnets* permitted the reader to feel a little of the problems of identifying coherent views across diversities of opinion. Diversity and colourful individuality were the charms of the texts – but also their implicit provocation. In the labour of reading, the interpretational task of pulling out majority convictions in scenes of such plurality was made experiential. Many are ready to believe, said Jethro Brown, that 'no means exist for securing the adequate expression of public opinion, and the opinion would be of little value even if such means could be found'.[19] How could 'public opinion' be secured for parliamentary purposes, particularly in a way that was useful to politicians whose responsibility was policy and action?

Was there really a meaningful thing called public opinion? What of diversities, differences, changes: public opinions? The difficulties of discerning coherent views across hosts of individuals, let alone of attending individually to and remembering the specificities of them, were glimpsed in the political playfulness of Victorian dramatic verse collections as collections. Each speaker proclaimed his or her individuality and asked to be heard – and in that individuality resided the dramatic poem's primary energy. But neither conversation nor debate was figured. No Millite movement towards conclusions determined an intellectual progress for most of the volumes (there is an argument to be had about *The Ring and the Book*'s relationship to Mill's faith in progress towards verities). In the reader's apprehension of the priority of individual perspectives over the coherence of a collective view the democratic challenge of representing many with few was, more often, glimpsed. 'If every minority had exactly as much weight in Parliament as it has in the nation, there might be a risk of indecision', remarked Walter Bagehot: anxious about democracy's capacity to stall action, his point came out as an embarrassing understatement.[20] In the world of the aesthetic, volumes of dramatic verse made visible a fraction of the difficulty involved in shaping multiple claims into majority opinions, the proper basis for political decision. 'Every minority', the collections seemed to insist, had the stage.

A fascination with collective opinion and communal voices gave new life, in verse, to the ballad, seemingly the possession of a community rather than an individual. Kipling and Davidson, writing ballads, toyed with the illusion of collectively owned perspectives, neither personal nor dependent on the private testimonies of individuals. There was, indeed, a pleasing irony in the title *Barrack-Room Ballads*, which, invoking a collective, folk form of verse, put it to the purposes of preserving individuals' narratives. Imagining others, the poets considered here represented versions of themselves too, playing out performances of private lives. Lyrics and autobiographical poems, including Davidson's fusion of confession and self-dramatisation in 'The Testament of John Davidson', gave to the corpora of dramatic writing companions of more self-reflective texts. Those representing others should not, after all, forget to represent themselves. But they were often complicated self-expressions. Michael Field, secretive behind the persona of Sappho, turned next to the testimonies of works of art in *Sight and Song* (1892). The function of that volume, they said, was 'to translate into verse what the lines and colours of certain chosen pictures sing in themselves; to express not so much what these pictures are to the poet, but rather what poetry they objectively incarnate'.[21] But if this was a deepening of their preference for masks and testimonies not their own, the poetry which followed next ventured into and upset more obviously autobiographical modes. From *Underneath the Bough* (1893), a lyric of apparent self-revelation intrigued the reader with an uncertainty of identities:

Sometimes I do despatch my heart
Among the graves to dwell apart:
On some the tablets are erased,
Some earthquake-tumbled, some defaced,
And some that have forgotten lain
A fall of tears makes green again;
And my brave heart can overtread
Her brood of hopes, her infant dead,
And pass with quickened footsteps by
The headstone of hoar memory,
  Till she hath found
  One swelling mound
With just her name writ and *beloved*;
From that she cannot be removed.[22]

The sonnet hardly allows an easy tracking of identity, a certainty about who is who: it deprives the reader of certainty and wholeness of knowledge about selves just as, in the filigree textures of its words, the final half-rhyme pointedly avoids the satisfaction of acoustic congruence. It is hard, indeed, to know exactly what is clinched in this poem. Is it about a lost part of an inner self, or a lost lover external to the self? What is at stake when the poet speaks of herself in the third person? Whose is the 'name' in the penultimate line? And what complications are added when the reader knows – as original readers could not – that the poet 'herself' is compound, is really 'their selves'? Representing the self is staged as a cryptic statement of identities hard to discern. And if representing the self is hard and mysterious, what indeed of the strange complexity of others?

Complicated testimony had been their starting-point, and that situated Michael Field in the main flow of late Victorian dramatic poetics as I have described it. The 'later Victorian voices' considered here made some of their most culturally resonant and aesthetically innovative declarations when allowing the reader to consider the nature of voices and how a poet and his or her personae might speak on behalf of others. Dramatic verse opened up the largest of questions about who was representable, whether representing others was really possible, whether some should not be represented and about how readers reacted to representations that were fragments of exceptionally complicated lives. These were powerful matters for verse throughout history, but for late Victorian dramatic poetry, they connected with a distinctive political environment. They were peculiarly apt for a state fortifying its conception of the democratic, slowly augmenting its electorate and debating with itself about the implications of representative government, of attending to the wills and choices of diversities, and entering a new parliamentary relationship with notions of 'public opinion'. Representative government as a political practice had further to go by the end of the nineteenth century. The suffragettes and Ireland, not least, made that clear. But the ideas about human representation in the realms of verse, to borrow Matthew Reynolds's formulation of Victorian poetry as complexly political sensitive,[23] were ones that reached their maturity in late Victorian dramatic poetry broadly defined. 'I call Democracy archaic', says Davidson's Sir Simon Simplex:

> just
> As manhood suffrage is atavic lust
> For folkmotes of the prime, whose analogue
> In travel was the train, a passing vogue. (lines 203–6)

Trains were, vogues or not, literally passing, travelling along the ringing rails of change. And Davidson's speaker's 'vogue' was apt in another way, reviving momentarily the echo of its etymology in the Italian *vogare*, to row, a verb caught up with a form of transport mechanisation had already displaced, as the car was replacing the train. Davidson's speaker offered witty rejection, possessed of the seductive charm of certainty. But if the genre in which he spoke was never so single-minded about democracy, it was also one remarkably alert to the very substance of his irascible pronouncements. Dramatic monologues and the span of nineteenth-century ventriloquising verse were caught up with ideas – assenting, critical, anxious, provocative – about representing others, however much, at the broadest level, they saluted a simple democratic principle in figuring non-authorial viewpoints. This was verse exploring anew an ancient theme of how men and women could be caught in language that was adequate to human complications and changefulness. But, in its own day, here also was verse in a suggestively searching relationship with the intellectual implications of a developing franchise, with all its queries about the individual view and the difficulties of taking it into account. Rarely had poetry, with its exceptional capacity to simulate the presence of speaking human voices, seemed more like a parliament about a parliament.

Notes

1. F. R. Leavis, *New Bearings in English Poetry: A Study of the Contemporary Situation* (Harmondsworth: Penguin, 1972), p. 4.

2. John Drinkwater, *Victorian Poetry* (London: Hodder and Stoughton, [1923]), p. 7.
3. I reference the most easily accessible of this poet's work, *Portraits and Other Poems*, ed. Christine Sutphin (Peterborough, Ontario: Broadview, 2000). All further quotations from Webster's poetry are from this edition.
4. See chapter 1 of *Crime and Punishment*.
5. See, for instance, Tennyson's 'St Simeon Stylites' (written 1833, published 1842) and Browning's 'Porphyria's Lover' (1836).
6. Rudyard Kipling, *The Complete Verse*, revised edition (London: Kyle Cathie, 2006), p. 315. All further quotations from Kipling's poetry are from this edition.
7. W. Jethro Brown, *The New Democracy: A Political Study* (London: Macmillan, 1899), p. 15.
8. *The Collected Works of John Stuart Mill*, General Editor John M. Robson, 33 vols. (Toronto: University of Toronto Press, 1963–91), vol. XIX, p. 404.
9. Lines 15–21; Michael Field, *Long Ago* (London: Bell, 1889).
10. J. S. Mill, *Collected Works*, vol. XVII, p. 227.
11. Line 36; *The Poems of John Davidson*, 2 vols. (New York: Gordon, 1977). All further references to Davidson's poetry are from this edition.
12. See, for instance, 'Tray' in *Dramatic Idyls*, first series (1879).
13. *The Times*, 6 October 1885, p. 9, column 2.
14. Lines 49, 65–72. I refer to an easily accessible edition of this poem: *Victorian Women Poets: An Anthology*, ed. Angela Leighton and Margaret Reynolds (Oxford: Blackwell, 1995).
15. Lines 1–4; Eugene Lee-Hamilton, *Imaginary Sonnets* (London: Stock, 1888), p. 28.
16. See Robert Langbaum, *The Poetry of Experience: The Dramatic Monologue in Modern Literary Tradition* (London: Chatto & Windus, 1957).
17. Lines 337–8; Eugene Lee-Hamilton, *The New Medusa and Other Poems* (London: Stock, 1882).
18. See Matthew Campbell, *Rhythm and Will in Victorian Poetry* (Cambridge: Cambridge University Press, 1999).
19. Brown, *The New Democracy*, p. vi.
20. Walter Bagehot, 'Parliamentary Reform' (1859) in *Essays on Parliamentary Reform* (London: Kegan Paul, Trench, 1883), p. 51.
21. Michael Field, *Sight and Song* (London: Bell, 1892), p. [v].
22. Michael Field, *Underneath the Bough* (London: Bell, 1893).
23. See Matthew Reynolds, *The Realms of Verse: 1830–1870: English Poetry in a Time of Nation-Building* (Oxford: Oxford University Press, 2001).

Chapter 39

Modernist and modern poetry: an overview

JASON HARDING

At the turn of the twentieth century, English poets might have been expected to take note of the clamour for political and sexual reform, or to gauge the effects of a period of unprecedented urbanisation and technological change. However, when Robert Bridges succeeded Alfred Austin as Poet Laureate in 1913, his intricately crafted poetry appeared less preoccupied by the need to confront modernity than by his meticulous study of classical quantitative metres. If a younger generation of poets, launched in 1912 by Edward Marsh's popular 'Georgian' anthologies, extended the subject matter and idioms of modern English poetry, their innovations were mild in comparison to the Modernist revolt inspired by the European avant-garde. Marinetti's Italian Futurist manifestos, for example, proposed a complete break with the cultural past, the dislocation of poetic syntax and reverence for the machine age of cars and aeroplanes. Partly as a response to Futurism's London publicity, the American émigré Ezra Pound organised an 'Imagist' manifesto, proclaiming a radical overhaul of the diction and metric of English poetry, followed by an anthology, *Des Imagistes* (1914). The radicalism of Pound's Imagist school was overtaken by the profound cultural upheaval which accompanied the First World War, dispersing their group momentum.

It was another American resident in London, T. S. Eliot, who theorised a way forward for post-war reconstruction. In 'Tradition and the Individual Talent' (1919), he argued for an impersonal modern aesthetic that selectively re-appropriated those elements of the literary past that could be made to live in the present. Oddly, Eliot's tradition needed to be actively fragmented before it could be inherited. Eliot rejected the extremist pure sound poems of Dadaism and what he perceived to be the debased romanticism of Georgian poetry, in favour of a return to the nervous and turbulent energies of seventeenth-century drama and lyric. His interventions in the advanced poetry coteries of London was decisive, preparing the ground for the 1922 publication of *The Waste Land*, a formidably difficult 433-line poem, complete with notes, praised by Pound as 'the justification of the "movement," of our modern experiment, since 1900'.[1] By the late 1920s, animated critical debate about what was called 'Modernist' poetry sought to identify not only its precise quality, but whether it constituted a reinvigoration or a destruction of English traditions. This chapter concentrates on Eliot and Pound as the poets chiefly responsible for the importation of Modernism into English poetry. The post-Romantic legacies of Yeats and Hardy are considered as alternative formulations of a modern poetic. The 'non-Modernist' current represented by Edward Thomas and Charlotte Mew, and the iconoclastic private visions of Robert Graves and D. H. Lawrence, are more briefly examined. This chapter closes with the regionally inflected modernisms of Hugh MacDiarmid and Basil Bunting.

Donald Davie contended that the break with the past represented by Modernist poetry was at bottom a change of attitude towards poetic syntax. For Davie, T. E. Hulme was the key theorist championing the unduly pessimistic idea, central to Symbolism, that grammatical syntax was inherently 'unpoetical'.[2] Instead, Hulme argued that modern poetry should seek to register immediate experience through a concentration on visual images as 'the very essence of an intuitive language'.[3] According to Hulme, the poet should avoid abstract concepts in favour of concretions, using a delicate interplay of arresting new images and rhythms close to the patterns of everyday speech, in order to evoke a fresh apprehension of lived experience. His polemical attacks on a lyrical afflatus in Romanticism and his advocacy of a new 'classical' poetry obscure the complex continuities his poetic practice shares with nineteenth-century predecessors. In 'Above the Dock', the moon, that mainstay of Symbolism, appears in the metaphor of a 'child's balloon, forgotten after play'. The inverted Romanticism of this homely image tethers the moon's mystical aura to the quotidian. The handful of poems Hulme wrote before his death in 1917 are a slender achievement, significant for the impetus they lent to Pound's Imagism.[4]

Pound himself credited Ford Madox Hueffer's derisory roll on the floor, rather than Hulme's aesthetics, as the jolt which caused him to abandon the archaic diction and well-worn poetical themes of his early volumes. At the time Pound christened the 'Imagiste' movement, he formulated a set of principles for writing modern poetry. His manifesto trumpeted three criteria: (1) 'Direct treatment of the "thing" whether subjective or objective'; (2) 'To use absolutely no word that does not contribute to the presentation'; (3) 'As regarding rhythm: to compose in the sequence of the musical phrase, not in the sequence of the metronome'. Despite the vague platitudes – what poetry of distinction seeks to elaborate verbiage? – and the brash tendentiousness – does *all* poetry composed in a recognisable metre tick with the monotony of a metronome? – these rules issued an Imagist rallying cry. 'In a Station of the Metro' is cited as the apotheosis of Pound's striving for an image presenting 'an intellectual and emotional complex in an instant of time':[5]

> The apparition   of these faces   in the crowd :
> Petals   on a wet, black   bough .[6]

The idiosyncratic typography is designed to shape the perception of these images: the ghostly apparition of faces from the underground gloom calls to mind the arrangement of petals on a dark branch. This chiaroscuro juxtaposes distinctly urban and pastoral images, rich in symbolic overtones. Critics continue to see the epitome of Modernist practice in this grain of Imagist poetry, although viewed in a broader cultural context the vivid superimposition of Oriental imagery – petals on a bough – on to an impressionist cityscape can appear a less radical departure from *fin de siècle* aestheticism than has commonly been assumed.

Perhaps Pound's finest work in a broadly Imagist vein is contained in his 1915 collection *Cathay*, a series of creative adaptations of certain classical Chinese poems derived from the notes of Ernest Fenollosa. These poems are riddled with mistaken assumptions and enact a wilful wrenching of the syllabic verse forms of the Chinese originals. Despite these differences, *Cathay* transmits to English poetry something of the exquisite imagery, concision and subtle evocation of Chinese poetic traditions. 'The River-Merchant's Wife: A Letter' presents a poignant tableau. A student of Browning's example in the dramatic monologue, Pound delineates with admirable tact the nuance, tone and dignified passion of this merchant's wife from the Tang Dynasty – a mask at the furthest extreme from the hectoring persona we are familiar with from Pound's oeuvre.

> You dragged your feet when you went out.
> By the gate now, the moss is grown, the different mosses,
> Too deep to clear them away!
> The leaves fall early this autumn, in wind.
> The paired butterflies are already yellow with August
> Over the grass in the West garden;
> They hurt me. I grow older. (lines 19–25)

There is a lot here that appears slipshod: the awkward repetition of 'moss' and 'different mosses'; the unidiomatic addition 'in wind'; the curious pre-autumnal yellowing of butterflies; a gawky rendering of the conventional verse form Li Po gracefully employs to unfold this *mise-en-scène*. Yet the essence of the wife's loneliness, smothered by the passage of time (symbolised by the moss growing over her husband's footprints), is conveyed by the halting line which registers her sight of 'paired butterflies': 'They hurt me. I grow older.' In moments like this, Pound's Imagist principles found their concrete embodiment.

Hilda Doolittle was the discovery of Pound's *Des Imagistes* anthology. The 'Hellenic' themes of her lapidary imagist poems are fraught with ambivalence, poised between submission to, or resistance towards, overpowering forces.[7] In 'Hermes of the Ways' the 'Dubious, / Facing three ways' (lines 16–17) winged messenger appears hermetically on the borderlines of sea, shore and forest. This pagan god, as fleet-footed as the wind which envelops the persona of the poet ('it whips round my ankles!' (line 29)), intensifies an uncertainty about how to define one's position: arguably a reflection of Doolittle's (or androgynous 'H.D.' as she was known) anxiety about her social-sexual identity. Shy, delicate line-breaks edge across physical and psychic boundaries – 'you have waited, / where sea-grass tangles with / shore-grass' (lines 52–4). At times, H.D.'s poetry offers a sharp riposte to masculine presumption, as in the imagined reproach Eurydice delivers to her husband Orpheus – 'so for your arrogance / I am broken at last, / I who had lived unconscious, / who was almost forgot' (lines 11–14; 'Eurydice'). The other male poet present at the launch of Imagism, Doolittle's sometime husband, Richard Aldington, also wrote self-consciously laconic poems on 'Hellenic' themes, but his free verse lacks the rhythmical subtlety and metaphorical reach of H.D.'s best work. The anger of his war poetry colours the insipidity of his Imagist style. The same is true of Ford. The writer Pound praised as 'the stylist' who impressed upon *les jeunes* the 'importance of good writing as opposed to the opalescent word',[8] was a more exacting critic of poetry than practitioner. Although Eliot described *Antwerp*, Ford's wartime lament for Belgian refugees as 'the only good poem I have met with on the subject of war',[9] his poetry was frequently hamstrung by an obtrusive use of rhyme. He was a conversational 'impressionist' not a terse imagist. Herbert Read's collection *Naked Warriors* (1919) deserves an honourable mention for the angular imagism of sequences depicting battle experience, but the dry intellectualism of his interwar 'metaphysical' poetry suffers from a lack of rhythmical variety necessary to carry the burden of ideas.

The technical hygiene of Pound's Imagist principles had an important impact on modern English poetry. Fortunately, however, his strictures were absorbed and then outgrown. A proscriptive doctrine rejecting discursive and metrical articulation forsook far too much. Pound moved forward from Imagism to the dynamic Vorticist stage of his career, and beyond to *The Cantos*. H.D. also exhibited development. Her later long poems meditate on crisply presented states of mind, especially the emotion of passionate love. Her ambitious *Trilogy*, composed during World War Two, bears comparison with *Four Quartets*, offering visions of spiritual renewal amidst the ruins of bombed London (mythopoeic insight reveals artefacts as numinous as those found in ancient ritual). Yet the music of H.D.'s fast-paced short stanzas never quite breaks free of the constriction of the tenets of Imagism. Eliot summed up the accomplishment of Imagism as 'critical rather than creative', eclipsing the excesses of Victorian style.[10]

According to Pound, Eliot had modernised himself on his own before he arrived in London. His contemporary models were French. A reading of Arthur Symons's *The Symbolist Movement in Literature* opened his eyes to a range of French poets writing in the wake of Charles Baudelaire; in particular, to the ironic poses of the dandy Jules Laforgue. The opening poem of his first collection, *Prufrock and Other Observations* (1917), flaunts Laforguean traits. The title of 'The Love Song of J. Alfred Prufrock' sets in opposition the incongruous associations of a 'love song' (which fails to get sung) with so unromantic a protagonist as J. Alfred Prufrock. The opening startles with sheer audacity:

> Let us go then, you and I,
> When the evening is spread out against the sky
> Like a patient etherised upon a table . . .[11]

It is customary to explain these lines in relation to Eliot's interest in the 'metaphysical conceit', but the figure is less a wittily ingenious parallel which sustains an argument than a surrealist gesture – an astonishing visual analogy which does not depend upon logic for its emotional effect. Eliot's precocity is breathtaking, the opening gambit of a young poet supremely confident of his voice. The poem re-inflects the meditations of those solitary *flâneurs* who people nineteenth-century French poetry. Baudelaire's desolate sense of isolation in the modern city is seasoned by Laforgue's penchant for wistful, languorous observation:

> Shall I say, I have gone at dusk through narrow streets
> And watched the smoke that rises from the pipes
> Of lonely men in shirt-sleeves, leaning out of windows? (lines 70–2)

The effect may be imagistic, but 'The Love Song of J. Alfred Prufrock' strikes deeper chords than Imagism. For the poem is a voyage of metrical discovery:

iambic gusts of desire are checked by sudden irregularities, indicative of a crippling loss of nerve in the presence of alluring but threatening women:

> We have lingered in the chambers of the sea
> By sea-girls wreathed with seaweed red and brown
> Till human voices wake us, and we drown. (lines 129–31)

The faltering anapaest 'We have língered' gives way to the assonantal erotic caress of iambs 'By séa-girls wréathed', before the expressive terminal pause of the closing line, after which Prufrock, awakened to society by 'human voices', drowns. Eliot became embroiled in contemporary debate about the unpoetical nature of free verse, but his art was a virtuoso display of consummate craft. The triumph of 'The Love Song of J. Alfred Prufrock' is intimate with its gestural phrasing; with its intermittent use of plangent rhymes; with its repetitions, ebbs and flows, and caesurae, whose counterpointed variations from the norms of accentual verse is misleadingly called 'free verse'.

By 1918, when free verse had become the vehicle for every aspiring Imagist, Eliot and Pound went back to school to the sculptural rhymes of Théophile Gautier's quatrains. The atmosphere of the distastefully witty quatrain poems Eliot collected in *Poems* (1920) darkens his tone: the invitations to prejudice are less forgiving and the satire is more biting – possibly the venting of a repressed fury over his wife's affair. The obliquely allusive air of these poems is thick with sexual intrigue. 'Burbank with a Baedeker: Bleistein with a Cigar' is a case in point. The poem's epigraph is a dense collage of allusions, all connected in some way or another with the great intertextual echo-chamber of Venice; for American readers of Henry James, a magnificent backdrop for European decadence. While the cultivated Jamesian should recognise a reference to Shakespeare's *Othello* – 'Goats and monkeys!' – even a visitor armed with a Baedeker might be forgiven for failing to decode the Latin inscription on a painting hanging in the Ca d'Oro. These displays of tourist knowledge mimic the disorientation felt by American pilgrims to Europe's thickly textured cultural sites, not least 'Bleistein', whose cultural pedigree is listed in abbreviated form: 'Chicago Semite Viennese' (line 16). The incitements implicit in this ethnic melting pot are intensified by abruptly splicing the architectural treasures of the Grand Canal with a snapshot of alien wealth:

> Declines. On the Rialto once.
>   The rats are underneath the piles.
> The Jew is underneath the lot.
>   Money in furs. The boatman smiles . . . (lines 21–4)

Notwithstanding a deliberate splintering of propositional syntax – creating uncertainty around the speaker of these lines and their interconnection – the quatrain's structure contemptuously implies that on this comparative rhetoric Jews (here allusion nods to the Venetian Shylock) are *beneath* disease-carrying vermin. The anti-Semitism is unmistakable, although it makes a huge difference whether one chooses to interpret these lines as a sly but complex compression of racist stereotypes (as Anthony Julius does), or as a caricature of the prejudices of Burbank (as Craig Raine contends), an American aesthetic snob in the Jamesian mould.[12]

Pound's experiments with quatrains issued in *Hugh Selwyn Mauberley* (1920): his testy farewell to London. While Eliot's broken-backed quatrains made notable use of enjambment to reposition rhymes at the beginning of lines, Pound makes full use of 'end weight' for the purposes of calculated satiric bathos:

> Conduct, on the other hand, the soul
> 'Which the highest cultures have nourished'
> To Fleet St. where
> Dr Johnson flourished;
>
> Beside this thoroughfare
> The sale of half-hose has
> Long since superseded the cultivation
> Of Pierian roses. (Section XII: lines 21–8)

F. R. Leavis was inclined to see such lines as a compelling diagnosis of the fate of 'minority culture' in a 'mass civilization',[13] but this is to place too much value on the sort of one-eyed cultural history that compares the worst of the present with the best of the past. Dr Johnson – the professional writer par excellence, who did not share Pound's idealism about patronage of the arts – is certainly an odd witness to call to support this thesis about London's rampant commercialism. And yet, *Hugh Selwyn Mauberley*'s sweeping denunciation of British culture from the age of Victoria to the post-war period laid a foundational myth of Modernism. Much depends on how far one sees this critique as dramatic monologue or thinly veiled autobiography. 'I'm no more Mauberley than Eliot is Prufrock', remarked Pound in a letter, unleashing more questions than answers,[14] for aspects of Eliot's hypersensitivity reappear transfigured in Prufrock, and it is natural to wonder about the slippage of idiom that has the effete poetaster 'Mauberley' refer to the First World War as a scrap involving 'an old bitch gone in the teeth' (line 90). Examination of the detail of the libellous vignettes contained in this sequence raise doubts about the efficacy of Pound's didacticism, which often seems preoccupied with exorcising those very faults exhibited by his own false starts (Pre-Raphaelite neo-medievalism and nineties Aestheticism) and litters the poem with a fair amount of frustratingly opaque allusion.

Although he came to resent British culture, Pound left an indelible mark on English poetry; not only through the example of his subtlety of rhythm, but indirectly through his influence on Eliot. The author of *Hugh Selwyn Mauberley* sorted through the jumble of drafts – discarding what he felt was extraneous baggage – published as *The Waste Land*. We are indebted to Pound for the structure of this sequence which exemplifies his post-Symbolist 'ideogrammatic method', placing multifarious poetic fragments in apposition without discursive narrative connections. *The Waste Land* is a medley of dramatic monologues, discrete lyrics, satiric quatrains, snatches of elegy, juxtaposed with syntactical lapses and yawning hermeneutic gaps. This experimental poetry frustrated generic expectations and demanded a new form of attention. After decades of critical exegesis, it is easy to forget how formless this method could appear to contemporaries. The notes Eliot added to the first book edition were devoured by readers. Under the cover of learned pedantry (at times clearly a parody of it), these notes helpfully identified recondite allusions. Yet Eliot's disingenuous remark that Jessie Weston's *From Ritual to Romance* would 'elucidate the difficulties' of the poem was seized upon as the solution to a cryptic work.[15] Eliot later retreated from claims that *The Waste Land* was representative of 'the disillusionment of a generation' ('I may have expressed for them their own illusion of being disillusioned' came the tart retort).[16] By then, critical orthodoxies had taken root which explicated a mythopoeic epic constructed around the symbolism of Weston's Grail legends. The texture of the poem is more loose-knit than this analogy suggests, offering fragile local recurrences and fugitive narrative developments. Michael Levenson has demonstrated the tension in the beginning of the poem between continuity and discontinuity:[17]

> April is the cruellest month, breeding
> Lilacs out of the dead land, mixing
> Memory with desire, stirring
> Dull roots with spring rain.
> Winter kept us warm, covering
> Earth in forgetful snow, feeding
> A little life with dried tubers.
> Summer surprised us, coming over the Starnbergersee (lines 1–8)

The repetitive phrasal syntax of the lines ending with participles ('breeding', 'mixing', 'stirring', 'covering', 'feeding') does the work of articulation, driving the poem towards full stops which check the rhythmical momentum. Seasonal regeneration is arrested by a pained recognition of 'dull roots' and 'a little life'. The sudden interpolation of an unattributed quotation from an unspecified (new?) speaker takes us in a different direction. The German place name is reinforced by later talk of Munich's Hofgarten and of an Austrian Imperial archduke, unavoidably raising awkward questions about the relation of the macabre title of this opening section, 'The Burial of the Dead', to the vitality of civilised life in post-war Europe. The disturbing effects of these lines do not indicate a communal sense of loss and potential renewal – a revamped Holy Grail – rather an awareness of the fragmented, polyglot experience of modern urban society, where miscommunication is inevitable: 'Bin gar keine Russin, stamm' aus Litauen, echt deutsch' (line 12) explains a shadowy voice to an audience that must strain very hard to understand.[18]

W. B. Yeats caught a crucial element of *The Waste Land* when he pronounced: 'I think of [Eliot] as satirist rather than poet.' Yeats lamented the 'rhythmical flatness' and 'monotony of accent'[19] evident in Eliot's travesty of Olivia's song in *The Vicar of Wakefield*, whereby Goldsmith's mellifluous iambic tetrameter ('When lovely woman stoops to folly, / ') is disrupted by the addition of an unaccented syllable and unsettled further by the trochaic inversion in the next line:

> When lovely woman stoops to folly and
> Páces about her room again, alone,
> She smoothes her hair with automatic hand,
> And puts a record on the gramophone. (lines 253–6)

Whereas the periphrasis of Goldsmith's 'folly' dare not mention the pre-marital sex leading to irrevocable shame, the corresponding folly in *The Waste Land* requires no pause for reflection, as the typist stumbles thoughtlessly onward. This episode began life as a series of Eliot's satirical quatrains until Pound scored out twenty-six lines and interlinked the rest as a verse-paragraph. Hugh Kenner thought the outcome a 'great *tour de force*';[20] others have winced at the arrogance which presumes to plumb the shallow depths of the sort of people who eat food from tins. If the animus towards the typist lacks an adequate objective correlative, biographical information is suggestive in light of the passages of marital hysteria dramatised in the poem. Vivien Eliot wrote of the strain on her husband, 'tired out by eight hours in the City, and who fills hot water bottles, and makes invalid food for his wretchedly unhealthy wife, in between writing' which brings us close to the state of mind which observed clerks and typists crossing London Bridge, and fantasised the nature of their sexual relations.[21]

According to Eliot's note, the prophet Tiresias, who recounts the tryst of the typist and clerk, is 'the most important personage in the poem, uniting all the rest'.[22] This assertion of a unifying voice, disguising Eliot's fear of personal revelation, is gainsaid by the final section 'What the Thunder Said'. This hallucinatory apocalypse of 'Falling towers' (Jerusalem, Athens, Alexandria, Vienna, London) and of invading 'hordes' sweeping across Eastern Europe (a nightmare of the Bolshevik Revolution)[23] was composed during a period of recovery in Lausanne. The feverish closing mimes, in stammering syntax, a breakdown of reason:

London Bridge is falling down falling down falling down

Poi s'ascose nel foco che gli affina
Quando fiam ceu chelidon – O swallow swallow
Le Prince d'Aquitaine à la tour abolie
These fragments I have shored against my ruins
Why then Ile fit you. Hieronymo's mad againe.
Datta. Dayadhvam. Damyata.

Shantih shantih shantih (lines 426–33)

The world-mind able to decipher this toppling tower of Babel discovers meaning in the interpenetration of allusions gesturing towards a sexual suffering as purgative as Arnaut Daniel's; a desire for the renewal of love as intense as the poet of *Pervigilium Veneris*; and a pose of melancholy disinheritance as affected as Gérard de Nerval's; all of which threatens to degenerate, in the tumult of grief, to the ferocious polyglot madness of Kyd's Hieronymo. This sound and fury is scarcely to be soothed by the appropriation of a chant, torn from its religious traditions, which marks the ending of an Upanishad. The *cri de coeur* – 'These fragments I have shored against my ruins' – reverberates after *The Waste Land*'s passion is spent.

Much has been made of Eliot's decision to join the Anglican Church in 1927 and his retreat from literary 'modernism' (a term he had never embraced). While it is correct to see a readjustment of values taking place in his prose criticism, it is wrong to see the poetry he wrote after his public profession of Christian faith as 'devotional' in the manner of George Herbert. The suite of poems that comprise *Ash-Wednesday* (1930), in spite of liturgical cadences and the allusions to Biblical exegesis indicative of a new religious – in this case Lenten – discipline, is structured upon essentially the same post-Symbolist techniques that govern the early poetry: the pronouns still denote elusive presences and the poetic syntax is no less a shadow dance upon the intellect.[24]

The same is true of the series of meditative poems collected as *Four Quartets*; a title advertising musical, post-Symbolist modes of articulation: a progressive development, variation and recapitulation of motifs. The theme of mastering, or being mastered by, the medium of language is introduced in 'Burnt Norton'. Strong stresses overturn any stabilising metre:

Words strain,
Crack and sometimes break, under the burden,
Under the tension, slip, slide, perish,
Decay with imprecision, will not stay in place,
Will not stay still. (lines 149–53)

The scepticism of *Four Quartets*' conviction makes it imperative to keep sincerity and irony clearly apart. 'Burnt Norton' maintains decorum through a philosophic and abstract cast of mind. Uncertainties of tone, however, are betrayed in the succeeding poems. 'East Coker' profanes a pietistic honouring of Eliot's Somerset ancestors with the tone-deaf thud of 'Dung and death' (line 46) – hardly an inviting prospect. 'The Dry Salvages' opens with the *faux-naïf* remark – 'I do not know much about gods' (line 1) – which Donald Davie thought would be embarrassing if spoken at a party.

The culminating poem of the sequence, 'Little Gidding', displays a tranquil assurance of style that facilitates virtuoso departures. The section set in the London Blitz after an air raid, in which the poet receives wisdom from the 'dead master', is written in an approximation of *terza rima*. This is Eliot's homage to the tender detail and masterful syntax of Dante's meeting with Brunetto Latini in *Inferno* xv. Other debts, to Shelley's post-mortem encounter with Rousseau in *The Triumph of Life* and to Arthur Hallam's haunting presence in Tennyson's *In Memoriam* vii, are also acknowledged. Above all, the meeting is Yeatsian phantasmagoria, summoning the ghost of the recently deceased poet whom Eliot belatedly recognised as the 'master' of the preceding generation. Once scolded for his pursuit of strange gods, Eliot now honours the wild old poet of 'The Spur' for his intensely passionate 'lust and rage'.[25] Numerous echoes of the astringent later Yeats are heard in the ghost's disclosure of 'the gifts reserved for age' (line 129):

First, the cold friction of expiring sense
Without enchantment, offering no promise
But bitter tastelessness of shadow fruit
As body and soul begin to fall asunder.
Second, the conscious impotence of rage
At human folly, and the laceration
Of laughter at what ceases to amuse.

> And last, the rending pain of re-enactment
>   Of all that you have done, and been; the shame
>   Of motives late revealed, and the awareness
> Of things ill done and done to others' harm
>   Which once you took for exercise of virtue. (lines 131–42)

Eliot was no different from everyman in having grounds for shame. This passage cannot be read, however, as Christopher Ricks suggests, as tacit redemption of his anti-Semitism: one of the 'things ill done'.[26] The lines are spoken with Yeats's life-affirming pride and not Eliot's accent of Christian humility. Perhaps the most telling moment of this 'dead patrol' with the Yeatsian alter ego is revealed in the admission: 'Too strange to each other for misunderstanding' (line 104).

Critics often patronise early Yeats as a dreamy minor poet of the Celtic Twilight who declined to come to terms with the modern world ('The Lake Isle of Innisfree' is cited as evidence); that is, until he emerged modernised following the winters he spent in a Sussex cottage with Pound, during the latter's Imagist phase. Yeats's oeuvre will not bear out this assertion that the master relearned his craft from the amanuensis. His poetic apprenticeship during the 1890s, in dialogue with members of the London Rhymers' Club, instilled a lifelong preoccupation with the technically perfect lyric wrought in strong syntax and with sonorous metre and rhyme. (Pound's free verse, according to Yeats, struggled to get 'all the wine into the bowl'.)[27] The slow ripening of Yeats's mature style is on display in the poetry itself. Successive volumes reveal a hardening of tone: thrilling lines enact the pang of unrequited love 'And now my heart is sore' (line 14, 'The Wild Swans at Coole')[28] and a shocked recognition of the new violence of Irish politics, 'A terrible beauty is born' (line 16, 'Easter 1916'). Yeats assumes a bardic voice in the roll-call of 'Easter 1916' ('I write it out in a verse – / MacDonagh and MacBride / And Connolly and Pearse' (lines 74–6)). His mythologising of the blood sacrifice of the Easter Rising, however, lacks full conviction as nationalist propaganda. The employment of half-rhymes ('not night but *death*' (line 66) with 'England may keep *faith*' (line 68)) is an index of the poet's ambivalence – an integrity of tone which owes as much to English Romanticism as to Irish nationalist ideals (Yeats grafted Shelley's phrase 'excess of love' on to his 'Bewildered' revolutionaries (lines 72–3)). Harold Bloom contends that Blake and Shelley were the singing-masters of Yeats's soul.[29] If Blake drew strength from the axiom 'Without Contraries there is no progression', Yeats's poetry was also energised by an occult knowledge of the conflict of opposites. He engaged with his wife in a steady round of spiritualist sessions. Eliot was sceptical that automatic writing could be ascribed to a 'friendly or impertinent demon'.[30] Still, Yeats's eclectic system of cones, gyres and phases of the moon, privately published as *A Vision* (1926), furnished metaphors and metaphysics for his poetry.

The most carefully orchestrated of his volumes, *The Tower* (1928), benefited from *A Vision*'s cosmology. The first line of the opening poem 'Sailing to Byzantium' – '*That* is no country for old men' (my emphasis) – announces in the ringing Irishness of its grammar and idiom (compare the clipped English of Auden's 'Look, stranger, at this island now'[31]) an intransigent renunciation of nature's 'dying generations' (line 3), figured in Ireland's teeming 'salmon-falls' and 'mackerel-crowded seas' (line 4), as well as a longing for the otherworldly realm of art. The rhyming pentameters of the *ottava rima* stanza take rapturous departures from the normative iambics:

> An aged man is but a paltry thing,
> A tattered coat upon a stick, unless
> Soul clap its hands and sing, and louder sing . . . (lines 9–11)

The emphatic pause after 'tattered coat upon a stick' prepares an enjambed metrical variation, 'unléss / Sóul', superseded by the rising feet of 'and síng, and lóuder síng' – an effect repeated in the incantatory 'gyre' of the succeeding stanza, which gathers the poet into the 'artifice of eternity'. The theme of 'Sailing to Byzantium' is the subject of Keats's great odes: the triumph of the artistic imagination over temporal suffering. Whereas Keats's nightingale appeared and disappeared as naturally as the leaves on a tree, Yeats's golden bird can appear too much of a mechanical contrivance. For Yeats (who viewed Byzantine mosaics in Ravenna, Venice and Sicily), Byzantium was an ideal of perfection, a vision of the Romantic imagination. This much is apparent from the Paterian prose he used to evoke Byzantium in *A Vision*.[32] But Yeats came to feel that 'Sailing to Byzantium' failed to present an adequate emblem of the 'artifice of eternity' (line 24).

In 1930 he revisited this topos in 'Byzantium'. The hectic rhythms of the new vision, interweaving long and short lines, recasts the spacious *ottava rima* of 'Sailing to Byzantium' in a verse-form expressive of a swift intensification, then release from, agonised longing. In the last stanza, mythological dolphins transport the souls of the dead to paradise, disembarking under the dome of the great cathedral Hagia Sophia, whose midnight gong tolls the after-life:

> Astraddle on the dolphin's mire and blood,
> Spirit after spirit! The smithies break the flood,

> The golden smithies of the Emperor!
> Marbles of the dancing floor
> Break bitter furies of complexity,
> Those images that yet
> Fresh images beget,
> That dolphin-torn, that gong-tormented sea. (lines 33–40)

'That dolphin-torn, that gong–tormented sea' is a powerful, haunting metaphor. Both the backs of the mythological dolphins and the resounding dome of Hagia Sophia, rise above the elements in this glittering dream of the intersection and perpetual conflict of the sacred and mortal. The dense symbolism of the Byzantium poems is connected to Irish politics, signalled by the poet's desire to leave behind, or transcend, intractable sectarian divisions ('bitter furies of complexity'). These poems are an admission of the old man's failure to make Ireland a holy land for her inhabitants; a young nation dominated by the Catholic middle class despised by patrician Protestant Yeats.

Eliot praised the 'greater clarity, honesty and vigour' of Yeats's poetry of old age.[33] Paradoxically, this clarity came in the form of masks, impossible other selves, such as the anti-self named 'Crazy Jane'. The provocative bluntness of her response to 'the Bishop' ('love has pitched his mansion in / The place of excrement' (lines 15–16)) is a defiant reassertion of instinctual life against the repressions of Catholic doctrine. In this late poetry, it is not always easy to separate magnificent rhetoric from histrionics. Yeats's adoption of the aristocratic pride of the Anglo-Irish ascendancy – mistaken for nobility of spirit – and his flirtation with eugenics and fascism certainly has repellent aspects. But Yeats's poetry is wiser than his politics. His dejection ode, 'The Circus Animals' Desertion', broods upon the dwindling power of the visionary gleam and the perils of a lifetime's search for the sublime among the unsorted junkyard of ordinary emotions:

> Now that my ladder's gone,
> I must lie down where all the ladders start,
> In the foul rag-and-bone shop of the heart. (lines 38–40)

A lifelong shaping and reshaping of his oeuvre warns against reductively reading any poem as a conclusion rather than as a dramatising of an exigent state of mind. Yeats's achievement resides in all 'Those masterful images' (line 33) born out of this struggle.

The pre-eminence of an Irishman and two American expatriate poets in histories of twentieth-century British poetry led Graham Hough to describe

Modernist poetics as 'a détour, a diversion from the main road'.[34] The prominence that Philip Larkin accorded to Thomas Hardy in his selection for *The Oxford Book of Twentieth Century English Verse* (1973) suggested a return of the native traditions connecting Victorian and modern 'English' poetry. Hardy's 'The Darkling Thrush', written on the dawn of the twentieth century, is full of transitional forebodings.[35] The archaic 'darkling' of the title alludes to the hope heard in the song of Keats's nightingale ('Darkling I listen'), and to Matthew Arnold's 'darkling plain', a twilight world caught between the demise of religious belief and the emergence of Darwinian values. Hardy's 'blast-beruffled' thrush (line 22) breaks into spondaic ecstasy – 'In a fúll-héarted evensong / Of jóy íllimited' (lines 19–20) – leaving the poet's wintry mindscape untouched by 'Some blessed Hope, whereof he knew / And I was unaware' (lines 31–2). This is not an indulgent pessimism, rather an expression of the strangely 'inhuman' detachment which typifies much of Hardy's best poetry. 'The Convergence of the Twain' is an instance: here fate collides with 'human vanity' (line 2) in the form of an iceberg and the *Titanic*. Inventive, intertwined triplets enforce due constraint on the human will.

And as the smart ship grew
In stature, grace, and hue,
In shadowy silent distance grew the Iceberg too. (lines 22–4)

Contemporaries censured Hardy's metric as capriciously gauche, and it is natural to wonder how much of his voluminous *Collected Poems* represents an unquestioned artistic success. The elegies to his first wife, Emma Gifford, have been granted this privilege, since what may appear as prosodic awkwardness is felt to denote honesty in dealing with piquant, melancholy memories. Although Hardy has sometimes been accused of stage-managing Emma's 'voiceless' ghost in performances of a self-protecting solipsism, quite the contrary is the case: her voice in these elegies is inescapably recriminatory. 'What have you now found to say of our past' (line 11), asks the poet in 'After a Journey'. 'Summer gave us sweets, but autumn wrought division?' (line 13) is a discomforting answer. Remembered details of their West Country courtship serves to reinforce the cooling of their sexual ardour into the resentments of domestic life.

The example of Hardy's bleak, weather-beaten mindscapes left an impression on five anthologies of *Georgian Poetry* (1912–22). If there is some justice in Eliot's complaint that the preoccupation of the Georgian poets with English rural landscapes was damagingly insular, he was unfair to damn them as simple-mindedly 'pleasant'.[36] Rupert Brooke's 'The Fish' is a dark, inscrutable ancestor of Ted Hughes's 'Pike'; Edmund Blunden's poems of country life are unmistakably post-lapsarian pastorals; and Walter de la Mare's mastery of nursery-rhyme rhythms do not express escapist fantasies; they are oddly disquieting recreations of childhood intimations of absence and death. In 'The Listeners', the traveller's uncertainty, 'Is there anybody there?', is received as eerily by the 'phantom listeners' as the interrogatives of Hardy's elegies: this world is no less indifferent to the faith and needs of the human enquirer.[37] All the same, set alongside *The Waste Land*, Georgian poetry does appear restricted in scope and lacking in curiosity about technique. The title poem of Charlotte Mew's *The Farmer's Bride* (1916), rejected from an anthology of *Georgian Poetry*, is composed in an experimental, rhyming irregular form. A Browningesque dramatic monologue, the poem narrates a farmer's frustrated erotic desire for his male-phobic wife – 'The brown of her – her eyes, her hair, her hair!' Mew's poetry has an element of decadent poise: unusual scenes of psychic abnormality and alienation threaten to destabilise her verse forms. In 'The Quiet House', cool interlocking rhymes imprison a middle-class speaker in her morbid introversion:

> The room is shut where Mother died,
>   The other rooms are as they were,
> The world goes on the same outside,
>   The sparrows fly across the Square,
>   The children play as we four did there,
>   The trees grow green and brown and bare,
> The sun shines on the dead Church spire,
>   And nothing lives here but the fire . . .[38]

Mew's brooding upon torturing sexual passions and estrangement from community drew praise from Hardy, whom she clearly admired.

Another poet who learned from Hardy's formal experimentation and turns of voice was Edward Thomas, arguably the most modern of the early twentieth-century 'non-Modernists'.[39] He revived English pastoral, modernising with seeming casualness and tentative 'ifs', 'yets' and 'buts', moments as rapt and visionary as Wordsworth's 'spots of time'. In a hiatus at Adlestrop train station, the poet ecstatically tunes into 'all the birds / Of Oxfordshire and Gloucestershire' ('Adelstrop', lines 15–16). The wartime composition of his poems sharpened receptivity to experience, as well as his thoughtful reflections upon it. In 'As the Team's Head-Brass', Thomas rewrites Hardy on the immemorial cycles of country life during the wartime 'breaking of nations'. The speaker's acceptance of fate, watching a 'stumbling team' (line 36) of plough-horses causing the earth to 'crumble and topple over' (line 35), gestures towards Flanders fields where countrymen are going 'over the top'. The calm effects of this poem, compared with Hardy's cosmic ironies, are deftly achieved. In common with Mew, Thomas explores squalls of desperate introspection. In 'Rain', assonantal drops of blank verse mirror a softly spoken death-wish:

> Like me who have no love which this wild rain
> Has not dissolved except the love of death . . . (lines 15–16)

Thomas was a quintessential 'Georgian' poet who wrote poems finer than any which appeared in the Georgian anthologies. Too often judged on criteria erected by Eliot's new poetic, Thomas's reticent unfolding of unexpectedly rapturous contemplations of rural place has been an evergreen presence in later British poetry.

The First World War casts its shadow over Thomas's poetry, but it would be reductive to think of him only as a war poet. He is incidentally one of the 'trench poets' of the Western Front crucial to the myth of the 'Great War' in British cultural memory. Although praised for his bitter realism, Siegfried Sassoon's satirical targets are painted with broad brush-strokes: 'scarlet Majors' who speed 'glum heroes up the line to death' do not allow great scope for analytical complexity.[40] Wilfred Owen, albeit a far more sophisticated poet, pitched his rhetoric equally high. The loss of innocence and the pity of war are tropes deployed to stimulate readers to feel the visceral horrors of trench warfare, but his Keatsian imagery revels in an excess of sensuous wounds. If 'Dulce et Decorum Est' declares that dying for one's country is the 'old Lie', similes figuring the dead soldier's face as 'a devil's sick of *sin*' and his traumas as 'Obscene as *cancer*' or 'incurable sores on *innocent* tongues' (my emphases) point less to the 'truth' of the First World War than to the intensity of his rhetorical address.[41] Not only is straightforward 'innocence' belied by the ferocity of Owen's poetry of pity, but a comparison of 'Strange Meeting' with Hardy's colloquial poem on the guilty killing of brother soldiers underscores the taste for melodrama. Yeats has incurred the wrath of British critics for condemning Owen's poetry as 'all blood, dirt and sucked sugar-stick'.[42] Generations taught to honour the pieties of Remembrance Day view Yeats's critique as an affront. Yet the private soldier Isaac Rosenberg put a quiet, ironical face on his war experience. In 'Break of Day in the Trenches' a 'sardonic rat' epitomises the grim absurdity of their wartime predicament. Rosenberg resists simple accusations of blame. In 'Returning, We Hear the Larks', tense soldiers are surprised by joy when it is birdsong, rather than shells, which falls from the air; although darkness masks the romantic proximity of beauty and death: 'Like a blind man's dreams on the sand / By dangerous tides'.[43] Rosenberg's poetry represents a modest development of technique. It should be recalled that Owen's jarring off-rhymes and expressive stress patterns propelled his attack on the insensibility of contemporaries to suffering on an appalling scale.

Robert Graves's wartime verse sought to recover sense from shock. He came to disown the Georgian elements of this apprentice work for a poetry drawn on more advanced 'Modernist' principles. The acerbic *A Survey of Modernist Poetry* (1927), written in collaboration with the American poet Laura Riding, dismissed Georgian and Imagist poetry as dead movements, unlike the Modernist poetic exhibited by *The Waste Land*, applauded for making no concessions to the general reader. Relatively conventional in terms of syntax, versification and structure, Graves offers fewer initial difficulties than Eliot, although the mythologising of his erotic goddesses can present barriers to the uninitiated. He is at his best in dry, urbane lyrics which contain inner conflict. The austere symbolism of 'Rocky Acres' offers a tough-minded allegory of the terrors and thrills of a cruel world. Graves's departure for Majorca signalled a wilful exorcising of his English, if not Celtic, cultural genealogy. Another visionary writer and exile, D. H. Lawrence, preferred the supposed authenticity of free verse as a pathway to unbridled freedom. R. P. Blackmur, however, lamented the unbuttoned 'plague of expressive form' disfiguring the art of this poetry towards prosaic flatness, the belligerently argumentative, or the weakly sentimental.[44] The emblematic poems of *Birds, Beasts and Flowers* – including the widely anthologised 'Snake' and tortoise poems – escape these failings by capturing in supple, open rhythms the vitality and variety of life. The freshness of his perception is thought-provoking. The late poem 'Bavarian Gentians' riffs disturbingly ('blaze of darkness', 'blue-smoking darkness', 'torches of darkness') on the deathly glow of sickroom flowers.[45] Lawrence's fearless, prophetic risk-taking is Blakean in its refusal to be enslaved by tradition.

The Modernism of C. M. Grieve (pen name Hugh MacDiarmid) exhibits a bold interweaving of nationalist and internationalist traditions. His remarkable 'Second Hymn to Lenin' is an angry diagnosis of contemporary political and economic ills, but the revolutionary fervour of his unorthodox communism is closer to the impassioned Russian poet Alexander Blok than to Lenin. The synthetic literary Scots (Lallans) of MacDiarmid's intoxicated Modernist epic *A Drunk Man Looks at the Thistle* fuelled a Scottish literary revival, even if his later return to English doubtless broadened his appeal. Unfortunately, this feisty nationalist who upbraided Yeats's ghost – 'I who am infinitely more un-English than you'[46] – commended himself to (in Davie's words) 'the malicious lethargy of non-Scottish readers'.[47] Basil Bunting was an English admirer, albeit a more painstaking craftsman. He had been a student in the atelier of Pound. Among his successes are Poundian free translations and adaptations of Latin, Persian and Japanese classics. Nevertheless, his finest work is as rooted as Wordsworth in the north of England. *Briggflatts*, titled after a Quaker meeting house in Cumbria, intones plain, effortful north-country music of vowel and consonant, well characterised as 'gruff, gritty and strong, deliberately modulated and melodious'.[48] The poem utilises Pound's method of 'luminous detail': dramatisations of Viking warriors and Celtic saints illustrate conflicting aspects of Northumbrian cultural mythology. Yet the five-part structure, tracing the cycle of the seasons, has a more clearly defined architecture than the monumental but sprawling *Cantos*. At the poem's winter end, constellations set over the Farne Islands, occasioning the poet to reflect upon a lost love, now as old as the years it has taken tonight's starlight to reach, and illuminate, the Northumbrian coast. 'The star you steer by is gone' encapsulates the poet's difficult task in carving a line out of the ocean of words, but also the wondrous relativity of limitless space–time which dwarfs sublunary love.

> Furthest, fairest things, stars, free of our humbug,
> each his own, the longer known the more alone,
> wrapt in emphatic fire roaring out to a black flue.
> Each spark trills on a tone beyond chronological compass,
> yet in a sextant's bubble present and firm
> places a surveyor's stone or steadies a tiller.
> Then is Now. The star you steer by is gone,
> its tremulous thread spun in the hurricane
> spider floss on my cheek; light from the zenith
> spun when the slowworm lay in her lap
> fifty years ago.[49]

The publication of this Modernist masterpiece in 1966 exemplifies the porous nature of period labels.

Notes

1. *Letters of Ezra Pound, 1907–1941*, ed. D. D. Paige (London: Faber, 1951), p. 248.
2. See Donald Davie, *Purity of Diction in English Verse and Articulate Energy* (Manchester: Carcanet, 1992), pp. 193–201.
3. T. E. Hulme, *Speculations*, ed. Herbert Read (London: Routledge, 1924), p. 135.

4. 'The Complete Poetical Works of T. E. Hulme' appeared as an appendix to Pound's *Ripostes* (1912).
5. *Literary Essays of Ezra Pound*, ed. T. S. Eliot (London: Faber, 1954), p. 4.
6. Ezra Pound, *Personae: Collected Shorter Poems* (London: Faber, 2001). Further quotations from Pound's poetry are from this edition.
7. H.D., *Collected Poems 1912–1944*, ed. Louis L. Martz (Manchester: Carcanet, 1984). Further quotations from H. D.'s poetry are from this edition.
8. *Literary Essays of Ezra Pound*, p. 371.
9. T. S. Eliot, 'Reflections on Contemporary Poetry', *The Egoist*, 4:10 (November 1917), p. 151.
10. T. S. Eliot, 'A Commentary', *The Criterion*, 16:65 (July 1937), p. 668.
11. T. S. Eliot, *The Complete Poems and Plays* (London: Faber, 1969). Further quotations from Eliot's poetry are from this edition.
12. See Anthony Julius, *T. S. Eliot, Anti-Semitism and Literary Form* (London: Thames and Hudson, 2003), pp. 92–110, and Craig Raine, *T. S. Eliot* (Oxford: Oxford University Press, 2006), pp. 164–9.
13. See F. R. Leavis, *New Bearings in English Poetry* (London: Chatto, 1932), pp. 138–51.
14. *Letters of Ezra Pound*, p. 248.
15. See *T. S. Eliot: Collected Poems, 1909–1962* (London: Faber, 1963), p. 80.
16. *Selected Essays of T. S. Eliot* (London: Faber, 1951), p. 368.
17. See Michael Levenson, *A Genealogy of Modernism* (Cambridge: Cambridge University Press, 1984), pp. 168–72.
18. 'I am not Russian, I come from Lithuania, a real German.' Eliot was drawing on a conversation with the Countess Marie Larisch.
19. W. B. Yeats, 'Introduction', *The Oxford Book of Modern Verse* (Oxford: Oxford University Press, 1936), pp. xxi–xxii.
20. See Hugh Kenner, *The Invisible Poet* (London: Methuen, 1960), pp. 142–6.
21. *The Letters of T. S. Eliot: Volume 1, 1898–1922*, ed. Valerie Eliot (London: Faber, 1988), p. 584.
22. Note to line 218, *T. S. Eliot: Collected Poems*, p. 82.
23. In the manuscript draft of line 369, 'endless plains' were 'Polish plains'.
24. For a fuller exposition of *Ash-Wednesday*, see Gareth Reeves's chapter in this volume.
25. In his 1940 Yeats memorial lecture, Eliot quoted the lines 'You think it horrible that lust and rage / Should dance attendance upon my old age'.
26. See Christopher Ricks, *T. S. Eliot and Prejudice* (London: Faber, 1988), pp. 39–40.
27. See Yeats, 'Introduction', *The Oxford Book of Modern Verse*, p. xxvi.
28. *Yeats's Poems*, ed. A. Norman Jeffares (London: Macmillan, 1989). Further quotations from Yeats's poetry are from this edition.
29. See Harold Bloom, *Yeats* (Oxford: Oxford University Press, 1970).
30. T. S. Eliot, *The Use of Poetry and the Use of Criticism* (London: Faber, 1964), p. 144.
31. W. H. Auden, *Selected Poems* (London: Faber, 1979).
32. See W. B. Yeats, *A Vision* (London: Macmillan, 1962), pp. 279–81
33. T. S. Eliot, *On Poetry and Poets* (London: Faber, 1957), p. 258.

34. Graham Hough, *Image and Experience* (London: Duckworth, 1960), p. 56.
35. Thomas Hardy, *The Variorum Edition of The Complete Poems*, ed. James Gibson (London: Macmillan, 1979). Further quotations from Hardy's poetry are from this edition.
36. See T. S. Eliot, 'Verse Pleasant and Unpleasant', *The Egoist*, 5:3 (March 1918), pp. 43–4.
37. Lines 1, 13; Walter de la Mare, *Collected Poems* (London: Faber, 1942).
38. Line 46; lines 50–7; Charlotte Mew, *Collected Poems and Prose* (London: Virago, 1982).
39. Edward Thomas, *Collected Poems*, ed. R. George Thomas (Oxford: Clarendon Press, 1978). Further quotations from Thomas's poetry are from this edition.
40. From 'Base Details', lines 2–3, in Siegfried Sassoon, *The War Poems* (London: Faber, 1983).
41. Lines 27, 20, 23, 24, in Wilfred Owen, *Collected Poems* (London: Chatto, 1963).
42. *The Letters of W. B. Yeats*, ed. Allen Wade (London: Rupert Hart-Davis, 1954), p. 874.
43. Line 4; lines 13–14, in Isaac Rosenberg, *Collected Poems* (New York: Schocken Books, 1949).
44. See R. P. Blackmur, *Language as Gesture* (London: Allen and Unwin, 1954), pp. 286–300.
45. Lines 5, 7, 9, in D. H. Lawrence, *The Complete Poems*, vol. II (London: Heinemann, 1964).
46. From 'In Memoriam James Joyce: In the Fall', line 47, in Hugh MacDiarmid, *Collected Poems* (London: Macmillan, 1967).
47. Donald Davie, *Under Briggflatts* (Manchester: Carcanet, 1988), p. 14.
48. Michael Hamburger, 'A Note', *Agenda*, 16:1 (Spring 1978), p. 100.
49. From 'Briggflatts: Part v', lines 86–96, in Basil Bunting, *Complete Poems* (Oxford: Oxford University Press, 1994).

Chapter 40

Hardy and Mew

RALPH PITE

Victorian versus Modernist

Critics concerned to locate Hardy's poetry within literary history have often focused on rhythm and metre. Bernard Richards stresses the naturalness of Hardy's rhythms and his nearness to Modernism: 'Hardy was evolving the concepts of a poetry that should be based on the rhythms of conversational speech during our [contemporary] period.'[1] Dennis Taylor, in his influential study, presents Hardy as sharing a Victorian preoccupation with prosodic theory.[2] Likewise, Donald Davie correlates Hardy's skills as a metrist with Victorian engineering, with 'the iron bridges and railway stations of engineers like Brunel and Smeaton'. He prefers Hardy's less dazzling and more irregular works, comparing them to Imagism, to music and to craft as opposed to industry. In all three critics, Victorian and Modernist are starkly opposed and that opposition repeats others: between metre and rhythm, mechanical and natural. Similarly, Davie's notorious reservations about Hardy's modesty endorse a literary history favourable to Modernism.[3] Hardy's work, though, does not respond well to this polarised historical account. He is neither a Modernist who rejects mechanical repetitiousness for 'moments of vision', nor is he a failed Modernist who retreats from the high claims of the visionary poet and carries on as a modest artificer of verses. His technical self-awareness and expertise were certainly remarkable but Taylor's elaborate cataloguing of stanza forms tends to give a distorted impression of extreme contrivance with its contrasting moments of 'naturalness'.

If Hardy were read without critics' insisting on a clash between metre and rhythm, their literary historical narrative would become less secure. The same history obscures connections between Hardy and his younger contemporary Charlotte Mew because both writers are caught on the same boundary between Victorian and Modernist poetic styles, placed in one or other camp, instead of among a group of contemporaries. Angela Leighton's feminist recuperation of Mew, for instance, placed her last in a nineteenth-century tradition, following after Elizabeth Barrett Browning, Christina Rossetti and others. Although Jane Dowson and Alice Entwistle have since broadened Mew's reach, praising her 'Saturday Market' for both its Modernism and its links to Rossetti,[4] this is rare. Mew is still positioned and her reputation hampered by critical attachment to the separation of Victorian and modern. Her and Hardy's distinctiveness are lost.[5]

Mew, Hardy and their contemporaries shared a distinctive relation to metrical pattern – they espouse neither adherence to regularity (whether resigned or nostalgic) nor Pound's desire to break the pentameter, occupying instead a position in between. In Hardy's case, this alternative positioning releases him from a false opposition between naturalness and intricate contrivance; it prevents his being seen as either an autodidact engineer or a clumsy though instinctively miraculous modern poet. He can re-emerge less overshadowed by the Victorians and less outshone by the Modernists.

Local ballads

Hardy's first volume of poetry, *Wessex Poems and Other Verses* (1898), includes a number of Napoleonic ballads – 'San Sebastian', 'Leipzig', 'The Peasant's Confession', 'The Alarm' – along with related pieces: 'The Sergeant's Song', 'Valenciennes', 'The Casterbridge Captains' and 'The Dance at the Phoenix'. These martial poems, all ballads or ballad-like in form, are little anthologised but, along with 'The Bride-Night Fire', they are the book's most explicitly local moments – the 'Wessex Poems' of Hardy's title.

Also included nearby in the book are two further ballads: 'Her Death and After' and 'The Burghers'. The first is set in Hardy's Dorchester (Casterbridge) and echoes in plot and topographical details *The Mayor of Casterbridge*; 'The Burghers' evokes Casterbridge through place names – 'Froom', 'Glyd'path Rise', 'the High-street to the West' – and again the story seems familiar. The protagonist learns he is being cuckolded and is given the chance of revenge. Like Angel Clare and Grace Melbury, among many others in Hardy, he must come to terms with a partner's infidelity.

Hardy subtitles the poem '(17–)', and period explains its stylised diction ('"Madam," I said / "Have you the wherewithal for this? Pray speak . . .') as well as its suggestions of Elizabethan drama, as mediated by the Romantic poets: 'Watch with thy steel', the friend declares, 'two righteous thrusts will end // Her shameless visions' – lines that could have been lifted from *The Cenci*.[6] Much more unusual, though, is Hardy's choosing to write 'The Burghers' in *terza rima*. By this, he conveys ballad material and local detail through the verse-form of Dante, whom Ruskin called 'the central man of all the world'. Amidst a sequence of narrative poems, all written in variants of ballad-metre, the *terza rima* is easy to miss and, equally, striking when it is observed.

The collocation of provincialism and high culture produces an effect Hardy sought repeatedly; in *Time's Laughingstocks* (1909), he entitled ballads tragedies: 'A Trampwoman's Tragedy', 'A Sunday Morning Tragedy' and 'The Flirt's Tragedy' are all written as ballads. Similarly, 'The Sacrilege' from *Satires of Circumstance, Lyrics and Reveries* (1914) is subtitled 'A Ballad-Tragedy'. These pieces, like 'The Burghers', reflect Hardy's novelistic concern to show how in 'sequestered spots outside the gates of the world . . . from time to time, dramas of a grandeur and unity truly Sophoclean are enacted in the real'.[7] Crossing poetic genres challenges established hierarchies of genre and form; it corresponds to the novels' preoccupation with the grandeur of people and communities that are systemically disparaged or culturally marginalised. Likewise, Hardy's prose writing frequent juxtaposes the exaggeratedly Latinate, whether in diction or syntax, with the plain and/or the dialectal; this clash jars (and intends to jar) readerly assumptions about relative status.

In this regard, Hardy did not abandon his novels' concern or their method throughout his poetic career. In *Moments of Vision* (1917), for example, 'Timing Her' is subtitled '(Written to an old folk-tune)' and its links to folk song are unmistakable:

Where is she now, O,
Now, and now, O,
Shadowing a bough, O,
Of hedge or tree
As she is rushing,
Rushing, rushing,
Gossamers brushing
To come to me?[8] (*CPW* II, p. 178)

'During Wind and Rain', later in the collection, deploys folk-song mannerisms with its refrains, 'Ah, no; the years O!' and 'Ah, no; the years, the years'. 'Timing Her' is more generous with its O's and Now's, and its repetitiveness appears oddly both compelled and carefree. The recurring lines of 'During Wind and Rain' cause an interruption verse by verse – wrenching away a sweet remembered scene just as it is being evoked and suddenly recalling instead the ruined present. It opens by remembering 'dearest songs' but within the stanzas song-lines rupture links with the past.[9] 'Timing Her' looks foolish by comparison with the anguished complexity that ballad elements lend to 'During Wind and Rain'.

Also in *Moments of Vision*, 'Lines: To a Movement in Mozart's E-Flat Symphony' approaches the same feverish energy as 'Timing Her', while also, like 'During Wind and Rain' declaring its concern for literary effect.

> Show me again the time
> When in the Junetide's prime
> We flew by meads and mountains northerly! –
> Yea, to such freshness, fairness, fullness, fineness, freeness,
> Love lures life on.
>
> (*CPW* II, p. 195)

Each stanza ends with a variation on these last two lines: 'Yea, to such surging, swaying, sighing, swelling, shrinking / Love lures life on', for instance. The effect in 'Timing Her' created by 'rushing, / Rushing, rushing, / Gossamers brushing' seems to be far simpler.

In the Mozart poem, Hardy stages a rise and fall, the five alliterative nouns of each penultimate line racing more and more quickly forward to a point of climactic excitement. This is followed by more reflective final lines in which trochees are replaced by the weightier spondee of 'Love lures'; the line hesitates, changing the intonation of its alliterative links. 'Lures' adds to this by hinting that love might be a trap (for life), before 'on' redirects the feeling, making the delay in the line feel like a morbid stasis which love alone can enliven. Love becomes a force refreshing age as well as youth – age as it remembers youth.

Retrospectively, then, 'Lures' shifts closer to a sense of playful cajoling, of *alluring*, so that 'freeness', which seems in contradiction with 'lures', comes into harmony with it. That love lures you into (a sense of) freedom could be a sad or grim irony. Hardy's lines hint at this feeling in order to show its being surpassed and forgotten: love draws the living forward into freeness, into a delight in the momentary. Indeed, to 'bodings, broodings, beatings, blanching, blessings, / Love lures life on': the blessings arise out bodings, out of fears and dangers. Without love's compelling power, life would play too safe. 'O make the most of what is nigh!' urges the spirit, singing to the tune played by 'The Musical Box' – a poem where Hardy's self-concern makes him deaf to the invitation. What the spirit sang, 'I did not hear in my dull soul-swoon – / I did not see' (*CPW* II, p. 225).[10]

'Timing Her', also preoccupied with grasping the moment, proves to be a comparably subtle work, although it uses different means, from the outset and throughout.

> Lalage's coming:
> Where is she now, O?

Turning to bow, O,
And smile, is she,
Just at parting,
Parting, parting,
As she is starting
To come to me? (*CPW* II, p. 178)

The question mark in the final line comes as a surprise, since the reader probably takes lines 3–8 as an answer to the question in line 2. When the lines turn out to have been a question all along, a new sense of anxiety is generated – this anxiety sets in motion what follows: a sequence of verses full of worry (that the woman may not come, that it's not really her who is coming and that nothing the speaker can offer is remotely good enough for her). A hint of such feelings had already appeared in line 4 because of its central comma: this punctuation does not enforce an interrogative mode, though it fits with it; consequently, questioning floats within the line. Furthermore, the comma separates the smile from the person smiling. Without the break, the line would enjoy her smiling more confidently, and 'Just' in the next line would remain a careless reference to her untroubled farewell. The pauses in line 4 allow line 5 to become edgy too, a tone that the repetition of 'parting, / Parting, parting' swiftly extends.

Features, then, that appear generically determined (the stylised pauses of a folk song) have consequences that counter the associations of that genre (an unselfconscious relation to the feelings expressed). Mannerisms and redundancies in language, which a reader might take to be simply stylistic indicators, become psychologically inflected, meaning that Hardy's ballad asks to be read within the terms of dramatic monologue. The implicit relation between words and music – the text of the poem and the 'old folk-tune' it is supposedly 'Written to' – is opened up to possibilities of interpretation. What has prompted and motivated the speaker to adopt this particular form becomes a relevant thought.

The complexity of the effects is heightened by Hardy's choice of name: Lalage, pronounced in three syllables, flows like Retty, Lizbie, Louie and Louisa, the other women Hardy addresses by name in the poems, but it is more refined.[11] The name derives from the Greek, λαλαγεῖν (lalagein), to babble, prattle (or, of a bird, to chirp); in Horace's odes (I.22 and II.5), Lalage is a girl not yet old enough for love, likened to a heifer and unripe grapes. Like the *terza rima* in 'The Burghers', the name Lalage seems too highbrow for lines 'Written to an old folk-tune'. Yet it is oddly appropriate too: the poem's extreme repetitiveness brings it close to babbling or prattling; the anxiety of the speaker seems youthfully excessive, as if this is calf-love. The name's particular associations allow for highly literary ironies which raise questions for the reader about the speaker's character and state of mind.[12] Meanwhile, the poem's exaggerated form troubles the decorum that the name invokes.

Lalage occurs in translations of Horace, naturally enough; Hardy could have come across the name in Decadent poetry too, in several contemporary Americans or from reading Coleridge.[13] The name brings with it, therefore, an aesthetic atmosphere of cultured feeling and delicate intensity, but Hardy's lines convey anything but that. The poem borders instead on the absurd, and its speaker is exposed to ridicule. Still, and strangely, genuine feeling emerges from the writing's detailing of a lover's ferocious anxiety: 'Yes, she is here now, / Here now, here now, / Nothing to fear now, / Here's Lalage!' (*CPW* II, p. 180) When Lalage, a figure who epitomises love's refinement, arrives in the poem's last lines, Hardy implies that true love can be 'here', in the experience of an unsophisticated person and in the whirl of unruly, undignified impulses he blurts out.[14]

The swing of the tide

Hardy's novels often sought to challenge the tourist's condescension and to establish the authenticity of the stereotyped. His plots and style both work towards these ends. Similarly, in 'Timing Her', the reader's disdain is invited and then rebuked; its apparent naivety tests the reader's self-complacency. Where, however, the novels seek the actuality behind and within what has been pigeonholed, Hardy's poems look to find again what's been forgotten and revive what has become mechanical. The stress is laid more on self-perception (across time) than on misperception (between social groups). So in 'Timing Her', words written to an old tune allow what is 'here now' to become, with extraordinary vividness, here and now. The stanzas' repetitions sound like clockwork ('Now, and now, O'), measuring out the minutes of the wait – timing her – but at the close they are transformed by Lalage's arrival.[15]

Throughout Hardy's poetry, clock-time threatens the vitality of the given instant.[16] 'How smartly the quarters of the hour march by', he writes in 'Copying Architecture in an Old Minster', 'That the jack-o'-clock never forgets; / Ding-dong'. In 'The Clock-Winder', 'The rheumatic clock' is 'Reposefully measuring / Each day to its end', even as the man himself speaks grief-stricken into the darkness:

So I wipe out one more,
My Dear, of the sore

Sad days that still be,
Like a drying Dead Sea,
Between you and me! (*CPW* II, pp. 171–2, 268–9)

There is a busy indifference in these mechanisms, a busyness that breeds indifference. Their never forgetting – to count out the hours – expresses their forgetfulness of the hours, and the ways in which these may truly count.

In 'An August Midnight', similarly, the 'shaded lamp and a waving blind, / And the beat of a clock from a distant floor' form the 'scene' where the speaker discovers four different insects gathering round his lamp. 'Thus meet we five, in this still place, / At this point of time, at this point in space' (*CPW* I, p. 184). The quiddity of this precise, actual moment seems to be realised in quite different terms from the steadily progressing time of the clock downstairs. Yet the word 'beat' allows also for a third sense of time, one in which measure and regularity enable the instant fully to be. In 'Tess's Lament', also from *Poems of the Past and the Present* (1901), Tess remembers:

'Twas there within the chimney-seat
He watched me to the clock's slow beat –
Loved me, and learnt to call me Sweet,
And whispered words to me.

Though there is something suspect about Angel Clare's observation of Tess, the 'clock's slow beat' works to allay fear, both Tess's own, following Alex's treatment of her, and the readers' on her behalf. The courtship was gradual – Angel 'learnt' – and it was shaped by the cyclical pattern of Tess's everyday life in which she 'would rise up stanch and strong / And lie down hopefully' (*CPW* I, p. 216).

'At Middle-Field Gate in February', a later poem, presents passion and structure as more completely at odds with one another.

The bars are thick with drops that show
As they gather themselves from the fog
Like silver buttons ranged in a row,
And as evenly spaced as if measured, although
They fall at the feeblest jog. (*CPW* II, pp. 220–1)

What condenses from the vague mist is 'as evenly spaced as if measured'; its neatness accompanies hints of tidiness and control (in the 'silver buttons') and of prim resolve (in 'gather themselves').[17] This makes a forlorn contrast with old days recalled in the third and final stanza.

How dry it was on a far-back day
When straws hung the hedge and around,

When amid the sheaves in amorous play
In curtained bonnets and light array
    Bloomed a bevy now underground!   (*CPW* II, p. 221)

The abandon of 'amorous play' is glimpsed in the contrast between evenly spaced buttons that gather themselves and the straws that 'hung the hedge and around' – scattered here and there, '*amid* the sheaves' not gathered '*from* the fog'. Rhythmically, too, the present seems mechanical – the first stanza tensely accommodates itself to the demands of a metrical structure, whereas the third moves more comfortably. The first lines initiate this difference: four exact iambics make 'The bars are thick with drops that show'; 'How dry it was on a far-back day' introduces an unaccented syllable midway ('on a') generating a heavier caesura (between 'was' and 'on'). That extra pause fits with the sense, which would divide the line into two halves ('How dry it was' 'on a far-back day'); the line becomes an exclamation dwelling on the past moment.

The poem's penultimate line, 'In curtained bonnets and light array' provides superfluous detail and its equivalent in the first stanza, 'And as evenly spaced as if measured', is also gratuitous. There, though, detail is introduced meticulously. Taut intricacy of description contrasts with carefree accumulation of detail and this corresponds to the clash between repression and delight. Delight, moreover, generates a rhythmic momentum made possible by the sequence of three postponements ('in amorous play' 'In curtained bonnets' 'and light array') before the main verb arrives: 'Bloomed'. The momentum of delay and climax fits the pattern of sexual love and makes a polemical point against the first stanza. Buttoned up and self-contained drops 'fall' just as easily as the bevy now underground – 'at the feeblest jog', in fact. There is no greater purity among the 'custom-straitened', only less joy.[18]

Metrical regularity seems in this poem to go along with a mechanisation of feeling, while irregularity interjects the transgressiveness of impulsive vitality. Dennis Taylor and Matthew Campbell both read Hardy's poetry in these terms – as the slow conquest of rhythm by metre. Hardy's natural voice – the voice of true feeling – is subjected incrementally but relentlessly to the constrictions of ageing and cultural decline. Campbell senses in Hardy the 'metres of the past sounding through the present and more substantial than the present'; he hears 'the sick and limping rhythms of the once vigorous rendered obsolete'.[19] Taylor identifies as crucial lines that are often criticised, those that seem both at odds with the metrical scheme and lame in rhythm. 'We try to read' a line like this, he says: 'according to its natural accents, but the rhythm strains to impose its pattern. The difficulty is functional for Hardy dramatises how his language and rhythm are being influenced by forces outside his control'. These forces freeze into metre what had been rhythmic; in parallel to this, impressions that 'begin as rich experiences . . . evolve and grow stealthily older until they end as "rigid frames", exposed skeletons, jarred by the changing world'.[20]

Hardy's metres are less ossifying than these readings would have it and vitality persists in his poetry both within and through its structures. Several of the 1912–13 poems, for instance, end by rediscovering rhythmical energy amidst and within the regularity of metre. Among these, 'The Phantom Horsewoman' opens with a portrayal of mechanical stasis:

Queer are the ways of a man I know:
He comes and stands
In a careworn craze,
And looks at the sands
And the seaward haze,
With moveless hands
And face and gaze, (*CPW* II, p. 65)

Each line here seems at once motionless and regular, like a clock ticking 'With moveless hands'. Separate actions remain separate, joined up only by 'and' after 'and'. Furthermore, the rhyme pattern starts awkwardly. Until line 4 completes the rhyme of 'stands' and 'hands', the only rhyme is between 'ways' and 'craze' and that falls out of place. After this, the pattern becomes rigidly mechanical (bcbcbc), and both qualities suit the man's condition.

What he sees, we learn in stanza two, is 'A phantom of his own figuring', which is visible here where he saw the woman in real life and is carried by him (the third stanza declares) 'In his brain . . . far from that shore'. The title says the phantom is a 'Horsewoman' but within the poem identification is delayed until the fourth stanza, which is also the last.

A ghost-girl-rider. And though, toil-tried,
He withers daily,
Time touches her not,
But she still rides gaily
In his rapt thought
On that shagged and shaly
Atlantic spot,
And as when first eyed
Draws rein and sings to the swing of the tide. (*CPW* II, p. 66)

The sequence of stanzas is consciously artful, even arch, taking up and playing on the gothic quality of the poem's title. The reality behind the melodrama is gradually disclosed – in the 'ghost-girl-rider' who is and is not 'the phantom horsewoman'. And though a ghost, this figure is less momentary and elusive than ghosts haunting 'The Voice' or 'After a Journey'; the man 'notes' her 'always' and 'everywhere . . . As if on the air' (*CPW* II, p. 66), like a presence interfused, who sings to the swing of the tide.

Up until this point, the stanza's rhythms have never settled into the metrical structure, not least because the man's consciousness has held them back. 'In his rapt thought' and 'And as when first eyed' both shatter the rhythmic assurance of lines surrounding them that refer to the woman: 'But she still rides gaily . . . On that shagged and shaly / Atlantic spot'. The final line, however, transforms this hesitancy; when it sweeps forward so confidently, the broken-up rhythm of 'And as when first eyed' turns into a preparatory crescendo, building up to (as it remembers) the long-distant moment of first seeing her. The singing he heard and still hears follows her drawing rein, her stopping and taking stock. This action makes her majestic; she seems in command of the space and of time, whereas the man, as he ages, has become mechanically subject to it: 'He withers daily'.[21] Her pausing (and her ability to pause) leads to the blending of her voice with the ocean's, a blending that the rhythms and internal rhyme recapture.

'I Found Her Out There', also in the 1912–13 sequence, ends on a similar note. The speaker has uprooted the woman during life and now 'laid her to rest / In a noiseless nest / No sea beats near'. Now 'She will never be stirred', he promises, 'In her loamy cell'. This act of apparent devotion is then turned back against itself and against himself, 'By the waves long heard / And loved so well'. The stillness he secures is a prison and a deprivation. Acknowledging that even his kindness is prolonged cruelty, the speaker finds comfort in a fanciful hope.

Yet her shade, maybe,
Will creep underground
Till it catch the sound
Of that western sea
As it swells and sobs
Where she once domiciled,
And joy in its throbs
With the heart of a child. (*CPW* II, p. 52)

Again the rhythm of the final line gains fluidity from its regularity; metre is one of the 'throbs' the poem delights in; it has the pattern amidst variety, the variety amidst pattern of the sea's 'swells and sobs'. This line too 'sings with the swing of the tide'. To the male speaker, the sea always looked more threatening: 'the ocean breaks / On the purple strand, / And the hurricane shakes / The solid land', the 'Atlantic smites', and the air is 'salt-edged' (*CPW* II, pp. 51–2).

Rest for him (and the rest he provides for her) consist in a sanctuary from violence. For her, rest is found in the sweet unrest of the sea's rhythms.[22]

The ending creates an echo with Hardy's earlier poem, 'I Look into My Glass', where he desires an unattainable 'equanimity'.

> Time, to make me grieve,
> Part steals, lets part abide;
> And shakes this fragile frame at eve
> With throbbings of noontide. (*CPW* I, p. 106)

The heart is as young as it ever was, only confined now within the speaker's fragile frame and his 'wasting skin' (*CPW* I, p. 106). It throbs as passionately as before, even though the body is too weak, too inelastic, to bear the turbulence of feeling. Both poems, then, recall from youth or project forward after death an ideal relation to intense feeling – one in which the heart beats with passion but the frame is not shaken by it. Elsewhere, Hardy locates such uncomplicated feeling in the Dorset past – in, for example, 'Afternoon Service at Mellstock' or in Mrs Edlin's impatience with Jude and Sue's anguished affairs. Her straightforwardness differs from Arabella's directness, because she remembers a time when passion was commonplace and accepted as commonplace, when people joyed in its throbs with the heart of a child.

Polygamous rhythm

This acceptance of passion – as something enviable and recoverable – extends to accepting its mobility. 'Over the Coffin', the fourteenth of the 'Satires of Circumstance', takes this idea to its logical conclusion. Over the body of a dead man, two women confront each other, 'His wife of old, and his wife of late'. The first explains why she has reappeared.

> 'Well, there was a word to be said by me! . . .
> I divorced that man because of you –
> It seemed I must do it, boundenly;
> But now I am older, and tell you true,
> For life is little, and dead lies he;
> I would I had let alone you two!
> And both of us, scorning parochial ways,
> Had lived like the wives in the patriarchs' days.'
> (*CPW* II, p. 148)

That is to say, polygamously – like Abraham, with two wives, or Solomon, with a thousand. 'Louie', a poem from *Human Shows* (1925), but written in July

1913, in the midst of Hardy's grief for Emma, similarly places two rival women together, the 'elect one' and 'Louie the buoyant . . . in gauzy muslin': 'Long two strangers they and far apart; such neighbours now!' (*CPW* III, p. 90).[23] Louie does not displace Emma and Hardy rejoices in that, yet in her gauzy muslin and with her 'life-lit brow' she is erotically attractive to him. Renewed love for one renews love for the other. 'I am forgetting Louie the buoyant', Hardy begins, 'Why not raise her phantom, too?' (*CPW* II, p. 90) There is no sense of betrayal here, rather the opposite – of recovering and obeying a (forgotten) loyalty to 'the other woman'. Moreover, the rhetorical question, in its casual self-confidence, suggests a feeling of elated liberation.

This apparently discordant note from 'Louie' serves curiously to bring out the sense of love triumphant that exists amidst the agonised 1912–13 sequence. 'At Castle Boterel' asks 'was there ever / A time of such quality, since or before, / In that hill's story'? The answer is resoundingly confident: 'To one mind never' (*CPW* II, p. 63). The following poem, 'Places' insists on that moment's lastingness:

> one there is to whom these things,
> That nobody else's mind calls back,
> Have a savour that scenes in being lack,
> And a presence more than the actual brings . . . (*CPW* II, p. 65)

'The Voice' can barely believe that the woman has returned 'as at first, when our day was fair' (*CPW* II, p. 56). 'After a Journey' ends with a bolder assertion on Hardy's part of that tentative hope: 'I am just the same as when / Our days were a joy, and our paths through flowers.' Hearing this, earlier lines in the poem sound firmer. Stanza two's melancholy question, 'Things were not lastly as firstly well / With us twain, you tell?', receive no answer, only instead the stanza's closing, terse shift away: 'But all's closed now, despite Time's derision'. The case seems to be closed, even if unresolved; and the speaker must simply face down the mocking voices of his own questions (recognising the vulnerability betrayed and created by silencing them). Yet, when the poem ends, all this is altered: 'closed' comes to mean 'forgiven and forgotten'. Time made a mockery of their early love but despite that, the love, the past has returned, and this makes a mockery of time. Something is at once completely finished ('closed') and starting again: 'I see what you are doing: you are leading me on', the next stanza begins. One stanza draws rein, the next starts singing again. The pulsating, systolic-diastolic rhythm, which has a regularity of its own, resists the 'unflinching rigour' of time's 'mindless rote' (*CPW* II, p. 60).

'Unflinching rigour' (*CPW* II, p. 64), used of time, widens in application to include the 'laws of men', the institutions that condemn polygamy.[24] Hardy encouraged Florence Henniker to read Shelley's *Epipsychidion* and hoped she would become his mistress; only her 'retrograde superstitions', he said, prevented that. He probably planned to set up a comparable *ménage à trois* with Florence Dugdale, his future second wife, while Emma was still alive. When as an old man, he fell in love with the young actress, Gertrude Bugler, he seemed not to recognise that this conflicted with love for his wife.[25] His novel, *The Well-Beloved*, and his poem of the same name, reflect then Hardy's understanding of love – that it shifted from one object to another and that flexibility was part of its vitality. The 1912–13 poems do not express regret over any sexual infidelity (although Hardy did fall in love several times during the marriage, causing Emma intense pain). Rather, the poetry's remorse centres on his not loving her well. The marriage made them loveless; had they been less strictly bound to each other, they would have been closer.[26]

It is unsurprising therefore that Hardy wrote several poems defending promiscuity and others defending those who forgive infidelity. In 'The Christening', the congregation cannot help delighting in the child brought into church, even though it has been born out of wedlock and the mother is scandalously unapologetic (see *CPW* I, p. 316).

'A Wife and Another', two or three poems further on in *Time's Laughingstocks*, explores this freedom from the position of the betrayed. The female speaker learns that her husband, coming home from war, will meet up with another woman before seeing her; she surprises the couple and finds out the woman is pregnant by her husband. But at this she feels, she says, no sense of victory, only sympathy. 'The ghastly disappointment / Broke them quite. / What love was theirs, to move them with such might!' In response, almost to her own surprise, she acts generously.

> Then, as it were, within me
>   Something snapped,
> As if my soul had largened:
>   Conscience-capped,
> I saw myself the snarer – them the trapped.
>
> 'My hate dies, and I promise,
>   Grace-beguiled,'
> I said, 'to care for you, be
>   Reconciled;
> And cherish, and take interest in the child.'

She leaves them, pretending blithely to the innkeeper that all is as it should be: 'He joins his wife – my sister.' This revelation is followed in the final stanza by a second:

> As I, my road retracing,
>   Left them free,
> The night alone embracing
>   Childless me,
> I held I had not stirred God wrothfully.
>
> (*CPW* I, pp. 319–20)

Her childlessness complicates her motives, raising the possibility of something underhand, as if in promising to 'cherish, and take interest' in the child, she were laying claim to it. Yet that possibility is raised only to be proved unfounded; there's a robust self-certainty in her telling of the story, and a candour in her willingness to leave 'them free' and 'be / Reconciled' – both qualities encourage the reader to take her at her word, and to notice the absence of self-pity, matched by the absence of self-congratulation. 'Grace-beguiled' takes none of the credit, but does so in part to ease the moment – to avoid the awkwardness of the couple's gratitude. That 'Something snapped, / As if my soul had largened' is the more telling and extraordinary statement. The lovers are 'Broke[n] quite' by being found out and now the abandoned wife snaps as well; for a brief moment, you expect rage or revenge. When she, instead, relinquishes her claim, the snap is of release; she breaks out of conventional structures, like a chrysalis opening to let free the butterfly, the soul.

In 'The Burghers' similar generosity follows from the same recognition. On the point of murdering his wife and her lover, the speaker is amazed at their love for each other.

> And then they saw me. Swift her gaze was set
>
> With eye and cry of love illimited
> Upon her heart-king. Never upon me
> Had she thrown look of love so thoroughsped! . . .
>
> . . .
>
> Blanked by such love, I stood as in a drowse,
> And the slow moon edged from the upland nigh,
> My sad thoughts moving thuswise: 'I may house
>
> And I may husband her, yet what am I
> But licensed tyrant to this bonded pair?
> Says Charity, Do as you would be done by.' (*CPW* I, p. 32)[27]

The lovers too are 'passive', like the forgiving husband and 'slow, as in surprise' they walk away at the end. Charity's command creates the fellowship it demands; as he helps his wife escape, the husband realises that he has 'Now grown wholly hers' (*CPW* I, p. 33). Throughout Hardy's work, moonlight's uncertainty allows for a generosity that the clarity of sunlight forbids; here its slowness calms him, preventing hasty revenge, imposing the different law of charity, which works with less rigour and to a more inconsistent, changeable, elastic rhythm. Once more, as the phantom horsewoman drew rein and then sang, so here the speaker falls into a drowse before being slowly led onward, in time with the moon, edging cautiously forward into the unfamiliar territory of love and forgiveness.[28]

Likewise, the opposition turns out to be not so much between love's freedom and marriage's imprisonment as between two forms of constraint: the husband sees himself as 'licensed tyrant to this *bonded* pair' – the bonding of love being as powerful as any tyranny.[29] Hardy revisits this thought in 'The Chapel-Organist', from *Late Lyrics and Earlier* (1922). The chapel elders, hearing of the organist's reputation and fearing scandal, dismiss her from the post. The organist, though she does not deny or feel guilt about her sexual behaviour, claims repeatedly that music is her one true love: 'I have craved minstrelsy more than lovers, or beauty, or gold.' She would rather die than not be allowed to play, and as she foresees her suicide, music's pre-eminence for her is declared again.

> I have never once minced it. Lived chaste I have not. Heaven knows it
> above! . . .
> But past all the heavings of passion – it's music has been my life-love! . . .
> That tune did go well – this last playing . . . I reckon they'll bury me here.
> Not a soul from the seaport my birthplace – will come, or bestow me . . .
> a tear. (*CPW* II, pp. 407–12)

Sex and music have always been different in degree not kind. Music has been erotic for her and she's loved all the tunes: 'I loved Old Hundredth, Saint Stephen's, / Mount Zion, New Sabbath, Miles-Lane, Holy Rest, and Arabia, and Eaton, / Above all embraces of body by wooers who sought me and won!' (*CPW* II, p. 409). The long list (its names like lovers) makes 'Above all embraces of body' sound like an afterthought. The organist appears faithful to the death, to the one thing she finds in many forms, to the well-beloved that plays in ten thousand places.

'The Thing is found': visionary rhythm

Charlotte Mew's 'Madeline in Church', published in *The Farmer's Bride* (1916), may have influenced 'The Chapel-Organist', since Hardy is known to have read and admired the volume. The return to dramatic monologue and the sheer length of 'The Chapel-Organist' were innovations for Hardy, at least as far as his two previous collections were concerned. Hardy's later volumes contain several poems close to Mew's style, in their use of rhyme within irregular stanza structures – 'A Spellbound Palace', 'Snow in the Suburbs' and 'Shortening Days at the Homestead', from *Human Shows*, for instance; 'The Mound' and 'Throwing a Tree' from *Winter Words*.[30] Mew's 'Fame' and 'The Sunlit House' are formally very near to these.[31]

Influence runs in the other direction most visibly in Mew's poems that employ and disrupt regular stanzas. 'The Farmer's Bride' is probably the most well-known of these, but 'Beside the Bed', 'The Pedlar', 'Pécheresse', 'A quoi bon dire' and sections of longer poems like 'In Nunhead Cemetery' are comparable. Mew's writing, like Hardy's (and in common with much Georgian poetry) plays within and against the structures of form – structures that betoken constraint, often, as with Hardy, marital constraint. The farmer's bride ran away from the bonds of marriage but the farmer and friends 'chased her, flying like a hare'.

> To Church-Town
> All in a shiver and a scare
> We caught her, fetched her home at last
> And turned the key upon her, fast. (*Mew*, p. 1)

There are numerous equivalents in Hardy to this rustic tale and its disclosure of (unwitting) oppression. Mew differs from Hardy's usual practice in not keeping to a regular stanza form – the first stanza has nine lines, the second has ten and a different rhyme-scheme, ending with a couplet that uses a new rhyme word ('last/fast'). More typically, Mew creates a distant rhyme with her last lines or makes a closing couplet repeat an earlier rhyme-sound. Here, the couplet assists the sense of forced enclosure, as if formally too a key were being turned.

The tone of the farmer's mind is evoked through this sudden imposition of formal strictness, then, and it is a characteristic achievement of Mew's poetry: within irregular structures, she makes regularity and its neatness serve dramatic ends. Hardy achieves similar effects, though most often while preserving at least the external appearance of structural regularity, and this formal difference reflects differences in temperament and relation to authority between the two poets. Nonetheless, both share a sense that 'Moments of Vision' take place and they employ comparable technical resources to convey how these occur within the mindless rote of time.

To remain within the natural, to not look beyond it (towards a transcendent or crucified God) and to seek in death to return to the earth is a recurrent set of connected impulses in Mew, which shows her affinity with Richard Jefferies and ruralist novelists like Mary Webb or Constance Holme.[32] 'Arracombe Wood' presents a rural figure 'at home' in nature: 'His heart were in Arracombe Wood where he'd used to go / To sit and talk wi' his shadder till sun went low' (*Mew*, p. 38). 'In the Fields', spoken in Standard English, conveys the strangeness of this intimacy to those educated into unfamiliarity with the natural.

Lord, when I look at lovely things which pass,
  Under old trees the shadows of young leaves
Dancing to please the wind along the grass,
  Or the gold stillness of the August sun on the August sheaves;
Can I believe there is a heavenlier world than this?
  And if there is
Will the strange heart of any everlasting thing
  Bring me these dreams that take my breath away?
They come at evening with the home-flying rooks and the scent of hay,
  Over the fields. They come in Spring. (*Mew*, p. 42)

Opening with echoes of Victorian hymnody, both in its formal ease (iambic pentameter strung together by lilting alliteration) and in its orthodox acceptance that nature 'passes', the poem is both arrested and drawn out when it voices a perception of stasis and internal accord: 'the gold stillness of the August sun on the August sheaves'. This hexameter line is busy with unaccented syllables and, at the same time, based firmly on a parallel between 'the August sun' and 'the August sheaves'. The energy that danced, pleasingly and responsively before, now seems contained. Metrically, it is more a change than a disruption – from pentameter to hexameter, native to classical – and one that fits with the nobility suggested by 'august'. It is odd to combine the two metres, perhaps, but both carry with them associations appropriate to the feeling in each and the transitions of feeling presented in the sequence. Metrical form is, therefore, again employed with a sense of its potential for dramatising emotion.

Mew, though, plainly goes much further than this in the rest of the poem. Line 5 is metrically a second hexameter but its stresses are lighter and have therefore to be forced, particularly in the case of 'there is'. Stress on the word 'is' establishes the hexameter's metrical pattern and a caesura between 'is' and 'a', giving a balance to the line that is at odds with the urgency of 'Can I believe there is'. Only when the next startlingly short line repeats 'there is' and slows the rhythm back into iambic regularity, does the previous line stabilise. Rather like Hardy's insistence on 'Here' and 'now' in the repetitions of 'Timing Her', Mew draws attention to elementals of language, to 'there is' and the question of heaven's actuality. The preciosity of 'heavenlier' is challenged by the interrupted and unadorned line that follows, giving the impression that vaguely religious speculations are being checked and rebuked by a more pressing, existential question. In that, a reason for praise (nature is so lovely it becomes hard to believe God could have created anything lovelier) turns into a source of fear: if heaven is our destiny, what will console us there for the loss of earth – of the 'lovely things which pass'?

The remaining four lines find these things again and reclaim them, repeating and altering the pentameter/hexameter pattern of the opening. The pentameter of lines 7 and 8 is less secure than it was before; the hexameter of line 9, similarly, is less noble than in line 4; a more domestic and warmer pastoral is evoked in rooks 'home-flying', something less pictorial and more lived emerges from the 'scent' of hay. Most importantly, perhaps, the hexameter line flows syntactically across the comma into the next line: 'They come . . . with the . . . rooks and the scent of hay, / Over the fields'. This final line is, moreover, in terms of rhythm and metre, the sixth line doubled. It has the same unpoetic simplicity – its plain indicatives working to echo and answer the doubts raised earlier in the plain question. Meanwhile, the diction seeks to keep 'dreams' in (and of) the earth which brings them: the 'heavenlier' is found as part of experience, and so intimately that 'heavenlier' seems too high-flown a word.

It is the affected, bourgeois character in Mew's drama 'The China Bowl' who believes 'The word is more horrible than the thing'; ordinary folk have kept in contact with a truer sense of things, both good and evil. They see lying politicians who are quite shameless until they are called liars, and 'many a woman playing the harlot, with pink rosy cheeks, turn white when she be called the name'.[33] Mew's poetry tries to get behind the distortions wrought by language so that, as in 'Moorland Night', 'The Thing is found'. Authentic experience requires solitude: it offers escape from the demands of others. What follows is not only a deathly stillness ('The Thing is found and I am quiet with the earth') but an unusual, unheard-of song as well: 'that bird's cry . . . The wild, long, rippling call' (*Mew*, p. 57).

In 'The Forest Road', this music, heard outside the window, 'on the road . . . makes all other music like the music in a dream'; it's 'like a stair, / A calling stair that climbs up to a smile you scarcely see'. To follow that music means leaving behind the beloved ('If I could leave you there – / If, without waking you, I could get up and reach the door – !'), leaving behind all the bonds of affection so as to follow:

> The road! the road!
> There is a shadow there: I see my soul,
> I hear my soul, singing among the trees! (*Mew*, pp. 24–5)

This is more high-pitched than 'In the Fields'; it portrays a thwarted passion for what is given, *brought* to the speaker of 'In the Fields' – for what in 'Moorland Night' is given found. These poems of elegiac fulfilment allow one to hear, however, the rhythm behind the fraught cries of the speaker in 'The Forest Road', the quiet apprehension that is registered at the poem's opening only to be blotted out by desire.

> The forest road
> The infinite straight road stretching away
> World without end: the breathless road between the walls
> Of the black listening trees: the hushed, grey road
> Beyond the window that you shut tonight
> Crying that you would look at it by day – (*Mew*, p. 23)

As the road is located among other things (between walls of trees, beyond the window), its qualities are elaborated in human terms; the infinite becomes breathless as descriptions respond to feelings and the pathetic fallacy imposes itself on the material. The word is therefore not only more horrible than the thing, it makes the thing more horrible itself, or at least makes it appear so.

The genuine is perceived as 'The infinite straight road', seen dispassionately and devotedly; fussy choosiness makes the other person shut the window and defer contact. The opening lines are Mew at her closest to Edward Thomas, both in her description of a road extending into a dark infinity and in the subtlety of the verbal music – the alliteration of 'straight' and 'stretching', the assonance of 'inf*inite*' and 'straight' both fashioning a counterpoint to iambic metre. But it is a further instance as well of her poetry's concern, like Hardy's, with the possibility of visionary rhythm – of a metre within which the thing is found.

Notes

1. Bernard Richard, *English Poetry of the Victorian Period* (London: Longman, 1988), p. 70.
2. Dennis Taylor, *Hardy's Metres and Victorian Prosody: With A Metrical Appendix of Hardy's Stanza Forms* (Oxford: Clarendon Press, 1988). Tim Armstrong's edition of Hardy's *Selected Poems* (London: Longman, 1993) gives stanza forms in all headnotes, employing Taylor's notation.

3. Donald Davie, *Thomas Hardy and British Poetry* (London: Routledge and Kegan Paul, 1973), pp. 17, 61–2; see pp. 49–56.
4. Angela Leighton, *Victorian Women Poets: Writing Against the Heart* (Charlottesville: University of Virginia Press, 1992), pp. 266–98; Jane Dowson and Alison Entwhistle, *A History of Twentieth-Century British Women's Poetry* (Cambridge: Cambridge University Press, 2005), p. 75. Jason Harding in 'Modernist Poetry and the Canon', in Alex Davis and Lee M. Jenkins (eds.), *Cambridge Companion to Modernist Poetry* (Cambridge: Cambridge University Press, 2007), pp. 225–43 is a fair-minded guide through these issues.
5. A superior periodisation is implied by Ian Fletcher's anthology, *British Poetry and Prose: 1870–1905* (Oxford: Oxford University Press, 1987); sadly, though it includes Mew it leaves out Hardy.
6. *The Complete Poetical Works of Thomas Hardy*, ed. Samuel Hynes (hereafter *CPW*), 5 vols. (Oxford: Clarendon Press, 1982–95), vol. I, pp. 31, 33.
7. Thomas Hardy, *The Woodlanders* (1887), ed. Dale Kramer (Oxford: Clarendon Press, 1981), p. 8. The first English edition included 'no less than in other places' after 'from time to time'.
8. Line 10 reads in the first edition, 'Now, O, now, O,' as did lines 26 and 58.
9. 'During Wind and Rain', *CPW* II, pp. 239–40; see also 'The Change' (*ibid.*, pp. 190–2), and its alternating refrains. The interlinking of poems within Hardy's collections is, unfortunately, little discussed.
10. These lines resemble a refrain, since the first stanza ends, 'Of the self-struck notes, I did not hear, / I did not see.'
11. 'Retty's Phases', 'To Lizbie Browne', 'Louie', 'To Louisa in the Lane', *CPW* I, p. 165; III, pp. 90, 110, 171–2.
12. Who is the real prattler here? Or, why does a prattling lover name his loved one prattler?
13. *Literature On-Line (LION)* gives 'Lalage' in Ernest Dowson, 'Amor Profanus', W. E. Henley, 'Of Ladies' Names' and, among several US poets, 'A Thanksgiving' from *Last Songs of Vagabondia* (1900) by Bliss Carman and Richard Hovey. Compare Coleridge's 'Names', 'Call me Sappho etc.' (*The Complete Poetical Works*, ed. E. H. Coleridge, 2 vols. (Oxford: Clarendon, 1912), vol. I, p. 318) with 'Call me Tess' in *Tess of the D'Urbervilles* (1891), chapter 20.
14. Compare *Lyrical Ballads* and Wordsworth's defence of repetition in the note to 'The Thorn' (*Lyrical Ballads*, ed. R. L. Brett and A. R. Jones (London: Methuen, 1963), pp. 288–9).
15. *CPW* II, p. 180; see also 'The Minute Before Meeting', *CPW* I, p. 287.
16. See *Far From the Madding Crowd* (1874), especially chapter 16, and Wolfgang Schivelbusch, *The Railway Journey: The Industrialization of Time and Space in the Nineteenth Century* (Berkeley: University of California Press, 1986).
17. In *Tess* chapter 14, buttons on labourers' trousers 'twinkled and bristled . . . as if they were a pair of eyes in the small of his back' (Hardy, *Tess of the D'Urbervilles*, edited with notes by Tim Dolin, introduction by Margaret Higgonet (Penguin: London, 1998), p. 86).

18. Amabel showed she had acquired 'custom-straitened views' when 'Her step's mechanic ways / Had lost the life of May's' (*CPW* I, p. 8).
19. Matthew Campbell, *Rhythm and Will in Victorian Poetry* (Cambridge: Cambridge University Press, 1999), pp. 220, 238.
20. Dennis Taylor, *Hardy's Poetry, 1860–1928* (London: Macmillan, 1981), pp. 4, 40, 93. The phrase 'rigid frames' is quoted from R. P. Blackmur's essay, 'The Shorter Poems of Thomas Hardy', *Southern Review*, 6 (1940).
21. Tennyson's 'Tithonus' stands in the poem's hinterland: 'I wither slowly in thine arms / Here at the quiet limit of the world' (lines 6–7).
22. John Lucas comments in his excellent essay, 'Beginning Again: Hardy's *Wessex Poems*' (*Starting to Explain: Essays in Twentieth-Century British and Irish Poetry* (Nottingham: Trent Books, 2003), pp. 15–32) that 'as memory becomes vocal so iambic gives way to, modulates into, the ripple of anapaest' (p. 29). See also Tom Paulin, *Thomas Hardy: The Poetry of Perception* (London: Macmillan, 1975), pp. 81–6.
23. Compare 'To Louisa in the Lane': 'Wait must I', he says, 'till with flung-off flesh I follow you.' *CPW* III, p. 172.
24. For 'laws of men' see 'At an Inn', a poem written with Florence Henniker in mind, *CPW* I, p. 90.
25. See Ralph Pite, *Thomas Hardy: The Guarded Life* (London: Picador, 2006), pp. 332–6, 401–3, 452–8.
26. See also 'Had You Wept' (*CPW* II, p. 96). Other voices advocated loosening marriage ties. Talcott Williams in 1900 remarked 'that monogamy is itself but an incident in . . . development of sexual relations which may, as other times come, breed . . . unions more flexible' ('The Historical and Ethical Basis of Monogamy', *The International Journal of Ethics*, 10 (1900), p. 166; Williams cites Letourneau's *The Evolution of Marriage* (1891)).
27. The ellipsis after 'thoroughsped' (line 30) is original; I have not quoted lines 31–3, hence the seeming disruption of the rhyme-scheme.
28. Taylor is right to suggest Coleridge's 'Frost at Midnight' as a key text for Hardy (Taylor, *Hardy's Poetry*, p. 5).
29. Compare 'A Conversation at Dawn', *CPW*, II, pp. 80–7.
30. Davie praises 'Snow in the Suburbs' and 'A Spellbound Palace' (*Hardy and British Poetry*, pp. 47–8); Tom Paulin praises, 'Last Look round St Martin's Fair' from *Human Shows* (*Poetry of Perception*, p. 169); neither critic mentions Mew.
31. Charlotte Mew, *Collected Poems and Shorter Prose*, ed. Val Warner (Manchester: Carcanet, 1997) (hereafter *Mew*), pp. 3, 34.
32. See 'Old Shepherd's Prayer', 'Not for that City', 'Do Dreams Lie Deeper', 'Moorland Night' (*Mew*, pp. 43, 45, 50, 57); Jefferies is quoted in the epigraph to Mew's short story, 'The Minnow-Fishers' (*Mew*, p. 90).
33. *Mew*, p. 122. The play was originally a short story; see Penelope Fitzgerald, *Charlotte Mew and Her Friends* (London: Collins, 1984), pp. 67–70, 112–13.

Chapter 41
Yeats

PETER VASSALLO

In Yeats's largely autobiographical novelette *John Sherman*, his eponymous hero, displaced in London, walking along the bank of the Thames, realises that the evocative scenery of an English landscape is alien to him. London, Sherman feels, could not be possessed by a young Irishman who finds himself gazing at the scene 'with foreign eyes' and the reason for this sense of alienation is that London could not be possessed because 'everything in London was owned by too many to be owned by anyone'. *John Sherman*, written in 1888 when Yeats was twenty-three, was an attempt to come to terms with his divided self – his Anglo-Irish identity. William Murphy perceived that the novella was based primarily on Yeats himself, who 'poured all my grievances against this melancholy London' where Yeats was living with his artist father.[1]

The loss of individuality in the metropolis brought about a twinge of nostalgia for Ireland, for the serenity of the Irish countryside. A wooden ball floating on a little water jet in a shop window in the Strand and the sound of dripping water suggested to Yeats the sound of a cataract with a long Gaelic name. This in turn evoked an old daydream about a lake where he had once gone blackberry picking – in actual fact the Lake of Innisfree, which occasioned one of Yeats's finest early lyrical poems. The assertive first line, 'I will arise and go now', is a remote resonance of the prodigal son's decision, in dejection, to leave a foreign land and return to the comfort of his father's house, and contrasts with the relaxed, musical modulations of the rest of the poem. The nostalgia here is an expression of the deep-seated yearning to return to the little island in Lough Gill remote from the 'pavements grey' of the metropolis. In a later poem ('Coole Park and Ballylee', 1931) Yeats counted himself as one of the last Romantics 'who chose for theme / Traditional sanctity and loveliness'[2] and this poem is an early expression of a Romantic longing to escape into the natural world of sights and sounds of his youth.

Nostalgia for Ireland and for the Irish oral tradition pervades his early poetry. It provided material for Romantic escapist poetry as well as an exploration of his identity as a poet brought up in the English mainstream tradition of Blake and Shelley and the Pre-Raphaelites but increasingly attracted to his own roots as an Irishman intent on tapping the resources of Celtic legend and folklore, which offered possibilities for the creative imagination. His early poetry was also a withdrawal into the arcane world of magic and enchantment. As he stated in the Preface to *The Celtic Twilight* (1893), every artist wants to 'create for himself a little world out of the beautiful, pleasant and significant things of this marred and clumsy world'.[3] From Ireland's heroic past and distant legends he wove his coat of embroideries tinged with languorous nostalgia. It was escapist poetry, in the Pre-Raphaelite mode, but composed with a sense of creating a national identity through the conscious forging of a link with a submerged past with its 'unbounded emotion and wild melancholy'.[4] Like Stephen Daedalus in Joyce's *A Portrait of the Artist* Yeats became increasingly aware of his mission as an artist 'to forge in the smithy of my soul the uncreated conscience of my race'.[5] Like Stephen, too, he was an Irishman brought up in a dominant English cultural tradition (the Anglo-Irish Protestant Ascendancy) who was seeking to tap the very source of Irishness which lay submerged, in his view, somewhere in the west of Ireland.

His early poetic works, *The Wanderings of Oisin and Other Poems* (1889) and *The Countess Cathleen and Various Legends and Lyrics* (1892), reveal his concern with Irish mythologies and traditional romance. In 'The Song of the Happy Shepherd' he puts forward the notion that past values, embodied in the Celtic legends, have significant relevance for the modern Irish poet profoundly concerned with his countrymen's sense of identity. The ancient myths of classical Greece ('the woods of Arcady' (line 1)) are no longer a source of inspiration concerned, as they once were, with 'grey truth' (line 4). A deeper truth perhaps could be sought in the alchemy of words (an 'echo-harbouring shell' (line 36)) which is the poet's means of articulating a deeper truth of the heart. The Celtic heroes of old are conjured up as examples of the indomitable spirit of Ireland: Fergus, King of Ulster, who abandoned his throne to seek self-fulfilment in hunting amid the peace of the woods; Aengus, a Celtic equivalent of Orpheus, who wanders continually in search of an elusive 'glimmering girl / With apple blossom in her hair' ('The Song of the Wandering Aengus', lines 13–14) and pursues his quest even in old age, yearning to kiss the enchanted woman of his dreams and pluck 'The silver apples of the moon, / The golden apples of the sun' (lines 23–4). These are hauntingly resonant verses inspired by the Celtic imagination. The elusiveness of the quest is enacted in the poem in the subtlety of the rhymed lines with their frequent enjambment. Yeats was fascinated by the story of Oisin with its blending of the medieval and the ancient Gaelic, in which the hero, the poet of the military order of the Fianna (of which Finn was chief) was seduced by the beautiful fairy Niamh, who led him to the enchanted country of the young. It has been suggested that 'The Wanderings of Oisin' (1889) might have been read as a political allegory in which the captive maiden Ireland is rescued from the power of England.[6] The link with Finn and the Fenians would have been noticed at the time of the publication of the poem in 1889. Again, in the versified account of the exploits of Cuchulain, Yeats assumes the role of a latter-day Druidic bard or story-teller reciting these heroic feats to his contemporaries. Cuchulain, the great warrior of the Canorian cycle, sustained Yeats's interest throughout his life and became, for the poet, an emblem of Irish resistance against impossible odds; the men who 'fought the good fight' had become gods and their undaunted spirit lived after them to inspire the living. In Yeats's imagination the dauntless spirit of Cuchulain fighting against the invulnerable tide, returns, much later, to inspire Patrick Pearse in his heroic resistance in the Dublin Post Office during the 1916 Easter Rising, when Pearse is imagined as summoning Cuchulain to his side in a moment of dire need ('The Two Statues'). The legend of Cuchulain is tapped to show the metamorphosis of the mild-mannered Pearse, a schoolmaster, into a determined latter-day Irish hero fighting against overwhelming odds. The Cuchulain myth also inspired Yeats's strange Dantean poem in *terza rima* 'Cuchulain Comforted' (composed towards the end of his life in 1939), in which, under the inspiration of Dante, antithetical notions of the after-life are expressed. In this poem the heroic Cuchulain finds himself a shade sitting among cowards who thread needles and sing. In Yeatsean terms the Irish hero had reached the phase of the 'shiftings' – epitome of his antithetical self, the complementary state of unity of being where the soul is submerged in collective existence with a group of bird-like shades (those who had lived a cowardly life).[7] This image is strongly reminiscent of Dante's 'Inferno', where the shades are described as peering in the 'waning dusk' like an old tailor at the eye of the needle, the celebrated scene in which Dante meets his former mentor Brunetto Latini.

'Apologia Addressed to Ireland in the Coming Times' was the young poet's attempt to establish his poetic credentials as a worthy successor of the nationalist poets Davis, Mangan and Ferguson, who sought inspiration in Ireland's 'primal world' of folklore and legends. The poem attempts to arouse a sense of national identity while seeking to transcend the limits of nationalism. The poem with its controlled rhetorical stance and rhythmic assurance was meant to blend the Druidic occult ('the dim wisdoms old and deep') with current political concerns ('the austere ways') in a manner which would be pleasing to Maud Gonne, the 'goddess' who at the time exerted such a vibrant fascination on the poet.[8] Maud Gonne's fanatical involvement in Irish nationalist politics, her agitation for revolt against British rule, deeply influenced Yeats and had a lasting impact on the drift of his poetry. The old Celtic embroideries were replaced, in Yeats's mythical coat, by a sense of urgency ('there's more enterprise / In walking naked' ('A Coat', lines 9–10)) in which he would abandon his concern with Celtic legends and engage with contemporary Irish politics. But while he was deeply enamoured of this modern Helen of Troy, he deplored her nationalist extremism and passionate demagoguery, which stirred up civil unrest by 'hurling the little streets upon the great' ('No Second Troy', line 4). 'No Second Troy' is an expression of Yeats's ambivalent feelings about Gonne's political fanaticism. On the one hand, he sees her as a latter-day Helen: as Helen brought destruction on the Trojans, so Gonne was a rabble-rouser teaching 'to ignorant men most violent ways' (line 3). On the other, he cannot help admiring her poise and her stern aspect. The poem celebrates an extraordinary woman of action, fiercely independent and self-assured who, in her classic dignity, has affinities with the goddess Diana ('with beauty like a tightened bow' (line 8)). In the questions in the last lines the poem enacts the tensions within Yeats himself as he sought to reconcile the conflicting emotions of admiration and reproof which Gonne aroused in him.

Another woman, Lady Augusta Gregory, was to exert a profound influence on Yeats's poetic development. Lady Gregory's friendship with Yeats and her generous patronage (he was a frequent guest at her manor house, Coole Park, County Galway) encouraged Yeats to explore the resources of Celtic folklore and to be involved in the setting up of an Irish national theatre, for she was determined to show that Ireland was not 'the home of buffoonery and easy sentiment' but the 'home of an ancient idealism'.[9] She was a natural folklorist and Yeats accompanied her occasionally when she went to collect stories in Galway and Clare. He later came to regard her as a member of his family, and in 'Estrangement' famously paid tribute to her as 'mother, friend, sister, and brother'.[10] For the poet she was a muse-figure, who represented the virtues of the Anglo-Irish aristocracy which, in his view, were essential to the formation of a modern Irish consciousness. Aristocrats like Lady Augusta Gregory, he was convinced, had a role to play in the creation of an Irish cultural revival based on patronage. His Italian visit in 1907 in the company of Lady Gregory made him all too aware of the power of ducal patronage in the Renaissance to sustain art and the life of the mind in miniature city states like Urbino and

Ferrara, the enabling of poets and artists to achieve artistic perfection through assiduous dedication. Castiglione's *The Book of the Courtier* ('the grammar school of courtesies' ('To a Wealthy Man', line 15)) with its insistence on courtly refinement, its advocating of astute self-fashioning and its emphasis upon 'sprezzatura' (a sort of studied patrician nonchalance), which she read to him in translation, was an immediate source of inspiration and sparked off the fantasy of the cultural appropriation of Renaissance Italy. Dublin, in Yeats's view, could in similar fashion become a centre of the arts sustained by the patronage of patriotic and influential women like Lady Gregory and her nephew, the public-spirited connoisseur and collector Sir Hugh Lane.

'To a Wealthy Man' (which was published in *Responsibilities*) was Yeats's attempt to join in the fray of public controversy on behalf of aristocratic patronage, and particularly in support of Hugh Lane's offer to bequeath his valuable collection of thirty-nine pictures to the city of Dublin on condition that they were suitably housed. These included invaluable works by Courbet, Corot, Degas, Manet, Monet, Pissarro and Renoir. The poet assumes the lofty patrician role of defender of Ireland's cultural values and heaps contempt on the philistines of his day (the 'Paudeens' and 'Biddys') who showed no regard for works of art. The poem is in effect a rhetorical plea addressed to potential patrons like Lord Ardilaun to ignore the popular will if they are to patronise and subsidise the arts in Dublin, in this case by giving their financial support to Hugh Lane's campaign for a permanent Dublin gallery. They are urged to follow the example of the ducal patrons of the Italian Renaissance, who, while lavishly promoting the arts, contemptuously disregarded the opinion of ordinary people, or 'onion sellers':

> What cared Duke Ercole, that bid
> His mummers to the market-place,
> What th'onion sellers thought or did
> So that his Plautus set the pace
> For the Italian comedies . . . (lines 9–13)

The great artistic movements and the revival of learning in Renaissance Italy, Yeats felt, were fostered by patrons like Duke Ercole d'Este, who were impervious to plebeian opinion and taste. Yeats's haughtily indignant poem, which was both a political manifesto and his own personal contribution to the prevailing cultural controversy, angered those like William Murphy, the newspaper magnate and proprietor of the Catholic *Irish Independent*, who strongly reacted by asserting the right of taxpayers to determine where their money went. Slum clearance, argued Murphy, from 'Paudeen''s point of view, was more important to the community than an art gallery housing 'all the pictures that Corot and Degas ever painted'.[11] Yeats's indignation at the philistinism and indifference of the predominantly Catholic middle class of Dublin is given expression in 'September 1913', where he laments the passing away of the romantic spirit of old Ireland, epitomised by the Irish patriot John O'Leary, which has been replaced by the insensitivity of shopkeepers who 'fumble in a greasy till / And add the halfpence to the pence' (lines 2–3). His disillusion with his fellow countrymen is conveyed in 'The People', where he expresses his yearning to escape from 'the daily spite of this unmannerly town' (line 3) and seek refuge among images of the past – the courtly images surrounding the Duchess of Urbino, Elisabetta Gonzaga, celebrated in Castiglione's *Book of the Courtier*. This indeed was a recurring image which seemed to haunt him when, later in 1922, he walked through the Gobelin-tapestried halls in the King of Sweden's palace, 'in excited reverie', to receive the Nobel Prize.[12] In Yeats's imagination this was a walk into the past, into the sumptuous court of Urbino where youth had 'imposed upon drowsy learning the discipline of its joy'.[13]

He was later to indulge his aristocratic concerns (and pretensions) in 'A Prayer for my Daughter', which extols the Renaissance virtues of courtesy and ceremony by equating aesthetic beauty with moral virtue, in the manner recommended by Cardinal Bembo in Castiglione's manual of courtly etiquette. He transposes this idealistic notion to the Anglo-Irish tradition of imposing country houses and gracious living now threatened by political turbulence. The poem, it should be recalled, was written in 1919 during the turbulence of the Anglo-Irish War between the Irish Republican Brotherhood and the Black and Tans, here symbolised by the howling storm outside. Yeats's prayer is that of paternalistic concern for a daughter who would grow into a beautiful woman but, he hoped, without that political fanaticism (an 'opinionated mind' (line 61)) which disfigured a lovely woman he once had known (a passing reference to Maud Gonne's fanatical involvement in politics). A similar theme of a civilised way of life threatened by impending violence is taken up again in 'Meditations in Time of Civil War', particularly in the first Section, 'Ancestral Houses'. The houses (Yeats has Lady Gregory's Coole Park in mind, as well as the Gore-Booths' mansion in Lissadel and his own ancient tower, Thor Ballylee) are emblems of the gracious patrician way of life which he considered an antidote to 'a mechanical / or servile shape' (lines 7–8) which was beginning to overshadow the present age. But the poem also expresses his perturbation at the realisation that these monuments to gracious living had been themselves brought into being earlier by violence:

> What if the glory of escutcheoned doors,
> And buildings that a haughtier age designed,

The pacing to and fro on polished floors
Amid great chambers and long galleries, lined
With famous portraits of our ancestors;
What if those things the greatest of mankind
Consider most to magnify or to bless
But take our greatness with our bitterness? (lines 33–40)

If greatness is dependent on bitterness (hatred, violence), the poem argues, it might disappear once violence has faded from the land, and civilised living will also vanish with the screaming of Juno's peacock, a forceful symbol used by Yeats to suggest the collapse of a civilisation. Hence his plea to the honey-bees (representing sweetness and light) to 'come build in the empty house of the stare' (line 145). Those 'bitter and violent men' (line 19) ensconced in bronze and marble now crave for its antithesis – the 'sweetness' and gentleness of gracious living which is enshrined in stone in the shape of those ancestral houses – 'buildings that a haughtier age designed'.

Yeats's passionate involvement with aristocratic ceremony is evident in two of his finest poems, both about responses to death. 'Upon a Dying Lady' is a moving tribute to Mabel Beardsley (Aubrey's sister), who even while dying of cancer courageously kept her 'old distinguished grace' (line 1) and nonchalance while she characteristically entertained her friends on Sunday afternoons with a gay mixture of moral and improper stories ('Thinking of saints and of Petronius Arbiter' (line 8)). Another remarkable poem, 'In Memory of Major Robert Gregory', celebrates the life and death of Lady Gregory's only son, who died in action on the Italian front in 1918. Beside the fireplace in Yeats's ancient Norman tower of Thor Ballylee (the old tower being a symbol of the soldier and the scholar), Yeats conjures up images of departed old friends who will not dine with him that night (he was profoundly interested in spiritualism and séances, and the effect of conjuration in the poem is strong): these friends include Lionel Johnson, the aloof scholarly poet; Synge, the playwright who sought inspiration in the Aran islands; Yeats's maternal uncle George Pollexfen, an eccentric astrologer; all remarkable Irishmen in their own way. Yeats focuses on Robert Gregory, a man who lived intensely and who succeeded in reconciling the antithetical attributes of soldier and artist, thereby achieving much-desired unity of being, and who is consequently mythologised as latter-day Irish version of Sir Philip Sidney, the accomplished Renaissance man.

Soldier, scholar, horseman, he,
And all he did done perfectly
As though he had but that one trade alone. (lines 78–80)

The aristocratic Robert Gregory, too, like Mabel Beardsley, could share in the 'discourtesy of death' (line 48). For Yeats, Gregory was the emblem of the complete man who succeeded in harmonising his self and anti-self, the man of action and the man of solitary contemplation, a synthesis which Yeats greatly desired as he strove to come to terms with his 'sense of bifurcated self'[14] in creating the antithetical characters of Robartes and Aherne in 'The Phases of the Moon', or those of Hic and Ille in 'Ego Dominus Tuus' and Self and Soul in the 'Dialogue of Self and Soul'. Through these personae, or embodiments of abstractions, Yeats sought to dramatise the tensions and characters within himself, constructing his mask ('the image of what we wish to become') in relation to his present self, forging poetry out of the conflict within himself.[15] He was aware of the necessity of fabricating his identity in relation to his readers. As he wrote in the section on 'Anima Hominis' in *Mythologies* (1918) 'If we cannot imagine ourselves as different from what we are and try to assume the second self, we cannot impose a discipline upon ourselves though we may accept one from others.'[16] His poetry grew out of the quarrel with himself as he sought to come to terms, not always successfully, with the contradictions within his personality, leading him to impose some form of order of experience on chaos. As a poet committed to the articulation of universal truths accessible through esoteric knowledge, the assumption of poetic masks served to protect himself against the Romantic temptation of direct or moralistic self-expression. It was also a strategy which allowed him to adapt to the changing shape of Irish nationalism as it evolved in the midst of political turbulence. For Yeats the mask was a literary artifice linked with the painfully acquired discipline of form which enabled him to transmute mundane biographical particulars ('the breakfast table') into artistic symbols ('phantasmagoria').[17] The poem which perhaps best illustrates Yeats's emerging system of deploying the poetic mask is 'Ego Dominus Tuus', a poem which was inspired by his reading of Dante's own allegorical account, in the *Vita Nuova*, of his conversion from man of the world to visionary poet when the Lord of Love takes over and becomes his master (the title taken from the *Vita Nuova* literally means 'I, [Love], am your master'). Dante, as Yeats argues through his surrogate, Ille, fashioned himself from his opposite self, which still remains attached to his earlier self. Dante's sublime poetry is based on the self, but through his poetic art transcends the bitterness of exile and leads to the exaltation of Beatrice.

> He set his chisel to the hardest stone
> Being mocked by Guido for his lecherous life,

Derided and deriding, driven out
To climb the stair and eat that bitter bread,
He found the unpersuadable justice, he found
The most exalted lady loved by man. (lines 32–7)

This is Yeats's fine poetic enactment of Dante's remarkable conversion conveyed in a philosophical dialogue about the transmutation of life into art. Dante's exaltation of Beatrice Portinari into a muse-figure who is sublimated into a moral and philosophical guide in *La Vita Nuova* and the *Divina Commedia* constitutes his poetics of conversion and the fashioning of a new self out of his earlier 'lecherous' life and his misfortunes. Like Dante, whom he admired, Yeats sought to chisel poetry out of the warring elements within himself. Similarly, and rather patronisingly, Yeats, through the persona of Ille, puts forward the notion that Keats sublimated his feeling of inferiority and social deprivation ('the coarse-bred son of a livery-stable keeper' (line 65)) into 'luxuriant song'.

Political events in Ireland were to impinge abruptly on his meditations on the nature of poetry and his insistence on the artfulness of art. 'Easter 1916' celebrates and yet questions the value of the Easter Rising of 1916, in which a group of armed Irish republicans occupied the General Post Office in Dublin and resisted for several days before surrendering to the British Army. The leaders Pearse and Connolly, and fourteen others, were executed. Another revolutionary, Constance Markiewicz (née Gore-Booth), Yeats's friend, was condemned to death but the sentence was later commuted to penal servitude. Yeats was in Gloucestershire at the time as a guest of William Rothenstein and his wife, and his initial reaction was one of dismay, for he felt that if the English Conservative Party had kept to the promise of the Home Rule Bill, the rebellion could have been averted. He confided to Lady Gregory that the Dublin events were a source of 'great sorrow and anxiety'[18] and he was trying to compose a poem on the tragic events which led to 'a terrible beauty' being born again. Maud Gonne for her part was rapturous and claimed in a letter to the poet from France that 'a tragic dignity' had returned to Ireland.[19]

'Easter 1916' is a complicatedly celebratory poem on an event which transformed the quotidian into the extraordinary, as ordinary men became suddenly invested with mythical status because of their single-minded devotion to a patriotic cause. The poem is divided into four stanzas or verse-paragraphs. The first concentrates on Yeats's memory of meeting some of the rebels and exchanging meaningless pleasantries, 'polite meaningless words' (line 6), in friendly banter near the Georgian Houses in the centre of Dublin (Yeats was then a member of the St Stephen's Green Club) in an atmosphere of jovial bonhomie ('where motley is worn' (line 14)) before the sudden and dramatic metamorphoses into the birth of 'a terrible beauty' (line 16).

The second verse-paragraph focuses on the leaders (not mentioned by name) and their part in the casual comedy which now has assumed tragic overtones. 'That woman' (line 23) is a reference to Constance Gore-Booth, daughter of the Gore-Booths of the great mansion of Lissadell, whom he had known and admired in his youth. The tone is ambivalent for, in singling Constance out as a heroine, he would seem to rebuke her for allowing herself to be carried away by political fanaticism. She, like Maud Gonne, allowed politics to disfigure her natural beauty ('her nights in argument / until her voice grew shrill' (lines 20–1)). The verse-stanza dwells on the metamorphosis of two sensitive men into heroic stature. The gentle Patrick Pearse ('This man' (line 25)), who was a schoolmaster and poet, and Thomas MacDonagh, Professor of English at University College, Dublin, both in their mild-mannered way, assumed the heroic role to which they were destined. Even Maud Gonne's coarse-grained husband Major John MacBride (Yeats's former rival, from whom Gonne had been estranged) is given a prominent place in the drama of Irish history, but is immortalised here as a 'drunken vainglorious lout' (line 33). The third stanza shifts into the metaphorical mode and the nature of heroism itself, which requires single-minded dedication to a cause which turns people's hearts into stone, in contrast with the perpetual flux of life which can be observed in the natural world of horses, moorhens which go by, minute by minute, while the stone lies stolidly still in the midst of the stream. This section elicited a strong reaction from Gonne, who writing to the poet from Paris, insisted that 'sacrifice had never turned a heart to stone'.[20] The last stanza reveals Yeats's ambivalence in celebrating this glorious event in Ireland's turbulent history and his conflicting feelings about the Easter Rising. The vapid, polite meaningless words of the opening stanza have now, by being translated into deeds, become a roll-call of honour for those whose unflinching determination has led to the supreme sacrifice. Yeats's original misgivings about the Rising, whether it was all premature and ultimately unnecessary, surface here at the very moment that he bestows praise on the rebel heroes. The expression 'where motley is worn' has now been transformed into 'wherever green is worn' (line 79), no longer a casual comedy but the tragic dignity of dying for one's beliefs ('green' being the colour of Ireland, synonymous with patriotism).

The uprising, for all its glorious heroism, may have been premature, for England, in Yeats's view, may have kept its promise in 1913 (but suspended in

1914 because of the outbreak of World War I) to pass a Bill granting Ireland Home Rule.

> Was it needless death after all?
> For England may keep faith
> For all that is done and said. (lines 67–9)

But doubts and misgivings are subsumed in the final flourish of the change that has come over Ireland as a consequence of patriotic self-sacrifice: '. . . changed, changed utterly: / A terrible beauty is born' (lines 80–1). Constance Markiewicz's name is, not surprisingly, omitted from the poet's roll-call. He had patronisingly dismissed her political involvement as 'ignorant good will' (line 18) and perhaps excluded her wilfully from a role which, he felt, was predominantly male. But he was to return to the subject of women's political role two years later in 'On a Political Prisoner', which is about Constance Gore Booth as it is about Maud Gonne. Constance Markiewicz, whose sentence of death was commuted to life imprisonment, was serving her sentence in Holloway Prison when the poem was written. The image of the seagull dominates the poem; the wild seagull tamed by Constance Markiewicz confined to the narrowness of her cell is contrasted with the untamed spirit of the woman whose involvement in politics changed her into a 'bitter abstract thing' (line 9), a far cry from the beautiful woman who, as Yeats recalls, rode, long ago, to the meet under Ben Bulben 'like any rock-bred sea-borne bird' (line 18). An impatient dynamic woman, she is now compelled to languish in a cell, patiently enduring the solitude of confinement. Later, in 'In Memory of Eva Gore-Booth and Con Markiewicz', he lingers nostalgically on the Lissadell mansion of the Gore-Booth sisters, both beautiful in their silk kimonos, whose beauty is eventually ravaged by time and political and social agitation, becoming 'withered, old and skeleton-gaunt' (line 12).

Later political events (the Anglo-Irish War and the Irish Civil War) impinge on the poet's consciousness as he meditates on his yearning for order and tranquillity in the isolation of his ancient tower and its gyrating winding stair – itself a double-edged symbol of serenity and violence. For Yeats, Thor Ballylee was a refuge for peaceful scholarly meditation in the manner of Milton's *Il Penseroso*, but as an ancient Norman tower built in times of strife by powerful overlords it also harbours ancestral memories of war where 'rough men at arms break upon the sleeper's rest' ('The Tower', line 70). 'Meditations in Time of Civil War' returns to the theme of impending violence, which cannot be isolated from his laborious stair and dark tower:

> We are closed in, and the key is turned
> On our uncertainty; somewhere

A man is killed, or a house burned,
Yet no clear fact to be discerned (vi, lines 6–9)

The first section, 'Ancestral Houses', had celebrated the gracious patrician way of life which was being swept aside by the 'mechanical or servile shape' (lines 7–8) of the present age. The final section, 'Phantoms of Hatred', enacts the poet's acquiescence in the grip of 'daemonic images' (line 200) as he turns away from the top of the tower and shuts the door. The theme of bitterness and violence is explored again in 'Nineteen Hundred and Nineteen', which opens in an elegiac mode by lamenting the passing away of 'many ingenious lovely things' (line 1). The mood shifts abruptly and the poem focuses sharply on the present turbulence – the atrocities committed in Ireland by the Black and Tans (mainly British soldiers demobilised from the First World War):

Now days are dragon-ridden, the nightmare
Rides upon sleep, a drunken soldiery
Can leave the mother murdered at her door,
To crawl in her own blood, and go scot-free;
The night can sweat with terror as before
We pieced our thoughts into philosophy,
And planned to bring the world under a rule,
Who are but weasels fighting in a hole. (lines 25–32)

The revival of the *ottava rima*, the stanza form favoured by Byron, Keats and Shelley, is one of Yeats's finest metrical achievements and is used here (and also in 'The Gyres', 'The Statues', 'Among School Children', 'The Municipal Gallery Revisited', 'The Circus Animals' Desertion') with consummate skill. The superb off-rhyme ('rule/hole') subtly conveys the poet's disillusion with contemporary Irish politics and its decline from idealism into bitter fighting. The image of dragon-ridden days merges, strikingly, with Loie Fuller's dance at the Folies Bergères in Paris, when she used lengths of silk wound round sticks to produce a dragon of air which whirled round the dancers on stage. As Frank Kermode has shown, the image of the dancer dominates Yeats's later work and is emblematic of the union between body and soul, form and matter, artist and soul, especially in the final stanza of 'Among School Children'.[21] But here, in the context of scenes of violence, the dragon dance leads to the 'barbarous clangour of a gong' (line 58). The poet's vision is that of the dance of death, where Salome's dance, which ultimately led to the beheading of John the Baptist, is conflated with that of the Sidhe, the Celtic goddesses who dwell in the wind, whirling round and round in their courses. The last stanza enacts the abruptness of the violence which erupts with dizzying motion to bewilder the poet. Such passages of intense visionary poetry can be discerned earlier, especially in the apocalyptic 'The Second Coming', where a civilisation (Christianity) has spiralled out of control to be replaced by its antithesis (the Antichrist), the rough 'beast' slouching towards Bethlehem to be born. The poem was composed (in 1919) in the aftermath of the First World War and expresses the apocalyptic vision of the end of civilised values which troubles the poet as he gazes apprehensively into the bleak future.

The initiation of a new age which ushers in an era of violence, 'some violent annunciation', is treated forcefully in 'Leda and the Swan'.[22] The rape of Leda, a mortal, by Zeus is presented ambivalently: the male aggressive sexual assault of the defenceless and terrified maiden on the one hand contrasts with Leda's seeming acquiescence on the other ('her loosening thighs' (line 6)). The questions in the poem would seem to suggest that it is through the violence of the sexual act, itself mitigated by the softness of the bird's feathers, that the mortal girl is apotheosised. The octave of this remarkable sonnet emphasises the brutality of Zeus's passion and Leda's helplessness, whereas in the sestet the focus is shifted to Leda's being 'caught up' (line 12) in his passion and her consequent sense of the 'strange heart beating where it lies' (line 8) at the moment of Zeus's 'indifferent' (line 15) withdrawal. Declan Kiberd interprets the poem allegorically in terms of an invading English occupier and a helpless ravished Ireland.[23] But the burning roof and tower would seem to suggest the violence which had suddenly erupted in Ireland as a result of political hatred (the Irish Civil War of 1922–3) at the time the poem was written.

Political events apart, Yeats was largely concerned with the subject of aesthetics and the struggle of the artist with himself. If the politics of the day demanded some form of active involvement as the poet (in 'The Statues') finds himself 'thrown upon this filthy modern tide' (line 29), art required isolation and detachment. But in his poetry Yeats is tormented by memories that prey upon him and by the fear of bodily decrepitude that turns people into caricatures ('old clothes upon old sticks' ('Among School Children', line 48)) of themselves, obsessed as he always is with the horror of ageing. Art is therefore not a refuge from life but an immersion into life. He strove in his later poetry to reconcile the opposites of action and contemplation by creating his own configuration of symbols, 'those masterful images', as he called them in 'The Circus Animals' Desertion' (line 33), which gave such vibrant resonance to his mature poetry. The pursuit of single-minded wisdom through such images afforded consolation from the threat of advancing 'decrepit age that has been tied to me / As to a dog's tail' ('The Tower', lines 2–4). But the artist engrossed in his art must labour at it incessantly, forgoing pleasure:

> The intellect of man is forced to choose
> Perfection of the life, or of the work,
> And if it take the second must refuse
> A heavenly mansion raging in the dark
> ('The Choice', lines 1–4)

'Among School Children' is a superb poem which moves from present actuality, through the labyrinth of memory, to images which take over and console the afflicted heart. Yeats, now 'a sixty-year-old smiling public man' (line 8), a Senator, visits a Montessori school, and one of the children vaguely reminds him of his beloved Maud Gonne, whose image floats before him like a present dream. But she is now transformed into a hollow-cheeked old woman, and he a scarecrow of a man, as he reflects on the indignity of old age. The poem then shifts gear and focuses on the ways in which mothers and nuns (surrogate mothers) worship images. If mothers could see their children at sixty, would they consider motherhood worthwhile, the poem asks. The great philosophers of old (Aristotle and Pythagoras) have been reduced to insignificance ('old clothes upon old sticks' (line 48)). The poet's consolation is that mothers and nuns worship images which are impervious to decay, being 'self-born', perfect and therefore un-ageing, mocking 'man's enterprise' (line 56) by their not being subject to change. In the final stanza the image of the dancer dissipates the poet's earlier reflections in an apostrophe which asserts the integrity of art and the subsuming of the artist into his artefact, like the dancer becoming one with the dance.

Yeats's fascination with complex symbols is best seen in the two poems 'Sailing to Byzantium' and 'Byzantium'. Both express Yeats's increasing concern with the dichotomy of body and soul, and the manner in which bodily decrepitude is transcended through art, the soul singing in spite of 'every tatter in its mortal dress' ('Sailing to Byzantium', line 12). Byzantium is Yeats's emblem of artistic perfection. As he wrote in *A Vision*, Byzantium was his symbol for the complete harmonisation of 'religious, aesthetic and practical life', those very aspects of his own complex personality which he sought to reconcile.[24] Byzantium, in Yeats's view, represented the Holy City of Art, the apogee of Eastern and Western art (splendid mosaics and golden artefacts) where the imagination, in Blakean fashion, transmutes ephemeral reality into immortal transcendence, the apotheosis of bronze and marble. The vitality of life (and sexuality, implied by the 'salmon falls' and 'mackerel-crowded seas'

('Sailing to Byzantium', line 4)) in the sensual music of time is contrasted with bodily decrepitude, which is only redeemed by the artistic soul which, fastened to the frail body ('dying animal' (line 24)), yearns for immortality ('the artifice of eternity' (line 22)). His imagination is fired by the Byzantine mosaics which had so impressed him in his earlier visit to Ravenna in the company of Lady Gregory (and later with his wife in Monreale, Sicily). The artefact, the golden bird, symbolises the reconciliation of opposites which the artistic world has created out of the natural. It stands for the poet who becomes one with his creation – an image of perfection. And yet eternity itself, the poem implies, is also a construct.

Obsessed as he always was with the occult and after-life, Yeats believed that he could communicate with the dead, and sometimes in the possibility of reviving old conversations with departed friends, especially those with whom he had shared interests in magic and the occult. And poetry was the medium in which this bond could be revived. As Seamus Heaney remarks, Yeats 'was always passionately beating on the wall of the physical world in order to provoke an answer from the other side'.[25] 'All Souls' Night', written at Oxford in 1920, is a fine example of his extraordinary ability to evoke the spirits of his departed friends in a setting appropriate for a séance. All were at one stage in their lives deeply involved in the pursuit of arcane knowledge. The mystical painter Horton, the actress and accomplished reciter of verse, Florence Farr Emery, who ended her life in a convent in Ceylon, and MacGregor Mathers, eccentric scholar of magic and the occult, are summoned around a table with two glasses of bubbling muscatel whose fumes nourish the visiting spirits. Their lives, passions and foibles are summed up as his friends are resuscitated in memory, enshrined in their own mysticism and obsession. This midnight encounter generates 'mummy truths' (line 86) concerning the after-life which the poet, in a moment of exaltation, is on the verge of revealing. In this poem and in others such as 'In Memory of Robert Gregory'; 'To a Shade'; 'In Memory of Eva Gore-Booth and Con Markiewicz', the spirits of the dead are conjured up to instruct the poet in the ineffable mysteries of the after-life, and this constant invoking of the supernatural was a means of raging against the obliterating power of death.

The noble dead are recalled in dignified *ottava rima* stanzas in 'The Municipal Gallery Revisited', as the poet gazes, 'heart-smitten with emotion', (line 17), at the portraits of his friends who, in life, were so meaningful to him. As his gaze focuses on Mancini's fine portrait of Augusta Gregory and that of John Synge, he pays tribute to their role in creating an Irish drama out of the simple lives and aspirations of the common folk. The message they impart, as they are immortalised on canvas, is that all art must ultimately derive its strength ('Antaeus-like' (line 44)) from contact with the earth. To gaze with admiration on these vivid portraits of his friends is to trace 'Ireland's history in their lineaments' (line 53). The celebration of people Yeats admired and their consequent mythologising is also evident in his fine poem 'Beautiful Lofty Things'. Yeats's visual memory focuses on the dignity and beauty of those people who mattered. From the patriot 'O'Leary's noble head' (line 1) to the sight of his father mollifying (and taunting) the rioting crowds after the performance of Synge's *The Playboy of the Western World*, to Standish O'Grady and his inebriated rhetoric ('high nonsensical' (line 6)), the poem shifts focus on to the two women who occupied a central place in his affections: Lady Gregory, seated by her ormolu table in all her dignity and refinement, telling a would-be assassin, with aristocratic nonchalance, where she could be found. The other woman, Maud Gonne, is in the process of being transformed into a mythic figure – the Greek goddess Pallas Athene – as she waits for a train at Howth station. Her image imprinted itself on his mind soon after they parted. Yeats and Maud Gonne, it should be recalled, had spent a day on the cliffs at Howth after his unsuccessful proposal to her.[26] His friends are here metamorphosed into heroic symbols, invested with the dignity and composure of Greek gods ('All the Olympians' (line 15)) who are destined, the poem suggests, to usher in a new heroic age – a phase in the history of Ireland which would not recur – unlike the 'unfashionable gyre' ('The Gyres', line 24) – 'a thing never known again' (line 15).

The sense of physical decrepitude creeping up on the poet, encasing a vigorous mind, compelled Yeats to write 'Under Ben Bulben', a poem which restates his deep convictions about life and death and 'all the complexities of mire or blood'. Invoking Shelley's enigmatic Witch of Atlas, who sees all human life shadowed on the waters of the Nile, and the wisdom of the Celts who in 'ancient Ireland knew it all' (line 16), Yeats asserts his own belief in reincarnation. A stridently assertive note is struck in quoting the bitter words of the patriot John Mitchel, who urged war with England as the 'truest moral force' (line 83) to accomplish fate in an indifferent nation.[27] The poem shifts from the politician's determined, uncompromising role to the single-minded stance of the artist who seeks ordered vision ('measurement' (line 41)) and perfection in his endeavour to 'bring the soul of man to God'. This artistic vision with its equipoise of the human and the divine ('profane perfection of mankind') is epitomised in Michelangelo's paintings in the Sistine Chapel as it is in earlier Renaissance art. The concluding stanzas, a sort of poetic last testament, express Yeats's admiration for the three classes of society which in his view have bestowed vigour and vitality on Irish life: the aristocrat, the poet and the peasant, and concludes with an exhortation to artists to compose that which is refined and well made and to discard the shoddy or the misshapen, modish verse which he disdainfully attributes to 'base born products of base beds' (line 73). Yeats's eugenist principles are evident here, as in his prose, where he thanks his ancestors for providing him with 'blood that has not passed through any huckster's loin'.[28] Only thus, he argues with a touch of the old arrogance, could the 'indomitable Irishry' (line 83) be preserved. The final stanza is a buoyant epitaph for posterity written, as it were, from a posthumous existence.

The sense of a life inexorably running out and the necessity to come to terms with his own failing poetic powers induced him to write one of his most powerful and moving poems. 'The Circus Animals' Desertion' is a superb poem about the poet's inability to tap the old sources of the imagination, those 'masterful images', which once bolstered his poetry and plays. One could perceive a similarity with Coleridge's 'Dejection: An Ode' which, paradoxically, is a fine poem on the poet's failing poetic powers. 'The Circus Animals' Desertion' projects mixed feelings of pride and disillusion as it enumerates old themes and lingers on the dazzling, arresting images which were so significant in sustaining the fresh impetus of Yeats's earlier poetry and plays. These images and metaphors were so deftly displayed, as he says in 'High Talk' – 'All metaphor, Malachi, stilts and all' (line 19).

The poem is typically Yeatsean in that it forges poetry out of the quarrel with himself combining, as Michael O'Neill has shown, a self-critique with a celebration.[29] There is the pride of the circus ring-master presenting his characters now on display as they perform, and transform, the ordinary (the quotidian) into the fantastic (the private world of symbols) – those poetic devices (tropes) which were skilfully manipulated to entertain, and dazzle, the reader. The poem surveys the old Celtic theme which inspired *The Wanderings of Oisin*, the warrior Oisin who is led to the island by the enchantress Niamh with whom he is infatuated. The allegorical islands are allegories of states of mind: 'infinite feeling, infinite battle, infinite repose'.[30] There is a shift to the legend of the Countess Cathleen, about whom Yeats had written a play in which the Countess (played by Maud Gonne ('The Circus Animals' Desertion', 'my dear', line 21)) barters her soul to the Devil to rescue the peasants from starvation. There is an implied rebuke in the parallel between the Countess's single-minded dedication to the peasantry and Gonne's fanatical devotion to the Irish cause. Other characters from his plays are evoked:

the Fool and the Blind Man, archetypal figures whose function (in *On Baile Strand*) is to comment wryly on the actions of the heroic characters Conchubar and Cuchulain, images that seemed to the poet to matter more than their source:

> And when the Fool and the Blind Man stole the bread
> Cuchulain fought the ungovernable sea;
> Heart mysteries there, and yet when all is said
> It was the dream itself enchanted me;
> Character isolated by a deed
> To engross the present and dominate memory.
> Players and painted stage took all my love
> And not those things that they were emblems of. (lines 25–32)

For Yeats the symbols gradually became more exciting than life itself, out of which they had evolved. But a revived moment of pride in these 'circus animals' that were placed on show to catch the eye of the reader gives way to an agonising moment of acquiescence in his having to be content with the raw material of life out of which he fashioned his poetry, those flickers of inspiration to be traced to the 'foul rag-and-bone shop of the heart' (line 40). In coming to terms with the original source of inspiration – the muse at her least inspirational ('that raving slut / Who keeps the till' (lines 37–8)) – he creates fresh powerful images of the quotidian, the bric-a-brac of daily living which assert themselves above the incoherence of life ('old kettles, old bottles, and a broken can' (line 36)).

'The Man and the Echo' dramatises such mixed feelings of diffidence and pride in a final self-assessment of Yeats's own poetic achievement as one of the last Romantics who has had to engage, as an Irishman, with 'this filthy modern tide' ('The Statues', line 28). A sleepless night in his old age leaves him prey to nagging self-questioning. Did his patriotic play *Cathleen ni Houlihan* contribute eventually to the execution of the leaders of the Easter Rising? Was he responsible for the mental disturbance of a girl (Margot Ruddock) he had once known? Could he have spoken out in favour of the preservation of a house (probably Lady Gregory's mansion at Coole, which had been sold to the Department of Forestry)? Speculations about the nature of death and immortality are fused with a sense of purging himself of guilt, by introspective analysis of some significant moments of his life (cleaning 'man's dirty slate' (line 25)). Man's apprehensive query – 'shall we in that great night rejoice?' (line 40) – is left unanswered by the oracular Echo which resounds from a magical 'cleft that's christened Alt' (line 1), a mountain in Sligo. Doubts and queries are set aside as the poem shifts to a mood of poignant resignation as the poet stoically awaits the end:

> Then stands in judgment on his soul
> And, all work done, dismisses all
> Out of intellect and sight
> And sinks at last into the night. (lines 33–6)

But then, at a moment of serenity, the 'spiritual intellect's great work' (line 16) is interrupted by the sound of pain and suffering ('a stricken rabbit' (line 47)) which distracts thought as it replaces the silent Echo.

Notes

1. *'John Sherman' and 'Dhoya'*, vol. xii of *The Collected Works of W. B. Yeats*, ed. Richard J. Finneran (London: Macmillan, 1991), p. 32; William Murphy, 'William Butler Yeats's *John Sherman*: An Irish Poet's Declaration of Independence', *Irish University Review*, 9:1 (Spring 1979), p. 93.
2. Lines 41–2; *The Collected Poems of W. B. Yeats* (London: Macmillan, 1967). All further quotations from Yeats's poetry are taken from this edition, unless otherwise stated.
3. *W. B. Yeats. Writings on Irish Folklore, Legend and Myth*, ed. Robert Welch (Harmondsworth: Penguin, 1993), p. 108.
4. W. B. Yeats, 'The Celtic Element in Literature (1898), in *Essays and Introductions* (London: Macmillan, 1961), p. 184.
5. James Joyce, *A Portrait of the Artist as a Young Man*, ed. J. Atherton (London: Heinemann, 1969), p. 235.
6. Notably by Elizabeth Cullingford, *Yeats, Ireland and Fascism* (London: Macmillan, 1991), p. 31, and Timothy Webb, *W. B. Yeats: Selected Poems*, ed. Webb (Harmondsworth: Penguin, 2000), in a note to *The Wanderings of Oisin* (Book iii), p. 231.
7. See Helen Vendler's perceptive interpretation in 'The Later Poetry', in M. Howes and J. Kelley (eds.), *The Cambridge Companion to W. B. Yeats* (Cambridge: Cambridge University Press, 2006), pp. 97–8.
8. Quoted in R. Foster, *W. B. Yeats: A Life*, 2 vols. (Oxford: Oxford University Press, 1997), vol. i, pp. 123, 27.
9. *Lady Gregory: Selected Writings*, ed. L. McDiarmid and M. Waters (Harmondsworth: Penguin, 1995), p. xvi.
10. *Ibid.*, p. xxiii; 'Estrangement', in vol. iii of *The Collected Works of W. B. Yeats*, ed. W. O'Donnell and D. Archibald (London: Macmillan, 1999), p. 353.
11. Quoted in Foster, *Yeats: A Life*, vol. i, p. 481.
12. *Autobiographies*, in *The Collected Works of W. B. Yeats*, vol. iii, ed. W. O'Donnell and D. Archibald (Basingstoke: Palgrave Macmillan, 1999), p. 400.
13. *Ibid.*

14. Richard Ellmann, *Yeats: The Man and the Masks* (London: Faber, 1960), p. 73.
15. W. B. Yeats, *Mythologies* (London: Macmillan, 1959), p. 333.
16. *W. B. Yeats, A Vision and Related Writings*, ed. A. Norman Jeffares (London: Arena, 1990), p. 42.
17. *W. B. Yeats. The Later Essays*, ed. W. H. O'Donnell (London: Macmillan, 1994), p. 204.
18. A. Norman Jeffares, *W. B. Yeats: A New Biography* (London: Hutchinson, 1988), p. 215.
19. *Ibid.*
20. R. F. Forster, *W. B. Yeats: A Life* II. *The Arch-Poet 1915–1939* (Oxford: Oxford University Press, 2003), p. 63.
21. Frank Kermode, *Romantic Image* (London: Routledge, 1961), p. 71.
22. A. N. Jeffares, *A New Commentary on the Poems of W. B. Yeats* (London: Macmillan, 1984), p. 247.
23. Declan Kiberd, 'Leda and the Swan', in *Inventing Ireland: The Literature of the Modern Nation* (London: Vintage, 1996), pp. 314–15.
24. Yeats, *A Vision*, p. 267.
25. Seamus Heaney, *The Redress of Poetry* (London: Faber, 1995), p 149.
26. Jeffares, *A New Commentary*, p. 381.
27. Quoted by Timothy Webb, in the notes to his edition of W. B. Yeats, *Selected Poems*, p. 296.
28. W. B. Yeats, *On the Boiler* (Dublin: The Cuala Press, 1939), p. 31.
29. Michael O'Neill, *Romanticism and the Self-Conscious Poem* (Oxford: Clarendon Press, 1997), p. 257.
30. Jeffares, *New Commentary*, p. 425 n.11 (quoting Yeats's letter to Katherine Tynan, 6 February 1889).

Chapter 42
Imagism

VINCENT SHERRY

On the evening of 17 July 1914, Ezra Pound and Amy Lowell faced each other from opposite ends of a long dinner-table in the Dieu-donné restaurant in London. The occasion brought together most of the poets included earlier that year in the anthology Pound had titled (in pseudo-French) *Des Imagistes*: H.D., Richard Aldington, F. S. Flint, Allen Upward and Ford Madox Hueffer (Ford), among others. The celebratory feeling turned to ritual toasts, but the accomplishments of Imagism(e) gave way in short course to questions about its very identity. Hueffer confessed that he was ignorant of what an Imagist was, or could possibly be (even so, he professed his doubts that Lowell qualified as one). Upward joked that all it took to be an 'Imagist' was to be named one by Pound. Aldington then objected that Imagism certainly existed, but only in the signal instance of H.D. (his wife), whose work discovered its proper company, not among the members of the contemporary avant-garde (the Vorticists had also gathered in the Dieu-donné), but with classical prosodists, with archaic Greek poetry in particular.[1]

The scene survives as an emblem of Imagism and, as a narrative for literary history, its parabolic fable. Here Pound and Lowell, sometimes behaving politely in public but usually not, face off in a test of strength for control over an initiative whose identity remains indeterminate. Any representative anthology of Imagism would reflect this uncertainty, showing more as a miscellany than a coherence. Even within the (assignably) Imagist oeuvre of individual poets the inconsistency is striking. Hueffer alternates a verse of horrible doggerel (as bad as the worst barrack-room ballad) with poems of exquisite urban impressionism. Aldington shifts from the songs of a neo-Hellenic ritual myth, which are remarkably adequate to a feeling of 'primitive' simplicity and impersonality, to lyrics of the sheerest personal grievance only a few rhythmic beats away from prosaic complaint. A vatic minimalism in H.D. is incandescent with vision in some poems; small, uninteresting things clot the prosody in others. Even the term Imagism, which frames a visual picture as the likely centre of poetic attention, fails to define the emphasis in much of the verse actually written.

The miscellaneous nature of this production, however, really indicates the experimental temper of Imagism. In the trial-and-error spirit of a novel prosody, it generated a good deal of surplus work. Of course 'surplus' is a term we impose retrospectively, as we read literary history backwards and exercise a principle of exclusion on writing that we judge to be less important in relation to those heuristic devices we call 'subsequent developments'. A linear model of literary history is positioned from the invented end-point of an exclusionary process. Nonetheless, Imagism can be seen as an energy coincident with the nascent poetics of High Modernism, as a force emerging in a fitful but highly eventful exchange with the major legacies of late Victoriana. If Imagism reveals a fault-line between the nineteenth and twentieth centuries, it also tells a story of continuity and change over the long turn of the century.

The most representative statement of Imagist poetics comes in the March 1913 issue of *Poetry* (Chicago). There is a descriptive essay titled 'Imagisme', attributed to Flint but composed jointly with Pound, which features these three injunctions:

1. Direct treatment of the 'thing,' whether subjective or objective.
2. To use absolutely no word that does not contribute to the presentation.
3. As regarding rhythm: to compose in the sequence of the musical phrase, not in the sequence of the metronome.[2]

Then comes the famous set of advisory mottoes, gathered under Pound's name as 'A Few Don'ts by an Imagiste', which, it turns out, he drafted originally as a rejection slip for the magazine's editors. That editorial function might encourage a misunderstanding of the principles of Imagism as an editorial cleansing action. But these 'Don'ts', which are more than a few,[3] also exceed negation as they reiterate and develop the dictates listed above. In this discursive synthesis, Pound projects the new ideals towards which Imagist poetry might aspire, offering the triple principle of direct musical presentation. These three words indicate the essential principles of Imagist poetics. Taken together, they represent the development of initiatives undertaken by the more advanced poetries of the preceding years. An understanding of the relation of Imagism to these predecessors is crucial to an assessment of its import in literary history.

Restoring Decadence

The most frequently credited precedent for Imagism is Symbolism (or, Symbolisme, which, in this modern French reference, echoes as the toney inflection dubbed into Imagiste and Imagisme). In one of the earliest, still most cogent accounts of French Symbolism, Edmund Wilson traces its poetics back to the American Poe and locates its motto and agenda in Mallarmé's famous saying – 'de la musique avant toute chose'.[4] As music above everything else, French Symbolism takes the action of poetic language to be not the representation of some prior reference but the direct presentation of the poem's own sensations and impressions. The poet handles the verbal counters as centres of immediate sensory experience, as material of musical plastic. The acoustic token prompts those imaginative associations which encompass the meaning, the sometimes misty significance, that 'symbol' claims as namesake for the school.

A poetry composed around these principles obviously resonates to a verse of 'direct musical presentation' in Imagism. Although Wilson was not studying Symbolism as a precedent for Imagism, it is nonetheless remarkable that the Symbolism he rebuilt around the musical value has simply dropped out of the critical account of Imagism. The occlusion has something to do with the false lead to the visual that is inscribed by the term 'Image'ism. But the misdirection also involves some of the literary and cultural values attached to Symbolist music. These values reside in the term which the authors of the first two major studies of Imagism, Glenn Hughes and Stanley Coffman, most notably suppress: Decadence. Coffman avoids the word entirely. Hughes reduces it to the status of a pseudo-counter. He labels it a 'so-called' reference – Decadence in this account being just one among a number of minor 'movements . . . that overlapped with and were submerged by "symbolism."'[5]

Decadence, it needs to be recognised, is not a 'movement', let alone a submergible one. It is a comprehensive sensibility, indeed a *weltanschauung*, one which includes a highly developed sense of its late historical day and which takes this presentiment of lateness, age or decline (*de-cadere* 'to fall away') as the basis for a broad range of artistic attitudes and practices. This sensibility coincides with apprehensions of decline in political and social history in the cultural capitals of Europe: a decaying aristocracy, an imperial outlook losing moral confidence even as it was gaining terrain and the emergence of 'the crowd' as a randomising force in the experience of urban modernity. These currents converge in an experience of lost dominance by a former master class which, whether or not the Decadents were actually members of it, was appropriated as an imaginative vantage for their representations. As an establishing circumstance, then, Decadence may be said to generate or include if not 'submerge' French Symbolism itself, which is 'decadent' in the evident sense that it represents a falling off from the dominant consciousness of nineteenth-century Romanticism, the mainstream values of late nineteenth-century literary culture: it eschews sincerity in emotional representation; it denies the truth value of poetic codifications; it rejects moral edification through literature. If Symbolism stands as a formative background for the poetics of Imagism, the meaning of this influence needs to be assessed in reference to the larger phenomenon of Decadence, which, as the larger phenomenon, provides the more highly signifying term.

In its well-established negative valence, Decadence stands as the pole opposing the fresher energies of Imagism. The negotiation, however, reveals a resisting reciprocity at least – a genealogy, a line of descent. A derivation with a difference, the exchange locates one of those sites where an outlook now identifiable as early Modernism extends the most important developments of the previous periods even – or especially – as it attempts to establish its independence. If modern-ism, after all, signifies the *ism* of the *modern*, the faith of the new, and 'decadence' invokes the old age of the world in its late stage of decay, the gravitational drag of this former century measures some of the historically determined content of Modernism – beginning with Flint's essay on contemporary French poets.

Published in August 1912, 'Contemporary French Poetry' gathers under its title a substantial (sixty-page) analytical anthology, which Flint ranges as a history of French poetry from Baudelaire to the present. The poetics of the verse he admires clearly anticipates the codes he will co-sign with Pound: this is poetry not of statement but of direct, musical, sensual evocation. Although he does not use the term 'Imagist', let alone 'Imagiste', the most significant action in the piece is the task of naming the poetics he is promoting. 'Symbolism', as a comprehensive category, offers a default term – with various prefixes attached to it or its epigones as partial apologies for the inexactness of the classification. Counters as awkward as 'neo-Mallarmism' make do, but will not do.[6]

The most conspicuous word is the one Flint takes great pains to exclude: Decadence, which he pushes out of the account in two signal positions. First, after opening with a census of poets writing in the aftermath of Baudelaire, and recognising that the most significant 'new spirit' to have 'found a voice . . . was called decadent', he relegates this designation immediately, in the next sentence, to the status of a remainder: 'It chose the designation *symbolist* as an alternative.'[7] The swiftness with which Flint accepts this alternative, which is entirely inadequate to the complexity of the case, bespeaks a nervousness and, in that, the edgy correctness of the name he would leave behind. And second, in his conclusion, where he addresses Futurism as the extreme type of the convention-dismaying energies of his chosen poets: '[T]o those who cry out against a great wind for its destructiveness, one must answer that great winds are the necessary sanitation of the earth. Degeneration? Rubbish!'[8] The judgment that Max Nordau attached to Decadence in his 1892 volume, *Degeneration*, haunts the identity of the poetry Flint admires. The nearly spasmodic quality in this rejection evinces that nervous concern which, in the twice-told action of his overture and closure, provides its own inverted testament to the power – as interesting and important as it is disturbing – of the connection he otherwise suppresses.

This connection with Decadence underlies a contemporary analysis of Imagism by (Margaret) Storm Jameson (in *The Egoist*, which ran a 'Special Imagist Number' in April 1915). It informs the essay in substance and style. While she does not name Decadence as such, she does not need to; the literary history she traces for Imagism emphasises just those themes of decline and decay that were attached to Decadence in polemics for and against it. That culture of controversy clings still to her own rather archly mannered rhetorical postures: 'Pray regard again the *degradation* of literature . . . the *descent* is prettily ordered', she remarks disingenuously on the movement from early modern to post-Victorian art. Within this literary history of decline she places Decadence understandably as a late or decayed Romanticism, and so reads Imagism as the last instalment of a long process beginning in Shelley, extending through Tennyson and cresting (if Decadence can be said to crest) in Swinburne. This trajectory is inscribed as the long dying fall in the Romantic poets' call for response to an ideal of nature that has faded through the nineteenth century.[9]

Whether Jameson disapproves or approves of Imagist poetry appears as a question not so important as the literary history she frames to explain it and the tone she adopts to respond to it. Seeing it as a decayed Romanticism, she adopts a voice of fond contempt that registers the status of a treasured but decrepit legacy. The dense involutions of her rhetorical pose register the tensions evident in the Decadent identity of Imagism – suppressed, expressed in deflected gestures, it is a truth as unexpected and uncomfortable as it is important.

Decadence appears in these duly complex representations in another one of the primary prose documents of Imagism, T. E. Hulme's 'Lecture on Modern

Poetry' (first delivered in 1909, again in 1914, as *Des Imagistes* was moving through the press).[10] Like Jameson, Hulme features 'decay' as the underlying force in the literary history he traces to situate his title subject. 'It must be admitted that verse forms, like manners, and like individuals, develop and die. They evolve from their initial freedom to decay . . .' He then repeats 'decay' as a refrain-word, as a continuous principle of English literary history: 'after the decay of Elizabethan poetic drama came the heroic couplet, after the decay of the couplet came the new lyrical poetry that has lasted until now'. The point of this emphasis lies in the attention he now forcibly draws to the literary sensibility of his own historical day: 'The latter stages in the decay of an art form are very interesting and worth study because they are particularly applicable to the state of poetry at the present day.' He expatiates:

> [poetry at the present day] resembles the latter stages in the decay of religion where the spirit has gone and there is a meaningless reverence for formalities and ritual. The carcass is dead, and the flies are upon it. Imitative poetry springs up like weeds, and women whimper and whine of you and I alas, and roses, roses all the way. It becomes the expression of sentimentality rather than of virile thought.[11]

From the effeminacy routinely attributed to Decadence through the attitudinised case of Wilde, to those tropes of overgrowth, which feature an overdoing of Romantic attitudes as a form of decay, the poetics and ethics of literary Decadence are evident in the strong caricature of this polemical negative. Accordingly, in the subsequent constructions of the 'Lecture', Hulme presents his proto-Imagist poetry as an intervention in the current Decadence. This poetry is to be pruned of the excesses of Decadent verbiage; it is attuned to a new range of sensory reference, the visual, which resists a Decadent poetics of music, music all the way, of music above everything else.[12] And while the poetry he extols (and writes) witnesses an interest in the possibilities of visualising through language, the 'Lecture' evidences an obsession with music that suggests, as with the revealing exertions in Flint's essay, the powerful presence of this enemy in the poetics he intends as riposte – a suggestion which the poems themselves bear out in richer detail.

Consider Hulme's instrumentation of syntax in 'The Embankment (The fantasia of a fallen gentleman on a cold, bitter night)':

> Once, in finesse of fiddles found I ecstasy,
> In the flash of gold heels on the hard pavement.
> Now see I
> That warmth's the very stuff of poesy.

Oh, God, make small
The old star-eaten blanket of the sky,
That I may fold it round me and in comfort lie.[13]

Normal word order is inverted several times, most strikingly in the first line. The words may thus function outside the constructive logic of grammatical statement. They are working as prompts, not only semantically but acoustically. And so the references to musical instruments, the conspicuous alliteration in the first line, the subtler consonance in the second between the feeling of the 'hard pavement' and the hard vowels of 'gold' and 'heels': the irregular syntax allows the imaginable sounds to be realised in the reader's 'inner ear'. The direct presentation of associative sensation like this, as the review of those 1913 documents in *Poetry* has suggested, establishes the method and directive of Imagist poetics, and this aim is realised as the syntax in 'The Embankment' orchestrates its images to a poetic whole that is, in every available sense of the term, musical, musical above everything else, musical all the way.

How is the visual content promised by the term Imagism negotiated by this proto-Imagist Hulme? He sets up the mechanics of the poetic image in a contemporary companion piece, 'Notes on Language and Style'. Here he depicts the image largely as a matter of 'poetic analogy', where visible images appear as the figurative terms of similes and metaphors. On this secondary level of elaboration, the visual image emerges as a decorative rather than essential element – a status he emphasises in according it the value of lightness, even capriciousness: 'Analogies in poetry, like the likenesses of babies, to be taken half-seriously, with a smile.' The visual similitude, he indicates, is really just a happy accident of perception, whose 'inspiration is a matter of an *accidentally* seen analogy or unlooked for resemblance . . . Fertility of invention means: remembrance of *accidental* occurrences noted and arranged (cf. detective stories)'.[14] In the poems, then, his 'visual images' appear characteristically as the humorously, sometimes surprisingly, always casually apprehended term of comparison. 'Like a red-faced farmer' goes his deflating trope for that old favourite, 'the ruddy moon'. More wistfully, even less imposingly, the moon in 'Above the Dock' is seen as 'but a child's balloon, forgotten after play'. Still lightly and comically, if more startlingly, he sees himself in passage 'to the final river' floating 'Ignominiously, in a sack, without sound / As any peeping Turk to the Bosphorus'.[15]

These chancy, sometimes hilarious 'accidents' characterise a poetic likeness that may be understood as a riposte to the 'Esemplastic Imagination' that Coleridge had proposed as the poetics of a visionary Romanticism. Hulme in fact uses 'plastic imagination' as a term elsewhere in the 'Notes', echoing Coleridge but only to take the edge of pretence off whatever '*esemplastic*' might mean – the example he provides for this 'plastic imagination' is 'two tarts walking along Piccadilly on tiptoe, going home, with hat on back of head'.[16] Hulme's visual wit is subverting Coleridge's High Romantic formulation and reducing it to the level of that lower imaginative activity which Coleridge called 'Fancy' and which, in his proscription, entails the mechanical elaboration of just such 'accidental' comparisons as Hulme features and enjoys. Hulme's claim to novelty in this proto-poetics of Imagism is thus strongly overridden with the practices of an inferior or decayed version of Romanticism, which is to say, by the spirit of the Decadence it otherwise contests. Indeed, he characterises the visual analogies of his Imagism, as a form of 'humour', as 'the decadent form into which all forms of literary expression can be shown to pass by degeneration of function'.[17]

Hulme's poems first attracted the 'Imagist(e)' tag when they appeared, in 1912, in the Appendix to Pound's volume *Ripostes*, where, in his gloss, Pound says nothing at all about any visual element in the poetry. He provides instead a tangled, mannered account of the origins of Hulme's verse in a so-called 'School of Images'. This is his formation for the 1909 *cénacle* that Hulme had convened with Flint, whose interest in recent French poetry is at once registered and ridiculed in Pound's characterisation.[18] In fact, Pound had taken little account of that national verse before now. As a formation, and in a moment dominated by a number of Continental 'isms', Imagisme appears as an assertion – dashing, dashed off – of French-ness most of all.

Pound invokes an alternative patria, however, in a couple of knowing jokes: in titling Hulme's *petit oeuvre* (there are five poems in all, none longer than nine lines) *The Complete Poetical Works of T. E. Hulme*; and in observing the sardonic chronology of an author 'publishing his *Complete Poetical Works* at thirty'.[19] The posthumous gesture in that title, which inters a young author's career virtually at its start, repeats a conceit that dominated the *English* 1890s – the decade of genius dying young, the so-called Tragic Generation. The conceit was realised through no shortage of examples, Aubrey Beardsley and Lionel Johnson and Ernest Dowson and, most memorably, Oscar Wilde. But it could be played on, too, in jests like *The Works of Max Beerbohm*, a title which, in 1896, lowered that twenty-four-year old's very small production (all *short* stories and essays) into an early crypt.

This conceit could be played on because it caught a presentiment working across the historical sense of this decade. Living in the last decade of the last century before the last century of the millennium, the sense of an ending that dominated this moment was echoed and reinforced in Britain with the figure of an ageing, long-dying queen, muse and icon for an ageing, long-dying empire. Coming into their maturity in the moment when history is winding down: here is the counter-rhythm special to the younger poets of this decade; growing up already and quickly dying, the paradox inscribes the wit and darkening jest of this brief generation, the model as well as the moment of English Decadence. That Pound invokes it as a reference for Hulme's poems suggests the continued relevance of a sensibility which Imagism reciprocates as much as resists. And while an end-of-empire-days feeling grew through the English nineties, calling up comparisons with the late age of Imperial Rome and echoing this presentiment in an ominously Latinate diction, the first anthology of Imagism will offer an answer to the Latinity of English literary Decadence in an alternative classicism.

Imagistes, and other Greeks

'It's straight talk, straight as the Greek!' Pound wrote of the H.D. poems he was sending to Harriet Monroe at *Poetry* in October 1912.[20] 'It will be seen from these that *Imagism* is not necessarily associated with Hellenic subjects', Monroe countered in her 'Editor's Note' to 'Imagisme' in the March 1913 issue,[21] where the Hellenic element was in fact so strong that Monroe, presenting herself as spokesperson for the 'modern' quality Pound had claimed for H.D.'s verse, felt obliged to issue this disclaimer about antique material. Together, Pound and Monroe define the significant counter-measure of this verse: its directness and intensity are associated with living speech but worked out in reference to, often in rhythmic mimicry of, the assignably archaic measures of Greek antiquity. 'And she also was of Sikilia and was gay in the valleys of Aetna, and knew the Doric singing', goes the epigraph (translated from the Greek) to *Des Imagistes*,[22] which, if it presents Hellenic song as the tuning fork for the poems to come, does so as writing on a page, the medium and register for the otherwise (to most readers) unspeakable Greek: we are, after all, just *looking at* these printed forms.

The tension goes to a question in the aesthetic identity of the initiative being fabled here. A myth of origins, as a song performed in the morning of the world, locates the revolutionary (going in a circle) impulse in Imagism, which is seeking the immediacy and directness of first words for its poetics of direct sensual experience. But the record of this incentive is overwritten with – as – a series of scripts: the Greek recedes from speaking immediacy even further as the language of English translation overshadows it. On this first page of Imagism, then, the palimpsestuous record of *litera*ture (letters on a page) locates the moment of its own writing at a late, an always later, day of history. It is a testament of the poetics of literary Decadence, which, as Linda Dowling has demonstrated, develops its highly writerly style as a response to contemporary understandings of the history of the language.[23] A shift from etymology to phonology relocated the unit of action in the development of words from semantic radicals (the root-and-branches scheme) to sound conglomerates (phonic molecules, as it were); these phonemic compounds changed according to rules that could only be formulated scientifically. In this model, the life of spoken language expired as soon as it hit the page, leaving printed words as mere shells, the fossilised remains, of their extinguished quick. This is the dead matter of language that Decadence takes hold of as carvable stuff, shaping and stylising it in ways that Beerbohm made famous for Pater's practice, 'that sedulous ritual wherewith he laid out every sentence as in a shroud'.[24] How powerful a precedent this sensibility remains in the substantiating struggle of Imagism's birth may be shown in the poems of this first anthology.

'The ancient songs / Pass deathward mournfully', Aldington writes in the first lines of 'Choricos'. Pound placed this poem as overture to the collection, and fittingly. The mythos of its rhetorical fiction commemorates the passing of that ancient music,

> From the green land
> Which lies upon the waves as a leaf
> On the flowers of hyacinth;
> And they pass from the waters,
> The manifold winds and the dim moon,
> And they come
>
> . . .
>
> In the silver days of the earth's dawning –
> Proserpina, daughter of Zeus. (*DI*, p. 7)

If the Imagist attempts to intervene in the dying fall of speech on to the page, thus to restore a sense of the music of spoken words in the reader's 'inner ear', his artistry works here to engage that finer audition of imagined sound. The parallelism of prepositional phrases – 'In the silver days of the earth's dawning' – offers its harmonic quality as a sort of second intention, in this secondary medium of print. Similarly, by placing 'manifold' and 'moon' at far ends of a line, he spaces out the alliteration, and, in the same line, submerges the vowel-rhyme to the internal assonance of 'wind' and 'dim'. It is a dense but hidden music. It is repeated in the locale of Hellenic myth in the second poem, 'To a

Greek Marble', where Keats's focus on the golden but frozen moment in 'Ode on a Grecian Urn' is recomposed to stress the lastingness of natural sounds:

When the fragile pipes
Ceased in the cypress shade,
And the brown fingers of the shepherd
Moved over slim shoulders;
And only the cicada sang. (*DI*, p. 10)

The music Aldington fables in the mythic garden endures in these lines as he quietly harmonises three disparate hard vowels into the one pleasing line of 'Ceased in the cypress shade', a consonance to which he contributes the further subtleties of slant internal assonance – 'fragile pipes', 'cicada sang'. And Aldington mythologises this poetic song as his riposte to the Rome of the Decadence, which, in the rhetorical fiction of his short poem 'In the Via Sistina', inverts the true muse of his poem, his poetics:

O daughter of Isis,
Thou standest beside the wet highway
Of this decayed Rome,
A manifest harlot. (*DI*, p. 15)

Similarly, in 'Sitalkas', H.D.'s first poem in the collection, the Hellenic site provides the ground for another ritual myth of poesis, which she observes in the curial manner of formulaic repetition:

Thou art come at length
More beautiful
Than any cool god
In a chamber under
Lycia's far coast,
Than any high god
Who touches us not
Here in the seeded grass.
Aye, than Argestes
Scattering the broken leaves. (*DI*, p. 20)

Where the repetitions – 'Than any cool god', 'Than any high god', 'than Argestes' – create the impression of a liturgical refrain, the speaking presence that is necessary to that fiction is not really claimed. The syntax and lineation resist it. Phrase-by-phrase, line-by-line, the language of the poem is shaped to a go-and-stop pattern that pauses always where the ritual plea – cresting, directed, momentous – would push it ahead. This may be taken as the effect of the Imagist's well-known attention to the individual line as the unit of composition. The freedom of *vers libre* brings this responsibility. And so this Imagist prosody – underplaying the musical effect as it undercuts the speakerly presence – works in the service once again of a finer audition, providing the reader's inner ear with this subtler music.

Like Aldington's, H.D.'s *is* the subtler music of Imagism. It is scored against those patterns of appliqué sound that Pound abjured as the Imagist resistance to fixed patterns of metre (the ignominious 'metronome') and end rhyme. It is designed, most important, not to attempt to out-shout the resistant medium of the page. Indeed, it may be heard as music *for the page*. Imagism may be read accordingly as a poetics that has taken the measure of the printed condition of literature. On this point, in fact, Hulme's 'Lecture' is adamant; he insists on a verse that is 'intended to be read in the study. I wish this to be remembered in the criticisms that are made on me.'[25] And that is the lesson of *literary* *Decad*ence (of *letters fallen* on to the page), with which Imagism is developing in due relation.

Another turn in this developmental curve shows in the poetry of F. S. Flint, whose signal position in the literary history of Imagism has been eclipsed, predictably but unfortunately, by the powerful personalities of Pound and H.D. The word to which his importance may be rightly scored is 'cadence', which appears as the title of his 1915 volume, *Cadences*, and which he glosses in his portion of the group-authored Introduction to the second of the annual *Some Imagist Poets* anthologies, where it offers a free-verse answer to conventional metrics.[26] If the impoverished Flint had less Greek than H.D. and Aldington (and Pound), he did have a little Latin, and the root his chosen word shares with that otherwise disputed name of *De-cadence* goes to a radical understanding indeed, a deep complicity that ensures the return of this repressed term. At his best, as his most defining measure, his verse features a 'falling away' as its signature rhythm, which writes out the major development his Imagism provides for the legacy of Decadence.

Flint's first poem in *Des Imagistes* shows this characteristic action in its master-cadence. Its rhythm, which rises and falls precipitously over its three verse-paragraphs, is built up and let down through a master manipulation of syntax and line-break. Opening with a lyric appeal to the apostrophised subject of London, it suspends the momentum as a series of rhetorical negatives leaves us waiting for the positive; but he also propels us forward through the fluid continuities of the soft enjambments:

London, my beautiful,
it is not the sunset

nor the pale green sky
shimmering through the curtain
of the silver birch,
nor the quietness;
it is not the hopping
of birds
upon the lawn,
nor the darkness
stealing over all things
that moves me.

The second of the three verse paragraphs provides a kind of medial hiatus, which expands the moment of dramatic waiting with emotions of longing and expectation – all in all, a rhythm rising within stasis,

But as the moon creeps slowly
over the tree-tops
among the stars,
I think of her
and the glow her passing
sheds on men,

so that, having paused and gathered and concentrated the forward orientation of the first verse paragraph in the second, Flint reaches a consummation in this third:

London, my beautiful,
I will climb
into the branches
to the moonlit tree-tops,
that my blood may be cooled
by the wind. (*DI*, p. 31)

The build-up and letting-go is not dissimilar to the structural rhythm of the Petrarchan sonnet, which accumulates the tension of the problem octave towards the 'turn' and release into the resolving sestet. In fact, Flint also cast this poem into sonnet form where, however, he loses its dramatic cadence, which becomes indistinct as the generic rhythm.[27] The contrast reveals the deeper conceit in his free-verse Imagism, especially in this climax. Just here, in the last line, as it were at the top of the wave, the rhythm comes to an exquisitely minimal figuration of, well, just the wind, and a cooling wind at that. This *falling off* conforms to '*cadence*' in the radical sense – in the specific, technical sense that is instinct with his own appropriation of the precedent of Decadence.

Of the five poems Flint contributed to *Des Imagistes*, only one other ('The Swan', *DI*, p. 35) finds a rhythm similar to the London piece. As though to recognise this as the distinctly Imagist 'cadence', Peter Jones included just these two poems (of those five) in his defining, retrospective anthology, *Imagist Poetry*.[28] The experimentation that retains an importance for literary history shows the negotiation with Decadence as one condition of its significance – as the intensifying condition of the most important verse in *Des Imagistes*.

Two of the poets who do not take up this eventful negotiation with Decadence are writing from a distant, an American, location. Lowell, for most notable instance, consistently misses the mark of the 'direct musical presentation' that is the rubric and standard of Imagism. Instead of converting the Symboliste emphasis on poetic music, *après* English Decadence in particular, into a distinctive prosody for the page, she tends typically towards a simple *visual representation*, which devolves all too often into an orgy of word-painting.[29] Certainly, William Carlos Williams paid attention to the page as a frame of visual reference for his reader. His experiments in verse lining turn this compositional space into a flexible medium, where he handles the language as a material of verbal plastic. None of this, however, in his 'Postlude' (*DI*, p. 39), which is really just an inventory of mythological allusion, a bad piece of classical pastiche. It seems to have been written in imitation of the neo-Hellenic dialect in which his friends Pound and H.D. were composing their Imagist verse. Not surprisingly, however, this American Continental is unable to share the motives his compatriots in London are following in giving their verse its ancient Greek turn. The European backgrounds and English location that explain the needs Pound and H.D. were serving in devising this alternative to the Latinity of Decadence are simply unavailable to him.

And James Joyce. Who, who, as a poet, might appear as a more incongruous accomplice among these Imagists?

> I hear an **ar**my ch**ar**ging upon the land,
> And the th**un**der of horses pl**un**ging; foam about their knees:
> **Ar**rogant, in black **ar**mour, behind them stand,
> Disd**ain**ing the r**ain**s [reins] with fluttering whips, the Charioteers.
>
> They cr**y** into the n**i**ght their battle name:
> I moan in sl**ee**p when I h**ea**r a**far** their whirling l**aughter**.
> They cl**ea**ve the gloom of dr**ea**ms, a blinding flame,
> Cl**an**ging, cl**an**ging, upon the heart as upon an **an**vil.
>
> They come sh**a**king in triumph their long gr**ey** hair:
> They c**om**e out of the sea and r**un** shouting by the shore. (*DI*, p. 40)

'I Hear an Army' shares a historical circumstance with the major poets of Imagism in England. The end-of-empire-days feeling that is one of the fostering conditions of literary Decadence, first Roman and then British, is recalled forcefully in this epic perspective. It recalls those northern European wastes, the channel- and battle-ground of fierce migrant tribes at the end of some perennially failing imperial reign. If an Irish political interest informs this historical fiction, Joyce scores his poetic music in accord with that of his companion talents in this volume – those Anglo-Americans, who have turned the poetics of literary Decadence, which admits the disintegration of voice in print and acknowledges the first claim of the page on the word, into the subtler acoustic of Imagism. This finer audition shows in the alternating pattern of end rhyme, where the muting effect of that sparer pattern is complemented by the concentration of *internal* assonance – internal both to the lines and to the words themselves, where the inner syllables form a recessed, a more distant, resonance to the reader's inner ear. Not that Joyce knew he was Imagist in this deep sense. The editor knew it, and, including this poem, builds out an understanding of the profounder historicity of Imagism in English literary culture.

Pound, moreover, follows Joyce in the sequence of *Des Imagistes*. Pairing their two poems, on face-to-face pages, he offers a conjunction more instructive by far than his fabled face-off with Lowell in the Dieu-donné. Joyce's historical fiction of falling empire, Roman as much as British, recalls the circumstance of a Decadent Latinity, to which the Imagist Pound offers the neo-Hellenic response in 'Doria' – a title which echoes to the call for the 'Doric singing' that he inscribed as legend and motto for the anthology:

> Be in me as the eternal moods
>   of the bleak wind, and not
> As transient things are –
>   gaiety of flowers.
> Have me in the strong loneliness
>   of sunless cliffs
> And of grey waters.
>   Let the gods speak softly of us
> In days hereafter . . . (*DI*, p. 41)

This bleak season clearly mirrors the late historical day of Joyce's poem, the declining time of empire, that time-zone of Decadence. Pound is pulling his own poem into that frame of reference and offering the now familiar Imagist response to it – important enough for him to republish this poem in *Des Imagistes*.

As a piece of signature Imagism, the poem uses the perspective of Greek antiquity to address emotions which, in any thesaurus of contemporary cultural codes, appear clearly as synonyms of Decadence. The stark solitude, which the poem offers as its dramatic emotion, reads as a sort of Byronic posture *in extremis* – at an extremity of late or exaggerated Romanticism, that is, as an attitude of Decadence. This is the poetic content of Imagism, which the new Hellenism is helping to sustain.

The integral role the new Hellenism plays in Imagism is borne out by the other poem Pound felt compelled to republish in *Des Imagistes*, 'The Return', which stages a rebirth of Homeric deities in a poetic fiction of lyric rapture:

> See, they return; ah, see the tentative
> Movements, and the slow feet,
> The trouble in the pace and the uncertain
> Wavering! (*DI*, p. 42)

The feeling of these gods' 'return' – hopeful but tentative, go-and-stop with the syntax breaking against the line-ends – is as convincing as the rhythm here is splendidly expressive. Our experience of this sensual dimension, however, is not keyed to syllable count, nor to the pacing or concentration of similar or related 'sounds'. The feeling of rhythm comes entirely through the enjambment. It is music for the eye of the reader. It exemplifies the visual prosody that Imagism has taken as the rule of its necessarily literary existence (as letters on the page) from that precedent of Decadence, to whose Roman deities it offers this alternative classicism.

The Imagist moment

The scene in the Dieu-donné may be located historically, too – in the high pathos of that particular moment, mid-July 1914. This is the Last Supper of Imagists, already in their early season, for, within several weeks, the war approaching from Eastern Europe will dissolve their bonds and shift their centre, which will not hold, to neutral America. Some of the reasons for this disintegration may have to do with the life-cycle of any literary movement, but the circumstances of immediate history also factor in strongly. The Imagist moment, I have been suggesting throughout this chapter, holds a firm and certain significance, and an appreciation of its coherence might be heightened with an understanding of how – and why – it comes apart in the years immediately following.

Whether Pound left Imagism because he had exhausted its resources or was incorporating these in the newer energies of Vorticism, the passing of organisational control to Lowell shows how strong a role his own editorial intelligence had played in drawing the poets he had gathered under the Imagist heading into a discernible identity. The group-authored Introduction to *Some Imagist Poets* (1915, first of three annual anthologies) reads like the proverbial letter-written-by-the-committee, replacing Pound's edgily negative 'Don'ts' with a set of literary platitudes. And the selection of poems shows no designing hand. Diminished if not missing entirely is the neo-Hellenic element that Pound had emphasised so consequentially. Few of Aldington's poems employ this resource, which, when it appears, appears just as a kind of relict; his lyric appeal shifts from the material of ancient song (renewed for the page) to the matter of personal story, barely rhythmical, hardly readable. Of the seven poems under H.D.'s name, only two have locations in Greek mythology, but this lower number coincides with initiatives now identifiable as the growing points of her own mature oeuvre. What these poems manifest is a well-managed, apparently calculated disproportion between a natural scene and the feelings projected into it. Speaking to a nature that does not answer as expected, H.D. is a Wordsworth who ramps up the language of emotional intensity in ratio to the failing authority of the natural subject to respond to, to correspond with, those feelings. It is another instance of Romanticism *in extremis*, at an extremity of literary history that is identifiable with the Decadence. This is the provoking circumstance of Imagism, but H.D. is now working at her own angle of relation to that provocation.

The loss of that original, integral conception may be followed as well through the external circumstances of history, that is, in the political and cultural eventuality of the First World War. If Imagism is a poetics of the private readerly space, the public Word of this Great War locates an antithetical register for the language of verse. Already by early 1915 the difference is told, and it occurs most notably in the wording of Aldington's references to archaic Greece – the verbal material that has grounded the distant music of the Imagist page. Those sound-effects belong to a different order entirely now:

> Zeus,
> Brazen-thunder-hurler,
> Cloud-whirler, son-of-Kronos,
> Send vengeance on these Oreads
> Who strew . . .[30]

Aldington is turning up the volume of imagined sound in a way that echoes most notably to the gigantism of mass war. He records this feature of the imaginative experience in the graphic, phantasmagoric prospect of '1915': 'A vast breast moves slowly, / The great thighs shift, / The stone eyelids rise.'[31] The colossus of Total War overwhelms the perceptual content of the Imagist poem, whose specificity of feeling is at odds with the generality – the ideological language – of the public war. Aldington traces this circumstance as the prospect in 'Whitechapel':

Noise;
Iron hoofs, iron wheels, iron din
Of drays and trams and feet passing;
Iron
Beaten to a vast mad cacophony.

In vain the shrill, far cry
Of swallows sweeping by;
In vain the silence and green
Of meadows Apriline;
In vain the clear white rain . . .

Noise, iron, smoke;
Iron, iron, iron.[32]

Where the 'clear white rain' presents the Imagist particular with exemplary specificity, the war impinges on this specialist (italicised) language and takes the poem back to a sphere of experience whose lexicon reads just as 'Iron, iron, iron'. The one word utters the generality of mass war, otherwise unspeakable in verse.

As for the other 'young men of 1914', then, 'Imagism' seems to be a victim of its short historical day. Yet it witnesses a considerable significance in the linkage it establishes between the Decadence of late Victoriana and the emergent poetics of Modernism. In the aesthetic values of that later canon, several points of Imagist influence are specifically evident: concision in imagery (of all senses), the crucial compositional unit of the line and the importance of music, of music above everything else, of music all the way. In a wider frame of reference, High Modernist poetry may be said to apply the Imagist principle of direct presentation to a new range of poetic materials, extending from the sensory to the rare and recherché: that peculiar combination of the recondite matter-of-fact is the enabling conceit of so much High Modernist verse. The rising rhythm of this musical obscurantism might be heard also as the dying fall of older standards of representation and statement – a not so distant echo after all of the Decadence that Imagism has restored if not reformed.

Notes

1. Claire Healey recreates this occasion from various sources in 'Amy Lowell Visits London', *The New England Quarterly* (September 1973), pp. 442–6.
2. 'Imagisme', in *Poetry* (March 1913), p. 199. The essay was Flint's, but Pound inserted these three points. See Christopher Middleton, 'Documents on Imagism from the Papers of F. S. Flint', *The Review* (April 1965), pp. 36–7.
3. *Poetry* (March 1913), pp. 200–7.
4. Edmund Wilson, *Axel's Castle: A Study in the Imaginative Literature of 1870–1930* (1931; repr. New York: Scribner's, 1969), esp. pp. 12–20.
5. Glenn Hughes, *Imagism and the Imagists* (London: Oxford University Press, 1931), p. 6; Stanley K. Coffman, Jr., 'Imagism and Symbolism', in *Imagism: A Chapter for the History of Modern Poetry* (Norman: University of Oklahoma Press, 1951), pp. 74–103. The suppression of the term begins in 1899, when Arthur Symons altered the wording of his pilot essay, 'The Decadent Movement in Literature', Harper's *New Monthly Magazine* (November 1893), pp. 858–67, to that of his book title, *The Symbolist Movement in Literature* (London: Constable, 1899). Frank Kermode accepts Symons's change of terms in *Romantic Image* (New York: Macmillan, 1957), pp. 108–11, while Hugh Kenner, in *The Pound Era* (Berkeley: University of California Press, 1971), valences 'decadence' entirely negatively and uses it to discount the importance of Pater and Symons to what is valid in Imagism, pp. 179–83.
6. F. S. Flint, 'Contemporary French Poetry', *Poetry Review* (August 1912), pp. 355–414; 365–6.
7. *Ibid.*, p. 357.
8. *Ibid.*, p. 411.
9. Margaret Storm Jameson, 'England's Nest of Singing Birds', *The Egoist*, 2 (1 November 1915), pp. 175–6.
10. The 'Lecture' is dated thus by Sam Hynes (ed.), *Further Speculations: T. E. Hulme* (1955; repr. Lincoln: University of Nebraska Press, 1961), p. xvii. Hynes places it as an essential precedent to the later 'Imagism' of Pound and Flint.
11. Hulme, 'A Lecture on Modern Poetry', in Hynes (ed.), *Further Speculations*, pp. 68–9.
12. *Ibid.*, pp. 70ff., esp. pp. 73–5.
13. As published in the 'Appendix' to Pound's 1912 *Ripostes*; repr. *Personae: The Shorter Poems of Ezra Pound*, ed. Lea Baechler and A. Walton Litz (New York: New Directions, 1990), p. 268.
14. Hulme, 'Notes on Language and Style', in *Further Speculations*, pp. 85, 84; emphases added.
15. In *Personae*, pp. 267–8.
16. Hulme, 'Notes on Language and Style', in *Further Speculations*, p. 82.

17. *Ibid.*, p. 85.
18. In *Personae*, p. 266.
19. *Ibid.*
20. *Selected Letters of Ezra Pound, 1907–1941*, ed. D. D. Paige (New York: New Directions, 1950), p. 11.
21. *Poetry* (March 1913), p. 198.
22. *Des Imagistes: An Anthology* (London: The Poetry Bookshop, 1914; New York: Albert and Charles Boni, 1914), p. 2. Poems in this collection will be cited as *DI*.
23. Linda Dowling, *Language and Decadence in the Victorian Fin de Siècle* (1986; repr. Princeton: Princeton University Press, 1989), pp. 46–103.
24. Max Beerbohm, 'Diminuendo', in *The Works of Max Beerbohm* (London: John Lane, The Bodley Head, 1896), p. 150.
25. Hulme, 'Lecture', p. 73.
26. *Cadences* (London: The Poetry Bookshop, 1915); *Some Imagist Poets, 1916: An Annual Anthology* (Boston: Houghton Mifflin, 1916), pp. viii–ix.
27. See *Imagist Poetry*, ed. Peter Jones (Harmondsworth: Penguin, 1972), p. 148.
28. *Ibid.*, pp. 75, 80; Jones takes other poems from various years of the annual *Some Imagist Poets* anthologies.
29. Only one of Lowell's poems appears in *DI* ('The Garden', p. 38); this visual proclivity is increasingly pronounced in the annual *Some Imagist Poets* anthologies.
30. *Some Imagist Poets: An Anthology* (Boston: Houghton Mifflin, 1915), p. 16.
31. *Some Imagist Poets, 1916*, p. 7.
32. *Ibid., 1916*, pp. 8–9.

Chapter 43

T. S. Eliot

GARETH REEVES

'Flinging itself at the last / Limits of self-expression': these lines from 'Opera', one of the early poems by T. S. Eliot in the notebook eventually published as *Inventions of the March Hare*,[1] convey a barbed attitude towards self-expression that was to be the hallmark of 'Tradition and the Individual Talent'. At the time 'still a fairly recent compound', as the notebook's editor Christopher Ricks remarks, 'self-expression' often occurs in scare quotes in Eliot's prose.[2] It is related to but not the same as 'introspection', the title Eliot gave to a short early prose-poem, also in the notebook, in which 'the mind' is observed 'six feet deep in a cistern' along with 'a brown snake with a tri-angular head' that has 'swallowed his tail [and] was struggling like two fists interlocked'.[3] The prose-poem wants to find a way to depict the actions of the mind, to objectify the subjective, while 'self-expression' claims no such objectivity. Fascination with and resistance to introspection intertwine in the prose-poem's appalled imagery of internal struggle.

Hence one way to read Eliot's 'Impersonal theory of poetry' is as defensive armoury against the demanding imperatives of introspection and its attendant terrors. The defensiveness is in such statements as the oft-quoted 'the poet has, not a "personality" to express, but a particular medium, which is only a medium and not a personality'.[4] And one can detect in the early poetry that attitude being worked towards and worked out. The poetry invariably reveals a meta-poetic awareness of itself as artistic *medium*, often involving the trope of stage or screen for the objectification of emotion, with attendant manoeuvres for distancing the self, such as sliding between first, second and third person pronouns, so that the self is both participant in and observer of experience. The approach signals a profound desire to apprehend the 'reality' (as in 'human kind / Cannot bear very much reality')[5] behind and beyond the miasma of self and everyday life – a beyond that, before his conversion to Christianity, Eliot tended to associate with F. H. Bradley's 'absolute', and after it definitively with God. This, in the words of another early notebook poem, 'Silence', 'is the ultimate hour / When life is justified'.[6] With reference to these lines Ricks cites Nietzsche's statement in *The Birth of Tragedy*, which Eliot had read: 'we have our highest dignity in our significance as works of art – for only as an *aesthetic phenomenon* is existence and the world eternally *justified*'.[7] The statement both denigrates life's diurnal self and makes great claims for the artistic vision of life.

The picture of the artist as self-divided, both participant and observer, is captured in an early four-part sequence of short poems, 'Mandarins', also in the notebook. Both creator and creation of his circumstances, the mandarin appears with 'intrepid dignity' as one 'indifferent' (a recurrent word in this and other early poems), to 'the crowds', who are 'Keen to appropriate the man' – thus anticipating Eliot's 'Coriolan': 'With fixed regardless eyes – / Looking neither out nor in – / The centre of formalities' (part 1). The mandarin is the type of Eliot's poet, caught amongst myriad experiences but apprehending an absolute, with whatever irony, his Nietzschean 'highest dignity' making aesthetic justification of 'The rest [which] is merely shifting scenes' (part 1). The result, in the words of another notebook poem, 'Interlude: in a Bar', is to make 'life' come across as 'immediate, and far'. 'Mandarins' 4 makes explicit the artistic mediation, both linguistic and, now, cinematic: 'Still one more thought for pen and ink! / . . . / How very few there are, I think, / Who see their outlines on the screen.'[8]

This epistemology, 'neither out nor in', with that accompanying screen, gets a more celebrated, and precise, elaboration in 'The Love Song of J. Alfred Prufrock': 'as if a magic lantern threw the nerves in patterns on a screen'. Ricks points out that according to the OED 'screen' was first used to mean cinema screen in 1910, and he also cites Robert Crawford's suggestion that a St Louis newspaper article, 'Seeing the Brain', illustrated with a head 'lanterned' or 'outlined' on a screen, inspired the line in 'Prufrock'.[9] The line conveys a sense of the poet's 'nerves' projected on to the 'screen' of the poem 'Prufrock' for the reader to see. The nervous system responds to external stimuli, and the poem-screen frames a projection of that inward response.

The epistemology is everywhere apparent in the linguistic procedures of Eliot's early poetry. 'To prepare a face to meet the faces that you meet', a line that is itself a verbal mirror, reflects the self-regarding air of the poetic medium which is 'The Love Song of J. Alfred Prufrock'. After the poem's self-reflexively divided opening address to 'you and I', the affected but affecting initial simile, 'When the evening is spread out against the sky / Like a patient etherised upon a table', says as much about the nervous system of the observing consciousness as it does about what is being observed. The first paragraph transfers on to things epithets of human awareness: 'The *muttering* retreats / Of *restless* nights . . .' (emphases added). The 'streets' turn into mental labyrinths to 'follow like a tedious argument / Of insidious intent', until they reach the final mental abstraction of 'an overwhelming question', which remains emphatically abstract by never being asked let alone answered. Much of the poem is filtered through a predisposed and ironically distancing consciousness 'immediate, and far', in lines that set up nervy repetitive patterns: 'For I have known them all already, known them all'; 'I know the voices dying with a dying fall'; 'And I have known the eyes already, known them all'; 'And I have known the arms already, known them all'. There are phrases implying the reduction of experience to the linguistic and verbal: 'That lift and drop a question on your plate'; 'For decisions and *revisions* which a minute will reverse' (emphasis added); 'The eyes that fix you in a formulated phrase'. The rhetoric is continually provisional, full of questions and conditionals, of future and past tenses, stage-managed by a fastidiously questioning consciousness: 'And indeed there will be time' twice, and variants thereof; 'Shall I say, I have gone at dusk . . .?'; 'Should I, after tea and cakes and ices . . .?'; 'And would it have been worth it' twice, and variants thereof.

Again, the elusive phrasing of the 'Preludes' (I–IV) sequence holds the very concept of 'consciousness', and the word, up for inspection: 'The morning comes to consciousness / Of faint stale smells' (II). But to whose consciousness? Or does the consciousness belong to the morning itself? Or perhaps this is a distinction without a difference, for 'You dozed, and watched the night revealing / The thousand sordid images / Of which your soul was constituted' (III) – 'as if a magic lantern threw the nerves in patterns on a screen' indeed, for these lines conceal as much as they reveal. They go round in circles, for the watcher discovers in the night whatever it is that constitutes her soul. The language of perception here ('revealing', 'images') enacts an objectification of the subjective, as the poetry itself goes on to imply a few lines later: 'You had such a vision of the street / As the street hardly understands.' A similar mindscaping scenario locates the 'soul' of 'Preludes' IV: 'His soul stretched tight across the skies / That fade behind a city block, / Or trampled by insistent feet . . .' The asyntactically surprising 'Or' throws the reader off-balance, and the 'stretched / trampled' parallelism makes the fleetingly nervy suggestion that the stretched soul is being trampled, rather than the 'block'. A little later the slippery genitive in the line 'The conscience of a blackened street' makes both street and city-*flâneur* the possessor of this conscience; and 'consciousness' shadows the word 'conscience', so that the mindscape flickeringly takes on a moral inflection. The flicker intensifies with the unexpected intrusion of the first person, right at the end of the sequence: 'I am moved by fancies that are curled / Around these images, and cling.' The effect destabilises not only the reader but also, it seems, the speaker, for the clinging imagery moves him from indifferently distant 'fancies' to 'The notion of some infinitely gentle / Infinitely suffering thing' – although even as that 'notion' is entertained, the very word intimates a dandyish resistance, no more than an entertaining. And so it proves, as the speaker instructs a worldly but indefinite 'you' to 'Wipe your hand across your mouth, and laugh' in order to contemplate 'The worlds [that] revolve'. The poet has taken a step back from his screen of nervous and nervy patterns, and the poetry wipes away the potentially deceptive vision to raise a defensive shield with a harder, unsympathetic simile about 'ancient women'. The poem moves sharply at the end here between the 'immediate' and the 'far'.

That double focus is at its sharpest in the stage-managed poem 'La Figlia Che Piange', with its Laforguean *dédoublement* in which, as A. D. Moody explains, 'the poet assumes a double presence, being at once the actor and the consciousness of his action'. The staging is managed in part by sliding between pronouns, 'your' giving way to 'her' and 'she', 'I' turning into 'him' and 'he', and then the two becoming one in 'we', and then, finally, 'they'. The verbs that begin the first five lines 'at once declare [the girl's] actions and direct them'.[10] The second stanza stands even further back, replaying the scene from a different perspective, moving from the original, ambivalent, present to an equally ambivalent past conditional: 'So I would have had him leave, / So I would have had her stand and grieve.' The ambivalence has the effect of 'mixing / Memory and desire' (*The Waste Land*, lines 2–3). When desire becomes uppermost, the tense moves unsettlingly back into the present, 'I should find': syntax requires 'I should have found', but the poem's 'consciousness' is compelled into a present beyond time. Tony Pinkney is alert to the poem's doubleness when he comments that 'the poet [is] simultaneously contemplative observer and dangerous participant in the dramatized situation',[11] but the danger of emotional involvement is averted by the very fact that the situation is being acted out mentally. The performance is highly poised and stagey, especially when the leave-taking is most dramatic: 'As the soul leaves the body torn and bruised, / As the mind deserts the body it has used'. Mental drama here turns into emotional melodrama, as the speaker almost admits when he wonders how the couple 'should have been' had they not parted: 'I should have lost a gesture and a pose' – 'aesthetic phenomenon' as justification indeed, but at what emotional expense? Consciousness directs the action on the mind's stage according to desire, but at the end the speaker turns on himself with Laforguean insouciance.

Another of Eliot's early self-reflexively stagey poems is 'Portrait of a Lady'. Here the situation is complicated by the fact that both protagonists, the speaker and the lady, who surreptitiously alters from 'you' to 'she', are at the mercy of their mental theatres. 'You have the scene arrange itself – as it will seem to do': this elusively double way of putting it has the protagonist both director of and actor in the drama. The aesthetics of the stage take over and take on the emotional dynamics. The poem unfolds in three set-piece scenes of familiar emotional patterns, 'Recalling things that other people have desired' (Part II). The 'atmosphere of Juliet's tomb' unashamedly makes Part I a theatrical setting. Whatever does or does not happen is according to a pre-arranged scenario: 'I have saved this afternoon for you.' The scene is 'Prepared for all the things to be said, or left unsaid'. The actors in this drama may have the illusion that they are free agents, but they have to choose from a pre-scripted repertoire: 'We have been, *let us say*, to hear the latest Pole' (emphasis added). When in Part II the lady quivers at youth's cruelty, that it 'smiles at situations which it cannot see', the speaker performs his allotted part and 'smile[s], of course'. When in Part III the script goes as expected and his 'self-possession flares up for a second; / *This* is as I had reckoned', a flash of self-awareness, that he is indeed playing a part, at once deflates: 'I feel like one who smiles, and turning shall remark / Suddenly, his expression in a glass. / My self-possession gutters; we are really in the dark.' The fearful craving to get behind the mirror of the self was the poet's lifelong obsession. But for now, for this poem, the defensive postures of the actor must suffice: 'And I must borrow every changing shape / To find expression' – a metapoetic moment that acknowledges what the poem is up to.

Existence becomes 'aesthetic phenomenon' in 'Portrait of a Lady' also by means of a running musical analogy. At first irony plays over the analogy, the poet gingerly fingering the Symbolist inheritance (Verlaine's 'Art Poétique': 'De la musique avant toute chose') as 'regrets' are 'caught' 'Through attenuated tones of violins / Mingled with remote cornets' (I). But soon the violins become insinuating and the cornets 'cracked' as the speaker's consciousness takes on a critical life of its own: 'Inside my brain a dull tom-tom begins / Absurdly hammering a prelude of its own' (I). The musical analogy then tracks the emotions: the lady's voice comes back to the poet discordantly 'like the insistent out-of-tune / Of a broken violin on an August afternoon', and the poet's aloof self-possession is only broken 'when a street-piano, mechanical and tired / Reiterates some worn-out common song' (II). And finally the analogy signals a characteristically Eliotic *dédoublement* in which the poet steps back to reflect on poetic and emotional gains and losses: 'This music is successful with a "dying fall" / Now that we talk of dying – / And should I have the right to smile?' Poetry as music takes on theatrical associations with the allusion to *Twelfth Night*; and this concluding self-reflexive question challenges the self-defensiveness of the whole performance which is the poem.

With all its evident textuality, its vacillations, abrupt transitions, disconnections and surprising connections, *The Waste Land* involves itself in complex ways in introspective struggle. At one time Eliot considered prefacing *The Waste Land* with 'Gerontion',[12] no doubt as a way of providing a unitary consciousness for the ensuing 'Thoughts of a dry brain in a dry season', the uncohering poetic fragments, as they must have appeared then to their author, that make up his startling brainchild. 'Gerontion' exposes the mind's tricky workings. The frequent reiteration of the word 'think' in the fourth verse-paragraph, at or near the end of a line, denotes a morbid propensity to deliberate, which appears to be the reason for the speaker's incapacity. The poem is self-defeatingly labyrinthine, enmeshed in its own thought processes. A comparable intense self-questioning characterises *The Waste Land*, which frequently betrays an awareness of its own procedures. It frames itself in self-aware gestures, near the start asking 'what branches grow / Out of this stony rubbish? . . . / . . . for you know only / A heap of broken images' (lines 19–22), and near the end saying, through the voice of the Fisher King, 'These fragments I have shored against my ruins' (line 430). The poem is attendant on its own birth-pangs, its effort to make sense out of the stonily intransigent material of memory.[13]

'This process of increasing self-consciousness . . . has as its theoretical goal what we may call *la poésie pure*', wrote Eliot.[14] The pressure of a Symbolist *poésie pure* is at the heart of *The Waste Land*'s yearnings towards an absolute, but the poem is continuously if sporadically aware of the possible deceptions, the whispering deceits, involved, as is evident in the epiphanic 'moment in and out of time' ('Dry Salvages' v) in the hyacinth garden. The episode presents a muse-figure at the opposite end of the inspirational spectrum from the woman who 'fiddled whisper music' (line 378), a spectrum that includes Madame Sosostris and the woman of the neurasthenic episode in 'A Game of Chess' – thus conforming after a fashion to Eliot's note to line 218 that 'all the women are one woman'. Memory and desire mix in the hyacinth girl episode (lines 35–41), the action of the poetry testifying to an intense struggle to locate the feeling. Yearning and desolation vie, yet the poetry would locate itself beyond, 'Looking into the heart of light, the silence'. It acts out an intense, trembling vacillation between fulfilment and void: 'I could not / Speak, and my eyes failed, I was neither / Living nor dead, and I knew nothing, / Looking . . .' The negatives suspended at the line-endings point up the emotional tension between 'profit and loss', in the words of 'Death by Water' (line 314).

Another moment of lyric intensity, the water-dripping song (lines 346–58), occurs in 'What the Thunder said', which Eliot, claiming it 'remained exactly as I first wrote it', evidently felt represented a breakthrough.[15] But though the song is arguably the nearest the poem gets to that theoretical goal of *la poésie pure*, its pellucid short lines emerging uncannily out of a congested, syntactically uncertain and haltingly expectant passage, it remains suspended in anticipation, the series of 'if' clauses getting resolved bathetically with the phrase 'But there is no water'. Yet there has just been water, sinuously articulated by the lines 'But sound of water over a rock / Where the hermit-thrush sings in the pine trees / Drip drop drip drop drop drop drop'. This music is present only momentarily before it gets dismissed, but nevertheless it is permanently present in the poetry, transcending memory and desire. Its conditional presence is an absolute of the poetry. Yearning and despair, fulfilment and frustration, come together and are left behind – but only for an instant.

Critics who have wanted to do justice to *The Waste Land*'s fleeting but powerful numinous moments and to the intimations of regeneration in 'What the Thunder said' – the 'damp gust / Bringing rain' (lines 393–4), the 'aethereal rumours' (line 415), the 'heart [that] would have responded / Gaily, when invited' (lines 420–1) – and reacting against early accounts of the poem as a vision of despair simply, have often read it as taking the first step towards Christian belief. This was Helen Gardner's approach, and that of Lyndall Gordon, who argues that Eliot's poetry traces 'a consuming search for salvation'.[16] From one point of view the argument is incontrovertible, but it inevitably employs hindsight: it knows the end of the search, that 'In my end is my beginning' ('East Coker' v), which indeed is the view the self-declared Anglo-Catholic poet himself was later to take. But from the perspective of the poem itself, the introspective view, Gardner's and Gordon's teleological approach runs the risk of denying the very nature of the poetry under examination, its enactment of not knowing where it is going.

Thus the poetry of 'What the Thunder said' is acute testimony to the fact that Eliot needed time in order to know what he really felt about, above all, Christianity. The first paragraph swells with surreal delirium, from the agony in the garden to post-apocalypse, without any sure sense of how it got there, either syntactically, chronologically or rhythmically. The uncertain syntax makes it impossible to tell if 'The shouting and the crying' and the 'reverberation / Of thunder of spring', with its intimations of regeneration, happen after 'the torchlight', 'the frosty silence' and 'the agony in stony places' of the first three lines, or if they are contemporaneous. The rhythmical deflation in the line 'He who was living is now dead' carries on into the next, 'We who were living are now dying', this effect paralleling the sense of incomprehension of the 'We' who are 'now dying' but why we cannot tell. These lines enact an emotional state akin to that of the Magi, in 'The Journey of the Magi', who, in the words of 'The Dry Salvages' II, 'had the experience but missed the meaning'. Of the paragraph's last three lines Ricks writes: 'Is the antithesis finished at "dying"? But then "dying" has not arrived at the endedness of "dead" . . . Is "With a little patience" a retrospect or a prospect?' The lines refuse to 'placate our impatience and settle the matter: no full stop after "dying" or after "patience" '.[17] Depending on whether one stops after the unpunctuated word 'dying' or reads on into the next line conveys either a new beginning and hope, or a diminuendo of hopelessness. In the space that succeeds this opening paragraph reader and speaker are suspended between 'living' and 'dying'. The abbreviated last line, 'With a little patience', sounds a disturbingly uncertain, nonplussed note, bewildered and bewildering, hesitating between conclusion and anticipation, stoicism and resignation, giving up and carrying on. But the passage does not dither, though it equivocates. It enacts patience, the sense of what it feels like not to know the outcome.

The poetry of 'What the Thunder said' repeatedly enacts patience. That is what happens with the water-dripping song, perpetually on the point of hearing the rain which does not fall. It is what happens on the journey to Emmaus, which provides the occasion for continual spectral apprehension and expectation. It is what happens notably in the responses to the thunder. The lines 'The awful daring of a moment's surrender / . . . / By this, and this only, we have existed' equivocate (lines 403–5). '[A]nd this only' is either a diminution ('only' meaning merely: 'this mere moment is all we have of significance to show for our lives') or an intensification ('only' meaning solely, uniquely: 'our lives are significant only by virtue of this supreme moment'); or rather it is both, the poetry holding in tense relationship two opposed attitudes, straining at each other. Diminution and intensification threaten to cancel each other out: entrapment tangles with release, in religious terms, damnation with redemption. Hence 'The awful daring of a moment's surrender' is inscrutably Janus-faced. One can either be defeated by dwelling on such intense memories, or be redeemed through them, as with the key a few lines later that can both lock and unlock. *The Waste Land*'s 'moment' is a decisive turning-point, but nothing has been decided. The only decisive thing is the firmness of the indecision, the poetry's precisely articulated patience.

Similarly, the second response to the thunder (lines 411–16) enacts the difficulty of breaking out of solipsism. Eliot's note to these lines quotes a passage from Bradley's *Appearance and Reality*: 'My external sensations are no less private to my self than are my thoughts or my feelings. In either case my experience falls within my own circle, a circle closed on the outside.' The struggle of introspection is the agonising aspect of the need to escape the self ('[O]nly those who have personality and emotions know what it means to want to escape from these things').[18] The poetry of the second response creates a closed circle of language. The syntax is locked in on itself, imprisoned; it is difficult to break out of the phrasing. But release is also audible. The line 'We think of the key, each in his prison', heard as a single unit of sense, closes the door, intimating the isolation of each of us. But then 'each in his prison / Thinking of the key', heard as another unit, opens the door, because for one isolated individual to think of the isolation of another momentarily breaks through the wall of isolation. But then the line 'Thinking of the key, each confirms a prison', read as another unit, closes the door again. In each case the line-ending can be heard as both a turning-point and a stopping-point. But the lines do not dither; they enact a resolutely scrupulous uncertainty. They are patiently possessed by the intransigence of their emotions.[19]

One of *The Waste Land*'s techniques to intimate thwarted religious longing, patience tried to breaking-point, is the truncated quotation, in particular the fragments shored from St Augustine: 'To Carthage then I came' and 'O Lord Thou pluckest' (lines 307, 310). The fact that the latter is preceded by the less truncated 'O Lord Thou pluckest me out' only goes to draw attention to the technique, the repeated phrasal fragmentation conveying emotional disintegration. Eliot uses the technique with greater deliberation in 'The Hollow Men', a poem which more consciously hovers longingly, if disconsolately, on the threshold of religious illumination. The last part of the poem quotes a fragment of the doxology from the Lord's Prayer, '*For Thine is the Kingdom*' (twice), and then, more stutteringly, 'For Thine is' and 'For Thine is the', thus registering emotional anticipation trailing off into dispiritedness, patience at a low ebb, endurance without prospect, and preparing the way for the parodic treatment, in the last four lines, of another doxology, 'Glory be to the Father', whose 'world without end' is turned into post- or non-apocalyptic bathos ('*This is the way the world ends*' thrice) before dying away with a '*whimper*'.

Greater still is the patient deliberation of *Ash-Wednesday*. This sequence enacts introspection's 'stops and steps of the mind' (III) with uncompromising emotional precision. The poem is, in the words of 'Journey of the Magi', 'no longer at ease here, in the old dispensation' and would move on. It apprehends Christian grace but would gain 'strength beyond hope and despair' (III), the strength to recognise that the poet may have had the experience and missed the meaning but that the meaning has not been, may never be, comprehended. The deliberation is, by its very nature, highly self-aware, spiritually and poetically. 'Teach us to care and not to care / Teach us to sit still': this lesson of fortitude towards the end of Part I is still to be learned towards the end of the sequence, where those words are repeated, but with the rider 'Suffer us not to mock ourselves with falsehood', in case the intervening long-suffering meditations have given vain hope. *The Waste Land* intuited patience; *Ash-Wednesday* works at it, with metaphoric contemplation, as it unfolds a series of spiritual states and stages. As argued earlier,*The Waste Land* frames itself in self-aware gestures, but *Ash-Wednesday* describes the task in hand more directly: 'Consequently I rejoice, having to construct something / Upon which to rejoice' (I). The joy is through gritted teeth at this stage in the sequence, but spiritual fortitude and the determination to make poetry out of it go hand in hand here.

Hence the 'Word', with a capital W, is the Logos, but God's Word can only be approached through the patient struggle with our words, the language of this fallen world. But the first paragraph of Part V, a heady whirl of words about (in both senses of that word) 'The Word without a word', inevitably finds this language inadequate to the task of locating the Word, for 'Against the Word the unstilled world still whirled / About the centre of the silent Word', the auditory pun emphasising the linguistically Babylonian confusion of this whirling world. Poetry attains its highest meaning in its opposite, silence ('Words, after speech, reach / Into the silence' ('Burnt Norton' V)) and so 'Where shall the word be found, where will the word / Resound? Not here, there is not enough silence' – and not therefore in this poetry you are reading, is the implication. But into this meditation, at this point in Part V and again later, the poet inserts words attributed to Christ on the cross: 'O my people, what have I done unto thee.' Isolated as a line on their own, surrounded by the silence of blank space, with their simplicity reaching beyond their fusion of anguish, accusation, sorrow and pity, these words, uttered by Christ on the point of death, approach the ineffable. And Part V ends with that quotation abruptly truncated – 'O my people' – as if reaching further into the silence: a decisive truncation, not the nervous truncations of *The Waste Land* and 'The Hollow Men'.

Eliot's poetic meditation on the Word was evidently prompted by the phrase (about the Nativity) 'the word within a word, unable to speak a word' that he gives as an instance of Lancelot Andrewes's 'flashing phrases which never desert the memory'. And, strikingly, Eliot's essay on Andrewes, 'the first great preacher of the English Catholic Church', gets a purchase on its subject almost entirely through the preacher's prose style, in which '[i]ntellect and sensibility were in harmony'. By way of demonstrating this harmony Eliot quotes the following (and much more) from F. E. Brightman's 'admirable criticism' on Andrewes: 'He does not expatiate, but moves forward: if he repeats, it is because the repetition has a real force of expression.' So when, taking his cue from Brightman, Eliot writes of Andrewes's sermons, 'this extraordinary prose, which appears to repeat, to stand still, but is nevertheless proceeding in the most deliberate and orderly manner', he could be describing the patiently deliberate new poetic style he was developing for the *Ash-Wednesday* sequence.[20] (The essay on Andrewes appeared in 1926; the *Ash-Wednesday* poems, originally published separately, began to appear in 1927.)

In particular he could be describing *Ash-Wednesday*'s opening lines, which enact the emotional tensions of turning back to and turning away from memory and desire – as well as the related tensions of poetic frustration and inspiration, of the 'turning' of a 'verse': 'Because I do not hope to turn again / Because I do not hope / Because I do not hope to turn'. This repeated truncating of a translated quotation (from the first line, 'Perch' io non spero di tornar giammai', of Guido Cavalcanti's heart-broken poem written in exile from his lady)[21] is, again, more deliberate than the emotionally disintegrating truncations of *The Waste Land* and 'The Hollow Men'. The repetitions that open *Ash-Wednesday* may appear 'to stand still', but they proceed purposefully in such a way as to question whether there is a difference between 'to turn again' and 'to turn'. At first any difference seems to be one of emphasis, but the intervention between the first and third lines of the more absolute line 'Because I do not hope' introduces a sense of resolution, acquired even this early in the sequence by the very act of repetition, of apparent standing still: since the 'turn[ing] again' has been to no avail, the poet determines not 'to turn' in the future. Already resignation has moderated, quietly and patiently, into resolution, anticipating in little the movement of the larger sequence. It seems the resolve is maintained at least into the third paragraph of Part I, where 'Because I do not hope' turns into 'Because I cannot hope', acknowledgment of hopelessness turning into recognition of the need to resist hope.

But backsliding is always imminent, so that even as the poet performs his verbal and mental revolutions and resolutions, he brings himself up short with the realisation that this very performance is at issue:

And I pray that I may forget
These matters that with myself I too much discuss
Too much explain
Because I do not hope to turn again
Let these words answer
For what is done, not to be done again . . .

Let these words 'Because I do not hope to turn again' with which the poem began, shorn of their repetitions with variation, suffice. But they do not, for Part I continues until it arrives at its inassimilable lesson, 'Teach us to sit still', and a Hail Mary. And the sequence continues until it arrives in Part VI at another repetition with variation of the 'hope' motif: 'Although I do not hope'. We, and the poetry, ponder the advance, in Hugh Kenner's words, 'from the zone of feeling dominated by "Because . . ." to the domain of "although . . .," from a ratiocinative submission ("Because I know . . ." "Consequently I rejoice . . .") in a place where "there is nothing again," to a tension among substantial presences . . . that has no place for "because" and "consequently."' That tension is elaborated in the bewitching paragraph of 'substantial presences' beginning 'And the lost heart stiffens and rejoices', in which, as Kenner further notes, 'every noun, verb and adjective pulls two ways', between memory and desire, renunciation and rebellion, transfiguration and delusion. 'The tension itself is a good', writes Kenner, so that when 'Teach us to care and not to care' is repeated from Part I, this time 'the resignation is of greater purity', since the poet has learned the lesson 'Suffer us not to mock ourselves with falsehood'.[22]

Redeeming the old, pre-Anglo-Catholic, self involves redeeming the poetry written by that self. '[H]aving to construct something', therefore, also entails the art of poetic re-construction and renovation, 'restoring / With a new verse the ancient rhyme' (IV). Thus some of the borrowings of *Ash-Wednesday* are from Eliot's old poetry, in particular *The Waste Land*. The 'stony rubbish' (line 20) and 'the desert' filled 'with inviolable voice' (line 101) of *The Waste Land* turn into the desert of renunciation of *Ash-Wednesday* II and into 'the last desert between the last blue rocks' of Part V and the 'blue rocks' at the poem's close, rocks amongst which we have to learn to endure and 'sit still', a revised and redemptive version of the Fisher King 'Fishing, with the arid plain behind me' (*The Waste Land*, line 424), shored up by poetic fragments – or at any rate potentially redemptive, for 'even among these rocks' the poet prays 'not to be separated' (thus echoing the Roman Catholic hymnal).

Crucially, *Ash-Wednesday*'s elusive visionary lady revises *The Waste Land*'s concatenation of muse-figures of differing and sometimes opposed natures. In *The Waste Land* the concatenation comes across as fortuitous, but

Ash-Wednesday, as if in response to this aspect of the earlier poem, merges its female figures with seeming deliberation in a way which, while mystifying, is central to the poem's spiritual search. While the hyacinth girl is fleetingly, if poignantly, ambiguous, in *Ash-Wednesday* such ambiguity is dwelt upon, for it is central to the spiritual states through which the sequence moves. Beginning in Part II as a mysterious figure 'withdrawn / . . . to contemplation', a Dantesque Beatrice (in the *Vita nuova*), 'Lady of silences' who, like the hyacinth girl but more definitively, fuses the contraries of memory and desire, of 'love satisfied' and 'love unsatisfied', she 'gathers divinity', in Kenner's words,[23] becoming associated with the Virgin Mary, 'the veiled sister' of Part V, to be addressed finally as 'Blessèd sister, holy mother'. In all this, the state of being mystified is what the poet must learn patiently to accept.

By the time of *Four Quartets* Eliot's poetry had become very aware of its customary procedures. Central to these, and indeed to his thinking on many topics, aesthetic, religious, social and political, is the ordering principle of 'pattern', a word that recurs throughout the *Quartets*. Pattern makes possible the organisation of multifarious experiences and emotions into a larger whole, and thus, as critics have long recognised, the reconciliation of opposites.[24] The two great opposites that the *Quartets* would reconcile are the temporal and the eternal. And it is remarkable how the sequence ponders what had been at the heart of Eliot's thinking since at least 'Tradition and the Individual Talent'. E. J. Stormon has summarised it as an awareness of the past 'both in its temporal perspective and as something persisting in the present': Eliot had a 'simultaneous perception of a time-dimension through which the past recedes and of a supra-temporal order in which the past never recedes'.[25]

Under these heads various opposites jostle in the *Quartets*: change and permanence, movement and stillness, speech and silence, past and future, the actual and the imagined. But although the sequence meditates on time and eternity, on history and the present, and on the intervention of the divine in human life, its idiom is poetry, not philosophy. Poetry, here allied in Symbolist fashion to music, is proposed as the great reconciler: 'Words move, music moves / Only in time', language is a temporal medium, but through 'the form, the pattern' of poetry, words 'reach' towards their opposite 'Into the silence' ('Burnt Norton' V). Discursiveness is one register of the *Quartets'* style, but the focus is more on mental landscape than on the validity of any particular proposition or argument. The sequence enacts the movement of words in time and the mind's alterations: 'The detail of the pattern is movement' ('Burnt Norton' V). Even in this ostensibly sociable poetry, much of it composed in an idiom befitting Eliot the Elder Statesman's public persona, introspection plays an important part.

Thus, as Gabriel Josipovici writes, 'This is a poem that grows by coils, not by marching forward in a straight line', a statement that can be applied to single passages as well as to the design of the sequence as a whole. In the opening section of 'Burnt Norton', which Josipovici calls 'the drama of a voice talking to itself',[26] and which meditates on time and memory and on what 'is the use of memory' ('Little Gidding' II), the poetry goes round in circles with deictic self-awareness: 'My words echo / Thus, in your mind.' The word 'present' occurs four times in the first ten lines, but without precision. But, we remember, 'if he repeats, it is because the repetition has a real force of expression' (Brightman on Andrewes): the repetition indicates how this mind is stuck in the 'present', of which it would make sense by looking before and after, but it cannot. Lines turn obsessively on themselves: 'Remaining a perpetual possibility' is either a hopeful line or a despairing one, or rather it is both, depending on how you hear the next line, 'Only in a world of speculation', which can mean 'merely' in such a world or 'solely' in such a world: 'a world of speculation' is something to be spurned ('merely') or to be desired ('solely'). The enjambment means that the line 'Only in a world of speculation' opens up the previous line in various, possibly contradictory ways, as the language listens to itself moving forward. What the next lines go on to present, to make 'present', is indeed a 'world of speculation', where the imagined and the desired become actual, in the here and now of the poetry: 'Footfalls echo in the memory / Down the passage which we did not take / Towards the door we never opened / Into the rose-garden.' Possibility has been made into actuality by the action of the poetry, by the sound of the voice's coiled meditation echoing in the mind *now*: 'Thus'.

After the ensuing lines have called up the visionary 'moment in and out of time' ('Dry Salvages' V) in the rose-garden, the poetry arrives at where it started, but with more certitude ('We had the experience but missed the meaning' ('Dry Salvages' II)). 'What might have been and what has been / Point to one end, which is always present': these lines, at the end of 'Burnt Norton' I, repeat lines already heard near the start. But whereas there they conveyed bewilderment and stalemate, here, in their new context, they sound purposeful. For although the poet has come to the conclusion that 'human kind / Cannot bear very much reality', at least that epiphany in the rose-garden has been, momentarily, realised, and a sense has therefore been achieved, through the action of the poetry, that everything is still to play for, that time is indeed, after all, 'redeemable'. The fact that we live in the 'always present' means that there is as much reason for hope as for despair, that possibilities are continually opening up, a process that the poetry enacts as it moves from line to line. This kind of poetry is the nearest language can get to creating the sensation that 'all is always now' ('Burnt Norton' v). Every moment – in the poem as well as in life – is a turning-point, an intersection of past and future, of actuality and possibility: 'the pattern is new in every moment' ('East Coker' II). Memory, at first potentially disabling, has become potentially liberating. The choice is ours as to what use we make of the present, whether we allow it to be a means of confinement or of emancipation – a lesson whose poetic enactment we have already witnessed most affectingly in *Ash-Wednesday*. That lesson gets a rather more definitive formulation towards the end of the *Quartets*, the poetry characteristically trying to make sense of what it has already enacted – the poetic equivalent of having had the verbal experience but not quite comprehended the meaning: 'This is the use of memory: / For liberation – not less of love but expanding / Of love beyond desire, and so liberation / From the future as well as the past' ('Little Gidding' III).

In the course of their coils the *Quartets* expand to apply this lesson to historical as well as to individual narrative – 'History may be servitude, / History may be freedom' ('Little Gidding' III) – and the backward look characteristic of the *Quartets* has Eliot revise his old poetic self so as to make private conform to public. The most remarkable instance is the *terza rima* passage of 'Little Gidding' II. This passage, evoking the bombing of London during the blitz, is also the occasion for some intensely personal poetry. The *mise-en-scène*, an amalgam of the *Inferno* and the *Purgatorio* of Dante, Eliot's lifelong poetic influence, is highly appropriate, because this 'moment in and out of time', this historical moment in wartime London and this ahistorical moment in a ghostly netherworld, becomes the occasion for defeat, or, if the right truths are learned from it, for purgatorial redemption. '[T]he dark dove with the flickering tongue' is a German warplane, but also recalls the Pentecostal dove and the Holy Spirit 'tongued with fire', and so destruction and the possibility of salvation merge in this image. The 'refining fire / Where you must move in measure, like a dancer' can be destructive or restorative. It paradoxically combines the fire of Hell and the fire of Purgatory. The home truths about the poet's lifetime dedication to poetry which are conveyed to him by the Dantean 'familiar compound ghost' are, again paradoxically, made the more searingly resonant by the fact that they are compounded from an echo-chamber of quotations from a host of writers, past and present, highly familiar to the poet, all members of his personal pantheon. This otherworldly doppelgänger comes up with some piercingly worldly-wise lessons about 'the gifts reserved for age'.

In the *terza rima* passage it is as if the poet is consciously formulating what he now recognises has always been at the heart of his poetry: 'So I assumed a double part'. As this chapter has argued, assuming a double part, seen at its most stagey – and 'part' conjures up the stage – in the *dédoublement* of poems such as 'La Figlia Che Piange', is the spirit informing Eliot's poetry early and late, enabling an objectification of emotion and probing of introspection. In the *terza rima* passage that spirit becomes an articulated and articulate strategy, the doubling signalled with great deliberation: 'Knowing myself yet being someone other'. The poetry hovers determinedly in the shady area between potentiality and actuality: ' "What! are *you* here?", / Although we were not.' And the self whom the poet encounters he must learn to face, to face up to, and so survive and live beyond: 'And he a face still forming'.

Notes

1. T. S. Eliot, *Inventions of the March Hare: Poems 1909–1917*, ed. Christopher Ricks (1996; San Diego: Harcourt, 1998), p. 17.
2. *Ibid.*, p. 121.
3. *Ibid.*, p. 60.
4. Eliot, 'Tradition and the Individual Talent', in *Selected Essays*, new edition (New York: Harcourt, 1950), pp. 7, 9.
5. Eliot, 'Burnt Norton' 1, *Four Quartets*, in *Collected Poems 1909–1962* (London: Faber, 1963). Unless otherwise indicated, quotations of Eliot's poetry are from this volume. Line references are given in parenthesis for *The Waste Land* only, following the practice of this edition.
6. Eliot, *Inventions*, p. 18.
7. As cited *ibid.*, p. 125.
8. *Ibid.*, pp. 19, 20, 51, 22.
9. *Ibid.*, p. 139, and Robert Crawford, *The Savage and the City in the Work of T. S. Eliot* (Oxford: Oxford University Press, 1987), pp. 8–9.
10. A. D. Moody, *Thomas Stearns Eliot: Poet* (Cambridge: Cambridge University Press, 1979), pp. 38, 39.
11. Tony Pinkney, *Women in the Poetry of T. S. Eliot: A Psychoanalytic Approach* (London: Macmillan, 1984), p. 56.
12. See Peter Ackroyd, *T. S. Eliot* (1984; London: Sphere, 1985), p. 117.
13. These sentences draw on my *T. S. Eliot's 'The Waste Land'* (New York: Harvester, 1994), p. 39.
14. T. S. Eliot, 'From Poe to Valéry', in *To Criticize the Critic* (London: Faber, 1965), p. 39.
15. Letter to Peter Russell, 19 May 1948, quoted in *The Waste Land: A Facsimile and Transcript of the Original Drafts*, ed. Valerie Eliot (London: Faber, 1971), p. 129.
16. Helen Gardner, *The Art of T. S. Eliot* (London: Cresset, 1949), throughout; Lyndall Gordon, *Eliot's Early Years* (Oxford: Oxford University Press, 1977), p. 2.

17. Christopher Ricks, *T. S. Eliot and Prejudice* (London: Faber, 1988), pp. 178–9.
18. Eliot, 'Tradition and the Individual Talent', in *Selected Essays*, pp. 10–11.
19. This and the previous paragraph draw on my *T. S. Eliot's 'The Waste Land'*, pp. 85–6, 91–2.
20. Eliot, 'Lancelot Andrewes', in *Selected Essays*, pp. 307, 302, 303, 307.
21. See Grover Smith, *T. S. Eliot's Poetry and Plays: A Study in Sources and Meaning* (1956; second edition, Chicago: University of Chicago Press, 1974), p. 140.
22. Hugh Kenner, *The Invisible Poet: T. S. Eliot* (1960; London: Methuen, 1965), pp. 225–6, 227.
23. Kenner, *Invisible Poet*, p. 231.
24. See especially Donald Davie, 'T. S. Eliot: The End of an Era', in *T. S. Eliot: 'Four Quartets': A Casebook*, ed. Bernard Bergonzi (London: Macmillan, 1969), p. 159; and Kenner, *Invisible Poet*, pp. 266–71.
25. E. J. Stormon, 'Virgil and the Modern Poet', *Meanjin*, 6 (Autumn 1947), pp. 13–14.
26. Gabriel Josipovici, '*Four Quartets*: A Commentary', *PN Review*, 19 (September/October 1992), pp. 46, 44.

Chapter 44

Owen, Rosenberg, Sassoon and Edward Thomas

MARK RAWLINSON

What Owen, Rosenberg, Sassoon and Thomas have most in common is being 'chained to a historical event, and an abnormal one at that'.[1] Chained both by their times, and by their reception. The seeming inevitability of their association, and of their relationship to literary Modernism, has much to do with how the Great War has been memorialised in English culture, and in particular with the role literature has acquired as a vehicle for the relaying of historical experience. Poetry's part in the popular and educational reproduction of what Ted Hughes called 'our number one national ghost' is exceptional, and has some striking consequences.[2] One is the distortion of the historical record by unrepresentative voices, another, the identification of war poetry as the acme of modern poetry. Rosenberg, Sassoon and Owen have all been 'novelised' in recent years, the most apt homage a culture increasingly hostile to the discourses of printed verse can afford.[3]

Reading these wartime writers as poets can put us at odds with assumptions put into circulation by the category of war poet, with all its political and ideological freight. In fact, to read more critically depends on reading more historically, with a less sentimental investment in the production of national history, to which Great War poetry has been conscripted. Of all the contexts we require in this respect, the most important – concerning evolving attitudes to war in prospect, actuality and memory – is the most elusive. Such attitudes are refracted by our own orientations to war as pageant or scourge, crusade or shambles. Anti-war sentiment has become culturally hegemonic, if far from politically efficacious. It has certainly changed the way the West goes to war, and it makes it difficult for us to credit the work required to make those famous poems of 1917. The narrative of the march to stalemate and mechanised slaughter, with its psychological subplot of disillusion, is now mythic in its generality, supplying the form of both poetry anthologies (with their admonitory inclusions of Brooke, Grenfell and other authors of bellicose verse) and an archetypal pattern of response to which war poets are expected to conform (making it difficult, for instance, to situate a poet like Charles Sorley). George Steiner noted long ago that 'the horror flatters attention', feeding a historical condescension that makes it harder to gauge why 'no one foresaw the scale of slaughter'.[4] 'We have to remember how they were taken by surprise', cautioned Hughes in 1965: remembering rather than simply recognising what was involved in creating the forms which could register other conflicts than 'the Great Adventure' and the 'Greater Game' scripted by Britain's imperial and Christian popular military culture.[5]

It is also important to be mindful of how the canonisation of a handful of war poets has distorted our account of what was felt, believed and written about 1914–18. Some correctives are to be found in the pages of Catherine Reilly's bibliography *English Poetry of the First World War* (1978), and in anthologies such as her *Scars upon my Heart* (1981, verse by women), and Dominic Hibberd and John Onions's important 1986 anthology, revised as *The Winter of the World* (2007), which brought historical and ideological clarity to the picture established by fiftieth-anniversary collections edited by Brian Gardner (still in print) and by the chairman of Chatto, I. M. Parsons, in the mid 1960s.[6] But that is another story, concerning the uses of verse for purposes patriotic, consolatory, humorous, topical or memorial (Reilly catalogues more than two thousand authors; Vivien Noakes, Rosenberg's most recent editor, superseding Parsons, has recently assembled an 'Alternative Book of First World War Poetry').[7] That we don't readily think of the canonical war poets as propagandists for particular attitudes to war (not unconnected with the casual and erroneous identification of writers like Sassoon and Owen with pacifism), is a further sign of a lack of critical watchfulness. This has been correctly diagnosed by James Campbell as substitutions of the poet for the poem in what appear to be attempts to make a virtue of Yeats's notorious claim about 'passive suffering' not being a fit subject for poetry.[8]

Reading Sassoon, Owen, Rosenberg and Thomas as war poets has diminished the extent to which, as comparison will show, they were distinct in their poetry, in their careers as writers and in their reception (as instanced not in the culture of war, but in their example to other poets). Each contributed something different to the verbalisation of the social and material conditions of modern industrial and popular warfare. However, the war made none of them writers, though it did transform the character of the oeuvres which would establish their names. Sassoon, surviving the war, was the only one to struggle with the public consequences of being a war poet, and it is significant that in his influential fictional memoir he suppressed this identity. The development of the poetry of Owen, Rosenberg and Thomas was arrested before they had a significant readership: each is a case study in significant poetic experiment, and it has taken the combined forces of the national ghost and the academic codification of poetic Modernism during the Cold War to distract us from just how radical were these brief periods of wartime creativity.

Siegfried Sassoon (1886–1967): 'scornful, harsh and discontented, / Mocking and loathing War'[9]

If Sassoon's earlier enlistment (August 1914) is a claim to priority, his status as a veteran war poet is reinforced by the specific impact of his poetry on Wilfred Owen (a master–disciple relationship which reprises the narrative of inter-generational initiation common to Great War fictions and memoirs), as well as by the fact that he survived to grow old. Thomas, born eight years before Sassoon in 1878, was a whole generation older than Rosenberg (b. 1890) and Owen (b. 1893). Another significant aspect of these generational relations is the relative conservatism of the verbal devices Sassoon employed in his incendiary campaign of protest, which continued beyond his supposed 'silencing' by a medical board in 1917. These issues are illustrated by the near-contemporaneous publication of Sassoon's 'Absolution' in *The Westminster Gazette* in March 1916 and of his 'The Redeemer' in *The Cambridge Magazine*, April 1916. The former was a Liberal paper founded by the publisher George Newnes, the latter a university periodical started by the undergraduate C. K. Ogden, later the creator of Basic English, in 1912. In wartime, it was geared up to monitoring the foreign press as a counterbalance to home propaganda (Ogden's critique of news management would feed into his work on semantics with I. A. Richards, and influenced Leavis's thinking on mass culture). The difference between readerships is coded in the difference between the poems, which for Sassoon would come to represent his pre- and post-front-line selves. The rhyming quatrains of 'Absolution' invoke, in a Hardyean conjunction, the lexicon of Christianity ('absolve', 'scourge') and the pagan fatalism of Housman ('happy legion'), to assert a transcendence of mortal fears in the wisdom and liberty of war. This feat is accomplished by the imperative voice rather than by elision or euphemism: 'Horror of wounds . . . must pass' (p. 15). Sassoon would later identify these manoeuvres with the feeling of having 'joined up' (p. 15). 'The Redeemer', presented to an audience self-selected by its liberty of mind on the subject of the war, deploys Christian motifs ironically and blasphemously, its status as 'first front-line poem' only seemingly at odds with its intricate Spenserian stanzas. These big, end-stopped paragraphs are capacious enough for Sassoon's descriptive experiments as he seeks verbal equivalents for an environment that you had to see and hear in order to believe (the pictorial as well as verbal art of the battlefield had been concerned for centuries with colourful, ordered and upright figures, not subterranean, clay-daubed forms 'floundering' in 'mire'). Two further aspects of 'The Redeemer' call for attention. The first is the problem of diction. At its most plangent, the poem transcribes an aural palette more musical than military: 'a bullet sang', 'a hollow bang', 'a rocket fizzed' (p. 16). Owen's 'Anthem for Doomed Youth', revised under Sassoon's direction at Craiglockhart, pursues a more effective relational approach to the sound worlds of poetry, worship and war:

> What passing-bells for these who die as cattle?
> – Only the monstrous anger of the guns.
> Only the stuttering rifles' rapid rattle
> Can patter out their hasty orisons.[10]

But Sassoon's handling of the Christ motif was more assured (and it weighed heavily on Owen). The 'blanching' light of a flare (many of Sassoon's poems use a brief period of nocturnal illumination to frame a scenario), 'lit the face of what had been a form': 'I say that He was Christ' (pp. 16–17). The identification, through the endurance of 'horror and pain', and the visual cue of a shouldered 'load of planks', is with the Christ of the passion, who saved men from sin. But it is an ephemeral redemption. As the flare sinks, 'all grew black as pitch' and the Saviour is invoked less poetically by a soldier in the benighted working-party: '"O Christ Almighty, now I'm stuck!"' The resolution of the poem on a curse has the effect of ironising the poet's hard-won analogy (and discounting the afflatus in 'Absolution'), as well as of challenging the authority and the nuance of the discourse of poetry. Two kinds of poem would develop from what Sassoon pulled off in 'The Redeemer', a longer-stanza, topographical-descriptive battlefield poem, and a shorter, colloquial and satiric form in which regularity of metre and rhyme vies with unpoetic or demotic discourse, underscoring the anger and seeming impropriety of the feeling expressed.

In 'The Poet as Hero', Sassoon explains why his 'ecstasies' (the Grail-stuff of poems like 'Absolution') have 'changed to an ugly cry'; his 'killed friends' haunt him, and he 'burn[s] to smite their wrongs' (p. 61). This was another *Cambridge Magazine* poem, printed in response to a letter of complaint about his earlier 'The Hero' and its conclusion that 'no one seemed to care' about blown-to-bits Jack, a proud mother's 'dead soldier' but also a 'cold-footed, useless swine'.[11] Sassoon realised the debt his ironical presentation of war owed to Hardy's *Satires of Circumstance*, an affiliation generalised by Paul Fussell in the seminal *The Great War and Modern Memory* (1975). But the 'absolution in my songs' (p. 61) was personal (Enoch Powell's verse from the Second World War is similarly haunted by guilt about the friends who did not survive). The 'ugly cry' has however often been misread as reasoned protest rather than spleen. '"Blighters"', a fantasy of vengeance on the performers ('prancing ranks / Of harlots' (p. 68)) and audience of music-hall turns, wishes a tank would materialise out of the jingoistic din to put an end to the mockery of corpses. This kind of jeremiad, in a more reflexive mode, recurs in the work of Owen, where, for example in 'Dulce et decorum est' or 'Mental Cases', the reader is cursed, or made complicit in the agonies of the poems' subjects. 'Base Details' and 'The General' are much anthologised poems which interweave demotic direct speech with four-square metres to present images of the incompetence and safety of the General Staff, motifs which have been staples of the post-1960s vision of the Great War, from *Oh, What a Lovely War* (1963) to *Black Adder Goes Forth* (1989). Written later at Craiglockhart hospital, verses such as 'Fight to a Finish' and 'Glory of Women' are by comparison vitriolic, redirecting front-line enmity towards home front institutions (the popular press, knitting socks for the troops). The latter takes the proud mother from 'The Hero' and, to make a symbol of womanhood's supposed ignorance of war, turns her into a German *Mutter* unwitting that her son's 'face is trodden deeper in the mud' (p. 100). This image, as readers of *Memoirs of an Infantry Officer* (1930) will recognise, is crucial in Sassoon's account of his own disillusionment with the heroic vision of war, a narrative turn hinging on the recognition of the humanity of the hated enemy. The poem falls well short of this generosity.

Sassoon suppressed his poetry-writing self in the characterisation of George Sherston, his alter ego in his trilogy of fictionalised memoirs (1928–36). Sherston, like Sassoon, makes a public protest about the conduct of the war (a letter to *The Times*) but is not granted an ironic vision of his progress from chivalric sport to political radicalism (in this sense, the memoirs purport to show us Fussell's satires of circumstance). This skewing of the record was only made good in *Siegfried's Journey* (1945), an autobiography focused on the literary contacts of the earlier war.

Wilfred Owen: 'Verse wails' ('1914')

Owen's development as poet, frequently adverted to as the signal case of the poet 'made a poet by the war', of war producing its own representation, can be recast by emphasising not the falling away of illusion, but his realising the gap between front-line experience in all its contradictions and any achieved concepts of war.[12] This came not just with the shock of combat, but with the discovery that writing the poem he felt he'd been desiring to write for years ('The Dead Beat', a sincere imitation of Sassoon) was not enough. Stephen Spender was the first to note just how various Owen's war poems were, but this still gets underplayed because of his role as cultural hero. Owen's achievement in less than twelve months of 1917–18 is as commanding in its ambition of renewal as it is morally, though his own sketch of a rationale for his wartime writing has, with its deprecation of poetry in favour of pity or compassion, cemented the priority of the latter achievement. When Virginia Woolf singled out Owen as a man for whom war was not 'a profession; a source of happiness and excitement', her evidence was taken from Blunden's edition which had reprinted an annotated table of contents for a volume of war poems Owen projected in the summer of 1918: 'The unnaturalness of weapons ... Inhumanity of war ... The insupportability of war ... Horrible beastliness of war ... Foolishness of war.' In Woolf's terms, Owen 'saves' his sex from uninterrupted solidarity over the sheer good of war, but this view both downplays Owen's insights into 'excitement' (in poems like 'Apologia pro poemate meo' and 'Spring Offensive') and discourages our curiosity about the forms within which he transcended the halting, inadequate locutions of 'horrible beastliness' and 'foolishness'. Woolf turns from words of witness to photographs, 'pictures of actual facts', as having true potential to unite men and women in feelings of war's 'abomination'.[13] Wilfred Owen also used images rather than words to confront civilians in Edinburgh with war, as recalled in one of Ted Hughes's weaker Great War poems, 'Wilfred Owen's Photographs'. But in retrospect, it is clear that it is not in the documentary visual image that the Great War has been remembered (there are no hegemonic photographic icons such as those with which the likes of Robert Capa, Joe Rosenthal, Eddie Adams or Huỳnh Công Út 'captured' later conflicts in Spain, the Pacific and Vietnam) but in the verbal figure.[14] Even a borrowed one – *dulce et decorum est* – may bear complex traces of the circumstances of its citation.

Owen's achievements are not essentially pictorial; it is the mind's eye, flinching from what is screened as dream-recurrence, and not the lens, which focuses the central acts of war in his poetry. The aerial battlescape in 'The Show', a bestial *paysage moralisé*, exhibits the limits of Owen's visual macabre ('pitted with great pocks and scabs of plagues' (line 5)). By contrast in 'Dulce et decorum est', the 'flound'ring' figure 'guttering, choking, drowning' is economically inset as a component of 'all my dreams' (lines 10, 16, 17), the nightmare repetition caught in the rhyming of 'drowning' on itself (four years before Eliot's 'so many, / I had not thought death had undone so many'[15]). Owen's synaesthetic image of drowning in a sea of green gas has become an archetype, as essentially modern as Eliot's yellow urban fog, and the inevitable reference point for a serviceman's verse about anti-bacteriological equipment in the Second Gulf War (1991).[16]

Owen's poems after Craiglockhart are primarily about combatants, and his authority as witness rests largely on his representation of the enlisted man and the subaltern in attitudes that have come to symbolise the futility of the Great War: maimed ('A Terre'), traumatised ('Mental Cases'), militarised ('Insensibility'), enduring ('Exposure'), dying ('Dulce et decorum est'), dead ('Asleep') and forgotten ('The Send Off'). But also killing ('Apologia pro poemate meo'). Owen could attempt a synoptic war poem, for instance in his appropriation of the Genesis story of Abraham and Isaac in 'The Parable of the Old Man and the Young' to figure the generational betrayal of 'half the seed of Europe, one by one' (line 16). However, the majority of his poems are conceived around a suffering consciousness, not an observing one. Some poems dramatise third-person experience ('Disabled'), others a first-personal witness or recall of such suffering ('The Sentry').

As James Fenton has demonstrated, Owen sustained his dedication to poesy through the war (the draft preface to the projected volume of war poems in May 1918 notwithstanding), and anticipated returning to earlier legendary themes when hostilities were over.[17] His verse declares its Romantic affiliations in its diction, rhyme and stanzaic forms (for instance a preference for the sonnet), as well as in its valuation of the poetical. Like Hardy, rather than Thomas, Owen worked within established technical frameworks to forge effects now associated with an idiomatic vision of modernity. By and large, Owen's longer stanzas and verse paragraphs are patterned in mixtures of quatrains and couplets; among his trials with rhyme, some plumb the bathos of Thomas Hood ('The Calls'). The consonantal rhyme (most commonly known as pararhyme) which he explored on occasions from late in 1917 provides the most productive case study of the interaction of the poet's craft and history. Owen was sparing with the potentially grotesque effects of vowel-shifts in rhyming pairs, whose first appearance is in 'From my Diary, July 1914', a sequence of recollections from the last days of peace. Here the pararhymes are line-initial, functioning not so much to frustrate expectations of consonance as to conjure happy (rather than Ovidean) metamorphoses, and erotic possibilities – Bees/Boys; Flashes/Fleshes. 'The Show' was drafted at the same time, a 'Vowel-rime stunt' (as he wrote to Sassoon)[18] which is again secondary, drawing on another document, this time Henri Barbusse's novel *Under Fire*

(1917), with its objectifying opening vision of the insect-like movements of massed soldiers. In the more usual line-terminal position, the pararhymes contribute not so much a dissonant effect, as one of an uncanny harmony amidst disorder: Death/dearth; hills/holes; spines/spawn. In the unique dramatic monologue, 'A Terre', pararhyme, including tercets – rat/rut/rot; sap/soap/man-soup – underlines the Hardyean ironies of the speaker, an auditory equivalent to the poem's improper juxtapositions, and its collapsing of the hierarchy of creation. As with 'The Show', the larger-scale patterning of pararhymes follows Owen's usual practice of varying quatrain and couplet rhyme schemes across unequal-length paragraphs. 'Miners', one of a handful of poems published in Owen's lifetime (in *The Nation*), disciplines these experiments to the regularity of strophic quatrains. An unusually indirect approach to the subject of civilian indifference to the predicament of soldiers in France, 'Miners' takes the occasion of a fatal explosion in a Staffordshire coal mine to contrast the poet's mindfulness of the human price of the fuel in his hearth with a vision of a post-war society's somnolent comfort: 'they will not dream of us poor lads / Left in the ground' (lines 33–4). He defended his rhymes to his cousin Leslie Gunston: 'I am doing in poetry what the advanced composers are doing in music'.[19] Just as 'Miners' picks up on 'A Terre''s theme of the conservation of matter (via an earlier vegetation of 'fronds'), so 'Exposure' develops the imagery of fireside repose as a contrast to the rain, cold and duration which reduce soldiers to another kind of suspension of life: 'All their eyes are ice, / But nothing happens' (lines 39–40): envelope quatrains, with a half-line burden, establish a less clangorous pararhyme, homing in on full rhyme. 'Futility', one of Owen's most finished poems, raises this variation on the technique to a new pitch. The first of two seven-line stanzas features a rhyme sequence – sun/once/half-sown/France/snow/now/know – which modulates undemonstratively among the times and places of individual and species history to resolve tentatively on a key verb in Owen's poetry, a word of great moral and political freight, 'know'. The second stanza withdraws the promise of certitude with a series of rhetorical questions forged into the tercet 'tall?/toil/all?' Owen's most famous pararhyme poem, 'Strange Meeting', reveals its earlier genesis in its development as a sequence of couplets distressed by pararhyme, and rhetorically pointing a visionary peroration:

> Now men will go content with what we spoiled,
> Or, discontent, boil bloody, and be spilled.
> They will be swift with swiftness of the tigress.
> None will break ranks, though nations trek from progress.
>
> (lines 26–9)

Despite the mantra-like succession of falling vowel-cadences, this poem still promises to transcend its occasion. This has not a little to do with the fact that it early turns its back on the landscape of war and features a disquisition on the poet and poetry, subjects supposedly outlawed by the Owen of the draft preface. This tendency to explore the sublime in war is taken a step further by the remarkable 'Spring Offensive', which succeeds both as a phenomenological narrative of battle and a metaphysical vision of violence's core in the sub- and super-human conduct of its perpetrators.

Edward Thomas: 'rumours of the war remote'[20]

Thomas is accidentally bound up with the myth of the war poet for reasons which should help explode it. He wrote in 'poetic form' only after the outbreak of war and his death makes him 'a lost voice'.[21] But his is not a battlefield verse, and most of it was written before Thomas embarked for France, where he served in a Royal Artillery battery, so cannot superficially be connected with the rhetoric or imagery of 'trench' poets. While Thomas recognised the American poet Robert Frost as the progenitor of his poetry, Frost suggested that enlistment 'helped [Thomas] make the other decision to be a poet in form'.[22] An exigent but professional writer of literary journalism and books on rural life, in the last three years of his life Thomas produced a body of poetry which, in figuring the changing landscapes of southern England, refined lyric and blank-verse forms and made them distinct from Georgian precedent in their inclusion of demotic speech rhythms and their nuanced registration of demographic and economic processes. Thomas is the formal bridge between the landscapes and sensibilities of Hardy and Auden, between an English modernity and English Modernism. John Moore, writing in the anxious build-up to the war against Hitler's Germany, suggested that the earlier war had released Thomas from a literary career as precarious as were the rural English lives he would catch in his poetry. War's impact on the publishing trade made the problem of feeding a family insoluble, hence not Thomas's 'fault'.[23]

Choice is a central issue in Thomas's 'This is no petty case of right or wrong' (written on leave at the end of 1915), but his treatment of agency in relation to historical crisis is altogether more subtle than the myth or these biographical assertions permit, though it could be argued it ends up in the same place. It is a poem particularly fascinating in view of the moral and ideological certitudes which shape much literary criticism of war poetry. Thomas is both assertorial and paradoxical. War isn't an issue of international justice or ethics to be sorted out by a statesman or a philosopher; jingoism in the mass media does not stir patriotism or enmity in the poet, except that a 'fat patriot' (line 5) is easier to hate than the Kaiser, who is here transfigured into a gong-banging forerunner of Yeats's 'King Billy' ('Lapis Lazuli'). The din of 'war and argument' (line 10; compare Sassoon's '"Blighters"') is no more to be 'read' or construed than 'the wind / Athwart the wood' (lines 11–12), a significant echo here of Housman's 'On Wenlock Edge the wood's in trouble', with its compression of Roman and modern, a model for the pageant of English military history which Thomas would, more modestly, recapitulate. But Thomas declares himself indifferent to the discriminations future historians will make when they rake the ashes of war for the education of some 'phoenix' post-war culture. Blank verse is supplanted at this point by rhyming couplets as, in the manner of a second, major-key theme becoming audible above the now exhausted variations on a first, Thomas declares allegiance to English dust. This is a deliciously ironic peroration: 'with . . . Englishmen / I am one' (lines 20–1), he writes, both united with the best and the worst, and in that line-initial declaration of insular selfhood, a poetic sensibility divided from Englishmen. Dust rhymed with trust; there is no choice here, but a faith which may lead from dust to dust. If the burial service resonates here as ambivalently as in Brooke's 'The Soldier' and 'The Burial of the Dead' from *The Waste Land*, then the transformative allusion to Romans 13:9, 'Thou shalt love thy neighbour as thyself' in the poem's last line, 'as we love ourselves we hate her foe' (line 26) is more akin to Eliot's methods. This is a poem which seeks as it were a pre-verbal and pre-ideological patriotism, a fellow feeling in a 'language not to be betrayed' ('I never saw that land before', line 22). But as we have seen, this ideal of an Edenic love of homeland uncorrupted by propagandist patriotism is undercut by its necessary complement of isolation and death.

The companion piece to this apparently public declaration is the poem 'Rain', which is imbued with the solitude-in-public which is the other side of the coin of the freedom from responsibility which has so often been claimed to follow from enlistment (this is the theme of Australian poet Frederic Manning's novel *Her Privates We* (1929), as well as of the writings, particularly *The Mint*, of Manning's admirer T. E. Lawrence). It was this dimension of Thomas's writing about war which served as a beacon for the Welsh poet and short-story writer of the Second World War, Alun Lewis, who pays direct and indirect homage in *Raiders' Dawn and Other Poems* (1942), in particular in the frequently anthologised 'All Day It Has Rained', a studied imitation, as well as a democratic updating, of Thomas's poem.

Like 'No petty case', another blank-verse paragraph, 'Rain' opens with a sentence that circles back on itself with internal rhymes on 'rain' and 'solitude', perfectly matching the curious temporality of Thomas's apprehension: 'that I shall die' (line 3) is not prophesied but remembered, as if that death is to be lived through again and again in the anticipation of battle. 'Like a cold water among broken reeds' (line 13), he is separate from the men drawn into war's maw, 'the living and the dead' (line 12). The equation of pain and sympathy in what has now become a prayer that 'none whom once I loved' (line 8) is so dissolved in solitude, gives us a different vantage on the question of compassion foregrounded by Owen's 'the poetry is in the pity' (draft 'Preface'), and in particular the complex relationship between pity and the self-affirmation which accompanies the contemplation of disaster. 'Rain' and 'No petty case' share themes and imagery with Owen's 'Futility', which itself echoes a Tennysonian juxtaposition of elegy and geology in the poet's ache of loss and the indifference of physico-chemical processes. But where the rhetorical questions in Owen's perfect lyric are a mantra holding at bay a Hardyean 'Hap' or randomness, Thomas's poems are unflinching in their unfolding of the implications of two variations of abandonment, one political, one psychological.

Comparisons with Owen's trench poetry are instructive. 'Digging (2)', Thomas's first post-enlistment poem, is also his 'Strange Meeting', where the subterranean encounter is enacted with the device of a 'time-capsule' in which are buried two clay pipes, one the poet's own, the other smoked by a soldier of Marlborough's army (Thomas had published his pot-boiling life of the Duke in 1914): 'The dead man's immortality / Lies represented lightly with my own' (lines 5–6). All is self-cancelling in this affiliation to military tradition. The mood of collected bemusement at the fatal rhyme of his life and that of the veteran of Blenheim is sustained in the poem's prehistoric coda, which introduces a natural equivalent to war, as 'the ancients . . . amazed to see' (line 8) the mastodon, '[o]nce laughed or wept' (line 10). The true legatee of this aspect of Thomas's writing about war is not Lewis, but the metaphysical Keith Douglas in his tragicomic vision of modern mechanised battle: 'the fool and the hero will be immortals'.[24] By contrast, Owen's way with the themes of historical tragedy and prehistorical process, in particular in the conceit of the burning coal in 'Miners', is to lament the victims of future forgetfulness, quite different from Thomas's playful planting of an archaeological anachronism.

Thomas's is not, then, a poetry that polemically opposes the distance between soldiers and civilians (which belied the 'strange proximity' of front line and home front). Instead it incorporates or models distances (historical, geographical, social) to grasp the war's significance in other ways. The war cannot be the more terrible for the banality of its impacts on life (though revealing the interpenetration of the domestic and strategic is also an important dimension of Ford Madox Ford's achievement in his novel sequence *Parade's End* (1924–8)), but it representations may be more resonant the less plangent it is.

In 'Roads', an example of Thomas's other leading formal innovation, the metrical and syntactic disruption of the internal structure of short-line quatrains to pattern mental and physical movement (another Hardyean preoccupation), a love of roads leads seemingly inevitably to war, just as '[n]ow all roads lead to France' (line 53). Rewriting Hardy's 'haunting' by the multitude in 'Wessex Heights', and in contrast to the threat of the 'crowds of ghosts among the trees' in Sassoon's 'Repression of War Experience' (p. 84), Thomas imagines the pattering of 'the dead / Returning' (lines 55–6) which counterpoints the heavy tread of the opposing stream of the (briefly) 'living' marching for France. The ghosts of Sassoon's troops are stuck overseas where they fell; Thomas, who has not been out, is kept company by the dance of the dead over upland roads, an image of a conscription into camaraderie which is both a fatal destiny and a release from pathological inwardness.

English writing of and about the Great War makes much of the contrast between the new landscape of war (which was desolate and abroad; no man's land), and the husbanded landscapes of home. Sassoon's southern England (in *Memoirs of a Fox-Hunting Man*) is a land of precarious plenitude; Thomas's was already a place of depopulation littered with the vestiges of human industry and hospitality. There is a historical logic in depicting the war as one more force reshaping the land, rather than its holocaust. In 'The sun used to shine', 'rumours of the war remote' (line 9) percolate unconsciously through the natural order, which reflects the militarised, armoured realm of war back at the strollers:

> . . . both stood disinclined
> For aught but the yellow flavourous coat
> Of an apple wasps had undermined;
>
> Or a sentry of dark betonies,
> The stateliest of small flowers on earth,
> At the forest verge; or crocuses
> Pale purple as if they had their birth
>
> In sunless Hades fields. The war
> Came back to mind . . . (lines 10–18)

The Homeric crocus, as much as the 'dark [purple] betonies' (reminding us, in their force, of D. H. Lawrence's deathly 'Bavarian Gentians'), and unlike John McCrae's poppy ('In Flanders' Fields'), which would become an official but ambivalent emblem of the Great War, symbolise a recurring pattern in human affairs: 'our eyes / Could as well imagine the Crusades / Or Caesar's battles' (lines 20–2).

This continuity, so signally at odds with Great War culture's motifs of cataclysmic discontinuities, is the formal and thematic keynote of 'As the team's head-brass', in which a deconstructed blank verse knits the interrupted dialogue of poet and ploughman as fitly as the field is patterned with furrows. And if the storm-felled elm makes the ploughman turn short of the headland, this no more stands for apocalypse than Thomas's supple metre boasts of breaking the pentameter. The poem strikes us as *sui generis*, its handling of speech patterns seemingly independent of the discoveries of the Browning–Pound–Eliot axis in the dramatic monologue, and closer in its sociology to a less bruited transatlantic affiliation (Frost, Williams). It has moved far beyond 'the man harrowing clods' of Hardy's 'In Time of "The Breaking of Nations"', which concludes that 'War's annals will cloud into night / Ere their story die' (although first published in 1915, this poem was first drafted as a response to the Franco-Prussian War nearly a half-century earlier).[25] Poems like 'Lob' have shown this continuity to be precarious in its dependence on the poet's undinned ear for the languages of nature and of rural community, and, given the brevity of his lease on life, his opportunity to reincarnate them in the language of poetry.

The ploughman's macabre internalisation of the wartime manpower shortage in reflecting on 'going out' – 'I could spare an arm. I shouldn't want to lose / A leg' (lines 20–1) – reverses the trope of the self-inflicted wound (in Owen and Sassoon an index of how badly soldiers want to get home, as well as an ironic gloss on the kinds of casualties war really creates). This ploughman's counter-factual conditionals are, the poet knows, akin to the philosopher's putative judgment in 'No petty case', an irrelevance (in *The Heart of England* Thomas had speculated that 'the ploughman's task' suited 'some well-balanced philosopher'; 'many a plain fellow must be turned into a fool by the immense monotony of similar furrows').[26] Envisaging a choice amongst apparently parallel but different universes cancels this one: if the ploughman's mate had not gone to France, the tree would have been moved:

> 'And I should not have sat here. Everything
> Would have been different. For it would have been
> Another world.' (lines 29–31)

Thomas's fatalism is quite distinct from the radical political programme polemically associated with the verse of Sassoon, an inheritor, in the view of the poet and critic Jon Silkin, of the first-generation Romantics, and Owen, Day Lewis's 'true revolutionary poet'.[27] In the ploughman's last word about 'another world' – 'Ay, and a better, though / If we could see all all might seem good' (lines 31–2) – it modulates into a resignation in the face of the inscrutable. In the final analysis, the war registers in Thomas's poetry as intensifying life's depths of sensuous experience and its crises, in a manner not dissimilar from Owen's bellicose sublime, the counterweight to his poetry of protest.

Isaac Rosenberg: 'human quagmire'

Isaac Rosenberg, like Owen, was living out of England when war was declared in August 1914. He enlisted unenthusiastically and non-patriotically at the end of 1915 – 'more men means more war'; 'the idea of killing upsets me a bit' – and, he would claim later, for mercenary reasons.[28] His first army poem, 'Marching – as Seen from the Left File', recalls the Futurist or Vorticist elements in the work of Slade School contemporaries, such as C. R. W. Nevinson or Mark Gertler[29] (and anticipates the 'human engine', and typist's 'automatic hand' in Eliot's 'A Game of Chess'):

> Like flaming pendulums, hands
> Swing across the khaki –
> Mustard-coloured khaki –
> To the automatic feet. (lines 4–7)

Alongside 'Returning, We Hear the Larks', that poem appeared in Harriet Monroe's *Poetry* (Chicago) in 1916. A painter, and the self-published author of poetry and a verse-drama on Jewish historical themes (Edward Marsh published extracts from *Moses* in *Georgian Poetry*), Rosenberg is now known primarily for half a dozen anthologised poems, and for being killed on the Western Front on 1 April 1918. Like Owen, though on a smaller scale (he continued to write on other subjects), Rosenberg did not write one kind of war poem, a sign of 'uneveneness' to some, but surely all evidence of the tension between a normative war aesthetic and a poet's multiple formal engagements with an existence which was a fascination and an abomination, numbingly dangerous *and* servile.[30] In a letter to Laurence Binyon, Rosenberg made a vow antithetical to Owen's subordination of poesis:

> this war, with all its powers for devastation, shall not master my poeting; that is, if I am lucky enough to come through all right. I will not leave a corner of my consciousness covered up, but saturate myself with the strange and extraordinary new conditions of this life, and it will all refine itself into poetry later on . . .'[31]

This was a wager in which the stakes were rather greater than 'evenness' of expression.

Rosenberg's poems reveal an utterly different ecology of war, and are altogether more populous than those of other soldier poets. His vision of no man's land is filled with non-human agents, from bugs to Amazons. Owen had recycled a pantheist conceit in 'A Terre', a dramatic monologue on the soldiers' 'philosophy', which foregrounds a *Wipers Times*, black-comic Romantic irony purporting envy of rat, microbe and daisy, alongside resignation that 'my fat' will be one with bud or grain: 'Shelley would be stunned' (line 45). But Rosenberg goes further in knocking the military male off his pedestal, placing him in a Darwinian (not Spencerian) competition for survival with arguably fitter creatures, more 'chanced . . . for life' (line 15).

'Break of Day in the Trenches' is a free-verse meditation that sutures two overdetermined symbols of the Great War, dawn, with its withdrawal of night's camouflage, and the poppy, nowadays compassion's badge. The rat's 'cosmopolitan sympathies' (line 8) mock the predicament of English and German hands which can only touch thus, indirectly, through a vector of disease (it is a conceit which rivals the Christmas Truce of 1914 and Owen's 'Strange Meeting' in troubling the 'versus' or border between enmity and fellowship). 'Returning, We Hear the Larks' opens like one of Sassoon's accounts of labour in no man's land: 'But hark! joy – joy – strange joy. / Lo! heights of night ringing with unseen larks' (lines 7–8). As if in an allegory of his vow to master war as a poet, he writes 'Death could drop from the dark / As easily as song' (lines 10–11). Rosenberg found it difficult to end poems; his openings are arresting, the development sometimes unexpected, but his codas seek a safe footing in a return to a recognisably poetic diction: 'a girl's dark hair', 'kisses where a serpent hides' (lines 15–16).

Consideration of Rosenberg's two poems about *Pediculus humanus corporis* juxtaposes stanzaic and free-verse treatment of another vector, the body louse (a blood-sucker, and hence a ready image for war itself, if it hadn't been such a disgusting, ubiquitous source of disease and discomfort). The regular quatrains of 'The Immortals' (a title Rosenberg's Second World War disciple Keith Douglas would take up in describing cavalry officers) insinuate an equation between a campaign of hygiene run amok, and the desperate repulse of the onslaught of the enemy. But 'my hands red in their gore' (line 6) are of course red in the blood the lice have sucked from his own body, so the frenzy of killing is doubly self-destructive. 'Louse Hunting' picks up the satanic motif but transfers it from the lice to the soldiers themselves, and the result is a less prosaically self-pitying presentation of the soldier. The free-verse lines share the vividness of

'Break of Day', but also its lack of cohesion. Unlike F. T. Prince's eponymous 'Soldiers Bathing' (1942), who call forth comparison with Michelangelo and Christ crucified, Rosenberg's 'Nudes – stark aglisten / Yelling in lurid glee' (lines 1–2) are fiends, part of a 'demons' pantomime' (line 13), closer to the theatricality of Douglas's 'Vergissmeinnicht' with its tank ordnance 'like the entry of a demon'.[32] 'Fiend' was applied to Germany and German troops from the outset, for instance by Robert Bridges in 'Wake Up, England!' (1914).[33] In his 'Apologia' and 'Spring Offensive', Owen uses the same vocabulary of 'glee' (line 4) and 'out-fiending' (line 41) to evoke the inseparable shame and glory of killing, but Rosenberg is more interested in the visual possibilities of the louse-infested shirt 'aflare' ('Louse Hunting', line 9) and the 'gibbering shadows' (line 16). Douglas's Second World War poetry would find inspiration in Rosenberg's depiction of militarised bodies in all sorts of postures – 'silhouettes agape' (line 15), 'gargantuan hooked fingers' (line 18) – which is most fully developed in 'Daughters of War' and 'Dead Man's Dump' (the later poet once likened poetry's capacity to surprise with seeing a man whose limbs were in positions you did not know). These capering soldiers are as in a spell cast by 'wizard vermin' (line 22), another inversion of the taxonomic hierarchy.

'Dead Man's Dump' appears to be another poem descriptive of no man's land, its opening reference to the limbers of wiring parties recalling Sassoon and also the sacralised warscapes of David Jones's woodcuts and his *In Parenthesis* (1937): 'their rusty freight, / Stuck out like many crowns of thorns, / And the rusty stakes like sceptres old' (lines 2–4). Indeed, it might be a compendium of the motifs associated with 'protest poetry', from death's armistice ('brutish men' (line 5) and 'brothers' (line 6) are 'huddled' (line 10) in painless repose) to entropy ('Earth . . . Fretting for their decay' (lines 14–16)). Rosenberg's angularly configured paragraphs are composed into a dramatisation of the moment of death, and this is prepared for by a mythic juxtaposition of those who have gone under and those who continue to bestride the earth. The interrogative mode is a clear point of contact with Owen's 'Spring Offensive', which wrestles with the same disjuncture between casualty and survivor, but finds resolution in the traumatised silence of the latter ('But what . . .'). Rosenberg's 'whats' equilibrate the mysteries of where go the 'God-ancestralled essences' emptied out of the 'soul's sack' (lines 24–5), and of the fate of those 'untouched' in body and thought, 'lucky limbs as on ichor fed, / Immortal seeming ever' (lines 33–4).

It is via the visceral, rather than the mythological, that 'Dead Man's Dump' achieves its own dislocation of temporality, its own timelessness (Fussell was quite right to observe that obscenity laws occluded the obscenity of war).[34] Rosenberg goes beyond the politicised framing of the putrid (Robert Graves's sole tactic in 'A Dead Boche' is a Courbetian realism: 'he scowled and stunk / With clothes and face a sodden green'[35]) with a more unsettling image of displacement or pollution. 'A man's brains splattered on / A stretcher bearer's face' (lines 48–9): bringing the audience face to face with the consequences of state violence has been a matter, in the twentieth century, of literalising such taboo-breaking contact. George Orwell knew this when he made O'Brien's icon of uninterrupted totalitarian power 'a boot stamping on a human face';[36] Pat Barker's reimagination of Rivers's sessions with Sassoon in *Regeneration* are counterpointed by the case of Burns, whose war neurosis stems from landing head-first, mouth-open on a German corpse (a programmed echo of Sassoon's own recorded memories of the face in the mud). Rosenberg's 'drowning soul', minus grey matter, is 'sunk too deep / For human tenderness' (lines 52–3), a recollection of Wordsworth's Ode, in which it is precisely mortal tenderness which limns the depths. That remoteness is a function of the presence of the dead, who collect about the place, in dumps like ordnance or material:

> They left this dead with the older dead,
> Stretched at the cross roads.
>
> Burnt black by strange decay
> Their sinister faces lie
> The lid over each eye . . . (lines 54–8)

Douglas's 'Vergissmeinnicht' pays homage to Rosenberg's having already said everything, by inscribing on the 'paper eye' of a dead German the way the survivor's 'content' at the enemy's 'decay' internalises the divisions of war.[37] But he does so within Owen's mode of return or recollection. Rosenberg persists in pursuing the moment, the core of violence, which so fascinated Douglas, giving 'Dead Man's Dump' the suspense and pathos of an emergency intervention, before withdrawing the humanising thread of contact: 'our wheels grazed his dead face' (line 79).

'Daughters of War' revokes the compensatory potential of salvage, with its vision from 'the root side', of the 'underside of things' (lines 3–4), the subterranean haunts of a race of Amazons. 'Somewhere they must have gone' (line 22), Rosenberg supposed in 'Dead Man's Dump'; here the souls of the slain dance naked in the 'huge embraces' (line 32) of the 'mighty daughters' (line 10). The transfiguration of the battlefield is also a haunting revaluation of the diction of Great War poetry:

> 'My sisters force their males
> From the doomed earth, from the doomed glee

And hankering of hearts.
Frail hands gleam up through the human quagmire, and lips of ash
Seem to wail, as in sad faded paintings
Far sunken and strange.' (lines 49–54)

Pathos is almost completely expunged from Rosenberg's myth of blood-lust, as a comparison with Owen's humanist subterranean elegy 'Strange Meeting' confirms. The latter, an arguably unfinished revision of verse about poetic collaboration with Sassoon, resolves its diagnosis of the world's deafness to the saving discourse of poetry in the transfigured embrace of the foemen. But for Rosenberg, humanity symbolised in the organs of speech and touch is twice remote, a mere apparition framed by some antique and unrecognisable art. This legend of war as transcendent experience – 'our corroding faces / . . . must be broken – broken for evermore / So the soul can leap out' (lines 29–31) – is without political or moral hope. Its estranging qualities culminate in a species of clear-sightedness; the war's lemming-like extinctions can have no logic superior to this paradox of a 'mortal tree of life' (line 14), or in contemporary terms, a Freudian death-drive. All else, as Keith Douglas would later concur, is just meat. But this is a vision whose undeceivedness comes at the cost of narrowness, the absence of the tension which animates 'Dead Man's Dump'.

The writers known as the major English poets of the Great War (Graves said 'Goodbye to All That', not least in the control he took of his *Collected Poems*) have, nearly a century on, usurped the role of historians of the conflict (military historians complain that Fussell's concept of a 'literary war' has been made literal by the teaching of the First World War in schools through poetry). It is as if Owen's sentiments in the draft 'preface' were realised, despite his worst fears of cultural amnesia. These poets' impact on the history of English poetry (its writing, not its pedagogy) is more modest, as if in keeping with Owen's statement ('Above all I am not concerned with Poetry').[38] Rosenberg and Thomas received homage from a later generation of war writers, though Thomas's importance as a relay in the tradition which connects Hardy with Heaney and Hughes cannot be overestimated (Glyn Maxwell's sequence of verse letters to Thomas being a case in point: 'Tell them how / You walked and how you saw, and how your pen / Did nothing more than that, / And, when it stopped, what you were gazing at').[39] Auden, a slavish imitator of Hardy and Thomas (see the *Juvenilia*) acknowledged Owen in *The Orators*, and tried out pararhyme after his own voice had started to be heard:

Or sit, the doors being shut,
'Twixt coffee and the fruit,
Touching, decline to hear
Sounds of conclusive war.[40]

English poetry of war has remained non-Modernist in its formal affiliations: F. T. Prince's 'Soldiers Bathing' and Tony Harrison's 'A Cold Coming' are written in unequal line couplets and leonine tetrameter couplets respectively. What connects Sassoon to Harrison the TV poet is the notion that poetry is a vehicle of a public discourse, rather than an elite, aesthetic or hermetic one, and this question of populism is the real key to the reception of the canonical war poets.

Notes

1. Philip Larkin, 'The War Poet', in *Required Writing: Miscellaneous Pieces 1955–1982* (London: Faber, 1983), p. 159.
2. Ted Hughes, *Winter Pollen: Occasional Prose*, ed. William Scammell (London: Faber, 1994), p. 70.
3. See Geoff Akers, *Beating for Light: The Story of Isaac Rosenberg* (Edinburgh: Juniper Books, 2006) and Pat Barker, *Regeneration* (London: Viking, 1991).
4. George Steiner, *In Bluebeard's Castle: Some Notes Towards the Re-definition of Culture* (London: Faber, 1971), p. 32.
5. Hughes, *Winter Pollen*, p. 72; Dominic Hibberd and John Onions (eds.), *Poetry of the Great War: An Anthology* (London: Macmillan, 1986), p. 11.
6. Brian Gardner, *Up the Line to Death* (London: Methuen, 1964), I. M. Parsons, *Men Who March Away* (London: Chatto and Windus, 1965).
7. Catherine Reilly, *English Poetry of the First World War: A Bibliography* (London: Prior, 1978); Vivien Noakes, *Voices of Silence* (Stroud: Sutton, 2006).
8. James Campbell, 'Combat Gnosticism: The Ideology of First World War Poetry Criticism', *New Literary History*, 30 (1999), p. 210.
9. Siegfried Sassoon, 'The Poet as Hero', in *The War Poems*, ed. Rupert Hart-Davis (London: Faber, 1983), p. 61. All further quotations from Sassoon's poetry are taken from this edition.
10. *The Poems of Wilfred Owen*, ed. Jon Stallworthy (London: Hogarth Press, 1985) lines 1–4. All further quotations from Owen's poetry are taken from this edition.
11. See Geoffrey Keynes, *A Bibliography of Siegfried Sassoon* (London: Rupert Hart-Davis, 1962).
12. C. Day Lewis, *A Hope for Poetry* (Oxford: Basil Blackwell, 1936), p. 15.
13. Virginia Woolf, *Three Guineas* (1938; Harmondsworth: Penguin, 1977), pp. 10–11, 13–14.
14. For a discussion of the war photograph, see Susan Sontag, *Regarding the Pain of Others* (London: Hamish Hamilton, 2003).

15. T. S. Eliot, *The Waste Land*, lines 62–3, in *The Complete Poems and Plays of T. S. Eliot* (London: Faber, 1969).
16. Unpublished material seen by the author.
17. James Fenton, *The Strength of Poetry* (Oxford: Oxford University Press, 2001), p. 37.
18. In *Selected Letters of Wilfred Owen*, ed. John Bell (Oxford: Oxford University Press, 1985), p. 300.
19. *Ibid.*, p. 531.
20. Edward Thomas, 'The sun used to shine', in *The Collected Poems of Edward Thomas*, ed. R. George Thomas (Oxford: Oxford University Press, 1981), p. 106. All further quotations from Thomas's Poetry are taken from this edition.
21. See Tim Cross, *The Lost Voices of World War One: An International Anthology of Writers, Poets and Playwrights* (London: Bloomsbury, 1988).
22. Thomas, *Collected Poems*, p. xv.
23. John Moore, *The Life and Letters of Edward Thomas* (London: Heinemann, 1939), pp. 216–17.
24. Keith Douglas, 'Sportsmen', in *The Complete Poems of Keith Douglas*, ed. Desmond Graham (Oxford: Oxford University Press, 1979), p. 116.
25. Thomas Hardy, *The Complete Poems*, ed. James Gibson (London: Macmillan, 1978), p. 543.
26. Edward Thomas, *The Heart of England* (1906; London: Dent, 1932), p. 25.
27. Jon Silkin (ed.), *The Penguin Book of First World War Poetry* (1979; Harmondsworth: Penguin, 1996); Day Lewis, *A Hope for Poetry*, p. 17.
28. *The Poems and Plays of Isaac Rosenberg*, ed. Vivien Noakes (Oxford: Oxford University Press, 2004), p. xliii. All further quotations from Rosenberg's poetry are taken from this edition.
29. Nevinson, 'Returning to the Trenches' (1914); Gertler, 'Merrygoround' (1916).
30. Jean Moorcroft Wilson, *Isaac Rosenberg: Poet and Painter* (London: Cecil Woolf, 1975), p. 195.
31. Noakes (ed.), *Poems and Plays*, p. xlvi.
32. Douglas, *Poems*, p. 111.
33. Hibberd and Onions (eds.), *Poetry of the Great War*, p. 3.
34. Paul Fussell, *The Great War and Memory* (Oxford: Oxford University Press, 1975), p. 334.
35. Hibberd and Onions (eds.), *Poetry of the Great War*, p. 70.
36. George Orwell, *Nineteen Eighty-Four* (Harmondsworth: Penguin, 1977), p. 215.
37. Douglas, *Poems*, p. 111.
38. *Poems of Wilfred Owen*, p. 192.
39. Glyn Maxwell, *The Breakage* (London: Faber, 1998), p. 27.
40. W. H. Auden, 'The crowing of the cock', in *The English Auden*, ed. Edward Mendelson (London: Faber, 1977), p. 24.

Chapter 45

Auden, Day Lewis, MacNeice, Spender: the thirties poetry

MICHAEL O'NEILL

The 1930s, construed for the purpose of this chapter as running from 1928 (when Auden's *Poems* were privately printed by Stephen Spender) to 1939 (the beginning of the Second World War and the date of Auden's departure for America), is an era in which fiercely individualist lyric voices emerge from and often in opposition to the complexity-laden bequests of Romantic, Victorian, Symbolist and Modernist poetry. These voices often inflect themselves through the process of responding to 'history', to use the period's domineeringly central term. This chapter will explore the work of three major poets of the 1930s, W. H. Auden, Louis MacNeice and Stephen Spender, and it will also, towards the close of the section on Auden, touch on the poetic achievement of C. Day Lewis.

W. H. Auden's early poems crackle with an urgency that can seem admonitory, even sinister. Their very acoustics are remarkable: curt, cold, intense, speaking from the heart's injuries as well as to the head's impulse to diagnose. Stephen Spender writes in evocative terms of 'terse syllables enclosed within a music like the wind in a deserted shaft'.[1] 'Syllables' are indeed 'enclosed within' the poetry's 'music'. Lines spring enigmatically and unforgettably into life, seeming to describe a landscape that is also a place we might meet in our dreams or nightmares. Poems can come across as pages torn from the screenplay of a chilling thriller: 'They ignored his wires. / The bridges were unbuilt and trouble coming', at the close of the octave of the unrhymed sonnet 'Control of the passes' is an example, the assonantally clustered 'trouble coming' looming with menace out of and fulfilling the incipient threat imparted to the short-vowelled sounds in 'ignored', 'bridges', and 'unbuilt'.[2] Words resonate in their void spaces; 'unbuilt', for example, means 'still to be built' and, in a wry reworking of Shelley's 'unbuild' at the close of 'The Cloud', 'changed back to the state before it was built'. The poet is spy predicting and foresuffering 'trouble coming', imminent 'trouble' that remains unspecified but that links the public and private; so, here, eros appears to be executed both by the servants of the State and by the inability of individuals to fulfil longing: 'They would shoot, of course, / Parting easily who were never joined'. The last line echoes the close of the enigmatic Anglo-Saxon poem 'Wulf and Eadwacer', suggesting a dark affinity between feudal and modern cultures. Yet it is the casual conversational flicker introduced by 'of course' after the gangster-like 'shoot' that does much to give the line a contemporary feel, miming as it does a bored acquiescence in violence. Other Auden poems of the era such as 'Doom is dark and deeper than any sea-dingle' also recall, yet make something disturbingly updated and relevant to the modern condition from, the diction, alliteration, stressed rhythms and mood of Anglo-Saxon poetry.[3] Auden fuses such effects with a variety of arresting poetic techniques: the use of a staccato, riddling, two-stress line patented by Laura (Riding) Jackson, for instance, compatible in 'This lunar beauty' with a laconic, even desolate lyric beauty that seems to hold its breath in a limbo space between 'Love' and 'sorrow'.

Here and elsewhere, Auden's adept deployment of pararhyme, a device picked up from Wilfred Owen, is in evidence. In 'Since you are going to begin to-day', that first line kick-starts an ironic scene of instruction, one that circles with bitter wit to the conclusion that 'Their fate must always be the same as yours, / To suffer the loss they were afraid of, yes, / Holders of one position, wrong for years'. The poem signs off with a pararhyming triplet in which the only affirmation ('yes') is hollow, the half-gleeful sense that 'Their fate' will be 'yours', that is, to be 'wrong for years.' The reader cannot but feel held and a little helpless, suddenly the 'you' on whom the poem trains its coolly unnerving fire. The writing is sufficiently sharp to pinpoint obstinate persistence in error, fluid enough to be both judge and latently complicit fellow traveller. 'Holders of one position' sounds fleetingly honourable, mimicking a bolstered self-approval in its initial stress, before the undercutting last three words.

'From the very first coming down / Into a new valley with a frown / Because of the sun and a lost way': this, the typical opening of an untitled poem (later 'The Letter'), might speak, at a subtextual level, of Auden's own poetic emergence 'Into a new valley'. The 'frown' worn by his early poems is induced by a metaphorically 'lost way'. The culture out of and about which the poet writes has lost its way in poems such as 'Who stands, the crux left of the watershed'. That opening line – presenting a momentary grammatical crux: is it a statement or a question? – illustrates the early poetry's ability to shape a landscape of unease, doubts, divisions. 'Who' names a subject position that will be occupied by an alienated onlooker, alter ego of the poet who tells him, 'Go home, now, stranger, proud of your young stock' at the start of the second of the poem's two verse-paragraphs. Auden's clipped blank verse collapses the shafts supporting any Wordsworthian assumption of harmonising accord between self and world, even as Wordsworth's own 'bleak music' in *The Prelude*,[4] distantly and in an estranged way, sounds through the poem's subterranean chambers. The post-industrial scenery of 'dismantled washing-floors' wins a tight-lipped approval, even admiration, but compassion is kept on a short leash; so a coffined miner 'Through long abandoned levels nosed his way', where death's 'levelling' tone dominates as 'nosed' twins human and animal. The second paragraph stresses the apartness of the 'stranger'; he is 'frustrate and vexed', 'cut off' from a land that 'will not communicate'. Yet a potent image that Auden uses to illuminate such cut-offness is double in effect: it haunts by persuading the reader that it is epiphanic, although it depicts a state in which revelation is not achieved: 'Beams from your car may cross a bedroom wall, / They wake no sleeper.'

Auden's phrasing ('They wake no sleeper') just about allows for a waking that might have happened, if only in some virtual space parallel to the poem's world. His political poetry is never merely documentary; it accommodates fears and hopes, and serves as a medium for 'scenting danger' ('Who stands') and for making 'action urgent' ('August for the people'). In many poems, historical crisis and imaginative response circle warily round one another. In the bewitchingly cadenced 'May with its light behaving', we are told that 'The real world lies before us', where the echo of the conclusion to *Paradise Lost* suggests that 'the real world' is distinctly post-Edenic, a place where, paradoxically, we are compelled to choose. The poem's delicately 'light' lyric measure sways deceptively between recognitions, much as 'light' itself sashays between meanings (including 'graceful', 'not violent', 'wanton', 'cheerful' and 'well provided with light'). 'The real world' includes, as part of its reality, the pleasure afforded to the senses by, say, the 'swan-delighting river'. The allusion, there, to Yeats's 'rook-delighting heaven' in the first line of 'The Cold Heaven' draws in a swarm of suggested comparisons and contrasts. Auden seems robustly empirical where Yeats's poem, 'Riddled by light', is intent on visionary experience, however painful. Yet Auden, too, is discontent with appearance. Whereas Yeats protests against 'the injustice of the skies',[5] Auden notes, disquietingly, that 'The unjust walk the earth.' The opaque conclusion appears to rebuke our yearning for 'love'; indeed, 'love' is ventriloquised as undercutting its sensuous appeal, even though it 'Urges' this undercutting 'upon our blood' as it tells us 'How insufficient is / The endearment and the look'. With brisk authority, Auden's definite articles consign 'endearment' and 'look' to the ranks of the 'insufficient'.

Patrons of the deftly caricatured 'Sport Hotel', 'the insufficient units', by whom Auden means an inadequate, ossifying upper class, have an important walk-on (or sit-down) role in 'Consider this and in our time'. They catch the panoptic eye of the poet as, with the ostentatiously detached gaze of 'the hawk' or 'the helmeted airman', he enjoins us to attend to 'this and in our time'. 'This' is the way things are 'in our time', a time in which division finds its slightly self-mocked yet talismanic emblem in the 'cigarette-end smouldering on a border / At the first garden party of the year'. Auden's technique, here and elsewhere, is to turn particulars into symptoms of a general disease: so, to be among the 'Seekers after happiness' is to be entrapped, as in a psycho-social labyrinth, by 'The convolutions of your simple wish', to share in an 'immeasurable neurotic dread'. The poet is master-diagnostician, seeming to have absorbed Marx and Freud yet not surrendering his authority to any guru, able to sense or hint at the link between an idle drink 'Within a stone's throw of the sunlit water' and an emergent crisis, 'A polar peril, a prodigious alarm', a line whose alliterative melodrama refuses to be dismissed as merely schoolboyish high-jinks.

Indeed, the threat communicated by Auden's early work, with its warning, as the final section of 'It was Easter as I walked in the public gardens' has it, that 'It is time for the destruction of error', exists in potent partnership with a vein of dark humour. It coexists, too, with a lyrical if often ironised vision of endings and renewals, compacted in the image which concludes this poem: 'deep in clear lake / The lolling bridegroom, beautiful, there'. That 'lolling bridegroom' appears at the close of an appositional run of figures who represent the 'old gang' and whose 'Death', the poem tells us, is required. Yet, set off from previous images by a semicolon, the bridegroom takes on (especially given the poem's Eastertide opening) a compelling suggestion of a potential or 'beautiful' resurrection.

Auden's style grows less elliptical in later poems of the decade as he strives, in words from his palinode to the thirties, 'September 1, 1939', to 'undo the folded lie'. Yet this is not to say that Auden grows more didactic. Rather, he moves from atmospheric menace to weighed if unpredictable and sometimes quirky meditation. The words just quoted follow the line 'All I have is a voice'. That concession or boast is strikingly different in its register from the tone adopted by the earlier, more impersonal voice issuing (say) the imperative-cum-(mock) prayer to 'look shining at / New styles of architecture, a change of heart' (in 'Sir, no man's enemy, forgiving all'). Even if that off-rhyme is shiningly eye-catching rather than dissonant, the desired 'change of heart' leaves unstated how the poet's own heart will change. In 'September 1, 1939', removed from England 'in one of the dives / On Fifty-Second Street', Auden is ready to concede and explore his subjectivity. The ironic, dazzling mimicry of authority voices in *The Orators* (tellingly subtitled *An English Study*) yields to an attempt, caught in the ever-shifting rhythms and rhymes of the poem's trimeters and eleven-line stanzas, to work through an analysis of what has led to war towards an authentic stance of difficult hope. 'Uncertain and afraid / As the clever hopes expire / Of a low dishonest decade' is how Auden describes himself and his era at the start, yet the poem embodies what it asserts, a tentative, tenacious belief in the capacity of the poet's 'voice' to illuminate. Indeed, among the triumphs of the poem (for all Auden's later disowning of it),[6] is its continual play of intelligence, modifications that expose to the light of critique, for example, the 'error bred in the bone' of longing 'to be loved alone'. The rhyme of 'bone' and 'alone' sympathises with what it suggests is a virtually ineradicable 'error'.

The poet names himself as an individual 'I', concluding with a prayer that he might 'Show an affirming flame'. The flame burns bravely; what it is 'affirming' will not resolve itself into a gem of wisdom and must be deduced from the tone of preceding lines. Indeed, Shelley-like (despite his professed dislike of Shelley, Auden can sound like his Romantic predecessor), Auden affirms the need to affirm, much as Demogorgon at the close of *Prometheus Unbound* places trust in hope's ability to create 'From its own wreck the thing it contemplates' (IV.574).[7] In the same long sentence Auden implies his fellowship with a band of privileged others, 'the Just'; he is 'composed like them / Of Eros and of dust'. For this Auden, deconstructor of dangerously reifying myths, 'There is no such thing as the State / And no one exists alone.' He himself would later find fault with his assertion that 'We must love one another or die', his 'must' possibly trading on the idea that the imperative driving such 'love' is akin to the 'Hunger' mentioned two lines before.[8]

Yet this 'Hunger' bespeaks an awareness that, in the face of 'international wrong' and given that we are 'Lost in a haunted wood', there are quasi-ethical commandments we ignore at our peril. It might be objected that Auden's own category of the 'the Just', introduced as 'Ironic points of light' in the last stanza, is itself merely an opportunist myth. 'Ironic' seems ineffectual, even to anticipate the later Auden's sense that there are vastly more important things than poetry. And yet if we can imagine these 'points of light' sparkling with pleasure at Auden's word-play in punning on 'lie' at the start of the last stanza, they are not merely fiddlers detached from European cataclysm. Rather, the very fact that 'the Just' can be imagined bears witness to the human need to believe in justice, and to this degree exemplifies the poet's determination to 'Show an affirming flame'.

'September 1, 1939', in its investigation of love, poetry, self and history, brings to a focus much of Auden's best work in the thirties. Auden tussles with these themes in the elegantly turned and deeply felt 'Out on the lawn I lie in bed'. Using the Burns stanza with alertness to tone and modulations of mood, the poem celebrates a moment of happiness. But the poem, refusing to see the private life as its own justification or as occurring in a vacuum, moves away from the initial enchanted 'ring' in which the poet sits to chart wider orbits. The major transition occurs as Auden, recalling many poets before him who have looked at the moon as glamorous if indifferent monitress of human fate,[9] says with unassertive resonance, 'She climbs the European sky.' The poem was written in 1933, the same year that Hitler came to power, and it is as though the pressure of history forced on Auden's generation a plainer, more coherent language than Modernist poets supplied. Eliot's 'What the Thunder said' fragments syntax and gives its hallucinatory imaginings over to a vision that includes terror, futility and boredom, interspersed with frail salvific hopes. 'Out on the lawn' positively manicures its syntax and steadies its imaginings as if to keep poetry in a position where it does not vanish into the pit opening up beneath 'European' culture. Auden remains ready to judge himself and his friends, who, as he observes with a flicker of self-irony, 'endure / The tyrannies of love'; other 'tyrannies' and their imagined redress, which takes the form of a conceit of a flood sweeping the status quo aside, mean that the enchanted moment at the beginning is perilously positioned, in danger from both political crisis and apocalyptic utopianism. All Auden's poise is needed to enter a plea for that enchantment's allowed continuance in the imaginary, post-deluvian new world. He hopes that 'this', so precious it defies definition, may 'to that strength belong; / As through a child's rash happy cries / The drowned voices of his parents rise / In unlamenting song'. The very form and grace of the writing, shown in the way 'unlamenting' brings into play yet fends off 'lament', value the 'drowned voices' that this subtly and knowingly self-divided poem concedes must be superseded.

Auden's balance in the poem, with its tremors of hope, is his own, but it has distinct parallels with effects achieved by other poets in the period. C. Day Lewis alludes to Auden's poem in his 'Song', where he conjures up the wraith of a lyric muse: 'Oh here and unlamenting / Her graceful ghost shall shine.'[10] As in other work, he reaffirms the lyrical nature of a gift forced by historical crisis to curb its grace-notes and go against its grain, sometimes to powerful effect. His poetry seeks to adjust to 'the entrance of a new theme' as he puts it in section 32 of his long poem *The Magnetic Mountain* (1933). This 'new theme' enters after Day Lewis has displayed his own exquisitely attuned 'ear' for a pastoral 'music'. The idea of 'England' calls up from him a poetry in touch with 'The slow movement of clouds in benediction'. In its own 'slow movement', as 'benediction' confers a measured, suggestive solemnity, the line reveals a default position to which Day Lewis's richly chorded imaginings wish to return.

In 'The Conflict' he composes an elegy for the lyric muse at a time inimical to lyric poetry. His verse-form – iambic quatrains with altering line-lengths that prevent the abba rhyme and off-rhyme scheme from growing mechanical – mirrors the poet's tilting feelings. On the one hand, Day Lewis rejoices in the fact that 'sorrow finds a swift release in song / And pride its poise'. On the other hand, such 'poise' discovers that the alliterating 'peace' that it bears witness to and bestows is precarious in the face of 'The red advance of life'; 'red' suggests a full-bloodedness denied to the poet and his way of life, and a Communist certainty. Although the poem commands, 'Move then with new desires', it capture memorably the poet's own, implicitly ghostly existence 'Between two fires'. It adapts for its disciplined, audibly dispirited ends a potent Romantic image when it asserts that 'private stars fade in the blood-red dawn'. No more than Emily Brontë in her 'Stars' is Day Lewis in love with what the earlier poet calls the day's 'hostile light'.[11]

Auden would not, one feels, allow himself so openly lyrical an expression of entrapment. More typical of his mid and late thirties poetry is a mood of complex or even, as in 'Spain 1937', desperate affirmation. 'Spain' presents 'history' initially in a virtuosic series of witty, charged vignettes, then as a voice unable to 'help' or 'pardon'. Responsibility for human beings is tragically ours, 'left alone with our day'. In 'Musée des Beaux Arts', Auden's deceptively informal phrasing and seemingly casual rhyming appear to praise the insight of 'The Old Masters' into 'suffering'. Yet the poem suggests, too, that, although the art work, 'Brueghel's *Icarus*, for instance', can report on, even startle us into seeing anew, the raggedy disconnected connections between ordinariness and terrible suffering, it can do little to change the nature of the world we inhabit. The ballad 'As I walked out one evening' glides its musical, unsettling way from sent-up Romantic cliché to glimpses of sexual trauma before settling for a wry, possibly queered reprise of standard Christian doctrine, if one hears 'crooked' as homosexual slang: 'You shall love your crooked neighbour / With your crooked heart'. It is in his sonnet sequence about the Sino-Japanese conflict (which began in earnest in 1937), 'In Time of War', and in his elegy, 'In Memory of W. B. Yeats', that Auden brings his oscillating feelings about art's limits and value to a point of complex resolution. 'Certainly praise: let the song mount again and again': the alexandrines of sonnet XIII in 'In Time of War' begin by mimicking a delight in spontaneous lyric overflow, before the poem reproves merely self-admiring song with the antithetical line, 'But hear the morning's injured weeping, and know why'. The finest poetry by Auden in the thirties emerges from a willingness to attend to both injunctions, the second of which is itself double, admonishing us both to 'hear' and 'know why', to attend and to analyse. In the poem for Yeats, Auden organises his elegy's three sections purposefully to offer different views of the dead poet, the significance of poetry and its relationship with history. Poetry, the poem famously or infamously tells us, 'makes nothing happen', yet it 'survives, / A way of happening, a mouth', especially in the work of a poet such as Yeats whose own rhyme of 'voice' and 'rejoice' in 'The Gyres' is graciously alluded to when Auden invites him, in the trochaic chant of the final section, 'With your unconstraining voice / Still persuade us to rejoice'. Auden's poetic voice in the thirties is 'unconstraining', even as and especially because it is acutely alert to all that constrains.

Louis MacNeice, like Auden, saw Yeats as a significant precursor. In his *The Poetry of W. B. Yeats*, he writes that 'Yeats and Rilke . . . insist, for all their recognition of misery and bewilderment and frustration, that the mainspring of Art, and even of Life, is *joy*.'[12] The chapter in question concludes by quoting the same lines from Yeats's 'The Gyres ('Out of Cavern comes a voice / And all it knows is that one word "Rejoice" ')[13] to which Auden alludes towards the close of his elegy for Yeats. MacNeice shares, in his individual way, the impulse to rejoice despite the evidence of 'misery and bewilderment and frustration'. MacNeice can be the darkest, most melancholy of poets, and yet his work seems always to be buoyed by an unsentimental, formally adroit insouciance. Indeed, the sadder the subject, the more bravura the formal response, the more flamboyant the airing of a rare lyrical inventiveness. 'Bagpipe Music' invites the decade, with its cares and its hedonisms, to go to hell in an explosively nihilistic yet stunningly impassioned handcart, accompanied by a flourishing skirl of pibroch music, or its metrical equivalent. The conclusion turns from hectic dance to cracked-voice dirge, but keeps its spirits up as it watches everything go down the chute: 'The glass is falling hour by hour, the glass will fall for ever, / But if you break the bloody glass you won't hold up the weather.'[14] There is an inflection not wholly removed from Yeatsian tragic sprezzatura here.

In 'The Sunlight on the Garden', a poem whose rhyming both at the end of lines and between the end of lines and the start of lines, mimes with virtuosic skill the wish and failure to 'cage the minute / Within its nets of gold', MacNeice invokes Antony's heroic posturing at the moment of death with wit and vividness in support of his own life-affirming stance. 'Posturing' rather than 'posture', since the writing cherishes, yet allows for the sad comedy of, Antony's characteristically moving but muddled attempt to go out on a high note. MacNeice settles for a less heroically 'grateful' note at his poem's close. 'Autobiography', a poem of 1940 (but illustrative of qualities apparent in many thirties MacNeice poems), makes of personal childhood 'misery' a bleakly mirthless and yet artistically exhilarating nursery rhyme. It moves from the account of the poet's father, a Church of Ireland minister, who 'wore his collar the wrong way round', to his mother, who suffered a nervous breakdown ('My mother wore a yellow dress; / Gently, gently, gentleness'), to his own sense of nightmare, isolation and terror ('The dark was talking to the dead; / The lamp was dark beside my bed'). A refrain, doubtless influenced by Yeats, chants, '*Come back early or never come*', and the poem is at once affecting and vigilant without being over-watchful: the way that 'Gently, gently, gentleness' croons its trochaic spell, for example, invokes the mother's protective voice and laments the irreparable loss of her vanished 'gentleness'.

Political pressures leave their impress on MacNeice's work, in the poetry about an Ireland towards which he feels irresolvable ambivalence in 'Valediction' '('I can say Ireland is hooey, Ireland is / A gallery of fake tapestries, / But I cannot deny my past to which my self is wed'), or in his *Autumn Journal*, the decade's major long poem, written after the diplomatic capitulation to Hitler of Munich 1938, or in 'Postscript to Iceland', in which he shows himself aware of 'Nations germinating hell'. Yet that poem, addressed to Auden, concludes with the spirit-braced, glass-raising gesture, 'Still I drink your health before / The gun-butt raps upon the door.' If the shift to octosyllabics in the final line carries menace, the 'lust for life' admired in Auden, and holding at bay that very thirties phenomenon 'the death-wish', animates MacNeice's poetry, too. In 'Snow', MacNeice emerges as the champion of the 'plural', the celebrant of 'The drunkenness of things being various'. 'To a Communist' uses snow as a figure for distinction obliterating 'unity': 'Snow's unity engrosses / Particular pettiness of stones and grasses' in that poem, where the off-rhyme stands up for 'Particular pettiness'. 'Snow' features not only snow but also the 'huge roses' and what lies, to employ a preposition vital to MacNeice's sense of chasms and links, 'between' them. The versification, long lines boisterously at odds with the decorum of the iambic pentameter, voices MacNeice's delight in chance connections and pattern-complicating differences. 'World', as he puts it, discarding any article that implies some kind of detached control, 'is crazier and more of it than we think, / Incorrigibly plural'; that final phrase sees plurality as unforgettable, but also delightfully mischievous, mimicking the way that one might speak with indulgent affectionateness of a person.

The MacNeice of the thirties is liberal where later Yeats is politically conservative; but he might have been talking partly about himself when he wrote of Yeats that 'Ireland means to Yeats something very specialized. It is not Ireland as the ordinary person knows it, yet it is something distilled from that Ireland.'[15] Actually, MacNeice's Ireland is in touch with the 'ordinary person', thanks to his conversational tones and sharp eyes, noticing, for instance, how in 'Belfast' 'The sun goes down with a banging of Orange drums.' But his evocation of a Northern Ireland upbringing in 'Carrickfergus' makes of his experience 'something distilled' because of the heart-catching, unmelodramatic way in which, without arresting the poem's flow, he implies that everything is coloured by memory: whether it be the 'bottle-neck harbour' (an early image of constriction, picked up towards the end in the 'prison ship for Germans'), or the alienating sense of being 'born to the anglican order, / Banned for ever from the candles of the Irish poor', or the recollection of 'long / Dummies hanging from gibbets for bayonet practice' in the First World War, as history makes its displaced impact on the child. The final stanza speaks of exile through education, the 'school in Dorset' an emblem of an adult world removed from a childhood, destined to stay with the poet in dreams and images.

Without wearing its authenticity on its sleeve, the poem persuades through its sense of fidelity to a particular person's memories. This fidelity to feeling is a major strength of *Autumn Journal*, in which MacNeice sets in tandem yet also tension historical crisis and the feelings and thoughts of the poet. With their varying swirl of rhymes (one per quatrain) and their sure, idiomatic rhythms, the twenty-four sections showcase MacNeice's intelligence, journalistic alertness and emotional mobility. They include two sections about Spain, the second (XXIII) of which is a report from Barcelona on the eve of the city's and fledgling Republic's conquest by Franco's Fascist army. MacNeice contrasts his 'niggling equivocations' with the courage of those fighting to save the Republic, 'The stubborn heirs of freedom'. What gives a typical energy to the writing is a metaphorical agility that is able to draw (for example) on at least four suggestive Biblical parallels. The poet sees the people as 'Condemned like the beasts in the ark', an image that prompts the faintest possibility of hope: 'Will there ever be a green tree or a rock that is dry?' Again, though 'the old order is gone and the golden calf / Of Catalan industry shattered', the 'golden calf' image suggests that a true object of admiration has risen from the ashes, namely the indomitable, unshowy human spirit. Moreover, at the section's centre is the image of cocks crowing, finally interpreted, after a self-implicating question involving the 'sour / Reproach of Simon Peter', as 'a whirr, a challenge, an aubade': a meaningless agitation of noise, a spur to conscience, a dawn promise that may be touched, in a more sombre way, by lament for the delights of a time that has gone. And the poet himself is a lamed Jacob wrestling with a 'Present' compared to 'a God who straddles over the night sky'. In another poet these associations would be portentous, inflated. Here and throughout the poem, MacNeice allows such intimations to emerge from and return naturally to the ongoing 'broken rambling track' of his remarkably deft verse.

Among Stephen Spender's finest poems of the 1930s are works responding to the Spanish Civil War, collected in *The Still Centre* (1939), his second major volume after *Poems* (1933); he also wrote a longer poem, *Vienna* (1934), that addresses with a terse, fractured, strong-line lyricism the idea of the 'real life', an idea that preoccupies his poetry in the period. In *Vienna* Spender seeks to locate such reality less in a numinous mysticism than in history, especially in the lives of those freedom-fighters celebrated in the poem.[16] But the value and meaning of 'inner worlds' obsess him. To his poetry's advantage, Spender was never able to subordinate his concern with inner experience to propagandist ends. He sympathised with the Spanish Republic, and yet in 'Two Armies' he exhibits, with great rhythmic sensitivity, feeling for both sides of those involved in the horror of war, as he updates Owen's sense of a shared, afflicted humanity: 'When the machines are stilled, a common suffering / Whitens the air with breath and makes both one / As though these enemies slept in each other's arms.' The imagining of deadly foes turning into sleeping lovers arises with ease from the calm introduced by 'stilled' and 'common suffering'; the effect is at once audacious and affecting.

In other Spanish poems, such as 'Thoughts during an Air-Raid' or 'Port Bou', what takes precedence over flag-waving is a sharp, even comic attentiveness to introspective experience. In the former poem, he tries to shut out the prospect of being just another victim recorded in 'statistics', but the ironic, lithely lumbering blank verse cannot wholly retain its stoic indifference ('Well, well, I carry on') when the poet imagines the 'obscene' thought that 'a bomb should dive / Its nose right through this bed, with me upon it'. The poem concludes with a sense of the necessary selfishness of each separate 'I', and yet the effect is less to mock narcissistically at such selfishness than to open out towards a more complex vision of 'that incommunicable grief / Which is all mystery or nothing'. Spender alerts the reader to his own understanding of Wordsworth's assertion in *The Prelude* that 'Points have we all of us within our souls, / Where all stand single'. This feeling for 'singleness' immediately catalyses in Wordsworth a sense of 'incommunicable powers',[17] but in Spender it prompts a wry, barely speakable, and potentially tragic glimpse of 'all mystery or nothing'.

Spender is determined to avoid the vacuum of the solipsistically private self and the opposite trap of supposing the individual is necessarily subordinate to the collective. 'Port Bou' supports Valentine Cunningham's point that in Spender's war poems 'the war crops up only incidentally, with a kind of inevitable naturalness'.[18] Spender finds himself in the port town, its harbour graphically imaged as a child holding a pet that 'watches the gap / To outer freedom in animal air', an image that hints at the speaker's longing for 'freedom', for himself and for those caught up in the war. The poem is hyper-aware, almost hypnotically so, of its own image-making activity: 'seeing an image I count out the coined words', writes Spender, but, as often in his work, the effect is to heighten and dramatise: here, his memory of the place, of the 'warm waving flag-like faces / of militia-men' in a lorry, of their 'old mother in a shawl – / The terrible machine-gun', and of his aloneness at 'the exact centre' of the town during firing practice when his 'body seems a cloth which the machine-gun stitches', recalling, in accord with the poem's topsy-turvy mingling of peace and war, 'a sewing machine'.

The result is an uncanny faithfulness to lived experience, at the time and in the process of recollection. Even when, in earlier poems, Spender seems to celebrate a utopian technological future in, say, 'The Pylons', he avoids propaganda, largely because of his readiness to speak what he feels, not what he ought to say. The poem's off-rhymes and elegiac syntax fortify the reader in the view that A. Kingsley Weatherhead is incorrect to say that 'the poet unwittingly captures our sympathy for the traditionally poetic'.[19] The final stanza holds a curtly usurpatory and progressivist 'This' in uneasy tension with 'our emerald country', and finally confers on 'This' associations borrowed from the old order, as Spender imagines new 'cities / Where often clouds shall lean their swan-white neck', an image and even cadence (compare the close of Wordsworth's 'Ode: Intimations of Immortality') that wittingly underscores the poet's wish not wholly to disown the past.

Above all, Spender's best thirties poems seek to inspire a change in consciousness, not by preaching Marxism, but by expressing what in 'Poetry and Revolution' he calls the artist's 'feeling for his own individuality, his isolation'.[20] In such poems as 'My parents kept me from children who were rough' he achieves a near-Blakean truthfulness to a state of soul. That is, he does not seek to justify, but to evoke, the boy's blend of snobbish fear and envy for 'the children who were rough', even if he permits some latent self-mockery to infiltrate the descriptions: 'I feared more than tigers their muscles like iron.' The poem's limber, powerful rhythms arrest the reader; they give to us, in a form that is seemingly unmediated yet skilfully ventriloquised, the child's vivid if distorted sense of class-difference. Again, in 'Moving through the silent crowd', a ballad-like poem behind which one may again sense the sponsoring voice of Blake's Songs, Spender breaks away from conventional pity for the unemployed, a familiar sight in the years after the Wall Street Crash and during the Depression. Instead, he probes and evokes his own motives and feelings as he writes, savouring a 'sense of falling light' but implying self-blame for doing so. At the close, the poet convicts himself for being 'haunted' by the poem's 'images' more than (he implies) the realities to which they correspond; then, finally, he concedes the 'emptiness' of his 'images'. But the concession stings one into an uncomplacent, renewed consciousness that between poetry and social reality there is a disturbing closeness and apartness. It is, in large part, for sparking such recognitions that Spender's poetry has continuing value.

Notes

1. Stephen Spender, *World Within World* (1951; London: Faber, 1977), p. 52.
2. Auden's prose and poetry are quoted from *The English Auden: Poems, Essays, and Dramatic Writings, 1927–1939*, ed. Edward Mendelson (London: Faber, 1977).
3. For relevant discussion, see chapter 2 of Chris Jones, *Strange Likeness: The Use of Old English in Twentieth-Century Poetry* (Oxford: Oxford University Press, 2006).
4. Book. XI, line 379; William Wordsworth, *The Major Works*, ed. Stephen Gill (1984; Oxford: Oxford University Press, 2008).
5. Quoted from *The Variorum Edition of the Poems of W. B. Yeats*, ed. Peter Allt and Russell K. Alspach (New York: Macmillan, 1957).
6. For discussion of Auden's 1964 rejection of the poem as 'infected with an incurable dishonesty', see Edward Mendelson, *Early Auden* (London: Faber, 1981), pp. 326–7 (quoted phrase on p. 326).
7. Shelley is quoted from *Percy Bysshe Shelley: The Major Works*, ed. Zachary Leader and Michael O'Neill (Oxford: Oxford University Press, 2003); for more on Shelley and Auden, see, among others, Carlos Baker, *The Echoing Green: Romanticism, Modernism, and the Phenomena of Transference in Poetry* (Princeton: Princeton University Press, 1984).

8. See the discussion in Mendelson, *Early Auden*, pp. 326–7; I read Auden's sense of the 'necessary' less as a quasi-Marxist recognition than as a moral recommendation.
9. Compare Keats's comparison between Moneta and the moon in *The Fall of Hyperion*, I.270–1, as one 'Who comforts those she sees not, who knows not / What eyes are upward cast'), *The Poems of John Keats*, ed. Miriam Allott (London: Longman, 1970).
10. C. Day Lewis's poetry is quoted from *The Complete Poems* (London: Sinclair-Stevenson, 1992).
11. Line 43; Emily Jane Brontë, *The Complete Poems*, ed. Janet Gezari (London: Penguin, 1992).
12. Louis MacNeice, *The Poetry of W. B. Yeats* (1941; London: Faber, 1967), p. 162.
13. *Ibid.*
14. Louis MacNeice's poetry is quoted from *Collected Poems*, ed. Peter McDonald (London: Faber, 2007).
15. MacNeice, *The Poetry of W. B. Yeats*, p. 46.
16. Spender's poetry is quoted from *New Collected Poems*, ed. Michael Brett (London: Faber, 2004). The two phrases from *Vienna* are quoted from p. 69, though the first occurs elsewhere in the work.
17. Lines 186–7, 188 in Wordsworth, *The Prelude* (1805), *Major Works*.
18. *The Penguin Book of Spanish Civil War Verse*, ed. Valentine Cunningham (1980; Harmondsworth: Penguin, 1983), p. 82.
19. A. Kingsley Weatherhead, *Stephen Spender and the Thirties* (London: Associated University Presses, 1975), p. 97.
20. Stephen Spender, *The Thirties and After: Poetry, Politics, People 1933–75* (Glasgow: Collins, 1978), p. 53.

Chapter 46

Dylan Thomas and the poetry of the 1940s

JOHN GOODBY

Forties poetry: definitions and defences

The political events of 1939 – the fall of the Spanish Republic, the Stalin–Hitler Pact and the outbreak of the Second World War – delivered a body-blow to the authority of the Audenesque style which had dominated thirties poetry. In January 1939 W. H. Auden (1907–73) himself had emigrated to the USA, and a shift from socio-political engagement to self-assessment and retrospection was discernible in his work as well as that of his followers. Those journals which had championed the Audenesque style, *Twentieth Century Verse* and *New Verse*, were wound up. Suddenly it was clear that events had outstripped even the direst prophecies of this poetry, insofar as these were cast in a realist style and rooted in a belief in the efficacy of rationality and collective action.

The sense of a sea-change in taste was confirmed by the publication of an anthology, *The New Apocalypse* (1939), edited by Henry Treece (1911–66) and J. F. Hendry (1912–86). Treece and Hendry spoke for a new poetic grouping (to which the anthology gave its name) which advocated an individualist, metaphysical, richly lyrical, anti-Audenesque poetic. Along with work by the group members, the anthology included poems by their chief inspiration, Dylan Thomas (1914–53), who, in Auden's absence, soon came to be regarded as the leading young British poet. Journals sympathetic to New Apocalypse appeared, among them Wrey Gardiner's *Poetry Quarterly* (1939–53) and M. J. Tambimuttu's *Poetry (London)* (1939–49). It was felt that, in Cyril Connolly's words, 'The flight of Auden . . . is also a symptom of the failure of social realism as an aesthetic doctrine . . . a reaction away from social realism is as necessary and as salutary as was, a generation ago, the reaction from the ivory tower.'[1]

Thomas, however, had come of poetic age with Auden in the crisis of the early 1930s, and both shared a 'vein of nervy apocalyptic jokiness'.[2] New Apocalypse, too, had 1930s roots; along with Thomas, it prized George

Barker (1913–91) and David Gascoyne (1916–2001), Yeats, the Surrealists, Jung, T. S. Eliot and D. H. Lawrence (from whose *Apocalypse* (1932) they took their name). 1939, then, marked a change in the response to a long-enduring crisis, rather than a disavowal of that crisis as such. The imminence of war precipitated the shift of emphasis from politics to myth, from cerebral irony to intuition, from collective struggle to the refashioning of the subject at the level of the body, psyche and language. As Stephen Spender (1909–95) noted during the Blitz, surrealism 'has ceased to be fantasy, its "objects" hurtle round our heads, its operations cause the strangest conjunctions of phenomena in the most unexpected places . . . [the] newest school of English poets signified this occasion by calling themselves "apocalyptics" '.[3]

That 'school' encouraged in turn a resurgence of native British neo-Romanticism, and a climate tolerant of poetic variousness. High Modernism made a comeback in David Jones's (1895–74) *The Anathemata* (1952; written 1946–51), Hilda Doolittle's (1886–1961) *Trilogy* and T. S. Eliot's (1888–1965) *Four Quartets*. Auden's social-discursive style was continued by Roy Fuller (1912–91). Women's poetry – the masterpieces of Edith Sitwell (1887–1964) and Lynette Roberts (1909–95) also belong to the 1940s – flourished as never before. Wartime Fitzrovia became England's only genuine twentieth-century Bohemia, as internationalism replaced thirties isolationism, and Rilke, Lorca and Cavafy brought new notes to English verse. In Egypt, soldier poets and expatriates – Bernard Spencer (1909–63), Lawrence Durrell (1912–90), Terence Tiller (1916–87) and Keith Douglas (1920–44) – created an independent literary outpost, with its own journals, coteries and East Mediterranean aesthetic.

Yet the 1940s also saw the savage ending and shattering of lives and careers. Along with Douglas, Alun Lewis (1915–44), Drummond Allison (1921–43) and Sidney Keyes (1922–43), died in the war, and many poets who survived it fell silent for a decade or more afterwards, some for good. The literary world, too, was altered: numerous long-established journals disappeared, and the pre-war life of a man of letters, supported by journalism and reviewing fees, became near-impossible. Several poets turned to non-literary work, often in the new media of film, radio and television, or tried to gain a foothold in academia. In higher education, and criticism more generally, there was a Leavisite emphasis on segregating 'high' from 'low' literature. The gap between Dylan Thomas's *Deaths and Entrances* (1946) and *Under Milk Wood* (1954), for example, reflects this newly fragmented, polarised scene. Significantly, while Thomas successfully balanced his roles as poet and public entertainer for a time, the conflict between them ultimately proved fatal, and his death in November 1953 is as good an end-date as any for the forties as a stylistic period.

The shape of forties poetry, then, is chaotic and difficult to understand. But the task of grasping its distinctiveness and achievement has been made immeasurably more difficult by the persistence of Movement stereotypes of a dire decade dominated by drunken Fitzrovian draft-dodgers and third-rate hysterical versifiers.[4] This not only travesties forties poetry, but does so in order to make exclusory claims on behalf of a narrowly defined 'English tradition' of plain-style, discursive poetry.[5] Forties poetry, which draws on surrealism and visionary Modernism, and concerns itself with the theme of mortality (and immortality), is, by such definitions, bad. Attempts to make it conform, such as F. R. Tolley's claim that it is 'typically, and, at its best, humanistic rather than apocalyptic', forget just how far traditional notions of human nature were unhinged by the Blitz, Auschwitz and Hiroshima.[6] In what follows, therefore, I take 'apocalyptic' as both a legitimate response and an accurate description of forties poetry, and argue that it is high time the poetic canon was expanded to include the best of it.

Voices prophesying war: Thomas and New Apocalypse

Auden had warned against 'surrender to / The apocalyptic dream' in his *New Year Letter* (1940), but New Apocalypse caught the mood of the generation that knew it had been 'bred to face death'.[7] Their unpublished manifesto of late 1938, 'Apocalypse, or, The Whole Man' explains their poetic as a rejection of mechanistic thought, including the 'ethereal [abstract] rationalism' of thirties poetry, Marxism's claim that human mastery of nature would eliminate myth and – as Spender had not quite grasped – the 'deliberate irrationalism' of surrealism.[8] Following the anarchist critic Herbert Read (1893–1968), it proposed that material drawn from the unconscious had to be subjected to conscious artistic shaping. Myth was crucial to this process because it was capable of reintegrating the fractured self to create the 'Whole Man' and able to pose questions 'which could not be neatly summarized or given fable-like clarity'.[9] Thomas was exemplary because he rigorously shaped his unconscious materials, and had a personal mythology based on the somatic drives and universal cycles of growth and decay: he was, in Hendry's words, 'the most organic of modern English poets'.[10] More, his verbal playfulness accorded with Treece's belief that for myth to perform its work, poetry had to reclaim its archaic musical powers, such that '[a]t times . . . music may take control [of poetry]'.[11]

But there were differences, reflected in Thomas's half-encouraging, half-mocking attitudes towards Treece, and his refusal to sign their New Apocalypse manifesto. Peter Riley notes that, rather than Thomas's 'passionate incantation compounding mind and body', in New Apocalypse poetry 'human existence itself is ... rendered sinister'.[12] Hendry's 'London before Invasion: 1940', for example, envisions the post-Dunkirk sense of historical breakdown, 'adrift' from past and future, far more negatively than Thomas:

> Flood-tides returning may bring with them blood and fire
> Blenching with wet panic spirit that must be rock.
> May bring a future tossed and torn, slippery as wrack.
> All time adrift in torrents of blind war. (Skelton, *Poetry*, p. 93)

In Treece and the weaker New Apocalypse poets, the result is tame symbolism and a strained, Grand Guignol tone. Indeed, none of the original Apocalyptics were able to realise the implications of Thomas's poetic, which was to 'push figuration beyond the bounds of rational location', in Riley's words, 'sett[ing] up poetry as a metalanguage, something which, like a painting or sculpture, uses materials of the world to create an entity which stands independently [of it]'.[13] While, in Thomas's work, obscurities can be decoded, the point is that they exist to temporarily delay comprehension, and so arrest perception at the level of verbal figuration. A line such as 'On the angelic etna of the last whirring featherlands' has a prose meaning, but before we work it out, it has created an imaginative space informed by a sense of how its figures become objects of attention in their own right, a verbal theatre where they operate without being fixed as symbols.[14] Thomas's word-play, like his universe, is also relativistic, and this helps subvert the portentousness that can so easily accrue to myth and organicism. Of the Apocalypse poets, however, it is arguable that only W. S. Graham (1918–86) fully understood this. There was, of course, some convergence: Thomas's poetry grew less obscure in the late 1930s, as marriage and war (which he often read into each other) demanded a more straightforward-seeming style.

Treece and Hendry edited two more anthologies, *The White Horseman* (1941) and *The Crown and the Sickle* (1943), the first of which triggered publication of *Eight Oxford Poets* (1941). This included Allison, Keyes and John Heath-Stubbs (1918–2006), and offered a more intellectualised neo-Romanticism that signalled the diffusion and mutation of New Apocalypse influence. Those associated with these developments also included Vernon Watkins (1906–67), W. R. Rodgers (1909–69), Norman McCaig (1910–96),

G. S. Fraser (1915–80) and Tom Scott (1918–95). As these names suggest, regionalist cultural movements used apocalyptic energies to advance their own agendas in the early 1940s, as did religious poets such as Kathleen Raine (1908–2003).

Ironically, the very success of New Apocalypse has made it easier for some critics to diminish its significance. In 1942 Herbert Read championed the group as 'The New Romantics', and this has often been taken to mean they were being supplanted by, or dissolved into, a new, broader grouping. But Read, like his contemporaries, understood the terms synonymously: with the agreement of Hendry and Treece, he had 're-brand[ed] the movement', thereby hitching it to the neo-Romantic current in painting, sculpture and music.[15] Indeed, New Apocalypse's high-water mark would be reached four years later, with Thomas's *Deaths and Entrances* (1946).

The Home Front, religion and the 'Blitz sublime'[16]

While the poetry-reading public of September 1939 craved war poets in the mould of Rupert Brooke, those who were called up took Wilfred Owen, Isaac Rosenberg and Siegfried Sassoon as their models. Yet the 'Phony War', Chamberlain's replacement by Churchill in May 1940, followed by the humiliation of Dunkirk and the fall of France, closed the gap between intellectuals and the population. Both became determined that, if victory was won, it must not be followed by a re-run of the miseries of the 1930s. In George Barker's words, 'My pig-faced kingdom with . . . an historical gait of trial and error', must 'Now answer History with a marvellous golden yes' (Skelton, *Poetry*, p. 49). The outcome of this, the best-selling Beveridge Report of 1942, pointed to the 1945 Labour government and a welfare state in which all citizens would be cared for 'from the cradle to the grave'. That this slogan echoes the basic terms of Dylan Thomas's poetry suggests just how a difficult thirties style could acquire a political charge and express profound social change.

Under wartime conditions, poetry flourished. It was the writing best equipped to deal with those experiences – love, death, mourning – which were now the common lot. Collections sold up to ten times as well as in peacetime, and numerous anthologies, miscellanies and journals appeared. Poetry came to reflect the inner and outer landscapes of war, its queasy blend of anxiety and solidarity under a regime of blackout, rationing, conscription, censorship and evacuation. Moreover, the Blitz, which began in September 1940, effectively turned civilians into combatants. By the winter of 1940–1, the blitzed city was as symbolic of the Second World War as the trenches were of 1914–18, and the distinction between 'Home' and 'Front', and hence the division between soldiers and civilians that bedevilled the First World War poets, had been substantially eroded (conversely, those in the forces never knew whether their loved ones were safe from air raids). 'War poet' no longer just meant one in uniform.

The Blitz also generated a desire to be reassured about permanent human values. Together with a heightened sense of the irrational, this made for an upsurge of religious poetry, reflected in a Penguin *Anthology of Religious Verse* (1942). Typically, the religious mood was Dostoevskyan and apocalyptic, exemplified by David Gascoyne's 'Ecce Homo', in whose 'Christ of Revolution and of Poetry' 'the rejected and condemned become / Agents of the divine' (Skelton, *Poetry*, p. 101). The irrational, uncanny aspects of the Blitz had other implications. Myth and magic could be used to figure the threat of the bombs, and the growing sense of the porousness of the boundary between the living and the dead. Concern with seepage between the two realms is apparent in the many poems about ghosts, revenants and doubles (though the best work in this vein was Elizabeth Bowen's short story 'The Demon Lover'). At the same time, the blackout came to symbolise lives put on hold, a wartime exile from some 'real' self and the ghosting of all relations.

To others, the Blitz purged national guilt (as in Eliot), or was an occasion for Marxist *schadenfreude*, as MacNeice's 'Brother Fire' (1942) hints:

> O delicate walker, babbler, dialectician Fire,
> O enemy and image of ourselves,
> Did we not on those mornings after the All Clear
> . . .
> Echo your thoughts in ours? 'Destroy! Destroy!'[17]

More generally, nihilism – what Gascoyne's 'Inferno' called 'Bottomless depths of roaring emptiness'[18] – alternated with an element of exhilaration. This response is part of what might be called the Blitz's Freudian-sublime aspect; a belief that it actualised a repressed psychic energy, and confirmed Freud's theory of the human subject. In the Blitz, so the argument went, the unconscious desire for destruction was made manifest, but so too were libidinal regressive urges, often Romantic-surreal in form. If religion and art were responses to its threat, so too was promiscuity; moreover, the Blitz created new opportunities for realising sexual promptings. As Spender rightly saw, surrealism, the art of fantasy and erotic desire, was now alive in the weird perspectives and paraphernalia of the blitzed city.

Dylan Thomas's Blitz elegies

Dylan Thomas's poems engage fully with the uncanny, anxious spaces of the besieged nation and its 'erotically-charged public sphere', which blurred espionage and affair, public and private.[19] Marital and martial overlap in 'Into her lying down head' (1940), for example, an anatomy of sexual jealousy haunted by 'colossal intimacies of silent / Once seen strangers or shades on the stair' and the wife's dream-lover who is 'the burning England she was sleep-walking' (*Collected Poems*, pp. 95–6). Yet, sexual love is also the 'immortal hospital' which alone is able to heal the fragmented self; 'There was a saviour' (1941) discovers in the excluded Other the only way to shatter the selfish pre-war self, and to free 'the / Unclenched, armless, silk and rough love that breaks all rocks' (pp. 105, 133). Even so, however he dealt with it, the war for Thomas was an ethical disaster, which could only be redeemed in and through the flesh.

This is clear in the elegies for children killed in the Blitz, 'Ceremony after a Fire Raid' (1944) and 'A Refusal to Mourn the Death, by Fire, of a Child in London' (1945). In them Thomas tests the elegiac mode by using the figure of the burning child, drawn from Southwell and Blake, to symbolise the greatest imaginable suffering inflicted on the greatest imaginable innocence. A need to bear public witness is reflected in their titles – a 'ceremony' and a newspaper headline – yet at the same time they also reveal Thomas's keen awareness, as a wartime scriptwriter for Ministry of Information films, of the dangers of performing official discourses of mourning, or of self-display in 'the strut and trade of charms / On the ivory stages' (p. 106).

'Among Those Killed in the Dawn Raid Was a Man Aged One Hundred' (1941) had already reflected these dangers in a substitute rite that exchanged the 'common cart' of Christianity for a pagan 'language of celebration that parodically compounds irony with affirmation'.[20] The last line – 'And a hundred storks perch on the sun's right hand' – alludes to the explanation of where babies come from offered to too-curious children, invoking a new birth for each of the hundred years 'lost', and 'Ceremony' takes this a stage further (p. 112). It opens by wrenching grammar to align the self with its audience ('Myselves / The grievers / Grieve / Among the street . . . A child of a few hours'), and announces his collective role in asking the dead girl to 'forgive / Give / Us your death that myselves . . . May hold it in a great flood / Till the . . . dust shall sing like a bird' (p. 107). It then proceeds to construct its 'ceremony' in anticipation of the transferred fulfilment of the child's lost genetic legacy. This appears in the poem's last section, the ceremony proper, in which part one's 'great flood' quenches the Blitz firestorm like some amniotic-sexual *tsunami* (the states are often confused by Thomas, and 'glory' is one of his words for orgasm):

> The masses of the infant-bearing sea
> Erupt, fountain, and enter to utter for ever
> Glory glory glory
> The sundering ultimate kingdom of genesis' thunder. (pp. 108–9)

For Steve Vine, 'Ceremony's ethics lie in the very extravagance of its rhetoric, which refuses to incorporate the death in realistic terms.'[21] The dark side of such rhetoric, however, is the silence Thomas always feared. 'A Refusal to Mourn' begins by refusing to mourn the child, until 'all humbling darkness / Tells with *silence*' a 'last light breaking' when the speaker will 'enter again' the mineral–vegetable–animal cycle of the 'round Zion of the water bead / And the synagogue of the ear of corn' (pp. 85–6). Only then can his mourning begin: to do otherwise would be to 'murder / The mankind of her going with a grave truth'. Typically, this end is rendered in paradoxically forceful verbs: the sea will 'tumble', the 'last light [tell]' (p. 86), and so on. Thomas wrests his severely qualified positives from a self-undoing language to avoid political, religious or sentimental exploitation of the death:

> Deep with the first dead lies London's daughter,
> Robed in the long friends,
> The grains beyond age, the dark veins of her mother,
> Secret by the unmourning waters
> Of the riding Thames.
> After the first death, there is no other. (p. 86)

Thomas defers mourning and then redefines it in terms of the perspective of vast cosmic cycles. His own entry into these will constitute a humanisation of them, as every human death does, and this will be his elegy for the child. In the meantime, she has already entered the continuum made up of 'the first dead' within a 'mother' earth. Although the Thames water is 'unmourning' it is 'riding' – charged, that is, with a sexual energy that ceaselessly vivifies dead matter. In this sense, the famous final line consoles by rejecting the 'second death' of the Book of Revelations.

Yet the line between consolation and despair is very fine. The poem refers to 'stations of the breath' (p. 86), invoking Henry Moore's famous drawings of shelterers in London Tube stations, especially children. These images are at the heart of the still-powerful 'Blitz myth' of national sacrifice, heroism and regeneration in a better future. Yet 'Zion' and 'synagogue' more obliquely point to the first reports, appearing as the poem was written, of the Nazi death camps. At this level, 'A Refusal to Mourn' deals with the unspeakable: it opens with the paradox of 'Never until' ('never' means 'not ever'; there can be no 'until' about it), and in its equally contradictory final line: a 'first' death presupposes a sequence, and an-'other' death (or why not 'After the *only* [or *one*] death . . . '?). The sense that there is no other death is thus haunted by that of 'there is nothing *but* death'. A myth of organic continuity is raised, but qualified by the possible failure of symbolic reparation – of language itself – in the face of Total War.

Theatre of War: the soldier-poets

Poets in uniform faced both the difficulty posed by the civilian redefinition of what war poetry was, and the anxiety of influence of the First World War poets. Unlike Owen and Sassoon, they knew they would not be shocked into memorable utterance – revelatory disillusionment could not occur a second time. Their problems were compounded by the war's mobility and its sheer scale.

Most responded by asserting the value of individual experience, stoically registering distinctness from the war machine as an act of faith in a better future, sharing in this the civilian fears of being made to act out of character. Submitting to military discipline meant playing a role, performing in the 'giant slapstick of modern war'.[22] In Henry Reed's 'Lessons of the War', the 'lessons' are not those of combat, but of the contrast between civilian and army life, with its risible yet insidious jargon, codes and rituals:

You must say, when reporting:
At five o'clock in the central sector is a dozen
Of what appear to be animals; whatever you do
    Don't call the bleeders *sheep*.   (Skelton, *Poetry*, p. 90)

The first war poem to attract widespread recognition, Alun Lewis's 'All Day It Has Rained' (1941), explores just such feelings of distance, of not quite fitting one's role. It describes a rainy day in an army tent, a hinterland between civilian life and combat. Sociable at first ('unbuttoning our braces, / Smoking a Woodbine'), the speaker thinks 'of the quiet dead and loud celebrities / Exhorting us to slaughter' and considers 'those whom we / For years have loved', before a quasi-visionary ending which recalls a walk to a local beauty spot

By Sheet and Steep and up the wooded scree
To the Shoulder o' Mutton where Edward Thomas brooded long
On death and beauty – till a bullet stopped his song.[23]

Beauty leads to death, the bullet-like ending suggests; Lewis identified with Thomas, and alludes to his poem 'Rain' in which, ominously, twilight and rain are emblems of death and the desire for death.

Lewis had turned to poetry to express 'the painful ease with which I feel the anxiety of a world at war', an oxymoron that sums up the split in him between a life of action and of fatalistic surrender to circumstance.[24] A teacher from the Cynon valley, devoted to his family and his wife Gweno, Lewis was a pacifist who rationalised joining up as a means of advancing the cause of socialism, and spoke of the need to 'educate *The People*', and advocated 'universal poems, not obscure modernities'.[25] But the clarity of 'All Day It Has Rained' was shadowed by expressionist intensities like those of 'The Sentry' (1940), with its opening line ('I have begun to die') read as another form of 'death and beauty', as is its conclusion that

> . . . the guns' implacable silence
> Is my black interim, my youth and age,
> In the flower of fury, the folded poppy,
> Night. (*Poems*, p. 28)

Lewis's first poetry collection, *Raiders' Dawn* (1942), sold well, as did his collection of short stories, *The Last Inspection* (1943). Putting his divisions to artistic use, stories such as 'Dusty Hermitage' and 'Ward "O" 3b' show how, as it was accentuated by war, he divided his split self between different characters. In his lyrics, however, this took the form of a stylistic dialogue between realism and Apocalyptic expressionism. The styles often cancel each other out, or conflict with the poem's subject, evidence of Lewis's risk-taking. Even so, the dissonance reflects on how the 'barren ugly coarse life of the army' sapped his certainties, increasing 'my trouble, this slipping away of individuality . . . my character [of having] no character'.[26] Although he had enlisted in the Royal Engineers to avoid killing, he was impelled, as if by the logic of the conflict, to transfer to a combat unit.

Posted to India in 1942, Lewis was immediately attracted to its brilliant, 'marco polo wonders'. Among them was his affair with a married woman, Freda Ackroyd.[27] His last and greatest story, 'The Orange Grove', a tale of an officer who escapes his role by usurping a dead man's name, echoes a letter to Freda in which Lewis tells of a dream of dying and returning to live with her freely, armed with a new identity. In this way he figured a desire to escape his own self-division and double life; and yet he seems increasingly to have found that the only route towards integration lay in death. His poems mirror this; 'Karanje Village' asks, 'When my sweetheart calls me shall I tell her / That I am seeking less and less of world?', while 'Burma Casualty' imagines death as a welcoming 'beautiful singing sexless angel' (*Poems*, pp. 130, 148). Lewis appears to wed his own melancholia to the fatalism and wretchedness of India, allowing it to both speak to him and overwhelm him.

In his last poem, 'The Jungle', a jungle pool offers 'To quench more than our thirst – our selves', but also 'a sinister content' where 'all fidelities and doubts dissolve'. Enclosed in foliage, the last of his retreats, his ideals are merely 'the vituperations of the just' in a 'world we could not change'. Like a suicide note, the poem requests forgiveness of those 'who want us for ourselves, / Whose love can start the snow-rush in the woods / And melt the glacier in the dark coulisse', a cool music which ends with 'The face distorted in a jungle pool / That drowns the image in a mort of leaves' (*Poems*, pp. 155, 156, 157). Beauty and death have fused into a death-urge. In the last two poems in the posthumous *Ha! Ha! Among the Trumpets* (1945), Lewis addresses Freda and Gweno directly; they seem to represent, respectively, his irreconcilable outer and inner, public and private, identities. Putting his affairs in order, Lewis had himself posted to the front line in Burma. There, on 5 March 1944, he shot himself.

Arguably, it was the fundamental sincerity and wholeness he so prized that had made Lewis vulnerable in the face of the war's performative demands. The pre-war attachments of Keith Douglas (1920–44) – rootless, unmarried, with only his mother for family – carried none of Lewis's personal or communal commitments. He nurtured a sense of being 'outcast', and a temperament at once rebellious and ritualistic, and his differently riven personality was held together by a modern version of traditional aristocratic discipline.[28] Douglas's poems give an impression of a strong will which is nevertheless committed to openness. In a 1940 essay he claimed, 'Poetry is like a man, whom, thinking you know all his movements and appearance you will presently come upon in such a posture that for a moment you can hardly believe it to be a position of the limbs you know.'[29] The defamiliarising effect Douglas extols is embodied in the supple but torqued syntax of the sentence that describes it. 'The Prisoner' (1940) exemplifies this trait:

> . . . today I touched a mask stretched on the stone-
> hard face of death. There was the urge
> to escape the bright flesh and emerge
> of the ambitious cruel bone. (*Poems*, p. 67)

The information that 'the urge' is not that of the speaker but the 'bone' is delayed until the final word, and 'emerge' is made to emerge at the line-end to form a couplet with 'urge' as a result, just as the 'bone' desires to emerge from the 'flesh' (and will after death). The manipulation gives 'bone's' adjectives, 'ambitious' and 'cruel', a sinister, Jacobean energy, and this is a kind of Revenger's poem, addressed as it is to an ex-lover. But they have a tragic cast too; the still-beloved face will become a skull.

Such poetry is essentially metaphysical. Emotion exists between the lines, as Douglas skirmishes around his sensibility, probing and retreating from it in order to contemplate more fundamental structures. In an essay written after his posting to North Africa in 1942, 'Poets in the War' (1943), he claimed that no poet had yet written well about the war, blaming its mobility and anxiety of influence. Yet although he echoes this in 'Desert Flowers' (1943) – 'Rosenberg I only repeat what you were saying' (*Poems*, p. 102) – in reality he was uniquely suited to deal with the high-speed, mechanised slaughter of the desert 'theatre'. 'Cairo Jag' (1943) opens by contrasting the middle-class 'Marcelle, Parisienne' brooding on 'her dull dead lover ... in a stink of jasmine', and the slum women 'offering their children brown-paper breasts / dry and twisted'. But at the end it pulls back further to juxtapose both against the battlefield 'a day's travelling' away, 'a new world' with 'gunbarrels ... split like celery' and 'all sorts of manure'

> ... you can imagine
> the dead themselves, their boots, clothes and possessions
> clinging to the ground, a man with no head
> has a packet of chocolate and a souvenir of Tripoli. (*Poems*, p. 97)

'Tripoli' is the dead man's equivalent of Cairo, making him the speaker's alter ego; but so surreal and absurd are the images that engross the speaker's sight that they thwart his development of this link. This lack of innerness has attracted hostile comment; Adam Piette claims that Douglas 'theatricalizes the ... deaths', that they 'mime his own pain and shock at seeing them' and that he 'writhes in pain at his own heartless (melo)dramatizing of other men's deaths, writhes in agony at his own lack of untheatrical feeling'.[30] Yet this rather naively (and '(melo)dramatically') assumes that death could be presented in some pure, un-'theatricalised' manner, and misrepresents Douglas's attempt to write about the already theatricalised experience of war as an inability to feel.

Douglas's distance is, in fact, an unwillingness to moralise. Writing to his friend J. C. Hall in 1943, he criticised the 'lyric ... approach' for being 'even less good than a journalese approach to the [war] subjects we have to discuss now'. He added that '[t]o be sentimental or emotional now is dangerous to oneself and to others. To trust anyone or admit any hope of a better world is criminally foolish, as foolish as it is to stop working for it. It sounds silly to say work without hope, but it can be done; it's only a form of insurance; it doesn't mean work hopelessly.'[31] Such forceful ambivalence can be seen in 'Sportsmen' (1943), which both mocks his fellow officers' insouciance (they treat battle as a fox hunt), and admires it. Mimicry – 'Peter was unfortunately killed by an 88 . . . he said: / it's most unfair, they've shot my foot off' – is indistinguishable from praise for 'obsolescent heroes' who perform 'attitudes of unconcern' even in death. The poem oscillates between the 'two legends' of 'stupidity and chivalry' as satire, elegy, slapstick and, in a final allusion to Roland's 'simple horn', myth (*Poems*, p. 110). The oscillation enacts the complex moods of the speaker, but avoids passing judgment.

The two most powerful presences in Douglas's work are the indifferent father-figure, or god, who reduces human beings to mere puppets, and an inner 'beast'. Both are related forms of the same 'deity'.[32] Douglas's poems often register a sense of being trapped between these figures, of performing their scripts. But there is always an ingenious relish also in maximising the freedom within such constraints. The drafts of 'Bête Noir', his final, unfinished, poem – and the striking ink drawings accompanying it of a man fighting a demon clinging to his back – show that, just before his death in Normandy in June 1944, Douglas had begun to challenge his inner division, and was about to make another poetic advance.

Regionalism and the pastoral mode

In the late 1940s the market for poetry subsided: new magazines now led brief existences, while established ones folded. A resurgence in Christian poetry reflected the conservative reaction to the reforms of the Attlee government, and verse drama also underwent one of its periodic revivals, with Christopher Fry's (1907–2005) *The Lady's Not for Burning* (1948) the best example. Both trends, however, were essentially archaising, and were petering out by the time of the Festival of Britain in 1951. In a separate development, poets pursued the alignment of neo-Romanticism with regionalism's protest against centralisation and the state. Regionalism presupposed an interest in local tradition and rural landscape, and had affinities with Romanticism, myth and organicist philosophy. In Northern Ireland, John Hewitt (1904–87) was its leading figure; in Scotland Norman MacCaig, Sidney Goodsir Smith (1915–75) and Tom Scott were prominent. The refusal of several of these poets to accept the nationalism-and-Lallans line of Hugh

MacDiarmid (1892–1978), the leader of the Scottish Renaissance, showed that such movements were not necessarily homogeneous.

This was true of Welsh poetry, the most thriving of all, which boasted, in *The Faber Book of Welsh Verse* (1944), David Jones, Alun Lewis, Vernon Watkins, Glyn Jones (1905–95), Lynette Roberts, R. S. Thomas (1913–2000), and Dylan Thomas. R. S. Thomas's 'The Peasant' (1944) challenges an Anglocentric state made over-mighty by war; 'Not to be stormed even in death's confusion', the peasant too 'is a winner of wars, / Enduring like a tree under the curious stars'.[33] Watkins's 'The Ballad of Mari Lywd' (1941) centres on a Welsh folk custom in which mumming groups bearing a horse's skull visit houses on New Year's Eve, challenging their inhabitants to rhyming contests, or even temporarily evicting them. It powerfully conveys the 'profane and sacred moment impossible to realize while the clock-hand divides the Living from the Dead', re-figuring in archetypal terms the dissolution of barriers experienced in the Blitz.[34]

Perhaps the most original of the forties Welsh poets was the Argentine-Welsh Roberts, whose 670-odd line *Gods with Stainless Ears* (written 1941–3, published 1951) aligns observation of nature, rural customs, air raids, miscarriage and domestic drudgery, with avant-gardism, as the opening of its fourth section, 'Cri Madonna', illustrates:

> I, rimmeled, awake before the dressing sun:
> Alone I, pent up incinerator, serf of satellite gloom
> Cower around my cradled self; find crape-plume
> In a work-basket cast into swaddling clothes
> Forcipated from my mind after the foetal fall . . .[35]

'Rimmeled', from Rimmel make-up, is a neologism meaning 'eyes black-ringed from sadness and sleeplessness, as if outlined in mascara', a result of the speaker's depression at the recent loss of her baby. 'Serf'-like in her crushed condition, clouded by 'gloom', she is an abject figure; 'forcipated' is from forceps, describing the poem, and the (mental) birth by which black cloth in a 'work-basket' becomes 'crape-plume' for the dead child, also alluded to in 'foetal [fatal] fall'. Roberts creates Anglophone equivalents of the effects of Welsh poetry (the reiterated *c*s and *f*s of lines three and five) – appropriately, because *Gods* is aligned with the sixth-century Welsh battle-epic, the *Gododdin*. Yet she is a non-nostalgic Modernist, and *Gods* ends with a futuristic episode and concern for the post-war world. She would claim, 'we need myth more than ever: but not blindly, only in relation to its scientific handling, in its relation to today'.[36] Though initially forbidding, the zig-zagging of *Gods'* verbal surface justifies itself in narrative terms as well as musically, its New Apocalyptic prioritisation of sound counterpointed by a scrupulous etymological passion.

Dylan Thomas's post-1944 style also shows an engagement with regionalism. Avoiding Roberts's nationalism, it engages with pastoral as that term is understood in William Empson's *Some Versions of Pastoral* (1935); namely, as 'putting the complex into the simple'.[37] 'In country sleep' (1947), 'Over Sir John's Hill' (1949), 'In the White Giant's Thigh' (1950) and 'Poem on His Birthday' (1951) are also haunted by the Cold War and present a natural world whose fragility is all the greater because of the threat of nuclear annihilation. The silence 'told' by the rich plenitude of 'all-humbling darkness' is now the void 'cyclone of silence' following 'the rocketing wind [which] will blow / The bones out of the hills' (*Collected Poems*, pp. 140, 146). Thomas explained that the first three poems were part of a sequence called *In Country Heaven*, a memorialisation of earth made by its former inhabitants after its destruction by nuclear war.

Similar fears inform work by Edwin Muir (1887–1959), and were sharpened by his journey across devastated post-war Europe to take up a British Council post in Prague in 1945. 'The Interrogation' is typical of his agile, lucidly unconsoling tone:

> We cannot choose
> Answer or action here,
> Though still the careless lovers saunter by
> And the thoughtless field is near.
> We are on the very edge
> Endurance almost done,
> And still the interrogation is going on.[38]

In 'The Labyrinth', a long unspooling single sentence – in the voice of a Theseus-figure, and imitating his thread – tells of one 'emerg[ing] from the labyrinth' (*Complete Poems*, p. 157) who continues to '[hear] my footsteps / Still echoing in the maze' and finds the world increasingly like 'the great labyrinth', 'as if the maze itself were after me' (p. 158). By the end, his claim that he 'has birdwings to fly free' (p. 150) of the maze is revealed as wishful thinking; Muir has fused the classical myth of the killer of 'the bull / . . . dead upon the straw' (p. 157), and the 1948 Stalinist coup in Prague, with impressive power. The most famous piece in this late mode is 'The Horses', an ecological parable poem set after 'the seven days' war that put the world to sleep', in which Muir's returning horses remind us of mankind's desperate, yet so often repressed need for the 'free servitude' (p. 227) of creaturely self-awareness.

Developing Dylan: W. S. Graham

The pastoral, mythic-allegorical elements of Dylan Thomas's and Muir's late poetry are present in the work of the poet who best developed the 'visionary Modernist' legacy, W. S. Graham. Born and brought up in Greenock, Graham lived in London in the 1940s, settling in Cornwall in 1955. *Cage Without Grievance* (1942), *The Seven Journeys* (1944; written 1941–2), *2nd Poems* (1945) and *The White Threshold* (1949), show him evolving the mature style which first flowered in *The Nightfishing* (1955; written 1950).

Unlike many of his critics, Graham was always comfortable with his debt to Thomas; indeed, in 'What is the Language Using Us for?' (1977), a meeting with 'a kind old uncle of mine', 'The King of Whales', affectionately alludes to him via a favourite Wales/whales pun.[39] He could do so because, as even *The Seven Journeys* (his earliest work) shows, he was adept from the start at creating his own version of Thomas's post-symbolic verbal 'theatre':

> Answering the abstract annals of unhero'd floes
> The chimes of sweet Elizabethan turtled air
> Guide their soul cirrus monuments of azure
> Round the skull's thundery cathedral adored in ice
> . . .
> Let me from a Celtic sex with granite my costume
> Rise like a bangled Messiah in a saga's beak
> And break the Arctic girl with no seal's barrier
> And set her madrigals round my flint wrists.
>
> (*New Collected Poems*, pp. 7–8)

As a note on the manuscript copy suggests – 'strange northern hardness against English softness' – the passage explores a sexualised definition of the self in terms of conflict and similarity between opposites.[40] Similarly, the poem's weird maritime and Arctic imagery derives from Thomas's use of the sea as a symbolic self-proving ground, in such poems as 'Ballad of the Long-legged bait' and the 'snowblind' 'A Winter's Tale' from *Deaths and Entrances*. Yet Graham defines himself in a style which is less monumental, more skittishly inclusive, one which will ultimately be more attached to the ordinary, and more explicit in its strategies (such as Jung's notion of the 'drowning voyage' that enables the birth of an integrated self, for example). Although it would be simplistic to say that what Thomas intuited, Graham systematised, it is striking that, as William Montgomerie has shown, *The Seven Journeys* effectively maps out Graham's life's work: 'The First Journey is Scottish . . . The Third Journey . . . [displays] aspects of water. The Fourth

Journey is through ice and snow, the Fifth suggests sex, the Sixth the sea.'[41] Indeed, it may have been omitted from his *Selected Poems* precisely because it was so programmatic.

Systematic experimentalism can be seen in *2nd Poems*, which also registers the influence of painting on his work; as he saw, the treatment of the poem as a word-pattern closely resembled the way twentieth-century painting styles, like Cubism, work to arrest the viewer's gaze at the surface plane. *The White Threshold* gives Graham's response to regionalism: Scots dialect and family, Greenock tenements, Lanarkshire pit-towns and the local countryside, all feature. It is a Blakeian vision of working-class life, obliquely outlining the way in which childhood energies are repressed in adulthood by authority in the form of 'poorhouse', police, drudgery and distant, uncaring government. These energies, however, may be reignited by love and an openness to language, which both represents and is that world: thus, his dead mother is described as 'Under (not ground but the words)' where she '[Rests] with the speaking hordes' (*New Collected Poems*, p. 101). The poems are pastoral, this often being signalled by simple forms, such as ballad, or tumbling three-stress lines:

> Listen. Put on morning.
> Waken into falling light.
> A man's imagining
> Suddenly may inherit
> The handclapping centuries
> Of his one minute on earth.
> And hear the virgin juries
> Talk with his own breath
> To the corner boys of his street.
>
> (*New Collected Poems*, p. 60)

Yet although evidently by a Scottish writer, the poems do not strive to project a Scottish identity. Graham saw poetry as most fully responsible – that is, political on its own terms – when treating what it is uniquely qualified to examine, namely the conditions of human communication and self-understanding in language.

As a voyage poem-sequence, *The White Threshold*'s title poem suggests how such conditions would become the subject of Graham's major works (the 'threshold' being the sea, the self and the poet's sheet of paper). With it the poetry shifts from establishing the validity of the linguistic surface to a metaphysical exploration of the paradox of a self constituted in language. This would make language the subject matter of the later poems, treating it as an animate, organic being; and the coherence of a self which can only be established and represented in unmasterable language would also be experienced as continually breaking down: madness and violence are never far away. Similarly, the later work evokes a sketchily defined muse-figure and a supernatural zone, both identified with the sexual drive, as necessary fictions. In all of these aspects, Graham's poetry develops that of Dylan Thomas.

Conclusion

The best poetry of the forties – which includes *The Anathemata*, *Four Quartets*, *Deaths and Entrances*, *Gods with Stainless Ears*, *The Nightfishing* and the best of Lewis, Douglas, Muir, Gascoyne and Barker – stands comparison with that of any other period of equal length in the twentieth century. Yet it is, above all, the variety and openness to different kinds of poetry which is the period's most significant aspect. This would be the most significant loss in the 1950s, when the radicalism of the 1940s was defused, women were returned to the home and traditional moral and spiritual values were reasserted. The Movement's response, as Andrew Crozier has remarked, was to limit poetry to 'an authoritative self discoursing in a world of banal, empirically derived objects and relations', the chief outcome of which was a dominant poetry that was largely 'a reserve for small verbal thrills, a daring little frill round the hem of normal discourse'.[42] Moreover, in so far as anxiety at Britain's reduced post-imperial power and purpose has continued to flourish, this discourse was able to ride out the disruptions of the 1960s and the expiration of Movement poetry as such, recharging itself after Auden's death with a re-mythicisation of Auden and the 'Auden Decade', and the consequent diminishment of Thomas and the visionary Modernist strain. A glance at the Faber list of today is enough to show that the publisher who embraced both Lynette Roberts and Walter de la Mare no longer exists.

Yet far from having been a chaotic dead end for British poetry, and despite the paucity of critical assessments, it is now apparent that the forties had a lasting if occluded impact on later British poetry. The vitalism of Ted Hughes (1930–98) and the radical metaphoricity of Sylvia Plath (1932–63), for example, not to mention their interest in the animal world or antenatal subjects, point directly to Apocalyptic modes and to Thomas. The Geoffrey Hill (1932–) of early poems such as 'Genesis', is likewise a product of the forties. More surprisingly, Roy Fisher (1930–) and Edwin Morgan (1920–) have both testified to Thomas's importance as an example. Through Graham, Thomas's linguistic experimentalism has passed to contemporary avant-garde figures such as Denise Riley (1948–). Moreover, Thomas's provincial assertiveness was exemplary for the 1960s revolt against the centre that included Seamus Heaney, Tony Harrison, Douglas Dunn and others. If the forties have been neglected in recent criticism, its own most important poetic sourcebook, Robert Graves's *The White Goddess* (1947), has been the most influential of the past half-century. All of which is a reminder that *British* poetry demands to be viewed as a dialogue between its components – national and regional, Dionysian and puritan, elite and populist, neo-classical and neo-Romantic, Modernist and social-realist – one productive of hybrids that confound attempts to assert singular narratives. In this sense it was forties poetry, not 'the English tradition', which set the pattern for today's pluralism.

Notes

1. Cited in *Poetry of the Forties*, ed. Robin Skelton (Harmondsworth: Penguin, 1968), pp. 17–18. Further quotations from this edition are cited parenthetically in the text as Skelton, *Poetry*.
2. Gabriel Pearson, 'Gabriel Pearson on Dylan Thomas', *The Spectator Review of Books* (20 November 1971), p. 731.
3. Stephen Spender, 'Some Observations on English Poetry Between Two Wars', in S. Schimanski and H. Treece (eds.), *Transformation* 3 (London: Lindsay Drummond Ltd, 1945), p. 3.
4. The best analysis (and rebuttal) of this discourse is to be found in James Keery's study '"The Burning Baby" and the Bathwater', published in nine instalments in *P. N. Review* between 2003 and 2006. This chapter is deeply indebted to Keery's pioneering work, and I hereby acknowledge a debt.
5. Donald Davie, cited in Tony Lopez, *The Poetry of W. S. Graham* (Edinburgh: Edinburgh University Press, 1989), p. 16.
6. F. R. Tolley, *The Poetry of the Forties* (Manchester: Manchester University Press: 1985), p. 213.
7. Linda Shires, *British Poetry of the Second World War* (London: Macmillan: 1985), p. 57.
8. The manifesto was published by Giles Goodland in *P. N. Review*, 154 (November–December 2003), pp. 22–5.
9. Skelton, *Poetry*, p. 26.
10. J. F. Hendry, 'Writers and Apocalypse', in *The New Apocalypse* (London: Fortune Press, 1940), p. 15.
11. Skelton, *Poetry*, p. 23.
12. Peter Riley, 'Thomas and Apocalypse', http://www.aprileye.co.uk/thomas.html, 3.
13. Peter Riley, review of W. S. Graham, *New Collected Poems*, *Jacket* 26 (October 2004), http://jacketmagazine.com/26/index.shtml, pp. 1–4.

14. Dylan Thomas, *Collected Poems: 1934–1953*, ed. Walford Davies and Ralph Maud (London: Dent, 1993), p. 78. Further quotations from this edition are cited parenthetically in the text.
15. James Keery, '"The Burning Baby" and the Bathwater', *P. N. Review*, 170 (July–August 2006), p. 62.
16. 'Blitz sublime' is Stuart Sillars's term for the mingled fear and excitement created by the spectacle of the bombing, in *British Romantic Art and the Second World War* (New York: St Martin's Press, 1991), p. 78.
17. Louis MacNeice, *Collected Poems* (London: Faber, 1979), p. 196.
18. David Gascoyne, 'Inferno', *Selected Poems* (London: Enitharmon, 1994), p. 82.
19. Lyndsey Stonebridge, 'Bombs and Roses: The Writing of Anxiety in Henry Green's *Caught*', in R. Mengham and N. R. Reeve (eds.), *The Fiction of the 1940s: Stories of Survival* (London: Palgrave, 2001), p. 59.
20. Steve Vine, '"Shot from the locks": Poetry, Mourning, *Deaths and Entrances*', in John Goodby and Chris Wigginton (eds.), *Dylan Thomas: New Casebook* (London: Palgrave, 2001), p. 140.
21. *Ibid.*, p. 154.
22. Karl Shapiro, in *The War Poets*, ed. Oscar Williams (New York: John Day, 1945), p. 27.
23. Alun Lewis, *Collected Poems*, ed. Cary Archard (Bridgend: Seren, 2007), p. 23. Further quotations from this edition are cited parenthetically in the text.
24. John Pikoulis, *Alun Lewis: A Life* (Bridgend: Seren, 1991), p. 227.
25. *Ibid.*, p. 102.
26. Pikoulis, *Alun Lewis*, pp. 115, 72.
27. *Ibid.*, p. 167.
28. Keith Douglas, *The Complete Poems* (Oxford: Oxford University Press, 1995), p. 105. Further quotations from this edition are cited parenthetically in the text.
29. *Ibid.*, p. 123.
30. Adam Piette, *Imagination at War: British Fiction and Poetry 1939–1945* (London: Macmillan, 1995), p. 18.
31. Douglas, *Complete Poems*, p. 124.
32. Shires, *British Poetry of the Second World War*, p. 118.
33. R. S. Thomas, *Selected Poems 1946–1968* (Newcastle: Bloodaxe, 1992), p. 11. Further quotations from this edition are cited parenthetically in the text.
34. *The Collected Poems of Vernon Watkins* (Ipswich: Golgonooza, 2000), p. 40.
35. Lynette Roberts, *Collected Poems*, ed. Patrick McGuinness (Bridgend: Seren, 2005), p. 60.
36. Nigel Wheale, 'Lynette Roberts: Legend and Form in the 1940s', *Critical Quarterly*, 36:3 (Autumn 1994), p. 7.
37. William Empson, *Some Versions of Pastoral* (London: Penguin, 1995), p. 25.
38. Edwin Muir, *The Complete Poems*, ed. Peter Butter (Aberdeen: Association for Scottish Studies, 1991), pp. 172–3. Further quotations from this edition are cited parenthetically in the text.

39. W. S. Graham, *New Collected Poems* (London: Faber, 2004), p. 202. Further quotations from this edition are cited parenthetically in the text.
40. Lopez, *The Poetry of W. S. Graham*, p. 35.
41. William Montgomerie, Introduction to W. S. Graham, *The Seven Journeys* (Glasgow: William Machellan, Poetry Scotland series, 1944), n.p.
42. Andrew Crozier, 'Thrills and Frills: Poetry as Figures of Empirical Lyricism', in *Society and Literature 1945–1970*, ed. Alan Sinfield (London: Methuen, 1983), p. 213.

Chapter 47
Larkin and the Movement

STEPHEN REGAN

Philip Larkin's place in the history of English poetry has been a matter of intense debate, but there is little doubt that Larkin was the most distinguished poet among that group of writers known as the Movement. Larkin claimed to have 'no sense at all' of belonging to a literary movement, but his work was widely regarded in the 1950s and 1960s as the most promising expression of a new set of thematic and stylistic preoccupations in English verse.[1] Larkin's poetry was anthologised with that of other Movement poets, including Kingsley Amis, Donald Davie, John Wain, Elizabeth Jennings, D. J. Enright and Thom Gunn, and these poets were grouped together in critical essays and reviews. Although the existence of the Movement has been treated with scepticism by some critics, and sometimes dismissed as a literary hoax or a journalistic publicity stunt, there is enough evidence in the poetry and prose of these writers to suggest a strong and genuine compatibility of interests. Blake Morrison, in the most authoritative account of the Movement to date, offers a compelling argument that, despite some obvious divisions and contradictions, 'there was considerable agreement and interaction, and out of these was established a Movement consensus'.[2]

It was in the pages of the influential London periodical the *Spectator* that claims on behalf of a new movement in English poetry in the 1950s began to appear. In a controversial review article, 'Poets of the Fifties', Anthony Hartley detected in the new poetry a prevailing outlook that was 'distrustful of too much fanaticism, austere and sceptical', and a set of stylistic preferences that included an avoidance of rhetoric, a cautious and subdued tone and a conversational idiom. Hartley's assertion that 'we are now in the presence of the only considerable movement in English poetry since the Thirties'[3] was echoed in the title of a later *Spectator* article, 'In the Movement', by its editor, J. D. Scott. The two articles insisted that the new poetry of the fifties was different in style and outlook from both the politically committed writing of the 1930s and the neo-Romanticism of the 1940s. Larkin's poetry was only briefly mentioned in the first of these *Spectator* articles, but its appearance in several anthologies in the 1950s gave further impetus to the idea of his involvement in a movement in English poetry of the time. The editors of *Springtime: An Anthology of Young Poets and Writers* (1953) presented Larkin as one of a number of poets in 'reaction against experiment for its own sake'.[4] Clarity and intelligibility were also the poetic virtues espoused in D. J. Enright's introduction to *Poets of the 1950s: An Anthology of New English Verse* (1955). Acknowledging 'a new spirit stirring in contemporary English poetry', Enright stressed the moderate political stance and 'chastened common sense' of his chosen poets, explaining their scepticism in terms of a widespread post-war cautiousness and uncertainty. The age demanded from these poets 'a fairly tough intelligence and an unwillingness to be deceived'.[5]

The anthology which was seen to herald and promote the work of the Movement most enthusiastically was Robert Conquest's *New Lines* (1956). Ironically, Conquest was at pains to play down any suggestion that he was promoting a definite group of writers with shared commitments: 'It will be seen at once that these poets do not have as much in common as they would if they were a group of doctrine-saddled writers forming a definite school complete with a programme and rules.'[6] Even so, Conquest's introduction came to be regarded as the manifesto of the Movement, strongly advocating a poetry 'free from both mystical and logical compulsions . . . empirical in its attitude to all that comes'.[7] Conquest's anthology was also largely responsible for promulgating the idea of the Movement as a concerted reaction against the excesses of 1940s Romanticism. The poets of that earlier decade were 'encouraged to produce diffuse and sentimental verbiage', while the new generation refused to abandon 'a rational structure and comprehensible language'.[8]

The qualities of clarity and intelligibility that came to be associated with the Movement are evident throughout the *New Lines* anthology. The poems of Elizabeth Jennings which open the collection are exemplary in their formal neatness and careful syntactical arrangement. 'The Island' swiftly establishes its control over diverse imaginative landscapes: 'All travellers escape the mainland here' (*New Lines*, p. 1). The explanatory voice, so familiar in the work of Larkin and other Movement writers, takes on a conversational tone as it expands across line-endings, varying its inflections as it moves from preposition to conjunction, and from verb to adverb, at the start of each new line. The tight alliterative patterning and the subtle, unforced rhymes enhance the impression of a rational, orderly syntax. 'The Island' has more to offer, however, than the satisfactions of the well-made poem. The island is not just an imaginary and physical escape, but a place of self-communing, where visitors explore an inward 'island strength'.

Like Philip Larkin's 'Here', the poem explores what it means to be 'here' in the most fundamental, ontological sense. If Movement poetry entails a readjustment of style in the interests of intelligibility, it also involves a readjustment of self and world that coincides with the broad intellectual context of post-war existentialism. The most compelling and enduring Movement poetry – that of Jennings, Larkin, Gunn and Davie – is a poetry profoundly concerned with knowledge of self, but knowledge of self intensified and complicated by changing post-war attitudes to political freedom, social class and religious belief. Jennings complicates the usual description of Movement poetry as agnostic or atheistic by subtly reconfiguring her philosophical inquiries in religious terms. In 'The Island' her existentialist travellers are 'Seekers who are their own discovery' (p. 2). In Jennings's later work, a more fully articulated Christianity sets her apart from her Movement contemporaries.

The idea of knowledge acquired through arrivals and departures, through experiential encounters with 'here' and 'there', gives a new resonance to Movement poetry. Journeying is a characteristic trope in a poetry habitually concerned with redefining identities and re-establishing boundaries in post-war society. It also provides the ideal metaphorical foil for imagined confrontations with poetic tradition. Kingsley Amis makes striking use of the journey motif in his defence of Movement modesty and restraint in 'Against Romanticism'. The poem is structured so that the poet-traveller leaves the safe woods and well-worn path behind, briefly encountering the wildly imaginative and exotically sensuous excesses of Romanticism along the way: 'A traveller who walks a temperate zone / – Woods devoid of beasts, roads that please the foot – / Finds that its decent surface grows too thin' (*New Lines*, p. 45). Familiar Movement virtues are clearly mapped at the outset. A 'decent' art (that single word embodies a host of ideological and aesthetic preferences) vies with a fumbling art of the nerves and the senses. Contrary to what its forthright title implies, the fascination of the poem has less to do with some easy polemical swipe against Romanticism than with the way in which Romanticism is so patently caricatured and knowingly overdetermined as to undermine the argument against it.

The Movement line that Amis articulates here resorts to comic hyperbole and innuendo ('legendary the taste / Of drinks or fruits or tongues laid on the tongue' (p. 45)), but it carries with it a more sensitive and subtle appreciation of the Romantic lyric, as with the skilful conflation of Keats's 'Ode on a Grecian Urn' and Shelley's 'Ode to the West Wind' in a single line: 'Melodies from shards, memories from coal' (p. 45). Romantic allusions are so deftly interwoven with the poem's counter-Romantic assertions that it becomes difficult to disentangle them. Amis's traveller is, in the first place, a modern counterpart to Shelley's 'traveller in an antique land' in 'Ozymandias', but the poem sets itself most obviously against Coleridge's 'Kubla Khan' ('the brain raging with prophecy' (p. 45)) and 'The Ancient Mariner' ('let the sky be clean of officious birds / Punctiliously flying on the left' (p. 46)). Michael O'Neill sums up Amis's complicated engagement with Romanticism very aptly in his claim that the poem 'seems more than half in love with the unruly energies that it seeks to curb'.[9]

Philip Larkin's representative traveller, cycling through 'suburb scrub' to a 'cross of ground' in 'Church Going',[10] has much in common with Amis's speaker, but he is not many miles away from 'the Boys' on motorcycles in Thom Gunn's 'On the Move'. Larkin, like Gunn, acknowledge how 'all our compulsions . . . Are recognised and robed as destinies' (p. 21). In Gunn's poem, 'One joins the movement in a valueless world'. His motorcyclists travel through towns that are 'home for neither bird nor holiness, / For birds and saints complete their purposes' (*New Lines*, p. 33). Larkin's cyclist is candidly inclined to wonder, while Gunn's goggled boys 'strap in doubt' (*New Lines*, p. 32) in a Nietzschean hurtling of the will, but both poems exemplify a Movement tendency in 'Reaching no absolute in which to rest' (*New Lines*, p. 33). The habitual association of travel with a philosophical readjustment to a changed world order explains why D. J. Enright's 'Waiting for the Bus' shifts suddenly from local mundanities to global uncertainties in its lament for lost hopes and unfulfilled ideals: 'Then have we missed the bus? Or are we sure which way the wind is blowing?' (*New Lines*, p. 53).

Criticism has tended to concentrate on what appears provincial, insular and introspective in Movement poetry; it has hardly begun to do justice to its cosmopolitan reach or its complex geographies of the imagination. Among the *New Lines* poems by Elizabeth Jennings are 'Afternoon in Florence', in which the city bathed in Tuscan light is half real, half dream, and 'Piazza San Marco', in which the play of mind over words is set against the sculpted beauty of 'those emotionless proud horses' (*New Lines*, p. 7). D. J. Enright's 'Evening in the Khamsin' and 'Baie des Anges, Nice' are vivid and colourful evocations of exotic landscapes, both of them acutely sensitive to the darkness and destruction inseparable from the preternatural beauty they apprehend: 'Proud mountain, luminous citron, azure coast – they do not grow / Without the shrivelling thunderbolt' (*New Lines*, p. 55). Elsewhere, America beckons in the Californian provenance of Gunn's 'On the Move' and in the proud New England whaling history of Conquest's 'Nantucket'. The Arctic landscapes of

Conquest's 'Near Jakobselv' prompt a deeply felt response that far exceeds the alleged reserve and ironic detachment of Movement verse: 'Perhaps this very newness and this isolation / May strike some hidden trauma in the heart / And make its rock gush water' (*New Lines*, pp. 80–1). For Donald Davie, Ireland proves amenable to the Romantic prospecting of his imagination, prompting one of his most accomplished lyrics, 'Woodpigeons at Raheny', in which the poet, lulled by the peace of a Capuchin monastery, attunes his voice to the crooning of a dove: 'I know the dove / Outsang me down the afternoon'.[11]

It is worth drawing attention to the imaginative uses of place in Movement poetry, not least because its principal opponents directed their most vehement criticism at what they perceived to be English insularity and provincialism. Charles Tomlinson complained that the *New Lines* poets 'seldom for a moment escape beyond the suburban mental ratio which they impose on experience', and he later suggested that the Movement had been an excuse for a calculated return to philistinism and aloofness: 'England seemed, in all senses, to be becoming an island, adrift from Europe and the past.'[12] For A. Alvarez, introducing *The New Poetry* in 1962, the Movement was part of a negative series of reactions against experimental Modernism, designed 'to preserve the idea that life in England goes on much as it always has, give or take a few minor changes in the class system'. The perpetuation of English gentility owes a good deal to 'the fact that England is an island; it is, literally, insulated from the rest of the world'.[13] Tomlinson and Alvarez were largely responsible for the propagation of a narrow and distorting criticism of Movement poetry. If they failed to recognise the full imaginative scope of that poetry, they also misperceived its place in the larger history of English literature, especially the role that Philip Larkin would play in consolidating and redirecting diverse traditions and influences in modern verse.

Along with the charges of English insularity and provincialism came the complaint that Movement poetry was intellectually tame and bookish, lacking any vital engagement with actual experience. Tomlinson's review of *New Lines* was titled 'The Middlebrow Muse' and it castigated the Movement poets for 'a total failure of nerve'.[14] Alvarez pointed out that, of the nine poets whose work appeared in *New Lines*, six were university teachers, two librarians and one a civil servant: 'It was, in short, academic-administrative verse, polite, knowledgeable, efficient, polished, and, in its quiet way, even intelligent.'[15] It is fair to say, of course, that some of the titles of Movement poems smack of bookishness or promise exercises in versified literary criticism. Thom Gunn's 'Autumn Chapter in a Novel', Kingsley Amis's 'Something Nasty in the

Bookshop', Donald Davie's 'Too Late for Satire' and John Wain's 'Eighth Type of Ambiguity' all carry traces of the academic interests of their authors. It is far more interesting, however, to consider the extent to which Movement poetry exceeds the cultural values and ideals of an aspiring lower-middle-class intelligentsia. In this respect, the question of audience is crucially important. Blake Morrison argues convincingly that while Movement poetry 'derives from and caters for an academic élite, it is frequently directed at a much broader readership'.[16] Often, the tension deriving from two seemingly different audiences gives certain poems an expansive energy and breadth of vision, as it does in Larkin's 'Dockery and Son' and Davie's 'Rejoinder to a Critic'.

A familiar Movement strategy is to begin the poem in mid-conversation, allowing readers to make what they will of the imagined dialogue. Larkin's rueful reflections on inheritance are prompted in the first instance by a recollection of the university-educated Dockery and his son, but like the college lawn, the poem 'spreads dazzlingly wide'. The speaker's brief stop at Sheffield, where 'I changed, / And ate an awful pie', effectively resituates him both geographically and culturally, opening the poem well beyond its initial academic confines to what we all might come to feel: 'Life is first boredom, then fear. / Whether or not we use it, it goes' (*Collected Poems*, p. 153). Davie's 'Rejoinder to a Critic' expands from a personal squabble over the place of feeling in poetry to a sombre and challenging reflection on literature and history that implicates both writers and readers in the aftermath of Hiroshima. The quotations from Coleridge and Donne invite a serious reconsideration of the function of poetry and the literary expression of intense personal feeling. The opening question, 'How can I dare to feel', is recognised at the end of the poem as a common dilemma of more than academic significance: 'How dare we now be anything but numb?' (p. 68).

If Davie and Larkin most clearly exemplify the poetic principles of the Movement as it gathered momentum in the 1950s and 1960s, they are also the poets who break most decisively with the Movement in later decades. Davie, by his own admission, appears as 'A pasticheur of late-Augustan styles' ('Homage to William Cowper', p. 8), and the classical restraint and propriety that the Movement poets often emulated are immediately apparent in his *Brides of Reason* (1955) and *A Winter Talent and Other Poems* (1957). Davie's stylistic preferences are strongly defended in his critical prose, especially in *Purity of Diction in English Verse* (1952) and *Articulate Energy: An Inquiry into the Syntax of English Poetry* (1955), both of which came to be seen as statements of Movement poetics. The opening poem in *Brides of Reason*, 'Among Artisans' Houses', conveys its admiration of eighteenth-century formal elegance through a stanzaic regularity and syntactical control reminiscent of Yeats (the title of the poem recalls Yeats's 'Ancestral Houses' and 'Among School Children'). Yeats's high estimation of eighteenth-century civility and his powerful contrasting sense of modern civilisation 'all broken down' and in 'decay' undoubtedly shape the poem, but it works impressively towards establishing an urgent and authentic Movement conclusion. A strong sense of moral evacuation is neatly conveyed through a slick and discomfiting closing couplet: 'Shortly, nothing will be seen / By which historians may fix / The moral shape of politics' (p. 13).

Moral vigilance and ironic distance are the keynotes of a good deal of Movement poetry, as it sedulously sets itself apart from both the political commitment of 1930s poetry and the neo-Romanticism of 1940s poetry. 'Creon's Mouse', like 'Rejoinder to a Critic', recognises the dangers offered by 'too much daring', but it diagnoses the quietism of contemporary civilisation not as fearful timidity but as principled abstention: 'A self-induced and stubborn loss of nerve' (p. 17). This is not to say that Movement poetry maintains a serene and even-handed political equipoise. It frequently voices anti-Establishment and anti-philistine sentiments with uncompromising vigour. With Davie, as with Larkin, the politics are complicated and contradictory, with compassionate liberalism often accompanying jaundiced conservatism. Davie's dissenting conscience prompts a scathing critique of social inequalities, but pulls back from any thoroughgoing radicalism. Like Scott Fitzgerald's narrator, Nick Carraway, in *The Great Gatsby*, the speaker in 'The Garden Party' is 'simultaneously enchanted and repelled'[17] by the moneyed ease of wealthy partygoers, but any sharper analysis of social class is diffused by a self-lacerating ruefulness and a poignant awareness of time passing: 'But theirs is all the youth we might have had' (p. 23).

Like Larkin, Davie was to find the experience of living in Ireland crucially formative in terms of clarifying his own uncertain relation to English culture. 'Demi-Exile. Howth' delicately registers the anguish of colonial history while carefully 'acknowledging no allegiance' (p. 15), but in 'Belfast on a Sunday Afternoon', the visitor is moved from scoff to scorn by the elaborately grim procedures of an Orange parade: 'No man is really crippled by his hates. / Yet I remembered with a certain scorn / Those "passionate intensities "of Yeats' (p. 21). If Davie remembers Yeats, he just as steadfastly remembers Auden, though the attitude in 'Remembering the Thirties' is a curious mixture of admiration and dissent. Auden's industrial landscapes are targeted in the reference to poems about 'abandoned workings' which show 'Worlds more remote than Ithaca or Rome' (p. 28). The main target, though, is 'courage', which (like 'daring') is apt to overplay its hand and prompt a poetry that looks embarrassingly naive and misconceived in retrospect. The image of courage as 'the weed / That beards the slag-heap with his hectoring' (p. 29) cleverly conflates Auden's northern landscapes with a critical view of dogmatic poetry, while punningly reflecting on Hector's Trojan adventures.

The declaration that 'A neutral tone is nowadays preferred' (p. 29) is so often cited as the definitive Movement response to the poetry of the 1930s that we might easily miss the casual allusion to Thomas Hardy's 'Neutral Tones'. Davie, like Larkin, finds himself attracted to both Yeats and Hardy, and there is much that looks forward to his categorical assertion in *Thomas Hardy and British Poetry* (1973) that 'in British poetry of the last fifty years the most far-reaching influence, for good and ill, has been not Yeats, still less Eliot and Pound, not Lawrence, but *Hardy* '.[18] *A Winter Talent and Other Poems* (1957) takes its cue from Hardy's *Winter Words*, while its opening poem, 'Time Passing, Beloved', echoes the closing line of 'Where They Lived': 'Time calls, "Pass below!"'[19] Hardy's example lies behind the imposing interplay of elaborately expanded lines and curtailed, diminished counterpoints in Davie's poem, but the poised rhetorical questions and the elegant parallel syntax are hallmarks of the Movement, similarly on display at the end of Larkin's 'Wedding-Wind' and 'Waiting for breakfast, while she brushed her hair': 'How can it end, / This siege of a shore that no misgivings have steeled, / No doubts defend?' (p. 40).

While Larkin affected scorn for 'foreign poetry', Davie was to embrace a cosmopolitan range of influences, including the works of Ezra Pound and the American Black Mountain poets. The tight stanzaic and syntactical structures of his early work begin to loosen as he turns to writing versions of the Polish *Pan Tadéusz* by Adam Mickiewicz in *The Forests of Lithuania* (1959), and then to the Russian of Boris Pasternak in *The Poems of Doctor Zhivago* (1965). Davie shows how Movement elegance might be profitably combined with Japanese sparseness in the beautifully poised lament, 'Ezra Pound in Pisa' (1969). By the mid 1970s, there is a new candour and stridency in the writing, perhaps in response to the poems of John Berryman and Robert Lowell, and a dark confessional manner comes through in the nervous, edgy diction of 'In the Stopping Train' (1977): 'I know who has to be punished: / The man going mad inside me' (p. 337). For all his exposure to American Modernism, however, Davie never entirely relinquishes his Movement reserve and decorum. 'Nashville Mornings' (1988) is a free-verse meditation on music and metaphysics, presided over by St Cecilia, and it suggests that Modernism and the Movement might occasionally discover some common ground in defending 'the ghetto of letters' against the pervasive noise of the popular: 'the appalling Rock and Country . . . the damnable steel guitar' (p. 473).

Davie inadvertently helped to promote a view of Larkin as a poet of narrowly English sentiments and limited imaginative perspectives by appropriating him for the Hardy tradition that he celebrated in *Thomas Hardy and British Poetry* (1973). Davie's description of 'a poetry of lowered sights and patiently diminished expectations'[20] might not sound like a compliment, but it can be seen at work in positive, aesthetically rewarding ways in Larkin's 'Born Yesterday', dedicated to Kingsley Amis's daughter, Sally. With typical Movement ambivalence, the title offers both a literal statement and a piece of proverbial wisdom cautioning against naivety. The poem belongs to a popular genre of verses addressed to children (Andrew Marvell's 'The Picture of Little T. C. in a Prospect of Flowers' comes to mind), but Larkin's vernacular idiom supersedes that venerable literary association and gives his poem a lively contemporary appeal: 'Well, you're a lucky girl.' The familiar debunking, anti-Romantic tendency in Movement writing is vigorously captured in the speaker's brisk dismissal of 'the usual stuff / About being beautiful, / Or running off a spring / Of innocence and love'. The word 'stuff' functions as it does in 'Toads', both as an embedded literary allusion, recalling 'such stuff as dreams are made on' in *The Tempest* (4.1), and simultaneously functioning as a dismissive contemporary colloquialism. The poem proceeds to lower its sights and prepare the child for a life of diminished expectations: 'May you be ordinary; / Have, like other women, an average of talents.' The true measure of the poem's achievement, however, is in the transition it makes to the uplifting rhetorical brio of the close, magnificently transforming ordinariness into a virtue and persuading us that dullness might be the precondition of happiness: 'If that is what a skilled, / Vigilant, flexible, / Unemphasised, enthralled / Catching of happiness is called' (p. 84). Here, as with other Larkin poems, including 'Mr Bleaney', 'The Whitsun Weddings' and 'High Windows', 'Born Yesterday' acquires its charge from an unexpected shift of perspective, from a downbeat empiricism to a much more intense and inquisitive speculation.

The key Movement word in that adjectival flurry at the end of 'Born Yesterday' is 'vigilant'. It defines an attitude to experience, a way of looking at life, which is prevalent in Movement poetry and is especially pronounced in Larkin's early work. The title of Larkin's first major volume of poems *The Less Deceived* (1955) derives from Ophelia's response to Hamlet's denial of love, 'I was the more deceived' (3.1), but the corresponding determination *not* to be deceived is clearly in keeping with both the vigilant social outlook of the post-war years and the philosophical empiricism that was prevalent at the time. The title poem, 'Deceptions', shares some of the insights of Alfred Ayer's influential *Language, Truth and Logic*, especially its insistence upon the 'fruitlessness of attempting to transcend the limits of sense experience' and the corresponding admission that 'our senses do sometimes deceive us'.[21] Contemplating the sexual assault on a Victorian working-class woman, as recorded by Henry Mayhew, the speaker of the poem moves from a hapless attempt to re-create the past through the senses ('Even so distant, I can taste the grief') to a final realisation of the impossibility of ever fully knowing and understanding the event. The intense combination of imaginative re-creation and imaginative failure is aptly conveyed through the painfully exact and yet strangely imprecise simile: 'All the unhurried day / Your mind lay open like a drawer of knives.' The negative prefix prompts its opposite, subtly conveying the contrast between a serene social exterior and a troubled psychological interior. The poem is acutely aware of its own stumbling efforts to make sense of violent outrage. 'I would not dare console you if I could' (p. 32) recalls Davie's 'How dare we now be anything but numb' (p. 68), its tense verbal condition underwriting its refusal of any easy moral stance. The speaker's reticence ('What can be said . . .?' p. 32) should not be confused with callousness or indifference. The awareness that 'readings will grow erratic' (p. 32) extends to its own limited comprehension, already hinted at in the plural title. The poem's painful, contentious response to sexual violence is heightened by an intense self-critical awareness of its own vulnerability and its own inadequacy as verbal artefact.

The violent discovery of 'fulfilment's desolate attic' is an extreme instance of a more general paradoxical embrace of desire and denial at work in *The Less Deceived*. 'Dry-Point', one of 'Two Portraits of Sex', turns out to be more concerned with sexual longing and frustration than with the art of etching. Lasting fulfilment is initially envisaged in the remote, but none the less domestic, image of 'a bare and sunscrubbed room', and then in the more distant but brilliant symbolist figure of 'a padlocked cube of light' (p. 37). The appeal of light in these images is simultaneously a reminder of the intangibility and inaccessibility of what we dream. The fondness for paradox in Larkin's poetry extends to questions of human freedom, most impressively in 'Poetry of Departures', in which the instinct to 'clear off' turns out to be part of our perpetual discontent with how things are, a kicking away of that ideal condition which we have so carefully constructed: 'a life reprehensibly perfect' (p. 86). If Davie's account of 'a poetry of lowered sights and patiently diminished expectations' seems peculiarly fitting here, it also sells short the intense dialogic qualities of Larkin's verse, its unrelenting insistence on seeing things from both sides of the fence. 'Wires' is prompted by the proverbial idea that the grass is always greener on the other side. The cattle in the poem are instinctively drawn to 'purer water / Not here but anywhere' (p. 48). The repetition of 'wires' across the two quatrains of the poem draws attention to the constraining rhyme scheme – abcd dcba – cleverly exercising containment, even as it evokes some abstract freedom beyond the wires.

If Larkin's poetry gains power from playing off starkly contrasting attitudes and differences of opinion against each other, it also makes decisive gains in terms of the vocal qualities and social registers that it introduces to post-war British poetry. The italicised vernacular '*He chucked up everything / And just cleared off*' in 'Poetry of Departures' is markedly different in tone and attitude from the later reported account of this action as an 'audacious, purifying, / Elemental move' (p. 85). 'Toads' is one of the most imposing examples of Larkin's finely poised rhetorical control over different vocal registers, shifting from its briskly emphatic and interrogative opening ('Why should I let the toad *work* / Squat on my life') to the carefully reasoned and reflective conclusion: 'I don't say, one bodies the other / One's spiritual truth; / But I do say it's hard to lose either, / When you have both.' The appealing style of 'Toads' derives in part from a combination of cliché ('cold as snow') and ostentatious artifice: ('Lecturers, lispers, / Losels, loblolly-men, louts'), but it also involves a more subtle collusion of diverse social registers: 'Their unspeakable wives are as skinny as whippets' (p. 89). It conveys the impression of vigorous colloquial speech through an ingenious arrangement of half-rhymes, often disguising these through a subtle variation in syllable count and stress (lanes/sardines; bucket/it; too/snow; toad-like/hard-luck). The opening rebellious instinct is elegantly contained, as it is in 'Poetry of Departures', but these are far from being defeatist poems. A pervasive irony and scepticism undercuts the solemn pronouncements with which these and other poems conclude, discouraging any easy political analysis.

The publication of *The Less Deceived* marked the achievement of a distinctive style that came to be seen not only as Larkinesque but as characteristic of the Movement: dry, ironic, colloquial, downbeat, but also given to a yearning for transcendence and affirmation. The maturing of Larkin's poetry was generated in part by his experiments with narrative perspective and narrative voice in his works of fiction in the 1940s, especially *Jill* (1946) and *A Girl in Winter* (1947), but it was also quickened by his early assimilation of a range of Modernist influences, including D. H. Lawrence, T. S. Eliot, W. H. Auden and Louis MacNeice. Larkin's early poetry shows how well he absorbed the experimental Modernism of his predecessors and near contemporaries. His ambitious free-verse composition, 'The Ships at Mylae', is one of several poems in which Larkin appears to be parodying, and not just imitating, the author of *The Waste Land*. 'Eliotian but amusing' is how he describes one of these early precocious pieces.[22] Larkin's poetry of the 1940s is much more diverse and eclectic than the limited range of poems included in *The North Ship* (1945) initially suggests. Among his *Collected Poems* (1988) are numerous poems that did not appear in any of his previously published volumes, including some that were selected for the unpublished typescript, 'In the Grip of Light' (1947).

'Midsummer Night, 1940' is distinctly Audenesque in its tense, wartime apprehension of geographical borders, moments of transition and private and public anxieties. 'Out in the lane I paused', written towards the end of 1940, recalls the solitary wartime musings of Edward Thomas in 'Rain' and 'The Owl'. The most accomplished of the early unpublished poems is Larkin's elegy for his father, 'An April Sunday brings the snow', a poem that was too personal and candid for inclusion in *The Less Deceived*. Echoing A. E. Housman's 'Loveliest of trees, the cherry now',[23] Larkin sensitively records how snow makes 'blossoms on the plum trees green' (p. 21). A more mundane but related image, a jar of jam made by his father, provides the impulse for the poem's insistent denial of traditional elegiac consolation: 'Behind the glass, under the cellophane, / Remains your final summer – sweet / And meaningless, and not to come again' (p. 21). Only two of the poems from the 1940s were eventually included in *The Less Deceived*. 'Going' is an ontological riddle in which death is equated with 'evening coming in' (p. 3; its original title was 'Dying Day'), while 'Wedding-Wind', written in the voice of a newly married woman, is a spirited Lawrentian *epithalamium* that vigorously captures both the excited elation and the troubled apprehension of marriage, as it turns from 'the night of the high wind' to 'perpetual morning' (p. 11, a double-edged phrase that manages to be simultaneously ecstatic and elegiac).

'Waiting for breakfast, while she brushed her hair', written towards the end of 1947, is a stark dramatisation, in the form of an *aubade*, of the choice between life and art, the lover and the muse. Larkin appended the poem to the 1966 reissue of *The North Ship*, claiming that it illustrated his turning from Yeats to Hardy, but the concluding lines in which the lover is sent 'terribly away' and the poet compelled to live 'Part invalid, part baby, and part saint' (p. 20) are nevertheless portentously Yeatsian. Like Davie, Larkin occasionally fuses Yeats's elevated style with a near-Augustan elegance and formality. 'At Grass' is modelled on 'The Wild Swans at Coole', but it confidently assumes its place in the tradition of English pastoral elegy. Extensively worked over in successive drafts at the end of the 1940s, the poem appeared in its final form in the privately published *XX Poems* in April 1951. It was given prominence both as the closing poem in *The Less Deceived* and as a favourite anthology piece (in *New Lines* and elsewhere), and it was frequently singled out by Alvarez and others as the quintessential Movement poem. The pastoral retirement of famous racehorses seems fitting to the needs of a post-war British society contemplating the end of Empire. There is nothing explicitly post-war or post-colonial in the language of the poem, though a vestigial military vocabulary – 'squadrons', 'stand at ease', 'field glass' (p. 29) – perhaps activates subliminal suggestions of a post-war context in the minds of some readers. More likely, as Blake Morrison points out, in 'allowing the horses to symbolize loss of power, Larkin manages to tap nostalgia for a past "glory that was England" '.[24]

'At Grass' shows Larkin to be a poet of consummate lyric skill. The alliterative phrasing of 'shade' and 'shelter', 'fable' and 'faint', is subtly deployed, as is the beautifully sibilant 'Silks at the start: against the sky / Numbers and parasols' (p. 29). As David Lodge has shown, the poem creates the impression of a predominantly realist, metonymic mode of writing, blending this with an elevated lyric intensity.[25] As with 'Mr Bleaney' and 'The Whitsun Weddings', the ending of the poem shifts into a new level of metaphoric discourse through a carefully articulated syntax. The slippage between stanzas effectively realises the new-found freedom and anonymity of the racehorses: 'their names live; they // Have slipped their names', before the pace slows down decisively and induces a mood of quiet contemplation: 'Only the groom, and the groom's boy, / With bridles in the evening come' (p. 30). The mellifluous archaic inversion in the closing line is enhanced by the telling half-rhyme between 'come' and 'home', and by the internal pararhyme in 'groom'. Whether read as a poem of 'post-imperial *tristesse* ' or as an allegory of fame and retirement, the curiously introverted human imaginings and 'seemings' that shape 'At Grass' make it more than just an animal poem.[26] The speaker who imagines that the horses 'gallop for what must be joy' (p. 30) has the same tentative, undemonstrative attitude to happiness as the speaker in 'Born Yesterday'.

It was 'Church Going', however, which came to be seen by many readers as the key Movement poem, not least because its ironic, self-deprecating speaker was reminiscent of the characters who inhabited Movement novels, including *Lucky Jim* (1954). As Blake Morrison observes, 'Church Going' was first published in a Movement periodical, the *Spectator*, and then in a Movement anthology, *New Lines*, before appearing in *The Less Deceived*, and it clearly demonstrates 'principles central to the Movement programme'.[27] John Wain and others have seen in the self-conscious antics of Larkin's speaker a distant glimpse of Jules Laforgue's clownish intellectuals, from whom T. S. Eliot's J. Alfred Prufrock descends, but John Betjeman's church visitor, 'Biking in high-banked lanes from tower to tower / On sunny antiquarian afternoons', seems just as likely a predecessor.[28] In typical Movement style, the punning title acknowledges both the familiar routine activity of 'going to church' and the steady erosion of traditional religious certainties. The relaxed narration of the opening line ('Once I am sure there's nothing going on') neatly contains both the casual apprehension of 'nothing going on' and the more profound metaphysical sense of being 'sure' of 'nothing'. In the same way, the comically dismissive 'God knows how long' and the apparently indifferent 'Someone would know: I don't' are accompanied by a more serious hunger for knowledge and by an evident capacity for wonder. The poem's spacious stanzaic structure, its subtle but insistent rhyme scheme and its interplay of colloquial conjecture with iambic pentameter create an impression of logical progression and careful reasoning. The effect is especially noticeable in the transition from the second to the third stanza. Having considered that 'the place was not worth stopping for', the speaker concedes, 'Yet stop I did' (p. 97), the pause between stanzas both enacting a momentary pause and initiating a crucial transition from solitary speculation to communal wonder.

James Booth underestimates the rhetorical power and expansive vision of 'Church Going' in reading its closing stanzas as 'a carefully staged' delivery of 'the mechanical rhetoric of Anglican religiosity'. Dogmatically insisting that the poem must be read as 'intended' – as an unequivocal rejection of theology – he argues that the poem's self-mocking performance 'becomes painful in the embarrassingly vacuous phrases "blent air", and "robed as destinies" '.[29] These phrases have a much more compelling function in the poem than Booth realises, subtly evoking Romantic ideas of aspiration and destiny that can be traced back through Yeats ('blent' is borrowed from Yeats, 'Among School Children') to Shelley's 'all-sustaining air'. Michael O'Neill has argued convincingly that the pervasive Romantic metaphor of air persists in modern poetry, providing a figurative space where ideas of transcendence can be simultaneously acknowledged and refuted.[30] This double responsiveness is a powerful and recurring element in Larkin's poetry, all the way from the 'blent air' of 'Church Going' to the negative sublimity of the 'deep blue air' in 'High Windows'.

The Whitsun Weddings (1964) shows Larkin consolidating Movement principles of clarity, rationality and coherence, but also moving ambitiously beyond the imaginative territory of his contemporaries. 'Here', the buoyant opening poem of the collection, immediately registers a new expansiveness of vision, 'Swerving east' towards the sun across the urban and rural landscapes of a rapidly changing post-war England. That powerful imaginative trajectory – 'swerving' – is itself the subject of the poem, alighting briefly on bustling town life before pushing on towards the 'bluish neutral distance' (p. 136) of sea and sky, and on to the mysterious final prospect of the mind. In a predictable Movement manner, the title signals the empirical co-ordinates of a real place and a real time, while prompting a more speculative and inquiring view of what it means to be 'here'. Even so, 'Here' far exceeds the range and subtlety of any earlier Movement poem. The town, with its 'ships up streets' and its 'slave museum' (Wilberforce House), is recognisably Hull, but the poem operates at a level far beyond descriptive realism, lifting its readers into the fabulously bright world of myth and fable: 'The piled gold clouds, the shining gull-marked mud' (p. 136). Larkin has clearly adopted both Auden's 'seamless wide-angled vision'[31] and MacNeice's fondness for compounds and catalogues – 'grain-scattered streets, barge-crowded water' (p. 136) – but the poem's soaring climax and its brilliant momentary capture of existential vistas beyond the quotidian are unmistakably his own: 'Here is unfenced existence: / Facing the sun, untalkative, out of reach' (p. 137).

'The Whitsun Weddings' acquires a similar momentum and rhetorical charge as it embarks on its imaginative journeying, following 'A slow and stopping curve southwards' to London. The casual observation of the solitary traveller ('That Whitsun, I was late getting away') is transformed into a shared sense of destiny ('There we were aimed' (p. 116)), as the weddings take on an unexpected ritualistic and anthropological significance akin to a rite of passage: 'a happy funeral . . . a religious wounding' (p. 115). The poem moves deftly from its empirical rendering of sights and sounds and smells, the hot cushions, the fish-dock, the buttoned carriage cloth, towards a rare moment of vision and illumination. The train journey is both an effective device for registering the changing industrial and pastoral landscapes of post-war England, and the subtle means of conveying particular angles of vision and perspective, from the sudden 'blinding windscreens' of cars on the street to the cinematic still of 'someone running up to bowl' (p. 114). The mundane events of 'a sunlit Saturday' are transformed into a strange and thought-provoking experience as the train races towards its destination and the bookish speaker is jolted into sympathetic identification with his fellow travellers. The condescension shown towards 'nylon gloves and jewellery-substitutes' gives way to a momentary glimpse of achieved community and togetherness in 'this frail / Travelling coincidence'. If the lasting appeal of 'The Whitsun Weddings' is due in part to its sunlit panoramic journey through an England readjusting to the changing realities of post-war society, it also derives from its poignant apprehension of the delicate hopes and desires of newly married couples confronting an uncertain future. The poem both swells and falls, holding in rapt suspension a romantic prospect of possible fulfilment and a realistic acceptance of impending disappointment, powerfully and memorably captured in the closing image of 'an arrow-shower / Sent out of sight, somewhere becoming rain' (p. 116).

Larkin's search for sustaining rituals and for a coherent social vision continues in *High Windows* (1974), but the late poems cannot conceal their implication in the growing ideological tension and economic turmoil of post-war Britain. The mood of national decline, prompted in part by the devaluation of the pound and the withdrawal of troops from Aden in 1967, prompts a brazenly outspoken poetry in which parody and polemic feature strongly. 'Homage to a Government' parades a calculated stylistic flatness: 'Next year we shall be living in a country / That brought its soldiers home for lack of money', while 'Going, Going' echoes the auctioneer's cry in a despondent narrative of the English countryside being sold to the highest bidder: 'And that will be England gone' (p. 171). Money threatens to displace all other forms of value. In 'Posterity', the poet's fictitious biographer, Jake Balokowsky, 'makes the money sign' (p. 170), and 'Annus Mirabilis' records how 'every life became / A brilliant breaking of the bank' (p. 167). Light verse is the appropriate medium for the shallow values of the time, but in 'Money' it modulates into a sublime sense of alienation and displacement: 'I listen to money singing. It's like looking down / From long french windows at a provincial town' (p. 198).

Amidst the despairing vision of financial collapse and social decline in *High Windows* there would seem to be little space for lyric beauty and romantic affirmation. When that lyric note is heard, it is all the more poignant and affecting, as if reclaiming an England that has already vanished, as in the exquisite pastoral elegy, 'Cut Grass': 'Cut grass lies frail: / Brief is the breath / Mown stalks exhale' (p. 183). As Tom Paulin perceptively notes, the opening line of 'Cut Grass' takes us back to the great pastoral poems of another Hull poet, Andrew Marvell, and the rhyming of 'rail' and 'fail' in 'Upon Appleton House'.[32] A lingering belief in the sustaining rhythms of English customs and seasonal rituals informs the seaside pastoral of 'To the Sea', which 'Brings sharply back something known long before' (p. 173), and it also shapes the rural vision of 'Show Saturday', though the closing line of this celebration of agricultural abundance wavers between affirmation and lament: 'Let it always be there' (p. 201). Elsewhere in *High Windows*, the ideal of communal endeavour belongs to the distant past, nostalgically and elegiacally represented by the funeral walkers in 'Dublinesque' and the miners shortly to lose their lives in 'The Explosion'.

The echoes of Joyce and MacNeice in 'Dublinesque', and of Longfellow and Lawrence in 'The Explosion', are indicative of Larkin's tendency in *High Windows* to play extravagantly with the voices of his poetic predecessors. 'Sad Steps' takes its bearings from Sir Philip Sidney's *Astrophil and Stella*, Sonnet 31, while 'Sympathy in White Major' is a jaunty parody of Théophile Gautier's 'Symphonie en blanc majeur'. What remains consistent in Larkin's style is its subtle manoeuvring between a downbeat colloquialism and an elevated lyricism. The title poem of the volume is one of the most striking examples of Larkin's ability to lift poetic language from grim and demotic observation into luminous reflection. Intimations of paradise and endless happiness prompt the speaker's comparison of his own relaxed attitude to religion with the sexual permissiveness of the 1960s: both apparent freedoms are equated with an illusory view of life as 'going down the long slide'. The poem envisages absolute freedom in more intense and compelling ways, as it slips from disgruntlement with social actualities into an enthralling vision of utter emptiness, holding these two perspectives in powerful juxtaposition. If the closing lines are poignantly aware of the futility and nihilism of their own escapist impulse, they nevertheless achieve a momentary perception of beauty and serenity. 'High Windows' is a final reminder that what sets Larkin apart from his Movement contemporaries is not only his formidable stylistic reach and virtuosity but his extraordinary way of capturing both the finely detailed quotidian surfaces of post-war British society and the sublime apprehension of absence and infinity: 'the deep blue air, that shows / Nothing, and is nowhere, and is endless' (p. 165).

Notes

1. Blake Morrison, *The Movement: English Poetry and Fiction of the 1950s* (Oxford: Oxford University Press, 1980), p. 4.
2. *Ibid.*, p. 6.
3. Anthony Hartley, 'Poets of the Fifties', *Spectator*, 27 August 1954, p. 260.
4. *Springtime: An Anthology of Young Poets and Writers*, ed. G. S. Fraser and Ian Fletcher (London: Peter Owen, 1953), p. 7.
5. *Poets of the 1950s: An Anthology of New English Verse*, ed. D.J. Enright (Tokyo: Kenyusha Press, 1955), p. 15.

6. *New Lines: An Anthology*, ed. Robert Conquest (London: Macmillan 1956), p. xv. All quotations of poetry from this edition will be cited parenthetically in the text.
7. *Ibid.*
8. *Ibid.*
9. Michael O'Neill, '"Fond of What He's Crapping On": Movement Poetry and Romanticism', in Zachary Leader (ed.), *The Movement Reconsidered: Essays on Larkin, Amis, Gunn, Davie and Their Contemporaries* (Oxford: Oxford University Press, 2009), pp. 270–91 (p. 283).
10. *Philip Larkin: Collected Poems*, ed. Anthony Thwaite (London: The Marvell Press and Faber, 1988), p. 98. All further quotations are from this edition of the poems.
11. Donald Davie, *Collected Poems*, ed. Neil Powell (Manchester: Carcanet, 2002), p. 38. All further quotations are from this edition of the poems.
12. Charles Tomlinson, 'Poetry Today', in Boris Ford (ed.), *The Pelican Guide to English Literature 7: The Modern Age* (Harmondsworth: Penguin, 1961; 1973), p. 472.
13. A. Alvarez (ed.), *The New Poetry* (Harmondsworth: Penguin, 1962: 1966), p. 25.
14. Charles Tomlinson, 'The Middlebrow Muse', *Essays in Criticism*, 7:2 (1957), p. 215.
15. Alvarez, *The New Poetry*, p. 23.
16. Morrison, *The Movement*, p. 109.
17. F. Scott Fitzgerald, *The Great Gatsby* (New York: Charles Scribner's Sons, 1925; 1953), p. 36.
18. Donald Davie, *Thomas Hardy and British Poetry* (London: Routledge and Kegan Paul, 1973), p. 3.
19. *The Complete Poetical Works of Thomas Hardy*, ed. Samuel Hynes, 5 vols. (Oxford: Clarendon Press, 1984), vol. II, p. 200.
20. Davie, *Thomas Hardy and British Poetry*, p. 71.
21. A. J. Ayer, *Language, Truth and Logic* (1936; London: Gollancz, 1960), p. 39.
22. Philip Larkin, *Early Poems and Juvenilia*, ed. A. T. Tolley (London: Faber, 2005), p. 21.
23. *The Collected Poems of A. E. Housman* (London: Jonathan Cape, 1977), p. 10.
24. Morrison, *The Movement*, p. 82.
25. David Lodge, 'Philip Larkin: The Metonymic Muse', in Stephen Regan (ed.), *Philip Larkin*, New Casebooks (Basingstoke: Macmillan, 1997), pp. 75–6.
26. Morrison, *The Movement*, pp. 82–3.
27. *Ibid.*, p. 229.
28. John Betjeman, *Collected Poems* (London: John Murray, 2006), p. 132.
29. James Booth, *Philip Larkin: The Poet's Plight* (Basingstoke: Palgrave Macmillan, 2005), p. 129.
30. Michael O'Neill, *The All-Sustaining Air: Romantic Legacies and Renewals in British, American, and Irish Poetry since 1900* (Oxford: Oxford University Press, 2007).
31. Philip Larkin, *Further Requirements: Interviews, Broadcasts, Statements and Book Reviews 1952–85* (London: Faber, 2001), p. 329.
32. Tom Paulin, *The Secret Life of Poems* (London: Faber, 2008), pp. 204–5.

Chapter 48

Three twentieth-century women poets: Riding, Smith, Plath

ALICE ENTWISTLE

In 1934, in common with thirty-nine other poets, Laura Riding was sent six questions by the editor of *New Verse*, Geoffrey Grigson. A collection of responses, hers among them, were published in the magazine on 11 October.[1] Grigson's final question was: 'As a poet what distinguishes you, do you think, from an ordinary man?' Riding responds: 'As a poet I am distinguished from ordinary men, first, in that I am a woman'. She goes on: 'poetry has been a male cult – where the mysteries were verse-rehearsals in sublimity. Those practice days are, however, over: poetry is now a direct matter.' Nervelessly confirming herself as the only 'other-than-male voic[e]', she concludes drily, 'But one woman goes a long way – in any capacity.'[2]

Both the eldest and the longest-lived of the three poets treated here, the American-born Riding can be said to have gone a long way in various respects. As Robert Nye testifies, this vital poet – first published in 1923 – was still writing a matter of weeks before she died aged ninety in 1991.[3] Her partnership with Robert Graves, which began in the twenties and ceased as World War II threatened, afforded her lasting fame in literary circles, although she would never achieve Graves's stature. However, as most commentators emphasise, Riding earned widespread respect on both sides of the Atlantic for the influence she exerted on English poetry and letters between the wars.[4] This extended beyond her productive collaboration with Graves on the Seizin Press, the publishing house they co-founded in 1928 and ran from their Mallorcan home until 1938; *Epilogue*, the journal they set up and co-edited; and several co-authored critical works, not least *A Survey of Modernist Poetry* (1927), the project that first brought Riding over to England at Graves's urging. There was also Riding's own critical writing, including *The Word Woman*, which, Elizabeth Friedmann and Alan J. Clark note, anticipated Simone de Beauvoir by almost two decades.[5] And then there was the effect of Riding's fastidiously self-sufficient poetics on some of the most distinguished figures of twentieth-century English poetry, not least W. H. Auden.[6]

As is often noted, Riding's delicate-boned lyrics have never fully escaped the shadow of their author's notoriously 'difficult' personality: there remain few sustained accounts of a challenging and original poetics.[7] Famously hostile to anthologies and apt to prickliness with the most determined supporter, the figure whom Ruthven dubs 'the Greta Garbo of modern poetry' herself did little to help.[8] Both Adams and Baker record her antagonism, echoing the exasperation that Graves's biographer, Martin Seymour-Smith, barely conceals.[9] Small wonder that when Riding appears in Janet Montefiore's viewfinder, an authoritative critical voice falters: 'I cannot even try to do justice to Laura Riding's *Collected Poems* without devoting this whole chapter to it. To pick out one or two sample poems from this important collection can give no idea of its scope and range; it seems best simply to alert readers to its importance.'[10] As Ruthven spots, Riding is also omitted from Montefiore's seminal *Feminism and Poetry* (1987).[11]

Riding's scope and range have undermined critical efforts to situate her. As Heuving notes, Riding has been labelled 'alternately a modernist, a New Critical and a postmodernist poet'; Susan M. Schultz anoints the same writer 'founder of a tradition that . . . include[s] John Ashbery . . . and the Language poets'.[12] Feminist critics find her no easier to locate. As Jane Dowson observes, Riding's poems typically 'appear to elude gender distinctness through their impersonality'; however, like Schultz, Dowson underlines an often highly theoretical interest in the problematic representation of female identity and experience.[13] Amid these ambiguities Riding's first published poem, 'Dimensions', seems both prescient and disingenuous. Notably absent from the 1938 *Collected Poems*, this prize-winning lyric[14] opens by coolly recommending:

> Measure me for a burial
> That my low stone may neatly say
> In a precise, Euclidean way
> How I am three-dimensional.

It concludes, more resolutely:

> Measure me by myself
> And not by time or love or space
> Or beauty. Give me this last grace:
> That I may be on my low stone
> A gage unto myself alone.
> I would not have these old faiths fall
> To prove that I was nothing at all. (RSP, p. 9)

Conversational, assertive, sceptical, this carefully wrought text makes a useful departure point as much for its sepulchral formalities (played out in the finality of the end rhymes on which it trades throughout, and most emphatically in its closing couplets) as its relative immaturity. Even so 'Dimensions' courts interest in the reticent figure to whom it becomes an ironically self-aware monument. Interestingly, the poem resonates with a judicious-seeming sketch of Riding by her fellow poet and publisher Nancy Cunard. When they met 'in London in 1929', Cunard recollects

> Her personality was very tense, dominating . . . Like a brooding, sultry day, there was electricity around, if not visible; a sense of contained conflict. And there was on the one hand, the terrific, clinical tidiness of everything in the London flat . . . On the other hand, there was an eerie atmosphere and the sense of distance between us . . . In this mystified state I could see two things, her quality and her meticulousness.[15]

From its opening lines, 'Dimensions' is almost mischievously 'meticulous', in both its formal elegance and thematic concern with construction, balance and architecture. Amid its materialities, however, the poem warningly renders itself and its 'eerie' subject increasingly remote. This is partly how the poem works to inscribe, while it contains and controls, those powerful tensions between now and later, unknowable chaos and empiricist order, presence which is (perhaps literary) life and absence, or rather spectrality, which is both death and literary burial.

If 'Dimensions' presages Riding's complex preoccupation with the 'self', it is tempting to discern within it the poet's own voice anticipating, with reproachful irony, her own literary sidelining. Another prescient-seeming poem, 'The Signature', does something similar. More explicitly literary and self-referential than 'Dimensions', this poem develops on the earlier text by gravely contesting the link between appearance and identity: 'The effort to put my essence in me / Ended in a look of beauty.'[16] The poem avoids revealing whose the effort is, but an apparently female speaker can neither entirely dismiss nor entirely duck responsibility for the 'look' itself, however 'cruel' and unsatisfactory it might seem as a way of establishing essence. In Riding's habitually 'metaphysical' mood, the speaker drily acknowledges the power and risks (of trivialisation: 'mere experiment') which attend 'a look of beauty'.[17] However, the 'sweetness' ascribed to an arguably female beauty proves profoundly disempowering in the long run:

> So I grow ghostly,
> Though great sincerity

First held a glass up to my name.
And great sincerity claim
For beauty the live image,
But no deathly fame:
The clear face spells
A bright illegibility of name. (PLR, p. 16)

The 'illegibility' flourished here can be read in several ways. If as the poem seems to argue 'beauty' (however 'sincerely' attributed) effaces identity, it must also corrode *literary* presence: social notoriety is expected to undermine the performative authority of signature. The poem seems to foresee how public persona ('the live image') menaces the survival of both literary identity and craft. To this day, critics differ on the value of Riding's work. For Montefiore, the 1938 appearance of *The Collected Poems* represents 'a landmark in twentieth-century poetry'.[18] Yet Ruthven notes Riding's absence from a range of influential critiques, including the works of Sandra Gilbert and Susan Gubar.[19]

As 'The Signature' reminds us obliquely, Riding herself helped render her 'name' unavailable in renouncing poetry and changing her authorial signature in 1941: 'illegibility' here might therefore connote freedom. Noting the influence of Gertrude Stein on Riding's poetry, Jane Marcus reads anti-essentialism into Riding's much-rewritten name:

> Her Jewish socialist father wanted her to be an American Rosa Luxemburg. But Laura Riechenthal went from Girls' High to Cornell . . . became briefly Laura Gottschalk, and went to New York to write poetry. The admiring Hart Crane [an early friend] first called her 'Rideshalk-Godding', then, cooling at her authoritative ways, termed her Laura Riding Roughshod. 'Riding' was the name she chose for herself as poet [prior to restyling herself] Laura (Riding) Jackson.[20]

In retrospect, just as the abstractions of a poem like 'I Am' can be read as warning against over-reliance on biography as a way into Riding's poetry, 'The Signature' foreshadows the 'bright illegibility' of its author's own eventually semi-parenthetical signature.

The Modernist compulsions of what 'Opening of Eyes' terms 'the mind's muchness' (PLR, p. 91), and the 'manyness' of what 'One Self' calls 'The recurring body' (PLR, p. 71), work in much the same way. The productive tension between singularity and multiplicity in what 'Opening of Eyes' later terms 'A single whole of seeing' (PLR, p. 92) has consequences for a sense of selfhood pathologised with Lacanian implications: 'With the face goes a mirror / As with the mind a world. / Likeness tells the doubting eye / That strangeness is not strange. / At an early hour and knowledge / Identity not yet familiar / Looks back upon itself from later, / And seems itself' ('With The Face', PLR, p. 187). Here, the metrical disturbances introduced by the shifting syllable-count reiterate the argument's difficulties: again and again, a rhythmic near-miss subverts the aural logic which the ear expects, just as the poem itself refuses (while appearing to confirm) the straightforward alignment of selfhood and 'identity'. So prodigal a sense of subjectivity bears, meanwhile, on a conventionally singular lyric voice: 'With the Face' seems to do the work of its own self-consciously refractive argument, the text holding itself reflectively apart, looking 'back upon itself' from a position outside the constellation of different referents (face / mirror; mind / world; strange / familiar) it nudges into productive orbit.

In poem after poem Riding constructs self and text alike in similarly provisional terms. One of her most replete short lyrics reads like an Elizabethan pastiche:

How well, you, you resemble!
Yes, you resemble well enough yourself
For me to swear the likeness
Is no other and remarkable
And matchless and so that
I love you therefore.

And all else which is very like,
Perfect counterfeit, pure almost,
Love, high animation, loyal unsameness –
To the end true, unto
Unmasking, self.

I am for you both sharp and dull.
I doubt thoroughly
And thoroughly believe.
I love you doubly,
How well, you, you deceive,
How well, you, you resemble.
I love you therefore. ('You Or You', PLR, p. 97)

Yet the same phrasings find a Donnean power, 'you' and 'I' drawn with contained passion into a series of manoeuvres around the definition and interpretation of motive and desire. The poem conflates its central pronouns in the aural and architectural symmetries linking and separating them in the visual patterning of the final embedded quatrain.

'You Or You' begs to be read as a meta-textual study of the frustratingly but also perhaps inspiringly contingent relationship between word and referent on which lovers, poets, poems and readers alike must depend. The addressee of so self-circling a monologue might in fact be the ever-powerful, self-resembling and yet 'perfect counterfeit' lyric construct and (or) its language, in all its loyal 'unsameness'. As a consequence, this love song proves and subverts the poet's own aesthetic powers of expression: 'I am for you both sharp and dull. / I doubt thoroughly / And thoroughly believe.' Such ambiguities reiterate Riding's problematising of the aestheticised 'You' who is the poem's central presence and silent interlocutor:

> Until 1940 . . . Riding directed her main energies towards creating a poetic equivalent of an invulnerable, perfect self – a self immune to the invasions of social, political, and even emotional impurities . . . Each poem says, in effect, 'This is the real me. The other one only holds the pen. She does my bidding so that I can come to perfect being in the poem.'[21]

Recalling the 'contained conflict' which Cunard had sensed in 1929, this critique also hints at Riding's conviction in the self-legitimating perfectibility of poetic language: 'She believed like Wittgenstein that the meanings of words could be pinpointed specifically in their sound and origins . . . Theoretically, the perfect self must be embodied in perfect language . . .'[22] One of her best-known poems urges: 'Come, words, away to where / The meaning is not thickened / With the voice's fretting substance' ('Come, Words, Away', PLR, p. 137). Paradoxically, that much-disparaged 'voice' can only be escaped, it seems, in the self-haunting aesthetics of the text: 'never shall truth circle so / Till words prove language is / How words come from far sound away / . . . / Centering the utter telling / In truth's first soundlessness' (PLR, p. 139). Riding's sense of professional responsibility to this dialectic is uttered at the close of the two-part 'Disclaimer of the Person' (concluding 'Poems of Final Occasion', in *The Complete Poems*), the 'taut community' of the poet-speaker interrogating a fractured subjectivity it stages in explicitly poetic terms:

> If I my words am,
> If the footed head which frowns them
> And the handed heart which smiles them
> Are the very writing, table, chair,
> The paper, pen, self, taut community
> Wherein enigma's orb is word-constrained
> Does myself upon the page meet,
> . . .

What thinks the world?
. . .
And what think I?
The world in me which fleet to disavow
Ordains perpetual reiteration?
And these the words ensuing. (PLR, pp. 259–60)

At the same time, the speaker-self's authorial direction of 'the words ensuing' slyly problematises the text's eponymous 'disclaimer'.

It is tempting to construct Riding's literary legacy in the light of her very public 'disavow[al]' of her own poetic craft; however, some studies recuperate her as an enabling figure. Georgina Taylor reads Riding's collaborative volume *The World and Ourselves* (1938) as having influenced the emergence of the 'counter-public sphere' of female literary Modernists circling American émigré poet H.D. in the early decades of the century: 'We begin with a group of people who know one another "through" one another . . . They rarely meet all at the same time, and perhaps only a few live in the same neighbourhood . . . But a thread of common interest is drawn from one to the other . . .'[23] Between them, Barbara Adams, Robin Peel and Deryn Rees-Jones notice such a thread in the BBC radio broadcast Riding made on April 1st, 1962.[24]

Alan Sinfield and Martin Booth argue radio's central role in post-war literary culture from the mid-century, not least in its hospitality to poetry.[25] In the sixties, BBC producer and poet George MacBeth embedded poetry in the schedules of the Third Programme and Home Service, in documentaries and popular fixtures like *The Poet's Voice* and *Poetry Now*: 'At the height of MacBeth's power at the BBC, *Poetry Now* had an estimated audience of 50,000 plus.'[26] With the BBC providing 'service of a kind that was then quite unfamiliar in the United States', Riding's approving of a reading of her poems in 1962 seems as unsurprising as the recording she made to accompany it.[27] Ironically, the programme was not well received, the Audience Research Panel underwhelmed: 'I listened to it all in a fog of incomprehension.'[28]

However, Peel and Rees-Jones between them argue that the April broadcast was productive, not least for revisiting Riding's 1941 'disclaiming' of her craft. Her talk argues that 'The equivalence between poetry and truth that I had tried to establish was inconsistent with the relation they have to each other as – the one – art and – the other – the reality.' Dismissing her entire oeuvre as 'poetry *in extremis*, poetry caught in and confronted with its factitious nature as a mode of linguistic expression', Riding confided: 'I came close to achieving in my poems, trueness of intonation and direct presence of mind in word. But, what I achieved in this direction was ever sucked into the whorl of poetic artifice, with its overpowering necessities of patterned rhythm and harmonic sound-play, which work distortions upon the natural properties of tone and word.'[29] The tone is warning, even proselytising. Yet Riding's determination to differentiate herself from her own literary history throws into stark relief the very different paths taken by two of her century's most influential writers, both also women. 1962 was the year in which that most flamboyantly 'factitious' of poets Stevie Smith would publish her *Selected Poems* to enormous acclaim. It was also the year in which another American self-exile called Sylvia Plath, refining her own inimitable 'whorl of poetic artifice', wrote many of her most powerful poems and made hesitant contact with Smith. Each challenges Riding's claim that poetry cannot 'truthfully' address a contemporaneous reality, finding her own way of engaging with the contingencies of her own socio-historic moment, and the particular literary-political complexities faced by the woman poet. Although, as Rees-Jones warns, there seems little point in over-playing the connections between the three writers, at the heart of a century in which the place and value of the woman writer was repeatedly called into question, it seems hard to avoid reading in Riding's self-censoring model an ironic frame for the extraordinary literary achievements of Smith and Plath respectively.[30]

Poetic recognition came slowly for Smith, also writing poetry throughout the twenties. Her first collection *A Good Time was Had by All* only appeared in 1937 (the year before Riding's prodigiously early *Collected Poems*); Smith produced five more collections to sometimes mixed reviews over the next two decades. Like Riding, however, Smith's singular lyric voice was as quick to draw attention as confound. Helen Spalding records that her first serious reader (identified merely as 'E. B.') greeted the 'bewildering conglomeration' of poems submitted to Curtis Brown in 1934 with scepticism: 'imitations of Milton: imitations of hymns (example "Gentle Jesus meek and mild"): ecstatic praise of Lawrence and Huxley and several valiant attempts to out-Sitwell the Sitwells'.[31]

If as Spalding says few of the poems 'E. B.' saw survive, the review resonates in struggling to characterise an idiom too gravely alive to the implications and shortcomings of its own expressiveness to suffer overdetermination. As the insouciant, self-deprecating refrain of 'The Songster' hints, poets depend on their audiences for survival:

> Miss Pauncefort sang at the top of her voice
> (Sing tirry-lirry-lirry down the lane)
> And nobody knew what she sang about
> (Sing tirry-lirry-lirry all the same)[32]

Time and again, Smith re/constructs the writer (often a poet, frequently female) in similarly provisional terms. In 'La Speakerine de Putney' these are straitened, with deflective but not uncompassionate deliberation, in close-rhymed couplets: 'This heap of ashes was a learned girl; / Oh how the ashes shift to the words' smoke-curl! / Blow wind, blow, blow away the frightful form, scatter / The false girl-form and the words' mutter' (SCP, p. 187). As a growing discourse testifies, Smith herself equally invites and resists identification with the reflexive subjects of poems like 'The Commuted Sentence': 'Here is all straight and narrow as a tomb / Oh shut me not within a little room' (SCP, p. 287); and 'Mrs Arbuthnot', a 'poet of high degree' whom death transforms into 'a heavenly comber': 'She runs with a comb of fire, / Nobody writes or wishes to / Who is one with their desire' (SCP, p. 492).

Smith's much-debated inscrutability has its price: Philip Larkin famously deems her 'almost unclassifiable' even as he robes her in the 'frivolous and vulnerable' attire he retrieves from her 1949 novel *The Holiday*. This review underestimates neither Smith's ambivalence ('As in Lear the silliness [is] part of the seriousness') nor her range: 'life, death, eternity, love, sin . . . continually recurring in different contexts and from different angles'. However, despite the 'completely original' qualities he acclaims, Larkin's title alone renders Smith inconsequential, her poetry girlish if occasionally disturbing whimsy.[33]

Certainly what Riding might have thought of as 'factitiousness', and Larkin calls '*bizarrerie*', has divided Smith's readers.[34] The 'doubly controlled tone' of a 'detached and critical frame of mind' was first admired by a percipient review of *A Good Time Was Had By All*.[35] Seamus Heaney is less persuaded by Smith's ludic unconventionalities: 'I suppose in the end the adjective has to be "eccentric".'[36] He has a point. Perhaps the most unnerving feature of Smith's irrepressible idiom is its carnivalesque destabilising of 'poetic' tradition, nourishing the 'play and fantasy' which Martin Pumphrey has painstakingly explored.[37] Other critics recuperate the naive-looking line-drawings – 'doodles' – with which Smith insisted whenever possible her work be illustrated.[38] Both features nuance her best-known poem, 'Not Waving But Drowning', its mordant treatment of its wretchedly clown-like subject – his dying gestures too easily mistaken, his moaned explanations unheard – part slapstick, part horror. The phlegmatic speaker, relaying the words of corpse and onlookers alike, is simultaneously effaced and incriminated by the Betjeman-esque platitudes ('Poor chap . . . larking') of the second crucial stanza and the self-marginalising conclusion: 'I was much too far out all my life' (SCP, p. 303). The apparent overlapping of author, speaker and subject is complicated by the poem's illustration of the upper body of a sharp-featured, androgynous figure with long sleek (wet?) hair, either emerging from or returning to a watery context, its gaze tellingly semi-averted.

Smith's texts offer a manifestly proliferative reading experience, conversing with interlocutors ranging from the 'Wanderer' poet to Edward Lear to women's magazines.[39] Amid lively critical interest in her poetic relations, variously, with Blake, Browning, Dickinson, Yeats, Auden and Sitwell, Smith's summoning of her near-contemporary Riding (there was barely a year between them) has largely escaped attention. They shared an interest in classical and European romance traditions, and in mythology and primitive narratives, especially fairy tale and ballad. Strictly speaking, neither can be defined as feminist, but both were openly impatient of a patriarchal literary establishment by which each felt judged and frustrated. Technically, Riding informs Smith's often cryptic (Steinian) repetitions. The refrain in 'Forgive me, forgive me' – opening rather than concluding three unpunctuated quatrains – undercuts the sincerity of a poem in which the melancholic courtly love song, inverted, asserts only its speaker's self-protective refusal of emotional relationship: 'Forgive me forgive me for here where I stand / There is no friend beside me no lover at hand / No footstep but mine in my desert of sand' (SCP, p. 23). The stagey rhetoric of 'Is it wise' recalls Riding more obviously (the question 'Is it wise' on which each stanza extends tersely rebuffed in each final line), as well as the abstracts it regulates: 'Melancholy', 'Mortality', 'Corruptibility' and 'Mutability' (SCP, p. 67). As here, however, Smith's abstractions refine Riding's example, serving both to collapse and widen the distance between speaker and audience. Undermined by her trademark balladic rhythms and banal-seeming rhymes, the high-flown never survives for long in this ruthlessly self-deprecating poetics.

Such, then, is the 'quizzical presence' Heaney finds, contentiously, 'eccentric'.[40] His adjective was immediately challenged by feminist scholars protesting Smith's literary marginalisation. Introducing her *Bloodaxe Book of Contemporary Women Poets* (1986), Jeni Couzyn identifies the central stereotype 'of the woman poet, who is generally considered a rare and rather inferior subspecies of the genus Great Poet', as: '*Miss Eccentric Spinster*', personified in 'Emily Dickinson, pale in her white dress behind closed doors; Edith Sitwell, raucous and purple-cloaked; Stevie Smith nervy in tweed skirt and ankle socks on the stage of the Festival Hall'.[41] Couzyn embeds Smith in an emergent female poetic canon even as she honours the poet's performativity. For Pumphrey, meanwhile, the constructedness of Smith's idiom, deploying 'indirection, inversion, paradox and riddle', only confirms this writer's 'constant manipulation of the culturally defined masks by which the self is known – to create a private space behind the surface of public experience'.[42]

Ironically, Heaney provides perhaps the finest portrait of Smith in performance, 'inviting the audience to yield her their affection and keeping them at bay with a quick irony. She seemed to combine elements of Gretel and of the witch, to be vulnerable and capable . . . with a hag's wisdom and a girl's wide-eyed curiosity.' In particular he captures something of Smith's aural expertise: 'her voice pitching between querulousness and keening . . . she chanted her poems artfully off-key, in a beautifully flawed plain-song that suggested . . . an embarrassed party-piece by a child half-way between tears and giggles, and a deliberately *faux-naif* rendition by a virtuoso'.[43] Heaney's depiction concurs with Pumphrey's Smith, restively sifting the imaginative and political possibilities enshrined in masks and masking; it also recalls the captivating live performances for which she would become renowned.

Severin argues that Smith's relaxed appearances at live events across the country owed much to some twenty years of radio-broadcasting experience.[44] Like her much-loved aunt, Smith listened enthusiastically to the 'wireless' throughout her life. Undoubtedly, radio played an important part in her professional maturation, nurturing an increasingly confident sense of herself as a public persona well before her professional stature and popularity were endorsed by the critical acclaim earned by *Selected Poems*.[45] Severin notices how Smith's broadcasting experiences helped to shape her poetry, besides securing her sense of public identity, partly in nudging her towards the carnivalesque realms of music hall and revue. A relatively late poem, however, recuperates the radio broadcast itself as a suggestively accommodating aesthetic space, laced with political as well as imaginative potency. 'The Listener', about a spoof radio programme (' "An encounter with mosquitoes in New Guinea" by Miss Cheeseman') only semi-humorously constructs the broadcast as a mesmerising in/accessible terrain tenanted by a mystical deity-like presence.[46] The poem riffs on the other/worldly nature of a territory both thrillingly exotic and reassuringly familiar: 'I fell to thinking of the animal kingdom / And experienced at once a relief of nervous tension. / For I thought, Their battles are as ours, as ours' (SCP, p. 451).

This text returns us to Riding's valedictory broadcast.[47] In one of the most significant and suggestive rereadings of Smith's 'discursive incongruities' to date, Huk complains that Smith has been read as 'an apologist for English/Anglican tradition . . . a Blakean Romantic, an Arnoldian Victorian, a royalist conservative, an Orwellian radical . . . a confessional would-be suicide, a religious poet, an anti-Semitic writer, a popular balladeer, an anti-feminist, a proto-feminist'. For Huk, Smith's work 'open[s] up to new interpretation when we realise that *all* and *none* of these voices are her own'. The socio-cultural 'incongruity' which Huk uncovers in re-embedding Smith in her own historical/political contexts liberates her from Riding's indictment; only with factitiousness could Smith have responded 'truthfully' to the socio-political, historical and aesthetic 'realities' of her time and place.[48]

Like Smith and Riding, Sylvia Plath has exerted a powerful grip on the popular imagination. Deborah Nelson asks us 'to imagine, for instance, a major Hollywood studio producing a film about any of her contemporaries, much less casting an A-list actor, Gwyneth Paltrow, in the feature role'.[49] A comparison might be made with Robert Enders 1978 biopic *Stevie*, starring Glenda Jackson. Like Smith's, Plath's literary stature today is evinced in a discourse increasingly interested in rereading itself. Having exhausted the literary possibilities of her death, Plath critics turned to the drama of her foreshortened life, with and without her poet-husband Ted Hughes; seemingly, they remain compelled by it.[50] Various additions to the primary works – a scholarly edition of Plath's *Journals*; a facsimile edition of *Ariel* and Hughes's award-winning *Birthday Letters*, explicitly concerned with the emotional history of his much-mythologised relationship with Plath – have re-ignited literary interest in Plath's biography.[51] However, in line with developments in the field of women's poetry as a whole, recent commentators have started probing the performative and socio-historically constructed nature of Plath's distinctive idiom.

The most established of these strands draws on poststructuralist re-understandings of the cultural practice of confession. Widely mobilised in the relatively new area of 'life-writing' this has led to re-evaluations of the 'confessional' school of poetry, as in Jo Gill's incisive recuperations of the work of Plath's friend and fellow poet Anne Sexton.[52] Plath's edgy performativity has started to win notice, as critics re-address the subtleties of her impressionistic, deceptively readable, 'poetic whorl', its proliferating imagery disciplined by elliptical syntax and phraseology. The subject of 'Gulliver' seems deliberately unclear, for example; is this text best understood as a self-admonishing dramatic monologue (the voice Gulliver's own) or a derisive rebuke from an intimate (perhaps, or perhaps not, Plath herself) taking advantage of her mythically gigantic subject's physically and politically compromised state? Or is its enigmatic speaker, even, in that ambiguous second person, somebody altogether different, for whom Gulliver becomes a witty or accusing analogy? The poem's sensualities do little to clarify its perspective, the gaze of its opening apparently as likely to be down as upward:

> Over your body the clouds go
> High, high and icily
> And a little flat, as if they

Floated on a glass that was invisible.
Unlike swans,
Having no reflections;

Unlike you,
With no strings attached.
All cool, all blue. Unlike you –[53]

The subject's physical incapacity is replayed in vision which proves unnervingly depthless ('Having no reflections'), and aurality which seems, under the pressure of linguistic alienation, just as inadequate. 'With no strings attached' the clouds by contrast float enviably, mockingly, free of the 'Winding and twining . . . petty fetters' constraining 'you'. The referent of the final lines ('The shadow of this lip, an abyss', PCP, pp. 251) is similarly unfixed: it might refer to and speak for subject or speaker, offering both to monumentalise and dislodge, consume and dismiss, or even bring enfranchising (sexual?) oblivion to their uncertain interlocutor.

'Gulliver' was written in early November 1962, around the time Plath, after a week of listening to 'the British Council's recordings of Stevie Smith reading her poetry', wrote to ask Smith if they could meet.[54] Rees-Jones exposes the degree to which Smith's idiom is implicated in Plath's refining of 'the performed self which eventually predominates in *Ariel*'.[55] However, Plath's interest in performativity predates her November sessions with Smith's recordings, reaching back – most immediately – to the radio play she had completed the preceding March, after the birth of her second child in mid January. As for Smith, broadcasting helped to embed Plath's developing sense of poetic identity, partly for financial reasons; it also affected her idiom.[56]

The 378-line verse-drama, 'Three Women: A Poem for Three Voices' (PCP, pp. 176–87) was commissioned by Douglas Cleverdon. The generic shift did not come out of the blue: in 1957 Plath describes working on 'a short-verse dialogue which is supposed to sound just like conversation but is written in strict 7-line stanzas rhyming ababcbc'. She goes on: 'I really think I would like to write a verse play, now. If I practise enough on getting colour into speech, I can write in quite elaborate rhymed and alliterative forms without sounding like self-conscious poetry.'[57] The largely unrhymed seven-line stanzas of 'Three Women' comprise a work which hovers between dialogue and a sequence of short lyric monologues and is arguably central to Plath's maturing interest in a self-protectively unfixed textual identity.

'Three Women' is set in a maternity ward. Steven Gould Axelrod characterises its three speakers: 'The first, by implication a wife and homemaker, has a baby boy and is contented; the second, a wife and secretary, miscarries and mourns; and the third, an unmarried student, gives her baby girl up for adoption.'[58] The poem interrogates the part which the experience of maternity, and especially parturition, plays in the public/private construction of female identity, by the speakers, their intimates and the institutions and networks of the wider socio-economic society. (For Axelrod, it protests against the 'sexist and hierarchical social arrangements' in and beyond hospitals and the medical profession, for example.[59]) At the same time, a generically hybrid construct mines the creative potentiality latent in the dramatic and dialogic relations between and among the three unnamed speakers. However, for all the structural space afforded by its length and semi-sequential nature, the poem retains (partly in its unvarying stanza-length) a powerful lyric economy.

The different perspectives of the three speakers, each universalising one version of maternity (the first happily fulfilled, the second painfully unrealised, the third poignantly frustrated), converge in their common struggle to understand their external and internal transformation through the intensely physical nature and sensations of their experiences. Absorbed in the implacable effort of labour, the first voice feels 'dragged by the horses, the iron hooves', a realisation recalled and transformed in the moment when 'I am drummed into use. / My eyes are squeezed by this blackness. / I see nothing' (PCP, p. 180). After the birth, the baby seems all indistinction ('a little, blind, bright plant') until, synaesthetically, 'One cry. It is the hook I hang on' (PCP, p. 183). The more tortured second voice rails, early on, against 'That flat, flat, flatness from which ideas, destructions, / Bulldozers, guillotines, white chambers of shrieks proceed' (PCP, p. 177); the third is likewise agonisingly caught between the palpable and the untouchable, her conflict uttered in graphically tangible terms: 'Her cries are hooks that catch and grate like cats.' The intensity heightens in the aural (assonantal and alliterative) 'hooks' and half-rhymes of a fresh stanza:

> I think her little head is carved in wood,
> A red, hard wood, eyes shut and mouth wide open.
> And from the open mouth issue sharp cries
> Scratching at my sleep like arrows,
> Scratching at my sleep, and entering my side. (PCP, p. 182)

Traversing the generic boundaries separating theatrical from poetic construct, 'Three Women' exposes and exploits the dialectical interchange between aural and visual, spoken and written, bodied and unbodied in the representation of identity. Here, selfhood is constantly in flux, despite each speaker's efforts to profile her manifestly fragile subjectivity. All three are and are not versions of each other and their author, herself not above conflating the processes of maternity and literary creation.

Plath's interest in the self as authorial / creative literary presence is mediated early in her writing career by precisely the physical sensations she summons in 'Three Women'. Her clinical-seeming interest in materiality, often mediated by the tactile senses of touch and taste, seems to offer her restless poetic intelligence imaginative anchorage, counterposing and counterposed by an equally immutable sense of insubstantiality and impalpability. Dedicated to Leonard Baskin, whom she befriended at Yaddo artists' colony in 1959, 'Sculptor' honours the delicate intercourse between the material ('Obdurate, in dense-grained wood') and the immaterial ('the bodiless / Come to barter') which sculpture registers and respects. The transfigurative process of this art form is gestured at in the barely realised figure of the sculptor himself, sketched as an earthy semi-deity, a sensor: 'Hands moving move priestlier / Than priest's hands, invoke no vain / Images of light and air' (PCP, pp. 91–2).

Like its silent subject, 'Sculptor' models a way of creating grounded in practicalities. Typically, for Plath, the interlocking senses of touch, taste and smell illumine those elements of lived experience which – apprehensible in and of themselves – remain out of reach and/or unbodied. The dialectical relationship between what is and is not perceptibly 'there' to the witnessing eye and mind, charges the emergent performativity of poems like 'The Lady and the Earthenware Head' (PCP, pp. 69–70), about the clay model of her own head Plath was given by a Smith College room-mate. A 1957 letter to her mother explains, 'It's been knocking about and I didn't have the heart to throw it away', before describing how Hughes and Plath eventually wedge the head 'in a gnarled willow, gazing out over the lovely green meadows . . . I like to think of leaving "my head" here, as it were . . . Every time I think of it now, I feel leaves and ivy twining around it, like a monument at rest in the midst of nature' (LH, p. 294). In the poem, by striking contrast, an object initially reassuring ('Stolidly propping thick volumes') becomes an 'effigy . . . / Lewdly beckoning', terrifyingly indestructible: 'An antique hag-head, too tough for knife to finish' (PCP, p. 70). In a journal entry written two days after the letter, the head is considered as a possible title-image for a first collection. Now, poised undecidably between the worlds of form and content, 'a terrible and holy token of identity' acquires an anti-subjective significance:

> This book title gives me such staying power (perhaps these very pages will see the overturn of my dream, or even its acceptance in the frame of the real world). At any rate I see the earthenware head, rough, crude, powerful and

> radiant . . . stamped with jagged black and white designs, signifying earth, and the words which shape it. (JP, pp. 193–4)

Freed of the jauntiness of Plath's letters home, the entry reinforces the implacable determination and anxieties of a developing sense of literary selfhood. The excerpt is highly reflexive, partly in the very material way in which the head – its textures ('rough, crude') and contours ('stamped') – is situated and read: the three words of the imagined book's title will, Plath nervously knows, 'shape' even as they are shaped into what will be to her a crucially public aesthetic signifier. Title and literary artefact both promise and imperil a sense of literary identity and authority 'in the frame of the real world'. It seems no accident that the same anxieties should inflect the poem Plath finally chose to title her first collection, *The Colossus*. Vestiges of the 'The Lady and the Earthenware Head' surely survive in the derelict materiality of the masculine visage which the speaker is now left struggling, in an intensely physical way, to understand: 'lips', 'throat', 'the weedy acres of your brow', 'the immense skull-plates' and 'bald, white tumuli of your eyes' (PCP, p. 129).

Written approximately two years after the earlier poem, for Rees-Jones among others 'The Colossus' defies the contingent yet also somehow imperviously (male-)gendered nature of literary authority. Whether, as Gill suggests, it is read as 'an allegory of Plath's self-constitution as a poet . . . a kind of manifesto . . . [or] a study of the psychoanalytic process itself', 'The Colossus' revisits the anxieties of its more naive precursor, refusing the patriarchal aesthetic it interrogates.[60] Often represented by his wife as colossally and provocatively masculine, Hughes stalks 'The Colossus' as plainly, in some ways, as his late father-in-law. The incipient tensions of Plath's literary relationship with Hughes were arguably prefigured in the moment when, at the Oxford party where they had just met, Plath bit Hughes 'long and hard on the cheek, and when we came out of the room, blood was running down his face' (JP, p. 112). If it registers Plath's passionate temperament, in retrospect the incident also hints at the professional anxieties which Rees-Jones uncovers in Plath's untiring efforts to establish herself as an authoritative literary figure in her own right. As her closest reader Hughes would always be Plath's nearest rival.

She may not have needed to worry in fact; as Vicki Bertram notes, 'Plath's words came to assume terrifying authority over Hughes' life; their capacity to judge and sentence unrivalled, perhaps, in the history of English literature.'[61] Re-inserting Hughes on his own terms in a literary-historical narrative which condemned, silenced, but never excluded him, Hughes's eighty-eight letter-poems write back to Plath's accusingly posthumous poetic voice. As Diane Middlebrook has shown, the material histories of the couple's compositions (frequently drafted on the back of the other's discarded drafts) were as entwined as their literary careers and poetic development.[62] Arguably Hughes's last collection re-appropriates a literary history which is already his own. And yet this now doubly posthumous literary relationship was never so straightforward: Hughes's version of the Oxford party ('St Botolph's') re/constructs him as impressionable victim of Plath's colonising creative imagination, in the 'swelling ring-moat of tooth-marks / That was to brand my face for the next month. / The me beneath it for good' (BL, p. 15). His conceit is disingenuous: Hughes's collection ensures that the last words can only now be his.

Hughes's equivocal figure returns us to Riding, to whose April broadcast Plath listened from her Devon home on the night of Frieda's second birthday. Like Adams and Peel, Rees-Jones discerns in Riding a muse-like figure, not least because of her centrality to Graves's *The White Goddess*, a work which Plath and Hughes discovered and used together; Rees-Jones like Peel speculates that Plath saw 'the relationship of Graves and Riding as some kind of a model of poetic partnership' for the meshing of emotional and literary in her own professional and personal life.[63] All three critics discern Riding's presence in the powerful poems Plath began to write in the weeks following the broadcast, many of them eventually published in *Ariel*. Although Peel reasons that the first of these, 'Little Fugue', was taking shape in the previous month, as Judith Kroll first remarked, this text's earliest draft is subtitled, significantly, 'On Listening to Laura Riding'.[64]

'Little Fugue' exemplifies the mobility of Plath's now maturing poetic imagination, its fugality less to do with formal efficiency (thirteen clipped quatrains of mostly end-stopped lines) than the interlocking motifs (the waving fronds of yew hedge, overcast sky, exploring fingers of the blind pianist and an ever-oppressive father-figure) which complicate our developing sense of their interrelationship. Its musical intelligence is palpable, from the control out of which its forensic study of sensory – and emotional – stunting (amputation) is conjured, through the increasing agitation of the central section, to the exclamations which, framing the ninth climactic stanza, end it dramatically on 'a silence!' Exorcistic, elegiac, in its quieter final stanzas the poem comes protectively to rest on the speaker's nearest, disquieting, immediacies: 'These are my fingers, this my baby' (PCP, pp. 187–9).

'Little Fugue' implicates Riding's broadcast in a critical moment in Plath's poetic development; Peel finds it resonating with several of the twelve poems aired in the broadcast. Peel's account seems as significant for weighing Plath and Riding's shared American-Jewish backgrounds, their common experiences of domicile in Europe, their nervous breakdowns and abiding sense of political responsibility (in contrast to both Hughes and Graves). The details nuance Peel's re-historicising of Plath's alienated figure, contextualising the socio-historic emphases he uncovers in the cuts and corrections of the text's unpublished drafts. As his work indicates, whatever Plath's motives for listening to Riding's broadcast in the first place, the highly wrought work she began producing in its wake, and would refine until her death the following spring, vigorously dismisses Riding's indictment of poetry as a vehicle for 'reality'.[65]

Amid the imponderable tensions of the Cold War, one of the 'realities' serving to confirm the views aired in Riding's 1962 broadcast might have been the space research programme presided over by the National Aeronautics and Space Administration (NASA), most visibly – in the early sixties – in the regular launches from Cape Canaveral, located not fifty miles from the seclusion of Riding's cottage in Wabasso, on the east coast of Florida.[66] It may not be coincidental that the first international satellite series, developed jointly by the UK and USA to record measurements in the ionosphere, was launched on 26 April 1962. The name selected for the series was 'Ariel'.

Notes

This chapter is indebted in numerous ways to the scholarship of my colleague Jo Gill, and to the patience of staff at the BBC Written Archives Centre, Caversham Park, Berkshire (hereafter WAC).

1. Laura Riding, 'An Enquiry', *New Verse* 1934 (11 October), pp. 2–5.
2. *Ibid.*, p. 5.
3. *A Selection of the Poems of Laura Riding*, ed. Robert Nye (Manchester: Carcanet, 1994), p. 7 (hereafter RSP). Riding publicly renounced poetry in 1941 on her marriage to her second husband, the literary journalist Schuyler Jackson, changing her authorial name to Laura (Riding) Jackson at the same time. Being only concerned with her poetry, I have opted for the former version.
4. Jeanne Heuving, 'Laura (Riding) Jackson's "Really New" Poem', in Margaret Dickie and Thomas Travisano (eds.), *Gendered Modernisms: American Women Poets and Their Readers* (Philadelphia: University of Pennsylvania Press, 1996), pp. 191–213 (p. 209). Riding's critical neglect has been examined by K. K. Ruthven, 'How to Avoid Being Canonized: Laura Riding', *Textual Practice*, 5:2 (1991), pp. 242–60 and Jo-Ann Wallace, 'Laura Riding and the Politics of Decanonization', *American Literature*, 64:1 (1992), pp. 111–26, among others.
5. Laura (Riding) Jackson, *The Word 'Woman', and Other Related Writings*, ed. Elizabeth Friedmann and Alan J. Clark (Manchester: Carcanet, 1994), p. 2. Interestingly Suzanne Clark summons Riding as critic rather than poet.

See *Sentimental Modernism: Women Writers and the Revolution of the Word* (Bloomington: Indiana University Press, 1991), p. 2. Deborah Baker echoes, 'While some memory of Laura Riding as poet prodigy of the 1920s may linger . . . her reputation was almost entirely superseded by Laura (Riding) Jackson's.' *In Extremis: The Life of Laura Riding* (London: Hamish Hamilton, 1993), p. xiii.

6. See Michael O'Neill and Gareth Reeves, *Auden, MacNeice, Spender: The Thirties Poetry* (Basingstoke: Macmillan, 1992), p. 25–31.
7. Baker, *In Extremis*; Barbara Adams, *The Enemy Self: Poetry and Criticism of Laura Riding* (Ann Arbor: University of Michigan Research Press, 1990); Joyce Piell Wexler, *Laura Riding's Pursuit of Truth* (Athens: Ohio University Press, 1979).
8. Ruthven, 'How to Avoid', p. 247.
9. Martin Seymour-Smith, *Robert Graves: His Life and Work* (London: Paladin, 1987), pp. viii–ix. For Riding's views on anthologies see Adams, *Enemy Self*, pp. 27, 29–31.
10. Janet Montefiore, *Men and Women Writers of the 1930s: The Dangerous Flood of History* (London: Routledge, 1996), p. 138.
11. Ruthven, 'How to Avoid', p. 255.
12. Heuving, 'Really New', p. 191; Susan M. Schultz, 'Laura Riding's Essentialism and the Absent Muse', *Arizona Quarterly*, 48:1 (1992), pp. 1–24 (p. 21).
13. Jane Dowson, *Women, Modernism and British Poetry 1910–1939* (Aldershot: Ashgate, 2002), pp. 155–8.
14. It was awarded the Nashville Prize in 1924 by the Fugitives, who numbered among them Allen Tate and Robert Penn Warren and acclaimed Riding 'the most promising poet of the year'. Adams, *Enemy Self*, p. 7.
15. Nancy Cunard, *These Were the Hours: Memories of My Hours Press, Réanville and Paris 1928–1931*, ed. Hugh Ford (Carbondale: Southern Illinois University Press, 1969), pp. 103–4. The Hours Press published Riding's *Four Unpublished Letters to Catherine* in 1930.
16. Laura (Riding) Jackson, *The Poems of Laura Riding*, ed. Elizabeth Friedmann, revised edition (New York: Persea Books, 2001), p. 16 (hereafter PLR).
17. Baker, *In Extremis*, p. 73; Ruthven, 'How to Avoid', p. 245.
18. Montefiore, *Men and Women Writers*, pp. 137–8.
19. Ruthven, 'How to Avoid', pp. 255–6. Among others he cites Hugh Kenner's *The Pound Era* (Berkeley: University of California Press, 1971), Bonnie Kime Scott's *Gender and Modernism* (Bloomington: Indiana University Press 1990).
20. Jane Marcus, 'Laura Riding Roughshod', *Iowa Review*, 12 (1981), pp. 295–9. Marcus cites Stein's 'I Am' ('I am because I say / I say myself / I am my name / My name is not my name') as evidence; the poem is a powerful intertext in both Riding's own 'I am' (PLR, p. 209) and 'Disclaimer of the Person' (PLR, pp. 251–60); see my discussion below.
21. Adams, *Enemy Self*, pp. 1–2.
22. *Ibid.*, p. 2.
23. Georgina Taylor, *H.D and the Public Sphere of Modernist Women Writers, 1913–1946: Talking Women* (Oxford: Oxford University Press, 2001), p. 196.

24. See Adams, *Enemy Self*, p. 48; Robin Peel, *Writing Back: Sylvia Plath and Cold War Politics* (Madison, NJ: Fairleigh Dickinson University Press, 2002), pp. 135–45; and Deryn Rees-Jones, *Consorting with Angels: Essays on Modern Women Poets* (Tarset, Northumberland: Bloodaxe Books, 2005), pp. 20, 118.
25. Alan Sinfield, *Society and Literature 1945–1970* (London: Methuen, 1983), p. 158; Martin Booth, *British Poetry 1964–1984: Driving through the Barricades* (London: Routledge and Kegan Paul, 1985), p. 88.
26. Booth, *Driving through the Barricades*, p. 92.
27. Peel, *Writing Back*, p. 133.
28. BBC Audience Research Report, 'Laura Riding', 1 May 1962 (LR/62/626); WAC.
29. Laura (Riding) Jackson, *The Laura (Riding) Jackson Reader*, ed. Elizabeth Friedmann (New York: Persea Books, 2005), p. 203.
30. See Jane Dowson and Alice Entwistle, *A History of Twentieth Century British Women's Poetry* (Cambridge: Cambridge University Press, 2005).
31. Frances Spalding, *Stevie Smith: A Critical Biography* (London: Faber, 1988), p. 89.
32. *The Collected Poems of Stevie Smith*, ed. James MacGibbon (Harmondsworth: Penguin, 1985), p. 30 (hereafter SCP).
33. Philip Larkin, 'Frivolous and Vulnerable', in *Required Writing: Miscellaneous Pieces 1955–1982* (London: Faber, 1983), pp. 153–8 (pp. 156, 154).
34. *Ibid.*, pp. 155–7; his italics.
35. Cited as *Granta*, 5 May 1937 in Spalding, *Stevie Smith*, p. 311 (footnote).
36. Seamus Heaney, 'A Memorable Voice', in *Preoccupations: Selected Prose 1968–1978* (London: Faber, 1980), pp. 199–201 (p. 201).
37. Martin Pumphrey, 'Play, Fantasy and Strange Laughter: Stevie Smith's Uncomfortable Poetry', *Critical Quarterly*, 28:3 (1986), pp. 85–96.
38. See, most recently, Romana Huk, *Stevie Smith: Between the Lines* (London: Palgrave, 2005), pp. 234–59.
39. Laura Severin, *Stevie Smith's Resistant Antics* (Madison: University of Wisconsin Press, 1997), pp. 52–7.
40. Pumphrey, 'Play, and Fantasy', p. 85.
41. Jeni Couzyn (ed.), *The Bloodaxe Book of Contemporary Women Poets: Eleven British Writers* (Tarset: Bloodaxe, 1985), p. 15.
42. Pumphrey, 'Play, Fantasy', pp. 85, 88, 95.
43. Heaney, 'Memorable Voice', p. 199.
44. Severin, *Resistant Antics*, pp. 119–22.
45. Spalding, *Stevie Smith*, pp. 204–7.
46. Staff at the WAC confirm that a Miss Evelyn Cheeseman made various natural history programmes, although none with Smith's title.
47. That Smith knew about the broadcast seems likely, given her long-standing friendship with Graves's niece, Sally Chilvers.
48. Huk, *Between the Lines*, pp. 3–5.
49. Deborah Nelson, 'Plath, History and Politics', in Jo Gill (ed.), *The Cambridge Companion to Sylvia Plath* (Cambridge: Cambridge University Press, 2006), pp. 21–35 (p. 21).

50. See Gill (ed.), *Cambridge Companion to Sylvia Plath*, pp. xi–xvi, 3–20.
51. Sylvia Plath, *The Journals of Sylvia Plath*, ed. Ted Hughes and Frances McCullough (New York: Anchor Books, 1998) (hereafter JP); *Ariel: The Restored Edition*, ed. Frieda Hughes (London: Faber, 2004); Ted Hughes, *Birthday Letters* (London: Faber, 1998) (hereafter BL).
52. See Jo Gill, 'Anne Sexton and Confessional Poetics', *The Review of English Studies*, 55:220 (2004), pp. 426–45, for example.
53. Sylvia Plath, *Collected Poems*, ed. Ted Hughes (London: Faber, 1981), p. 251. Hereafter PCP.
54. Rees-Jones, *Consorting with Angels*, pp. 120–1.
55. *Ibid.*, p. 122.
56. According to Peel, 'before she died, Plath had agreed to appear in three discussion programs to be recorded in May 1963. Each program would have earned her 30 guineas . . . when the average weekly wage for women was seven guineas'. Peel, *Writing Back*, p. 133.
57. Sylvia Plath, *Letters Home: Correspondence 1950–1963*, ed. Aurelia Plath (London: Faber, 1976); 6 August 1957, p. 324 (hereafter LH).
58. Stephen Gould Axelrod, 'The Poetry of Sylvia Plath', in Gill (ed.), *The Cambridge Companion to Sylvia Plath*, p. 86.
59. *Ibid.*, pp. 86–7.
60. Jo Gill, 'The Colossus and Crossing the Water', Gill (ed.), *The Cambridge Companion to Sylvia Plath*, pp. 94–5.
61. Vicki Bertram, *Gendering Poetry: Contemporary Women and Men Poets* (London: Pandora Press, 2005), p. 139.
62. See Diane Middlebrook, *Her Husband: Hughes and Plath – A Marriage* (New York: Viking, 2003).
63. See Adams, *Enemy Self*, pp. 48–9; Peel, *Writing Back*, pp. 135–7; Rees-Jones, *Consorting with Angels*, p. 22.
64. See Judith Kroll, *Chapters In A Mythology: The Poetry of Sylvia Plath* (New York: Harper and Row, 1976), p. 47. See also Adams, *Enemy Self*, p. 48; Peel, *Writing Back*, p. 135; Rees-Jones, *Consorting with Angels*, p. 22.
65. Peel, *Writing Back*, p. 145.
66. Baker, *In Extremis*, p. xi.

Chapter 49

Hughes and Heaney

EDWARD LARRISSY

Hughes and Heaney in one chapter? Various arguments to do with nationality or poetic fashion might lead one to expect, let us say, Ted Hughes and Thom Gunn, or Seamus Heaney and Patrick Kavanagh. Indeed, the former coupling was promoted by Faber, who published both Gunn and Hughes in a well-known and much-used joint selection. In retrospect, as we shall see, the combination seems less plausible than it once did. But interpretations which assume the dominance of a cultural and national framework are destined to inaccuracy and limitation. The structure of publishing arrangements and the reading habits of poets in Britain and Ireland from the 1960s to now are such that one simply cannot take the first steps in accounting for poetic relationships and influence without looking at the two countries together. And while there is now some evidence that Ireland as a whole is looking more and more to America, the period with which we are concerned in this chapter was characterised by the substantial overlap of matters poetic in Ireland and Britain – including in the question of what American poets to read. Hughes was an acknowledged influence on Heaney, and became a good friend. Heaney, like Hughes, was published by what was then unquestionably Britain's premier poetry publisher, Faber. Together, they edited one of the most popular and influential poetry anthologies of the late twentieth century, *The Rattle Bag* (Faber, 1982). Hughes was always interested in Celtic mythology and folklore, and most of all in Ireland and Irish literature. Both poets understood and drew inspiration from the traditional life of country people, and from the way nature was encountered by them. Both poets nursed a strong sense of national and poetic tradition. Both poets were concerned to uncover the ancient roots of their cultures, revealing violence as well as beauty. Both poets explored the symbolisation of gender and the specific powers and fallibilities of the male poetic imagination. None of this, of course, is to deny the influence of specifically Irish models on Heaney: that of Patrick Kavanagh, for instance, is undoubtedly important. Indeed, this is a notable instance of Irish readers looking to different lights from British ones, since Kavanagh had been largely ignored by British readers until recently, when the editorial labours of Antoinette Quinn have made his work available in Penguin. Nor should one suggest that Heaney is subdued to the influence of Hughes. While it is clear, as Roland Mathias says, that 'the first third of *Death of a Naturalist* . . . is pretty clearly a response to the new climate . . . initiated by Ted Hughes', it is, as he also says, 'no less obvious that the momentum of Heaney's writing was very different', with little of Hughes's 'biological ferment', and far more anxiety about nature's ugliness.[1] Nevertheless, as one looks back at the milieu out of which these two poets emerged, it is possible to discern the outlines of a literary history which helps to explain the similarities in their preoccupations. In particular, it is possible to suggest that Hughes's work, like that of contemporaries such as Larkin, Gunn, Davie and Hill, however dissimilar they may seem at first sight, arises out of, and responds to, the anxieties of British nationhood after the Second World War. It looks as if Heaney, learning from Hughes (and also from Hill) was able to graft some appropriate techniques and themes on to the different troubles and identity problems of Northern Ireland.

Ted Hughes's first published collection, *The Hawk in the Rain* (1957), was accepted into an environment where a revolution against the neo-Romanticism of the 1940s and of Dylan Thomas had recently been enacted. The poets associated with 'The Movement' – Larkin, Gunn, Davie, Kingsley Amis, Elizabeth Jennings, John Wain – had been announced and represented in Robert Conquest's anthology *New Lines* (1956). The manner of these poets was rational, discursive, orderly, ironic and urbane. This was even the case with a poet such as Gunn, who nevertheless celebrated the role of the will to power in human society and relationships. Yet this will to power only held significance and value if supported by reason, not least in the sense of choices rationally pondered in an absurd universe, conscious of the limits within which effective action is possible. As we have seen, Hughes was bracketed with Gunn by their publisher and in the public mind, and it is possible to see how this occurred. In Hughes's *The Hawk in the Rain*, there is a certain frankness about the violence of nature, not least in the depiction of human love as the product of animal will: 'There is no better way to know us / Than as two wolves, come separately to a wood' ('A Modest Proposal').[2] And there is a sense of the fatuity and weakness of the self that surrendered to respectability. These things find echoes in the work of Gunn.

Yet despite this affinity, there is much in what Keith Sagar claims when he says that Kingsley Amis's poem, 'Against Romanticism', 'reads like a prophetic attempt to keep Ted Hughes at bay'.[3] On the one hand, Amis attacks what he sees as vagueness (the 'abstract noun') and a taste for the supernatural ('tickled up with ghosts') in Romanticism, and even allowing for Hughes's interest in the esoteric, this does not seem quite right as a description of him. On the other hand, Amis's desire for 'Woods devoid of beasts, roads that please the foot' belongs in a different mental universe from that of Hughes.[4] As Sagar points out, Hughes was unaware of the *New Lines* poets, with the exception of Gunn, whom he admired.[5] If Amis's 'Against Romanticism' was partly aimed at Dylan Thomas, and if it reads in part like an attempt to keep Ted Hughes at bay, we should entertain the possibility that has been concealed from us by the vagaries of literary history: namely, that Hughes exhibits the influence of Dylan Thomas. It is plain enough in an early poem like 'The Little Boys and the Seasons' (*CP* 8–9), or in the title poem of *The Hawk in the Rain* itself, where the speaker is described as a 'Bloodily grabbed dazed last-moment-counting / Morsel in the earth's mouth' (*CP* 19). Here the accretion of alliteratively supported components of a complex adjectival phrase is similar enough to Thomas. Or consider the last stanza of 'Egg-Head': 'opposing his eye's flea-red / Fly-catching fervency to the wheel of the sun, / Trumpet his own ear dead' (*CP* 34). Seamus Heaney has offered a salutary corrective to accounts of poetic influence in this period which do not give his rightful importance to Thomas.[6] He was the poet all were reading, and his importance to Hughes emerges also from his letters.[7]

Yet there seems to be no true approximation in *The Hawk in the Rain*, nor indeed in subsequent books, to Thomas's recurring patterns of birth, spiritual rebirth and death, evoking the cycles of nature and in doing so constantly referring to the Christian mythos, albeit with reference to Blake and Wordsworth. On the face of it, with Hughes, at least up until *Crow* (first edition 1970), we are offered observations which do not gesture towards myth. The topic of relations between man and woman is instructive on this point: they are central to *The Hawk in the Rain*, and indeed to Hughes's work as a whole. Sometimes they suggest the predatory, as we have seen in the case of 'A Modest Proposal', and this is also the case with 'Incompatibilities' ('Desire's a vicious separator'; *CP* 28). Sometimes, on the other hand, Hughes evokes the manners of courtly love, as in 'Song': 'O lady, when the wind kissed you / You made him music for you were a shaped bell' (*CP* 24). Just as men may become alienated from nature, and become pompous fools, like the 'Famous Poet' (*CP* 23–4) or the man in 'The Man Seeking Experience Enquires His Way of a Drop of Water' (*CP* 34–5), so women, fleeing from sexuality, may become pitiably weak, like the woman in 'Secretary', who lies 'with buttocks tight, / Hiding her lovely eyes until day break' (*CP* 25). Nature never loses its poise, never becomes ridiculous: that is a matter for humanity, its ego and its accompanying mirror of vanity: 'He smiles in a mirror, shrinking the whole / Sun-swung zodiac of light to a trinket shape / On the rise of his eye' ('Meeting'; *CP* 35). The ills of civilisation notably include modern warfare: there is a whole sequence of war poems near the end of *The Hawk in the Rain*. And it is modern rather than ancient warfare which seems to be at fault: the pilot, in 'The Ancient Heroes and the Bomber Pilot', imagines the exploits of ancient warriors in bloody detail, but though he can pulverise cities at the flick of a wrist, he feels a sense of awe at the idea of even one of these warriors returning (*CP* 47–8). The contrast is between remote mechanised warfare and hand-to-hand battle in a society full-heartedly immersed in the warrior-code.

Now in all of this it has long been known that Hughes felt himself to be responding to the influence of Robert Graves's *The White Goddess*.[8] The influence makes itself felt in the poetry in the insistence on the purity of true love between man and woman, and the relationship between being in love and poetic inspiration, and in the suggestion that modern civilisation, not least in the practice of mechanised warfare, has gone astray. It is as if Dylan Thomas had given Hughes permission to allude to this myth in the way that Thomas himself alludes to a Romantic and visionary version of Christianity. Yet unlike in Thomas, we are not presented with something that we can identify as the outlines of a myth: it would be quite hard for the reader to deduce from *The Hawk in the Rain* the ascendancy of Graves over Hughes's imagination. And the same is perhaps even truer of the powerful and assured volume he next presented to the world: *Lupercal* (1960).

Here there is far less of the contorted syntax Hughes inherited from Thomas. Rather, there is an intensity of concentration on the subject, conveyed more often now with simpler syntax but powerfully vivid descriptive metaphors. Thematically, much remains the same. As in *The Hawk in the Rain*, nature goes her brutal way incognisant of the finer feelings professed by humanity. And yet, as most readers and critics have readily conceded, there is much anthropomorphism in Hughes. A poem such as 'Hawk Roosting' (*CP* 68–9) may well be the most powerful imagining conceivable of the mind of a hawk, but it is surely more human than hawkish. The hawk, when it describes its 'Inaction' as 'no falsifying dream' is extremely eloquent and socially conscious, and seems to have picked up some of its philosophy from Ted Hughes. It has also been influenced by Darwin: 'It took the whole of Creation / To produce my foot, my each feather.' Darwin's thought is even more evident in 'Pike' (*CP* 84–5): 'The jaws' hooked clamp and fangs / Not to be changed at this date; / A life subdued to its instrument'. The description of the poet's work in Hughes's account of poetic creativity, *Poetry in the Making*, is illustrated by the task of 'Capturing Animals', and this idea helps to explain the ingenious accuracy to be found in some of Hughes's descriptive imagery.[9] But, as with the shamanism upon which his efforts were partly modelled, the encounter seems very much a two-way process. For his part, Hughes brings with him the consciousness of a twentieth-century man whose upbringing in the mining town of Mexborough occurred, like that of D. H. Lawrence (another favourite), on the boundaries of the industrial and rural worlds. Perhaps for that reason, Hughes's Darwinian nature is often conceived in terms of the mechanical or industrial. Looking back to *The Hawk in the Rain*, one notes that the jaguar hurries 'Through prison darkness after the drills of his eyes / On a short fierce fuse' (*CP* 19–20). And in 'October Dawn', from the same volume, the ice puts 'plate and rivet on pond and brook; / Then tons of chain and massive lock' (*CP* 37). In 'November', the speaker stays on 'under the welding cold . . . / In the drilling rain' (*CP* 81–2), while in 'Thrushes', in a good example of Hughes's mechanised Darwinism, those birds possess 'bullet and automatic / Purpose', are 'more coiled steel than living' and are 'Triggered', 'streamlined', and possess 'efficiency' (*CP* 82). When we reach the Crow poems, we find that this bird is also sometimes mechanical, with a 'trapsprung' head ('Crow Tyrannosaurus'; *CP* 215). In *Season Songs* the swifts are a 'Shrapnel-scatter' ('Swifts'; *CP* 315), and in 'Earth-numb' from *Moortown* (1979), the salmon possess an 'electrocuting malice' (*CP* 541).

Of course, another way of looking at this mechanical imagery is to concede that it is the most unaffected contemporary language in which to convey the relatively automatic character of natural processes and animal behaviour. Hughes remains fascinated not only by this broad picture, but also by the continued existence of amoral nature just below the surface of civilised human codes. This fascination leads to the distilling of a myth. In *Lupercal*, a stoat, caught and nailed to a door, re-emerges, 'thirsting, in far Asia, in Brixton' ('Strawberry Hill'; *CP* 63), becoming a universal principle – a kind of Crow.[10] In *Wodwo* (1967) this movement towards a unifying myth is accelerated. Hughes seeks to embody the primeval life force in terms that transcend the use of animals. In 'Theology' (*CP* 161), for instance, we have the first of Hughes's poems based on Genesis, this one, like some others, being about Adam and Eve and the serpent. In 'Gog' (*CP* 161–4) it is the ancient giant who represents the vital force. As for the 'wodwo' of the book's title, this is another mythical creature (drawn from the pages of *Sir Gawayn and the Green Knight*), half beast and half man.

Crow exhibits the ruthless – and sometimes squalid and amoral – greed and lust one has learned to associate with earlier Hughes creatures and mythological figures. But while he is a kind of summation of these tendencies, he is far more than that. His resourceful cunning, and the blackly comic stories Hughes tells about him, align him with the Trickster, a clownish, subversive figure frequently to be found in the tales of Native Americans and Siberians, who works against the plans of the benevolent Creator.[11] Interestingly, as Sagar points out, the Trickster may sometimes be identified with the Raven.[12] Even so, his cleverness and perversity align Crow with the human world. Jung, another influence on Hughes, was interested in the Trickster stories.[13] But there is probably another Jungian connection with *Crow*. Jung liked to explain depression in terms of the processes described in alchemy, whereby the amalgam of opposites (mercury and sulphur, representing solar and lunar), when heated, entered into a dark stage which ultimately should lead to the creation of the philosopher's stone. This dark stage was identified with melancholy ('black bile'), and represented a temporary death to be followed by a resurrection. Jung noted that melancholy might be called 'the head of the raven'.[14] Indeed, it might also be compared to a crow:

> My soul and spirit fast are sinking
> And leave a poison, black and stinking.
> To a black crow am I akin,
> Such be the wages of all sin.[15]

The association of Crow with a transient stage of melancholy is connected to the fact that the book is more than merely an assemblage of blackly humorous tales. It gestures towards the status of myth and presents the outlines of a cyclical development. The most obvious reminder of this fact lies in the number of poems which offer a reworking of Genesis. In this, as in the plan for accompanying illustrations by Leonard Baskin, one can see the influence of Blake, in particular of *The Book of Urizen*.[16] Even so, there appears to be no one version of the myth – at least, not one that could account for all the detail provided: indeed, in this character of existing in different versions, the Crow story may exhibit its postmodernity.[17] Crow also represents Britain, for the Celtic god Bran was associated with the crow.[18] Thus *Crow* also represents a more emphatic formulation of the way in which Hughes's exploration of violent nature had always been undertaken from within a specifically British tradition: for instance, in 'Pike', when the speaker contemplates the frightening depth of the dark pool, he remarks: 'Stilled legendary depth: / It was as deep as England' (*CP* 85). This aspect of *Crow* is an influence on Heaney's Bog

Poems. As for its status as poetry, *Crow* has always evoked doubts in its readers, on grounds such as those advanced by Kevin Hart: '[i]t might be said that the poems try to efface themselves as poems in order to give the impression of anonymous myth or legend. The poetic yield is certainly thin.'[19]

A consideration of *Crow*'s reworking of Genesis is a good way of understanding the sequence as a whole, since the differences from the Bible are so extreme and so starkly eloquent. Thus, 'Lineage' (*CP* 218) opens with the lines 'In the beginning was Scream / Who begat Blood.' Later lines include 'Who begat Adam / Who begat God / Who begat Nothing'. Nothing begat 'Never / Never Never Never' who begat Crow, 'Screaming for Blood / Grubs, crusts / Anything / Trembling featherless elbows in the nest's filth'. God is displaced into a natural process in which he possesses the unique distinction of producing meaninglessness: out of which emerges Crow, the very emblem of the combined absurdity and amorality of the universe. Yet in 'Crow's Theology' (*CP* 227) we discern the outlines of a slightly different version. Here, Crow entertains the idea that there are 'two Gods – One of them much bigger than the other / Loving his enemies / And having all the weapons'. One God is humanity's fantasy of the finer feelings. The other, referred to in the lines quoted, is the amoral life force, and the sense in which he loves his enemies has been explained earlier in the poem: 'Crow realised God loved him – / Otherwise he would have dropped dead.' Not surprisingly, then, the life force sustains life, but the God of Christianity is a different matter altogether.

The outlines of a fundamental myth have more to do with a goddess than a god. For *Crow* hints at a way out of melancholy in terms that Graves would have recognised. A retelling of the story of Oedipus, 'Song for a Phallus' (*CP* 248–50), ends with Crow unsuccessfully attempting matricide. His failure bears witness to the power of the Great Mother, for all that happens is that 'He found himself curled up inside / As if he had never been bore.' The refrain, 'Mamma Mamma', confirms the mother's power. The attempted rejection of the mother, and by extension of woman, is futile and dangerous to humanity, as in 'Revenge Fable' (*CP* 244–5): 'There was a person / Could not get rid of his mother.' So 'he pounded and hacked at her / With numbers and equations and laws / Which he invented and called truth'. He also tries to obliterate her with 'Bulldozers and detergents' and with 'Rifles and whisky and bored sleep'. Thoughts such as these are consistent with Graves's analysis of masculine religions and traditions, not least Judaeo-Christianity, which he claims are founded in fear of the feminine, and which are supposed to have suppressed the cult of the Goddess. Patriarchal religion may lead to the desecration of nature, to arid rationalism, to the glorification of war and to laws which oppress women. Hughes's own interpretation of the archetypal character and actions of the Goddess can be understood from his *Shakespeare and the Goddess of Complete Being*, for he thought that Shakespeare's work provided, in its totality, a detailed exploration of most of the central topics of this supposed myth.[20]

If *Crow* represents the low point of a brief cyclic myth, with only a hint as to the means of recovery, *Gaudete* (1977) is far more explicit about the change of heart which is necessary. Much of the book consists of narrative poems, consecutive sections of an allegorical tale. This is followed by a series of terse, gnomic lyric poems.

The story concerns one Nicholas Lumb, the vicar of a parish in the south of England who, travelling to a Northern industrial town (the very symbol of modern malaise), encounters a beautiful woman who is sick, and whom he must heal. But first he must heal himself. He is required to go through a ritual in which he is tied to an oak, after which both man and oak are flogged, and then he has to kill a bull, though the bullet enters his own head as well as the bull's. Thus he comes to embody in himself the animal and vegetable world of nature, becoming a 'changeling', although he is also giving expression to the repressed side of his original self. In this condition, he fascinates and inflames the women of his parish, but the result is that he elicits the customary resentments and jealousies among both the women and the men. One of these, Major Hagen, sounds like a personification of the most malignant patriarchal tendencies. His 'perfunctory campaign leatheriness' has been 'pickled in mess-alcohol'.[21] His rifle is the 'slender goddess' of his 'devotions', his 'bride' (*G* 24). It is a mechanical and destructive symbol of the phallus, symbolising that his most binding attachment is to a brutalised form of his own sexuality. With this rifle he shoots Lumb (*G* 167). The latter is re-born 'in the west of Ireland, where he roams about composing hymns and psalms to a nameless female deity' (*G* 9).

While this deity may be identified with the White Goddess, it is significant that there are references to Plath: 'You knocked the world off, like a flower-vase. // It was the third time. And it smashed' (*CP* 364; *G* 185–6). (There is a common misconception that Hughes refrained from comment on Plath until he wrote *Birthday Letters* (1998).) The relation of his own experience to the myth of the Goddess shows Hughes convicting himself of error. And indeed, a change of poetic manner is the corollary of this. The violent metaphors and blunt diction of Hughes's early work are clearly involved in the kind of male aggression he now repudiates, just as, at the thematic level, there had been hints of misogyny or disgust: in 'Soliloquy' the speaker predicted that, when buried, he would thank God to be lying beside women 'who grimace / Under the commitments of their flesh, / And not out of spite or vanity' (*CP* 26). In 'Fragment of an Ancient Tablet', from *Crow*, we are presented with an epitome of woman: 'Above – her perfect teeth with a hint of a fang at the corner . . . Above – a word and a sigh. / Below – gouts of blood and babies' (*CP* 254). Stylistically, the lyric poems from the Epilogue to *Gaudete* enact completeness of being, combining passionate personal address and Goddess symbolism with the kind of vivid description at which Hughes had always excelled. At the thematic level, Hughes's work now celebrates the recovery of the right relationship of man and woman, as in *Cave Birds: An Alchemical Cave Drama* (1978), the subtitle of which refers to the alchemical marriage of opposite principles: near the end of the sequence, bride and groom 'bring each other to perfection' (*CP* 438).

In his subsequent development, Hughes never returns to the violently forceful manner of his earlier poems. Those in *Moortown*, for instance, describing life on the farm, are happy to reduce the quantity of metaphor in favour of a more relaxed unfolding of context. The benign concern for nature to be found in these poems suggests that Hughes's work may in future offer material for ecological criticism.[22] When he touches on the matter of Plath, he is capable, precisely because of this less commanding style, of some memorable effects, as in the incomparable 'Black Hair' (*CP* 858), a hitherto uncollected poem from the 1990s, in which he recounts how he had wrongly thought of Plath's brown hair as black, comparing it to the hair of a 'Red Indian': it was also extraordinarily fine, 'So fine I could hardly feel it / As I stroked it through those days she lay / Vanishing under my fingers'. Nor could he see it correctly, of course, until she had indeed vanished in death. The austere irony and pathos of these lines are typical of some of the better poems of Hughes's later years, which, when added to what he had already accomplished in the various manners of his early poems, of *Crow*, and of *Gaudete*, help to consolidate one's sense of the variety, as well as the significance, of Hughes's achievement.

Seamus Heaney's indebtedness to Hughes in his first complete volume, *Death of a Naturalist* (1966), is evident – perhaps nowhere more so than in 'Trout', where the fish 'hangs a fat gun-barrel' and 'darts like a tracer-bullet'.[23] Here, the use of mechanical imagery to describe the violent energy of a beast conveys an unmistakable sense of the debt. It is felt more generally in the harshness or bluntness of the frogs from 'Death of a Naturalist': 'Right down the dam gross-bellied frogs were cocked / On sods . . . The slap and plop were obscene threats. Some sat / Poised like mud-grenades, their blunt heads farting' (*DN* 16). The course of many of the poems in this volume, in conformity with its title, is one in which the speaker recounts his transition from pleasant, often childish, illusions about nature, to an unsentimental recognition of a harshness to which the tough language is appropriate. Alongside Hughes, we must recognise the influence of Patrick Kavanagh upon this attitude, for Heaney's depiction of a rural way of life, with its potato-digging and drowning of surplus kittens, is more conscious of a whole society than is early Hughes. It corresponds to what Heaney himself finds in Kavanagh's works, quoting Kavanagh: 'the usual barbaric life of the Irish country poor'.[24] The comprehensiveness of Heaney's account may also owe something to a less poetic source, namely E. Estyn Evans's *Irish Folk Ways*.[25] The rejection of illusions that might be thought Romantic is, among other things, the rejection of the vision of rural existence to be found in Dylan Thomas, in a poem like 'Fern Hill'. Long after he wrote *Death of a Naturalist*, Heaney reflected, in his lecture 'Dylan the Durable?', on the shortcomings of 'Fern Hill' as a 'poem of loss': he was thinking there of its lack of 'an intonation arising from the "years that bring the philosophic mind"'.[26] Yet in his youth, 'Thomas had gradually come to represent a longed-for, prelapsarian wholeness . . . where the song of the self was effortlessly choral and its scale was a perfect measure and match for the world it sang in.'[27] In *Death of a Naturalist*, Heaney shows the untenability both of the song, and of a world supposed to be matched by it.

Behind Thomas stand Blake and Wordsworth. It was also shrewd of Heaney to detect Blake's influence on Kavanagh.[28] The movement of the poems in *Death of a Naturalist* conforms to a transition from Innocence to Experience. As for Wordsworth, the resonance in Heaney is not merely with the radiant vision, but also with Wordsworth's unsparing depiction of the rigours of the life of country people, in poems such as 'Michael'.[29]

Discussing the influence of the lecturer and critic Philip Hobsbaum on Heaney and other young poets at Queen's University, Belfast, in the 1960s, Blake Morrison remarks that 'it is clear that [Hobsbaum] favoured a poetry that combined the wit and metrical tightness of the Movement with the power and physicality of Ted Hughes, a combination his young Derry protégé achieved only too well'.[30] Yet the comparison with the Movement should not be taken too far: the Movement poets prized not only wit and metrical tightness, but also the development of poetic argument. This has never been predominantly Heaney's way of unfolding complexity. While there are other influences than Hughes, then, Heaney seems far more similar to Hughes than to a Movement poet. Those who would shield the early Heaney from the imputation that he enthusiastically adopted roughness find no support from him, for he freely avows that the influence of Hobsbaum encouraged him to convey the 'bleeding hunk of experience'.[31] Furthermore, Heaney's poems, early and late, tend to be spaces for the exploration of associations within a narrative framework, however tenuous. 'Blackberry Picking' tells the story of how the blackberries the children picked swiftly grow a fur of mould. Heaney's language imparts a dense, descriptive richness to the story of how, on top of the can of blackberries, 'big dark blobs burned / Like a plate of eyes', until, having filled the bath with berries, the children find the mould. But no more than in Hughes is Heaney's descriptiveness to be associated with an uncomplicated notion of objectivity. His nature is part of a human universe, and in the poems of *Death of a Naturalist* we occasionally hear the voice of the discomfited child intrude: the speaker in 'Blackberry Picking', for instance, remarks that 'It wasn't fair / That all the lovely canfuls smelt of rot' (*DN* 20).

Heaney's manner changed in the years between the publication of *Death of a Naturalist* and that of the so-called Bog Poems which appeared in *Wintering Out* (1972) and *North* (1975). In these, and in other poems of the same period, we find a rhythmically looser, short-lined form without capitals at the beginning of lines. It seems that Heaney may have learned from Robert Lowell's comparable formal transformation, in the service of something emotionally direct, in some of the poems from *Life Studies* and *For the Union Dead*. In 1970–1, Heaney was a visiting Professor at the University of California, Berkeley, at a point when Lowell's star was in the ascendant. He later spoke of how Lowell's poetic resources 'proved themselves capable of taking new strains, in both the musical and stressful sense of that word'.[32] After the clotted or hacking consonants of his earlier work, Heaney seems to be trying for something more quietly associative. He thinks of the contrast in gendered terms:

> In the masculine mode, the language functions as a form of address, of assertion and command, and the poetic effort has to do with conscious quelling and control of materials, a labour of shaping; words are not music before they are anything else, nor are they drowsy from their slumber in the unconscious, but athletic, capable, displaying the muscle of sense. Whereas in the feminine mode the language functions more as evocation than address, and the poetic effort is not so much a labour of design as it is an act of divination and revelation; words in the feminine mode behave with the lover's come hither instead of the athlete's display, they constitute a poetry that is delicious as texture before it is recognised as architectonic.[33]

This description does indeed conform with a relative looseness and freedom to be found in these new poems: a languorous caressing of choice words, a relative lack of intrusive figures and alliterative bluntness, a surrender to association: such qualities are to be found in 'Anahorish', from *Wintering Out*, which is about a place near Heaney's boyhood home:

> *Anahorish*, soft gradient
> of consonant, vowel meadow
>
> after-image of lamps
> swung through the yards
> on winter evenings[34]

The Bog Poems themselves consist of a series of ruminative but startling responses to the sight of mummified corpses of Iron Age people exhumed from the Danish bog which had preserved them. They appear to have been the victims of ritual killings, and Heaney had read a study of them, *The Bog People* (1967) by P. V. Glob. Similar mummified corpses had been exhumed from the extensive bogs of Ireland, but the title of *North*, the volume in which some of these poems appear, conveys Heaney's intention to make something of the North European distribution of these bodies. Although it is not known which peoples inhabited Iron Age Denmark, the presence in *North* of a poem about 'Viking Dublin' indicates a reference to Ireland as historically the home of a violent warrior-code comparable to that of the Vikings, and indebted to the many Viking colonies to be found there, though the Viking age is several hundred years later than that of the bog bodies discussed by Glob.[35] More surprising is another connection alluded to in the very title of *North*: Heaney proposes an imaginative parallel between ancient North European violence and that of the Northern Irish Troubles, by the early 1970s in full swing.

The comparison is not permitted to rest at a general level. Thus, going back to *Wintering Out*, Heaney compares the experience of driving around Jutland with being in Northern Ireland, and asserts that out there, 'In the old man-killing parishes / I will feel lost, / Unhappy and at home' (*WO* 48). Whatever one might think about the comparison between Ireland and Jutland (whether in the present or the Iron Age), it does need to be recalled that in Northern Ireland the political affiliation of the neighbouring village through which one was driving could be alien, as well as relevant to one's personal safety. An even closer comparison is developed in 'Punishment', in which Heaney compares the retribution meted out to a young Iron Age woman for adultery (he assumes) with that suffered by young Northern Irish Catholic women who went out with squaddies (*N* 37–8). The latter might be tarred and feathered, and he goes so far as to compare the 'tar-black face' of the Iron Age 'adulteress' to those of the latter-day 'betraying sisters' who are 'cauled in tar'. From the point of view of an objective history, there is little here that convinces. But the Bog Poems insist on their status as subjective interpretation: in 'Punishment', for instance, statements are preceded by 'I can feel' and 'I can see'. This subjective interpretation has aspects which are not immediately apparent from a reading of the poems alone. The connection between Iron Age Denmark and modern Ireland has to do with a cruel, feminine religion:

> You have a society in the Iron Age where there was ritual blood-letting. You have a society where girls' heads were shaved for adultery, you have a religion centring on the territory, on a goddess of the ground and of the land, and associated with sacrifice. Now in many ways the fury of Irish Republicanism is associated with a religion like this, with a female goddess who appeared in various guises. She appears as Cathleen ni Houlihan in Yeats's plays; she appears as Mother Ireland. I think that the republican ethos is a feminine religion, in a way. It seems to me that there are satisfactory imaginative parallels between this religion and time and our own time.[36]

So far, then, we have encountered the feminine twice in this discussion of Heaney: once with 'the lover's come hither', and once in the guise of a goddess of cruel sacrifice. This is Graves's ambivalent goddess interpreted in the light of very specific Irish problems.[37] The cruel goddess is associated with both Celtic and Norse cultures. Yet in a discussion of Hughes, Heaney remarks that 'His consonants are the Norsemen, the Roundheads in the world of his vocables, hacking and hedging and hammering down the abundance and luxury and possible lasciviousness of the vowels.'[38] In 'Traditions', from *Wintering Out*, he describes how the Irish 'guttural muse / was bulled long ago / by the alliterative tradition' (*WO* 31), an idea which makes the Gaelic passive and feminine, and more associated with the 'vocables' which, rising from the back of the throat, contribute to the 'guttural' effect. The Gaelic vowels are 'hacked' by Germanic alliteration. This makes the invasion of Germanic verse, of which Anglo-Saxon alliterative measure is a subsection, an enactment of the larger rape committed on Ireland by England: 'Ralegh has backed the maid to a tree / As Ireland is backed to England' ('Ocean's Love to Ireland', *N* 46). Heaney's feminine religion seems to comprise the opposites of passive and active, Celt and Teuton, male and female, and in this large respect it seems appropriate to Northern Ireland, rather than simply to Ireland. The part of Heaney that imitates Hughes's hacking consonants wishes to identify with the particular Hiberno-English idiom of Northern Ireland rather than with the Irish language: as he says in 'Traditions', 'We are proud / of our Elizabethan English ... we "deem" or we "allow"' (*WO* 31). This is also the side of Heaney that leads him to make the highly regarded translation of *Beowulf* (1999).

Subsequent to *North*, Heaney's treatment of the Troubles is less demonstrative, but often possesses a profound resonance, as in a number of poems from *Field Work* (1979) such as 'The Toome Road' or 'The Strand at Lough Beg (In Memory of Colum McCartney)'. The latter is a melancholy and densely reflective elegy for his cousin, shot in a random sectarian murder. Yet to some extent poems such as this are given their context by the sequence of ten sonnets ('Glanmore Sonnets') in the central pages of the book, where the world of politics and the exigencies of a particular historical period are relegated in favour of the larger context of nature: its rhythms, its unexpected happinesses, the fact of death.[39] This relegation finds a biographical correlative in Heaney's move, in 1977, from Belfast to County Wicklow, near Dublin, and the subject matter is found in the countryside there.

In *Sweeney Astray* (his translation of the medieval romance *Buile Suibhne* ('The Frenzy of Sweeney')), and in the contemporaneous volume *Station Island*, the topic of escaping from the violence of the North is again broached.[40] The hero of *Sweeney Astray*, Sweeney, a king from County Antrim in Ulster, insults St Ronan and is driven into a life of wandering. In his introduction, Heaney refers to 'the quarrel between free creative imagination and the constraints of religious, political and domestic obligation'.[41] The desire for freedom of imagination receives intellectual support in the sequence 'Station Island', from the volume of that name, which is structured around the stages (called 'stations') in the perambulations of pilgrims around the island of St Patrick's Purgatory in Lough Derg. Heaney solicits the comparison of the stages of Dante's *Purgatorio*, and in the final poem the shade of Joyce appears, like the shade of Brunetto Latini, and proffers this advice: 'That subject people stuff is a cod's game ... it's time to swim // out on your own and fill the element / with signatures on your own frequency' (*SI* 93–4).

Nevertheless, there are indications that this removal from a concentration on the North is strange and troubling. 'Away from It All' contrasts a lobster fished from its tank for the consumption of the speaker and his companion with those that were left behind: 'And I still cannot clear my head / of lives in their element ... / and the hampered one, out of water / fortified and bewildered' (*SI* 17). Heaney's removal from Northern Ireland may seem 'fortifiying', but is bewildering and possibly disabling, this poem suggests. On the whole, though, the prospect is optimistic, and is one where the powers of the poet – imaginative, sensitive, verbal – are given pride of place. These powers act through the 'echo soundings, searches, probes' recommended by the shade of Joyce (*SI* 94). This means moving on from the Celtic goddess and her feminine religion, and that, indeed, is what Heaney explicitly does in 'Sheelagh na Gig', also from *Station Island*. A Sheelagh na Gig is an obscene female figure sculpted on early medieval churches in Ireland (where possibly it originated), western England and western France. The one Heaney depicts is at Kilpeck in Herefordshire, near to the Welsh border. It seems fair to assume that the figure derives from a Celtic religious cult, and no doubt Heaney was aware of this possibility. Towards the end of the poem, he describes her as 'grown up, grown ordinary'. She enjoins him to 'look at me to your heart's content / but look at every other thing', and adverts to the other carved figures under the eaves of the church: 'here is a leaper in a kilt, / two figures kissing, // a mouth with sprigs, / a running hart, two fishes' (*SI* 49–50) There is a world out there to be explored by means of the poet's 'echo soundings, searches, probes'.

The dense complexity of the human relationship to the world – the world of people, the world of natural processes – is something that it is the poet's calling to explore on behalf of us all. That complexity is alluded to in the title of a sequence of twelve-line poems from Heaney's 1991 collection, *Seeing Things*. As he explains, 'In the game of marbles, squarings were all those anglings, aimings, feints and squints', those 'Hunkerings, tensings, pressures of the thumb' that were permitted before you would shoot.[42] These 'squarings' sound somewhat like the 'echo soundings' from 'Station Island'. And if there Heaney came face-to-face with the shade of Joyce, here he is inclined to give its due to the notion of the spirit's immortality. As he asks in 'Squarings xxii', 'Where does the spirit live? Inside or outside / Things remembered, made things, things unmade?' (*ST* 78). Could it be that 'a marble bust' is proof of the spirit, being 'perfected form'? (*ST* 78). In 'Squarings xlvi', he asks if music was once proof of God's existence, and replies in a manner that is almost affirmative: 'As long as it admits things beyond measure, / That supposition stands' (*ST* 106). It is this world itself which is the nurse of form and measure, understood in all the complexity that makes a requirement of 'squarings'. Yet measure itself is the very thing that indicates the existence of things beyond measure. Hence the ambiguity in the title *Seeing Things*. The similarity with Yeats's thought is noteworthy. The same ambiguity informs the title of his next collection, *The Spirit Level* (1996). Subsequent work has rendered the question more urgent, in the shadow cast by mortality, but Heaney has never retreated from his high estimate of the worth of balance and 'measure' in the relation between mind and the world; or from a sense that, even if one rejects a literal understanding of the transcendent, its terms are the most cogent ones we have for speaking of that balance. This desired balance can be seen as a resolution of the two apparently contrasting poles of his earlier work: that of the first poems, which enacted a detailed realisation of physical experience, and that of the more exploratory mode which made itself particularly felt in *Wintering Out* and *North*. In reality, both modes were characterised by a tendency to unfold mental associations in detail. Heaney's work after *North* has sought to integrate complexity of association, organised reflection, and compelling realisation of the world of nature. The result has been a meditative and verbally rich poetry of experience.

Notes

1. Roland Mathias, '*Death of a Naturalist*', in *The Art of Seamus Heaney*, fourth edition (Dublin: Wolfhound Press, 2001), pp. 11–26 (pp. 14, 15).
2. Ted Hughes, *Collected Poems*, ed. Paul Keegan (London: Faber, 2003), p. 27. Future references to this edition are given in the text as '*CP*' followed by the page number.
3. Keith Sagar, *The Art of Ted Hughes*, reprint of second edition with updated bibliography (Cambridge: Cambridge University Press, 1980), p. 13.
4. Kingsley Amis, 'Against Romanticism', in *A Case of Samples* (London: Victor Gollancz, 1956), pp. 30–1.
5. Sagar, *The Art of Ted Hughes*, pp. 13–14.
6. Seamus Heaney, 'Dylan the Durable? On Dylan Thomas', in *The Redress of Poetry: Oxford Lectures* (London: Faber, 1996), pp. 124–45 (p. 124).
7. *The Letters of Ted Hughes*, ed. Christopher Reid (London: Faber, 2007), pp. 15, 16, 52, 67.
8. Sagar, *The Art of Ted Hughes*, p. 14; Terry Gifford and Neil Roberts, *Ted Hughes: A Critical Study* (London: Faber, 1981), p. 19.
9. 'Capturing Animals' is a section from Hughes's book *Poetry in the Making* (1970), the whole of which was republished in *Winter Pollen: Occasional Prose* (London: Faber, 1994), p. 10.
10. Edward Larrissy, *Reading Twentieth-Century Poetry: The Language of Gender and Objects* (Oxford: Blackwell, 1990), p. 129.
11. Sagar, *The Art of Ted Hughes*, p. 114.
12. *Ibid*.
13. *Ibid*, p. 113.
14. Stuart Hirschberg, *Myth in the Poetry of Ted Hughes* (Portmarnock: Wolfhound Press, 1981), p. 155.
15. C. G. Jung, *Alchemical Studies* (vol. XIII of *Collected Works*,) ed. and trans. G. Adler and R. F. C. Hull (Princeton: Princeton University Press, 1968), p. 229.

16. See letter to Leonard Baskin, 15 December 1969, in *Letters*, pp. 300–1. For Blake and Hughes see Edward Larrissy, *Blake and Modern Literature* (Basingstoke: Palgrave, 2006), pp. 12–13, 91–2.
17. Larrissy, *Blake and Modern Literature*, pp. 91–3.
18. Sagar, *The Art of Ted Hughes*, p. 106: Sagar refers to 'England', but the myth of Bran forms part of Celtic British tradition predating even the origins of the idea of 'England'.
19. Kevin Hart, 'Varieties of Poetic Sequence: Ted Hughes and Geoffrey Hill', in Neil Corcoran (ed.), *The Cambridge Companion to Twentieth-Century English Poetry* (Cambridge: Cambridge University Press, 2007), pp. 187–99 (p. 192).
20. Ted Hughes, *Shakespeare and the Goddess of Complete Being* (London: Faber, 1992).
21. Ted Hughes, *Gaudete* (London: Faber, 1977), p. 24. Not all the poems in *Gaudete* are reproduced in the *Collected Poems*, so reference will also be made to the original edition. Future references will appear in the text as *G* followed by the page number.
22. See Terry Gifford, 'Laureate of Nature: The Poetry of Ted Hughes', in *Green Voices: Understanding Contemporary Nature Poetry* (Manchester: Manchester University Press, 1995), pp. 114–39. This book also contains a chapter on Heaney.
23. Seamus Heaney, *Death of a Naturalist* (London: Faber, 1966), p. 39. Subsequent references to this volume are given in the text as *DN*, followed by the page number.
24. Seamus Heaney, *Preoccupations: Selected Prose 1968–1978* (London: Faber, 1980), p. 124.
25. E. Estyn Evans, *Irish Folk Ways* (London: Routledge, 1957).
26. Heaney, *Redress of Poetry*, pp. 142, 143.
27. *Ibid.*, p. 133.
28. Heaney, *Preoccupations*, p. 119.
29. On Heaney and Wordsworth, see Hugh Haughton, 'Power and Hiding Places: Wordsworth and Seamus Heaney', in *The Monstrous Debt: Modalities of Romantic Influence in Twentieth-Century Literature*, ed. Damian Walford Davies and Richard Marggraf Turley (Detroit: Wayne State University Press, 2006), pp. 61–100.
30. Blake Morrison, *Seamus Heaney* (London: Methuen, 1982), pp. 29–30.
31. James Randall, 'An Interview with Seamus Heaney', *Ploughshares*, 5:3 (1979), pp. 7–22 (p. 15).
32. Seamus Heaney, *The Government of the Tongue* (London: Faber, 1988), p. 132.
33. Heaney, *Preoccupations*, p. 88.
34. Seamus Heaney, *Wintering Out* (London: Faber, 1972), p. 16. Subsequent references to this volume are given in the text as *WO*, followed by the page number.
35. Seamus Heaney, *North* (London: Faber, 1972), pp. 21–4. Subsequent references to this volume are given in the text as *N*, followed by the page number.
36. Seamus Heaney, 'Mother Ireland', *The Listener*, 7 December 1972, p. 790.
37. Compare Fran Brearton, 'Visions, Goddesses and Bog People: Yeats, Graves and Heaney', in Ian Firla and Grevel Lindop (eds.), *Graves and the Goddess: Essays on*

Robert Graves's 'The White Goddess' (Selinsgrove, PA: Susquehanna University Press; London: Associated University Presses, 2003), pp. 152–65.

38. Heaney, *Preoccupations*, p. 154.
39. Seamus Heaney, *Field Work* (London: Faber, 1979), pp. 15, 17–18, 33–42.
40. Seamus Heaney, *Sweeney Astray* (London: Faber, 1984); Seamus Heaney, *Station Island* (London: Faber, 1984). Subsequent references to the latter are given in the text as *SI*, followed by the page number.
41. Heaney, *Sweeney Astray*, p. iv.
42. Seamus Heaney, *Seeing Things* (London: Faber, 1991), p. 57. Subsequent references to this volume are given in the text as *ST*, followed by the page number.

Chapter 50
Hill

ANDREW MICHAEL ROBERTS

Geoffrey Hill is widely regarded as the greatest English poet of the period 1950 to the present (many would say the greatest English-language poet). This claim rests on a unique range of qualities: the seriousness and intensity of his poetry; its intellectual depth and sensuous vividness; its melding of high thought, evocative description and wry humour; its profound engagement with many of the traditions of English poetry (as well as aspects of European and American poetry); its combination (over nearly sixty years and twelve major volumes) of formal experiment and creative development with continuity of ethical and aesthetic principles. His essays, though less frequently admired and less influential than his poetry, are of a depth, scope and originality to place them in the company of those critical writings of great poets, such as Coleridge and Eliot, which can inform our reading of their poetry, but also of all poetry, by the interaction they exhibit between creative and critical thought. But, above all, Hill's reputation rests on the sheer power of his words. He achieves effects of sublime beauty, of agonising sorrow, of tragic indignation, of complex abstract thought, even of self-mockery, bitterness, reproach, unmatched by any other poet of our age. There are some readers and critics who dislike Hill's poetry, for what they take to be his political or aesthetic stance, or because they regard his poetry as excessively mannered or misanthropic, but his mastery of technique is hard to deny; and, for Hill, technique and ethics are one.

A crucial aspect of Hill's importance as a poet is his seriousness. This does not mean lack of humour: a strong comic vein is a submerged presence in the early work and very evident in the later. Nor does it mean portentousness or self-importance, though these are hostile misreadings to which his seriousness may be liable. Rather it means that Hill regards the poet's responsibility to and for language as a matter of ethical and political import, and regards the poet as, in this sense, not a leader or legislator (he rebukes Pound for this delusion in 'Our Word is our Bond'), but as exemplary (a key word in Hill's ethics).[1] Here is precisely a point where Hill's seriousness can easily be misread. To regard oneself as exemplary might be, in one sense of that word (as in 'I was an exemplary pupil'), the height of smug self-satisfaction. Hill does not mean it in that sense, but rather as implying 'of value as an example' or 'exemplifying with particular intensity' – and this can be exemplification of failure as well as success. Hill's reflexive critique, his self-mocking irony, his willingness (especially in later work such as *Speech! Speech!*), to project an absurd, clowning, persona when the work requires it, means that he 'makes an example of himself' in the punitive, as much as the self-congratulatory, sense:

> Decency, duty,
> fell through the floorboards (*applause*). I cannot
> do more now than gape or grin
> haplessly. On self-advisement I erased
> WE, though I is a shade too painful . . .[2]

The poet's failures are as exemplary as his successes, the two being woven together in the fabric of language. The point is that so much of ethics, politics, justice and injustice, care and cruelty (so much, in sum, of human life), takes place in and through language. The poet is not a legislator, and though he can express ethical and political judgments, his voice is no louder than many other competing voices in contemporary society. His or her special power lies in the depth and rigour of engagement with the material of language, its responsible and irresponsible use, its potential for good or harm. In conversation with Rowan Williams, Hill remarked that 'tyrants need a language drained of its complexities', and it is such simplification that he holds poetry should resist.[3] As he puts it in his recent poem, 'On Reading *Crowds and Power*', 'that which is difficult / preserves democracy; you pay respect / to the intelligence of the citizen'.[4] Poetry is valuable (I take this to be Hill's view) in so far as it uses language with the greatest possible intensity and responsibility (two qualities which obviously risk coming into conflict). In so far as it does this it makes a stand (which has the potential to change at least individual awareness), against the many coercive, simplistic, manipulative, oppressive and dishonest uses of language which afflict contemporary culture. It is this position that gives Hill's work its seriousness.

Hill's poetry is rich in cultural and historical reference, and diverse in the historical periods and aspects of human experience with which it engages. Nevertheless, it is persistently concerned with certain matters: the history of Europe in the twentieth century, in particular the two World Wars; English history more generally; the corruption of language by power, greed, self-interest and indifference; the psychology of political power; the importance and fragility of the 'common weal'; the lives of poets and artists, especially those who have resisted tyranny or otherwise shown exemplary courage and determination; the obligation and debt owed by the living to the dead, and the importance of historical understanding; the obligation to attend to the suffering of others and the impossibility of doing this adequately, at least in words; the psychology of faith and belief, and the struggle between faith and scepticism; the exploration of various forms of Christian sensibility; the beauties of the (primarily English) landscape; the risk of contemporary British life declining into media-dominated triviality, ignorance and callousness; the relationship between culture and barbarism; the envy of music and its transformative power; the vicissitudes of the poetic imagination, its exhilaration and self-hatred, and its roots in childhood experience.

Hill was born in 1932, growing up in rural Worcestershire, the son of a village policeman and descended on his mother's side 'from artisans in the traditional cottage-industry of nail-making'; his parents had both left school at 13.[5] He gained a grammar school place and went on to university, one of an increasing number of children from English working-class backgrounds to follow this path in the 1940s and 1950s. Hill read English at Keble College Oxford and began to attract notice as a poet with a Fantasy Press pamphlet in his final year as an undergraduate. Various aspects of his early life may be noted as of significance for his poetry. The beauties of the English landscape, its mythic qualities and its historical imbrication with the oppressions and conflicts of the English class system, are recurrent presences in his work, notably in *Mercian Hymns*, in 'An Apology for the Revival of Christian Architecture in England' and in *The Orchards of Syon*. Section 62 of *The Orchards of Syon* begins: 'Myth, politics, landscape; with language / seeding and binding them', one of many passages where Hill gives a terse poetic summary of key aspects of his own work.[6] Hill has been much concerned with matters of power and just or unjust authority, and has commented that 'I'm glad and proud of being born into the English working class.'[7] He has spoken of gazing, like A. E. Housman, at the hills of Shropshire and Wales in the distance, and his poetry shares with the (very different) poetry of Housman a powerful concatenation of landscape, memory, longing, loss and elegy.[8] *The Orchards of Syon* in particular contains many powerful and vivid evocations of landscape, scenery and weather. A wartime childhood, described in *Mercian Hymns* ('I loved the battle-anthems and the gregarious news'), clearly played a part in the development of some of Hill's greatest preoccupations: wars, suffering and atrocities (especially of twentieth-century Europe); the debt owed by the living to the dead; the problems of survivors giving credit to those who did not survive.[9] He sang in an Anglican church choir for most of his boyhood, and the Church of England hymnal, the Book of Common Prayer, and musical form and aesthetics more generally, are of importance to his poetry.

Hill's start as a published poet in 1952 coincided with the early days of what was to become 'the Movement', as well as with the fashionability of Empson's poetry. A substantial selection from Hill's first volume, *For the Unfallen* (1959) was included in Alvarez's *The New Poetry* (1962), which sought to champion a 'new seriousness', associated with psychoanalysis and the 'mass evil' of the Holocaust.[10] Seriousness and the horrors of war were indeed to remain central to Hill's poetry, but from the outset he distanced himself from the confessionalism of Lowell and Berryman who, together with Ted Hughes (and in the 1965 edition, Plath and Sexton), were Alvarez's key exhibits. Indeed, Hill's poetry has always had more to differentiate it from that of his contemporaries than it has had in common. It exemplifies, however, Eliot's theory of originality or Harold Bloom's idea of the strong poet, in that Hill's originality is fed by a rich dialogue with many other poets, though not, in general, his contemporaries. The physicality of certain of his metaphors, a muscularity of style and a powerful use of myth led to early comparisons with Ted Hughes and Seamus Heaney. These qualities are very apparent in the first poem of Hill's *Collected Poems*, 'Genesis', which begins with a sort of muscular creativity – 'Against the burly air I strode / Crying the miracles of God' – and goes on to evoke the violence of nature and various mythic creatures such as Leviathan and the phoenix, before asserting that 'There is no bloodless myth will hold.'[11] But Hill's poetry integrates the cerebral and the sensuous where Hughes tends to set them in opposition.[12] Hill does share with Heaney a concern with political violence and the poet's guilt in representing it: Hill's reflexive suspicion of the fascination of violence is evident at least as early as 'The Martyrdom of Saint Sebastian', introducing a relentlessly self-critical edge.[13] But Hill's Christian sense of sin and error as deeply embedded in language itself, so generating a struggle with recalcitrant words, is very different from Heaney's more fluent and discursive self-questioning, and the centrality of direct biographical reference in Heaney's work marks a large distance in aesthetics. Individual affinities, limited in scope, can be noted in Hill's poetry: the suspicion of writing and fascination with English landscape as a record of the past which he shares with Roy Fisher, for example. But during a period when movements, groups and generations were the fashion in mainstream poetry publishing and reviewing, and when the cultural politics of form have been articulated round an opposition of 'mainstream' and 'alternative' poetry, Hill's work has evolved in a manner largely unresponsive to these categories and constructions. He has been notably resistant to fashion and never remotely belonged to any group. As he said in a 1981 interview: 'I've not found that anybody's expectations have led me to qualify or modify my own work.'[14]

Certain key aspects of Hill's aesthetics can be understood in relation to the English poets who are of greatest importance to him, including many of the canonical figures of English poetry. Throughout his career he has maintained his allegiance to Milton's assertion that poetry should be 'simple, sensuous and passionate', and his belief that this requires a unity of intellect and passion, not their separation (a view which connects him to the Metaphysicals, especially, of course, as understood by Eliot).[15] In 1981 he commented that 'Of the Metaphysicals, I believed I most admired Donne, but I was probably more haunted by Vaughan and Herbert.'[16] Hill's affinities to Donne may be seen in his address to metaphysical issues in a language which combines a certain formality with a tone of vigorous speech, as in the following lines from the sonnet sequence, 'Funeral Music':

> If it is without
> Consequence when we vaunt and suffer, or
> If it is not, all echoes are the same
> In such eternity.[17]

Vaughan and Herbert, along with the Spanish Counter-Reformation poetry which inspired 'The Pentecost Castle', and the English recusant sensibility of Robert Southwell and John Dowland (imitated and parodied in 'Lachrimae'), underlie and inform Hill's rich use of paradox, itself a form of cerebration which points beyond the cerebral, and a use of language which evokes what is or might be, 'beyond' words, as when Hill explores the paradoxes of selfhood in 'selfless raptures that are all his own', or evokes the tension of faith and doubt: 'I founder in desire for things unfound. / I stay amid the things that will not stay.'[18] The prevalence of paradox (or lines which give the feel of paradox) frequently reflects this counterpoising of the temporal and the permanent : 'Even now one is amazed / by transience: how it / outlasts us all.'[19] Hill has written about Vaughan's use of paradox and repetition in terms of a 'metaphysical phonetics', and his own use of sound repetition, like Vaughan's, uses such techniques to combine the 'absolute' and 'contingency', as when he revolves a poem reflecting on the deaths of World War I pilots on the multiple meanings of the word 'incredible': [20]

How swiftly they cease to be
incredible
            how incredible
the sudden immortals –[21]

Among the English Romantic poets, Coleridge, Wordsworth and Blake are of particular importance to Hill, and the legacy of Romanticism is one that Hill has both written about in his criticism and written through in his poetry. In a crucial early lecture and chapter, 'Poetry as "Menace" and "Atonement"', he distinguishes between the Romantic elements of his own desire to resist the current of his times, and what he sardonically sees as a fashionable Romanticism of the 1970s, which endowed the poet with a specious vatic connection to 'non-human' 'energies, powers, presences'; a critique which distances him from the neo-Romantic myth-making of Ted Hughes as much as from Charles Olson (who is mentioned).[22] Presumably this, in Hill's view, would be a use of language which sacrificed responsibility for intensity. Hill has criticised ideas of self-expression and spontaneity in poetry as misreadings of Wordsworth's 'Preface' to the *Lyrical Ballads*, adding that 'I distrust any "creative" dogma which regards language as an outmoded hindrance to the freedom of self-expression, a weird obstacle between the strident authorial "personality" and the audience's acquiescent passivity.'[23] And in *Speech! Speech!* he proclaims:

Either the thing moves, RAPMASTER, or it
does not. I disclaim spontaneity,
the appearance of which is power.[24]

The enjambment ('it / does not') recalls the much-debated enjambment of 'September Song' ('it / is true').[25] But where the latter figures an epistemological and ethical *mise en abyme* (simultaneously asserting and revoking the truth of the elegy in which it occurs), the effect in *Speech! Speech!* is one of mimetic hesitation in rhythm, producing emphatic, polemical stresses (particularly on 'not'). Early Hill can be evidently Wordsworthian: the ending of 'Genesis' would surely not have been written without the Lucy poems: 'Though Earth has rolled beneath her weight / The bones that cannot bear the light.'[26] Many of his comments on Romantic poets focus on semantic effects which are also social and ethical acts. One such is Wordsworth's expressive shift of rhythm from stanzas 8 to 9 of the 'Immortality' ode, a formal 'break' which represents 'a resistance [to social and conventional pressures] proclaimed', showing that rhythm is 'capable of registering, mimetically, deep shocks of recognition'.[27] Another is Keats's shift on 'forlorn' from the penultimate to the final stanza of 'Ode to a Nightingale', which for

Hill shows the discovery within language of the risks of a drift from actuality towards mere 'expansive gesture', and a return upon and revocation of that risk, so that 'what is revoked is an attitude towards art and within art'.[28] Hill produces a technically comparable effect in 'Funeral Music', where a line which is metaphorical at the end of the fourth sonnet is repeated with a literal meaning at the start of the fifth sonnet. This self-critical strain within Romanticism is one which Hill has associated more generally with Coleridge, who is particularly important for his sense of the ethical responsibilities of the poet. A powerful and persistent anxiety in Hill's work, about the ethical risks attendant upon aesthetic pleasure, has been more than once referred by Hill himself to a phrase in Coleridge's notebooks ('Poetry – excites us to artificial feelings – makes us callous to real ones').[29] Coleridge is also an important influence on Hill's sense of the corruption of language in a corrupt society, the pressures this imposes on the poet (Hill has quoted Coleridge's dictum, 'our chains rattle, even while we are complaining of them') and the need for the redeeming power of the secondary imagination.[30] Hill has written of the primary imagination as 'an ideal democratic birthright' of which 'the majority is deprived . . . in exchange for a mess of euphoric trivia', so that 'the secondary imagination, the formal creative faculty, must awaken the minds of men to their lost heritage . . . of perception'.[31] Hill's reading of Romanticism is, then, as a self-critical spirit. Its lessons for his own poetry are everywhere apparent in his technique of mimetically inhabiting or performing social, historical and psychological conditions (sentimentality, cruelty, voyeurism, the trivial cacophony of media), so as to critique them from within; indeed, simultaneously to discover and critique them within language: 'that obsessive self-critical Romantic monologue in which eloquence and guilt are intertwined'.[32] In the early work this takes place particularly through double meanings, where one undercuts another: an example which Hill has analysed himself is the phrase 'Our God scatters corruption', from 'Annunciations'.[33] In the later work the crucial technique is ironic performance: self-interruptions, humorous asides and elaborately staged mock debates with real or imagined enemies and friends within and outside the self of the poetic persona.

Of the Modernist poets, it is Eliot with whom Hill has the most obvious affinities: a concern with history, especially English history; the sense of living in a corrupt society; a strongly Christian imagination; a longing for transcendence and a fascination with music and silence; ironic treatment of the self in poetry. The last of these is connected with a certain allegiance that Hill has maintained to Eliot's idea of impersonality in poetry, though from the first he sought to modify Eliot's terms (suggesting that Eliot's 'escape from personality' should be read as 'transcendence of personality'), and since 2000 he has explicitly revised his view of the place of the self in poetry, abandoning his early view that the 'objective' and the 'subjective' are completely incompatible in poetry, in line with what he now sees as 'the qualifications that Eliot himself would have entered'.[34] Hill however has also explicitly measured his distance from Eliot, and particularly the late Eliot, on various occasions. As early as 1977, stigmatising the language of the post-war verse-plays as 'aloof and ingratiating, unambiguous yet ambivalent', Hill wrote of the need for the poet, '[a]s Eliot well knew', to 'turn back' from the lure of music and silence to the wrestle with words.[35] More recently Hill has been sharply critical of the language of *Four Quartets*, arguing that 'Eliot's poetry declines over thirty years from pitch into tone', where pitch (as in 'Prufrock') signifies a properly poetic intensity of linguistic pressure, a heuristic ambiguity, as against the complacent vagueness or complicity with cliché characterising 'tone'.[36] In Hill's own poetry, the elusive protagonist of 'The Songbook of Sebastian Arrurruz' has obvious affinities with the ironic, self-conscious personae of the *Prufrock* volume, though Pound's 'Hugh Selwyn Mauberley' is also an influence. Pound is important for Hill's sense of the corruption of language, and the idea of dogged resistance to what '[t]he age demanded'.[37] Indeed, Hill has drawn on the range of Modernist strategies for complicating and questioning the self. The word-play and mythic doubling in *Mercian Hymns* has Joycian elements as well as recalling the Yeatsian antithetical mask, and Yeats's use of the mask for a dramatised dialogue of self and other may contribute, along with the belligerence and divided self of Berryman's persona in *Dream Songs*, to the self-mocking performative personae of the poet in *Speech! Speech!*, a volume whose cacophony of fragmented voices also owes something to *The Waste Land*, though its final destination is not 'peace' (Eliot's 'Shantih shantih shantih'), but self-obliteration: 'At least pass me the oxygen. Too late. / AMOR. MAN IN A COMA, MA'AM. NEMO. AMEN.'[38] Yeats's rhetorical power is an influence on Hill, though one he views with caution: as he comments in relation to 'The Circus Animals' Desertion': 'How is it possible . . . to revoke "masterful images" in images that are themselves masterful?'[39] Hill indeed attempts a masterful parody of Yeatsian rhythms in 'Quaint Mazes', ending his first stanza on 'those muddy-hued and midge-tormented ghosts': the comic echo of Yeats's 'Byzantium' ('That dolphin-torn, that gong-tormented sea'[40]), is acknowledgment both of debt and of distance.[41] Elements of black and scatological humour connect Hill to Swift; a bitter satirical vein to Pope; and a strain of the prophetic to Blake. His poetic influences are many, and include French, German, Spanish and Eastern European poets, as well as American poets.

An understanding of creative processes and critical debates in terms of the language of Christian theology is a strong link to Hopkins, as also is the use of rhythm and stress (including stress marks borrowed from Hopkins's sprung rhythm) in *Speech! Speech!* in particular. The Bible and Christian liturgy are pervasive influences in Hill's work (his *Collected Critical Writings* even includes a separate *Index of Biblical Passages*). The grandeur and simplicity of Hill's early poetry surely owes much to the King James Bible: 'So with sweet oaths converting the salt earth / To yield, our fathers verged on Paradise'; 'Do words make up the majesty / Of man, and his justice / Between the stones and the void?'[42] The work of theologians such as Karl Barth and T. H. Green has been important to aspects of his thought about the ethics of writing. Hill's has a fundamentally Christian sensibility, in that his thought works through the main Christian paradigms, such as the Fall, the Resurrection, redemption and grace: it is not just that he writes about these concepts, but that he thinks with them. This has been the case throughout his career, even while his overt statements in relation to the Christian faith have moved from a certain tortured hesitation towards more definite affirmation. In 1981 he commented that 'I would not wish to describe myself as an agnostic', proposing instead, as a description of 'the area in which my poetry moves' the formulation 'a heretic's dream of salvation expressed in the images of the orthodoxy from which he is excommunicate'.[43] In a 1998 lecture, however, he simply referred to himself as 'a Christian'.[44] Central to his understanding, I take it, is that sin (and the Fall, or original sin) remain crucial concepts in history, politics and sociology as much as ethics, a position which sets him apart from much contemporary thought which is implicitly or explicitly scientific, post-Christian humanist, or postmodern. Whether one regards this as a strength or weakness in Hill's thought will depend to a great extent on one's own views. What can be said is that, in an age in which faith and the intellect often find themselves at odds, because of the growth of anti-rational fundamentalism, Hill remains a serious and deep thinker in the traditions of intellectual Christian theology. Gravity, or weight, as a metaphor for sin and its effects, has been a persistent thread in Hill's poetry and prose, with Karl Barth's theology and Simone Weil's *Gravity and Grace* being important influences. Hill's stress is, as ever, on language, so that in 'Poetry as "Menace" and "Atonement"' he links 'the "density" of language', with which the poet must grapple in the act of writing, with the 'specific gravity of human nature as such' (Barth's description of sin).[45] Fourteen years later he writes, with a combination of assertion and caution, that 'I cannot myself see any way of escaping complete assertion to the doctrine of original sin, which, in the contexture of this argument, may be understood as no more and no less than "the imperfection which marks all human effort, especially where it aims to avoid it".'[46] Music and painting are clearly of great importance to Hill, formally and conceptually. The earlier poetry, in particular, is full of musical titles, allusions and influences. 'Locust Songs', 'September Song', 'Funeral Music', 'The Songbook of Sebastian Arrurruz', *Mercian Hymns* and 'Two Chorale-Preludes' all have music in their titles (indeed, Hill describes 'Funeral Music' as 'ornate and heartless music punctuated by mutterings, blasphemies and cries for help').[47] The poems of *Tenebrae* draw extensively on musical models: 'Lachrimae' on Dowland's composition of the same title and 'The Pentecost Castle' on variations on a folk tune by Antonio de Cabezón.[48] In 1981 he spoke of his 'Schopenhauerian and Nietzschean' feelings about music, his 'envy of the composer', because of the sensuous possibilities of music and its 'iconic presence' when performed.[49] *Scenes from Comus* represents a more extended thematic use of music, with Hill's work alluding to Hugh Wood's symphonic composition of the same title, 'Scenes from Comus: Op. 6', which in turn is inspired by, but also subverts, Milton's masque.[50] He has written a number of powerful poems about painting and painters, including 'A Pre-Raphaelite Notebook' and 'Terribilis est Locus Iste: Gauguin and the Pont-Aven School' and in 'In Ipsley Church Lane' 1, writes that 'More than ever I see through painters' eyes' – a claim borne out by the detailed visual evocation, especially of the effects of light and weather, of which his poetry is capable.[51] In a BBC Radio programme he spoke about the powerful impact upon him of the Gauguin painting, *The Vision after the Sermon*, a detail of which was chosen for the cover of his 1985 *Collected Poems*.[52] Hill's influences and intertexts are highly diverse. He has alluded to the choreography of Mark Morris (with whom Hill's wife, an opera librettist, has worked), as a formal influence: 'Morris is like Dryden in the way he can move rapidly from broad satire to pointed farce to tragic resonance and back.'[53] Equally, though, film, television and radio have emerged recently as strong aesthetic influences, particularly in the later work. Hill has acknowledged film as a likely formal influence, and in his most staccato work, *Speech! Speech!* writes of 'That caught-short trot-pace of early film', asking 'did minds / adjust automatically then?'[54] This in part repeats an effect he used earlier, in *The Mystery of the Charity of Charles Péguy*, where the technical and aesthetic qualities of the film medium acquire metaphorical force in relation to history as itself imbricated with representation:

> Violent contrariety of men and days; calm
> juddery bombardment of a silent film
>
> . . .

> The brisk celluloid clatters through the gate;
> the cortège of the century dances in the street;
> and over and over the jolly cartoon
> armies of France go reeling towards Verdun.[55]

The nature and significance of the self or personality has been one of Hill's main grounds of contention with the poetry and culture of his time. Hill's critique of 'self-expression' has many points of contact with the critique of 'voice' in Language poetry (such as Charles Bernstein or Bob Perelman) and British 'linguistically-innovative' poetry (such as Tom Raworth or Denise Riley), though Hill addresses the issue in ethical-aesthetic rather than political-aesthetic terms. Hill's understanding of the appropriate role of the self in poetry is central to many aspects of his poetic technique, as it is to many of his critical arguments. It is also a focal point for various stages in the development of his poetry. In both technique and critical stance there is a certain shift from an early allegiance to impersonality in poetry to a later acceptance of a more explicit role for the self. However, the underlying aesthetic stance evolves rather than changes, and is based on a series of distinctions between forms or conceptions of the self which have real value in poetry and in thought (sometimes referred to by Hill as 'selfhood'), in that they engage in a mutual process of shaping and discovery with language; and forms or conceptions of selfhood which are commodified, clichéd, naively self-congratulatory, or subordinate to the demands of public performance, social convention or literary fashion (of which the television 'personality' might stand as the epitome). As Hill puts it succinctly in his 1981 interview: '[t]he crux of the matter turns upon creative expression of personality versus commodity exploitation of personality'.[56] Generally, though, he is hostile to the whole concept of 'expression', arguing that '[s]elfhood is more vital, recalcitrant, abiding, than self-expression' and that '[a] great deal of the [bad poetic] work of the last forty years seems to me to spring from inadequate knowledge and self-knowledge, a naïve trust in the unchallengeable authority of the authentic self'.[57] The precise terminology is clearly not the real point; the real point for Hill is that selfhood is complex and elusive; it is something we discover with difficulty (and which the poet, in particular, discovers in his or her struggle with language); it should not be treated as a commodity. As in so much of Hill's poetics and ethics, the insistence on language is crucial.

The first few poems of *For the Unfallen* include some rather chilly, distanced forms of the poetic 'I': as prophetic poet in 'Genesis', and 'Merlin', or as anonymous soul struggling for Christian redemption in 'God's Little Mountain' and 'The Bidden Guest'.[58] But much of that volume and the next, *King Log*, inscribes no version of the self whatever, creating an autonomous linguistic structure, a condensate of historical experience. However, from the time of 'The Songbook of Sebastian Arrurruz' Hill experiments with forms of persona, mask or double, as ways of alienating the self from spurious or complacent centrality: the bracketed 'I' of 'September Song', the child-poet doubled with eighth-century tyrant in *Mercian Hymns*; the exploration of the poetic vocation and sensibility via the celebration, commemoration or translation of the work of other poets: *The Mystery of the Charity of Charles Péguy*, 'Two Chorale-Preludes', and other poems. *Canaan* in certain ways returns to the historical perspectives of *For the Unfallen*: there are some relatively personal poems, such as 'Pisgah' (a memory of Hill's father), but the dominant modes are philosophical, historical and satirical, and the pronoun is as likely to be an impersonal 'one' or a collective 'you/we/us' as 'I': 'One sees again how it goes'; 'You foretold us, hazarding the proscribed tongue / of piety and shame.'[59] Publicity for *The Orchards of Syon* described it as the fourth and final part of 'a single great poem, a kind of high-modernist Divine Comedy', comprising *Canaan*, *The Triumph of Love*, *Speech! Speech!* and *The Orchards of Syon*. However, the crucial shift seems to come rather with *The Triumph of Love*, which both inaugurates a series of book-length poems (continuing into *Scenes from Comus*), and handles matters of the personal, the autobiographical and the self in a wholly new way, which those following volumes develop and refine. In these later volumes, especially *The Triumph of Love* and *Speech! Speech!*, an element of performance becomes significant, as Hill deploys a shifting, ironic persona to engage in polemical battles and ironic banter with imagined interlocutors, including imagined critics and readers. The title of his second collection of essays, *The Enemy's Country*, and the cover image of *Speech! Speech!* (a caricatured audience credulously applauding), suggest something of his sense of the public and literary realm as a place marred by aggressive hostility and specious enthusiasm. In *The Triumph of Love*, those who might see Hill as a 'Shameless old man, bent on committing / more public nuisance', or a 'Rancorous, narcissistic old sod' are met with a corresponding defiance: 'And yes – bugger you, MacSikker et al., – I do / mourn and resent your desolation of learning.'[60] In *Speech! Speech!* Hill's persona engages in a prolonged verbal battle with a 'Rapmaster' who represents the voice of hostile criticism but also commodified contemporary culture. This performative element complicates the question of the role of the self in Hill's poetry. In a 2000 lecture subsequently published as the first part of *Alienated Majesty*, Hill discusses nineteenth-century American thinkers, particularly Emerson, William James and Josiah Royce, and seeks to distinguish rigorous thinking, which may include 'self-apprehension' and 'attentive self-scrutiny', from a portentous, vacuous or lazy rhetoric of public performance: a 'public self-awareness', which is part of a 'professional personality', or a 'cultural personality'.[61] Yet Hill's persona in *The Triumph of Love* and *Speech! Speech!* makes a public performance of 'self-awareness'. However, it is done with a parodic, self-mocking stance, and therefore continues in a new form the technique which Hill employed to explore political cruelty in *Mercian Hymns* and national sentimentality in 'An Apology'; a technique of inhabiting that which is subject to analysis and critique to produce what might be termed an internalised critique. It is, indeed, something more than a technique: it is something approaching a philosophy of both criticism and poetry, one which Hill has described, in the words of F. H. Bradley, as the imperative to 'get within the judgement the condition of the judgement' – achieving a form of objectivity, not through attempting to stand outside the subject, but through a full acknowledgment that 'the theorist [and the poet] is . . . part of the world he examines'.[62]

The importance of the past and memory is a central theme of Hill's work. He has frequently argued for the centrality of a sense of the past as a 'vital dimension of intelligence', stressed the ethical importance of acknowledging our debt to the dead and criticised contemporary Britain as 'a nation / with so many memorials but no memory'.[63] He is also a powerfully evocative poet of personal memory, with a poignancy reminiscent at times of Hardy, and as with Hardy, the emotional intensity of his attachment to the past creates a play of presence and absence, a chasm of death and loss across which the memory and imagination seek to make connections, or find connections gripping them unsought.

> Dear one, be told
> you chose impenetrable absence; I became
> commonplace fantasy's
> life-sentenced ghost.[64]

The Mystery of the Charity of Charles Péguy, in the course of paying tribute to the Catholic socialist French poet killed at the Battle of the Marne in 1914, articulates a sense of the absurdity and horror of history, with its seemingly meaningless repetitions of violent conflict. History is personified as 'supreme clown, dire tragedian', who

> commands the stage wielding a toy gun,
> rehearsing another scene. It has raged so before,
> countless times; and will do, countless times more.[65]

The emotional power of memory, refracted through Péguy's mystical invocation of an ideal France, here has ambivalent political and epistemological status. Arguably exploring at one remove his own ambivalence about English landscape and its ideological representations in the discourse of national identity, Hill uses his lyrical gifts and a subtle note of parody to evoke a 'dream of France' which is at once a genuine utopian ideal and a dangerous nationalistic fantasy:

> three sides of a courtyard where the bees thrum
> in the crimped hedges and the pigeons flirt
> and paddle, and sunlight pierces the heart-
>
> shaped shutter-patterns in the afternoon,
> shadows of fleur-de-lys on the stone floors.[66]

The mannered stanza enjambment of 'heart- / shaped' flirts with but then refuses the kitsch poignancy of sunlight which 'pierces the heart'. Delicately poised between evocation and parody, Hill's poem seeks to diagnose pastoral sentimentality by inhabiting its language with a self-critical edge of parody. Hill's response to the mysterious power and unavailability of the past is finally to return to language, to the poet's responsibility to language as a form of witness to history: flawed, ambiguous but necessary. The final line of *Péguy*, registering the inevitable intertextuality of language by being in quotation marks, reads 'in memory of those things these words were born', reminding us that words too have a life history.[67]

Hill's poetry moves between formality and informality, between complexity and simplicity, between enigma and directness of utterance. These seemingly opposed pairs are intimately connected in his understanding of language as an ethical and political phenomenon. In response to the pressures which power, corruption and commodification place on language, the poet seeks to use poetic form to place words under corresponding, resistant pressure (semantic, aesthetic and ethical), to wrest back some control from 'this heaviness which is simultaneously the "density" of language and the "specific gravity of human nature" ', to maintain a quest for poetic truth amidst the multiple threats of 'The Enemy's Country'.[68] Form and formality are the means of creating this pressure; complexity and enigma are some of the costs imposed by the process; simple, direct utterance is the prize which it at times attains, since in the face of the corruption of language, simplicity can only speak in a space briefly cleared for it by the wrestle with dense, 'compacted' material: 'That I mean what I say | saying it obscurely'; 'I'm wresting myself into simplicity.'[69] Hill's formality has included virtuoso handling of poetic form itself: sonnets, sonnet sequences, prose poems (*Mercian Hymns*), visual poetry (particularly in *Canaan*), dramatic monologues, the brief lyric and the book-length sequence. The combination of the formal and the informal at times joins with a seemingly casual allusiveness to give the impression of a shared familiarity with historical material, as when a line in the sonnet sequence 'Funeral Music' refers to the Wars of the Roses: 'Oh, that old northern business'.[70] Such use of deictics is frequent: 'This not quite knowing what the earth requires'; 'This our egregious masking – what it entails'.[71] This is one among a number of persistent stylistic features of the poetry which can be identified. Another is reflexive comments, whether self-exhortations or self-criticisms, expressive of a certain mannered self-consciousness. In earlier work these comments often express anxiety, guilt or failure: 'This is plenty. This is more than enough'; 'The dead keep their sealed lives / And again I am too late.'[72] In more recent work defiance and wry self-mocking humour are more to the fore: 'Some believe / we over-employ our gifts'; 'Right, one more time!'; 'Hazardous but press on. Enjambment / drags'; 'I know that sounds / a damn-fool thing to say.'[73] The interjected question, appeal or comment to the reader or imagined interlocutor has become frequent: 'Now / move to the next section'; 'As to whether there persists – enlighten me / – a dialectic'; 'Quiet – I'm still trying'; 'ask me to explain'.[74] Often the poetry combines abstract and sensuous registers, juxtaposing philosophical (or theological) language with physicality of image and a vividly evoked sensuous world. Double layers of meaning recur, often in ironic relation to each other, and word-play, punning and sound resemblances are used to open up issues of meaning and fine distinction. A play on semantic distinctions and the etymological significance of words ('by definition // not by default') can at times take a comic form: 'give the old / bugger a shove / gentleman a shout'.[75] Apposition, in a broad sense of that term, is a persistent feature of Hill's poetic structure. This can include informal, fragmentary note-like discourse:

> Need to see proof that P. slid Coriolanus
> through to Italia; whether he admired him.
> If hated, for what reason or whatever
> runs off the track of reason. He was a *Lear* man
> (I do know that) possibly thanks to Melville.[76]

But it also extends to fluid lyric utterance:

> Two nights' and three days' rain, with the Hodder
> well up, over its alder roots; tumblings
> of shaly late storm light; the despised

ragwort, luminous, standing out,
stereoscopically, across twenty yards,
on the farther bank.[77]

Appositional structures or series of fragments extend from startling juxtapositions at the level of the clause to a collage-like structure of disparate sections in the long sequences of *The Triumph of Love*, *Speech! Speech!*, *The Orchards of Syon* and *Scenes from Comus*.

There is a strong strain of irony in Hill's poetry, especially in the often humorous reflexive connotations of his lines. To start his *Collected Poems* with a poem entitled 'Genesis' I take to be more irony than hubris; it is more evidently self-mocking irony to interrupt the first lines of *Speech! Speech!* with the tabloid-headline language of the 'PEOPLE' declaring his project a 'non-starter'.[78] A poignant tragic irony ends 'Funeral Music', a masterful sequence of blank verse sonnets imagining the world-view, beliefs, doubts, resolution, suffering, humanity and longing of knights engaged in the Wars of the Roses:

If it is without
Consequence when we vaunt and suffer, or
If it is not, all echoes are the same
In such eternity. Then tell me, love,
How that should comfort us – or anyone
Dragged half-unnerved out of this worldly place,
Crying to the end 'I have not finished'.[79]

Hill's mastery of the power of Shakespearean blank verse draws contemporary relevance here from his ability (which is also a Shakespearean ability) to conjoin the rhetoric of the heroic with the sense of the rhythms of human thought and human voice. The grandiloquence of the first two lines quoted is subtly inflected by a note of hesitation, introduced by the enjambment between 'without' and 'Consequence', which also allows the other sense of 'without' (as outside) to flicker across the lines. The accomplished variation of the iambic line – the dactylic 'Consequence', the trochee of 'If it', the strong spondees of 'Dragged half' and especially the first two syllables of 'have not finished' – provide a classic syncopation of metrical effect and semantic emphasis. 'Then tell me, love' flickers between an appeal to a lover and an apostrophe to the spirit of love itself. The phrase 'or anyone' suddenly widens the meditation to include twentieth- (or indeed twenty-first) century readers as well as fifteenth-century noblemen, and Hill somehow brings off the feat of a reflexive meaning (the sequence ends but is 'not finished') which does not detract from the poignancy of the phrase as the final thoughts or words of a dying man. Here, as so often in Hill's poetry, the inaccessibility of plenitude of experience (in this case the impossibility of conveying in language the reality of death) becomes a source of meaning in itself.

Since this is a history of English poetry, it may be fitting to end by moving from Hill's feat of historical imagination in 'Funeral Music' to his continued belief that poetry can, with whatever difficulty, transcend historical circumstances. A passage near the conclusion of Hill's monumental 2008 *Collected Critical Writings* brings together many key aspects of his thought as a poet, as well as a critic, including a belief in poetic truth, allegiance to a strong but not dependent relationship between poetry and history, a complex sense of self and otherness (here explored through the concept of 'alienation'), and a troubled sense of the condition of the poet:

> the poem – the true poem, the poem that has got within its judgement the condition of the judgement – is not exhausted by the uses to which it is put; it is alienated from its existence as historical event. This intolerable condition, rejected, may lead a poet to a political aesthetics; embraced, to an apolitical one; these twin betrayals . . . haunt modernist poetics.[80]

While developing in new and startling ways, Hill's poetry continues to assert and exemplify 'the authority of the right, true poem', yet always in productive contention with 'the imperfection which marks all human effort'.[81]

Notes

1. Geoffrey Hill, *Collected Critical Writings*, ed. Kenneth Haynes (Oxford: Oxford University Press, 2008), pp. 146–69.
2. Hill, *Speech! Speech!* (Washington, DC: Counterpoint, 2000), p. 3.
3. 'Geoffrey Hill in Conversation with Dr Rowan Williams, Archbishop of Canterbury', Geoffrey Hill and his Contexts, conference held at Keble College, Oxford, 2–3 July 2008.
4. Hill, *A Treatise of Civil Power* (London: Penguin, 2007), p. 47.
5. Interview with John Haffenden, *Quarto*, 15 (March 1981), pp. 19–22, reprinted in *Viewpoints: Poets in Conversation with John Haffenden* (London: Faber and Faber, 1981), pp. 76–99 (pp. 76, 77).
6. *The Orchards of Syon* (Washington, DC: Counterpoint, 2002), p. 62.
7. 'The Art of Poetry', Geoffrey Hill interviewed by Carl Phillips, *The Paris Review*, 154 (Spring 2000), pp. 272–99 (p. 298).
8. *Viewpoints*, p. 80.

9. *Mercian Hymns* (London: André Deutsch, 1971), n.p. (section XXII).
10. *For the Unfallen* (London: André Deutsch, 1959); *The New Poetry*, ed. A. Alvarez (1962; revised edition, Harmondsworth: Penguin, 1966), pp. 28, 27.
11. 'Genesis', in *Collected Poems* (Harmondsworth: Penguin, 1985), pp. 15–16.
12. See Martin Dodsworth, 'Ted Hughes and Geoffrey Hill: An Antithesis', in Boris Ford (ed.), *The New Pelican Guide to English Literature* (Penguin: Harmondsworth, 1982–8), vol. VIII: *The Present* (1983), pp. 281–93.
13. Section VI of 'Of Commerce and Society', in *For the Unfallen*, p. 53.
14. *Viewpoints*, p. 81.
15. 'Poetry as "Menace" and "Atonement"', in *The Lords of Limit: Essays on Literature and Ideas* (London: André Deutsch, 1984), p. 1; *Viewpoints*, p. 80.
16. *Viewpoints*, p. 79.
17. *King Log* (London: André Deutsch, 1968), p. 32.
18. 'Damon's Lament for his Clorinda, Yorkshire 1654', section 2 of 'An Apology for the Revival of Christian Architecture in England'; 'Pavana Dolorosa', section 5 of 'Lachrimae or Seven tears figured in seven passionate Pavans', in *Tenebrae* (London: André Deutsch, 1978), pp. 23, 19.
19. 'Scenes with Harlequins', *Canaan* (London: Penguin, 1996), p. 20.
20. *Critical Writings*, pp. 323–7, 326.
21. 'To the Nieuport Scout', in *Canaan*, p. 27.
22. *Critical Writings*, p. 17.
23. A Sermon Delivered at Great St Mary's University Church, Cambridge, 8 May 1983, p. 1.
24. *Speech! Speech!*, p. 46.
25. 'September Song', in *King Log*, p. 19.
26. 'Genesis', in *For the Unfallen*, p. 17.
27. *Critical Writings*, p. 91.
28. *Ibid.*, p. 7.
29. *Ibid.*, p. 5.
30. *Ibid.*, p. 151.
31. *Ibid.*, p. 101.
32. *Ibid.*, p. 5.
33. *King Log*, p. 15. For Hill's commentary, see Kenneth Allott (ed.), *The Penguin Book of Contemporary Verse*, second edition (Harmondsworth: Penguin, 1962), pp. 391–3.
34. *Viewpoints*, p. 87; 'The Art of Poetry', p. 282.
35. *Critical Writings*, p. 11.
36. *Ibid.*, p. 377.
37. Ezra Pound, *Hugh Selwyn Mauberley*, in *Collected Shorter Poems* (London: Faber, 1968), p. 188.
38. *Speech! Speech!*, p. 60.
39. *Critical Writings*, p. 5.
40. *Yeats's Poems*, ed. A. Norman Jeffares, revised edition (London and Basingstoke: Macmillan, 1991), p. 364.

41. 'An Apology for the Revival of Christian Architecture in England', in *Tenebrae*, p. 22.
42. 'Locust Songs', 'Three Baroque Meditations', in *King Log*, pp. 16, 46.
43. *Viewpoints*, p. 98.
44. *Critical Writings*, p. 401.
45. *Ibid.*, p. 17.
46. *Ibid.*, p. 362.
47. *King Log*, pp. 16, 19, 51–63; *Tenebrae*, p. 35; 'Funeral Music: An Essay', in *King Log*, pp. 67–8.
48. *Viewpoints*, pp. 91–2.
49. *Ibid.*, p. 91.
50. *Scenes from Comus* (London: Penguin, 2005).
51. *Tenebrae*, pp. 37, 38; *Without Title* (London: Penguin, 2006), p. 6.
52. 'Postscript: Picturing the Word', BBC Radio 3, 18 August 1999.
53. 'The Art of Poetry', p. 296.
54. *Ibid.*, pp. 285–6; *Speech! Speech!*, p. 17.
55. *The Mystery of The Charity of Charles Péguy* (London: Agenda Editions and André Deutsch, 1983), p. 10.
56. *Viewpoints*, p. 87.
57. Sermon, p. 2; 'The Art of Poetry', pp. 282–3.
58. *For the Unfallen*, pp. 15–17, 20, 18, 21.
59. 'Pisgah', 'Of Constancy and Measure', 'De Jure Belli Ac Pacis', in *Canaan*, p. 52, 68, 32.
60. *The Triumph of Love* (Harmondsworth: Penguin, 1999), pp. 19, 20, 63.
61. *Critical Writings*, pp. 493, 501, 493, 496, 497.
62. *Ibid.*, pp. 561 and 562, quoting F. H. Bradley and William Empson.
63. 'Under Judgment': interview with Blake Morrison, *The New Statesman*, 8 February 1980, pp. 212–14 (p. 213); *The Triumph of Love*, p. 40.
64. *The Orchards of Syon*, p. 65.
65. *Péguy*, p. 9.
66. *Ibid.*, p. 12.
67. *Ibid.*, p. 28.
68. *Critical Writings*, pp. 17, 171.
69. *Scenes From Comus*, pp. 9, 11.
70. *King Log*, p. 27
71. 'Citations I', in *A Treatise of Civil Power*, p. 2; *Scenes From Comus*, p. 18.
72. 'September Song', in *King Log*, p. 19; 'Tristia: 1891–1938: A Valediction to Osip Mandelshtam', in *King Log*, p. 38.
73. *Speech! Speech!*, p. 1; *The Orchards of Syon*, p. 70; 'Ars', in *Without Title*, p. 62; 'Coda', in *A Treatise of Civil Power*, p. 50.
74. *The Triumph of Love*, p. 10; 'Discourse: For Stanley Rosen', in *Without Title*, p. 25; *Scenes From Comus*, pp. 31, 6.
75. *Scenes From Comus*, p. 11; *The Triumph of Love*, p. 38.
76. *Without Title*, p. 51.

77. *The Orchards of Syon*, p. 20.
78. *Speech! Speech!*, p. 1.
79. *King Log*, p. 32.
80. *Critical Writings*, p. 580.
81. Interview with Hermione Lee, *Book Four*, 2 October 1985, Channel Four Television; *Critical Writings*, p. 362.

Chapter 51

Mahon, Longley, Muldoon, McGuckian, Carson, Boland and other Irish poets

STEPHEN REGAN

The Northern Irish Renaissance that brought Seamus Heaney and other poets to prominence in Belfast in the 1960s has been much debated, but another story might begin in Dublin in the 1960s with the meeting at Trinity College of Derek Mahon, Michael Longley and Eavan Boland. As Northern Protestants, Mahon and Longley found confirmation of their own complicated sense of belonging in the poetry of Louis MacNeice, while Boland, as a Catholic in the Republic, sought space for her voice in a culture of female passivity and in a poetic tradition still dominated by W. B. Yeats and Patrick Kavanagh. In the intellectual ferment in Dublin in the 1960s, the three poets would share a deep and sustaining interest in the classics and in modern European and American literature, drawing on these resources in ways that would reshape and redirect contemporary Irish poetry. This would be a well-travelled, international poetry. Mahon's work would be written in London and New York, but also reflect upon his time in France and Italy; Longley would return to Belfast, but also draw inspiration from summers spent in Mayo and from memories of a visit to Japan; and Boland, having already spent part of her childhood in London, would eventually settle in California.

For Mahon and Longley, the replenishment of the imagination through the contemplation of isolated landscapes and seascapes became a salutary and necessary activity as sectarian violence disrupted any secure sense of attachment to Ulster. Poetry might be elevated and energised by a bold encounter with the ferocious political energies of the Troubles, but in such a precarious context it also ran the risk of exhaustion and extinction. For both authors, writing poetry was, in itself, an exemplary act, an expression of vital creativity at the very time that civil liberties were being threatened and curtailed. The early publications of Mahon and Longley coincide with the campaign for civil rights in Northern Ireland in 1968 and 1969, and they seem to anticipate the decades of violence that would follow. Mahon's first volume of poems, *Night-Crossing* (1968), registers the philistinism and bigotry of a culture hostile to poetry, while countering the attendant disappointment with a compensating display of formal elegance and lyric assurance. The title refers to the mail boats that crossed the Irish Sea at night, and it carries with it suggestions of metaphysical unease, an intellectual journey in the dark, as well as hints of physical danger. Like Heaney's *Door into the Dark* (1969), it teeters on the edge of a darkness that has political as well as philosophical possibilities.

Mahon found his poetic voice at the grave of Louis MacNeice in a finely judged obituary, written just a year or so after the poet's death in September 1963. 'In Carrowdore Churchyard' is distinguished by its deft combination of elegiac gravitas and playful irony, skilfully recalling MacNeice's own poetic procedures. The poem gently acknowledges the elegiac convention of looking backwards and forwards simultaneously, extending this through its subtle word-play ('You lie past tension now'), and giving new life to dead clichés ('down to the ground', 'hard as nails') so that the churchyard setting takes on a more 'humane perspective'. MacNeice's cultural achievements in both Irish poetry and the classics are fittingly summed up in the passing reference to the ninth-century Gaelic poem, 'The Blackbird at Belfast Lough', and 'a phrase from Euripides'. Echoes of several poems by MacNeice, including 'Snow', 'Casualty' and 'Brother Fire', pay tribute to his dazzling talent, as the elegy moves from the grip of winter to a spring that is 'coming round / Igniting flowers on the peninsula'. The 'bombed-out town' alludes to MacNeice's experiences as a fire-watcher during the London Blitz, though it seems to look forward uncannily to bombings in Belfast during the Troubles. For all its playful ironies, 'In Carrowdore Churhyard' fulfils the vital obligation of all serious elegies in its ritualistic cleansing of the past and its assertion of new life, not least in poetry itself: 'Rinsing the choked mud, keeping the colours new'.[1] MacNeice's influence is powerfully at work, as well, in the startlingly sophisticated diction and syntax of 'An Unborn Child' whose birth is ironically envisaged as a departure and an ending: 'give / Or take a day or two, my days are numbered'. The precursor here is 'A Prayer before Birth', but Mahon leaves himself latitude for 'a free hand' in the cave of making, demonstrating his astonishing facility with the dramatic monologue.

MacNeice's satirical treatment of suburban civilisation is recalled in 'Glengormley', as Mahon caustically introduces his own provincial locale with a deflationary echo of Sophocles's *Antigone*: 'Wonders are many and none is more wonderful than man / Who has tamed the terrier, trimmed the hedge / And grasped the principle of the watering can.' The poem recalls the legend of Finn McCool in its recollection of giants who 'tore up sods' and 'hurled them out to sea', but 'the new era' which it celebrates is one no longer troubled by monsters and one that has no need for saints and heroes, even if the hesitation between the final two stanzas reveals a lingering sympathy for 'The unreconciled, in their metaphysical pain' (p. 26). The new suburban order is seen ironically as the apotheosis of the heroic struggles of the past, though the closing attitude is one of reluctant acceptance: 'By / Necessity, if not choice, I live here too' (p. 14). The speaker in 'Spring in Belfast' is more explicit and less ironic about his disaffected condition. Despite the apparent solidarity in 'Walking among my own', the poem is soured by its observation of an ungenerous morality ('the squinting heart') and a harsh religion ('The cold gaze of a sanctimonious God'). There is a prominent echo of *Paradise Lost* in the self-instructive line, 'One part of my mind must learn to know its place', but the poem closes with a Yeatsian reduplicative syntax in which an attitude of reluctant attachment once again prevails: 'this desperate city / Should engage more than my casual interest, / Exact more interest than my casual pity' (p. 13).

The publication of *Lives* in 1972 coincided with the escalation of violence in the North, including the Bloody Sunday shootings of thirteen civilians by the British Army in Derry. Mahon's poetry responds in complex ways to the changed political circumstances of the time, both intensifying the anguished metaphysical questions that it asks and simultaneously exposing itself to scrutiny. 'Rage for Order' is painfully alert to charges of aesthetic indulgence and detachment, prompting a fierce act of self-interrogation: 'Somewhere beyond / The scorched gable end / And the burnt-out / Buses there is a poet indulging his / Wretched rage for order' (p. 47). The poem appears to treat with scepticism the aesthetic credo of Wallace Stevens and the structuring role of the imagination in 'The Idea of Order at Key West', but poet and inquisitor are ultimately one and the same, and both are in need of 'Terminal ironies' (p. 48). Some of Mahon's finest rhetorical effects derive, ironically, from his attempt to imagine a world in which poetry has been displaced entirely. 'As It Should Be' is spoken by an assassin who applauds the cold instrumentality of 'a world with method in it' (p. 49). As the poet withdraws from the barbarism of his times, carefully cultivating his art and waiting patiently for the end, his models are Constantine Cavafy and Samuel Beckett.

The extremes of aesthetic detachment and political terror are starkly juxtaposed in the haunting title poem of *The Snow Party* (1975). The seventeenth-century Japanese poet, Bashō, is invited to a ceremony which culminates in the contemplation of falling snow. 'Elsewhere', we are told, 'they are burning / Witches and heretics' and 'Thousands have died.' Without disturbing the seemingly tranquil surfaces of its haiku-like tercets, the poem offers an implicit criticism of the cold aesthetic of Yeats's 'Lapis Lazuli'. Where Yeats's musicians 'begin to play', here 'there is silence' (p. 63). If Mahon is a masterful exponent of aesthetic disengagement, he is also the most severe critic of intellectual solipsism, frequently exposing his own high-minded artistic ideals to withering mockery. In 'The Last of the Fire Kings', which mixes anthropology with spy films and science fiction, the speaker has grandiose notions of being 'Through with history' (p. 64). Articulating the dilemmas and frustrations of the poet, the fire king seeks to perfect his 'cold dream / Of a place out of time', imagining himself among the decadent 'frugivorous inheritors' in H. G. Wells's novella *The Time Machine*. His fate, however, might well be the less glorious one of inhabiting 'a world of / Sirens, bin-lids / And bricked-up windows' (p. 65). In the extraordinary closing poem of the volume, 'A Disused Shed in Co. Wexford', Mahon presents a powerful political parable on behalf of the forgotten victims and outcasts of history. Taking as its setting the 'burnt-out hotel' (p. 89) in J. G. Farrell's novel of the Irish Civil War, *Troubles* (1970), the poem also looks back from the German concentration camps in Poland to the collapse of ancient Rome ('Lost people of Treblinka and Pompeii!' (p. 90)). The imaginative brilliance of the poem is in its depiction of desperate, abandoned people as a 'thousand mushrooms' (p. 89) crowding to the light of a keyhole. In giving voice to what he calls elsewhere 'The Mute Phenomena' of the world, Mahon aligns his apocalyptic and eschatological vision with a sensitive reckoning of our heedless ecology: 'Already in a lost hub-cap is conceived / The ideal society which will replace our own' (p. 82).

One of the salient and persistent features of Mahon's poetry has been its impulse to imagine other states of being or to reflect upon 'The lives we might have led' (p. 60, 'Leaves'). At the local level, this makes for rueful reflection on origins and destinations, as with the appropriately titled 'Afterlives', in which the speaker wonders if staying behind in Belfast and living it 'bomb by bomb' might have enabled him to learn 'what is meant by home' (p. 59). In other places, the instinct to re-invent himself brings with it a tremendous imaginative resilience and creativity, as with 'Courtyards in Delft', the opening poem of *The Hunt by Night* (1982). Here, the poet dreams himself into the pure, sunlit canvas of Pieter de Hooch, imagining himself as 'A strange child with a taste for verse' (p. 106). While he dwells on the exquisite aesthetic pleasures of things ('The ceiling cradled in a radiant spoon' (p. 105)), his 'hard-nosed companions dream of war', bringing to the surface the subtle hints of a shared Dutch and Irish Protestant Orangery. 'The Globe in North Carolina', the closing poem of the volume, both testifies to the rich imaginative resources to be found in geographical displacement and signals the poet's metaphysical homelessness, as he waits in the dark with insects, 'Listening to that lonesome whistle blow' (p. 142). The poems in *The Hudson Letter* (1995) emerge from an extended stay in America, with the loose epistolary style corresponding to the daily rhythms of a Manhattan 'resident alien' (p. 190). If the Hudson letters keep open a dialogue with John Keats and Hart Crane, they also turn with shaming invective on America's inhumanity to man. The homeless at the end of the final letter call out with voices that echo the cries against abandonment in 'A Disused Shed in Co. Wexford': 'We have been too long in the cold. – Take us in; take us in!' (p. 222). The epistolary style has produced a noticeable relaxation in Mahon's recent work. If there are dark visions of ecological ruin in *Harbour Lights* (2005) and *Life on Earth* (2008), there is also abundant imaginative vitality.

Michael Longley's verse letter 'To Derek Mahon' recalls their time in Belfast in 1969, archly depicting them as 'Two poetic conservatives / In the city of guns and long knives'.[2] Part of a series of 'Letters' in his second book, *An Exploded View* (1973), the poem recalls the *Letters from Iceland* of MacNeice and Auden, and it shows an early shared love of islands and seascapes. A more troubling and immediate sense of place is evident in the quotation from Keith Douglas which prefaces the letters: 'returning over the nightmare ground / we found the place again' (p. 53). Douglas and the earlier war poets, Edward Thomas and Isaac Rosenberg, were important influences on Longley as he searched for a way of writing that was resilient enough to withstand the shock of war. Already, however, Longley had proved himself to be a poet whose lyric aptitude was tempered by a deeply elegiac impulse. His strengths as an elegist would sustain his work throughout the Troubles. The key poem in his first collection of poems, *No Continuing* City (1969), is 'In Memoriam', in which his father's death prompts an intimate poetry of mourning: 'Let yours / And other heartbreaks play into my hands' (p. 30). The candid, unguarded address and the personal intimacy are distinguishing characteristics for which Longley has been greatly admired.

If Mahon is alert to the ironic urbanities of MacNeice, Longley is attracted to the tender eroticism of the poet who could write so candidly to his lover in 'Mayfly', 'I want always to be near your breasts.' The influence is apparent in the closing invocation of 'The Linen Industry': 'And be shy of your breasts in the presence of death'. In many ways, 'The Linen Industry' (from *The Echo Gate*, 1979) is the quintessential Longley poem, amply demonstrating his skills as love poet and elegist, but also his fidelity to detail as naturalist and botanist. At the same time, the poem is sensitively attuned to its Ulster roots and the deep losses that the province has suffered, along with the 'dying trade' of the linen industry. Longley's trademark is to be found in the delicate lyric grace with which he matches the rhythms of work and the rhythms of love ('Pulling up flax after the blue flowers have fallen'), and in the sudden but unforced epiphany in which a linen bow is transformed into an emblem of ephemeral beauty: 'A butterfly attending the embroidered flowers' (p. 143). There is a generosity of spirit and an appealing sociability that endears Longley to his readers, even in his most intimate love poems. 'Swans Mating' is a love poem born of a desire to share a privileged 'Heraldic moment' of beauty and power, but the special nature of that moment is extended to the reader: 'Even now I wish that you had been there.' The casual colloquialism acquires a new rhythmic charge and opens into the dazzling epiphany of the female swan: 'Her feathers full of water and her neck / Under the water like a bar of light' (p. 47).

The title of *An Exploded View* points initially to a open architectural perspective (as used in 'Skara Brae'), but it prompts reflection on the explosive circumstances through which Longley was living in Belfast in the early 1970s. 'Kindertotenlieder' (taking its title from Mahler's song cycle) insists that 'There can be no songs for dead children', but despite its brevity the poem seeks to accommodate the infant victims of the Troubles. In this sense, the children are 'unrestricted tenants' of the poet's mind, but the adjective has an appalling resonance in terms of number. In the same way, the initial childlike impression of 'fingerprints / Everywhere, teethmarks on this and that' (p. 61) takes on a disturbing surrealist dimension in the context of 'an exploded view' (p. 39). 'Wounds' is at once an elegy for Longley's father, 'a belated casualty' of the Ulster Division at the Somme, and the unnamed victims of sectarian violence, with the poet's personal loss (verified in the release of 'secrets' from his father's head), authorising his role as spokesman for the community. The memory of 'the London-Scottish padre / Resettling kilts with his swagger-stick' after the Battle of the Somme prompts in the poet a similar need to restore the dignity of the dead in his own time, including 'Three teenage soldiers' with 'their flies undone'. The closing reflection on the cold-blooded murder committed by 'a shivering boy' seems appalling in its blunt inadequacy – 'I think "Sorry Missus" was what he said' (p. 62) – but the qualifying 'think' both declares the poet's own uneasiness as the arbiter of such events and insists on his urgent need to understand the motivation behind them.

The 'two pictures' (p. 62) from his father's head have a parallel in a much later poem, 'Björn Olinder's Pictures' (in *The Weather in Japan*, 2000), in which

Longley recalls the husband of a Swedish friend, Britta Olinder, needing to look at two pictures when he was dying, one of them a seascape showing 'A glimpse of immaculate sand that awaits our footprints' (p. 268). Some of Longley's most imposing and memorable writing, including 'The Linen Workers' (*The Echo Gate*, 1979), 'The Ice-cream Man' (*Gorse Fires*, 1991), 'Ceasefire' and 'The Fishing Party' (*The Ghost Orchid*, 1994), have been written in an elegiac mode that manages to find such glimpses of redemption and renewal, despite the prevailing pain and anguished disbelief. 'The Linen Workers' opens with the grotesque surrealism of Christ's 'exposed canines' against 'a wintry sky' but seeks some restoration of dignity, if not consolation, in a careful ritualistic re-ordering of the personal effects of the dead, tantamount to burying his father 'once again' (p. 119). The figure of the father reappears in 'Ceasefire' (first published in *The Irish Times* two days after the IRA ceasefire on 31 August 1994), with Priam receiving the body of his dead son, Hector, from Achilles. The Homeric narrative is distilled into a modified sonnet, in which the closing couplet depicts 'what must be done' (p. 225) without any heavy-handed polemic or premature rejoicing.

Eavan Boland shares with Derek Mahon a strong sense of dislocation and uprootedness, but the experience of being 'outside history' is not, for her, a desirable aesthetic standpoint. Much of her work (especially *In a Time of Violence*, 1994) is concerned with restoring to Irish history its missing female perspective. 'That the Science of Cartography Is Limited' looks back to the unrecorded suffering of the Famine, while 'The Dolls Museum in Dublin' recreates the events of Easter 1916. The poems in *Night Feed* (1982) and *In Her Own Image* (1980) had been concerned with finding a space in poetry for the suburban domestic experience of motherhood, but *Outside History* (1990) signalled a new political direction in her writing. If Boland's work derives from an initial uncertainty about her own authority in relation to the English language and the English literary tradition, it is also informed by the experience of being a woman writer in a culture where women have tended to serve as passive images and emblems of the nation rather than the creators of poetry. In her literary memoir, appropriately titled *Object Lessons*, she asks what is needed for a woman to become the convincing subject rather than the passive object of a poem. How can a woman poet retain and redefine the element of the erotic, which so often provides the energy and impulse in poetry, without being in herself the object of desire? One way forward is for the woman poet to explore those objects of memory that carry indelible and intimate traces of herself. 'The Black Lace Fan My Mother Gave Me' is one such object, allowing the poet to re-create the youthful romance of her parents during a heat wave in pre-war Paris. The fan itself is faded and violated by time, and it seems to offer little insight into 'what happened' in the past. The object of memory, however, encourages the poet to 'improvise', and the opening of the fan is transformed into a blackbird's wing, renewing the promise of romance in the heat of the present: 'Suddenly she puts out her wing. / The whole, full, flirtatious span of it.'[3] *The Lost Land* (1998) and *Code* (2001) show her bringing her abiding interests in language, nation and sexual politics to fruition: 'I also am a daughter of the colony. / I share their broken speech, their other-whereness.'[4]

Paul Muldoon's *New Weather* (1973) seemed to indicate in its title a perceived change in the poetic environment in Northern Ireland. 'Wind and Tree', from which the title is taken, has subtle intertextual links with Robert Frost's 'Tree at My Window'. If Muldoon is drawn to the American poet's sleight of hand, he also shares his conviction that a poem is a temporary stay against confusion, a momentary clarification. The early Muldoon is quizzical, teasing and enigmatic. The voice of the poet as weather prophet speaks out of a community now well accustomed to suffering and sacrifice: 'Yet by my broken bones // I tell new weather'.[5] What Muldoon has also brought to Irish poetry is a new playfulness, often arising from misprision and misunderstanding, and often informed by subtle sexual allusions and innuendoes. The child in 'Duffy's Circus' hears a 'long-drawn-out cry' and from 'under a freighter' watches 'a man sawing a woman in half' (p. 66). Illusion and illusionism (and even the illusion of illusionism) feature prominently in Muldoon's work, as does a pervasive interest in mixed and metamorphic states of being, perhaps to be expected of the poet of *Mules* (1977).

What makes the title poem of *Why Brownlee Left* (1980) so notable is its performance of a mysterious disappearing act within the familiar Irish poem of rural life and labour made popular by poets such as Patrick Kavanagh and Seamus Heaney. At the same time, the poem skilfully fuses English lyricism with Irish metrics, creating a sonnet in which rhyme and rhythm follow a playful syllabic variation. Brownlee's funereal black horses are seen 'Shifting their weight from foot to / Foot, and gazing into the future' (p. 84). The ostentatious enjambment and the enterprising half-rhyme of 'foot to' and 'future' maintain the suspense surrounding Brownlee's leaving, without ruling out the possibility that he is already in the earth. The playful ambivalence and teasing obliquity do not necessarily rule out a purposeful engagement with the politics of the Troubles. 'Lull' ostensibly refers to a period of IRA ceasefire, contemplating both the beneficent calm implied by 'lull' and the consequences of being 'lulled' into a false sense of security. The poem's paradoxical 'eternal interim' invites despair, momentarily relieved by the opportunistic rhyme at the end of a chain of Northern Irish place names – 'Tyrone, Fermanagh, Down and Antrim' (p. 81) – crossing the sonnet with the Irish *dinseannchas* tradition.

Quoof (1983) marked a new phase of radical experimentation with language and form in Muldoon's work, as well as an increasing eclecticism and self-reflexiveness that were recognisably 'postmodern'. At the same time, the poems began to turn increasingly towards the United States, where Muldoon would eventually settle. The title poem reflects upon the intimacies and estrangements that language can beget, tracing the 'family word / for the hot water bottle' – 'quoof' – from an Irish homestead to a hotel room in New York City. The half-rhyme of 'English and 'language' (p. 112) ironically carries the poem's expression of the difficulties and failures of communication in the most intimate circumstances. Fragmentation, hallucination and intertextuality predominate in poems that are nevertheless responsive to contemporary Irish politics. What might occasionally look like evasion or digression is not without political significance in challenging and subverting established narratives, destabilising fixed positions, and prompting new perspectives. 'Gathering Mushrooms' has a powerful intertextual relationship with Mahon's 'A Disused Shed in Co. Wexford' and also with Heaney's poems of paternal labour, but the measure of its accomplishment is to be found in the mesmerising psilocybin-induced vision, in which the poet's head is transformed into that of a horse that shakes its 'dirty-fair mane' and speaks on behalf of the IRA hunger-strikers: '*Lie down with us and wait*' (p. 106). The hunger-strikes are recalled in 'Aisling', in which the traditional female personification of Ireland in the dream poem is presented as an anorexic, venereal goddess who leaves the speaker waiting anxiously for the '*All Clear*' (p. 126). Contamination reappears in *Meeting the British* (1987), the title poem of which shows Muldoon extending his interest in the cultural encounter between the British and the Native Americans. The sheer range and ambitiousness, as well as the immense confidence, of Muldoon's work at this time is evident in '7, Middagh Street', which playfully assembles prominent poets and artists in W. H. Auden's New York residence, rearranging the best-known lines of Yeats and others in a scintillating parodic pastiche: 'Both beautiful, one a gazebo' (p. 189).

Further confirmation of Muldoon's international stature was to follow in *Madoc: A Mystery* (1990), the ambitious title poem of which takes its bearings from Robert Southey's 'Madoc' and the utopian desires he shared with Coleridge to found a 'pantisocracy' in America. Foregrounding its own metapoetic features, the poem nevertheless provides a critique of the philosophical ideals underpinning imperialist politics. One of the most striking developments in Muldoon's career has been his emergence as a writer of extraordinary elegies, including his 'Incantata' (*The Annals of Chile*, 1994), which draws on Irish terms of endearment to seal its imaginative reunion with the artist Mary Farl Powers: 'that you might reach out, arrah, / and take in your ink-stained hands my own hands stained with ink' (p. 341). *Moy Sand and Gravel* (2002) includes 'Herm' (in memory of Ted Hughes) and closes with a Yeatsian meditation, 'At the Sign of the Black Horse, September 1999', in which he contemplates his sleeping son in the aftermath of a storm. *Horse Latitudes* (2006) opens with a sequence of nineteen sonnets in which personal battles are measured against a history of warfare from Bannockburn to Baghdad, and it closes with 'Sillyhow Stride', ostensibly in memory of the rock musician, Warren Zevon, but also recalling the death by cancer of his sister, Maureen.

Since the 1980s, and especially since the publication of *The Irish for No* (1987) and *Belfast Confetti* (1989), Ciaran Carson has acquired a reputation as a master of the long line, a poet who cannily crosses the English lyric with the endlessly digressive narratives and tall tales of the Irish story-teller or *seanachie*. That long line is allied to an unflinching and remorseless way of seeing. Frequently it conveys the bewildering experience of mapping a city that keeps on changing, as in 'Turn Again', but it also suggests the unremitting effort of an imagination that refuses to be quelled by violence, the existential persistence of a voice that goes on talking at the same time as it sceptically undermines its own ostensible desire for meaning and order. 'Belfast Confetti' renders the world as text in a radical attempt to represent violence: 'Suddenly, as the riot squad moved in, it was raining exclamation marks, / Nuts, bolts, nails, car-keys. A fount of broken type.'[6] Carson's Belfast is a city in which surveillance and interrogation are routine, and one of the consequences is an intense self-consciousness about the operations of language as revelation and concealment. This interest persists throughout *First Language* (1993) and *Opera Et Cetera* (1996), and it resurfaces in *For All We Know* (2008): 'As our promise was never to be betrayed by our words / so we became our own shadowy police watching us' (p. 496). A new Imagist style influenced by William Carlos Williams coincides with a more peaceful, post-ceasefire impression of Belfast in *Breaking News* (2003) – 'beside the motorway / a black taxi / rusts in a field / of blue thistles' (p. 431) – but in other poems the British Army helicopter is a pervasive image.

In the late 1990s, a new lyric intensity pervaded Carson's work and found its most creative expression in a prolific series of sonnets. Significantly, it was the twelve-syllable or alexandrine line of the French sonnet that Carson found most appealing. His versions of sonnets by Charles Baudelaire, Stéphane Mallarmé and Arthur Rimbaud in *The Alexandrine Plan* (1998) provided the blueprint for the immensely ambitious sequence of seventy-seven alexandrine sonnets in *The Twelfth of Never* (1999). Repeatedly, the sonnets in *The Twelfth of Never* dissolve the myths that have hardened around historical events and their monumental dates, allowing dream and fantasy to wash over the fixed and fossilised terrain of sectarian politics, and countering the violence of both revolutionary insurrection and imperial power with images of peace and sleep. Like Muldoon, Carson turns his parodic gaze on poetic tradition itself, mixing genres and registers and intertextual allusions with impressive ease and fluency. The personification of Ireland as Roisin Dubh or Dark Rosaleen is a recurring motif in several sonnets which adopt the nationalist emblems of the Irish Rebellion of 1798 and present themselves as variants of the familiar *aisling*. '1798' powerfully conveys the seductive glamour of nationalist iconography, while also subtly decommissioning its rebel emblems, exchanging them for the delicate Japanese image of snowy blossoms in a closing glimpse of peace.

Medbh McGuckian marks the 1798 bicentenary in *Shelmalier* (1998), a volume that recalls the deaths of Irish patriots and brings her own political consciousness to the fore. This might seem like a dramatic reversal of her early preoccupation in *The Flower Master* (1982) and *Venus and the Rain* (1984) with what looked like a carefully demarcated area of female interest and influence, including horticulture, the weather and domestic interiors. In fact, the obliquity and opacity of the poems are unchanged, even if the later volumes appear to be more historically and politically charged. *Had I a Thousand Lives* (2003) is prefaced by Yeats's remarks on the saintly life of Robert Emmet and by a tribute from his fellow patriot, Thomas Russell. 'To My Disordered Muse' suggests a changing poetic sensibility, one that is now prepared to contemplate political execution, while other poems, such as 'The Corduroy Road', draw a parallel between the victims of the Irish famine and those of the Holocaust. Even so, working back through McGuckian's poetry, what becomes apparent is how consistent her poetic procedures have been, and how the realm of the aesthetic has always been the primary concern of her work. *Drawing Ballerinas* (2001) is instructive in this respect, carrying on its cover a quotation from Matisse: 'I may not be in the trenches, but I am in a front line of my own making.' The title poem commemorates the death of a neighbour in an explosion in 1972, recalling Matisse's remark that he managed to survive the war by drawing ballerinas. Many of McGuckian's poems, including those in *Marconi's Cottage* (1991) and *On Ballycastle Beach* (1988), are perhaps best understood in terms of a studied artistic concentration comparable to a Matisse painting. Titles such as 'Blue Vase', 'The Blue She Brings with Her' and 'Woman with Blue-ringed Bowl' clearly demonstrate her care for colour and composition. *Captain Lavender* (1994) is prefaced with a quotation from Picasso: 'I have not painted the war . . . but I have no doubt that the war is in . . . these paintings I have done.' 'The Albert Chain' is one of a number of poems deriving from McGuckian's work with political prisoners in Long Kesh, an experience encouraged by her father, who died in 1992: 'I am learning my country all over again, / how every inch of soil has been paid for / by the life of a man, the funerals of the poor.'[7] The conclusion of the poem returns to a more introspective and syntactically complicated verse, as if reminding us of the poet's own prison house of language, her weighing of aesthetic and political priorities and the 'unjust pursuit of justice / that turns one sort of poetry into another' (p. 89).

The artistic pursuit of justice is one of the motivating impulses in the work of Tom Paulin, from *In a State of Justice* (1977) to *The Invasion Handbook* (2002). From the outset, his poems have demonstrated a shrewd and circumspect political intelligence, combining a bold depiction of 'gunfire, night arrests and searches'[8] with a sensitive discernment of how petrifying violence intrudes into personal and domestic spaces: 'An oleograph of Pity in each kitchen. / My heart is stone. I will not budge' (p. 14, 'Ballywaire'). Too often, Paulin has been caricatured as a pugnacious *politico*, without there being sufficient awareness of the brilliant polyvocal qualities of his poetry, or any acknowledgment of the skilful rhetorical contrivance behind the voices in his verse. Little attention has been given to the meditative lyricism that defines so many memorable poems in *The Strange Museum* (1980): the glimpse of peace in the unrhymed sonnet, 'In the Lost Province', the elegiac mood of 'The Harbour in the Evening' and the wonder of being alive in 'A Lyric Afterwards'. Paulin's disaffected Ulster Protestantism was tempered by his growing interest in the eighteenth-century republican spirit of the United Irishmen and this combined with a lively enthusiasm for vernacular verse to produce the powerful, compelling poems in *Liberty Tree* (1983). Although criticism fastened on 'Desertmartin' with its deep disdain for 'a culture of twigs and bird-shit / Waving a flag it loves and curses' (p. 43), the most impressive poem in the collection is 'The Book of Juniper' with its uplifting 'dream / of that sweet / equal republic' (p. 51). An anguished contemplation of the political future of Ulster in the context of the Anglo-Irish agreement fuels the poems of *Fivemiletown* (1987), including the ambitious meditative poem looking back to the Thirty Years

War, 'The Caravans on Lüneburg Heath'. Paulin's later work in *The Wind Dog* (1999) shows a sparkling inventiveness, with a rainbow-inspired return to 'the lingo-jingo of beginnings'.[9]

The work of Paulin's close contemporary, Bernard O'Donoghue, is distinguished by its combination of colloquial ease and an unerring instinct for finding the miraculous and the sacred in everyday events. 'A Nun Takes the Veil' adopts the first-person voice of a novitiate nun who recalls seeing and hearing a car 'for the first time ever' on the morning that she leaves home for the convent.[10] That 'morning's vision' takes on the force of revelation as she falls asleep, 'With the engine humming through the open window' (p. 4). There is a generous and humane vision in O'Donoghue's poems. They are sensitively alert to our capacity for cruelty and violence (as with 'O'Regan the Amateur Anatomist'), but also profoundly aware of our instinct for survival and solidarity. 'The State of the Nation' declares the need for eternal vigilance as it contemplates both local and global instances of displacement and annihilation. The speaker imagines Irish travellers mysteriously disappeared from their encampment, and he waits in braced attention for any sound of their return. The touching image of ponies 'bringing home / Hay, a clutch of eggs, unminded pullets' (p. 13) both registers desolation and simultaneously restores a sense of life and fullness to the scene in its marvellous particularity. 'The Iron Age Boat at Caumatruish' shares with the poems of Seamus Heaney a strong interest in archaeological remains, but also an awed awareness of the miraculous. The opening of the poem, recalling doubting Thomas in the presence of Christ, is both resoundingly reverential and playfully practical in its homage to the Iron Age boat: 'If you doubt, you can put your fingers / In the holes where the oar-pegs went' (p. 42). The repetition of that phrase, 'if you doubt', creates a litany in praise of Iron Age culture, and it shows a poet supremely in control of his medium, drawing easefully and effectively on Irish myth and Irish landscape. Along with the best of Irish writing in the past forty or fifty years, Bernard O'Donoghue's poetry perpetually reaches for the extraordinary and the exceptional without ever losing sight of the trials and the tribulations of here and now.

Notes

1. Derek Mahon, *Collected Poems* (Dublin: Gallery Press, 1999), p. 17. All further quotations are from this edition of the poems.
2. Michael Longley, *Collected Poems* (London: Jonathan Cape, 2006), p. 58. All further quotations are from this edition of the poems.
3. Eavan Boland, *Outside History* (Manchester: Carcanet, 1990), p. 11.

4. Eavan Boland, *The Lost Land* (Manchester: Carcanet, 1998), p. 16.
5. Paul Muldoon, *Poems 1968–1998* (London: Faber, 2001), p. 5. All further quotations are from this edition of the poems.
6. Ciaran Carson, *Collected Poems* (Oldcastle: Gallery Books, 2008), p. 93. All further quotations are from this edition of the poems.
7. Medbh McGuckian, *Selected Poems* (Oldcastle: Gallery Books, 1997), p. 88. All further quotations are from this edition of the poems.
8. Tom Paulin, *Selected Poems* (London: Faber, 1977), p. 14. All further quotations are from this edition of the poems, unless otherwise stated.
9. Tom Paulin, *The Wind Dog* (London: Faber, 1999), p. 22.
10. Bernard O'Donoghue, *Selected Poems* (London: Faber, 2008), p. 4. All further quotations are from this edition of the poems.

Chapter 52

Contemporary poetries in English, c.1980 to the present I: the radical tradition

PETER BARRY

Anyone offering a single phrase to describe a specific period in the history of contemporary poetry risks delivering a hostage to fortune. But the 1982 Penguin anthology *Contemporary British Poetry*, edited by Blake Morrison and Andrew Motion, took that risk, and has frequently been criticised for declaring that in 'much of the 1960s and 70s . . . very little – in England at any rate – seemed to be happening'. Among the loudest critics of the Morrison/Motion verdict were the poets of what is known variously as the 'parallel' or 'alternative' or 'neo-Modernist' or 'experimental' or 'radical' tradition, on which the present chapter concentrates. For these poets, the decade of the 1970s had been the heroic age, the high period of what came to be called the British Poetry Revival, during which, for six years, the Revivalists had taken over the National Poetry Centre and its journal *Poetry Review*.[1] By contrast, the 1980s and the early 1990s, I will risk saying, was for them a period of demoralised re-grouping, when their secure oppositional identity had been undermined, when a number of publishing ventures had foundered, and when the new electronic media which revitalised the scene in the later 1990s had not yet come into being. Thus, the traditionalists, in the 1980s, seemed to have triumphed – in 1994 a 'New Generation' of such poets was launched by the Poetry Society and a consortium of presses with much fanfare – poetry, the publicists claimed, had become the new rock-and-roll. Furthermore, the Martians had landed,[2] and the tricksy, decentred 'secret narratives' of James Fenton and Andrew Motion pleased a public which seemed to enjoy a moderate amount of narratological teasing with its poetry.[3] Likewise, the fey whimsicality of Paul Muldoon appealed, then as now, to readers with a sweet poetic tooth. The poetry readings associated with the 'New Gen' promotion achieved a degree of prominence, and a similar promotional formula (that is, a group of youngish poets going 'on tour' together to a succession of towns and cities) was used to promote new poets from the enterprising Bloodaxe Books stable. The early 1990s, then, exacerbated the sense of exclusion, elected isolation and, at best, challenging marginalisation, felt by the 'radicals', as I will call them here, for contemporary poetry in general seemed to have taken off again, and they seemed to have been left behind.[4]

The foregoing reads the post-1980 period in UK poetry using a 'divergence' model which sees an increasing polarisation taking place over the period between 'radical' and 'mainstream' poetries. A 'convergence' model, by contrast, would see in the 1980s a mainstream which is tiring of its allegiance to the conventional 'lyric I' and is no longer content with 'straight' accounts of personal experience, ego-based, overheard 'private' reflection, and the never-ending exploration of individual subjectivity. Having seen off the radicals, say the convergence modellers, mainstream poetry was beginning to dress up in some of their clothes – verbal play, experimentation with linguistic registers, politicised and gendered poetics, 'content-specific' poetries, multiple-meaning strands, 'hard-edged' image techniques and so on. Whether the divergence or convergence model best represents the situation within contemporary poetry during this period is still disputed, and it increasingly seems that both divergent and convergent forces were at work, and that mapping the cross-currents is a complex business. But we do not have to have already taken a definitive position on this issue to ask a key question of the post-1980 period – to what extent did those of the radicals who had already established their presence in the 1970s respond to the undoubtedly changed situation of the 1980s and 1990s by producing work which further enhanced their reputations?

By the start of the 1980s the radical poetry scene was dominated by several well-established writers who had all produced a major long work in the 1960s or 1970s. These included: Allen Fisher, whose *Place* sequence first appeared in substantial consolidated form in 1974, when his own Aloes Books published *Place Book One* (I–XXXVII); Iain Sinclair, whose *Lud Heat* was first published by his own Albion Village Press in 1975; Roy Fisher, whose poetry–prose hybrid *City* first appeared in conventional book form in his Fulcrum Press *Collected Poems* in 1968; Barry MacSweeney, whose collection *The Boy from the Green Cabaret Tells of his Mother* (Hutchinson, 1968) had become well known when he was nominated by the publishers for the Oxford Chair of Poetry that year, and he had since moved into small presses with *Brother Wolf* (1972), and *Black Torch* (1973), of which Book II appeared in 1980; Denise Riley, whose poetry and linked writing about feminism and poetics had been prominent since the 1970s; and J. H. Prynne, whose *Kitchen Poems* (Cape Goliard, 1968) and *The White Stones* (Grosseteste Press, 1969) had established his lasting reputation. As might be expected, the progress of these figures in the post-1980 period has been various.

Allen Fisher, firstly, remained active as a poet, and continued to be a major influence, but he diversified increasingly into art, performance and installation work, though also taking on a series of poetic projects of ever greater scope and complexity. Thus, 'The Art of Flight' project occupied him for fifteen years, and *Gravity as a Consequence of Shape* since 1982.[5] Each of his major works comprises a series of interlinked composites, and the catalogue description of *Gravity* tells us that its 'subjects bridge biotechnology and quantum physics through a system of urban gardening and leaking streets'. While the 'urban gardening and leaking streets' are familiar aspects of the loco-specifics that made *Place* so successful, the 'biotechnology and quantum physics', and the like, had always been counter-balanced in the earlier work by more 'grounded' elements, such as those streets and gardens. There was, for instance, the garden in which the apples thump the grass as they fall and the streets which make up the eastern sector of Coldharbour Lane, about which the poet writes to Lambeth Council, enclosing a copy of the *Ley Hunter Magazine*, and asking them to stop pulling down houses there.[6] South London has a vivid presence in *Place*, which frequently mentions actual streets, pubs, bus routes, historical incidents, local legends, local archaeological finds and so on. In the later work, by contrast, the 'grounding' becomes more fleeting and evanescent, as if it is thought less important. This is not to say that biotechnology and quantum physics have no place in poetry – only that a poet needs to fillet out (say) a limited number of dominant biotechnological images or ideas which can be used to suffuse the whole mix and orientation of the subject matter. In other words, the biotechnology (or whatever) needs to be highly specific and tightly edited. This kind of specificity is achieved to some extent in 'Brixton Fractals', the first of the five books in *Gravity*, in which Fisher suggestively uses the notion of fractals. Fractals are shapes that are patterned, but in ways too irregular to be described in terms of conventional Euclidean geometry, and in such a way that parts of the structure have the same form as the structure as a whole (a characteristic known as 'self-similarity'). Fractal forms are common in nature, but their combination of irregularity and patterning seems to be the source of Fisher's interest in them, for socially and intellectually they are forms which combine opposed characteristics within themselves.

The 'Brixton Fractals' sequence consists of some eighty pages and contains fourteen poems, of which the last is 'Birdland', itself containing five unnamed parts. 'Birdland' often seems to be hovering at a considerable height above the streets – sometimes literally – 'Beneath helicopters / Brixton abandoned / challenges the closure of meaning', the fourth part begins.[7] Here the image is familiar – the streets are a palimpsest built and rebuilt (literally) over, the urban text becoming more and more difficult to decipher, so that it is an open-ended text, self-deconstructing and expressing the intentions of no transcendent author at all. 'Endless destruction / makes Brixton', the poet says in the second section, which is really the same thing (p. 81). When it does seem to be at street level, the mode of writing is a kind of 'cool denotation' of people noticed ('On the edge / of death High Road, the Busker / starts up a reel, it begins as dance interlaced / with anger', p. 81). The next stanza starts with a glimpse of a harassed-seeming citizen who expresses her annoyance at bickering children: 'A woman came down the walkway / lost in transport / exploded her language at a kid / with a stick / restrained by another who breaks / the rod across his leg' (pp. 81–2). The sense of quiet desperation, of lives lived at the deprived edges of society, is strong, and the high-rises with their drab walkways and an overall air of pointlessness seem vividly present: on the speaker's way back there's more:

> One hour later someone has dragged
> a felled lime onto the walkway
> It makes a green path
> A pack of dogs surround this, yelp
> out of phase. (p. 82)

But the final section of 'Birdland' returns to that sense of generalising overview which always seems to outweigh the concrete specifics in 'Brixton Fractals'; it begins 'The imaginary takes over from laughter, / it is a joy without words, a riant [smiling, cheerful] spaciousness / become temporal. / The demonstrative points to an enunciation, / it is a complex shifter straddling the fold of / naming it, and the autonomy of the subject' (p. 83). Here the register of 1980s 'theory' and linguistics ('the demonstrative', 'enunciation', 'shifter', 'the autonomy of the subject') is brought into play – not *used*, exactly, to establish precise meanings, but *utilised* to exemplify a way of making meanings. The final lines of 'Birdland' are:

> Subjection to meaning gets
> replaced with morphology. I become a mere
> phenomenal actualisation moved through a burning gap.
> The irrational state insists on control. (p. 83)

Part of the general sense of 'Brixton Fractals' is this feeling of entrapment, as structures of control and surveillance become ever more impersonal and pervasive, while the sequence as a whole claims to be the expression of a form of resistance to these forces. Thus, the author himself describes 'Brixton

Fractals' in his preface to *Gravity* as 'a technique of memory and perception analysis', presumably, therefore, seeing it as part of a technique for opposing these forces. The 'Resources' note for this single poem 'Birdland' lists 'Halliburton, Kristeva, Mallarmé, Reid', the first being a book about Heidegger and the last a biography of the mathematician David Hilbert. There is an element of information-overload here – though 'Brixton Fractals' studies systems, it never seems to consider the poem itself as a system which, in the end, can only bear so much scientific and technological reality. 'Brixton Fractals', then, on its first appearance in full as a free-standing book in 1985, and later as the first of the five books which became *Gravity*, gave an indication of how far Allen Fisher would move from the pioneering psychogeographical notations of the early phases of *Place* in the 1970s, to works which tend to survey intellectual and social territories in a rather more abstract way.

The other London 'urbanist' writer who was already prominent by 1980 was Iain Sinclair, whose *Lud Heat* appeared in 1975. Indeed, of the cluster of figures who produced influential and trend-setting work in the 1970s, Iain Sinclair stands out, with *Lud Heat* almost seeming to define the period. But this London book, its territories bounded by the City and East End churches of Nicholas Hawksmoor, was not followed up by any poetic work of equal cohesion in Sinclair's later history. *Suicide Bridge*, first published in 1979, is a related work which uses similar methods and format, which is to say, a mix of prose and poetry, the focus on a specific locale and its myths and histories and the use of a 'mosaic' or 'open field' method of accumulating juxtapositions of material. But the overall effect is much more diffuse in this later work, and the 'anchoring' effect of that tight grid of Hawksmoor churches is much missed, the tone becoming more portentous, with too many 'voice-over' pronouncements on the nature of myth and suchlike. Thus, we are told that 'The need for the old myth is a confession of our failure to handle the world, to be on terms with the life-spill of this moment' and 'Myth is breech: faces backwards. The Siamese twin is place. They are sown together & cannot be separated, dependent systems. Man is the messenger substance between them.'[8] This kind of thing is saying it rather than doing it, and to the mix has been added a whole technological dimension – terms such as 'tachyonic voltage' are found (p. 149), and there are quotations (pp. 158–9) from early Hawking on the structure of space–time. The problem, again, is that a long poetic structure must have both clearly defined central concerns and a definite destination, but this one seems to have neither, since a concern with 'the mythology of myth and place' (publisher's description) is too vague to constitute a centre, and it is impossible to imagine reaching a definite conclusion (or, better, providing a convincing sense of an ending) on issues so nebulous.

In *Lud Heat*, by contrast, the centre had been both the Hawksmoor churches and their surroundings, and the figure of the young poet himself, whose work as a GLC gardener took him to those places (in which he is photographed in the illustrations which were included in the original edition). In *Suicide Bridge* this identifiable figure has disappeared, being replaced by the over-confident 'voice-over', and the Sinclair of *Suicide Bridge* seems already to have begun the glide into both fiction writing in general and the urban-based, prose-quest narratives in particular which will form the bedrock of his highly successful subsequent career as a writer. He continues to write and edit poetry, but nothing of his has ever approached the force of his pioneering *Lud Heat*. Instead, Sinclair was the sponsor of a major epic sequence on London mystical themes, based on material from the 1970s, which appeared belatedly in 1995 – Aidan Dun's *Vale Royal* (Goldmark, 1995). This epic piece is centred upon the region of King's Cross, and has a powerful drive and energy which are very apparent in the poet's own performance of the work on the two CDs which accompanied the original publication, though it perhaps lacks variety of tone and treatment, remaining at a high bardic pitch of intensity throughout. Dun's later sequence, *Universal* (Goldmark, 2002), abandons the tight London focus of his previous work in favour of a 'journey through transculture: London, the West Indies, North Africa, India' (publisher's prospectus), seeking the origins of creative and performative impulses and capabilities. Thus, the trajectory is similar to that of Allen Fisher and Iain Sinclair, into ever broader intellectual concerns which do not seem to lend themselves to cogent poetic organisation, and this later work has not received the notice or acclaim accorded to the earlier poem.

Arguably, the movement from a precisely 'loco-specific' work to a much broader geographical canvas in a subsequent work is also seen in the case of Roy Fisher, another of these key figures well established by the 1970s, though Fisher manages the transition better. Fisher's *City* had a similarly tight focus to *Place* and *Lud Heat*, in his case on a range of perceptions of the city of Birmingham, and he continued the mode of tightly disciplined urban provincial explorations into the 1970s, 1980s, and 1990s, with the sequence 'Handsworth Liberties' (1978), and then the epic-scale *A Furnace* (1986) and the sequence 'Six Texts for a Film' in his 1994 collection *Birmingham River*. Hence, the readers created by *City* were retained, and though their interests and tastes were stretched further, they were not challenged to make a kind of quantum leap and become either techno-scientific polymaths in order to keep up with the work (as in the case of Allen Fisher), or else out-and-out mystics (as with Aidan Dun). Roy Fisher is above all a long-poem poet, and his shorter poems are often strangely uneven, quirky or self-deprecatingly jokey. This apparent anxiety about perhaps seeming too serious and 'intellectual' is a problem reflected in the inappropriate titles given to his various volumes of Collected Poems, the first of which was subtitled 'The ghost of a paper bag', and the two most recent (from Bloodaxe) being *The Dow Low Drop* and *The Long and the Short of It*. He does have occasional successes with short poems, a powerful example being 'A Sign Illuminated', which is about the Birmingham Corporation illuminated bus which, during Fisher's childhood, used to emerge rather spookily from the depot on occasions of national celebration to tour the city and suburbs. It was an antique vehicle in which the silhouetted driver 'sat exposed above the engine', and the poem ends with the information that it 'possessed no / route number, passengers or conductor; was less / than a bus, let alone less than lit up'.[9] The piece has a vivid solidity of mood and image, yet the ending gives it a typically 'Fisherian' conceptual twist which complicates the whole, in a satisfyingly tight and controlled way. But this piece is cognate with Fisher's core Birmingham material, and could easily be a residual fragment from *City*.

But, to repeat, Fisher's hold on the broader poetic canvas is very sure, and that is indisputably where his reputation rests. At the risk of delivering a hostage to fortune, I would claim that *A Furnace* is his masterpiece, though the difficulty of this text is formidable – it can often seem 'fugitive from all exegesis', to quote a line from the text itself (*The Long and the Short of It*, p. 73). Indeed, reading it brings home vividly both the challenge and the risky allure, of explicating contemporary poetry from the radical side of the spectrum. Initially, it is like standing at the foot of a daunting wall of words, a sheer cliff-face that seems to have no visible footholds at all. Furthermore, usually the ascent has not been previously attempted, so there are no known routes, no useful bits of gear and tackle left on the climbing face by predecessors. Edging out along a precarious shelf of words induces feelings of vertigo (like those described in the Denise Riley poem quoted later), and explicating these radical contemporary texts is the extreme sport of literary criticism. In the case of *A Furnace*, there are in fact, predecessors whose work is very useful,[10] but once above the tree-line of critical commentary, so to speak, it becomes apparent that what is needed is a planned collaborative expedition by a co-ordinated team, in which the terrain could be mapped out in a systematic way, section by section. Broad surveys from helicopter height are useful, but this text needs line-by-line explication and annotation, like *The Waste Land* or *The Cantos*.

However, at the start *A Furnace* reassuringly signals its relationship to *City* with the beautifully sustained 'Introit' section which acts as its prelude, the speaker being on the top deck of a trolley-bus crossing towards the outskirts of the city in hazy November sunshine, 'the trolley wires / chattering and humming from somewhere else' above his head. The speaker contemplates the processes of thinking, seeing, realising – preoccupations which are so much the essence of Fisher:

Whatever
approaches my passive taking-in,
then surrounds me and goes by
will have itself understood only
phase upon phase
by separate involuntary
strokes of my mind, dark
swings of a fan-blade
that keeps a time of its own

(*The Long and the Short of it*, p. 52)

It might seem at this stage that we are in for a re-run of *City*, but the poem's initial geographical focus is the West Midlands as a whole, rather than just its urban core, and it therefore follows the outward-moving trajectory of *City*, which, when reread, shows a remarkable centrifugal tendency that constantly takes it outwards to the regions on the edge of the city where the surrounding countryside begins to encroach. Thus, the geography of *A Furnace* is regional, conceptual and trans-historical. It is much taken, for instance, with the ancient stones of Brittany, with pre-historic burial chambers and with places where one civilisation is built on top of another – first an ancient settlement, then a Greek city, then a Roman, then a medieval trade centre, then a modern industrialised city. The poem seems to be preoccupied with questions such as: where does the creative and organisational impulse come from? What is the nature of the energies which take it through these transformations? A city produces a Marx or a Hitler, but why? What are the factors which are in play? Described thus, the concerns seem as vast as Allen Fisher's, so what is it that creates the feeling that the poem can somehow contain and *embody* them, making the bitterly difficult slog of explication in the end worth it? It is partly that the poem constantly touches solid objects, envisions specific places, so that the reader (at the end of Part 1) can, for instance, walk into the deep cleft known as Lud's Church in the Staffordshire countryside which is linked with the Green Chapel that features in *Sir Gawain and the Green Knight*, or can see the rust on semi-derelict industrial installations, those unburied carcases of deceased industrial enterprise which seemed to litter the environs of every city in the country in the 1970s and 1980s: this, for instance, is the area of the Saltley Viaduct just outside Birmingham, formerly the scene of massed railway depots and interchanges, now fenced off and weed-infested, and viewed in Sunday morning sunlight:

> Arcanum, Forbidden
> open space, marked out with
> tramlines in great curves among blue
> Rowley Rag paving bricks. (p. 57)

The Rowley Rag is the volcanic stone quarried in the West Midlands, evoking a vast timescale and the forces which form a landscape and make it subsequently conducive to one industry rather than another. The area now looks as if blasted again by those same volcanic forces, not a place 'for stopping and spying', says the poet:

> The single human refuge
> a roadside urinal, rectangular
> roofless sarcophagus of tile and brick,
> topped round with spikes and
> open to the sky. (p. 57)

The financial and commercial gods had spoken, smiting the land and transferring production to the other side of the world. The Fisher Kings of these blighted waste lands are pursued – we come upon the 'wonderful carcase', 'pitiable and horrific' (pp. 57, 58) of these industrial giants, and wonder what the disease can have been that killed them. Fisher is almost alone among British poets of the post-industrial era in noticing what had happened and wondering why. Such descriptions are found almost nowhere else in contemporary poetry: the post-war dismantling of the cities was recorded by documentary photographers – such as Jimmy Forsyth in Newcastle and Shirley Baker in Salford – but the poets of the time mostly seem to have been occupied elsewhere. There are exceptions, and a number of poets I have written about elsewhere charted the process of urban decay and breakdown in the 1970s and 1980s – including: Edwin Morgan's sequence 'Glasgow Sonnets' (in his *From Glasgow to Saturn*, 1973); Ken Smith's *Fox Running* (1980) and 'The London Poems', in his collection *Terra* (1986); the sequence 'Drumming' by Ken Edwards (1982); Peter Reading's book *Perduta Gente* (1989); Robert Hampson's *Seaport* (1995); John Barnie's *The City* (1993); and Bill Griffiths's *The Book of Spilt Cities* (1999).[11]

Barry MacSweeney is another radical poet whose post-1980 work has added significantly to his stature, and he too has followed a similar trajectory, outwards from a decaying urban provincial centre (the Newcastle of

Hellhound Memos, 1993) to a broader regional focus (the Cumbria/Northumbria of *Pearl*, 1995).[12] *Hellhound Memos* shows Newcastle at the height of its industrial decline, presenting it as a kind of Dantean netherworld which has descended into some even deeper abyss – violence and addiction abound, and, as an early reviewer said, the city seems filled with Ecstasy dealers and joyriders; it's a 'Fauvist metropolis. // The world with hate and envy raging' (p. 242); 'Week-kneed sunk in my blueness, my sun / your sun. My fuck-up, your fuck-up. / My rain, your rain. // All aboard and welcome' (p. 225). The pace and drive of the sequence is relentless and exhilarating, but it is also more than somewhat manic ('I don't care what the damage is. Or the waste', p. 227). What saving grace there is comes from a sense of the countryside beyond the city, which so often seems to be close in British provincial cities – surrounding hills are visible from the city centre, outlying dales and moors are just a bus ride away, or it is just a short ferry trip to the other side of the river where ramblers and cyclists over generations have spent their weekends. Thus, *Hellhound Memos* constantly refers to wildflowers and foliage, using their local names and evoking their reputations as soothing balms or as folk remedies, so that a kind of ironic, exalted pastoral tone seems to soothe the urban damage:

> we fled into the dales and yarns, the yearns,
> the raw grass which greened our thighs and knees.
> The sun was like a bucketful of gold! (p. 235)

Interwoven with the language of anxiety and excess is a vocabulary of loving botanic precision – in the final poem it is mentioned that 'the lanceolate leaves, still / fragrant, ready for the pan, are quivering under the fjord blasts tonight' (p. 242). 'Lanceolate' is a botanical term which designates leaves 'having the general shape of a lance; much longer than wide, with the widest part lower than the middle and a pointed apex' (*Wiktionary*). Carefully picked during the day out in the countryside, they are readied for cooking, as the wind rises outside and the speaker empathises with the plants that bear the brunt of the blast. In *Hellhound Memos*, then, a poet who had been over-hyped at various points in his career finally produces the goods, transcending the dark glamour of his alcoholism, presenting us with a finely judged enactment of loss of control rather than with loss of control itself, and producing that best of all virtues in a long poem, the knowledge of when to stop.

Pearl, appearing two years later, moves further out into that surrounding countryside – a Northumbria and Cumbria which is partly of the mind, producing a myth of innocence in the mute child whom, says the blurb,

'MacSweeney [when himself a child] taught to read and write on a slate in the rain.' MacSweeney is frequently thought of as the protégé or pupil of Basil Bunting, and *Pearl* therefore as the poetic child of Bunting's Northumbrian epic *Briggflatts*, but a recent article argues persuasively that the connections between the two have probably been over-emphasised: 'The similarities between *Pearl* and *Briggflatts* are particularly visible for several reasons: they occupy analogous positions in each poet's career; evoke their author's passionate regard for his individually distinct landscape; utilise memories of formative sexual experience as central motifs and represent maturely developed and personalised assessments of a particular place.'[13] The *Pearl* sequence of poems charts Pearl's joyous entry into language and the speaker's sexual awakening, and the echoes of hurt and healing are vividly rendered in images and sensations. Whereas the speaker of *Briggflatts* is the misty-eyed rememberer of first love who is now in his old age, the speaker in *Pearl* often *is* Pearl, convincingly given the words she lacks, and MacSweeney's often successful attempts to re-create her subjectivity are much more convincing than (for instance) better-known acts of poetic ventriloquy such as Tony Harrison's creation of his skinhead personae in *V*. MacSweeney's strategic design is surer, in that the words on the page are not actually meant to be Pearl's spoken words, but represent words thought or felt:

> I held myself in a corner laughing
> when they moved around their pretty vowels and consonants.
> Outside, are they blisters of hurt on the moon?
> Or the rims of craters before you fall defeated
> with the dogs on your blood.
> Will I return forty years from now – 1998 –
> to find the chalkboard frozen, nibs
> broken, inkwell shards scattered to four walls,
> by Irish gales through shattered windows, and
> no one ready to pick up a pen to say this:
> sentences are not for prisoners only.[14]

Pearl takes up about one-third of MacSweeney's last book, *The Book of Demons*, the remainder being the sequence which gives it its overall title. It contains some further Pearl poems, but overall it has no central magnetic track to ground and orientate its ferocious and self-destructive energies, and that makes it a lesser achievement than *Hellhound Memos* and *Pearl*. These poems are MacSweeney's 'Crack-Up Essays', and it is difficult to believe there could have been any way back from them. Though the seething mists of self-loathing and despair clear from time to time, revealing moments of beautiful and poignant calm ('Standing on a January morning hunched together on a gatepost / when snow starts / is like I hope heaven will be', p. 84), the sequence as a whole cannot be ranked with the two earlier ones. But no matter, for the Boy from the Green Cabaret had already fulfilled his early promise – his future stature will rest on *Hellhound Memos* and *Pearl*, and in them he has produced more of real poetic substance than have many poets whose life demons were less destructive than his.

Many of the poets thus far considered have associations with the so-called 'London' wing of the avant-garde of the 1970s, and this is often set against the 'Cambridge' wing, conveniently represented by the 1987 anthology *A Various Art*, edited by Andrew Crozier and Tim Longville, in the Paladin Poetry series for which Iain Sinclair was series editor. The series as a whole sought to represent poets who 'have chosen to work outside the customary institutions of British poetry'. Except for telling us that most of the included poets had started writing in the 1960s, Crozier's guarded introduction to the volume reveals little about the 'Cambridge' 'group', except that they were not really 'Cambridge' (which is just one of several places mentioned) and were not really a 'group' (having merely 'become aware of one another's presence' and of their 'shared reaction to current taste'). What made them at the beginning 'identifiable to one another' was their common interest in the American poetic tradition, 'not that of Pound and Eliot but that of Pound and Williams'. Nothing so vulgar as 'polemic apology or manifesto' is offered in the introduction, because the poets assembled do not claim to be 'anything amounting to a school'. However, towards the end of the introduction, the word 'language' occurs frequently, though the sentences containing this word never quite make sense. Thus, the collection manifests 'a poetry deployed towards the complex and multiple experience in language of all of us': the poets collected 'set their writing towards a range of languages, ordinary, scientific, traditional, demotic, liturgical, and so on', and have a commitment to 'the discovery of meaning and form in language itself'.[15]

Of those already discussed, the collection contains Roy Fisher and Iain Sinclair, and other prominent contributors are Anthony Barnett, David Chaloner, Andrew Crozier himself, Veronica Forrest-Thomson, John Hall, John James, Tim Longville, Douglas Oliver, John Riley and Peter Riley. In so far as there might be said to be a typical poem by this 'school', it could be this one:

> Street lights reflected in the wet
> on the way back though the rain stopped
> before we went out.
> Lost on the outer rim of some

barely perceptible whirling, I float
slowly in toward the other.
A blight from England's present-day
covers me. I can hardly move my mind.
Is that any way to speak?
What we want indeed! He comes in
and states exactly what he wants,
a bacon sandwich and a cup of tea.
If you count up the different senses of 'you' in the text
(including these two)
You may reach some interesting conclusions.

This perhaps indicates what might be meant by a poetry which is committed to 'the discovery of meaning and form in language itself', and it is possibly indicative of the practice of poets who 'set their writing towards a range of languages'.[16] But there is, perhaps, a rather higher degree of uniformity of technique and attitude among these poets than the editor allows in his introduction (in spite of the title of the anthology), for the above 'poem' is actually a composite made up of lines taken from five different poems by Andrew Crozier, John James, Douglas Oliver, Peter Riley and Nick Totton – yet the joins are by no means obvious.[17] Indeed, a tentative verdict on 'Cambridge' would be that the conscious orientation of poets towards 'language' (that is to say, just 'language', not some specified variety of images, metaphors, ideas, things, events – or even just words) inevitably tends to produce a certain thinness of effect. A kinder way of putting this would be that 'Cambridge' poets write best when furthest away from following the precepts of their (albeit very tentative and ever so British) manifesto, although they are not unique in that, for such is usually the case with poetic manifestos. Perhaps we might even proffer a kind of homeopathic principle, maintaining that whatever the poetics, it will probably be improved by a certain amount of dilution. In his typically modest way, Crozier does not announce a Revolution of the Word, just a slight touch on the tiller to take poetry a little more in the direction of 'the complex and multiple experience in language of all of us'. But whether 'language' is a fruitful goal for a poet to steer towards is open to question – it can easily become more of a gaol than a goal.

Still, two 'Cambridge' names which certainly do stand out – the first as being on the periphery of the 'school', the second as being all too near the centre – are those of Denise Riley and J. H. Prynne. Riley's affiliations are various: as a feminist theorist her work links back to the writing of the 1960s and 1970s, as a poetic experimentalist she has distinct affinities with other women innovator poet-performers of her own generation, like Maggie O'Sullivan, Wendy Mulford and Geraldine Monk,[18] and as a 'critical-creative' practitioner, writing both poetry and criticism, she has been an important figure in the spread of creative writing courses in UK higher education. Her reputation was consolidated with the publication of her *Mop Mop Georgette: New and Selected Poems 1986–1993* (1993), and her *Selected Poems* (2000), both from Reality Street. She is featured in all the defining anthologies of the radical movement, and discussed in all the accounts of contemporary poetry which recognise radicalism as a distinct area of the contemporary poetic spectrum. Sheppard's description of her in *The Poetry of Saying* makes her sound very 'Cambridge' in the sense just discussed – 'her work . . . seems muted, the ironical play with voice and self more often attenuated by traditional rhetorical figures'.[19] Yet she would not blend so unnoticeably as the others into the composite 'Cambridge' poem constructed earlier. While it is true, on the one hand, that she does the 'Cambridge' thing (foregrounding aspects of 'the self and the lyric "I" as constructed in language' as Keith Tuma puts it[20]), it is also true that she somehow does it much more seriously, not as if regarding the language games of the rest of us from a vantage point of strangely privileged superiority, as most of the male poets in Crozier's anthology often seem to do. In one of her best poems, for instance, 'Wherever you are, be somewhere else', the language first constructs the illusion of solid reality before it deconstructs it, enacting the terror of the annihilation of self in a convincing way before talking about dissolving selves and the like:

> Draw the night right up over my eyes so that I
> don't see and then I'm gone; push the soft hem
> of the night into my mouth so that I stay quiet
> when an old breeze buffets my face to muffle
> me in terror of being left, or is that a far worse
> terror of not being left. No. Inching flat out
> over a glacier overhanging blackness I see no
> edge but will tip where its glassy cold may stop
> short and hard ice crash to dark air.[21]

When the speaking voice(s), at the conclusion of the poem, admits its inadequacies and incapacities and earnestly seeks something from us, it is far more persuasive than most of the others in the Crozier anthology at convincing us that this is a real crisis rather than just a philosophical crux, in other words, that it is not just a language game in which, always from a safe distance, the speaker calmly exposes our everyday linguistic naivety with his (nearly always his) lecturer's laser pointer – on the contrary, this speaker needs something from us:

> Stop now. Hold it there. Balance. Be beautiful. Try.
> – and I can't do this. I can't talk like any of this.
> You hear me not do it.

Prynne, by contrast, is less often anthologised than Riley, being fastidious about such appearances (he declined an invitation in the 1970s to appear in Mottram's *Poetry Review*, and would not agree to being in Keith Tuma's Oxford anthology of twentieth-century British and Irish poetry) but his work is prominently discussed in all the relevant critical sources, and Randall Stevenson's Volume XII of the *Oxford English Literary History* caused a stir by seeming to put him forward as the most important living British poet. The attention given to his work increased dramatically with the publication of his *Collected Poems* by Bloodaxe in 1999: the *TLS*, says Stevenson, described Prynne's later work as a series of 'impenetrable enigmas', though in his view Prynne does provide clues for his crossword puzzles, such as his comment in *Conductors of Chaos* that 'within the great aquarium of language the light refracts variously and can bounce by inclinations not previously observed' (I do not myself find this comment particularly helpful).[22] A brief row in 2004, when Stevenson's book appeared, described him as preferring Prynne to Larkin, which he did, and calling Prynne the most significant poet of the twentieth century, which he did not quite.

Any evaluation of Prynne, however, needs to be conducted at (so to speak) poem level, rather than at the generalised level of seeking out broad principles of language use, or exploring images like that of the aquarium in which linguistic light is bent or refracted and bounces in unpredictable ways. The poem 'One Way at Any Time' is unusual among Prynne's work in providing a single long 'take' on an identifiable scene; it is set inside a busy transport café, where lorries and vans are seen passing beyond the steamed-up windows, and commonplace events happen – the waitress leans over to take the speaker's plate before he has finished, and snatches of conversation are heard from those at adjacent tables. There is a brief exchange with the speaker by one of the other customers, but mostly the speaker notes his surroundings and thinks about language in the Cambridge way described in Crozier's preface. For instance, he notes the inscriptions on the sides of vans and lorries ('Through the steamed-up windows it says / "Thermal Insulation Products" I can't see / where it's come from' and 'McCormick International rumbles past / in truly common dialect'). What is notable about what is noted, however, is not quite clear. When the waitress tries to take the plate, 'the man opposite without think- / ing says must be on piecework'. But what does the speaker think the other speaker *ought* to be thinking? The one form of language designated in the poem which the speaker does not register any awareness of *as* a register is his own (actually rather ordinary) poetic diction, as when, speaking of the same man opposite, he tells us that 'his / regular false teeth gleam like sardines'. The poet-speaker is, apparently, happy with his simile and pleased to have spotted the falseness of the teeth, and he goes on, 'But / the twist here is that it's all in that yokel / talk they have for the rustics and this man / is in overalls'. All but the speaker himself are laid bare by accent or garb, or even by not speaking, like 'his boy about nine silent / beside him'. Someone says he 'left by six', and the speaker notes primly, 'and I don't know whether a.m. or p.m.' as if noting the man's inability to use a middle-class 'elaborated code' which does not rely on implicitness.[23] The poem is certainly an embodiment of the brief set out in the introduction, for it offers us 'a poetry deployed towards the complex and multiple experience in language of all of us'. But it also shows how this formula leads to a certain inhuman aridity, producing a kind of Mass Observation poetry of the overheard, in which the overhearers never overhear themselves. I have discussed this matter in some detail to illustrate the point that the 'language' agenda in poetry is by no means always a radical or progressive one. Overall, then, however we define the 'radicalism' of the 'parallel tradition', we would do well to steer clear of the dead end of seeing it as entailing chiefly a certain attitude to language. Language itself is not the point – it is a stance towards content, towards the human subject and towards the nature of social experience which counts.

Notes

1. *The Penguin Book of Contemporary British Poetry*, ed. Blake Morrison and Andrew Motion (Harmondsworth: Penguin, 1982). The simplest map of the poetry of that period sees a 'Mainstream' dominated by the conservative poetics of the 'Movement', and an oppositional 'Margins' dominated by the radical poetics of the British Poetry Revival, as identified by Eric Mottram in his essay 'The British Poetry Revival, 1960–75', reprinted in Robert Hampson and Peter Barry (eds.), *New British Poetries: The Scope of the Possible* (Manchester: Manchester University Press, 1993), pp.15–45. Randall Stevenson neatly characterises the fundamental dichotomy between these two groupings as 'Movement or Revival' (the title of chapter five in his *The Last of England?*, vol. XII, 1960–2000, of *The Oxford English Literary History* (Oxford: Oxford University Press, 2004). Others have disliked the self-marginalisation implicit in adopting the term 'Margins', and have preferred to use terms such as 'the parallel tradition', or 'the alternative tradition', which

are not much of an improvement in that respect, or else 'the neo-Modernist tradition', which emphasises a claimed continuity of 'project' between these poets and the British and American poets of the High Modernist period. For an excellent account of some of the differences between 'BPR' poetry and the rest, see Ken Edwards, 'The Two Poetries', *Angelaki*, 3:1 (April 2000), pp. 25–36. Also extremely useful are: Peter Middleton's chapter, 'Poetry after 1970,' in Laura Marcus and Peter Nicholls (eds.), *The Cambridge History of Twentieth Century Literature* (Cambridge: Cambridge University Press, 2004); the chapter 'Linguistically Innovative Poetry 1978–2000', pp. 142–67, in Robert Sheppard, *The Poetry of Saying* (Liverpool: Liverpool University Press, 2005); and 'Innovative Poetry in English', pp. 121–38, in Tony Lopez, *Meaning Performance: Essays on Poetry* (Cambridge: Salt Publishing, 2006). For an overview account of the nature of 'BPR' writing, see the chapter 'The British Poetry Revival – Some Characteristics', pp. 123–43 in Peter Barry, *Poetry Wars* (Cambridge: Salt Publishing, 2006).

2. The 'Martian' vogue for visual metaphor was initiated by Craig Raine's prize-winning poem 'A Martian Sends a Postcard Home' (the title poem of his 1979 collection). James Fenton introduced the term in the article 'Of the Martian School' (*The New Statesman*, 20 October 1978). Christopher Reid and David Sweetman were other poets identified as members of the 'school'.
3. In an earlier piece I described the 'secret narrative' genre as involving 'the use in poetry of obliquely told, often fragmented and unanchored narratives, emotive but obscure in character, often with highly-coloured colonial, or historical settings'. See Peter Barry, *Contemporary British Poetry and the City* (Manchester: Manchester University Press, 2000), p. 56. The name 'secret narrative' comes from Andrew Motion's volume *Secret Narratives* (Edinburgh: Salamander Press, 1983), and a representative 'secret narrative' poem is Motion's 'Open Secrets' in his collection *Dangerous Play: Poems 1974–1984* (London: Penguin, 1984), p. 11.
4. For anthologies mainly devoted to the work of the radicals, see: Andrew Crozier and Tim Longville (eds.), *A Various Art* (London: Paladin, 1987; 1990); Gillian Allnutt, Fred D'Aguiar, Ken Edwards and Eric Mottram (eds.), *The New British Poetry: 1968–1988* (London: Paladin, 1988); Iain Sinclair (ed.), *Conductors of Chaos: A Poetry Anthology* (London: Picador, 1996); Ric Caddel and Peter Quartermain (eds.), *Other British and Irish Poetry since 1970* (Middletown, CT: Wesleyan University Press, 1999); Nicholas Johnson (ed.), *Foil: An Anthology – Poetry, 1985–2000* (Exbourne, West Devon: Etruscan Books, 2000); Keith Tuma (ed.), *Anthology of Twentieth-Century British and Irish Poetry* (New York: Oxford University Press, 2001); and Jerome Rothenberg and Pierre Joris (eds.), *Poems for the Millennium: Volume Two – From Postwar to Millennium* (Berkeley, CA: University of California Press, 1998).
5. The last named is now published in part as *Gravity* (Cambridge: Salt Publishing, 2004), described as 'the first five books of poems from the sequence *Gravity as a Consequence of Shape*, started in 1982 and scheduled for completion in 2005'. 'Birdland' is the final section of 'Brixton Fractals', which is the first book of the

five books which make up *Gravity*. The sequence *Place* was republished in full by Reality Street Editions in 2005.

6. See Allen Fisher, *Place* (Hastings: Reality Street Editions, 2005), pp. 133, 157. Further quotations are from this edition.
7. See p. 82 in the 2004 edition of *Gravity*, from which all quotations from 'Brixton Fractals' are taken.
8. *Lud Heat and Suicide Bridge* (London: Vintage Books, 1995), p. 149. Further quotations are from this edition.
9. *The Long and the Short of It*, p. 168. Further quotations are from this edition.
10. See, for instance, chapters 9 and 11 in John Kerrigan and Peter Robinson (eds.), *The Thing about Roy Fisher: Critical Studies* (Liverpool: Liverpool University Press, 2000).
11. All discussed in Barry, *Contemporary British Poetry and the City*.
12. First published by The Many Press in 1993, and reprinted in Iain Sinclair's *Conductors of Chaos*, to which pages numbers given here refer.
13. Rebecca A. Smith, 'Barry MacSweeney and the Bunting Influence: "A key figure in his literary universe?" ', *Jacket*, 35 (2008), http://jacketmagazine.com/35/smith-macsweeney.shtml, accessed 5 May 2008.
14. Barry MacSweeney, *The Book of Demons* (Newcastle upon Tyne: Bloodaxe, 1997), p. 30; further quotation from this edition.
15. Crozier and Longville (eds.), *A Various Art*, pp. 11, 12, 13, 14.
16. *Ibid.*, pp. 14, 13.
17. There are three lines by each of these, in the order listed.
18. For an influential collection of this kind of writing see: Maggie O'Sullivan (ed.), *Out of Everywhere: Linguistically Innovative Poetry by Women in North America and the UK* (Hastings: Reality Street Editions, 1996).
19. Including Hampson and Barry (eds.), *New British Poetries*, pp. 175–6; Tony Lopez, *Meaning Performance*, throughout, and Sheppard, *The Poetry of Saying*, pp. 163–4.
20. Tuma, *Anthology*, p. 748.
21. The poem quoted is in Iain Sinclair, *Conductors of Chaos*, pp. 392–3.
22. Quoted in Stevenson, *Oxford English Literary History*, vol. XII, p. 234.
23. Crozier and Longville (eds.), *A Various Art*, p. 250.

Chapter 53

Contemporary poetries in English, c.1980 to the present 2

JAMIE MCKENDRICK

More than thirty years ago, in his lecture 'Englands of the Mind', Seamus Heaney broached the subject of specifically 'English' poetry in relation to Ted Hughes, Philip Larkin and Geoffrey Hill: 'All three are hoarders and shorers of what they take to be the real England.'[1] In Heaney's reading these poets all brought to a head contrasting strains of a plural, contested, national identity. Since then, the entity of the United Kingdom has taken steps in the direction of increasing devolution, with regional parliaments in Scotland, Wales and Northern Ireland. The poetry of these three regions has often alluded to its cultural, and sometimes asserted its linguistic, distinctiveness. Inevitably, what this difference defined itself against was England (and English), and a supposed cultural hegemony, and yet whatever characterised 'English' poetry remained undefined, certainly unanthologised. Within the so-called Scottish Renaissance, figures such as Hugh MacDiarmid, Iain Crichton Smith, Norman McCaig, Edwin Morgan, the Gaelic poet Sorley MacClean and later Douglas Dunn, showed how vigorous and various this independence could be. The last forty or so years have seen the emergence of two remarkable generations of poets from Northern Ireland – the first including Seamus Heaney, Derek Mahon and Michael Longley, and the second, Paul Muldoon, Tom Paulin and Ciaran Carson. Whatever the forces that brought such a number of talented poets there to the fore, from the early 1970s onwards, the impact on British poetry has been momentous.

In the 1982 anthology, *The Penguin Book of Contemporary British Poetry*, the effect was startling – so much over there and so little here! Though had Heaney's triumvirate been included, comparison might have seemed more balanced. In speaking of an extended 'imaginative franchise' and 'the ludic' elements shared by their poets, the anthologists were bravely trying to bridge a chasm.[2] On the English side of this divide were, among others, the 'Martian' poets Craig Raine and Christopher Reid (so-called after Raine's poem 'A Martian Sends a Postcard Home'). Both poets shared a delight in the surfaces and appearances of things and in inventive simile, a procedure for which, as other critics have noticed, MacCaig might be considered the unacknowledged legislator. Clearly, metaphor and simile, the techniques of likening two or more disparate objects have been a perennial resource of poetry – famously in Donne's compasses and lovers, Herbert's pulley and the soul's attraction to God – but where the Metaphysical poets often compared the concrete to the abstract, Martian poetry showed little interest in the abstract and almost exclusively likened one to another concrete thing, or often several at once, so you could say that vehicle and tenor already started off with much in common. Characteristic of this method is Raine's 'The Grocer' which posts an epigraph from Joyce – 'the Kingdom of God cometh not with observation' – almost as a defiantly unheeded caveat:

> His cheesewire is a sun-dial selling by the hour.
> He brings it down at four and five o'clock,
> the wooden T gripped like a corkscrew.[3]

Whereas the first metaphor is showy and decorative, the simile that follows is more dynamic and economic. It might not be the Kingdom of Heaven but there's an element of the mustard seed. Although his work can be seen at its most elegant in *A Free Translation*,[4] Raine subsequently pushed against what might be considered a kind of ivory miniaturism in his long poem *History: The Home Movie*, though it is still most effective in the heightened details which often occlude the ambitious scheme of the poem: 'At the perforated line // of portholes, heavy, clamped, / faces like bottled fruit'. It domesticates the abstraction of history, by playing the story of his wife's family, the Pasternaks, against that of his own family, but the result is more like a photo album than a movie. Though many of the stills are striking, their effect can be undermined by reifications which may be intended to shock the complacent reader but come across as merely heartless: 'the full moon hangs up / her radical mastectomy', or 'The boy has chicken pox: / hard white blobs of candle grease / windows of translucent fat / suet crusts, cigarette burns, / craters.'[5] Even in translation, the contrasting use of metaphor in another intensely visual poet such as Tomas Tranströmer is instructive: 'and the banner of Baltic herring swayed in the depths. // And the swarm of smallpox caught up with him / clustered onto his face'.[6]

Reid's poems, which emerged in tandem with Raine's, also frequently employed couplets and eye-catching similes: in 'Baldanders' a weightlifter 'carries his pregnant belly / in the hammock of his leotard // like a melon wedged in a shopping bag' and is later seen as 'Glazed, like a mantelpiece frog' and finally as 'the World Champion (somebody, answer it!) / Human Telephone'.[7] There is an appealing affect and humane whimsy in this work but by his third book, *Katerina Brac*,[8] he had begun to put the *ostranye* techniques of Martianism to more interesting effect, writing in the persona of an East European woman poet. The estrangement proves durably liberating, and the poems work on several levels – as a coherent 'other' voice which implicitly criticises the perspectives of British poetry, as a vehicle to explore strangeness within the world and also as a witty commentary on the unexpected or inadvertently 'poetic' effects of translation – perhaps in homage to the Polish Zbigniew Herbert and Tadeusz Rosewicz or the Czech Miroslav Holub. Reid's later work has continued to develop, and ranges from curt and deftly ironic poems to longer tours de force such as 'Two Dogs on a Pub Roof'[9] (with its 'woof' rhyme running throughout) or 'Bollockshire', a devastatingly witty anathema on rural England. *For and After*,[10] which imaginatively extends the work of *Katerina Brac*, proves him also to be a gifted translator, subtly attentive to a variety of tones and voices.

Reading the couplets of Hugo Williams's short poem 'The Butcher'[11] in this anthology, one might be encouraged to think that he was a junior Martian poet; but actually he is from an altogether different planet, whether older or younger is hard to say, but certainly more sparing in its use of metaphor. What would not be apparent from this selection is the quality that would make him the author of poems such as 'Keats', which imagines an amorous encounter with a bag lady: 'She shows me / her business card, an empty sardine tin / attached to a chain around her neck'[12] or 'When I Grow Up' in which the straightforward language unleashes an anarchic and lacerating humour:

> When I grow up I want a thin piece of steel
> inserted into my penis for some reason.
> Nobody's to tell me why it's there. I want to guess.

The suggested site of these indignities is 'a National Health Hospice / somewhere in Manchester'[13] – evidently for the Southerner a place of exile worse than Scythia.

Reminiscence about such unpromising topics as prep schools, hairstyles and clothes fashions had somehow found a lyrical poet of lost time and human pathos. 'God give me strength to lead a double life' is the effortlessly resonant pentameter that begins 'Prayer', a poem about adultery. The irony of a prayer made to school oneself in vice has an appealing sacrilege to it, but the poem allows for the further irony that pursuing an affair, and living with the regrets it causes, does call on a certain kind of moral fortitude. In *Billy's Rain*,[14] where this poem is to be found, and its indoor sequel *Dear Room*,[15] a foundered extra-marital relationship is both relived, re-enacted and poignantly anatomised.

With his internationalist perspective and experience as a war correspondent, James Fenton, also showcased in that anthology, is willing to entertain a much more dramatic and global field of reference, as far off as the killing fields of South-East Asia and with murder as near to home as Staffordshire. Though many of the poems in Fenton's first two books have a formality reminiscent of Auden, the form has what seems to be a deliberate externality, as though its original purposes had become vacated and it remained an uninhabited, almost reproachful, shell, so the mismatch between form and content amounts to a metaphysical unease. 'A Staffordshire Murderer', though written in neat quatrains, scrupulously avoids the pentameter, and its formal veneer and internal irregularity help to build up a sinister vision of the English Midlands in which the Quaker George Fox crying out 'Woe to the bloody city of Lichfield', in belated witness to the martyrs of Roman Britain, and his challenge to the 'Steeple-house', is made co-eval with towpaths and helipads, and with a murderer who 'sees the point of you as no else does'.[16] The unsettling political passion in these poems seems to have moved increasingly towards the private in his more recent work, especially in his love poems, which have an artful simplicity. As these are celebrations of homosexual love, though, it could be argued that they have not entirely lost a political edge.

Andrew Motion, too, has little in common with the other English poets in his anthology. His predominant note is elegiac, from an early poem which deals with his mother's death after a riding accident to a more general sense of a lost England. It is a privileged England of country houses and tree-lined drives, but no less intensely felt and described for that. His syntax has a lithe intelligence that suggests his early critical work on the poetry of Edward Thomas has borne fruit. Poems such as 'Serenade' in the sequence 'A Long Story', which returns to the question of his mother's death, show what a considerable poet he is. The detail is finely realised and every slow phrase is plotted across the emotions:

> poor dumb creature nobody blamed,
> or could easily like any more either, which meant nobody
> came to talk to her much in the spot she eventually found
> under the spiky may tree in the field, and still less
> came to shoe her, so her hooves grew long and crinkled
> round the edges like wet cardboard (except they were hard) . . .[17]

With the plainest language, these lines themselves mournfully grow 'round the edges' and carefully evoke the texture of things; their sustained emotional freight is individual enough not to be overshadowed by Larkin's 'At Grass', a poem which it might superficially resemble.

Eleven years after Motion and Morrison's, another anthology appeared: *The New Poetry*. More than twice the length of the former, and with fifty-five poets rather than the former twenty, it takes up where the other left off. This inclusionary ethos may be admirable (showing regional as well as ethnic diversity in Britain's poetry) and yet there is little that stands comparison with the best of the earlier anthology. The editors, who claim 'the new poetry emphasises accessibility, democracy and responsiveness', have their first problem with Peter Reading, given prominence both in the introduction and selection. Reading's mordantly terminal satire on contemporary England has little truck with anything as palliative as 'democracy and responsiveness' and is deeply sceptical about 'the art's significance as public utterance'[18] (two claims the introduction makes for its characteristic poets) – as one can see from this caustic advert in *Ukulele Music*: '[Squirrelprick Press is producing my / latest, *Blood Drops in Distich*, / hand-deckled limp-covered rag, / Special Edition of ten]'.[19] His stance is for the most part bleakly misanthropic, though there are moments of comic tenderness, for example in his portrayal of Viv the cleaner in the same book.

Regarding the impact of Northern Irish poetry, the deceptive straight-faced qualities of Muldoon's poems as well as his continuous, cunning play on idiom have found a host of British imitators, and *The New Poetry* offers no shortage of examples. And yet, without the tense backdrop of the Troubles, this manner quickly descends into jokey mannerism. Imagine the roundabout octave of Muldoon's poem 'The Sightseers'[20] without its deadly sestet and you can see how the possibility of bathos haunts this legacy. Clearly though, it is not just political circumstances that make Muldoon, and the other Northern Irish poets, figures of such importance. David Harsent, though older than Muldoon, is someone on whom the Irish poet's influence has been productive. In *Marriage* (2002) the skewed and inventive rhyming is of a piece with the whole perspective, and his *Legion* (2005) is a haunting and original collection. Perhaps his earlier translations from the Sarajevan poet Goran Simic have helped him write this convincing sequence of poems from an unspecified war zone. Alan Jenkins is another poet whose deft rhyming and sense of form may owe some debt to Muldoon, but whose concerns are very much his own, and based in a vision of England, of literary London and the south coast.

Michael Hofmann is one notable talent which that anthology signals. From his first book *Nights in the Iron Hotel* (1984), perhaps the most impressive debut volume since Tom Paulin's *State of Justice*, his poems have seemed set apart, at odds with the general currents of British poetry. Alight on any of his poems and you find an unmistakable stylistic signature. Take the ending of 'On the Margins' from *Acrimony*:

> We hear the hoarse, see-saw cries of the donkeys
> grazing in the churchyard, mother and daughter,
> and the first mosquitoes, bouncing up and down,
> practising their verticals like a videogame. Next door,
> his green clothes hung on pegs, Eric, the rustic burr,
> is taking his bath, whistling and crooning happily
> in his timeless, folkloric voice. I pat your nakedness.
> In evil whispers, I manage to convince you.[21]

The donkeys' cries are punningly 'hoarse', and 'see-saw' is inventively onomatopoeic (including 'Eeyore'), leading on to the mosquitoes 'bouncing up and down'. The finely observed analogy with early videogames has a hint of the 'Martian' but does not seem to want to stop for applause. This slightly crazed and sardonic pastoral is completed with the green man Eric, 'the rustic burr', who will presumably stick; 'timeless', in passing, gathers up a surplus meaning of out of time or tuneless. The finale is sex, prepared for by the 'see-saw' and 'bouncing', but the poem delights in its errant, polyvalent particles as much as it gives a trenchant glimpse of a moneyed countryside, 1980s social mores and of the nature of the relationship it treats. What is utterly his own is the sheer excess of verbal play, the way it allows language to generate and multiply levels of meaning. It finds spaces within phrases, twists and spins within words, things that had been passed over unsuspected before Hofmann. These effects would not be apprehensible without the exact linguistic scruple and intellectual mobility he brings to his lines.

England is just one site for Hofmann's migratory imagination, which also inhabits, with the same restless particularity of vision, Germany and the United States (the other countries he lives and works in). 'Dean Point' offers a particularly enervated vision of England. It could, of course, be an industrial premise anywhere, but it is sited at what seems to be a Cornish Gabbro mine. The reader, however, is deliberately left uncertain as to what is being processed in this ransacked landscape shaped, on a Dantesque model, by 'three of four turns of a gigantic screw'. From an ecological point of view, the poem speaks of a complicity of ignorance – again and again 'the mess of possibilities'[22] is explored to no avail, confronting a set of unreadable forensic signs, and even the sea seems to have long abandoned any Keatsian 'priestlike task / Of pure ablution round earth's human shores'.[23] Impotent, it deposits some sea-weed like a 'bloodied thighbone' (an almost humorous, Gothic touch) and 'spends itself a little way onto the sand'.[24] It is like a study in Marxian alienation, in which only waste products are visible, and even these are out of bounds, and it signals an England even more bereft than the eighties London scenes which *Acrimony* described with such verve and in such metallic detail.

Among other poets who have learned from Muldoon, Simon Armitage's work stands out. One characteristic poem, from his acclaimed first book *Zoom*, begins:

> I have not bummed across America
> with only a dollar to spare, one pair
> of busted Levi's and a bowie knife.
> I have lived with thieves in Manchester.

Something of a manifesto, this has a swaggering Northern exoticism to it, but the poem moves on to give its real credentials: 'I held the wobbly head of a boy / at the day centre, and stroked his fat hands.' I don't think the England visible in these lines had really made its way into poetry before. A love poem like 'Night Shift', from the same book, shows Armitage's capacity for emotion without sentimentality: 'and in this space we have worked and paid for / we have found ourselves, and lost each other'. At times his early work plays obsessively on idiom and favours a riff of parallel phrases over the *mot juste*, but then in 'Ivory' this gallimaufry of synonyms is the rhythmic motor of the poem: 'No more malarkey, / no baloney. No more cuffuffle / or shenanigans; // all that caboodle / is niet dobra'.[25] Its linguistic surfeit is the whole point – a mixing pot of American, Irish and English slang ending up in a Russian cul-de-sac. These earlier poems have a confident, rhythmic energy that sets them against the mannerly and muted ironies more often met with in British verse. What is surprising is that for a poet of such popular appeal, his poems, whilst often humorous, make few concessions to facile effects. Armitage's work is often linked with that of another gifted poet, Glyn Maxwell, with whom he has collaborated, but where Maxwell's inventive and deliberately jolting syntax keeps the reader in a state of anticipation, Armitage's poems are in a more accessible vernacular – abounding in jokes and contemporary reference. Increasingly, though his subject matter ranges from the South American rainforest to outer space, he has begun to explore an England of his own mind, a persistent and neglected place.

Armitage (born 1965), the most popular poet of his generation, shares a confident play on idiom and a pithy demotic with Carol Ann Duffy (born 1955), the most popular of hers; though it is unlikely either one has influenced the other. She can be seen at her best in 'Mrs Midas', a poem that delivers a continuous ripple of invention both in language and imagery. The book it is part of, *The World's Wife*,[26] plays many variations on the same theme, essentially a debunking of the masculine, the phrasing rarely less than punchy and memorable. Although it comprises a series of dramatic monologues, most of the voices are similar and sound pretty much like Duffy's own, so a reader drawn to that voice will find much to admire.

Sean O'Brien has long been exploring a dysfunctional England of his own: a defeated landscape, a *paysage demoralisé*, only occasionally relieved by a utopian glimpse of what the place might be like, free of the weight of the past: 'It is somewhere / In moments of weakness at Worcester Shrub Hill / Or in Redditch or Selby you wished / You could enter. You already had. This is it, / The good place, unencumbered by meaning' in 'Somebody Else'. A few lines later the faint idyll has been snuffed out: 'were you moved / To halve a gravestone you might find / That *England 2pm* was written through it'. This is a terminal, sardonic advance on Larkin's equally time-specific 'Sad Steps': 'Four o'clock . . .' O'Brien's poem ends in an angry though moving compassion:

> When will you learn? What could it mean,
> Conspiracy, when everyone conspires
> Against themselves and does not know it?

A poem like 'Essay on Snow' from the same book shows that this emotion is capable of real lyricism among 'Untrodden parks and freezing underpasses' – 'There is a bird somewhere. Its voice // Is like chipping an icicle'.[27] He has such an extensive wardrobe of dour, state-of-the-nation props, such a vast repertoire of grim effects, that he can effortlessly access any telling detail. Often the details are arresting, as in the opening of 'Boundary Beach': 'Invalids, perverts, and chambermaids born to be duped', everything is murderous and glowering, like 'the constable sat in the kitchen, his collar undone, / As he wiped his moustache free of mustard'. There is a kind of cataloguing impulse which can make the poems seem like a list of national ailments, but at the same time it takes courage and intelligence to write these head-on diagnostic poems about England. He is also able to shape memorable lines with great frequency: 'The rotundas of the mercantile retired / Glint with speculation. Telescopes are aimed . . .'[28] This ('Dundee Heatwave') has an Audenesque authority and music which is equally evident in his latest book, *The Drowned Book* (2007).

Jo Shapcott's poetry explores a slant, side-on England, and it seems right that her last book, *Tender Taxes* (2002), should combine a celebration of the Welsh borders with the borderless re-workings into English of the Prague-born German Rainer Maria Rilke's poems in French. Displacement and disruption of perspective have been qualities of her work since her first book *Electroplating the Baby* (1988), which begins in China ('Hubei Province Tornado') with the flight of an 'umbrella-holding woman' and sites her poems in the realm of wonders, but wonders recounted in a level, natural tone.[29] Her poem 'Phrase Book' shows some of the ways in which Shapcott undermines any fixity of viewpoint in her narratives. It intercuts archaic phrases from a language book with the military and media idiolect of the first Gulf War, and overlays them upon glimpses of a love affair. This palimpsest technique is daringly unresolved. The confident, dated phrases which speak of England's cultural superiority to the unspecified foreigners – 'Let me pass please. I am an Englishwoman' – against a backdrop of war, suddenly open out on to vistas of insecurity and vulnerability, but the real victims of the ongoing war are hidden by a technocratic language. The skin with which the poem begins, and which is celebrated in the glimpsed sexual scene ('when I raised my body to his mouth') is the universalised subject of violence as well as love, which may well be the 'word' the speaker of the poem has yet to learn in this other language.[30] The poem purposefully disturbs the reader by setting these images side by side, or one above the other. The England of her poems is a country deprived of the old certainties, and no worse for that. Despite the presence of numerous place names her relation to England is shorn of atavism and rootedness in any locale; it is destabilised, made labile, even at times turned into a cartoon encounter as when 'Tom and Jerry Visit England', but this turns out to be not just a playful critique of American cartoons but also a study of the entrapment and limitations of a poem.

Alice Oswald seems to have emerged from a Hughesian Deep England, a Devonshire terrain, and her poems tend to spurn the city and look for their roots in the natural world. Her first book is full of sonorous and seasonal abstractions: like the opening quatrain of her sonnet 'Prayer':

> Here I work in the hollow of God's hand
> with Time bent round into my reach. I touch
> the circle of the earth, I throw and catch
> the sun and moon by turns into my mind

which multi-tasks gardening with cosmic juggling. These timeless poems, barely touched by the modern world, can make the Georgians look impossibly modern. Children's rhymes and the ballad tradition are used to curious effect, as in 'Woman in a Mustard Field':

> The sun was rude and sensible
> the rivers ran for hours
> and whoops I found a mustard field
> exploding into flowers[31]

Lines as questionable as these (why 'rude and sensible', why only 'for hours', why exactly 'whoops'?) make her second book *Dart* (2002) all the more extraordinary: an ambitious long poem which plaits the voices of the river with those who work on it. Possibly that sense of other voices than her own, other tones of voice than the vatic, have made the poem more fluent and formally explorative. Inventively, it combines Coleridgean marginal summaries, song-like lines and sections of prose for some of the characters. Behind it lies the ghost of Hughes's poetry, including his book *River*, but the writing is more freehand, choric and plurilingual. If it misses much of Hughes's power, it is free of the violence that marks his work and the biological imperatives he insists on: '*Only birth matters* / say the river's whorls.'[32]

Woods etc. is a partial return to the lyric manner of the first book, but its poems are more complex and various. Nature still remains the one authenticating source and the writing has a tendency to dismiss those who work in offices as having 'tiny thoughts and authorities'. Something of the manner of Hughes's 'Wodwo', an elemental, half-formed, questioning consciousness, infuses many of these poems, as in the minimally punctuated, lower-case opening of 'Sea Poem':

> what is water in the eyes of water
> loose inquisitive fragile anxious
> a wave, a winged form
> splitting up into sharp glances[33]

Paul Farley, brought up in a 1960s Netherley estate in Liverpool, has a very different England to offer and one perhaps more familiar to most of us – a threatening urban wilderness bordering on a straggly, thorny countryside, 'the larder of the shrike'. There are some unusual connections between the England he describes and that of Larkin. A poem like 'An Interior'[34] seems to acknowledge its debt to a Larkin forebear, 'Home is so Sad', which begins 'Home is so sad. It stays as it was left', and grinds to a verbless halt in its masterly last line 'The music in the piano stool. That vase.'[35] In Farley's poem, this reappraisal of a home left behind is made consciously:

> I'm not listening. My eyes have found
> the draining board, its dull mineral shine,
> the spice rack, still exactly how I left it,
> knives, a Vermeer vinyl table-mat.[36]

So far, the poem looks like Larkinland, with the artful substitution of a class difference: no piano, but artistic aspiration in a vinyl mat. But Farley's poem does not end where Larkin had pinned his own vision, but begins there, easily throwing off what a poetry audience might expect as distaste for a crass facsimile, and instead uses it as a starting-point for a meditation on art, on the child's as well as the adult's wonder at how things are made. It pushes on to a sense of the artist's 'excitement', an emotion that the Larkin poem would never countenance, would close off. Rather than a reflex imitation of a formula, the reader might discover in Farley's poems a deliberate consciousness of literary tradition and a desire to extend and transform it. Farley is a poet with other influences, notably Derek Mahon, whose lines often resurface in Farley's poems, but transmuted. What I am suggesting here is that there is nothing lazy and involuntary about Farley's appropriation of, and allusion to, his poetic predecessors, but something of a mortal struggle going on: one that makes room for a significantly different poetic consciousness. As Mahon subjected Northern Ireland's internecine state of war to the rigours of a cold universe, a kind of wondrous but indifferent starry backdrop, Farley's poems are always listening out for lost histories behind the urban wasteland. There is a kind of cosmic static or background hum the poem tries to tune into.

After the generation of MacDiarmid, Scotland has seen the emergence of considerable talent in the last decades. The prolific and original poet Edwin Morgan has continued to experiment with poems that range from computer-generated lyrics to the traditional sonnet. His latest book, *The Book of the Dead* (2007) shows no diminishing of talent and energy. Eight Scottish poets were selected among the twenty poets of the 1993 'New Generation' promotion. Whatever the merits of that strange affair, the ratio indicated a justifiable northward shift of focus. Since that promotion, therefore not included, Robin Robertson has published three collections, and his poems look more consistent and forceful than several poets who were. As do those of Kate Clanchy, another Scot who has little in common with them (except perhaps with Kathleen Jamie) and who writes in a movingly direct and imaginatively resonant style about personal experience.

Jamie's fifth book of poems *The Queen of Sheba* (1994) had already established her as one of the best poets of her generation, especially with the Scots poems such as 'Skein o Geese' and 'Arraheids': 'They urnae arraheids / but a show o grannies' tongues, / the hard tongues o grannies / aa deid an gaun.'[37] Her two latest books, *Jizzen* (1999) and *The Tree House* (2004), have consolidated this reputation. To adapt Wendell Phillips's remark about liberty, the price of her lyricism is constant vigilance. The 'hard tongues' of her language allow her poems about the natural world to be held in balance against the human and allow her access to a voice (whether in Scots or English) that can be both plain-speaking and intensely celebratory. In 'St Bride's', a series of images of childbirth are woven together, alternately drawn from the domestic and the natural world:

Consider
the hare in jizzen: her leveret's ears
flat as the mizzen of a ship
entering a bottle. A thread's trick . . .

The word 'jizzen', Old Scots for 'child-bed' (from Latin *iacere* – 'to lie'), has not had such prominent airing in a poem since Hugh MacDiarmid's A *Drunk Man Looks at a Thistle*: 'Mary lay in jizzen / As it were claith o' gowd.' The effect could easily have been strained and recherché, but the precise image of the leveret's slicked back ears is animated by the internal rhyme with 'mizzen' and by the curious effect of the simile which describes a precisely reversed activity: entering rather than leaving. By way of these intricate similes within metaphors, the poem delivers a final image which is both shockingly raw and matter-of-fact in its physicality:

and a last sharp twist for the shoulders
delivers my daughter, the placenta
following, like a fist of purple kelp.[38]

The three stressed monosyllables, 'last sharp twist', give way to three arduous trisyllabic words ('delivers . . . placenta / following') before returning to the final monosyllables 'fist' and 'kelp', the first internally rhyming with 'twist'. Much of her work shows these beautifully weighed acoustics together with a spare intensity of observation.

Don Paterson's first book,[39] published just after *The New Poetry*, puts in the shade most of the work that was included. A poem like 'An Elliptical Stylus' is specifically concerned with class and not with nation, but as the title – with its oblique reference to the art of writing suggests – this is also a poem about poetry, its aspirations and its audience. It tells the story of the poet as a boy accompanying his father to a store in search of a stylus that will play in stereo and the humiliation of his father at the hands of the technically knowledgeable salesman. The last stanza reads:

> We drove back slowly, as if we had a puncture;
> my Dad trying not to blink, and that man's laugh
> stuck in my head, which is where the story sticks,
> and any attempt to cauterize this fable
> with something axiomatic on the nature
> of articulacy and inheritance,
> since he can well afford to make his *own*
> excuses, you your own interpretation.
> But if you still insist on resonance –
> I'd swing for him, and every other cunt
> happy to let my father know his station,
> which probably includes yourself. To be blunt.

This sudden turning on the reader recalls the end of Baudelaire's 'Au Lecteur': 'Hypocrite lecteur, mon semblable, mon frère', but whereas the French poet accuses his readers of a complicit 'ennui', Paterson associates his with the mocking salesman, and aggressively sides with his father against them. The poem's second stanza even wittily imagines the different inheritance Paterson might have had 'Supposing I'd been *his* son' and drafts a fussy elegy praising that father's technical know-how. There is a feasible objection that Paterson's (supposedly) middle-class readers might be more likely to look down on the 'smirking' shop assistant than on Paterson's father with his 'ancient, beat-up Phillips turntable', whether or not that offers them any 'excuses'. This is a bitter poem about class, and the barriers of entry to culture are symbolised by the elliptical stylus through which the 'music billowed into three dimensions'. Paterson's father 'who could appreciate the difference' is barred both by money and prejudice from a cultural inheritance that is his right. And yet, bitter as it is, the aggression at the end is more cathartic, and imaginatively challenging, than the kind of class grudge savoured by many poems of Tony Harrison.

Harrison's sixteen-line Meredithean sonnets in *The School of Eloquence* often house a decidedly non-literary diction within traditional metres and give a voice to the suppressed and excluded, in barbed celebration of 'mute ingloriousness' ('On Not Being Milton'). As he enacts a battle between upbringing and education, Harrison plays an at times virtuosic literary artistry against loathing of what, in his phonetically class- and conflict-ridden 'Them & [uz] (II)', he calls 'Littererchewer'. The effect is arresting, but it also involves a sense of elegiac arrest. In 'Book Ends (1)', Harrison commemorates his father thus: 'Back in our silences and sullen looks, / for all the Scotch we drink, what's still between's / not the thirty or so years, but books, books, books.'[40] A carefully careless rhyme with the 'smithereens' to which the father's life has been reduced, 'between's' holds in painful suspension a permanent ambivalence. Harrison, like MacNeice in 'Snow', exploits the ambiguity of 'between': father and son are at once sharers (if only of 'silences', 'sullen looks' and 'Scotch') and divided by 'books, books, books'. Affecting as its treatment by Harrison can be, it is not the kind of question that will detain Paterson as a poet for long, as the terms of British class conflict are entrenched and static, and Paterson's net is cast wider.

His second book, *God's Gift to Women* (1997) can bear comparison with the best that has been written in this period, and *Landing Light* (2003) shows no slackening of intent. A poem from the former such as 'The Chartres of Gowrie' shows how his tracing of negative forms can take on an utterly convincing and eerie life, and the monosyllabic last line displays a characteristic power and resonance:

> at Errol, Grange, Longforan and St Madoes
> they stand dumb in their doorframes, all agog
> at the black ship moored in the sea of corn.[41]

Paterson, from the outset, has had an impressive linguistic range and, like his friend the American poet Michael Donaghy (1954–2005), also a musician, a pitch-perfect sense of traditional form. Muldoon's virtuoso refashioning of the sonnet has not discouraged Paterson, and his own sonnets (as well as his masterly translations of Antonio Machado's and Rainer Maria Rilke's) stand among the best of the age.

Mick Imlah's *Birthmarks* (1988) showed unusual formal accomplishment, especially in his use of the dramatic monologue, cunningly laid with trip-wires and sudden depths. The comic bravura of the half-rhymes in his poem 'Cockney' show that, already, he had little to learn from Muldoon. In the succeeding twenty years of silence, it might have seemed as though he had been left behind by his more productive contemporaries, but the publication of *The Lost Leader* (2008) shows this to be very far from the case. The book is a compendious, subtle meditation on the nature and matter of Scotland, from the historically well-worn to the most arcane. Its patriotism is nothing if not ambivalent, as can be seen in 'The Empty Tumbler', which plays havoc with two of MacDiarmid's finest poems ('Empty Vessel' and 'The Bonnie Broukit Bairn') and implicates the Scots in the British Empire. Another, richer strand to the book can be seen in the elegy 'Stephen Boyd', where the poised avoidance of sentimentality makes the warmth of feeling all the more touching. A unique blend of the ironic and the elegiac make for a quicksilver mobility of tone. Characteristic of the book is an effortless command of period detail, as in his portrait of 'Roseberry', in which the skill of the writing is easily the equal of the figure's own wit, pathos and panache:

> And I suppose we will cheer for anything
> that lets us own a bit of its victory,
> even if it is stricken or so struck
> it can't get to the window to wave back
> or utter a word to clinch the occasion.[42]

Sport and war, the traditionally masculine pursuits, weave in and out of the poems, as here with the notion of victory and the crowd like football fans. Although the book treats Scottish history from its murkiest beginnings to the present day, the tone is never less than contemporary and the achievement formidable.

Jackie Kay's first book, *The Adoption Papers* (1991), has a dramatic cast of three voices, the Highland birth mother, the white adopting mother and the black adopted girl, signalled by different typefaces. Much of her poetry, like this book, has a dramatic aspect, a sure feel for the give-aways of voice and cadence. But particularly here, in this extended work, which explores prejudice as well as heartfelt searching (on questions of race, identity and belonging) there is a lyric momentum. The warm, forthright quality of her writing is also audible in more recent poems: 'Somehow yesterday it felt much better, / you lying into the home telephone', from a poem about betrayal, and in 'Late Love': 'How they strut about, people in love, / how tall they grow, pleased with themselves / . . . / They don't remember who they have been.' In the same book, an effective poem, 'Things Fall Apart', about her born-again, African birth-father ('Christianity had scrubbed his black face with a hard brush') meets deep disappointment with restraint.[43]

The period is also rich in other perspectives on Britain, such as the childhood perception of English mores in Moniza Alvi's poem 'Neighbourhood': 'Next door they were always fighting / calling each other Mr and Mrs.' The poem continues with a Larkinesque vision of 'families with bitten / trickles of children / who pushed prams full of babies', but rather than resting on a note of judgmental scrutiny it ends in an alarming and touching image of a boy 'bruised with dirt, never at school' wandering out of his house 'wearing a hard brown plastic wig'.[44] She was born in Pakistan but brought up in England, and her poems are continually enriched with this dual perspective, each of those countries described with the same relish and wonder, neither one more exotic than the other.

Born in London, but having grown up in Guyana, Fred D'Aguiar explores his Caribbean heritage in *Mama Dot* (1985) and *Airy Hall* (1988) but his work also registers with humour and finesse the fraught contours of black experience in contemporary Britain. Returning in 'Home', he must 'resign to the usual inquisition', courtesy of H. M. Customs, and to the dubious welcome of a cockney cab driver who 'begins chirpily / but can't or won't steer clear of race, / so rounds on Asians. I lock eyes with him / in the rearview when I say I live with one.'[45]

If the last thirty years of poetry from Great Britain do not easily sustain comparison with the poetry of Northern Ireland, nor often reach the accomplishment of Larkin or Hughes, it certainly affords a more various, and admits a more socially and politically challenging, perspective than either of those monumental figures did. [46]

Notes

1. Seamus Heaney, *Preoccupations*, new edition (London: Faber, 1984), p. 150.
2. *The Penguin Book of Contemporary British Poetry*, ed. Blake Morrison and Andrew Motion (Harmondsworth: Penguin, 1982), pp. 20, 12.
3. Craig Raine, *The Onion, Memory* (Oxford: Oxford University Press, 1978), p. 5.
4. Craig Raine, *A Free Translation* (Edinburgh: Salamander, 1981).
5. Craig Raine, *History: The Home Movie* (London: Penguin, 1994), pp. 139, 170, 216.
6. Tomas Tranströmer: *New Collected Poems*, translated by Robin Fulton (Newcastle upon Tyne: Bloodaxe, 1997), p. 176.
7. Christopher Reid, *Arcadia* (Oxford: Oxford University Press, 1979), p. 22.
8. Christopher Reid, *Katerina Brac* (London: Faber, 1985).
9. Christopher Reid, *Expanded Universes* (London: Faber, 1996).
10. Christopher Reid, *For and After* (London: Faber, 2003).
11. Hugo Williams, *Symptoms of Loss* (Oxford: Oxford University Press, 1965).
12. Hugo Williams, *Dock Leaves* (London: Faber, 1994), p. 5.
13. Hugo Williams, *Self-Portrait with a Slide* (Oxford: Oxford University Press, 1990), p. 1.
14. Hugo Williams, *Billy's Rain* (London: Faber, 1999).
15. Hugo Williams, *Dear Room* (London: Faber, 2006).
16. James Fenton, *The Memory of War: Poems 1968–1981* (Edinburgh: Salamander Press, 1982), p. 46
17. Andrew Motion, *Public Property* (London: Faber, 2002), p. 19.
18. *The New Poetry*, ed. Michael Hulse, David Kennedy and David Morley (Newcastle upon Tyne: Bloodaxe, 1993), p. 16.

19. Peter Reading, *Ukelele Music* (London: Secker and Warburg, 1985), p. 57.
20. Paul Muldoon, *Quoof* (London: Faber, 1983).
21. Michael Hofmann, *Acrimony* (London: Faber, 1986), p. 15.
22. Michael Hofmann, *Corona, Corona* (London: Faber, 1993), p. 25.
23. *The Poetical Works of John Keats*, ed. H. Buxton Forman (Oxford: Oxford University Press, 1922), p. 486.
24. Hofmann, *Corona, Corona*, p. 25.
25. Simon Armitage, *Zoom* (Newcastle upon Tyne: Bloodaxe, 1989), pp. 20, 14, 74.
26. Carol Ann Duffy, *The World's Wife* (London: Picador, 1999).
27. Sean O'Brien, *Ghost Train* (Oxford: Oxford University Press, 1995), pp. 1, 2, 17.
28. Sean O'Brien, *HMS Glasshouse* (Oxford: Oxford University Press, 1991), pp. 15, 23.
29. Jo Shapcott, *Electroplating the Baby* (Newcastle upon Tyne: Bloodaxe, 1988), p. 9.
30. Jo Shapcott, *Phrase Book* (Oxford: Oxford University Press, 1992), pp. 26–7.
31. Alice Oswald, *The Thing in the Gap-Stone Stile* (Oxford: Oxford University Press, 1996), pp. 38, 14.
32. Ted Hughes: *New Selected Poems 1957–1994* (London: Faber, 1995), p. 257.
33. Alice Oswald, *Woods etc.* (London: Faber, 2005), pp. 38, 3.
34. Paul Farley, *The Ice Age* (London: Picador, 2002), p. 42.
35. Philip Larkin, *Collected Poems* (London: Faber, 1988), p. 119.
36. Farley, *The Ice Age*, p. 52.
37. Kathleen Jamie, *Mr and Mrs Scotland are Dead* (Newcastle upon Tyne: Bloodaxe, 2002), p. 137.
38. Kathleen Jamie, *Jizzen* (London: Picador, 1999), p. 45.
39. Don Paterson, *Nil Nil* (London: Faber, 1993), pp. 21–2.
40. Tony Harrison, *Selected Poems* (Harmondsworth: Penguin, 1984), p. 126.
41. Don Paterson, *God's Gift to Women* (London: Faber, 1997), p. 11.
42. Mick Imlah, *The Lost Leader* (London: Faber, 2008), p. 72.
43. Jackie Kay, *Darling: New and Selected Poems* (Newcastle upon Tyne: Bloodaxe, 2007), pp. 171, 164, 178.
44. Moniza Alvi, *The Country at My Shoulder* (Oxford: Oxford University Press, 1993), p. 11.
45. Fred D'Aguiar, *British Subjects* (Newcastle upon Tyne: Bloodaxe, 1993), p. 14.
46. For reasons of brevity this survey has failed to mention numerous poets whose work would naturally occur in a fuller or even a differently slanted approach, especially the older generation, including Anne Stevenson, Fleur Adcock, Roy Fisher, Alan Brownjohn, John Fuller and E. A. Markham. Southern Irish poets, long resident in England, such as Bernard O'Donoghue, Matthew Sweeney and Maurice Riordan, all merit serious attention and, like them, there are many English and other Scottish poets with as good a claim on such as survey as several I have included, whilst the poetry of Gwyneth Lewis, Stephen Knight and Oliver Reynolds would easily dispel any impression this chapter might have left that Welsh poetry in English could be overlooked.

Bibliography

Introduction

Grierson, Herbert and J. C. Smith, *A Critical History of English Poetry* (Harmondsworth: Penguin, in association with Chatto and Windus, 1962).
Saintsbury, George, *A History of English Prosody*, 3 vols. (London: Macmillan, 1923).

1 Old English poetry

Alexander, Michael, *The First Poems in English* (London: Penguin, 2008).
Bessinger, J. B. and S. J. Kahrl (eds.), *Essential Articles for the Study of Old English Poetry* (Hamden, CT: Archon Books, 1968).
Bjork, R. E. and J. D. Niles (eds.), *A 'Beowulf' Handbook* (Lincoln: University of Nebraska Press, 1997).
Bradley, S. A. J, *Anglo-Saxon Poetry* (London: Everyman, 1982).
Crossley-Holland, Kevin, *The Anglo-Saxon World: An Anthology* (Oxford: Oxford University Press, 1999).
Fulk, R. D. and Christopher Cain, *A History of Old English Literature* (Oxford: Blackwell, 2003).
Godden, M. and M. Lapidge (eds.), *The Cambridge Companion to Old English Literature* (Cambridge: Cambridge University Press, 1991).
Gordon, R. K., *Anglo-Saxon Verse* (London: Everyman, 1926).
Greenfield, S. B. and D. G. Calder, *A New Critical History of Old English Literature* (New York: New York University Press, 1986).
Hamer, Richard, *A Choice of Anglo-Saxon Verse* (London: Faber and Faber, 1970).
Heaney, Seamus, *Beowulf* (London: Faber and Faber, 1999).
Jones, Chris, *Strange Likeness: The Use of Old English in Twentieth-Century Poetry* (Oxford: Oxford University Press, 2006).
Krapp, G. P. and E. V. K Dobbie (eds.), *The Anglo-Saxon Poetic Records*, 6 vols. (New York: Columbia University Press, 1931–53).
Mitchell, Bruce, *An Invitation to Old English and Anglo-Saxon England* (Oxford: Blackwell, 1995).
Mitchell, Bruce and Fred C. Robinson, *A Guide to Old English*, seventh edition (Oxford: Blackwell, 2007).
Muir, B. J. (ed.), *The Exeter Anthology of Old English Poetry* (Exeter: University of Exeter Press, 1994; second edition 2000).

O'Keeffe, K. O'Brien, *Reading Old English Texts* (Cambridge: Cambridge University Press, 1997).
Orchard, Andy, *A Critical Companion to 'Beowulf'* (Cambridge: Brewer, 2003).
Pulsiano, Phillip and Elaine Treharne (eds.), *A Companion to Anglo-Saxon Literature* (Oxford: Blackwell, 2001).
Raw, B. C., *The Art and Background of Old English Poetry* (London: Arnold, 1978).
Shippey, T. A., *Old English Verse* (London: Hutchinson University Library, 1972).
Shippey, T. A. and Andreas Haarder, *Beowulf: The Critical Heritage* (London: Routledge, 1998).
Stanley, Eric, *Imagining the Anglo-Saxon Past: The Search for Anglo-Saxon Paganism and Anglo-Saxon Trial by Jury* (Cambridge: Brewer, 2000).
Swanton, Michael, *English Literature before Chaucer* (London: Longman, 1987).
Tolkien, J. R. R., *'The Monsters and the Critics', and Other Essays*, ed. Christopher Tolkien (London: George Allen and Unwin, 1983). Essay written 1936.
Wrenn, C. L., *A Study of Old English Literature* (London: Harrap, 1967).

2 The *Gawain*-poet and medieval romance

Editions

Andrew, Malcolm and Ronald Waldron (eds.), *The Poems of the Pearl Manuscript: 'Pearl', 'Cleanness', 'Patience', 'Sir Gawain and the Green Knight'*, Exeter Medieval Texts, and Studies, fifth edition (Exeter: University of Exeter, 2007). Translation published separately, *The Poems of the Pearl Manuscript in Modern English Translation* (Exeter: University of Exeter Press, 2008).
Barron, W. R. J. (ed. and trans.), *Sir Gawain and the Green Knight* revised edition (1974, Manchester: Manchester University Press, 1998). Includes prose translation.
Benson, Larry D. (ed.), *King Arthur's Death: The Middle English 'Stanzaic Morte Arthur' and 'Alliterative Morte Arthure'*, Exeter Medieval English Texts and Studies (1974, Exeter: University of Exeter Press, 1986).
Brewer, Elisabeth (ed.), *'Sir Gawain and the Green Knight': Sources and Analogues*, Arthurian Studies 27 (Woodbridge: D. S. Brewer, 1973, 1992).
Cawley, A. C. and J. J. Anderson (eds.), *Pearl, Cleanness, Patience, Sir Gawain and the Green Knight*, Everyman Classics (London: Dent–Everyman's Library, 1976).
Gordon, E. V. (ed.), *Pearl* (Oxford: Clarendon Press, 1953).
Sands, Donald B. (ed.), *Middle English Verse Romances*, Exeter Medieval English Texts and Studies (1966; Exeter: University of Exeter Press, 1986).
Tolkien, J. R. R., and E. V. Gordon (eds.), *Sir Gawain and the Green Knight* (1925; revised edition Norman Davis, Oxford: Clarendon Press, 1967).

Verse translations of *Sir Gawain and the Green Knight* and other poems

'Sir Gawain and the Green Knight', 'Pearl' and 'Sir Orfeo', trans. J. R. R. Tolkien, ed. Christopher Tolkien (1975; London: HarperCollins, 1995).
'Sir Gawain and the Green Knight', 'Patience', and 'Pearl': Verse Translations, trans. Marie Borroff (New York: W. W. Norton, 2001). Original translation of *Sir Gawain*, 1968.

Pearl. A Modernised Version of the Middle English Poem, trans. Victor Watts, ed. Corinne Saunders and David Fuller, intro. Kathleen Raine (London: Enitharmon, 2005). Includes original text

Translations of *Sir Gawain and the Green Knight*

Armitage, Simon (trans.), (London: Faber, 2007).

Harrison, Keith (trans.), intro. and annotated Helen Cooper, Oxford World's Classics (Oxford: Oxford University Press, 1998).

Hughes, Ted, *Selected Translations*, ed. David Weissbort (London: Faber, 2006).

Merwin, W. S. (trans.), (Tarset: Bloodaxe, 2003). Includes original text.

O'Donoghue, Bernard (trans.), Penguin Classics (London: Penguin, 2006).

Vantuono, William (trans.), (Notre Dame, IN: University of Notre Dame Press, 1999). Includes original text.

Winny, James (ed. and trans.), (Peterborough, Ontario: Broadview, 1992). Includes original text.

Recordings

In Middle English

Sir Gawain and the Green Knight

Read by Trevor Eaton (Wadhurst: Pavilion Records, 1992).

Read by Paul Piehler *et al.* (Vancouver: Golden Clarion, 1965). Abbreviated.

Read by Thomas Rendall *et al.* (Adelaide: Chaucer Studio, 1990).

In translation

Sir Gawain and the Green Knight, Pearl and *Sir Orfeo*

Read by Terry Jones, trans. J. R. R Tolkien (London: Harper Collins, 2006).

Sir Gawain and the Green Knight

Read and trans. by Simon Armitage (Faber: London, 2008).

Read by Jasper Britton, trans. Benedict Flynn (Redhill, Surrey: Naxos Audiobooks, 2008).

Critical studies

Barron, W. R. J., *English Medieval Romance*, Longman Literature in English Series (London: Longman, 1987).

Trawthe and Treason: The Sin of Gawain Reconsidered. A Thematic Study of 'Sir Gawain and the Green Knight', Publications of the Faculty of Arts of the University of Manchester 25 (Manchester: University of Manchester Press, 1980).

Brewer, Derek and Jonathan Gibson (eds.), *A Companion to the 'Gawain'-Poet*, Arthurian Studies 38 (Cambridge: D. S. Brewer, 1997).

Condren, Edward I., *The Numerical Universe of the 'Gawain-Pearl' Poet: Beyond Phi* (Gainesville: University Press of Florida, 2002).

Cooper, Helen, *The English Romance in Time: Transforming Motifs from Geoffrey of Monmouth to the Death of Shakespeare* (Oxford: Oxford University Press, 2004).

Davenport, W. A., *The Art of the 'Gawain'-Poet* (London: University of London, Athlone Press, 1978).

Pound, Ezra, *The Spirit of Romance* (London: Peter Owen, 1910). Revised edition 1952.

Putter, Ad, *An Introduction to the 'Gawain'-Poet*, Longman Medieval and Renaissance Library (London: Longman, 1996).

'Sir Gawain and the Green Knight' and French Arthurian Romance (Oxford: Clarendon Press, 1995).

Saunders, Corinne (ed.), *A Companion to Romance: From Classical to Contemporary*, Blackwell Companions to Literature and Culture (Oxford: Blackwell, 2004).

Thompson, Raymond H. and Keith Busby (eds.), *Gawain: A Casebook*, Arthurian Characters and Themes Series (New York: Routledge, 2006).

Electronic resources

http://alliteration.net/Pearl.htm. Includes verse translation of sections of *Sir Gawain* by Paul Deane, 1999.

www.luminarium.org/medlit/gawain.htm. Includes editions of *Sir Gawain* by Tolkien and Gordon, 1967 and Ross G. Arthur, 1999, prose translation by W. A. Neilson, 1999, and prose translation by Jessie L. Weston.

3 Late fourteenth-century poetry (Chaucer, Gower, Langland and their legacy)

Editions

Benson, L. D. (ed.), *The Riverside Chaucer* (Oxford: Oxford University Press, 1988).

Macaulay, G. C. (ed.), *The Complete Works of John Gower: The English Works*, 2 vols. (Oxford: Clarendon Press, 1901).

Schmidt, A. V. C (ed.), *Piers Plowman: A Parallel Text of the A, B, C and Z Versions* (Harlow: Longman, 1995).

Critical studies

Burrow, J. A., *Ricardian Poetry: Chaucer, Gower, Langland, and the 'Gawain' Poet* (London: Routledge and Kegan Paul, 1971).

Muscatine, Charles, *Poetry and Crisis in the Age of Chaucer* (Notre Dame, IN: University of Notre Dame Press, 1972).

Schmidt, A. V. C., *The Clerkly Maker: Langland's Poetic Art* (Cambridge: D. S. Brewer, 1987).

Yeager, R. F., *John Gower's Poetic: The Search for a New Arion* (Cambridge: D. S. Brewer, 1990).

Journals

The Chaucer Review, 1– (1966–).

The John Gower Newsletter, 1– (1989–).

Studies in the Age of Chaucer, 1– (1979–).

The Yearbook of Langland Studies, 1– (1987–).

4 Langland: *Piers Plowman*

Aers, D., *Piers Plowman and Christian Allegory* (London: Arnold, 1975).
Burrow, J. A., 'The Action of Langland's Second Vision', *EC*, 15 (1965), pp. 247–68.
Thinking in Poetry: Three Medieval Examples (London: Birkbeck College, 1993).
Chamberlin, J. C., *Medieval Arts Doctrines on Ambiguity and their Place in Langland's Poetics* (Montreal: McGill-Queen's University Press, 2000).
Colledge, E. and J. Walsh (eds.), *A Book of Showings to the Anchoress Julian of Norwich*, 2 vols. (Toronto: Pontifical Institute, 1978).
Davlin, M. C., *A Game of Heuene: Word Play and the Meaning of 'Piers Plowman'* (Cambridge: Brewer, 1989).
Kaske, R. E., 'Holy Church's Speech and the Structure of *Piers Plowman*', in B. Rowland (ed.), *Chaucer and Middle English: Studies in Honour of R. H. Robbins* (London: Allen and Unwin, 1974), pp. 320–7.
'The Use of Simple Figures of Speech in *Piers Plowman* B', *SP*, 48 (1951), pp. 571–600.
Kean, P. M., 'Langland on the Incarnation', *RES*, 15 (1964), pp. 241–61.
Lawlor, J., *Piers Plowman: An Essay in Criticism* (London: Arnold, 1962).
Lewis, C. S., *The Allegory of Love* (London: Oxford University Press, 1936).
Martin, P., *Piers Plowman: The Field and the Tower* (London: Macmillan, 1979).
Salter, E., *Piers Plowman: An Introduction* (Oxford: Blackwell, 1962).
Salter, E. and D. Pearsall (eds.), *Piers Plowman* (London: Arnold, 1967).
Schmidt, A. V. C., *The Clerkly Maker: Langland's Poetic Art* (Cambridge: Brewer, 1987).
Piers Plowman: A New Translation of the B-Text (Oxford: Oxford University Press, 1992).
The Vision of Piers Plowman, second edition (London: Dent, 1995).
Schmidt, A. V. C. (ed.), *Piers Plowman: A Parallel-Text Edition of the A, B, C and Z Versions*, vol. I: Text (London: Longman, 1995).
Simpson, James, *Piers Plowman: An Introduction to the B-Text* (London: Longman, 1990)
Smith, B. H., *Traditional Imagery of Charity in 'Piers Plowman'* (The Hague: Mouton, 1966).
Smith, G. G., *Elizabethan Critical Essays*, 2 vols. (London: Oxford University Press, 1904).
Spearing, A. C., 'The Art of Preaching and *Piers Plowman*', in *Criticism and Medieval Poetry*, second edition (London: Arnold, 1972), pp. 107–34.
Medieval to Renaissance in English Poetry (Cambridge: Cambridge University Press, 1985).
'Verbal Repetition in Piers Plowman B and C', *JEGP*, 62 (1963), pp. 722–37.
Warner, L. 'The Ur-B *Piers Plowman* and the Earliest Production of C and B', *Yearbook of Langland Studies*, 16 (2002), pp. 3–39.
Zeeman, N., *'Piers Plowman' and the Medieval Discourse of Desire* (Cambridge: Cambridge University Press, 2006).

5 Chaucer: *Troilus and Criseyde* and *The Canterbury Tales*

Benson, L. D., *The Riverside Chaucer* (Oxford: Oxford University Press, 1988).
Brewer, D., *Chaucer: The Critical Heritage*, 2 vols. (London: Routledge and Kegan Paul, 1978).
Kindrick, R. L., *The Poems of Robert Henryson* (Kalamazoo: Medieval Institute Publications, 1997).

Muscatine, Charles, *Medieval Literature, Style and Culture* (Columbia: University of South Carolina Press, 1999).

Peterson, C., *St Erkenwald* (Philadelphia: University of Pennsylvania Press, 1977).

Stockton, E., *The Major Latin Works of John Gower* (Seattle: University of Washington Press, 1962).

6 Late medieval literature in Scotland: Henryson, Dunbar and Douglas

Henryson

Fox, Denton (ed.), *The Poems of Robert Henryson* (Oxford: Clarendon Press, 1981).

Gray, Douglas, *Robert Henryson* (Leiden: Brill, 1979).

Wheatley, Edward, *Mastering Aesop: Medieval Education, Chaucer, and His Followers* (Gainesville: University Press of Florida, 2000).

Dunbar

Bawcutt, Priscilla, *Dunbar the Maker* (Oxford: Oxford University Press, 1992).

Bawcutt, Priscilla (ed.), *The Poems of William Dunbar*, 2 vols. (Glasgow: Association for Scottish Literary Studies, 1998).

Mapstone, Sally (ed.), *William Dunbar, 'The Nobill Poyet': Essays in Honour of Priscilla Bawcutt* (East Linton: Tuckwell Press, 2001).

Douglas

Bawcutt, Priscilla, *Gavin Douglas: A Critical Study* (Edinburgh: Edinburgh University Press, 1976).

Bawcutt, Priscilla (ed.), *The Shorter Poems of Gavin Douglas*, revised edition (Edinburgh: Scottish Text Society, 2003).

Coldwell, David F. C. (ed.), *Virgil's Aeneid Translated into Scottish Verse by Gavin Douglas*, 4 vols. (Edinburgh: Scottish Text Society, 1957–64).

General

Bawcutt, Priscilla and Hadley Williams, Janet (eds.), *A Companion to Medieval Scottish Poetry* (Cambridge: D. S. Brewer, 2006).

Clancy, Thomas Owen and Pittock, Murray (eds), *The Edinburgh History of Scottish Literature I: From Columba to the Union* (Edinburgh: Edinburgh University Press, 2007).

Jack, R. D. S (ed.), *History of Scottish Literature I: Origins to 1660 (Mediaeval and Renaissance)* (Aberdeen: Aberdeen University Press, 1988).

Mapstone, Sally (ed.), *Older Scots Literature* (Edinburgh: John Donald, 2005).

7 Sixteenth-century poetry: Skelton, Wyatt and Surrey

Griffiths, Jane, *John Skelton and Poetic Authority* (Oxford: Clarendon Press, 2006).

Hadfield, Andrew, *Literature, Politics and National Identity: Reformation to Renaissance* (Cambridge: Cambridge University Press, 1994).

Hardison, O. B., *Prosody and Purpose in the English Renaissance* (Baltimore: Johns Hopkins University Press, 1989).
Heale, Elizabeth, *Wyatt, Surrey and Early Tudor Poetry* (London: Longman, 1998).
Jones, Emrys (ed.), *Henry Howard, Earl of Surrey: Poems* (Oxford: Clarendon Press, 1964).
Meyer-Lee, Robert J., *Poets and Power from Chaucer to Wyatt* (Cambridge: Cambridge University Press, 2007).
Muir, K. (ed.), *Life and Letters of Sir Thomas Wyatt* (Liverpool: Liverpool University Press, 1963).
Rebholz, R. A. (ed.), *Sir Thomas Wyatt: The Complete Poems* (Harmondsworth: Penguin Books, 1978).
Scattergood, John (ed.), *John Skelton: The Complete Poems* (New Haven: Yale University Press, 1983).
Sessions, W. A., *Henry Howard. The Poet Earl of Surrey: A Life* (Oxford: Oxford University Press, 1999).
Walker, Greg, *John Skelton and the Politics of the 1520s* (Cambridge: Cambridge University Press, 1988).

8 Spenser

Alpers, Paul J. 'How to Read *The Faerie* Queene', *Essays in Criticism*, 18 (1968), pp. 429–43.
Burrow, Colin, *Edmund Spenser* (Plymouth: Northcote House, 1996).
Craig, Martha, 'The Secret Wit of Spenser's Language', in Paul J. Alpers (ed.), *Elizabethan Poetry: Modern Essays in Criticism* (Oxford: Oxford University Press, 1967), pp. 447–72.
Bartlett Giamatti, A. *Play of Double Senses: Spenser's* Faerie Queene (New York: Norton, 1975).
Gless, Daryll J., *Interpretation and Theology in Spenser* (Cambridge: Cambridge University Press, 1994).
Greenblatt, Stephen J., *Renaissance Self-Fashioning from More to Shakespeare* (Chicago: University of Chicago Press, 1980).
Hadfield, Andrew, *Spenser's Irish Experience: Wilde Fruyt and Salvage Soyl* (Oxford: Clarendon Press, 1997).
Hadfield, Andrew (ed.), *The Cambridge Companion to Spenser* (Cambridge: Cambridge University Press, 2001).
Hamilton, A. C. (ed.), *The Spenser Encyclopedia* (London: Routledge, 1990).
McCabe, Richard A., *Spenser's Monstrous Regiment: Elizabethan Ireland and the Poetics of Difference* (Oxford: Oxford University Press, 2002).
Maley, Willy, *A Spenser Chronology* (Basingstoke: Macmillan, 1994).

9 Sidney, Shakespeare and the Elizabethan sonnet and lyric

Bates, Catherine, *Masculinity, Gender and Identity in the English Renaissance Lyric* (Cambridge: Cambridge University Press, 2007).
Booth, Stephen, *An Essay on Shakespeare's Sonnets* (New Haven: Yale University Press, 1969).
Dubrow, Heather, *Echoes of Desire: English Petrarchism and its Counterdiscourses* (Ithaca, NY: Cornell University Press, 1995).
Edmondson, Paul and Stanley Wells, *Shakespeare's Sonnets* (Oxford: Oxford University Press, 2004).
Ferry, Anne, *The 'Inward' Language: Sonnets of Wyatt, Sidney, Shakespeare and Donne* (Chicago: University of Chicago Press, 1983).

Henderson, Diana E., 'Love Poetry', in Michael Hattaway (ed.), *A Companion to English Renaissance Literature and Culture* (Oxford: Blackwell, 2000), pp. 378–91.

Lever, J. W., *The Elizabethan Love Sonnet*, second edition (London: Methuen, 1966).

Marotti, Arthur F., ' "Love Is Not Love": Elizabethan Sonnet Sequences and the Social Order', *ELH*, 49 (1982), pp. 396–428.

Roberts, Sasha, 'Shakespeare's *Sonnets* and English Sonnet Sequences', in Patrick Cheney, Andrew Hadfield and Garrett A. Sullivan, Jr. (eds.), *Early Modern English Poetry: A Critical Companion* (Oxford: Oxford University Press, 2007), pp. 172–83.

Roche, Thomas P., *Petrarch and the English Sonnet Sequences* (New York: AMS, 1989).

Schalkwyk, David, *Speech and Performance in Shakespeare's Sonnets and Plays* (Cambridge: Cambridge University Press, 2002).

Schiffer, James (ed.), *Shakespeare's Sonnets: Critical Essays* (New York: Garland, 1999).

Spiller, Michael R. G., *The Development of the Sonnet: An Introduction* (London: Routledge, 1992).

Vendler, Helen, *The Art of Shakespeare's Sonnets* (Cambridge, MA: Harvard University Press, 1997).

10 The narrative poetry of Marlowe and Shakespeare

Cheney, Patrick (ed.), *The Cambridge Companion to Christopher Marlowe* (Cambridge: Cambridge University Press, 2004).

Dobson, Michael and Stanley Wells (eds.), *The Oxford Companion to Shakespeare* (Oxford: Oxford University Press, 2001; reprinted 2005).

Edmondson, Paul and Stanley Wells, *Shakespeare's Sonnets* (Oxford: Oxford University Press, 2004).

Marlowe, Christopher, *The Complete Plays*, ed. Frank Romany and Robert Lindsey (Harmondsworth: Penguin, 2003).

The Complete Poems and Translations, ed. Stephen Orgel (Harmondsworth: Penguin, 1971).

The Poems, ed. Millar Maclure (London: Methuen, 1968).

Shakespeare, William, *The Complete Poems and Sonnets*, ed. Colin Burrow (Oxford: Oxford University Press, 2002; reissued 2008).

The Complete Works, ed. Stanley Wells, Gary Taylor, John Jowett and William Montgomery, second edition (Oxford: Clarendon Press, 2005).

11 Seventeenth-century poetry 1: poetry in the age of Donne and Jonson

Bald, R. C., *John Donne: A Life* (Oxford: Oxford University Press, 1970).

Fowler, Alastair (ed.), *The New Oxford Book of Seventeenth-Century Verse* (Oxford: Oxford University Press, 1991).

Martz, L. L., *The Poetry of Meditation*, revised edition (New Haven: Yale University Press, 1964).

Post, Jonathan F. S., *English Lyric Poetry: The Early Seventeenth Century* (London: Routledge, 1999).

Riggs, David, *Ben Jonson: A Life* (Cambridge, MA: Harvard University Press, 1989).

Smith, Rosalind, *Sonnets and the English Woman Writer, 1560–1621* (Houndsmills: Palgrave, 2005).

12 Seventeenth-century poetry 2: Herbert, Vaughan, Philips, Cowley, Crashaw, Marvell

Bath, Michael, *Speaking Pictures: English Emblem Books and Renaissance Culture* (London: Longman, 1994).

Davidson, Peter (ed.), *Poetry and Revolution: An Anthology of British and Irish Verse, 1625–1660* (Oxford: Clarendon Press, 1998).

Fowler, Alastair, *The Country House Poem: A Cabinet of 17th-Century Estate Poems and Related Items* (Edinburgh: Edinburgh University Press, 1994).

Healy, Thomas F., *Richard Crashaw* (Leiden: Brill, 1986).

Lange, Marjory E., *Telling Tears in the English Renaissance* (Leiden: Brill, 1996).

Potter, Lois, *Secret Rites and Secret Writing: Royalist Literature, 1641–1660* (Cambridge: Cambridge University Press, 1989).

Saintsbury, George (ed.), *The Lives of John Donne, Sir Henry Wotton, Richard Hooker, George Herbert and Robert Sanderson* (London: Oxford University Press, 1927).

Shell, Alison, *Catholicism, Controversy and the English Literary Imagination, 1558–1660* (Cambridge: Cambridge University Press, 1999).

Warnke, Frank Joseph (ed.), *European Metaphysical Poetry* (New Haven: Yale University Press, 1974).

Wiseman, Susan, *Drama and Politics in the English Civil War* (Cambridge: Cambridge University Press, 1998).

13 Milton's shorter poems

Editions

Carey, John (ed.), *John Milton: Complete Shorter Poems*, second edition (London and New York: Longman, 1997).

Revard, Stella P. (ed.), *John Milton: Complete Shorter Poems* (Oxford: Wiley-Blackwell, 2009).

Critical studies

Bevington, David and Peter Holbrook (eds.), *The Politics of the Stuart Court Masque* (Cambridge: Cambridge University Press, 1988).

Brown, Cedric C., *Milton's Aristocratic Entertainments* (Cambridge: Cambridge University Press, 1985.

Bush, Douglas *et al.* (eds.), *A Variorum Commentary on the Poems of John Milton*, 2 vols. (New York: Columbia University Press, 1970–2).

Freeman, James A. and Anthony Low (eds.), *Urbane Milton: The Latin Poems, Milton Studies*, 19 (1984).

Haan, Estelle, *From Academia to Amicitia: Milton's Latin Writings and the Italian Academies* (Philadelphia, PA: American Philosophical Society, 1998).

Lewalski, Barbara K., *The Life of John Milton: A Critical Biography*, revised edition (London: Blackwell, 2003).

Leishman, J. B., *Milton's Minor Poems* (Pittsburgh, PA: University of Pittsburgh Press, 1969).

Martz, Louis L., *Poet of Exile: A Study of Milton's Poetry* (New Haven, CT: Yale University Press, 1980).

Revard, Stella P., *Milton and the Tangles of Neaera's Hair: The Making of the 1645 Poems* (Columbia: University of Missouri Press, 1997).
Smart, J. M. (ed.), *The Sonnets of Milton* (Glasgow: Maclehose Jackson, 1921).
Tuve, Rosamond, *Images and Themes in Five Poems by Milton* (Cambridge, MA.: Harvard University Press, 1957).
Wittreich, Joseph A., Jr., *Visionary Poetics: Milton's Tradition and his Legacy* (San Marino, CA: Huntington Library, 1979).

14 Milton: *Paradise Lost, Paradise Regained, Samson Agonistes*

Editions

Fowler, Alastair (ed.), *John Milton: Paradise Lost*, second edition (London and New York: Longman, 1998).
Knoppers, Laura Lunger (ed.), *The 1671 Poems: Paradise Regain'd and Samson Agonistes*, in *The Complete Works of John Milton*, vol. II (Oxford: Oxford University Press, 2008).
Lewalski, Barbara K. (ed.), *John Milton: Paradise Lost*, revised edition (Oxford: Blackwell, 2003).

Critical studies

Achinstein, Sharon, *Milton and the Revolutionary Reader* (Princeton: Princeton University Press, 1994).
Bennett, Joan, *Reviving Liberty: Radical Christian Humanism in Milton's Great Poems* (Cambridge, MA: Harvard University Press, 1989).
Bowra, C. M., *From Virgil to Milton* (London: Macmillan, 1945).
Evans, J. M., *Paradise Lost and the Genesis Tradition* (Oxford: Clarendon Press, 1968).
Fish, Stanley, *How Milton Works* (Cambridge, MA: Harvard University Press, 2001).
Surprised by Sin (1967; Cambridge, MA: Harvard University Press, 1997).
Knoppers, Laura Lunger, *Historicizing Milton* (Athens: University of Georgia Press, 1994).
Labriola, Albert C. and Michael Lieb (eds.), *The Miltonic Samson, Milton Studies*, 33 (1996).
Lewalski, Barbara K., *The Life of John Milton: A Critical Biography*, revised edition (Oxford: Blackwell, 2003).
Milton's Brief Epic: The Genre, Meaning, and Art of Paradise Regained (London: Methuen, 1996).
Paradise Lost and the Rhetoric of Literary Forms (Princeton, NJ: Princeton University Press, 1985).
Lieb, Michael, *Milton and the Culture of Violence* (Ithaca, NY: Cornell University Press, 1994).
Loewenstein, David, and Albert C. Labriola (eds.), *Paradise Regained in Context: Genre, Politics, Religion, Milton Studies*, 42 (2002).
McColley, Diane, *Milton's Eve* (Urbana: University of Illinois Press, 1983).
Norbrook, David, *Writing the English Republic: Poetry, Rhetoric, and Politics* (Cambridge: Cambridge University Press, 1999), pp. 438–67.
Quint, David, *Epic and Empire: Politics and Generic Form from Virgil to Milton* (Princeton: Princeton University Press, 1992).
Parker, William R., *Milton's Debt to Greek Tragedy in Samson Agonistes* (Baltimore: Johns Hopkins University Press, 1937).
Pope, Elizabeth M., *Paradise Regained: The Tradition and the Poem* (Baltimore: Johns Hopkins University Press, 1947).

Radzinowicz, Mary Ann, *Toward Samson Agonistes: The Growth of Milton's Mind* (Princeton, NJ: Princeton University Press, 1978).

Rajan, Balachandra (ed.), *The Prison and the Pinnacle* (Toronto: University of Toronto Press, 1973).

Stein, Arnold, *Heroic Knowledge: An Interpretation of Paradise Regained and Samson Agonistes* (Minneapolis: University of Minnesota Press, 1957).

Teskey, Gordon, *Delirious Milton: The Fate of the Poet in Modernity* (Cambridge, MA: Harvard University Press, 2006).

Webber, Joan, *Paradise Lost: Milton and His Epic Tradition* (Seattle: University of Washington Press, 1979).

Wittreich, Joseph A., Jr., *Calm of Mind: Tercentenary Essays on Paradise Regained and Samson Agonistes* (Cleveland, OH: Case Western Reserve Press, 1971).

Interpreting Samson Agonistes (Princeton: Princeton University Press, 1986).

15 Restoration poetry: Behn, Dryden and their contemporaries

Atkins, George Douglas, *The Faith of John Dryden: Change and Continuity* (Lexington: University Press of Kentucky, 1980).

Barash, Carol, *English Women's Poetry: 1649–1714: Politics, Community and Linguistic Authority* (Oxford: Clarendon, 1996).

Gillespie, Stuart (ed.), *John Dryden: Classicist and Translator* (Edinburgh: Edinburgh University Press, 2001).

Goreau, Angeline, *Reconstructing Aphra: A Social Biography of Aphra Behn* (Oxford: Oxford University Press, 1980).

Hammond, Paul, *Dryden and the Traces of Classical Rome* (Oxford: Oxford University Press, 1999).

John Dryden: A Literary Life (Basingstoke: Macmillan, 1991).

Hammond, Paul and David Hopkins (eds.), *John Dryden: Tercentenary Essays* (Oxford: Oxford University Press, 2000).

Hopkins, David, *John Dryden* (Cambridge: Cambridge University Press, 1986).

Hughes, Derek and Janet Todd (eds.), *The Cambridge Companion to Aphra Behn* (Cambridge: Cambridge University Press, 2004).

Spencer, Jane, *Aphra Behn's Afterlife* (Oxford: Oxford University Press, 2000).

Wiseman, S. J., *Aphra Behn* (Plymouth: Northcote House, 1996).

Zwicker, Steven N. (ed.), *The Cambridge Companion to John Dryden* (Cambridge: Cambridge University Press, 2004).

16 Dryden: major poems

Brower, Ruben, *Alexander Pope and the Poetry of Allusion* (Oxford: Oxford University Press, 1963).

Empson, William, *Using Biography* (Cambridge, MA: Harvard University Press, 1984).

Hill, Geoffrey, *The Enemy's Country* (Stanford, CA: Stanford University Press, 1991).

Hume, Robert, *Dryden's Criticism* (Ithaca, NY: Cornell University Press, 1970).

Macdonald, Hugh, *John Dryden: A Bibliography of Early Editions and of Drydeniana* (Oxford: Clarendon, 1939).

Ohlmeyer, Jayne and Steven Zwicker, 'John Dryden, the House of Ormond, and the Politics of Anglo-Irish Patronage', *Historical Journal*, 49.3 (2006), pp. 688–9.

Ricks, Christopher, *Allusion to the Poets* (Oxford: Oxford University Press, 2002).

'Dryden's Triplets', in Steven N. Zwicker (ed.), *The Cambridge Companion to John Dryden* (Cambridge: Cambridge University Press, 2004), pp. 92–112.

Swift, Jonathan, *Jonathan Swift*, ed. Angus Ross and David Woolley (Oxford: Oxford University Press, 1984).

Winn, James A., *John Dryden and his World* (New Haven: Yale University Press, 1987).

17 Swift

Editions

Swift, Jonathan, *Complete Poems*, ed. Pat Rogers (Harmondsworth: Penguin, and New Haven: Yale University Press, 1983).

Poems, ed. Harold Williams, 3 vols., second edition (Oxford: Clarendon, 1958).

The Essential Writings of Jonathan Swift, ed. Claude Rawson and Ian Higgins (New York: Norton, 2009).

Critical studies

Barnett, Louise K., *Swift's Poetic Worlds* (Newark: University of Delaware Press, 1982).

Berwick, Donald M., *The Reputation of Jonathan Swift, 1781–1882* (1941; New York: Haskell, 1965).

Ehrenpreis, Irvin, *Swift: The Man, His Works, and the Age*, 3 vols. (London: Methuen, 1962–83).

England, A. B., *Energy and Order in the Poetry of Swift* (Lewisburg, PA: Bucknell University Press, 1980).

Fischer, John Irwin and Donald C. Mell (eds.), *Contemporary Studies in Swift's Poetry* (Newark: University of Delaware Press, 1981).

Jaffe, Nora Crow, *The Poet Swift* (Hanover, NH: University Press of New England, 1977).

Johnson, Maurice, *The Sin of Wit: Jonathan Swift as a Poet* (Syracuse, NY: Syracuse University Press, 1950).

Mell, Donald C. (ed.), *Pope, Swift, and Women Writers* (Newark: University of Delaware Press, 1996, 1998).

Rawson, Claude, *Order from Confusion Sprung: Studies in Eighteenth-Century Literature from Swift to Cowper* (London: Allen, and Unwin, 1985; paperback edition Atlantic Highlands, New Jersey: Humanities Press, 1992).

Rawson, Claude (ed.), *Jonathan Swift: A Collection of Critical Essays* (Englewood Cliffs, NJ: Prentice Hall, 1994).

Schakel, Peter J., *The Poetry of Jonathan Swift* (Madison: University of Wisconsin Press, 1978).

Vieth, David M. (ed.), *Essential Articles for the Study of Swift's Poetry* (Hamden, CT: Archon, 1984).

Williams, Kathleen (ed.), *Swift: The Critical Heritage* (London: Routledge, 1970).

Woolley, James D., *Swift's Later Poems: Studies in Circumstances and Texts* (New York: Garland, 1988).

18 Poetry of the first half of the eighteenth century: Pope, Johnson and the couplet

Barnard, John (ed.), *Pope: The Critical Heritage* (London: Routledge, 1973).

Boswell, James, *Life of Johnson* (1791), ed. George Birkbeck Hill, and L. F. Powell, 6 vols. (Oxford: Clarendon Press, 1934–64).

Bradford, Richard, *Augustan Measures: Restoration and Eighteenth-Century Writings on Prosody and Metre* (Aldershot: Ashgate, 2002).
Brower, Reuben A., *Alexander Pope: The Poetry of Allusion* (Oxford: Clarendon Press, 1959).
Erskine-Hill, Howard, *The Augustan Idea in English Literature* (London: Arnold, 1983).
The Poetry of Opposition and Revolution: Dryden to Wordsworth (Oxford: Clarendon Press, 1996).
Erskine-Hill, Howard (ed.), *Alexander Pope: World and Word*, second edition (Oxford: Oxford University Press for British Academy, 1998).
Griffith, R. H., *Alexander Pope: A Bibliography*, 2 vols. (1922, 1927; London: Holland Press, 1962).
Johnson, Samuel, *Poems*, Yale Edition of the Works of Samuel Johnson, vol. VI, ed. E. L. McAdam (New Haven: Yale University Press, 1964).
Mack, Maynard, *Alexander Pope: A Life* (London: Yale University Press, 1985).
Collected in Himself: Essays, Critical, Biographical, and Bibliographical on Pope and Some of his Contemporaries (Newark: University of Delaware Press, 1982).
Mack, Maynard (ed.), *Essential Articles for the Study of Alexander Pope*, revised and enlarged edition (Hamden, CT: Archon, 1968).
Mack, Maynard and James A. Winn (eds.), *Pope: Recent Essays* (Hamden, CT: Archon, 1980).
McLaverty, James, *Pope, Print and Meaning* (Oxford: Oxford University Press, 2001).
Piper, William Bowman, *The Heroic Couplet* (Cleveland, OH: Press of Case Western Reserve University, 1969).
Rogers, Pat, *Essays on Pope* (Cambridge: Cambridge University Press, 1993).
Grub Street: Studies in a Subculture (London: Methuen, 1972).
Pope and the Destiny of the Stuarts (Oxford: Oxford University Press, 2005).
(ed.), *The Alexander Pope Encyclopedia* (Westport, CT: Greenwood Press, 2004).
Spence, Joseph, *Observations, Anecdotes and Characters* (1820), ed. James M. Osborn, 2 vols. (Oxford, Clarendon Press, 1966).
Stack, Frank, *Pope and Horace: Studies in Imitation* (Cambridge: Cambridge University Press, 1985).
Pope, Alexander, *Correspondence*, ed. George Sherburn, 5 vols. (Oxford: Clarendon, 1956).
The Dunciad (1728) and The Dunciad Variorum (1729), ed. Valerie Rumbold (Harlow: Pearson Longman, 2007).
The Dunciad in Four Books, ed. Valerie Rumbold (Harlow: Longman, 1999).
Prose Works of Alexander Pope, ed. Norman Ault, and Rosemary Cowler, 2 vols. (Oxford: Blackwell, 1936–86).
Twickenham Edition of the Poems of Alexander Pope, ed. John Butt, Maynard Mack *et al.*, 11 vols. in 12 (London: Methuen, 1939–69).

19 Eighteenth-century women poets

Barash, Carol, *English Women's Poetry, 1649–1714: Politics, Community and Linguistic Authority* (Oxford: Clarendon, 1996).
Doody, Margaret Anne, 'Women Poets of the Eighteenth Century', in Vivien Jones (ed.), *Women and Literature in Britain 1700–1800* (Cambridge: Cambridge University Press, 2000), pp. 217–37.
Egerton, Sarah Fyge, *Poems on Several Occasions* (London: J. Nutt, 1703).
Fairer, David, *English Poetry of the Eighteenth Century* (London: Longman, 2003).

Fairer, David and Christine Gerrard (eds.), *Eighteenth-Century Poetry: An Annotated Anthology*, second revised edition (Oxford: Blackwell, 2003).

Ferguson, Moira, *Eighteenth-Century Women Poets: Nation, Class, and Gender* (Albany: State University of New York Press, 1995).

Gerrard, Christine (ed.), *A Companion to Eighteenth-Century Poetry* (Oxford: Blackwell, 2006).

Greene, Richard, *Mary Leapor: A Study in Eighteenth-Century Women's Poetry* (Oxford: Clarendon Press, 1993).

Grundy, Isobel, *Lady Mary Wortley Montagu: Comet of the Enlightenment* (Oxford: Oxford University Press, 1999).

Landry, Donna, *The Muses of Resistance: Labouring-Class Women's Poetry in Britain, 1739–1796* (Cambridge: Cambridge University Press, 1990).

Lonsdale, Roger (ed.), *Eighteenth-Century Women Poets: an Oxford Anthology* (Oxford: Oxford University Press, 1989).

Montagu, Lady Mary Wortley, *Essays and Poems and 'Simplicity, a Comedy'*, ed. Robert Halsband and Isobel Grundy (Oxford: Clarendon Press, 1977, revised editon 1993).

Prescott, Sarah and David E. Shuttleton (eds.), *Women and Poetry, 1660–1750* (Basingstoke: Palgrave Macmillan, 2003).

Thomas, Claudia N., *Alexander Pope and his Eighteenth-Century Women Readers* (Carbondale: Southern Illinois University Press, 1994).

Tillotson, Geoffrey, Paul Fussell and Marshall Waingrow (eds.), *Eighteenth-Century English Literature* (New York: Harcourt, Brace and World, 1969).

Yearsley, Ann, *Poems on Several Occasions* (London, 1785).

20 Longer eighteenth-century poems (Akenside, Thomson, Young, Cowper and others)

Akenside, Mark, *Poetical Works*, ed. Robin Dix (London: Associated University Presses, 1996).

Barrell, John, *English Literature in History 1730–80: An Equal, Wide Survey* (London: Hutchinson, 1983).

Blom, T. E., 'Eighteenth-Century Reflexive Process Poetry', *Eighteenth-Century Studies*, 10 (1976), pp. 52–72.

Brown, Marshall, *Preromanticism* (Stanford, CA: Stanford University Press, 1991).

Cowper, William, *Poems*, ed. John D. Baird, and Charles Ryskamp, 3 vols. (Oxford: Clarendon Press, 1980–95).

Doody, Margaret, *The Daring Muse: Augustan Poetry Reconsidered* (Cambridge: Cambridge University Press, 1985).

Dowling, William C., 'Ideology and the Flight from History in Eighteenth-Century Poetry', in Leo Damrosch (ed.), *The Profession of Eighteenth-Century Literature* (Madison: University of Wisconsin Press, 1992), pp. 135–53.

Eliot, T. S., 'Poetry in the Eighteenth Century', in Boris Ford (ed.), *The New Pelican Guide to English Literature Vol. 4: From Dryden to Johnson* (Harmondsworth: Pelican, 1982), pp. 228–34.

Fairer, David, *English Poetry of the Eighteenth Century 1700–1789* (London: Longman, 2003).

Griffin, Dustin, *Regaining Paradise: Milton and the Eighteenth Century* (Cambridge: Cambridge University Press, 1986).

Havens, R. D., *Milton's Influence on English Poetry* (Cambridge, MA: Harvard University Press, 1922).

Jacobus, Mary, *Tradition and Experiment in Wordsworth's Lyrical Ballads 1798* (Oxford: Oxford University Press, 1976).

Nicolson, Marjorie Hope, 'The Microscope and English Imagination', in *Science and Imagination* (Ithaca, NY: Cornell University Press, 1956), pp. 155–234, 164–9

Sitter, John E., *Literary Loneliness in Mid-Eighteenth Century England* (Ithaca, NY: Cornell University Press, 1982).

'Theodicy at Mid-Century: Young, Akenside, and Hume', *Eighteenth-Century Studies*, 12 (1978), pp. 90–106.

Terry, Richard, 'Transitions and Digressions in the Eighteenth-Century Long Poem', *Studies in English Literature*, 32 (1992), pp. 495–510.

Thomson, James, *The Seasons*, ed. James Sambrook (Oxford: Clarendon Press, 1981).

Young, Edward, *Night Thoughts*, ed. Stephen Cornford (Cambridge: Cambridge University Press, 1989).

21 Lyric poetry: 1740–1790

Barry, Paul, *Language, Music and the Sign: A Study in Aesthetics, Poetics and Poetic Practice from Collins to Coleridge* (Cambridge: Cambridge University Press, 1987).

Bate, W. J., *The Burden of the Past and the English Poet* (Cambridge, MA: Belknap, 1970).

Bloom, Harold, *The Anxiety of Influence* (New York: Oxford University Press, 1973).

Fairer, David, *English Poetry of the Eighteenth Century* (Harlow: Longman, 2003).

Rollins, H. E. (ed.), *The Keats Circle* (Cambridge, MA: Harvard University Press, 1965).

22 Romantic poetry: an overview

Abrams, M. H., *The Mirror and the Lamp: Romantic Theory and the Critical Tradition* (New York: Oxford University Press 1953).

Bate, Walter Jackson, *From Classic to Romantic: Premises of Taste in Eighteenth Century England* (Cambridge, MA: Harvard University Press, 1946).

Bayley, John, *The Romantic Survival: A Study in Poetic Evolution* (London: Constable, 1957).

Beer, John, 'Literature'; in Boris Ford (ed.), *The Romantic Age in Britain* (Cambridge: Cambridge University Press, 1992), pp. 56–117.

Bloom, Harold, *The Visionary Company: A Reading of English Romantic Poetry*, revised edition (Ithaca: Cornell University Press, 1971).

Curran, Stuart, *Poetic Form and British Romanticism* (New York: Oxford University Press, 1986).

Furst, Lilian R., *Romanticism*, Critical Idiom Series (London: Methuen, 1969).

Kermode, Frank, *Romantic Image* (London: Routledge and Kegan Paul, 1957).

McFarland, Thomas, *Romanticism and the Forms of Ruin: Wordsworth, Coleridge, and Modalities of Fragmentation* (Princeton: Princeton University Press, 1981).

McGann, Jerome, *The Beauty of Inflections: Literary Investigations in Historical Method and Theory* (Oxford: Clarendon Press, 1985).

Man, Paul de, *The Rhetoric of Romanticism* (New York: Columbia University Press, 1984).

Mellor, Anne K., *Romanticism and Gender* (New York: Routledge, 1993).

O'Neill, Michael, *Romanticism and the Self-Conscious Poem* (Oxford: Clarendon Press, 1997).

Wolfson, Susan J., *Formal Charges: The Shaping of Poetry in British Romanticism* (Stanford, CA: Stanford University Press, 1997).

Wordsworth, Jonathan, Michael Jaye and Robert Woof, *William Wordsworth and the Age of English Romanticism* (New Brunswick, NJ: Rutgers University Press, 1987).

23 Blake's poetry and prophecies

Beer, John, *Blake's Humanism* (Manchester: Manchester University Press, 1968).

Blake's Visionary Universe (Manchester: Manchester University Press, 1969).

William Blake: A Literary Life (New York: Palgrave Macmillan, 2005).

Blackstone, Bernard, *English Blake* (Cambridge: Cambridge University Press, 1949).

Bloom, Harold, *Blake's Apocalypse: A Study in Poetic Argument* (Garden City, NY: Doubleday, 1963).

Bronowski, Jacob, *William Blake: A Man without a Mask* (London: Secker and Warburg, 1944).

Damrosch, Leopold Jr., *Symbol and Truth in Blake's Myth* (Princeton: Princeton University Press, 1980).

Erdman, David V., *Blake – Prophet against Empire* (Princeton: Princeton University Press, 1969).

Frosch, Thomas, *The Awakening of Albion: The Renovation of the Body in the Poetry of William Blake* (Ithaca, NY: Cornell University Press, 1974).

Frye, Northrop, *Fearful Symmetry: A Study of William Blake* (Princeton: Princeton University Press, 1947).

Gardner, Stanley, *Infinity on the Anvil: A Critical Study of Blake's Poetry* (Oxford: Blackwell, 1954).

Gillham, D. G., *Blake's Contrary States: The 'Songs of Innocence and of Experience' as Dramatic Poems* (Cambridge: Cambridge University Press, 1966).

Glen, Heather, *Vision and Disenchantment: Blake's 'Songs' and Wordsworth's 'Lyrical Ballads'* (Cambridge: Cambridge University Press, 1983).

Lowery, M. R., *Windows of the Morning: A Critical Study of William Blake's 'Poetical Sketches'* (New Haven: Yale University Press, 1940).

Mee, Jon, *Dangerous Enthusiasm: William Blake and the Culture of Radicalism in the 1790s* (Oxford: Clarendon Press, 1992).

Mellor, Anne Kostelanetz, *Blake's Human Form Divine* (Berkeley: University of California Press, 1974).

Mitchell, W. J. T., *Blake's Composite Art: A Study of the Illuminated Poetry* (Princeton: Princeton University Press, 1978).

Otto, Peter, *Blake's Critique of Transcendence: Love, Jealousy and the Sublime in 'The Four Zoas'* (Oxford: Oxford University Press, 2000).

Paley, Morton D., *Energy and the Imagination: A Study of the Development of Blake's Thought* (Oxford: Clarendon Press, 1970).

The Traveller in the Evening: The Last Works of William Blake (Oxford: Oxford University Press, 2003).

Percival, M. O., *William Blake's Circle of Destiny: A Study in the Interpretation of Blake* (New York: Columbia University Press, 1938).

Thompson, E. P., *Witness against the Beast: William Blake and the Moral Law* (Cambridge: Cambridge University Press, 1993).

24 Wordsworth and Coleridge: *Lyrical Ballads* and other poems

Abrams, M. H., 'On political readings of *Lyrical Ballads*', in Michael Fischer (ed.), *Doing Things with Texts: Essays in Criticism and Critical Theory* (New York: Norton, 1989), pp. 364–91.

Bate, Walter J., *Coleridge* (London: Weidenfeld and Nicolson, 1968).

Beer, John, *Coleridge's Poetic Intelligence* (Basingstoke: Macmillan, 1977).

Gill, S., *William Wordsworth: A Life* (Oxford: Clarendon Press, 1989).

Glen, Heather, *Vision and Disenchantment: Blake's 'Songs' and Wordsworth's 'Lyrical Ballads'* (Cambridge: Cambridge University Press, 1983).

Hartman, Geoffrey H., 'Wordsworth, Inscriptions, and Romantic Nature Poetry', in Frederick W. Hilles and Harold Bloom (eds.), *From Sensibility to Romanticism: Essays Presented to Frederick A. Pottle* (New York: Oxford University Press, 1965), pp. 389–413.

Wordsworth's Poetry, 1787–1814, new edition (New Haven: Yale University Press, 1971).

Holmes, Richard, *Coleridge: Early Visions* (London: Hodder and Stoughton, 1989).

Jackson, J. R. de J. (ed.), *Coleridge: The Critical Heritage* (London: Routledge and Kegan Paul, 1970).

Jacobus, Mary, *Tradition and Experiment in Wordsworth's 'Lyrical Ballads' (1798)* (Oxford: Clarendon Press, 1976).

Johnston, Kenneth R., and Gene W. Ruoff (eds.), *The Age of William Wordsworth: Critical Essays on the Romantic Tradition* (New Brunswick, NJ: Rutgers University Press, 1987).

Newlyn, Lucy, *Coleridge, Wordsworth, and the Language of Allusion* (Oxford: Clarendon Press, 1986).

Perry, Seamus, *Coleridge and the Uses of Division* (Oxford: Clarendon Press, 1999).

Perry, Seamus (ed.), *Coleridge's Notebooks: A Selection* (Oxford: Oxford University Press, 2002).

Roe, Nicholas, *Wordsworth and Coleridge: The Radical Years* (Oxford: Clarendon Press, 1988).

Ruoff, Gene W., *Wordsworth and Coleridge: The Making of the Major Lyrics, 1802–1804* (London: Harvester Wheatsheaf, 1989).

Wordsworth, Jonathan, Michael C. Jaye and Robert Woof (eds.), *William Wordsworth and the Age of English Romanticism* (New Brunswick, NJ: Rutgers University Press, 1987).

25 Wordsworth's *The Prelude* and *The Excursion*

Bromwich, David, *Disowned by Memory: Wordsworth's Poetry of the 1790s* (Chicago: University of Chicago Press, 1998).

Bushell, Sally, *Re-reading The Excursion: Narrative, Response, and the Wordsworthian Dramatic Voice* (Aldershot: Ashgate, 2002).

Fry, Paul H. *Wordsworth and the Poetry of What We Are* (New Haven: Yale University Press, 2008).

Gill, Stephen (ed.), *William Wordsworth's The Prelude: A Casebook* (Oxford: Oxford University Press, 2006).

Hartman, Geoffrey H., *The Unremarkable Wordsworth* (London: Methuen, 1987).

Wordsworth's Poetry, 1787–1814 (Cambridge, MA: Harvard University Press, 1987).

Johnston, Kenneth R., *The Hidden Wordsworth: Poet, Lover, Rebel, Spy* (New York: Norton, 1998).

Wordsworth and The Recluse (New Haven: Yale University Press, 1984).

Lindenberger, Herbert Samuel, *On Wordsworth's Prelude* (Princeton: Princeton University Press, 1963).

Liu, Alan, *Wordsworth: The Sense of History* (Stanford, CA: Stanford University Press, 1989).
Ricks, Christopher, *The Force of Poetry* (Oxford: Oxford University Press, 1984).
Wordsworth, William, *The Excursion*, ed. Sally Bushell, James A. Butler and Michael C. Jaye (Ithaca, NY: Cornell University Press, 2007).
The Five-Book Prelude, ed. Duncan Wu (Oxford: Blackwell, 1997).
The Fourteen-Book Prelude, ed. W. J. B. Owen (Ithaca, NY: Cornell University Press, 1985).
The Prelude, 1798–1799, ed. Stephen Parrish (Ithaca, NY: Cornell University Press, 1977).
The Prelude, 1799, 1805, 1850, ed. Jonathan Wordsworth, M. H. Abrams and Stephen Gill (New York: Norton, 1979).
The Ruined Cottage and The Pedlar, ed. James Butler (Ithaca, NY: Cornell University Press, 1979).
The Thirteen-Book Prelude, ed. Mark L. Reed (Ithaca, NY: Cornell University Press, 1991).
William Wordsworth, ed. Stephen Gill (Oxford: Oxford University Press, 1984; reprinted 1990).

26 Second-generation romantic poetry 1: Hunt, Byron, Moore

Byron, Lord, *The Complete Poetical Works*, ed. Jerome, J. McGann, 7 vols. (Oxford: Clarendon Press, 1980–93).
Cox, Jeffrey, N., *Poetry and Politics in the Cockney School: Keats, Shelley, Hunt and their Circle* (Cambridge: Cambridge University Press, 1998).
Cronin, Richard, *The Politics of Romantic Poetry: In Search of the Pure Commonwealth* (Basingstoke: Macmillan, 2000).
Hunt, Leigh, *The Poetical Works of Leigh Hunt* (London: Edward Moxon, 1832).
Mole, Tom, *Byron's Romantic Celebrity: Industrial Culture and the Hermeneutic of Intimacy* (Basingstoke: Palgrave, 2007).
Moore, Thomas, *The Poetical Works of Thomas Moore*, 10 vols. (London: Longman, Orme, Brown, Green, and Longmans, 1840).
Roe, Nicholas, *Fiery Heart: The First Life of Leigh Hunt* (London: Pimlico, 2005).
Vail, Jeffrey W., *The Literary Relationship of Lord Byron and Thomas Moore* (Baltimore: Johns Hopkins University Press, 2001).

27 Byron's *Don Juan*

Barton, Anne, *Byron: Don Juan* (Cambridge: Cambridge University Press, 1992).
'*Don Juan* Transformed', in Andrew Rutherford (ed.), *Byron: Augustan and Romantic* (London: Macmillan, 1990), pp. 199–220.
Beatty, Bernard, *Byron's Don Juan* (London: Croom Helm, 1985).
Bevis, Matthew, *The Art of Eloquence: Byron, Dickens, Joyce* (Oxford: Oxford University Press, 2007).
Bone, Drummond, '*Childe Harold's Pilgrimage* IV, *Don Juan* and *Beppo*', in Drummond Bone (ed.), *The Cambridge Companion to Byron* (Cambridge: Cambridge University Press, 2004), pp. 151–70.
Cooke, Michael G., '*Don Juan*: The Obsession and Self-Discipline of Spontaneity', in Harold Bloom (ed.), *George Gordon, Lord Byron: Modern Critical Views* (New York: Chelsea House, 1986), pp. 101–16.

Curtis, Paul M., 'Byron and Digression', in Jane Stabler (ed.), *Byron Studies* (London: Palgrave Macmillan, 2007), pp.60–80.
England, A. B., *Byron's Don Juan and Eighteenth-Century Literature* (London: Associated University Presses, 1975).
Graham, Peter, *Don Juan and Regency England* (Charlottesville: University of Virginia Press, 1990).
Jump, J. D., *Byron's 'Don Juan': Poem or Hold-All?* (Swansea: University of Swansea Press, 1968).
McGann, Jerome J., *Don Juan in Context* (London: John Murray, 1976).
Punter, David, '*Don Juan*, or the Deferral of Decapitation: Some Psychological Approaches', in Nigel Wood (ed.), *Don Juan*, Theory and Practice Series (Buckingham: Open University Press, 1993), pp. 124–49.
Ricks, Christopher, *Allusion to the Poets* (Oxford: Oxford University Press, 2002), pp.121–56.
Ridenour, G. M., *The Style of Don Juan* (New Haven: Yale University Press, 1960).
St Clair, William, *The Reading Nation in the Romantic Period* (Cambridge: Cambridge University Press, 2004).
Stabler, Jane, *Byron, Poetics and History* (Cambridge: Cambridge University Press, 2002), pp. 1–17, 106–97.

28 Second-generation Romantic poetry 2: Shelley and Keats

Shelley

Bloom, Harold, *Shelley's Mythmaking* (New Haven: Cornell University Press, 1959).
Clark, Timothy, *Embodying Revolution: The Figure of the Poet in Shelley* (Oxford: Clarendon Press, 1989).
Cronin, Richard, *Shelley's Poetic Thoughts* (Basingstoke: Macmillan, 1981).
Hogle, Jerrold E., *Shelley's Process: Radical Transference and the Development of His Major Works* (New York: Oxford University Press, 1988).
Keach, William, *Shelley's Style* (New York: Methuen, 1984).
Leighton, Angela, *Shelley and the Sublime* (Cambridge: Cambridge University Press, 1984).
O'Neill, Michael, *The Human Mind's Imaginings: Conflict and Achievement in Shelley's Poetry* (Oxford: Clarendon Press, 1989).
Sperry, Stuart M., *Shelley's Major Verse* (Princeton: Princeton University Press, 1988).
Wasserman, Earl R., *Shelley: A Critical Reading* (Baltimore: Johns Hopkins University Press, 1971).
Webb, Timothy, *Shelley: A Voice Not Understood* (Manchester: Manchester University Press, 1977).
Weinberg, Alan M. and Timothy Webb (eds.), *The Unfamiliar Shelley* (Farnham: Ashgate, 2009).

Keats

Barnard, John, *John Keats* (Cambridge: Cambridge University Press, 1987).
Bate, Walter Jackson, *John Keats* (Cambridge, MA: Harvard University Press, 1963).
Bennett, Andrew, *Keats, Narrative and Audience: The Posthumous Life of Writing* (Cambridge: Cambridge University Press, 1994).

Bush, Douglas, *John Keats: His Life and Writings* (London: Weidenfeld and Nicolson, 1966).
Fermanis, Porscha, *John Keats and the Ideas of the Enlightenment* (Edinburgh: Edinburgh University Press, 2009).
Ricks, Christopher, *Keats and Embarrassment* (Oxford: Oxford University Press, 1976).
Roe, Nicholas, *John Keats and the Culture of Dissent* (Oxford: Clarendon Press, 1997).
Sperry, Stuart M., *Keats the Poet* (Princeton: Princeton University Press, 1973).
Stillinger, Jack, *The Hoodwinking of Madeline, and Other Essays on Keats's Poems* (Urbana: University of Illinois Press, 1971).
Vendler, Helen, *The Odes of John Keats* (Cambridge, MA: Harvard University Press, 1983).

29 Third-generation Romantic poetry: Beddoes, Clare, Darley, Hemans, Landon

Abbott, Claude Colleer, *The Life and Letters of George Darley, Poet and Critic* (London: Oxford University Press, Humphrey Milford, 1928).
Arnold, Matthew, *The Poems of Matthew Arnold*, second edition, ed. Kenneth and Miriam Allott (London: Longman, 1979).
Barfoot, C. C. (ed.), *Victorian Keats and Romantic Carlyle: The Fusions and Confusions of Literary Periods* (Amsterdam: Rodopi, 1999).
Barrell, John, *The Idea of Landscape and the Sense of Place, 1730–1840: An Approach to the Poetry of John Clare* (Cambridge: Cambridge University Press, 1972).
Bate, Jonathan, *John Clare: A Biography* (London: Picador, 2003).
Beddoes, Thomas Lovell, *The Works of Thomas Lovell Beddoes*, ed. H. W. Donner (London: Oxford University Press, 1935; repr. New York: AMS Press, 1978).
Berns, Ute and Michael Bradshaw (eds.), *The Ashgate Research Companion to Thomas Lovell Beddoes* (Aldershot: Ashgate, 2007).
Bloom, Harold, *The Visionary Company: A Reading of English Romantic Poetry* (London: Faber and Faber, 1962).
Brisman, Leslie, 'George Darley: the Poet as Pigmy', *Studies in Romanticism*, 15 (1976), pp. 119–41.
Chilcott, Tim, *A Publisher and his Circle: The Life and Work of John Taylor* (London: Routledge and Kegan Paul, 1972).
Clare, John, *The Oxford Authors: John Clare: A Critical Edition of the Major Works*, ed. Eric Robinson and David Powell (Oxford: Oxford University Press, 1984).
Poems of the Middle Period, 1822–1837, vol. 1, ed. Eric Robinson, David Powell and P. M. S. Dawson (Oxford: Clarendon Press, 1996).
Darley, George, *Selected Poems of George Darley*, ed. Anne Ridler (London: Merrion, 1979).
Donner, H. W., *Thomas Lovell Beddoes: The Making of a Poet* (Oxford: Blackwell, 1935).
Frye, Northrop, *A Study of English Romanticism* (New York: Random House, 1968; repr. London: Harvester, 1983).
Haughton, Hugh, Adam Phillips and Geoffrey Summerfield (eds.), *John Clare in Context* (Cambridge: Cambridge University Press, 1994).
Hemans, Felicia, *Selected Poems, Prose, and Letters*, ed. Gary Kelly (Ontario: Broadview, 2002).
Jack, Ian, 'Clare and the Minor Poets', in *English Literature 1815–32: Scott, Byron and Keats* (Oxford: Clarendon Press, 1963), pp. 130–84.

Landon, Letitia Elizabeth, *Selected Writings*, ed. Jerome McGann and Daniel Riess (Ontario: Broadview, 1997).

Leader, Zachary, 'John Taylor and the Poems of John Clare', in *Revision and Romantic Authorship* (Oxford: Clarendon Press, 1996), pp. 206–61.

Mellor, Anne K., *Romanticism and Gender* (New York and London: Routledge, 1993).

O'Neill, Michael, '"A storm of ghosts": Beddoes, Shelley, Death and Reputation', *Cambridge Quarterly*, 28.2 (1999), pp. 102–15.

Richardson, Alan, '*Death's Jest-Book*: "shadows of words"', in *A Mental Theater: Poetic Drama and Consciousness in the Romantic Age* (University Park: Pennsylvania State University Press, 1988), pp. 154–73.

Robinson, Eric and Geoffrey Summerfield, 'John Taylor's Editing of John Clare's *The Shepherd's Calendar*', *The Review of English Studies*, 14:56 (1963), pp. 359–69.

Sales, Roger, *John Clare: A Literary Life* (Basingstoke: Palgrave, 2002).

Snow, Royall H., *Thomas Lovell Beddoes, Eccentric and Poet* (New York: Covici-Friede, 1928).

Tibble, J. W. and Anne, *John Clare: A Life* (London: Cobden-Sanderson, 1932; second edition 1972).

30 Women poets of the Romantic period (Barbauld to Landon)

Barbauld, Anna Laetitia, *Selected Poetry and Prose*, ed. William McCarthy and Elizabeth Kraft (Peterborough, ONT: Broadview Press, 2002).

Hemans, Felicia, *Felicia Hemans: Selected Poems, Letters, Reception Materials*, ed. Susan J. Wolfson (Princeton: Princeton University Press, 2000).

Landon, Letitia Elizabeth, *Letitia Elizabeth Landon: Selected Writings*, ed. Jerome J. McGann and Daniel Riess (Peterborough, Ontario: Broadview Press, 1997).

O'Neill, Michael and Charles Mahoney (eds.), *Romantic Poetry: An Annotated Anthology* (Oxford: Blackwell, 2008).

Robinson, Mary, *Mary Robinson: Selected Poems*, ed. Judith Pascoe (Peterborough, Ontario: Broadview Press, 2000).

Rowton, Frederic, *The Female Poets of Great Britain, Chronologically Arranged, with Copious Selections and Critical Remarks*, ed. Marilyn L. Williamson, Facsimile edition (1853; Detroit: Wayne State University Press, 1981).

Smith, Charlotte, *The Poems of Charlotte Smith*, ed. Stuart Curran (Oxford: Oxford University Press, 1993).

31 Victorian poetry: an overview

Armstrong, Isobel, *Victorian Poetry: Poetry, Poetics and Politics* (London: Routledge, 1993).

Buckley, Jerome Hamilton, *The Victorian Temper: A Study in Literary Culture* (London: George Allen and Unwin, 1952).

Byron, Glennis, *The Dramatic Monologue* (London: Routledge, 2003).

Campbell, Matthew, *Rhythm and Will in Victorian Poetry* (Cambridge: Cambridge University Press, 1999).

Christ, Carol T., *The Finer Optic: The Aesthetic of Particularity in Victorian Poetry* (New Haven: Yale University Press, 1975).

Cronin, Richard, Alison Chapman and Antony H. Harrison (eds.), *A Companion to Victorian Poetry* (Oxford: Blackwell, 2002).

Douglas-Fairhurst, Robert, *Victorian Afterlives: The Shaping of Influence in Nineteenth-Century Literature* (Oxford: Oxford University Press, 2002).
Erickson, Lee, *The Economy of Literary Form: English Literature and the Industrializing of Publishing, 1800–1850* (Baltimore: Johns Hopkins University Press, 1996).
Griffiths, Eric, *The Printed Voice of Victorian Poetry* (Oxford: Clarendon Press, 1989).
Harrison, Antony H., *Victorian Poets and the Politics of Culture: Discourse and Ideology* (Charlottesville: University Press of Virginia, 1998).
Jackson, Holbrook, *The Eighteen Nineties* (London: Grant Richards, 1913).
Langbaum, Robert, *The Poetry of Experience: The Dramatic Monologue in Modern Literary Tradition* (London: Chatto and Windus, 1957).
Leighton, Angela, *Victorian Women Poets: Writing Against the Heart* (London: Harvester Wheatsheaf, 1992).
Reynolds, Matthew, *The Realms of Verse 1830–1870: English Poetry in a Time of Nation-Building* (Oxford: Oxford University Press, 2001).
Shaw, W. David, *The Lucid Veil: Poetic Truth in the Victorian Age* (Madison: University of Wisconsin Press, 1987).

32 Tennyson

Collins, Philip (ed.), *Tennyson: Seven Essays* (Basingstoke: Macmillan, 1992).
Culler, A. Dwight, *The Poetry of Tennyson* (New Haven: Yale University Press, 1977).
Douglas-Fairhurst, Robert and Seamus Perry (eds.), *Tennyson among the Poets: Bicentenary Essays* (Oxford: Oxford University Press, 2009).
Eliot, T. S., 'In Memoriam' (1936), in Frank Kermode (ed.), *Selected Prose of T. S. Eliot* (London: Faber, 1975), pp. 239–47.
Griffiths, Eric, *The Printed Voice of Victorian Poetry* (Oxford: Clarendon Press, 1989), pp. 97–170.
Jump, John D. (ed.), *Tennyson: The Critical Heritage* (London: Routledge, 1967).
Martin, Robert Bernard, *Tennyson: The Unquiet Heart* (Oxford: Oxford University Press, 1980).
Mazzeno, Laurence W., *Alfred Tennyson: The Critical Legacy* (New York: Camden House, 2004).
Page, Norman (ed.), *Tennyson: Interviews and Recollections* (London: Macmillan, 1983).
Perry, Seamus, *Alfred Tennyson* (Tavistock: Northcote House, 2005).
Richardson, James, *Vanishing Lives: Style and Self in Tennyson, D. G. Rossetti, Swinburne and Yeats* (Charlottesville: University Press of Virginia, 1988).
Ricks, Christopher, *Tennyson* (London: Macmillan, 1972).
Sinfield, Alan, *The Language of Tennyson's 'In Memoriam'* (Oxford: Blackwell, 1971).
Stott, Rebecca (ed.), *Tennyson*, Longman Critical Readers (London: Longman, 1996).
Tennyson, Hallam, *Alfred, Lord Tennyson: A Memoir by his Son*, 2 vols. (London: Macmillan, 1897).
Tucker, Herbert, *Tennyson and the Doom of Romanticism* (Cambridge, MA: Harvard University Press, 1988).

33 Elizabeth Barrett and Robert Browning

Chesterton, G. K., *Robert Browning* (London: Macmillan, 1903).
Gibson, Mary Ellis (ed.), *Critical Essays on Robert Browning* (New York: G. K. Hall, 1992).

Karlin, Daniel, *The Courtship of Robert Browning and Elizabeth Barrett Browning* (Oxford: Clarendon Press, 1985).
Kelley, Philip, Ronald Hudson and Scott Lewis (eds.), *The Brownings' Correspondence*, 16 vols to date (Winfield: Wedgstone Press, 1984–).
Langbaum, Robert, *The Poetry of Experience: The Dramatic Monologue in Modern Literary Tradition* (London: Chatto and Windus, 1957).
Leighton, Angela, *Elizabeth Barrett Browning* (Brighton: Harvester, 1986).
Markus, Julia, *Dared and Done: The Marriage of Elizabeth Barrett and Robert Browning* (New York: Knopf, 1995).
Mermin, Dorothy, *Elizabeth Barrett Browning: The Origins of a New Poetry* (Chicago: University of Chicago Press, 1989).
Pollock, Mary Sanders, *Elizabeth Barrett and Robert Browning: A Creative Partnership* (Aldershot: Ashgate, 2003).
Ryals, Clyde de L., *The Life of Robert Browning: A Critical Biography* (Oxford: Blackwell, 1993).
Tucker, Herbert F., *Browning's Beginnings: The Art of Disclosure* (Minneapolis: University of Minnesota Press, 1980).
Woolford, John (ed.), *Robert Browning in Contexts* (Winfield: Wedgstone Press, 1998).

34 Emily Brontë, Arnold, Clough

Emily Brontë

Gezari, Janet, *Last Things: Emily Brontë's Poems* (Oxford: Oxford University Press, 2007).
Tayler, Irene, *Holy Ghosts: The Male Muses of Emily and Charlotte Brontë* (New York: Columbia University Press, 1990).
Wordsworth, Jonathan, 'Wordsworth and the Poetry of Emily Brontë', *Brontë Society Transactions*, 16 (1972), pp. 85–100.

Arnold

Buckler, William E., *On the Poetry of Matthew Arnold: Essays in Critical Reconstruction* (New York: New York University Press, 1982).
Culler, A. Dwight, *Imaginative Reason: The Poetry of Matthew Arnold* (New Haven: Yale University Press, 1966).
O'Neill, Michael, ' "The Burden of Ourselves": Arnold as a Post-Romantic Poet', *Yearbook of English Studies*, 36.2 (2006), pp. 109–24.
Woolford, John, 'Arnold on Empedocles', *Review of English Studies*, 50 (1999), pp. 32–52.

Clough

Bailey, Suzanne, ' "A Garland of Fragments": Modes of Reflexivity in Clough's *Amours de Voyage*', *Victorian Poetry*, 31 (1993), pp. 157–70.
Cronin, Richard, 'Byron, Clough, and the Grounding of Victorian Poetry', *Romanticism*, 14.1 (2008), pp. 13–24.
Kenny, Anthony, *Arthur Hugh Clough: A Poet's Life* (London: Continuum, 2005).

35 Dante Gabriel Rossetti and Swinburne

Buchanan, Robert, 'The Fleshly School of Poetry: Mr D. G. Rossetti', *Contemporary Review*, 18 (1871), pp. 334–50; reprinted in David G. Riede (ed.), *Critical Essays on Dante Gabriel Rossetti* (New York: G. K. Hall, 1992); pp. 24–39.

Hallam, Arthur Henry, 'On Some Characteristics of Modern Poetry and on the Lyrical Poems of Alfred Tennyson', in *The Writings of Arthur Hallam*, ed. T. H. Vail Motter, (London: Oxford University Press, 1943), pp. 182–98.

Henderson, Philip, *Swinburne: Portrait of a Poet* (New York: Macmillan, 1974).

Hyder, Clyde K. (ed.), *Swinburne: The Critical Heritage* (New York: Barnes and Noble, 1970).

Keats, John, *Letters*, ed. Hyder Edward Rollins, 2 vols. (Cambridge, MA: Harvard University Press, 1958).

Louis, Margot K., *Swinburne and his Gods: The Roots and Growth of an Agnostic Poetry* (Montreal: McGill-Queen's University Press, 1990).

McGann, Jerome, *Dante Gabriel Rossettis and the Game That Must Be Lost* (New Haven: Yale University Press, 2000).

'Rossetti's Significant Details', *Victorian Poetry*, 7 (1969), pp. 41–54.

Swinburne: An Experiment in Criticism (Chicago: University of Chicago Press, 1969).

Mansel, H. L. 'Sensation Novels', *Quarterly Review* (April 1863).

Maxwell, Catherine, *Swinburne* (Tavistock, Devon: Northcote Publishers, 2006).

Myers, F. W. H., *Essays: Modern* (London: Macmillan, 1885).

O'Gorman, Francis, 'Clough's Difficulties', *Yearbook of English Studies*, 36.2 (2006), pp. 125–38.

Pater, Walter, 'Poems by William Morris', *Westminster Review* (October 1868), pp. 300–12.

Rees, Joan, *The Poetry of Dante Gabriel Rossetti: Modes of Self-Expression* (Cambridge: Cambridge University Press, 1981).

Riede, David G., *Dante Gabriel Rossetti and the Limits of Victorian Vision* (Ithaca, NY: Cornell University Press, 1983).

Dante Gabriel Rossetti Revisited (New York: Twayne, 1992).

Swinburne: A Study of Romantic Mythmaking (Charlottesville: University Press of Virginia, 1978).

Rooksby, Rikky, *A. C. Swinburne: A Poet's Life* (Aldershot: Ashgate, 1997).

Rosenberg, John D., 'Introduction', *Swinburne: Selected Poetry and Prose* (New York: Modern Library, 1968).

Rossetti, Dante Gabriel, *Collected Poetry and Prose*, ed. Jerome McGann (New Haven: Yale University Press, 2003).

Correspondence, ed. William E. Fredeman, 9 vols. (Cambridge: D. S. Brewer, 2002–8).

Swinburne, Algernon, *Letters*, ed. Cecil Y. Lang, 6 vols. (New Haven: Yale University Press, 1959–62).

Poems, 6 vols. (London: Chatto and Windus, 1904).

William Blake: A Critical Essay, ed. Hugh J. Luke (Lincoln: University of Nebraska Press, 1970).

36 Christina Rossetti and Hopkins

Christina Rossetti

Arseneau, Mary, Antony H. Harrison and Lorraine Janzen Kooistra (eds.), *The Culture of Christina Rossetti: Female Poetics and Victorian Contexts* (Athens: Ohio University Press, 1999).

D'Amico, Diane, *Christina Rossetti: Faith, Gender, and Time* (Baton Rouge: Louisiana State University Press, 1999).

Harrison, Antony H., *Christina Rossetti in Context* (Brighton: Harvester Press, 1988).

Jiménez, Nilda, *The Bible and the Poetry of Christina Rossetti: A Concordance* (London: Greenwood Press, 1979).

Kent, David A. (ed.), *The Achievement of Christina Rossetti* (Ithaca, NY: Cornell University Press, 1987).

Leighton, Angela, 'Christina Rossetti', in *Victorian Women Poets: Writing Against the Heart* (New York/London: *Harvester Wheatsheaf*, 1992), pp. 118–63.

McGann, Jerome J., 'Christina Rossetti's Poems: a New Edition and a Revaluation', *Victorian Studies*, 23 (1980), pp. 237–54.

'The Religious Poetry of Christina Rossetti', *Critical Inquiry*, 10 (1983), pp. 133–41.

Marsh, Jan, *Christina Rossetti: A Literary Biography* (Harmondsworth: Penguin, 1994).

Mayberry, Katherine J., *Christina Rossetti and the Poetry of Discovery* (Baton Rouge: Louisiana State University Press, 1989).

Packer, Lona Mosk, *Christina Rossetti* (Cambridge: Cambridge University Press, 1963).

Rees, Joan, 'Christina Rossetti: Poet', *Critical Quarterly*, 26:3 (1984), pp. 59–72.

Rosenblum, Dolores, *Christina Rossetti: The Poetry of Endurance* (Carbondale: Southern Illinois University Press, 1986).

Thomas, Frances, *Christina Rossetti* (London: Virago, 1994).

Gerard Manley Hopkins

Allsopp, Michael E. and David A Downes, *Saving Beauty: Further Studies in Hopkins* (London: Garland, 1994).

Ball, Patricia M., *The Science of Aspects: The Changing Role of Fact in the Work of Coleridge, Ruskin and Hopkins* (London: Athlone Press, 1971).

Bender, Todd K., *Gerard Manley Hopkins: The Classical Background and Critical Reception of his Work* (Baltimore: Johns Hopkins University Press, 1966).

Bottrall, Margaret (ed.), *Gerard Manley Hopkins: Poems – A Casebook* (London: Macmillan, 1975).

Boyle, Robert (S J), *Metaphor in Hopkins* (Chapel Hill: University of North Carolina Press, 1961).

Brown, Daniel, *Hopkins's Idealism: Philosophy, Physics, Poetry* (Oxford: Clarendon Press, 1997).

Cotter, James Finn, *Inscape: The Christology and Poetry of Gerard Manley Hopkins* (Pittsburgh: University of Pittsburgh Press, 1972).

Ellis, Virginia Ridley, *Gerard Manley Hopkins and the Language of Mystery* (Columbia: University of Missouri Press, 1991).

Fennell, Francis L. (ed.), *Rereading Hopkins: Selected New Essays* (Victoria: University of Victoria Press, 1996).

Griffiths, Eric, *The Printed Voice of Victorian Poetry* (Oxford: Clarendon Press, 1988).

Johnson, Margaret, *Gerard Manley Hopkins and Tractarian Poetry* (Aldershot: Ashgate, 1997).

Lichtmann, Maria, *The Contemplative Poetry of Gerard Manley Hopkins* (Princeton: Princeton University Press, 1989).

MacKenzie, Norman H., *Excursions in Hopkins* (Philadelphia: St Joseph's University Press, 2008).

A Reader's Guide to Gerard Manley Hopkins (London: Thames and Hudson, 1981; second edition Philadelphia: Saint Joseph's University Press, 2008).

Mariani, Paul, *Commentary on the Complete Poems of Gerard Manley Hopkins* (Ithaca, NY: Cornell University Press, 1970).

Martin, Robert Martin, *Gerard Manley Hopkins: A Very Private Life* (London: HarperCollins, 1991).

Milroy, James, *The Language of Gerard Manley Hopkins* (London: André Deutsch, 1977).

Milward, Peter (SJ), *Commentary on G. M. Hopkins' 'The Wreck of the Deutschland'* (Tokyo: Hokuseido Press, 1968).

A Commentary on the Sonnets of G. M. Hopkins (Tokyo: Hokuseido Press, 1969).

Mortimer, Anthony, *The Authentic Cadence: Centennial Essays on Gerard Manley Hopkins* (Fribourg: Fribourg University Press, 1992).

Nixon, Jude, *Gerard Manley Hopkins and His Contemporaries: Liddon, Newman, Darwin, and Pater* (New York: Garland, 1994).

Phillips, Catherine *Gerard Manley Hopkins and the Victorian Visual World* (Oxford: Oxford University Press, 2007).

Plotkin, Cary H., *The Tenth Muse: Victorian Philology and the Genesis of the Poetic Language of Gerard Manley Hopkins* (Carbondale: Southern Illinois University Press, 1989).

Roberts, Gerald (ed.), *Gerard Manley Hopkins: The Critical Heritage* (London: Routledge, 1987).

Saville, Julia F., *A Queer Chivalry: The Homoerotic Asceticism of Gerard Manley Hopkins* (Charlottesville: University Press of Virginia, 2000).

Storey, Graham, *A Preface to Hopkins* (London: Longman, 1981).

Thornton, R. K. R., *Gerard Manley Hopkins: The Poems* (London: Edward Arnold, 1973).

Waterman Ward, Bernadette, *World as Word: Philosophical Theology in Gerard Manley Hopkins* (Washington, DC: The Catholica University of America Press, 2002).

White, Norman, *Hopkins: A Literary Biography* (Oxford: Clarendon Press, 1992).

Hopkins in Ireland (Dublin: University College Dublin Press, 2002).

Hopkins in Wales (Bridgend: Poetry Wales Press, 1998).

Zanniello, Tom, *Hopkins in the Age of Darwin* (Iowa City: University of Iowa Press, 1988).

Zonneveld, Sjaak, *Random Grim Forge: A Study of Social Ideas in the Work of Gerard Manley Hopkins* (Assen, Maastricht: Van Gorcum, 1992).

Hopkins Quarterly is a journal devoted to Hopkins and his circle. *Victorian Poetry* also frequently publishes articles about his work.

37 Later Victorian voices 1: James Thomson, Symons, Dowson, Lionel Johnson, Housman

Beckson, Karl, *Aesthetes and Decadents of the 1890s*, revised edition (Chicago: Academy Chicago, 1981).

Bristow, Joseph (ed.), *The Fin-de-Siècle Poem: English Literary Culture and the 1890s* (Athens: Ohio University Press, 2005).

Evans, Ifor, *English Poetry in the Later Nineteenth Century*, second revised edition (New York: Barnes and Noble, 1966).

Fletcher, Ian (ed.), *British Poetry and Prose 1870–1905* (Oxford: Oxford University Press, 1987.

Rodensky, Lisa (ed.), *Decadent Poetry from Wilde to Naidu* (London: Penguin, 2006).
Thornton, R. K. R. and Marion Thain (eds.), *Poetry of the 1890s* (Harmondsworth: Penguin, 1997).

38 Later Victorian Voices 2: Davidson, Kipling, 'Michael Field' (Bradley and Cooper), Lee-Hamilton, Kendall, Webster

Primary

Blyth, Caroline (ed.), *Decadent Verse: An Anthology of Late Victorian Poetry, 1872–1900* (London: Anthem, 2008).
Thornton, R. K. R, and Marion Thain (eds.), *Poetry of the 1890s* (Harmondsworth: Penguin, 1998).

Secondary

Armstrong, Isobel, *Victorian Poetry: Poetry, Poetics and Politics* (London: Routledge, 1993).
Bristow, Joseph (ed.), *The Fin-de-Siècle Poem: English Literary Culture and the 1890s* (Athens: Ohio University Press, 2005).
Christ, Carol T., *Victorian and Modern Poetics* (Chicago: University of Chicago Press, 1986).
Sloan, John, *John Davidson, First of the Moderns* (Oxford: Clarendon Press, 1995).
Thain, Marion, *Michael Field: Poetry, Aestheticism and the Fin de Siècle* (Cambridge: Cambridge University Press, 2007).

39 Modernist and modern poetry: an overview

Cianci, Giovanni and Jason Harding (eds.), *T. S. Eliot and the Concept of Tradition* (Cambridge: Cambridge University Press, 2007).
Davie, Donald, *Modernist Essays: Yeats, Pound, Eliot* (Manchester: Carcanet, 2004).
With the Grain: Essays on Thomas Hardy and Modern British Poetry (Manchester: Carcanet, 1998).
Leavis, F. R., *New Bearings in English Poetry* (London: Chatto, 1932).
Levenson, Michael, *A Genealogy of Modernism* (Cambridge: Cambridge University Press, 1984).

40 Hardy and Mew

Davie, Donald, 'Hardy's Virgilian Purples', *Agenda*, 10:2–3 (1972), pp. 138–56.
Elliott, Ralph W. V., *Thomas Hardy's English* (Oxford: Basil Blackwell and Andre Deutsch, 1984).
Gifford, Henry, 'Hardy's Revisions (*Satires of Circumstance*)', *Agenda* 10:2–3 (1972), pp. 126–37.
McSweeney, Kerry, 'Hardy's *Poems of 1912–13*: A Presence More than the Actual', *Victorian Poetry*, 33:2 (1995), pp. 191–220.
Rees-Jones, Deryn, *Consorting With Angels* (Newcastle upon Tyne: Bloodaxe, 2005).
Rees-Jones, Deryn (ed.), *Modern Women Poets* (Newcastle upon Tyne: Bloodaxe, 2005).
Shires, Linda, 'Hardy and Nineteenth-Century Poetry and Poetics', in Phillip Mallett (ed.), *Palgrave Advances in Thomas Hardy Studies* (Basingstoke: Palgrave, 1984), pp. 255–78.

41 Yeats

Brown, Terence, *The Life of W. B. Yeats: A Critical Biography* (Oxford: Blackwell, 2001).

Cullingford, Elizabeth, *Gender and History in Yeats's Love Poetry* (Cambridge: Cambridge University Press, 1993).

Yeats, Ireland and Fascism (London: Macmillan, 1981).

Ellmann, Richard, *Yeats: The Man and the Masks* (Oxford: Oxford University Press, 1979).

Foster, Roy, *W. B. Yeats: A Life* I. *The Apprentice Mage 1865–1914* (Oxford: Oxford University Press, 1997).

W. B. Yeats : A Life II. *The Arch-Poet 1915–1939* (Oxford: Oxford University Press, 2003).

Howes, Marjorie and John Kelly (eds.), *The Cambridge Companion to W. B. Yeats* (Cambridge: Cambridge University Press, 2006).

Jeffares, A. Norman, *A New Commentary on the Poems of W. B. Yeats* (London: Macmillan, 1984).

W. B. Yeats: Man and Poet (London: Routledge, 1949).

Kiberd, Declan, *Inventing Ireland: The Literature of the Modern Nation* (London: Vintage, 1996).

O'Neill, Michael, *Romanticism and the Self-Conscious Poem* (Oxford: Clarendon Press, 1997).

O'Neill, Michael (ed.), *The Poems of W. B. Yeats: A Sourcebook* (London: Routledge, 2004).

42 Imagism

Altieri, Charles, 'Objective Image and Act of Mind in Modern Poetry', *PMLA*, 91 (January 1976), pp. 101–14.

Coffman, Stanley K., Jr., *Imagism: A Chapter for the History of Modern Poetry* (Norman: University of Oklahoma Press, 1951).

Davie, Donald, 'Syntax as Unpoetical: T. E. Hulme', in *Articulate Energy: An Enquiry into the Syntax of English Poetry* (New York: Harcourt Brace, 1958), pp. 1–13.

Dowling, Linda, *Language and Decadence in the Victorian Fin de Siècle* (1986; repr. Princeton: Princeton University Press, 1989).

The Egoist: An Individualist Review, 'Special Imagist Number', 2 (1 May 1915), pp. 70–82.

Hough, Graham, *Image and Experience: Studies in a Literary Revolution* (Lincoln: University of Nebraska Press, 1960).

Hughes, Glenn, *Imagism and the Imagists* (London: Oxford University Press, 1931).

Jameson, Margaret Storm, 'England's Nest of Singing Birds', *The Egoist: An Individualist Review*, 2 (1 November 1915), pp. 175–6.

Kenner, Hugh, 'Imagism', in *The Pound Era* (Berkeley: University of California Press, 1971), pp. 173–91.

Kermode, Frank, 'The Image', 'Arthur Symons', 'T. E. Hulme', in *Romantic Image* (New York: Macmillan, 1957), pp. 43–8, 107–18, 119–37.

Martin, Wallace, 'The Sources of the Imagist Aesthetic', *PMLA*, 85 (March 1970), pp. 196–204.

Middleton, Christopher, 'Documents on Imagism from the Papers of F. S. Flint', *The Review* (April 1965), pp. 35–51.

Pondrom, Cyrena, 'Selected Letters from H. D. to F. S. Flint: A Commentary on the Imagist Period', *Contemporary Literature*, 10 (Autumn 1969), pp. 557–86.

Schneidau, Herbert, *Ezra Pound: The Image and the Real* (Baton Rouge: Louisiana State University Press, 1969).

43 T. S. Eliot

Ackroyd, Peter, *T. S. Eliot* (1984; London: Sphere, 1985).
Bergonzi, Bernard (ed.), *T. S. Eliot: 'Four Quartets': A Casebook* (London: Macmillan, 1969).
Crawford, Robert, *The Savage and the City in the Work of T. S. Eliot* (Oxford: Oxford University Press, 1987).
Eliot, T. S., *Collected Poems 1909–1962* (London: Faber, 1963).
Inventions of the March Hare: Poems 1909–1917, ed. Christopher Ricks (1996; San Diego: Harcourt, 1998).
Selected Essays, new edition (New York: Harcourt, 1950).
To Criticize the Critic (London: Faber, 1965).
The Waste Land: A Facsimile and Transcript of the Original Drafts Including the Annotations of Ezra Pound, ed. Valerie Eliot (London: Faber, 1971).
Gardner, Helen, *The Art of T. S. Eliot* (London: Cresset, 1949).
Gordon, Lyndall, *Eliot's Early Years* (Oxford: Oxford University Press, 1977).
Josipovici, Gabriel, '*Four Quartets*: A Commentary', *PN Review*, 19 (September/October 1992), pp. 44–51.
Kenner, Hugh, *The Invisible Poet: T. S. Eliot* (1960; London: Methuen, 1965).
Moody, A. D., *Thomas Stearns Eliot: Poet* (Cambridge: Cambridge University Press, 1979).
Pinkney, Tony, *Women in the Poetry of T. S. Eliot: A Psychoanalytic Approach* (London: Macmillan, 1984).
Reeves, Gareth, *T. S. Eliot's 'The Waste Land'* (New York: Harvester, 1994).
Ricks, Christopher, *T. S. Eliot and Prejudice* (London: Faber, 1988).
Smith, Grover, *T. S. Eliot's Poetry and Plays: A Study in Sources and Meaning* (1956; second edition, Chicago: University of Chicago Press, 1974).

44 Owen, Rosenberg, Sassoon and Edward Thomas

Bergonzi, Bernard. *Heroes' Twilight: A Study of the Literature of the Great War* (London: Constable, 1965).
Fussell, Paul, *The Great War and Modern Memory* (1975; Oxford: Oxford University Press, 2000).
Hibberd, Dominic and John Onions (eds.), *Poetry of the Great War: An Anthology* (London: Macmillan, 1986).
Hynes, Samuel, *A War Imagined: The First World War and English Culture* (London: Pimlico, 1992).
Khan, Nosheen, *Women's Poetry of the First World War* (New York: Harvester, 1988).
Silkin, Jon (ed.), *The Penguin Book of First World War Poetry* (1979; Harmondsworth: Penguin, 1996).

45 Auden, Day Lewis, MacNeice, Spender: the thirties poetry

Fuller, John, *W. H. Auden: A Commentary* (London: Faber, 1998).
Gelpi, Albert, *Living in Time: The Poetry of C. Day Lewis* (Oxford: Oxford University Press, 1998).
Hecht, Anthony, *The Hidden Law: The Poetry of W. H. Auden* (Cambridge, MA: Harvard University Press, 1993).

Hynes, Samuel, *The Auden Generation: Literature and Politics in England in the 1930s* (London: Faber, 1976).

Mendelson, Edward, *Early Auden* (London: Faber, 1981).

Longley, Edna, *Louis MacNeice: A Study* (London: Faber, 1988).

McDonald, Peter, *Louis MacNeice: The Poet in His Contexts* (Oxford: Clarendon Press, 1991).

O'Neill, Michael and Gareth Reeves, *Auden, MacNeice, Spender: The Thirties Poetry* (Basingstoke: Macmillan, 1992).

Smith, Stan, *W. H. Auden* (Oxford: Blackwell, 1985).

Smith, Stan (ed.), *The Cambridge Companion to W. H. Auden* (Cambridge: Cambridge University Press, 2004).

46 Dylan Thomas and the poetry of the 1940s

Douglas, Keith, *The Complete Poems* (Oxford: Oxford University Press, 1995).

Graham, W. S., *New Collected Poems*, ed. Matthew Francis (London: Faber, 2004).

Hewison, Robert, *Under Siege: Literary Life in London 1939–45* (London: Methuen, 1988).

Keery, James, '"The Burning Baby" and the Bathwater', parts 1–9, *P.N. Review*, 151 (May–June 2003), p. 54; 152 (July–August 2003), pp. 57–62; 154 (November–December 2003), pp. 22–5 and 26–32; 156 (March–April 2004), pp. 40–2; 159 (September–October 2004), pp. 45–9; 164 (July–August 2005), p. 5761; 170 (July–August 2006), pp. 59–65; 171 (September–October 2006), pp. 56–62.

Lopez, Tony, *The Poetry of W. S. Graham* (Edinburgh: Edinburgh University Press, 1989).

Shires, Linda M., *British Poetry of the Second World War* (London: Macmillan, 1985).

Sillars, Stuart, *British Romantic Art and the Second World War* (New York: St Martin's Press, 1991).

Skelton, Robin (ed.), *Poetry of the Forties* (Harmondsworth: Penguin, 1968).

Thomas, Dylan, *Collected Poems: 1934–1953*, ed. Walford Davies and Ralph Maud (London: Dent, 1989).

Tolley, A. T., *The Poetry of the Forties* (Manchester: Manchester University Press, 1985).

47 Larkin and the Movement

Booth, James, *Philip Larkin: The Poet's Plight* (Basingstoke: Palgrave Macmillan, 2005).

Booth, James (ed.), *New Larkins for Old: Critical Essays* (Basingstoke: Macmillan, 2000).

Cooper, Stephen, *Philip Larkin: Subversive Writer* (Brighton: Sussex Academic Press, 2004).

Hartley, George (ed.), *Philip Larkin 1922–1985: A Tribute* (London: The Marvell Press, 1988).

Morrison, Blake, *The Movement: English Poetry and Fiction of the 1950s* (Oxford: Oxford University Press, 1980).

Regan, Stephen, *Philip Larkin* (Basingstoke: Macmillan, 1992).

Regan, Stephen (ed.), *Philip Larkin*, New Casebooks (Basingstoke: Macmillan, 1997).

Swarbrick, Andrew, *Out of Reach: The Poetry of Philip Larkin* (Basingstoke: Macmillan, 1995).

48 Three twentieth-century women poets: Riding, Smith, Plath

Adams, Barbara, *The Enemy Self: Poetry and Criticism of Laura Riding* (Ann Arbor: University of Michigan Research Press, 1990).

Dowson, Jane and Alice Entwistle, *A History of Twentieth-Century British Women's Poetry* (Cambridge: Cambridge University Press, 2005).

Gill, Jo (ed.), *The Cambridge Companion to Sylvia Plath* (Cambridge: Cambridge University Press, 2006).
Heuving, Jeanne, 'Laura (Riding) Jackson's "Really New" Poem', in Margaret Dickie and Thomas Travisano (eds.), *Gendered Modernisms: American Women Poets and Their Readers*, (Philadelphia: University of Pennsylvania Press, 1996), pp. 191–213.
Hughes, Ted, *Birthday Letters* (London: Faber, 1998).
Huk, Romana, *Stevie Smith: Between the Lines* (London: Palgrave, 2005).
Jackson, Laura (Riding), *The Laura (Riding) Jackson Reader*, ed. Elizabeth Friedmann (New York: Persea Books, 2005).
The Poems of Laura Riding, ed. Elizabeth Friedmann, revised edition (New York: Persea Books, 2001).
Middlebrook, Diane, *Her Husband: Hughes and Plath: A Marriage* (New York: Viking, 2003).
Peel, Robin, *Writing Back: Sylvia Plath and Cold War Politics* (Madison NJ: Fairleigh Dickinson University Press, 2002).
Plath, Sylvia, *Ariel* (London: Faber, 1965).
Ariel: The Restored Edition, ed. Frieda Hughes (London: Faber, 2004).
Collected Poems, ed. Ted Hughes (London: Faber, 1981).
Letters Home: Correspondences 1950–1963, ed. Aurelia Plath (London: Faber, 1976).
The Journals of Sylvia Plath, ed. Ted Hughes and Frances McCullough (New York: Anchor Books, 1998).
Pumphrey, Martin, 'Play, Fantasy and Strange Laughter: Stevie Smith's Uncomfortable Poetry', *Critical Quarterly*, 28:3 (1986), pp. 85–96.
Rees-Jones, Deryn, *Consorting with Angels: Essays on Modern Women Poets* (Tarset, Northumberland: Bloodaxe Books, 2005).
Severin, Laura, *Stevie Smith's Resistant Antics* (Madison: University of Wisconsin Press, 1997).
Smith, Stevie, *The Collected Poems of Stevie Smith*, ed. James MacGibbon (Harmondsworth: Penguin, 1985).
Me Again: The Uncollected Writings of Stevie Smith (London: Virago, 1988).
Selected Poems (London: Longman, 1962).
Spalding, Frances, *Stevie Smith: A Critical Biography* (London: Faber, 1988).

49 Hughes and Heaney

Brearton, Fran, 'Visions, Goddesses and Bog People: Yeats, Graves and Heaney', in Ian Firla and Grevel Lindop (eds.), *Graves and the Goddess: Essays on Robert Graves's 'The White Goddess'* (Selingsgrove: Susquehanna University Press; London: Associated Universities Press, 2003), pp. 152–65.
Corcoran, Neil, *The Poetry of Seamus Heaney: A Critical Guide*, second revised edition (London: Faber, 1998).
Feinstein, Elaine *Ted Hughes: The Life of a Poet* (London: Weidenfeld and Nicolson, 2001).
Gifford, Terry, *Green Voices: Understanding Contemporary Nature Poetry* (Manchester: Manchester University Press, 1995).
Hart, Kevin, 'Varieties of Poetic Sequence: Ted Hughes and Geoffrey Hill', in Neil Corcoran (ed.), *The Cambridge Companion to Twentieth-Century English Poetry* (Cambridge: Cambridge University Press, 2007), pp. 187–99.

Haughton, Hugh, 'Power and Hiding Places: Wordsworth and Seamus Heaney', in *The Monstrous Debt: Modalities of Romantic Influence in Twentieth-Century Literature*, ed. Damian Walford Davies and Richard Marggraf Turley (Detroit: Wayne State University Press, 2006), pp. 61–100.

Hirschberg, Stuart, *Myth in the Poetry of Ted Hughes* (Portmarnock: Wolfhound Press, 1981).

Ingelbien, Raphaël, 'Mapping the Misreadings: Ted Hughes, Seamus Heaney, and Nationhood', *Contemporary Literature*, 40:4 (1999), pp. 627–58.

Larrissy, Edward, *Reading Twentieth-Century Poetry: The Language of Gender and Objects* (Oxford: Blackwell, 1990).

Morrison, Blake, *Seamus Heaney* (London: Methuen, 1982).

Parker, Michael, *Seamus Heaney: The Making of the Poet*, second edition (Basingstoke: Macmillan, 1994).

Sagar, Keith, *The Art of Ted Hughes*, reprint of second edition with updated bibliography (Cambridge: Cambridge University Press, 1980).

50 Hill

Bloom, Harold (ed.), *Geoffrey Hill* (New York: Chelsea House, 1985).

James, Stephen, *Shades of Authority: The Poetry of Lowell, Hill and Heaney* (Liverpool: Liverpool University Press, 2007).

Knottenbelt, E. M., *Passionate Intelligence: The Poetry of Geoffrey Hill* (Amsterdam: Rodopi, 1990).

McDonald, Peter, *Serious Poetry: Form and Authority from Yeats to Hill* (Oxford: Clarendon Press, 2002).

Milne, W. S., *An Introduction to Geoffrey Hill* (London: Bellew, 1998).

O'Neill, Michael, *The All-Sustaining Air: Romantic Legacies and Renewals in British, American, and Irish Poetry since 1900* (Oxford: Oxford University Press, 2007).

Ricks, Christopher, 'Geoffrey Hill and "The Tongue's Atrocities" ' and 'Clichés', in *The Force of Poetry* (Oxford: Oxford University Press, 1984), pp. 285–318, 356–68.

Roberts, Andrew Michael, *Geoffrey Hill* (Tavistock: Northcote House, 2004).

Robinson, Peter (ed.), *Geoffrey Hill: Essays on his Work* (Milton Keynes: Open University Press, 1985).

Sherry, Vincent, *The Uncommon Tongue: The Poetry and Criticism of Geoffrey Hill* (Ann Arbor: University of Michigan Press, 1987).

Silkin, Jon, 'The Poetry of Geoffrey Hill', in Michael Schmidt and Grevel Lindop (eds.), *British Poetry since 1960* (Manchester: Carcanet, 1972), pp. 143–64.

Wainwright, Jeffrey, *Acceptable Words: Essays on the Poetry of Geoffrey Hill* (Manchester: Manchester University Press, 2005).

51 Mahon, Longley, Muldoon, McGuckian, Carson, Boland and other Irish poets

Boland, Eavan, *Object Lessons* (London: Vintage, 1996).

Brearton, Fran, *Reading Michael Longley* (Tarset: Bloodaxe, 2006).

Campbell, Matthew (ed.), *The Cambridge Companion to Contemporary Irish Poetry* (Cambridge: Cambridge University Press, 2003).

Corcoran, Neil (ed.), *The Chosen Ground: Essays on the Contemporary Poetry of Northern Ireland* (Bridgend: Seren Books, 1992).
Goodby, John, *Irish Poetry Since 1950* (Manchester: Manchester University Press, 2000).
Haughton, Hugh, *The Poetry of Derek Mahon* (Oxford: Oxford University Press, 2007).
Longley, Edna, *The Living Stream* (Newcastle upon Tyne: Bloodaxe, 1994).
Matthews, Steven, *Irish Poetry: Politics, History, Negotiation* (Basingstoke: Macmillan, 1997).
Reeves, Gareth, 'Tom Paulin: Writing from the Edges', in Alison O'Malley Younger and John Strachan (eds.), *Essays on Modern Irish Literature* (Sunderland: Sunderland University Press, 2007), pp. 135–41.
Wills, Clair, *Improprieties: Politics and Sexuality in Northern Irish Poetry* (Oxford: Clarendon Press, 1993).

52 Contemporary poetries in English, *c.*1980 to the present 1: the radical tradition

Critical Studies

Hampson, Robert and Peter Barry (eds.), *New British Poetries: The Scope of the Possible* (Manchester: Manchester University Press, 1993).
Lopez, Tony, *Meaning Performance: Essays on Poetry* (Cambridge: Salt Publishing, 2006).
Sheppard, Robert, *The Poetry of Saying* (Liverpool: Liverpool University Press, 2005).

Anthologies and collections

Crozier, Andrew and Tim Longville (eds.), *A Various Art* (London: Paladin, 1987).
Fisher, Allen, *Place* (Hastings: Reality Street Editions, 2005).
Fisher, Roy, *The Long and the Short of It: Poems 1955–2005* (Newcastle upon Tyne: Bloodaxe, 2005).
MacSweeney, Barry, *The Book of Demons* (Newcastle upon Tyne: Bloodaxe, 1997).
O'Sullivan, Maggie (ed.), *Out of Everywhere: Linguistically Innovative Poetry by Women in North America and the UK* (Hastings: Reality Street Editions, 1996).
Prynne, J. H., *Poems* (Newcastle upon Tyne: Bloodaxe, 2005).
Riley, Denise, *Selected Poems* (Hastings: Reality Street Editions, 2000).
Sinclair, Iain, *Lud Heat and Suicide Bridge* (London: Granta Publications, 1998).
Sinclair, Iain (ed.), *Conductors of Chaos: A Poetry Anthology* (London: Picador, 1996).
Tuma, Keith (ed.), *Anthology of Twentieth-Century British and Irish Poetry* (New York: Oxford University Press, 2001).

53 Contemporary poetries in English, *c.*1980 to the present 2

Davie, Donald, *With the Grain: Essays on Thomas Hardy and Modern British Poetry*, ed. and intro. Clive Wilmer (Manchester: Carcanet, 1998).
O'Brien, Sean, *The Deregulated Muse* (Newcastle upon Tyne: Bloodaxe, 1998).
Rees-Jones, Deryn, *Consorting with Angels: Essays on Modern Women Poets* (Newcastle upon Tyne: Bloodaxe, 2005).
Robinson, Alan, *Instabilities in Contemporary British Poetry* (Basingstoke: Macmillan, 1988).

Index